DATE DUE

			PRINTED IN U.S.A.

CLIFFS NOTES

HARDBOUND LITERARY LIBRARIES

EUROPEAN LITERATURE LIBRARY

Volume 1

French Literature

12 Titles

ISBN 0-931013-20-8

Library distributors, hardbound editions:
Moonbeam Publications
18530 Mack Avenue
Grosse Pointe, MI 48236
(313) 884-5255

MOONBEAM PUBLICATIONS
Robert R. Tyler, President
Elizabeth Jones, Index Editor

FOREWORD

Moonbeam Publications has organized **CLIFFS NOTES**, the best-selling popular (trade) literary reference series, into a fully indexed hardbound series designed to offer a more permanent format for the series.

Hardbound volumes are available in a **BASIC LIBRARY**, a 24 volume series. The current softbound series (over 200 booklets) has been divided into five major literary libraries to help researchers, librarians, teachers, students and all readers use this series more effectively. The five major literary groupings are further subdivided into 17 literary periods or genres to enhance the use of this series as a more precise literary reference book.

Hardbound volumes are also available in an **AUTHORS LIBRARY**, a 13 volume series classified by author, covering 11 authors and over 70 Cliffs Notes titles. This series helps readers who prefer to study the works of a particular author, rather than an entire literary period.

**CLIFFS NOTES HARDBOUND
LITERARY LIBRARIES**
1990 by
Moonbeam Publications
18530 Mack Avenue
Grosse Pointe, MI 48236
(313) 884-5255

Basic Library - 24 Volume
ISBN 0-931013-24-0

Authors Library - 13 Volume
ISBN 0-931013-65-8

Bound In U.S.A.

EUROPEAN LITERATURE LIBRARY

Volume 1

French Literature

CONTENTS

CANDIDE

NOTES

mes K. Lowers, Ph.D.
epartment of English
niversity of Hawaii

Cliffs® Notes

INCORPORATED

LINCOLN, NEBRASKA 68501

Editor

Gary Carey, M.A.
University of Colorado

Consulting Editor

James L. Roberts, Ph.
Department of Englisl
University of Nebraskc

ISBN 0-8220-0283-3
© Copyright 1965
by
C. K. Hillegass
All Rights Reserved
Printed in U.S.A.

1990 Printing

Cliffs Notes, Inc.   Lincoln, Nebraska

CONTENTS

INTRODUCTION

A Voltairean, as defined by Ernest Benot, philosophical writer and one-time director of the Ecole normale superior, in his *Etudes et pensées* (1884) is:

> a man who prefers to see clearly in all matters; in religion and in philosophy, he believes willingly only what he understands, and he admits that there are things he does not know; he values application above speculation, simplifies ethics as well as doctrine, and tries to direct it toward useful virtues; he likes a moderate political system that preserves 'natural liberty, the liberty of conscience, of speech and of the individual, reduces evil as much as possible, procures the greatest good, and places justice among the highest benefits; in the arts, he admires above all moderation and truth; he has a deadly hatred for hypocrisy, fanaticism and bad taste; he does not limit himself to detesting them, he fights them to death.

The man who inspired these words, often called the Father of the French Revolution, may indeed have had limitations as regards his personal life, but he did emerge as the leading apostle of tolerance and freedom in the eighteenth century, which has been called the "century of Voltaire."

Voltaire is the name he adopted in his maturity; his real one was Francois Marie Arouet. He was born on November 21, 1694, in Paris, the fifth child of his middle-class parents, who were natives of Poitou. Voltaire's father was a rather prosperous lawyer and notary who became treasurer to the Chambres des Comptes. A sickly child, Francois was not expected to live. And it must be admitted that, like Alexander Pope, whom he was to meet and with whom he corresponded, his life could be described as "one long disease." Yet he was to live that life energetically and to survive until May 30, 1778.

The Abbé de Châteauneuf, Voltaire's godfather, took special interest in the boy. Among other things he introduced him to deism. The Abbé, noted for his skepticism and wit, also taught him to recite lines from the satirical and shocking poem *Moisade*.

Voltaire's father was determined that his son should study law, and the lad was enrolled in the Jesuit College of Louis-le-grande in 1704. He remained there until his seventeenth year, winning many academic prizes. Evidence of his precocity is also found in the fact that the gifted Ninon de Leclos, one of his father's clients, was sufficiently impressed by the young man to will him 2,000 francs for the specific purpose of buying books. At the Jesuit college Voltaire received a sound liberal education, developed his ability as a writer, and trained his critical sense. Of significance also is the fact that he gained considerable theatrical training, for the Jesuits continued the Renaissance tradition of having plays in Latin and the vernacular performed by their charges.

Voltaire had already demonstrated his ability to write verse and was determined to become a great poet. But his father had little faith in literature as a means of earning a good living, and he insisted that his son continue to study law. The young man complied, but only in a perfunctory way.

All his life Voltaire was to demonstrate his ability to make friends among the influential, and he knew that the right circle in prerevolutionary France was the aristocratic one. Therefore, he was elated when his godfather, the sophisticated Abbé de Châteauneuf, introduced him into the daringly liberal society of the Temple, where he was welcomed by such freethinking aristocrats as the Duke de Sully, the Duke de Vendôme, the Prince de Carti, and other persons of high rank as well as by men of letters. To Voltaire the Temple was a society of "princes and poets." Determined to distinguish himself among the latter, he wrote satirical verse, and, since the surest way to fame in literature at that time was to become a tragic poet, began planning a tragedy in verse. It may be added that Voltaire exercised that charm of which he was always capable and became quite a gallant and favorite of the ladies.

At this point Voltaire's father, alarmed not only because his son was neglecting his legal studies but because the society the young man now kept was notoriously libertine, forced him to leave Paris. This was the first of the many "exiles" he was to experience. He was sent to Holland as a page to the French Ambassador. The result, however, was an unfortunate love affair with a respectable young lady whose Protestantism was not acceptable to Voltaire's father. The young man found himself back in Paris again. The year was 1713.

By this time Voltaire had won quite a reputation for his satirical verse and prose. But his gift was to get him into trouble from time to time throughout his life. When he was publicly accused of writing libelous poems his father again sent him away from Paris, this time into the country, where for nearly a year he was the guest of the Marquis de Saint-Ange. He spent his time writing essays and working on his first tragedy, certainly not in studying law.

Mention has been made of Voltaire's ability to make friends, but it should be noted that he was something of a past master at making enemies, largely because of his sensitivity and the fact that he took almost malicious pleasure in using his sardonic wit to attack those with whom he did not agree. He demonstrated both capacities when he was allowed to return to

Paris. He was introduced to the Court de Seaux, a famous literary and political salon, over which the attractive Duchess du Maine presided. It was apparently the duchess who got Voltaire to write lampoons against her enemy, The Regent, Orleans. So, in May, 1716, Voltaire once more was forced to leave Paris for a time, going first to Tulle and later to Sully. He was not back in Paris very long when he faced more trouble. Two especially offensive libels appeared, *Puerto Regnanto* and *J'ai vu*. And this time Voltaire, suspected of being the author, was sent to the Bastille on May 16, 1717. He was to remain there for eleven months and then to be exiled to Châtenay and elsewhere. While occupying the room that came to be known by his name in the famous prison, Voltaire revised his tragedy, which was entitled *Œdipe*, and began work on his epic poem *L' Henriade*, which celebrated the deeds of Henry IV of France. It is notable that these two earliest works reveal Voltaire as a man dedicated to freedom and justice as he understood those concepts. A dominant theme in the play is the tyranny of the priesthood; the epic poem is memorable for the plea for tolerance.

It was on his release from prison that Voltaire adopted the name by which he is now known universally, Aurot de Voltaire. The aristocratic particle *de* is of special interest, since he belonged to a bourgeois family. This indeed points to the fact that he was determined to rise in the world. The most common explanation of the name is that it is an imperfect anagram of Arouet, l.j. (le jeune), but other explanations have been advanced. Some have believed that it was an older name on his mother's side of the family; still others argue that it was derived from his schoolboy sobriquet, *le volontaire*.

The tragedy *Œdipe*, first acted in November, 1718, was an immediate success, enjoying a run of forty-five days. Now Voltaire was welcomed back to Paris as a gifted tragic poet. But his reputation for writing lampoons and other satiric verse directed against public figures was too great for him to avoid new difficulties. He was falsely accused of being the author of the La Grange-Chancel libels, the *Philippiques*, which were virulent satires directed against the Duc d' Orleans. This time he was guest of the Duc de Villars, maréchal of France and famous war hero. While living with the maréchal and harmlessly making love to the duchess, Voltaire commenced gathering material for his historical works.

By the end of 1725, Voltaire was flourishing, enjoying as he did the patronage and friendship of the Duke of Richelieu. Then his fortunes turned again. The arrogant Chevalier du Rohan, obviously jealous of Voltaire's popularity, taunted him about his adopted name. There followed a harsh exchange between the two, and the Chevalier subsequently had his lackeys attack his foe. When the latter challenged him to a duel, the Chevalier had his opponent sent to the Bastille. Voltaire was imprisoned only for a fortnight, but when released he again faced exile.

Voltaire had met Henry St. John, Viscount Bolingbroke in the early 1720's when the Englishman was himself in exile. The two became firm friends, and Voltaire, always a great letter writer, corresponded with him regularly. It was perhaps this relationship which led the Frenchman to spend most of the next three years in England. The consensus is that this period in Voltaire's life was of the greatest importance to him. John Morley, one of his better known English biographers, went so far as to say that the English Deists formed Voltaire's mind. This, no doubt, is an exaggeration, in view of the Frenchman's apprenticeship to the Abbé de Châteauneuf, his admiration of Henri Bayle, and the evidence found in his growing list of publications. But certainly Saintsbury did not exaggerate when he wrote as follows (*Encyclopaedia Britannica,* 11th edition):

> Before the English visit, Voltaire had been an elegant trifler, an adept in the forms of literature popular in French society, a sort of superior Dorat or Boufflers of earlier growth. He returned from that visit one of the foremost literary men in Europe.

The cultural and intellectual climate of England at this time (1726 to 1729) delighted the young Voltaire. He was welcomed in Tory and Whig circles alike. Among his friends and acquaintances were the leading literary figures of the day, among them Pope, Swift, Gay, Young, and Thomson. He was to record his respect and admiration for the author of *A Tale of a Tub* and the newly published *Gulliver's Travels,* a work which was not without its influence on *Candide.* But especially he revered Alexander Pope, with whom he had so much in common — the satiric gift, wit, great facility at versifying, the critical temperament and, yes, the vindictiveness, the inability to suffer a fool gladly.

While in England, Voltaire learned to read and write the language fluently. He read avidly the works of Bacon, Shakespeare, Milton (whose allegory of Death and Sin he found unacceptable), Newton, and Locke (whose views on tolerance particularly were acceptable to him). His new-found interest in Shakespeare was to lead him to begin writing his own Roman play, *Brutus.* Later he was to establish himself as a dedicated Newtonian and to write a treatise on Newton's system. Voltaire also collected materials or his *Lettres philosophiques sur les Anglais,* in which he interpreted most favorably English culture for his countrymen and contrasted it with that of France. Gustave Lanson, the noted French literary historian, called these English Letters the first bomb thrown at the *ancien régime.* It is clear that Voltaire had only admiration for England and Englishmen. In contrast to the France he had known he found freedom and tolerance in his temporary home. This was the man who declared that he might disapprove of what an individual said but that he would defend to his own death the individual's right to say it. Little wonder that he so admired the island kingdom. As regards the exile in England, one more thing may be reported. He brought out an English edition of *L'Henriade,* dedicating it to the English Queen. It was a great success, the author realizing some 1000 pounds from subscriptions alone.

Voltaire, however, remained a Frenchman and a Parisian. However much he enjoyed the sojourn in England, he yearned to return home. In the spring of 1729 he secured permission to do so. But not too much time passed before Voltaire again experienced difficulties. In 1733 the publication of the English Letters and the satirical poem *Temple du Goût* enraged many people of influence. The first, while lauding the English, attacked the French government and the Church; the second satirized contemporary writers, especially J. B. Rousseau, the man who had once predicted that Voltaire was to make a great name for himself. The government issued a warrant for Voltaire's arrest, and his house was searched. By that time, however, the author of the two offensive works was at Cirey in Lorraine, an independent duchy, the guest of Emilie de Breteuil, Marquise du Châtelet, with whom he had been intimate during the previous year. The relationship between her and Voltaire was to last for some sixteen years and marks the next important stage in his long career.

Mme. du Châtelet, twelve years Voltaire's junior, was in many ways a remarkable woman. Short of temper, often difficult, *persona non grata* in fashionable society, she nevertheless had her attractions. A woman of keen intellect, she was devoted to mathematics, science, and philosophy. Particularly was she dedicated to the optimistic philosophy of Leibnitz; and, assisted by Voltaire she spent much of her time writing an exposition of the German's conclusions. She shared Voltaire's enthusiasm for Newton, and while her companion worked on an exposition of the Newtonian system, she translated the *Principia* into French, adding a commentary.

These were indeed productive years for Voltaire. Among other works, he completed a treatise on metaphysics, wrote six plays, completed two poems—*Le Mondain,* a satire against the Jansenists, whose doctrine had much in common with Calvinism, and the philosophical *Discours sur l'homme.* He also labored on the *Siècle de Louis XIV* and his universal history, *Essai sur moeurs.*

Once the Regent had died, Paris again beckoned to him. After 1743 he found himself in favor at Court, thanks largely to Richelieu and Madame de Pompadour, who admired the dramatist Voltaire. When a new work, *Poème de Fontenay* (1745), proved to be a success, he was rewarded by being made the royal historiographer and received a substantial pension. The post had been held earlier by Racine and Corneille. It was about this time that he turned to another type of writing, the philosophical tales, among which *Candide* was to become best known. He also continued to write plays, now in competition with Crébillon, with whom he was to engage in a bitter quarrel. In 1746, finally, Voltaire was elected to the French Academy; most certainly he had attained maturity as a literary artist and *philosophe.*

Nothing could stop the audacities of Voltaire's pen. In his bitingly satirical *Trajan est-il content?* there were obvious references to Louis XV himself. In 1748 he found it expedient to find refuge with the Duchess de Sceaux, and somewhat later he joined Mme. de Châtelet at Lunéville. In September 1749, his close friend Mme. de Châtelet, died while giving birth to a child, the father of whom was neither her husband nor Voltaire. Again he had reached the crossroads in his eventful life. What to do now? He could not return to Paris, especially because of the continuing feud with Crébillon.

Frederick the Great, whom Voltaire had once met and with whom he had been corresponding regularly for some time, had been urging the Frenchman to come to Potsdam, where the Prussian King had established his Academy and was anxious to add another star to his galaxie of *philosophes*, the intellectuals of Europe. So Voltaire took up his residence at Potsdam in 1750. There, the recipient of a generous pension, he completed his most ambitious historical work, the *Siècle de Louis XIV;* wrote a new philosophical tale, *Micromégas,* which illustrates the influence of Swift's *Gulliver's Travels* upon his own fiction; and worked on his universal history.

Unfortunately, the friendship of Frederick and Voltaire did not flourish; both could be difficult individuals in their respective ways. Voltaire was offended by elements in the King's personal life and found him to be particularly arrogant. What ultimately led to the break in their relationship, however, was Voltaire's attack upon the President of Frederick's cherished Academy of Science. Entitled the *Diatribe du Doctor Akakia,* it was published without permission; and despite his assurance that all copies would be destroyed, Voltaire took malicious pleasure in seeing to it that the work circulated. As a result he suffered the indignity of being arrested at Frankfort and having his baggage searched. No longer could he stay in Germany under the patronage of the man whom he had once eulogized as a Horace, a Catullus, a Maecenas, a Socrates, as Augustus and as the Solomon of the North. This brings us to the last stage in Voltaire's long career.

Aware that he would not be welcome back in Paris, especially because his sojourn in Germany was looked upon as an insult to his fellow countrymen, Voltaire took up residence in Geneva, where in most respects the air of freedom was purer. He was now a wealthy man. He had inherited sums of money from his father and brother, he had been given pensions by the French and Prussian kings, and he had gained more money from many of his works (particularly his plays). Early in young manhood he had demonstrated his skill in speculation. Indeed, had he chosen to concentrate on finance rather than literature, he very well could have emerged as a Rothschild. He purchased a château near Geneva and called it Les Délices, his "summer palace." He bought another residence at Monrion, Lausanne, which he called his "winter palace." As busy as ever as a writer, he nevertheless found time to encourage the local manufacturers, particularly the watchmakers. It was here that he wrote *Candide,* as well as a tragedy and much verse. Polemical works also came from his pen, for he continued the attack upon religion with his war cry "Écrasez l'Infame."

Although Voltaire did find greater tolerance in Switzerland, his relations with the Calvinists were not harmonious. Specifically, they were shocked to learn that he had built a private theater at Les Délices and frequently staged plays. So, retaining possession of that château, he bought the château and demesne of Ferney, in France, quite close to the Swiss border; he moved there in 1760 and lived with his niece, Mme. Denis. Here indeed he flouished as a manorial lord, served by as many as sixty persons. He was extremely hospitable and welcomed the many distinguished visitors from all parts of Europe who came to see and talk with the now widely famous man. He remained in residence at Ferney for twenty years.

Although he continued to the end to write on literary subjects, they received less attention. All his life he had been convinced that all literature should teach, and he had used drama and tales for that very purpose. His works demonstrate his sustained interest in religious, political, social, and philosophical questions. But now he was not content merely to use belletristic literature as his medium. He became the active champion of tolerance and justice, emerging as an eighteenth century Zola. Most notable in his *Traité sur la tolerance* (1763), which he wrote in defence of Jean Calais, who had been tortured and executed as a result of a religious controversy. This was effective enough so that Calais was recognized as the victim of judicial murder. The death of the young Chevalier de la Barre for alleged sacrilege led Voltaire to write another powerful tract which was effective in clearing the Chevalier's name. To note just one other example, he came to the rescue of one Sirven, a French protestant declared guilty of the murder of his Roman Catholic daughter and who had been banished as a then penniless criminal. Voltaire succeeded in having the sentence reversed. Little wonder that he was hailed as the apostle of freedom, as well as intellectual potentate of Europe.

Voltaire began his literary career as a tragic poet, if one excepts minor verse; he was to end it as one — and to end it triumphantly. In the spring of 1778 his last play, the tragedy *Irene,* was accepted for performance in Paris, and the old man was determined to be present at the Première. His return to the city from which he had been exiled time and again created a sensation. He was honored by the French Academy as its most distinguished member. But his rapidly failing health made it impossible for him to witness the great success of his tragedy on the opening night. He was able, however, to attend the sixth performance and to receive the acclaim of an enthusiastic audience.

Voltaire, the long-time valetudinarian who now was eighty-four years of age, died on May 30, 1778. Typically, the man who had erected a Catholic Church on one of his estates (having the inscription "Deo erexit Voltaire" placed upon it), and who in his last years played chess regularly with a Jesuit, refused Extreme Unction and absolution. There was thus difficulty relating to his burial, and his body was hastily interred at the abbey of Scellières in Champagne barely before the interdict of the bishop. But thirteen years later the body was brought back to Paris for repose in the Pantheon, the famous church which is the French equivalent of Westminster Abbey.

It is clear that Voltaire was a brilliant, complex individual. He manifested great charm which won him many friends among influential members of both sexes; he also possessed almost a genius for making enemies. For he was a man who liked to oppose. Witness his quarrel with J. B. Rousseau and the completely uncalled-for one with Crébillon. And surely it was not all Frederick the Great's fault that Voltaire did not flourish at Potsdam. There is a comparable contrast with reference to his reputation. Goethe praised him in superlatives, speaking of his genius, his "eagle's sweep of vision," his "vast understanding"; for the great German the Frenchman was "perfection indeed." One dissenter was the pensée-writer Joseph Joubert, who believed that Voltaire lacked compassion—a curious judgment on the man who came to the defense of such victims of intolerance as Calais, Sirven, and the Chevalier de la Barre. We shall find that the critical estimates of *Candide* also vary markedly, but the consensus is that, of its kind, the tale is unsurpassed.

Reference has been made to various works by Voltaire, giving an indication of his breadth. Indeed one must turn to a Lope de Vega or a Daniel Defoe to find as prolific a writer. It is now desirable to provide a short survey of the works. They are properly described as "vast and various" by Saintsbury and may be easily classified as to type.

First are the tragedies and comedies, some fifty to sixty in all. As has been indicated Voltaire was a dramatist early and late, beginning his literary career with a tragedy and ending it with one. *Nanine* has been called his best comedy, although, curiously enough, this man with such a superior wit was not too well at home in this *genre*. *Zaïre* (1732) and *Mérope* (1741) have been placed among the superior plays of the entire Classical School in France.

The second grouping is that of the non-dramatic poems. He was an indefatigable writer in this area. It will suffice to note three here. First is the heroic epic *L'Henriade,* an ambitious work modelled after Virgil's *Aeneid* and written in alexandrine couplets. Next is the scandalous but often amusing *La Pucelle* (surreptitiously printed in 1755; first authorized edition, 1755); this is actually a burlesque attacking the reputation of Joan f Arc. It was one of the several works (including *Candide*) the authorship f which Voltaire for a time denied. The third poem which deserves notice, articularly because of its close relationship to *Candide,* is *Désastre de isbon,* published in 1756, the year following the terrifying earthquake. his poem will call for sufficient attention in the section entitled "Back-round to *Candide*" below. It is true that Voltaire lacked what may be alled the true passion, but his verse is memorable for technical virtuosity nd superior diction—and quite often for superior wit.

A third classification is that of the historical works, which, excepting 'oltaire's correspondence, are most voluminous. Mention has been made f the *Siècle de Louis XIV* and to *Essai sur les moeurs,* chiefly remarkable or the amount of private, personal information Voltaire was able to include a them. His short monographs on Charles XII and on Peter the Great, as vell as the *Annales de l'empire,* deserve mention. In this field Voltaire was ompetent enough, but there is no danger of anyone confusing him with an :dward Gibbon.

Voltaire wrote a great deal on the subject of physics in which he dem-nstrated considerable knowledge; but it is to the philosophical works that ve now turn, to two in particular: the *Dictionnaire philosophique,* which is argely made up of material which he had prepared for the *Encyclopédie,* of vhich Diderot may be considered the guiding spirit; and the ambitious ʳraité de Metaphysique. The first is a prime source for Voltaire's religious ind political views; the second, which did not really succeed, merely proves hat Voltaire, however intellectual he may have been, was not a philosopher n the sense that Locke or Leibnitz was.

Still another division is that of critical and miscellaneous writing. In ›amphlet after pamphlet he demonstrated superior ability as a journalist. ʳhe ones in defence of Calais and others are prime examples. The best of iis several critical works is his *Commentaire sur Corneille.*

Logically the prose tales should have been discussed after the plays ind the poems. But it is desirable to conclude this introduction with a liscussion of them, since *Candide* is the best known philosophic tale, one :hat has been called "the most remarkable fruit of Voltaire's genius." The iuthor, who believed that all literature should teach, used the tale as a vehicle for his profoundest views on politics, religion, and philosophy. Besides *Candide,* memorable among them are *Zadig* (1747), first published inder the title of *Memnon,* in which the young hero, like Candide, travels far and wide, and experiences great dangers. The special interest of this :ale is that Voltaire concluded it on a completely optimistic note. *L'Homme aux quarante écus* (1768) attacks certain political and social practices of eighteenth century France. A few are out-and-out lampoons on the Bible. *Histoires des voyages de Scarmentado* (1756) has been described by Gus-tave Lanson as a kind of preliminary sketch of *Candide.*

Apparently aware that *Candide* would shock and offend many readers, Voltaire did not acknowledge authorship of the tale at first. He gave the work the fictitious subtitle: "Translated from the German of Dr. Ralph, with the additions found in the doctor's pocket when he died at Minden, in the year of grace 1759." Its immediate and sustained popularity is indicated by the fact that forty-three editions appeared between 1759 and 1789. A second part, or sequel was published with the original first in an English edition and erroneously attributed to Voltaire. Further evidence of the popularity of the work is found in the attention given to it by critics from the very start.

In a letter to Voltaire dated February 23, 1759, Nicholas-Claude Theirot praised him as the "most excellent author and inventor of quips and jests" and said that his "book is snatched from hand to hand." Theirot went so far as to predict that Voltaire's work would live for a century and considered it "more like Lucian, Rabelais, and Swift than all three put together." In the same year Friedrich M. Grimm expressed his views in a letter. He too appreciated the wit and gaiety in *Candide,* but deplored what he considered the author's bad taste, referring to the "vulgarity, indecent talk, and filth without disguise to make them bearable." For him *Candide* was no more than a *plaisanterie.* But for many others, like Mme de Staël, it was the serious work of a scoffing philosopher.

The same division in critical estimates of the tale is to be found abroad. We have Boswell's word for it that Samuel Johnson, literary dictator of his age, never tired of expressing his admiration for *Candide,* which in its "plan and conduct" is so much like his own philosophical tale, *Rasselas.* But to the poet Edward Young, whom Voltaire had met in England, *Candide* was no more than "bold trash." So with the romanticist William Wordsworth, who referred to it as:

> ...this dull product of a scoffer's pen,
> Impure conceits discharging from a heart
> Hardened by impious pride.
>
> (*The Excursion,* II, 484-486)

Carlyle's name may be added to those who either dismissed the tale as a kind of joke or deplored Voltaire's cynicism. Carlyle denied that the Frenchman had one great thought and described the work as "mere logical pleasantry."

The pendulum has, however, swung far in Voltaire's favor as the years have advanced. William Hazlitt, refuting Wordsworth, flatly declared that "*Candide* is a masterpiece of wit"; Henry Brougham (in *Lives of Men of Letters,* 1856) praised it as "most extraordinary"; John Morley, perhaps best known among the many biographers of Voltaire, writing at the end of the nineteenth century, admired its "fresh and unflagging spontaneity." In our own century G. Lytton-Strachey and Aldous Huxley are among the many who have hailed *Candide* as a masterpiece. Mr. Ira O. Wade has provided the correct explanation of why there should have been such widely divergent views of the tale: *"Candide* is...in its inner substance not wholly optimistic, or pessimistic, or skeptical or cynical; it is all these things at the same time" *(Voltaire and Candide,* 1959, p. 319). Whether viewed favorably or unfavorably, *Candide* remains a classic. Theirot wrote that it would live a hundred years; it has already survived for well over two hundred and will continue to live as long as there is an intelligent reading public.

CHAPTER 1*

SUMMARY AND COMMENTARY
CANDIDE'S BACKGROUND AND FIRST MISFORTUNE

Summary

The story begins in Westphalia at the castle of the high and mighty Baron of Thunder-ten-tronckh, his three-hundred fifty pound wife, their beautiful young daughter Cunégonde, and an unnamed son. Living happily at the Castle is Candide, whose name points to his character—that of one who is simple of mind and (adds Voltaire ironically) sound of judgement. Prominent in the baron's ménage is the tutor, Doctor Pangloss, a man revered as a profound and learned philosopher, Pangloss firmly believed and taught that everything in the world was necessarily for the best end: it was all a matter of recognizing the sufficient reason and accepting the logic of cause and effect. Thus, for him and his disciples, this is indeed "the best of all possible worlds." If Candide had had his wish, he would have first chosen to be the powerful baron, second the lovely Cunégonde, and third the wise Pangloss.

The significant incident in this first chapter involves Pangloss' illicit relations with a still unnamed chambermaid. Cunégonde herself witnessed with great interest the act, which took place in a little wood on her father's estate. So intrigued was she with this lesson in "experimental physics" and the demonstration of sufficient reason involving cause and effect that she was determined to experiment herself with the cooperation of Candide. The opportunity presented itself when the two found themselves behind a screen. But, alas, My Lord, the Baron discovered them. Cunégonde received a slap on the face, but poor Candide was literally kicked out of the Castle. He was now an exile from his best of all possible worlds in Westphalia.

Commentary

It has been held that the pompous Baron of Thunder-ten-tronckh is one of the representations of Frederick the Great, with whom Voltaire had such close relations for so long a time. Later, as we shall see, it is the

---

* Although Roman Numerals are used to identity chapters in most editions, Arabic ones are used in these *Notes* as a matter of convenience.

Baron's son who appears to be identified as the Prussian ruler. Here the original identification is justified in view of the fact that the son is said to be very much like his father. The latter is depicted as one who is inordinately vain and all-powerful. He is always addressed as "My Lord"; all those who serve him laugh appreciably at his stories.

Among the more ingenious theories is that Candide to some extent represents Voltaire here, as he does elsewhere in the tale from time to time. The Frenchman is said to have suspected that he was illegitimate, and he began life sufficiently optimistic and satisfied with the world. It has further been suggested that the fair Cunégonde is none other than Mme. de Châtelet herself. And it has been said that the Cunégonde-Candide affair represents the common passion of Frederick's sister for Baron Trenck.

The name of the oracle of the Baron's castle, Pangloss, derives from the Greek and means "all tongues." It may be added that *nigology,* part of the title of Pangloss' impressive subject matter, may very well derive from the French *nigaud,* which means "booby." Thus Voltaire's mockery and satire make an early appearance in *Candide.* It is surely going too far to say that Pangloss is a caricature of Gottfried Wilhelm Leibnitz, the great German philosopher and mathematician, for whom Voltaire had expressed admiration on more than one occasion; but Pangloss' optimistic philosophy is a caricature of that of Leibnitz's as it was systematized by Christian Wolff (1679-1754) and popularized widely in the *Essay On Man* (1733-34) by Alexander Pope. The philosophers and the poet will be discussed below in the section on the background to *Candide.*

One should be aware that, whereas the main target of Voltaire's attack remains the optimistic philosophy which held that all is for the best, he did not neglect to satirize other things, including excessive pride and the essential littleness of man. Thus, according to rumor, the Baron's sister refused to marry her lover who had only seventy-one divisions on his coat of arms indicating the degrees of nobility. Actually the maximum number which an aristocrat could possess was much less than this. And what of the Baron himself? A measure of his greatness was that *his* castle had a door and a window, and a piece of tapestry hung on the wall of his great hall. One is reminded of Swift's Lilliputian emperor who was taller by the length of a thumbnail than any of his subjects.

CHAPTERS 2-3

CANDIDE AND THE BULGARIANS

Summary
Candide was now reduced to a state of misery as, in the freezing cold, he dragged himself toward the neighboring town, nearly dying from

unger and fatigue. At the door of an inn two uniformed men addressed im. Strangely enough they offered to buy him food and to give him money mply because he was five feet five in height. "Men are made to help each ther." explained one, and Candide was moved and delighted to hear this onfirmation of Doctor Pangloss' teaching. They induced the youth to rink to the health of the Bulgarian King, and then announced that he was soldier in the King's army — a hero whose glory and fortune were assured.

For one so honored the treatment Candide received was rather star-ling. He was placed in irons and taken to the regiment, where he was put nrough endless drills and nearly beaten to death. One day he ran away, but efore he had covered many miles four of his "fellow heroes" overtook him, ound him, and put him in a dungeon. Offered a choice, he understandably hose to be beaten unmercifully thirty-six times by the whole regiment ather than to be shot. As Voltaire described the punishment, the callow outh might have been wiser to have accepted death. But, just at the time vhen it seemed that he could not survive, the King of the Bulgarians ap-eared, made inquiries, and granted Candide a pardon. Three weeks later, he youth, restored to good health, was able to join his fellow soldiers in he war against the Abarians.

In the third chapter Voltaire described the "glories" of war — the well-rilled troops, the martial music, and the "heroic" butchery, from which Candide hid himself as best he could. And while both kings were having heir *Te Deums* sung, he decided the time was ripe for him to reason else-vhere about the cause and effect. He made his way over heaps of dead and lying men before reaching an Abarian village. It was in ashes, having been urned in accordance with the rules of international law. Candide saw at irst hand how the horrors of war could be visited on the innocent civilians. Women, children, old men — none had escaped.

Candide fled to another village, which proved to be a Bulgarian one, and found that it and the inhabitants had received the same treatment. At ast he escaped from the theatre of war. Never did he forget Mademoiselle Cunégonde. When he reached Holland, he optimistically believed that he would be as well treated as he once had been in Westphalia; for were not he Hollanders Christian? But the starving youth found little charity. One native threatened him with prison when he asked for alms; another, a mili-tant Protestant, excoriated him when he did not provide the expected an-swer as regards the Pope. It remained for an Anabaptist — a man who had not even been baptized — to play the role of the Good Samaritan. His gen-erosity and kindness reaffirmed in Candide faith in the wisdom of Doctor Pangloss: all must be for the best in this best of all possible words.

At this point in the action, Candide met a beggar covered with sores. The beggar's eyes were lifeless and the tip of his nose had been eaten away by disease. His mouth was twisted and he was racked by a violent cough. He spat out a tooth with every spasm.

18

Commentary

The two chapters summarized above are most notable for anti-war satire. Voltaire was appalled by the slaughter and waste which characterized the Seven Years War, in progress at the time he wrote. This conflict has its place in the background to *Candide* and will be discussed later. The Bulgarians are the Prussians. Long since, critics and editors of the tale have pointed out that Voltaire chose that name to refer to his one-time patron, Frederick the Great, whom he suspected of being a pederast. The French word *bougre* (cf. English *bugger*) derives from *Bulgare*. Voltaire chose the term *Abarians,* the name of a Scythian tribe, to represent the French. But in Chapter 2, the author first pokes fun at the drillmastership of Frederick the Great, and implies that the "heroes" are made into mere automatons. Writing with studied casualness, he depends as usual upon irony. His description of the slaughter and destruction incidental to war is absolutely devastating, and his irony reached the apex when he told how the rival kings retired to their respective camps to sing praises to God.

Notable also is Voltaire's offensive against religion as he found it practiced in his day. As the account of the Anabaptist's warmth and generosity indicate, Voltaire found the Church suspect when its clergy and laymen failed to be tolerant and merciful. It is of some relevance to recall that in his *English Letters,* he had kind words to say about the Baptists, whose practices seemed to him to be closer to those of the primitive Christians than did those of other sects. It is quite interesting that Voltaire should have chosen an Anabaptist as his Good Samaritan: apparently, deist that he was, he believed strongly in justification by works. Particularly he deplored the extremes of religious zealots.

In the category of antireligious satire, may be included what Voltaire had to say about free will. Basic to the Christian doctrine, certainly to Roman Catholicism, is the proposition that man, endowed with reason, can and must make his choice between good and evil. The well-meaning Candide found that, although he knew war to be evil, he had no choice as regards becoming a soldier or not. The best that he could do was to hide when the hostilities began.

To be sure Voltaire does not neglect his major thesis—the attack upon optimistic philosophy—he inserts the introduction and description of the pitiable beggar who made his appearance at the end of Chapter 3.

CHAPTERS 4-6

CANDIDE AND PANGLOSS REUNITED

Summary

Irony of ironies! The diseased, pathetic beggar turned out to be that confident exponent of optimism, the learned Doctor Pangloss, and he had a most dismal report of what had been happening in the best of all possible worlds. Candide's adored Cunégonde was dead. After having swooned and then revived, Candide might well have asked, "Ah, best of worlds, where are you?"—especially when he learned that she had been repeatedly ravished and then disemboweled by Bulgarian soldiers, who had cut the Baroness to pieces, smashed the head of the Baron, killed his son, and destroyed everything—more evidence of the heroics of warfare.

Once more Candide swooned. When he revived, he inquired of his mentor the cause and effect, the sufficient reason, which had reduced Pangloss to such a pitiable state. He learned that, his mentor and Paquette, pretty attendant of the Baroness, had become intimate. But earlier Paquette had become infected with a social disease as a result of relations with a learned Franciscan. Pangloss then traced the infection back to companions of Columbus, who first brought it from the New World. "Wasn't the devil the root of this strange genealogy?" asked Candide. But he is assured that all was logical and for the best: had not Columbus and his men sailed to the New World, Europe would not now enjoy chocolate or cochineal; the reason had been sufficient. And is it not marvelous how the disease has spread?

Again the charitable Anabaptist came to the rescue. Pangloss was cured, suffering only the loss of one eye and one ear. The optimistic philosopher became his bookkeeper. With Candide the two made a trip to Lisbon. En route, Pangloss expounded his philosophy to his benefactor, but the latter remained unconvinced of its validity: men were not born wolves, yet they had become wolves and sought to destroy each other. But Doctor Pangloss assured him that private misfortunes make up the general good; the more misfortunes there were, the more all was well. At this point the ship began to endure a frightening tempest as it sailed in sight of the Port of Lisbon.

Crew and passengers alike were terrified as the ship tossed helplessly in the turbulent waters. No one commanded, none of the crew cooperated. Only the Anabaptist endeavored to help, but a frightened sailor struck him a hard blow and from the force of it he himself fell overboard. Caught on a masthead, he seemed to be lost. The good Anabaptist rescued him and lost his own life in the action. Candide wanted to sacrifice himself when he saw his benefactor die, but Pangloss convinced him that a wise Providence had arranged all this so that the Anabaptist would not survive. For the Doctor all things continued to be for the best. And at that moment the ship split open. Everyone perished except Candide, Pangloss, and the heartless sailor who had been saved by the Anabaptist. The first two reached shore on a plank.

No sooner had they reached Lisbon than they experienced, with all the others in the city, a terrific earthquake in which many thousands lost their lives and the city itself was left in shambles. Even Pangloss was at a loss to explain the sufficient cause for that catastrophe. As for Candide, he was sure that the end of the world had come. The sailor whom the Anabaptist had saved lost no time looking for money, getting drunk, and enjoying the favors of any girls he could find among the ruins. Reproved by Pangloss, he replied that he was a sailor who four times had renounced Christianity in Japan (as required by the Japanese who resented the presence of European traders), and who had only contempt for Pangloss and his universal reason.

While Pangloss reasoned about the cause of the earthquake, the injured Candide pleaded for succor; at last the confident philosopher brought him a little water. On the next day the two found some food and worked to relieve the surviving victims of the earthquake. Pangloss, of course, gave everyone philosophical comfort. He was challenged by a little dark man who charged that it would seem Pangloss did not believe in Original Sin; for if all is for the best, then there could be no fall and punishment. But Pangloss glibly defended his position.

Since three-fourths of Lisbon had been destroyed, the wise men in Portugal, especially the scholars at the University of Coimbra, decided that auto-da-fé was called for if total ruin were to be avoided, and that the spectacle of people ceremoniously burned by slow fire should take place at once. Among the victims was a Biscayan charged with having married the godmother of his godchild, and two Portuguese known to have eaten chicken only after removing the bacon (thus proving that they were Jews and enemies of Christendom). Later Pangloss and Candide were seized and imprisoned, the former guilty of having spoken, the latter of having listened — obviously capital offenses. A week later, each was given a paper mitre and a sanbenito (yellow robe which heretics condemned to the stake were required to wear). Mitre and robe alike were adorned fearsomely with flames and devils. The two marched in procession and heard a morning sermon followed by vocal music. Candide was flogged in time to the music; the Biscayan was burned at the stake; and, contrary to usual procedure, Pangloss was hanged. But on the same day another terrible earthquake occurred.

Little wonder that Candide, reviewing all the things that had happened since he was turned out of the Baron's castle, should wonder what other worlds were like if this one was the best. As he was being flogged and preached to, absolved, and blessed, an old woman appeared. She bade him to take courage and then to follow her.

Commentary

In Chapters 4-6, Voltaire especially attacked intolerance, injustice, and cruelty in the Church as he saw it. Once more he made a tacit plea for the use of reason and the rejection of superstition. He first leveled his critical guns at individual members of the Church who ignored their sacerdotal vows and failed to follow vocation. The social disease which Pangloss caught from Paquette was traced to a "very learned Franciscan" and later to a Jesuit. There are anti-religious satire and a rejection of the Providential theory (that of a benign God who remains concerned with the condition of mankind) in the details relating to the charitable Anabaptist, who continued to be his brother's keeper at the cost of his life. The brute whose life he had saved swam safely to shore.

Primarily it is the account of the auto-da-fé which is most devastating. The term, a Portuguese one, means "act of faith." This was the *Sermo generalis,* an assembly convoked for the purpose of trying and, if deemed necessary, passing sentence on individuals charged with heresy. To the masses, and to many others, the name suggested the very worst horrors of the Inquisition. It is essentially this concept that Voltaire presented in his tale. The author's mockery and irony are evident throughout. Note, for example, his account of the "pathetic sermon followed by some beautiful music" heard by the condemned Biscayan, the two Portuguese, Pangloss — and by Candide, who was flogged in time to the music. Note further Pangloss' earlier discourse with the man familiar with the Inquisition. This incorporates one of Voltaire's objections to the philosophy of optimism; for him it contradicted the doctrine of the Fall of Man.

The Lisbon earthquake and fire took place on November 1, 1755. As many as 30,000 people were killed and the city reduced to ruins. This was the crucial event which led Voltaire to make his two strongest attacks on philosophical optimism, in *Poème sur le désastre de Lisbonne,* written shortly after the disaster occurred, and in *Candide.* The poem, so important as part of the background of the tale, will be discussed later.

Voltaire achieved one of his several climaxes in the story when he had his young hero bewail the fact that he had to witness the hanging of his "dear Pangloss" and the drowning of his "dear Anabaptist, best of men," and to learn that the pearl of young ladies, Madamoiselle Cunégonde, had been disemboweled — all without learning the necessary cause thereof.

CHAPTERS 7-10

CANDIDE AND CUNÉGONDE REUNITED

Summary
The old woman led Candide to a hovel, provided ointment for his wounds, gave him food and drink, and arranged to get for him a suit of clothes and an acceptable bed. Candide found himself overwhelmed by her

charity, and he endeavored to kiss her hand. But it was not *her* hand that he should kiss, he was informed enigmatically. She voiced a short prayer for his well being and promised to return on the next day.

Despite his misfortunes, Candide was able to eat and sleep. In the morning the old woman reappeared with breakfast for him. For the next two days she attended him. Although Candide repeatedly asked her who she was and why she should be so kind to him, the woman would not enlighten him. Toward evening she returned and told him to come with her in silence. She took him to an isolated country house surrounded by gardens and canals. In response to her knock, a little door was opened, and Candide followed her up a hidden staircase and into a gilded boudoir. She then left him. Candide was nonplussed; for a moment he considered that his whole life had been a wicked dream, and that the present moment was a wonderful dream.

Once more the old woman came back, this time assisting into the room a trembling woman, majestic in bearing, who gleamed with precious stones. Her face is veiled, and the old woman commanded Candide to lift the veil. Behold, the strange woman turned out to be his adored Cunégonde. Speechless in their surprise, both swooned and then were revived by the useful old woman, who had the tact to leave them to themselves.

Candide had many questions to ask Cunégonde. Yes, he learned, she had been ravished and wounded, but she obviously had survived the ordeal. Her father, mother, and brother, however, had been killed. Before she would complete her story, she insisted that Candide tell his, and she listened to it most sympathetically.

Cunégonde's story was quite as melodramatic as Candide's. She provided the details of the Bulgarian's attack on the castle of Thunder-ten-tronckh and the slaughter of her father, mother, and brother. She herself had been repeatedly raped and then stabbed with a knife in the side. Candide expressed the hope that he would be allowed to see the scar. "You shall," replied Cunégonde, and then she resumed her story.

A Bulgarian captain had appeared, took compassion on the wounded girl, killed the guilty soldier, had her wounds dressed, and took her to his quarters as prisoner of war. For some time she performed menial work for the captain, who found her to be quite attractive. And Cunégonde conceded that he was not without his attractions but added that he had little philosophy, since he had not been schooled by Doctor Pangloss. Having lost both his money and his taste for the young lady after three months, the captain sold her to an amorous Jew named Don Issachar, a man who traded in Holland and Portugal. But Cunégonde successfully resisted his efforts to win her favors, and to tame her he had brought her to this country house which rivaled the Westphalian castle in splendor.

At Mass one day the Grand Inquisitor himself took much interest in her, and he sent word that he had secret matters to discuss with her. At his palace, when Cunégonde identified herself as a lady of high rank, he reproached her for being in the possession of an Israelite. On the Grand Inquisitor's behalf, Don Issachar was asked to yield her to that high-ranking official. But the Israelite was not without his influence, for he was, among other things, court banker. He refused to comply. The Grand Inquisitor's passion for Cunégonde would not let him give up the attempt to gain her for himself. Finally, Don Issachar agreed that the two men would share her and the house. The Jew was to have her on Monday and Wednesday, his rival to have her on Sunday. The design for living did not make for complete tranquility; but, more important, so far Cunégonde had succeeded in resisting both men, whose love became more ardent for that very reason.

It was to prevent earthquakes and to frighten Don Issachar that the Inquisitor had decided to "celebrate" an auto-de-fé, Cunégonde explained. At that assembly she was an honored guest, and was among those served refreshments between Mass and the executions. She was appalled to witness the burnings, but was utterly horrified to see first the hanging of Pangloss and then the flogging of the naked Candide. She found herself too weak to cry out in protest. One thought possessed her: Doctor Pangloss had deceived her when he had called this the best of all possible worlds.

It was Cunégonde who had instructed the old woman to find her lover and bring him to the house in the wood. She expressed her joy at meeting him again, and the two sat down to supper. But soon Don Issachar arrived. It was Sunday, and he had come to enjoy his rights.

The Jew was in a choleric fit when he found Candide with Cunégonde. He denounced her as a "bitch of a Galilean" who was not satisfied with the love of two men. Drawing out a long dagger, he attacked Candide. Again in danger of losing his life, the usually gentle youth met the attack with his sword and killed his opponent. Cunégonde was terrified: if the law came, both she and her lover would be hanged. Candide replied that, if Pangloss had not been hanged, he would tell them what to do. Had he not been a great philosopher? In the absence of Pangloss, the two consulted the old woman.

As the old woman began to counsel the two, My Lord the Inquisitor arrived; it was an hour after midnight and his turn to visit the fair Cunégonde. He viewed the complete tableau: the flogged Candide, now armed with a sword; the slain Israelite; the frightened Cunégonde. Candide, fully aware of the new danger, hesitated only momentarily and then killed the Inquisitor, tossing his body beside that of the Jew.

Cunégonde knew that she and Candide had no chance to be pardoned; they would be excommunicated. Especially was she surprised that the kindly Candide could have killed one Jew and an Inquisitor in two minutes. Candide could only reply that when a person has been flogged and is in love and is jealous, he is out of his mind.

It was the old woman's turn to speak next. She informed them that there were three Andalusian horses in the stable and Candide should get them for the flight from the Jew's house. She pointed out that Cunégonde had money and jewels to cover the expenses. She herself would ride one of the horses, despite the fact that she had only one buttock. The plan was carried out.

Not long after they had left, the Holy Hermandad (an association founded in Spain with its own police force to track down criminals) came to the house and discovered the two bodies. The body of Don Issachar was tossed on a dump; that of the Grand Inquisitor was buried in a beautiful church. Already Candide, Cunégonde, and the old woman had reached a little town in the Sierra Morena mountains and were resting at an inn.

Cunégonde found that someone had stolen her money and jewels: they were now destitute. The old woman was sure that the thief was a reverend Franciscan father who had occupied the same inn as they had in another village. Candide recalled that Pangloss had often proved to him that the goods of the earth belong to all men. According to this principle, he concluded, the priest should have left them part of the money and jewels.

Again it was the old woman who came up with a plan. Let them sell one of the horses. She will then ride with Cunégonde, and the three will reach Cadiz. And so it was. They arrived to witness the equipping of a fleet and troops which were to be sent to Paraguay to suppress the militant Jesuit Fathers who were accused of inciting one of their tribes to rebel against the Kings of Spain and Portugal. Now Candide was able to put to use his knowledge of military drill, and he so impressed the Spanish general that he was given command of an infantry company. With Cunégonde, the old woman, two valets (for he was now a Captain), and the two valuable horses, he embarked for South America.

During the voyage the philosophy of Doctor Pangloss was the subject of much discussion. Candide was sure that in the New World they would find the one where all is for the best. But Cunégonde, recalling all they had suffered, remained dubious. As for the old woman, she insisted that neither of the lovers had suffered as much as she had—a statement which amused the skeptical Cunégonde. The old woman was then ready to tell her story.

Commentary

The first thing to be noted is the adroit way in which Voltaire effects his transitions to a new episode and how he maintains suspense. The old woman appears like a *deus ex machina* just at the critical moment when Candide had no idea which way to turn. Note further the time that elapsed and Candide's repeated inquiries before the discovery of Cunégonde's identity.

Next, it is apparent the experiences of Cunégonde, in their violence and melodramatic quality, parallel those of Candide and provide counterpoint. In character also the two lovers complement each other. Both continued to revere Doctor Pangloss; and, although Cunégonde was beginning to feel much less sure than Candide, neither completely abandoned the optimistic philosophy inculcated by their mentor. Note that Candide's discovery of Cunégonde parallels his discovery of Pangloss: he had thought that both were dead. With fine irony, Voltaire had Cunégonde say that it pleased Heaven to send the Bulgarians to her father's castle; she still accepted the concept of necessary cause and effect, basic to the optimistic philosophy. The author achieved irony and witty understatement when he put these words in Candide's mouth: "We are going to another universe; no doubt it is in that one that all is well. For it must be admitted that one might groan a little over what happens in the physical and the moral domain in ours." Groan a little — this to describe the reactions of a young man who had endured so much! Clearly life, with all its cruelities and injustice was educating him, but how slowly. But if Cunégonde continued to worship Pangloss and to voice his profound views, she was not so sure as she had been that he was right.

These chapters also carry forward the anti-Church satire. This is obvious enough with reference to My Lord, the Grand Inquisitor, a prominent official of the Church. Thus, it is at a Mass that his illicit passion for Cunégonde first developed. He competed with an Israelite for her favors and even agreed to share her with his rival. Significant also is the fact that one of his two reasons for deciding to "celebrate" an *auto-da-fé* was to frighten the non-Christian Don Issachar. And when the police of the Holy Hermandad found the bodies of the Inquisitor and the Jew, the former was given burial with the full ceremony of the Church, whereas the body of the Jew was thrown on a rubbish heap as if it were the carcass of a dog. Add to all this the fact that, in all probability, a Franciscan priest had robbed Cunégonde of her money and jewels.

The responsibility of the Jesuits for the revolt in Paraguay was, for Voltaire (who never endorsed political revolution) new evidence of injustice within the Church: men of the cloth especially should render unto Caesar the things that are Caesar's. As early as 1605 the Jesuits had succeeded in establishing a kind of *imperium in imperio* in the little South American country and had drilled the natives in the use of arms, although they did not yet control the government. With the powerful assistance of Zabala, governor of Buenos Aires, however, the anti-Jesuit and quasinational party was crushed in 1735. In 1750, Ferdinand VI of Spain ceded

26

to the Portuguese both the district of La Guayra and a territory of some 20,000 square miles east of Uruguay. The Jesuits actively resisted, and it took the combined forces of Spain and Portugal to defeat them. The revolt referred to in *Candide* occurred in 1756 and provides a good example of how topical the tale is in many respects.

CHAPTERS 11-12

THE OLD WOMAN'S STORY

Summary
    The old woman revealed herself to be the daughter of Pope Urban X and the Princess of Palestrina, and until the age of fourteen she had lived in a castle which far exceeded in splendor any German castle. Indeed, her dresses were worth more than all the magnificence of Westphalia. And, of course, she was a peerless beauty, admired by all.

    She had been betrothed to the most handsome sovereign Prince of Massa-Carrara, and the elaborate festivities appropriate for the nuptials were prepared. But just when the marriage was to take place, the Prince was poisoned by his jealous mistress and died in frightful convulsions. Her despairing mother then decided to take the girl to an estate near Gaeta, and with their entourage the two set sail on a galley lavishly appointed. Enroute they were attacked by pirates, and their own soldiers proved to be cowards. All were subjected to appalling indignities. Male and female alike were stripped naked, the pirates showing amazing skill in this process. But if all this was almost unbearable, what followed was worse. The pirates' search of their captives was shockingly thorough as they looked for jewels perhaps hidden somewhere in the bodies of the helpless group. The girl, her mother, the ladies of honor—all were taken as slaves to Morocco. The girl was ravished by the pirate captain, an abominable Negro, who was convinced that he did her great honor. The old woman was content, at this point, merely to stress the heartlessness of the pirates. No need for details, she said, for these are things so common that they are not worth speaking about.

    Slaughter was everywhere when the group arrived in Morocco. The fifty sons of Emperor Muley Ismael had formed fifty factions, which produced fifty civil wars. The carnage extended over the entire empire. One of the black factions, hostile to pirates, seized their stolen treasure, and then fought furiously for possession of the women. The terrified girl saw all the Italian women and her mother torn, cut, and massacred. The pirate captain kept the girl hidden behind him and, with his scimitar, killed all who approached him. Finally the members of both factions were killed, and the girl lay dying on a heap of bodies. Similar scenes took place throughout Morocco; but none of the living failed to say the five daily prayers ordained by Mohammed.

The poor girl managed to crawl away and, reaching an orange tree beside a stream, swooned from sheer fright, exhaustion, despair, and hunger. For some time she was unconscious, languishing between life and death. Then, becoming aware that someone was pressing her body, she awoke to see an attractive looking white man, who was bewailing the fact that he had been emasculated. Astounded and happy to hear her native language spoken, if surprised at the words she heard, the girl endeavored to console the stranger by telling him that there are worse misfortunes than that which he endured. Briefly she recounted the horrors she had experienced, and then she fainted. The man took her to a nearby house, had her put to bed, waited on her, and in his turn sought to console her. He was overwhelmed by her beauty and told her that never before had he so regretted his state of emasculation. Then he told his story.

He had been born in Naples and became one of the 3,000 boys who, every year, were emasculated. Some died as a result, but others went on to become beautiful singers or even to govern states. He had survived to become a musician in the Chapel of My Lady the Princess of Palestrina — his young audience's mother! And the two then knew that in early childhood they had been reared together.

The two exchanged reports of their experiences. The honest eunuch, as Voltaire called him, told her that he had been sent to the King of Morocco to conclude a treaty involving munitions, arms, and ships "to help exterminate the trade of the other Christian countries." His mission had been concluded; he now planned to take her back to Italy. Again he groaned over the fact that he was a eunuch.

The "honest" eunuch took her instead to Algiers and sold her to the Dey (governor, ruler or pasha). There a terrible plague, described by the old woman as being worse than an earthquake, broke out. She became one of its victims. She, the daughter of a pope, a girl who, at the age of fifteen had endured poverty, slavery, and repeated rape; who had seen her mother cut into quarters — she was now dying of the plague in Algiers. But she did live, although the eunuch, the Dey, and nearly all the ladies of the seraglio perished. She was sold to a merchant who brought her to Tunis, and then sold successively at Tripoli, Alexandria, Smyrna, and Constantinople. Finally, she was bought by the Aga of the Janizaries (a high officer of the Turkish Sultan's guards), whose immediate commission was to defend the city of Azov against the Russians. The gallant Aga took his entire seraglio with him.

The slaughter on Turkish and Russian sides alike was very great, and Azov was put to fire and sword, neither age nor sex being spared. Only the fort, where the members of the seraglio were lodged, protected by two eunuchs and twenty Janizaries, remained. The Russians sought to starve them out; and the determined but starving Janizaries ate the two eunuchs rather than surrender. A few days later they were about to eat the women. But a pious, compassionate imam (Mohammedan priest) persuaded them to restrain themselves and to cut off only one buttock from each of the ladies. The horrible operation was performed, just before the Russians arrived in flat-bottomed boats and slaughtered the Janizaries. Fortunately, there were French surgeons available, and one of them took care of the ladies. Not only did he cure them but he was most consoling: it was a law of war for them to be so treated.

The girl and her companions were sent to Moscow, where she was given as a slave to a Boyar (Russian nobleman), who made her his gardener and saw to it that she was beaten daily. But the Boyar himself was broken on the wheel with some other noblemen for some petty offense, and the girl was able to escape across the whole of Russia. She traveled far in Western Europe, working as a servant in various cities, including Rotterdam. Once most beautiful, she had indeed grown old in misery. Many times she had wanted to end her life, but she still loved it. For this clinging to life is one of the evidences of man's stupidity. Man caresses the serpent that devours life until it has eaten up his heart. Among the very few who loathed their lives and had the courage to commit suicide, she cited the case of the German professor Robeck, author of dissertations on the futility of life, who drowned himself in 1739 at the age of sixty-seven.

The old woman had made her point. Most things are relative. Cunégonde, a baron's daughter, had indeed suffered much. But evil pervades the world, and others have suffered, often to a far greater extent. After all, how many have been deprived of a buttock? Her concluding advice is that one should get what enjoyment he can and learn from others in life's journey. Nowhere will Cunégonde find a person who has not often cursed his life and contemplated suicide.

Commentary

The old woman's story is one of the several examples of digression so characteristic of the romantic tale of adventure, but it provides the author with new opportunity to attack the Leibnitzian optimistic philosophy as well as to shoot his barbs of satire at other targets. The prime evidence of pervading evil in this section of *Candide* is the carnage of warfare. Voltaire had already established his strong views on war in the account of the Bulgarian-Abarian conflict; now he reinforced them; the conflict depicted here was far more brutal than that of Western Europe. The girl arrived in Morocco to find it swimming in blood as brother fought brother in the worst kind of war, a civil one. The anti-war satire was carried forward in the account of the conflict between the Turks and the Russians with its attendant horrors, especially those visited upon the helpless civilians.

Voltaire did not relent in his running battle against religion and the Church. The old woman, we learn, turned out to be the illegitimate daugher of a pope. Of great interest is a note which first appeared in an 1829 edition of *Candide,* one which has been attributed to Voltaire himself, despite the late date of publication: "Note the author's extreme discretion! So far there has been no pope named Urban X; he is afraid to ascribe a bastard daughter to a known pope. What circumspection! What delicacy of conscience." If these are not Voltaire's words, they at least are quite Voltairian and provide a good example of his sardonic wit.

Voltaire scored a hit again, this time against warring popes who maintained armies when he described the soldiers who were expected to defend the ladies as being more cowardly than the Pope's soldiers.

Yet one must not conclude that, in the realm of religious satire, Voltaire, the man reared in the Church and educated by Jesuits, attacked only Catholicism. His satire was more general when he told how the eunuch had been sent on a mission to Morocco to conclude a treaty for exterminating the trade with other Christians: people who professed to adore the Prince of Peace violently opposed each other. And it is religion in general, not merely Christianity, in which Voltaire found fatal shortcomings. This is made clear when he told how the devout Mohammedans, amid the violence of warfare, never failed to say the five prayers daily as prescribed by their faith. It is further emphasized in the account of the "pious, compassionate" holy man who persuaded the starving Janizaries to slice off one buttock from each of the ladies of the Aga's seraglio rather than to kill them: "Heaven will be pleased with you for so charitable an action."

As before, Voltaire, the man whose pronounced views did so much to prepare the way for the overthrow of the *ancien régime,* directed his satire also against the illogical appeal to custom and the law to justify man's inhumanity to man. With what irony did he have the fifteen-year old girl learn that the pirates, in carrying out the indecent search of the ladies, were only following "a custom established from time immemorial among civilized nations that roam the seas"—a custom followed by My Lords the Knights of Malta. And it is the French surgeon, a man of apparent good will, who assured his patients that the sort of atrocity they had endured was common enough: it was the law of war. It will be observed that, in the reference to the Knights of Malta, Voltaire works in anti-religious satire as well.

Finally, in the last of these two chapters, the author introduced the theme of despair, one often discussed among the deists and children of the Enlightenment. Injustice, intolerance, and the avariciousness of mankind caused so much of the evil which spread throughout the world; evil derived also from nature itself, which, to borrow the words of the Victorian Alfred Lord Tennyson, could be red in tooth and claw. Death, it would logically seem, would be embraced as a welcome relief by any intelligent person. Thus ran the argument. The old woman stated that, in the course of her trying life, she had seen a prodigious number of people who loathed their existence, but only twelve who had the courage to end it. Since the Church holds despair to be an unforgivable sin—the rejection of the re ligious virtue hope—one can see the extent to which Voltaire went in his rejection of orthodoxy. Nor did Christian stoicism provide an answer for him.

CHAPTERS 13-16

ADVENTURES IN BUENOS AIRES, PARAGUAY, AND THE LAND OF THE OREILLONS

Summary

The old woman had advised Cunégonde to get the passengers to tell her their adventures. The latter did so and found that the pessimistic argument was correct. Candide expressed regret that Pangloss was not present to voice his optimistic philosophy and that he would now offer the learned doctor a few objections.

The vessel landed at Buenos Aires, where Cunégonde, Captain Candide, and the old woman called on the proud, often overbearing governor Don Fernando d'Ibarra y Figueroa y Mascarenes y Lampourdos y Souza. His chief passion was women. Struck by the beauty of Cunégonde, he asked her if she were married to Candide. And Candide, alarmed by what seemed to be implied, stated that the Madamoiselle was engaged to him and implored His Excellency to perform their wedding ceremony. In response, the insolent Governor ordered Candide to go pass his company in review. He then announced that on the next day he would marry Cunégonde. The young lady asked for a few moments to consult the old woman before making up her mind.

The old woman's advice was practical enough: the high born Cunégonde now was destitute; she could retrieve her fortune by becoming the wife of the greatest lord in South America. Was it for Cunégonde, the old woman asked, to pride herself on an invincible fidelity, when the many misfortunes she had experienced conferred rights? The old woman herself would have had no scruple about marrying My Lord Governor.

While the woman spoke, a small vessel entered the port, bringing an alcaide (municipal officer) and some alguazils (police officers). From them it was learned that a Franciscan father indeed had stolen Cunégonde's money and jewels. When he tried to sell some jewels, the jeweler recognized them as belonging to the Grand Inquisitor. Before he was hanged the culprit confessed. The flight of Cunégonde and Candide was known to the town officials, who had then followed them to Cádiz and on to Buenos Aires. When the old woman learned that her companions were being sought by Spanish police, she consoled the young lady: she was not guilty of murder, and she now would be protected by His Lordship. The old woman sought out Candide and urged him to flee. So again the callow youth was to be parted from the incomparable Cunégonde. Where could he go?

We now learn that Candide had brought with him from Spain as his valet one Cacambo, a man of mixed blood and wide experience. In fact, he had been at various times a choirboy, sacristan, monk, merchant's agent, soldier, and lackey. He was loyal and devoted to Candide. When he learned of his master's plight, he quickly saddled the two Andalusian horses and urged Candide to run for it. Candide shed appropriate tears for Cunégonde, whom he had expected to marry immediately. But Cacambo urged him not to worry about her: women were never helpless; God looked after them. So Candide placed himself in the hands of his servant, who told him that, sent to fight the Jesuits, they would instead join the warring Fathers. The Jesuits, he was sure, would welcome a captain who could drill Bulgarian style, and Candide would prosper. The youth learned that Cacambo had been in Paraguay previously; he had been a servant in the College of the Assumption, and he was quite familiar with the Jesuits' government, which he described as most admirable; in truth he knew nothing so divine as the Fathers!

At the first barrier, the two sought an audience with My Lord the Commandant. Candide and his servant were permitted to appear before him only after having been disarmed and their horses seized. Since Candide proved to be a German, not a Spaniard, the Jesuit leader, who had been at parade following Mass, deigned to meet him in a splendid, ornate arbor, where an excellent breakfast served in golden vessels had been prepared.

The Reverend Father Commander, a very proud young man, saw to it that the two were given back their arms and horses. While Cacambo left to feed the horses, Candide sat down at the table, after first having kissed the hem of the Commander's robe. The Jesuit, questioning Candide in German, learned that his guest was from Westphalia and had been born in the castle of Thunder-ten-tronck. There follows another one of those surprising discoveries so typical of the tale: the Commander revealed himself as the brother of the fair Cunégonde—the man who, in Candide's words, had been killed by the Bulgarians. How happy Pangloss would have been, had he not been hanged, exclaimed the naive Candide. As for the Commander, he thanked God and St. Ignatius a thousand times.

Candide next informed the Commander that his sister lived and was in good health, that she was with the Governor of Buenos Aires, and that he (Candide) had come to make war against the Jesuits in Paraguay. Germans as they were, the two remained long at the table, the Jesuit Baron especially talking at length, as he recalled the day when he saw his mother and father killed and his sister raped. Assuming that he had been killed, the Bulgarians had placed his body in a cart along with those of other victims to be taken for burial. A Jesuit discovered that he still lived and rescued him and his fortunes then turned for the better.

Candide will have remembered, the Commander continued, that he was very pretty. As a result of his physical endowments, the Superior had become very fond of him. He was made a novice and later sent to Rome. Ultimately he was among the young German Catholic recruits to be sent to Paraguay. In the new country his advancement was rapid. He became a subdeacon and a lieutenant and finally a colonel and a priest. The Spanish troops, he assured Candide, would be soundly beaten and excommunicated.

The Baron never tired of embracing Candide, whom he called his brother and savior. Perhaps, he said, they could enter Buenos Aires as conquerors and be reunited with Cunégonde. Nothing would have pleased Candide more, and he then revealed the fact that he expected to marry the Baron's sister. Now the Baron, who had been so effusive toward Candide, became enraged, and he denounced the hapless youth as an insolent wretch. How could Candide have had the impudence to marry *his* sister with seventy-two divisions on her coat-of-arms! The petrified young man endeavored to reason with the Jesuit Baron, telling how he had rescued her from a Jew and the Grand Inquisitor and adding that Doctor Pangloss had always told him that men are equal. He concluded firmly that he intended to marry Cunégonde.

The Baron could not restrain himself. He struck Candide on the face with the flat of his sword, and the youth, drawing his own weapon, paid back the blow with a thrust to the hilt into the Jesuit's body. Appalled that he again had been placed in a position where he was impelled to perform a violent act, Candide bewailed his lot: he, the kindest man in the world, had now killed three men, two of them priests.

Standing at the door of the arbor, Cacambo had observed all this. He came running to his master's side and told him that they must sell their lives dearly. He remained his calm self; after all, he had seen much violence before. Cacambo put the robe of the Jesuit Baron on Candide, gave him the dead man's head gear, and had him mount one of the horses. As they dashed away the clever servant cried out: "Make way, make way for the Reverend Father Colonel!"

The two rode safely beyond the barriers which had been erected for the defense of Paraguay. Cacambo had taken care to bring along provisions and, after riding deep into the unknown country, the two dismounted. Beginning to eat some of the food, Cacambo urged his master to do likewise. But Candide exclaimed that he could not be expected to eat ham since he had just killed the son of My Lord the first Baron and now knew that he would never see Cunégonde again. He was sure that remorse and despair were his lot for the rest of his days. And what, he asked, will the

Journal de Trévoux say? (The reference is to the Jesuit publication which was founded in 1701.) But nevertheless he did eat.

Hearing some cries uttered by young women, the two jumped to their feet in alarm. The sound, they discovered, came from two naked girls who were pursued by monkeys that bit at them as they ran. Candide, moved by compassion, killed both animals with his double-barreled Spanish gun. God be praised, he said to Cacambo; this good deed would make up for the sin of killing an Inquisitor, a Jew, and the Jesuit Baron. And perhaps this action would win them advantages in this strange country. But the girls did not rush forward to thank their rescuer; instead they wept and tenderly embraced the two dead monkeys. "I was not expecting such goodness of soul," said Candide, and then he was informed that he had killed the girls' lovers. He was incredulous, but once more Cacambo enlightened him: after all monkeys were one-quarter men. Why should it be strange that in some countries the ladies became emotionally attached to monkeys? Then Candide recalled that Pangloss had told him of such unions, but he had believed that all he had been told belonged to the realm of fable. As Cacambo remarked, now he knew better.

The two next retired into the woods, where they ate and slept. They could not move when they awoke, for during the night the native Oreillons had bound them with ropes of bark. Fifty naked Oreillons, armed with arrows, stone clubs, and hatchets, surrounded them. Nearby other natives attended a great caldron of boiling water, while still others prepared spits. All shouted that they would be avenged by eating a Jesuit. Cacambo blamed the girls for their sad plight. Candide, looking at the caldron and spits, knew that they were about to be roasted or boiled; and he wondered what Doctor Pangloss would have said if he saw what the pure state of nature was like.

Cacambo, as we have seen, never lost his head. He consoled his master, saying that he knew a bit of the native's language and would talk with them. And so he did, most reasonably. He argued with the Oreillons that a Jesuit should be devoured, for national law taught us to kill our neighbors, and all people behave accordingly. But, he continued, the natives would not want to eat their friends. He then convinced them that they should verify the facts before deciding to treat him and Candide as enemies. And the facts were verified, whereupon Candide and his servant were treated most hospitably. At last the Oreillons conducted the two to the border of their country, shouting joyfully: "He's not a Jesuit!" Candide wondering about this latest experience, decided that the pure state of nature must be good, since his life had been spared, once his captors learned that he was not a Jesuit.

Commentary

Chapters 13-16 are particularly interesting because in them Voltaire described two Utopian states of sorts. It has been argued that life at the castle in Westphalia was Utopian for Candide prior to the difficulty which led to his expulsion. But the Utopias in this section are more easily identified as such. The first is the Jesuit Utopia in Paraguay, where the Fathers had established a theocratic tyranny. One might very well call it a counter-Utopia, because it was an ideal state only if one were a Jesuit in the country. It was Cacambo who, not without irony, first described the Utopia in glowing terms: "It is an admirable thing, this government. *Los Padres* (the Fathers) have everything and the people nothing; it is a masterpiece of reason and justice." The splendor in which the Jesuits of Paraguay lived was well illustrated by the description of the Commandant's arbor with its colonnade in green and gold marble. And it will be recalled that Candide was served an excellent breakfast prepared in vessels of gold, whereas the native Paraguayans ate corn in wooden bowls out in the open fields under the blazing sun. Yes, for *Los Padres,* life was indeed Utopian as long as the theocratic government survived.

The second Utopia in this section is that of the Oreillons, who existed in a pure state of nature, uncontaminated by man-made Western civilization; Jesuit Paraguay was beyond the borders of their land. All this relates to the concept of the Noble Savage which became increasingly popular in the latter half of the eighteenth century. The idea was that nature itself was benign and good; let man live in a state of pure nature and he in turn will be good. Pangloss had embraced this philosophy of primitivism, as we learn from Candide. The name *Oreillons* derives from the Spanish *Orejones,* which indicates "pierced ears" or "big ears." Voltaire remained ironical in his account of these Utopians. Understandably Candide began to question all that had been taught him about "natural" man when it appeared that Oreillons were going to boil or roast him. But, once his life was spared because he was not a Jesuit, he was no longer doubtful. The obvious conclusion is that the primitive people are no better nor no worse than so-called civilized people. Both are capable of great cruelty.

To be sure Voltaire did not lose any opportunity for anti-religious satire. Warring churchmen especially were his target here. It was a nice touch for him to report that the Jesuit Commandant had been to Mass and then had hurried to the parade ground. The intelligence that the practical, ingenious Cacambo had been successively a choirboy, sacristan, and monk, as well as merchant's agent, soldier, and lackey has its place in carrying forward the satire. And in Chapter 13, we learn that a Franciscan in truth had stolen Cunégonde's money and jewels and was hanged when the jewels were recognized as having belonged to another Churchman, the Grand Inquisitor. Related to all this is Voltaire's rejection of the Providential theory, that of a benign Deity who is constantly concerned with the lot of mankind. This is implicit in Cacambo's remark that Cunégonde would be safe: women are never helpless, for God looks after them. Recall all that had happened to Cunégonde since the Bulgarian attack on her father's castle. Finally, when Cacambo was made to say that it is natural for one to kill his enemies, Voltaire underscored his belief that so many people give only lip service to the religion they profess.

Voltaire once more found the opportunity to satirize wittily inordinate pride and vanity. Note the pretentious list of names used by the Governor of Buenos Aires, who never dreamed that Cunégonde or any woman would reject his offer of marriage. He spoke to his men "with the noblest disdain, his nose in the air, his voice raised pitilessly." Add to this the Jesuit Baron's reaction to Candide's announcement that he expected to marry the aristocratic Cunégonde — he, a commoner and she a Baron's daughter with seventy-two quarterings to the family coat of arms!

Personal satire finds a place in these chapters. It will be remembered that, in the person of the original Baron in Westphalia, Voltaire was poking fun at Frederick the Great. And we were told that the son, whom we now have met as the Jesuit Commandant, was much like his father. Therefore, the portrait of that son in Chapter 15 again includes satire of the Prussian King. This is true not only with reference to a preoccupation with military activities, especially drill and parades, but with reference to the alleged moral character of Frederick. The Jesuit Baron told Candide that he had been a "pretty" youth whom the Superior of the Jesuit house found most attractive and who advanced him accordingly. And when he learned the identity of Candide, his words and actions were those one would expect a man to reserve for a woman whom he adored; he never tired of embracing Candide.

The episode involving the monkeys has its place in the realm of satire. It may well be said that Voltaire was pointing up the bestiality in mankind. According to Cacambo, monkeys are one-fourth human. Voltaire apparently had in mind the traditional view of man, who on the hierarchical scale occupied a place equidistant between that of the beast (representing the rejection of reason) and that of the angel (representing pure reason). If this be true, then the love of the young ladies for the monkeys could represent man's rejection of reason and his descent on the hierarchical scale.

Last, Voltaire's account here makes it only too clear that he found evil essentially unavoidable. The basically good, well-meaning Candide found it necessary again to kill a man, and another churchman at that. He thus was responsible for the death of three men, this innocent who had been schooled to believe that all is for the best in this best of all possible worlds.

CHAPTERS 17-18

CANDIDE IN THE COUNTRY OF ELDORADO

Summary
    At the frontiers of the Oreillon country, Cacambo told Candide that
this hemisphere was no better than the other and that they ought to go back
to Europe. Candide, rudely awakened regarding the world he knew in
Western Europe, had been sure that the New World would be that best of
all possible ones. But he replied that return would be impossible: in Westphalia the war continued; in Portugal he would be burned at the stake. Yet
if they remained in South America, he continued, they would risk being
put on the spit and roasted. The one imponderable was that he could not
leave this part of the world where Cunégonde lived.

    Cacambo proposed that they go to Cayenne, where they would find
Frenchmen who might help them and take pity on them. They started out
on the arduous journey, crossing mountains and rivers and meeting bri-
gands and savages. Their horses died of fatigue, and for a month they lived
on wild fruits. At last they came to a little river bordered with coconut
trees, which provided them with food. Cacambo spotted an empty canoe
on the beach and suggested that the two fill it with coconuts and then drift
with the current. A river, he explained, always led to some inhabited spot.
Candide agreed to this plan. The trip was not without its hazards, and at
last their canoe was smashed on the reefs. With difficulty they continued
afoot, finally coming to a vast open country bordered by inaccessible
mountains. On the roads were splendidly ornate carriages in which were
men and women of singular attractiveness and which were drawn rapidly
by big red sheep.

    As he surveyed the scene Candide concluded that this strange country
was even better than Westphalia. Children dressed in gold brocade were
playing quoits. And the quoits were made of gold, emeralds, and rubies
which would have been an ornament to a mogul's throne. Cacambo was
sure that the children were sons of the King. When the village schoolmaster called to the children, Candide was no less sure that he was the tutor
of the royal family. The children went from their game to the school, leaving the priceless quoits lying on the ground, whereupon Candide picked
them up and ran to the tutor with them. He made the tutor understand by
means of signs that the quoits had been forgotten. But the tutor, smiling,
merely threw them to the ground and walked away. Candide and Cacambo
did not fail to pick them up. Both were surprised that these "King's children" should have been reared to despise gold and jewels.

    They next approached the first house in the village and found a crowd
of people at the door, heard pleasant music, and enjoyed the odor of

cooking. Cacambo discovered that the people spoke his native tongue, Peruvian. When the two entered what they now took to be an inn, he served as interpreter.

Two boys and four girls dressed in cloth of gold invited them to sit down at the host's table, and they were served a sumptuous dinner of many strange and rare dishes. Most of the guests were merchants and coachmen. All were extremely polite and tactfully asked many questions. When the dinner was over, Cacambo and Candide thought that they should pay their bill for the dinner. So Cacambo threw on the host's table two of the golden quoits, at the sight of which the host and hostess laughted heartily.

"We can readily see that you are foreigners," said the host, and he asked their pardon for having laughed. He referred to the golden quoits as the "pebbles of our highways," and explained that in this country payment was not required since the government paid for the upkeep of all hostelries. He concluded by apologizing for what he called a bad meal and assured the two that they would fare better elsewhere.

Candide listened in amazement to Cacambo's translation of the host's remarks. Both he and his companion were sure that at last they had found the one country where indeed all was best. Candide now admitted that, whatever Doctor Pangloss had said, things were really pretty bad in Westphalia.

In order that Cacambo might satisfy his curiosity about the country, the friendly host took him to see an elderly retired courtier. This man lived in a modest home, one with only a silver door and gold paneling in the apartments, which were adorned only with rubies and emeralds. He received the two visitors on a sofa stuffed with humming bird feathers, served them drinks in diamond vases, and proceeded to tell them about himself and the kingdom. They learned that their host was one hundred and seventy-two years old and that his father had taught him the history of the country. That country had been the ancient kingdom of the Incas, who imprudently had left it to conquer part of the world and were finally destroyed by the Spaniards. But the wiser Incan Prince remained in this country, and, with popular consent, ruled that no others should leave it, thus their innocence and happiness were preserved. The Spaniards had learned something about the country, which they call Eldorado. And an Englishman named Walter Raleigh nearly reached it a hundred years ago, but the inaccessible rocks and precipices protected the land, so that the inhabitants were sheltered from the rapacity of Europeans.

Candide and Cacambo learned a great deal about the form of government, women, public spectacles, and arts. Then the youth asked if the Eldoradoans had a religion. To be sure they had, and they worshipped the only God, not two or three. No, they did not pray to him because they did not have to; they had all they wanted, but they did sing hymns of thanksgiving. Nor was there a separate priesthood; all were priests. They would have been crazy to have monks "to teach, to dispute, to govern, to intrigue, and to have people burned for not being of their opinion." Candide was in ecstasy, for he had heard of nothing like this in Westphalia or elsewhere in Europe. Travel was indeed enlightening.

At last the good old man ordered a carriage drawn by six sheep, gave the travelers twelve servants, and directed them to visit the King, who would welcome them. In only four hours Candide and his valet arrived at the palace, the most remarkable edifice imaginable. They were received by twenty beautiful girls and accorded every courtesy. As they were being conducted to the throne room, they learned that they were not expected to grovel or in other ways demean themselves before His Majesty. The custom was to embrace him and kiss him on both cheeks. They were most graciously received, invited to supper, and conducted about part of the town with its great squares paved with precious stones. To his surprise, Candide learned that neither law courts nor prisons were needed for these happy, law-abiding people. What most impressed him, however, was the Palace of Sciences with its many instruments for mathematics and physics. Later, the royal supper completed the wonderful experiences of the day. What amazed Candide was the King's witty conversation.

For a month the two remained in Eldorado, but Candide pined for his lovely Cunégonde, and he was sure that Cacambo must have a lady love in Europe. Why, he asked, should they not take their twelve sheep laden with the "pebbles" of Eldorado and return? Wealthy as they would be, they would fear no one, and they could recover Mademoiselle Cunégonde easily. Cacambo agreed. But the King warned them that they were being foolish: when a person is reasonably well off, he should not grow restless. Yet he conceded that he had no right to detain foreigners; such an action would be tyrannical, for all men are free. To help them on the arduous journey out of Eldorado he ordered the necessary supplies and equipment that would get them beyond the mountains. They would be accompanied to the borders of the country. When Cacambo asked that they be given "a few sheep loaded with victuals, pebbles, and some of the country's mud," the King, greatly amused, granted the request, although he declared that he could not understand the European's obsession for the yellow mud. So the travelers were able to leave this fabulous land, riding on two big red sheep and leading a pack of twenty others laden in the manner requested. Candide was content. Now he had enough wealth to ransom Cunégonde. First he and Cacambo would head for Cayenne and then see what kingdom they could buy.

Commentary

Voltaire learned of the fabled land of Eldorado by reading Sir Walter Raleigh's account in *The Discoverie of the Large and Rich and Beautiful*

Empire of Guiana, first published in 1595. If he did not read the account in English, he could have found it available in the *Voyage de Francois Corréal aux Indes Occidentales,* Volume II (Paris, 1722). Raleigh described a fabulous country, one possessing towering mountains and immense treasures, so that the name came to be used metaphorically of any place where wealth could be acquired rapidly. In his Eldorado, also, the ruling princes were descended from the once-powerful Incas, famed for their magnificent civilization. Various travel books may well have influenced Voltaire as well. And no one who wrote of a Utopia could avoid owing a debt to Sir Thomas More, the author of the first modern one. In More's work he could have found a completely happy people who, without Divine Revelation, recognized one God to whom they sang hymns of adoration, but did not presume to petition when they had more than they needed to satisfy their wants — a people who considered gold and precious gems to be mere baubles for children to play with. The benign philosopher-ruler also flourished in More's Utopia, wherein the well-planned cities and impressive public buildings and works bore testimony to an enlightened government. But More's account of the fabled land is remarkably circumstantial. One learns the width of streets and comparable details. Thus, like Swift in *Gulliver's Travels,* he secures the willing suspension of disbelief on the reader's part through verisimilitude. The landscape of Voltaire's Eldorado, like that of Milton's Hell, remains most impressive but rather indefinite most of the time — and that is another way in which a reader, for the time being, is led to accept it as believable; it is left to him to fill in the details imaginatively.

Eldorado is Voltaire's ideal world, one that he knew could never exist, but which provided him with the means to point out grievous shortcomings of the real world — how very far short of perfection it really was; and this was another way in which he attacked the doctrine of philosophic optimism. Of course, it may well be argued that, given a land rich enough that all have plenty, most people would be Utopians devoid of rapacity. For if indeed avarice is the root of all evil, as Chaucer's Pardoner insisted, there existed no such root in Voltaire's Utopia and therefore none of the evils found elsewhere. So it would seem that the superior civilization of the Eldoradoans does not really redound to their credit: they simply have been incredibly lucky, but there is more to it than this. Voltaire used his Utopia to provide emphatic contrast with what Candide had experienced elsewhere — in Westphalia, where life once seemed ideal to the youth, thanks especially to Pangloss' arguments; elsewhere in Europe, where he experienced the horrors of war, a devastating earthquake and the terrifying work of the Inquisition in Portugal; and in South America, where he had witnessed more warfare and tyranny. In short, intolerance, rapine, utter cruelty everywhere, to say nothing of what he learned from the story of the old woman. The experiences in Eldorado also provided an illuminating contrast with what Candide will experience after leaving the country. Perhaps the most significant point which Voltaire wished to make was that the

Utopians were Utopians primarily not because they occupied a land of plenty but because they were dedicated to Right Reason at all levels of private and public activity.

It is true that the lowliest subject enjoyed the benefits of what seemed to be the ideal Welfare State. Merchants and coachmen, others of even lowlier status, were looked after by an enlightened government. But the point is that all were wise enough to work and to be satisfied with their lot and, unlike their Incan ancestors, remain in Eldorado and not attempt the conquest of other lands. To look forward to the most important lesson Candide was to learn from his varied, often harrowing, experiences, the Eldoradoans had learned to cultivate their gardens; thus they lived in comfort and safety. Practically all critics find in Voltaire's creation of an ideal society all the virtues of the perfect state: belief in one god, tolerance, wisdom, liberty, happiness, an enlightened government. As Mr. William F. Bottiglia has pointed out (*Voltaire's Candide: Analysis of a Classic,* Vol. VII of *Studies on Voltaire and the Eighteenth Century,* ed. Theodore Besterman, 1959), "the key trait is not tolerance as the ground of liberty but deism as the ground of an unanimously cultivated social and practical morality which produces all the other traits." For Voltaire deism was the true faith. It was based on fundamental, universal principles with which God had endowed all men and which were lastingly valid. When he had the wise old man expound this belief to Candide and Cacambo, Voltaire was indicting institutional religion, just as his description of the Eldoradoan government was a criticism of governmental systems elsewhere.

Among the points of interest in this section is personal satire. It has been reasonably argued that the pebbles, at one level, represent the sums of money that Voltaire had received from Frederick the Great during his stay in Prussia. And, most ingeniously, it has been argued that the big red sheep, which as we shall see later Candide loses, represented Frederick's literary works bound in sheepskin which Voltaire was forced to relinquish to the officials at the time of the distressing Frankfort incident.

The host, the old man, and the King represent respectively the commoner who is an intelligent conformer, the intellectual leader or *philosophe,* and the statesman. One may reasonably assume that each in turn represents the voice of Voltaire expressing earnest opinions.

Most ironic is the fact that the now happy Candide and Cacambo resolved to be happy no longer. Five reasons have been advanced for their determination to leave Eldorado: (1) the country provided neither end nor consummation; (2) Candide's vanity manifested by his desire to impress others with an account of his experiences; (3) Candide's restlessness—his continuing inability to be content to "cultivate his garden"; (4) his desire for power and superiority to be purchased with the wealth he would bring along; (5) his deep love for Cunégonde. The last reason, strictly in the romantic tradition, is the only really valid one. Obviously Candide's education was incomplete; he remained sufficiently callow and was not ready to assume the status of a Utopian.

CHAPTER 19

CANDIDE IN SURINAM

Summary
Heartened by the thought that they were now wealthy, Candide and Cacambo found the first day of their journey pleasant. The love-sick youth wrote Cunégonde's name on the trees. But then new difficulties arose. On the second day two sheep, laden with treasure, were lost in a bog; two others died of fatigue a few days later. After days of travel, just two sheep were left. Candide pointed the moral: the riches of the world are perishable; only virtue and the joy of seeing Cunégonde again lasted. Cacambo agreed, but added that they still had the two sheep and much wealth. And in the distance was the Dutch possession, the town of Surinam. Surely their happiness was about to begin.

Near the town they saw a Negro in rags lying on the ground. His left leg and right hand were missing. Candide addressed him in Dutch and was told that he was waiting for his master, Mynheer Vanderdendur. Further, Candide learned that this same master had punished the Negro by maiming him as he did all servants or slaves who offended him. The Negro recalled that his mother, when she sold him into slavery, assured him that he was making his parents' fortune. So far from doing so, he continued, he had only helped to increase his Dutch master's fortune. Dogs, monkeys and parrots had a happier lot than the slaves. The Dutch "fetishes," as he called them, converted him to Christianity, assuring him every Sunday that white and black alike were the children of Adam. "You must admit that no one could treat his relatives more horribly," the Negro concluded.

Candide invoked the name of Pangloss and declared that he must renounce optimism, which he now saw as "a mania for insisting that everything is all right, when everything is going wrong." The sight of the maimed Negro made him weep.

In Surinam, they first asked a Spanish captain if any ship in the harbor could be sent to Buenos Aires. The captain offered to give them passage for a fair price, and a meeting at an inn was arranged. At that meeting Candide, with his free and open disposition, told the captain all that had happened to him. When the captain learned that the youth wanted to rescue Cunégonde, he declared that he would never take Candide to Buenos Aires because if he did both would be hanged since the lady was the Governor's favorite. Candide, crushed by this decision, drew Cacambo aside and instructed him to go to Buenos Aires with gold and jewels and to pay what price he must for the release of Cunégonde. Candide himself would take another ship to the free state of Venice, where he would have no fear of Bulgars, Abars, Jews, or Inquisitors. Although grieved at the thought of leaving his master, Cacambo agreed to the plan. "A fine man, that Cacambo," wrote Voltaire.

A master of a large ship who introduced himself to Candide turned out to be Mynheer Vanderdendur. He agreed to take the youth to Italy for 10,000 piasters, but when Candide readily agreed to pay that amount, the Hollander successively raised the price to 30,000, aware as he was that Candide's sheep must be laden with immense treasures. Candide paid the fare in advance. The two sheep were put aboard, and the young man followed in a small boat to join the ship in the harbor. But the unscrupulous captain set sail without him. "Alas!" cried Candide. "That's a trick worthy of the Old World!" The loser of enough to enrich twenty monarchs, he disconsolately turned back to shore.

The distraught Candide went to see a Dutch judge to seek redress. In his excitement he pounded loudly on the judge's door and shouted. So the judge promptly fined him 10,000 piasters before listening to him and promising to investigate the case when the captain returned. The judge then charged Candide another 10,000 piasters for expenses. For the youth this was the last straw; he had been victimized by both the captain and the judge. The wickedness of man was now only too apparent to him. Finally, he managed to secure passage on a French ship headed for Bordeaux. And he announced that he would pay the fare and provide sustenance and money to any truly unfortunate man, one most disgusted with his lot in Surinam. Among the great numbers who applied, Candide selected twenty, assembled them in an inn, and had each relate his story, assuring them that he would choose the one most deserving pity. As he listened, he recalled what the old woman had told him on the way to Buenos Aires, and he thought much of Pangloss, whose system he now found to be suspect. He was sure that if indeed all goes well, it was only in Eldorado.

Candide selected a poor, long-suffering elderly scholar, who, among other things, had been persecuted because the preachers of Surinam believed him to be a Socinian, whose doctrine had been condemned by the Inquisition in 1559 since it rejected several orthodox tenets, notably the divinity of Christ, the Trinity, and eternal punishment.

Commentary

In this chapter Voltaire continued his savage satirical attack upon philosophic optimism, denying that public disasters and individual tribulations were no more than part of a cosmic plan from which good ultimately emerged. Although Candide tried desperately to cling to the faith Doctor Pangloss had taught him, he found the effort to be increasingly difficult. After all, he had been robbed by the rascally captain and then victimized by the judge who represented law and order in the land. But the fact that Candide sought legal redress pointed to the conclusion that Voltaire did not seek to excuse the world's evils and that he believed man should fight to prevent it.

The plight of the Negro underscores cruelty at the personal level once more. And the fact that the slave had been converted to Christianity, his master's faith, provided another example of Voltairian irony—Christianity, the religion which teaches love of one's fellow man and stresses the idea that we are all God's children. Finally, with the introduction of the long-suffering scholar, who will prove to be a most interesting character, Voltaire again struck out at intolerance and implied that there was still no place for free thought in this troubled world.

CHAPTERS 20-23

THE ADVENTURES OF CANDIDE AND MARTIN

Summary
    Candide and Martin, as the old man identified himself, set sail for Bordeaux, and the topic of moral and physical evil was the dominant one discussed by the two during the voyage, for both had suffered much. But Candide had one thing to sustain him: the hope of seeing Cunégonde again, and he still had some Eldoradoan gold and diamonds. Especially at the end of a meal he inclined toward Pangloss' philosophy once more.

In the course of their discussion Martin told Candide that he was not a Socinian but a Manichean (one who, according to an ancient Persian system, believed that man's soul, sprung from the kingdom of light, seeks escape from the body, the kingdom of darkness). He conceded that, in view of what he had seen, God must have abandoned the world to some malevolent being—with the exception of Eldorado. Martin then summed up the miseries of the world—personal injustice and cruelties; a million regimented assassins sweeping over Europe as one nation warred against another; the envies, cares, and anxieties even in supposedly cultured cities. Candide insisted that there was *some* good in the world, but the pessimistic Martin only replied that he had never seen it.

In the midst of their discussion they heard the sound of gunfire and, along with others aboard the ship, saw two ships, one French, fighting about three miles away. One of the ships was sunk; and Candide and Martin saw a good hundred men implore the Heavens for help and then go to their deaths. Martin pointed out that this incident illustrated how men treated each other, and Candide conceded that there was something diabolical in what they had seen. As he spoke, a red object was seen moving toward their ship. To the great joy of Candide, it turned out to be one of his big sheep. It was then revealed that the Dutch captain's ship was the one which had been sunk. The enormous wealth the captain had stolen had gone to the bottom of the sea. Candide was sure that all this proved that crime was sometimes punished. But, asked Martin, why should so many blameless creatures have had to die? God, he concluded, punished the guilty captain, but the devil drowned the others.

The two continued their discussion. Despite the pessimism of Martin, Candide did not lose hope; he had found one of his sheep; now he was sure that he would be reunited with Cunégonde.

When they sighted France, Candide inquired whether Martin had ever been there. The latter answered affirmatively and then provided an unflattering description of the French and especially of the citizens of Paris. In some parts of the country, he said, half the people were mad; elsewhere they were too crafty; still others were rather gentle and stupid. And in every province the chief occupations were love making, malicious gossip, and talking nonsense. As for Paris, it was a mixture of everything found in the provinces. Martin had heard that the Parisians were a very refined people but was not yet convinced that they were.

Candide at first had no desire to tarry in France; he wanted to take the shortest route to Venice. Martin accepted his invitation to accompany him. Martin's logic was impeccable: Candide had money; Martin had none; he had heard that Venice welcomed the rich. And then their philosophical discussion was continued. Nothing that Candide had experienced surprised the old scholar. He had lived too long and seen too much. He believed that man had always been bloodthirsty, greedy, lecherous, hypocritical, foolish, and so on. And he insisted that man no more changed his character than does a predatory bird. Candide objected, as he introduced the subject of free will. When the ship reached Bordeaux, the discussion was still in progress.

At Bordeaux Candide remained long enough only to sell some Eldorado pebbles and purchase a good two-seated carriage, for he could no longer do without Martin. Since he could not take the sheep along, he regretfully gave it to the Academy of Science, which was particularly interested in sheep with red wool. He had intended to leave France as quickly as possible, but since all the travelers he met on the road said they were going to Paris, he decided to visit that famous city. Candide had just put up at an inn when he became ill from fatigue. Two doctors, many "intimate friends," and two pious and charitable ladies gave him every attention, for they had noticed his big diamond ring and his strongbox. Martin observed that once in Paris he fell ill but had no one to attend him. "I recovered," he concluded. Thanks to the medicine and bloodlettings, Candide became worse. A clergyman who was a regular visitor asked him for a "note payable to the bearer in the next world"; that is, a document signed by a non-Jansenist priest certifying that he was not a Jansenist. (For a time in Paris extreme unction was refused to anyone who did not have such a document). Candide became incensed, and the two began to quarrel, whereupon Martin took the clergyman by the shoulders and shoved him out of the room. A police report was made of the commotion.

Fortunately, Candide recovered. A number of distinguished people came to supper during his convalescence and gambled with him for high stakes. It was no surprise to Martin that his young friend never held any aces. Among those who showed him Paris was an abbé, a scheming, parasitical individual who sought out strangers, told them scandalous gossip, and offered them pleasure at any price. First he took Candide to see a tragedy and the two were seated near several wits. One of these quibblers insisted that Candide should not have wept because the play was impossible. Tomorrow, he said, he would bring Candide twenty pamphlets written against the dramatist. Candide was informed by the abbé that five or six thousand plays had been written in France, but that only fifteen or sixteen were any good. "That's a lot," said Martin.

Since an actress who had played the role of Queen Elizabeth reminded Candide of his Cunégonde, the young man was attracted to her. The abbé offered to take him to her residence. In response to Candide's inquiry as to how Queens of England were treated in France, the abbé told him that they were respected when they are beautiful and thrown into the garbage dump when they are dead. The youth was shocked, especially when Martin confirmed what the abbé had said. The abbé continued his critical description of Paris and its citizens with characteristic malice.

Because the abbé knew that one of his obscure station was not welcome at the home of the actress, he made an excuse and suggested that Candide come with him to visit a lady of quality in whose house he would learn much about Paris. And the abbé did conduct Candide and Martin to the lady's house, where a faro game was in progress. Voltaire described the play in sufficient detail—the tenseness of the players, the attempts to cheat, the characters of the players. So occupied were these people that no one greeted Candide and his companions. Meanwhile the abbé had secured the attention of the self-styled Marquise de Parolignac. (The name derives from *paroli* and refers to the practice of letting one's winnings ride on the next draw in a card game). She smiled at Candide and gave Martin a nod, and then she offered the youth a seat at the gambling table. Only two draws were required for him to lose 50,000 francs, but he appeared so unconcerned that the servants took him to be an English milord. Supper followed, with the usual unintelligible chatter, witticisms, false rumors, bad reasoning, a little politics, a great deal of slander, and even some discourse on literature, most of it adversely critical, reference being made to the "enormous mass of abominable books." Particularly there was a fairly long discussion of what constituted a good tragedy by one especially impressive and apparently well-informed scholar. Candide thought that he must be another Pangloss, and he asked the man if he subscribed to the optimistic philosophy. The scholar did not — quite the contrary, for everything was going wrong in the country. He referred to wide-spread ignorance of rank and responsibility and the senseless quarrels — an endless war. "Janesenist against Molinist, Parliament against the Church, men of letters against their fellow writers, courtiers against courtiers, financiers against the people, wives against their husbands, relatives against relatives." The naive Candide again invoked the name of Pangloss and voiced his confidence that all was for the best, arguing that the apparent evil was no more than shadows in a beautiful picture. Martin could not restrain himself. "Your hanged philosopher was an arrogant jester," he exclaimed.

After supper the Marquise invited Candide to her boudoir, where, in the course of their conversation, he was properly courteous, but he had his difficulties. The lady told him that now he should no longer love Cunégonde (for he had told her all about her) since he had now seen the Marquise. "Your passion for Cunégonde began when you picked up her handkerchief; I want you to pick up my garter." Candide complied and at her further request put it on her. The Marquise pointed out that she was according him unusual privileges, for she usually made her lovers languish for two weeks. When she praised the diamonds on his hands, the gallant Candide gave them to her. As he left the house, he was conscious-stricken for having been unfaithful to Cunégonde, and he received the consolations of the abbé. As for the latter, he could have fared better. He had received only a small share of the 50,000 francs Candide had lost at cards and of the diamonds Candide had given to the Marquise. But determined to get more at the expense of the youth, he redoubled his amiable attentions. Particularly did he manifest an appreciative interest in Cunégonde. Candide lamented the fact that he had never received a letter from her, whereupon the abbé, having listened attentively, took his leave. Surprisingly enough, on the next morning Candide did receive a letter from his beloved. She was in Paris! The Governor of Buenos Aires had taken everything, but she still had his heart. When he read that she had been ill, Candide was greatly concerned, torn as he was between inexpressible joy at having heard from her and then learning that she was not well.

Candide and Martin went to the hotel where Cunégonde was supposed to be staying. When the young man tried to draw back the bed curtains and asked for light, he was restrained by the maid. He addressed [the fake] Cunégonde but was informed that she could not speak. The lady behind the curtains *did* put forth her hand, which Candide bathed in tears and filled with diamonds. Moreover, he left a bag full of gold on the arm chair. At this tender moment, two officers appeared and arrested Candide and Martin on suspicion.

"This isn't the way travelers are treated in Eldorado," said Candide. And Martin declared that he was more a Manichean than ever. The two were taken to a dungeon. Candide provided a bribe of sufficient size to secure their release. "Ah, sir," said one of the officers, "if you'd committed every crime imaginable, you'd still be the most honest man in the world!" But why, asked Candide, were all strangers arrested? The abbé provided the answer. It was all because a beggar from Artois heard some people talking nonsense, which was enough to make him try to commit parricide. Candide was shocked at the monstrosity of the people and was eager to get out of a country where monkeys harassed tigers. He pleaded to be taken to Venice, but the officer's brother, after receiving three diamonds, took them to Portsmouth, England. Candide was not in Venice, to be sure, but he felt that he had been delivered from hell.

Voicing the names of Pangloss, Martin, and his dear Cunégonde, Candide vehemently asked what kind of a world this was. Martin replied that it was something insane and abominable. The English, he continued, had their own type of madness, and he made reference to the war between France and England in America (the French and Indian War). He described the English as being extremely moody and morose.

When they arrived in Portsmouth, the two witnessed the execution of a rather stout man who, blindfolded, knelt on the deck of a naval vessel. Four soldiers each fired three bullets into his head, to the great satisfaction of the large crowd of spectators. Candide learned that the man was an admiral whose crime was that he had not killed enough men, that he had not closed with the French enemy. "Then why was not the French admiral killed?" asked Candide. He was informed that in England it was considered good to kill an admiral now and then "to encourage the others." So shocked was Candide that he immediately arranged passage to Venice. "God be praised," he exclaimed when they arrived in that city. Trusting Cacambo as he did, he was sure that he would see his Cunégonde again and that all would be well.

Commentary
Of primary interest in these chapters is the old philosopher, Martin. In important ways he stood for the attitude of Pierre Bayle, just as Pangloss did for Leibnitz. A word about Bayle is therefore in order. Voltaire had discovered him early, and particularly after the Lisbon earthquake his letters were filled with eulogies of him as the leading opponent of optimistic philosophy. Bayle (1647-1706), lexicographer, philosopher, critic, had been a Protestant who became a Catholic and then reverted to Protestantism. At last, in faith he became a Pyrrhonian (an adherent to the system of gnosiology, which treats of the sources, limits, and validity of knowledge, and which inculcates skepticism). In a word, he was an absolute skeptic. Voltaire was especially attracted to him because he was a champion of tolerance in opinion. His attack on superstitions, his view of morality as being independent of religion, were set forth at sufficient length, especially in his *Pensées sur la comòte* (1682) and his greatest work, the *Dictionnaire*

historique et critique (1697), which was enlarged in 1702 and supplemented in 1704-6 by *Réponses aux questiones d'un provincial,* wherein he paid close attention to philosophical and theological subjects which called for free investigation. These works recommended themselves to the *philosophes,* among whom Voltaire was numbered, in the author's espousal of the sovereignty of reason and his effort to remove all obstacles to its supremacy. Voltaire made Martin a Manichean who believed in two nearly equal forces of good and evil: God punished the vicious Dutch captain, but the Devil was responsible for the deaths of so many innocent people. Thus Voltaire was not arguing that evil prevailed everywhere. After all, there were men of good will like the youthful Candide; and others like the Anabaptist and the old woman and the faithful Cacambo who were humane individuals. But to ignore the extent of evil manifested at both private and public levels and to tell one's self that ultimately good emerged from it was to blind one's self to reality.

Years before Pope was to write his *Essay on Man,* the dictum "Whatever is, is right" had been defended by Archbishop William King in his *De origine mali* (1702). Bayle provided the most eloquent and telling rebuttal. How, he asked, can evil occur if the creator is infinitely good, infinitely wise, infinitely powerful? Thus Bayle emphatically rejected providentialism, as does Martin in this section. For Martin, summing up his long experiences, most men are predatory animals, cruel and unscrupulous. And if the guilty are occasionally punished, the innocent in great numbers suffer.

It is of interest to learn that Voltaire did not readily reject the optimistic philosophy. In the first of his philosophical tales, *Zadig* (1747), he was not without optimism. His hero, like Candide, experienced great difficulties in his travels. He was nearly strangled in Babylon, barely escaped being roasted to death in Barra, was impaled by bonzes in Serendip, and enslaved in Egypt. Understandably, he questioned the theory of providentialism. But he finally was told by an angel that there is no evil in the world from which good does not arise. The Voltaire of *Candide,* published twelve years later, no longer could accept this point of view. He rejected the views of Leibnitz, Wolff, Bolingbroke, and Pope: there was overwhelming evidence that all was not for the best in this world.

It was inevitable that Voltaire would have Candide and Martin visit Paris before going on to Venice and the possible reunion with Cunégonde. This gave him the chance to satirize the foibles and vices of the town. First were the unscrupulous, parasitical fortune hunters in the persons of the contemptible group, including a cleric, who sought to capitalize on Candide's illness and convalescence. They remind one of the vultures in human form who fawned over the wealthy Volpone in Jonson's well-known comedy. The difference is that Volpone, the Fox, was fully aware of their intentions and succeeded in turning the tables on them. The young, inexperienced Candide could not hold his own against the group who sought to victimize him.

The avaricious abbé who conducted Candide and Martin about Paris, showing him life in so-called high society at the theater and the salon, was a particularly well-realized character. There was sufficient viciousness in the urban world Voltaire described, what with its cheats, its purveyors of slander, its bogus aristocrats, its officers of the law who are only too easily bribed, its courtesans. But the beaux, fops, and would-be wits who peopled the scene are reminiscent of those depicted in Alexander Pope's *Rape of the Lock.*

It is Voltaire the literary critic who proved most interesting in this section. In other works, for example the satiric *Le Pauvre Diable* (1758) he had attacked the "writing rabble." Having himself been the target of adversely critical remarks made by would-be critics, Voltaire made the most of the chance to castigate the breed. In order to provide evidence of the critic's intellectual limitations, he quoted him as denouncing the playwright as "a man who does not believe in innate ideas." Voltaire himself followed Locke's view of the mind as originally *tabula rasa,* a blank slate or tablet, rather than Descartes' theory of innate ideas.

On two occasions, the author provided some personal satire. When Candide asked the abbé what he meant by 'hack' the abbé replied: "A man man who writes for cheap rags. A F----." The reference is to Fréron (whose name in full is provided in some translations), a journalist with whom Voltaire carried on a bitter feud. And when the abbé asked the Marquise what she thought of Archdeacon ——'s essays and was told that they were a deadly bore, the reference is to the Abbé Trublet, another enemy of Voltaire's.

Other points of interest in this chapter included the following. Satire of religion and churchman was sustained. A cleric was prominent among those who harassed Candide as he lay ill; and, of course, it was another self-interested churchman who conducted Candide and Martin to the theater and to the Marquise's residence. Martin spoke not only of the "writing rabble," but also of the "convulsionary rabble," a hit at the Jansenists, who indulged in manifestations of religious ecstasy or mania, like those of the Holy Rollers today. To be noted also is the name Marquise de Parolignac. *Paroli* has been explained above; the suffic *-gnac* was common in southwest France, from which area came many impoverished and spurious nobility. Finally, bribery among legal officers was illustrated by the incident where Candide secured his release from prison for a price. Clearly the Paris Voltaire described was corrupt at practically every level of society.

The significant experience Candide and Martin had in England was their witnessing the execution of an English naval officer. The execution actually took place on March 14, 1747, and the unfortunate man was Admiral George Byng, who was courtmartialed and found guilty of losing a naval battle to the French in the previous year. Voltaire had tried to intervene to save his life. So, far from being a digression, the report of this incident had its place in the development of the author's major thesis.

CHAPTERS 24-26

CANDIDE IN VENICE

Summary
Immediately upon reaching Venice, Candide began searching for Cacambo. Every day he had all the ships and boats investigated, but he learned no news of his servant. As he explained to Martin, after his long journey from South America he had met only a tricky abbé from Périgord. He was sure that Cunégonde was dead, and he regretted that he had not remained in Eldorado rather than returning to this "accursed Europe," where all was illusion and calamity. Martin, as frank as ever, called his companion a simpleton for believing that a half-breed valet with so much wealth would have fulfilled the mission assigned to him. Martin advised Candide to forget both Cacambo and Cunégonde. As the old scholar continued, the young man's melancholy increased.

Candide noticed a young Theatine arm-in-arm with a young lady in the Piazza San Marco. They were an attractive and apparently a very happy couple. Turning to Martin, Candide argued that there at least were two happy creatures. But Martin was sure that they were among the unfortunates who people this world. To settle the question, the young man invited the monk and the pretty girl to dine with Martin and him, and the invitation was promptly accepted. Hardly had they entered Candide's room at the inn than the girl recognized her host and identified herself as Paquette, the baroness' maid with whom Pangloss had had a love affair. She stated that she had heard of the frightful misfortunes that had happened to all at the baron's castle in Westphalia. She herself had fared quite badly. And then she told her story.

After Paquette had been forced to leave the service of the baroness, she became successively the mistress of a doctor who killed his jealous wife; and of a judge, who had freed her from prison, where she had been remanded as a possible accomplice to the murder. A rival soon took her place, and she was obliged to become a common prostitute, the profession she was following in Venice. She dwelt at some length on the degradation she had to endure with only a frightful old age to look forward to. Martin remarked that he had certainly won half of his wager. Candide asked Paquette why it was, in view of her sad lot, that she appeared so gay, so happy. "That is still another of the miseries of the trade," she replied. "Yesterday I was robbed and beaten by an officer, and today I have to appear in a good humor to please a monk." Candide then conceded that

Martin was right. He turned to the monk, who, he said, seemed to enjoy a destiny that everyone must envy and who appeared content with his status as a Theatine. But Friar Giroflée (for that was his name) protested that he wished all Theatines were at the bottom of the sea. He himself would have liked to burn the monastery and turn Turk. A younger son, his parents had forced him to leave a greater fortune to the older brother whom he detested and to become a monk. Jealousy, discord, rage characterized life in the monastery. Oh, to be sure, a few bad sermons had brought him some money, half of which the prior stole from him, the rest serving him to keep girls.

Now Candide had to admit that Martin had won the entire wager. He gave Paquette 2,000 piasters and Giroflée 1,000 — sure that the money would make both happy. But Martin was not so sure: perhaps the money would lead them to greater unhappiness. Observing the fact that he often found again people whom he had been sure were lost forever, Candide now believed that there was a good chance of his finding Cunégonde. Martin remained pessimistic; for him happiness in this world was a very scarce commodity. Candide called his attention to the singing gondoliers; surely they were happy. Let Candide see them at home, said Martin, with their wives and brats of children; then he would think otherwise. He conceded that the lot of a gondolier was probably a better one than that of the Doge (the city's chief magistrate). Candide then said that the Venetians spoke of Senator Pococurante, who lived in a palace on the Brenta and who received foreign visitors graciously, as one who was reputed to be a man who never knew grief. Martin expressed a desire to see such a rarity, and Candide immediately arranged for them to visit the senator on the next day.

Both Candide and Martin were quite impressed by the palace and the surrounding gardens and the statuary. The noble Pococurante, a man of about sixty, received them hospitably, if with little enthusiasm. Candide praised the beauty, grace, and skill of the two pretty girls who served them refreshments. The sophisticated senator remarked that sometimes he enjoyed their favors, for he "tired of the town ladies, their coquetries, their follies..." When Candide expressed admiration for the original Raphaels and other paintings, Pococurante spoke disparagingly of them; he did not find them true to nature. And when Candide voiced his high approval of the music provided for him, his host held forth on the limitations of contemporary music, especially operatic tragedies. Martin was in full agreement with his host. When they inspected the impressive library, Pococurante had as pronounced ideas on the limitations of such acknowledged greats as Homer and Milton; he preferred Virgil, Tasso, and Ariosto. So with reference to Horace: the Roman writer had his virtues, but also serious limitations. Since he had never been brought up to judge anything for himself, Candide was astonished at what he heard; but again Martin was in full agreement with his host. The tenor of the conversation remained the same as reference was made to Cicero, to the eighty volumes of the Academy of Sciences, and to Italian, Spanish, and French drama.

Particularly interesting was the discussion of English literature. Pococurante agreed with Martin that the English had the privilege of writing what they thought about, whereas in "this Italy of ours" people wrote only what they did not think. He would be glad of the freedom of English geniuses, but added that passion and factionalism corrupted all that was estimable in that precious freedom. He dismissed Milton as "a barbarian who writes a long commentary on the first chapter of Genesis in ten books of harsh verses" and as a "crude imitator of the Greeks."

Candide was rather disturbed by these frank, original estimates of the literary greats, but was convinced that his host was a great genius: "Nothing can please him." When he and Martin left, Candide remarked that they had indeed met the happiest of all men, one who was above everything he possessed. But insisting that Pococurante was disgusted with everything he possessed, Martin argued that their host was nothing of the sort. So Candide concluded that only he was a happy person – or he would be if and when he saw Cunégonde again. But weeks passed with no sign of Cacambo. Depressed as he was, the youth did not even notice that Paquette and the Friar had not bothered to come and thank him.

One evening Candide, followed by Martin, went to a hotel to dine. Before they could sit down, a man with a very dark complexion came up to him and told him to be ready to leave. It was Cacambo. Candide learned that his valet was now the slave of a man who awaited him and that Cunégonde was in Constantinople, He told the young man to have supper and then be ready for their departure.

In a state of great excitement and mixed emotions Candide joined the calm Martin at a table with six foreigners who had come to spend the Carnival in Venice. Cacambo was pouring a drink for one of them. He and the other servants or slaves informed their masters that their ships were ready for departure; each left promptly after delivering his message. But the sixth slave had another kind of intelligence for his master. "Your Majesty," he said, "they won't give you any more credit, nor me either. You and I could be imprisoned. I'm going to look after myself. Farewell." Those seated at the table remained silent for a time. Finally, Candide asked how it happened that all six were kings. Each identified himself. They were Achmet III, one-time Grand Sultan, who had been deposed by his nephew; Ivan, former Emperor of all the Russias, dethroned when still an infant; Charles Edward, King of England, whose dethroned father had ceded his rights to his son; the King of the Poles, whose father had had similar experiences; another King of the Poles, one who had twice lost his kingdom; the now destitute King of Corsica, to which royal position he had been elected. The sixth King's story so moved the others that they gave him money for clothes. Candide gave him a diamond worth 2,000 sequins, much to the surprise of their Royal Highnesses, who wondered how a commoner was able to be so generous. Candide assured them that he was not a king and had no desire to be one. As all prepared to leave, four other Most Serene Highnesses who had lost their states by the fortunes of war arrived. But now Candide was concerned only with going to find his dear Cuñegonde in Constantinople.

Commentary

In these chapters Voltaire added further examples of the misfortune and evil to be found everywhere; no individual, however lowly or exalted, could escape them. Particularly with reference to Paquette and Friar Giroflée, somewhat less so with reference to Senator Pococurante, appearances were deceiving. The young couple seemed to be completely carefree and happy, absorbed as they were in each other. Nothing could have been further from the truth. Both were miserable, pathetic creatures. The Senator, living like a manorial lord, sought out by visitors from all over Europe, had not found tranquility either. And it was Martin, functioning as usual as a kind of chorus, who drew the appropriate conclusion in each case.

Voltaire introduced an amusing bit of irony in his choice of names in this section. Candide described Friar Giroflée as one on whose face the flower of youth shone. The Friar's name means "gillyflower"; that of Paquette means "daisy." The author also satirizes the individual who entered the religious life by default and was anything but a dedicated spirit. Friar Gironflée was one of the many younger sons in better class families, who, according to the law of primogeniture, could not inherit their father's estate. Their only recourse was to try to find places in one of the Three Estates — the military, the government, the Church. For they could not lower themselves by becoming farmers or tradesmen. Little wonder that many who entered the Church were utter misfits.

Senator Pococurante proved to be a most interesting character, what with his impressive palace, the well-planned gardens, the objets d'art, and large library. His name means "caring little" — and that is the key to his character. Voltaire, perhaps playfully, identified himself with the Senator. And, it will be recalled, he lived in manorial splendor with his sixty retainers at Les Délices and Ferney. On occasion Voltaire expressed his boredom of such a placid life — he who seemed to have loved a good fight. The Senator's views on literature are not to be taken strictly as those of the author; but they often reflect his sense of weakness in the great and his skepticism as regards what may be called "received opinion," that which Candide had depended upon. It comes as a shock to hear Milton described as "that barbarian who writes a long commentary on the first chapter of Genesis in ten books of harsh verses." Voltaire did object especially to the Sin-Death allegory in *Paradise Lost,* but one wonders how Milton's magnificent blank verse, to be found even in the books which are heavily doctrinal, could be called harsh. As for Pococurante's dislike of Homer, it may be pointed out that most neo-classicists (Pope a notable exception) preferred Virgil. Ariosto and Tasso, the epic poets of the Italian Renaissance, were long-time favorites of Voltaire's.

One last point. The six kings whom we meet in this section were actually historical ones. When Voltaire referred to the four others who enter near the end of Chapter 26 as "Most Serene Highnesses," he indulged himself in more mockery. His point was that there is little if any serenity to be found anywhere, even if one were a king.

CHAPTERS 27-30

THE CONCLUDING ADVENTURES OF CANDIDE

Summary

Cacambo had made arrangements for Candide and himself to sail aboard a ship commanded by a Turkish captain under orders of the Sultan Ahmed. Both prostrated themselves before his "miserable Highness." En route, Candide, in whose breast, hope sprang eternal, contemplated the lot of the six kings he had met in Venice and compared their lot with his own, now that he was flying to the arms of Cunégonde. He assured Martin that Pangloss had been right: "All is well." Martin could only express his hope that the youth was right. Unlike his companion, he saw nothing extraordinary in the fact that they had dined with six dethroned rulers; such dethronements were common enough.

Candide turned to Cacambo and asked him many questions about Cunégonde. What was she doing? Was she still the peerless beauty? Had Cacambo bought her a palace in Constantinople? He was told that the lady was a lowly servant in the household of a former sovereign named Ragotsky (actually a former prince of Transylvania). Much worse she had lost her beauty. Candide gallantly declared that, ugly or beautiful, it was his duty to love her. But how, he asked, had she been reduced to such an abject state? Did not Cacambo have vast wealth in his possession? The valet told of the ransom he had had to pay to the Governor of Buenos Aires, and of the large sums which he had been forced to turn over to the pirates. He himself was a slave to the deposed Sultan.

Candide consoled himself with the thought that he still had a few diamonds left and that he would be able to rescue Cunégonde. But now he wondered if his lot were not really worse than that of the six kings. He assured Martin that Pangloss would have been able to provide an answer. But Martin was convinced that there were millions far worse off than Candide and the deposed rulers.

When they arrived at Bosporus, Candide secured the freedom of Cacambo and, without waste of time, headed for the shores of the Propontis to find Cunégonde. Again there occurred one of those amazing coincidences. Two galley slaves turned out to be none other than Doctor Pangloss and the Jesuit Baron, Cunégonde's brother! "Is it a dream?" asked Candide. "Is that My Lord Baron, whom I killed? Is that Doctor Pangloss, whom I saw hanged?" Then he made immediate arrangements with the Levantine captain for ransoming the two. Since they were "dogs of Christian convicts," one a baron and the other a metaphysician, the price was an exorbitant one; but Candide did not protest. He also paid the captain to take them all to the nearest port.

Candide introduced Martin and Cacambo to the Baron and Pangloss. They all embraced; they all talked at once. When they reached port, Candide sold a diamond worth a hundred thousand sequins for 50,000 and immediately paid the ransom for the two former galley slaves. He sold more diamonds, and they all set out in another galley to deliver Cunégonde, now a kitchen slavey in the household of the Prince of Transylvania.

Again Candide implored the Baron's pardon for having given him the great sword thrust through the body. "Let's say no more about it," said the Baron, and he admitted that he had been a little too hasty himself. He then told his story. After having been cured of his wound by the brother apothecary of the Jesuit College, he was carried off by a party of Spaniards and imprisoned in Buenos Aires just after his sister left; next he was chosen to go to Constantinople and serve as almoner with the Ambassador of France. A week after he had assumed his duties he met a very attractive young page to the Sultan. Since it was very hot, the two bathed together. But in Turkey it was a capital crime for a Christian to be found naked with a young Moslem. A cadi (magistrate or judge) sentenced the Baron to be given one hundred lashes on the soles of his feet and condemned him to the galleys. This was unjust enough, he concluded, but why should his sister be in the kitchen of a refugee Transylvanian prince?

Next Candide turned to Pangloss and asked how it happened that he had survived. Yes, he had been hanged rather than burned because of the heavy downpour of rain. A surgeon had bought his body, took it to his home, and dissected it. No one had been worse hanged than Pangloss. The Holy Inquisition's Executor of High Operations, a subdeacon, did burn people marvelously, but he was a rank amateur at hanging. The wet rope had slipped badly and had become knotted. And thus Pangloss was still breathing. He had cried out loudly when the doctor made an incision in his body, and the frightened man fled, convinced that he had been dissecting a devil. When the doctor's wife came running into the room, she was more frightened than her husband, over whose prone body she stumbled as she ran. "My dear," she said, "what are you thinking of, dissecting a heretic? Don't you know that the devil is always in those people?" When Pangloss heard her say that she would summon a priest quickly to exorcise him, he shuddered and cried out for them to take pity on him. Finally, the "Portuguese barber," as Pangloss called him, recovered enough courage to sew up Pangloss. Further, he found Pangloss a job as lackey to a knight of Malta who was going to Venice. But since the knight was penniless, Pangloss entered the services of a Venetian merchant and went with him to Constantinople.

One day he entered a mosque where an old iman (holy man) and a very seductive appearing young devotee were present. The girl dropped the beautiful bouquet she had placed between her uncovered breasts. The gallant Pangloss retrieved and replaced it, but took so long in doing so that the iman grew angry. Recognizing Pangloss as a Christian, he cried out for help. And, like the baron, Pangloss was taken before a magistrate and given the same sentence his fellow-sufferer had received. In the galley were four young men from Marseilles, five Neapolitan priests, and two monks who told the baron that what had happened to him was a daily occurrence. The baron and Pangloss argued about who had suffered most, the latter insisting that it was far more permissible to replace a bouquet on a woman's bosom than to be stark naked with the page of a sultan, when Candide appeared and ransomed them.

"Well, my dear Pangloss," said Candide, "when you were hanged, racked with blows, and rowing in the galleys, did you still think that all was for the best?" And the philosopher assured the youth that he was still of his first opinion, arguing that Leibnitz can not be wrong.

En route to the house of the Prince of Transylvania on the shore of the Propontis, Candide, the baron, Pangloss, Martin, and Cacambo talked at length about their adventures, reasoned on the contingent and noncontingent events of the world, argued about causes and effects, moral and physical evil, and free will and necessity. When they landed at the Prince's house they saw Cunégonde and the old woman hanging towels on a line to dry. The baron paled at the sight of his once beautiful sister. She was now dark-skinned; her eyes were blood shot; her cheeks wrinkled; her arms red and rough. No longer did she have the enticing figure he had remembered. She embraced her brother and Candide, who in turn embraced the old woman. Candide ransomed both women.

The old woman, never without a plan, suggested that they buy a small farm in the neighborhood and await a better destiny. Poor Cunégonde, who did not know that she had grown ugly, reminded Candide of his promise to marry her. "I shall never endure such baseness on her part or insolence on Candide's," exclaimed the baron. He could not bear the thought that his sister's children would be barred from the aristocracy. Although Cunégonde threw herself at his feet and wept bitter tears, he was adamant. Candide called him the maddest of madmen and reminded him of all he had done for his sister. The baron replied, "You may kill me again, but you shall not marry my sister while I am alive."

Candide really had no desire to marry Cunégonde, but the baron's arrogance and Cunégonde's pleading made him determined to do so. He consulted Pangloss, Martin, and the faithful Cacambo. Pangloss prepared a fine memoir by which he proved to his own satisfaction that the baron had no right to interfere, that she could make a morganatic marriage. Martin thought that the baron should be thrown into the sea. Cacambo decided that the baron should be returned to galleys and then be sent by the first ship to the Father General in Rome. All but Cunégonde, who had been told nothing, approved of the plan. So they had the pleasure of trapping a Jesuit and punishing a German baron for excessive pride.

It would seem that Candide, married to Cunégonde and living with two philosophers and the prudent Cacambo, would now lead a pleasant life. But the Jews had so cheated him that he had nothing left but the little farm. His wife became uglier and more shrewish every day. The old woman, now an invalid, became more intolerable than Cunégonde. Nor was Cacambo happy. He was overworked and bewailed his fate. Pangloss was disappointed because he was not flourishing at some German university. As for Martin, his pessimism was more pronounced than ever, but he accepted his lot patiently.

Candide, Martin, and Pangloss spent much of their time arguing about metaphysics and morality and watching the sights. They often saw Turkish officers of all ranks on farm boats which took them into exile; and they saw other officials arriving to take their places, ones who would later be exiled. They saw "properly impaled heads" being taken to the Sublime Port (the gate of Sultan's palace). These sights redoubled the discourse of the three. But the boredom increased, and the old woman proposed a question: was it worse to be raped a thousand times by Negro pirates, have a buttock cut off, run the gauntlet of the Bulgarians, and be flogged and hanged in the *auto-da-fé*, be dissected, row in the galleys—in short, to undergo all the miseries they had experienced—or stay where they were and do nothing? A great question, as Candide remarked, one that called for reflection. Martin was sure that it was man's lot to live in a state of anxiety and boredom. Candide disagreed, but asserted nothing. Pangloss admitted that his life had been filled with suffering, but he still defended his position that everything was wonderful, even if he himself did not believe so.

When th · saw Paquette and Giroflée, in a state of utter misery, coming to the far , Martin was absolutely convinced that his dark view of life was the correct one. The two had squandered the money Candide had given them; they had quarreled and then become reconciled to each other; they had been put in prison, from which they had escaped. Now the Friar had made good his threat to turn Turk, and the pathetic Paquette endeavored, unsuccessfully, to ply her trade everywhere. Martin told Candide that he had known that the young man and Cacambo would dissipate their wealth, that they were no happier than these two most recent arrivals. As for Pangloss he greeted Paquette by telling her that she had cost him the end of his nose, an eye, and an ear.

This new adventure led them to philosophize more than ever. In an attempt to get some answers to basic questions, they consulted a very famous dervish, one considered to be the best philosopher in Turkey, and posed this question to him: why was such a strange animal as man ever created? The dervish replied that they were meddling in matters which were no concern of theirs, that it does not matter if there is a horrible amount of evil on earth. "When His Highness sends a ship to Egypt, is he bothered about whether the mice in the ship are comfortable or not?" All they should do, the dervish continued, was to hold their tongues. Pangloss was crushed. He had hoped to reason with this man about effects and causes, the best of all possible worlds, the origin of evil, the nature of the soul, and pre-established harmony. But the dervish slammed the door in the face of his visitors.

Meanwhile, the news had gone round that in Constantinople the authorities had just strangled two viziers of the Divan (ministers of state) and impaled several of their friends. The catastrophe had created quite a stir for a few hours. Upon returning to the farm, Pangloss, Candide, and Martin met an old man relaxing under a bower of orange trees. They asked him the name of the mufti who had just been strangled. The old man professed to know nothing; he had always assumed that those who meddle with public affairs sometime suffer and deserve to do so. As for him he contented himself with cultivating his garden. Then he invited the three into his house and provided them with refreshments. His two daughters perfumed the visitors' beards. Candide was most impressed. He was sure that his good Moslem must have a vast estate but learned that his host possessed only twenty acres. "I cultivate them with my children," said the Turk. "Work keeps away three great evils: boredom, vice, and need."

As he went back to the farm, Candide pondered deeply what the old man had said. He informed Pangloss and Martin that the man had made a life for himself which was far better than that of the six kings they had met in Venice. Pangloss held forth at his usual length, appealing to Biblical and secular history, to prove that great eminence is always dangerous. "I also know," said Candide, "that we must cultivate our garden." His philosopher friend agreed. "Let us work without reason," added Martin. "It is the only way to make life bearable." And so the little society entered into this laudable plan — Cunégonde, Paquette, Friar Giroflée included.

That irrepressible optimist Pangloss sometimes repeated his belief that all events were linked together logically in this best of all possible worlds.

He argued that had not Candide been expelled from a fine castle and experienced so many difficulties he would not now be enjoying candied citrons and pistachios. "That is well said," replied Candide, "but we must cultivate our garden."

Commentary

In these last three chapters Voltaire managed to bring together the leading characters in *Candide* and to provide a good resolution of the eventful story. Almost to the very end the emphasis remained on man's irrationality, intolerance, cruelty, avarice. Much of this was illustrated by the narratives of the Jesuit Baron and of Pangloss, whose account of his experiences with the "Portuguese barber" and his wife, however gruesome the details, provided the most hilarious bit of low comedy to be found in the tale. Leading up to the final injunction that one must learn to cultivate his garden, Voltaire especially stressed the evils visited upon those in public life: the plight of the six kings, whom Candide cannot forget, as well as the strangulation and impaling of the viziers and the indications that their successors would fare no better. The good old man presumed "that in general those who meddle with public affairs sometimes perish miserably, and that they deserve it...." Voltaire, one remembers, had had his difficulties in court and aristocratic circles; he had experienced imprisonment and exile. Finally he retired to his estates near Geneva and at Ferney, where he indeed "cultivated his garden," working diligently to the very end of his long life.

A deist, Voltaire believed in a god; the arrangements of the universe presupposed a designer. But to suppose that God intervenes in the affairs of the world was to him superstition. The key passage in which he made clear his point of view is the following:

> Pangloss was the spokesman and said to him, "Master, we have come to ask you to tell us why such a strange animal as man was ever created."
> "Why are you meddling in?" said the dervish. "Is that your business?"
> "But Reverend Father," said Candide, "there is a horrible amount of evil on earth."
> "What does it matter," said the dervish. "whether there is evil or good? When His Highness sends a ship to Egypt, is he bothered about whether the mice in the ship are comfortable or not?"
> "Then what should we do?" said Pangloss.
> "Hold your tongue," said the dervish.

And when Pangloss expressed the hope that he and the dervish might discuss effects and causes, the nature of evil, and pre-established harmony — in short Leibnitzian philosophy — the dervish shut the door in his face. Voltaire had lost faith in systematic philosophy.

In the first two of these three chapters, as in the earlier ones, Candide's attitude vacillated, but he had never entirely abandoned the optimistic faith taught to him by Pangloss. However, in the final chapter, after the conversation with the old man who owned the twenty acres of cultivated land, he finally became convinced that man cannot understand the evil in the world. Therefore man should not make it worse by vain perplexities. He should attend to the counsels of moderation and good sense and let the narrow bounds of his knowledge at least teach him restraint. Above all let him find support in work, even if he does not see to what it tends. In a word, let him cultivate his garden. Only then will life become meaningful and a modicum of happiness be realized. Fundamentally, the aim in life is not the pursuit of happiness, as the romanticist believed.

This is the main point Voltaire made in the final chapter and indeed in the entire tale. But there are many other facets of interest in these last chapters. To the very end, Voltaire continued his anti-clerical satire. Friar Giroflée, still the profligate, did become a Turk; and the Jesuit Baron was punished for his arrogant pride by being sent back to the galleys and then to Rome. There was no place for him in the garden the others planned to cultivate. Voltaire wrote of their "pleasure in trapping a Jesuit." Pangloss' remarks about the Holy Inquisition's Executor of High Operations, who, although expert at burning people, proved to be most inept at hanging them was part of the satire directed against the Church.

It is to be noted also that, as regards the baron, Voltaire returned to personal satire directed against Frederick the Great. Not only did the baron continue to be ridiculously proud of his lineage and to refuse under any conditions to see his now ugly and destitute sister marry a commoner who was willing to look after her, but the episode involving the young page pointed to Frederick's alleged sexual aberrations. Personal also was the statement that Candide had been victimized by Jews: Voltaire himself had suffered financial losses from the bankruptcies of Jewish bankers.

BACKGROUND TO *CANDIDE*

THE PHILOSOPHY OF LEIBNITZ

No attempt here is made to present in detail an account of the philosophy of Gottfried Wilhelm Leibnitz (1646-1716), which Voltaire called "optimism," the term he used as the subtitle to *Candide,* but only to call attention to the points relevant to an understanding of the philosophical tale. In the summaries and commentaries are repeated references to the Leibnitzian ideas. Pangloss referred to the German as "the most profound metaphysician of Germany" and, in view of his constant use of Leibnitzian terms and concepts, he has often been identified with the German philosopher. To that extent, as has been pointed out above, through the character of Pangloss, Voltaire satirized Leibnitz. But the great philosopher and mathematician, the man who was co-discoverer with Newton, yet independently, of differential calculus, was anything but such a ridiculous figure.

Although as early as 1733, Voltaire had written in a note in *Temple du goût* that no man of letters had done Germany greater honor and that Leibnitz was more universal than his revered Newton, it was not until 1737 that he really became interested in the philosophy. In that year Frederick the Great wrote to him enthusiastically about the works of Christian Wolff, the man credited with systematizing Leibnitz's views. His mistress, Mme. du Châtelet, was a dedicated Leibnitzian, and during his stay at Cirey, Voltaire, although concentrating largely on Newton, took part in the study and lengthy discussions of the German's philosophy.

Early and as late as 1756, Voltaire had praise for Leibnitz. Thus in the letter to Koenig, the German mathematician, dated November, 1752, he expressed admiration for the philosopher's manner of thinking and his tendency to scatter the "seeds of ideas." And in the *Siecle de Louis XIV* (1756) he wrote approvingly of the man. But fundamentally Voltaire was suspicious of all attempts at systematic philosophy. In 1737 he wrote to Frederick the Great: "All metaphysics contain two things: all that intelligent men know; second, that which they will never know." Certain views he did share with Leibnitz. He too believed in a Supreme Being who created the universe and whose glory is manifest in the Heavens and on the earth; and he rejected the idea that the world was entirely mechanical or determined or material. The record shows that he did not reject optimism without a struggle. Among his works which indicate a tendency to hold on to an optimistic view of life are *Mondain* (1736), *Discourse en vers sur l'homme* (1736-41), *Micromégas* (1739), *Le monde comme il va* (1746), and *Zadig* (1747). But it was indeed a struggle for him. For example, the idea that human events can be explained by providentialism he could not accept. Deist as he was, his God was an absentee one, to use Carlyle's phrase. In a letter written in the late 1730's he used the analogy of the mice in the ship's hold and the complete indifference of the ship's master—the very same analogy he repeated near the end of *Candide*. By 1741, Voltaire had spoken out clearly against the major tenets of Leibnitzianism. He wrote: "Frankly, Leibnitz has only confused the sciences. His sufficient reason, his continuity, his plenum (all-embracing whole of the universe), his monads, are the germs of confusion of which M. Wolff has methodically ha⁺ ꞓd fifteen volumes in quarto which will put the German heads more than ever in the habit of reading much and understanding little." Moland, ed., Voltaire, *Œuvres complétes* (Paris, 1877-1885, XXXVI, P. 50) Quoted by G. R. Havens, ed., Voltaire, *Candide and L'Optimisme* (1934, p. xxxvi). Although he had some praise for Leibnitz in the *Siecle de Louis XIV* (1756), he also called him *"un peu charlatan."*

The two main points of Leibnitzian philosophy are that God is beneficient and that, in creating the world, He created the best possible one. It should be realized that the philosopher did not argue that the world was perfect or that evil was non-existent. What he did mean was that, thanks to God's goodness and His constant concern with his creation, that which is moral and right finally emerges: it is the ultimate reality. It is all a matter of being able to see the Divine plan in its entirety and not to judge by isolated parts. Leibnitz held that nature moves in an orderly way; that its laws are immutable; that any deviation would upset the universe. Matter he defined as an indivisible something. His name for it was *monad*. All matter, according to his theory, was composed of monads, and these rise on a hierarchical scale from the lowest to the highest. And thus he accounts for the principle of continuity and being in the Great Chain of Being.

By the time he came to write *Candide*, Voltaire's wide reading and experiences provided him with sufficient reason for rejecting these ideas. The phrase "all is well," a refrain in *Candide*, voiced again and again by the young hero and Pangloss, his teacher, is scorned; "the best of all possible worlds" becomes a grim joke. The belief that everything forms a chain and that each individual must keep his place in that chain is dismissed as sheer nonsense. Voltaire also rejects the belief that personal evil only contributes to the general good, that human events are wholly in terms of providentialism, and that harmony is pre-established.

ALEXANDER POPE'S ESSAY ON MAN

The work which more than any other popularized the optimistic philosophy, not only in England but throughout Europe, was Alexander Pope's *Essay on Man* (1733-34), a rationalistic effort to justify the ways of God to man philosophically. As has been stated in the introduction, Voltaire had become well acquainted with the English poet during his stay of more than two years in England, and the two had corresponded with each other with a fair degree of regularity when Voltaire returned to the Continent. Voltaire could have been called a fervent admirer of Pope. He hailed the *Essay of Criticism* as superior to Horace, and he described the *Rape of the Lock* as better than *Lutrin*. When the *Essay on Man* was published, Voltaire sent a copy to the Norman abbot Du Resnol and may possibly have helped the Abbot prepare the first French translation, which was so well received. The very title of his *Discours en vers sur l'homme* (1738) indicates the extent Voltaire was influenced by Pope. It has been pointed out that at times he does little more than echo the same thoughts expressed by the English poet. Even as late as 1756, the year in which he published his poem on the destruction of Lisbon, he lauded the author of *Essay on Man*. In the edition of *Lettres philosophiques* published in that year he wrote: "The *Essay on Man* appears to me to be the most beautiful didactic poem, the most useful, the most sublime that has ever been composed in any language." Perhaps this is no more than another illustration of how Voltaire could vacillate in his attitude as he struggled with the problems posed by the optimistic philosophy in its relation to actual experience. For in the Lisbon poem and in *Candide* he picked up Pope's recurring phrase "Whatever is, is right" and made mockery of it: *"Tout est bien"* in a world filled with misery!

Pope denied that he was indebted to Leibnitz for the ideas which inform his poem, and his word may be accepted. Those ideas were first set forth in England by Anthony Ashley Cowper, Earl of Shaftesbury (1671-1731). They pervade all his works but especially the *Moralist*. Indeed, several lines in the *Essay on Man,* particularly in the first Epistle, are simply statements from the *Moralist* done in verse. Although the question is unsettled and probably will remain so, it is generally believed that Pope was indoctrinated by having read the letters which were prepared for him by Bolingbroke and which provided an exegesis of Shaftesbury's philosophy. The main tenet of this system of natural theology was that one God, all-wise and all-merciful, governed the world providentially for the best. Most important for Shaftesbury was the principle of Harmony and Balance, which he based, not on reason, but on the general ground of good taste. Believing that God's most characteristic attribute was benevolence, Shaftesbury provided an emphatic endorsement of providentialism.

Following are the major ideas in *Essay on Man*: (1) a God of infinite wisdom exists; (2) He created a world which is the best of all possible ones; (3) the plenum, or all-embracing whole of the universe, is real and hierarchical; (4) authentic good is that of the whole, not of isolated parts; (5) self-love and social love both motivate man's conduct; (6) virtue is attainable; (7) "One truth is clear, WHATEVER IS, IS RIGHT." Partial evil, according to Pope, contributes to the universal good. "God sends not ill, if rightly understood..." According to this principle, vices, themselves to be deplored, may lead to virtues. For example, motivated by envy, a man may develop courage and wish to emulate the accomplishments of another; and the avaricious man may attain the virtue of prudence. One can easily understand why, from the beginning, many felt that Pope had depended on Leibnitz.

The key passage is found in Epistle I, lines 281-294, which appropriately may be quoted here:

> Cease then, nor ORDER Imperfection name:
> Our proper bliss depends on what we blame.
> Know thy own point: this kind, this due degree
> Of blindness, weakness, Heav'n bestow on thee.
> Submit. In this, or any other sphere,
> Secure to be as blest as thou canst bear:
> Safe in the hand of one disposing Pow'r,
> Or in the natal or the mortal hour.
> All Nature is but Art, unknown to thee;

All Chance, Direction which thou canst not see;
All Discord, Harmony, not understood;
All partial Evil, universal Good:
And spite of Pride, in erring Reason's spite,
One truth is clear, WHATEVER IS, IS RIGHT.

POÈME SUR LE DÉSASTRE DE LISBONNE

On November 1, 1755, a terrifying earthquake occurred in Portugal and Spain. It occasioned the greatest of suffering in at least twenty towns and cities; hardest hit was Lisbon. An estimated number of 30,000 to 40,000 people were killed in the catastrophe, 15,000 of them in the city of Lisbon, where the destruction to property was appalling. Inevitably this event posed a most serious problem for the theologians and those who subscribed to the philosophy of optimism. The former, depending upon the concept of Original Sin and present-day wickedness, attributed the earthquake to God's wrath visited upon sinful people. The Protestant clergy in Northern Europe argued that the quake had occurred because most of the people of Lisbon were Roman Catholics. Among the Catholics, the anti-Jesuit and pro-Jansenists especially were vocal. And in Portugal's capital city the clergy believed that the shock was the result of divine anger at the presence of Protestants. Alleged heretics were forcibly baptized, and an *auto-da-fé* was instituted with the aim of preventing more earthquakes. Voltaire was pre-eminent among the *philosophes* who sought another answer.

We have seen that Voltaire's pessimism had become more pronounced as the years advanced. Long before the earthquake he had rejected general optimism. Among other things, his attitude, no doubt, had been influenced by his age and continued illness, the death of Mme. du Châtelet, the Berlin-Frankfort experience, and his rejection by Louis XV and the court which had led to his exile in Switzerland. (Cf. Wade, *op. cit.*, p. 143). There was also the outbreak of the Seven Years War, which will be discussed briefly below. But for Voltaire the great earthquake provided incontrovertible proof that the *tout est bien* doctrine was nonsense. All thinking men, he was convinced, would no longer look for a safe life in this world under the guidance of a benign and concerned deity who would reward the virtuous. Voltaire was more than ever sure that accident played a major part in life, that man was basically weak, helpless, ignorant of his destiny. He might well hope for a happier state, but that was the logical limit of his optimism.

Voltaire's correspondence immediately following the earthquake provides complete evidence of the extent of his concern. On November 24, 1755, he wrote to one of the Tronchin brothers in Lyon that it now would be hard to see how the laws of motion lead to such awful catastrophes in the "best of all possible worlds." Again he commented how mere chance often determined the fate of the individual. He wondered what the clergy would say, especially the officials of the Inquisition, if their palace still stood in Lisbon. Voltaire expressed the hope that the Inquisitors had been crushed like the others, for that would teach mankind a lesson in tolerance: the Inquisitors burn some fanatics, but the earth swallows the holy man and heretic alike. In a letter to M. Bertrand, dated four days later, he again discussed the earthquake and asked whether Alexander Pope would have dared to say that all is well if he had been in Lisbon on the fateful day. In other letters Voltaire also challenged both philosophy and religion.

Poème sur le désastre de Lisbonne was written during the early days of December, 1755. It was a work of accretion, the final version published in 1756 was one hundred and eighty lines in length.

Voltaire's poem properly may be called an indispensable introduction to *Candide;* in both works he came to grips with reality. Practically every question advanced in the poem appears at least implicitly in the prose tale. Both are savage attacks upon optimism. Aside from form and medium, the essential difference between the two works lies in the fact that irony, mockery, ridicule, high spirits, and broad humor have no place in the poem. Voltaire was deadly serious throughout, and the tone is one of deep pity for the lot of mankind in a world where both the innocent and the guilty are pawns of fate. Quite as interesting as the poem itself is the preface which Voltaire provided. In the words of Mr. Ira O. Wade (*op. cit.,* pp. 56-57), "He seems here to have bundled together the ideas of Plato, Pope, Bolingbroke, Shaftesbury, and Leibnitz and to have labelled the package *Tout est bien.*" He emphatically renounced Alexander Pope and endorsed the skeptical views of Pierre Bayle. He argued that the English poet's belief in optimism set up a fatalistic system which demolished a whole category of widely accepted ideas such as that relating to free will. If indeed this is the best of all possible worlds, Voltaire continued, there was no such thing as Original Sin; human nature could not be corrupt and it follows that man has no need for a Redeemer. The student will recall that this is the point made at the end of Chapter 5 in *Candide,* wherein Pangloss engaged in a colloquy with "a familiar of the Inquisition." Voltaire also declared that if all misfortunes contribute to the general good, man has no need for future happiness and that he should not seek to find out the causes of moral and physical evil. Moreover, if such is the case, man is as unimportant in the eyes of God as are the very animals that seek to devour him. And this, of course, is the complete negation of the dignity of man. To Voltaire man was not part of a chain, assigned a place in the hierarchical scheme of things: at least he had hope in the future. Voltaire also opposed the idea of a logical chain of events; the earthquake provided sufficient evidence for him to reject the concept of universal order which was an uninterrupted succession and a necessity. Neither Pangloss nor his pupil could subscribe to their creator's point of view. Voltaire concluded that optimism, so far from being a source of comfort, was a creed of despair.

The poem is available in an excellent translation by Tobias Smollett and others in *The Works of Voltaire* (Paris, 1901), from which quotations are made. It is the humanitarian Voltaire, a man deeply moved, who posed the question, can we indeed say that innocent victims were being punished for sin by a just God?

> And can you then impute a sinful deed
> To babes who on their mothers' bosoms bleed?
> Was then more vice in fallen Lisbon found,
> Than Paris, where voluptuous joys abound?
> Was less debauchery to London known,
> Where opulence luxurious holds the throne?

He rejected the charge that selfishness and pride had made him rebel against suffering:

> When the earth gapes my body to entomb,
> I justly may complain of such a doom.

Why, asked Voltaire, could not an omnipotent God achieve His purpose in another way? The earthquake could have occurred in some distant unpopulated area. And should one conclude that the victims should die consoled by the thought that the terrifying event occurred for the general good? God he respected, but he loved weak mortals.

In the poem, as in the preface, Voltaire rejected the doctrine of necessity; it provided no comfort for him. He came close to absolute despair when he wrote that all living things seem to be doomed to live in a cruel world, one of pain and slaughter. How then could one believe in providentialism. How could one say *Tout est bien*? Voltaire's frightening conclusion is that man knows nothing, that nature has no message for us, that God does not speak to him. Man is a weak, groping creature whose body will decay and whose fate is to experience one grief after another.

> We rise in thought to the heavenly throne,
> But our own nature still remains unknown.

The student will recall the pessimistic reply of the dervish to Pangloss, who expressed the desire to probe the meaning of life and man's destiny.

Voltaire sent a copy of the poem to Jean Jacques Rousseau. The answer he received is that which would be expected from the man who was confident that nature was beneficent and who endorsed providentialism. Rousseau's letter was sent on August 18, 1756. He criticized Voltaire for seeking to apply science to spiritual questions, and he argued (as all optimists did) that evil is necessary to the existence of the universe and that particular evils form the general good. Rousseau implied that Voltaire must either renounce the concept of Providence or conclude that it is, in the last analysis, beneficial. Voltaire avoided controversy with the man who was to become his leading adversary; he pleaded illness. The particular significance of all this is that Rousseau, as he tells us in the *Confessions,* remained convinced that Voltaire had written *Candide* as a rebuttal to the argument he had made.

OTHER SOURCES OF INFLUENCE

Voltaire's anti-war views, his hatred of war with all its brutalities, are quite prominent in *Candide.* In Western Europe, in South America, in Morocco, and in Turkey warfare occurred with all its attendant horrors. Voltaire was particularly depressed by the Seven Years War, which began in 1556, the year after the Lisbon earthquake, and was still raging in Europe and in the New World when he wrote *Candide.* The Seven Years War, of course, was the name given to the conflict which arose from a coalition of Austria, France, Russia, Sweden, and Saxony against Prussia, with the aim to destroy, or at least to weaken appreciably, the growing power of Frederick the Great. Historians may point out that the war led to the emergence of Germany as a great modern power, and that it laid the foundations of the British Empire, what with English victories on the American continent. But to Voltaire it was a hideous crime. In the Battle of Prague (May 5, 1756) alone, the Germans lost 20.8 per cent of their strength; there was a comparable number of casualties on the other side. And inevitably the civilian population in the theatre of war suffered greatly.

Voltaire had endeavored to play the diplomat and to bring together Frederick the Great and the Duc de Richelieu in hope that peace could be secured; he failed. On October 11, 1557, he wrote to Mme. de Saxe-Gothe that 20,000 men had already died in a quarrel in which no one was interested. And he wrote many other letters on this subject. In one addressed to M. D'Alembert he declared that those who get themselves killed in the service of kings are terrible fools. One remembers that, while serving with the Bulgars, Candide did his best to hide himself during the conflict. So, far from depicting him as a coward in this episode, Voltaire expected his readers to applaud the youth's behavior.

Deserving brief notice also is the *Essai sur les meurs* (1753-56), which Voltaire began writing during the Cirey period. This work was an attempt, rather successful in consideration of the time in which it was written, to produce a universal history. M. Morize (*Candide,* 1913) stated that the abstract generalizations of the *Essai* become persons and incidents in the philosophical tale. For example, the *Essai* includes material on the French colonies in America; the Jesuits in South America; the Anabaptists; the treatment of captured Christians by the Moors; and comparable material. Indeed, throughout *Candide* are found details the origin of which may be traced to the earlier work.

As regards *Candide,* the source hunters have been indefatigable, citing earlier narratives which, in one way or another, have affinities with the philosophical and/or satirical tale. These include the seventeenth and eighteenth century pastoral and heroic-gallant romances which were so popular. There were also the novels of travel, some of which have been held to have made contributions to *Candide.* These include Fénelon's *Télémaque* (1699); Lesage's widely popular *Gil Blas* (1715-1735), the great picaresque romance memorable for animation of narrative, fluidity, and precision of style; and Montesquieu's *Letters persanes* (1721; additions 1754), the imaginary correspondence of two Persian princes in which are recorded what they observed and experienced in France and their reflections which provided the opportunity for satirical comment on contemporary society and political institutions.

Not to be ignored are Voltaires own philosophical tales written prior to *Candide,* and most particularly *Histoire des voyages de Scarmentado* (1756), which M. Lanson called a kind of preliminary sketch for *Candide.* As Mr. Havens has pointed out (*op. cit.,* p. lxiv), there are in this short prose narrative significant elements which anticipate several found in Voltaire's masterpiece. The *Histoire* also has as its framework the rapid journey of adventure and disappointment peculiar to most of the author's fiction. The hero visited many of the same countries Candide did — France, England, Spain, Holland, Turkey, and North Africa. Moreover, certain plot elements closely resemble ones in *Candide.* The lady Fatele, with her three suitors, Scarmentado among them, suggests Cunégonde with her three — Candide, the Grand Inquisitor, and Don Issachar. Scarmentado witnessed an execution just as Candide did that of Admiral Byng. Finally, both protagonists had experiences with pirates and both became involved in the Inquisition. In the words of Mr. Havens, "The parallels are numerous enough and definite enough to show a real connection in Voltaire's mind between the two works."

STRUCTURE AND STYLE

The narrative technique used by Voltaire in *Candide* dates back as far as the Milesian tales, which were short, erotic narratives first collected in the second century, A.D. These became the source of such Decadent Latin works as Apulius' *Golden Ass* and Petronius' *Satyrican,* copies of which Voltaire had in his library. Related works certainly include the late Greek romances, filled as they were with melodramatic incidents involving the separation of families and lovers, shipwrecks, near-miraculous reunions and discoveries; the pastoral romances, many of which included just this sort of material, and the heroic-gallant romance to which reference has already been made. But basically the structure of *Candide* is that of the picaresque narrative. The problem of the author is to provide the main character or characters with an inciting incident and then to start him or them off on the road to adventure. And that is exactly what happened in *Candide*. Related works, as far as structure is concerned, are Oriental narrative, especially the *Arabian Nights* (available in Galland's excellent translation into the French, *Mille et une nuits* [1747], a copy of which was in Voltaire's library); and the medieval Renard the Fox stories, which originated in Germany and which swept Europe. But the one work which generally is recognized as having given impetus to the type of narrative wherein the hero travels far and wide and has many startling adventures, the one which flourished originally in Spain but soon won popularity in France and throughout Europe, was the sixteenth century *Amadis de Gaula*. *Don Quixote* (1605, 1615) is the acknowledged masterpiece in this tradition.

Strictly speaking, however, the picaresque novel (as the adjective indicates) is the story of roguery. But the technique which it popularized recommended itself to writers of other types of narrative.

So in *Candide* one finds a hero living in his Utopia, the castle of the Baron Thunder-ten-tronckh. Voltaire then posed the basic problem: is this indeed the best of all possible worlds, as his naive hero firmly believed? To answer that question an inciting incident is provided — Candide's amatory play with Cunégonde, which leads to his expulsion from his Westphalian paradise. What follows is a conflict between hope and despair, as the hero experiences one thing after another. And each experience constitutes for the reader, if not until the end for Candide, a refutation of the doctrine of optimism: the brutal treatment at the hands of the Bulgars; the horrors of warfare; the tempest and earthquake; the Inquisition, where he witnessed the hanging of Pangloss and was flogged within an inch of his life; the slaying of the Jew and the Grand Inquisitor, and the stabbing of Cunégonde's brother; the loss of most of his Eldoradoan wealth; the rapacity of Parisian society. In addition, by means of digressions, well justified since each adds to the accumulating evidence against optimism, Candide heard the frightening story of the old woman's sufferings and the disheartening experience of Paquette and Giroflée. Yet even after the appearance of Martin (as late as Chapter 19), he never entirely abandoned hope, although he understandably began to question Pangloss' teachings, especially when that would-be savant reappeared as an abject beggar, ravaged by disease. The series of adventures, therefore, were stages in the education of young Candide. Since he was a slow learner, the series was necessarily a long one, each adventure marked by its own climax — and anticlimax — until the very end of the story, when Voltaire provided the major climax. Up until then, romantic Candide remained hopeful: he could always look forward to the reunion with his incomparable Cunégonde. But when that longed-for event finally took place, he found that his beloved had lost all her beauty; and as they lived together as man and wife she became increasingly shrewish. Best of all possible worlds? His last hope was destroyed. There remained for him only to adopt a kind of stoical retreat: henceforth he would cultivate his own garden, his own little plot of ground.

Admittedly the structure is simple, even obvious, enough; but it exactly served Voltaire's purpose. Candide's experiences, and those of others which were recorded at any length, provide the *reductio ad absurdum* to the facile conclusions of Leibnitz, Wolff, and Alexander Pope. For Voltaire, so far from this being the best of all possible worlds, it too often is a vale of tears; evil abounds. Nor can evil be explained away by saying that, in accordance with the Divine plan, evil contributes to ultimate goodness. Candide's repeated loss of even a modicum of happiness almost as soon as he acquires it points to the fact that Voltaire, structurally, employed the cumulative method as the formula of presentation in his narrative.

"God preserve me from ever being the possessor of a complete Voltaire," wrote Joseph Joubert (*Pensées et lettres,* 1842; trans. H. P. Collins, 1925, p. 214). Especially he denied that Voltaire possessed the emotion of pity. But like practically all other commentators, he had only the highest praise for his countryman as a stylist. "The finest ages of literature have always been those when writers have weighed and counted their words," Joubert also wrote (*op. cit.,* p. 137). He ranked Voltaire very high among those writers. From generation to generation praise of the Frenchman's style has increased, particularly as manifest in his acknowledged masterpiece, *Candide.* Quite properly most critics emphasize the rapidity and absolute clarity. Gustave Lanson stressed these virtues and praised Voltaire for his rejection of all heavy, dull fashions of expression (*L'Arte de la prose,* 1908, p. 155). Lytton Strachey, himself a gifted writer of lucid prose, testified as follows: "Voltaire's style reaches the summit of its perfection in *Candide*...His prose is the final embodiment of the most characteristic qualities of French genius" (*Landmarks in French Literature,* 1912, p. 163). Strachey identified these qualities as clarity, simplicity, and wit. He went on to say: "Compared to the measured march of Bousset's sentences. Voltaire's sprightly periods remind one of a pirouette. But the pirouette is Voltaire's — executed with all the grace, all the ease, all the latent strength of a consummate dancer" (*op. cit.,* p. 165). The testimony of one other critic may be added. In his edition of *Candide* (1960), Mr. William H. Barber pointed out that the very structure of the work demanded that he [Voltaire] write in a pungently concise style, and added: "The many minor characters must be hit off in a phrase, situation must be presented in a sentence or two, journeys accomplished, intervals of time passed over, without the reader losing the sense of furious pace..." (p. 35). Indeed words, phrases, clauses rush along at full speed page after page. And Voltaire managed to sustain this style without leaving his reader with the impression that the pace was too fast to convey the sense of reality. To be sure he did slow down on occasion and introduced more elaborate, wordy sentences. But when he did so, it was usually for purposes of satire and irony, as we shall see later.

It was most appropriate that Voltaire, at the end of his career should have received the accolade as the most brilliant member of the French

Academy. It must be conceded that he attained this honor as a *philosophe*. But originally the Academy was dedicated to the perfection of the French language, and remained so dedicated well into the eighteenth century. *Le mot juste* — the right word — could have been its motto; and Voltaire deservedly has been hailed early and late as one who complied. Moreover, no one had a finer sense of sentence rhythm. If precision, clarity, and rapidity are the first elements of his style which deserve notice, quite as important are the satirical, the ironical elements; these deserve separate discussion in the next and final section.

There remain to comment on and to illustrate other stylistic virtues. Most works suffer through translation, and it must be admitted that *Candide* is no exception. But it has suffered much less than others. In his detailed discussion of the sentence structure and pattern in *Candide*, Mr. Ira O. Wade (*op. cit.*, pp. 243 ff.), has pointed out that short sentences abound, ones with the so-called normal pattern of subject-verb, subject-verb-object. And when modifiers are added to one or more of these elements, the sentence never expands beyond modest proportions. Consider the very opening paragraphs:

> In the castle of Baron Thunder-ten-tronckh in Westphalia, there once lived a youth endowed by nature with the gentlest of characters. His soul was revealed in his face. He combined sound judgment with great simplicity of mind; it was for this reason, I believe, that he was given the name of Candide.

> The baron was one of the most powerful lords in Westphalia, for his castle had a door and windows. Its hall was even adorned with a tapestry. The dogs in his stable yards formed a hunting pack when necessary, his grooms were his huntsman, and the village curate was his chaplain. They all called him "My Lord" and laughed when he told stories.

Voltaire used the device of the formulaic story. It is as if this were a folk or fairy story with its "once upon a time" beginning. This is the art that conceals art. But Voltaire does more than add modifying elements to avoid monotony and excessive predication which leads to it. He could and did build up his sentences to a greater degree so that the story (What happens next?) did not become more important than its meaning. Note the final paragraph in Chapter 22, for example, when Candide, disillusioned by his experiences in Paris, prepared to leave, having managed to bribe the officers of the law to relieve him from custody:

> "I can take you only to Lower Normandy," said the officer. He immediately had the irons removed, sent his men away and took Candide

and Martin to Dieppe, where he left them in the hands of his brother. There was a small Dutch ship in the harbor. The Norman, who, with the help of three diamonds, had been made into the most obliging of men, embarked Candide and his retinue on this ship, which was about to sail for Portsmouth, in England. It was not the way to Venice, but Candide felt that he had been delivered from hell and expected to resume his journey to Venice at the first opportunity.

Here is a good example of effective loose sentences, each illustrating adroit use of coordination and subordination. Also apparent is Voltaire's success in keeping the pattern symmetrical and sustaining the rhythm.

Voltaire found most effective ways to provide concluding statements. Recall Pangloss' account of what happened at the castle when the Bulgars stormed it; note particularly his final remark. Candide had just been informed that Cunégonde was dead and had asked if she died as a result of his being kicked out of the beautiful castle —

"No," said Pangloss, "she was disemboweled by Bulgar soldiers after having been raped as much as a woman can be. They smashed the baron's head when he tried to defend her, the baroness was hacked to pieces, my poor pupil treated exactly the same as his sister. As for the castle, not one stone was left standing on another; there's not one barn left, not one sheep, not one duck, not one tree. *But we were well avenged, because the Abars did the same to a nearby estate that belonged to a Bulgar lord.*

Judicious repetitions are another stylistic device of which the author was master. *Tout est bien* — "All is well" — of course is a refrain line throughout the work; but there are many other examples, two of which may serve as illustrations here. Time and again the repetition of the word *for* (*car*) served as means of inciting derisive laughter at the supposed logic of Leibnitzian philosophy. Following the tempest and the disastrous earthquake in Lisbon, Pangloss attempted to justify his optimism by assuring his companions that things could not be otherwise: "For," he said, "all is for the best. For if there's a volcano at Lisbon, it couldn't be anywhere else. For it's impossible for things not to be where they are. For all is well." It will also be noticed that Voltaire handled dialogue expertly.

The above quotations point to the fact that Voltaire's style is a satiric, ironic one. And it is to this aspect of it that we now turn.

SATIRE AND IRONY IN *CANDIDE*

Largely because of *Candide,* Voltaire ranks with Jonathan Swift as one of the greatest satirists in literature. Satire may be defined as the particular literary way of making possible the improvement of mankind and his institutions. The satirist adopts a·critical attitude and usually presents his material with wit and humor. Aware of grave limitations in the institutions which man has erected, he may seek through laughter to effect a remodeling rather than the demolishing of them. Voltaire is to be identified as such a satirist, and he sought a most thorough-going remodeling of human behavior and institutions.

Basically satire is of two kinds: that which follows the tradition of Horace, which is mild, urbane, good-natured, and which aims to correct by means of tolerant, sympathetic laughter; and that of Juvenal, which is biting, vituperative, derisive, and which is filled with moral indignation at the corruption and evil of man and his institutions. To put it another way, one may say that Horatian satire sports with folly, and that Juvenalian satire attacks crimes or at least offenses deemed to be anti-social. Obviously the latter type, if it invites laughter at all, invites scornful laughter. Both types of satire are found in *Candide*. And the significant thing is that even when Voltaire was most aroused he employed the light touch and achieved a tone often of gaiety that is deceptive to the literal-minded reader who accepts the tale as an exaggerated account of the protagonist's adventures and no more. For Voltaire's primary device as a satirist is that of irony, applying it not only to statement but also to event, situation, and structure.

Irony is a rhetorical device by means of which the writer's or speaker's actual intent is expressed in a manner carrying the opposite meaning. Quite often, as in Voltaire's work, it is characterized by grim humor. Usually the writer sets down words of praise to imply blame, and words of blame to imply praise, the former practice being more common. As a literary device, irony is effective because it calls for restraint. The satirist who depends upon it never descends to railing or to sarcasm; he expects his audience to get the point. One can understand why Thierot lauded Voltaire as the "most excellent author of quips and jests" and that both Baron Grimm and Mme. de Staël stressed the comic aspects of *Candide* while not ignoring the underlying seriousness of the tale.

As the summaries and commentaries have shown, it is hoped, the targets of Voltaire's satire are many and varied. First in importance, to be sure, is philosophical optimism; others include religion, kings and the State, war, avarice, social pride, and folly of one kind or another. In the moral order, dishonesty, sham, prostitution, and all the grave and petty inhumanities of man against man are assailed, just as in the natural order disease, cataclysms, and malformations are. For his purpose Voltaire depended especially upon exaggeration; but he also used the contrasting device of understatement, often in the form of litotes, which is understatement whereby something is affirmed by stating the negative of its opposite—a common device in ironic expression. Related to it is euphemism, a figure of speech in which an indirect statement is substituted for a direct one. Euphemistic terms have been used by many writers to avoid bluntness or offense, but they reveal a tendency to be insincere and sentimental. Voltaire, as we shall see, used them ironically with fine comic effect to advance his satire of injustice, crime, and folly. Caricature and parody, ways in which the author exaggerated details of one sort or another for the same purpose, also must be noticed. There remains to cite specific examples of these devices which Voltaire used so expertly.

To repeat, Voltaire's primary purpose in writing *Candide* was to demolish the theory of Optimism, and for this purpose exaggeration served him best. As Miss Dorothy M. McGhee has made clear (*Voltairian Narrative Method,* 1933, Part IV, Chapter II), he opposed gross absurdity with absurdity—the doctrine repeatedly voiced by Pangloss and echoed by his disciples versus the conclusions to be drawn from the fantastic experiences which are recorded. In Miss McGhee's words (p. 112), "This heaping of event upon event yields first place...to the fact that exaggeration was the means by which the author sought to attain irony." Candide is driven from what for him and others at the baron's castle was "the best of all possible worlds." The carnage of the Bulgar-Abar conflict, the tempest and earthquake, the apparent death of Cunégonde and the actual death of her parents, the experiences during the Inquisition—these and all other salient events are described in exaggerated terms.

The superlative is dominant from the very beginning. Life at the castle of Thunder-ten-tronckh is utopian, a life of perfect happiness. It is a "most beautiful castle." Candide is introduced as the "gentlest of characters" who combined rather sound judgment with great simplicity of mind. The baron is a great, powerful lord in Westphalia; the baroness is the best of all possible baronesses; Cunégonde is the perfect beauty. Pangloss is presented as an oracle, the wisest philosopher in the realm. Already the absurd is opposed to the absurd. We learn that this most beautiful and agreeable of all possible castles, as Voltaire calls it in the last sentence in the chapter, is crude enough, what with its one door and window and its one tapestry. The baroness is obese; the baron obviously a primitive character. But all this exaggeration, all the superlatives prepare the reader for the dire events which are to follow. Similarly in the account of that never-never land, Eldorado, and the description of Don Issachar's residence in the woods, with its spacious gardens and magnificent appointments, Voltaire again used exaggeration as a prelude to adverse fortune.

The author used a variety of forms to oppose Optimism. The formula "best of all possible worlds" appears again and again only to be refuted with satiric and ironic sting. One of these forms involves a type of understatement. Candide is master of it—inadvertently so. Often, after experiencing terrible danger and suffering, his immediate reaction is that Doctor Pangloss might possibly—just possibly—begin to doubt his own philosophy. After hearing the old woman's story in all its horrible detail, he remarks: "It's a great pity that the wise Pangloss was hanged, contrary to custom, in an auto-da-fé: he would have told us admirable things about the physical and moral evils that cover the earth, and I would have felt strong enough to venture a few respectful objections." Recall also his immediate reaction when he learned that the Oreillons, believing him to be a Jesuit, intended to roast or boil him and then eat him: "All is well, I won't argue about it; but I must admit that it's a cruel fate to have lost Lady Cunégonde and then be roasted on a spit by the Oreillons." At the inn in a Spanish village, the old woman expressed her conviction that a Franciscan Father had stolen Cunégonde's money and jewels. Candide remarked that he should have left them enough to finish their journey. There is ironic understatement also to be found in the account of Candide's losses at cards in Paris. The youth was puzzled because he never held any aces; but, wrote Voltaire, Martin was not surprised. It is often through just such laconic statements that the author achieves witty understatement.

Voltaire had a natural tendency toward euphemism, and examples of this rhetorical device are plentiful in *Candide*. Doctor Pangloss was inevitably euphemistic as he voiced the clichés of Optimism to prove that even great evil leads to good. In matters relating to Church and State, the euphemistic cliché also served Voltaire's purpose. The account of the Inquisition, for example, provided him with wonderful opportunities for satirical, euphemistic comment. One should recall the almost ceremonial politeness of the dark-skinned inquisitor when he inquired into Pangloss' views at the end of Chapter 5. The plight of Pangloss and Candide was described in a manner no less ceremonious (Chapter 6).

They were separated and each was placed in *an extremely cool room where no one was ever bothered by the sun.* A week later they were both dressed in sanbenitos and paper mitres...Thus attired, they walked in a procession and *heard a deeply moving sermon, followed by beautiful polyphonic music.* Candide was flogged in time to the singing, the Biscayan and the two men who had refused to eat pork were burned, and Pangloss was hanged, although this was not customary (The italics are this author's).

The incongruity of the scene is pointed up by the formal euphemistic terms in which it is described, and so with reference to Cunégonde's experiences as a spectator at the Inquisition (Chapter 8). The Grand Inquisitor, whose illicit passion for her had been aroused when he saw her at Mass, did her "the honor of inviting her to attend. She had a very good seat" and enjoyed the refreshments served to the ladies between Mass and the executions. It is as if she were attending a fashionable social event!

Cacambo's glowing praise of the Jesuits' government in Paraguay provides another example. "Their government is a wonderful thing. The kingdom is already more than seven hundred fifty miles across, and it's divided into thirty provinces. The Fathers have everything, the people nothing; it's a masterpiece of reason and justice. I don't know of anyone as divine as the Fathers...."

The Bulgar-Abar conflict gave Voltaire quite as good a chance for satire in which he made the most of euphemism (Chapter 2). Having recruited Candide into the service of "the most charming of kings," one of the recruiting sergeants said: "You're now the support, the upholder, the defender and the hero of the Bulgars: your fortune is made and your glory is assured." Immediately after this high-flown speech, Candide was put in irons and taken to a regiment. In this entire episode euphemism as opposed to reality abounds. We read of the gay uniforms, the stirring music — and learn the grim facts of warfare (Chapter 3):

> Nothing could have been more splendid, brilliant, smart or orderly than the two armies. The trumpets, oboes, drums and cannon produced a harmony whose equal was never heard in hell. First the cannons laid low about six thousand men on each side, then rifle fire removed from the best of worlds about nine or ten thousand scoundrels who had been infesting its surface.

After the terrible carnage, Te Deums were sung in each camp: the properties were carefully observed — thus Voltaire's view of "glorious war."

One other quite amusing and effective use of euphemism deserves to be noticed. In the first chapter the beautiful and innocent Cunégonde observed Pangloss and Paquette in a most compromising situation. Voltaire successfully strove to avoid calling a spade a spade:

> One day as Cunégonde was walking near the castle in the little wood known as "the park", she saw Doctor Pangloss in the bushes, giving a lesson in experimental physics to her mother's chambermaid, a very pretty and docile little brunette. Since Lady Cunégonde was deeply interested in the sciences, she breathlessly observed the repeated experiments that were performed before her eyes. She clearly saw the doctor's sufficient reason, and the operation of cause and effect.

Exaggeration, understatement, and euphemism obviously lend themselves to caricature and parody, of which we now take particular notice. Out-and-out caricature is apparent in the characterizations, however brief, of the baron and baroness in Chapter 1. The learned Doctor Pangloss, early and late, is a notable caricature — and so the Jesuit Baron, what with his protestations of undying devotion and then his complete volte-face. The Governor of Buenos Aires, with his multiple proper names, his insufferable pride, provided another example. The entire deflating effect in Chapter 1, with its contrast of naiveté and dogmatism, is sheer parody — especially the mock tragedy of Candide's expulsion from the castle.

In the discussion of the background to *Candide,* reference was made to seventeenth and eighteenth century romantic fiction, especially the pastoral romance and the heroic-gallant adventure narratives, most of them of almost interminable length. Voltaire, who could no more stomach these than could his illustrious predecessors, Molière and Boileau, objected to both style and content, as he made clear in his *Siecle de Louis XIV*. With reference to style, the chief aberrations were those of préciosité. In origin *l'esprit precieux* was the search for elegance and distinction in manners, style, and language. Its devotées sought for new expressions, particularly metaphorical ones; they avoided low or barbarous terms, and — to their great credit — pursued clarity and precision. At its very best *préciosité* stood for sensitivity in taste and sentiment. But it had a narrowing tendency, and the style of the typical romantic writer easily led to excess. The pages of their works were filled with eloquent protestations of undying love, torrents of tears, swooning heroines, sudden recognition scenes, violent deaths, journeys from one country to another. In *Candide* Voltaire no doubt enjoyed himself parodying the *genre:* his hero traveled far and wide; Pangloss was hanged but survived; Cunégonde was reported to have been disemboweled, yet she reappeared; there were deaths of adversaries and flights to temporary safety. The extravagant discourse of the Jesuit Baron perhaps best illustrates caricature and parody in the narrative. When he first met Candide in Paraguay and found out the youth's identity, he was most effusive. "The baron never tired of embracing Candide," we read. And then the reversal follows immediately. When the baron learned that the youth expected to marry his sister, his mood changed, but his discourse and actions were no less extreme: "You insolent wretch! How impudent of you even to think of marrying my sister, who has seventy-two generations of nobility behind her!" Later when Candide and the baron, whom Candide had not really killed, met again, the baron said "You can kill me again, but you'll never marry my sister while I'm still alive." Fully to appreciate the extravagance of his words, one must recall all that had happened to both the baron and his sister — the one now a woman whose beauty had completely faded as a result of her suffering, the other just rescued by Candide from the galleys.

QUESTIONS

1. What are three examples of surprising discoveries in *Candide?* In reference to such discoveries, with what popular fiction does Voltaire's narrative have affinities?

2. What evidence is there that Voltaire's attack upon religion was not limited to Christianity or even to Catholicism?

3. What are the chief elements of personal satire in *Candide?*

4. What episodes reflect Voltaire's experiences at Potsdam?

5. To what extent may Candide at times be identified with Voltaire himself?

6. With what other character has Voltaire been identified? Why?

7. What are three notable examples of exaggeration—one of setting, one of character, one of action?

8. Voltaire has been denounced as a scoffer, a cynic. Is there any evidence that he had not lost his faith in mankind?

9. What views of literature find a place in *Candide?*

10. What chiefly do you find ironic in the author's account of the Inquisition?

11. What do you consider to be Martin's function in *Candide?*

12. In view of Voltaire's relentless attack upon religion, what did he himself believe?

13. Optimism, religion, and war are chief targets of Voltaire's satire. At the social level what else did he satirize?

14. Voltaire's comic gift has been widely recognized. What are three episodes which especially illustrate this gift?

15. How may the old woman's story, a long digression, be justified structurally?

16. What are the chief characteristics of Voltaire's style?

17. What are two examples of caricature in Candide? Of parody?

18. In what special way does the Eldorado episode serve in the author's attack on optimism?

19. What place does the rhetorical device of euphemism have in *Candide?* Illustrate.

20. Discuss these two quotations central to an understanding of *Candide:*
(1) "All is for the best,"—"in the best of all possible worlds."

(2) "We must cultivate our garden."

SELECTED BIBLIOGRAPHY

Paperback of Candide in English: The student should consult the current catalogue of paperback books in print. Among the many available, the following are particularly useful because of their introductions containing biographical and critical material and their notes:

Blair, Lowell, tr. *Candide.* Introduction by André Maurois Bantam Books, Inc.

_____. *Candide.* Introduction by Alex Szogy. Dual Language Books. Bantam Books, Inc.

Butt, John, tr. *Candide.* MacMillan. Acorn Books.

Gay, Peter, ed. and tr. *Candide.* St. Martin's Press, N.Y.

Redman, Ben Ray, ed. *The Portable Voltaire.* Viking Press, N.Y.

The following books, some of which include the text of *Candide* in English, are quite useful:

Aldington, Richard. *Candide, or Optimism.* 1939.

Besterman, Theodore. *Voltaire Essays and Another.* 1962.

Brailsford, Henry N. *Voltaire.* 1935.

Flowers, Ruth Cave. *Voltaire's Stylistic Transformation of Rabelaisian Satirical Devices.* 1951.

Milton P. Foser, ed. *Candide and Ots Critics.* 1962.

Havens, George R. *Selections from Voltaire,* with explanatory comment upon his life and works. 1925.

_____, ed. *Candide and L'Optimisme.* 1934.

Lanson, Gustave. *Voltaire.* 1906. (In French)

Littel, Philip, ed. *Candide.* 1951.

Maurois, André. *The Living Thoughts of Voltaire.* 1939.

McGhee, Dorothy M. *Voltarian Narrative Devices.* 1933.

Meyer, Adolph. *Voltaire: Man of Justice*. 1945.

Torrey, Norman L. *Voltaire and the Enlightenment*. 1931.

_____. *The Spirit of Voltaire*. 1938.

Wade, Ira O. *Voltaire and Candide*. 1959.

THE COUNT OF MONTE CRISTO

NOTES

Including
- *Life of the Author*
- *Character Sketches*
- *Brief Plot Synopsis*
- *Summaries and Commentaries*
- *Suggested Essay Questions*
- *Select Bibliography*

by
Arnie Jacobson
University of Nebraska

Cliffs Notes
INCORPORATED
LINCOLN, NEBRASKA 68501

Editor

Gary Carey, M.A.
University of Colorado

Consulting Editor

James L. Roberts, Ph.D.
Department of English
University of Nebraska

ISBN 0-8220-0326-0
© Copyright 1985
by
C. K. Hillegass
All Rights Reserved
Printed in U.S.A.

1990 Printing

Cliffs Notes, Inc.   Lincoln, Nebraska

CONTENTS

THE COUNT OF MONTE CRISTO
Notes

LIFE OF THE AUTHOR

Dumas, the author of *The Three Musketeers* and *The Count of Monte Cristo,* among scores of other novels, was born on July 24, 1802. His father was somewhat of an adventurer-soldier, a mulatto, and was not a favorite of Napoleon because of his staunch republicanism. Therefore, on his father's death in 1806, when Alexandre was only four, the family was left in rather severe financial straits. The young boy's formal education was scanty, most of it provided by a priest, and as soon as he could qualify, Alexandre entered the services of a lawyer. As he grew older, he became close friends with the son of an exiled Swedish nobleman, and the two of them began to dabble in vaudeville enterprises. Later, as a young man, Dumas went to Paris and secured a position as a clerk to the Duc d'Orleans; this was a marvelous stroke of good fortune, for the Duc would soon become king, and Dumas would write a superb *Memoir* about his many and varied mishaps while he was employed by the future king.

At the same time, Dumas and his old friend, Leuven, produced several melodramas. When he was twenty-two, however, a melodrama of his own making presented itself: Dumas found himself the father of an illegitimate son by a dressmaker, Marie Labay; when the boy was seven, Dumas went to court to get custody of him, and succeeded.

Professionally, this was an extremely happy time for Dumas; for six years, he and Leuven had been collaborating on plays, and their legitimate dramas had been staged to much popular acclaim. Then in 1829, Dumas' *Henri III et sa cour (Henry III and His Court)* was produced; it was Dumas' first spectacular triumph. The Duc was so fond of it that he appointed Dumas the librarian of the Palais Royal.

The Revolution of 1830 interrupted Dumas' playwriting, and for a pleasant and amusing account of these years, one should consult Dumas' *Memoirs* for many rich and humorous anecdotes (not worrying unduly about the degree of truth in them, of course). Then, because Dumas was implicated in some "irregularities" during a noted French general's funeral, he suddenly decided to "tour" Switzerland; as a result, we have another long series of delightful *Memoirs*, this time issued as travel books. It should be noted, though, that Dumas always retained his affectionate relationship with the Duc, and that he eventually returned to France, where he composed many first-rate, long-running plays.

Dumas' well-known collaboration with Auguste Maquet began in 1837 and resulted in a series of historical novels in which Dumas hoped to reconstruct the major events of French history. For example, the Three Musketeers are united in order to defend the honor of Anne of Austria against Richelieu. This particular novel in the series was so popular that Dumas immediately composed two sequels and, by coincidence, *The Count of Monte Cristo* was also written during this same period, with the help of collaborators.

In fact, Dumas, with the aid of collaborators, turned out so much fiction and miscellaneous writing that it has been remarked that "No one has ever read the whole of Dumas, not even himself." We know now, however, that Dumas' assistants only provided him with rough plotlines and suggested incidents to him. He himself filled in the outlines, and all of his novels' manuscripts are in his handwriting.

Like so many creative and productive men, Dumas' life ended in a series of personal and financial tragedies. He built a strangely beautiful and impressive French Gothic, English Renaissance hybrid mansion and filled it with a multitude of scavenger-friends; both home and hangers-on were tremendous drains on his purse, as was the construction and upkeep of his own theater, the Theatre Historique, built specifically for the performance of his own plays.

In 1851, Dumas moved to Brussels, as much for his political advantage as it was to escape creditors – despite the 1,200 volumes which bore his name – and he died not long after a scandalous liaison with an American circus girl, a situation that he might well have chosen as a fictional framework for his demise.

Dumas' son, Alexandre Dumas *fils,* is remembered today chiefly for his first novel, *The Lady of the Camellias,* which was the basis for the libretto of Verdi's opera *La Traviata,* as well as for the plot of one of Hollywood's classic films, *Camille,* starring Greta Garbo.

CHARACTER SKETCHES

The Count and His Friends

Edmond Dantès (alias the Count of Monte Cristo; his other aliases are Sinbad the Sailor, Abbé Busoni, and Lord Wilmore)

Dantès is the dashing and romantic hero of the novel; at the age of nineteen, he is falsely imprisoned for a crime which he did not commit and is kept in the horrible dungeon of the Chateau d'If, where he undergoes unbelievable hardships and sufferings that would destroy an ordinary man. While imprisoned, Dantès hears a fellow prisoner digging a tunnel, and so he too begins digging. When the two men finally meet, the other prisoner turns out to be a learned Abbé, who teaches Dantès many languages, sciences, history, and other subjects. They become as father and son, and when the Abbé is about to die, he reveals to Dantès the hiding place of a long-secret buried treasure, consisting of untold wealth in gold coins, diamonds, and other precious jewels.

After fourteen years of bitter imprisonment and hardships, and after a very daring and miraculous escape, Dantès is able to discover the buried treasure on the island of Monte Cristo, and so he buys the island. He becomes the Count of Monte Cristo and dedicates himself to becoming God's avenging angel. The rest of his life is spent, at first, performing acts of goodness and charity for the good people whom he has known. Then he devotes his life to bringing about God's retribution against the evil people who were responsible for his imprisonment. The largest portion of the novel deals with his unique methods of effecting this revenge against his enemies, who became, during Dantès' fourteen years of imprisonment, very powerful and very wealthy people.

Monsieur Dantès, *pere*

Edmond Dantès' old father, for whom he has a deep devotion – so deep, in fact, that part of the revenge which he takes against his enemies is due to the fact that their treatment of his father caused him to die of starvation. Likewise, those people, like Monsieur Morrel, who treated Dantès' father kindly when he was in despair, come into the good graces of Monte Cristo and are rewarded by him.

Monsieur Morrel, a shipbuilder and shipowner

This is a kindly man interested only in doing good for others and for his family. At the beginning of the novel, when the captain of one of his ships dies en route home, Monsieur Morrel is so impressed with the way that the young, nineteen-year-old Edmond Dantès takes over the captainship of the *Pharaon* that he makes him captain of the ship. This act causes the antagonism of others. Likewise, when Dantès is imprisoned, Monsieur Morrel risks his reputation by continually applying for Dantès' release, even though politically it is an extremely dangerous thing to do. When he learns of the death of Edmond Dantès' father, Morrel arranges the proper ceremonies. Later, upon learning about these facts, the Count of Monte Cristo is able to return the favors triple-fold, for not only does he save Monsieur Morrel's life, but he is able to recover Monsieur Morrel's fortune.

Julie Morrel Herbault

Monsieur Morrel's daughter, who first meets the Count of Monte Cristo as "Sinbad the Sailor"; he sends her on an errand to obtain monies which will save her father's business.

Maximilien Morrel

The son of Monsieur Morrel who will later become not merely a close young friend of the Count of Monte Cristo, but because of his nobility of soul and his devotion and loyalty, he will become the Count of Monte Cristo's spiritual "son" and the recipient of a great deal of the Count's fortune. Thus, virtue is highly rewarded.

Cloclès

A long-time employee in the Morrel firm who remains loyal to the firm, despite its financial difficulties.

Abbé Faria

The wise, learned, and lovable political prisoner in the Chateau d'If; he is a remarkable and ingenious person, capable of creating some digging tools out of virtually nothing. He writes the life history of a noble Italian family, the Spada family (who possessed such great wealth that, after the family suffered poisoning, their fabulous treasure remained hidden for centuries until the Abbé Faria was able to decipher the secret message giving the location of this treasure, which Faria, in turn, reveals to Dantès). Faria becomes Dantès' spiritual "father" and teaches Dantès not only worldly matters of languages, science, and mathematics, but also spiritual matters. His death in the Chateau d'If provides Dantès with his daring means of escape.

Cesare Spada

A member of the Spada family living in Italy in the fourteenth century; he amassed such a huge fortune that the expression "rich as Spada" became a common saying, thus evoking much envy for such great wealth. Spada was poisoned – but not before he secretly buried his great wealth on the island of Monte Cristo. Centuries later, the Abbé Faria worked as secretary to the last surviving member of the family, Cardinal Spada, who still possessed a breviary with some papers dating back to the fourteenth century. When Abbé Faria was writing a history of the family, he discovered the clues which led him to the whereabouts of the secret treasure that later becomes the source of great wealth for Dantès, the Count of Monte Cristo.

Haydée

This is the daughter of the Ali Pasha, whom Fernand, alias Baron de Morcerf, betrayed and sold into slavery. She became the "property" of the Count of Monte Cristo. At Morcerf's trial, she is able to testify as to Morcerf's villainy and thus convict him. Eventually, Monte Cristo begins to fall in love with her and at the end of the novel, they sail off into the horizon: "On the dark blue line separating the sky from the Mediterranean," the white sail carries the Count and Haydée away.

Bertuccio

Early in his life, Bertuccio had been betrayed by Villefort, when he requested punishment for the murderer of his brother, and Villefort, having no respect for Bertuccio's Corsican heritage, ignored Bertuccio's request. This refusal prompted Bertuccio to swear a vendetta against Villefort. Some years later, Bertuccio traced Villefort to the Chateau of the Saint-Mérans, where Villefort was burying alive his and a lady's child (the lady will later be revealed to be the Baroness Danglars). After stabbing Villefort and thinking that he killed him, Bertuccio took the box, assuming that it contained money or gold or something else valuable. To his dismay, a live infant was inside, whom Bertuccio took home to his sister-in-law. The woman raised the child and called him Benedetto; later, his alias is Andrea Cavalcanti.

Bertuccio was involved in a smuggling ring which used Caderousse's inn as a hiding place. One time, Bertuccio was hiding in Caderousse's inn when he overheard the story about Abbé Busoni (alias Monte Cristo) giving Caderousse a diamond; Caderousse sold the diamond, then killed the diamond merchant and his own wife. Bertuccio was falsely arrested for the murders, and he pleaded with the judge to find Abbé Busoni, who could verify his story.

A search was made and eventually, Abbé Busoni came to the prison, listened to Bertuccio's confession, including the details about his alleged murder of Villefort. Abbé Busoni managed to free Bertuccio and recommended that he enter the employment of the Count of Monte Cristo. Thus, when the Count takes Bertuccio to the Chateau of the Saint-Mérans, he knows from Bertuccio's confession to Abbé Busoni that this is the place where Bertuccio attempted to murder Villefort, and therefore, he extracts yet another confession, which is identical to the first. For Monte Cristo, this is proof that he has Bertuccio's total allegiance.

Luigi Vampa

Chief of a large gang of bandits, whose headquarters are in the ancient catacombs outside of Rome. Some years earlier, Monte Cristo met Vampa when the bandit was still a young shepherd, and they exchanged gifts which should have made them lifelong friends, but apparently Vampa forgot because he later tried to capture the Count only to be captured *by* the Count. The Count could have turned Vampa over to "Roman justice," which would have quickly snuffed out his life, but instead, the two men parted friends, with the condition that

Vampa and his band would always respect the Count and all of the Count's friends – this is how the Count was able to so easily rescue Albert de Morcerf. Of course, there is always the suspicion (or knowledge) that the Count "arranged" the kidnapping in the first place, so as to make Albert indebted to him, because it is through Albert's obligations that the Count will be introduced to all of his enemies in Paris, including Albert's father, who betrayed Edmond Dantès many years ago. Vampa also serves the Count by kidnapping Monsieur Danglars at the end of the novel and holding him prisoner until the Baron is forced to spend all of the five million francs that he embezzled from charity hospitals. Again, every indication points to the Count of Monte Cristo's arranging the kidnapping, thus effecting his final revenge against Danglars.

Signor Pastrini

The owner of the Hotel de Londres in Rome who arranges for the meeting between the Count of Monte Cristo and Albert de Morcerf, a meeting which the Count anticipates so that his introduction to his enemies can be effected.

Peppino

An agent of Luigi Vampa, he is deeply indebted to the Count of Monte Cristo for saving his life. Peppino was sentenced to death, and the Count used his wealth (he gave one of the three enormous emeralds from his treasures to the Pope, who installed it in his tiara) and his influence to buy a pardon for Peppino, just minutes before Peppino was to be executed.

Ali, the Count's mute Nubian valet

He serves virtually no function in the novel except to lasso Madame de Villefort's runaway horses, thus obligating the Villeforts to the Count.

Jacopo

Dantès first meets Jacopo when he escapes from the Chateau d'If. Swimming toward a ship which he hopes will rescue him, he is approaching the vessel when his strength gives out. He is pulled out of the water by Jacopo, who then lends him a pair of pants and a shirt. Thus, Monte Cristo is indebted to Jacopo for saving his life and is symbolically aligned with him by sharing Jacopo's clothes.

Later, when Monte Cristo pretends to be wounded on the island of Monte Cristo, Jacopo proves his devotion and loyalty to the Count by volunteering to give up his share of the smuggling bounty in order to look after his friend. Thus, Monte Cristo now knows that he has found a loyal and devoted friend whom he can fully trust to help him once he has recovered the treasure of the Spada family. Later, Jacopo is fully rewarded for his loyalty to the Count by being made, among other things, the captain of Monte Cristo's private yacht.

Enemies of the Count (and their families and friends)

Gaspard Caderousse

He is one of the original conspirators who falsified facts in a letter and thereby framed Edmond Dantès. He never came to Dantès' aid when he was imprisoned, and later, the Count of Monte Cristo comes to him disguised as the Abbé Busoni and learns about the entire nature of Caderousse's conspiracy against Dantès, as well as Caderousse's rampant duplicity. Busoni rewards Caderousse for his narration, hoping that Caderousse will become an honest man. However, Caderousse's greed is too strong, and he continues to rob and murder until one evening, while attempting to rob the Count's house, he is killed by an accomplice, just as the Count reveals that he is Edmond Dantès.

Monsieur de Villefort

Villefort is described early in the novel as the type of person who "would sacrifice anything to his ambition, even his own father." And throughout the novel, whenever political expediency demands it, he denies his own father, who was a Bonapartist and therefore opposed to the ruling royalty. When it is discovered that Edmond Dantès has a letter from the island of Elba, where Napoleon is confined, to be delivered to Villefort's father (Monsieur Noirtier), Villefort, in order to protect his own interest, has Dantès imprisoned in the impregnable fortress of the Chateau d'If, from which there is no escape. (Villefort is the prosecuting attorney, with great powers of life and death.) In addition, Villefort closes his ears to the entreaties of the elder Dantès, as well as to Monsieur Morrel, who tries on several occasions to plead for Dantès' release.

Because of his political ambitions, Villefort is willing to have an innocent man imprisoned for life. Thus, he becomes the central enemy against whom the Count of Monte Cristo effects revenge. During Dantès' fourteen years of imprisonment, Villefort uses all sorts of conniving means to achieve the powerful post of Deputy Minister of France; he becomes the most powerful law enforcement man in the nation. He has also made a politically advantageous marriage to the daughter of the Marquis and Marquise de Saint-Méran and has one daughter, Valentine, by that marriage. He later takes a second wife and has one son, Edouard, by her. He also has had an affair with a woman who becomes the Baroness Danglars, and Villefort uses his wife's family mansion (Monte Cristo later purchases this mansion) to conceal his mistress (the woman who will become Madame Danglars) while she is pregnant. When the child is born, Villefort announces that the child is stillborn and takes the child in a box to the garden, where he plans to bury him alive. However, an assassin who has a vendetta for Villefort stabs him and, thinking that the box contains treasure, he takes it, only to find that it contains an infant who is ultimately raised by him and his sister-in-law. The boy is named Benedetto, and he will later be brought back to Paris by Monte Cristo as Prince Cavalcanti and will accuse his own father, Villefort, of all of his dastardly deeds. This is part of Monte Cristo's revenge: a son whom the father tried to kill as an infant becomes the instrument of Divine Justice and accuses and destroys the evil father.

Renée, the first Madame de Villefort, née Mademoiselle Saint-Méran

The mother of Valentine. Her marriage to Villefort was "politically" arranged, and she does not appear in the novel.

Valentine de Villefort

Valentine is the daughter of the first Madame de Villefort and is, therefore, the granddaughter of the Marquis and Marquise de

Saint-Méran, whose fortune she is due to inherit. This fortune causes extreme envy in her stepmother. Valentine, like her brother, Edouard, and Albert de Morcerf and Eugénie Danglars represent the innocent persons who are trapped by the evil machinations of one or both parents. Valentine's mother, as far as we know, was an innocent person, and Valentine herself represents the absolute purity of young womanhood who will attract the pure love of the noble Maximilien Morrel. She unknowingly also attracts the enmity of her wicked stepmother, who tries to poison her. Since it is the Count of Monte Cristo who recognizes the stepmother's envy and greed and because he instructs her in the use of poison, the Count undergoes his greatest change as a result of his exposure to some of the children of his enemies. Prior to the realization that his beloved friend, Maximilien, loves Valentine, The Count had begun his revenge with the biblical philosophy that the sins of the father will be visited upon the later generations, even unto the fourth generation. Therefore, he is not concerned that Valentine's stepmother might poison her; this would be proper punishment for the wicked father. It is only when Maximilien Morrel reveals that Valentine is his true love that the Count undergoes a significant change of heart, and because of the Count's love for Maximilien, he sets a plot in motion that will save the life of the daughter of his most hated enemy. To do so, however, he must ask her to undergo such tremendous terrors as being entombed alive, until she is reborn into happiness with Maximilien at the end of the novel.

Héloise, the second Madame de Villefort

Early in the novel, in Paris, the Count of Monte Cristo became acquainted with Madame de Villefort, and in an intimate conversation, he discussed with her his extensive knowledge of poisons, particularly a poison known as "brucine" which, taken in small doses, can cure a person but which, taken in larger doses, will kill one. Since Madame de Villefort has a child named Edouard, she becomes insanely jealous of the large fortune which her stepdaughter, Valentine, will inherit from the Marquis and Marquise de Saint-Méran. Likewise, Valentine is to inherit most of Monsieur Noirtier's fortune, making her one of the wealthiest heiresses in France. In Madame de Villefort's desire to possess the wealth that Valentine is to inherit, she poisons both the Marquis and the Marquise (and during the process, one of the servants, Barrois), and then she believes that she has also successfully poisoned Valentine. Later, when her husband accuses her of the poisonings and demands that she commit suicide or else face public execution, she poisons both herself and their nine-year-old son, leaving Villefort totally distraught. Thus, the Count's revenge is complete against the cruel and inhuman Monsieur de Villefort.

Edouard de Villefort

The young nine-year-old son of the second Madame de Villefort and her husband. He is merely an innocent pawn caught in a vicious power struggle. The death of this innocent young boy causes the Count of Monte Cristo to re-evaluate his belief in the rightness of the "sins of the father being visited upon the son." The Count feels deep remorse over the death of the young boy, and he tries to save his life, but on failing to do so, he places the innocent, dead boy beside the body of his dead mother.

Monsieur Noirtier

Villefort's very strong-willed father, who is the source of great embarrassment to Villefort and a threat to his ambitions. Monsieur Noirtier was one of France's leading Bonapartists (supporters of Napoleon), and his political views, his power in the Bonapartist party, and his influence make him a thorn in the side of his son, an opportunist who is willing to support whichever political party is in power. It is because of a letter carried by Edmond Dantès and addressed to Monsieur Noirtier and sent from someone on the Isle of Elba (probably Napoleon himself), that Villefort is persuaded to imprison Edmond Dantès so that no royalists (supporters of the king) will ever know that Villefort's father is so intimately associated with Napoleon. Later in the novel, when Monsieur Noirtier is paralyzed, he is able to communicate only with his servant, Barrois, and with his beloved granddaughter, Valentine, whom he tries to warn about the intricate plots surrounding her because of her pending inheritance.

Monsieur Danglars, later Baron Danglars

When we first meet this envious and devious man, we are immediately aware that he has a jealous hatred for Edmond Dantès simply because Dantès is younger, more capable, more assured, and self-confident and because he is a thoroughly good-natured young man of nineteen, with complete openness, honesty, and frankness. Danglars is the one who conceives of the conspiracy against Dantès, and he is the one responsible for writing the treacherous, anonymous note which sends Dantès to prison for fourteen years. The note and the handwriting are permanently engraved in Dantès' eyes, and years later, he is able to confirm Danglars' evil duplicity by another sample of his handwriting, in addition to the somewhat reliable testimony which Caderousse tells to the Abbé Busoni, an alias for the Count of Monte Cristo. By various illegal means, Danglars first ingratiates himself into the family of a prominent banker, later marries the banker's widow, and by using illegal banking methods, he quickly becomes an extremely wealthy man. The Count of Monte Cristo, however, is even more clever, and he gradually involves himself in Danglars' finances to the point that Danglars eventually goes bankrupt. But he does manage to confiscate five million francs in bank notes, and he flees to Italy, hoping to have them cashed. He is captured by the bandit chief Luigi Vampa, an old friend of the Count of Monte Cristo, and then he is gradually stripped of all his five million francs. He is finally freed by the bandits, but he is now an old and broken man, and, worst of all, he is penniless. The Count's vengeance has at last been effected.

Baroness Danglars

She is the wife of Danglars, but they have lived separate lives for over seven years, and both have their own separate lovers. At present, her lover is Lucien Debray, an officer in Baron Danglars' banking establishment, who is collaborating with her to manipulate stocks and bonds so that they can accumulate large sums of money. When their scheme is over, because Danglars is on the verge of bankruptcy, young Lucien divides the money and then drops Madame Danglars as his mistress. Madame Danglars also figures prominently in another aspect of the plot. Earlier, she had an affair with Monsieur Villefort, the Count's archenemy, and she retired to Villefort's wife's family estate to have their child in secrecy. The estate is later purchased by the Count of Monte Cristo, and her son, whom she thought to be dead, is paid by the Count of Monte Cristo to pretend to be the wealthy

Prince Cavalcanti. As such, her illegitimate son becomes engaged to her own legitimate daughter, Eugénie.

Eugénie Danglars

The daughter who is first engaged to Albert de Morcerf and then, in another arranged marriage, to the bogus Prince Cavalcanti, alias the criminal Benedetto, who is actually her mother's illegitimate son. She abhors the idea of marriage and bondage and wants to live as a liberated woman in charge of her own destiny. When her fiancé is exposed as a fraud and a murderer, she and a girl friend escape; they hope to reach Rome by a circuitous route. Her disappearance is one of the final blows to the pride of her villainous father.

Fernand Mondego, alias the Count de Morcerf

In his youth, Fernand was a simple fisherman and a sometime smuggler who was in love with the woman whom Edmond Dantès was engaged to, Mercédès Herrera. Because Mercédès loved Fernand as a brother, Edmond Dantès trusted him. However, it is Fernand who actually mailed the letter condemning Dantès, hoping all the while that if Dantès was arrested, he would then be able to marry Mercédès. By evil means, he was able to use his smuggling skills and his treachery in warfare to eventually be made a Count and awarded an immense sum of money. Sometime during his rise to power, he married Mercédès, who had waited a long time for Dantès, but finally abandoned hope. Fernand gained most of his wealth by betraying a high authority named Ali Pasha, whose daughter he sold into slavery, and who is now the paramour of the Count of Monte Cristo. When all of his treachery is exposed and he discovers that his wife and son have deserted him, Fernand shoots himself.

Mercédès Herrera, later the Countess de Morcerf

She is the innocent victim of many of the above machinations. She loved only Edmond Dantès, and when he seemingly disappeared forever, she attempted to care for his father. When the elderly Dantès died, she had no place to go, and so she succumbed to pressure and married Fernand. As the Countess de Morcerf, she became an educated and distinguished but unhappy woman. She is the only person who knows that the Count of Monte Cristo is really Edmond Dantès. When she discovers the full extent of her husband's treachery, she leaves his house without any of his wealth (giving all her money to charity hospitals), and she returns to the small house which once belonged to Edmond Dantès' father, there to live out her life in deep prayer.

Albert de Morcerf

When the young Viscount Albert was visiting Rome, he happened to be staying in the same hotel where the Count of Monte Cristo was staying. They became close acquaintances, and when Albert was kidnapped by a gang of bandits, whose chief was Luigi Vampa, a man deeply indebted to the Count of Monte Cristo, the Count was able to rescue Albert before the bandits put him to death. Thus, young Albert was indebted to Monte Cristo forever for saving his life. Because of Albert's obligation to him, the Count was later able to be introduced to all of his enemies in Paris, including Albert's father, Count de Morcerf (alias Fernand), who betrayed Dantès many years ago. Albert, however, apparently inherited all of his mother's goodness and none of his father's treachery. Eventually, Albert wins the love and respect of the Count of Monte Cristo, and even though the Count is on the verge of killing Albert in a duel after he is challenged and insulted by Albert, the Count's willingness to recognize Albert's goodness is another example of "an exception" to his belief in the "sons of the father rightly inheriting their father's guilt."

Benedetto, alias Andrea Cavalcanti

Being the illegitimate son of the immoral Madame Danglars and the corrupt, ambitious, and despicable Villefort, Benedetto represents almost pure evil. It is only by luck that he was not buried alive as an infant, but as his father, Villefort, was about to bury him, Bertuccio saw the box that Benedetto was in and mistakenly believed it to be filled with treasure. Bertuccio hoped to revenge himself on Villefort, and so he stabbed him and took the baby to his sister-in-law. Benedetto lived with her and made her life miserable. Then one day, he tied her up, beat her, and stole all of her money. Later, he was caught and found himself in prison, with Caderousse as a cellmate. By the time of the story, Monte Cristo has tracked him down and has paid him to disguise himself as a wealthy Italian nobleman so that he can use Benedetto in his larger, ultimate plan for total revenge against the traitorous Baron Danglars (by having him become engaged to Eugénie Danglars) and by exposing Villefort as the would-be murderer of his own infant son.

The Marquis and the Marquise de Saint-Méran

The first in-laws of Villefort, whose granddaughter, Valentine, will be the sole inheritor of their fortune, thus arousing the envy of the second Madame de Villefort, who poisons both the Marquis and the Marquise so that Valentine can inherit their fortune immediately and she can then poison Valentine, insuring that Edouard, Valentine's half-brother, will come into an immense fortune.

Monsieur de Boville

He is the Director of Prisons, from whom Dantès buys financial notes which are invested in Monsieur Morrel's shipping firm. Dantès is also able to secretly extract Villefort's note condemning him to what Villefort believed would be a life of isolated imprisonment. Boville is also involved in devastating financial transactions with Danglars.

Doctor d'Avrigny

The attending physician to the Villeforts, who is convinced that the Marquis and the Marquise de Saint-Méran were poisoned. After the death of Barrois, whom the doctor is certain was the victim of the same poison, he threatens Villefort with a police investigation, but is persuaded to keep the matter quiet. With Valentine's "seeming" death, d'Avrigny joins Maximilien in demanding punishment for the "supposed" murderer.

Lucien Debray

A young man in Monsieur Danglars' office who is having an affair with Madame Danglars; Debray and Madame Danglars are using certain information to destroy Danglars' fortune while increasing their own fortune tremendously.

Franz d'Epinay

One of the many men about town; he is a friend of Albert de Morcerf. Franz accompanies Albert to Rome, where he acts as an emissary between the bandits and Monte Cristo after Albert is captured by the bandits.

BRIEF PLOT SYNOPSIS

Edmond Dantès, a handsome, promising young sailor, skillfully docks the three-masted French ship, the *Pharaon,* in Marseilles after its captain died en route home. As a reward, Dantès is promised a captainship, but before he can claim his new post and be married to his fiancée, Mercédès, a conspiracy of four jealous and unsavory men arrange for him to be seized and secretly imprisoned in solitary confinement in the infamous Chateau d'If, a prison from which no one has ever escaped. The four men responsible are:

1. Fernand Mondego, who is jealous of Mercédès' love for Dantès;
2. Danglars, the purser of the *Pharaon,* who covets Dantès' promised captainship;
3. Caderousse, an unprincipled neighbor; and
4. Villefort, a prosecutor who knows that Dantès is carrying a letter addressed to Villefort's father; the old man is a Bonapartist who would probably be imprisoned by the present royalist regime were it not for his son's, Villefort's, influence. Villefort fears, however, that this letter might damage his own position, and so he makes sure, he thinks, that no one ever hears about either Dantès or the letter again.

For many years, Dantès barely exists in his tiny, isolated cell; he almost loses his mind and his will to live until one day he hears a fellow prisoner burrowing nearby. He too begins digging, and soon he meets an old Abbé who knows the whereabouts of an immense fortune, one that used to belong to an immensely wealthy Italian family.

Dantès and the Abbé continue digging for several years, and from the Abbé, Dantès learns history, literature, science, and languages, but when at last they are almost free, the Abbé dies. Dantès hides his body, then sews himself in the Abbé's burial sack. The guards arrive, carry the sack outside, and heave the body far out to sea.

Dantès manages to escape and is picked up by a shipful of smugglers, whom he joins until he can locate the island where the treasure is hidden. When he finally discovers it, he is staggered by the immensity of its wealth. And when he emerges into society again, he is the very rich and very handsome Count of Monte Cristo.

Monte Cristo has two goals – to reward those who were kind to him and his aging father, and to punish those responsible for his imprisonment. For the latter, he plans slow and painful punishment. To have spent fourteen years barely subsisting in a dungeon demands cruel and prolonged punishment.

As Monte Cristo, Dantès ingeniously manages to be introduced to the cream of Parisian society, among whom he goes unrecognized. But Monte Cristo, in contrast, recognizes *all* of his enemies – all now wealthy and influential men.

Fernand has married Mercédès and is now known as Count de Morcerf. Monte Cristo releases information to the press that proves that Morcerf is a traitor, and Morcerf is ruined socially. Then Monte Cristo destroys Morcerf's relationship with his family, whom he adores. When they leave him, he is so distraught that he shoots himself.

To revenge himself on Danglars, who loves money more than anything else, Monte Cristo ruins him financially.

To revenge himself on Caderousse, Monte Cristo easily traps Caderousse because of his insatiable greed, then watches as one of Caderousse's cohorts murders him.

To revenge himself on Villefort, Monte Cristo slowly reveals to Villefort that he knows about a love affair that Villefort had long ago with the present Madame Danglars. He also reveals to him, by hints, that he knows about an illegitimate child whom he fathered, a child whom Villefort believed that he buried alive. The child lived, however, and is now engaged to Danglars' daughter, who is the illegitimate young man's half-sister.

Ironically, Villefort's wife proves to be even more villainous than her husband, for she poisons the parents of Villefort's first wife; then she believes that she has successfully poisoned her husband's daughter by his first marriage. With those people dead, her own son is in line for an enormous inheritance. Villefort, however, discovers his wife's plottings and threatens her, and so she poisons herself and their son.

At this point, Dantès is half-fearful that his revenge has been too thorough, but because he is able to unite two young people who are very much in love and unite them on the Isle of Monte Cristo, he sails away, happy and satisfied, never to be seen again.

SUMMARIES AND COMMENTARIES

Chapters 1–6*

ACCUSATION AND ARREST

Summary

The time: February, 1815. The place: Marseilles, France. The *Pharaon,* a three-masted sailing ship coming from Italy, is docking. Like all dockings, this one attracts a large crowd, but this particular ship draws a great crowd because it belongs to a wealthy man of Marseilles, Monsieur Morrel. Strangely, there is a quiet, solemn air about the approaching ship, even though the pilot seems to have her in perfect control. Suddenly, we see a man being rowed out to the ship, where he hails a tall, dark, and slender young man, Edmond Dantès, on board the *Pharaon.* The man in the rowboat is Monsieur Morrel, the ship's owner, and he inquires about the gloomy mood of the sailors; he is told that their captain died of brain fever, but that the cargo is safe. The handsome young man then gives orders to lower the top sails and invites Morrel aboard. Monsieur Danglars, the purser, comes forward to give Morrel further information about the voyage.

Danglars, a rather melancholy, oily man of about twenty-five, laments the loss of the ship's captain, a man who spent his life at sea. Morrel remarks that a life at sea doesn't necessarily guarantee one's worth as a sailor; he cites young Dantès' obvious skill and relish for sailoring. Danglars' face darkens. Dantès, he says, took command of the ship with no authority and then lingered a day at the Isle of Elba instead of sailing on a straight course for Marseilles. Morrel calls to Dantès and asks him if this is true. Dantès explains that he was carry-

---

*Chapter divisions correspond to Lowell Bair's translation: Bantam Books, 1956.

ing out an order of the late Captain Leclère – to deliver a package to a Marshal Bertrand.

Whispering, Morrel asks Dantès about the health of Napoleon, and Dantès explains that Napoleon inquired about the ship and its cargo and that he was pleased to discover that the ship belonged to Morrel. This news pleases Morrel, and he praises Dantès for stopping at Elba. But he warns him to tell no one about the parcel which he delivered. Dantès then leaves to greet a customs officer, and Danglars steps forward, criticizing the handsome young Dantès and asking Morrel about a letter which the captain gave Dantès along with the packet. Sharply, Morrel asks Danglars how *he* knew about the packet. Danglars tries to explain, but it is obvious that he was eavesdropping; thus, he hastily excuses himself and says that he was wrong to even mention the letter.

Morrel invites Dantès to dinner, but the young man cannot accept; his father awaits him, as does his fiancée, Mercédès. Morrel asks Dantès about Leclère's letter, and the sailor is puzzled. Leclére, he says, was "unable to write."

Then he asks for two weeks' leave – to be married and to go to Paris. He is granted the request; moreover, says Morrel, Dantès shall be the new captain of the *Pharaon* when he returns from Paris – that is, if Morrel can convince his partner to agree to the captainship. Morrel then questions Dantès about the character of Danglars, the purser of the *Pharaon,* and Dantès' answer is immediate: Danglars is no friend of his; however, as a purser, he is quite satisfactory, and if Morrel is satisfied with Danglars, then Dantès will respect the purser.

At home, Dantès' sudden appearance causes his father to go terribly pale. Dantès, in contrast, is exultant! He is a captain at nineteen, with a large salary, plus a share in the profits, and he is soon going to be married to the woman he adores! Noticing that his father is obviously very weak, he discovers that his father has very little money. Dantès had left with a debt to Caderousse, a neighbor, and after Dantès sailed, Caderousse demanded full payment, which amounted to almost the full sum that Dantès left for his father.

Caderousse enters, hoping to gain information about Dantès' new post and also to mock Dantès for refusing to flatter Morrel and accept his invitation to dinner. Dantès, however, dismisses Caderousse's criticism and hurries off to see his fiancée, wincing that Caderousse once did the family a great favor long ago. Caderousse leaves, meets

Danglars, and the two men go to a tavern to drink wine and speculate about Dantès' future.

Not far away is the village of the Catalans, a community of closely knit Spanish people living near Marseilles. Mercédès lives in this village, and at present, Fernand, a young man from her village, is trying to convince her to marry him. Mercédès is frank with him, declaring her love for Dantès, but Fernand begs her to marry him instead. Dantès appears, and he and Mercédès fall into each other's arms. Fernand leaves and is stopped by Danglars and Caderousse. They invite him for a drink and then make him drunk with wine and thoughts of revenge. Dantès and Mercédès pass the tavern, and Dantès is so happy that he invites all three men to his wedding. After the wedding, he reveals, he must go to Paris to deliver a letter which he received on Elba. Danglars is overjoyed with this news; a plot to foil Dantès' promise of happiness begins to form.

Next day, Dantès' official appointment as captain of the *Pharaon* is made in the tavern amidst much celebrating. But when the thunder of three loud knocks is heard, all is quiet. Four armed soldiers and a corporal enter. Dantès is arrested – with no explanation.

Meanwhile, in one of the aristocratic residences of Marseilles, another betrothal is being celebrated by several enemies of Napoleon. At the center of this scene is Monsieur de Villefort, who describes Napoleon as *more* than a man; he was, Villefort says, a symbol, the personification of equality. Those assembled are obviously royalists, and they chide Villefort about his attitude toward Napoleon. Villefort flashes with anger: his *father* may be a Bonapartist, but *he himself* is the antithesis of his father.

At that moment, a servant enters and whispers that a Bonapartist plot has been discovered: Edmond Dantès has been charged as the traitor responsible for delivering correspondence between "the usurper" and the Bonapartist party of Paris.

Villefort leaves to question Dantès, and at the police commission, he meets Morrel, who pleads Dantès' innocence, which is unnecessary, for as Villefort questions Dantès, he sees that the young man is utterly candid and frank – and innocent. Villefort gives Dantès the accusatory note; Dantès, he says, has jealous and dangerous enemies. Dantès then tells Villefort that the letter was entrusted to him to give to a certain Monsieur Noirtier. Villefort pales; Noirtier is his father. He makes Dantès swear that no one knows the contents of the letter, then he apparently frees him, hoping fervently that no one can link him, Villefort, with any traitorous plot of his father's.

Dantès leaves, but instead of being escorted to freedom, he is shut behind the iron doors of a prison. A police van then comes for him, and he is placed in a boat, despite his protests. He is rowed to the Chateau d'If, an infamous prison because of its brutality and its impossibility of escape, and then he is taken to the dungeon, where they throw "madmen with madmen."

Commentary

The greatness and the enduring popularity of *The Count of Monte Cristo* is mainly accounted for by the narrative force of the novel. In very simple terms, the novel tells an exciting story in an engaging and straightforward narrative—a narrative that grasps and involves the reader in the action. This novel is, in literary terms, a "well-made Romantic adventure story." By "well-made," we mean that very early in the novel, Dumas sets up his characters, even though they are one-dimensional and predictable, and places them in situations where their actions are such that the reader will respond to them with sympathy or with revulsion and dislike. Thus, in the opening scenes, Danglars is presented as a troublemaker, a jealous and envious person for no other reason than pure jealousy and spite. He makes all sorts of false insinuations against Dantès in order to disgustingly ingratiate himself before the owner of the ship, Monsieur Morrel. In contrast to Danglars' sniveling and sycophantish behavior, Dantès is open and aboveboard in all his dealings. He immediately evokes trust in everyone except the envious Danglars, and it is Dantès' excellent qualities which win the complete confidence of the shipowner Morrel; in fact, as we learn later, Dantès has won the total allegiance of Monsieur Morrel, for he will risk his business in order to intercede for the imprisoned Dantès.

In the "well-made novel," we are immediately attracted to the hero and are likewise repulsed by people like Danglars and his cohort, Caderousse, the dishonorable neighbor who forced Dantès' old father into virtual starvation by demanding the return of a loan which Caderousse had made to Dantès. Early in the novel, therefore, the forces of good are aligned against the forces of evil and destruction. And in this alignment, Mercédès' friend Fernand becomes a willing partner in the conspiracy to frame Dantès (Fernand mails the accusatory letter), and, consequently, in these first six chapters, we have met all four enemies (Danglars, Caderousse, Fernand, and Villefort), against whom Dantès will ultimately seek revenge for his fourteen years of imprisonment.

By the term "Romantic," we mean a novel that is filled with high adventure, one in which the hero possesses the most noble of qualities and where he is often put to various tests and survives these tests superbly. It is a novel that does not focus on intricate character analysis, but emphasizes, instead, the narrative plot element, and the success of this type of novel is measured by how much it engages or captures the reader's interest in the adventures set forth.

In the first six chapters, Dumas has created his main character, or hero, has shown his superb qualities and capabilities, has presented him as a loyal friend to the late captain and as an honorable man of his word. Dumas has involved his character innocently in a political intrigue about which Dantès knows nothing. Furthermore, he is exposed to an overly ambitious official, Monsieur Villefort, who "would sacrifice anything to his ambitions, even his own father"; in addition, Villefort marries a woman whom he doesn't love in order to advance his financial and political future, and Villefort also uses Dantès as another instrument to further his career when he lies to the king that Dantès is a dangerous rebel involved in a treasonous plot against the king. These false accusations and political concerns cause Dantès to be sentenced to life imprisonment in the infamous Chateau d'If, a fortress legendary for its severe punishment and for its impossibility of escape. Until the time of this story, no prisoner had ever successfully escaped from this fortress, therefore making Dantès' escape a feat of great daring and magnitude.

The reader, of course, responds emotionally to Dantès' plight. While we do not now know who the author of the note is, we can assume that the jealous and spiteful Danglars is the perpetrator since he is the only person to know about the letter which Dantès was to deliver to Monsieur Noirtier. And ironically, if the letter had not been addressed to Villefort's father, an avid Bonapartist, then Villefort, a royalist, would not have used Dantès so badly, but Villefort's ambitions force him to remove anyone who might influence his desperate desire to rise to power. If Dantès knows the contents of the letter, or even the name of the addressee, then Villefort knows that he will be "ruined, ruined forever." Therefore, it is absolutely necessary to do away with Dantès forever, and thus by the end of the sixth chapter, the noble

Dantès is falsely imprisoned with no hope of escape and no hope of making contact with anyone in the outer world. In a rather catatonic state, he argues with a guard in the prison, and as a result, he is placed in a dungeon. These first six chapters, then, have shown the hero to be a person of potential greatness and honor being reduced to a hopeless prisoner with no hope for release and no contact with the outer world.

Chapters 7 – 12

DANTÈS' IMPRISONMENT

Summary

In his study at the Tuileries in Paris, King Louis XVIII jokes about Bonaparte's partisans causing "trouble" in the south of France – that is, he jokes about it until Villefort's arrival is announced. Villefort brings news of "dire importance" about a traitorous conspiracy: Napoleon has manned three ships, has left Elba, and is undoubtedly sailing for France. Villefort, carefully avoiding all names, says that he learned of this plot from a man (Dantès) whom he immediately ordered to be arrested when he learned that this man planned to carry a message to a dangerous Bonapartist in Paris (actually, Villefort's own father).

At that moment, the Minister of Police arrives and announces that Bonaparte landed near Antibes two days ago and is now marching on Paris. Louis is so angered that he is unable to speak, but in gratitude, he removes the Legion of Honor cross from around his neck and bestows it on Villefort because of Villefort's patriotic zeal. Later, and not without a little envy, the Minister of Police comments that Villefort has made "a magnificent beginning," and that his "fortune is assured." Villefort, we gather, is already impatient for the promising future that seemingly lies ahead for him.

Napoleon returns to France, ousts Louis, and begins what will be his Court of the Hundred Days. Normally, Villefort would probably have suffered the same fate as King Louis, but because of the influence of Villefort's father at Napoleon's court, Villefort retains his post. When Napoleon is defeated at Waterloo and Louis returns to the throne, Villefort is able to use his own influence to reinstate himself politically, and he decides to marry a woman whose family will further his political ambitions.

Meanwhile, Dantès remains a prisoner and knows nothing about Napoleon's return and his crushing defeat, or about Louis' return to Paris. Mercédès lives in absolute despair and is saved from suicide only because of her strong faith. Likewise, Dantès himself so despairs of ever gaining freedom that, finally, he too is on the brink of suicide. All hope seems to be absolutely denied to him. Thus, he decides to starve himself to death.

It is while Dantès is numb with hunger and illness that he hears a curious, animal-like scratching outside his cell, within the earth or within the foundations of the prison. It is not rats, he discovers; it is the famous old "mad Abbé Faria," who, it is believed, knows the location of a fabulous treasure. The Abbé has been imprisoned for twelve years and now believes that he will finally be able to burrow his way to freedom.

The Abbé and Dantès become fast friends, and as the Abbé teaches Dantès languages, history, and science, they begin to make elaborate plans to cooperate in tunneling out of the prison. After some years, they begin their labors, carefully and secretly digging through the earth beneath the foundation of the prison. Finally, they believe that they are almost ready to escape, but the Abbé cannot continue; he collapses in a cataleptic seizure. He simply cannot go on. He urges Dantès to do so, but Dantès cannot; he refuses to desert his friend. Dantès' loyalty so impresses the Abbé that when he recovers, he tells Dantès about the hidden treasure. It actually exists, the Abbé insists, and in the fourteenth century, it belonged to the famous Spada family, for whom the Abbé worked. Since there is no family remaining, the treasure now belongs to whoever finds it. It is buried, the Abbé says, in a cave on the little island of Monte Cristo.

Dantès urges Faria to resume their plans for escape and although he is very weak, the Abbé does, but again he collapses, this time in fearful and harrowing spasms, and then lies unconscious. Dantès tries to revive him, as he did before with the Abbé's potent medicine, but this time, it is to no avail.

Panicking, Dantès scurries along the secret passageway back to his own cell and waits until he thinks that it is safe to return to the Abbé's cell. When he does so, he carefully removes a stone from the cell wall and sees the Abbé's corpse encased in a shroud. His future plans crumble; he cannot think of escape any longer. He and the Abbé have been like brothers, working long and difficult hours in order to reach freedom. Now Dantès is alone. Yet a small flicker of the possibility of escape remains in Dantès, and clutching at freedom like a drowning man, he takes the Abbé's body back along the secret corridor, lays it out on his own bed, toward the wall, replaces the stone leading to their secret passageway, and hurries back to the Abbé's cell, where he stitches himself into the Abbé's shroud. And none too soon, for the prison guards arrive and lift up Dantès' stiffened body. Ominously, one of them comments that the corpse seems unusually heavy, and for an instant, Dantès is filled with fear, but nothing more is said as they carry him out of the prison. Then Dantès hears the sound of waves breaking against the rocks of the Chateau d'If.

"What miserable weather," one of the guards remarks, and they both laugh. Dantès hears a heavy object being dropped on the ground, and then he feels the sudden pain of a heavy rope being knotted around his ankles. There is more laughter, and then Dantès is heaved far out into the depths of the fierce, icy sea – the "cemetery," Dantès realizes, of this abominable prison.

Commentary

In these chapters, we have two main concerns: first, Chapters 7 and 8 are concerned with establishing the greed and the ambition of Villefort, and second, the experiences of Edmond Dantès as a prisoner in the dungeon of the Chateau d'If. Clearly, Villefort's ambitions are largely responsible for Dantès' imprisonment, and here, we also see additional evidence that "he [Villefort] would sacrifice anything to his ambition, even his own father." Villefort's ambitions *also* lead him to postpone his marriage to the daughter of the Marquis de Saint-Méran – if Napoleon regains power; if that happens, he will marry someone whom his father would know since his father is one of the most prominent Bonapartists in Paris; otherwise, Villefort will marry the royalist Saint-Méran's daughter – if Napoleon is again exiled. Villefort's ambition caused him to imprison Dantès, and later, because of Dantès' sense of "justice," his ambition will be his downfall.

During the early years of Dantès' imprisonment, Dantès suffers almost every stage of human emotion that can be imagined. He begins his term of imprisonment with pride and hope, being fully conscious of his innocence, but then his pride and hope are replaced by *doubt,* which is followed by fervent prayers to God. Then his soul becomes dark, and his despondency turns into wrath. In utter despair, Dantès finally decides upon suicide by starvation.

The greatness of a novel is often related to the universal appeal of that novel. For example, Dumas creates very vividly here the idea of a trapped animal which wishes desperately to escape, and we, the readers, respond completely to Dantès' desperate plight and his determination to escape because it is a basic aspect of human nature to sympathize with a trapped animal, whether it is a dog tied on a leash or a human being chained to a chain gang. Correlated with this universal idea is another scene that is now famous to almost everyone in the Western world—that is, in imprisoned solitude, one hears the faint beginnings of contact with another person.

After six years of virtual isolation in prison, Dantès finally hears an unusual and curious noise, the constant and continual scraping sounds of a prisoner trying to escape. The ray of hope that escape is possible restores Dantès to life. This scene, of course, is famous because it, or variations of it, have been the plot of many later books and untold movies about the attempted escape of innocent prisoners. Every detail of this scene has been so often repeated that it is difficult to conceive that this is the original version of the story. One can only be stunned at Dantès' realizing the *possibility* of human contact after being isolated for a full *six years.*

His contact with the Abbé Faria will be the most important contact that Dantès will ever make. For eight years, he will be a constant companion with a man who possesses one of the finest minds of that time; this is an immense stroke of good fortune for Dantès, who is himself a quick student with many natural endowments, a prodigious memory, a keen intellect, a mathematical turn of mind, the poetic strain which is in every sailor, and the ability to quickly master languages. Within a year, in addition to the French, Greek, and Italian which Dantès already knows, he adds Spanish, English, and German. Also, Dantès quickly learns history, sciences, and basic human psychology, all of which will serve him perfectly in times to come. For example, Dantès observes the psychological and analytical mind of the Abbé when, by simply questioning Dantès, the Abbé is able to identify the persons of Danglars, Caderousse, and Fernand as the people who betrayed Dantès; the Abbé is also able to determine the relationship between Villefort and Monsieur Noirtier, Villefort's father, fully explaining the motivations which prompted Villefort to have Dantès imprisoned.

The purpose of the plan to escape and the completion of the plan come at a time when both men *could* have escaped except that the Abbé has one of his rare cataleptic seizures. His life is saved by some miraculous drops which he has, but he is so weakened that he is no longer able to carry through with his plans for escape. Thus, he sends Dantès on to escape by himself, but Dantès refuses. The point of this narration is to test Dantès' loyalty – that is, the loyalty of the hero. Dantès' refusal to escape, his refusal to desert his beloved friend (or father figure) shows him to be a person essentially noble of heart and worthy of the secret which the Abbé will now share with him. In works of Romantic fiction, the hero is tried and tested and must be proven to be true and dependable. Dantès easily passes these tests; had he not been found to be true and loyal and noble, he would have escaped empty-handed, but now that he has proven himself to be noble-hearted and devoted, the Abbé will reveal the secret of the hidden treasure to him.

In a realistic novel or in real life, such virtue is not necessarily rewarded. However, in a Romantic novel, virtue is always rewarded and vice is always punished. Consequently, once Edmond Dantès has proved himself to be loyal, faithful, and trustworthy to the Abbé, he is given the history of the Spada family and the secret of the immense treasure which is hidden on the island of Monte Cristo. (One should note that the method which Abbé Faria used to discover the treasure – that is, a document written in invisible ink which becomes legible under heat – is a literary device that has now become commonplace since this novel was published.)

With the possibility of an immense fortune coming to him, Dantès thinks of "all the good a man could do for his friends with such a fortune, and at those moments, [his] face would darken because he remembered the oath of vengeance he had sworn, and he thought of how much harm a man could do to his enemies in modern times with such a fortune." When Dantès escapes, he will use his immense fortune for both purposes – to reward his friends, and to punish his enemies.

Dantès' escape from the Chateau d'If is perhaps the most daring and the most famous escape scene in all of literature. The imagination, the fortitude, and the ingenuity of the escape is equalled only by the courage and desperation that it would take to exchange places with a dead man, concealing oneself in a heavy canvas bag, not knowing if you were going to be buried alive, burned, or otherwise done away with. Few people could be so desperate that they would be willing to face such unknown terrors without resorting to utter panic. Dantès' calmness in the face of such terror and adversity is the very stuff of which Romantic heroes are made. And the difficulty of the escape is correlated with the pleasure that the reader has when that escape has been effected.

Dantès' fourteen years of imprisonment represent a major portion of his life. Now thirty-three, the age at which Christ rose from the dead, Dantès escapes from prison, and he figuratively "rises from the dead" as he cuts through the burial shrouds and emerges naked into a new world as a reborn man.

Chapters 13 – 19

MONTE CRISTO'S GENEROSITY

Summary

Stunned and almost suffocating, Dantès manages to rip open the shroud-sack with a knife, and then he cuts himself free from the cannon ball that is tied around his feet. But he is still not safe. The waves around him churn and rise like phantoms. Finally, however, Dantès is able to reach the small island of Tiboulen, where, exhausted, he falls asleep on its jagged, rocky shoreline. Briefly, he wakes long enough to see a small fishing boat smashed against the rocks, its crew lost. Then, in almost disbelief, he sees a single-masted Genoese ship approaching, and snatching up a cap from one of the drowned crew of the fishing ship, he hails the tartan and is taken aboard. He tells the captain that he is Maltese, and he explains that he has a six-inch beard and foot-long hair because of a vow that he made to Our Lady of Piedigrotta. He is given trousers and a shirt and is hired on as a sailor.

Fourteen years have passed since Dantès entered prison as a handsome young stripling of nineteen. He is now thirty-three. What has happened to his beloved Mercédès in these fourteen years? And what has happened to his father? to Danglars? Fernand and Villefort? His dark eyes flash with hatred at the thought of these last three names. His spirits brighten, though, when he suddenly sees an island appear amidst the soft pink rays of the rising sun. It is the Isle of Monte Cristo, the isle of his immense, secret fortune.

Two and a half months pass, and Dantès becomes a skillful smuggler (for the boat which rescued him was a smuggler's ship). His strategy is to remain a smuggler long enough so that he can avoid all suspicion when he finally decides to sail for Monte Cristo and claim his hidden fortune. Fate lends a hand to Dantès when the captain of the smuggling ship decides to dock at Monte Cristo and make an illegal exchange of goods with a ship from the Levant.

On the island, Dantès pretends to be hunting for goats, and he does actually kill one and sends it back to camp with Jacopo, a sailor who has befriended him. Then, in order to be able to remain on the island, Dantès pretends to have hurt his leg. Reluctantly, his comrades leave him, but as soon as their ship is at sea, Dantès searches for the treasure and, with difficulty, he finally finds it in a second cavern beyond the cave which he first entered. The cask which he unearths is filled with gold coins, unpolished golden ingots, and diamonds, pearls, emeralds, and rubies. Dantès is giddy and wild. He feels on the brink of madness. All of these incalculable, fabulous riches are for him and him alone!

Six days later, the smuggling ship returns, and Dantès boards it, carrying several carefully concealed diamonds. In port, he exchanges them for a small yacht, sails for Monte Cristo, and places his immense fortune in an especially built, secret compartment on board the yacht. Then he boldly sails into the port of Marseilles with an English passport.

The narrative now moves to the south of France, to an inn that is owned by Dantès' old neighbor, Caderousse. Caderousse is visited by Dantès, disguised now as Abbé Busoni, an inquisitive priest who says that he is the executor of Dantès' will; accordingly, he asks Caderousse numerous questions about what happened to Dantès' three "friends" – Caderousse, Danglars, and Fernand – and also about the fate of Mercédès, Dantès' former fiancée. Caderousse is cautioned by his wife not to be so candid, but Caderousse loves to talk; besides, he has become very cynical about life. Thus, not knowing that it is Dantès to whom he is speaking, he reveals that:

(1) Monsieur Morrel risked his life trying to legally set the "rabid Bonapartist" (Dantès) free.

(2) Dantès' father is dead, so he has no use for Dantès' money.

(3) Danglars was no friend to Dantès; in fact, he instigated Dantès' arrest; *he* doesn't deserve Dantès' money.

(4) Fernand has been friendly with Danglars ever since he mailed Danglars' denunciation of Dantès; furthermore, he himself compromised all nationalistic and moralistic principles in order to have himself made a Count; he now lives in Paris with his wife, the beautiful Mercédès.

(5) Villefort married well, has received many honors, and is wealthy.

The "priest" (Dantès) tells Caderousse that "God's justice" demands that Caderousse be given a fabulous diamond, worth fifty thousand francs. In exchange, the "priest" asks for the "red silk purse" that Morrel, the shipowner, left full of money on Dantès' father's mantle, a purse that is now in Caderousse's possession. The "priest" then takes the purse and leaves, and Caderousse and his wife are dumbfounded at their sudden, miraculous good fortune.

Next day, Dantès, again in disguise, this time as an English gentleman, acts as a representative from the firm of Thomson and French and makes inquiries about the firm of Morrel and Son. He is told that they are rumored to be on the brink of bankruptcy. Therefore, Dantès purchases a very large account, which Morrel will soon have to pay off. Still in disguise, Dantès visits Morrel; during the visit, Morrel is told that his only remaining ship, the *Pharaon,* has sunk in a hurricane. The few half-naked sailors in Morrel's office are paid their wages and are discharged. Morrel can do no more. He has no money. But at that moment, the disguised Dantès tells Morrel that the bill which will soon be due does not have to be repaid until three months later. Morrel is so choked with emotion that he can barely speak. Before leaving, Dantès tells Julie, Morrel's daughter, that sometime in the future she will receive a message from "Sinbad the Sailor," and that she must do exactly as "Sinbad" tells her to do – "no matter how strange."

Because of the generous financial postponement offered him, Morrel is able to remain financially solvent – but only barely so. Therefore, he goes to Marseilles to ask the millionaire Danglars to guarantee a loan for him. Danglars refuses, and Morrel returns to Marseilles, overcome with humiliation and despair.

Morrel tells his family that this time, they're "lost," and Morrel fully intends to commit suicide; he tells his son, Maximilien, that if he were to live without paying his bills, he would be disgraced. If he kills himself, however, he will die – and be remembered – as "an unfortunate but honorable man." His son reluctantly understands and allows his father to be alone.

At the very moment that Morrel lifts a pistol to his mouth, his daughter cries out that they are saved! She says that she went to a house in the Allées de Meilhan, which the note from "Sinbad" asked her to do, and there she found an old red silk purse; inside it was a bill for two hundred and eighty-seven thousand, five hundred francs, marked *paid!* There was also a "diamond the size of a walnut" in the purse, alongside a small piece of parchment, which read "Julie's dowry." Then, suddenly, Julie and her father hear a voice crying out that the *Pharaon* is coming into port. Morrel's strength fails him, but the news is absolutely true: an exact duplicate of the lost *Pharaon*, with a full cargo, is ready to dock.

Unnoticed, a handsome and smiling gentleman calls out to Jacopo to bring a boat; then the two men row toward a beautifully rigged yacht. On board, the handsome gentleman looks out to sea and bids a formal farewell to "kindness, humanity and gratitude." Henceforth, he will be an agent of vengeance and will "punish the wicked." He gives a signal, and the yacht puts out to sea.

Commentary

Even the most elemental reader will recognize the Romantic technique of having the hero escape during a storm – the cliche, of course, is that the storm outside is correlated with the storm raging in the breast of the hero. Here too, the noise of the storm ironically masks Edmond Dantès' cry for freedom, and it is also ironic that Dantès is rescued by smugglers and that the young smuggler Jacopo will ultimately become the captain of the yacht of the Count of Monte Cristo, another indication that the Count is always generous with those who have been kind to him.

Edmond Dantès has been in prison for fourteen years, and during that time he has not shaved nor had a haircut, yet he is able to successfully account for these matters by his ingenious story that he made a religious vow not to cut his hair for ten years.

When Dantès does cut his hair, he is drastically changed. He entered the Chateau d'If with the round and smiling face of a happy young man. Now his oval face has lengthened, his lips have taken on a line of firm resolution, and his eyebrows now possess a thoughtful wrinkle; his eyes are of deep sadness with occasional flashes of dark hatred, and his skin has grown wan and pale. Thus, Dantès' physical attributes have changed to the point that his old enemies will not recognize him, and, consequently, he will be able to move among them with complete anonymity, effecting his revenge without suspicion. (As we later discover, only Mercédès, the woman he was about to marry when he was arrested, recognizes him, and she does not reveal his secret.)

More important, Edmond Dantès has changed inwardly. Because of the tutelage of Abbé Faria, he has mastered many languages, he has learned much history and politics, he has studied mathematics and the sciences, and he has been exposed to treachery and betrayal by honorable men in high places. Thus, the deep learning that Dantès has acquired is now reflected in his face by an expression of intelligent self-confidence. Certainly, he is no longer the trusting and naive young man that he was at the beginning of his imprisonment fourteen years ago.

In Chapter 15, we have the search for buried treasure. Here, Dumas appeals to a very basic instinct in human nature by having Edmond Dantès discover a secret treasure of untold value – diamonds, rubies, emeralds, pearls, and gold coins of immense value are now in his possession. The universality invoked is that most people have, at some time or other in their lives, harbored a dream of discovering a buried treasure, or else they have dreamed that they might, in some way, become the sudden recipient of untold wealth. This human desire can be found in works from Homer's *Iliad* (when the hero Achilles is offered all sorts of valuable prizes if he will return to war) to Stevenson's *Treasure Island,* and to modern-day TV shows, which give away large sums of money. The search for buried treasure is one of the many universals that Dumas uses to involve his reader in his exciting adventure story.

In order to stay on the island of Monte Cristo, Dantès has to create an ingenious ruse to persuade the smugglers to leave him there. But

Dantès' plan *almost* fails because Jacopo wants to stay with him — even though that would mean that Jacopo would sacrifice his rather significant share in the smuggling profits. Thus, this particularly unselfish act is a correlation to Dantès' resolve to remain with the ailing Abbé Faria, and in a lesser way, Jacopo will also be rewarded for his unselfishness and for his devotion to Dantès; he will become the trusted servant and friend that Edmond Dantès needs so badly at this time in his life.

In Chapters 15 and 16, Dantès discovers what has transpired during his imprisonment. Then he goes to his old neighbor, Gaspard Caderousse, and all of the projections of Abbé Faria about Dantès' "friends" are confirmed by Caderousse — that is, Danglars wrote the letter of betrayal, and it was mailed by Fernand — both of whom are now wealthy and titled men of France. In addition, Dantès learns of all the wrongs which were perpetrated against him, and of the people like Monsieur Morrel who risked his own life trying to obtain Dantès' release.

This section illustrates particularly well how thoroughly Dantès has learned the basic psychology of mankind during his tutorials with Abbé Faria; that is, in his disguise as Abbé Busoni, Dantès shows a diamond worth fifty thousand francs to Caderousse, suggesting that the diamond is to be divided between Dantès' four old friends and Dantès' father. Dantès, however, is absolutely certain that Caderousse, because of greed, will tell the exact (and damning) truth about Danglars, Fernand, and Villefort. Dantès' father is dead and is of no matter to Caderousse. And, as is apparent to both the reader and to Dantès, Caderousse convicts himself of the most base treachery in his narration so as to get full and sole possession of the diamond; ultimately, he will murder a jeweler from Paris, as well as his own wife, and thereby enter upon a career of all sorts of crime until he is finally apprehended by Abbé Busoni (alias the Count of Monte Cristo).

Chapter 17 serves a double purpose. By buying financial notes (two hundred thousand francs worth) which would aid his old friend and benefactor (Monsieur Morrel) from the Director of Prisons, Monsieur de Boville, Dantès is able to gain access to all the prison records and thus confirm whose handwriting assigned him to supposedly life imprisonment; the handwriting is Villefort's.

During Caderousse's narration, it is furthermore discovered that *all* of Dantès' enemies have prospered and are now among the most powerful and the most wealthy men of France. It would have been an easy or simple task of revenge if all of his enemies had remained simple and unpretentious people. Instead, all except Caderousse have prospered tremendously, and thus, Dantès' task of revenge will be more involved. That is, their wealth, their political influence, and their power make the Count's task of revenge much more complicated and difficult, but also, to use the common cliche, "the bigger they are, the harder they fall." Dantès, of course, will finally be able to topple the most powerful, the most wealthy, and the most influential men of France by using slow and deliberate subterfuges. If readers are ever tempted to sympathize with the victims, they should always keep foremost in mind how Edmond Dantès suffered in prison for *fourteen* long and miserable years as the result of their treachery.

At the end of Chapter 19, Dantès has now used his wealth to perform all sorts of good deeds – to reinstate Monsieur Morrel and to re-establish the Morrel family name. The rest of the novel will show how Dantès (now about to assume the identity of the Count of Monte Cristo) effects his revenge upon his enemies. As Dantès himself expresses it: "And now farewell to kindness, humanity, and gratitude. Farewell to all sentiments that gladden the heart. I have substituted myself for Providence in rewarding the good. May the God of Vengeance now yield me His place to punish the wicked!"

Chapters 20-21

MONTE CRISTO'S REVENGE

Summary

The scene now changes dramatically. We are in Rome, where two new characters appear: Franz d'Epinay (a young baron) and Albert de Morcerf (a good-looking viscount). The young men are fretting because they have come to Rome to find romance and laughter during the carnival season, but strangely, all of Rome's carriages and horses have been rented. The two young men are furious; men of their class do *not* "run around Rome on foot like lawyers' clerks." Nevertheless, they decide to deliver their "letters of introduction" to all of Rome's first families and make plans, if need be, to costume themselves as colorful "Neapolitan harvesters" and ride around in a festive and be-ribboned oxcart. But at the last minute, the two men are saved by a stroke of good fortune: the hotel-keeper tells them that the "very great" Count of Monte Cristo has heard of their plight and has offered them two seats in *his* carriage, as well as two seats in *his* window above the square where most of the merriment will take place.

When Franz and Albert meet Monte Cristo, they are in awe of him and of his palatial quarters and his princely generosity. In addition, both men are startled by Monte Cristo's enthusiastic invitation to join him in witnessing a public execution from a window over-looking the execution site. Both Albert and Franz survive the ordeal, but they are both greatly distraught. Immediately before the execution, Monte Cristo talks of little else except the justice of slow and painful revenge; the guillotine, he feels, offers death too quickly and too pain-lessly. In contrast to instantaneous decapitation, however, Franz and Albert witness a singularly savage execution: a man is bludgeoned with a mace, his throat slit open, and his stomach trampled on until jets of blood spurt from his mouth like fantastic ruby-colored foun-tains. Curiously, the other prisoner on the block, a bronzed and hand-some young man with a wild, proud look in his eyes, is pardoned at the last minute – as Monte Cristo prophecied earlier that he would be.

Hurriedly, the two men and Monte Cristo don their carnival cos-tumes and join the festivities. Albert is soon rewarded with romance; a masked lady in a carriage tosses a bouquet of violets to him, and on the second day of the carnival, she tosses another bouquet to him; then Albert is rewarded with an invitation to a rendezvous with the mysterious lady. He goes to the appointed street, but at the moment when all of the carnival candles are suddenly extinguished in a dramatic finale, he is kidnapped.

Franz receives a note demanding a great deal of money and threat-ening Albert's life if the sum is not paid. In desperation, Franz asks Monte Cristo for a loan, explaining that a man waits below for the ransom money. Monte Cristo goes to the window and speaks to the fellow. It is Peppino, the handsome, tanned youth who was pardoned earlier, and who, it turns out, "owes his life" to Monte Cristo. He explains that his master, the notorious Luigi Vampa, kidnapped Albert. Monte Cristo immediately tells Peppino to take them to Vampa at once.

Deep in the bowels of Rome's catacombs, Monte Cristo accuses Vampa of breaking his vow *never* to molest a friend of the Count's. Vampa, more like a gallant gentleman than a bandit, profusely apologizes to Monte Cristo and immediately releases Albert. Later, Albert asks Monte Cristo how he can ever repay him for saving his life, and Monte Cristo answers that he would like to be introduced into Parisian society. Albert, of course, promises to do so, and he sets a date for their next meeting—in Paris, in exactly three months. The two men shake hands on the agreement, and Monte Cristo leaves. Franz turns to Albert and says that Monte Cristo is indeed a strange man; he feels uneasy about the Count's coming to Paris.

Commentary

These two transitional chapters show Edmond Dantès now totally metamorphosed into the noble, distinguished, and very rich Count of Monte Cristo. Quite a number of years have passed since the episode with Monsieur Morrel, and we can only gather from later facts that the Count has traveled extensively and performed many acts—such as acquiring Ali, his mute valet, Bertuccio, his steward, and Haydée, his "slave-mistress." And note that although it seems that the Count is "accidentally" staying in the same hotel with Albert de Morcerf and Franz d'Epinay, and although it seems to be a "miraculous" rescue of Albert, there is every indication (virtual proof, in fact) that Monte Cristo has arranged these things to happen so that he can "seemingly" come to the rescue of these two young (and prestigious) Parisian gentlemen. In other words, the Count of Monte Cristo wants Albert to become so indebted to him that Albert will introduce him into Paris society, and thereby introduce him to the very enemies against whom he plans his revenge. The first and simplest obligation which Albert owes to Monte Cristo is, of course, the loan of a carriage when one was "suddenly impossible to obtain" during Rome's carnival season. But the major obligation occurs when Monte Cristo "saved Albert's life" after he was "captured" by the bandit Luigi Vampa, a person who is also obligated to the Count. Albert is obligated to such an extent, therefore, that he will gladly introduce Monte Cristo to prominent Parisian society, where Monte Cristo will begin his slow revenge against those who are responsible for his long years of brutal imprisonment.

In this section also, we discover Monte Cristo's philosophy of revenge and death. Since the Count could obviously hire an assassin, or in other ways bring about the *immediate* death of his enemies, we should note that he does *not* believe in a quick and easy death for a person who has made others suffer for a long and extended period of time. As he says, "If a man has tortured and killed your father, your mother, your sweetheart, one of those beings who leave an eternal emptiness and a perpetually bleeding wound when they are torn from your heart . . . do you think society has given you sufficient reparation because the man who made you undergo long years of mental and emotional suffering has undergone a few seconds of physical pain?" In other words, Monte Cristo does *not* want quick revenge—he wants *slow* and *deliberate* vengeance: "For slow, profound, infinite, and eternal suffering, I'd try to avenge myself by inflicting similar suffering—an eye for an eye, and a tooth for a tooth." Thus, Monte Cristo will bring revenge upon his enemies slowly and very deliberately, making those who made him suffer, suffer in turn, for a very long time.

Chapters 22–26

CADEROUSSE'S VILLAINY

Summary

In Paris, three months later, Albert impatiently awaits the arrival of Monte Cristo for a luncheon party. The first guest to arrive is Lucien Debray, the tall, blond Secretary to the Minister of the Interior (we discover later that he is Danglars' wife's lover). Among the other guests is Captain Maximilien Morrel, a tall, dark, and broad-chested young man who is the only son of Monsieur Morrel, the owner of the lost *Pharaon*, which Monte Cristo financially "resurrected" and thereby saved Morrel's shipping firm. Young Morrel, it is revealed, once saved a nobleman's life in Constantinople, and because Morrel's father's life was once "miraculously" saved, Maximilien tries to do "some heroic action" every year.

Albert then tells his guests about his own "miraculous" rescue by the Count of Monte Cristo. One of the guests says that no such "Count" exists; he knows *all* of Europe's nobility, and he has *never* heard of the

Count *nor* of the island of Monte Cristo. But, at the very stroke of ten-thirty, Monte Cristo is announced.

Over lunch, Monte Cristo impresses them all with his pillbox, fashioned out of a magnificent, hollowed-out emerald; then he tells them of his daring adventures with Luigi Vampa, the bandit king, and mentions that his steward, Bertuccio, was once a bandit and that he, Monte Cristo, was influential enough to save the life of the handsome Peppino, Vampa's bandit-liaison. In turn, Albert tells Monte Cristo about his fiancée, Eugénie Danglars (the daughter of the purser on the *Pharaon*, that Dantès was once to have commanded). The young men enjoy the story and are so impressed by Albert's guest that they plead to be allowed to help Monte Cristo secure a lodging, but the Count tells them that he already has a Paris address – 30 Champs Elysées (Paris' most famous boulevard). They are all stunned at such costly originality, and thus, they beg to introduce him to a Parisian mistress of their choice. But Monte Cristo says that he has already chosen a mistress; she is his "slave," whom he bought in Constantinople, and who speaks nothing but modern Greek. Clearly, Monte Cristo is one of the most extraordinary men whom any of the young Parisian noblemen have ever known.

After the others have gone, Albert shows Monte Cristo around his apartment, pointing out an oil portrait of his mother dressed as a Catalan fisherwoman. Monte Cristo admires the portrait (it is a stunning likeness of the beautiful and beloved Mercédès, who is, we will learn, Albert's mother; Albert's father is Fernand, who "bought" his title of Count de Morcerf as soon as he was rich enough to afford it). Later, in the salon of Albert's parents, Monte Cristo meets Mercédès and his old rival, Fernand. Fernand apparently does not recognize the immensely wealthy and distinguished Monte Cristo, whom he knew years ago as Edmond Dantès (we discover later that Mercédès recognized Dantès immediately). Both of the Morcerfs are deeply grateful to Monte Cristo for saving Albert's life, but Mercédès is obviously stunned when she first sees Monte Cristo. She explains her unusual behavior as only that of any mother who suddenly meets the man who has saved her son's life. Monte Cristo, however, is even paler than Mercédès, and he soon excuses himself, explaining that he has yet to see his new house in Paris. After he leaves, Mercédès questions her son: does Monte Cristo like Albert? Is Albert fond of Monte Cristo? Albert defends Monte Cristo with great fervor, not noticing that his mother is deeply absorbed in her own thoughts, her eyes closed.

When Monte Cristo returns to his city residence, he prepares to sign the necessary papers to buy his "country house," and we discover that instead of its being outside of Paris, it is *in* Paris, in the suburb of Auteuil, opposite the Bois de Boulogne, an enormous park within the city environs of Paris. (This house will be the scene of one of Monte Cristo's most startling "revelations.")

Bertuccio, Monte Cristo's steward, is clearly but unexplainably upset when he hears the word "Auteuil"; later, he crosses himself fearfully when he learns that he will have to live in the house with Monte Cristo. The Count questions Bertuccio about his unnatural fear of the country house, and we learn that:

(1) The house formerly belonged to Saint-Méran, the father of the woman who was Villefort's first wife. She died, but Villefort continued to make mysterious visits to this house, where he kept a young lady. Bertuccio went to the house, hoping to murder Villefort, the public prosecutor, because Villefort refused to find the murderer of Bertuccio's brother.

(2) At the house, Bertuccio saw Villefort come out with a spade and bury a small box. Bertuccio stabbed Villefort and uncovered the box. Thinking that it might contain money, he found, instead, a newborn baby boy. He took the child to his sister-in-law, and he remembers that the baby's swaddling clothes were marked with a crown and the initials *H* and *N*.

(3) The years passed, and when the boy was eleven, Bertuccio feared that he was becoming irredeemably perverse. Then one night, Bertuccio was almost arrested by customs officers, but was able to escape and flee to an inn run by a clever scoundrel, Caderousse. Bertuccio spied Caderousse bargaining with a jeweler, trying to get as much money as possible for a magnificent diamond that Caderousse and his wife swore was a gift from a sailor named Edmond Dantès.

(4) The jeweler finally gave Caderousse forty-five thousand francs and hurried away amidst a violent thunderstorm. He returned, soaked to the skin, and asked for a bed. The Caderousses fed him, and later in the night, Bertuccio heard a pistol shot and a terrible shriek. He got up and saw Caderousse covered with blood and clutching the diamond; he disappeared into the darkness. Upstairs, Bertuccio found the corpse of Madame Caderousse, as well as that of the jeweler, a

kitchen knife plunged in his chest. Immediately, Bertuccio was arrested by the customs officers who followed him.

(5) Five days before Bertuccio's trial, Abbé Busoni came to prison and vouched for the truth of Bertuccio's story about the diamond. Meanwhile, Caderousse was arrested, confessed everything, and was sentenced to hard labor for life. Bertuccio was released and sought out Monte Cristo, as the Abbé told him to do. He has been Monte Cristo's trusted steward ever since.

Bertuccio's story finally finished, Monte Cristo and his steward return to Paris.

Dantès' plans for revenge have begun. He has spun a web of deception and has already caught Fernand, his old rival for Mercédès, and, in addition, he has found Mercédès, and he has ferreted out Danglars, as well as Monsieur Morrel's son, Maximilien—and he has also cornered Villefort, who did *not* die when Bertuccio stabbed him. (Villefort, remember, named Dantès as a traitor to the state and signed Dantès' indictment; Danglars wrote the initial letter condemning Dantès, and Fernand mailed the letter. Because of these men, Dantès almost died during his fourteen years in prison.) Now, Dantès (as the awesome Monte Cristo) will create more "coincidences" so that he can ingratiate himself to certain other people and make them *all* feel "deeply obligated" to him.

First, Monte Cristo begins his revenge on Danglars and his wife. Danglars presents his wife with two handsome, dappled grey horses which are supposedly the finest horses in Paris. Monte Cristo sees the horses, admires them, and orders his steward to buy them. Bertuccio obeys, and then Monte Cristo goes to visit Danglars, where the two men discuss finances. Monte Cristo convinces him to open a checking account for him so that he can draw instant cash up to six million francs. Danglars finally agrees, although reluctantly, with a pale and nervous smile. Monte Cristo then meets Danglars' wife and discovers that she is being entertained by young Debray, whom Monte Cristo met earlier at Albert's luncheon. Debray glances out the window and sees Madame Danglars' prize horses harnessed to Monte Cristo's carriage. Madame Danglars is furious with her husband for selling the horses, and Monte Cristo feigns ignorance of the whole affair. Later, Monte Cristo sends a note of profuse apology to Madame Danglars and returns her horses with a gift of large, awesome, flashing diamonds in each of their silver rosettes.

Next, Villefort's wife, Héloise, borrows these fabulous horses from Madame Danglars, and Monte Cristo arranges to have the horses "run away." Then, "by accident," Monte Cristo's mute Nubian servant, Ali, is able to stop the horses dramatically in front of Monte Cristo's house, and the Count is able to administer a few drops of a potent liquid (the same that Abbé Faria used in prison) to rally the faint young Villefort child, Edouard. Héloise is absolutely bewitched by Monte Cristo, and she says that she is in his debt forever because of his "goodness and generosity."

That evening, Villefort visits Monte Cristo to thank him for saving his wife and his son. The two men talk, and Monte Cristo reveals that he has made a study of all men in all countries on all continents. He knows all their virtues, all their vices, and all their weaknesses. He tells Villefort that men are, at heart, "ugly creatures." Unlike other men, however, Monte Cristo belongs to no country, nor is he identifiable as being a certain "kind" of man. He is extraordinary. He fears no one because he is able to determine immediately whether a man is sufficiently advantageous enough to be useful to him. All men, he says, have committed "either errors or crimes," and long ago, Monte Cristo set himself up as Providence, as it were, to "reward and punish." Arrogantly, Villefort remarks that while Madame de Villefort may see herself as merely the Count's "eternal friend," he – that is, Villefort – wants Monte Cristo to recognize that *he* is "*not* an ordinary man. Not at all."

Commentary

Six months later, and after many years of preparation in which the Count of Monte Cristo seems to know *every detail* about his enemies, we are now presented with his first direct meeting with his enemies, and we learn the various methods which he will use to get each one of them either obligated to him or involved with him in some financial way. Thus, we can assume again that, as he himself announced, the reason for his so-called "rescue" of Albert de Morcerf was so that he would be able to meet intimately with Albert's father, Count de Morcerf, alias Fernand Mondego, his old rival for Mercédès.

At the breakfast (brunch by today's standards) that Albert has arranged for the Count, Maximilien Morrel unexpectedly is there and, moreover, the Count learns that Maximilien's sister, Julie, has been happily married for nine years; therefore, we know that the Count would now be around forty-one or forty-two years old, and we may assume that during these intervening years, Monte Cristo has spent his time investing his money, increasing his knowledge of his enemies, and establishing his power in the world at large. It is particularly ironic that the Count is described at the breakfast party as being the "savior" of young Albert, and that Maximilien is there as the "savior" of another of the guests. This will allow the Count to become friends with Morrel and, ultimately, become his protector.

Among the young group, the Count is quite outspoken. He explains that his steward, Bertuccio, was probably once a smuggler who is now obligated to him; that his valet is a mute Nubian whose life he once saved; that his mistress is a woman he bought out of slavery; and that the people who kidnapped Albert Morcerf are people for whom he once performed acts requiring gratitude—for example, he kept Luigi Vampa from being captured by the Italian police, and it was he who saved Peppino's life during the carnival in Rome.

After the party, Albert introduces the Count to his parents, who acknowledge their deep indebtedness to him for having saved their son's life. Monte Cristo's old acquaintance Fernand (Count de Morcerf) does not recognize him, of course, but we are made aware that Mercédès does indeed recognize the Count as her fiancé of long ago, Edmond Dantès, but she will keep his secret until much later in the novel, only to reveal it to her son to keep him from dueling with the Count.

In the history that Bertuccio relates of his own life and experiences, we must remember that the Count of Monte Cristo has already heard all of these experiences; unknowingly, Bertuccio confessed them to the Count when Monte Cristo was disguised as the Abbé Busoni. Consequently, the Count has already heard Bertuccio's story and has arranged to buy the house which Bertuccio talks about. Monte Cristo wants to *test* Bertuccio's veracity and *insure* that Bertuccio will always be totally and completely loyal to him. Through Bertuccio's story, we learn of the almost total depravity of Caderousse and of the baseness of Benedetto, the son of the present Madame Danglars (the mysterious "lady" at Auteuil) and Villefort.

By the end of this section, Monte Cristo has also involved himself with Danglars—by means of letters of investment—to the tune of six million francs—and he has rescued Madame de Villefort and her son,

Edouard, from the runaway carriage which the Count caused to be a runaway carriage so that he could rescue it. Thus, he has deeply obligated the Villefort family to him.

When Villefort himself comes to express his appreciation to the Count for having saved the lives of his wife and their son, the Count is once again able to express his views concerning rewards and punishments. The Count maintains that if he were, like Christ, offered anything in the world which he could choose, he would reply: "I have always heard of Providence, yet I have never seen it or anything resembling it, which makes me think it does not exist. I want to be Providence, for the greatest, the most beautiful and the most sublime thing I know of in this world is *to reward and punish.*"

At the end of this section, then, Monte Cristo has not encountered quite all of his enemies, but he has made those whom he has encountered extremely obligated to him in one way or another, and he will continue to follow his philosophy of *slowly* avenging himself.

Chapters 27 – 38

THE SECRET OF BENEDETTO'S BIRTH

Summary

At home, Monte Cristo visits Haydée, his soft and beautiful slave girl; he reminds her that they are in Paris now. Therefore, she is free to dress as a Westerner, meet other people, especially other men, and fall in love if she pleases – but Haydée says that she will *never* find a more handsome man than the Count. She loves only him, and she will never, ever leave him. Minutes later, Monte Cristo alights at the residence of Monsieur Morrel's daughter, Julie, who is now Madame Emmanuel Herbault; young Maximilien Morrel, we learn, also lives here. Inside, Monte Cristo notices a red silk purse, lying on a black velvet cushion inside a hollow crystal globe, alongside a handsome diamond in another crystal globe. (This is the diamond which Monte Cristo secretly presented for Julie's dowry.)

Maximilien and his sister relate the history of their strange and wonderous good fortune; their "angel," as they call the mysterious person who is responsible for all their material magnificence, is an Englishman representing the firm of Thomson and French of Rome.

Monte Cristo half-teases them that perhaps he knows their "angel"; the mysterious man might be a certain Lord Wilmore, who is known to perform deeds of immense, anonymous generosity. His where-abouts, however, are unknown. Maximilien then says that Morrel, their father, told them that he was convinced that their secret bene-factor was none other than Edmond Dantès. The Count suddenly grows deathly pale, hurriedly pays his compliments to the Herbaults, then excuses himself. Afterward, Julie remarks that she is absolutely sure that she has heard the Count's voice before.

The Count arrives at the Villefort residence ostensibly to repay Villefort's visit, but he learns that Villefort is dining with the chan-cellor, and so he decides to spend the time visiting with Villefort's wife, his teenage daughter Valentine, and his son Edouard. Edouard is mutilating a beautiful picture album until his mother snatches it from him, and Valentine stays only briefly, but for the few moments that Monte Cristo sees her, he is very impressed with her gracious and forthright manner.

When Monte Cristo and Madame de Villefort are alone, he re-minds her that they spoke together once before; they were in Italy, and because Monte Cristo had used his knowledge of chemistry to cure a hotelkeeper of jaundice, he acquired an instant reputation as a "great doctor." Madame de Villefort questions Monte Cristo closely about medicines and poisons. She reveals to us – and to Monte Cristo – that she herself knows a great deal about poisons. And before Monte Cristo leaves, she has managed, she thinks innocently, to make him promise to send her some of his potent liquid which he used to rouse Edouard after he fainted during the "run-away accident." Monte Cristo warns Madame de Villefort that "one drop restores life . . . but five or six drops kill." The next day, she receives the potion.

Several days later, when Albert (Mercédès' son) and Debray (Madame Danglars' lover) call on Monte Cristo, they immediately notice that the Count's house on the Champs Elysées has already acquired the palatial air of Monte Cristo himself. Albert has come for a specific reason: he wants to talk to Monte Cristo about his expected engagement to Eugénie, the elder daughter of Danglars. Eugénie is, Albert confesses, "too rich for me." Such wealth, he says, frightens him. His mother (Mercédès) is also against his marrying Eugénie. But his father (Fernand) is hoping that Albert *will* marry Eugénie. Mean-while, Monte Cristo seems strangely agitated; he speaks of the Danglars' fabulous wealth, and suddenly Albert suggests to Debray that since he is the minister's secretary, he could teach an invaluable lesson to the speculating-prone Madame Danglars – an especially good lesson if she is soon to be Albert's mother-in-law. Albert suggests that Debray drop a fabricated rumor about a certain political situation that will make certain stocks a wise investment; then, next day, Beauchamps, the journalist, can publish a refutation of that rumor, and the stocks would collapse, and Madame Danglars will lose a good deal of money. Several "doses of this medicine" will make the woman "more cautious." Albert (but *not* Monte Cristo) is totally oblivious to Debray's deep embarrassment. (If Debray were to do this, of course, he would be betraying his mistress and, as we will find out later, he would be creating financial disaster for himself because Madame Danglars splits her "winnings" with Debray.) Not surprisingly, Debray cuts his visit to Monte Cristo short.

Afterward, Monte Cristo proposes to Albert that perhaps he, Monte Cristo, should have a dinner party and invite the Villeforts and the Danglars – but *not* the Morcerfs. That way, Monte Cristo can spare Albert's mother (Mercédès) the pain of seeing her son with Danglars' daughter, Eugénie. "I wish to avoid that [pain to Mercédès] at all costs," Monte Cristo tells Albert. Albert, of course, is extremely grateful and says that he will tell his mother about Monte Cristo's thoughtfulness. Meanwhile, Albert will arrange matters so that it will be *impossible* for him and his family to dine with Monte Cristo – because of a "previous commitment." The Count then tells Albert that he is going to meet with a Major Cavalcanti and assist Cavalcanti's son, Andrea (in actuality, this is Villefort's and Madame Danglars' bastard son, Benedetto), to make his entrance into Parisian society. Albert jokes, yet seriously, that Monte Cristo should *also* assist Andrea to make the acquaintance of Eugénie. (Remember, however, that Eugénie is Andrea's – Benedetto's – half-sister; they share the same father, Villefort.)

That night at seven, Major Cavalcanti meets with the Count, and it is immediately clear that Cavalcanti is an imposter whom Monte Cristo is grooming for a "role," for which he is being paid an enormous sum. Monte Cristo furnishes him a birth certificate for his "son," Andrea, as well as a trunk of suitable clothing for himself. Then Monte Cristo introduces Cavalcanti to his "son," a tall blond man with flashing black eyes and a red beard. The two men agree that they must play their parts well. Monte Cristo then instructs his two "actors" to be at his house on Saturday for a dinner party. The secret web of revenge that Monte Cristo is weaving is clearly well planned, because he is preparing a series of slow and extremely painful acts of revenge upon his enemies.

We now eavesdrop on the Villefort home, where Maximilien Morrel is at a grilled iron gate. Rendezvousing with Valentine Villefort, he learns how unhappy she will be if she is forced to marry Franz d'Epinay; Maximilien vows that he will love no one else but Valentine – no matter what happens. Then, hearing voices, Valentine returns to the house where her grandfather (Monsieur Noirtier, the Bonapartist, now a paralyzed mute) is revising his will with commands from his eyes. Two notaries have been summoned. The old man's fortune, we learn, is large, almost a million francs, all of which he intends to leave to the poor – if Valentine marries Franz. Villefort (a royalist, as opposed to a Bonapartist) is furious with his father, but he knows that the old man is not *only* politically stubborn; he is stubborn by nature, and so he instructs the notaries to make the will according to Noirtier's wishes.

Leaving his father's room, Villefort learns that he and his wife have a guest: the Count of Monte Cristo, who reminds them that he expects them for dinner on Saturday at his country home in *Auteuil*. Villefort pales at that word, and even more so when Monte Cristo tells them that his "country home" once belonged to the Saint-Mérans (Villefort's former in-laws); Villefort, remember, used this house as a rendezvous site with the present Madame Danglars; in addition, Villefort believes that he buried their newborn baby alive in what is now Monte Cristo's garden. This is the house, then, where Benedetto – "Andrea Cavalcanti" – was born.

That Saturday, Monte Cristo's guests arrive – Maximilien Morrel, Lucien Debray (Madame Danglars' lover), the Danglars (the Baron, looking extremely pale and dreamy; he speaks to a cactus, and it pricks him), the "Cavalcantis" (father and son, resplendent in new finery), and the Villeforts (Monsieur Villefort is "visibly agitated").

Privately, Bertuccio (Monte Cristo's steward) excitedly tells his master that Madame Danglars is the pregnant woman whom he saw having a rendezvous with Villefort – the man whom Bertuccio was positive that he killed! The Count explains to his steward that Bertuccio's knife lodged between the wrong ribs. Then Bertuccio spies young Cavalcanti—and realizes that the young man is Benedetto, the child who was such a menace to Bertuccio's late sister-in-law!

Bertuccio staggers back to the dining room, scarcely believing his eyes, but he is able to serve dinner. And over the many opulent and exotic dishes, Monte Cristo tells his guests of the strange history of the house. Villefort begins drinking rapidly, particularly when Monte Cristo asks them all to view a "peculiar bedroom," where one's imagination might conjure up a dark night when someone might carry away "some sinister burden." At these words, Madame Danglars half-faints and asks for no more stories. Monte Cristo suggests, instead, that perhaps this room could just as well have been a bedroom for a wondrous birth! At this, Madame Danglars groans and faints. (Remember that she gave birth to Benedetto—that is, Andrea Cavalcanti—in this room and that Villefort stole away to bury the infant alive.) Villefort cries out that Madame Danglars is ill and should be taken to her carriage.

Instead, Monte Cristo takes her to another bedroom, administers a drop of his potent red liquid, and she regains consciousness. Then Monte Cristo tells them all that a crime was indeed committed in this house and that one of his workmen unearthed a wooden box containing the skeleton of a newborn baby. Madame Danglars and Villefort both tremble visibly. Cavalcanti remarks that in *his* country, the criminals would have had their heads cut off. Villefort makes a comment, but only barely, in a voice "scarcely human." Then Monte Cristo reminds his guests that they must return to their coffee. Villefort whispers to Madame Danglars that she must meet him tomorrow at his office.

Shortly afterward, the guests begin to depart. And as Andrea Cavalcanti is about to climb into his carriage, he is stopped by a bearded, ragged man with glittering eyes and teeth as sharp and white as a wolf's—it is Caderousse, and he addresses Andrea by his real name, Benedetto. Andrea quickly ushers Caderousse into his cab and tells the driver that the two men need to talk in private. Then, as Andrea drives away, Caderousse reminds him that he used to share his soup and beans with Andrea in prison; now he expects the same from Andrea, *or Benedetto!* Moreover, he needs money *now,* and so Andrea gives it to him, of course, but he touches his pistol meanwhile. And Caderousse, in turn, fingers his long Spanish knife. It is a stand-off, and so Andrea agrees to take Caderousse into Paris. When they are on the outskirts of the inner city, Caderousse snatches Andrea's hat, grabs his groom's overcoat, and leaps out of the cab, vanishing down a side street.

When the Danglars arrive home, young Debray tries to comfort Madame Danglars, but Monsieur Danglars abruptly sends him home so that he can rail at his wife in private because of her speculation debts—which have *also* cost Danglars a small fortune. He knows that Madame Danglars gambles with her "allowance" and then splits the profits with Debray. Now Danglars wants *Debray* to pay him the exact amount that Danglars has lost. Danglars names Debray outright as his wife's lover, and he accuses his wife of taking some very bad financial advice from Debray. But it was advice which Danglars followed also. He announces to his wife that he knows about *all* of her lovers— from Villefort to Debray—and he has never complained before, but heretofore, none of them cost him money. Now, Debray has caused him to lose an enormous amount of money; he will no longer be silent, and Debray must pay up. If Debray goes bankrupt, then he can leave Paris—as all bankrupts do. Danglars leaves then, and his wife collapses, in *utter* disbelief of all of the disasters that have suddenly enveloped her.

Next day, Danglars notes that young Debray's carriage does *not* arrive when it usually does, and that "by coincidence," his wife leaves in her carriage. Mid-afternoon, Danglars drives to Monte Cristo's residence on the Champs Elysées. He tells the Count about a series of financial disasters that have befallen him, and then he asks what he should do about a new problem—Cavalcanti's request for credit. The Count changes the subject. He suggests that young Andrea Cavalcanti has been brought to Paris to find a wife to share his immense fortune. Danglars intimates that he would be willing to speculate with his daughter's (Eugénie's) future if she weren't "unofficially" engaged to Albert (Mercédès' son). Monte Cristo then asks about Albert's father's past (Fernand's past, that is), and Danglars recalls a dark, mysterious "secret" concerning the "Ali Pasha affair." Monte Cristo urges Danglars to solve this mystery—especially if this man might someday be Eugénie's father-in-law, and Danglars agrees to do so—and to tell Monte Cristo if he learns, perchance, "some scandalous piece of news."

Commentary

The middle portion of the novel deals with many diverse matters. Mainly, we are concerned with the Count's involving his enemies in one way or another with their eventual downfall. The first two chapters deal with the Count's relationship with his "slave," Haydée, and his deep, fatherly affection for her and her deep devotion to him as a man. Likewise, Monte Cristo pays a visit to the grown children of Monsieur Morrel, the shipowner, the Count's first benefactor. At Julie's house, where Maximilien lives, Monte Cristo hears that both Julie and Maximilien long to discover the name of their family's secret benefactor and that their father died believing that their benefactor was Edmond Dantès.

Monte Cristo then visits the Villefort residence, and he is received as the "savior" of Villefort's wife and son. Monte Cristo reminds Madame de Villefort that they once met in Perugia (Italy), when the Count was healing a servant and a hotelkeeper, and he reveals his knowledge of medicinal herbs, especially poisonous ones. And while the Count is explaining how one drop of his liquid brought her son back to life, but that a few more drops would have killed him, Madame de Villefort's curiosity is aroused out of all proportion to the discussion; she wants some of Monte Cristo's "medicine" (poison) for her own use. At the end of their conversation, the Count acknowledges that he's convinced that "the seed I have sown has not fallen on barren ground." This is a part of his plan for slow revenge. Significantly, Madame de Villefort will prove to be the ultimate villainess of this novel; she will deliberately poison three people and will attempt to poison even her own stepdaughter.

The Count's revenge becomes more complicated when he includes Benedetto in his scheme. Benedetto is the illegitimate son of Villefort and Madame Danglars, and Monte Cristo is paying Benedetto to pretend to be the extremely wealthy son of an Italian nobleman because ultimately, the Count will intrigue Baron Danglars into arranging a marriage between Benedetto (alias Andrea Cavalcanti) and Danglars' daughter, who is (unbeknownst to Andrea) Benedetto's half-sister. Throughout this novel, we must always remember that the Count wants his revenge to be slow and *deliberate*; an immediate or quick revenge would not do justice to the suffering which he himself has undergone.

We also learn that Maximilien Morrel, the son of the Count's first employer, and Valentine de Villefort, the daughter of the Count's worst enemy, are in love with each other. And furthermore, we discover that while Maximilien feels that the Count is especially favorable in his cause, Valentine, on the contrary, feels a dislike for the Count because she senses that he has completely ignored her and her plans in order to use her in some way. (This is not found in some of the abridged editions.) Both feelings are indeed true. The Count will take no interest in Valentine until he discovers that Maximilien is deeply in love with her, and then he will leave no stone uncovered to help her.

Monsieur Noirtier is introduced in these chapters. We first heard of him when Edmond Dantès was supposed to deliver a letter to him (allegedly from Napoleon) and was arrested by Villefort for carrying that letter. Now, years later, Noirtier is paralyzed, and when he discovers that his beloved granddaughter is about to be forced by her parents into a marriage with Franz d'Epinay, the old man is horrified because we discover later that Noirtier was the person who killed Franz' father years ago in a political duel. Noirtier is also aware, even though he is paralyzed, that Valentine is being used by Madame de Villefort because of Valentine's wealth, and therefore, Noirtier decides to cut her out of his will for her own protection. Shortly, his fears will be proven to be entirely correct as we see that Madame Villefort tries to poison Valentine so that Valentine's money will revert to her father, who will leave everything to his son.

Coincidences abound in Romantic novels, so the readers should not be surprised to discover that Caderousse, who now reappears in the plot, was an old cellmate of young Benedetto. Their relationship will lead directly to the death of Caderousse because of Caderousse's extreme greed.

The Count continues his plan of exacting slow and deliberate punishment for those guilty of causing him such extreme torment and suffering. Thus, he gives the party at his chateau in Auteuil, fully aware of the horrors perpetrated there by Villefort and the Baroness Danglars. As he shows them the rooms and projects stories about one of the rooms, he is actually describing the birth of the infant child that the Baroness had by Villefort, and when he mentions how the workmen discovered the bones of an infant child buried in the garden, he is of course referring to the child of the Baroness and Villefort. His punishment is directed toward both the Baroness Danglars and Villefort, and the reader should repress all sympathy for these two people – for they are *guilty* of bearing an illegitimate child and then of attempting to kill it by burying it alive.

The Count further involves Danglars in financial intrigues by using his loyal friend Jacopo (the person who saved the Count from drowning alongside the smuggling ship) to borrow large sums from Danglars and thus having established excellent credit, to borrow a million francs and then disappear. At the end of this section, the Count causes further dissension by revealing to Danglars the means whereby he can obtain damaging information about Morcerf's activities during his Greek campaigns in Yanini, the campaigns which allowed him to become so immensely wealthy and powerful. By the end of this section, therefore, the Count has set into motion many different techniques by which his enemies will all be entrapped.

Chapters 39 – 44

DEATH BY POISONING

Summary

When Danglars saw his wife leaving in her carriage – without Debray – he never suspected that she was leaving to meet her old lover, Villefort. Of course, however, *she* never suspected the extent of the bad news which Villefort would have for *her*. Villefort tells her very straightforwardly that they are both in extremely serious trouble. He reminds her that Monte Cristo mentioned a baby's skeleton having been unearthed. That would have been impossible, Villefort says, because while he was burying the newborn baby, he was stabbed by a Corsican and left for dead. Afterward, he was critically ill for three months, but when he was able to travel, he returned to Auteuil and dug up the entire garden area, searching for the makeshift casket. There was no casket nor was there a baby's corpse. Someone dug it up and is now waiting to make them both pay for their crime.

Madame Danglars screams: "You buried my child alive!" Villefort loathes these accusations and tries to frighten her. Perhaps *she* talked in her sleep . . . perhaps she is to blame. Whatever the reason for their present predicament, someone *now* knows about them both. "We are lost," he says. But he vows to discover who Monte Cristo is and why he lied about the baby's corpse being "accidentally" discovered – when indeed it was not.

Later, after Madame de Villefort and Valentine leave for a ball, Villefort shuts himself in his study. But before he has time to work at his papers, his former mother-in-law arrives. Her husband, Saint-Méran, has just died. The old lady is so distraught that Villefort has her put to bed, where she falls into a feverish sleep. When she rouses, she questions Villefort closely about Valentine's upcoming marriage. She is surprised that Franz, Valentine's fiancé, does not object to marrying the granddaughter of a fervent Bonapartist. After all, she says, Franz' father was assassinated only a few days before Napoleon returned from exile in Elba. Villefort tries to dismiss the old lady's worries; Franz, he says, was "only a child" when all that took place. Old Madame Saint-Méran, however, urges Villefort to marry his daughter to Franz as soon as possible. She says that she is certain that she is going to die. Last night, she saw a white "form" do something with her orangeade glass. And abruptly, she asks for the glass and empties it in a long, single swallow. An hour later, the old lady is dead.

Villefort is hysterical at the attending doctor's cross-examination. The old woman could not have died of poison, as the doctor states. Why would anyone want to poison her? Her sole heiress is Valentine – and Valentine is absolutely incapable of murder. But the doctor is *certain* not only that murder was committed, but that the poison used was brucine, a red liquid which he has been administering in very small doses to Villefort's father. One drop of that potion is a medicine; several drops are deadly poison.

Meanwhile, Valentine takes her beloved Maximilien to meet her grandfather, old Noirtier. He obviously approves of the young man as a husband for Valentine, but signals for them to wait, instead of eloping. He has plans for them.

Two days later, Monsieur and Madame de Saint-Méran are buried in a vault beside Renée, Valentine's mother. Then Villefort makes immediate plans for his daughter's marriage to Franz d'Epinay. The formal papers are ready to be signed when a message arrives from Villefort's father, old Noirtier. He wishes to see Franz immediately. So Franz, Valentine, and Villefort all hurry to the old man's room. There, by means of eye signals, a secret packet of old papers, tied in a black ribbon, is brought forth from Noirtier's desk. Franz is directed to read the papers.

He cries out when he sees that they are dated on the very day that his father was assassinated. There was, he reads, a secret club of Bonapartists during Louis XVIII's reign. Unfortunately, it was erroneously believed that Franz' father was a secret Bonapartist, and thus he was blindfolded one day and taken to one of the secret meetings of the Bonapartists. Among the matters discussed were the details of Bonaparte's return, including the mention of a certain letter carried on Morrel's ship, the *Pharaon* (the ship on which we first met Edmond Dantès. This "message" was also the message which Danglars used to indict Dantès and send him to prison for fourteen long, torturous years).

When Franz' father could no longer listen to plans for overthrowing the king's government, he spoke out loudly and said that his loyalty would *always* be to Louis — never to Bonaparte. Thus he was blindfolded again and was taken away and forced to fight a fair duel with old Noirtier, who killed him honorably. D'Epinay's death was no assassination.

Franz sinks lifelessly into a chair. The grandfather of his fiancée killed his own father! Villefort opens the door and flees in order not to choke the life out of his mute old father, who has just ruined Valentine's chance for marrying the wealthy Franz d'Epinay.

But Valentine, happy and frightened at the same time, kisses her grandfather and goes to the iron grill to speak of what has happened to her beloved Maximilien. "We're saved," she tells him, but she states that she will not reveal the full story until she is his wife.

Next day, Monsieur Noirtier has a new will made up, leaving Valentine his entire fortune. Valentine will soon be a very rich woman, with three hundred thousand francs a year.

Meanwhile, just as Valentine is planning for her marriage to Maximilien, another proposed marriage is being shattered. Morcerf (Fernand) comes to discuss his son's upcoming marriage to Eugénie Danglars with Danglars. Danglars tells Morcerf that "certain new circumstances have arisen"; Eugénie will *not* marry Albert. Morcerf proudly bites his lip at Danglars' arrogance. He asks for an explanation. "Be grateful that I don't give you one," snarls Danglars.

For a very short time, Maximilien is a very happy man. He is so very much in love with Valentine that he is scarcely able to believe in his happiness, expecially as he listens to Valentine tell him about the details of her future plans. Her grandfather has given her and Maximilien his blessing and, in eighteen months, Valentine will be of legal age and can marry Maximilien.

Just then, Valentine notices that Noirtier's old servant, Barrois, who has been standing in the background, is looking very tired. She offers him a glass of lemonade from her grandfather's tray. Gratefully, he empties the glass. In a few moments, he begins to stagger and his facial muscles begin to twitch violently. "Call the doctor," cries Valentine. D'Avrigny comes at once. Barrois rallies briefly, but then he is seized with an attack even more intense than the first one. The doctor discovers that Barrois has drunk some of the lemonade meant for Noirtier, and after Barrois falls dead with a loud cry, d'Avrigny reminds Villefort that the Saint-Mérans *also* died suddenly – and, moreover, that Madame Saint-Méran died of brucine poisoning, the same poison that has just now killed Barrois. Villefort cries out. But d'Avrigny says that he knows the symptoms of brucine poisoning very well. He performs a colored paper test and proves that brucine was indeed used.

"Death is in my house!" moans the public prosecutor. The doctor corrects him. "*Murder* is in your house," he says. Only the fact that Noirtier was taking graduated doses of brucine saved him, the doctor states. By accident, Noirtier was immune. But clearly, d'Avrigny believes that the poison was meant for Noirtier – and the evidence points to Valentine because *she* prepared the lemonade and would gain all of Noirtier's fortune if he were dead.

Villefort is furious with the doctor, but d'Avrigny is unmoved. He simply washes his hands of the Villeforts. If Villefort harbors criminals, or murderers, in his home, he wants nothing more to do with the family. He bids Villefort a final goodbye.

Commentary

This section continues the involvements which began earlier – that is, the complications before the plot begins to resolve itself. For example, the Count's plan to slowly become involved with his enemies in order to manipulate matters so that they, the enemies, begin to suffer has already been extremely effective. Madame Danglars meets with Villefort the next day in order to relive some of the horrors that they had originally perpetrated when Villefort tried to bury their son alive. But Villefort is even more concerned now because he knows that the Count did *not* discover the body of an infant; after Villefort recovered from the stab wounds, he returned to the garden and dug up the entire area, and he has lived all these years with the knowledge that his and Madame Danglars' son is alive somewhere in this world. Madame Danglars is horrified that Villefort would sink so low as to try to bury their child alive, and the grisly irony will soon be made clear when their son (once, supposedly dead) becomes unofficially engaged to Eugénie Danglars, his half-sister.

With the deaths of the Marquis de Saint-Méran and then of the Marquise de Saint-Méran, evil in the Villefort household is beginning to assert itself. In both deaths, Doctor d'Avrigny suspects the use of poison – brucine – which the Count of Monte Cristo had talked about earlier to Madame Héloise de Villefort and had obliged her by sending her some. But in both deaths, it was Valentine who unknowingly administered the fatal potion, and finally, with the death of Barrois, it seems frighteningly clear to Doctor d'Avrigny that once again, Valentine is involved, because she brought the drink to her grandfather, old Noirtier, and Barrois accidentally drank it. All of the circumstantial evidence points to Valentine as the culprit in the deaths of these three old people. The doctor believes that the poison was intended for Villefort's father so that Valentine could inherit all of her maternal and paternal grandparents' monies. This causes Villefort to undergo deep and desperate grief – but not nearly so deep and desperate as Edmond Dantès underwent during his fourteen years of imprisonment.

Since Valentine is in love with Maximilien Morrel, but is honorably engaged to young Franz d'Epinay, there must be a way to honorably break the engagement. To do so, Noirtier reveals through some old documents that date back to 1815 that it was he who, for political reasons, killed Franz' father in an honorable duel over a difference in political philosophy. Thus, when Franz sends a letter breaking off the engagement, this is another blow, another bit of suffering for Villefort. The Count of Monte Cristo's desire for long and slow revenge is gradually being effected.

Chapters 45 – 46

THE DEATH OF CADEROUSSE

Summary

Andrea Cavalcanti returns to his hotel and discovers that Caderousse has been there looking for him. Moreover, Caderousse refused to take his "allowance." Reading the note that Caderousse left, Andrea fears that Caderousse plans to make trouble. He is right. Caderousse wants to see Andrea immediately. Therefore, Andrea dons a disguise and goes immediately to Caderousse's room.

Caderousse demands more money, and Andrea refuses him. Caderousse says that if Andrea really wanted more money, he could easily get it from Monte Cristo, his benefactor. Then, suddenly inspired by the thought of the wealthy Monte Cristo, Caderousse begins to question Andrea in detail about Monte Cristo's house on the Champs Elysées; Andrea answers in detail, and it is very clear that Caderousse means to rob Monte Cristo's house.

The two men part, and the next day, Monte Cristo receives a note informing him that his house will be robbed and, furthermore, that the thief will try and break into the desk in the Count's dressing room. The note ends with the information that this thief will be no ordinary thief; this thief will be an "enemy" of the Count. Monte Cristo's curiosity is sufficiently aroused so that he sets a trap.

He wants all of his staff moved to his house in Auteuil, and he wants the house on the Champs Elysées left exactly as it is – except that the shutters on the ground floor are to be closed. When that is finished, Monte Cristo and Ali slip into a side door and go up to Monte Cristo's bedroom to wait. It is half-past nine. At a quarter to twelve, Monte Cristo hears a faint noise, then another, and then a third; then he hears the sound of a diamond cutting the four sides of a pane of glass. (This is the diamond from a ring that Caderousse finagled from Andrea.)

Monte Cristo signals to Ali, and in the near-darkness, they see a man entering through an open window. He is alone. Ali touches the Count's shoulders, Outside, another man has climbed onto a hitching post to watch. Meanwhile, the thief methodically goes about his work, trying to unlock the desk with his collection of "nightingales" (assorted keys). Unable to find the correct key, Caderousse turns on a dim light. Monte Cristo can scarcely believe his eyes. He motions to Ali not to use any weapons. Quickly then, he dons his disguise as the Abbé Busoni, and taking a lighted candle, he steps into the room. "Good evening, Monsieur Caderousse," he says.

Caderousse is speechless. The Abbé wonders aloud why Caderousse is trying to rob the Count's house. Has prison taught him nothing? Clearly, he says, Caderousse is still very much himself — that is, he is Caderousse the murderer, referring to the jeweler who bought the diamond which Abbé Busoni gave to Caderousse and who was later killed because of the diamond. Caderousse, the Abbé infers, always wants *more*. Earlier, he wanted the enormous diamond *and* the money, so he killed the jeweler. Now, he is breaking into the home of a very wealthy gentleman.

"It was poverty," Caderousse gasps, "Poverty drove me to all this." No, Monte Cristo tells him. Poverty does *not* drive a man to use a *diamond* to cut through the pane of a window. Caderousse pleads for pity, and the Abbé offers him pity if he will but tell the truth. Caderousse agrees, and he begins to tell the Abbé about his years in prison, but when he begins to describe his relationship with Benedetto, he begins to lie, and so the Abbé *forces* him to confess what Andrea's role is in deceiving Parisian society. The Abbé states that he will reveal the truth about Andrea's fraudulence. Caderousse panics; if the Abbé does that, Caderousse will have no more money. Drawing a knife, he lunges at the Abbé, striking him in the middle of the chest, but the knife bounces back, its point blunted. Monte Cristo wore a metal vest, expecting this very thing. Monte Cristo then wrenches Caderousse's arm until he agrees to write a letter to Danglars exposing Andrea. Then he releases Caderousse, who climbs out of the window. During his escape, he is stabbed three times. He makes no sound; he simply slumps to the ground.

Slowly and painfully raising himself on one elbow, he calls out for the Abbé. Monte Cristo comes and forces Caderousse to write one more note, this time naming Benedetto as the man who stabbed him. Caderousse does so, then looks at the Abbé and accuses him of allowing Benedetto to stab him. Not I, says the Count, it was "the justice of God in Benedetto's hand." He tells Caderousse that God gave him health, good work, and good friends and that he squandered them all in laziness and drunkenness.

"I need a doctor," cries Caderousse, "not a priest!" Monte Cristo continues: "God sent an enormous diamond to you, and you became a murderer when you sought to double your good fortune. In prison, you were given a chance to escape and begin a new life when you were slipped a file by myself, but once free, you blackmailed Benedetto, then tried to rob Monte Cristo's house. Then you tried to kill *me!*"

He urges Caderousse to repent, but Caderousse refuses. So Monte Cristo takes off his disguise and orders Caderousse to look long and hard at him. "Oh, my God," Caderousse cries out, "Forgive me, Lord!"

Ten minutes later, the Abbé Busoni is found praying for the soul of the deceased.

Commentary

We saw earlier that Caderousse is a person of exceptional greed, and that the Count of Monte Cristo has given him ample opportunity to revise his values. But greed is too strong within Caderousse. Thus, he not only uses his knowledge of Benedetto's prison background, but he also uses his knowledge of Benedetto's fraudulent deception of the Count in order to gain access to the Count's house.

Benedetto, however, is as vicious a criminal as Caderousse is. While he is seemingly willing to betray his benefactor by giving Caderousse the floor plans of the count's house, he in turn informs the Count about Caderousse's intended break-in. And not content with these basic provisions, he later follows Caderousse to the Count's house, and when Caderousse does try and escape, he stabs his former fellow criminal.

When the Count recognizes Caderousse as the thief, he quickly changes to his disguise as the Abbé Busoni, taking the precaution to add heavy metal armor under his priestly frock. Thus, when Caderousse turns on the Abbé, his benefactor, and tries to kill him, the Count realizes that there is *no hope* for Caderousse. As the Count earlier maintained, he always wanted to play the role of Providence—meting out rewards and punishments. Now, the Count, in the disguise of the Abbé, allows Caderousse to leave, knowing full well that someone is lying in wait for Caderousse. Monte Cristo is, as it were, leaving everything to Providence. He tells Caderousse: "I want what God wants. . . . If you arrive home safely, leave Paris, leave France, and wherever you are, and as long as you behave honestly, I'll see that

you receive a small pension, because *if* you arrive home safely, then
. . . I'll believe that God has forgiven you, and I'll forgive you also."
The Count/Abbé cannot bring himself to actually kill Caderousse, but
he is willing to leave Caderousse's fate to the hands of Providence.

Before Monte Cristo allows Caderousse to leave, he forces him
to write a letter to Danglars, revealing that Andrea Cavalcanti is really
the criminal known as Benedetto; this will be a letter which will cause
intense pain for another of the Count's enemies. Once again, we will
see the Count effecting punishment by slow suffering, which he
believes his victims deserve. After the stabbing, the Count gets a
signed confession from Caderousse that Benedetto was the person who
stabbed him. Thus, the Count has now further entrapped yet another
of his enemies.

Before Caderousse dies, Monte Cristo tells him about his immorality, of the many opportunities he had to become a good and honest
man and about the many men whom he betrayed; then Monte Cristo
reveals that he is really Edmond Dantès, one of the oldest friends
whom Caderousse has betrayed. Caderousse is finally able to view
Monte Cristo as a savior, someone far superior to most earthly men.
He says, "You are the father of men in heaven and the judge of men
on earth. I refused to acknowledge you for so long, O my God! Forgive
me, Lord, forgive me." It is as though he is seeing in the Count the
aura of divine justice; then he dies, ending a chapter in the life of
one of Monte Cristo's oldest enemies.

Chapters 47 – 54

THE DEATH OF MORCERF

Summary

One morning, Albert and Beauchamp (the journalist) call on
Monte Cristo, and it is soon clear to the Count that Albert is out of
sorts, so he invites him to go away with him to his new estate in
Normandy, on the coast of France. Albert accepts the invitation, and
when he arrives there, he is once more in awe of the Count – and
of his new estate. From the terrace overlooking the sea, Albert sees
Monte Cristo's yacht, proudly at anchor in the bay. That night, Albert
falls asleep, lulled by the sound of waves breaking on the shore.

The following day, after shooting a dozen pheasants and catching a number of trout, Albert's idyllic interlude is cut short. Albert's valet arrives breathlessly from Paris, utterly exhausted from having traveled so far so quickly; he has a letter of urgent importance. Albert reads the first few lines and half-collapses. Monte Cristo murmurs omnisciently that "the sins of the father shall be visited upon the children." His insight is uncanny. The true identity of Albert's father has been revealed in the Paris press, as well as the fact that years ago when Fernand (de Morcerf) was supposedly defending Ali Pasha's fortress, he betrayed Ali Pasha to the Turks. (We learn later that not only did Fernand betray Ali Pasha, but that he assassinated him.) The implication is that "Count" de Morcerf (who bought his title), a member of the French Parliament, is both a *traitor* and a *fraud.* Albert leaves immediately for Paris. He is terribly confused. His father has such public stature that this scandal, he fears, will soon "echo all over Europe." He is correct.

Albert's father, meanwhile, reports to the Chamber totally unaware of the incriminating article that has just been published. Within minutes, one of his peers opens the floor for debate on the matter of Ali Pasha's assassination and what role Colonel Fernand Mondego (Morcerf's real name) played in it. Morcerf pales immediately, and then his entire body is rocked with a horrible shudder. There is a unanimous demand for an immediate investigation into the entire matter, and that evening, Morcerf presents himself before a twelve-member commission. His defense is that he was Ali Pasha's most trusted confidant; to be accused of betrayal is a grave error, for Morcerf *tried* to defend Ali Pasha, he says, but found him dead and his wife and daughter gone. Furthermore, he resents this *anonymous* attack on his honor.

The commission then produces a witness to substantiate the charges against Morcerf. Monte Cristo's slave-girl, Haydée, offers as evidence her birth certificate and her "bill of sale." She is Ali Pasha's daughter, she says, sold by Fernand (de Morcerf) to a slave merchant after her father was assassinated. At last, she says, she has the opportunity to avenge her father's murder. She identifies Morcerf by saying that her father's assassin has a wide scar on his right hand; immediately, Morcerf hides his hand and sinks into a chair, crushed by despair. Then, tearing open his coat, he flees from the room. Within moments, the commission finds him guilty of felony, treason, and dishonor.

When Albert hears of this decision, he vows to "find the denouncer" of his father. Beauchamp, the journalist, mentions that Danglars recently questioned his "correspondent" in the East about Ali Pasha's betrayal. Albert seizes on the news with vehemence and anger. He will fight Danglars, he says, and either he or Danglars "will be dead before the end of this day."

At first, Danglars shrinks with fear when he is confronted by Albert, but when he realizes that Albert's anger is totally irrational, he very cleverly suggests that it is Monte Cristo who is to blame for Albert's father's defamation. It was Monte Cristo, he says, who told him to investigate "the Ali Pasha affair" – which he did – and reported his findings to Monte Cristo immediately. Albert realizes that Danglars sounds like a man who has been used only as a "tool," and so he vows to go immediately to Monte Cristo and confront him with the charges.

The Count is unavailable when Albert calls, but Albert is told that Monte Cristo plans to go to the opera that evening, so Albert decides to attend the opera also and therefore sends word to Franz, Debray, and Maximilien to meet him there. He plans to use them as witnesses. Later, Albert questions his mother, Mercédès, about Monte Cristo. Mercédès cannot believe what her son tells her; she pleads with him to stay with her instead of going to the opera, but she is unsuccessful.

Monte Cristo arrives late, but Albert sees him enter, and during the intermission, he hurries to Monte Cristo's box. He shouts threats at the Count and makes an ugly scene, but Monte Cristo is undaunted; if Albert wants to duel, he will oblige him. He promises Maximilien that he will kill Albert tomorrow. Then he sits back and enjoys the rest of the opera.

Later, Mercédès visits Monte Cristo and agonizingly pleads for her son's life; then it is clear that she knows that Monte Cristo is Edmond Dantès. She begs him for pity – because of her. The Count refuses, revealing what a villain Fernand was – to help send Monte Cristo to prison for fourteen long, torturous years. Mercédès pleads with him, "the man [she] still loves," *not* to become the murderer of her son. Finally, Monte Cristo agrees not to kill Albert. Instead, he tells Mercédès, he will allow Albert to kill *him.* Gratefully, Mercédès leaves Monte Cristo. The Count is puzzled by Mercédès' seeming indifference to his own, certain death. He curses the day that he vowed to revenge himself on his enemies.

Next morning, Maximilien (Monte Cristo's "second") and Emmanuel

(Julie Morrel's husband) arrive for Monte Cristo. They tell the Count that he will fire first, since he is "the offended party." Maximilien fears that Monte Cristo is not a good shot, and so the Count attaches an ace of diamonds to a plank and instantly shoots *each* of the four corners of the diamond in the center of the card. Maximilien cries out to the Count for mercy for Albert, but seemingly, the Count's decision will not be swayed. Yet, he says, despite the marksmanship that Maximilien has just seen, it will be Monte Cristo, and *not Albert*, who will be carried back.

The three men arrive at the appointed hour, and when Albert arrives—at a full gallop—he leaps off his horse and, before his own witnesses, he apologizes for his conduct. He knows now that his father, Fernand Mondego, *did* betray Ali Pasha. But, far worse than that was his father's betrayal of Edmond Dantès. Because of the enormity of Fernand's crime, Albert can only thank Monte Cristo for not deciding on more painful vengeance than he did.

Monte Cristo realizes that Mercédès has told her son everything; obviously she planned to do so all along, after Monte Cristo promised *not* to kill Albert. The two men shake hands on Albert's apology, and Albert returns home and begins to pack his belongings, including the portrait of Mercédès as a Catalan fisherwoman. But he discovers, to his surprise, that his mother is *also* packing. The two vow to make a complete break with their pasts, and Mercédès advises Albert to use the name of "Herrera," her father's name, instead of Morcerf.

Albert replies that if Monte Cristo was able to endure his own misery, unhappiness, and injustice, then he, Albert, can do the same. So he and his mother make ready to leave. Just then, Bertuccio, Monte Cristo's steward, delivers a letter to Albert from the Count. Albert is told to claim three thousand francs (money which Edmond Dantès buried twenty-two years ago, when he believed that he would marry Mercédès); the money lies buried in the garden of Dantès' father's house in Marseilles. Mercédès reads the letter and accepts the Count's offer. She'll take the money to a convent with her.

At home, Monte Cristo learns that Maximilien is deeply in love with someone, and so he tells him goodbye and asks him not to forget to call on the Count if ever the need arises. Maximilien agrees to do so. Shortly thereafter, Morcerf (Fernand) arrives to speak with Monte Cristo. He wants verification that his son actually *apologized* to Monte Cristo—instead of dueling with him. He cannot understand why.

Because, Monte Cristo says, "there was another man guiltier than I." Monte Cristo then names Fernand, labeling him an "enemy." Fernand challenges Monte Cristo to a duel, this time with swords. But Monte Cristo first identifies Fernand for *what* he is: Fernand, he says, deserted the French army on the eve of Waterloo; he served as a spy in Spain; he assassinated Ali Pasha, and he unscrupulously managed to become Count Morcerf. Fernand is livid. He demands to know who Monte Cristo is so that he can pronounce his name aloud as he plunges his sword into the Count's heart. Monte Cristo leaves the room and returns dressed as a young sailor. Morcerf's teeth begin to chatter; he leans against the wall, and then he slides out of the room, crying out in terror, *"Edmond Dantès!"*

Fernand returns home just in time to see his wife and son leaving together. Their carriage door closes, and Fernand is alone. Moments later, a shot rings out so violently that one of the frames in the bedroom window is shattered.

Commentary

These chapters show how the Count effects his plan for revenge against his old enemy, Fernand, the man responsible for mailing the letter which imprisoned Dantès for fourteen years. His first act is to remove Fernand's son, Albert, from the environs so that Fernand will not be able to turn to his "beloved son" for solace. We see again the Count's very strong religious belief that the "sins of the father shall be visited upon the children to the third or fourth generation." Consequently, all the time that Monte Cristo has been seeing Albert, he has remained aloof, knowing that this young man, however charming, is nevertheless the son of one of his most detested enemies.

The damaging information about Morcerf's treacherous behavior at the battle of Yanina and his betrayal of his benefactor (Ali Pasha) is information that was given to the press by Danglars, partly because Danglars has never liked Count de Morcerf – even when they were young together and especially since the Count was able to buy a higher title than the one that Baron Danglars has. But more important, Danglars wants some reason to break off the marriage between Albert and Eugénie Danglars because he wants to align himself with a much larger fortune through young Andrea Cavalcanti, but who (unbeknownst to Danglars) is an imposter as well as the illegitimate son of Danglars' wife.

These chapters show that the Count's carefully laid plans are now beginning to pay off. We must, therefore, review the Count's philosophy: if a man has made you suffer for an untold number of years, then you are not right in revenging yourself instantaneously; you are obligated, as it were, to make your enemy endure prolonged suffering. Thus, Count de Morcerf must first face the humiliations of being called a traitor in the newspaper, of being charged to defend himself before the Chamber of Deputies (of which he is a very proud and feared member), and then he must face the direct accusations of Haydée, whom Morcerf obtained by treachery when he betrayed Haydée's father, then sold her as a slave girl, along with her mother, who soon died. Moreover, he must hear the Chamber of Deputies vote him guilty by a unanimous voice vote. He is now a man in *complete* public disgrace.

If the reader will remember that this is a Romantic novel, written for an audience believing in personal honor and integrity, then Albert de Morcerf's actions against the Count of Monte Cristo won't seem so strange. It is not that Albert ever questions his father's dishonorable actions – all noble families have things to hide – but it is dishonorable for any man to make public these dishonorable actions. Thus, Albert feels that Monte Cristo is totally accountable: Albert remembers that Monte Cristo knew everything, for he bought Ali Pasha's daughter, and then knowing everything about the "Ali Pasha" affair, he urged Danglars to write to Yanina. Finally, he took Albert to Normandy with him just at the moment when he knew the disaster was to occur. Thus, it now seems to Albert that Monte Cristo planned everything and that he was in league "with his father's enemies."

When Albert questions his mother about his father's enemies, he wonders about Monte Cristo because the Count has "always refused to eat or drink anything in our house . . . and as you know, Mother, the Count is almost an Oriental and, in order to maintain full freedom to avenge themselves, Orientals never eat or drink anything in the house of an enemy." Now, earlier scenes in the novel (often omitted in abridged versions), in which the Countess de Morcerf (Mercédès) would pick grapes and offer them to the Count who refused, or when Mercédès would bring the Count tempting morsels which he would always refuse, become clear when we realize why Monte Cristo always refused to eat what was offered to him. Note too, that in this present scene, when Mercédès comes to plead with the Count for the life of her son, this is not by any means the first time that they have acknowledged by indirect signs that they are indeed the old lovers of years ago, but this is the first time that they call each other by their real names. When Mercédès tells Monte Cristo that Albert attributes Fernand's misfortunes to him, the Count reiterates his basic belief: "What has happened to his father is *not* a misfortune: It's a *punishment.* I haven't struck him down: Providence has punished him." Thus, as with the death of Caderousse, the Count believes strongly in the efficacy of Providence. When Mercédès pleads for the life of her son, the Count tells her of Fernand's betrayal and says that he, Monte Cristo, is only acting in the name of God – "You're asking me to disobey God, who brought me back from a living death in order to punish them. Impossible . . . I suffered for fourteen years, I wept and cursed for fourteen years, and now I tell you, Mercédès, I must have vengeance!"

Finally, the remembrance of Monte Cristo's past love for Mercédès conquers his desire for vengeance; Monte Cristo agrees not to kill Albert, but he lets it be known to Mercédès, and later to Maximilien, that he *will* allow Albert to kill him. This is the only *honorable* course that he can take, for no longer can he adhere to his credo that the "sins of the father must be visited upon the son."

Fernand's death comes after he has confronted the Count with a demand for a duel; when the Count reveals that he is Edmond Dantès, Fernand can barely stagger home, and when he arrives there, he discovers that his wife and son – the only people whom he has ever loved – have totally rejected him and are leaving his house, carrying absolutely nothing that belongs to him. With this knowledge, Fernand shoots himself, thus ridding the Count of Monte Cristo of the second of his four enemies.

Chapters 55 – 67

THE MADNESS OF VILLEFORT

Summary

Leaving Monte Cristo, Maximilien walks to the Villefort residence. He meets Valentine and is immediately concerned about her health. She seems disoriented. Valentine tells him that she is "slightly indisposed," but that she is gaining strength; she has been taking slow, but increasing doses of her grandfather's medicine (brucine). She says that she'll be fine; only minutes ago, she drank a glass of sugared water.

Madame Danglars and Eugénie arrive to announce Eugénie's engagement to "Prince" Cavalcanti, a title that somehow "sounds better" to Madame Danglars than does "Count." Eugénie protests her engagement; she does *not* look forward to marriage and becoming "a wife or a slave of a man." She wants to be free, and she *needs* to be free, she says. Valentine leaves the room and collapses on the landing, where Maximilien finds her and carries her to old Noirtier's room. There, Valentine suffers another attack, and this time she becomes so cold and so lifeless that Doctor d'Avrigny is called.

Maximilien goes immediately to Monte Cristo. He says that he fears that Valentine has been murdered. Monte Cristo instructs Maximilien to "be strong" and not to "lose hope."

Back at the Villefort residence, Doctor d'Avrigny announces guardedly that Valentine is still alive, and Villefort suggests that Valentine be put in her own bed. Then he exits. Doctor d'Avrigny stays behind with Noirtier and questions the old gentleman about Barrois' (Noirtier's servant's) death. Noirtier tells the doctor, with signs, that Valentine was poisoned by the same person who killed Barrois, and moreover, that Barrois was poisoned *by accident;* he drank a glass of liquid that was meant for Noirtier. The doctor then asks Noirtier if it was he who began giving Valentine increasingly potent doses of brucine – to make her immune if someone tried to poison her. Noirtier signals *Yes,* it was indeed he. The doctor leaves then and goes to Valentine's room, where he discovers an Italian priest – Abbé Busoni (Monte Cristo, in disguise).

Three days later, the Danglars' mansion is all aglitter with guests adorned with diamonds, rubies, and other precious stones. Eugénie Danglars is announcing her engagement to young Cavalcanti to an enormous crowd of her father's friends. At exactly nine o'clock, Monte Cristo arrives and soon after, a notary calls for the signing of the wedding contract.

Baron Danglars signs, then hands the pen to the representative of Major Cavalcanti (the Major himself has disappeared). Madame Danglars sighs; she wishes that Monsieur Villefort were here, whereupon Monte Cristo steps up and says that, unfortunately, he is the cause of Villefort's absence. Andrea Cavalcanti (Benedetto) immediately pricks up his ears. Monte Cristo continues, and he says that the vest on the murdered Caderousse has been examined and that a piece of paper was found in one of the pockets. It was a letter addressed to Baron Danglars. Monte Cristo speculates that the letter might have concerned a plot against Danglars, so he sent the vest and the letter to the public prosecutor, Villefort.

The notary then announces that the signing of the contract will once again resume; just then, an officer and two gendarmes enter the salon and ask for Andrea Cavalcanti, "an escaped convict accused of murdering another escaped convict by the name of Caderousse." A search begins for young Cavalcanti, but he seems to have disappeared.

Upstairs, Eugénie makes plans to flee with her friend Louise d'Armilly. She says that she *loathes* men and intends to leave Paris immediately! Then she cuts off her long black hair and dons a man's suit of clothes. Louise is speechless at Eugénie's daring; they quickly hire a cab and escape into the night. Monsieur Danglars has lost his daughter.

"Andrea Cavalcanti" is a clever young man. Before escaping, he detours through the room where the "wedding jewels" are on display. He seizes the most valuable ones, then he cajoles a cab driver to whisk him as fast as possible out of the city (ostensibly to try and catch a friend in another carriage); then, after he alights, he smudges dust on one side of his overcoat and asks to rent a horse (his own horse threw him in the darkness, he says). All of his plans work, and by 4 a.m., he has settled himself in a rented room and is ready for a good sleep, after having consumed a cold chicken and some excellent wine. He is absolutely certain that no one will capture him, for he plans to depart early, travel through a forest, and then cross the French border.

Unfortunately, Andrea sleeps later than he expected to – and when he peers out the window, he sees three gendarmes arriving at the inn. Hastily, he writes a note to the innkeeper, making it sound as though he had to leave in shame because he had no money. He leaves a handsome tie pin behind as payment for board and room, then he climbs up the chimney and onto the roof. He is afraid, however, that while the gendarmes are searching the rooms in the inn, they might look out of an upper window and spy him on the roof. Thus, he slips down a chimney where there is no smoke. Imagine his surprise, when he drops down the chimney and onto the hearth of a bedroom – and two young ladies rise up out of their bed and scream for help. One of them is Eugénie Danglars – the woman he was supposed to marry – and the other is her friend Louise! Eugénie tells Andrea to climb back up the fireplace, but one of the gendarmes has already seen Andrea through the keyhole and breaks open the door and arrests him. Andrea is taken back to Paris and imprisoned.

Back at the Villefort residence, Valentine has still not recovered. She seems to see phantoms in her fevered, delirious state. One night in particular, she seems to see a human figure approaching her bed; the figure takes her drinking glass, samples the contents, then speaks: "Now you may drink." It is the Count of Monte Cristo. He explains to her that he has been keeping guard over her, ascertaining *who* has come into her room, *what food* has been prepared for her, and *what liquids* Valentine has been given to drink. He says that, just now, he emptied the glass by her bed – which was filled with poison – and refilled it with a therapeutic potion. Valentine is confused and distraught: Monte Cristo obviously knows *who* her poisoner is.

He does indeed, and he tells Valentine to pretend that she is asleep and she will see for herself who is trying to murder her. Then Monte Cristo hides.

Madame de Villefort, Valentine's twenty-five-year-old stepmother enters; she empties a flask into Valentine's glass, then silently withdraws. Valentine is dazed with horror and disbelief, as Monte Cristo explains Madame de Villefort's motives: when Valentine is dead, he says, the huge fortune that was to be Valentine's inheritance will revert to her father (Villefort), who will leave it all to Edouard – the one true love in Madame de Villefort's life. Valentine can scarcely believe that her stepmother is so diabolical, so she asks the Count what she must do. He tells her that "no matter what happens . . . if you awaken in a tomb or a coffin, keep your head and say, 'Maximilien is watching over me.' " Then he gives her a pill the size of a pea, bids her goodbye, and tells her that she is saved. Valentine gradually falls asleep, looking like "an angel lying at the foot of the lord."

In the morning, a nurse enters and shrieks. Seemingly, Valentine is dead. Villefort enters and sinks to the floor, his head on Valentine's bed. Madame de Villefort arrives and is speechless. She is *sure* that the glass by Valentine's bed was empty, but now it is one-third *full!* And Doctor d'Avrigny is studying it, she thinks, in order to punish her. D'Avrigny then makes a little experiment with a drop of nitric acid, and immediately, the potion changes color. "Aha!" he exclaims. Madame de Villefort crumples to the floor unconscious.

Maximilien appears and is transfixed; then he lifts up old Noirtier *and* his wheelchair and brings them both into Valentine's room. Noirtier looks as though he is on the verge of an epileptic seizure, and Maximilien vows that he will be Valentine's avenger. Villefort, in secret to Maximilien, confesses that he knows who the murderer is, and he asks for three days before Maximilien begins his vengeance. On his way out, the doctor sees Abbé Busoni, who agrees to attend to all last rites. (Busoni, remember, is Monte Cristo in disguise.)

Next day, Monte Cristo visits Danglars and asks for five million francs. Danglars, who has been boasting about the immense fortune of his firm, is panic-stricken, but finally he pays the Count, who leaves. Within moments, Monsieur de Boville is announced, and *he also* asks for five million francs from Danglars; tomorrow, his books are being examined. Danglars promises to have the money ready by noon the next day. Of course, however, he won't. He writes a letter to his wife, then takes about fifty thousand francs, his passport, and closes the door behind him.

Valentine's funeral procession is especially painful for Maximilien, and afterward, he retires to his room, lays out his pistols, and begins to write a suicide note. He is interrupted by Monte Cristo, who successfully begs him not to commit suicide. The Count tells him to *live* — with hope. Then, as proof of his compassion for Maximilien's future, he reveals who he actually is — Edmond Dantès, the "savior" of the Morrel shipping firm. Dantès says that within a week, all matters which now seem hopeless will be resolved. Then, in exactly one month, they will meet and be happier than Maximilien can even imagine. Maximilien agrees to Monte Cristo's proposition and also to his invitation to move into the Count's house with him.

Coincidentally, Albert and Mercédès have chosen to live in a rooming house that contains an apartment that is being used by Debray and Madame Danglars for their affair. Madame Danglars assures Debray that her husband's farewell note is final. He will *never* return to Paris nor to her. She has been abandoned. Debray becomes very nervous. He reminds her that she is rich, rich beyond measure, and then, business-like, he announces that it is time for them to reconcile their individual financial balances. At this point, Madame Danglars carefully conceals the pain which Debray's words give her and hurries away, scorning him for allowing her to leave "like a servant with a paycheck."

Upstairs, Albert tells his mother that he has enlisted in France's military forces. She sobs out of fear for him, but Albert manages to get her to promise that she will "live to hope." He will henceforth use her maiden name in his new life, and he tells her further to make plans to go to Marseilles and claim the money which Edmond Dantès saved long ago and buried to be used after he was married to Mercédès.

From a secret vantage point, Monte Cristo wonders if he can ever bestow happiness on these innocent creatures who have, by association with him, become victims of his vengeance.

In the maximum security unit in the prison of La Force, Benedetto lives in great optimism. He is certain that Fortune will soon be kind to him.

Villefort continues to work feverishly on the legal case involving the murderer of Caderousse, and before he leaves for court, he asks his wife straightforwardly *where she keeps her poison*. She is thrown off-guard and tries to evade the question. Villefort then accuses her of murdering three people and of watching them die. But he tells her that "as public prosecutor" and because of the possibility that her execution would "taint the Villefort name," he will be merciful to her. He swears that he will administer only "justice." (We feel that he wants the poison in order to force her to drink it and thereby save him, Villefort, from a court scandal.) Madame Villefort falls at her husband's feet, and Villefort tells her that he must go; he is due in court to demand the death penalty for a murderer. If she is still alive when he returns home, he vows that she will be in prison by nightfall.

The "Benedetto Case" produces a great sensation all over Paris. Everyone, it seems, knows about "Cavalcanti"; his splendid adventures are recounted in copious detail in the newspapers, alongside stories about his life in prison. Because Benedetto is handsome and suave, most people believe that he is the living reincarnation of a Byronic hero and is the tragic victim of Injustice and Misunderstanding.

Benedetto's actual day in court, however, is far different from the Romantic gossip that surrounds him. He begins the session by confessing that he murdered Caderousse. He is asked his name, but he says that he cannot say what his name *really* is; he does not know. He only knows what his father's name is: that name is Villefort.

A thunderous explosion of surprise rocks the courtroom. Villefort slumps half-unconscious in his chair, and a woman in one corner of the courtroom faints (this is Madame Danglars, hidden behind a veil). Andrea still doesn't fully understand what is taking place. All he knows is that he was born in Auteuil, he says, on September 27, 1817, and that his father immediately picked him up, told his mother that her new baby was dead, and then buried the baby alive in the garden. Benedetto has learned these facts from a Corsican who stabbed Villefort, then opened the grave that Villefort had just deposited the baby into, and took the boy to his sister-in-law to raise. This baby was born with such a "perverse nature" that he grew up evil and turned to crime—loathing and cursing his father for condemning him to hell—"if he had not lived . . . and to poverty if—by a miracle—he lived." He still doesn't know who his mother is and he doesn't want to know.

A shrill cry arises from the courtroom, and the woman who fainted earlier succumbs to a violent fit of hysteria. As she is being carried from the courtroom, her veil falls aside: it is Madame Danglars.

"Look at Villefort! There is the proof!" Benedetto cries, pointing to the staggering, disheveled public prosecutor who has torn his cheeks with his fingernails. In a choked voice, his teeth chattering, Villefort confesses that everything that Benedetto has said is true. He, Villefort, is guilty. Then he lunges mindlessly out of the courtroom.

Villefort realizes that his life is now ruined. He writhes inside his carriage. He acted like a god of Justice to his wife; he sentenced her, as it were, to death. Now, trembling with terror and remorse, he realizes that Madame de Villefort became a criminal *only* because "she touched me"—in other words, his own criminal nature "infected her." And he dared to accuse and condemn *her!* He prays that she is still alive. They must flee from France immediately. The scaffold is waiting for them both.

Sighing with hope, he sees nothing amiss at home. He calls again and again to his wife, and finally he finds her, pale and staring at him from her boudoir. "It's done," she moans and falls to the floor. Desperately, Villefort calls out for Edouard. Icy sweat breaks out on his forehead, and his legs begin to tremble. He sees his son lying on a sofa in the boudoir. Villefort leaps over the corpse of his wife and fervently kisses Edouard's cold cheeks. The boy is dead.

At that moment, Abbé Busoni enters; he has come to pray for

Valentine's soul, he says. Villefort steps back in terror. The voice coming from the Abbé is *not* Busoni's. Monte Cristo tears off his disguise and stands before Villefort, daring him to recognize him. With an anguished shriek, Villefort acknowledges that the man before him is Edmond Dantès. "Is your vengeance complete?" he cries, grabbing Dantès' wrist and leading him to where Madame de Villefort and Edouard lie. Then he utters a loud shriek, followed by a burst of laughter, and runs down the stairs. Later, Monte Cristo sees him digging in the ground with a spade. "I must find my son," Villefort gasps. He is mad.

At home, Monte Cristo calls to Maximilien and tells him that they are leaving Paris tomorrow. He hopes that he hasn't caused any more suffering in his unrelenting quest for vengeance.

Commentary

This section, while focusing on the downfall of Villefort, also continues with Monte Cristo's slow and deliberate entrapment of Baron Danglars. Dumas leaves the scene of the Villefort family so that we can witness Danglars' slow and painful downfall. After everyone except Andrea Cavalcanti has signed the marriage contract before the huge gathering, Baron Danglars is told that the murdered man, an escaped convict, was carrying a letter addressed to the Baron, and that the murdered man's name is Caderousse. Upon hearing the name of his old fellow conspirator, Danglars is visibly upset, and then he is horrified when the police raid his house in search of young Cavalcanti—"an escaped convict from the prison at Toulon, and he's also accused of murdering another escaped convict by the name of Caderousse." The Baron is left in a state of consternation and shock. In addition to his crumbling financial structure, his entire social life has been slowly and painfully deteriorating. Now, it has collapsed before his eyes. His daughter, Eugénie, was forced into two unwanted engagements (first, to Albert de Morcerf, whose father is now dishonored; then, to Andrea Cavalcanti, who turned out to be a criminal), and she has taken advantage of the confusion to run away (by a circuitous route) to Rome so she can live the life of a free and unhampered artist. Thus, in addition to everything else, Baron Danglars has lost his only daughter.

Later in this section, Danglars will become desperately confused by his failing financial affairs, especially when Monte Cristo suddenly withdraws five million francs and, at the same time, Monsieur de Boville arrives to collect another five million francs owed to charity hospitals. In desperation, Baron Danglars embezzles all the money he can put his hands on and, totally disgraced, he leaves France – but with a considerable amount of money, money which he clearly worships more than he does his family.

This section focuses primarily on the destruction of Villefort, 'as we watch Monte Cristo's slow punishment erode Villefort's arrogance – first, he must endure the illness of his beloved daughter Valentine, and then, he must accept her "death," after Monte Cristo gives her a mysterious pill which puts her into a state resembling death. Villefort is deeply grieved and almost inconsolable upon hearing that his daughter is dead, and he must further face Maximilien's and Dr. d'Avrigny's charges that Valentine was murdered, in addition to enduring the disgrace of having "a crime committed in my own house." Villefort is also horrified to discover through his father, Monsieur Noirtier, that the murderess is *his own wife!* Then he must face the horror of confronting his wife and demanding her suicide – or else he will have her sentenced to public execution. He tells her, "I am going to the Palace of Justice now to demand the death penalty for a murderer. If I find you alive when I return, you will be in prison by nightfall."

In addition to Danglars' shock at the humiliating revelation that Andrea Cavalcanti (alias Benedetto) is a criminal, this news will bring about Villefort's total destruction, and it will further emphasize Monte Cristo's belief that "the sins of the father are visited upon the son" since the evil and corrupt Andrea is actually the son of Villefort; in addition, poetic justice can be seen in the fact that the son will accuse the father of attempting to bury him alive when he was an infant. This reveals to us that Villefort is capable of the most horrible sin and atrocity known to civilized man – that is, of coldly and deliberately burying one's own child alive. Poetic justice occurs when the son whom the father tried to kill returns to publicly destroy his own father. Ultimately, however, we must remember that the Count of Monte Cristo has arranged *all* of this for the sake of punishment and justice.

But Villefort's slow punishment is not yet complete. When he arrives home, repentant of his demand that his wife kill herself, he discovers that she has already taken the poison and is now dying.

The ultimate horror is revealed when Villefort discovers that his wife has also poisoned their son, who is already dead. Then Abbé Busoni, who is visiting Monsieur Noirtier, reveals that he is, first, the Count of Monte Cristo, and then he forces Villefort to recognize him as Edmond Dantès, whom Villefort "condemned to a slow and hideous death," thereby depriving Dantès "of love, freedom and fortune." Villefort is barely able to withstand the horror of it all. He leads Dantès to the dead young Edouard, asking him, "Is your vengeance now complete?" Villefort then loses his mind and wanders through the garden in complete madness, searching for his dead son. The Count has once again gained his revenge against yet another of his enemies.

This section shows the first basic and fundamental change in Monte Cristo; until now, he has functioned under the theory that "the sins of the father are visited upon" subsequent generations. For this reason, he would have dueled with and killed Albert de Morcerf because Albert is the son of a hated enemy, but Monte Cristo *did* see a certain nobility in Albert, in spite of his treacherous father. Likewise, when Maximilien asks Monte Cristo to help Valentine, the daughter of his dreaded enemy Villefort, Monte Cristo is horrified to discover that so noble a young man as Maximilien could love such a descendant: "You love Valentine? You love that daughter of a cursed breed?" And yet he, out of his devotion to the young Maximilien, is persuaded ultimately to devote himself to saving and preserving Valentine for Maximilien. Finally, when Monte Cristo is confronted with the death of the young nine-year-old Edouard de Villefort, he doubts "for the first time" that he has a right to do what he has done. He hopes that "God grant that I haven't done too much already." Monte Cristo now seems to be satiated with his desire for revenge, even though he has arranged for the final destruction of Danglars in the next section.

Chapters 68 – 72

THE COLLAPSE OF DANGLARS

Summary

As Monte Cristo and Maximilien leave Paris, the Count asks young Morrel if he regrets coming with him. Maximilien, of course, confesses his terrible and agonizing grief for Valentine, but Monte Cristo urges him to remember that, above all, the friends whom one loses to death are in our hearts forever – *not* in the earth. He asks Maximilien to give up his gloomy mood. The two men then make a sea journey that is characterized by one of the Count's passions – that is, speed. And even Maximilien allows himself to feel the intoxication of the wind in his hair.

After they have docked at Marseilles, Maximilien goes to the cemetery where his father is buried, and Monte Cristo goes to call on Mercédès, who is living in the house that Dantès' father once lived in. (Mercédès, we are told, found the money that Dantès buried twenty-four years before.) She is sitting in an arbor, weeping when the Count finds her. He tells her that Albert did the right thing when he joined the military service, that he will now become strong through adversity. Staying in Marseilles would only have made Albert bitter. Mercédès is profuse in her gratitude for all that Dantès has done, but he demurs; he was only an agent of God, he says, bringing disaster and suffering on the villains who were responsible for his captivity, his long years of imprisoned solitude, and his measureless sorrow. He is only a single part of a great design. He tells Mercédès that perhaps some day she will let him share his wealth with her, and she agrees to accept his generosity – but only with Albert's permission. Then she touches the Count's trembling hand and tells him *au revoir* (until we meet again) instead of goodbye. As she looks away toward the harbor, her eyes are not on the Count's slowly diminishing figure; instead, they are on a single, tiny ship far in the distance that carries her son away from her. Yet in her heart, a small voice murmurs, "Edmond! Edmond!"

Monte Cristo can think of only one thing; he may never see Mercédès again. Once, he was so cocksure and confident. Now he has doubts. Introspectively, he wonders if he was right to follow the trail of vengeance for ten years. But only briefly does he question his actions. He instantly delights in the beauty of the day, the sky, the boats, and the harbor. But again, the dark mood of memory envelops him as he recalls a certain ship in this very harbor, the ship that carried him away to the horrible prison of Chateau d'If.

The Count hires a nearby pleasure boat and has it take him to the old prison, which, since the July Revolution, has been used only as a curiosity of terror and punishment. It is empty now. A cold pallor sweeps through the Count as he steps ashore. He secures a guide and asks to be taken to his old cell. He is curious if there are any stories connected with this particular cell, and he is stunned to discover that he is filled with fear when he hears a complete stranger recount all of the details of the imprisonment of Edmond Dantès, "that dangerous man," and the details about the imprisonment of "a poor priest who went mad" (Faria). He listens in a cold sweat as his guide tells him about the secret passageway which the two men made, of Faria's illness and his death, and about Dantès' daring and ingenious escape from the supposedly inescapable Chateau d'If.

Monte Cristo asks to see the cell of this "poor, mad priest," and afterward, overcome with emotion, he tips the guide twenty-four gold francs (symbolically, one franc for every year since he was imprisoned). The guide is confused at such generosity, so he decides impulsively to show Monte Cristo "a sort of book written on scraps of cloth." This is the book that Faria painstakingly wrote, into which he poured all the treasures of his knowledge and wisdom. In it, Monte Cristo sees the phrase "'Thou shalt tear out the teeth of the dragon and trample the lions underfoot,' sayeth the Lord." This, then, is holy proof! This is a sign that stills Monte Cristo's questioning heart. Here, God justifies and *demands* vengeance! He impulsively buys the book made from scraps and strips of cloth, puts ten thousand francs in a wallet, and makes the guide promise not to open the wallet until after he has departed. Then he calls to a boatman and orders him to sail for Marseilles immediately. His victory is complete! He has no more doubts.

Monte Cristo meets Maximilien, still in the cemetery, and tells him to meet him on the Isle of Monte Cristo on *the fifth of October*. A yacht will be waiting to take him there. Then, if Maximilien is still convinced that he must commit suicide because of his unrelieved suffering for Valentine, the Count will give him permission to die. He will even help him. But for now, he must *hope* and *live*. Monte Cristo bids him farewell.

Meanwhile, Monsieur Danglars is joyously making his escape from Paris. He secures five million francs from the firm of Thomson and French (Monte Cristo's firm), and note in this chapter who the employee is in the back room of the firm: it is Peppino, the handsome and tanned bandit whom Dantès secured a pardon for long ago. In addition, there is mention of Luigi Vampa, the bandit king who kidnapped Albert de Morcerf. Clearly, they are both a part of Monte Cristo's scheme to make Danglars (the former purser on the *Pharaon*) suffer for his part in unjustly imprisoning Edmond Dantès.

When Danglars finishes his banking transactions, a carriage is waiting for him, and he is whisked away from Rome just before nightfall; then the carriage halts and sets off again. Suddenly, Danglars realizes that he is being taken *back* to Rome. The carriage stops, and Danglars is ordered out. He is taken along a twisting route and into a cavern, half-open like an eyelid, and to a cell made from a hollowed-out rock. Obviously, his abductors do not mean to kill him, despite the fact that he recognizes the villainous Luigi Vampa among the bandits. He falls asleep that night confident that *if* he is ransomed, the sum will be paid.

In the morning, Danglars calls out for food, but, to his surprise, he learns that he must pay for it: 100,000 francs *per meal.* He tries to protest, and he tries to fast, but two weeks later, his cash flow is exhausted, and he is almost mad with hunger and frustration. What *do* they want from him? He thinks of death sometimes with longing; he is that miserable. Finally, when all of his money is gone, he begs Vampa for *only* the opportunity to live – here in these caves, if necessary. He wants only the opportunity to have enough to eat. He groans in pain, and then he hears a deep and solemn voice asking, "Do you repent?" The voice comes from a figure hidden in the shadows who is wearing a cloak. Danglars cries out that he *does repent!* Then Monte Cristo steps forth and forgives Danglars, but tells him that he, Monte Cristo, is *not* a Count. Instead, he is the man whom Danglars betrayed and dishonored years ago: he is Edmond Dantès.

Danglars gasps, cries out, and falls to the floor. When he recovers, he is free; he has been abandoned along the roadside. He bends down to drink from a brook and is stunned: his hair has turned white.

Commentary

In these chapters, Monte Cristo begins to put his life into its proper perspective. He bids farewell to Paris, believing that "the spirit of God led me there, and He has led me out triumphant. He alone knows that I now leave without hatred or pride, but not without regret; he alone knows that I have not used the power which He entrusted to me either for myself or for vain causes. Now my work is completed, my mission accomplished. Farewell, Paris, Farewell!" Then he visits Mercédès and leaves her with peace and understanding between them and with the implication that he will constantly watch over the future fortune of her son, Albert de Morcerf. He then visits the infamous Chateau d'If and after generously tipping the guide, he is given the book that Abbé Faria wrote on strips of cloth. His delight at finally possessing the Abbé's manuscript is immeasurable.

Then Dumas returns our attention to Monte Cristo's revenge against Danglars. If we remember that Fernand (Count de Morcerf) loved his wife and son more than anything else, and that his ultimate punishment occurred when they denied him and left his house empty-handed, and if we remember that Villefort cherished his public image and ambition more than anything else, and that ultimately he was publicly ruined, then we must also remember that Danglars loves nothing so much as he loves money. Consequently, Monte Cristo arranges matters so that Danglars is constantly losing money, but even so, Danglars is able to leave France with over five million francs by embezzling and stealing from various sources, particularly from charity hospitals.

Danglars arrives in Rome, totally unaware that Monte Cristo has informed (1) the banking firm of Thomson and French; (2) Peppino, the person whom Monte Cristo saved earlier from execution; and (3) Luigi Vampa, the Italian bandit who specializes in kidnapping (earlier, he kidnapped Albert de Morcerf). Therefore, when Luigi Vampa kidnaps Danglars and forces him to pay for his food or else starve—100,000 francs for one chicken—this *demand for money* crucifies Danglars more than would any *physical* pain. Finally, Monte Cristo reveals himself to Danglars: "I am the man you betrayed and dishonored, the man whose fiancée you prostituted, the man on whom you trod on the way to fortune, the man whose father you caused to die of hunger, the man you condemned to die of hunger but who now forgives you because he himself needs to be forgiven. I am Edmond Dantès."

This revelation is too much for Danglars, because when he is released with only a pittance of his fortune remaining, his hair has turned completely white. Now, the Count of Monte Cristo is finally revenged against all of his enemies.

Chapter 73

EPILOGUE

Summary

October has finally come. It is evening. A light yacht is sailing toward a small island, and a tall, dark young man asks if the island ahead of them is the Isle of Monte Cristo. It is, and a shot suddenly flashes loudly from the island. The young man answers it with a shot from his carbine, and ten minutes later, the yacht is anchored, and the young man, Maximilien Morrel, wades ashore, where he is greeted by Monte Cristo.

Maximilien tells the Count that he has come "to die in the arms of a friend who will smile at me during my last moments of life." He fears that his sister, Julie, would burst into tears and that his brother-in-law would snatch his gun away. Clearly, Maximilien is still so morose over Valentine's death that he doesn't want to go on living. In his own words, he has "come to the end of the road," and he can go no further. He checks his watch; he has three more hours to live.

"Come," says the Count, and leads Maximilien to a grotto, which magically becomes a deeply carpeted, underground palace. An odor of sweet, exotic perfume envelops them, while around them, marble statues hold baskets of flowers and fruit. Monte Cristo proposes that the two of them spend Maximilien's last hours "like the ancient Romans."

"No regrets?" he asks Maximilien. "Not even about leaving me?" A tear glistens in Maximilien's eye. Monte Cristo asks him if he isn't afraid of losing his soul, and Maximilien answers that his soul is no longer his own, meaning that it belongs to Valentine. Monte Cristo says that he has long regarded him as a son, but that he hoped for a son who would enjoy life as few people ever could because of untold wealth. "You can have *anything* you want," he tells Maximilien, "Only live!"

But Maximilien is coldly resolute. Only a miracle will save him. Therefore, Monte Cristo goes to a cabinet and takes out a small silver box, in which there is a still smaller golden box, which contains a substance that the Count offers to Maximilien on a spoon. "This is what you asked for, and this is what I promised you," he says. Then he takes a second spoon for himself and dips into the golden box, saying wearily that he too is tired of life.

Maximilien cries out that if the Count were to kill *himself,* it would be a crime, for the Count has faith and hope. Then he quickly bids Monte Cristo farewell, promising to tell Valentine how very good and generous the Count has been to him. He swallows the mysterious substance, and the room suddenly seems to dim, the marble statues become gauzy, and the incense becomes only a whisper. Maximilien thanks Monte Cristo one last time, then he falls lifelessly to the floor. His eyes flicker, and he seems to see a hazy image of Valentine. Is this heaven? Is this death? No sound comes from Maximilien's lips, but his soul cries out to Valentine, and she rushes to him.

"He is calling you," Monte Cristo tells Valentine. "You and Maximilien must never leave one another again. Now I give you back to one another, and may God bless you, and despite all of my acts of vengeance, may He take into account these two lives that I have *saved!*"

Monte Cristo turns to Haydée and tells her that he is entrusting her future to Valentine and Maximilien; but Haydée says that she will die without Monte Cristo. She loves him as she loves life and as she loves God; Monte Cristo is the "finest, the kindest, and the greatest man on this earth!" The Count realizes now that God is, as it were, offering Haydée to him so that he can be happy. He puts his arm around Haydée's waist and leaves, just as Maximilien awakens and is reunited with Valentine.

Next morning at dawn, Jacopo gives Maximilien a note from Monte Cristo. In it, Monte Cristo tells Maximilien that in life, there is neither happiness nor unhappiness. One can only compare one with the other, and one must have suffered terrible despair if one is ever to know ultimate bliss. Both Maximilien and Valentine have known the depths of unhappiness; therefore, they will now know bliss. Monte Cristo asks them both to be happy and to do two things in order to ensure happiness for them: *wait* and *hope.*

On the far horizon, where a hard blue line separates the sky from the Mediterranean, a tiny white sail can be seen. Maximilien bids farewell to Monte Cristo, "my father!," and Valentine bids farewell to Haydée, "my sister!" Then she turns to Maximilien and reminds him that perhaps one day they may see them again — if they only *wait* and *hope,* the two words containing all of human wisdom.

Commentary

Almost every nineteenth-century novel of this period had a final chapter that brought the story to a very neat ending, tidying up all the loose narrative strands. In this final chapter, Monte Cristo puts his beloved young friend Maximilien to a final test to see whether or not his suicide intent is superficial or whether there is indeed the deep love that he suspects. He has held Maximilien in suspense concerning the supposed death of Valentine because "there is neither happiness nor unhappiness in this world; there is only the comparison of one state with another. Only a man who has felt ultimate despair is capable of feeling ultimate bliss." Since Monte Cristo himself felt ultimate despair, we must happily conclude that with his realization of his love for Haydée and Haydée's love for him, that he has at last found "ultimate bliss."

SUGGESTED ESSAY QUESTIONS

1. Consider the four enemies of Edmond Dantès and discuss how the punishment that the Count of Monte Cristo inflicts upon them is related to their deepest ambitions.

2. Using Monte Cristo's concept that great suffering requires prolonged punishment rather than instantaneous death, discuss the justice of the punishment that he inflicts on each of them.

3. Using Albert, Valentine, and Edouard, how does Monte Cristo's theory of "the sins of the fathers must be visited upon subsequent generations" undergo a dramatic reversal?

4. Discuss the metamorphosis of Edmond Dantès from a handsome, naive, and idealistic young man into the sophisticated and aristocratic Count of Monte Cristo.

5. This novel is often considered to be one of the greatest adventure stories in Western literature, yet in reality, it is a novel of intrigue and mystery. Discuss the discrepancy.

SELECT BIBLIOGRAPHY

BASSAN, FERNANDE. *Alexandre Dumas, pere, et la Comedie-Francaise.* Paris: Lettres Modernes, 1972.

BELL, A. CRAIG. *Alexandre Dumas, a Biography and Study.* London: Cassell, 1950.

COOK, MERCER. *Five French Negro Authors.* Washington, D.C.: Associated Publishers, 1943.

GORMAN, HERBERT SHERMAN. *The Incredible Marquis, Alexandre Dumas.* New York: Rinehart, 1929.

HEMMINGS, FREDERICK WILLIAM JOHN. *The King of Romance: A Portrait of Alexandre Dumas.* London, 1929.

LUCAS-DUBRETON, JEAN. *La Vie d'Alexandre Dumas, pere.* Paris: J. Lucas-Dubreton, 1916.

MAUROIS, ANDRE. *Alexandre Dumas: A Great Life in Brief.* New York: Knopf, 1955.

_____. *The Titans.* New York: Hopkins, 1957.

MUNRO, DOUGLAS. *Alexandre Dumas, pere.* New York: Garland, 1981.

PARIGOT, HIPPOLYTE LOUIS. *Alexandre Dumas, pere.* Paris, 1902.

REED, FRANK WILD. *Alexandre Dumas, Benefactor.* New York: Colophon, 1935.

ROSS, MICHAEL. *Alexandre Dumas.* London: Newton Abbot, 1981.

SIMON, G. M. *Histoire d'une Collaboration.* Paris, 1919.

STOWE, RICHARD. *Alexandre Dumas.* New York: Twayne, 1976.

THOMPSON, JOHN A. *Alexandre Dumas, pere, and the Spanish Romance Drama.* Louisiana State University Press, 1938.

NOTES

NOTES

CYRANO DE BERGERAC

NOTES

including
- *Introduction and Life of Rostand*
- *List of Characters*
- *Synopsis of the Play*
- *Summaries and Commentaries*
- *Character Analyses and Critical Commentaries*
- *Review Questions and Essay Topics*
- *Bibliography*

by
Estelle and LaRocque DuBose
Department of Languages and Literature
Western State College of Colorado

Cliffs Notes

INCORPORATED

LINCOLN, NEBRASKA 68501

Editor

Gary Carey, M.A.
University of Colorado

Consulting Editor

James L. Roberts, Ph.D.
Department ,of English
University of Nebraska

ISBN 0-8220-0346-5
© Copyright 1971
by
C. K. Hillegass
All Rights Reserved
Printed in U.S.A.

1990 Printing

Cliffs Notes, Inc.   Lincoln, Nebraska

CONTENTS

CHARACTER ANALYSES

CRITICAL COMMENTARY

REVIEW QUESTIONS AND ESSAY TOPICS

BIBLIOGRAPHY

Cyrano de Bergerac Notes

INTRODUCTION

The classical tradition of French drama was formalized in the seventeenth century, and the eighteenth century was an imitation of the seventeenth. During this time, the plays were usually centered around characters from history—most often Greek or Roman history or literature—and were of a psychological nature. Any action which was violent or shocking, such as a battle, was simply told about and never re-enacted on stage. Aristotle's unities were closely observed—that is, the action took place within a time span of no more than 24 hours, in one geographical location, and concerned one main character.

The state of French drama during the nineteenth century was as tumultuous as was the state of French politics. Victor Hugo broke the restrictive chains of French classicism with the famous "Preface" to *Cromwell* (1827), the manifesto of romanticism. Over the next 25 years his dramas employed action as well as other dramatic devices denied to the classicists. During this period of literary and political upheaval, the schools of romanticism, naturalism, symbolism, and realism developed in France. Yet *Cyrano de Bergerac* does not really fit into any of these categories. Some have considered it a revival or culmination of romantic drama, but it did not truly revive this school nor continue it. *Cyrano* was presented in 1897 for the first time, half a century after Hugo's last effort, and is not a part of any school or movement.

Rather, *Cyrano* seems an outgrowth of the medieval French literature—the songs of the troubadours. Most notable of these were the *Chanson de Roland* and *Roman de la Rose*. The tales of Roland concerned a hero, brave, noble, loyal, and steadfast, who avenges any affront by killing the offender, and whose word is his bond. The *Roman de la Rose* is the prime example of the other kind of popular literature of that period, the type which idealized Woman and Love. The love in these tales was respectful, submissive, almost religious. *Cyrano* combines these two genres in its central character and its story. Rostand himself came from southern France where these tales originally developed and where the historical Cyrano de Bergerac had his roots.

Cyrano can also be considered as a virtuoso play, one written to exploit the talents of a particular actor. (See the section of this study guide entitled, "*Cyrano* as a Virtuoso Play," for a more complete examination of this question.) Previously, Rostand had written *La Samaritaine* for Sarah Bernhardt, but that play did not meet with the popular or critical approval which *Cyrano* was to achieve. The fact that *Cyrano* has outlived the actor for whom it was supposedly written, and that many actors have played the lead role successfully surely outweighs the fact that the play might not have been written had not Rostand known an actor who was perfect for the role. More than many artistic efforts, *Cyrano* is a perfect blending of the author's personality, philosophy, and subject, resulting in a work of art that is enjoyable in and for itself, and which has been continually popular since its first performance.

LIFE AND WORKS OF ROSTAND

Edmond Rostand was born in Marseilles, France, on April 1, 1868. When he was twenty-two years old, he married the poet, Rosemond Gerard, and presented his first book, a volume of poems, to her as a wedding gift.

His first play, *Les Romanesques*, which concerned two young lovers, appeared four years later. And the next year, 1895, *La Princesse Lointaine*, was produced. It was the story of the Provençal poet, Rudel. Rostand's next play was *La Samaritaine*, written for the popular French actress, Sarah Bernhardt. Most critics did not like it because one of the characters — and a minor one, at that — was Christ.

Cyrano de Bergerac made its first appearance in 1897 with the actor, Coquelin, in the title role and was presented for 500 consecutive performances. It was the most popular play of the era, and since its first performance there has hardly been a time when it was not in production somewhere in the world. For, although the play is typically French, it is highly popular in other countries, even when it is translated poorly or cut unmercifully.

Rostand's next play, *L'Aiglon,* was about Napoleon's heir. It was too French for foreign audiences, who did not always revere Napoleon as much as did the French, and even in France it was never as popular as *Cyrano*. After its production, Rostand retired to the country for ten years to write *Chantecler*. It received some acclaim, but Paris audiences did not like it nearly so well as they had *Cyrano*.

Rostand was elected to the French Academy at the age of thirty-three, the youngest member at that time. After the production of *Chantecler,* he was raised to Commander of the Legion of Honor and received a "Grand Diploma."

When World War I began, Rostand volunteered for service, but was refused. He consoled himself by writing patriotic poetry. One poem, praising America, was dedicated to Sarah Bernhardt, and another was occasioned by the sinking of the *Lusitania*.

Rostand was never robust, his health being one reason that he retired to the country, and he died in Paris on December 2, 1918. He left one drama, *La Derniere Nuit de Don Juan,* with an unfinished prologue which further illustrated his idea of the unattainable ideal being more desirable than the real or practical.

In the dedication to *Cyrano de Bergerac,* Rostand says that he would like to dedicate the play to the spirit of Cyrano, but since that has passed on to Coquelin, the actor, he dedicates it to Coquelin. Because the actor who plays Cyrano is so very crucial to the success of the play—all the other characters are merely supporting roles—it is fortunate that an actor whom the author considered perfect for the role was able to introduce it.

LIST OF CHARACTERS

Characters whose names are followed by an asterisk are known to have been historical personages.

Cyrano de Bergerac*

The main character of the play. He is a soldier, poet, philosopher, and scientist—a man of immense courage, versatility, and talent. He has an enormous nose and is very sensitive about it. He is an expert swordsman and challenges anyone who mentions his nose. He jealously guards his intellectual freedom, even though he suffers poverty. His integrity and innate nobility of spirit are the theme of the play.

Christian de Neuvillette

Cyrano's comrade-in-arms. A handsome man of noble spirit and generosity. He is in love with Roxane, but unable to express his love in such a way as to be acceptable to her. He is not stupid, but is actually inarticulate.

Roxane (Madeleine Robin)*

The beautiful girl with whom both Cyrano and Christian are in love. She falls in love with Christian's beauty and (though she is unaware of it) Cyrano's mind. She is described as a *précieuse*, which, in seventeenth-century France, meant a person highly affected in language, manners, and dress. To the *précieuse*, what a person *was* was not so important as what he *appeared* to be. Some of them, wishing to appear witty, are said to have rehearsed repartee amongst themselves before going to a party. Molière wrote a play, *Les Précieuse Ridicules*, making fun of them. Christian is afraid that Roxane, being a *précieuse*, would not love a plain-spoken man.

Comte de Guiche*

The villain of the play, Richelieu's nephew, who wants Roxane as his mistress, and wishes her to marry Valvert. Solely for revenge against Christian and Cyrano, he sends the Gascony Guards to almost certain death.

Le Bret*

Cyrano's friend and confidant.

Ragueneau

A poet who runs a bakery shop where other poets congregate.

Lise

Wife of Ragueneau.

Carbon de Castel-Jaloux*

The commander of the Gascony Guards.

Lignière*

A poet, Cyrano's friend. Cyrano single-handedly routs the one hundred men sent to kill Lignière.

Valvert

A *précieuse* who insults Cyrano by referring to his nose. He is the man De Guiche wants Roxane to marry. It is to him that the famous speech of insults is addressed, and it is he with whom Cyrano duels while composing a poem.

Montfleury*

An actor, one of Roxane's suitors. He has incurred Cyrano's displeasure and has been forbidden by Cyrano to act on the stage for three weeks.

Bellerose*

Manager of the theater which Cyrano closes by not allowing Montfleury to act.

Jodelet*

A comedian in the same theater.

Cuigy*
Brissaille* } Friends of Cyrano.

Soeur Marthe
Soeur Claire } Nuns in the convent where Roxane goes to live.

Mère Marguérite de Jésus

Mother Superior at the same convent.

A NOTE ABOUT SCENE DIVISION

Since many of Rostand's devices are confined to and isolated within the space of a scene or two, the authors feel that discussing the play in elements of one entire act at a time would be too broad a basis from which to work, and would lead to confusion on the part of the student. Act II, for example, contains so many dramatic devices, moods, and characters that it would be very difficult to discuss without some reference point, such as scene divisions.

Since many English-language editions of *Cyrano de Bergerac* are not divided into scenes, an explanation of the scene division used here would seem to be in order.

The scene divisions used are the traditional ones: in general, the scenes end or begin when a character of some importance to the plot either exits or makes an entrance. The student using an

English-language translation should have no trouble recognizing the divisions between the scenes if he refers to the exit or entrance of an important character or, simply, to the action described for a particular scene. The student using one of the French-language editions will in all likelihood find that the scene division used here is identical to that used in his copy of the play.

BRIEF SYNOPSIS

The curtain rises to disclose the interior of a theater. Several spectators are present, waiting for the play to begin, and their conversation informs us (erroneously) that this is the famous theater in which Corneille's *Le Cid* was introduced. The play tonight is Baro's *Clorise,* and the leading actor is Montfleury.

Ragueneau and Le Bret enter, and Lignière calls attention to the fashionable people who are present. They wonder where Cyrano is, since he has forbidden Montfleury to act on the stage. When Roxane enters, Christian points her out to Le Bret as the woman with whom he is in love, even though he does not know her name and has never talked to her. Lignière says that De Guiche is also interested in Roxane, and though she is resisting him he is a very powerful and vindictive man. He is also married.

Before the play-within-a-play begins, Christian goes to warn Lignière (who has left the theater) that his latest poem has offended a highly-placed person who has stationed a hundred men near Lignière's street to ambush and murder him.

The curtain rises and Montfleury enters on stage. As he begins to speak, Cyrano's voice interrupts and tells him to leave the stage. Cyrano offers to fight anyone who wishes to defend Montfleury, but there are no volunteers. When the manager of the theater asks Cyrano if he is also going to force him to refund the money of the patrons, Cyrano tosses a bag of gold to the stage, and the manager is happy.

An affected gentleman who wishes to insult Cyrano says, "Your nose is very — large." Cyrano describes to him what a number of different types of people might have said about his nose. Then he says that while they duel, he will compose a *ballade* and thrust on the last line. He proceeds to do just that.

When almost all the spectators have left the theater, Cyrano confesses to Le Bret that he is in love with his cousin, Roxane. Then Roxane's duenna comes in and makes an appointment with Cyrano for the next day. He is ecstatic, and when he learns of Lignière's plight he happily goes off to fight the one hundred men lying in wait for the poet.

The next morning, Cyrano waits for Roxane in Ragueneau's pastry shop. He writes a letter, thinking that he may simply hand it to her when she arrives and leave without waiting for her answer. When she comes, she confesses that she is in love — with Christian. Cyrano, broken-hearted though he is, promises that he will look after Christian for her. All of Paris is talking of his exploit of the previous night in routing the one hundred men sent to murder Lignière. De Guiche comes and offers to be Cyrano's patron, but Cyrano refuses.

Christian joins the Cadets of Gascogne, the famed Gascony Guards, and he and Cyrano become friends. He confesses to Cyrano that he loves Roxane, but that he is afraid that he cannot express himself well enough to win her love. Cyrano gives him the letter which he himself had written to Roxane and tells him to send it to her in his own name. This is the beginning of the deception. Cyrano writes beautiful letters and makes up impassioned speeches which Christian memorizes. Roxane falls in love with Christian's borrowed eloquence.

At last, however, Christian tires of his role as Cyrano's mouthpiece. The company is leaving for the siege of Arras, and before he goes he wants to woo Roxane with his own words. But he has underestimated the strength of her attachment to beautiful language and gets nowhere with her. Cyrano saves the day for him by hiding under the balcony where Roxane stands and whispering words which Christian repeats. Soon, however, Cyrano's enthusiasm makes this unbearable and he speaks aloud —but Roxane does not know that it is he and not Christian who is speaking.

A monk brings a letter from De Guiche to Roxane, saying that he is sending the regiment on ahead, but that he is remaining behind for one night in the expectation of meeting Roxane secretly. Roxane pretends that the letter directs the monk to marry her to Christian immediately, which he does while Cyrano detains De Guiche. The marriage is not consummated, however, because the Guards leave for the front, on the orders of De Guiche, to fight at the siege of Arras.

During the siege, Cyrano finds a way through the lines and risks his life to get letters to Roxane, purportedly from Christian. Much to the surprise of everyone, Roxane appears, bringing food and news, which makes Cyrano's hopes soar. She has come, she says, to confess that at first she loved Christian for his beauty, but that now, because of his letters, she has fallen in love with his spirit and his wonderful mind. This is a much deeper and truer love, and she is ashamed that she has been so shallow.

Christian is an honorable man and he wants Cyrano to tell Roxane the truth. Just as Cyrano is about to do so, Christian's body is carried in; he has been killed by the first shot fired in the battle.

Nearly fifteen years elapse, and we find the mourning Roxane in a convent. She has always carried Christian's last letter next to her heart. Cyrano comes to her each week and gives her a witty resumé of the week's gossip. Today, however, he is late. One of Cyrano's enemies has managed to injure him by having a lackey drop a heavy log on Cyrano's head as he passed beneath a window. Cyrano is mortally wounded, but still comes just at sunset, as always, to give Roxane her news of the outside world. He sits in his usual chair and begins, but then asks to read Christian's last letter. Roxane gives it to him. As he reads, she realizes that it is too dark for him to see the words and that this was the voice she had heard under her balcony on her wedding night. As Cyrano dies, Roxane says that she has loved only once, but has lost her love twice.

SUMMARIES AND COMMENTARIES

ACT I – SCENE 1

Summary

The curtain rises to show the interior of a dimly-lighted theater. Some cavaliers enter without paying and practice fencing; they are followed by two lackeys who sit on the floor and begin gambling; a middle-class man and his son enter; then a pickpocket and his accomplices come in. Through conversations we learn that this is the theater where Corneille's *Le Cid* was first performed, and that the play tonight is Baro's *Clorise*, and that its star is Montfleury.

Commentary

This opening scene is a very good example of two things: the playwright's problem of providing his audience with necessary information, and Rostand's craftsmanship in dealing with the problem. While the novelist can give descriptions, explanations, and background material in many ways, the playwright has only the dialogue and setting—and sometimes the latter must be explained in the dialogue if it is especially significant.

Notice the many types of people—those who come to play cards, to picnic, to flirt, to steal, and even a few honest souls who really want to see the play—whom Rostand introduces in this brief scene. But he is not only describing a cross-section of seventeenth-century French society; he also manages a comment on that society by having the two cavaliers enter the theater without buying tickets. Overall, he gives the very distinct impression to the audience that this is an exciting period in the history of the French theater. And, since the student of French civilization automatically thinks of Corneille, Molière, and Racine when he thinks of seventeenth-century France, what better place to begin a play set in that period than in its most famous theater? (*Le Cid* was not actually introduced in this theater, however.)

Apart from all the information conveyed, there is also the mood of the play, which must be established at the beginning. Rostand does this with his setting, for there is a distinct excitement in a theater before a play just as there is before a symphony or opera when the musicians are tuning their instruments.

If the playwright's problem at the opening of a play were simply that of conveying information and establishing mood, it would be relatively easy to solve. But one must remember that the playwright must not only capture the attention of the audience, but must also hold its interest for the full course of the play. The air of anticipation created by the setting in this scene is added—and the element of suspense is introduced—to the scenes immediately following.

ACT I – SCENES 2-3

Summary

Christian is introduced in Scene 2 by the poet, Lignière. The poet/baker, Ragueneau, enters dressed in his Sunday best, and talks with Lignière. He asks about Cyrano, who has forbidden Montfleury to act, but who has not yet appeared. Ragueneau describes Cyrano's nose as well as his reputation as a swordsman. When Roxane enters the theater, Lignière tells Christian, who has fallen in love with her without knowing her identity, who the lady is. He also tells Christian that De Guiche, who is married to Richelieu's niece and is very powerful, wants Roxane to marry a complaisant courtier, Valvert, so that De Guiche can make her his own mistress. In Lignière's opinion, Christian hasn't a chance with the lady.

After Lignière leaves the theater, Christian learns from a pickpocket that Lignière has written a poem which has offended some powerful person. This highly-placed man plans to have the poet killed and has hired a hundred armed men to waylay Lignière on his way home. Christian goes off to find Lignière and warn him.

Montfleury goes onto the stage and begins his first speech, the prologue of the play, but he is interrupted by the voice of Cyrano telling him to stop. He makes several attempts to continue his speech, but is interrupted by Cyrano each time.

Commentary

It may seem that nothing much happens during the first three scenes. People wander in and out, we are given snatches of conversations, and in Scenes 2 and 3 Christian and Lignière come and go, as does Ragueneau. Actually, these characters are giving us information which we will need later in order to understand the play.

As in Scene 1, there is a variety of characters introduced. The marquis who comments that Christian is handsome enough, but not really in the latest fashion, is an excellent example of the *précieuse* attitude (an attitude, prevalent in seventeenth-century France, that what a person *appeared* to be was more important than what he really *was*). Our knowledge of the marquis—he is vain, and affected in language, manners, and dress—will help us to understand that of Roxane, since she is also one of the *précieuse*.

We are told of the political climate in France and of the worsening relationship with Spain, which prepares us for the later mention of the forthcoming battle of Arras. Duels were fought then, and we discover that an insult in a poem was sufficient cause for murder. We may rightly assume that the theater is important since members of the Academy are present. (The French Academy is composed of very distinguished intellectuals who are, among other duties, the arbiters of the French language.

Their rank is higher than any other in France today—for purposes of seating arrangements at official dinners, for example—though the Academy has lost much of its former prestige.)

By the end of Scene 3 we have been introduced to the three men who are in love with Roxane, and their characters have been explained. Christian is an "honest, brave soldier" who fears that he will not have the words to win her. De Guiche is powerful and arrogant. Cyrano is a noble, brave man, "an exquisite being."

Roxane is introduced as well, and so we have the conflict of the play: De Guiche's interest in Roxane, Christian's love for her, and Cyrano's love for Roxane.

It might, perhaps, be worthy of mention here that Rostand represented most of his characters who have historical counterparts according to the generally reputed personality of the character. Montfleury's obesity was satirized by both Molière and the historical Cyrano, and Lignière refers to him as a "hippopotamus."

The groundwork for the events which occur toward the end of Act I is laid in the knowledge that Lignière is in danger. We are also prepared for Cyrano's appearance: he has a huge nose which no one dares mention to him, even by implication. The interest shown in him arouses our own interest and curiosity. If such a character had appeared without preparation, he might well have seemed merely ridiculous. In other words, we are now prepared for the delightful events in Scene 4.

ACT I – SCENE 4

Summary

Montfleury tries to continue his speech, but is repeatedly interrupted by Cyrano. The audience jeers Cyrano, who offers to fight anyone who will come forward in Montfleury's defense, but no one comes. Montfleury leaves the stage. The theater manager points out to Cyrano that if he does not allow the play to proceed, the manager will have to refund the money to the patrons. Cyrano tosses a sack of gold to him, which is obviously more than adequate to cover the loss. Cyrano is not worried by the fact that Montfleury has a powerful patron who may be angry at Cyrano's preventing the performance.

The vicomte, Valvert, says to Cyrano, "Your nose is, hmm . . . is . . . very . . . hmm . . . big." This leads to one of the memorable moments of the play in which Cyrano, with great wit and charm, suggests what many types of people might say about his nose. After this tirade by Cyrano, De Guiche tries to lead the vicomte away, but the foolish man delays long enough to sneer at Cyrano for not wearing gloves. Cyrano replies that his elegances are moral ones. Then he announces that he will fight a duel with the vicomte and that, while they are fighting, he will compose a *ballade* (a poem consisting of three stanzas of eight lines each, concluding with a four-line refrain). At the end of the refrain, he says, he will end the duel with a thrust. He does exactly as he has promised.

When the hall is almost empty, Le Bret asks why Cyrano has not eaten dinner. He confesses that he has no money. Le Bret asks about the sack of gold that Cyrano threw to the theater manager, and Cyrano confesses that that was his month's income — he has nothing left. "What foolishness," says Le Bret. "But what a beautiful gesture!" Cyrano replies.

Commentary

The first three scenes of the first act have accomplished, among other things, the setting of the play and the introduction of nearly all of the major characters, including Cyrano. But Cyrano does not appear on the stage during these three scenes. All we know about him — who and what he is, as well as the size of his nose — comes from the dialogue of no less than half a dozen other characters. This preparation is extremely important, for if we were not so well prepared beforehand — if, for instance, Cyrano were to be visible on stage at the rise of the opening curtain — our reaction to this apparently ludicrous character would be completely different from what it is. As it is, we have heard a great deal about Cyrano in these early scenes, and Scene 3 ends with Cyrano on stage (but hidden by the crowd) speaking to Montfleury.

Scene 4 begins with Cyrano making himself visible to the audience. Notice that there is not necessarily a curtain nor any break in the action between scenes. And here is an excellent example of Rostand's dramatic technique. When a major character makes an important entrance, the eyes, as well as the interest of the audience must be directed to that character. A standard device for accomplishing this is by having a minor character precede the major character on stage and announce his arrival. Rostand's device is enormously more effective. Cyrano's presence on stage is indicated only when he speaks his first line to Montfleury, and suspense is heightened as the audience tries to locate the speaker. In case some of the audience still do not know where to look for Cyrano, Rostand has Cyrano raise his arm and wave his cane. *Now* we know exactly where he is, and the attention of the audience is riveted to the spot. And *now* we are finally allowed to see the man for whose entrance we have been so well prepared.

This long scene is not only exciting from both the intellectual and physical standpoints, but it serves to refine our knowledge of Cyrano's character. And it is his character and personality which make most of the events in the play seem real and logical regardless of how unlikely they might appear otherwise. In other words, given Cyrano's character, there is a "willing suspension of disbelief" on the part of the audience.

Cyrano's extreme sensitivity about his nose (the historical Cyrano is supposed to have been just as touchy) is made clear when he challenges the vicomte to a duel and doubly insults him by besting him in the duel and composing a poem at the same time.

Cyrano is highly intelligent, talented, brave, impetuous, and sensitive. He is more than that: after the duel we learn that he has no money left. His comment that tossing the bag of gold onto the stage to reimburse the theater manager was a beautiful gesture tells us that the "beau geste" means more to him than bread. He is extremely idealistic and has a very dramatic temperament.

From the discussion about the patron of Montfleury, we learn that all artists are expected to have a patron—one who supports his protégé with money and position. Cyrano has no patron. He stands alone, beholden to no man, independent, unafraid and unprotected.

ACT I – SCENES 5-7

Summary

As Cyrano eats the frugal "meal" provided by the adoring little orange-girl, Le Bret warns him that his rash actions are making powerful enemies, but Cyrano refuses to be seriously concerned. He says, "I have decided to be admirable in everything." He then confesses that he is in love with his cousin Roxane, but that he is so ugly that he is afraid to try to win her hand. The only thing he fears is having his nose laughed at; for her to laugh at him would be a blow he dare not risk.

In Scene 6 Roxane's duenna enters the theater and asks Cyrano to meet Roxane. Elated, he makes an appointment to meet her at Ragueneau's pastry shop the next morning at seven o'clock. Cyrano is ecstatic; he feels invincible; he feels that he needs to fight whole armies.

Brissaille enters with the drunken Lignière, saying that Lignière is in trouble. Lignière explains that his poem has gotten him into difficulties; Cyrano orders his entourage to follow and watch, but not to interfere. He will defend Lignière himself because he once saw his friend perform a lovely romantic gesture. Cyrano leaves the stage twenty paces ahead of the rest—officers, comedians, actresses, and musicians—pausing only to explain that it was necessary to send a hundred men to kill Lignière because it is well known that he is a friend of Cyrano's.

Commentary

In these three scenes Rostand finishes giving the audience the problem on which the plot turns. We already know that Christian is in love with Roxane and that he is afraid that he is not sufficiently eloquent to win her hand. Now we have the knowledge that the fabulous Cyrano also loves her—and he certainly has the language at his command to win a woman of her type—but he fears that she would not love him because of his physical oddity: his enormous nose.

The act ends on a very hopeful note, as far as Cyrano's love for Roxane is concerned. We see how a little encouragement in this direction increases his already monumental dash and daring. He gladly goes to fight a hundred men. The fact that Lignière is in trouble was carefully prepared for earlier, so this is no surprise. And we know that Cyrano is just the sort who would gaily and pompously lead his admirers to watch him fight a hundred men.

Although Cyrano does not appear until Act I, Scene 3—and actually only his voice is heard in Scene 3—he has been described, and we are thoroughly prepared for him. Also, by the time Cyrano makes a physical appearance in Scene 4, Rostand has so completely established the character that we are more delighted than surprised by his extravagances. Rostand has, in addition, established so much sympathy for his main character that we hope that Roxane is going to confess her love for him and not merely warn him of some plot or give him some other cousin-ly message. This is one of Rostand's most artful strokes, and one of his secrets of making fantastic, romantic nonsense believable.

ACT II – SCENES 1-2

Summary

Act II takes place in the pastry shop owned by Ragueneau, who was introduced in Act I. Ragueneau's wife, Lise, has more business sense and less love of poetry than her husband—she has made sacks out of the poems his friends have left in payment for food. Two children make a small purchase, and Lise wraps their pastries in the pages of poetry. When his wife is not looking, Ragueneau calls the children back and trades them three more pastries for the poems.

Commentary

These short scenes serve to establish the personalities of Ragueneau and his wife, Lise, as well as the fact that there is a conflict between them. Ragueneau seems to be almost a caricature of Cyrano — a man who loves the gallant gesture, the bravado of the soldier, and the sensitivity of the poet. Ragueneau reappears throughout the play as a friend and admirer of Cyrano, and since Act III will open with the tale of Ragueneau's own drama, Rostand very economically prepares us for that in these scenes.

Ragueneau is a "utility" character in the play. In Act I, he gives the audience various bits of important information; in Act II, he provides an appropriate setting for the occurrences which take place in that act; in Act IV, he serves in the capacity of coachman; and in Act V, he is the necessary old friend of Cyrano. How much more interesting it is for these to be combined into one character with a personality and history instead of being portrayed by a series of faceless actors. Moreover, the preparation for Ragueneau's tale gives the audience an opportunity to become accustomed to, and to enjoy, the setting of the little pastry shop — which, incidentally, Rostand envisioned as a very complicated and interesting set. If he had had any really important action take place at the very beginning of the act, it might well have failed to make the proper impression upon an audience absorbed in the scenery.

ACT II — SCENES 3-4

Summary

Cyrano enters and Ragueneau congratulates him on the duel in the theater the night before. But Cyrano is not interested in

anything except his meeting with Roxane. He asks Ragueneau
to clear the place out when he gives the signal, and Ragueneau
agrees. A musketeer enters who will be mentioned again later.

The poets come in, for their "first meal," as Lise says. They
are all excited about the feat of the evening before—one man
against a hundred, and no one knows who the brave one was.
Cyrano is writing a love letter to Roxane and is not at all interested in the conversation around him. He does not sign the letter,
because he plans to give it to Roxane himself.

The poets flatter Ragueneau by asking for his latest poetic
effort—a recipe in rhyme.

Cyrano constantly asks the time, and the hour finally arrives
for his meeting with Roxane. The poets are rushed to another
room so that Cyrano can see her alone.

Commentary

These scenes contain several elements of interest: Lise's
sarcasm about the poets, the comedy of Ragueneau's recipe in
verse, and the fact that the poets are buzzing with talk of
Cyrano's various exploits of the previous evening. Cyrano himself, however, is the most interesting element. He is concerned
only with the letter he is writing to Roxane—the one he has
carried in his heart for years—and in the fact that he will soon see
her and at last declare his love for her. He cares about nothing
else. The brave hero is as excited as a schoolboy.

In the first act, our attention has been directed to Cyrano's
bravado and his true courage, but now we are seeing a completely different facet of his personality. He is so nervous about
his forthcoming confrontation with Roxane that he simply
ignores the opportunity to submit himself to the adulation of
the poets.

ACT II – SCENES 5-6

Summary

Cyrano fills the "poetry-sacks" with pastry for Roxane's duenna, who goes into the street to eat, then he and Roxane, who are cousins, reminisce about their childhood games. She tenderly bandages his injured hand with her handkerchief while she tells him shyly that she is in love with someone in his regiment. Cyrano's hopes rise. Then she adds that this man is young, fearless—and handsome.

Cyrano asks if she has spoken with him. "Only with our eyes," she replies. But Cyrano asks, "What if he is a savage— uncultured, unlettered?" Roxane declares that no one with such beautiful hair could fail to be eloquent.

She has come to Cyrano because Christian, her love, has joined Cyrano's regiment. She knows that it is the custom to provoke an outsider to a duel, since the regiment is composed entirely of men from Gascony. She wants Cyrano to protect Christian, and he promises to do so.

Commentary

In the beginning of this scene, Rostand very skillfully builds up the hopes of Cyrano and the audience. Roxane commences quite naturally with childhood memories and, until she pronounces the word, "handsome," there is really no reason to believe that she is not going to confess her love for Cyrano. This, of course, makes Cyrano's disappointment more acute. Promising to protect Christian is a bitter pill for him to swallow. This promise, however, is preparation for what is to follow.

Cyrano never seems to feel that Roxane should be any different than she is—only that *his* nose is at fault. Since he and Roxane have known each other so long, Cyrano may see qualities in his lady love which are not readily apparent to others. It does not seem possible that one of his intelligence and sensitivity should be in love with a woman totally committed to the shallowness and pretentiousness of the *précieuse* philosophy.

ACT II – SCENES 7-8

Summary

The Gascony Guards enter, proud of Cyrano. There is also a poet who wants to immortalize the exploit, and a newspaper editor who wants to interview Cyrano. The little pastry shop is suddenly full and noisy. Cyrano, of course, cares nothing for poets and reporters. When Le Bret asks about his interview with Roxane, Cyrano simply tells him to be quiet. De Guiche, Richelieu's powerful nephew who wants Roxane for his mistress, offers the services of himself and his uncle. Cyrano refuses, though he has written a play which he would like to see produced. As De Guiche leaves, he asks Cyrano if he knows of Don Quixote. Cyrano acknowledges that he recognizes himself. De Guiche tells him that the arm of the windmill could cause his downfall, but Cyrano refuses to be intimidated.

Le Bret chides Cyrano for throwing away such a brilliant opportunity. Cyrano describes the life of a protégé in disparaging terms. He wants to be free, to sing, to dream. He still refuses to discuss Roxane.

Commentary

Scene 7 gets the cadets on stage and shows their admiration of Cyrano. Cyrano, in refusing De Guiche's offer so cavalierly, is in a sense throwing away another bag of gold. This, however, is more than an extravagant gesture; it is also a dangerous one since De Guiche is a powerful man who does not like to be crossed.

Cyrano's impassioned defense to Le Bret of intellectual freedom is a beautiful speech, altogether in character, and as impractical as Ragueneau's attitude toward the poets. One might say, however, that it is just such impractical attitudes as this one in the play which have caused *Cyrano* to be continuously popular through the years. It is these ideas which have caused men to rebel, even up to our present day.

ACT II – SCENES 9-10

Summary

Christian enters and talks with the Guards, and the other cadets tell him that he must under no circumstances mention or imply the word "nose" in Cyrano's presence. The cadets ask Cyrano to tell them about the fights of the evening before. Averse as he was to telling reporters or poets about his exploits, he enjoys telling his friends. While Cyrano is talking, Christian continually interrupts him by interjecting the word "nose" into the story. Cyrano becomes more and more furious but, knowing that Christian is the man whom he has promised to protect, he cannot give vent to his anger. At last, he can stand it no longer. He sends everyone out and explains that he is Roxane's cousin. Christian confesses that he is afraid that he will lose Roxane because he cannot speak and write well – he is only a simple soldier. Roxane is so refined that she will surely not love him. Cyrano says that together, with Christian's looks and Cyrano's genius, they make one perfect hero. Roxane will suffer no disappointment. He gives Christian the unsigned letter he had written, telling him to send it as his own – he has but to sign it.

Commentary

Rostand establishes once and for all that Christian is no coward by having him try very hard to impress the cadets. He has been warned about the subject of Cyrano's nose, so he does his best to provoke the famous swordsman to a duel. There is humor in Cyrano's dilemma.

Cyrano's guess proves to be true. Christian confesses, in effect, that his brain-power is not the equal of his physical beauty. Cyrano generously gives the letter to him, beginning the deceit which will last for nearly fifteen years. Rostand brings this ridiculous situation about so carefully that it seems almost logical. He has prepared us for everything. The unsigned letter is at hand.

Is Cyrano being generous? Does he merely want Roxane to have what she wants? Does he really think that she could be happy as the wife of the brave but simple soldier? On the other hand, perhaps he really meant his defense of freedom speech in Scene 8. Perhaps he realizes subconsciously that what he needs is not a wife, but an unrequited love. His motive is one we will never know. Rostand nowhere implies that Cyrano ever adopts any of the false values of the *précieuse* and we must assume that his conscious motive is pure and noble. Perhaps he feels that Christian is worthy of Roxane. Or maybe his disappointment is so acute that for the moment he feels defeated. While there are many possible explanations, the play is a better one for leaving a few questions unanswered.

ACT II – SCENE 11

Summary

The cadets re-enter, and much to their surprise find Christian still alive. The musketeer, deciding that one can now make fun of Cyrano's nose with impunity, tries his hand at the game. Cyrano knocks him down.

Commentary

Throughout this act, Cyrano's emotions have run the gamut from elation to depression, and the emotions of the audience have followed in close pursuit. In addition to setting up the situation of the play, Rostand has gotten his audience involved with Cyrano, the man. The playwright has made us hope that his main character's dream of love will come true, only to have those hopes dashed to earth. And he has added the irony that Cyrano must not only protect the man who is taking his love from him, but must also help him to win the girl through deception. And so, by the end of the act we are in need of the comic relief furnished by this scene and the two which precede it.

In the previous two scenes, Cyrano is caught in the dilemma of having to accept the insults of the man he has sworn to protect. This internal struggle which goes on as he tries to recount his exploits over Christian's interruptions is a source of high humor for the audience. And the act ends on an even more humorous note when the musketeer misinterprets the situation. Since Cyrano does not kill the musketeer, but simply knocks him down for his insult, it is obvious that Rostand's intention was to end the act on the much-needed light note.

ACT III – SCENE 1

Summary

Act III, entitled "Roxane's Kiss," takes place in the street under Roxane's balcony. It opens with Ragueneau telling Roxane's duenna that his wife, Lise, ran off with the musketeer. He tried to hang himself, but Cyrano saved him and brought him to Roxane to be a steward in her household.

Cyrano enters, followed by musicians whom he keeps correcting. He explains that he won them for a day with a bet over a fine point of grammar. Roxane tells Cyrano that Christian is a genius: he will be quiet and distracted for a moment, then say the most beautiful things. Cyrano teases her about some of Christian's speeches.

Commentary

The fact that Cyrano saved Ragueneau's life is characteristic of Cyrano. Lise's defection is a logical result of the relationship shown in Act II between her and Ragueneau (even the musketeer was introduced – see Act II, Scenes 3 and 4, as well as Scene 11). This enables Rostand to keep Ragueneau in the play and gives the baker good reason to be a loyal friend to Cyrano.

Note that Cyrano, the Renaissance man, has won the musicians in a dispute over a point of grammar—("I was right, of course.")—and is now correcting the musicians. He knows grammar and music, writes poetry, and is a superb swordsman. New facets of his personality, and new abilities, are continually being shown to us.

Cyrano enjoys teasing Roxane about Christian's (really his own) beautiful speeches, and hearing her hotly defend each word. Though writing for someone else, he still has an author's pride in his creation. It seems that this is a game to him, a way to exercise his fertile brain and facile wit, and that he gives little or no thought to the consequences. He may, of course, be convinced that since they do love each other, as each has confessed to him, playing Cupid is the noblest, most generous and extravagant gesture he can make. He is, after all, a modest man in some ways.

ACT III — SCENES 2-3

Summary

De Guiche enters and tells Roxane that he has come to say goodbye. He has been placed in command of Cyrano's regiment. She tells him that if he really wants to hurt Cyrano, he should leave him and the other cadets behind, while the rest of the regiment goes on to glorious victory. De Guiche sees in this a sign that Roxane loves him (De Guiche) and suggests a rendezvous at a monastery. She makes De Guiche believe she is consenting; she has managed to keep Christian out of the war.

Cyrano comes out of the house and asks Roxane on what subject she will ask Christian to speak tonight. She replies that tonight he must improvise on the subject of love.

Commentary

For the sake of Christian, Roxane plays the coquette with De Guiche, and very skillfully. We are shown how powerful

De Guiche is, and how much vengeance he would take for a slight, for Cyrano has only refused De Guiche's offer to be his patron. He does not hesitate to use this threat of revenge against Cyrano (and Christian, too, though he does not know about Christian's relationship with Roxane) to influence Roxane.

When Roxane tells Cyrano that Christian's subject for the evening will be to improvise on love, he sees an opportunity to work in all the beautiful phrases he has been saving up for just such an occasion.

ACT III – SCENE 4

Summary

Christian refuses to memorize speeches tonight. He is tired of pretense: he knows enough, he says, to take a woman in his arms. He knows that Roxane loves him, and refuses to continue this uncomfortable and demeaning role.

Commentary

We have already seen, in Act II, that Christian is no coward, though he lacks the facility with words that Roxane demands of a lover. Here we see that he has moral courage as well. Cyrano is not the only noble character in this play. If Christian had never protested the deception which he and Cyrano are perpetrating upon Roxane, we would think much less of him, and it is necessary that he be a noble idealist, though of course much less so than Cyrano. Without this protest, he would seem a rather despicable character. This scene makes his plight a tragic one, for he feels that he can accomplish his purpose by means of his own capabilities when, in fact, he cannot. Thus, the scene also raises the situation above the comic or the opportunistic aspect it might otherwise have had.

Summary

Christian tells Roxane, "I love you." "That," she replies, "is the theme. Embroider."

Of course, poor Christian can think of nothing else to say. Roxane goes inside in disgust. Christian asks Cyrano to help him. Cyrano hides under Roxane's balcony and whispers to Christian, who repeats the words aloud to Roxane. At last, Cyrano is carried away and speaks aloud eloquently himself, but Roxane still believes it is Christian who is doing the speaking.

Commentary

Second only to the famous one in *Romeo and Juliet*, this is probably the most famous balcony scene in literature. In fact, one wonders if Rostand might not have had in mind a parody of Shakespeare's well-known scene as he began writing this. At any rate, it contains many elements of interest. There is some amusement in Cyrano's whispering to Christian. There is poignancy in poor Cyrano's winning Roxane's love, not for himself, but for Christian. There is irony in the fact that he talks to her of honesty, of doing away with artificiality. We wonder if Cyrano could have won her love if he had written eloquent letters in his own name and spoken for himself – and perhaps brought her to a more mature sense of values.

Summary

A monk comes by, looking for Roxane's house, and Cyrano misdirects him. Christian wants Roxane's kiss, climbs the balcony, and kisses her. The monk returns. He is delivering a letter from De Guiche to Roxane. De Guiche has sent his regiment on but has stayed behind himself. The letter instructs her that he is coming to see her. She tells the monk that De Guiche's letter orders that she and Christian be married immediately. She pretends that this is against her will and the monk is completely convinced. The monk, Christian, and Roxane go inside for the ceremony, while Cyrano waits outside to divert De Guiche.

Commentary

It might be worthwhile at this point to remind the reader briefly about the traditional practices of scene division. This section, as well as the preceding section, describes portions of the play which are very closely knit. Then, why divide each of the sections into three scenes? As mentioned earlier, it is traditional in drama to begin and end scenes with the entrance and exit of a reasonably important character, and such is the case here. Though there are no real interruptions in these sections, there are certain entrances and exits which would be marked as scene divisions in some texts. If the student is using a text without scene divisions, he can easily locate the portion of an act dealt with in the summaries by simply comparing the actions described with his text.

Roxane is very quick-witted in these scenes. She seems a little hasty in her wish to marry a man she sent away a short time earlier because he could not embroider upon the theme of love. The fact that De Guiche is pressing her may have something to do with her decision. At any rate, Rostand has managed to make the whole thing quite believable. We already know of De Guiche's desire for Roxane and of his power. This seems a simple and logical way out of all the difficulties Roxane and Christian would have if they married in a more conventional manner. It is necessary that they be married to explain Roxane's behavior in Acts IV and V.

ACT III – SCENES 11-12

Summary

Cyrano has climbed to the top of the wall, and when De Guiche enters, Cyrano swings from a branch and drops down in front of him. He tells De Guiche that he came from the moon and asks where he is. In spite of himself, De Guiche is amused. When Cyrano says that he has invented six ways to travel to the moon, De Guiche is curious enough to listen to what they are. Then, after telling him the six ways, Cyrano says, in his own voice, that the quarter of an hour is up, and the marriage completed. He believes there is nothing De Guiche can do about the marriage. De Guiche, however, gains revenge by sending the cadets to the front immediately.

Commentary

The brilliant bit of nonsense in Scene 11 is an opportunity for Cyrano to show off yet another of his interests — science. But, before the reader begins to feel that Rostand is exaggerating Cyrano's varied interests, he should remember that among the many talents of the historical Cyrano was that of writing science-fiction.

Poor Cyrano not only wins the lady for Christian, but must stall De Guich while the couple is being married. He promises that "Christian" will write to her often. Since Rostand has De Guiche on the scene, has prepared us for his anger, and has already introduced the war, he encounters no difficulty in separating the young couple immediately, before they have a moment alone together. Thus, Roxane never has an opportunity to know her husband without Cyrano's words to make him seem more facile of tongue.

ACT IV — SCENE 1

Summary

This act takes place in the camp of the Gascony Guards at the siege of Arras. The soldiers are all suffering from hunger, for while the French are besieging Arras, the Spanish have encircled them and no supplies can be brought to them through the lines. Cyrano, at great risk to his life, has found a way to get across the lines and he does so in order to send "Christian's" letters to

Roxane. The reason that he does not bring food on any of these trips is that it would be too bulky for him to carry and still be able to evade the Spaniards. Cyrano says that he thinks there must be a change soon, that the company will either eat or die: the Spanish are planning something.

Commentary

Act III has been a light, often humorous, act. Now, however, the mood undergoes a very definite change. This scene sets that mood by showing us the state of the war and indicating that the situation at Arras is very serious. The atmosphere of gloom deepens throughout the act, with only one touch of lightness.

How typical that Cyrano's dangerous journeys through the enemy lines are made for spiritual and not physical reasons! Keeping the promise of frequent letters, which he made for Christian in Act III, Scene 12, does not seem sufficient justification, especially since he cannot bring food back with him. (And we can be sure that, with his friends approaching starvation on the other side of the lines, he would not avail himself of the opportunity to eat.) Perhaps he feels that once the war is over he will never have another chance to tell Roxane of his love, and he wants to do that more than anything else, even if he must sign Christian's name to his own letters.

ACT IV – SCENES 2-3

Summary

The cadets complain of hunger. Cyrano tries to entertain them with his wit, but when even he cannot cheer them up, he asks an old piper to play some familiar Provencal songs for them and speaks to them of home. When Carbon protests that Cyrano is making them cry, Cyrano responds that it is nobler to cry from homesickness than it is to cry from hunger, because homesickness is moral and hunger is physical.

Commentary

These scenes provide Rostand the opportunity to work in some of the lovely folk songs from southern France, and they also point up Cyrano's leadership among the cadets. It is he who is resourceful enough to cheer them. The observation that it is nobler to cry from homesickness than hunger is an interesting bit of philosophy. It is also good psychology as well, since a desire to live to return home is more likely to sustain them than self-pity.

ACT IV – SCENE 4

Summary

De Guiche enters. He says that he knows the cadets do not like him. The cadets continue smoking and playing cards as if they were not paying any attention to De Guiche. They do not want him to know how miserable they are. He tells them of his action in the war the day before. Cyrano, however, knows every detail. He knows that when De Guiche's life was in danger, he flung off his officer's scarf so he would not be recognized. Cyrano picked up the scarf, and now exposes De Guiche's cowardice by producing it. De Guiche mounts the parapet and waves the scarf, explaining that, with the aid of a spy, he has arranged for the Spanish to attack at the position from which he signals. At the same time, the French armies will mount their own attack against the weakest position of the Spaniards. De Guiche admits that, by ordering the attack on the Gascony Guards, he serves both the king and his own rancour.

Christian says that he would like to put his love for Roxane into one last letter. Cyrano hands him a letter he has ready. Christian notices that a tear has splashed on the letter, and Cyrano explains that the letter was so beautiful that he himself was carried away with emotion.

The sentinel announces that a carriage approaches and the cadets line up, preparing a salute.

Commentary

De Guiche is certainly not a pleasant character, but he is at least honest. The attack which he has arranged for at this position will probably turn into a massacre of the Gascons. The cadets show their dislike for him quite openly, and Cyrano has shown that his own courage exceeds that of De Guiche by retrieving De Guiche's scarf from the most dangerous part of the battlefield. It is another touch of irony in the play that Cyrano's displaying of the scarf is the action which makes De Guiche come to a definite conclusion about inviting the attack.

Rostand has established that Cyrano manages to get through the lines to send letters, but at very great risk on his life. Surely, if it were at all possible to get food in, he would do so. Thus, when a coachman arrives, declaring that he is in the service of the king of France, it is certainly cause for amazement.

This business is ridiculous, but absolutely essential for the development of the plot. Rostand does it about as well as it could be done, inasmuch as he thoroughly prepares the audience for everything explainable and makes a thorough surprise of what is not logical.

ACT IV – SCENES 5-7

Summary

When the carriage comes to a halt, everyone is astonished to see Roxane alight from it. She has charmed her way through the Spanish lines and gaily explains that this siege has gone on too long. De Guiche and Cyrano try to convince her to leave, but she refuses.

The cadets are introduced to Roxane. She gives them her dainty handkerchief to use as a banner. She has managed to bring a carriage-load of gourmet food with her and, with Ragueneau's help, she dispenses it to the cadets. They eat hungrily, but hide the food when De Guiche returns.

De Guiche announces that he has brought a cannon for the cadets. He says that if Roxane will not leave the encampment and return to safety he will stay, too. Cyrano cautions Christian to remember about all the letters written to Roxane in Christian's behalf.

Commentary

Though absolutely necessary to the plot, this is one of the weakest points of the play. The only thing more ridiculous than Roxane's arrival on the scene is her explanation of how she managed the feat. The student of drama—particularly the student of playwriting—could learn a great deal about dramatic structure by attempting to re-write Act IV in summary form. The problem would be to accomplish the same thing as Rostand in terms of plot, but to avoid the more far-fetched elements such as those contained in these scenes.

At this point in the play, it would be well to re-assess Roxane's behavior. It is possible that one might mistakenly believe her to be shallow, frivolous, and self-centered. But this is not true. Although she is all these things on the surface, she is also extremely intelligent and sensitive. It is true that she came to see Christian, but apparently an equally important reason was to bring the food for the company of cadets. She flirted her way through the Spanish lines and concealed the food very cleverly. Also, she was not shallow when she managed to keep Christian's regiment at home for a time and deceive De Guiche. It must be remembered that she truly does appreciate Cyrano's poetry, and because of the letters he has written, true love has bloomed within her for the first time. We are seeing a new dimension of Roxane, quite different from the *précieuse* we were introduced to.

De Guiche and Cyrano have one thing in common—they both love the same woman; only for her do they join forces. In Scene 7, Rostand begins to change the audience's mind about De Guiche and show us that he is not really all bad. He is at least sincere in his concern for Roxane. If she insists upon staying for what he is sure will be her death, he, too, will commit suicide by remaining with her. Thus does Rostand begin to imply that, at least at this point in his life, De Guiche's heart is filled more with love for Roxane than with lust. Rostand then brings the audience's attention back from the war to the letters.

ACT IV – SCENE 8

Summary

Roxane tells Christian that she has made the dangerous journey to come to him because of the letters which he has written to her. She says that she began to know his mind and soul the night when he spoke to her under her balcony. And the letters were so powerful and so sincere, that she now wants to ask his pardon for loving him only for his physical beauty. She feels now that that was an insult, for his mind and his spirit are so much more beautiful. In reading his letters she has learned to love him for better reasons, more deeply than before. His physical appearance now means nothing to her.

Commentary

This is the reason that Roxane has to make an appearance on the battlefield. Without this scene the play would be meaningless. Christian *must* learn that it is Cyrano whom Roxane actually loves. We also now discover that Roxane's character has begun to undergo a very definite change. She is capable of more maturity than Cyrano gave her credit for. His persuasive powers are greater than he knew, for he did not dare trust his ability to woo her for himself. And now she is married to Christian.

ACT IV – SCENE 9

Summary

Christian tells Cyrano that Roxane loves not him, but Cyrano, for she loves the author of the letters and the man who spoke to her under her balcony. Since she is unaware of this, Christian wants Roxane to be told the truth so that she may choose between them. He calls Roxane and exits, leaving Cyrano to explain the fraudulent situation. Cyrano begins to unravel the story, but just when his hopes are aroused, Christian's body is carried on stage; he has been killed by the first bullet fired in the battle. This bullet also destroys Cyrano's hopes; he can never tell Roxane the truth now, especially after she discovers a letter on Christian's body. It is addressed to her, covered with Christian's blood and, although Roxane does not know it, Cyrano's tears.

Commentary

Christian has all the virtues except eloquence. He behaves nobly. One wonders why he never before guessed that Cyrano loves Roxane. Perhaps he was blinded by his own love for her, or perhaps we should credit Cyrano's glib tongue and forceful personality with the successful deception.

Christian has to die, of course. Cyrano's despair over an unrequited love can hold an audience's attention for only a limited amount of time. And what sort of climax can the play have if the war ends with Cyrano, Christian, and Roxane all still alive? What sort of relationship would develop then between these three? Rostand very cleverly makes De Guiche, Roxane, and Christian show the noblest and most mature sides of their characters in this act, and at this moment we are especially sympathetic to Christian.

ACT V – SCENE 1

Summary

The final act takes place in the courtyard of a convent. The sisters are awaiting Cyrano's arrival. We learn that he is poor, often hungry, and that he visits Roxane, who took refuge here after Christian's death, every Saturday.

Commentary

This subdued scene, which takes place more than fourteen years after the incidents which closed Act IV, gives the audience an opportunity to become accustomed to the setting and to learn the situation. As noted elsewhere, this is a characteristic quality of the scenes which open the various acts of the play.

The nuns explain the situation as it has existed for nearly fifteen years. They also give a clear and very endearing picture of Cyrano's visits to Roxane, who is still grieving for Christian. The nuns love Cyrano and enjoy telling him their little pecadillos and being teased by him. They know that, while he may not be a good Catholic (could Cyrano ever conform to anything except his own notions of chivalry?), he is the best and noblest of men. He takes it upon himself to bring a smile to Roxane's face. Cyrano is a ray of sunshine in her life and in the lives of the nuns. He hides his poverty with his pride, his wit, and his charm.

ACT V – SCENES 2-3

Summary

Roxane is talking to De Guiche, who is now the Duc de Grammont. Roxane has lived in the convent in mourning for all these years, always carrying "Christian's last letter" next to her heart. Le Bret enters. They worry about Cyrano, who always seems to be cold, hungry, and alone, and whose writings have made him new enemies.

De Guiche admits that, in spite of all he has and all that Cyrano lacks, Cyrano in his poverty is the better and happier man. In other words, things of the spirit are of more value and are nobler than material things. De Guiche then calls Le Bret aside and tells him that Cyrano is in danger of his life.

As Roxane walks with the duke, Ragueneau enters hurriedly. He tells Le Bret that Cyrano has had an "accident" — someone has dropped a heavy log of wood on his head as he passed beneath a window. Ragueneau has carried Cyrano to his room. The two men hurry to him.

Commentary

We learn that, while De Guiche has mellowed, Cyrano is much the same. Independent, outspoken, fearless, witty, he has antagonized many important men with his satires. This is reminiscent of Lignière, in Act I. Ragueneau is still the "utility" character, a faithful friend of Cyrano.

Notice that De Guiche praises Cyrano before he hears of the accident. The friends (and the former enemy) have been faithful to each other. While this is some fourteen years later, it is worth remembering that Roxane must have been quite young at the beginning of the play and could hardly be more than about thirty-five years old now. In those times, when the aging process was faster and the life expectancy much shorter, she would be, at the very least, approaching middle age. Nonetheless, De Guiche and Cyrano still look upon Roxane as a beautiful and desirable woman. There is irony in the fact that the letter which Roxane carries next to her heart is the one which Cyrano gave to Christian in Act IV, and which was found on Christian's body.

ACT V – SCENE 4

Summary

Roxane is alone. Two nuns bring Cyrano's favorite chair and place it under the tree in the courtyard. The leaves are falling and Cyrano is late. This is so unusual that Roxane is worried about him. Then a sister announces his arrival.

Commentary

As Cyrano was a faithful writer, he is now a faithful visitor. His weekly visits to Roxane considerably brighten her self-imposed retirement. The nuns also obviously look forward to seeing Cyrano. He is the sort of man who could be very popular and tactful, and the nuns' attitudes toward him are altogether in character. One may also contrast Cyrano's constancy with the apparent neglect which De Guiche has shown Roxane.

Rostand uses some rather obvious symbolism here. The leaves are falling from the tree, indicating the approach of winter when everything dies, at least for a while. Cyrano, too, is fast approaching his end.

ACT V – SCENE 5

Summary

Roxane works on her tapestry, and does not notice that Cyrano is pale. Sister Marthe, whom he teases as usual, thinks that his pallor is caused by hunger. Cyrano begins his witty, amusing account of the week's gossip, then nearly faints for a moment. He asks to see Roxane's last letter from Christian. Roxane gives it to him, and he reads it aloud. Roxane recognizes the voice which she heard under her balcony so long ago. She realizes that it is dark, that Cyrano could not be reading the letter but must be quoting from memory. She understands the deception at last, and knows that it is Cyrano whom she loved.

Commentary

Rostand has carefully prepared the audience for the significance of the letter. The scene is poignant, thoroughly romantic, and thoroughly in character for Cyrano. He could not have told her earlier that the husband she mourned was not the author of the letters or of the romantic speeches. He has lived his life as he wished, content with seeing her once each Saturday, and free to write what he wanted. Roxane cannot be told the truth, she must divine it. Through all the years she has been faithful to Christian (really to Cyrano), and this must have pleased Cyrano.

ACT V – SCENE 6

Summary

Le Bret and Ragueneau enter. Cyrano says that he has barely missed everything in life – including a noble death. Ragueneau says that Molière has stolen a scene from one of Cyrano's plays and that it has been very well received. Cyrano says that that is the way his life has been — Molière has the genius, Christian had the beauty. Cyrano compares himself and Roxane to the fable of "Beauty and the Beast," then thanks Roxane for her friendship. He dies praising his unsullied white plume — his integrity.

Commentary

Cyrano did not lack any quality which would have given him a more successful life, but he lacked the right combination of qualities. He was notably self-confident with a sword or pen in his hand, but was so ashamed of his ugliness that he did not try to win Roxane. He did not lack genius, since we see that the stolen act of his play is very popular, but he refused to try to get along with the "right" people.

In fact, Cyrano prized his independence, his unique and unfettered style, above any worldly success. Just as it is nobler to weep for a spiritual reason than a physical one, so it was nobler to live for his moral and spiritual principles than for physical or worldly success. As he remarked in Act I, his elegances are spiritual, or moral, ones. De Guiche acknowledged this earlier in this act, when he admitted that with all his wealth and power, he was not as good nor as happy a man as Cyrano.

Rostand has managed this last act without any of the melodrama of Act IV. Cyrano's death is gentle, dignified, in character, logical, prepared for, and truly romantic. He does not really regret his life, and he dies with the satisfaction that the one recognition he wanted most — Roxane's — is his.

CHARACTER ANALYSES

CYRANO DE BERGERAC

Cyrano is, first and last, an idealist. He is not, however, a blind idealist. He does not expect tangible rewards for his idealistic behavior. When he throws his money to the players (Act I) he knows full well that he will be hungry, but the *beau geste* means more to him than material things—even food and drink. His own comfort never is a motive for action with Cyrano.

This idealist with his eyes open can also be a very intelligent man. He can disdain the very precise "establishment" rules because he does have such intelligence and competence. He can beat these people at their own game, though he does not often choose to play their game. For instance, Cyrano won the musicians for an evening because he had won a bet about grammar. At the time in which the play was set, grammar was a complicated and extremely technical subject. Cyrano knows all the rules for polite behavior and speech, but these do not matter to him as much as matters of the spirit.

Cyrano is as careless of personal danger as he is of personal comfort. He is truly a brave warrior. He remains calm and cheerful in the most trying of circumstances. He is such a good swordsman that he can fight off a hundred men. In battle he is brave, but he is also brave in the much more difficult situation presented by the siege. He never loses his courage, his good humor, his ability to cheer the other men. It is important to note that he is cool and collected when other brave soldiers become despondent. He is true to Roxane and Christian unto death. He never reveals that he wrote the letters which Roxane has accepted as coming from Christian. He always visits Roxane with delightful bits of gossip.

Cyrano never was successful in a worldly way. His play was never produced, though some of it was used by another. Even as a mature man he is often hungry, though he well knows that his talents could make him rich and famous if he chose to use them for that purpose. He is extremely versatile, and knows a great deal about many subjects. He simply does not ever choose to be rich or famous—he prefers to be right in his own eyes. He is inner-directed, in that the opinions and standards of the world really do not matter to him. He rebels by not playing the game;

he never adopts another's standards for his behavior; he is true
to himself and his ideals.

This lack of change in the character could be a basis for
criticism. Rostand has not created a growing, evolving personality. He did not try to do so. Cyrano was, at the beginning of the
play, the epitome of the romantic idealist, and he remains so to
the end. He is a perfect example of the type. The flaws of the
character grow directly and logically from the perfection of the
type. Cyrano is uncompromising, idealistic, faithful, brave, consistent, disdainful of acclaim and wealth, intelligent to the point
of brilliance, creative, imaginative, witty, knowledgeable. Any
change in the character would be a compromise of some sort.
This is why Cyrano remains the perfect example of the romantic
idealist—anything added to or subtracted from the character
would make him less so.

ROXANE

The character of Roxane is difficult to accept at first. She is
a romantic idealist, but seemingly not of the depth of character
or intelligence of Cyrano. She is, rather, a *précieuse*. Her attention is on the surface of things, just as Cyrano's is on the roots.
She seems as shallow as he is deep.

The character of Cyrano and that of Roxane offer many
parallels. She, too, loves the *beau geste.* She goes to the battlefield with food, and to see her husband. She, too, is faithful until
death. She, too, turns her back on the world, to retire to the convent to mourn her lost husband.

Cyrano and Roxane have many of the same ideals, though
Roxane seems to see only the surface. She is attracted to Christian in the first place by his physical qualities, but she then
attributes to him all the qualities that Cyrano has in such
abundance, and she mourns Christian for these very qualities.
When Cyrano dies and she learns the truth, she says that she has
lost her love twice. One can only assume that she was blind to

Cyrano's true character because of her memory of Christian as she thought he was; she still sees Cyrano as the friend and companion of her childhood. Nevertheless her years of mourning are for the nobility of soul that she believed she had lost when Christian died, and not for the surface values of the *précieuse* she once was.

Both Roxane and Cyrano, then, are consistent, faithful, uncompromising characters, and both are dedicated to their ideals rather than worldly rewards. Both live in a dream world by choice.

DE GUICHE

In contrast to the two idealists, Roxane and Cyrano, we have De Guiche. He is a worldly, sophisticated cynic. He is motivated by personal desires rather than ideals. His own comfort means more to him than any noble idea. He takes revenge on Cyrano and Christian for having stolen Roxane from him by sending the regiment to almost certain death.

De Guiche would use anything at hand—power, influence, position, wealth—to get what he wants. He wanted Roxane because she was so beautiful; he would certainly not have married her with the idea of remaining forever faithful and devoted to her, even if he had not already had a wife. What he wanted was a rich and beautiful mistress.

De Guiche is the only character in the play who changes or develops, with the possible exception of Christian. In the last act De Guiche has mellowed considerably, to the extent that he has developed respect for both Roxane and Cyrano. He has learned to respect their spiritual values, though he does not completely share them, and he has learned that worldly rewards are not everything.

If Rostand had shown De Guiche undergoing a greater change than this, we would be very suspicious; if he had shown him not changed at all, we would be a little disappointed.

De Guiche is not able to adopt these ideals for himself, but he no longer is contemptuous of them in others.

De Guiche admits that Cyrano is probably a happier man than he is, though to all appearances De Guiche has everything a man could want. He is concerned about Cyrano and the threats to Cyrano's life: this is the same man who once sent Cyrano's entire regiment to what appeared to be certain death.

De Guiche has always had qualities of intelligence, wit and courage, but he lacked the nobility of character and dedication to ideals that Cyrano had. He is honest enough to admit that Cyrano may well have been right to choose the ideal, while realizing that the life of dedication to the ideal is not for him to embrace, himself.

In De Guiche, Rostand has treated a living, evolving human rather than a type. He is the villain of the piece, because he does try to win Roxane by devious means and because he does take his revenge. Yet he does not seek to evade the fire of battle himself, and he grows to admit that he was wrong, which takes some nobility of character.

If Rostand had given us a villain who was as purely villainous as Cyrano was a purely heroic hero, what a boring play it would be! The fact that De Guiche does develop and does show a brave spirit under fire contributes to the believability — if not to the realism — of the play. Also, with De Guiche's admission that his own views of life might be wrong, we have further subtle support in believing that Cyrano's views might be right.

CRITICAL COMMENTARY

CYRANO DE BERGERAC AS ROMANTICISM

Since *Cyrano* is so often referred to as a romantic play, a discussion of romantic and romanticism seems to be in order.

Three aspects of the words, "romantic" and "romance" should be considered by the student of *Cyrano:* romance, meaning a medieval, chivalric tale; romantic, as used in English literary criticism; and Romantic, as used in French literary criticism.

Romance, as a medieval tale, was a French literary form. During the middle ages, when the chivalric tradition was paramount in the minds of the upper classes, the chivalric tale developed. These tales concerned the daring deeds of the knights, and the relationship of the knights to their ladies. Many men were away from home during the crusades, and the tradition of the *chevalier servant* developed. This is particularly illustrated in *Roman de la Rose,* in which the *chevalier servant* loved his lady from afar. He wrote poetry, he served her in every way possible, but he never touched her.

The term "romantic" in English criticism most often refers to a treatment of a theme. Romantic treatments are sometimes sentimental, idealistic rather than realistic; Victorian literature is largely romantic, for example. The romantic attitude is quite different from the restrained neoclassical attitude. Reason, order, balance are earmarks of neoclassicism, while a wild, free exuberance is characteristic of romanticism.

French literary critics use the word "Romantic" to indicate the literary period from about 1827 to 1847. Hugo pioneered this period, and broke the rules of classicism forever. (See the section of this study guide entitled "Nineteenth-Century French Drama.") The freedom from the unities was exhilarating to the writers and audiences at the time. Vigny translated Shakespeare during the period, and Shakespeare became a hero of the Romantic movement in France. When critics said that *Cyrano* heralded a revival of the Romantic movement, or Romanticism, they were referring to a revival of this period. In actual fact, *Cyrano* was not a revival or a copy of the Romantic period plays; it is far superior to most of them.

Cyrano is a truly romantic play, harking back to the tales of chivalry; Cyrano is the perfect *chevalier servant*. This is a completely French play, a completely French hero. It is not at all like the romantic plays of Shakespeare, for example, and it follows few, if any, of the traditions of the French Romantic period. It is a spark of genius, growing out of French literary tradition, but not tied to any school.

NINETEENTH-CENTURY FRENCH DRAMA

During the Renaissance, France was slavishly following the classic patterns in its drama, particularly those laid down by Aristotle in his famous definition of tragedy. Plays observed the unities — of place (only one setting), time (twenty-four hours), and action (everything in the play points toward one major conflict). There was no violence on stage; battles and fights were told about, sometimes at great length. The plays concerned an important and heroic character, usually Roman or Greek, although one of the first French classic plays was *Le Cid*, by Corneille, which dealt with Spanish history. The heroes of these plays always had a tragic flaw and were dogged by fate. The plays were in verse. Racine, in the latter part of the seventeenth century, wrote such beautiful and perfect plays after this model that French drama of the eighteenth century was simply repetitious.

Romanticism was heralded in 1827, when Hugo published his "Preface" to *Cromwell*. He felt that although many of these classic plays were beautiful, they no longer expressed current tastes and needs in the theater and that there was a lack of development in the drama because of this slavish imitation. The first Romantic play to be performed in Paris was Hugo's *Hernani*, in 1830. Before the play was produced, he did all that he could to insure its success by reading it to his many friends. On opening night, the theater was full. Hugo had many supporters, and the classicists were also there in full force. Early in the play one of the characters drew his sword on stage, a breach of one of the cardinal rules of classic drama. The result of this defiance of the principles of the classic play was that a riot erupted in the theater, spreading rapidly to the streets of Paris. It was several hours before the gendarmes were able to subdue the warring classicists and romanticists. Later, this incident was to be called "The Battle of *Hernani*"; and it is interesting to note that the people who objected to showing violence on stage (among other things) were the ones who resorted to violence in the stalls of the theater.

The Romantics freed the French drama from the two unities of place and time. Hugo retained the unity of action, feeling that this was an artistic necessity. Local color was important in Romantic plays. The setting was more often Spain, though several plays were written about England and English historical characters, such as Cromwell and Mary, Queen of Scots. Violence was permitted on stage. The play often—indeed, usually—concerned a couple in love. Shakespeare was translated by Vigny during this period and became one of the idols of the French Romantics.

This new freedom in French drama was the beginning of much of the later development of drama in France and the world. Nineteenth-century France was not in a mood for much experimental drama, but the way was paved for the twentieth-century experimenters. The audiences in the nineteenth century in France were bourgeois, and they demanded entertainment of a rather light vein for their evenings at the theater. Consequently, with no intellectual (and wealthy) patrons to foot the bills for the playwrights, the theater became more commercial.

Some later developments in France in the latter part of the nineteenth century were naturalism and symbolism. Naturalism aimed at showing social conditions as they really were—usually as sordid as possible. Symbolists did not think that anything should be shown if it could be hinted at or symbolized. Closet drama, or static drama, was a development of this period. As little action as possible was shown on the stage, and the plays sometimes became very conversational.

Cyrano was written in 1897, and some people said that it marked a revival of Romanticism. It is a historical play. There is much local color in the various sets. There is action on the stage—

the sword fight in Act I is certainly violent, but it is also witty. It would be very difficult to imagine Cyrano without this display of his wit and courage and impromptu poetry. Very little else is shown, however, of violence. The fight with a hundred men is told about, as only the flamboyant Cyrano could tell it.

One of the earmarks of Romanticism is idealism. Certainly Cyrano is an idealistic person, and ideal takes precedence over common sense in his scheme of things.

Rostand never tried to imitate his success with *Cyrano*. Though there were other authors who did try to imitate it, it was not the revival of Romantic drama. It really did not belong to any school of drama which was current when it was written. Actually, if more of the truly Romantic plays had been of the quality of *Cyrano*, the period might have lasted longer.

Rostand does not seem to have been imitating the Romantics, though he used the freedom they had given to the French stage. He found an historical character who inspired him, an actor who could play the part, and the play resulted. While *Cyrano* is truly romantic in almost every sense of the word except that which denotes the French Romantic period, it does not fit into any school. It stands alone.

CYRANO AS A VIRTUOSO PLAY

Many critics have called *Cyrano* a virtuoso play, saying that it was written especially to capitalize upon the sundry talents of the famous French actor, Constant Coquelin. There is, of course, a precedent for thinking that Rostand wrote *Cyrano* with Coquelin in mind; he had previously written *La Samaritaine* specifically for Sarah Bernhardt. In addition, the dedication of the play, which reads, "It was to the soul of CYRANO that I intended to dedicate this poem. But since that soul has been reborn in you, COQUELIN, it is to you that I dedicate it," has also been pointed to as evidence that the play is a virtuoso play. If this dedication were written prior to production or publication of the play in the hope that such flattery would entice Coquelin to play the leading role, then it may well support this view. If, on the other hand, the dedication were written after production of the play, then it is more likely to be simply Rostand's way of thanking Coquelin for a job well done.

Another area which must be examined in any attempt to decide whether or not *Cyrano* was a virtuoso play is concerned with the main character of the play. In most, if not all, virtuoso plays the character is created to fit the abilities of the chosen actor. In *Cyrano*, Rostand did not create a character for Coquelin; indeed, he did not even distort the character of the historical Cyrano. If anything, the real Cyrano is less believable than Rostand's character. The only exaggeration of the character on stage is the size of his nose, and this is necessary in order that the audience may be able to see that the nose really is quite prodigious. One might object that the main character in *La Samaritaine* is a well-known character, Mary Magdalene. However, very little is known about Mary Magdalene, so Rostand was free to create a character to fit the unique capabilities of an actress such as Sarah Bernhardt.

Actually, *Cyrano* was probably the result of the happy conjunction of three things: the existence and availability of a virtuoso actor such as Coquelin, the re-discovery of the historical Cyrano, and the personality and ability of a playwright such as Rostand. As a man of the theater, Rostand was certainly acquainted with Coquelin and with the actor's great histrionic talent. That the playwright was interested in history is attested to by his choice of subjects for most of his other plays, and it is quite obvious that he was familiar with the recently discovered material dealing with his character's historical counterpart. And Rostand's own poetic and romantic nature might easily have created a desire in him to act as the catalytic agent which would bring the actor and the story together on the stage. In all probability, what happened was that Rostand's interests and personality made him want to write a play based upon the person whose exploits as a poet and soldier had just been brought to light. At the same time, luckily, he recognized in Coquelin the perfect actor to play the role.

Perhaps the final determination of whether or not *Cyrano* is a virtuoso play rests on the answer to one question: "Would Rostand have written *Cyrano* if there had been no Coquelin to play the part?" We shall never know the answer to that question. And that is unfortunate, because a playwright does not write a virtuoso play in the same way that he writes any other play. In a virtuoso play, the playwright includes bits of dialogue, action, even entire scenes for the sole reason that his chosen actor can do those particular things exceptionally well. And often these elements contribute nothing to characterization or plot. In reading *Cyrano*, the student might do well to examine it carefully and decide for himself whether or not the internal evidence indicates that Rostand inserted such elements.

THE PLAY AS HISTORY

During his lifetime, Edmond Rostand was in revolt against the important movements of his age—naturalism, symbolism, and Ibsenism—and all of his plays illustrated his idea that an illusion or unattained ideal is superior to real life. Although his plays, particularly *Cyrano de Bergerac*, are undeniably romantic, the Romantic movement in drama had been over for almost fifty years before Rostand wrote, and although anything as popular as *Cyrano* was naturally imitated, Rostand did not spark a general revival of Romantic drama. What he did do was to prove that historical drama was, and still is, a viable theme for the modern stage. Most of the characters and events in *Cyrano*—the conflict with Montfleury, for instance—are historical.

In *Cyrano*, Rostand had an opportunity to blend all his unique talents, interests, and spirit to produce a masterpiece; none of his other works, including the unfinished *La Dernière Nuit de Don Juan* (The Last Night of Don Juan), demonstrated his talents so well. In *Cyrano*, his southern spirit of exuberance, his lyricism, his fascination with unrequited love, all blended so well with the historical Cyrano's exploits that Rostand found in him the perfect subject. This seems almost to be a play of the seventeenth century rather than of the nineteenth century.

The historical Cyrano—Savinien Cyrano de Bergerac—was born near Paris on March 6, 1619. His parents, who were prominent but not noble, came from the town of Bergerac in southern France. And so, when he became old enough to care, Cyrano added "de Bergerac" to his name for the sole purpose of impressing people. He did, indeed, have an enormous nose, and on one occasion actually did describe it as preceding him by a quarter of an hour. In fact, he was such a renowned swordsman that no one else would have dared to make such a remark; many men died for much less. He entered the military profession, fighting and sustaining wounds at Arras. He retired because of his wounds and became a philosopher at the College de Beauvais in Paris.

The historical Cyrano wrote poetry, political pamphlets defending Mazarin, some plays — Molière really did use two scenes written by Cyrano—belles-lettres, and science fiction. His books on voyages to the moon and sun show his interest in science, and many of his ideas are startlingly modern. He was a Renaissance man—dashing, courageous, gallant, and intellectual. Like the Cyrano of the play, the real Cyrano was a man of many talents, high courage, and equally high spirit. He guarded his intellectual freedom and made many enemies, and he was destitute until he found a patron who suited him. Unlike the Cyrano of the play, however, he did find such a protector. And, like the Cyrano of the play, he was fatally wounded by a falling object— a stone, actually, instead of the log of wood mentioned in the play—which may have been dropped by an enemy. Some sources say that the accident, if it was one, happened in the house of his patron. He died on July 28, 1655. There is no record of such a romance as appears in the play, but Rostand has invented one which admirably suits the character and is dramatically necessary.

The real Cyrano, of course, was as much a man of his own time as Rostand was *not* a man of his own time, and perhaps that is what lends a note of authenticity to the drama. However foreign the ideas of Cyrano may be to any generation or country, they seem to strike a responsive chord in many and varied audiences. Cyrano is true to his own ideals and to himself, though he never really loses sight of reality or expects his quixotic behavior to be rewarded in any worldly way. He is true to himself merely for the sake of being true to himself—the ultimate idealism.

THEME AND IRONY IN *CYRANO DE BERGERAC*

Irony may be loosely defined as a distinct difference between what appears to be and what is. Since the main idea of *Cyrano de Bergerac* is the conflict between appearance and truth, it is obvious that theme and irony are closely woven in the play.

Irony is, of course, one of the most intriguing of literary devices. It has been in use at least since the early Greek dramatists, and it has seldom failed to capture the interest of an audience. And that is one of the major reasons that *Cyrano* has remained popular for so many years. Here are just a few of the ironies of the play:

It is ironic that Christian's beauty makes him appear to Roxane to be all that she thinks her heart desires, and it is ironic that Cyrano's ugly appearance hides from Roxane that which she truly desires—beauty of soul.

It is ironic that Roxane confesses to Cyrano, not her love for him, but for Christian. And it is doubly ironic when she begs Cyrano to protect the man she loves.

It is ironic that it is Cyrano's deception which makes possible the blossoming romance between Roxane and Christian. And it is even more ironic that when Christian tries to be honest, he fails hopelessly, and it is Cyrano's words and Cyrano's presence which enable Christian to marry Roxane.

It is ironic that Christian is killed before Roxane can be told what only Christian and Cyrano know—that the man she loves is, in reality, Cyrano. And this irony is compounded by the fact that it is Cyrano's letter which Roxane carries next to her heart, "like a holy reliquary," during her years of mourning.

The crowning irony—certainly, at least, for Cyrano—is that he is dying, not with "steel in my heart and laughter on my lips," but murdered by "a lackey, with a log of wood!" "How Fate loves a jest!" he says.

And, finally, there is irony in Roxane's discovery—too late—that it is Cyrano whom she has loved for so long. "I never loved but one man in my life, and I have lost him twice."

All these ironies and the many, many more that are to be found throughout the play add up to the great irony that appearance is not always truth, and truth is not always clothed in appropriate appearances. The eternal nature of this theme is one explanation for the continued success of the play. Another reason could be the suitability of the ending to the characters.

Imagine Cyrano as a husband. Imagine Roxane as a wife. Their romance, with Cyrano playing the part of the *chevalier servant*, could go on for all their lives; their marriage would have been miserable. But Cyrano did not really want to marry Roxane. She was lovely, and he loved her for exactly the same reasons that Roxane loved Christian. Christian is the only major character in the play who makes any attempt at being honest. He wants very much for Roxane to love him for himself. Neither Roxane nor Cyrano have any desire to face reality, however. They are happy in their make-believe world.

The historical Cyrano once killed a monkey. The monkey's owner, who operated a puppet show in Paris, had dressed the monkey as Cyrano, even down to a false nose. Cyrano heard of it, went to the puppet show and ran the monkey through with his sword. The owner sued, and Cyrano said that since the whole affair had taken place in the make-believe world of the theater, he would pay in kind. The judge accepted his payment—an ode eulogizing the monkey.

Just as the real Cyrano paid in the coin of the make-believe realm of the theater, so the emotions in the play are altogether theatrical—divorced from reality. The audience senses that this flamboyant character could never accept mere reality. He demands more from life. He fulfills the adolescent dream of an unrequited, tragic love. He is realistic enough to know that he could not have his cake and eat it too. He enters the pact with Christian with relish because it allows him to escape humdrum reality and to continue a delightfully boyish relationship. He is allowed to be misunderstood and tragic and to write beautiful love letters without the usual result of marriage and daily problems.

Just as *Huckleberry Finn* owes part of its charm to the return to childhood, so does *Cyrano*. These are children, not adults. Cyrano never faces adulthood, with its responsibilities, where he would not be able to toss his month's income away as a gesture. He would not want to pass up the *beau geste* because of duty. And Roxane enjoys her role as the grieving widow, solaced by visits from the attentive Cyrano.

In summary, *Cyrano* pleases audiences because it satisfies the adolescent dreams which are a part of all adults; it pleases because it is well-constructed and because the characters are consistent and romantic; and it pleases because there is harmony in the theme, characters, plot, and language. The ending is sad and bittersweet, but it is the only possible ending. It satisfies because any other solution to the ironic dilemma would be unromantic; a romantic play must have a romantic ending.

There is no jarring note in this play. The theme, plot, and characters are theatrical but somehow believable, because they are childhood dreams. The most fantastic thing about the play is that it is based on an historical character who was every inch as romantic and unrealistic and boyish and charming as the Cyrano in the play. The play has harmony and unity throughout, and allows us to live for a while in a make-believe world. The ending satisfies because any other solution to the ironic dilemma would be unthinkable.

STAGECRAFT OF ROSTAND

Cyrano de Bergerac could easily have been melodramatic if it were not for the fine balance of the play: the actions and settings are well-matched; the interest of the audience is held by color and excitement until the characters develop; and the costumes suit the setting, the mood, and the action.

Act I, in the theater, is lively and colorful. Act II is also in a public place, and many people appear on stage. The third act, on a darkened street, is very quiet. Cyrano's good deed — holding De Guiche's attention while Roxane and Christian are married — is performed in near darkness. Act IV again has the cadets on stage. The battlefield setting is not gay and cheerful, as are the first two settings, but it is still colorful. Act V is in the quiet courtyard of the convent. If Acts III and V were contiguous, the audience might well grow bored, but the color of Act IV provides contrast if not actual relief.

As interest in the characters develops, the settings have less intrinsic interest, and do not distract. The darkness of Act III is in keeping with Cyrano's dashed hopes and is necessary for the deception as well. And it is worth noting that, in Act V, most of the costumes — specifically, Roxane's mourning dress and the nuns' habits — are black, foreshadowing and complementing the idea of (Cyrano's) death.

REVIEW QUESTIONS AND ESSAY TOPICS

1. Point out ways in which Rostand shows Cyrano's personality, accomplishments, and character.

2. What is Rostand's attitude toward Roxane?

3. Is the appearance of De Guiche necessary in Act V? Why does Rostand include him in this act?

4. Discuss various ways in which Rostand prepares the audience for Cyrano's death and the resolution of his relationship with Roxane.

5. Does Cyrano have a "tragic flaw"? If so, what is it?

6. What purpose does Ragueneau have in the play?

7. In what ways does Rostand express the idea that the spiritual is nobler than the physical in life?

8. Is Cyrano's gesture of throwing away the bag of gold (Act I) characteristic of him? Is it symbolic? Does he do similar things elsewhere in the play? Discuss his character in the light of this gesture.

9. Discuss the ways in which each of these characters changes between his first appearance and his last in the play: De Guiche, Roxane, Ragueneau, Christian, Cyrano.

10. Discuss the dramatic contrasts in Act II.

11. Discuss Rostand's method of building suspense in Act I before the appearance of Cyrano.

12. Is Cyrano more tragic because of his nose? Considering Cyrano's nose, how does Rostand manage to keep Cyrano from being a comic character?

13. What can a reader learn about customs and society in seventeenth-century France by reading this play?

14. How does Rostand relate Cyrano's duel with the vicomte to the plot?

15. Is Cyrano a tragic or pathetic character?

16. Does Rostand make Cyrano a believable character?

17. Does the attitude of the cadets shed any light on Cyrano's personality?

18. Why does Rostand have Roxane marry Christian?

19. Point out Rostand's uses of irony in the play.

20. Why does Cyrano give Christian the letter in Act II and deceive Roxane?

21. Is Christian the antithesis of Cyrano? Is De Guiche? Is Ragueneau?

22. Where and how does Rostand use the dramatic device of comic relief in the play?

23. Do you think Cyrano's conduct toward Roxane was admirable or foolish? Why? Would Rostand agree with you? Why?

24. Is Rostand saying in this play that we should not overestimate the effect of our bad qualities, or put too much importance on them?

BIBLIOGRAPHY

There is a scarcity of book-length material in English dealing with either Edmond Rostand or his plays. The few books which have been written on the subject are no longer in print, but the student may be able to locate one or two such items if he has access to the library of a large university. The following is a list of several essays on Rostand and/or *Cyrano de Bergerac,* which appear in books more readily available.

BEERBOHM, SIR MAX. "Cyrano de Bergerac" and "Cyrano in English." *Around Theatres.* New York: Simon and Schuster, 1954.

BENNETT, ARNOLD. "Rostand." *Things That Have Interested Me*. New York: George H. Doran Co., 1921.

BERMEL, ALBERT (ed.). "Romantics: E. Rostand." *Genius of the French Theatre*. New York: New American Library, 1961.

CHANDLER, F. W. "Romanticists: Claudel, Richepin, Maeterlinck, Rostand." *Modern Continental Playwrights*. New York: Harper and Brothers, 1931.

CHESTERTON, G. K. "Rostand." *Five Types* (also, *Varied Types*). New York: Henry Holt and Company, 1911.

————. "Romance of Rostand." *Uses of Diversity*. London: Methuen and Co., 1920.

CHIARI, JOSEPH. "Edmond Rostand." *Contemporary French Theatre*. New York: The Macmillan Co., 1959.

CLARK, B. H. "Edmond Rostand." *Contemporary French Dramatists*. Cincinnati: Stewart and Kidd Co., 1915.

DUCLAUX, A. M. F. R. "Edmond Rostand." *Twentieth Century French Writers*. Freeport, N.Y.: Books for Libraries Press, 1966. (Reprint of 1919 edition.)

ELIOT, T. S. " 'Rhetoric' and Poetic Drama." (1919) *Selected Essays*. New York: Harcourt, Brace & World, 1950.

GOSSE, SIR EDMUND W. "Rostand's Plays." *More Books on the Table*. London: W. Heinemann Ltd., 1923.

HALE, EDWARD EVERETT, JR. "Rostand." *Dramatists of Today*. (6th ed., rev.) New York: Henry Holt and Company, 1911.

HAMILTON, CLAYTON MEEKER. "Edmond Rostand." *Conversations on Contemporary Drama*. New York: The Macmillan Co., 1924.

————. "Edmond Rostand." *Seen on the Stage*. New York: Henry Holt and Company, 1920. (A different essay from the preceding.)

JAMES, HENRY. "Edmond Rostand." *The Scenic Art*. New Brunswick, N.J.: Rutgers University Press, 1948.

LAMM, MARTIN. "First Symbolists." *Modern Drama*. Tr. by Karin Elliott. New York: Philosophical Library, 1953.

MOSKOWITZ, SAMUEL. "Cyrano de Bergerac: Swordsman of Space." *Explorers of the Infinite*. Cleveland: World Publishing Co., 1963.

NATHAN, G. J. "Rostand." *The Magic Mirror*. New York: A. A. Knopf, 1960.

NICOLL, ALEX. "Neo-Romanticism in the Theatre." *World Drama*. London: Harrap, 1965.

PHELPS, WILLIAM LYON. "Edmond Rostand." *Essays on Modern Dramatists*. New York: The Macmillan Co., 1921.

————. "Postscript: Rostand and France." *Twentieth Century Theatre*. New York: The Macmillan Co., 1918.

ROSENFELD, PAUL. "Edmond Rostand." *Men Seen*. New York: L. MacVeagh, The Dial Press, 1925.

SMITH, HUGH ALLISON. "Edmond Rostand." *Main Currents of Modern French Drama*. New York: Henry Holt and Company, 1925.

WALLEY, HAROLD R. "The Virtuoso Play." *The Book of the Play*. New York: Charles Scribner's Sons, 1950.

A few of the better editions of *Cyrano de Bergerac*, both in French and in English, available in this country in paperback are as follows:

The Leslie R. Méras edition of *Cyrano*, among the best available in French. It was published in 1936 by Harper Brothers, and is now in paperback.

Another French version edited by Oscar Kuhns and Henry Ward Church, published by Holt, Rinehart and Winston in 1960. Available hardbound or in paperback.

There are several translations available. One of the best is by Brian Hooker, in the Bantam paperback edition, and also in the Modern Library edition.

There are also several collections of plays which include *Cyrano:*

ROSTAND, EDMOND, and WILLIAM SHAKESPEARE. *Romeo and Juliet; Cyrano de Bergerac.* New York: Noble's Comparative Classics Series, 1965. (Revised edition). This is placed first in the list rather than in its proper alphabetical order because it may be of special interest, due to its specific aim of comparing the two plays.

GOLDSTONE, RICHARD H. (ed.). *Mentor Masterworks of Modern Drama: Five Plays. (Cyrano de Bergerac, Our Town, Pygmalion, The Crucible, Enemy of the People).* New York: New American Library, 1969.

POPKIN, HENRY. *Four Modern Plays, Series 2. (Rosmersholm, Cyrano de Bergerac, The Importance of Being Earnest, The Lower Depths).* New York: Holt, Rinehart and Winston.

WATSON, E. BRADLEE, and BENFIELD PRESSEY (eds.). *Contemporary Drama: Nine Plays. (The Hairy Ape, Street Scene, Abe Lincoln in Illinois, The Silver Cord, Justice, What Every Woman Knows, The Circle, RUR, Cyrano de Bergerac).* New York: Charles Scribner's Sons, 1941.

NOTES

LES MISERABLES

NOTES

including
- *Life of Victor Hugo*
- *Hugo the Writer*
- *Synopsis*
- *Summaries and Commentaries*
- *Review Questions and Essay Topics*
- *Selected Bibliography*
- Les Miserables *Genealogy*

by
Amy L. Marsland, Ph.D.
Harpur College
State University of New York

and
George Klin
Dept. of Foreign Languages
Atlantic Community College

Cliffs Notes

INCORPORATED

LINCOLN, NEBRASKA   68501

Editor

Gary Carey, M.A.
University of Colorado

Consulting Editor

James L. Roberts, Ph.D.
Department of English
University of Nebraska

ISBN 0-8220-0735-5
© Copyright 1968
by
C. K. Hillegass
All Rights Reserved
Printed in U.S.A.

1991 Printing

Cliffs Notes, Inc.   Lincoln, Nebraska

CONTENTS

Les Misérables Notes

LIFE OF VICTOR HUGO

Victor Hugo was born on February 26, 1802, the son of a Breton mother and a father from northeastern France. His works show the influence of both racial strains: the poetic mysticism which marks Celtic literature from the Arthurian romances to Chateaubriand and the earthy vigor of the peasant of Lorraine.

Although Hugo later claimed he descended from a family of the minor nobility, his father, General Joseph Léopold Hugo, was the son of a carpenter, and like many men of the Napoleonic era, he rose through valor and merit to power and influence in Napoleon's citizen army.

General Hugo was attached to the entourage of Joseph Bonaparte, and his duties took him to Naples and to Spain. Victor visited him in Italy at the age of five and went to school in Madrid in 1811. Traces of these exotic memories will be found in his later poetry and plays. However, Mme. Hugo, a strong-minded and independent personality, did not like the unstable existence of an army wife and in 1812 settled in Paris. Here her three sons, of whom Victor was the youngest, received their first orderly education.

As a result of this estrangement, General Hugo formed a liaison that took on a permanent character, and after Waterloo the Hugos arranged a separation. General Hugo, however, refused to leave his sons with their mother and sent them to a boarding school.

Victor Hugo suffered, but not acutely, from this separation from his mother. He was already, at fifteen, in love with a neighbor's daughter, Adèle Foucher, and was planning a brilliant literary career so that he could marry her. An excellent student in literature and mathematics, in 1817 he received an honorable mention from the Académie Française for a poem entered in a competition, and in 1819 he won first place in another national poetry contest.

When his mother died in 1821, he refused to accept any financial support from his father and endured a year of acute poverty, but in 1822 his first volume of verse, *Odes at Poésies diverses*, won him a pension of 1,000 francs a year from Louis XVIII. On the strength of this he promptly married Adèle, and during the following years four children were born to the Hugos.

Already in 1824 Hugo was a member of the group of Romantic rebels who were attempting to overthrow the domination of classical literature, and in 1830 he became one of the leaders when his historical drama *Hernani* won the theater audience and broke the stranglehold of the classical format on the stage. It also made him rich, and during the next 15 years six plays, four volumes of verse, and the novel *Notre Dame de Paris* (The Hunchback of Notre Dame) established his position as the leading writer of France.

His connection with the stage also had effects on his personal life. In 1831 a rupture developed in the Hugo household when Sainte-Beuve, one of Hugo's closest friends and a well known Romantic critic, fell in love with Adèle Hugo and received some encouragement. The next year Hugo met a young actress, Juliette Drouet, who in 1833 became his mistress and quit the stage. Supported by a modest pension from Hugo, she became for the next fifty years his unpaid secretary and traveling companion.

In 1843 the failure of Hugo's last drama, *Les Burgraves,* and the death of his eldest daughter, drowned on her honeymoon, caused him to abandon poetry temporarily for politics. This sharp change of direction in Hugo's career was paralleled in the lives of a number of other Romantic authors, for instance, Lamartine and George Sand. In the face of a rapidly growing and changing French society, plagued by social problems of all kinds, many writers came to feel that it was not enough simply to write beautiful and moving works of art but that their talents should be more directly applied in helping the poor and oppressed. In effect, this changing mood marks the end of the Romantic era in French literature and the opening of the Realistic-Naturalistic period.

Originally a royalist like his mother, Hugo's reconciliation with his father in 1822 broadened his political views and he was, by this time, a moderate republican. He was made a peer of France in 1845 and made a number of speeches on social questions of the time.

With the revolution of 1848 and the founding of the Second Republic, Hugo was elected deputy to the Constitutional Assembly. Three years later, when Louis Napoleon abolished the republic by a coup d'etat and reestablished the Empire, Hugo risked his life trying vainly to rally the workers of Paris against the new emperor and had to flee to Brussels disguised as a workman.

The next 19 years of Hugo's life were spent in exile, first on the island of Jersey, then on Guernsey. His family and Mlle. Drouet accompanied him into exile. From his island in the English channel Hugo continued to inveigh against the man he considered the perverter of republican liberties, and 1852 and 1853 saw the writing of the satires *Napoléon le Petit* and *Les Châtiments*. He also turned again to poetry and the novel, publishing the philosophical *Les Contemplations* and the remarkable "history of man's conscience," *La Légende des Siecles*. Three novels also occupied him: *Les Misérables*, first begun many years before; *Les Travailleurs de la Mer* (1866), and *L'Homme qui rit* (1869).

Following the Franco-Prussian War and the fall of the Empire in 1870-71, Hugo returned to Paris. It was a triumphal return: he was greeted at the station by an immense crowd and was accompanied through the streets to his hotel amid shouts of "Vive Victor Hugo!" He remained in Paris throughout the siege of the city, and the revenues from the first French publication of *Les Châtiments* bought two cannons to defend the city. In 1871 the death of one of his sons took him for some time to Brussels; he then returned to Guernsey until the death of another son brought him back to Paris in 1873. He was elected to the Senate in 1876, but two years later poor health forced him to return to the tranquility of Guernsey. His later years were saddened not only by the death of his sons but by that of Mme. Hugo in 1868 and of Mlle. Drouet in 1882.

Hugo himself died in 1885 at the age of eighty-three. His last wishes were, "I leave 50,000 francs to the poor. I wish to be taken to the cemetery in the hearse customarily used for the poor. I refuse the prayers of all churches. I believe in God."

Despite the austerity of his wishes, his funeral was the occasion of a national tribute to France's greatest writer. His body lay in state under the Arc de Triomphe guarded by horsemen with flaming torches, while twelve poets watched around his bier. On the day of the funeral, a million spectators followed his cortege, and the Pantheon, a church under Napoleon III, was once again transformed into a national sepulcher to receive his remains. He lies there today, amid France's great men.

Victor Hugo has frequently been criticized for vanity of character and shallowness of mind. The vanity of which he was accused is largely justified by the immense scope of his talents, unparalleled in literary history since Shakespeare and Goethe. It is true that he was not a profound thinker, but his devotion to "the good, the beautiful and the true," if uncritical, was instinctive and sincere. The people of France whom he loved have judged him better than the critics, and he remains to this day one of France's best-loved authors.

HUGO THE WRITER

Hugo's career, covering as it does most of the nineteenth century, spans both the Romantic and the Realist movements, but it cannot be said—despite Hugo's initial fame as a Romantic poet—to belong to one movement more than the other. His superb use of the colorful and significant detail, which produces exoticism in *Les Orientales* and local color in *Notre Dame de Paris*, becomes, when applied to the modern scene in *Les Misérables*, the sheerest realism. He is never, like Stendhal and Flaubert, objective and impassive in the face of the scene he describes, but he is always more interested in the external world than in the inner world of his own feelings; and the passionate spirit with which he describes what he sees is no more "romantic" than Zola's. If the themes of his poetry are often Romantic, his concern for art and technique makes him a brother to the Parnassians; and the epic quality of all his work links him with Chateaubriand and de Vigny, on the one hand, and with Zola, on the other. Only as a dramatist can he be considered purely a Romantic.

POETRY

Victor Hugo is among the greatest poets of a century of great poets. He claims this place not only because of the immense volume of his production, spread over nearly sixty years, but because of the variety of his themes and techniques.

Hugo's poems deal with an unusually wide range of themes. Romantic love and the evocation of nature are, of course, among them; but he also deals ably and movingly with current events of the day, descriptions of exotic and historic scenes, philosophy, parenthood and grandparenthood. His satires are as powerful as his lyrics; no strain is foreign to his lyre.

As a poetic technician, Hugo is a great innovator. He is one of the first to move away from the classical tradition of the Alexandrine couplet (which, nevertheless, he can handle magnificently) toward more complex and subtle forms of verse borrowed from the Middle Ages and from his own rich imagination. He reshapes not only the form, but the vocabulary of poetry, and injects it with a new variety and richness.

In contrast with most poets who are skilled in the use of only two or three poetic devices, Hugo is master of all. He is a splendid rhetorician but is also adept in the music of poetry. And he employs not only the music of skillful phrasing but the sound of the words themselves to awaken and charm the inner ear of the imagination. When in *L'Expiation* he writes "Après une plaine blanche, une autre plaine blanche," not only the repetitive phrase but the flat echo of the open vowels call up the image of Russia's endless expanses.

He is also a master of imagery, not only simile and metaphor, but symbol. He advises poets to interpret their "interior world of images, thoughts, sentiments, love and burning passion to fecundate this world" through "the other visible universe all around you" (*Pan*, 1831); and he can almost always find a vivid and exact natural parallel to the landscape of his soul. In all these respects, he is the precursor and inspiration for the poets who follow: Baudelaire, the Parnassians, and the Symbolists are all to a large extent his disciples and his debtors.

DRAMA

In the Preface to *Cromwell* of 1827-28, Hugo serves as spokesman for the Romantic movement in attacking classical drama and in laying down the precepts of the new drama to be. He condemns the rigidity of both classical format and language: the unities of time, scene, and action, and the false and formal elegance of speech. He calls for a richer and more flexible verse, which will more closely approximate the rhythm of everyday speech, and a more flexible format, which will allow comedy and tragedy to mingle in Shakespearean fashion, just as they do in life itself. Weary of the eternal Greek kings and Roman heroes of the classical stage, he suggests that more recent history may also provide suitable themes for drama and that a bourgeois or a bandit may also sometimes possess enough nobility to transform a stage.

These precepts he exemplified in his own plays, some of which are in prose as well as in verse and which generally deal with some dramatic episode from European history. The subjects of *Marie Tudor* and *Lucrezia Borgia* are self-explanatory. *Hernani* — which quite literally caused a riot at its first performance — sets at odds a noble Spanish bandit and Charles V, Emperor of Spain; in *Ruy Blas* a valet, through the love of a queen, temporarily becomes head of state.

We cannot today appreciate Hugo's plays as wholeheartedly as did his contemporaries. His plots with their disguises and recognitions seem a little too melodramatic; his daring adventurers and his perfect, passionate, unattainable heroines are two-dimensional. Nevertheless, particularly in their historical accuracy of incident and decor, they represent a great stride toward realism in the drama; and in the stage's own terms, some of them are still "marvelous theater."

THE NOVEL

Hugo wrote several novels, but the only three that have continued to be much read today are *Les Misérables; Notre Dame de Paris;* and *Les Travailleurs de la Mer,* the story of a young fisherman who fights the sea to salvage a wreck and win the girl he loves but who gives her up when he learns she prefers another man.

Les Travailleurs de la Mer is read chiefly for its magnificent evocations of the sea, but *Notre Dame de Paris* is known the world over. Set in medieval Paris, it is one of those Romantic historical novels inspired by Sir Walter Scott, and on more than one score it bears comparison with *Ivanhoe*. Both are popular classics; both have suspenseful and melodramatic plots; and both contain character sketches which, despite their lack of depth, have remained vivid and memorable for a century. Just as every English school child knows Rowena, Rebecca, Ivanhoe, and Sir Brian de Bois Guilbert, so every French reader knows the poor but beautiful gypsy Esmeralda with her little goat; the alchemist-priest Claude Frollo, who desires her; and Quasimodo, the "hunchback of Notre Dame," who loves her and tries to save her.

The chief fascination of *Notre Dame de Paris,* however, lies in its powerful and living recreation of the Middle Ages. Hugo consulted many historical archives and accounts in his research for the novel, but the scenes of Paris life seem the work not of a scholar but of an eyewitness.

Les Misérables has many of the same qualities as *Notre Dame de Paris*, but it is a far more complex creation. As early as 1829 Hugo began to gather notes for a book that would tell the story of "a saint, a man, a woman, and a child," but over the years it became enriched by a throng of new characters and multiple accretions from Hugo's philosophy and experience. When it was finally published in 1862 it had attained, both in quality and quantity, an epic sweep.

In both thought and feeling, *Les Misérables* is far more profound than *Notre Dame de Paris*. In writing it, Hugo came to grips with the social problems of his own day; and this demanded much reflection upon the nature of society and, therefore, upon the nature of man. In 1830, the average life expectancy of a French worker's child was two years. Hugo, unlike many of his contemporaries, did not consider this statistic as "inevitable," or "the fault of the parents," but evaluated it in human terms, and cried out that suffering of such magnitude was intolerable and that such conditions must be changed through social action. What social action he considered desirable he shows us indirectly by portraying children who need to be fed, men who need jobs, and women who need protection; but also directly through M. Madeleine, who serves as an example of the ideal employer, and through the students of the 1832 revolt who demand legislation that will make possible equal education, equal opportunity, and genuine brotherhood among men.

But to support this social action Hugo must be convinced, and convince others, that the poor, the outcast — the *misérables* — are worth saving: that even the most impudent, scruffy street gamin has something to contribute to society, that even the most hardened convict is capable of great good. And the most appealing and enduring quality of *Les Misérables* is the fact that it is permeated by this unquenchable belief in the spiritual possibilities of man.

Plot and Structure

Like that of *Notre Dame de Paris*, the plot of *Les Misérables* is fundamentally melodramatic; its events are often improbable and it moves in the realm of the socially and psychologically abnormal. But this melodrama is deliberate; Hugo has chosen an extreme example, the conversion of a convict into a saint, to illustrate a general truth: that man is perfectible.

Moreover, within this general framework, the sequence and interrelation of the events are credible, and the structure is very carefully plotted. Like a good play, it opens on a situation of high suspense, rises to two increasingly tense climaxes at the ends of Part Three and Part Four, and arrives at a satisfactory and logical denouement in Part Five. Its two themes, the struggle between good and evil in the soul of one man and society's struggle toward a greater good, are skillfully interwoven, and Hugo effectively immortalizes this struggle in our imaginations by a number of striking visual tableaux.

Character

Psychological subtleties are not Hugo's forte. He does not, probably cannot, delve into the baffling paradoxes, the complexities, the idiosyncracies of the soul. His gift is for the fundamental truth. Valjean is a simple character dominated by one powerful emotion: *caritas* (charity — active, outgoing love for others). He helps a prostitute, protects his workers, gives constantly to the poor. His very *raison d'être* is literally love, since his existence revolves around Cosette and when she leaves him he dies.

Javert is the watchdog of the social order. Marius is the incarnation of the romantic lover. Enjolras is the incorruptible revolutionary. All of Hugo's characters can be briefly described — in other words, labeled.

But this simplicity has its own value. It allows the writer to analyze in depth a particular emotion, like a scientist studying an isolated germ. No one has captured better than Victor Hugo the arduous path of virtue or the poignancy of love. Valjean's deathbed scene has brought tears to the most sophisticated reader.

Of course, Hugo's truth is the poet's not the psychologist's. He takes great liberties with reality. His characters do not always evolve in convincing steps. Valjean's conversion is almost miraculous, Thénardier's degradation unmotivated. They are larger than life. Marius loves passionately, Valjean is a modern saint, Thénardier a Satanic villain.

But these are superficial criticisms. Hugo only distorts details: he scrupulously respects the basic integrity of the character. *Les Misérables* is the archetypal representation of eternal human emotions such as love, hate, and abnegation.

Style

Style is the reflection of the man and it is therefore not surprising that a writer of Victor Hugo's enormous vitality should abandon classical restraint. Hugo revels in language. Ideas are stated and restated. Places are exhaustively described. Characters do not speak, they harangue, lament, eulogize. No doubt, Hugo's exuberance is excessive. His antitheses occasionally grow tiresome. His discourse can degenerate into verbiage. His pronouncements sometimes sound hollow, or worse, false. But the defect is minor, for Hugo suffers only from an overabundance of riches. His style is a mighty organ.

He is at home in every idiom from the argot of the underworld to the intellectual tone of student discussion. He captures the slangy sarcasm of the gamin, the eloquence of the idealist, the lyricism of the lover. His expository prose, fed by an insatiable curiosity, deals with a range of subjects rarely encountered in a novel. Hugo writes with an absolute command of the *mot juste*, about history, logistics, philosophy, religion. and political morality.

He remains, of course, the greatest word painter in the French language. In *Les Misérables* no less than in his poetry, he justifies his claim of being "the sonorous echo of the universe." Countless vignettes and a few bravura pieces such as the description of the Battle of Waterloo invest his novels with a heightened sense of reality. Few writers can rival the vividness and eloquence of Hugo's style.

SYNOPSIS

Jean Valjean, after spending 19 years in jail and in the galleys for stealing a loaf of bread and for several attempts to escape, is finally released. But his past keeps haunting him. At Digne he is repeatedly refused shelter for the night. Only the saintly bishop, Monseigneur Myriel, welcomes him. Valjean repays his host's hospitality by stealing his silverware. When the police bring him back, the bishop protects his errant guest by pretending that the silverware is a gift. With a pious lie, he convinces them that the convict has promised to reform. After one more theft, Jean Valjean does indeed repent. Under the name of M. Madeleine he starts a factory and brings prosperity to the town of Montreuil.

Next, Hugo introduces the pathetic young girl Fantine. Alone and burdened with an illegitimate child, she is on the way back to her home town of Montreuil, to find a job. On the road she entrusts her daughter to an innkeeper and his wife, the Thénardiers.

In Montreuil, Fantine finds a job in Madeleine's factory and attains a modicum of prosperity. Unfortunately she is fired and, at the same time, must meet increasing financial demands by the Thénardiers. Defeated by her difficulties, Fantine turns to prostitution. Tormented by a local idler, she causes a disturbance and is arrested by Inspector Javert. Only Madeleine's forceful intervention keeps her out of jail. She catches a fever, however, and her health deteriorates dangerously. Death is imminent and M. Madeleine promises to bring her daughter, Cosette, to her.

Madeleine, however, is faced with serious problems. A man has been arrested as Jean Valjean and is about to be condemned for his crimes. After a night of agonizing moral conflict, Madeleine decides to confess his past. At Arras, the seat of the trial, he dramatically exonerates the accused. A few days later he is arrested by Javert at Fantine's bedside. The shocking scene kills the young woman.

That same night Valjean escapes, but he is quickly recaptured and sent to Toulon, a military port. One day he saves a sailor about to fall from the rigging. He plunges into the sea and manages to escape by establishing the belief that he has drowned. He uses his precarious freedom to go to Montfermeil, the location of the Thénardiers' inn. After burying his money in the woods, he frees Cosette from the Thénardiers' abominable guardianship and takes her into the protective anonymity of Paris.

In Paris he lives like a recluse in a dilapidated tenement, the Gorbeau House, in an outlying district. In spite of his precautions, however, Javert manages to track him down. Valjean is forced to flee abruptly. After a hectic chase and imminent capture he finds a miraculous refuge in a convent. With the cooperation of the gardener, Fauchelevent, a man whose life he has saved in the past, Valjean persuades the prioress to take him on as assistant gardener and to enroll Cosette as a pupil. Valjean and Cosette spend several happy years in the isolation of the convent.

Hugo now turns to another leading character, Marius. Marius is a seventeen-year-old who lives with his grandfather, M. Gillenormand, a relic of the Old Regime. In a nearby town Georges Pontmercy, Marius' father, a hero of the Napoleonic wars, lives in retirement. M. Gillenormand, by threatening to disinherit Marius, has forced Georges Pontmercy to relinquish custody of his son. He has completed the estrangement by communicating his aversion for Pontmercy to Marius. Consequently, the young man reacts almost impassively to his father's death. A fortuitous conversation reveals to Marius the depths of his father's love for him and, indignant at his grandfather's deception, he leaves home.

He takes refuge in the Latin Quarter and falls in with a group of radical students, the Friends of the A.B.C. Marius, who under his father's posthumous influence has just switched his allegiance from the monarchy to Napoleon, falls into a state of intellectual bewilderment. Material difficulties increase his unhappiness. Finally he manages to create a tolerable existence by finding a modest job, living frugally, and withdrawing into his inner dreams.

His peace is shattered when he falls passionately in love with a beautiful young girl in the Luxembourg Gardens. She is Jean Valjean's ward, Cosette. Too timid for bold actions, he courts her silently. A fatal indiscretion ruins his nascent love affair. He quizzes the doorman where the girl lives and a week later she moves without leaving an address. For a long time Marius is unable to find a clue to his sweetheart's whereabouts and is overcome by despair.

Coincidence puts him back on the track. One day curiosity impels him to observe his neighbors through a hole in the wall. He glimpses a family—father, mother, and two daughters—living in unspeakable squalor. Soon after he witnesses the entrance of a philanthropist, M. Leblanc, and his daughter. To his immense surprise, the daughter is Cosette. His jubilation is replaced by consternation when he discovers that his neighbors are planning to draw M. Leblanc into a trap the same evening. Marius contacts the police and on the instructions of Inspector Javert returns to his room.

When Leblanc comes back, Marius' neighbor identifies himself as Thénardier, ties up his victim, and demands an exorbitant ransom. The plot fails with the timely arrival of the inspector. In the confusion of the arrest Leblanc escapes.

Once again, the young girl has vanished. But Thénardier's daughter, who is selflessly in love with Marius, manages to find his sweetheart for him.

After worshiping Cosette from afar, Marius summons the courage to declare his love. Cosette reciprocates. For a whole month the couple lives a chaste and secret idyll, secret because Cosette intuitively guesses Valjean's hostility to the man who is usurping his place.

Marius' happiness is unwittingly shattered by Valjean who, disturbed by a secret warning and the growing popular unrest in Paris, has decided to take Cosette to England. As a first step he moves to a hideaway prepared for this kind of emergency.

Absorbed by his love, Marius has been unaware of the deteriorating political situation. Now his private crisis is echoed by the crisis of an imminent insurrection. His friend Enjolras directs the erection of a barricade in front of the Corinth wine shop. The first enemy he has to deal with is found within the rebels' ranks. It is Javert, who is unmasked as a spy and tied up to await execution.

Marius, driven by despair, decides to seek death in the insurrection. He joins the fighters at the barricade and fights valiantly to the end. Valjean also joins the insurgents, but for special reasons. He has discovered Marius' relationship with Cosette and his role in the revolution. For Cosette's sake he decides to protect the life of the man he abhors.

Before the final assault, Valjean volunteers to execute Javert. Instead he spares the inspector's life and sends him away. Then Valjean returns to the barricade as the few surviving defenders are driven inside the wine shop. He seizes the seriously wounded Marius, disappears into a manhole, and undertakes a heroic and harrowing passage through the sewers of Paris. Unfortunately, Javert arrests him at the exit. However, he allows Valjean to take Marius to his grandfather and later, in a quandary, he releases Valjean. But he cannot forgive himself for this breach of duty and commits suicide.

Marius' life has a happier epilog. He recuperates from his wounds and overcomes his grandfather's hostility to his marriage. The marriage, however, is a mortal blow to Valjean. He has confessed his past to Marius, and the latter, in spite of his magnanimity, slowly estranges Cosette from Valjean. Marius does not know that Valjean is the man who saved his life in the sewers. Without Cosette, Valjean's life loses its meaning and he slowly withers away. Thénardier, however, unwittingly reveals to Marius that Valjean is his savior, and Marius and Cosette arrive in time to console Jean Valjean on his deathbed.

LIST OF CHARACTERS

Monseigneur Charles François-Bienvenu Myriel

Saintly bishop whose compassionate treatment causes the reformation of the ex-convict Valjean. He is also called "M. Bienvenu."

Mlle. Baptistine

Sister of the bishop.

Mme. Magliore

Housekeeper for the bishop and his sister.

Jean Valjean

Ex-convict still pursued by the law, who strives for moral perfection and achieves a kind of sainthood in his love for the little orphan Cosette. He is also known as M. Madeleine and M. Leblanc.

Little Gervais

Chimney sweep from whom Valjean steals a coin, his last criminal act for which Javert inexorably trails him.

Fantine

A beautiful waif of unknown parentage who comes to Paris at the age of fifteen. She falls in love with Tholomyès and bears an illegitimate child, Cosette. Forced to give up her child, Fantine is crushed and ultimately destroyed by adversity.

Cosette

Illegitimate daughter of Fantine, originally named Euphrasie. She has a wretched childhood as the ward of the brutal innkeeper Thénardier, but later finds happiness in Valjean's devoted care and in the love of a young man.

Félix Tholomyès

A student, Fantine's lover and father of Cosette.

Thénardier

An evil innkeeper who mistreats Cosette during her childhood, lures Valjean into an ambush, and commits various other crimes. He is also known as Jondrette and Fabantou.

Mme. Thénardier

A virago whose sweeping malevolence spares only her husband and her two daughters.

Eponine

Older daughter of the Thénardiers. As a child she is spoiled at Cosette's expense; later she becomes a ragged, hungry adolescent. Her love for Marius first endangers, then saves his life.

Azelma

Second daughter of the Thénardiers. Spoiled at first, her life becomes as miserable as her sister's.

Gavroche

The Thénardiers' oldest son, a typical Paris gamin. He dies heroically at the barricades in the revolution of 1832.

Two little boys

The Thénardiers' youngest children. Given by their parents to an acquaintance, Magnon, they wander the streets of Paris after she is arrested. Gavroche's protection gives them temporary solace.

Inspector Javert

An incorruptible policeman. He makes it his life's work to track down Jean Valjean.

Fauchelevent

Valjean, as Madeleine, saves his life; Fauchelevent later is gardener at the convent of the Little Picpus and gives shelter to Valjean and Cosette.

Bamatabois

An idler of the town who torments Fantine by putting snow down her back.

Champmathieu

The man accused of being Jean Valjean, on whose behalf "Madeleine" reveals his true identity.

Sister Simplicity

A nun who lies to save Valjean from Javert.

Boulatruelle

An old roadworker, ex-convict, and minor associate of the underworld chiefs. He is constantly seeking buried treasure in the forest near Montfermeil.

The Prioress

Head of the convent where Valjean and Cosette live for several years.

Mestienne and Gribier

The two gravediggers. Mestienne, friend of Fauchelevent, dies suddenly, and his place is taken by Gribier, nearly causing Valjean to be buried alive.

M. Gillenormand

Relic of the Enlightenment, he is hostile to the romantic love and liberal politics of his grandson Marius.

Mlle. Gillenormand

Gillenormand's daughter, a lackluster old maid whose interests are limited to devotional practices.

Marius Pontmercy

An idealistic student who falls passionately in love with Cosette and later marries her.

Colonel Georges Pontmercy

Marius' father, an officer of Napoleon's, named by him a colonel, a baron, and an officer of the Legion of Honor.

Lieutenant Théodule Gillenormand

M. Gillenormand's grandnephew. He is asked to spy on his cousin Marius.

Magnon

Friend of Mme. Thénardier. She bears two illegitimate boys, for whom M. Gillenormand, her former employer, pays all expenses. When the boys die, the Thénardiers gladly give her their two youngest sons in exchange for a share of the money.

M. Mabeuf

An old horticulturist and bibliophile, now a churchwarden. He is instrumental in revealing to Marius the truth about his father. Later, driven by destitution, he dies a heroic death at the barricades.

Mother Plutarch

Servant of M. Mabeuf; shares his poverty to the end.

Montparnasse
Claquesous   The four chiefs of the Paris
Gueulemer   underworld, occasionally asso-
Babet   ciated with Thénardier.

Enjolras

An uncompromising political radical who dies courageously as the leader of a group of student insurrectionists.

Grantaire

Enjolras' friend. He is a drunken cynic who redeems a useless existence by sharing Enjolras' death before a firing squad.

Combeferre

Friend of Enjolras and second in command of the student insurrectionists.

Courfeyrac

A student. With Enjolras and Combeferre, he helps incite and lead the insurrection.

Jean Prouvaire

A friend of Enjolras and one of the group of revolutionaries. He is rich, sensitive, and intelligent.

Bahoral

A law student and revolutionary. He is good-humored and capricious, and refuses to be serious in his studies.

Joly

A student. A hypochondriac, he is nevertheless a gay and happy companion.

Bossuet

A student revolutionary. Although he signs his name "Lègle (de Meaux)," he is called Bossuet (Bald), Laigle (The Eagle), and occasionally Lesgle.

Feuilly

A self-taught worker, and an ardent insurrectionist.

Le Cabuc

Shoots a porter during the insurrection and is executed by Enjolras. May actually have been Claquesous.

SUMMARIES AND COMMENTARIES

PART ONE: FANTINE

Book I

Summary

In 1815, M. Charles François-Bienvenu Myriel has been Bishop of Digne for nine years. He is seventy-five years old and lives only with a sister Baptistine, ten years younger than he, and an old servant, Madame Magloire, the same age as his sister.

The bishop's background destined him to a worldly career. His father was a counselor at the Parlement of Aix and was grooming his son to be his successor. The young man married at eighteen and cut an impressive figure in society. But the Revolution changed his destiny. Exile, his wife's death, the destruction of the ancient order, perhaps some private grief, turned M. Myriel toward the priesthood.

M. Myriel became a priest of ineffable goodness. His appointment as bishop by Napoleon was a blessing to his diocese. He turned over his vast and sumptuous palace to the sick and converted the hospital into his own Spartan residence. The only luxury that he has retained from a more comfortable past are a few silver pieces: six knives and forks, a soup ladle, and two candlesticks.

Not only the resources of the church, but most of his own, are used for the benefit of the indigent. Out of a salary of 15,000 francs, 14,000 are earmarked for charity. For the sake of the poor the bishop willingly hazards his reputation. He requests funds for the maintenance of a carriage, risking criticism for this extravagance, in order to give the money to orphans and foundlings. His sacrifice does not prevent him from visiting his flock on foot, by donkey, or by some other modest means of transportation. Tirelessly he ministers to the sick, consoles the dying, and preaches the moral life. He does not demand the impossible and never condemns hastily. His front door is always unlocked, a perpetual invitation for those in need.

Only a few events interrupt his saintly daily routine. On one occasion, he consoles a convict during his last night on earth and attends his execution. The experience leaves him with a lingering impression of horror and doubts about the social order.

The bishop's pastoral duties involve him in another experience that illustrates his unflinching zeal. Eager to visit an isolated parish village, he ventures alone into the mountains where the bandit Cravatte has his hideout. At the village, he wants to sing a Te Deum but finds the parish too poor to provide the necessary episcopal ornaments for the service. Help comes from an unexpected source: the thief Cravatte sends him a trunk filled with the treasures he has stolen from another church, Notre Dame of Embrun. The bishop uses them for his service, but we are left in suspense as to whether he then returns them to Embrun or sells them and gives the funds to the hospital.

Humble with the underprivileged, M. Bienvenu (as his parishioners call him because of his kindness to them) can be cutting with the complacently wealthy. He refutes the amoral materialism of a senator with a sarcastic sermon, an ironic compliment.

His irony is reserved exclusively for the selfish, however, and he treats honorable opponents with consideration and courtesy. When he hears of the serious illness of G., a member of the Convention of 1793 that sent so many to the guillotine, he feels compelled to pay him a pastoral visit, and in a long conversation marked by mutual respect the two argue the value of the Revolution. With uncommon understanding, the bishop acknowledges its merits and, in a reversal of roles, concludes by asking the conventionist's blessing.

Commentary

It is often the case that the opening lines of a book set the keynote for the whole. Here, it is the Bishop of Digne who sets the spiritual keynote for *Les Misérables*.

A truly good man or woman is one of the most difficult characters for a writer to portray convincingly. Notice that in describing the bishop, Hugo does not simply tell us "This man is a saint." Instead, he introduces him to us gradually and lets us form our own conclusions. We learn first what people say about his past. Then we see him in action, giving away his palace and his income; and we hear him speak — simply and wisely to his parishioners, gaily to his sister, wittily to the great. In Chapters 5-9 we penetrate further into his private life and learn that he lives as unpretentiously in his bedroom as he does in

24

public, and that his sister and servant love and revere him even more than his parishioners. To add more conviction still to this straightforward account. Hugo lets us read at firsthand the bishop's personal budget and his sister's letter to an old friend, and subjects him to two difficult tests: a test of courage with Cravatte, the thief, a test of charity with G., the conventionist. And when, finally, we are given a glimpse of his inner thoughts we are not surprised at the radiance we find there.

Most of all, however, it is the touch of humor—even of the sardonic—which Hugo gives M. Myriel that makes him believable. The bishop is not above a bit of larceny in a good cause, nor is he free from personal and class prejudice. But he is constantly being changed by what he believes; his inner light changes his own personality as well as that of those around him.

The bishop is also important to Hugo as a social symbol. A man of the Old Regime, he has accepted his loss of privilege without bitterness, and though a student of the divine, he is not blind to the flaws in human law. In his sympathetic treatment of both the bishop and the conventionist G., and in showing that a reconciliation between them is possible, Hugo is indirectly urging his readers to put progress above party and to unite to lift from the poor the terrible burden that, more than 80 years after the Revolution, they are still suffering.

Book II

Summary

At the beginning of October, 1815, a disreputable-looking traveler enters Digne on foot. In spite of his money, he is repeatedly refused food and shelter for the night with harsh words and threats. A fierce hound routs him from a doghouse when he mistakes it for a worker's hut. Despairingly he sums up his plight with the pathetic cry, "I am not even a dog!"

On the advice of a kindly passerby he tries the door of Monseigneur Myriel. He bluntly introduces himself as Jean Valjean, an ex-convict recently released from prison. To his surprise the bishop welcomes him warmly, inviting him to share his supper, giving him advice, and finally offering him a bed for the night. Even more remarkable, he treats Valjean with unfailing courtesy and ignores the stigma of his past.

Valjean's past is a tragic story. Originally a primitive but uncorrupted creature, when he was twenty-six years old he was condemned to a five-year jail term for stealing a loaf of bread to feed his widowed sister and her large family. Repeated attempts to escape lengthened his sentence to 19 years. In jail, the merciless treatment he endured corrupted his fundamental potentialities for good into an implacable hatred for society. The continuous hostility he has encountered since his release has only confirmed this hatred.

The bishop's kindness moves Valjean profoundly but does not regenerate him. Rising stealthily in the middle of the night, the ex-convict steals his host's silver from a cupboard above the sleeping man's head—indeed, he is prepared to kill the bishop if he wakes. The police, however, catch him when he is making his escape and bring him back to the bishop. This time his crime will bring him life imprisonment. However, Monseigneur Myriel pretends that the silverware is a legitimate gift and in a gesture of supreme kindness, even adds his candlesticks to it—the only objects of value he has left. As Jean Valjean is leaving he exacts his reward, "Don't forget," he tells the astonished man, "that you promised me to use this silver to become an honest man."

Still Jean Valjean's conversion is not complete. On a deserted road, he steals a coin from an itinerant chimney sweep, Little Gervais. But this last contemptible act sickens him of himself, and in a paroxysm of remorse he resolves to amend his life.

Commentary

When we first meet Jean Valjean, he is in fact less than a dog. A dog may be a useful animal; Jean Valjean is a dangerous one. Even before he went to the galleys he was more animal than man, moved only by an instinctive loyalty to those of his own litter, as brutishly ignorant of evil as of good. For Hugo, the fact that Valjean has educated himself in prison is promising; at the moment, however, education has only served to make him vicious.

The penal laws of the nineteenth century seem absurd to us, but they stem from the primitive mores of tribal society when most property is held in common and theft is a crime often punishable by death. Under the influence of utilitarian philosophy, which considered environment rather than original sin to be the most important element in character formation, thinking men in the eighteenth and nineteenth centuries began to take a new look at the legal system, and to call for milder laws and a prison system which would rehabilitate rather than degrade the offender. Hugo shares these enlightened views, and in

26

fact his desire for reform of the penal system was the original inspiration for *Les Misérables*.

Impressive is the skill with which Hugo uses an external visual impression to evoke an internal conflict. Hugo was artist as well as writer, and in the scene in the bishop's room he gives us no sound, almost no motion. What we see, what we remember, is a darkness in which a threatening weapon hangs, the gleaming oval of the bishop's face, and between the two, the glimmer on the arms of the crucifix — an unforgettable pattern of black and white which symbolizes the unending conflict between good and evil, within and without, in man and in history.

The episode of the bishop's candlesticks is justly famous. The situation is dramatic, the psychology profound, and the artistry superb. Giving us only glimpses into the chaos in Jean Valjean's mind, Hugo deliberately awakens empathy by forcing us to provide our own explanations for Valjean's previous urge to murder, his theft, and his headlong flight.

Jean Valjean's conversion is completely convincing. He believes a totally hostile world surrounds him; the bishop has shown him good in it; but before he can change, he must see the evil in himself. Confronted by Little Gervais, he reacts with automatic cruelty — and then realizes that what the world has done to him he has done to someone even more defenseless. If he continues as he is, he will become one of those he hates; he has no choice but to change.

Book III

Summary

In this book we are introduced to one of the most pathetic characters in the novel, Fantine. A young girl of humble origins, she has retained her candor and compassion in the libertine company she keeps. Although she has taken a lover, Félix Tholomyès, she treats her affair with the romantic intensity of a first love. One summer day of the year 1817, Tholomyès arranges an outing in the country for Fantine and three more lighthearted couples. The day is spent in carefree amusements and concludes with a dinner in a restaurant, accompanied by banter and laughter.

But the festivities are marred by a macabre incident. An old horse dies before the eyes of the students and their girls. For Tholomyès it is only an occasion for a pun, but Fantine is touched by the nag's death.

The event seems to be the knell of her happiness. The men steal away from the restaurant and leave behind only a callous goodbye note — they are deserting their mistresses. Fantine's life is shattered, for she has had a little girl, Cosette, by Tholomyès and he has left her without resources.

Commentary

Victor Hugo was one of the earliest supporters in France of the "Shakespearean" approach to drama: mingling comedy with tragedy, and the sublime with the grotesque, to create a powerful contrast. Here, following the shadows and sufferings of Jean Valjean in Book II, he introduces youth, gaiety, and spring in the persons of Fantine and her companions on their student frolic; the effect of each tableau is heightened by the other.

However, the contrast is only apparent. In fact, we are about to begin another cycle of descent, despair, and regeneration, and as Jean Valjean plays out for us the fate of Man, Fantine and her baby will trace the fate of Woman and Child as they descend into the dark world of "les misérables."

In the earlier part of the nineteenth century, Balzac and the historical novelists developed the technique of the "significant detail," precise external description which nevertheless gives many clues to the inner nature of the person being described. We are so accustomed to this technique today that we automatically fill in any suggestive gaps in the text and find a writer like Hugo — who gives us the significant detail (Fantine's modest yet charming openwork blouse contrasted with the low necks of the other girls) but then goes on to explain its inner meaning (the purity and idealism of Fantine's passion contrasted with theirs) — old fashioned and boring. However it must be remembered that Hugo was not writing for college students or for a literary coterie; he wanted to reach the masses and was willing to say the same things in as many different ways as necessary to carry his message home, regardless of the esthetic effect. Hugo, in fact, was always willing to sacrifice his art to his conscience.

28

Book IV

Summary

In her distress, Fantine decides to return to her home town, Montreuil, taking with her her little girl, who is now two or three years old. On her way she becomes acquainted with Mme. Thénardier, an innkeeper's wife who is watching her two little daughters play at her doorstep. Misled by Mme. Thénardier's obvious affection for her children and unwilling to expose herself and Cosette to the shame that will result if she returns home an unmarried mother, Fantine entrusts her daughter to Mme. Thénardier.

It is an unfortunate decision. Mme. Thénardier is a vile and brutal creature whose affections are limited to her husband and her two daughters. Her husband is even worse than she. For him Cosette is nothing but an object for exploitation. He makes increasingly difficult financial demands on her mother and treats the child like a servant. Ill-fed, cold, and ragged, she becomes ugly and hostile.

Commentary

Artistic unity is complete in the confrontation of Fantine and Mme. Thénardier. The scene is a halfway house on Fantine's road to Montreuil; but she herself is at a halfway house, half Virgin with Child, half unmarried mother, on her road to Calvary. Mme. Thénardier too is at a halfway house, still capable of tenderness in the romantic dreams of her youth and in her love for her children, but under her husband's influence she has begun to lapse into brutality. Fantine's love for Cosette will save the child, but Cosette is also the agent who will bring about Mme. Thénardier's spiritual doom. Provided with a helpless victim, the innkeeper's wife will give way to all her worst instincts, and Cosette will totally corrupt her.

Book V, Chapters 1-7

Summary

In 1818 Montreuil becomes much more prosperous than it has previously been, thanks to a mysterious stranger, M. Madeleine, who has established a flourishing industry which he runs not only efficiently but with much humanity. He has become a father to his workers and to the whole community. His unfailing generosity has won him the post of mayor.

In 1821 a shadow is cast on M. Madeleine's good fortune. The local paper carries the announcement of M. Myriel's death. The next day, Madeleine appears dressed in black with a mourning band in his hat.

Somewhat later, M. Madeleine endears himself further to the town by a heroic exploit. As he walks down the street he sees one of his few enemies, Father Fauchelevent, caught under the wheels of his own cart. Immediate action is imperative. Madeleine offers a generous reward to induce the bystanders to lift the carriage, but the task requires Herculean strength and no one will volunteer. Faced by Fauchelevent's iminent death, Madeleine reluctantly undertakes the rescue himself and in one supreme effort manages to lift the carriage sufficiently to free the victim.

Paradoxically, Madeleine's heroism is to have ominous results for himself. It awakens the suspicions of his chief of police, Inspector Javert, for Madeleine's strength reminds him of Jean Valjean, an ex-convict he had known in Toulon.

This Javert is described at some length by Hugo. He is the epitome of the devoted police officer, incorruptible and relentless. He renders blind obedience to all constituted authority, and by the same token, condemns any and all lawbreakers to legal damnation.

Commentary

The transformation of Jean Valjean into M. Madeleine is improbable, coincidental, and comes out of the same formula box as The *Count of Monte Cristo;* nevertheless it is psychologically and artistically satisfying. We recognize, as Hugo does, that it is not enough for Jean Valjean to have experienced a spiritual conversion; this conversion must be tested in action; and the wider the field of action, the more satisfactory the test.

In any case, Hugo makes it clear that this transformation is not intended to be a happy ending. Jean Valjean is still in jeopardy, still, like Fantine, at a halfway house, as is shown by the presence of Javert.

Once every few hundred years, an author manages to delineate a character at once so individual and so universal that he becomes a new archetype in literature. Chaucer developed Pandarus; Victor Hugo created Javert. With consummate artistry Hugo blends Javert's history, his external appearance, and his inner nature to paint for us an unforgettable and terrifying portrait of a man-bloodhound, an inexorable and incorruptible police agent—a contradiction in terms in those days, when police forces were largely made up of "mouchards," or informers themselves involved in the criminal world.

What is most terrifying about Javert, however, is neither his persistence nor his purity but the fact that like a robot he decides always according to the letter of the law and not its spirit. Because of this, he makes both Fantine and Jean Valjean suffer acutely, but in the long run their weakness proves spiritual strength, and Javert's strength a spiritual weakness.

Book V, Chapters 8-13

Summary

Fantine has readily found a job in M. Madeleine's factory. Unaware of her child's plight, she feels a momentary surge of optimism as her fortune improves. Even though she is not very skillful, she earns enough to make ends meet. She rents a little room and furnishes it on credit. But clouds gather quickly on her peaceful horizon. Her letters to the Thénardiers arouse the curiosity of the town's busybodies. A certain Mme. Victurnien, a woman of malevolent piety, undertakes to investigate the mystery and discovers Fantine's secret.

Unbeknown to Madeleine, Fantine is abruptly fired by his assistant as "immoral." Unable to leave town because of her debts, she works at home, sewing coarse shirts for the soldiers of the garrison. Her ill-paid occupation earns her 12 sous a day and her daughter's board costs 10. Fantine works interminable hours and economizes desperately. In addition she suffers the opprobrium of the whole town. At first she cannot face the accusing fingers. Soon, however, she adopts a defiant attitude that rapidly becomes brazen.

Her situation grows worse. Overwork undermines her health. She is racked by a dry cough and contracts a fever. Her debts accumulate and the Thénardiers hound her unmercifully. One day they send her a frightful letter. Cosette needs a new wool skirt for the winter. It costs at least 10 francs. That night Fantine goes to the barber and sells him her hair for 10 francs and spends it on a skirt. Her mutilation causes her joy rather than regret. "My child is not cold any more," she thinks, "I dressed her with my hair." Unfortunately her sacrifice does Cosette no good. The Thénardiers have invented the story of the skirt to extort more money from her. Furious at having been unwittingly outsmarted, they give the skirt to their daughter Eponine and Cosette continues to shiver in the cold.

Misfortune also begins to take a moral toll. Fantine mistakenly attributes her troubles to Madeleine and begins to hate him. She has a sordid affair with a beggarly musician who beats her and then abandons her.

One day a new blow increases her misery. The insatiable Thénardiers bill her for 40 francs to cure a fever Cosette has supposedly contracted. Fantine tries to ignore their exorbitant demand, but not for long. One day Marguerite, Fantine's neighbor, finds her sitting on her bed overwhelmed by grief. When the candle suddenly lights Fantine's face, it reveals a gaping hole where her two front teeth had been. The desperate mother has sold them.

Fate now persecutes her relentlessly. She is reduced to the bare necessities of existence. Exhausted, she surrenders to dirt and rags. Creditors plague her. Bad health and endless work sap her vitality. Competition from cheap prison labor reduces her income to a pittance. The crushing blow comes from the Thénardiers. Now they want 100 francs and Fantine becomes a prostitute. But this is not the last ignominy. She is destined to drink her cup of pain to the dregs.

In January, 1823, a certain Bamatabois, one of the local idlers, amuses himself by insulting a wretched creature soliciting on the street. Exasperated by her indifference, he sadistically pushes some snow down her back. Fantine, for it is she, retaliates with an explosion of fury, scratching and swearing. Suddenly Javert makes his way through the crowd and peremptorily arrests her. At the police station, despite her pleas, he condemns her to six months in prison.

Without warning M. Madeleine enters and quietly interrupts the execution of the order. Fantine, still laboring under her mistaken impression of him, spits in his face. Undeterred, Madeleine carries through his merciful deed. Javert, of course, is stupefied by this outrage to authority and refuses to carry out his superior's order. It is only when the mayor explicitly invokes his authority that Javert is forced to set Fantine free. Fantine, before this titanic struggle that holds her fate in the balance, feels an upheaval in her soul. Finally, when

Madeleine promises her financial help and the return of her child she falls to her knees and faints.

Commentary

Fantine's degradation is skillfully portrayed, and every detail of Hugo's rather lengthy earlier description of her carries weight here, as the golden hair becomes a cropped stubble, the voluptuous lips give a gap-toothed grimace, and the dainty white blouse turns into a patched bodice topped by a dirty cap. The final touch of the snowball down the back is in the best traditions of realism, which involves us in the scene by an almost photographic accuracy of impression rather than by any commentary. By comparing M. Bamatabois and Félix Tholomyès in his essay on dandies, however, Hugo subtly underlines the point that Fantine's last torment, like her first, is the work of masculine vanity and callousness. The snowball incident was actually seen by Hugo in 1841. He waited over 20 years to find exactly the right place to use it in fiction.

The scene in the police office is again a graphic rather than a literary one, and in posing and lighting the three principal characters Hugo may have been influenced by a theme common in medieval painting — the struggle between an angel and a devil for the possession of a cringing soul. Indeed in their taste for local color and specific detail, as opposed to general truths, the Middle Ages and the nineteenth century are much alike.

Books VI-VIII

Summary

Fantine catches a high fever and Madeleine has her transported to the infirmary he has endowed. True to his word, he also writes the Thénardiers telling them to send Cosette. They, of course, sensing a profit, raise their financial demands; Madeleine immediately meets them. Unfortunately, Fantine is not getting better in spite of the nuns' devoted care. One day the doctor ominously recommends that Cosette be sent for as quickly as possible. Madeleine, armed with a note from Fantine, decides to get Cosette himself from the Thénardiers, who so far have stubbornly refused to give her up.

However, catastrophe is about to descend upon both Madeleine and Fantine. Unbeknown to the mayor, Javert has investigated Madeleine's past. Now Javert comes to see him with a surprising request: he wants to be relieved of his duties as inspector. He has in his own eyes committed an unpardonable transgression: he has accused Madeleine of being the ex-convict Jean Valjean. But the real Valjean has just been found; he now goes under the name of Champmathieu and has been arrested for stealing some apples by climbing the walls of an orchard and breaking off a branch. The identification is positive; not only has he been recognized by three of his fellow inmates, but Javert himself swears that the accused is Valjean. He is, in fact, leaving for Arras to testify at the trial, which is to take place the next day.

After Javert's departure, Valjean goes to the infirmary, stays with Fantine longer than usual, and recommends her to the special care of the nuns. Then he goes to a stable and rents a sturdy horse and carriage for 4:30 the next morning.

Until the arrival of the carriage he spends an agonizing, sleepless night. Irrationally he locks the door and blows out the candle. For one long hour, his head burning, he contemplates with horror the abyss into which he is about to slip. Then, with immense relief, he resolves to let fate have her way, to sacrifice Champmathieu to his own security. Later, however, the reproachful image of the bishop looms before him and he decides to give himself up. He puts his affairs in order, but the battle is not yet over: doubts and fearful visions weaken his resolve. He changes his mind again, this time even more definitely because the new solution seems morally right. He convinces himself that the welfare of many others – Fantine, Cosette, the whole town – depends on his staying out of prison. But his conscience returns to the assault, more imperious, more inflexible, until it seems like a real voice filling the room. For five endless hours he undergoes this torture, like Christ at Gethsemane.

At three o'clock he falls asleep, exhausted. But nightmarish dreams disturb his rest. He sees his dead brother, finds himself in a deserted village, among enigmatic crowds. He is abruptly awakened by his servant announcing the arrival of the carriage. For a moment he listens in an uncomprehending stupor. Then he says the fateful words: "All right, I'm coming down."

Driven by a mysterious compulsion, Valjean drives furiously to Arras. On the way, the wheels of a coach going in the opposite direction strike his, but he does not stop. At daybreak he has left Montreuil far behind. Several hours later he stops at Hesdin to feed his horse and let him rest, only to find out his wheel has been broken in the accident.

Valjean, however, will not give up. He wants to take the stagecoach. Impossible. He tries to borrow a horse. None available. He attempts to rent a carriage. There aren't any. Now he allows himself a long sigh of relief. He has done his best.

But fate has decided that he is not to be spared his tragic confrontation. Suddenly, an old woman approaches him and offers him an old wreck of a carriage. He accepts and goes on. Late in the evening after innumerable difficulties, Valjean reaches Arras.

At Arras, Valjean sets out for the courthouse. He makes his way through a crowd of sinister-looking lawyers and attempts to get into the courtroom. But the place is packed. There are only a few seats left behind the presiding judge reserved to public officials. Reluctantly, Valjean requests admission as mayor of Montreuil. Thanks to his widespread reputation, he is welcomed with great deference. He steps into the judge's chamber and, overcome by panic, flees, only to return once more with a sense of doom. Hypnotized by the copper handle of the door, he opens it like an automaton and finds himself in the courtroom. In the semi-darkness he discovers the accused and has the anguished vision of himself back in jail, a reversion to the degenerate and wretched creature he had been. Terrified, he sinks into a seat and hides his distress behind a pile of boxes.

Then he proceeds to watch the horrible spectacle of an innocent man crushed by the weight of evidence and the formidable apparatus of the law. Before the inexorable questions of the prosecutors, Champmathieu has only one pathetic defense: bewilderment.

Dramatically, the mayor interrupts the proceeding by confessing that he, and not Champmathieu, is Jean Valjean. He turns to the convicts and gives them such personal details about themselves that they are forced to recognize him. The audience is so stunned that nobody stops Madeleine-Valjean from leaving the courtroom; indeed, someone even opens the door for him.

Back in Montreuil, Valjean goes directly to the infirmary. Sister Simplicity is surprised by his unannounced arrival, but even more by his appearance, for his hair has turned snow white.

He enters Fantine's room and observes her thoughtfully while she sleeps. She, too, has changed. The approach of death has given her an ethereal glow, an inexpressible serenity. When she wakes up she looks at Madeleine without surprise and with a touching faith asks "And Cosette?" He mumbles an inadequate reply; luckily, the doctor comes to his aid and tells Fantine that her daughter is here but will not be allowed to visit her mother until Fantine feels better. The lie comforts Fantine, but with growing excitement she begins to talk about her daughter. Suddenly she stops and points behind Madeleine. He turns around and sees Javert, who with an expression of demoniac joy orders the mayor to come with him.

When Valjean fails to comply, the policeman grabs him by the collar. Valjean does not resist but, in a quiet voice, asks Javert privately for three days to go and bring back Cosette. Javert refuses, sneeringly and loudly, and Fantine realizes that her daughter has not arrived and that the mayor is a criminal under arrest. She suffers a convulsion and the shock kills her.

In Valjean's eyes, Javert has murdered her, and he is overcome by a terrible silent anger. Defying Javert, he says a silent goodbye to the dead woman and whispers a promise in her ear. Then he places himself at Javert's disposal.

The news of Valjean's arrest spreads quickly through Montreuil. The town to which he has brought prosperity unanimously rejects him. Only his old servant remains faithful. In the evening, as she sits musing over his tragedy, Valjean suddenly appears, explains that he has broken a bar of the jail window, and asks her to get Sister Simplicity. In his room, with closed shutters, he then packs up Little Gervais' coin and the bishop's candlesticks.

Sister Simplicity faithfully answers the summons and Javert, of course, follows soon after. In spite of the protestations of the servant, he resolutely climbs the stairs. Sister Simplicity falls to her knees and begins to pray, and continues to pray as Javert enters. His first impulse is to withdraw, but his professional conscience urges him on. Twice he asks the sister whether she has seen Valjean and twice she who has never lied answers "No." The categorical denial of such a holy person satisfies Javert and he insists no further.

An hour later, Valjean is walking quickly toward Paris. As for Fantine, she is thrown in a common grave to suffer the promiscuity of the dead as she had suffered the promiscuity of the living.

Commentary

Jean Valjean is sometimes spoken of as a "Christ figure," and Hugo, when he compares M. Madeleine's silent inner struggle with that in the Garden of Gethsemane, seems to underline this similarity, but it is not really an accurate comparison. Jean Valjean is a man from beginning to end and nowhere more human than here when he tries to use fate, accident, and his own responsibility to others as arguments to avoid his Calvary. Even when he does go to Arras, it is not so much the result of a conscious decision to sacrifice himself to another as out of the instinctive knowledge, which his dream has brought him, that if he does not go he will have no life left worth living. He will be spiritually dead.

The courtroom scene in which he declares his identity forms a perfect conclusion to Part One and is the exact counterpart of the meeting between Jean Valjean and the bishop early in the novel. Now, however, Champmathieu is the ignorant benighted victim persecuted by society, while Jean Valjean's suddenly white hair underlines the fact that he has inherited the saintliness of the Bishop of Digne.

PART TWO: COSETTE

Book I

Summary

Before resuming his story, Hugo acquaints the reader with such peripheral matters as the topography of Waterloo, a description of the farm of Hougomont, where Napoleon encountered his first setback, certain military considerations, and the emperor's personality.

Only then does the author launch into the long chronological narration of the Battle of Waterloo. It is the morning of June 18, 1815. In spite of the rain of the previous night which interferes with his plans, Napoleon exudes confidence. The army is in position, his strategy is decided. He gives the order to attack, expecting to deliver his usual stunning blow. But the British prove to be unusually stubborn opponents, and Napoleon suffers staggering losses in forcing Wellington to retreat on the Mont Saint Jean plateau.

The emperor orders Milhaud's cuirassiers, a formidable regiment 3,000 strong, to crush the enemy. Headed by Marshal Ney, they gallop like a massive juggernaut toward the British forces. But fate intervenes, putting in their path a sunken road impossible to detect from a distance. The troops fall headlong into it, carried on by their own impetus. Men and horses serve as a living bridge for their comrades to cross. The British assemble their artillery and proceed to shell the survivors.

The remainder of the regiment, however, continues the charge and hurls itself furiously on the enemy; in spite of the deadly calm efficiency of the British infantry, the regiment slices deep gaps in the British formations. Wellington orders his cavalry to attack from the rear, and suddenly the assailant becomes the defender, and the charge becomes a general slaughter. In one minute the cuirassiers lose 600 men, and the British formations are reduced from thirteen to seven.

Both sides are seriously weakened, but Wellington's losses are the greatest. His cavalry is destroyed, his artillery largely disabled, and panic begins to infect his ranks. At five o'clock, he is forced to the somber admission "Blucher [that is, reinforcement by the Prussian army which was supposed to join him earlier in the day] or the night."

Miraculously, a few minutes later, a line of bayonets sparkles on the horizon. Blucher's army, held up by the rains of the previous day, has arrived. This new intervention turns the tide of battle. Caught between Prussian shells and the bullets of the reinvigorated British, the French offensive turns into a rout, into disaster, into extermination.

Still the French do not succumb. Napoleon sends his picked troops, the Imperial Guard, against the British; marching resolutely against the enemy in the tide of universal retreat, it is mowed down rank by rank. Ultimately the whole Guard is destroyed: "Not one man misses his appointment with suicide." After this, panic is complete, and the French army turns into a disorganized mob which sweeps over the countryside pursued by Blucher's troops, who give no quarter.

One incident remains to be told, unimportant to the course of history, but illustrative of man's undying spirit. At the end of the battle an obscure officer named Cambronne is one of the few men still resisting. To the British exhortations to surrender he answers with one eloquently obscene word.

After the French defeat, the field is abandoned to the scavengers. Among the most industrious we find a certain Thénardier, who methodically proceeds to strip the dead. Suddenly a hand grabs him from behind. It is a dying officer clutching him for help. Calmly

Thénardier removes him from the cadavers and pockets his valuables. The officer, a man called Pontmercy, ironically believes Thénardier has saved his life and, asking his name, says he will never forget him.

Commentary

For some critics this description of the Battle of Waterloo is simply a typical example of nineteenth-century long-windedness, but in fact it is a vital part of *Les Misérables*. The society that persecutes Jean Valjean is not irrevocably cruel; it is capable of change, and of radical change in the interest of the poor and oppressed, as the Revolution showed. Napoleon I, dictator though he was, was a child of that Revolution and consolidated some of its liberal social advances. With his defeat at Waterloo and the consequent restoration of the Bourbons, social progress was checked; Jean Valjean, Fantine, Cosette, and thousands of others like them were again neglected. But their fate is not inevitable; history may again intervene to reverse the effects of Waterloo, and it is one of Hugo's purposes in writing *Les Misérables* to encourage it to do so.

Furthermore, Hugo uses the battle scene to warn us that his stage and his cast of characters is about to widen and that we shall meet not only characters from Book I, like Thénardier, but others yet unknown to us, of whom Pontmercy is the forerunner.

Finally, the epic quality of this book underlines the epic quality of the novel as a whole. The same capricious fate thwarts indifferently the plans of Napoleon I and M. Madeleine; the men of Waterloo and Jean Valjean struggle against their destinies with the same blind determination and terrible valor. From the moment when Hugo leads us, unsuspecting, through the gate of the farm of Hougomont with its brave bird singing and its banks of violets, we are in the hands of a great poet, who is as sensitive to the nuances of war as to those of everyday life and sees in both alike pity and horror, irony and beauty.

Book II

Summary

Valjean does not enjoy his freedom long. Several days after his prison break he is recaptured and sent to the galleys in Toulon. However, just a few days following Valjean's escape an incident takes place around Montfermeil that is not unrelated to our story. Every day an old roadworker, Boulatruelle, quits his job early and wanders in the most remote spots of the forest as if he were looking for something. To superstitious old women he is looking for the devil's treasure, for according to a legend, Satan has chosen the forest to hide his gold. A few skeptics, however, such as Thénardier — who is now innkeeper at Mont-fermeil — suspect that he is attracted by something more substantial than Satan's gold. Thénardier had the schoolmaster ply Boulatruelle with wine and extract a bit of intriguing information.

One morning as he was going to work, Boulatruelle had stumbled upon a hidden spade and pickaxe. Later, he had encountered a man whom he recognized as a fellow convict from years past, carrying a little chest. Interesting coincidence: the police had speculated that after his escape Jean Valjean had been in the vicinity of Montfermeil.

Toward the end of October of the same year, 1823, a ship docks at the Toulon shipyard for repairs. This routine operation is marred by a dramatic incident. A sailor working in the rigging high above the ship suddenly loses his footing and barely manages to avoid a fatal fall by grabbing a rope. But he remains in a perilous situation: incapable of climbing to the yard, he dangles like a stone at the end of a string. No one dares to help him and he seems doomed to plunge to his death.

Suddenly a convict, assigned to the ship, dashes to the riggings and climbs them with the agility of a cat. In a flash he is on the yard. For just a second he stops to gauge the distance to the end of the yard; then he runs to it, ties a rope around it, and lowers himself to the desperate man like a spider going after a fly. When he is within reach he attaches a rope to the sailor's body and lifts him to safety.

But the rescuer himself is not so fortunate. On the way back to his work gang he seems to lose his balance and drops into the sea. Four men immediately launch a boat to rescue him, but he has disappeared without leaving a trace. The next day the local papers announce Jean Valjean's death.

Commentary

The incident of Jean Valjean's heroic rescue of the sailor is taken from a friend's eyewitness account of a similar rescue by a convict which actually took place at Toulon. Writers of the Realistic school frequently took material from contemporary events — Flaubert's *Madame Bovary*, for instance, is based on a newspaper account of the suicide of a country doctor's wife—and Hugo in this same chapter uses fake newspaper reports to give "authenticity" to his account.

In fact the use of newspaper reports, false or true, in a novel does not necessarily add conviction. No amount of "real life" stuffing will save a novel that is not artistically and psychologically sound. But where the novel is otherwise satisfying, such devices do add powerfully to the *illusion* of authenticity.

Criminals sent to the galleys, as every reader of historical fiction knows, were used as oarsmen on those wooden men-of-war which, though they had sails, needed oar power to maneuver in a calm or in a crisis. The prisoners were exposed to every inclemency of weather and, chained to their benches, often went down with the ship. However, since such ships were outmoded early in the eighteenth century, it may surprise the reader to find Jean Valjean on one in 1823. In fact the "galériens" no longer ply the oars, but work for the navy shifting stores and repairing vessels at navy yards in Marseilles, Toulon, Rochefort, and Brest; and they sleep at night in shore prisons.

Book III

Summary

It is Christmas Eve at Montfermeil. At the Thénardier inn, the husband is drinking with the customers and the wife is supervising the meal. Cosette is at her usual place, huddled under the table near the chimney. Ragged and barelegged in her wooden shoes, she is knitting woolen socks for Eponine and Azelma, the Thénardier daughters. Upstairs a new Thénardier baby, a boy, is wailing; but his mother detests him and pays no attention.

Cosette muses somberly as she knits. Four travelers have arrived unexpectedly and she has had to fill their pitcher with water. That means the supply is probably exhausted, a situation fraught with anxiety for Cosette. She may have to go out in the black of night to fill the pail at the distant spring. Unfortunately, her worst fears are realized. A traveling salesman furiously complains that his horse has not been given anything to drink, and Mme. Thénardier consequently orders Cosette to bring back water. As an afterthought she hands her a coin to buy a loaf of bread.

The beginning of the trip is relatively reassuring, since the center of the town is filled with carnival stands whose candles give off a protective light. It even holds a brief and poignant pleasure. One of the shops contains a magnificent doll, which Cosette contemplates for a moment in delirious admiration.

But as she leaves the confines of the fair the night grows darker and the last glimmers of light vanish at the edge of the forest. The countryside is transformed into a nightmarish vision, a world of ghosts, animals, and unknown terrors. So great is Cosette's terror she does not notice her coin fall into the spring as she feverishly fills her pail.

The return trip is agonizingly slow. Every few steps she stops to put down her inhumanly heavy burden and rests. Suddenly the pail becomes weightless. A man has come up from behind and like a rescuing angel, has silently taken the handle from her grasp. A stranger just arrived from Paris, the man appears weary and grieved, and his clothes indicate a genteel poverty. After getting off the stagecoach, he has plunged into the forest instead of entering the village, and so has noticed Cosette.

The stranger accompanies her to the inn and on the way elicits her pathetic story. When she gives him her name, Cosette, he seems to receive a shock. When they arrive at the inn, on Cosette's timid suggestion he gives her back the pail to save her from a beating by the irascible Mme. Thénardier. Mme. Thénardier greets Cosette crossly and the stranger, on account of his unprepossessing appearance, with insolence. But he is indifferent to his reception and to the wine Cosette has automatically brought him; all his attention seems concentrated on the child.

Suddenly Mme. Thénardier remembers the bread. Cosette, desperately attempting to avoid her wrath, pretends the bakery was closed. But now she cannot find the coin to give it back. The stranger intervenes once more; pretending to pick up a coin from the floor, he gives the woman a 20-sou piece he has taken from his pocket. His kindness does not stop there. He notices that Cosette is diligently knitting while the Thénardier girls are playing without a care. Moved to compassion, he buys the unfinished socks for the exorbitant sum of five francs and relieves Cosette of her dreary task.

Little girls need toys to fill their leisure, however, and Cosette has none. When the Thénardier children abandon their doll for a moment to play with the cat, Cosette surreptitiously grabs it; but when the theft is discovered, Mme. Thénardier erupts with the violence of a storm.

Cosette wrings her hands in desperation and terror. The stranger then does an incredible thing. He steps out of the inn and returns with the magnificent doll from the village shop, which he hands to Cosette. The assembly is stunned, Mme. Thénardier is speechless, and Cosette contemplates the doll with awed veneration.

After his dramatic intervention, the man returns to his reverie and much later retires to his room, escorted by a now obsequious Thénardier. Before he retires, however, he performs one last good deed. The Thénardier girls have placed their little shoes near the chimney and a tender mother has put a 10-sou coin in each. Next to them stands a worn, muddy wooden shoe, empty. The traveler puts a shining gold louis in it and steals off to bed.

The next day the stranger reveals the purpose of his trip. He offers to relieve Mme. Thénardier of Cosette, and she eagerly accepts. Her husband, however, is more greedy. He plays the affectionate father, unwilling to abandon the child he cherishes. The stranger has to pay him 1,500 francs before he will relinquish her. The stranger takes Cosette's hand, and she trustingly follows him out of the inn.

But the happy ending is spoiled by one last complication. Egged on by his wife, the insatiable Thénardier runs after the pair to see if he can extort yet more money. Valjean—for of course it is he—plays his trump card and shows the innkeeper Fantine's note. When Thénardier still tries to follow from a distance, Valjean raises his cane menacingly and disappears into the forest with his precious charge.

Commentary

Once again the Thénardiers appear in our story, and we realize that they are and will remain an integral part of the novel. In contrast to Jean Valjean, who represents man rising from animality to sainthood, the Thénardiers are losing their humanity and becoming savage brutes. In describing them, Hugo uses the common realistic and naturalistic technique of presenting selected details of external appearance, and letting these suggest the truth of the inner man. By the time he has finished painting Mme. Thénardier's stature, her energy, her great voice, her freckles, her beard, and her jutting tooth, we can see for ourselves she is a monster, and Hugo does not need to tell us so.

With the innkeeper, Hugo extends his exploration somewhat beyond Thénardier's surface appearance. He adds details of manner, gesture, and speech that are characteristic of the man, and he even goes so far as to say Thénardier is a hypocritical crook. None of these facts, however, goes beyond what a shrewd observer might deduce about the innkeeper on modest acquaintance, and Hugo is very careful never to take us "inside" Thénardier. "We believe," he says about the details of the man's past; it is a guess, not a statement; and he concludes, "There was some mystery in Thénardier." It is just this, in fact, that makes him so terrifying a personage.

As for Cosette, Hugo sums up the history of her last five years in terms of the most common and vivid of childhood experiences — fear of the dark. The intensity of her fear is so great, however, that we recognize without being told that it is the expression of a thousand other unexpressed real terrors. Her fear of the night is only the outward mark of the fear kindled in her by her total solitude and inhuman treatment.

There were many such abandoned children in nineteenth-century France, rejects of an industrialized society that no longer had any use for them. Fantine herself was an abandoned child, and like Cosette, her name meant only "little one"; but she was raised by the village to which she belonged because in an agricultural society a child can always earn its keep: tend sheep, feed chickens. In the nineteenth-century city, however, there was no way for a small child to help carry the family's economic burden, and it was often abandoned to allow the parents to work.

Cosette is fortunate that she is useful at the inn; for Mme. Thénardier has exactly the temperament of those infamous nineteenth-century baby-nurses who, when their payment for the care of an unwanted baby did not come, promptly tied the infant up in brown paper and dropped it in a river.

Hugo has compensations for Cosette, however. Her St. Nicholas may be only an old convict, but he comes with exactly the right fairy-tale gifts — the biggest doll in the world and a gold piece down the chimney. What is more, her Christmas miracle is to be a lasting one. It is one of the oldest stories in the world Hugo tells here, but it is always a satisfying one.

44

Book IV —
Book V, Chapters 1-5

Summary

In Paris, Valjean takes refuge in a dilapidated house in an outlying district. The only other tenant is an old woman who also performs the functions of caretaker. Passing off Cosette as his granddaughter and himself as a bourgeois ruined by unlucky investments, he lives quietly and at last happily. He lavishes on the little girl his immense reservoir of long-suppressed affection and she responds with equal love. He teaches her to read or simply watches her undress her doll. Cosette plays, chatters, and sings.

The world seems to have forgotten Jean Valjean, but he continues to take infinite precautions. He only goes out at night, sometimes with Cosette, sometimes alone, always choosing back alleys and deserted neighborhoods. His only contact with society is a visit to church or giving charity to a beggar.

He does not, however, remain undisturbed long. The old caretaker, tirelessly inquisitive, watches his every move. One day through a crack in the door she catches him taking a 1,000-franc bill from the lining of his coat. A moment later he approaches her and asks her to go change it, saying it is a dividend he has just received. But as he only goes out at night after the post office is closed, his explanation is highly suspicious. A few days later the room is momentarily deserted and the old woman creeps in to examine the intriguing coat. The lining is filled with paper — no doubt more bills — and the pockets with such incriminating objects as needles, scissors, and a collection of wigs.

On his nightly walks, Valjean has regularly been giving a few cents to an old beggar who sits at a nearby well. One evening as Valjean is ready to give his customary alms, the beggar raises his head and Valjean, petrified, seems to see the familiar face of Javert. The next night he returns to confirm his suspicion, but it is the same harmless beggar he knows from before.

However, in the evening a few days later Valjean hears the front door open and shut, and someone climbs the stairs to stand in front of his door. The next morning he hears footsteps again and through the keyhole sees Javert's formidable silhouette. That evening he makes a roll of his ready cash and taking Cosette by the hand, departs from the lodgings.

Commentary

A nineteenth-century novel is meant to be savored slowly, not rushed through to find out "what happens next"; and Chapter 1 of Book IV is a good example of the pleasures it can offer a reader willing to linger. Not only does Hugo give us a fascinating historical portrait of a section of Paris in 1823 and again in the 1860s, and a perceptive and witty comment on the magical swiftness with which faster transportation changes the look and feel of our environment, but a poetic evocation of a particular type of city area—a "hell of monotony"—which still fits perfectly our interstitial areas today with their rows of concrete gas stations, used car and trailer lots, and neon signs.

Hugo's city, however, is never truly urban, never the dense center of commercial and social relationships we find portrayed in Balzac or Zola. If Hugo's nature sometimes—as with Cosette at the spring— seems to take on the attributes of a person, his city equally often takes on the aspect of the countryside. When Jean Valjean needs a banker, he relies on a tree; but conversely, the maze of Paris streets is for him a jungle whose trees are lampposts and whose clearings are squares. There are times when Hugo sees Paris still with the eyes of the boy who grew up across from the Feuillantines Park in the middle of the city —as a wonderful place in which to play hide and seek.

Book V, Chapters 6-10

Summary

Jean Valjean maneuvers through the back streets of Paris like a hunted deer. He has no destination, no plan; he simply wants to throw Javert off the scent. Instead of leading him to freedom, his labyrinthine escape route brings him to a police station, where Javert picks up three allies and gives the alarm.

Valjean beats a hasty retreat and momentarily confuses his pursuers. When he reaches the Austerlitz Bridge he is detained at the tollgate and consequently observed by the gatekeeper. He continues his headlong flight, but Cosette's exhaustion impedes his progress. Then, tragically, he is trapped. The street he is following forms a "T" with another street, terminating on the right in a dead end and barred on the left by a police lookout. Behind him, invisible but terribly present, Javert inexorably advances.

Frantically casting around for an avenue of escape, Valjean notices a vast building which might possibly serve as a refuge. But the windows are barred, the pipes rickety, the doors unyielding. In his desperation, he decides to climb the walls, and miraculously finds a rope to aid him — the rope that lowers and raises the gas street-lanterns so that they can easily be lit. He cuts it, ties it around Cosette's body, takes the other end between his teeth, throws his shoes and socks over the wall, and then climbs it like a cat-burglar at the spot where the wall forms an angle with another building.

When he reaches the top, he pulls Cosette up, jumps on the roof of a building leaning against the wall, clambers down what appears to be a linden tree, and winds up in a garden. Outside Javert's voice barks imperative orders. The garden in which Valjean has arrived is vast and depressing. He distinguishes a big building with barred windows and, in the distance, the silhouette of other buildings. Suddenly an eerie sound breaks the silence, a hymn sung by an ethereal choir.

The winter wind begins to blow and Cosette shivers; Valjean wraps her in his own coat and then starts out to explore the grounds. As he peers through one of the windows, a macabre sight paralyzes him with terror. In a deserted room a human form is lying prone on the floor, motionless, covered with a shroud, its arms in the shape of a cross.

He returns to Cosette panting with fright, and sits down next to her; she has fallen asleep. His loving contemplation of the child is broken by the ringing of a little bell and he sees a man limping alone in a melon patch, bending and rising rhythmically, accompanied by the sound of the bell. Valjean has no time to examine the mystery, for he suddenly notices that Cosette's hands are nearly frozen. She is not dead, as he at first fears, but her breathing is shallow. There is obviously an urgent need to find her warmth and a bed.

Valjean does not hesitate. He goes straight to the man in the garden and shouts to him, "A hundred francs if you give us shelter for the night." Unexpectedly, the stranger answers, "Well! It's you, M. Madeleine!" and continues to chat with Valjean like an old friend. Valjean, astonished, recognizes Fauchelevent, the old man whose life he saved when he was trapped under a cart. Fauchelevent explains that they are in the garden of the convent of Petit-Picpus, where he is gardener. He is still very grateful to "M. Madeleine" for saving his life, and left Montreuil before Valjean's true identity was discovered, so he readily agrees not only to keep Valjean's secret, but to harbor him and Cosette.

A warm bed in his cottage brings Cosette back to consciousness, and a glass of wine and a frugal meal revive Valjean.

While they rest, Hugo explains Javert's uncanny arrival on the scene. There is really no mystery about it. When Valjean "drowned," the police suspected he might really have escaped and would, like many fugitives, head for Paris. Javert was called to Paris to assist with the hunt because he knew Valjean by sight, and his subsequent zeal and intelligence earned him an appointment to the Paris police force. Some time later, Javert came upon the report of the kidnaping of a little girl from her guardians, the Thénardiers, at Montfermeil. He suspected it was Jean Valjean who had taken Cosette away and subsequently learned that at the Gorbeau House there lived an old bourgeois whose "granddaughter" came from Montfermeil. Thoroughly suspicious now, he disguised himself as the old beggar one evening and identified Jean Valjean.

Commentary

Once again we see Jean Valjean fleeing, as he fled from Digne and from Montreuil; but this time something in his silhouette is different—he is carrying a child as he flees. No longer the solitary thief, he takes on the appearance of a St. Christopher, a man defined not by what he is but by what he carries and how he bears his burden. But as Hugo points out, Jean Valjean's burden is in itself its own reward. In taking on Cosette, he expects responsibility, but what he gets is love. Jean Valjean may be an apprentice saint, but as a social human being he is stunted because his criminal past has cut him off from the society of others. Cosette too has been stunted by cruelty and neglect. Together, however, they can form their own society and expand in heart and soul through the experience of loving each other.

Throughout Part Two Hugo's palette is somber, and in both the episode of Cosette's trip to the well and that of the "night hunt" we have scenes of darkness only fitfully touched by light which resemble the scene in the bishop's bedroom in Part One. However there is a contrast in mood and movement between the two darkness scenes in Part Two. The total darkness at the well is sinister, and Cosette escapes it by moving into the moonlight where she meets Jean Valjean, then into the firelight at the inn where he protects her. In the "night hunt," it is the fitful moments of light which reveal Jean Valjean to his pursuers that are sinister, and the total darkness into which he plunges on the other side of the wall in the Rue Droit Mur spells safety.

Books VI-VII

Summary

Hugo pauses in his story to give a long description of the convent in whose garden Jean Valjean now finds himself: its founding, its inhabitants, its activities, even the colors in which its walls are painted. In the chapter following, he gives his own personal views on the subject of monastic institutions.

Commentary

Because, according to the tenets of realism, environment is one of the most important factors in forming character, a detailed description of the character's environment is common. Hugo had all the details he gives us here about convent life from Juliette Drouet; they are all accurate, and for someone interested in convent life, even fascinating. But fifty pages of convent is, for the ordinary reader, far too much.

Hugo does have two practical aims, however, in discussing the convent at length. He wants us to understand thoroughly this atmosphere, which will add its gift of humility to the charity Bishop Myriel taught Jean Valjean and which for so many years will protect Cosette's innocence while not depriving her entirely of feminine mischief such as eating forbidden fruit (the orchard apples and pears) and reading forbidden books (the Rules of St. Benedict.)

He also, in an age when a single church and a Divine Monarchy still vie for French loyalty with an irreligious democracy, wishes to state his position on the religious question. Hugo as a modern man finds convents unnatural and unproductive, but as a poet, he cannot help admiring the sublimity of the monastic sacrifice. And if the convent stultifies, so does pure materialism: there is no Progress without an Ideal. What he himself would prefer is a more active, a more secular form of salvation, the striving for social utopia.

Book VIII

Summary

Valjean realizes that with Javert back on his trail he is lost if he goes back into the outside world. It is imperative that he remain in the convent. But even with Fauchelevent's loyal assistance the difficulties are insuperable. He cannot wander very far in this community of women. He cannot even stay hidden, for the convent has boarding students, whose tireless curiosity would soon betray the fugitives. Valjean's only hope is to be officially accepted by the nuns under some plausible alias. But to return in a normal way, he must first leave the convent undetected.

Both men fruitlessly examine the problem until Fauchelevent is summoned by the prioress. She gives him a confidential mission. A nun, Sister Crucifixion, has died that morning. Her last wish was to be buried in the vault under the altar. As this is against the law, a bit of subterfuge is required to carry out her request. The prioress asks Fauchelevent to come back before midnight, after the coroner's visit, to nail down the coffin and bury it in the vault. Later he is to accompany an earth-filled casket to the cemetery to throw the authorities off the track. As he listens to the instructions, Fauchelevent, who is not without peasant shrewdness, has been suggesting that he has a brother who could usefully help him in the garden and a niece who might become a nun if she were allowed to go to school at the convent. Satisfied with Fauchelevent's cooperation, the prioress gives him permission to bring his supposed brother and niece to the convent to live.

When Fauchelevent tells Jean Valjean what has just taken place, the ex-convict has a hair-raising idea. He himself will occupy the false casket, and at the cemetery Fauchelevent can get his friend Mestiennes, the gravedigger, drunk and free Valjean. As for Cosette, she will simply be carried out by Fauchelevent in a basket on his back.

The next day at sunset Fauchelevent confidently follows the funeral procession to the Vaugirard cemetery. Everything is going well and Valjean's confident courage has reassured him. At the gate an unexpected *contretemps* strikes him like a thunderbolt. He is greeted not by the alcoholic Mestienne, but by a replacement, Gribier; Mestienne has just died. In his bewilderment, Fauchelevent can think of nothing better than to continue with the original plan, but the new gravedigger is a teetotaler and virtuously refuses Fauchelevent's repeated urgings to come and have a drink with him.

Valjean has weathered his ordeal well, has suffered stoically through the long procession, the descent into the grave, and finally the lugubrious funeral services. But when he hears the earth falling on the casket and understands its implications, he faints.

Above ground, desperation has brought inspiration to Fauchelevent. He has noticed a white card in the gravedigger's pocket, his pass to enter and leave the cemetery after sunset. Fauchelevent steals the pass skillfully, then brings the loss to his companion's attention. Gribier is terrified, for the loss incurs a large fine. Fauchelevent helpfully suggests he go home and look for it, offering to guard the grave. The gravedigger, overwhelmed with gratitude, shakes his hand and dashes away. Valjean is soon freed and the fake burial completed. The two men leave the cemetery without further difficulty.

An hour later, two men and a little girl present themselves at the gate of the convent. Valjean makes a good impression on the prioress, and Cosette's homeliness seems to predestine her to become a nun. Valjean is installed as assistant gardener and Cosette is accepted as a student. Life for Valjean is henceforth to be confined within the walls of the convent, but he is satisfied with it. His work gives him serenity and he finds consolation in Cosette's daily visits. She too is happy. Laughter, like sunshine, dissipates the winter in her heart. In this fashion, several years go by.

Commentary

Part Two as a whole has presented technical problems for Hugo. Its plot comprises only three events: Valjean's escape and rescue of Cosette; his flight from Javert; and his discovery of a new refuge in the convent. This is very little action to stretch over nearly 300 pages, and Hugo uses various devices to maintain the reader's interest: cumulative suspense, deliberate mystifications, and unexpected dramatic confrontations only later explained in flashbacks.

When Jean Valjean comes to the inn, there is no real reason why he cannot simply present Fantine's note and take Cosette away directly. Instead, Hugo has him approach the problem in a subtler manner, so that for several chapters the reader does not know whether he will succeed in rescuing the child or not. Interest is sustained, and the rescue when it comes is much more emotionally satisfying.

Hugo also deliberately mystifies us at three points in Part Two. Valjean falls from the mast at Toulon, but it is a long time before we are quite sure that he has survived and made good his escape. Boulatruelle suspects a man of burying treasure in the woods, but again we do not know for sure that it is Valjean, and that he has secreted the wealth he gained as M. Madeleine, until much later in the book. And finally, the strange sights and sounds Valjean sees after he has climbed over the wall into the convent garden are deliberately chosen to alarm and puzzle us, and to pique our curiosity.

The flashback is a legitimate dramatic device, almost as old as the novel itself, and Hugo uses it here and in many other places in *Les Misérables* to good effect. To explain Javert's appearance immediately he enters upon the scene would be to weaken all the dramatic effect of his irruption into Valjean and Cosette's peaceful life and would destroy the unity and steadily mounting suspense of the discovery-chase-escape sequence. As it is, crisis follows crisis until Valjean disappears over the convent wall; and then, satisfied that he is safe, we are prepared to hear an explanation of Javert's presence.

The suspense in Chapter 8 is also very effectively maintained, and the working out of a complex criminal escape plot against the background of a convent also gives Hugo an opportunity for one of the dramatic contrasts both he and the reader enjoy.

PART THREE: MARIUS

Book I

Summary

Hugo opens this section with a sentimental tribute to the Parisian gamin, or street urchin. The gamin is for him a pearl of innocence hidden under outer depravity and squalor. He uses slang, talks to prostitutes, frequents bars, wears rags, sings obscene ditties, and sneers at religion. Yet for all his apparent immorality he elicits admiration. His skepticism mocks sham and convention. It is served by a lively wit and a picturesque vocabulary. At times, when he is sufficiently aroused, the gamin rises to the sublime. To use Hugo's image, this handful of mud becomes Adam when it is sparked by the divine breath. And he is happy in spite of his wretched poverty. The street is for him an ever-exciting domain full of marvels, fraught with adventures. In the evening he loses himself in the magic of the theater.

Nine years have elapsed since the events related in the second part. Hugo now introduces Gavroche, a boy of eleven or twelve—gay, free, hungry, slightly larcenous, dressed in hand-me-downs, a typical Parisian urchin. There is a tragic background to his life, however. He has been callously abandoned by his parents, brutally kicked out of the nest. Yet in spite of the estrangement, every few months he goes to see his mother in the Gorbeau House. The visit is invariably depressing. Gavroche is greeted by abysmal poverty, hunger, and worse, indifference. The conversation is laconic and matter-of-fact:

> — Where have you come from?
> — The street.
> — Where are you going?
> — Back to the street.
> — Why did you come?

Commentary

By now we are used to Hugo's dramatic technique of shifting us abruptly from the known to the unfamiliar, in a plot dislocation that is more apparent than real, and we are confident that if we are patient he will eventually bring us back to Jean Valjean.

The problem of the abandoned child has already been evoked with Cosette. Hugo reverts to it here by introducing Gavroche, who is — in more ways than one, as we shall see — a sort of little brother to Cosette but even more unlucky than she. Where misfortune stupefied her, however, it has only sharpened Gavroche's wits.

In 1830 the average life expectancy of a bourgeois' child was eight years; of a worker's, two. This statistic goes a long way to explain the phenomenon of the Paris gamin: those children who survive parental neglect and the urban death rate have already proved themselves remarkably flexible and sturdy and are, in a sense, the pick of the crop. With keen observation and tender empathy Hugo portrays their courage and their sufferings, their irreverence and their audacity, and glorifies them as symbols of that spirit which makes Paris the capital of the world. And finally, he uses them as a telling argument in favor of universal schooling; if they, unlettered, show so much ingenuity, intelligence, and wit, what could they not achieve with education?

Books II-III

Summary

In the neighborhood around the Temple there lives a curious character, M. Gillenormand, vestige of another age. His ninety years have in no way diminished his vigor. He walks straight, drinks with gusto, speaks loudly, sleeps soundly, snores vigorously. He has given up women, but not without some lingering regrets. When a former maid in the house tries to claim he is the father of her baby boy, he flatly denies it, but pays for the child's keep just the same, and for that of his little brother later on.

He is authoritarian and cannot brook contradiction. He still beats his servants in the grand old tradition and even punishes his fifty-year-old unmarried daughter. He has retained the Enlightenment's cynicism about the world. Europe, to him, is a civilized version of the jungle. Of course, he finds contemporary society particularly repulsive. He declares peremptorily: "The Revolution is a bunch of rascals."

M. Gillenormand has outlived most of his relatives. He still has, as we have just mentioned, an old maid daughter, a lackluster creature. In her youth she dreamed of a rich husband, prominence, an imposing butler. Now she has turned into a prude and a bigot. She defends with a heavy fortress of clothing an unthreatened virtue. She fills her day with religious practices, says special prayers, belongs to the Association of the Virgin, and venerates the Sacred Heart. She is, moreover, abominably stupid.

Her younger sister, now dead, was her exact opposite. She breathed poetry, flowers and light, dreamed of falling in love with a remote heroic cavalier, and married the man of her dreams. She has left behind a son, Marius, who lives with M. Gillenormand. Marius is a sensitive child who trembles before his gruff grandfather, for the latter speaks to him severely and sometimes raises his cane to him. Secretly, however, M. Gillenormand adores the child.

Even though the boy lives under his grandfather's care he is not an orphan. His father lives in very straitened circumstances in the little town of Vernon. Practically a hermit, he has only one occupation: the cultivation of a magnificent garden.

This humble and peaceful retirement, however, is the poignant conclusion to a stormy existence. The father, Georges Pontmercy, was for most of his life a soldier in Napoleon's army. He had a heroic career, distinguishing himself in all the Emperor's campaigns. He captured a British ship, was severely wounded, and won the highest military decoration. At the debacle of Waterloo he achieved the peak of valor by capturing the flag of the Lunebourg battalion. The emperor, delighted, shouted, "I'm making you a colonel, a baron, an officer of the Legion of Honor."

The Restoration did not look with favor on one of Napoleon's staunchest partisans, and Pontmercy was retired on half pay. Worse, the reactionary M. Gillenormand detests him, calls him a "bandit" and pressures him into giving up his son under the threat of disinheriting the child. Marius knows that he has a father, but he is completely indifferent to him. From the disapproval his name evokes in his royalist environment, he has gathered that his father is a man to be ashamed of.

He is tragically mistaken. Georges Pontmercy was not only a heroic soldier, he is a loving father. Unable to bear total separation from his child, he periodically comes to Paris and stealthily enters St. Sulpice church to watch his son at mass. His sacrifice has brought him a small consolation. It has won him the friendship of the curate of Vernon, M. l'abbé Mabeuf. This priest is a brother of the churchwarden of St. Sulpice, who has noticed Pontmercy, his scars, and his tears, during his secret visits to the church. On a visit to his brother at Vernon, Mabeuf recognizes Pontmercy; the two brothers pay the colonel a visit and learn his story. This confidence has created a friendship based on mutual admiration.

In 1827, Marius has just turned seventeen. One evening as he comes home his grandfather hands him a letter.

— Marius, says M. Gillenormand, you are to go to Vernon tomorrow.
— Why?
— To see your father.

The colonel is ill and has asked to see his son. Marius is not anxious to go, because he feels that his father has deserted him. Nevertheless he sets out for Vernon the next day. He is too late, however. Georges Pontmercy is dead. Marius is not grief-stricken: he feels only the sadness caused by the death of any stranger. He leaves 48 hours later, taking with him a note, his only legacy from his father.

The note reads, "To my son: The Emperor named me baron on the battlefield of Waterloo. Since the Restoration questions the title I won with my blood, my son will take it and bear it. It goes without saying that he will be worthy of it." On the back, the colonel adds: "At the same battle of Waterloo, a sergeant saved my life. The man is called Thénardier. Lately I believe he has been running an inn in the vicinity of Paris in Chelles or Montfermeil. If my son meets him he will be as helpful as he can."

One day Marius' indifference to his father is shaken by a fortuitous encounter with the churchwarden who knew and admired Georges Pontmercy. A casual conversation brings Marius the momentous revelation of his father's selfless love and the explanation of his apparent neglect. Marius is stunned. The next day he asks his grandfather's permission to leave for three days. What he does will be explained later. On his return he goes straight to the library and asks for the collection of the newspaper *Le Moniteur*. He devours it and everything else he can read concerning the Republic and the Empire. He hardly ever comes home. The old man, judging from his own past, suspects a love affair. It *is* something of the sort. Marius has begun to worship his father.

His emotional upheaval is accompanied by a transformation in his political views. The Revolution which in the past seemed to him one of the darkest chapters of history now impresses him with its battle for civil rights for the masses; the Empire becomes the standard-bearer of democracy in Europe. Likewise, Marius reconsiders his ideas about Napoleon, who ceases to be the monster of Marius' childhood and is transformed into the victorious captain who swept away the last remnants of the Old Regime. One stormy night, overwhelmed by the majesty of the hour, Marius completes his conversion by the fervent exclamation, "Long live the Emperor!" He is now entirely his father's son; he goes to a printer on the Quai des Orfevres and orders visiting cards with the inscription "Baron Marius Pontmercy."

At the same time, Marius draws away from his grandfather. He has always found him uncongenial; now his dislike becomes more specific. He blames the old man for the stupid prejudice that deprived him of a father's love. He becomes distant and cold, and frequently takes short trips away from home. During one of these he goes to look for Thénardier, his father's rescuer. But Thénardier has gone bankrupt, the inn is closed, and its owner has disappeared.

Marius' periodic absences have aroused the curiosity of Mlle. Gillenormand, especially since she scents a juicy scandal. She sends another nephew, Théodule, who has never met his cousin, to find out what Marius is doing. Théodule does not obey, but accidentally finds himself on the same coach and travels with Marius to Vernon.

At Vernon, both young men get off the coach, and Marius buys a beautiful bouquet from a flower vendor. Théodule follows him, expecting to observe a tender rendezvous. Instead he finds a somber tête-à-tête with a tomb. Marius has taken his flowers to a cross on which is inscribed the name, "Colonel Baron Pontmercy."

Théodule does not report what he has learned, but later on, M. Gillenormand investigates Marius' room and discovers Pontmercy's note to his son and the visiting cards. When Marius returns, there is a heated confrontation and bitter words are exchanged, words too bitter to be forgotten. Marius leaves his home forever. With 30 francs in his pocket, his watch, a few clothes, and only vague plans in mind, he sets out for the Latin Quarter.

Commentary

M. Gillenormand is an exceptional human being, as tough for an old man as Gavroche for a gamin, but in quite a different social sphere. Gavroche belongs to the slums of the nineteenth century, the octogenarian to the salons of the eighteenth, and everything about him, from his profanity to his bed hangings, breathes the atmosphere of another age. He has all the virtues of the eighteenth-century upper classes — their elegance, gaiety, and charm — and their worst failing, callous class egoism. M. Gillenormand is not, however, cruel or mean; he is generous with money, kind enough to support two bastards who are not even his, and in fact he and his grandson are very much alike. Unfortunately, their differences grate on particularly sensitive points. Marius' attitude to his fellow man, as we shall see, is more fraternal than patriarchal; he believes it is a virtue to feel strongly, while M. Gillenormand thinks it is in bad taste; and the egoism of youth is as stubborn as the egoism of age.

Even so, no separation would have come between them except for an accident of history. M. Gillenormand has an emotional horror of everything that has to do with the Revolution, and Marius cannot endure to deny a second time a father he has already involuntarily neglected. Like many Frenchmen of their age, Marius and his grandfather suddenly and unhappily find themselves on opposite sides of the widening chasm between the Old Regime and the young Republic.

Book IV

Summary

As his cab takes him without destination through the streets of the Latin Quarter, Marius is hailed by a fellow student, Bossuet. He tells him of his difficulties, but Bossuet though full of goodwill, is unable to help, since he himself is homeless. Another classmate, Courfeyrac, however, comes to the rescue and suggests a room in the Hotel de la Porte Saint Jacques, where he himself lives. With the spontaneity of youth, the two students immediately become friends.

This friendship is to have a profound effect on Marius' intellectual life. Courfeyrac belongs to a radical group, the Friends of the A.B.C. (This is a serious pun; the pronunciation of A.B.C. in French is the same as *abaissé*, the oppressed.) Inevitably, he introduces his new friend and Marius is caught up in a tide of new ideas. Nothing is respected in these wild and irreverent discussions. Not even Napoleon is spared. When the word "crime" is applied to his empire, Marius, usually reserved, explodes in a passionate harangue and eloquently defends Napoleon's career. But his concluding question, "What is greater than Napoleon's conquests?" is squelched by a quiet retort, "To be free."

Marius' new convictions are shaken, but not enough to make him embrace the more radical ideas expounded around him. He suffers from intellectual uncertainty and isolation. Material difficulties aggravate his unhappiness. He has no job and he proudly refuses help from home. To pay his most pressing bills he sells his few possessions and leaves the hotel. These measures are mere palliatives, however.

Commentary

Having reassured us somewhat by explaining the Colonel Pontmercy who appeared out of nowhere in Part Two, and by connecting Marius with him, Hugo now takes us to meet yet a third group of unknown characters, the Friends of A.B.C. However, all these strangers— Gavroche, Marius, Enjolras and his friends, and even M. Mabeuf of Book V—are only apparently introduced at random. All their destinies are converging on one historic moment where they will also become entangled with the fate of Jean Valjean.

Hugo describes each member of the student group with affection and understanding; and the assortment of temperaments he portrays —Enjolras the militant, Combeferre the genial philosopher, Prouvaire the artistic idealist, Feuilly the intelligent workman, Courfeyrac the "good guy," Bahorel the irrepressible, Bossuet (Laigle) and Joly the misfits, and Grantaire the cynic—can be duplicated in student activist groups today. Enjolras is a particularly interesting study, since he is one of the first portrayals in literature of that characteristic nineteenth-century

58

angel of death, the political idealist, the flawless fanatic, the "pure" Marxist or anarchist. What really justifies the attention Hugo devotes to these young men, however, is that they are all going to die.

It will be noted that Marius' political evolution follows that of Hugo himself—from the royalism of his Breton mother to the mildly liberal Bonapartism of his heroic father to a firm devotion to Republican principles.

Books V-VI

Summary

After he exhausts his last resources, Marius finds life cruel. He suffers in body and soul. He has no bread and no fire, and his clothes are shabby. He bears the insolence of shopkeepers, the laughter of working girls, taunts, humiliation. At one point his coat wears out and he has to accept cast-offs from his friends. But poverty is a crucible that destroys the weak and tempers the soul of the strong. Marius proves himself firm in the face of adversity and slowly manages to create a bearable existence. He earns a modest living as a literary factotum, writing prospectuses, annotating editions, translating newspapers, and compiling biographies. He lives in a monkish room in the Gorbeau House—the same building once occupied by Cosette and Jean Valjean. He eats frugally and never drinks wine.

Marius is at peace with the world, for his austere way of life is in keeping with his ascetic temperament. He lives like a hermit, avoiding even his own family. Unaware that his grandfather secretly regrets his behavior, Marius never goes to see him. He has given up his circle of student friends, cultivating only Courfeyrac and the old churchwarden, M. Mabeuf, who knew his father. Solitude suits him. It allows him to abandon himself to a life of contemplation that provides him with moments of veritable ecstasy. Marius is in the process of becoming a visionary.

Consequently, he is completely indifferent to any woman whom chance puts in his path. For a year now on his regular walks in the Luxembourg Gardens he has frequently encountered an old man with a pleasant countenance and the modest air of a Quaker, accompanied by a little girl thirteen or fourteen years old. Marius is favorably impressed by the "father," but finds the "daughter" of no interest.

Then, for no particular reason, he interrupts his visits to the park and does not see the unknown couple for six months. A momentous event has taken place during his absence. The ugly duckling has become a swan, and the little girl has become a ravishing young woman. So striking is the transformation that Marius has to observe her attentively to make sure it is the same person. Yet this new beauty does not at first dispel his indifference.

Later, however, their eyes meet, and Marius' whole life changes. In this one glance he finds a depth, a mystery, a charm, that intoxicates him. Suddenly he is ashamed of his old clothes, and the next day he appears at the Luxembourg Gardens resplendent in his new suit. Resolute, proud of his appearance, he walks toward the bench on which the young girl sits with her father. As he draws near, however, his emotions overwhelm him and he has to turn back. Once again, he attempts the difficult adventure and this time manages to pass the bench, but not without acute embarrassment. Then he sits down at a respectable distance, and a quarter of an hour later, leaves in a trance. That night he forgets to have supper.

For two weeks he continues to stroll past the bench, nothing more. Then a cataclysmic event takes place. M. Leblanc, as Marius has decided to call the old man on account of his white hair, decides to take his daughter for a walk and they stroll in front of Marius. Ineffable moment: he is dazzled by the pensive and gentle look she gives him. Her beauty reminds him of an angel, of the heroines of Petrarch and Dante. He is floating on clouds and painfully aware of the dust on his boots.

When he is not in the Luxembourg Gardens, Marius is, like all lovers, afflicted with a touch of madness. He is alternately thoughtful and uproariously gay. He embraces strangers. He makes remarks out of context. A whole month goes by, and he never misses a day at the Luxembourg. But restrained by timidity and caution, he does not again parade in front of the bench. With apparent casualness, he stands near a statue or tree, exhibiting himself to the young girl and sending her tender looks. She, in turn, manages to return his glances with meaningful looks of her own while talking to her father.

A few miscalculations, however, put an end to Marius' discreet courtship. One day M. Leblanc changes benches and Marius follows. Then he comes without his daughter and Marius, by leaving immediately, makes it obvious that he has been interested in her. He has picked up a handkerchief initialed "U" which he thinks she has dropped, and he has christened her "Ursula" in his private thoughts; and finally he tries to follow "Ursula" to her home. This last mistake is irreparable. He asks the doorman about her; the doorman tells "M. Leblanc" of the inquiry; and a week later, the old man and the girl have disappeared without a trace.

Commentary

The description of how Marius lives on 700 francs a year is a passage straight out of Balzac's type of realism, and it has all the mathematical fascination of a well-worked-out equation. Marius however is not, and never will be, one of Les Misérables. Unlike Gavroche and Jean Valjean, he does not expect suffering from life; he chooses it, and thereby adds a halo of glory to the rosy glow of youth that already surrounds him. Marius' natural environment is not the slums but the Luxembourg Gardens; he belongs to the world of the wealthy, the leisured, the fortunate, and no matter how shabby his pants, he always wears them like a gentleman.

In Marius, Victor Hugo is painting his own portrait as a young man — the same political views, appearance, and youthful struggles — but it is a fair portrait, unretouched. Hugo recognizes what is admirable in Marius — his integrity, his generosity, his imaginative fervor, his genuine idealism, and his capacity for feeling; but he does not extol them beyond measure, and he does not fail to point out Marius' faults: the unconscious cruelty with which he makes his grandfather suffer and the humor as well as the beauty of his grand passion. To fall in love forever, without a word spoken, on the strength of a single glance, is sublime — but it is also incredibly stupid, and so, in some respects, is Marius.

Book VII

Summary

In this book, Hugo introduces us to a number of Paris criminals; in particular, to Babet, Claquesous, Gueulemer, and Montparnasse, who governed the Paris underworld from 1830 to 1835. Gueulemer is a stupid strong man, thief, and murderer. Babet is a former tooth-puller who has also sold plaster busts and shown freaks at fairs; he is thin, supple, and absolutely without morals. Claquesous is a ventriloquist behind a mask; Montparnasse is young, good-looking, and ruthless.

Thanks to their various skills and their close relations, they have practically a monopoly of crime in the department of the Seine. With them work a number of other minor criminals, of whom Boulatruelle — the ex-convict we already met at Montfermeil — is one.

Commentary

In an epic description which perhaps may owe something to Dante's *Inferno*, Hugo now introduces us to the world that lies even below that of Les Misérables — the lowest depths of the criminal poor. The study of criminal life fascinated many nineteenth-century authors. Balzac has several novels in which the master criminal Vautrin appears; Dickens has his Fagin; and a number of popular French authors like Eugene Sué made adventures in the underworld their stock in trade.

Like most nineteenth-century reformers, Hugo is an environmentalist; that is, he believes that man is, on balance, naturally inclined to good, and that the evil in him is a product of his treatment by society. Crime, he says at the end of Chapter 2, will vanish with enlightenment. However, Hugo the writer is wiser than Hugo the theoretician; and in Book VIII he will invalidate everything he has said in Book VII by showing us a man whose criminality is not the result of his environment, and who is villainous as naturally as he breathes.

Book VIII

Summary

Summer passes, then fall. Winter comes. Neither M. Leblanc nor the young girl have reappeared at the Luxembourg Gardens. Marius is overwhelmed by an immense despair and a profound listlessness. One day he goes to a dance hall with the vague hope of encountering his lost love. The inevitable disappointment leaves him more depressed than ever, weary of people, obsessed with his anguish. Another day he has a strange encounter. He meets a man with long white hair who much resembles M. Leblanc but who is dressed as a workingman. Perplexed, Marius decides to investigate the mystery. But the passerby disappears before he can follow him.

On February 2, Marius witnesses a depressing scene that seems to be in keeping with his somber mood. He is passed by two girls, emaciated, ragged, barefoot. They are running, and from a word or two he overhears, Marius gathers that they are fleeing from the police. In her haste one of them drops an envelope and Marius picks it up. Before he can call them, they are out of earshot. He puts the envelope in his pocket and forgets it.

Undressing in the evening, he comes upon the envelope and examines it. In it he finds four letters addressed to prominent people, containing pleas for money and signed with the names of four different petitioners. But certain signs indicate the same author wrote all four. The handwriting, the paper, a peculiar tobacco odor, the spelling mistakes, are all identical. However, none of the letters bears an address, so Marius dismisses the mystery from his mind.

The next day as he is working, someone knocks on his door, and a young girl enters. She is no more than fifteen, but misery has already made her haggard. She gives Marius a letter from her father, Jondrette, asking for money. The face of the girl is not absolutely unknown to Marius. He seems to remember that he has seen her somewhere before. She calls Marius by name. He could not doubt that she means him, but who is this girl? How does she know his name? Even though Marius has been living in the house for some time, he has had, as we have said, very few occasions to observe his squalid neighborhood. His mind has been elsewhere, and where the mind is, there also are the eyes.

The letter from Jondrette is in the same handwriting as those in the packet Marius had picked up the day before. While Marius ponders the coincidence, the young girl frolics boldly around the room, sings, examines Marius' possessions, looks in the mirror. Finally, she tells him how handsome he is and accompanies her compliment with a meaningful look. Ignoring the hint, Marius hands her the package she has lost. Her manner changes; she is incredibly grateful and pours out to him a tale of constant hunger, suffering, hallucinations, and suicidal thoughts. Touched, Marius gives her his last five francs, and she thanks him in a flood of revolting but pathetic slang.

When she has left, Marius reflects on the depths of misery and degradation to which society allows a human being to sink. As he muses, he notices a triangular hole near the ceiling in the wall that divides his room from the Jondrettes'. Compassion is a spur to his curiosity, and he climbs on a dresser to observe his wretched neighbors. What he sees is a den: "abject, dirty, fetid, infected, dark, sordid." At a table sits a fairly old man who resembles both a shady businessman and a bird of prey. He is in the process of writing another begging letter and ranting against the injustices of life. Near the chimney sits his wife, a virago of indeterminate age. A listless, wan girl – the second fugitive of the day before – is resting on an old mattress.

Marius is about to leave his observation post when the older daughter walks in. She announces the imminent arrival of a potential benefactor, whom she has accosted during one of his frequent visits to St. Jacques Church. The father springs into action and orders various actions taken to worsen the squalid appearance of the room. He tells his wife to put out the fire, the younger daughter to break the seat of a chair, the eldest to break a window. The room is suitably devastated when the philanthropist walks in.

His entrance causes Marius an incredible shock. It is "M. Leblanc" and he is accompanied by his daughter, who is as lovely as ever. Meanwhile Jondrette, posing for this occasion as Fabantou, an actor down on his luck, launches into an emotional lament. As he details his real and pretended misfortunes, he stares hard at the visitor, as if trying to remember a familiar face. The latter, moved by the evident misery of the family, hands Jondrette five francs and a package of clothing, and promises to return at 6 P.M. with money for his rent.

Marius is an indifferent eyewitness to the whole scene. His only interest is the young girl. A moment after she leaves he runs after her. He reaches the street just in time to see her depart in a cab. He hails another, but since he has no money on him, the driver refuses to take him. In despair he turns back to his room. As he is about to climb the stairs he notices Jondrette in deep conversation with a man of menacing appearance. It is one of the most notorious hoodlums in the neighborhood.

As he mournfully enters his room, he is followed by Jondrette's older daughter. Marius is piqued at her, since by giving her his last five francs he has lost the opportunity to follow his elusive sweetheart. His resentment is particularly unfair, for the young girl's visit is motivated only by compassion and gratitude. She has noticed Marius' depressed air and is offering her help. Marius asks her to discover M. Leblanc's address. The young girl agrees, although with a sadness that Marius does not notice.

Alone again, Marius plunges into a poignant reverie. He is disturbed by Jondrette's excited comments about M. Leblanc and his daughter. Hoping to obtain some vital information, he jumps back on his observation post. He learns that Jondrette has recognized in M. Leblanc an old acquaintance, although obviously not a friend, since his wife greets the news with venomous rage. Jondrette, however, is pleased by the discovery, since he thinks he will be able to extort vast amounts of money from this old man. He has evidently hatched a sinister plot, judging from the ominous instructions to make up a fire which he gives his wife. Then he leaves to further perfect his trap.

Marius quickly resolves to checkmate whatever mischief Jondrette is planning. After a brief hesitation, he quietly sets out for the police station. On the way he overhears a conversation between two disreputable characters which confirms his suspicion that a net is closing around M. Leblanc. At the police station he is met by an inspector of impressive height with a piercing gaze. The interrogation is incisive and to the point. After his briefing, the policeman requests Marius' passkey and tells him to return home immediately. He is to observe the execution of the plot and, when the trap is about to be sprung, to shoot in the air as a signal to the police. As Marius leaves, as an afterthought the inspector gives him his name: Javert.

A little later Courfeyrac and Bossuet, Marius' student friends, run into him on the street. But he is unaware of their presence, as he is intently following Jondrette. The latter, not suspecting he is being followed, enters a hardware store and comes out with a chisel. Then he disappears into the shop of a man who hires out carriages. Marius gives up his spying to return home before the house is locked up for the night. On his way to his room he glimpses four men lurking in one of the empty apartments. But fearing to be seen, he refrains from investigating.

In his room he hears Jondrette returning, then giving various instructions and sending the two girls into the street as lookouts. He climbs back on the dresser and peers through the hole. The room is illuminated by an eerie red glow produced by a sizable stove full of burning coal, with a chisel in the middle of the fire. In a corner he notices two piles, one of old pieces of iron, the other of rope, which upon close examination turns out to be a ladder. Jondrette places two chairs at a table, lights his pipe, and waits.

The church bells strike six and, as agreed, M. Leblanc comes in. His first act is to hand Jondrette more money for his rent and his immediate needs. While he thanks him profusely, Jondrette manages to give his wife a disquieting order, "Send away the cab." Jondrette and Leblanc sit down and Jondrette holds his attention with talk while, unobtrusively, a man enters the room behind the old man's back.

Warned by a kind of instinct, M. Leblanc turns and perceives the new arrival. Jondrette explains him away as a neighbor, and the same explanation covers the arrival of three more sinister figures.

Then he explodes his bombshell: "Do you have your wallet? I'll settle for a thousand crowns." Leblanc, alarmed by this blackmail, stands up with his back to the wall and stares at him suspiciously. Like a cat playing with a mouse, Jondrette turns to more innocent conversation. Suddenly three armed men walk in and Jondrette ceases his pretense. In a thunderous voice he says to Leblanc: "Do you recognize me?" Leblanc, pale but far from intimidated, retreats behind the table and steels himself for action, declaring he does not know Jondrette. Jondrette cries, "I am not Fabantou. I am not Jondrette. I am Thénardier."

The revelation leaves Leblanc unmoved, but not Marius. He is stunned, for he finds himself confronted by an impossible dilemma: save Thénardier and sacrifice an innocent man or call the police and betray his father's trust. He has no time to deliberate, for events move rapidly. Thénardier savors his triumph with hysterical glee, pouring out a flood of reproaches, threats and boasts; Leblanc calmly replies that Thénardier is mistaken, he is not a rich man, and they have never met before. But, as Thénardier turns around to speak to one of his accomplices, the prisoner springs to the window and nearly escapes. It takes three men to bring him back and, after a titanic struggle, he is tied to one of the beds.

Thénardier then sends the gang out and tries another tactic. Shrewdly he points out to Leblanc that in spite of his danger he has never called for help. Can it be that he is afraid of the police? With elaborate casualness, he moves to give the old man a view of the red-hot chisel; and proposes a bargain—200,000 francs for Leblanc's freedom. With the smile of a "grand inquisitor," he invites Leblanc to write a letter to his daughter asking her to come to him; she will serve as a hostage to insure that Leblanc pays the money. Silently, Leblanc writes, signs his name, and gives his address. Convulsively, Thénardier grasps the letter and sends his wife out with it to get the girl. They wait in a long and dreadful silence until Mme. Thénardier returns in a fury. They have been duped: Leblanc has given them a false address.

While she has been gone, however, Leblanc has used a miniature saw hidden in a hollow coin in his pocket to cut his bonds, and he is free except for one leg. He leaps to his feet and defies them, seizing the red-hot chisel in one hand. "You will never make me write what I do not want to write," he cries, and disdainfully puts the chisel to his own arm, watching it burn without a quiver; then he flings the chisel out of the window. The gang falls upon him, and Thénardier, deciding there is nothing left to do but kill him, takes a knife from the drawer.

Marius is in an agony of indecision, but he can no longer delay — it is Leblanc or Thénardier. Suddenly he has an inspiration; During her visit that morning. Thénardier's daughter had written on a piece of paper to show her education, "The cops are here." Marius grabs it and throws it through the crack in the wall. The gang reacts just as he has hoped. They rush to the window in a disorderly panic.

But their escape is foiled by Javert's dramatic appearance. His authority reduces them to a flock of sheep. Thénardier alone among the men offers some resistance; he aims a pistol at Javert, but the gun misfires. In bestial fury, his wife hurls a rock at the inspector, who simply ducks. The police put handcuffs on the gang, and the three masked men are identified: they are Gueulemer, Babet, and Claquesous, three of the four bandit chiefs of Paris. His prisoners secured, Javert looks around for the victim, but in the confusion he has vanished. "The devil!" says Javert. "He must have been the best catch of the lot."

The next day Gavroche goes to see his parents, impertinent and carefree as usual. He finds the door to their apartment closed, and an old lady whom he has just insulted informs him that his whole family is in jail. He greets the news with a casual, "Ah!" and with a song on his lips returns to the wintry street.

Commentary

Hugo has an instinct for innocence; with sexually mature women characters he is sometimes uneasy as a writer, but with the girl-woman his touch is unerring. Confronted by the elder Jondrette girl, with her torn bodice, her harsh voice, and her abominable argot, he looks beyond the surface and shows us hunger, grief, modesty, shame, courage, a longing for affection and even for respectability. Through her and her sister, he gives us a vivid illustration of his thesis that "le misère de l'enfant" is the most appalling of all.

However, this is not his only purpose in introducing them. Where his plot is concerned, he is taking up again, on a deeper, more human level, the Cinderella theme treated at the beginning of Book II. These two creatures in rags were once the spoiled darlings, Eponine and Azelma; the "ugly sisters" have become ugly indeed, and when Cosette appears before her erstwhile tormentors in silk cloak and velvet hat she takes a crushing revenge, though she is quite unaware of it. The irony of their meeting is mingled with tragedy: Eponine and Azelma were, at Montfermeil, and are still, only children and no more deserve their present fate than Cosette deserved her ill-treatment at the inn. All three have been equally victims of Thénardier.

Thénardier is the most enigmatic of the characters in *Les Misérables*, and during most of Book VIII he has us, like Marius, standing on tiptoe with an eye to the peephole to see what he will do next.

"Evil" is not an exact adjective for Thénardier, nor is "criminal," though he is both. "Perverse" describes him more precisely; he is incurably perverse, and his perversity ruins his own life as well as that of others. He is not without intelligence and education, and when we saw him last he was proprietor of his own inn, with 1,550 francs of debts, of which Jean Valjean had just relieved him by buying Cosette. There was no reason why he could not have led a reasonably prosperous life. However, even then, far from being content with his luck, he followed Jean Valjean to extort more funds and was nearly killed by the goose that laid the golden egg. As Jondrette, he behaves in exactly the same way: in the hope of one extra franc of charity, he destroys two francs' worth of chair, window, and fire—not to speak of injuring Azelma; and when he is assured of regular help from Valjean-Leblanc, he throws it away in the vain hope of wringing his whole fortune from the ex-convict. Never satisfied with what he has, each failure leaves him poorer and more embittered.

The most dangerous thing about him, however, is the power of his fantasy to obscure the truth. When he tells Valjean in Part Two how fond he is of Cosette, how much he will miss her, we have to think twice to reestablish the real facts; and when he rails against society in the garret, he almost convinces us that it is the world and not himself who is responsible for all his troubles. In his presence, even Jean Valjean's image becomes distorted, and from behind the facade of the philanthropist emerges again the figure of the convict, complete with prison ruses, secret escape coin, and superhuman strength. As for Marius, Thénardier's old lie on the field of Waterloo has him so confused he does not know whether or how to come to Jean Valjean's aid. This, however, is the least of Marius' unwitting sins against Cosette's foster-father; by notifying the police, he has put Javert back on Jean Valjean's track again.

68

The "recognition scene," in which one character turns out to be other than he appears, has been a common device for achieving dramatic surprise since the Greeks; with the superb nonchalance of a great writer, Hugo tops off Part Three with a quintuple recognition scene. We have, of course, suspected for a long time that the Jondrettes are really the Thénardiers, but the confirmation is satisfying; and there is even some genuine surprise in our realization that Gavroche is the baby we heard wailing, neglected, at the inn when Jean Valjean came to find Cosette.

Les Misérables is, like a drama, divided into five sections, and its inner structure parallels that of a drama as well. The first act is a highly suspenseful exposition; the second one—as all too often on the stage, unfortunately, drags; the fourth and fifth are reserved for climax and denouement. At the end of the third act, most dramatists like to provide a subclimax, only slightly less powerful than that at the end of the fourth. This is the pattern of most of Shakespeare's tragedies, and it is the pattern Hugo follows here, bringing together, at almost exactly the midpoint of the book, all his key characters in a dramatic confrontation. The confrontation is, however, inconclusive for all of them and we are left in the expectation of a more decisive encounter later on.

PART FOUR: ST. DENIS

Book I

Summary

Hugo interrupts his narrative to give a historical sketch of the background and beginning of the July Monarchy, which was established by the Revolution of 1830. After Napoleon fell, he was followed by the two Bourbon kings Louis XVIII and Charles X, who reigned from 1814 to 1830. This period was known as the Restoration, and it was marked by a great longing for peace, a great weariness after the heroic days of the Republic and the Empire. However, the people were not so passive that they did not demand the retention of the freedoms won by the Revolution. These the Bourbons grudgingly granted, but they acted in bad faith. When, in 1830, Charles X felt himself sufficiently strong to do so, he attempted to abrogate his concessions. It was a grievous miscalculation. The nation rebelled and the king was deposed and exiled.

Unfortunately, the revolution was captured by opportunists. Pleading the need for peace and order, they restored the monarchy. Their choice fell upon Louis Philippe, a representative of the Orléans, the younger branch of the royal family. While the move was designed to protect the privileges of the bourgeoisie against the people, it was, however, not a complete retrogression. It confirmed certain democratic gains, though it stopped short of giving the people full sovereignty.

The hybrid character of the revolution is illustrated by the king it selected. Louis Philippe, nicknamed Egalité (equality), was, in spite of his royal ancestry, sympathetic to liberal ideas. Unlike his predecessors, he had been on the side of the people during the events of 1789 and had even participated actively in them. During his reign, he not only respected the prerogatives of his subjects but actively concerned himself with their welfare. He frequently intervened, for instance, in favor of political prisoners. Nevertheless the beginning of the king's reign was not auspicious. On the one hand, Louis Philippe was attacked by the conservatives who could not resign themselves to the loss of their privileges. On the other, he was not acceptable to the republicans, for whom any monarchy, however enlightened, was a betrayal of their ideal.

Behind the visible resistance, a quieter, more pervasive opposition was growing to the whole concept of monarchy and government by the propertied classes. Socialist thinkers were critically reexamining the whole structure of society and undermining its old foundations. Thus, two years after the overthrow of the Bourbons, radical ideas, international tensions, and popular discontent already were forming heavy clouds on the political horizon. In April, 1832, the situation has become explosive. The Saint Antoine section, the most volatile in Paris, is openly planning revolution. Discussion groups examine the legitimacy of the government; militants gird for action. Extremists manufacture bullets, and the police report that a veritable arsenal is being collected.

Inevitably, the revolutionary fever spreads. Secret societies, increasingly defiant, proliferate and spread like a cancer through the body politic. First Paris is infected, then the provinces. Marius' old friends take an active part in the seditious activities. A.B.C. leader Enjolras dispatches his lieutenants to various groups of students and workers to organize them for the revolution. Enjolras reserves for himself the group known as La Cougourde. On his way to meet them, he mulls over the situation and optimistically foresees a glorious uprising leading to the ultimate emancipation of the people.

A slight disappointment, however, mars his grandiose vision. In passing he decides to inspect the work of his friend Grantaire, the cynic who has only become a revolutionary out of admiration for

Enjolras. Instead of haranguing the workers whose revolutionary fervor he was supposed to excite, Grantaire is engaged in an absorbing game of dominoes with them.

Commentary

Hugo's long discussion of the political evolution of France from 1815 to 1832 is primarily a republican political document. It is intended to hearten French republicans by reminding them that, despite many checks, republicanism has steadily gained ground in the nineteenth century and to encourage his readers to oppose the Empire, which subverted the Republic of 1848. And as usual, Hugo, the political exile, is a very effective propagandist. The book, however, also serves as an introduction to the revolt of 1832, which will involve most of the characters we have met so far in *Les Misérables;* and the activity of Enjolras and his group foreshadows this important plot development.

Books II-III

Summary

After Thénardier's arrest, Marius immediately leaves his room and moves in with Courfeyrac, who receives him with the simple hospitality of a true friend. Marius has two reasons for the move. First, the viciousness he has witnessed makes him loathe the Gorbeau tenement; and second, he does not want to testify against Thénardier. As the months go by, Marius sinks back into a state of depression. The happiness that he has glimpsed has again vanished. This time the loss of his beloved seems irreparable; he cannot find even the most tenuous link with her. He is disturbed, also, by her "father's" equivocal behavior. The old gentleman's refusal to call for help, his quiet escape, are highly suspicious.

Material difficulties compound his misery. Once again Marius is plagued by poverty. Too discouraged to work, he has quit his job and abandons himself to a dangerous reverie that increases his lethargy. Absorbed by the vision of his lost love, he contemplates impassively his inexorable disintegration. Unfit for practical activities, he is only capable of absurd and romantic gestures. In a notebook he writes ethereal love letters destined never to be read. Because the Thénardiers called the girl he loves "the Lark," her Montfermeil nickname, he makes regular pilgrimages to an isolated area called "the Field of the Lark."

Hugo now takes us to visit Javert, who is not happy. Thénardier's prisoner, who would probably have been an interesting prize for the police, has vanished, and two of the gangsters — Montparnasse and Claquesous — have slipped between his fingers too. The latter's escape is particularly humiliating, since it was engineered in the police vehicle itself. The rest of the gang are also far from inactive. One of its imprisoned members, Brujon, is engaging in suspicious maneuvers. He dispatches three messages to confederates on the outside. One day a guard catches him in the act of writing a letter, but the letter disappears before the guard can seize it.

The next day a note wrapped in a ball of bread reaches Babet, one of the leaders of the Patron-Minette gang. From Babet, it goes to Eponine, who inspects the house in the Rue Plumet. As an answer Eponine returns a biscuit, which in the mysterious code of the underworld means "nothing doing." This abortive criminal plot has totally unexpected consequences. It acquaints Eponine with Cosette's whereabouts, and this piece of information soon changes the latter's destiny and that of her lover Marius.

Marius' old friend Mabeuf, the churchwarden, has been suffering a decline which resembles that of Marius himself. His major source of income, his book *Flora of Cauteretz,* is not selling at all. His experiments on indigo are a failure. His breakfast is reduced to two eggs, and often it is his only meal. One peaceful evening, Mabeuf sees a strange apparition. Exhausted from his day's work on his indigo experiments, he rests in his garden with a book in his hands while he anxiously studies his magnificent rhododendron, threatened by drought. He would like to water his flowers, but he doesn't even have the strength to unhook the chain from the well. Unexpectedly, he has a bizarre visitor, a ragged, undernourished girl who proceeds to water his whole garden for him. As a reward she asks for Marius' address and disappears as soon as she has learned it.

A few days later Marius, restless and unable to work, has gone on his usual pilgrimage to the Field of the Lark. Sadly he is thinking of "her," and his sadness is aggravated by self-reproach. His reverie is broken by Eponine's appearance. She addresses him in a babbling mixture of delight, naive questions, explanations, and compassion. The girl is obviously and pathetically in love with him. At last, since he shows no interest in her as a person, she tells him that she knows Cosette's address. Marius is ecstatic and, blinded by love, ignores the tragic effect his happiness has on Eponine. He is concerned only with his sweetheart's safety and makes Eponine promise she will not reveal the address to her father. She reminds him that he has promised her a reward, and he gives her five francs. Somberly she drops it with the comment, "I don't want your money."

In the suburb of Saint Germain is located an unobtrusive little house, the former love nest of an eighteenth-century magistrate. Among its features, there is a secret exit onto another street which allowed the amorous but prudent judge to visit his mistress without arousing suspicion. In October, 1829, Jean Valjean has rented the long-vacant house under the name of Fauchelevent, reopened the secret passageway, and installed Cosette and an old servant, Toussaint, in this new residence. In spite of his happiness in the convent he decided after much thought to leave Little Picpus. He felt that he owed it to Cosette to provide her with a normal life in spite of the dangers this would present to his personal safety. As an added precaution, he has rented two other old apartments in Paris as potential retreats; one is that to which Marius previously traced Cosette.

Except for a few luxuries for Cosette the pair lives modestly and above all discreetly. They take walks in the Luxembourg Gardens, go to mass, give generously to the beggars at the door of the church, and visit the poor and sick. Valjean serves in the National Guard, an obligation that he welcomes, since it gives him an aura of respectability. Buoyed by Cosette's companionship, Valjean enjoys the simplicity of his new life.

The young girl is happy too. Her garden is a world of endless discoveries. In Valjean she finds an interesting friend who shares with her the fruits of his wide readings; he is her universe, both father and mother to her, and she fusses over his cold room and his Spartan diet. She hardly remembers her past and has completely forgotten her mother, for Valjean never mentions her. A mysterious instinct warns her that her origins are a subject better left unmentioned.

But unsuspected dangers threaten their tranquility. Cosette is about to enter adolescence, an age of temptations and longings for which she is completely unprepared. Her ignorance, carefully protected by the convent, only enhances the intensity of desires that she experiences without understanding. Valjean, a bachelor quite unused to women, is unable to help her.

One day Cosette suddenly realizes that she is very pretty. What her mirror has hinted is confirmed by the comments of a passerby and the observations of the old servant Toussaint. With inexpressible satisfaction she realizes that her skin is a satiny white, her hair lustrous and beautiful, her blue eyes splendid. Valjean, however, is dismayed by her beauty; he is dimly aware that any change threatens his happiness and that another may some day steal Cosette from him. Nevertheless, he does not prevent her from ordering an elegant new wardrobe nor from parading her gracefulness in public.

It is at this time that Cosette meets Marius in the park. Subconsciously she notes his good looks, his air of intelligence, his gentleness. Then their eyes meet, and his glance produces the same effect on her as hers on him. Love, in turn, unleashes a multitude of incomprehensible and contradictory emotions in her. At first she is angry at Marius' apparent indifference, then she boldly approaches him in the park. Later melancholy overtakes her, and she suffers the traditional sleeplessness, agitation, and fever. Still her love remains distant, "a mute contemplation, the deification of a stranger."

Valjean, too, is aware of Marius. Unlike Cosette, he views him as a threat and lays traps for him. He changes benches, drops his handkerchief, comes alone to the park. When Marius' reactions betray his interest in Cosette, Valjean grows hateful and ferocious and watches him like "a hound looking at a thief." When Marius makes the mistake of questioning the doorman, Valjean moves to the Rue Plumet without leaving a trace. Cosette accepts her fate without complaint; indeed, she has no vocabulary to express any of the feelings she now experiences. But she falls into a profound despondency which becomes deeper as the separation from Marius lengthens. Valjean notices her sadness and is heartbroken, but he does not know how to cure it. Tragically, Cosette and her foster father come to hurt each other deeply in spite of their mutual love.

One morning a somber incident deepens their gloom. As is their wont, they are taking a walk to enjoy the glory of sunrise. For a moment they are consoled by the serenity of the hour. Then a harsh noise disturbs their peace: it is the forerunner of a dreary spectacle, a long convoy of prisoners. A mass of convicts, sinister and dehumanized, are being transported to the galleys on seven tumbrils escorted by rows of equally sinister guards. The scene is one of degradation, brutality, misery, and filth. Valjean is petrified by this vision from his past, and the sensitive Cosette is equally frightened.

Commentary

In these two books, through many rapid changes of scene, Hugo is maneuvering all his characters toward a crisis and preparing also for the denouement of the love story in the next part. Five of his characters — Marius, M. Mabeut, Eponine, Cosette, and Jean Valjean — are undergoing a period of sorrow and doubt. For Marius, this period of inactivity and passivity is a prelude to a violent reaction which will once more reunite him with the realities of life and decide his destiny for good or ill. The despair of Eponine and M. Mabeuf, which has more valid causes, will also produce dramatic decisions and drastic consequences. Cosette's unhappiness deepens and strengthens her feeling for Marius, and by learning to bear sorrow with patience, she matures from girl into woman. As for Jean Valjean, his anger and grief are a normal response to the foreknowledge that yet one more sacrifice will soon be demanded of him, and this the greatest sacrifice of all.

Skillfully, Hugo uses Eponine not only to win our sympathy but to further plot and character development. A waif just out of prison, she is a figure pathetic enough to cause any bourgeois to subscribe promptly to public education and child welfare, but she also serves as a link between the criminals, Marius, M. Mabeuf, and Cosette and Jean. Finally, her love for Marius, which Marius ignores, points up the egoism of his blind devotion to his unknown love — a devotion that has already made him idle and neglectful of his own future. Marius, young hero though he is, is far from perfect — perfection is a privilege that will ultimately be reserved for the elderly Jean Valjean.

Jean Valjean, however, is right to fear him, just because he is young and in love and because nature is therefore on his side. Good parenthood always ends in a painful separation because it is a parent's function to prepare the child to leave home and become a good parent in his turn. Jean Valjean has courageously taken the first step in this direction already by taking Cosette out of the convent and allowing her the liberty to choose what her future life will be. Nature, in making her beautiful, takes the next step; Marius is simply the inevitable conclusion of a normal series of developments.

The garden of the Rue Plumet is the image of Cosette's spirit — innocent, beautiful, and wild — and Jean Valjean has until now been privileged to share its springtime joy. Cosette's true companion, however, is on his way, and once he arrives Jean Valjean will again be shut out in the shadows of his past, as the scene with the convicts at the Barrière du Maine implies.

Summary

During the period when both he and Cosette are unhappy, Valjean makes his historic visit to the Thénardiers. When he comes back the next day with an ugly wound on his arm that keeps him in bed with a fever for a month, Cosette cares for him with angelic devotion. Their renewed intimacy fills Jean Valjean with delight and Cosette, for her part, finds a distraction in her new responsibilities and satisfaction in her father's improvement. Then April comes, and spring is an infallible balm for a young and delicate soul.

One evening Gavroche, tired of a two-day fast, decides to go on a food-hunting expedition. In investigating an apple bin in a garden, he overhears a conversation between M. Mabeuf and his old servant, Mother Plutarch. She is reminding him there is no food in the larder, and no one will give them credit because they owe money everywhere.

This doleful exchange compels Gavroche to abandon his designs on the apple bin and to think about this poverty even greater than his own. He is distracted from his meditations by a puzzling and alarming sight. An old gentleman is strolling toward him, unaware that he is being followed by Montparnasse, Gavroche's underworld friend. Before the urchin has a chance to intervene, the thief pounces on his intended victim. But he has underestimated his opponent. To his immense humiliation, he is beaten to the ground and held as if by a vise. Without letting go, the passerby gives him a sobering lecture, a preview of his potential fate as a convict in a living hell. Then he hands Montparnasse his purse and quietly resumes his walk. Montparnasse is stunned — a fatal paralysis. Gavroche sneaks up on him like a cat, steals his purse, and drops it in Mabeuf's garden. Mabeuf cannot believe his eyes as the purse falls from the sky before him.

Cosette continues to recover from her heartbreak. She seems to have forgotten Marius, and begins to take an interest in a handsome young officer who struts daily in front of her garden, and who is really Théodule, a grandnephew of M. Gillenormand. Cosette has more resiliency than Marius, who seems to be trapped in his dream of love.

One evening during one of Valjean's periodic absences Cosette has a disquieting experience. She hears what sounds like a man's footsteps in the garden. The next evening she hears the same footsteps and then sees a shadow, a terrifying shadow topped by a man's hat. By the time she turns around, the shadow has disappeared. When Valjean comes back she tells him of her alarms. He, deeply preoccupied, spends the next three nights in the garden. The third night he calls her down to show her the explanation of the mystery: the shadow of a near-by chimney which might easily be mistaken for that of a man.

A few days later, however, a new incident occurs. Cosette is sitting, in the melancholy of nightfall, on a bench near the garden gate. Slowly she gets up, strolls through the garden, and returns to her seat. On the spot she just vacated on the bench there now lies a stone. This time she is genuinely frightened, all the more so since her father has gone on one of his nocturnal walks. Feverishly she runs inside, barricades the house, and spends a restless night.

In the morning, the sun dissipates her apprehension and she dis-misses the incident as a nightmare. But when she returns to the garden she finds that the stone is real. Fright gives way to curiosity and she examines the stone more closely. Under it she discovers a notebook containing a kind of prose poem celebrating the splendors of love. Cosette intuitively recognizes the author of the letter and simultane-ously the truth about her own emotions. Her love for Marius had be-come an ember, but never died. Now it blazes up again to a bright new flame. At that moment the handsome lieutenant passes by and Cosette finds him supremely unpleasing.

During her evening stroll in the garden she has the sudden feeling of a presence behind her. She turns her head and sees Marius, gaunt and spectral. She is overwhelmed by his humble, poignant declaration of love and reciprocates with her own. They kiss and are transported out of this world. After a long moment of silent ecstasy, they proceed to mutual confessions of their deepest feelings. Two souls melt into one. Only after their reunion is complete do they ask each other their names.

Commentary

In character portrayal, Hugo prefers to reveal personality through simple feeling and direct action, and seldom indulges in the lengthy and complex psychological analysis of such later nineteenth-century writers as Marcel Proust. Jean Valjean's lecture to Montparnasse on laziness is one of his rare excursions into abstract psychology, and it is a remarkable one. Hugo, like the medieval church, recognizes that sloth, as opposed to occasional holiday idleness, is a mortal sin. Man's only lasting happiness lies in work, and the refusal to work leads to the total destruction of the personality. The passage is interesting, too, because it is one of the rare occasions on which Hugo gives us an insight into Jean Valjean's thinking. Indeed, Valjean cannot properly be said to think; rather, he turns things over and over in his mind until a conclusion evolves, and the conclusion is usually remarkably wise.

The reunion of Marius and Cosette is unquestionably one of the most touching scenes in literature despite, or perhaps because of, the touch of humor with which Hugo introduces it. While Marius is dying for love, Cosette has almost forgotten him — but not for long. With superb suspense, Hugo brings him closer and closer to her, as a sound of footsteps, a shadow, a letter, and finally Marius himself. Nor does Hugo spare any of the resources of his art to enhance the drama of their meeting and mutual avowals. The essence of his poetry has gone into Marius' love letter; the garden in springtime offers the perfect setting for first love; and Cosette's poignant cry, "O ma mère!" seems to set the seal of heaven itself on their union.

Book VI

Summary

After 1823, the Thénardiers had two more sons whom the mother hated and managed to get rid of in a very efficient way. A friend, Magnon — the woman who had persuaded M. Gillenormand to support them — lost her two illegitimate sons in an epidemic. In order to conserve her income she needed replacements; and these Mme. Thénardier provided, to their mutual convenience. The children benefit temporarily from the exchange. Magnon treats them kindly because of the money they represent. But she is implicated in the Thénardier affair and arrested. The children are left to wander alone in the streets of Paris.

One cold spring day of 1832 Gavroche is standing in front of the window of a barbershop. He is waiting for a propitious moment to steal a cake of soap which he hopes to sell in the suburbs. While Gavroche is preparing his bit of larceny, two little boys enter the shop to ask for help and are harshly rebuffed. Touched by their tears, the urchin takes them royally in tow, and leads them in the rain to a baker's, where he manages to extract a small coin from his pocket and buy them and himself a piece of bread. On the way he has passed a girl in rags and given her the woman's shawl he wears for warmth over his shoulders.

After their casual meal, the boys and Gavroche resume their walk until they meet Montparnasse, wearing dark glasses. Their conversation is brief, inhibited by the arrival of a policeman. At last the waifs reach the Place de la Bastille, where Gavroche has a unique domicile, the inside of the statue of an elephant which has been neglected by the authorities. Gavroche shows the children how to get in by climbing one of the elephant's legs and entering through a hole in his belly. The older boy follows Gavroche and the younger one, more timid, is carried up the ladder.

Once inside, Gavroche closes the hole and lights a candle. He comforts the frightened children with a mixture of gruffness and solicitude. Then he shows them his bedroom, a kind of cage made of metal trellis to protect him against the army of rats who share his quarters. At the thought of rats, the children begin to cry again, so he cheers them by painting a picture of all the delights he has in store for them — shows, swimming, and mischief. After he blows out the candle, the older boy falls asleep; but his brother is still terrified of the rats, which are excited by the presence of human flesh. Gavroche gives him a reassuring hand and soon all three are asleep, oblivious to the harsh world outside.

At dawn, Gavroche is awakened by Montparnasse. The latter needs his help and Gavroche follows him without a question. They go to La Force prison to help Brujon, Thénardier, and Gueulemer, who are planing an escape.

With a providential nail, Brujon has that night managed to make a hole in a chimney, and with Gueulemer he has climbed to the roof. Then they lower themselves with a rope they have brought along. A few minutes later they join Montparnasse and Babet, who has escaped some time before.

Now it is Thénardier's turn. He drugs his guard with doped wine and with a metal pin breaks his chains. But he is not out of danger yet. His friends have left him a piece of rope too short to reach the ground and he must seek a different avenue of escape. With the mysterious instinct of despair he finds his way to the roof of a building outside the prison walls. But his prodigious effort is futile: he is too weak and the ground is too far below for him to climb down the facade of the building. Suddenly he notices his confederates below debating whether or not they should give him up and leave. Afraid to speak, he signals by throwing them his hitherto useless piece of rope.

At the instigation of the others, Gavroche with careless courage climbs a rickety pipe to the roof and carries his father another, longer rope. No sooner has Thénardier reached freedom than he and the rest of the gang begin to discuss a subject that had earlier been debated in prison: a possible coup against Valjean, Rue Plumet. Then they disband, and as Thénardier departs Babet says to him, "Did you notice the boy who brought you the rope? I think he was your son." "Bah," says Thénardier, "do you think so?" and the subject is forgotten.

Commentary

Gavroche provides us with an excellent example of Hugo's technique in character development. Hugo introduces him to us first simply as a member of a species, the Paris gamin, and gives us to understand that he possesses the courage, impertinence, and ingenuity of his kind, but he says little about Gavroche as an individual. He remains for us only the silhouette of a boy with his hands in his pockets who passes us in the street whistling. In Part Four, however, Hugo begins to fill in this outline with precise details of speech and behavior. Gavroche wears a woman's shawl and gives it away on a cold day; he steals soap and buys little boys bread; he helps criminals escape, but steals from them to help poor old men; and he lives in an elephant. He becomes a contradictory, colorful, lively personality, totally unlike anyone but himself.

But this realistic character study also carries social and spiritual overtones. The picture of Gavroche aiding his little brothers and his father, quite unaware of their relationship to him, underlines a social tragedy — the disintegration of the family under the pressures of poverty. And his comment on his two little lost wards, "All the same, If I had children, I would take better care of them that that," is a masterpiece of dramatic and social irony. This waif of the streets, to whom society has never given any material help or moral training, has a far deeper compassion for childhood, and a far sharper sense of his moral responsibility toward the unprotected, than an average adult French citizen like the barber.

Gavroche is also, however, a spiritual symbol. Without comment and without sentimentality, Hugo through him unfolds to us the natural simple Christianity of the gospels. With cheerful patience Gavroche makes fun of his own troubles, but he is keenly sensitive to the sufferings of others. Hungry, he feeds M. Mabeuf; cold, he clothes the shivering girl he meets on the street. Whatever he has, he shares with the poor;

he suffers little children to come unto him; he is kind to those who despitefully use him; and he even manages, against all odds, to honor his father and mother. Unlike Jean Valjean, who has to struggle with himself to achieve good, Gavroche comes by it naturally—even gaily; but neither is inferior to the other. Both are types of the Christian spirit triumphing over adversity.

Book VII

Summary

In Book VII, Hugo digresses to defend his use of slang. Slang, he concedes, is a horrible, pestilential language. But the novelist no more than the scientist can exclude any phenomenon from his field of inquiry, however unpalatable. Slang in its purest sense is the weapon of the have-nots against the establishment. Hence its preservation is of sociological interest. Furthermore, the study of slang is a means of curing the misfortune that has engendered it.

The spirit of slang, admittedly, is evil. "It is a dressing room in which the language disguises itself because it has some evil deed to do." But let us be merciful to it and to those who speak it, for human existence seems to indicate that none of us is free of guilt. The universal unhappiness of mankind seems to suggest that all of us are carrying the burden of divine retribution.

Slang, besides its ethical interest, has a literary value. It is the poetry of evil. It is a kind of geological formation whose numerous layers contain the fossils of various foreign words. It coins evocative expressions, it creates metaphors, it freely reshapes the language. Slang is dynamic, ever changing. It is the mirror of a soul, for a close study of it reveals the psychology of the underworld.

Commentary

Victor Hugo is not the only nineteenth-century novelist to immortalize slang in his pages. Zola, Balzac, Dickens—all frequently use slang and dialect in their novels to add authenticity and realism to the speech of their characters. This was, however, still considered an innovation, and not always a desirable one. Many people in the nineteenth century were still horrified to find such "vulgar" language in a work of art, so Book VII is really a document setting forth Hugo's views on a lively literary controversy.

In the sixteenth century, the poets of the French *Pléiade* introduced a number of new dialectal and technical words into the French literary vocabulary in order to make the French language more flexible and more representative of the wider world of the Renaissance. The classical writers of the seventeenth century, however, adopted the doctrine that true art dealt only with the noble and the beautiful, and expressed it in universal and general terms. In accordance with this view, they purified literary language of most of its colorful "special" terminology, and writers of the eighteenth century narrowed the vocabulary yet further to the point of monotony. The early Romantics, in their revolt against classical strictures on art, rebelled against restrictions on vocabulary too.

Hugo was one of the leaders of this movement, and almost single-handed brought about a complete revolution in the concept of "poetic" vocabulary. "I have put the red bonnet of the Revolution on the old dictionary," he said, and in language he used any word that pleased him — exotic, learned, archaic, technical, or vulgar — as long as it conveyed his meaning more effectively. Here, he defends slang because it seems to him a colorful expression of the poetry of the people, the authentic voice of their courage and their defiant despair. Today, thanks to Hugo and others like him, there are no censored words in literature, and writers have a freer artistic vocabulary than ever before.

Books VIII-IX

Summary

During the month of May, Marius visits Cosette every evening in the garden and they live an idyll of chaste adoration. They exchange trivial observations charged with emotion. They laugh lightheartedly. Marius pays Cosette admiring compliments and Cosette confesses her love. They simply enjoy the plenitude of existence. Valjean is completely unaware of Marius' visits. The young man comes when the old man has retired. Cosette is extremely amenable, never objecting to Valjean's plans and suggestions.

Unfortunately, complications are about to disturb the perfect simplicity of the couple's lives. One day Marius meets Eponine. Egoistic like all lovers, he has completely forgotten her. He finds the meeting awkward and she, for different reasons, is embarrassed too. They exchange only a few words. The next day Marius sees Eponine again. He avoids her, but she follows him to the Rue Plumet and hides in a dark corner outside the gate, lost in unhappy thoughts.

Soon after, six men meet in front of the house. It is Thénardier's gang, planning to carry out the robbery of Valjean's house which they had first discussed in prison. Eponine abruptly leaves her hiding place and, as a diversionary tactic, she embraces her father and greets his accomplices. When cajolery proves ineffective, she turns to defiance. Alone, this frail creature challenges the entire gang, and even when threatened with death, declares she will rouse the whole neighborhood at the first hostile move. Her firmness alarms the thieves, who reluctantly abandon their project and scatter in the night.

But misfortune, checked in one direction, attacks in another. While Eponine stands guard outside, Cosette gives Marius a piece of news that is the equivalent of a death sentence. Jean Valjean, alarmed by a sense that he is watched, has decided to take her to England. Confronted by this catastrophe, Marius makes a desperate resolution. He will go to see his grandfather and appeal to his pity. Had he seen M. Gillenormand recently, Marius might be more hopeful, for the old man has been undergoing a transformation. His self-righteousness has given place to sorrow and he thinks about Marius with more affection and less bitterness. The sudden realization that their separation may be permanent has cut him to the heart.

Marius' unexpected visit provokes an immense longing for reconciliation which, alas, the old man cannot express. He greets Marius with his usual severity and his grandson responds with constraint. Angry at himself for his inept behavior and at Marius for his obtuseness, he vehemently refuses him permission to marry. His answer is a long, bitter, sarcastic diatribe climaxed by an irrevocable: "Never!"

In his distress Marius cries out: "Father!" and this word proves the open sesame to the old man's heart. Abruptly he is transfigured, embraces Marius, seats him in an armchair, and listens with the deepest sympathy to his love story. But no amount of understanding can quite bridge the gap between the libertine eighteenth-century grandfather and the romantic nineteenth-century grandson. To the grandfather, Marius' love affair is only a youthful escapade, and he suggests that he make Cosette his mistress. Marius is deeply offended by this suggestion and leaves indignantly. M. Gillenormand, thunderstruck, believes that this time the rift is irreparable, and he sinks into an agony of grief that transcends tears.

Meanwhile Valjean, sitting on a slope in the Champ de Mars, is pondering the new dangers that are threatening his safety. Several times he has seen Thénardier roaming the neighborhood. The political unrest has made the police extremely vigilant, and he is afraid of becoming an accidental victim of their investigations. Finally, a fresh and enigmatic inscription on his garden wall adds to his preoccupation; "16 Rue de la Verrerie" is simply Marius' address, which he has written on the wall so that Cosette will know where to find him, but to Valjean it is a sinister sign. As he ponders, a note from the ever-watchful Eponine falls in front of him. It contains one significant word: "Move." This is the last straw; he decides to obey the note's warning.

Marius leaves his grandfather's house in a state of absolute despair. His rational faculties have abandoned him and, like a robot, he walks the streets for hours. The next day, after a restless night, he resumes his wanderings; but without really knowing why, he takes Javert's pistols with him. Obsessed by his pain and the thought of his last rendezvous with Cosette, he is only dimly aware of the rumblings of the uprising.

At nine o'clock in the evening he arrives at the garden to say good-bye to his love forever. But he is to be denied this last consolation. Jean Valjean has already taken Cosette away, and Marius falls on the bench like a man who has received a mortal blow. Then, through the trees, a dim figure whispers a message. "Monsieur Marius, your friends are waiting for you at the barricade in the Rue de la Chanvrerie."

M. Mabeuf is also in despair. He has been sinking to the last stages of destitution. Gavroche's purse has done him no good, since in his naive honesty he has taken it to the police. His indigo experiment has been a total failure. The plates of his books have been sold to a pawnbroker. He cannot even afford his starvation diet, and he has been forced to the supreme sacrifice of selling his rare books. The promised help of a cabinet member proves a disappointment. At last he is reduced to disposing of his most precious volume, a book by Diogenes Laertius, to buy medicine for his sick servant. When he hears shots in the direction of the Arsenal, he takes his hat and goes out.

Commentary

Skillfully, Hugo here begins to draw all his characters together towards the climax of the revolution. Not all will be on the same side: Javert, for instance, will be there as a police officer, and Valjean as an angel of mercy; and even among the revolutionaries motivations will differ widely. Marius will fling himself into it because he has lost the only thing in life he cares about; M. Mabeuf because he simply cannot afford to go on living; and even among the Friends of the A.B.C. the emotions are not entirely political. This only adds to the realism of the events, however, and to the credibility of their actions.

In French, a climax is known as a *noeud,* or knot, and the denouement is the untying of that knot. Hugo in the last two parts has given us an excellent example of the aptness of the term. At the beginning of Part Three, the lives of most of the characters of *Les Misérables* were single threads scattered all over Paris and its nearby villages. Thénardier with his colonel at Waterloo, Cosette and Marius, Enjolras and Gavroche, appeared to have nothing whatever to do with one another. Gradually Hugo has tied these threads together, knotting Marius and Cosette together by Eponine, Valjean and Javert by Thénardier, Gavroche and M. Gillenormand through the little lost boys. Now he throws a final loop about them, and, like the fine dramatist he is, draws them all gently toward a common center.

Book X

Summary

An insurrection is a sudden conflagration that spreads without pattern, fed by every disappointment, from disillusioned idealism to vile resentment. But for all its destructiveness it is not *ipso facto* reprehensible. Insurrections are wrong when they are an attempt of the minority to frustrate the general will. When they serve the aims of democracy they become sublime. "Insurrection," says Hugo, "is sometimes resurrection." According to this distinction, and in spite of appearances, the uprising of 1832 was legitimate. Furthermore, it gave rise to such acts of heroism that even its critics speak of it with respect.

When a situation is sufficiently combustible, it takes but a spark to light the fires of revolt. In 1832 the occasion is provided by the burial of General Lamarque, hero of the Empire and later a political leader of the left. On June 5, the funeral procession crosses Paris followed by a seditious crowd, armed and prepared for action. The dimensions of the popular unrest worries the government. It has posted 24,000 soldiers in Paris and 30,000 in the suburbs. Near Austerlitz Bridge, someone—no one knows who—fires three shots, and the storm breaks. A vast and lethal improvisation changes Paris into an armed camp. Flags are unfurled, weapons requisitioned, arms factories pillaged. In less than an hour 27 barricades go up in the Halles district alone. The center of Paris, transformed into an impregnable citadel, becomes the heart of the insurrection.

The authorities retaliate by mobilizing all their forces, including the National Guard. But the military leaders hesitate to give the order to attack. A dreadful feeling of suspense hangs over the city, for the population senses that it is not a few disgruntled acts of protest, but a large-scale uprising, that is in prospect.

Commentary

Hugo's account of the revolt of 1832 is taken from his own memories of the uprising as it appeared from the passage du Saumon, where he himself was stationed; from the experiences a friend, Jules Resseguier, recounted to him; and from a book on the revolt, *Le Cloitre Saint-Mery*, by Ray-Dusseuil. In this book there appear a real gamin and a real student who play the roles and suffer the fates of Gavroche and Enjolras in the novel, but as we have seen, Hugo has made both full-fledged characters in his book. As is natural with such sources, the whole account breathes the realism and immediacy of eyewitness testimony.

The chapters on the revolt form a counterpart to the book on Waterloo, and Hugo uses the same mingled irony and pathos, poetry and action, to arouse our emotions. Chapter 3 is an excellent example of his technique. He has already compared the coming rebellion to the natural phenomenon of a gathering storm, and he describes the progression of the revolt here in terms of the same metaphor. He describes first the "rumors" among the populace—the first faint rumblings of thunder on the horizon; then the massing, aligning, and remingling of the mob behind the cortege that, watched by the hidden eyes of fearful women and children, resemble the rapid shifting and massing of the thunderclouds; and finally the shots that, like the first lightning bolt, open the sky for the deluge. Interspersed with these images are precise and convincing details of conversation, visual impressions, and incidents, and two observations that underline the historic irony and grandeur of the moment: the Duke of Reichstadt, Napoleon's heir, is dying at the same moment the crowds are considering him as their next king; and Lafayette, hero of the American War of Independence, serves as rallying-point for this new insurrection in the cause of freedom.

86

Books XI-XV

Summary

Gavroche decides to go to war. Without much ado he steals an old pistol from a junk shop and swaggers down the street to the accompaniment of a song from his vast repertoire. Unfortunately, the pistol does not have a hammer. Gavroche, however, is above this or any other disappointment. If his gun is less than lethal, his monolog becomes inflammatory. If he cannot afford a piece of cake, he gets immense pleasure from tearing up billboards or insulting a bourgeois. He has a choice reply to the indignant remarks of three old crones. He hurls a stone through the windows of the barber shop whose proprietor treated his two proteges so callously. Life is a continual adventure.

Now he is about to embark on his supreme adventure. At the Saint Jean market he meets Enjolras' group and decides to join forces with them. As they march, new recruits, workers, artists, students, swell their ranks. In the Rue Lesdiguières, they enlist a most unlikely firebrand, the gentle M. Mabeuf. His mind in a trance, but his posture militant, he follows the tumultuous crowd. Near the Rue des Billettes a tall graying man joins them.

As he passes in front of his own house, Courfeyrac takes advantage of the situation to grab some money and a suitcase. On the way out, he has a few words with a young worker who is waiting for Marius. The worker follows him.

Adjoining the Halles, in a decrepit neighborhood of labyrinthine and somber streets, we find the Rue de la Chanvrerie. One end is blocked by a row of tall houses in which the ancient Corinth wine shop is located. The street would be a dead end if it were not for a narrow passage, the Rue Mondétour, which leads out of it. Inexplicably, since the food is poor, the wine atrocious, and the decor rudimentary, the Corinth has become the hangout of the Friends of the A.B.C.

On June 5, two inseparable friends, Laigle (Bossuet) and Joly, are having lunch at the Corinth. They are joined by Grantaire, who takes his nourishment in liquid form. Indifferent to the trouble brewing outside, he is earnestly trying to do justice to two bottles of wine. Alcohol proves to be a melancholy muse and he rambles on wryly about the imperfections of man and God. "I hate mankind," he avers. Books are a proliferation of trivia. Women sacrifice their virtue to greed. Brutal self-interest governs international relations. God is an unimaginative creator who must forever correct his work through revolutions, great men, and assassinations. The universe is a shabby place and everything is going wrong.

After his sweeping condemnation, Grantaire attacks his second bottle. He is about to launch into another diatribe when a nine-year-old urchin brings Laigle a cryptic message from Enjolras: "A.B.C." It is his invitation to Lamarque's funeral. But the three companions prefer wine to politics and at two in the afternoon their table is strewn with empty bottles. Grantaire especially is drinking with a vengeance. He has replaced wine with a potent mixture of brandy, stout, and absinthe. Suddenly a tumult interrupts the drunken conversation. Through the window Bossuet spots Enjolras and his armed men looking for a place to erect a barricade. He suggests the space in front of the Corinth. *In vino veritas.* The location is strategically perfect.

In a flash, the houses and streets are stripped. Soon a rampart higher than a man blocks the street. Everyone participates feverishly except Grantaire, who merely looks on and perorates incoherently. Enjolras, irritated, dismisses him with a cutting remark. But Grantaire refuses to leave, promises to sacrifice his life, and collapses in a drunken stupor. Under Enjolras, Combeferre, and Courfeyrac's energetic direction the fortifications are rapidly completed. To the original barricade has been added another one, closing one side of the Rue Mondétour.

The barricide is now manned by about 50 defenders. They are a motley aggregation, including every age, all kinds of faces, an indescribable combination of arms and costumes. Among these disparate strangers reigns a spirit of perfect fraternity. Gavroche is the life of the party. A perpetual motion machine, he is everywhere. He encourages a worker, goads a student, stings everybody. Only one shadow mars his enthusiasm: he is unhappy with his useless gun.

At dusk the barricade is finished. The men are ready, the sentinels posted, and in the deepening silence the rebels wait calmly. So remarkable is their *sang-froid* that the younger men recite love poems. Gavroche alone is preoccupied. The man from the Rue les Billettes has a disturbing familiarity. Finally, dumbfounded, the young boy finds the key to the mystery. When Enjolras approaches him to send him on a reconnaissance mission, Gavroche gives him a stunning piece of information: "Do you see the tall man?" "Well?" "He's a spy."

Enjolras immediately interrogates the suspect, who haughtily admits his double identity. His papers confirm his confession. It is Javert, and his orders are to spy on the insurrectionists. He is tied up and condemned to be shot just before the capture of the barricade. Gavroche, exultant, goes out to reconnoiter, but not before laying claim to Javert's gun: "I'm leaving you the musician, but I want the clarinet."

Revolutions, while they breed heroism, also bring out the dark side of man. Thus it happens that a certain Le Cabuc conceives the idea of posting a sniper on top of a tall building. But the fearful tenants have locked the door. Le Cabuc tries fruitlessly to break it down. Attracted by the noise, the porter sticks his head out the window. When he refuses to unlock the door, Le Cabuc shoots him. Without a moment's hesitation Enjolras grabs the killer by the shoulder and forces him to kneel, gives him a few minutes to prepare himself for death, and executes him. To a silent audience he delivers a funeral oration in which he expresses horror for his necessary act and hopes for a future where the reign of love will replace that of death.

Meanwhile Marius, overwhelmed by despair, interprets the voice that has called him to join his friends at the barricade as an order from destiny. Driven by a death wish, he makes his way through the crowd, eludes the troops, and finds himself in a no-man's land, an immense, dark vacuum. Only the agonized voice of Saint Merry's tocsin disturbs the silence.

In the total darkness Marius spots the red light of a torch and goes toward it. He reaches the Rue de la Chanvrerie barricade, but before he steps inside, he stops to examine the flux of contradictory emotions that surge in his heart. First he is proud to imitate his father's bravery; then he shudders at the ignoble nature of the conflict in which he is about to participate. But his despair, his duty to his friends, show him no alternative. Finally an illuminating thought sweeps away his hesitations. Wars are not judged by the identity of the opponents, whether they are foreigners or compatriots. All wars are internecine, since we are all brothers. Wars find their justification in their ideal. Consequently, Marius' cause is just, since he is about to fight for freedom.

At ten in the evening the long wait of the revolutionists at the barricade ends. Gavroche sings a warning and regains the barricade, out of breath after his patrol. The rebels take up their combat positions. A moment later they hear the growing sound of steady, unhurried footsteps. A disembodied voice asks: "Who goes there?" At the reply:

"French Revolution," a heavy volley shakes the barricade and knocks down the flag. One man volunteers to put it up again: Mabeuf. Like a specter he climbs the barricade, to the awe of the spectators. With a cry of "Long live the Republic!" he falls back, cut down by a bullet.

While the insurrectionists pay Mabeuf their last respects, the army attacks and manages to climb over the rampart. Gavroche and Courfeyrac are in mortal danger. In the nick of time Gavroche's assailant receives a bullet in the forehead and Courfeyrac's is hit in the chest. Marius has joined the fight in a spectacular manner. Immediately a soldier takes aim at him, and his death seems inevitable, but a young worker puts his hand on the barrel of the soldier's gun and saves Marius' life at the expense of his own.

The other insurgents are being pushed back by the army swarming over the barricade. Most of them have taken refuge inside the wine shop. A sudden thundering threat imposes a cease-fire. Marius is standing on top of the wall with a torch in his hand, ready to put it to a powder keg. "Go away," he cries, "or I'll blow up the barricade." The soldiers who are scrambling on the barricade, impressed by his earnestness, retreat in disorderly haste.

The joy of the besieged is dampened by a sobering discovery. Jean Prouvaire, one of their bravest comrades, has been made prisoner. Combeferre suggests that Jean be exchanged for Javert. The plan proves futile, however: no sooner has Combeferre stopped speaking than a vibrant voice cries, "Long live France! Long live the future!" followed by the report of a rifle. Jean Prouvaire has been executed.

While everybody's attention is engaged by the main barricade, Marius decides to inspect the small one, which is completely deserted. He is about to return to his comrades when a weak voice calls, "Monsieur Marius!" He is startled because he recognizes the voice: it is the same one which that morning had called him to the barricades. Shocked, Marius discovers Eponine crawling toward him. She has a wound in her hand, for she was the worker who deflected the bullet aimed at him. But she also has a mortal wound in her body, for she took the full impact of the shot. Marius takes her head in his lap and listens to her pathetic confession, her happiness at finding him at the supreme moment, her jealousy that made her lure him to the barricade in the hope of his death, her change of heart that saved his life at the last moment. She also tells him that she is Gavroche's sister and that she has a letter for Marius.

After Eponine dies, Marius gently kisses her on the forehead as he has promised. He enters the inn to open the letter she has given him, for he feels the impropriety of reading it beside her body. It is a note from Cosette informing him of her departure from the Rue Plumet. He is momentarily elated by this proof of love, but only momentarily, since the possibility of their marriage remains as remote as ever. He resigns himself once more to death and makes his last dispositions. He writes a note to Cosette to be delivered by Gavroche. This way he will kill two birds with one stone: assure his sweetheart of his love and save the urchin. Then he leaves instructions to have his body delivered to his grandfather.

Gavroche, afraid he will miss the great encounter, is reluctant to accept the errand. He undertakes it only because he intends to return immediately rather than wait until the next day as Marius has suggested.

On June 4, just before the insurrection, Valjean moves to his retreat in the Rue de l'Homme Armé. So deep is his alarm that he overrides Cosette's unprecedented objections. Once installed in his new quarters, he feels reassured, for the Rue de l'Homme Armé is located in an obscure and neglected neighborhood. Cosette, on the other hand, is deeply distraught. She spends the day in her room and appears only for dinner. Then, pleading a headache, she leaves the table.

Cosette's chagrin does not disturb Valjean's tranquility. He is in an optimistic mood and has radiant visions of renewed happiness in England. A heartbreaking discovery shatters his dream. On the table there is a mirror which reflects Cosette's blotter and rights its inverted message: Cosette's letter to Marius. At first, Valjean refuses to accept the evidence, but the message remains inexorably in the mirror.

Now he who has never yielded to temptation feels himself weakening, for the supreme test is the loss of one's beloved. The voice of the devil is particularly insistent, well-nigh irresistible, when love is concentrated in one person, when one single being is the object of an affection usually divided among brother, mother, and wife, and when a stranger threatens to destroy that love. Jean Valjean, in the tragic despair of old age, succumbs to hatred and goes to sit on the doorstep and contemplate the depth of his misfortune.

There Gavroche finds him, and, touched as always by the radiance of childhood, Valjean engages him in conversation. He hands him some money and indulgently allows him to break a few streetlights. Then with a little lie he persuades the urchin to hand him Marius' letter and tell him where Marius is. Gavroche disappears into the night, breaking another streetlight by way of goodbye.

Gripped by an overwhelming emotion, Valjean hurries to his room and reads Marius' words: "I am dying. When you read this my soul will be near you." His first reaction is an ugly feeling of triumph, of exultation at fate's convenient solution to his problem. But the mood quickly subsides and an hour later he makes his way to the Halles in the uniform of the National Guard.

Returning to his post, Gavroche is singing a love song with unquenchable good humor. On the way he spots a drunken man sleeping it off in a cart, and he requisitions the vehicle for the revolution. He deposits its occupant on the pavement and leaves him a receipt in the name of the Republic. Unfortunately his triumphal march is also very noisy and attracts the attention of a sergeant of the National Guard. Gavroche favors him with a few choice insults and shoves the cart into his stomach. The soldier falls, his gun goes off, and his comrades, rushing to his rescue, fire wildly in all directions for the next 15 minutes. From a safe distance, Gavroche enjoys his handiwork, then goes on his way with a disrespectful gesture and a farewell song.

Commentary

In this section, the revolt claims its first lives. The deaths of M. Mabeuf and Eponine, however, have their splendor as well as their tragedy. M. Mabeuf has deliberately committed suicide rather than endure the shameful humiliation of starving to death, and his gesture has its reward. After a lifetime in which he has vainly sought the respect and admiration of his fellow citizens by study and science, his last moments in the incongruous role of freedom fighter win him a lasting glory. As for Eponine, she too has in a sense committed suicide by turning on herself the bullet meant for Marius. For her as for M. Mabeuf, the future held nothing but shame and suffering, and her brief instants in Marius' arms are probably the only moments of real happiness she has experienced since childhood.

The deaths of Le Cabuc and the porter, however, cast a more somber light on this scene of violence. War brings out the baser as well as the nobler instincts in man, and the innocent suffer. Enjolras' prompt punishment of the criminal and his touching vision of a more perfect world temper somewhat the horror of this motiveless assassination, and the fact that he is willing to execute one of his own men also serves to underline the absolute purity and rectitude of his ideals, but Hugo never lets us forget the lolling head of the innocent corpse in the background.

In fact the scene at the barricades by night is another of the masterly tableaux in black and white that gives *Les Misérables* much of its power over our imaginations. This time, however, the light comes not from the moon but from a flaring torch that illuminates a splash of scarlet in the background. When Marius arrives he sees dimly beyond the gathered insurgents "a sort of spectator or witness who seemed to him unusually attentive. It was the porter killed by Le Cabuc. . . . A long trail of blood which had flowed from that head ran down in a scarlet network from the window to the level of the second floor, where it stopped."

Once again Jean Valjean makes one of his extraordinary decisions, expressed in actions rather than words or thoughts. But the meaning of that decision is, like his decision in Part Two to go to Arras, ambiguous until the last moment, and ambiguous perhaps even to Valjean himself.

His hatred for Marius is real, and so is his delight at the thought that the revolution may eliminate him from Cosette's life. Jean Valjean is not a milksop, and his conversion by the bishop did not, as we have seen, guarantee him the exercise of perfect and effortless goodness for the rest of his life. There is, and always has been, evil in him — as there is in any man — and if he falls prey to it, the unusual strength and cunning that have made him a remarkably good man will make him an appallingly evil one. Marius was not wrong to mistrust him after the scene in Thénardier's garret; his unusual potentialities will always make him a frightening as well as an impressive personality.

Valjean puts on his National Guard uniform and leaves the house. Why? To join the Guard and make sure Marius dies or simply to make his way safely through the streets? Hugo does not tell us, and perhaps Valjean himself does not know. But, as at M.-sur-M., if his conception of what he is about to do is not clear, his instinctive knowledge of what he is *not* about to do does not fail him.

PART FIVE: JEAN VALJEAN

Book I, Chapters 1-10

Summary

The barricade, on the Rue de la Chanvrerie, far from yielding, has been fortified. The wounded have been bandaged, lint prepared, and new bullets made. On the other hand, food has run out and the defenders are beginning to suffer from hunger. Since there is no food, Enjolras forbids the men to drink.

Dawn is coming, and the insurgents, unwilling or unable to sleep, are chatting. The conversation does not reflect their desperate position. Its tone is optimistic: humorous, literary, or philosophical. This mood, however, is shattered by Enjolras, who brings back from his reconnaissance the disastrous news that a large force has been assigned to take the barricade and that the populace as a whole has not joined the uprising. Optimism gives way to despair, but not to defeatism. The insurrectionists swear to fight to the last man.

But Enjolras refuses to accept such a sacrifice. He brings out four National Guard uniforms that he has laid aside for just such an emergency. They will provide a safe passage out for four men. No one, of course, wants to go, but Combeferre points out the uselessness of heroism and calls on the family men to leave and carry on the fight by protecting young girls from prostitution and children from hunger. In a sublime competition of generosity, each married man then pleads with the others to go. Finally five are taken out of the ranks—but there are only four uniforms. At this moment, a fifth uniform drops on top of the others. It is that of Jean Valjean, who has just entered the barricade. He is welcomed as a friend and a savior.

At this supreme moment, Enjolras is immune to fear; instead, he is carried away by a utopian vision of the future and predicts the reign of equality, justice, and liberty—the enlightenment to be brought about by education, the harmony to be born from their sacrifice. Marius does not share Enjolras' exaltation. He is still numb with grief and the world has for him the unreality of a dream. Even the arrival of Cosette's "father" makes little impression on him.

The drama of the night has driven Javert from everyone's mind. After the departure of the five married men Enjolras suddenly remembers him, gives him a glass of water, and ties him more comfortably on the table. The action attracts Valjean's attention, and he recognizes his old enemy. Javert turns his head and without surprise recognizes Valjean.

At daybreak, the attack begins with the thundering rattle of an approaching piece of artillery. A cannon appears and Enjolras yells: "Fire!" The rain of bullets misses its target and the cannon moves forward; but its first shot falls harmlessly on the pile of debris that forms the outer section of the barricade. Simultaneously with the shell, Gavroche lands in the barricade with a cheerful, "Present!" His arrival is hailed with delight by his comrades but with dismay by Marius, who had hoped to spare him this ordeal. Gavroche, however, knows no fear and with insouciant courage requests a gun.

The cannoneers rectify their aim and ricochet grapeshot off the wall. This time they are more successful: two insurgents are killed, three wounded. Enjolras carefully points his gun at the sergeant commanding the battery, squeezes the trigger, and kills him. But he feels no sense of triumph, only grief at the death of his enemy. The cannoneers, however, prepare to fire again. A mattress is needed to absorb the shots. Valjean spots one protecting a window and, with prodigious marksmanship, shoots at the ropes holding it and cuts it down. Unfortunately it falls outside the barricade. Coolly, Valjean steps out in range of enemy fire and retrieves it.

At dawn of this same day, Cosette wakes after a sweet dream of Marius. Believing he has received her letter and will soon come to see her, she rises and dresses quickly, and goes to her window to watch for Marius. Finding she cannot see the street from there, she cries for a short time, then hears the sound of cannons. Cosette does not recognize the sound and becomes absorbed in watching a family of martins nesting just below her window.

Commentary

Jean Valjean, ex-convict and wanted man, is out of place among the forces of "law and order." Arriving at the wine shop, he takes off his uniform and jumps the barricade.

Once inside, Valjean instantly belongs there. He is the right man, arrived at the right time with the right gift. And it is perfectly fitting that he, who has been one of Les Misérables and who has spent much of his life helping them privately and secretly, should at the moment of reckoning act openly on their behalf. Neither Javert nor Marius are truly among the "misérables," however, and his attitude toward both of them remains ambiguous.

The short chapter concerning Cosette is a welcome relief from the agonies and excitement of the insurrection.

Summary

The assailants of the barricade keep up their fire, hoping to provoke a riposte, exhaust the defenders, and then charge. But Enjolras does not fall into the trap. Impatient and curious, the army dispatches an observer to a roof overlooking the barricade. Valjean hits him squarely in the helmet and does the same to his successor. Bossuet asks why he did not kill him; Valjean does not answer.

Another cannon is brought up, and the attack suddenly becomes destructive. Aimed at the top of the barricade, it shatters the paving stone, and the flying fragments force the insurgents to withdraw. The wall, left undefended, is now ripe for an assault. Enjolras sees the danger and orders the artillerymen put out of commission. A well-aimed salvo kills two-thirds of them, but it is a Pyrrhic victory. Too many bullets have been wasted.

Gavroche casually decides to remedy the situation. Like a housewife doing her shopping, he grabs a basket, jumps outside the protective wall, and empties into his basket the cartridge-bags of the dead soldiers lying in the street. He is temporarily protected by a thick curtain of smoke, but his boldness leads him too close to the enemy line; the soldiers notice him and begin to shoot. Undeterred he continues his harvest; in fact he stands up straight and sings a little ditty. As the bullets rain around him, he jumps, darts, disappears, reappears, plays a frightening game with death. Finally his magic fails him, and he falls wounded. Gavroche, however, will not die without a swan song. He manages to sit up and sing another stanza of his mocking song. Then another bullet, this time fatal, cuts him down.

As Gavroche falls on his face and stops moving, two waifs are wandering hand in hand through the deserted Luxembourg Gardens. They are the two brothers whom, unknown to himself, Gavroche took under his wing. Today, June 6, 1832, the gardens are an earthly paradise, a riot of flowers, birds, and insects, bathed in sunshine. But to this festive tableau the two little boys add a somber accent, for they are hungry.

Their solitude is disturbed by a prosperous bourgeois accompanied by his six-year-old son, who is listlessly eating a brioche. The father is giving his offspring such edifying instruction as the maxim "The wise man is happy with little." When his son tires of his brioche he advises him to feed it to the swans, to teach him compassion. With laudable thrift he tries to attract their attention before the brioche sinks. Then the noise of the insurrection grows louder and the father, as prudent as he is wise, takes his son home. As soon as the pair is out of sight, the older Thénardier boy fights the swans for the soggy brioche and shares it with his brother. It is their meal, both food and drink.

Back at the barricade, Combeferre and Marius run out to retrieve the basket and carry back the child's body. Gavroche's cartridges are distributed to the men, 15 apiece. Valjean refuses his share. Paradoxically, as the situation grows more hopeless, the occupants of the barricade become calmer. They seem to ignore the imminence of death. The tranquility, however, only masks an apocalyptic mood. The barricade fighters experience the ultimate emotions, anticipate the future, sink to unplumbed depths of feeling, touch eternity.

At noon Enjolras orders paving blocks brought up to the windows of the wine shop and has axes readied to cut down the stairs and bars to barricade the door. He has, however, one last job before they retreat: to execute Javert. Valjean offers, as he puts it, "to blow his brains out." His offer is readily accepted. As the bugles sound outside he cocks his pistol. But to the last Javert retains his calm bravado and observes sarcastically: "You are no better off than I am."

As the besieged rush to the defense of the barricade, Valjean leads his prisoner outside and over the side wall, out of sight of the rest. Javert calmly invites Valjean to take his revenge, but instead the ex-convict cuts his bonds. "You are free," he tells him, and adds, "I live under the name of Fauchelevent, at No. 7, Rue de l'Homme Armé." Javert is not an easy man to surprise, but Valjean's incredible behavior stuns him. He leaves slowly, then turns around to once again invite Valjean to kill him; Valjean orders him to go away. After Javert's departure Valjean fires his gun in the air and announces that the execution has been carried out.

Meanwhile, Marius too has slowly recaptured the memory of Javert and their previous encounter. Enjolras confirms his identity, and at this precise moment he hears the pistol shot and Valjean's announcement. Marius is filled with a sensation of cold horror.

At this point Hugo breaks off to discuss, in Chapter 20, the failure of the general populace to rise in 1832. He is convinced that in the long run the natural, inevitable direction of mankind is forward, but he recognizes that this march is not steady. Sometimes a specific generation places its own happiness above the general welfare. Hugo is not severe toward this selfishness; he recognizes the individual's right to prefer his own interests to those of humanity. In general, he observes, people are resistant to the more violent forms of progress such as revolutions and insurrections. They are afraid of violence and incapable of understanding the ideals that motivate them. But self-interest, however understandable, must not and will not be man's guiding principle. Paris' rejection of the insurgents was a temporary aberration, a sickness. Mankind is basically healthy. With all its relapses, failure of nerve, intermittences, it is surely marching toward its ultimate apotheosis.

At the barricade, the government troops launch an open assault. The insurgents retaliate vigorously and once more they push back the assailants. Marius and Enjolras are the two poles of the resistance. On one side Marius exposes himself impetuously. On the other side, Enjolras, more self-controlled, fights with deadly efficiency.

For a while the military situation remains a stalemate. The rebels in their almost impregnable fortification fend off the enemy. But they cannot defeat an inexhaustible supply of troops. Gradually the successive waves of soldiers sweeping over the wall wear them down. Their weapons are gone. Many are killed, almost all are wounded. Their defense is a magnificent epic. It invites comparison with Homeric deeds or medieval heroes.

The inevitable breakthrough finally takes place. The infantry makes a breach in the middle. At last, after an eternity of heroism, a few begin to weaken. First they try to take refuge in one of the houses, and then fling themselves inside the Corinth. Enjolras, the dauntless warrior, covers their retreat and manages to bar the heavy door. Marius, however, has not been able to follow the others. He begins to faint and, as he falls, feels himself supported by a vigorous hand.

Now begins the assault of the wine shop. If possible, the defense becomes even more ferocious. Paving blocks rain from all sides. Shots are fired from the cellar and the garret. When all else fails, the rebels resort to horrible weapons, bottles of nitric acid. The battle is no longer

Homeric. It is Dantesque. When the soldiers finally manage to break into the wine shop, they find only one man standing, Enjolras. His execution is immediately ordered. Enjolras crosses his arms and serenely accepts his death. So magnificent is his courage that the enraged attackers suddenly fall silent.

The silence has an unexpected result. Grantaire, dead drunk, has slept through the most savage moments of the battle. But the unusual quiet wakes him up. With the peculiar gift of some drunkards, he is not only awake but completely lucid. He takes in the whole situation at a glance. As the firing squad prepares to shoot, he cries, "Long live the Republic!" and takes his place next to Enjolras. "Kill two birds with one stone," he suggests. Then he gently asks Enjolras: "You don't mind?" A second later, Enjolras is backed against the wall pierced by bullets and Grantaire is lying at his feet.

Meanwhile, Jean Valjean has picked up Marius as he falls and carried him off with the swiftness and agility of a tiger. Around the corner from the Corinth he finds a temporary haven, but it is unfortunately also a trap. Behind him is a wall, in front a squad of approaching soldiers. His only avenue of escape is underground. As he looks wistfully downward he suddenly notices an iron grating covering a shaft resembling a well. His bitter knowledge of escape techniques stands him in good stead and in an instant he lowers Marius to the bottom of the shaft. He finds himself in a kind of subterranean corridor. The feeling is strikingly reminiscent of his descent into the convent with Cosette. The tumult of the outside world has abruptly vanished to be replaced by a profound peace, an overwhelming silence.

Commentary

Upon the sacrifice of women and old men follows the sacrifice of children and heroes, and the tragic atmosphere deepens. Eponine and M. Mabeuf wanted to die; the Friends of the A.B.C. did not, though they accept their fate with gaiety and courage. Indeed, they had a great deal to live for: 40 years of shaping a better world; and it is just this dream of a fuller life that brings them to their deaths. Moreover, Hugo suggests, through her indifference to their dream France has lost the flower of their generation. Each of them was a young man of intelligence and ability, and in the revolution they have given proof of their ability in action as well as thought, of bravery as well as brilliance. Even Grantaire, cynic and drunkard, dies as gracefully, as courteously, and as courageously as his friends.

The death of Gavroche is an even greater tragedy, for he possessed the talents of all of them combined: courage and ingenuity, humility and joy, wit and compassion; and society had even less time to profit from his gifts. The world is poorer without him—a truth that Hugo underlines by the vignette of the two lost boys scrabbling for the swans' bread after his death.

Only Jean Valjean and Marius escape, and this is not really due to any deliberate act of will or heroism on Valjean's part. He has made no attempt to shield Marius during the battle; indeed, he seems rather to be waiting for fate to decide whether it will be Cosette's father or Cosette's lover who survives. In any event, it is Javert's unexpected presence that decides the question. As the situation evolves, it becomes apparent that it is not in Valjean's nature to kill Javert in cold blood; and if he cannot kill Javert, he has lost Cosette anyway. Marius survives, Valjean picks him up, and carries him off—not out of kindness to Marius, but because it is perhaps the last gift he will ever be able to give his child.

And yet the self-sacrifice implicit in the rescue of his rival is genuine. Physically, he could have killed the snipers on the roof, could have killed Javert, could have left Marius to die. Morally, he cannot, and this was as true when he arrived at the barricade as when he left it. The obscure forces of character in him have not changed; they have simply emerged, tough and unscathed, from the ultimate test. Jean Valjean has been a good man for so long that he cannot do evil even when he would.

**Book II—
Book III, Chapters 1-9**

Summary

A city has in its sewers a valuable resource, says Hugo, for it has been proved that human excrement is the richest fertilizer. Man's waste of this resource is a mad prodigality. Paris, for instance, literally throws away 25 million francs a year. Not only does it neglect a precious asset, but it contributes to its unsanitary condition by poisoning the water. To perpetuate this waste Paris has erected a spectacular structure, the sewers, a gigantic sponge, an underground city with its squares, streets, and crossroads.

Besides their physical interest, the sewers are also psychologically fascinating. Throughout history they have been the scene of many dramas; countless pursuits have taken place in them. The sewers are a mirror of human vices. The garbage they harvest bears witness to man's fallibility and speaks out against his pretensions. Broken bottles speak of drunkenness; clothes that have been worn at the Opera are rotting in the mud.

Except for a dim light filtering through openings in the sewer vault, Valjean is surrounded by blackness. Nevertheless he must plunge into this vacuum, for Marius' condition is alarming. Valjean must trust almost entirely to chance, for he has no landmark. The only clue in the sewers' layout is their slope. He knows that the sewers descend toward the Seine. He therefore chooses to proceed uphill, for he does not want to emerge near the river among the crowd.

Valjean advances like a blind man, feeling the wall with one hand and holding Marius on his back with the other. After a little while, thanks to the parsimonious light glimmering through a distant manhole, he gets a vague impression of his surroundings. While the light provides some mental comfort, it is of no practical help whatsoever. Even with the best visibility no one can find his way in this vast labyrinth, this unexplored territory. Valjean, in spite of his fortitude, cannot help contemplating with horror the perils of his situation. Will he find an exit? Will he find it in time? Will he stumble on some insurmountable obstacle? Will he die of starvation, and Marius of loss of blood?

Then he makes a disturbing observation. Instead of climbing, he is now going downhill. He wonders apprehensively whether his calculations were wrong and he is going in the direction of the Seine after all. It is too late to retrace his steps and Valjean continues to advance. Without knowing it, he has made the right decision. The sewers empty not only in the Seine but also in the outer sewer. For a half hour Valjean continues to walk without resting, trusting almost entirely to chance. The only rational decision he can make is to choose the larger corridors on the assumption that the smaller ones will lead to a dead end.

Suddenly Valjean notices his shadow in front of him, profiled against a reddish background. Dumbfounded, he turns around and sees a ball of fire in the distance. It is the lantern of a police patrol, for the authorities have readily surmised that some of the insurgents might try to escape through the sewers. Valjean, too exhausted to understand the full gravity of the situation, nevertheless flattens himself against the wall and remains motionless. The police conclude that they have heard an imaginary noise and proceed to the neighborhood of the insurrection. Just in case, they fire a parting shot, but it hits the vault above Valjean's head. Slowly darkness and silence recapture the sewers. When the patrol is safely gone Valjean resumes his march.

It must be said to the credit of the police that not even extraordinary events like an insurrection distract them from their customary enforcement of the law. Thus during June 6 in the afternoon on the right bank of the Seine near the Invalides Bridge a policeman is shadowing a thief. They are proceeding without haste, keeping an equal distance between them. But the fugitive, beneath his calm, feels the hostility and fear of a tracked animal. The policeman hails a passing cab and orders it to follow.

The chase takes the two adversaries to a ramp leading to the Champs Elysees. It seems likely that the thief is going to take the ramp, for the Champs Elysees is a wooded area tempting to a fugitive. To the surprise of the policeman, he avoids the exit and continues straight ahead. His decision is inexplicable, since the bank terminates in a dead end when the river makes a bend. When he comes to the end of the road the thief ducks behind a pile of debris. The policeman quickens his step, expecting to trap his quarry. When he too rounds the debris he discovers to his surprise that his prey has vanished. The thief has disappeared into the opening of a sewer. But this disappearance is not without an element of mystery, for to open the grating the outlaw needed a key that could only be obtained from the authorities. Though he has been outwitted, the policeman with the blind persistence of a hunting dog takes up a meaningless vigil.

In the sewer, Valjean refuses to rest, but he is encountering increasing difficulties. The ground is slippery. The low vault forces him to march bending over. Hunger and, above all, thirst torment him. In spite of his strength the inevitable exhaustion begins to take its toll. At three o'clock Valjean arrives at the outer sewer. There he is confronted by vital decisions. He has to choose among the several corridors that join at this point and he picks the wider one. Then he must decide whether to go downhill or uphill. He prefers to descend, on the assumption that the downward march will lead him to the Seine. His luck serves him well and saves his life. The other direction would have taken him to a dead end or an inextricable jungle.

Shortly after, Valjean is forced to make a halt. He deposits Marius tenderly on a bank, feels his heart beating, and bandages his wounds as best he can. Then he contemplates Marius with inexpressible hatred. After reading the note in Marius' pocket giving instructions to deliver his body to his grandfather's, and eating a piece of bread he also finds there, Valjean resumes his march with Marius on his back. Night is falling and the openings are getting rarer. The obscurity proves to be a near disaster, for it camouflages dreadful traps known as "fontis," mud-holes in the ground of the corridors with all the dangers of quicksand. They hold for their victims a similar death, unexpected, lonely, inexorably slow. In addition, they have their own refinements: darkness, filth, fetidness. Sewers add degradation to the final agony.

Jean Valjean feels the pavement disappearing under his feet, plunging in a pool of water and a bed of mud. Of necessity, he goes forward and sinks with every step. Soon he is forced to throw his head back and hold up Marius' at arm's length. At last, on the verge of death, he touches solid ground and climbs out of the mire. He stumbles on a stone and falls to his knees. This position of prayer turns his thoughts toward God. In a fervent dialog he purges his heart of hate. The journey now becomes torture, for Valjean's strength has completely abandoned him. At every few steps he has to pause to catch his breath. Once he is forced to sit down and he is almost unable to get up.

Suddenly he feels a surge of energy, for in front of him he spots the beckoning light of an exit. He rushes toward it like a soul fleeing from hell. When he reaches it he has, alas, a shattering disappointment. The grating is locked. Maddened by a tantalizing glimpse of Paris and freedom, Valjean shakes the bars frantically, but it is as futile as trying to pull the teeth of a tiger. He collapses to the ground drained of hope. Valjean feels himself caught in death's web.

As darkness invades his soul, Valjean feels a hand on his shoulder and hears a whisper, "Share and share alike." He is dumbfounded to find a man in this forgotten place, even more startled to recognize Thénardier. However, he immediately regains his presence of mind and notes that Thénardier does not recognize Valjean through the mask of blood and mud. Thénardier, taking him for a murderer with his victim, proposes a characteristic deal. For half of the profit he'll open the grating. He starts a conversation by way of getting Valjean to betray himself, but Valjean maintains a stubborn silence. At last, Thénardier returns to the original subject, in terms that allow no evasion: "How much did the guy leave in his pockets?"

Valjean for once is without funds, and he can offer only 30 francs. Dissatisfied, Thénardier searches him and in passing manages to tear off a piece of Marius' jacket for later identification. He takes the 30 francs, completely forgetting the terms of the deal. He inspects the outside and silently opens the door, letting Valjean out. For a moment Valjean is overwhelmed by the majestic serenity that greets him, the reassurance of twilight, the immensity of the starry sky, the murmur of the river. Then he senses a presence behind him and recognizes Javert's ubiquitous figure.

Javert, however, is not a superman. He has been looking for Thénardier, not Valjean; at first, in fact, he does not recognize his perennial quarry. It is Valjean who identifies himself and offers no resistance to Javert's iron grip. He asks just one favor, to be allowed to take Marius home. Contrary to his behavior at M.-sur-M., Javert consents and calls his waiting cab. The trip is like the funeral procession of three cadavers.

Commentary

A book could be written about the fascination Paris sewers hold, not only for twentieth-century tourists, but for much nineteenth-century literature. Hugo, however, sums up neatly their persistent attraction for the inquiring mind: their technical ingenuity, their participation in the romance of "secret passageway," their grim summation of human existence.

Hugo skillfully weaves them into the epic pattern of his novel. They not only serve as counterpart to the passage in which he describes the "underworld mine" of criminal Paris, but provide him with a structural, picturesque, and psychological climax to a long sequence of similar scenes. Jean Valjean had fled alone in fear, carrying the beloved burden Cosette; now he flees with Marius, carrying hatred and despair on his back. He has experienced many scenes of darkness: darkness lit by a crucifix in the bishop's chamber, darkness lit by the moon with Cosette at the well, darkness lit by a flaring torch at the barricades; but now the darkness is total and absolute.

And the darkness is within his soul as well. He has saved Marius, but this has not freed his spirit. He is still drowned in hatred, and there is not a glimmer of comfort or hope upon the black path before him. Like Aeneas, like Dante, Valjean has descended into hell; but it is only a last stage on his journey into light, and as he emerges from the

104

sewers he emerges, through prayer, from his spiritual torment also.

The deeper significance of this emergence into the light of the friendly stars is underlined by the presence of Thénardier and Javert, standing like Charon and St. Michael upon the threshold of a better life. Thénardier has always been Valjean's criminal alter ego, and even now for a moment Thénardier's evil magic seems to work again, making us wonder whether Valjean has not after all really killed Marius. But in the face of this new Valjean, Thénardier's influence ebbs, and he meekly opens the door to freedom. Javert the avenging angel is a more implacable doorkeeper, but judgment must always precede paradise on Resurrection Day.

Book III, Chapters 10-12 – Book IV

Summary

Night has fallen when the cab reaches its destination. The house is asleep. Javert knocks and has Marius' body, as he imagines it to be, transported upstairs. While M. Gillenormand's servants go for the doctor and prepare bandages, Javert leaves unobtrusively, accompanied by Valjean. In the cab, Valjean risks one more request. He asks for permission to see Cosette. This request, too, is quietly granted.

When they arrive at the Rue de l'Homme Armé, Javert dismisses the cab. The procedure is a little unusual, but Valjean assumes that he is to be taken on foot to the police station. Unusual too is Javert's discretion in allowing his prisoner to see Cosette alone. On the landing Valjean, weakening at the prospect of a heart-wrenching tête-à-tête, stops for a minute and distractedly looks out of the window. The lamplight reveals a deserted street.

At M. Gillenormand's, a camp bed is set up for Marius at the doctor's orders. A careful examination reveals no fatal wound. Marius is not out of danger, however. His loss of blood has exhausted him, his collarbone is fractured, his head has been injured by sword cuts, and he may have a skull fracture. The doctor, feverishly working to stop the bleeding, looks pessimistic.

In spite of all efforts to keep the news from him, M. Gillenormand is awakened by the commotion and appears, ghost-like in his white nightgown. When he sees his grandson, apparently dead, he is overcome by an immense grief which quickly rises to a paroxysm of despair. In his hysteria he accuses Marius of having got himself killed in revenge. Then he turns his wrath on the liberals and babbles reminiscences of Marius' golden childhood, followed by murmured laments on Marius' wasted life and his own lonely old age. At this moment, Marius slowly opens his eyes and M. Gillenormand faints.

Javert slowly walks away from Valjean's house. For the first time in his life he is in the throes of indecision. As he meditates painfully, he reaches the Seine and leans on the parapet, absentmindedly contemplating its swirling waters. To arrest Jean Valjean is personal ingratitude, but to let him go is an inconceivable breach of duty. A more introspective man might be able to solve the dilemma. But Javert, a mental automaton governed by rigid principles, has always avoided thinking. Now, however, a new, unprecedented, unacceptable idea is forcing its way into his consciousness. There is a higher law than the judicial apparatus. A man can be an outlaw and still be virtuous. Valjean must be respected, not only for his latest act of generosity, but for all the good he did as M. Madeleine. Javert is entering a new moral universe; his narrow, uncomplicated world is crumbling. He is "an owl forced to gaze with the eye of an eagle."

But Javert's myopia is incurable. He cannot reject the values of a lifetime and survive. He cannot reconcile himself to his own act. For him, the freeing of Valjean is a clear violation of the law, hence inexcusable. Incapable of executing what he considers his duty, Javert must find some other way of making peace with his intransigent conscience. At last he sees a way. Firmly he enters a nearby police station, takes some writing material, and addresses to the prefect various recommendations for the improvement of the police administration. Then he returns to his previous position at the Seine parapet. The night is pitch black. The streets are deserted. The river is invisible and only betrays itself by the sound of its rushing whirlpools. Javert contemplates for an instant the precipice, takes off his hat, climbs the parapet, and disappears into the gaping obscurity.

Commentary

Thénardier has given Valjean his physical freedom; Javert completes the task by giving him his legal freedom. Spiritually, Valjean has already freed himself and is now truly M. Leblanc: the "white" man, the man with no name, who belongs only to God. A single force has brought him out of the slough of ignorance and evil: the power of love. Love, first, for the bishop; then love of Cosette; and finally, as he shows on the barricades, love of mankind.

In contrast, Javert has always feared and mistrusted love. It twists things, changes things: it is not "in order." Lost, lonely bloodhound that he is, he feels safe only with what is tangible, organized, immutable; if he loves anything, it is the law that has always kept a warm place in a corner for him and told him exactly what to do next. Now, in a revelation like that on the road to Emmaus, he discovers that the law is not enough, that there is a more powerful force to which even the law must bow and which can make even him, Javert, go against his conscience. He sees the light of love, but it is too shattering for him to endure.

"Justice," of which Javert is a personification, says critic Georges Piroué, "cannot accept into its corpus the foreign body of contradiction;" only the divine justice based on charity can do this, and in fact constantly renews itself by so doing. The reign of justice must be destroyed before the reign of charity can begin, and Javert must die so that Jean Valjean may live. His death, however, is not so much a defeat as a transformation. By loving Javert, Valjean has destroyed him, but he has saved him too; and divine justice will reward Javert's crime against human justice.

Books V-VI

Summary

Marius' recovery is long and difficult. Suffering from a concussion, racked by delirium, covered with infected wounds, he remains at death's door for several weeks. As long as he is in danger, M. Gillenormand does not leave his bedside. Another man, a white-haired gentleman, also takes an interest in the convalescent. He comes daily to inquire about the state of his health.

It takes Marius six months to recover. The lapse of time has cooled all political passion and Marius receives a *de facto* amnesty. His gradual recovery fills his grandfather with ecstasy. M. Gillenormand celebrates his cure by giving his servant three louis, singing a licentious eighteenth-century song, and even, according to an eyewitness, praying.

Marius himself is not so happy. He is still obsessed by the thought of Cosette, and he has resolved not to accept the gift of life without love.

He is determined to marry Cosette even if it means defying his grandfather. And he is convinced that all M. Gillenormand's new affection is still conditional on Marius' compliance with his wishes. Finally, angrily, he announces his plans to marry. M. Gillenormand, incredible though it seems to Marius, is enchanted and expresses the greatest enthusiasm for Cosette. Their interview ends with a complete emotional reconciliation, and Marius even calls M. Gillenormand by the magic name of "Father." The old man arranges for an immediate visit from Cosette and even painfully suppresses a diatribe against the Revolution.

Cosette appears in a state of happy bewilderment, ecstatic, blushing, shy before so many bystanders. Fauchelevent-Valjean, dressed with sober correctness, stands quietly to one side with a smile that expresses more poignancy than joy. M. Gillenormand greets him courteously but mispronounces his name with aristocratic negligence. Overcome by emotion, Marius is unable to speak, but Cosette in an uninterrupted monolog pours out her anxiety, her love, her joy.

M. Gillenormand seems happiest of all. He hovers over the couple, marvels at Cosette's beauty, and courts her charmingly. Valjean, until now so quiet he has been forgotten, now intervenes. Without any theatrics he announces that Cosette is rich. He has at her disposal almost 600,000 francs, which he lays down on the table. M. Gillenormand is thunderstruck, but Cosette and Marius are too much in love to pay any attention to such a trivial detail.

The marriage is set for February. The two old men, each in his fashion, work for the happiness of the young couple, Valjean quietly takes care of all practical details and solves a problem Cosette is not even aware of. To spare her the stigma of illegitimacy, he passes her off as Euphrasie, the daughter of the real Fauchelevent.

Gillenormand's services, while not as valuable, are more dramatic. He raids the family heirlooms to offer the girl a shimmering collection of bibelots and jewels. He is as earnest about his frivolities as other men are about more serious matters, for to Gillenormand luxury is not merely a way of life, it is a philosophy. It is only through frills and superfluities, he says in effect, that life becomes a banquet. He waxes particularly eloquent about weddings. He contrasts the dull ceremony of the nineteenth century with the elegance, the sauciness, and the revelry of the eighteenth. His description of a wedding is a canvas inspired by Fragonard, Watteau, and Boucher.

Cosette is to be installed in the handsomest room in the house, which, moreover, is to be luxuriously redecorated. Mlle. Gillenormand, who had nothing but contempt for the young couple when she thought they would be poor, now plans to leave them all her money. Cosette comes to visit Marius daily with Valjean as chaperon. Marius tolerates him as Cosette's father but avoids any intimacy. They discuss only such neutral subjects as politics and education. Marius remembers still that when he last saw Valjean the old man was about to shoot a policeman, but as Valjean never refers to the events of the insurrection Marius cannot accuse him openly.

Marius is also preoccupied by the problem of Thénardier. Despite the man's viciousness, Marius still feels an obligation to carry out his father's last wishes. His investigation, however, fails to unearth Thénardier: all the man's associates have either disappeared or died; Thénardier himself has been condemned to death and has dropped out of sight.

Marius feels that he also owes a debt of gratitude to the unknown stranger who saved him and brought him home, but he too cannot be found. Neither the cabdriver nor the police can provide any information about him. Marius is bedeviled by a series of puzzles: why did a total stranger save his life? Why didn't the policeman in the cab arrest him? Why has his savior not appeared to claim a reward, or at least an expression of thanks? Throughout Marius' stubborn search Valjean keeps silent. Even when he hears Marius' awed reconstruction of what the escape through the sewers must have cost his rescuer, he does not utter a word.

The wedding, while it is not the mad extravaganza M. Gillenormand has dreamed of, is nevertheless a heartwarming and happy event. Only one incident mars it: Valjean has had a slight accident a few days before and, with his arm in a sling, is unable to sign any of the wedding documents. The "accident" is fortunate, since Valjean's signature as Fauchelevent would be illegal.

On the way to church the nuptial procession has to take a street filled with carriages and Mardi Gras maskers. At one point a traffic jam causes a halt, and a carriage overflowing with revelers also stops in the other line of traffic. They are a ragged, disreputable lot, noisy and sarcastic. In the midst of the general hilarity two of the maskers, an old Spaniard with an enormous nose and gigantic mustache, and a thin young girl, carefully observe the wedding party. The man is particularly interested in the father of the bride, whom he seems to recognize. He is consumed by curiosity and urges his indifferent companion, Azelma, to find out more about them.

With their marriage vows, Marius and Cosette are transfigured. They accomplish that miracle, the realization of a dream, and all the bitterness they have endured only enhances their present happiness. Back at Gillenormand's, the wedding banquet is gay. Flowers fill the house, the dining room is ablaze with lights, crystal, and precious metal. Three violins and a flute play Haydn quartets.

Valjean slips quietly away, but nothing can dim the happiness surging in the room. M. Gillenormand, champagne glass in hand, delivers an epicurean sermon, praises love, preaches joy, and enthusiastically acknowledges the eternal domination of woman. He makes of marriage the ultimate form of piety. Led by the grandfather's contagious exhilaration, the wedding feast reaches a crescendo of gaiety. At midnight the newlyweds take their leave and the houses lapses into silence.

When he leaves the party, Valjean pauses outside for a moment to listen to the muted gaiety of the banquet. Then he returns home along the same route by which he has escorted Cosette to see Marius during the past three months. In the apartment he wanders from one empty room to another, attentive to the heightened sound of his footsteps. Then he goes to his bedroom and removes the perfectly sound arm from its sling. His eyes fall on the suitcase containing the clothes Cosette wore when she left Montfermeil. Slowly he pulls them out and spreads them on the bed. Memories of his first meeting with Cosette throng to his mind, and he buries his head on the bed and sobs heartbreakingly.

All his life Valjean has waged with his conscience Jacob's fight with the angel. In spite of the ferocity of the struggle, his conscience has always won. But tonight he faces the supreme challenge. He must decide whether to impose his presence on Cosette and Marius, whether to associate his dark and illegal existence with the luminous young couple. Valjean cannot accept the renunciation that his heroic lucidity dictates. Cosette is his life raft and he cannot yet resign himself to drowning. Isn't there a limit to man's sacrifice, he wonders? Can God demand absolute annihilation? As on a previous occasion with the Champmathieu affair, Valjean contemplates his fateful alternatives through the long night.

Commentary

One by one, Hugo untangles his complications and brings them to a tidy conclusion. Jean Valjean is safe, Marius is healthy, M. Gillenormand and his grandson become completely reconciled, Cosette and Marius are united. Only one problem remains: the antipathy between Jean Valjean and Marius. And it is a genuine problem. Marius is young and callow, and fails to appreciate Valjean at his real value, it is true; but he also has extremely good reasons to mistrust him. It is hard to feel comfortable with your father-in-law when you have met him in a den of thieves and heard him shoot a policeman.

Valjean is fully aware of this problem, but he cannot help Marius. To reveal that he is the young man's rescuer would be to burden him with an uncomfortable debt of gratitude; and the explanations it would entail would saddle Cosette, too, with the details of a dark past from which he has done his best to shield her. The only solution is for him to vanish, but he cannot bring himself to do it. His struggle, however, is qualitatively unlike any he has undergone before. At Arras, at the barricades, the good in him struggled with the evil; now he undergoes a conflict between two goods, his human love for Cosette and the spiritual nobler love that demands he surrender his earthly joys for her ultimate salvation and his own. Neither choice can be a wrong one.

Books VII-IX

Summary

Late the next morning Valjean returns to the Rue des Filles du Calvaire and asks for Marius. His somber and weary air makes a strange contrast with the festive appearance of the living room. Marius greets him with the greatest cordiality. He seems to insist on disregarding the strain that has existed between them and invites Valjean to make his home with him. Valjean interrupts by blurting out that he is an ex-convict. As corroboration, he shows him his perfectly sound hand and explains the subterfuge as a means of avoiding the signing of legal documents. Appalled, Marius urges him to continue, and Valjean complies by briefly stating his background, his meeting with Cosette, and his love for her—the depth of which he does not reveal, however. His confession ends with a reference to the 600,000 francs, which he explains as a trust.

Marius is puzzled by this unnecessary honesty. Valjean answers by explaining the tyranny of his confession, which demands nothing less than absolute truth, which rejects the most compelling excuse. He cannot bear to be befriended under false pretenses. Poignantly, he refers to the tragic destiny that requires him to be despised by others in order that he may respect himself. Marius is crushed by Valjean's revelations, but is magnanimous enough to shake his hand.

The painful conversation is interrupted by Cosette's charming intrusion. She gossips, coaxes her father to smile, pleads for permission to remain. When Marius asks her to leave them in privacy, she goes, with playful reproaches and threats. Cosette's visit reminds Valjean of the emotional impact his confession will have on her, and, his face bathed in tears, he longs for death. Marius instantly promises to keep it a secret from her and offers him a reward for managing Cosette's money so scrupulously. His magnanimity, however, is mixed with aversion and he suggests that Valjean stop seeing Cosette. At first Valjean agrees, but then blanches at the magnitude of the sacrifice. He who in the past has asked nothing for himself now humbly pleads with Marius not to separate him permanently from her. He invokes his immense love, promises to come rarely and remain unobtrusive. Marius understands this pathetic plea and reluctantly allows Valjean a nightly visit.

When Valjean goes, Marius is the prey of mixed emotions, but dismay is dominant. He wonders whether he has been too lenient with Valjean, whether he should have investigated the old man more carefully. Apprehensively, he wonders if he has not paid too dearly for his happiness, if his whole life is to be tarnished by this infernal shadow. He has, certainly, a measure of esteem for his father-in-law. His scrupulous administration of Cosette's fortune has been admirable. His confession, so painful and so dangerous for himself, indicates a certain nobility of spirit. But Marius cannot forget the Thénardier incident nor Valjean's revenge on Javert at the barricades.

Beyond the practical considerations, Valjean poses a metaphysical problem for Marius. How can Cosette have achieved such innocence in daily contact with such evil; how could such an impure tool have created a work of such purity? God's methods are unfathomable. Ultimately, Marius' lasting impression is one of revulsion, and relief that Valjean is willing to retire into the background. In spite of his enlightenment, Marius still retains the prejudices of his time in regard to criminal matters. He does not yet understand the cruelty, even the immorality, of the French penal system, which for a single crime brands a man for life.

The next evening at dusk Valjean is respectfully greeted by a servant and introduced into a neglected, dank room on the ground floor. Two armchairs have been installed with a worn bedside rug by way of carpet. Cosette enters and greets him with the most tender affection. But Valjean remains stubbornly reserved. He refuses to kiss her, refuses her invitation to dinner, even addresses her formally as "Madame." Cosette is puzzled and disturbed by Valjean's eccentricity, especially his insistence that he be called Monsieur Jean. She pleads with him to return to their former intimacy and scolds him affectionately. Briefly Valjean yields to the poignant temptation to call Cosette "tu" ("thou," the familiar form of address), but he regains his self-control and departs with a respectful "Madame."

Cosette resigns herself to Valjean's bizarre ways. She has the room cleaned up, but otherwise accepts their painful estrangement. The rest of the household simply dismisses Valjean as an eccentric. No one suspects the agony he is suffering.

In the next few weeks Cosette's new life, new social engagements, her absorption with Marius, make the loosening of old ties easier for her. For Valjean, however, love will not die. He cannot resist the temptation to lengthen his visits. Cosette's accidental return to the word "father" brings him to the brink of tears. But the gulf between them continues to widen. Every gesture of familiarity is gradually dropped. Valjean's happiness is reduced to an hour a day of contemplation or reminiscence.

One day in April, moved by the rebirth of nature, Marius and Cosette go back on a little pilgrimage to the garden of the Rue Plumet and forget all about Valjean. Valjean is not discouraged by this involuntary snub. To prolong his visit, he even resorts to the stratagem of praising Marius. Cosette, delighted to talk about her husband, does not notice the passage of time. But Marius subtly manages to shunt Valjean aside. When the old man's visits last too long, a servant is sent to remind Cosette that it is time for dinner. At the end of April the fire is not lit in the fireplace. When Cosette orders the fire relit, the chairs are moved to a far corner.

One evening Cosette reports that Marius has asked her whether she could live on his income alone. Valjean concludes, to his great distress, that Marius suspects Cosette's money really comes from him and that it is tainted. At last Marius makes his hostility brutally clear. He has the chairs taken away, and Valjean, unable to delude himself any longer, stops coming. Cosette in her new marital happiness scarcely notices his absence. However, she does send her maid to inquire, and

Valjean generously pretends that he has been busy and is about to take a trip.

During the last months of spring and the first months of summer, 1833, Valjean takes a daily walk in the direction of the Rue des Filles du Calvaire. He is in a complete trance. When he approaches his destination he slows down, and when he reaches the street he stops. He stares ahead yearningly at his forbidden paradise and a tear slips down his cheek. Gradually, like a pendulum whose oscillations grow shorter, he abbreviates his walks.

Hugo points out that Marius feels it a matter of husbandly duty to separate Valjean from Cosette; new and mysterious information has confirmed his darkest suspicions of the old man. Cosette is almost equally blameless. Marius exerts a magnetic influence on her and almost involuntarily she yields to his wishes. In any case, her neglect of her father is only superficial; under the surface her love is as deep as ever. She does occasionally inquire about Valjean, but he encourages the estrangement by pretending to be out of town. Besides, what is known as the ingratitude of children is merely the fulfillment of the scheme of nature. It forces the young to look to life and to neglect the generation that represents the past and is journeying toward the grave.

The pendulum finally comes to a halt. One day, Jean Valjean merely takes a few steps, sits down on a milestone and returns home. The next day he does not leave his room. The following day he does not get out of bed. His janitress, who prepares his meager meal, finds the dish untouched. A week elapses and Valjean does not leave his bed. The janitress' husband, when he hears the news, pronounces the case hopeless, and the doctor, after his visit, conforms his diagnosis. He announces that Valjean is suffering from the loss of a loved one.

One evening Valjean has trouble finding his pulse. Driven by a supreme compulsion, he puts on his clothes with extreme difficulty, takes out his valise and spreads Cosette's clothes on the bed. Then he lights the bishop's candlesticks. The effect is disturbingly funereal. Every movement drains his strength. He catches a glimpse of himself in the mirror and finds he has aged 30 years. At last, after a tremendous effort, he manages to sit down and in a trembling hand writes Cosette a last letter. It contains a reassuring explanation of the source of his fortune. Suddenly he is overcome by an immense despair, by an overwhelming yearning to die in Cosette's presence. At that moment he hears a knock on the door.

One evening, as Marius has been working in his study, he has received a letter that promises important revelations about an individual living with Marius; the tobacco odor and handwriting immediately remind him of Thénardier. Happy to be able to settle his debt at last, Marius orders Thénardier sent in; but he can scarcely recognize him, for Thénardier is thoroughly disguised. Upon Marius' curt invitation to speak, Thénardier explains he wants to retire to an isolated village in Panama, but he needs money. If Marius will provide it, he will provide Marius with a secret. He tells Marius, to whet his appetite, that his father-in-law is a thief, a murderer, and an ex-convict named Jean Valjean.

Contemptuously, Marius tells him he knows that already and further demoralizes Thénardier by revealing all he knows about the former innkeeper's own background. Giving Thénardier a 500-franc bill to settle his debt of gratitude, he goes on to say that he believes Valjean had M. Madeleine arrested, stole his money, and killed Javert. Thénardier, better informed on this point than Marius, regains lost ground by triumphantly announcing that Valjean and Madeleine are the same person. With a flourish he pulls out two newspapers which confirm his allegations.

Belatedly, it begins to dawn on Marius that he has misjudged Valjean, but Thénardier insists he is, nevertheless, a thief and a murderer. To prove it, he recounts his own version of the adventure in the sewer. According to him, Valjean was there to dispose of the body of a young man whom he had murdered for his money. There he met a fugitive who provided him with a key to get out, but not before the fugitive had torn off a piece of clothing from the murdered man; and Thénardier, to clinch his case, produces a piece of black rag. Marius, dazzled by the revelation of the magnificent truth, reaches blindly into the closet and throws a black suit at Thénardier's feet. Proclaiming that he is the supposed victim, he fits the torn piece of cloth neatly into the rent in his suit. Accusingly, he turns on Thénardier and catalogs all the sins of his past life, but offers him 4,500 francs now and 20,000 the next day if he will leave and never return. Thénardier accepts and departs — to become a slave trader in America, Hugo tells us.

In feverish haste, Marius takes Cosette and speeds with her in a cab to Valjean's home. On the way, he reveals the whole story of her father's life to Cosette and comments rapturously on its ineffable saintliness. The young couple arrive in time: Valjean still lives. Choked with emotion, Cosette rushes toward him and embraces him; Marius calls him "father." Valjean is incoherent with joy. To Cosette, tenderly nestled on his lap, he pours out his immense love and poignant longing. Cosette responds with affectionate reproaches and Marius with profound gratitude and admiration. Firmly but respectfully, he declares they have come to take Valjean home with them, and Cosette paints a radiant picture of their future life together.

Valjean listens as if to a magnificent symphony, and a tear comes to his eyes. Then, sorrowfully, he announces he is dying. Cosette and Marius, heartbroken, refuse to accept the truth. Valjean, however, in the spirit of abnegation that has characterized his whole life, exhorts them to accept the wisdom of God's decision and urges them to look forward to their future happiness.

The doctor arrives and confirms the verdict. Valjean settles his earthly and spiritual affairs and, with an unexpected renewal of strength, walks to the wall, takes down the crucifix, and sits down again. He reassures Marius as to the legitimacy of his wealth, and requests an anonymous tombstone; and his last moments are filled with happy memories. He evokes Cosette's childhood, their humble pleasures, their adventures. He tells Cosette about her mother, and asks her to forgive the Thénardiers. In the presence of the two people he loves, he dies happy.

In the Père-Lachaise cemetery there is a neglected and anonymous tombstone. Time, vegetation, and the elements are slowly destroying it. Only an unusual epitaph in pencil gave it a transitory distinction.

> He sleeps. Although fate was very strange to him,
> He lived. He died when he lost his angel;
> It happened simply, as naturally as
> The night falls when the day goes away.

Commentary

Characteristically, Jean Valjean decides to speak the bitter truth about himself and conceal the sweet. Although he considers this being honest with Marius, it is not really honesty; but he has no choice. An ex-convict cannot say "I am a good man" and be believed; he has lost his credibility.

His confession clears the air temporarily, but it does not really solve anything. Some readers feel that the continuing struggle over Cosette is unworthy of Jean Valjean, that a proper hero ought simply to have gone away; but to think so is to misunderstand Jean Valjean and Hugo's vision of him. In the first place, as Hugo has been saying all along, to do right is never easy; and in the second place, when Valjean thinks of disappearing, it is not going away he has in mind; it is death. Cosette is the only thing he loves in this world, and if he gives her up he will die. And Jean Valjean, as we have seen, has a very powerful instinct for survival. He remains to the last no incredible saint, but a thoroughly human figure.

His final renunciation is a defeat, but thanks to Thénardier, it is also a victory. Through the maze of lies this man has woven about himself and everyone who comes in contact with him, the truth accidentally emerges — as it always does if a lie goes on long enough. Thénardier, evil though he is, must eventually also contribute to the apotheosis of the good; this is the law of life as God has planned it.

And so Jean Valjean, having sacrificed his last happiness, has it returned to him a hundredfold; the lonely man, the outcast, dies surrounded by the happiness he has created, and the solitary celibate has been the progenitor, through Marius and Cosette's children, of a fruitful and contented posterity. No man can ask for a happier ending.

One knot, however, Hugo has left without untangling: no one has adopted the two little lost boys Gavroche left unprotected. An oversight, perhaps; or perhaps it was intentional. Perhaps he wanted his readers to remember, every night as they tumbled into bed, that somewhere out in the cold and darkness there were still two little lost boys, and many more like them, hungry and unprotected. And that, his unspoken conclusion seems to say, is *your* business.

REVIEW QUESTIONS AND ESSAY TOPICS

1. *Les Misérables* is one of the most widely read novels of all time. How do you explain its appeal?

2. Trace Victor Hugo's numerous antitheses.

3. Comment on Hugo's preface: "As long as there shall exist, by virtue of law and custom, a social damnation artifically creating hells in

the midst of civilization and complicating divine destiny with a human fatality . . . books like this cannot be useless."

4. "My belief is that this book will be one of my major achievements, if not my major achievement." Do you agree with Victor Hugo's appraisal of his own work?

5. To those who accuse Victor Hugo of implausibility Baudelaire answers: "It is a novel constructed like a poem, where each character is an exception only by the hyperbolic way he represents a generality." Elaborate.

6. One of Victor Hugo's most poignant and recurrent themes is what François Mauriac calls "the desert of love," that is, unfulfilled love. Trace Hugo's variations on this theme.

7. One of Hugo's editors Marius-François Guyard, claims to see a solid framework behind the apparent disorder of *Les Misérables*. What is your estimate of the novel's structure?

8. To what extent is Javert a symbol and to what extent an individualized characterization?

9. Thénardier is an absolutely evil man. Can such a character be considered realistic? Is he convincing?

10. Diderot defines one form of genius as the tendency to see abstract ideas only through their concrete manifestations. How does Victor Hugo illustrate this definition in *Les Misérables*?

11. Discuss *Les Misérables* as a realistic novel.

12. It has been said that Jean Valjean's dominant emotion is *caritas* (charity — active, outgoing love for others), but that it is not his only passion. Discuss some other emotions that Jean Valjean experiences in the course of the book and show how they conflict with or reinforce his *caritas*.

13. What are the principal social evils Victor Hugo is attacking in *Les Misérables*?

14. What social reforms does Victor Hugo advocate, directly or indirectly, in *Les Misérables*?

15. What is Hugo's view of human nature? Does he believe it is naturally good or vitiated by original sin, or does he take a position somewhere between these two extremes?

16. Marius has been described as a typical young Romantic of his era. Discuss him and compare him with other Romantic heroes in books, plays, or poems of the Romantic period which you may have read.

17. Explain Cosette's function in the novel in regard to character development, plot development, and theme.

18. What are Hugo's principal weapons as a propagandist? Discuss the effectiveness of each.

19. Gavroche is considered one of the most memorable characters in French literature. Analyze the techniques Hugo has used to make him so.

20. Discuss the Romantic elements in *Les Misérables*.

SELECTED BIBLIOGRAPHY

GRANT, ELLIOTT M. *The Career of Victor Hugo.* Cambridge, Mass.: Harvard University Press, 1945.

GUIER, FOSTER. *The Titan Victor Hugo.* New York and San Francisco: Vanni, 1955.

HUGO, VICTOR. *Le Post-scriptum de ma vie.* Translated with a study of the last phase of Hugo's genius by LORENZO O'ROURKE. New York and London: Funk & Wagnalls, 1907.

JOSEPHSON, MATTHEW. *A Realistic Biography of the Great Romantic.* Garden City, N.Y.: Doubleday, Doran, 1942.

MAUROIS, ANDRE. *Olympio: The Life of Victor Hugo.* Translated by GERARD HOPKINS. New York: Harper, 1956.

MOORE, O. H. "Realism in Les Misérables," *PMLA*, LXI (March, 1946), 211-28.

Les Misérables Genealogy

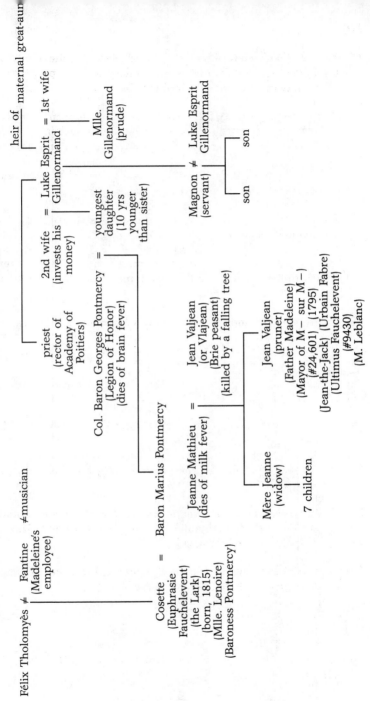

Les Miserables Genealogy

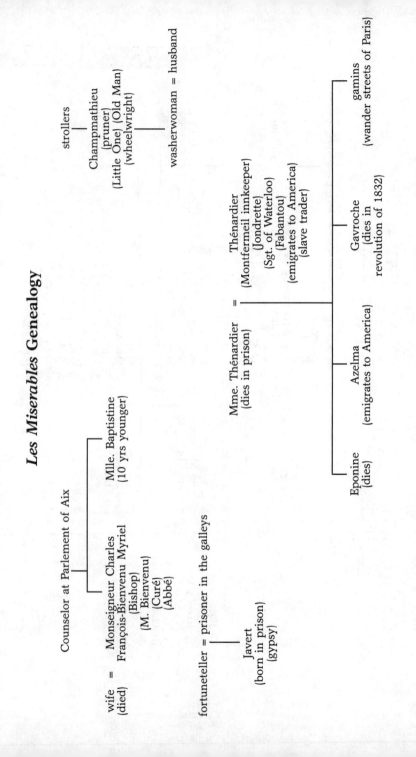

MADAME BOVARY

NOTES

including
- *Introduction to the Novel*
- *Brief Synopsis of the Novel*
- *List of Characters*
- *Chapter Summaries and Commentaries*
- *Character Analyses*
- *Flaubert's Life and Works*
- *Questions for Review*

by
James L. Roberts, Ph.D.
Department of English
University of Nebraska

REVISED EDITION

Cliffs Notes

INCORPORATED

LINCOLN, NEBRASKA 68501

Editor	Consulting Editor
Gary Carey, M.A.	*James L. Roberts, Ph.D.*
University of Colorado	*Department of English*
	University of Nebraska

Cliffs Notes, Inc.   Lincoln, Nebraska

CONTENTS

MADAME BOVARY

INTRODUCTION

Gustave Flaubert's masterpiece, *Madame Bovary,* was published in 1857. The book shocked many of its readers and caused a scandalized chain reaction that spread through all France and ultimately resulted in the author's prosecution for immorality.

Since that time, however, *Madame Bovary* has been recognized by students of literature as being the forerunner and model of our most prevalent and influential literary genre, the realistic novel. It is now considered a book of great intrinsic worth and one which contains an important and moving story. In addition, it provides a standard against which to compare the works and writers that have followed it. It is impossible to understand or appreciate modern European and American fiction without an acquaintance with *Madame Bovary.*

A SUMMARY OF *MADAME BOVARY*

Charles Bovary, the only son of a middle-class family, became a doctor and set up his practice in a rural village. He made a marriage of convenience with a woman older than himself. Upon his wife's death, Bovary married an attractive young woman named Emma Roualt, the daughter of one of his patients. For a while Emma was excited and pleased by her marriage, but because of her superficial romantic ideals she was soon bored and disillusioned by her new life. As a result of her dissatisfaction she became ill.

For the sake of her health the Bovarys moved to a new town, where their daughter was born. Emma's unhappiness continued, and she began to have romantic yearnings toward Leon, a young law clerk. After Leon left the town in order to attend law school, Emma's boredom and frustration became more intense. She was negligent of her duties as a wife and mother. None of Bovary's efforts to please her were successful, and she did not value or understand his devoted love for her.

Finally Emma had an adulterous affair with Rodolphe, a local landowner. When he abandoned her, she became seriously ill. After her recovery Emma encountered Leon in Rouen and began to carry on an affair with him. In order to afford weekly trips to the city to see Leon and to satisfy her other whims, Emma spent her husband's money freely and incurred many debts. She kept these secret from Bovary and managed to obtain a Power of Attorney so that she would have full control over their financial affairs.

Eventually her unpaid bills went long overdue and a judgment was obtained against her by her creditors. She owed a vast sum of money, and the sheriff's officers arrived to confiscate the family property. Emma tried frantically to raise the money and finally turned to both Rodolphe and Leon, but neither was willing or able to help. Out of shame and despair, she poisoned herself. Shortly afterwards her husband, now a ruined and broken man, also died, leaving their daughter to a life of poverty.

THE MAIN CHARACTERS

(For a more full analysis of these characters, see section on *Character Analysis*.)

Charles Bovary

A country doctor. He lacks intelligence and imagination; he is naive and unaggressive and has the most conventional and mundane interests.

Emma Bovary

She is portrayed as an irresponsible, immature, and neurotic woman who is unable to adjust to the realities of her life.

Homais

The apothecary at Yonville. He stands for the new middle-class spirit and "progressive" outlook that Flaubert detested so much.

Rodolphe
Emma's first lover, a shrewd bachelor who lives on his estate near Yonville.

Leon
Emma's early friend and later her second lover.

THE SECONDARY CHARACTERS

Marquis d'Andervilliers
A nobleman who invites the Bovarys to a ball at La Vaubyessard, his chateau.

The Blind Beggar
A hideously deformed creature whom Emma encounters several times on the road between Rouen and Yonville, and who passes beneath her window when she is dying. His ugly appearance and ghastly song horrify her whenever they meet. He has been interpreted as a symbol of either Death or the Devil.

Berthe
The daughter of Charles and Emma Bovary.

Binet
The tax collector at Yonville.

Maitre Bocage
Leon's employer at Rouen.

Bournisien
The priest at Yonville. He is a good-natured and simple man but utterly lacking in intelligence, perception, or sophistication. He accepts and defends all the dogmatic and outmoded aspects of official Church thought and never dares to question anything. He has no understanding of the real needs of his parishioners. He represents the ignorance and inadequacies of the rural clergy in Flaubert's time and serves as an effective counterpoint to Homais.

Mme. Bovary the Elder

Charles' mother. In order to compensate for the unhappiness of her marriage, she has been an overly protective and indulgent mother. When her son becomes an adult, she is grasping and domineering and tries to run his life for him. She is jealous of Charles' affection for his wife, and as a result, she and Emma do not get along well.

M. Bovary

Charles' father. He is a former army officer who was forced to resign from the service. He is tyrannical, cruel, and boastful; he spends and drinks too much and is an unfaithful husband.

Canivet

A doctor from a neighboring town who is called in by Bovary after the operation on Hippolyte, during Emma's various illnesses, and at the time of her poisoning. He is hardly more competent than Bovary, but he condescends to him as an inferior, and is smug about his own skill and reputation.

Felicite

Emma's maid.

Maitre Guillaumin

The lawyer at Yonville for whom Leon originally worked. Emma asks him for help near the end of the novel.

Maitre Hareng

A sheriff's officer.

Heloise

Bovary's first wife.

Hippolyte

The servant at the inn on whom Bovary and Homais unsuccessfully operate.

Hivert

The coachman at Yonville.

Homais
The apothecary at Yonville. He is one of the most successful supporting characters in the novel, because there is a complete identity between his function as a character and his function as the representative of a type. He stands for the new middle-class spirit and "progressive" outlook that Flaubert detested so much. Homais' intellect is limited, and he is poorly educated, but he is pretentious and puffed up with self-esteem. His talk consists of cliches and half-truths, and he demonstrates all the limitations and prejudices of the new bourgeoisie. For example, he is an avowed agnostic and an exponent of Voltaire, yet he is fearful and superstitious in the face of death. Furthermore, he is cowardly and irresponsible, as is shown in the aftermath of the episode concerning the operation on Hippolyte, and though he professes equalitarian principles, he is himself status conscious. Some of the best comic scenes in the novel are the conversations between Homais and his rival, the priest. Flaubert's pessimism is illustrated by the ending of the novel, where Homais' advancement and personal triumph are described.

Mme. Homais
The apothecary's wife; she is a simple and placid woman.

Justin
Homais' teen-age assistant. He is secretly in love with Emma and is seen crying on her grave near the end of the novel. He is naïve and innocent, but ironically it is Justin who is responsible for giving Emma the arsenic.

Lagardy
A well-known tenor whom the Bovarys hear at the opera in Rouen; he is also famed as a lover, and Emma's interest in him serves as an introduction to her meeting with Leon.

Lariviere
A great doctor from Rouen who arrives too late to save Emma's life, and who is consulted on other occasions. He is a brilliant and highly skilled physician and is contemptuous of his less capable colleagues and of such pretentious fools as Homais. He is coldly superior and aloof in his bearing, yet he is the only doctor in the

novel to express real sympathy for the suffering of his patients and to show a sense of professional dignity and integrity. Biographers have determined that in this character, Flaubert portrayed his own father.

Mme. Lefrancois

The owner of the inn at Yonville.

Mlle. Lempereur

The teacher in Rouen who is supposedly giving piano lessons to Emma.

Catherine Leroux

An aged peasant woman who is awarded a prize at the Agricultural Show. Her humility and dedication are meant to stand in sharp contrast to Emma's way of life.

Lestiboudois

The general handyman and church sexton at Yonville.

Lheureux

An unscrupulous moneylender and commission merchant at Yonville who entices Emma into debt by playing on her weaknesses and fears. He eventually forces the Bovarys into bankruptcy, thus precipitating Emma's suicide.

Lieuvain

The representative of the Prefect; he makes a speech at the Agricultural Show. His platitudes about patriotism, progress, duty, religion, and the nobility of agriculture serve to illustrate Flaubert's attitude toward the bourgeoisie, and are also an effective counterpoint to the platitudes about love that Rodolphe is whispering to Emma at the same time.

Nastasie

Bovary's first maid; she is fired by Emma after the ball.

Roualt

Emma's father. He is a simple and nearly illiterate peasant, but he is the only character of any significance in the novel who is genuinely warm and unselfish.

Tuvache
> The mayor of Yonville.

Vincart
> A banker who works with Lheureux in his financial transactions.

PART I – CHAPTER 1

Summary
> At the age of fifteen, Charles Bovary struck his schoolmates as a shy and clumsy country lad. He did not have great intelligence or wit but was a diligent and industrious student. He was quiet; however, he mixed well with the other boys.

> His father was a former army surgeon who had been forced to leave the service as a result of some scandal. He was a handsome and unscrupulous man who had married Charles' mother in order to get his hands on her large dowry. After the marriage, he wasted most of the money in foolish speculations, drinking, and amorous affairs. He had always been a cruel and unfaithful husband. In middle age he continued to mistreat his wife and was a bitter, stern, and boastful man. He and his wife eventually acquired and lived on a small farm.

> Charles' mother had once loved her husband deeply, but her unfortunate marriage had cooled this affection and had turned her youthful gaiety and optimism into nervous moodiness and spite.

> After their son's birth, the two Bovarys had often clashed about his rearing, and Charles' boyhood was one of inconsistencies and contradictions. His mother had been overly fond and doting, while his father had attempted to inure him to the rigors of life through austere treatment.

> Eventually Charles was sent to a secondary school and then studied medicine. Although he worked hard at first, his lack of great intelligence and a natural tendency to laziness caused him to fail his examinations. His mother attributed this to unfairness on the part of the examiners, and the news was kept a secret from his

father. The following semester, after much hard work, Charles was able to pass. While at the university he had his first real taste of freedom and engaged in several typical student adventures.

After he became a doctor, Charles' mother found him a practice in the village of Tostes, and a wealthy wife in Heloise, an ugly widow who was several years older than he. Charles had hoped that marriage would bring him freedom, but soon found his wife to be as grasping and domineering as his mother had been. Nevertheless, his medical practice prospered.

Comment

A.

Flaubert is presenting in rapid sketches the essential nature and characteristics of some of the background figures, and is preparing us for later actions. For example, it is important to see from the very beginning that Charles is a rather ordinary person with no special talents. He must work exceptionally hard for anything that he achieves. Furthermore, we see that Charles is easily ruled by his mother and later by his wife. He is obedient, diligent, and hard working, but possesses no natural talents.

B.

Flaubert is going to present a novel about the provincial middle-class society. He is interested in this first chapter with presenting a basic picture of the typical country background against which the story takes place.

C.

Note the tremendous contrast between Charles and his father. The father has a dash of charm and imagination that is missing in Charles. The son is more closely aligned with his mother whose main concern is with meeting the bills and getting by in life.

D.

Charles' first marriage is very important in relationship to his later marriage with Emma. First, we see that his wife is able to make him walk a tight line. She is easily able to control him even though she possesses none of the "loveliness" of Emma. She was a real shrew who made life very difficult and unpleasant for Charles. She is so antagonistic that Charles will naturally be more receptive to Emma's charms.

PART I – CHAPTER 2

Summary
Late one night Charles was awakened with a request to come 18 miles out in the country and set a broken leg. He sent the messenger on ahead and promised to follow in a couple of hours. At four in the morning, Charles set out on the journey, trying to search his memory for everything he knew about fractures.

When he arrived at the farm house, he was admitted by a charming young lady. Upon seeing the patient, he was greatly relieved to find a simple fracture with no complications. Mademoiselle Emma came in and assisted with preparing bandages. Charles was struck by the beauty of her flashing brown eyes which appeared to be almost black. When he had finished, she led him into the dining room where he ate and talked with Mademoiselle Emma about the patient. Upon leaving, he promised to come back in three days. But instead, he found himself returning the next day and went twice a week regularly in spite of the long ride. In about eight weeks, the patient was able to walk about.

During the entire episode, Charles never questioned himself as to why he went so often to see the patient, but his wife did. She made inquiries and found out that the patient had a daughter who had been brought up in a convent and was known to give herself airs. After much complaining, nagging, and pleading, Charles' wife finally extracted a promise from him that he would not go there again.

As time passed, Charles' mother and wife both began to pick at him incessantly. Suddenly it was learned that the lawyer who had been administering Heloise's estate had absconded with nearly all her money. Furthermore, it was discovered upon investigation that her remaining property was of little value and that the woman had lied about her wealth prior to the wedding. Bovary's parents had a violent argument about this, and Heloise was very upset. About a week later she had a stroke and died.

Comment

A.

In this chapter, we meet Mademoiselle Emma. But Flaubert is interested in presenting her from a distant view, that is, we hear about her first from other viewpoints. He is saving his personal or direct introduction of Emma until a later chapter and is here presenting Charles' and Heloise's view of Emma. This technique is called the delayed emergence. It functions to arouse the reader's interest in the main character.

B.

It is a part of Charles' character that he is not even aware of why he went so often to see his patient. It might even be said that he was surprised when his wife accused him of going solely to see Mademoiselle Emma. Denied of the privilege of seeing her, Charles determined that he could then justifiably love her at a distance.

C.

Again, note that Charles' present wife is such a shrew, is so bad and so demanding and so ugly ("Her dresses hung on her bony frame."), and is so unpleasant that by contrast Emma seems like an angel to Charles. Thus Charles' miserable experiences with his first wife prepare him to be so indulgent and yielding to Emma later in his life.

D.

The reader who is not aware of Flaubert's method of evoking a scene is missing a large measure of the greatness of this novel. The reader should select a passage, such as Charles' arrival at his patient's house, and examine the careful way in which Flaubert makes you feel this scene. His choice of language and careful description paints an accurate description of what he is writing about. The technique that Flaubert uses may be compared to that of a camera coming slowly in for a close shot and then moving subtly away for another shot.

PART I–CHAPTER 3

Summary

Sometime after, Roualt paid Charles a call to settle his bill and to offer his condolences. He invited Bovary to visit at the farm. Charles accepted the offer and became a frequent guest at the Roualt house. In these circumstances, Bovary's interest in Emma matured, and soon he found himself in love with her.

Emma's father had never been a very good farmer. He had debts and constantly drank the best cider rather than sending it to the market. Thus, when he realized that Charles was interested in Emma, he resolved to give his consent, especially since Emma had never been very good around the farm. Thus Charles' proposal was accepted.

Charles and Emma decided that the wedding would take place as soon as Charles was out of mourning. He visited often and they discussed the details of the wedding. Emma would have preferred a midnight wedding with torches, but her father would not stand for that. Instead, there was a traditional wedding with a party which lasted sixteen hours.

Comment

A.

We should note with what delight Charles observes everything that Emma does. He is charmed with her looks, her way of talking, her actions, and everything about her. He can find no fault with her. This attitude or view toward his future wife will essentially continue during his entire married life, making it easy for Emma to commit her indiscretions.

B.

Flaubert begins already to offer little hints as to Emma's character. We see that her father thinks of her as rather useless around the farm and is not sorry to lose her in marriage. Emma's romanticism, which will later be seen to be the cause of her tragic life, is here suggested by her desire to have a midnight wedding with torches. This is the first hint that Emma is a person who seeks something of the strange and marvelous, something that will break the monotony of living in a dull world.

PART I – CHAPTERS 4 & 5

Summary

The wedding was a gala affair with many friends and relatives present. There was much good fun; the only unpleasant note was the sullen attitude of Bovary's mother who resented not having had a hand in the plans or preparations. Charles' great happiness was apparent to all who saw him, and Emma too seemed pleased by her marriage. After two days at Roualt's farm, the couple returned to Tostes.

Charles proudly led Emma into her new house, the furnishings and arrangement of which are described in great detail. Emma discovered her predecessor's wedding bouquet on display in the bedroom, where Bovary had thoughtlessly left it. She indulged in some morbid thoughts, but her sorrowful mood passed quickly in the excitement of the moment. In the days that followed, Bovary's every thought was with his wife, and all his efforts were devoted to pleasing her. He took her for walks and enjoyed fulfilling her every whim. He had never known that life could be so pleasant. But Emma wondered why she had not attained the happiness she expected from marriage and what happened to such words as "bliss," "passion," and "ecstasy;" words which had sounded so wonderful when read in books.

Comment

A.

Chapter 4 devotes itself to creating a realistic picture of a country wedding. Flaubert, in a few masterful strokes, makes us feel the entire provincial life. Scenes such as these account for Flaubert's title as the first master of perfect realism.

B.

In both chapters, the reader should note how utterly Charles dotes on Emma. His dogged devotion accounts for his later blindness to Emma's faults and his later desire to fulfill her every whim.

C.

Emma's desire to change the house should not be seen as a touch of individuality on her part. Rather, she will be seen to be constantly desiring a change, thinking that in every change she will find the happiness that she is seeking.

D.

The first blow to Emma's romantic nature comes when she sees the still preserved bridal bouquet held over from Charles' first marriage. This takes away from the sentimentality she is trying to attach to her own bouquet.

E.

At the end of Chapter 5, Emma's true nature is beginning to emerge. She is already disillusioned because marriage is not as great in real life as it was in her books. She is disappointed because she has not found all of the "bliss, passion, and ecstasy" that she had read about in novels. This idea will now be developed as the main theme of the book. That is, the contrast Emma finds between the realistic world and her dreams of what life should be.

PART I – CHAPTER 6

Summary

Emma recalls her thirteenth year, when her father took her to the convent to live. She enjoyed the convent at first; she liked talking with the nuns and she enjoyed answering the difficult questions correctly. But she soon relinquished herself to the languid atmosphere of the convent and found herself admiring the beauty of the chapel rather than listening to the lessons. She gave herself over to romantic notions concerning the church and dreamed of the "sick lamb" and the metaphors of a "betrothed spouse, heavenly lover, marriage everlasting," and she listened only to the romantic melancholy of the lamentations.

There was an old maid who came to the convent and who would sing romantic ballads to the girls on the sly. Emma then read voraciously from tales of romance involving lonely meetings, secret encounters, gloomy forests, and troubles of the heart. She became enthusiastic over Sir Walter Scott and dreamed of living in some romantic palace where a cavalier with a white plume could come galloping up and rescue her.

When her mother died, Emma had a lock of her dead mother's hair mounted and wrote her father that when she died she would like to be buried in the same grave. She gave her time to reading romantic, sentimental poetry and while enjoying the mysteries of the church, she rebelled against the discipline.

When her father took her from the convent, she enjoyed managing the servants for a while, but soon tired of it and longed for the convent. When Charles appeared, she found it difficult to believe that the quietness and dullness of her romance was what she had read about in the novels.

Comment

A.

The earliest chapters have been concerned with Emma only from an indirect view. Now Flaubert is ready to present his view or analysis of Emma. As pointed out earlier, this technique — a delayed emergence of the main character — serves to heighten the reader's interest in hearing about the main character.

B.

This chapter presents Emma as an incurable romantic, a person who lives in a dream world, in a world of fiction rather than in the real world. She is a dreamer and a sentimentalist. When young she had read *Paul and Virginia*, a highly sentimental and romanticized view of life and love. This novel of idyllic love contributed to Emma's dreamy sentimentalism. The chapter then proceeds to show how a person already endowed with a strong degree of sentimentality was placed in a type of life in the convent which nourished her already excessive tendency toward this type of sentimentalism. In religion she searched for the unusual, the mystic, the dreamy. In the convent, she read stories of romance while being unable to see the real world. She concentrated her attention upon the beautiful and artistic rather than finding the basic elements of a natural life. Novels read on the sly only increased the value of the romance by being forbidden. Thus, left alone with her dreams, she developed into a dreamy girl who wanted all the elements of romantic fiction to come alive in her own life. She longs for old castles, for romantic lovers charging up to a balcony on a white horse, for moonlight meetings in far-away places. She feels the need of excitement and mystery, and cannot tolerate the normal life of everyday living. Thus, when Charles comes calling, she cannot understand why her life wasn't suddenly filled with passion, bliss and ecstasy.

C.

Another of Emma's characteristics is suggested in this chapter: Emma's constant need for a change. She at first enjoyed being out of the convent and at home managing the servants, but then grew rapidly tired of this and longed again for the convent. Thus throughout the novel, Emma will begin one project and drop it only to begin another, always in the constant search for something new and exciting.

PART I – CHAPTER 7

Summary

Emma wondered if the honeymoon was actually to be the finest part of her life. She wondered why she couldn't be standing in a Swiss chalet with a husband in a dashing outfit of velvet, soft boots, peaked hat, etc. As Charles' outward attraction for her increased, she began inwardly to detach herself from him. As she observed Charles, she noted that he simply trudged through every day. His talk was dull, he provoked no emotions in her, he had no desire to do or see anything, and he couldn't even explain a riding term in one of her novels. Ideally, she dreamed of a man who would introduce her into a multitude of activities and passions, who would inspire her to live to the fullest. And when she perceived that Charles was perfectly content simply to be with her, she hated him for his placid immobility and contentment.

Charles, on the other hand, found no fault with his wife. She was an excellent manager and played the piano with skill. All her acts gave him pleasure, and in every way he was content with his life and good fortune. Whenever Mrs. Bovary visited, however, he was confounded by the coldness between his wife and mother. Emma resented the older woman's advice or interference, and the mother was jealous of her son's affection for his wife.

Meanwhile, Emma continued to crave the exalted and passionate love which she sadly felt had been denied her. She criticized herself for ever having married and suffered from envy of the imagined happiness of the girls with whom she had gone to school.

One September the Bovarys were invited to a ball at the chateau of the Marquis d'Andervilliers, whom Charles had treated. The Marquis was far above them in social rank but wanted to demonstrate his gratitude for the service Bovary had done him. Emma looked forward to this unique event with great eagerness.

Comment

A.

Emma continues her dreaming of another life and another husband. She pictures to herself a fabulous life with another person, and begins to detach herself from Charles. The contrast between her dreams and her life is brought out rather concisely in two paragraphs, the first describing Charles' commonplace banalities, his slow plodding ways, his lack of emotional stimulation and his contentment, whereas in her dreams, she sees a man sweeping her off her feet and introducing her to all the intense passions of life. Finally, to observe her dull husband being content with a snack, falling into bed, and snoring fills her with indescribable longings for another life.

B.

This chapter then begins to depict the complete contrast between Emma and Charles. His plodding nature and his routine ardors and embraces destroyed all the excitement in life for Emma. She becomes increasingly irritated with his coarse ways and his dullness. This chapter then marks the beginning of her life of waiting for something exciting to happen. Her entire life will be characterized by her unfilled longing and incessant waiting for some excitement to enter into it. Her disappointment prompted her first words to be spoken in the novel: "O God, O God, why did I get married?"—previous to this statement, we have heard about Emma and about her thoughts, but significantly, these are her *first* spoken words.

C.

The excitement that Emma has been waiting for comes in the form of an invitation to La Vaubyessard. This will soon become one of the high points of her life.

PART I – CHAPTER 8

Summary

The chateau was a building of stately proportions, situated on a large and prosperous estate. The many rooms were filled with expensive and artistic furnishings and decorations. The ball was attended by all the aristocracy and gentry of the surrounding area.

Emma was overjoyed at the opportunity of being able to move freely in such noble company. During their stay at the chateau she constantly berated Bovary, whom she felt looked like a country buffoon and whose presence embarrassed her. Emma dressed and attempted to behave as if she too were a great lady and mingled with the other guests. All night she basked in the reflected glory of those around her. The ball and the people at it seemed to be transported from out of the novels and dreams she had long cherished. Emma was so ecstatic she never noticed that most of the guests ignored her. The high point of her evening came when a man known only as "Vicomte" danced with her.

On the trip home Emma suffered from bitter disappointment that she, who was so obviously entitled to preferment, could not live this way all year round. In her disillusionment she saw Bovary as a clumsy, simple oaf. Back home her frustration caused her to be cross with him, and in a fit of pique she fired the maid, despite the woman's devotion and good service. Each day Emma attempted to recall the great events of the ball, but in time they became vague memories.

Comment

A.

This chapter presents in reality all of the grand elegance that Emma had dreamed and read about. Here then are her dreams turning into reality. Everything that she dreamed of is here: the grand dinner, the magnificent ball, the elegant dances, the discussions of far away people and even an old man who had slept with the queen, and a young lady carrying on an intrigue with a young man. And finally, Emma's being requested to dance with a Viscount testifies to her own superiority over her upbringing.

B.

This chapter focuses almost all of the attention on Emma. It is important here to see that Emma *does* possess the necessary qualities so as to blend in with an aristocratic world. Unlike Charles who stands limply around for five hours watching a game he doesn't understand, Emma is moving graciously and rather charmingly amid this aristocratic society. Even though she does not attract people to her, she seems to blend in. Her invitation to dance with the Viscount and her ability to learn the dance attest to her acceptance. Thus, Emma's later degradation should be contrasted to the success she attains here, and by the comparison, Emma's later plight will be seen to be more pathetic.

C.

Note the cigar box that Charles found. Emma will later dawdle over this as a reminder of her experience at the ball and convince herself that it belonged to the Viscount.

D.

Returning to her own drab surroundings, Emma can barely tolerate the dull routine of everyone doing the same dull things. She therefore loses herself in her reveries about the ball.

PART I—CHAPTER 9

Summary

Emma buried herself in her fantasies and dreamed of living in Paris, among the nobility. She visualized life in the capital as a constant round of balls, parties, amours, and other exciting things. She read novels and travel books voraciously and studied maps of the city. Much of her time was spent planning imaginary trips, adventures, secret meetings, and visits to the theater or opera. The reality of life at Tostes became unbearable to her, and she was even more critical of Bovary.

At first Emma attempted to add little touches of elegance to her humdrum life, such as fancy lampshades and silver, but this soon became an unsatisfactory solution to her craving, even though it pleased Charles. Emma's despair became more intense when she finally was forced to realize that there would be no further invitations to the chateau, and in her depression she gave up her music, sketching, and other pursuits. She was often sad and lonely, and during the long winter her plight became worse. She seemed to cultivate her unhappiness and self-pity by concentrating on her unattainable aspirations, and by finding so little with which to oocupy herself. Most of her time was now spent staring down from her window at the village street. She was sullen and rarely spoke to Charles.

As her condition became even worse, Emma's moods began to fluctuate between extreme forms of behavior. Sometimes she was very active, sometimes lethargic and slovenly, sometimes nervous and stingy, sometimes capricious and temperamental, but always she was unpredictable and difficult to get along with. Soon she became physically ill. None of Charles' worried efforts to cure her were successful, and he took her to Rouen, to see the medical professor under whom he had studied.

This learned doctor recommended a change of scene for the sake of Emma's health, since it was evidently a nervous disorder and she complained so much of disliking Tostes. Despite the fact that he had built a flourishing practice in the village, Charles was willing to sacrifice all for Emma's welfare. After making some inquiries, he decided to move to the town of Yonville, which was located in a nice area and where a doctor was needed.

While Emma was helping with the packing, she pricked her hand on her old bridal bouquet, which was now dried up, frayed and yellow with dust. She threw it into the fire and watched it burn. By the time they moved to the new town, Emma was pregnant.

Comment

A.

Perhaps no chapter in the novel presents Flaubert's essential theme and meaning as well as does this concluding chapter of Part One. Flaubert vividly depicts the exhausting and enervating results of a woman who expends all her energy in dreams and futile longings. The chapter opens with Emma's recalling the events of the ball, reliving certain episodes and then progressing to envisioning new incidents which might have happened. She wastes, then, her energies in imagining that the cigar case belonged to the Viscount, that he is now in Paris and is pursuing a life of intrigue and excitement. She fritters away her time and energy by tracing walks through Paris on a map she bought, she imagines shopping in Paris, she subscribes to Paris magazines and she dreams of the Viscount. But Flaubert is able to make us all see that Emma's frustrated longing for a different type of life is a quality that we all possess. Thus he universalizes Emma's longings so as to make an indirect comment concerning this type of wasted and futile activity.

B.

Emma constantly contrasts her real environment and surroundings with those she conjectures in her dreams. The real then seems completely intolerable: "The nearer home things came, the more she shrank from all thought of them." In her dreams, new and exciting things happen every day, but in her real life in Tostes, the same things happen over and over again, so that "the whole of her immediate environment — dull countryside, imbecile petty bourgeois, life in its ordinariness — seemed a freak, a particular piece of bad luck that had seized on her." Therefore, she tries to introduce some elegance into her life; she hires a fourteen-year-old girl and tries to teach her how to become a "lady's maid."

C.

Emma's frustration and longings cause her to give up her piano, her needle work, drawing, care for the house and all other useful activity. Instead, she fritters away her time in daydreaming. Rather than making herself useful in some way, she drains herself of all her energy by these longings for another life. In waiting for something to happen, she becomes a pathetic (almost tragic) case of a woman who exhausts herself in these futile longings until she is physically sick. In other words, she indulges in her own misery until her self-indulgences cause her sickness. She has had a fleeting glimpse at emotions that transcend the dull routine life at Tostes, and her intense longings for these more sublime emotions cause her sickness. The pathos of Emma's life is that she does possess enough sensitivity to be aware of feelings and emotions greater than those of Charles, but is unable to find a suitable outlet for these emotions.

D.
　　Emma's plight is symbolically depicted in the discovery and burning of her bridal bouquet. What was once to be the symbol of a new and exciting life filled with new emotions now is seen as a faded, frayed, dusty object on which she pricks her finger. Thus, the burning of the bridal bouquet signifies the end of her marriage and prepares us for her promiscuity later on. It is not just the end of a marriage, but also the end of her life at Tostes, because now that they are moving, Emma can perhaps be reawakened to a different life.

PART II – CHAPTERS 1 & 2

Summary
　　Yonville was a market town located in the center of a farming district, not far from Rouen. The main features of the surrounding region and of the town itself are described in some detail. Various inhabitants of Yonville, including Madame Lefrancois, the innkeeper, Hivert and Artemise, her servants, Binet, the tax collector, and Homais, the apothecary, make their first appearances in this chapter.

　　Homais, with whom Bovary had corresponded before deciding to move to Yonville, was an outspoken and pretentious fellow of some education and status. He was always eager to impress people by his knowledge and sophistication, although in fact he did not possess much of either.

The Bovarys and Felicite, their new maid, arrived in Yonville after a very tiring trip and an accident in which Emma lost her pet greyhound. She was in her usual irritable mood.

Bovary and his wife dined at the inn. They were joined at the table by Homais and his boarder, Leon, a shy young man who was the town lawyer's clerk. During the meal Homais devoted most of his attention to Bovary, seeking to awe him by his extensive acquaintance with science and local affairs. Meanwhile, Emma and Leon fell into conversation. He shared many of her romanticized notions and was also an avid reader of sentimental novels. An immediate rapport sprang up between them. Their talk consisted of platitudes and conventionalities, but they each interpreted them as sensitive and profound observations.

Later on the Bovarys took possession of their new house. Emma recalled the other places in which she had lived and been unhappy. She hoped that the future would bring an improvement in her life.

Comment

A.

Flaubert's masterful description and rendition of the town is a masterpiece of realistic writing. It captures all of the mediocrity of a small town. And what Flaubert never says directly, but depicts through his descriptions is that this town is just about the same as was Tostes. Yonville is just as monotonous, routine, and boring as was Tostes. Here, nothing has changed in years and nothing will change. So suddenly, we realize that this town will depress Emma as much as did Tostes.

B.

We meet the chemist Homais for the first time. He will develop into a stereotype. It will suffice here to begin to note certain characteristics which make up the stereotype. 1) He is the man who professes to keep up with the times. 2) He feels it is his duty to ridicule the church, therefore aligning himself with the advanced thinkers of the world. 3) He has accumulated many facts which he enjoys reciting, but the reader should note that his facts are of a trivial nature.

C.

Emma's first meeting with Leon is an exciting event for her. For the first time in her life, she has met a person who shares the same interest in literature, music, and related subjects. She immediately feels that they are kindred spirits and an immediate rapport sprang up between them. But the reader should note that their talk consisted of platitudes and conventionalities, but they each interpreted them as sensitive and profound observations.

PART II – CHAPTER 3

Summary

All the next day Leon thought about Emma, for their meeting had been a very special event to him. This was the first time that the bashful youth had ever spoken to a lady at such length, and he was surprised at his own eloquence.

In the days that followed, Homais was of great assistance to Bovary in establishing himself, although it must be said that the druggist's motives were partly selfish. Charles was a bit gloomy, because his medical practice was slow in starting and he had financial worries. The cost of moving had been high, he had lost money on the sale of the house at Tostes, and there was now a child on the way. However, the thought of having a baby Emma to love also, and to watch grow, was a source of great joy to him.

Emma had originally been surprised by her pregnancy but was now accustomed to the idea. She was eager to have the child, although all the preparations made her impatient since they could not afford the kind of layette she insisted was necessary. She hoped the baby would be a boy, for she felt that only a man could have the freedom and strength to overcome the constraints that had always so frustrated her.

The child was born, and after much discussion the name of

"Berthe" was selected. There was a gay christening party, and Bovary's parents visited at Yonville for a month.

One day Emma decided to visit the baby at the home of its wet nurse. She was still weak after her confinement and was beginning to feel faint, when she encountered Leon. She asked him to accompany her. Leon consented and by nightfall, rumors had spread through the town that Madame Bovary was compromising herself.

After seeing the child, Madame Bovary was pestered with lots of trivial requests from the nurse. She quickly consented to give the woman more supplies and even some brandy for the woman's husband. Then she and Leon took a long stroll along the river. Even though they didn't say very much to each other, both were aware of a strange bliss and a deeper communication. After Leon left her, he thought how radiantly she stood out, especially amid all the banalities of Yonville.

Comment

A.

When Emma first learned she was pregnant, she thought that this could be a new experience for her, could fill her empty life with excitement, especially if it were a boy. But when the girl was born, she soon lost interest in it. Again this shows Emma's erratic nature, her inability to maintain an interest in any aspect of life. Her reaction differs significantly with Charles' and the difference emphasizes the growing breach between them. Charles thinks that with the birth of the child, he will have been through the entire range of human experience.

B.

Emma's indiscretion in asking Leon to accompany her, foreshadows her later promiscuities. We have seen that Emma possesses an impetuous nature, and this quality will also contribute to her series of indiscretions.

C.

Emma's encounter with the nurse foreshadows her handlings with the various tradesmen which will later take her so deeply in debt. It seems that Emma would rather give in than discuss the needs of the nurse. Later, her financial troubles are a result of her impetuousness and her failure to consider her needs.

PART II – CHAPTERS 4 & 5

Summary
During the winter Emma's favorite pursuit was to sit at the window and watch the street. She often saw Leon as he passed and had a new and unknown feeling at those moments.

Homais lived across the street and was a frequent caller, especially at mealtimes. He enjoyed gossiping about Bovary's patients and discussing science, philosophy, and politics with the doctor. It was the druggist who always did most of the talking.

On Sundays the Bovarys usually visited the Homais family. Leon was always there, and a bond rapidly developed between him and Emma. They used to sit together and discuss fashions or books while the others played cards or dozed.

Leon began to grow confused and was tormented by these meetings. He was uncertain whether Emma responded to his feelings for her. He was afraid to displease her by remaining silent about his love, but he did not have the courage to declare himself.

One Sunday in February, Homais and his children, the Bovarys, and Leon went on an outdoor excursion. Emma watched the men with interest and decided that she was disgusted by Charles' commonplace appearance and personality.

That night she suddenly realized that Leon loved her. This novel idea pleased her, and she began to complain to herself about the cruel fate which had separated the two of them. Later that week Leon paid her a visit, on some weak pretext. They were both shy and their conversation was stilted, for they feared to express their real feelings to each other.

As time passed Emma began to lose weight through worry. She found a delicious pleasure in contemplating her affection for Leon and contrasting it with her sensible, though unsatisfying role of the virtuous wife. She was herself as a martyr to marital fidelity. Emma became irritable again and was exasperated by Bovary's placid ignorance of her torments. She blamed him for all her troubles and in addition was overly tolerant in judging herself and her behavior. She dreamed of running away with Leon but then doubted his love for her. She wished that Bovary were a cruel husband so that she would have an excuse to be unfaithful. Her nervousness and tension often caused her to engage in fits of weeping.

One day while she was dreaming of Leon, Monsieur Lheureux, a draper, paid her a visit in order to show her some of his wares, especially scarves and little ornaments. He then slyly let her know that he was also a moneylender in case she ever needed to borrow a little money.

As Emma came to the realization of her love for Leon, she tried to compensate for her frustrated love by being the ideal wife, mother and housekeeper. But while she was being the model wife, "she was all desire and rage and hatred."

Comment

A.

In these chapters, Flaubert is developing the love between Emma and Leon, a love that will not be consummated until the third part of the novel. Emma's love causes her to despise her husband, then she turns into the model wife trying to compensate for her lack of love, and finally turns to moods of despair. This again emphasizes Emma's lack of stability and her constant fluctuation between opposite extremes. These moods foreshadow her later sickness and ultimately her suicide.

B.

Monsieur Lheureux is here introduced. He is the moneylender who will unscrupulously play on Emma's weaknesses and will be the cause of her suicide. His portrayal here already suggests his obsequious personality.

PART II — CHAPTER 6

Summary
One evening the tolling of church bells made Emma recall her childhood and school days. She mused about the solace she had often found then through religious devotions and set out for the church, hoping that there she might resolve her present problems and gain some inner peace.

She met the curé, Abbe Bournisien, near the entrance, where he was attempting to control the mischievous children of his catechism class. Emma attempted to explain to the priest her need for spiritual help, but the priest's attention focused more on the young boys who were misbehaving. He was also more interested in telling Emma about his problems within the parish than he was in listening to her. After several attempts on Emma's part to explain her dilemma, she finally sighed in despair: "O God, O God!" The Abbe immediately thinks she has some physical ailment, and advises her to go home immediately and have a cup of tea. Then "it suddenly struck him: 'there was something you were asking me. What was it, now? I can't recall.'" Emma responds that it was nothing and then leaves as the Abbe goes in to teach catechism to the group of boys.

She continued to be very jumpy and tense. That same evening, in a fit of nervous annoyance, she pushed the baby away from her. Berthe fell and cut herself. Emma screamed for help and claimed that the child had been hurt accidentally while playing. After some confused excitement, Bovary and Homais (who always appeared whenever anything of interest happened) managed to calm her and take care of Berthe.

Leon found that his position in Yonville remained perplexing and intolerable. He adored Emma, but saw no future in his love for a married woman. He decided to go to Paris to study law, something he had long spoken of doing. The idea of being alone in the capital frightened him, but he saw no other alternative. After a while though, he began to imagine with great joy the Bohemian adventures he would have there.

Leon made his arrangements and the day finally came for his departure. When he bid farewell to Emma, they were both restrained and shy, although their eyes and gestures communicated a wealth of emotional meanings. After he had gone, Homais and Bovary discussed the dangers and temptations of life in the city. Emma listened silently.

Comment

A.

When Emma thinks of the consolation she had at the convent, she fails to remember that she was also terribly dissatisfied there. Emma is actually looking for some experience that will fill her void and occupy her so that she will not think about her misery. In other words, she is using religion as a substitute for real experiences and as a way of forgetting her present misery.

B.

In this brief scene between Emma and the priest, Flaubert offers a masterful condemnation of the church in a very subtle way. The priest is so occupied with his own insignificant occupation that he does not have time to perceive Emma's distress. In fact, he thinks that she needs a cup of tea rather than spiritual guidance. His devout devotion to details renders him incapable of recognizing Emma's spiritual need and thus he fails in his greater mission as a Priest.

C.

This chapter presents the departure of Leon without a physical consummation of their love. But the length of this mutual attraction and Emma's many reflections about it make her more receptive for her next encounter. In other words, she regrets her timidity in not letting Leon know of her love so that now she is emotionally prepared to respond more openly to the advances of Rodolphe. It can also be said that both Emma and Leon have progressed in their education so that when they next meet, they will not be so bashful and timid.

PART II – CHAPTER 7

Summary

After Leon had gone, Emma began a period of secret mourning. She drifted about aimlessly and was often melancholy. She saw Leon in her imagination as the hero of all her dreams and remembered their walks and conversations. She reproached herself for not having responded to his love, and he became the center of all her thoughts. In her misery, she began again the strange and unpredictable behavior that had marked her in Tostes. Her moods constantly changed, and she was often giddy and nervous.

One day Rodolphe Boulanger, a handsome and wealthy landowner, brought one of his servants to be treated by Bovary. While there he saw Emma and was immediately attracted by her good looks and ladylike bearing. Boulanger was a suave bachelor, both coarse and shrewd. At once his thoughts turned to Emma's seduction, and he began to lay his plans.

Comment

A.

Emma's long melancholy and regret over not having seized her opportunity with Leon actually cause her to become sick. She then goes into one of her spending sprees, justifying her spending by feeling she has sacrificed so much by being faithful to Charles. These are the same types of spending sprees which will later lead her into heavy debts.

B.

Note again Emma's erratic actions. She would take something up, leave it, go to something else only to leave it, etc. It seems that nothing fulfills her. Flaubert's description of Emma's actions and looks implies that Emma fits ironically into the tradition of the courtly love. The "vaporish airs," the fact that she was "pale all over, white as a sheet," and given to spells of dizziness are all characteristics of the courtly love tradition or are signs of disappointed or unfulfilled love.

34

C.

Emma is, after all, essentially middle-class, but she is also more than this. In a sense, she raises herself above the town because unlike others, she is vaguely aware that there are emotions of a higher and purer nature than those with which she finds herself surrounded. This realization does raise Emma in our estimates although this is also the ultimate cause of her tragedy.

D.

Note that Rodolphe is able to see through Emma immediately. He sees her boredom, recognizes that she dislikes her husband and her present life, and realizes that she is "gasping for love" and is ready for a love affair. What we know is that this is true, but partly because she regrets not having an affair with Leon.

PART II CHAPTER 8

Summary

At the time of this story, the annual Agricultural Show for the Prefecture of the Seine-Inferieure was held at Yonville. Everyone looked forward to the fair with great enthusiasm; when the long awaited day finally arrived, Yonville was crowded with visitors from all the surrounding farms and towns. There were exhibits and contests of many kinds, and everything had a carnival aspect. The most important event of the day was the speech and presentation of awards by a representative of the Prefect.

According to his carefully calculated plan, Rodolphe took advantage of the excitement of the day to renew his acquaintance with Emma. They went walking together and spoke about a variety of things. Rodolphe took every opportunity to drop some hint about his love for Emma. He gradually leads her toward the city hall so that they can be alone.

Meanwhile the representative from the Prefect arrived, and even though the people expected the Prefect himself, they were still honored by this man. However, in trying to pay homage to him, the battalion of men confused their orders and everything ended in confusion. While he spoke about the government, Rodolphe begins to hint to Emma his affections for her. And while the speech is going on in the background about the morality and government, Rodolphe begins to declare his love for Emma and to insist that his feelings are nobler than common morality. He continues to declare his love for her in high sounding language while the representative of the Prefect awards prizes to various people.

After the awarding of the prices, Emma separates from Rodolphe and does not see him again until that night at the banquet and later at the fireworks. She was complimented by his attentions, but had constantly acted as she thought proper for a respectable, married woman. As the fireworks were being set off, Emma watched Rodolphe. She was not even aware that the fireworks had gotten wet and wouldn't go off. Later, however, Homais wrote a glowing account of the entire day's activities.

Comment

A.

The inexperienced reader will often overlook the greatness of this particular chapter. It is often referred to when the subject of Flaubert's greatness is being discussed. It will profit the reader to re-read the chapter and observe many of the following factors: the number of things that are contrasted; the use of subtle irony, especially in passages that seem to be simply description; the elaborately described show, the gold medal won by the old peasant woman, and the subtle but damning description of the pompous dignitaries; and the use of foreshadowing, especially in the way in which Emma is able to see unknowingly her whole pathetic life unfold before her in symbolic events.

B.

Use of Contrast and Description: There are so many masterfully descriptive passages, it will suffice to point out only one. In the first part of the chapter, Flaubert is describing all the animals that are gathered together for the show. Most of the details of this description suggest symbolically that this animal world is the same world in which the action of the entire novel is being played.

The animals are described in the same manner in which people will later be described. For example, later in the chapter, when Flaubert is describing the feast, the same type of description is used for both the animals and the people. They were both herded into a small place with noses together, sweating and stuffing themselves. One could even maintain that the animals are described in terms of people and the people are described in terms of animals, emphasizing the nature of the people that Flaubert is dealing with.

C.

Use of Irony: The speech of the representative of the Prefect is filled with cliches and pompous platitudes. The speaker says only what every other speaker has been saying for years, but yet his speech is highly praised.

Rodolphe's speech to Emma, delivered against the background of the general prizes being awarded, is a masterpiece of irony. First, we hear about the old peasant woman who is winning a prize for fifty-four years of faithful service and fidelity as a servant. At the same time, Emma is planning on being unfaithful and on beginning a love affair with Rodolphe whom we know can never be faithful to any person very long.

It is a further stroke of irony that his false speeches of passion such as "I stayed with you, because I couldn't tear myself away..." are spoken during the awarding of the first prize in *manure*. Subtly speaking, Rodolphe's speech is just so much manure, but Emma is not capable of recognizing it.

D.

Foreshadowing: In the discussion of Lheureux's being the cause of the downfall of a certain man, we are warned that Emma will herself get into trouble because of her dealings with this man. He is even described here as a wheedling, grovelling creature.

The tremendous waste of human energy in preparing for the show indicates how the energies of Emma are wasted throughout the entire novel.

Emma's view of the ancient *Hirondelle* as it approaches the town, foreshadows her degradation and involvement with Leon later in the novel, as this coach will be instrumental in her love affair.

E.

Homais' role in the entire pageant and his essay sent to the paper afterwards reaches the height of the comic absurd. First of all, from all of the description, the entire day was a failure if not a fiasco. The dignitary was late and when he finally arrived he was only a representative of the Prefect; the presentation of arms was sloppy, confused, and ridiculous; the speeches were dull; there were not enough seats; the feast was long and noisy and badly served and too crowded; the fireworks were damp and would not go off, and it rained during the proceedings. But Homais' account of the day written for the newspaper was so frankly false that his exaggerations seem the height of the comic. And ironically speaking, an earlier description of Homais' says that he "had the right form of words for every conceivable occasion."

PART II – CHAPTERS 9 & 10

Summary

During the next six weeks Rodolphe did not see Emma. This interval was also planned by him, acting on the theory that "absence makes the heart grow fonder." He had carefully analyzed her personality and decided to take advantage of all her frustrations and weaknesses.

When Rodolphe finally called at the Bovary house, Emma, who had thought about him often and was insulted by his lack of attention, was unresponsive. But Rodolphe was so eloquent in amorous language that she soon forgot her affected annoyance at his absence and was overcome by sentiment. When Charles came in, Rodolphe suggested that perhaps riding would be good for Emma. He offered to lend them a horse, but Emma refused. After Rodolphe had gone, Charles convinced Emma to accept Rodolphe's offer and even wrote to Rodolphe himself requesting the horse.

The next day Emma and Rodolphe went for a ride together. He led her to a beautiful and deserted glade in the nearby forest. When they had dismounted, Rodolphe again spoke of his passion for her. Emma was frightened by his intensity but quickly forgot all her good intentions and gave herself entirely to him. When she returned home that night she was radiant with joy. In her new happiness she identified herself with all the daring and romantic heroines of literature whom she had always envied and admired. She unbelievingly repeated to herself over and over again, "I have a lover—a lover."

From this day on the affair between Emma and Rodolphe progressed with great speed. They frequently exchanged love letters and had many secret meetings. Rodolphe was always in Emma's thoughts. She often slipped from her house in the early morning while Bovary was still asleep in order to surprise Rodolphe and have a few extra hours with him.

After a while, Rodolphe, who was a practical and realistic man, became concerned about Emma's imprudent behavior. He spoke to her about this, claiming to be worried lest she compromise herself, and soon she too became nervous. She began to be troubled by feelings of guilt. The pair took precautions to keep their correspondence hidden and worked out an arrangement so that Rodolphe could meet Emma at night in her garden or even in her house, once Bovary had fallen into his usual deep sleep. Rodolphe began to visit her several times each week.

He was sometimes troubled by her wildly romantic fancies and feared that she would do something irrational or impractical, in accord with her silly ideas. He thought of ending their relationship but procrastinated because of the great physical appeal she had for him. So far as Emma's love for him was concerned, Rodolphe cynically doubted her sincerity and had no compunctions about using or abandoning her. Emma, on the other hand, considered him the one great love for whom she had always yearned and surrendered herself to him with complete devotion.

As time passed, Emma became unhappy about both her marriage and adultery. She was often negligent of her duties and then, in a moment of guilty realization, would engage in a brief spurt of activity or maternal affection. Her guilt kept bothering her, and for a short period she even decided to repent and reform. She derived a strange pleasure from her masochistic decision to assuage her guilt through self-sacrifice, for her affection for Rodolphe had not lessened. In order to end the affair, she was cold to him and she planned to force herself to love and assist Bovary.

Comment

A.

Emma is a woman of romantic longings. We saw earlier that she longed for a man who "should know about everything; excel in a multitude of activity, introduce you to passion in all its force, to life in all its graces, you into all mysteries," (see Chapters 6 and 7 of Part I), and now Rodolphe comes to call after a six week's absence, and tells her things she "had never been told before." Here then is the romantic dream come true. *But,* in reality, he is not the knight in shining armor. He is, after all, a thirty-four year old farmer. But to Emma who has lived in boredom so long and who has longed for some type of escape, he is the fulfillment of her dreams. After she surrenders to him, she then thinks of all the heroines of books and compares her shoddy seduction in the woods to those of the romanticized heroines of her novels. She is convinced that her affair has all the "passion, ecstasy and delirium" of the fictionalized accounts in romances. Emma then attempts to make her shoddy affair conform to those of fictionalized accounts. She insists that they leave letters for each other in secret hiding places. She comforts him about absurd insignificant events and when once she thinks she hears Charles coming, she expects Rodolphe to grab his pistol so as to defend himself. She insists upon exchanging miniatures, locks of hair, and even rings. Even Rodolphe realizes the degree of sentimentality that Emma is attaching to their love affair.

B.

Emma never realizes that Rodolphe is simply using her for a pretty mistress. Even though they are having their affair now in Charles' consulting room, she fails to realize how shoddy the affair is and continues to force their affair into the pattern of a great love.

C.

Ironically, it was Charles who originally assured the success of the love affair by insisting that Emma accept Rodolphe's offer of the riding horse. Of course, we have seen earlier that Charles, due to the horror of his first wife, can see no fault in Emma.

D.

Chapter 9 ends with Rodolphe's admonition to Emma that she is compromising herself by her visits to his cabin. This foreshadows his rejection of Emma. We know from the beginning that this is to be only a brief love affair for him, but as he reminds her of her position, we note already that he is beginning to tire of her.

PART II – CHAPTER 11

Summary

One day it was learned that a doctor in Rouen had published a remarkable new surgical procedure for curing clubfoot. Emma and Homais urged Charles to carry out the new operation on Hippolyte, the crippled servant at the inn. Emma hoped in this way to advance Bovary in his career and thus satisfy her desire to be a good wife; she had many daydreams about the wealth and increased prestige to which his success would entitle them. Homais expected to gain personal repute from his own part in the operation and to bring more business to Yonville (and himself) as word of the cure spread. Neither Homais nor Emma was particularly concerned with the safety of the operation or the well-being of Hippolyte.

Bovary was dubious about the new technique and was unwilling to cooperate, but, under the combined pressure of Emma and Homais, finally gave in. Moreover, nearly everyone in the town, including the mayor, was a staunch advocate of the new operation, for they had all been convinced by Homais of its advantage to them. Their ceaseless prodding continued until Bovary was ready to proceed. Hippolyte was terrified and confused by the whole idea, but he was a simple youth and was induced to volunteer his body for the sake of Yonville and Science.

The operation was carried out by Homais and Charles in the local inn. At first it seemed a success, but Hippolyte soon became ill and suffered terrible pain. It was discovered that his leg was infested with gangrene. Bovary was very upset and unable to act; so a consultant was called in from another town. The doctor sternly admonished Bovary for his foolish treatment and amputated the patient's leg. Homais, meanwhile, disclaimed any responsibility, and Emma was disgusted by what she interpreted as a further demonstration of Charles' stupid incompetence. In fact, however, the fault was not entirely Bovary's although no one recognized this. Some of the blame also belonged to the specialist who had published an untested and undependable "cure."

Bovary and Emma were both depressed by this incident, although for different reasons. He was ashamed of what he had done and felt that he had been irresponsible. She reproached herself for ever having had faith in him and decided that she was now absolved of any responsibility to her husband. Her passion for Rodolphe flared up again, and she saw him that night for the first time in many days. Charles, in his simplicity, assumed that Emma's depression had been caused by sympathy for him and was gratified by her demonstration of devotion.

Comment

A.

This chapter interrupts the progress of the love affair. At the end of the last chapter, Emma had begun to repent of her love for Rodolphe. Now she turns to Charles, and when Homais suggests the operation, she encourages it thinking that if Charles were famous she could respect him. Through it all, Homais and Emma never give any thought to Charles or to Hippolyte, but instead see in the operation how they could personally benefit from the fame. *We* know, and later in retrospect Emma realizes, that Charles is not capable of such an operation, and it is only through the goading of Emma and Homais that he ever consents. The operation having failed, Emma now repents of her past virtue. In other words, Charles' ineptitude and stupidity now give her full justification to carry out her affair with no tinge of recrimination. Thus this interlude functions to again convince Emma of Charles' ignorance and to justify her infidelity.

B.

The description of the operation, the gangrene with its smell, the interest of the crowd, and the suffering of Hippolyte are all masterfully rendered. And the absurdity of Homais' letter composed immediately after the operation should be compared with the equally absurd letter describing the agricultural show in chapter 8.

PART II – CHAPTERS 12 & 13

Summary

The liaison between Emma and Rodolphe began again and now evolved with greater ardor. As her passion for Rodolphe increased, Emma found that she disliked Bovary even more, and she began to speak vaguely of leaving him someday. When she was not with Rodolphe, Emma suffered from boredom and was irritated by all of Charles' mannerisms and acts. She began to feel sorry for herself because of her unhappy marriage and found some solace in catering to her material desires. She fell an easy victim to the wily merchant, Lheureux, who cajoled her into many purchases that she could not afford.

Rodolphe, meanwhile, was growing tired of Emma. The novelty of her love was wearing off, and her ridiculous whims annoyed him.

Bovary's mother paid the family a visit. She and Emma had their usual fight, though Emma was finally induced by Charles to apologize. She was mortified by this and when she saw Rodolphe that night, Emma asked him to take her away from all her misery. He reminded her of the baby, and as an afterthought, Emma decided to take the child with her.

In the next few days Bovary and his mother were amazed and pleased at the changes that came over Emma; she was quiet and docile now and seemed a new person. But at her secret meetings with Rodolphe, Emma was planning to run away and start her life again. The happiness that such plans gave her added new highlights and softness to her beauty. She was so gentle and lovely that Bovary was reminded of the first days of their marriage, and his love for her and Berthe deepened. Emma's thoughts, though, were always far off, contemplating exotic lands and adventures.

Despite Rodolphe's procrastination, the final plans for their departure were made. He and Emma would leave Yonville separately, meet in Rouen, and then go on together to Paris. On the night before the day selected, they met in Emma's garden to make the last arrangements. Emma was in high spirits and seemed more beautiful than ever. Rodolphe was reserved and thoughtful. After leaving her he argued with himself for a while. The problems and burdens of life with Emma, he decided, would not be worth the sensual pleasure she could offer him.

That night Rodolphe sat at his desk and mused for a while about the many women he had known. After some trouble he composed a letter which he felt would end their affair with the fewest complications. He wrote her that he loved her very much (which was not true) and that this was why he was abandoning her. He said that the life he could offer would provide her only with pain and indignity, and he could not bear to do this. And, he thought, this was really not too far from the truth after all. Much satisfied with his work, Rodolphe went to sleep.

Emma received this note the next morning and became faint from shock. In her confusion she dropped the crumbled up letter in the attic and forgot about it. Rodolphe had told her that he was leaving Yonville to protect her from him, and a few moments later she saw his carriage drive by. This awful reminder of what had just happened was like a blow to her heart. She screamed aloud and fell unconscious.

Emma became seriously ill. She had a high fever and delirium for 43 days and was often close to death. Bovary never left her side and neglected all his affairs to care for her. Specialists were called in from Rouen and elsewhere, and every effort was made to cure her, but for a long time nothing had any success.

By October Emma began to regain her strength. She still had fainting spells and weak periods, but she was able to move around a little, and was clearly on the road to recovery.

Comment

A.

These two chapters present the passionate renewal of Emma and Rodolphe's love affair after the disappointing interlude connected with Hippolyte's foot. Emma's romanticism now forces her to bring the romance to a climax. She is not satisfied with having an affair with Rodolphe. She insists that they flee together to some strange land. This emphasis on flight is another romantic concept. And while she is insisting that they go away, she begins to go deeper in debt to Lheureux by ordering expensive gifts for Rodolphe and the necessary things for the trip.

B.

After Emma receives Rodolphe's letter, she immediately begins to think of suicide. This foreshadows her actual suicide later on.

C.

Emma's sickness caused by her betrayal suggests that perhaps she felt a love for Rodolphe that is indeed deeper than that of a common woman. Perhaps Flaubert is here indicating that Emma, in spite of her romanticism, is capable of a deep devotion. But most critics prefer to read this scene as Emma's reaction to the loss of her dream and the realization of the emptiness and uselessness of life without her dream. Her sickness, therefore, is simply a result of the betrayal and the loss of her ideal which brings to her the realization that she must continue the empty life that she had lived before her encounter with Rodolphe.

D.

It should be noted here that in spite of Charles' dullness and stupidity, he does possess a dogged devotion to Emma. He gives up his practice and remains by her side during her entire illness. Of course, it could be said that his devotion is the same that an animal would have for his master, but it is, nevertheless, a redeeming characteristic in Charles' otherwise flat personality.

PART II—CHAPTERS 14 & 15

Summary
In addition to his concern about Emma, Charles was also bothered by financial worries. The illness had been very expensive, and other bills were piling up. Moreover, Lheureux suddenly presented him with a statement of Emma's debts. Not knowing what else to do, Bovary borrowed money from Lheureux and signed several notes at a high rate of interest.

All through the winter months Emma's convalescence continued. During a crisis in her illness, Emma's religious sentiments had reawakened. Now she was very devout and spent much of her time reading religious books or conversing with the priest.

By spring Emma was relatively strong again and returned to her household duties. Her religious feelings remained firm, and everyone was surprised by her new generosity, spirituality, and stern principles.

One day at Homais' suggestion, Bovary decided to take Emma to the theater at Rouen. He hoped that such an outing would be good for her health. Emma was not eager to go, but Bovary was so persistent that she agreed. On the day of the trip they excitedly left for the city.

Emma was embarrassed and upset by Charles' behavior and appearance all that afternoon. She wanted very much to seem a sophisticated, cosmopolitan lady, and she felt that he was just a country bumpkin. She was tense and self-conscious wherever they went. Despite this, however, Emma enjoyed the opera, *Lucie de Lammermoor,* very much. She found that the story reminded her of events in her own life.

During the intermission they were both surprised to encounter Leon, who now lived and worked in Rouen. The three went to a cafe together, where Bovary and Leon talked at length about Yonville, their mutual friends, and old times. Leon also told them a little about his present position and his experiences at the university. Emma was impressed by Leon's suave, citified manners and dress. When they discussed the opera they had just left, Leon at first ridiculed it until he learned that perhaps Emma could stay over to see the second part again. He then praised the opera so highly that Charles suggested that Emma stay while he return to his practice. In any case, before they separated, the Bovarys and Leon arranged to meet again the next day.

Comment

A.

After Emma's recovery from her illness, she falls back into the old established neurotic pattern of taking up something (this time religion) only to drop it for something else. She gave herself so completely to religion that even the curé thought she went too far. Then she began charity work even though her own household needed attention.

B.

Once at the opera, Emma becomes immersed in the romantic world on the stage. She begins to identify with the heroine and she is entranced with the tenor. Here Flaubert's art is very subtle. The objective description of the artist says little, but implies that the artist is false. Like Emma, he misrepresents art. He uses tricks to cover up for his lack of art. There is "something of the hair dresser and the toreador" about him. Thus, Emma is lost in this false and sentimental world of cheap art.

C.

The scene at the opera prepares the reader and also Emma for the reintroduction of Leon. The romantic elements of the opera provide an apt meeting place to rekindle their attraction to each other.

PART III – CHAPTER 1

Summary

While attending law school in Paris, Leon was a model student. But he did experience a new way of life even though he remained quiet and respectable. And now that he has returned to Rouen, he has brought with him many of the manners and sophistication that he learned in Paris. He dressed and acted in the Parisian style and felt especially self-confident in Rouen, where he considered himself to be a sophisticate among the local provincials.

At first in Paris he had often thought about Emma, but gradually she became a blurred memory. Now his old feelings for her were reawakened. He visited Emma at her hotel the next day while Bovary was out.

She and Leon were pleased by this opportunity to see each other in private, and they held an animated conversation for several hours. Their old intimacy was renewed, although both withheld several personal details of their recent experiences. Emma and Leon recalled their sad parting in Yonville and the times they had spent together there and discussed with a new frankness their mutual affection. Before leaving, Leon kissed Emma, and they arranged to have a secret meeting at the cathedral the next day.

In the morning, Leon arrived punctually at the place of the rendezvous. Emma was late and tried at first to avoid him, for she hoped to prevent herself from falling in love with him again. She tried to pray but her mind was not on it. Then she readily accepted an invitation from the beadle of the church to see the various parts of the cathedral. Leon suffered the sightseeing as long as possible and then pulled Emma away from the church and into a carriage he had sent for.

The carriage driver could not understand why two people would want to ride aimlessly about the countryside on such a pretty day with all the curtains pulled. Every time he made an attempt to stop, he was severely reprimanded by Leon. They were together in the carriage so long that Emma missed the Hirondelle that was to take her back to Yonville. She had to hire a special hack to catch the Hirondelle before it reached Yonville.

Comment

A.

Chapter 1 presents Leon's background so as to show how he

has changed during the interim. He is no longer so retiring and bashful. Paris has given him a sense of self-assurance which will allow him now to approach Madame Bovary. But we should also note that even though both he and Emma have changed, their talk is still filled with commonplace romantic cliches and platitudes.

B.
Flaubert's description of the church where Leon is to meet Emma is a masterpiece of realistic description and subtle suggestion. Flaubert describes the church (particularly the chancery) in terms of a lady's boudoir where the church (or Emma) is waiting to "gather the confession of her love." These descriptions sum up everything about Emma's own religion — a religion which Emma sees only in her own way. Thus, after Emma enters, she immediately attempts to pray, but her thoughts are not on religion but instead on herself and her relationship with Leon. Throughout the entire scene, it is ironic that both Emma and Leon are seething with a burning passion while the slow bungling guide shows them through the cold ancient church. Their view of the huge, magnificent church should be contrasted with the final scene, that of Emma and Leon riding in a small closed carriage while consummating their love. The carriage is even described as being "sealed tighter than a tomb," and if the image is extended, this is the beginning of Emma's last fated episode which will lead to her suicide.

PART III — CHAPTERS 2, 3, & 4

Summary
On her return to Yonville, Emma learned that Bovary's father had died. Charles was very upset, particularly because he had not seen the man in a long time. Emma felt no sorrow but made the usual sympathetic gestures, which her husband misunderstood and appreciated very much. After a while, Mrs. Bovary came to stay with them. Emma was polite and attentive but was annoyed because the necessity for being kind to the mourners distracted her from thoughts of Leon.

At about this time Lheureux made another appearance and presented Emma with her unpaid bills. He also managed to sell her some more high priced merchandise. When Emma expressed a worry about managing to pay, he suggested that she get a Power of Attorney from Bovary. That way, he said, she would not have to bother her husband with "petty" financial matters and could find a convenient method to settle her debts.

Emma convinced Bovary of the wisdom of this scheme without too much trouble, since he had no idea of the true amount of their debts. Emma even induced him to use the services of Leon, instead of the local attorney, for drawing up the papers, and Bovary trustingly arranged to send her alone to Rouen to take care of this business.

Emma spent the next three days in Rouen with Leon. He rented an expensive hotel room for the occasion, and this short period was like a honeymoon for them. They went to some of the best restaurants and places of entertainment and spent most of their time in lovemaking and romantic pursuits.

Leon became completely involved in his affair with Emma; he neglected his work and saw little of his friends. The arrival of her letters became a major event in his life, and he even paid a few visits to Yonville, either in secret or on various false pretexts, to see her.

Emma, meanwhile, was getting even more deeply enmeshed in financial obligations to Lheureux. In order to see Leon more often, she began to show a renewed interest in the piano, and soon got Bovary to arrange for her to take a weekly lesson with a teacher in Rouen.

Comment

A.

Before Emma can continue with her affair with Leon, she is interrupted by the death of her father-in-law. Then she must think of some plan whereby she can get back to Rouen and Leon. Monsieur Lheureux gives her the pretext. Knowing how easily he can convince Emma to buy things from him, he tells her to get Charles' power of attorney. His plan is to eventually foreclose on everything and thereby make a large profit. But his suggestions offer to Emma a pretext for going to Rouen to consult with Leon. So she convinces Charles that she should handle everything.

B.

The very short Chapter 3 covers the three days Emma spent with Leon in Rouen. The three days were described as "a real honeymoon." But the readers should remember that this is the *third* one. The episode is described in romantic terms of bliss and joy. For these few days, the image of beauty and innocence was restored to Emma, but the scene ends on an uglier note. Amid her renewed joys, she is reminded of her sordid affair with Rodolphe by hearing the boatman relate how Rodolphe had taken the same ride last week with some other lady.

C.

The short fourth chapter shows Emma and Leon continuing in their plans to make their meetings definite, and to meet at least once a week. This of course means that Emma will have to go deeper in debt.

PART III – CHAPTERS 5 & 6

Summary

On the days of her lessons, Emma occupied all her time with Leon. Each week they had a passionate reunion, as if they had been separated for an age instead of for a few days. These visits were joyous events for both of them and were marked by profound emotional and romantic feelings. As their affair progressed, they viewed each other as if they were the idealized figures of sentimental fiction and attempted to enact all that once they had only imagined.

Emma's departure was always a sorrowful moment, and the happiness she gained from seeing Leon disappeared as soon as the coach left Rouen. At home Emma was irritable and tense. She lived only for her next meeting with Leon and spent the week reading romantic books and reliving her memories, in order to keep her ardor at a high pitch.

Once she was nearly caught in her lie when Bovary ran into her supposed piano teacher and the woman did not recognize Emma's name. However, she was able to show Charles falsified receipts for the lessons and soon convinced him that nothing was wrong. Another time Lheureux saw her and Leon together in Rouen. She was afraid that he would tell Bovary, but instead the crafty merchant used her fright to force her into signing additional notes and selling some of Bovary's father's estate at a loss. Meanwhile, Emma was regularly being presented with other unpaid and overdue bills. She was confused by all this and unable to settle matters; so she attempted to ignore her creditors. She borrowed more and more from Lheureux, for as she became more worried and frightened, she also became more extravagant. She seemed to have no conception of the obligations incurred from borrowing money and hoped to forget her troubles through the possession of all sorts of wasteful luxuries. As a result, she went heavily into debt.

Despite her torrid affair with Leon, Emma was rapidly becoming unhappy again. Nothing meant anything to her any more except her Thursday in Rouen. She indulged in complicated sentimental excesses and wild flights of fantasy. In the desperate hope of finding happiness, she became voluptuous and greedy and tried to experience every kind of sensual pleasure. Nothing satisfied her, and her frustration increased. Her behavior perplexed Leon, particularly when she tried to force him to dress or act in certain ways or to quit his job in order to ensure his permanent devotion to her.

In the earliest stages of this affair, Emma had found contentment, and her mellow mood was reflected at home where she had been a considerate and dutiful wife. Now she was impossible to get along with again. Once she stayed overnight in Rouen with Leon and did not bother to inform Charles of her whereabouts. He was very worried and set out to find her. Later on she managed to convince the poor man that he was at fault for worrying and inquiring about her, and that there was nothing wrong with her strange behavior.

During Leon's visits to Yonville he had dined at the house of Homais, his old landlord. In return for this hospitality he felt obligated to invite Homais to Rouen. Homais eventually accepted the invitation and decided by coincidence, to come on the same day that Emma usually went to the city.

Once in Rouen, Homais sought out Leon and insisted that the young man accompany him to a restaurant and other places. Leon was not too assertive, and Homais easily quieted all his objections. Meanwhile, Emma waited impatiently in the hotel room. Leon managed to slip away from Homais for a little while to see her, but there was a nasty scene. She refused to listen to his excuses and accused him of such ridiculous things as preferring Homais to her. She returned to Yonville in a state of anger and began mentally to seek out all Leon's weaknesses.

After a while Emma realized that Leon was not really to blame for his conduct, but her awareness of his faults remained. She began to see that he was not the ideal figure she had imagined, and this thought troubled her. Their relationship was already shaky, and now it began to depend almost entirely on sensuality and various outside diversions that had once been secondary to their emotional feelings. In a frantic effort to regain the security of happiness, Emma sought to dominate all aspects of Leon's life. He resented her demands, and their moments of contentment were briefer than ever.

One day a debt collector called on Emma to get payment on one of her notes to Lheureux. Emma did not fully understand the meaning of his visit and made some feeble promises. The next afternoon she was served with a legal notice from the sheriff of the district. Emma was terrified and went to Lheureux. He was curt with her. After a while he relented, and though he claimed he could not afford the risk, he finally lent her more money on stiff terms and again tricked her into buying some expensive merchandise.

Emma was aroused by this experience and began an economy campaign. She cut down on household expenses, urged Bovary to get money from his mother, purchased little items in Rouen for resale to the ladies of Yonville, and secretly collected the money that was owned Bovary by his patients. She told her husband nothing about the real state of their finances. Despite all her efforts, Emma was unable to stop borrowing and continued to run up debts.

With this new burden added to her other troubles, Emma became temperamental and slovenly. The Bovary house was a melancholy place because she sold so many things to raise money; the mending and washing were undone, and the needs of the child were usually ignored. Emma had few friends any more and spent most of her time locked in her room. Bovary was worried and tried to comfort her, but she refused to speak with him and was unresponsive to all his clumsy advances.

Emma continued seeing Leon in Rouen and insisted on spending those days extravagantly. Leon often could not afford to entertain her in the style which she demanded; so she provided him with money, even when it meant pawning some of her possessions. Leon's family and friends had been urging him to end the affair, since they were concerned about its adverse effect upon his career and reputation. Now that Emma was becoming so moody and difficult, he started to agree with them and began to view her as a burden. Their relationship went on, but both of them often felt a secret disgust for each other, and even their lovemaking was now usually a source of boredom. In addition, Emma degraded herself by frequenting disreputable places and keeping low company, although she was ashamed afterwards. Her tastes and fancies became decadent and corrupt.

At last Emma was served with a court order, enjoining her to pay the sum of 8,000 francs or suffer confiscation of her household property. She ran to Lheureux and made wild promises, but he callously refused to help her any longer and sent her away.

Comment

A.

These two chapters present Emma's entry into another love affair and her forthcoming destruction. These two chapters evoke many comparisons and contrasts. In the beginning of the affair, she again saw herself as the "woman in love of all the novels, the heroine of all the dramas, the shadowy 'she' of all the poetry-books." This was the same as in the beginning of her romance with Rodolphe. But along with this similarity, we see Emma going to meet her lover by "going through alleyways and emerging" in disreputable parts of towns. Strong hints of ugliness pervade these meetings.

But as the affair progresses, we suddenly realize that the role Emma played with Rodolphe is suddenly reversed. Now Leon is in the place of Emma and Emma is playing the role that Rodolphe earlier acted. Now Emma is the experienced partner introducing the young and inexperienced Leon into love making and as Rodolphe used to come to her, now she goes to Leon. At the end of the day, it is Emma who must dress and make the journey home. Finally, even Leon realizes that he has "become her mistress rather than she his."

B.

During the first part of their relationship, Emma thought that she had found what she had been searching for during her whole life. But as the relationship progressed, she gradually began to realize that she couldn't look at Leon realistically. "Idols must not be touched; the gilt comes off on our hands." And she also realizes that she had made him seem to be more than he is. Then she wonders what causes "this inadequacy in her life." At home she would try to read romantic fiction hoping that the idealized heroes would re-awaken a love for Leon. But she had to finally admit that she was tired of him. She "had rediscovered in adultery all the banality of marriage." This discovery then seems to leave Emma more empty than ever.

C.

During her affair with Leon, she has continued to neglect her business and is steadily becoming more entangled in financial affairs. Flaubert seems to be correlating Emma's deteriorating moral sense with her financial deterioration. She becomes the pathological liar both about her affair with Leon and about the financial debts. And as the love affair begins to fail, her debts begin to confront her as though they were analogous to her entangled love life.

D.

Even in the early parts of Emma's affair with Leon, an ominous note appears. It is in the form of the old beggar, whom Emma often meets immediately after leaving Leon. The ugliness and vulgar appearance, the degradation of this old blind beggar contrast well with the artificial bliss with which Emma has enfolded herself, and also serve to foreshadow the depths of degradation to which Emma is falling. He can even be said to be symbolic of the ugly death that Emma is soon to face. Emma then sinks to her lowest shortly after this when she goes to a masquerade party and ends up with low class clerks in an inferior eating house.

PART III – CHAPTER 7

Summary

In the morning the sheriff's officers arrived and made a complete inventory of the household furnishings and goods, but Emma managed to maintain a stoic attitude all the time they were there. They left a guard on the premises, but she kept him hidden in the attic where Bovary would not see him. That evening Bovary seemed worried, and Emma fearfully imagined that he knew, but he said nothing. She was particularly resentful that she bore all the responsibility in this matter and that Bovary was innocent. As the night passed, she occupied herself in making plans to raise the money.

The next morning Emma went to Rouen and called on several bankers, but they all refused to make a loan to her. She asked Leon for help, but he protested that he could never raise such a large sum and became angry when she suggested that he steal the money from his employer. Finally, in order to quiet her, Leon promised that he would see his friends, and if he could raise the sum she required, he would bring it to Yonville.

On Monday, Emma was horrified to discover that a public notice of the sheriff's confiscation and auction had been posted in the market place. She went to see Guillaumin, the town lawyer. He offered to help her, but made it clear that he expected favors from her in return. Emma was insulted by his forwardness, shouted that she was not for sale, and left in a fury.

Bovary was not home and still did not know what had taken place. Meanwhile, the entire town watched expectantly to see what would happen next. Emma felt weak and afraid; she kept hoping that Leon would gallop up with the money but really had no confidence in this possibility. She was bitter and frightened. Suddenly an idea came to her—Rodolphe—and she set out for his estate. She planned to take advantage of his supposed love for her and get the money from him. It never occurred to her that what she was planning to do was actually prostitution; exactly what she had so angrily refused when Guillaumin had made the same suggestion.

Comment

This chapter presents Emma's frantic efforts to obtain money from almost any source. She first goes to her latest lover, Leon; but since Leon is rather anxious to break with Emma, he proves to be of little help. In fact, he hurriedly gets rid of Emma by promising to do something the next day. Her failure is again represented by the appearance of the blind man. This time Homais gives the man a lecture and Emma throws him a half crown piece, the "sum of her wealth." Now she is totally destitute.

At the suggestion of her maid, Emma goes to see the lawyer, Monsieur Guillaumin, who supposedly was infatuated with Emma. He offers to give her the money, but she is expected to sleep with him. Emma is horrified and leaves in disgust. There is here a nobility in Emma's make-up. For all of her love affairs, she has never prostituted herself and totally rejects the idea. All of her love affairs have been an attempt to fulfill her dreams.

PART III—CHAPTER 8

Summary

Rodolphe was surprised to see Emma. They talked about the past for a while, and she was able, as planned, to arouse his old interest in her. She told him about her debts and asked him to lend her several thousand francs. Rodolphe began to understand the reason for her strange visit and calmly told her that he had no money available. Emma knew he was lying. She lost her temper and left.

Now Emma realized that the situation was hopeless. She walked through the fields without seeing and had dazed memories of incidents in her life. Then she became lucid again and decided what she had to do. She ran to Homais' shop and induced the servant, Justin, to let her into the attic. There she opened a jar of arsenic and ate a large quantity of it, while the frightened boy watched. She went home again, for the first time in a long while feeling at peace.

Meanwhile, Bovary had learned about the sheriff's confiscation. He searched frantically for Emma, but no one knew her whereabouts. When he returned home, he found her resting in bed. She gave him a letter which he was not to read until the next day.

In a short time Emma was torn by spasms of nausea and became violently ill. Despite his concern, she would tell Bovary nothing; so he opened her letter and discovered to his horror that she had poisoned herself. He called for help and soon the news spread through the town.

Homais came to his assistance, and they sent for doctors from Rouen and a neighboring town. Bovary was too upset to do anything and sat at Emma's bedside crying. She wept also and for once was tender to him. The other doctors and the priest arrived, but nothing could be done. After a few more hours, Emma died in great pain.

Comment

A.

When Emma arrives at Rodolphe's house to ask for money, the reader should remember that they haven't seen each other for over three years. Thus when he first sees Emma, all of his old desires for her are re-awakened and Emma is aware that she has some effect on him. Thus in his refusal to give her money, Emma feels that this is again a betrayal of her love. Flaubert intimates that Emma's desire to kill herself comes, not from her desperate financial condition and not from the weak Leon's refusal, but from a larger sense of betrayal by Rodolphe. To Emma, who has devoted her life to a search for perfect love, this second betrayal by Rodolphe makes life not worth living. Her reactions and her state of mind immediately after leaving Rodolphe are practically the same as when he first betrayed her. And as she was sick for forty-three days on the first time, she decides now to take her life. Thus Emma's suicide is motivated by her sense of betrayal by the one man whom she might have loved. Flaubert perhaps is suggesting that Emma was capable of a profound love. If she was not, then at least, she possessed a dream of love which was worth living for and when this dream was betrayed, there was nothing left but suicide.

B.

It is a bit of Flaubert's irony that Justin is directly responsible for Emma's death. This is ironic because he is the one character in the book who has demonstrated a constant, undeviating love for Emma. His love for Emma exists on a plane which Emma herself never felt and never achieved; thus it is ironic that the person who most loved and adored her was also the one responsible for her death. That is, had he not loved her so much, he would never have been intimidated enough so as to give her the keys to the secret room where the arsenic was kept.

C.

Emma's death reflects the pathetic misuse of her life. As she has spent her life longing for the unattainable and had failed miserably, so in death she longed for a simple but beautiful death. But instead, her death is one of horrible suffering and ugliness, and the ugliness of her death is emphasized by the appearance of the blind man, the symbol of her degradation in life.

D.

Emma's last act is that of taking extreme unction, and this act captures the essence of the novel. Here she returns to the religious fold, but her return is in terms of sensuousness. The kiss that she gives to the crucifix is not one given to God but it is more of an erotic, sensual kiss. And when the priest anoints her, Flaubert subtly reminds the reader that this woman is a sensualist: the priest anoints the eyes "that had coveted all worldly pomp" then the nostrils and mouth "that had uttered lies, that had curled with pride and cried out in lewdness;" then the hands that "had delighted in sensual touches," and finally the feet which were "so swift...when she was running to satisy her desires, and that would now walk no more." Thus the final picture of Emma is that of the sensualist looking in death for the supreme sensual desire.

E.

Many critics have suggested that with the appearance of Dr. Lariviere we have our only admirable character in the novel. Perhaps this characterization is influenced by Flaubert's own father. He does contrast to the other characters, in view of the fact that he is coldly analytical, but yet his presence indicates that he cares for humanity. He does express real sympathy for his patients; and his sense of intelligence, his professional dignity, and his integrity set off all the other characters as being petty and stupid.

PART III – CHAPTERS 9, 10 & 11

Summary

It took Charles a long time to recover from the initial shock of Emma's death. His mother arrived and helped to put affairs in order, and thought that now Emma was gone she would be reinstated in Charles' affection. Emma's father also showed up for the funeral, but was too emotional to be of help. The priest and Homais sat up all night with the body and performed certain rites which they thought appropriate. The priest had a difficult time convincing Charles that the burial should take place soon. Charles gave directions for Emma to be buried in her wedding dress and quarrelled with his mother about the expense of some parts of the funeral.

As soon as the funeral is over, old Roualt goes home without even seeing little Berthe. Later that night the sexton sees Justin by Emma's grave and thinks that he now knows who has been stealing his potatoes.

In the days which followed, Bovary was contacted by all Emma's creditors. Her debts included not merely those of Lheureux, but many bills to business concerns, tradesmen, and other people.

Their total constituted a vast amount. Bovary tried to collect the fees due him in an effort to pay but learned that Emma had already done so.

In the meantime, Leon became engaged to a young woman of good family. Bovary sent a letter of congratulations to Leon's mother, in which he remarked, innocently, that the news would have pleased his late wife.

One night Bovary came across the letter from Rodolphe that Emma had lost in the attic a long time before. He read it, but assumed that there had been a platonic affection between them and was not concerned. He idealized Emma's memory and was pleased to learn that another had also admired her.

In an attempt to pay his debts, Bovary had to sell nearly all the furniture, but even this amount was not sufficient. For sentimental reasons, though, he refrained from taking anything from her bedroom and kept it just the way it was before her death. Mrs. Bovary had come to live with him, but they had a quarrel over the possession of one of Emma's shawls and she left his house. The servant left also, taking most of Emma's wardrobe with her.

Bovary began to live in seclusion. He avoided his old friends and neglected his practice. Homais, who had once been so close, and who was now a power in the community, shunned him, claiming that there was too big a gap in their social positions.

Bovary often sat in Emma's room, examining her possessions and recalling their life together. One day he opened her desk and discovered the letters from Rodolphe and Leon. He read them with an air of disbelief and was very distressed when he realized their meaning and was forced to acknowledge that Emma had been unfaithful. After this he was always gloomy and seemed a broken man. He rarely left his house and kept away from people.

Once he had to go to Rouen to sell his horse in order to raise more money. He met Rodolphe there and the two men had a drink together in a cafe. Rodolphe felt guilty and tried to make small talk. Finally Bovary told him that he knew the truth, but that he no longer held any grudge against him. The fault, Bovary said, was with Destiny.

The next day Bovary died quietly while sitting in his garden. His house and remaining property were sold on behalf of his creditors, and there was just enough left over to send Berthe to stay with her grandmother. Mrs. Bovary died later that year and Roualt was seriously ill; so Berthe was then sent to an aunt's house. This woman was very poor, and the little girl ended up working in a cotton mill.

Comment

A.

The final chapters are concerned with showing the effect of Emma's death on various people. The greatest effect is on Charles who mourns her death for a long time before he discovers the letters from Rodolphe and Leon. Then he slowly deteriorates in despair and poverty and inertia. Obliquely, Emma's death probably has the greatest effect on little Berthe, since at the age of seven she is sent into the cotton mill to earn her own living. In contrast, the people whom she most loved, Rodolphe and Leon, are not at all affected by her death. Justine who loved her with the purest love, is accused of stealing potatoes because he returned to cry at her grave.

B.

The last chapter is filled with many ironies. That Charles would want to bury Emma in her wedding dress (symbol of purity) is ironic in view of Emma's infidelities. The actions of the chemist and the priest are developed to show how their every act is not for someone else's benefit but for their own advancement. Homais' receipt of the cross of the Legion of Honor suggests the pettiness of the society against which Emma revolted.

C.

So in the final analysis, as seen against the society in which Emma lived, Emma becomes a rather sympathetic character. She was a woman who had a full conviction of her dreams and was willing to risk everything for them. She had a glimpse of a life and of emotions that exist outside this narrow provincial world, but her tragedy lies finally in the fact that she could find no object in this world worthy of her dreams.

CHARACTER ANALYSIS

Emma Bovary

(For additional help in analyzing Emma, see especially the comments after the following chapters: Part I, Chapters 6 and 9; Part II, Chapters 9 and 10.)

Emma's early life influenced her entire approach to life. She was born with a natural tendency toward sentimentality. She preferred the dream world to the real world. Rather than being brought up in the realities of everyday living, she was sent when very young to a convent where she indulged in daydreams and in sentimentalizing about life. Here at the convent, she began reading romance novels which affected her entire life. In religion, she searched for the unusual, the mystic, and the beautiful rather than for the real essence of the church. Being basically a dreamy girl, she developed into the extreme romantic who spent her time longing and sighing for old castles, secret meetings, and intrigues. She closed her eyes to the real world and attempted to force life to conform with her romantic fiction. She constantly felt the need for excitement and could not endure the dull routine of everyday living.

After her marriage, Emma continued in her search for excitement. She could not tolerate her marriage because it did not fit into the fictionalized accounts that she had read about. She missed the bliss, ecstasy, and passion that she hoped she would find in marriage. And rather than devoting herself to living life, rather than facing reality, she hid herself in her dreams and expended all of her energy in futile longings. She was continually dissatisfied with her life and searched constantly for ways to change things.

Thus, since life refused to conform to her romantic picture, Emma began to alternate between various things in the hope that her unfulfilled longings would be satisfied. She tried everything. She redecorated the house, she took up reading, subscribed to Parisian magazines, helped at charities, knitted, painted, played the piano, and engaged in a multitude of other activities. But with each thing she attempted, she soon became bored and rejected one activity for another. This frenzied search for excitement exhausted her until she made herself physically sick.

Charles' own sense of complacency and his dullness only added to Emma's misfortune. Thus when she met Leon, she felt that she had found her soul mate. She was unable to see that her thoughts and his were both part of the same romantic concept expressed in platitudes and cliches. She mistook superficiality in Leon for profundity. They became platonic friends. After he left, Emma felt that she had missed something, that something had been denied her. Therefore, later when she meets Rodolphe, she is ready to give herself to him readily. She had longed for someone who would "know about everything, excel in a multitude of activity," and who would introduce her "to passions in all its force, to life in all its graces," and initiate her "into all mysteries." Thus, when Rodolphe appears and begins his frank, daring and passionate exclamations of love, Emma feels that she is now experiencing these passions and these elemental forces. He is then the fulfillment of her dreams. For the first time, she feels that her life now has all the "passion, ecstasy and delirium" of the romances which she had read.

Emma's nature will not allow her to remain in one situation. She begins to want to change things. As she changed from knitting to painting, etc., so now she wants to change things with Rodolphe. She insists that they run off together. This insistence causes Rodolphe to drop her.

After her recovery from Rodolphe's betrayal, Emma meets Leon again and gives herself to him rather readily. She is still searching for that noble passion. But true to Emma's nature, she soon begins to tire of Leon and becomes once again bored with life. She found in "adultery all the banality of marriage."

Thus Emma Bovary was a middle class woman who could not stand the middle-class life. She spent her entire life in an attempt to escape from this middle-class existence by dreams, love affairs, and false pretentions.

Emma possesses one quality that the other characters do not have. She has a dream of life that allows her to look for ideals and feelings greater than she is. Even though these ideals might be superficial, she is aware that there are feelings greater than those found in her middle-class surroundings. And in spite of her infidelities, she could not give herself in prostitution in order to solve her financial situation. She remained true to her dreams and she died by her dreams. After her second interview with Rodolphe, she felt that she had been betrayed anew and felt that only in death could she find the peace and fulfillment that she had been searching for. Thus, she tried to live by her dreams, and when that failed, she died by them without ever compromising her vision of something greater than she.

Charles Bovary

Charles is the dull, unimaginative country doctor. From the opening chapters, we are made aware that Charles must work very diligently at something that comes easily for others. He lacks the dashing imagination that characterizes his father, the elder Bovary. His constant struggle to achieve almost anything is a part of his essential nature. He has no natural talents and must work twice as hard as others in order to achieve the simplest results.

In his school, we saw that when he relaxes he gives himself over to aimless wanderings and ultimately fails his examinations. Furthermore, he is the type who can be easily controlled by a woman. First, his mother ruled his life completely for him, even arranging a marriage for him with a woman about twenty years older than he. Thus his first wife was able to rule him rather easily. But these women make it exceptionally easy for Emma to control Charles and to get her way in every matter.

Charles functions as a complete contrast to Emma. His plodding nature and his routine ardors and embraces suggest his insensitive nature. He is content with the commonplace activities and is too dull to notice Emma's dissatisfaction. He assumes that

Emma is as happy as he is, and he is incapable of detecting any subtle differences in their life. Whereas Emma burns to experience everything in life, Charles feels that with the birth of his daughter, he has now gone through the complete list of human experiences. His contentment with his life only makes life more unbearable for Emma.

Charles' only attribute is his devoted love for Emma. His every concern is directed toward her happiness and his love and devotion are completely unselfish. When Emma is sick, he leaves all else and devotes himself entirely to her recovery. He is, then, capable of unselfish feelings whereas Emma is concerned only with herself.

Charles is, then, the dull commonplace little man, the typical representative of the insensitive and unimaginative human being. He was intended by Flaubert to personify many of the most appalling aspects of provincial, middle class society.

Leon

When Emma first meets Leon, she feels that she has found a kindred spirit. But we know that Leon is as superficial as is Emma. Both are distinguished from the other members of the society because both strive for some feelings that transcend this society. But both are also trapped in their own romantic dreams.

At first Leon is terribly shy and unsure of himself. He is inexperienced in the world of women and love. He has lived too long in a world of sentimental romantic fantasy. Thus when confronted with Emma, he cannot bring himself to tell her of his real feelings. His fears overcome him, and he is afraid of being ridiculous.

After Leon has been to Paris, he gains more confidence in himself. When he returns to Paris, he retains many of the Parisian manners and "airs," giving the impression that he is really the master of any situation. Thus when he meets Emma again after three years separation, he has acquired a thin veneer of sophistication, but he is still a shallow and weak young man. Even though he begins a love affair with Emma, he realizes himself that he is not the master of the situation. He is unable to act in an aggressive or decisive manner and allows Emma to lead in their relationship.

Furthermore, Leon also serves to illustrate the divergence between Emma's dreams and her reality. She forces Leon to conform to her idealized concept of a lover. She refuses for a long time to face reality, and the contrast between Flaubert's objective description of the weak, fluctuating Leon and Emma's idealized conception of him underlines Emma's predicament.

Rodolphe

Rodolphe is the only person in the novel who understands Emma. He is basically a shrewd and cynical bachelor who has spent his time studying the psychology of women with the sole purpose of seducing them. When he first met Emma, he knew immediately that she was bored with her husband and was ready for a love affair. He met her often enough to get her excited with his straight, direct declarations of love. He knew that she wanted to hear fanciful exaggerated things, and he accommodated her. Then he disappears for six weeks so as to let Emma worry and fret. When he reappears, it is no trouble to carry out the seduction.

But Rodolphe is not interested in any affair for very long. He is interested only in his own sensual enjoyment and his only worry is how to break off his love affairs after he tires of them. His attraction toward Emma is founded only on her good looks and her sensuous appeal. Thus, he has no qualms about seducing her and later abandoning her. He is even able to rationalize his motives so well that he feels no guilt about the episode. Upon learning of Emma's death, he has no feelings one way or another. He is, therefore, the unemotional, sensuous individual concerned only with his own pleasures.

Homais

The apothecary at Yonville. He is one of the most successful supporting characters in the novel, because there is a complete identity between his function as a character and his function as the representative of a type. He stands for the new middle-class spirit and "progressive" outlook that Flaubert detested so much. Homais' intellect is limited, and he is poorly educated, but he is pretentious and puffed up with self-esteem. His talk consists of cliches and half-truths, and he demonstrates all the limitations and prejudices of the new bourgeoisie. For example, he is an avowed agnostic and an exponent of Voltaire, yet he is fearful and superstitious in the face of death. Furthermore, he is cowardly and irresponsible, as is shown in the aftermath of the episode concerning the operation on Hippolyte, and though he professes equalitarian principles, he is himself status conscious. Some of the best comic scenes in the novel are the conversations between Homais and his rival, the priest. Flaubert's pessimism is illustrated by the ending of the novel, where Homais' advancement and personal triumph are described.

CRITICAL PROBLEMS

THEME AND INTENT

Madame Bovary is a study of human stupidity and the "romantic malady," the despair and unhappiness faced by those who are unwilling or unable to resolve the conflicts between their dreams and idealized aspirations and the real world; in modern terms, one might say it is a study of a neurosis. Furthermore, it examines middle-class conventions and the myth of progress, exposing weaknesses and hypocrisies, and it deals with the inability of the different characters to communicate with each other. In all of these aspects, this novel is as pertinent in the mid-twentieth century as when it was written. The costumes and settings may change, but people do not, and human problems remain the same. As a matter of fact, some critics have pointed out the close relationship between Emma Bovary and the heroine of Sinclair Lewis' *Main Street,* for provincial life is the same everywhere, and these two women, despite their differences, are afflicted by many similar problems and frustrations.

Flaubert's characters are all ordinary people and are very much like ourselves and our neighbors. Nothing about them is romanticized or exalted, so that it is possible for the reader to see himself in a new and harsher light, and he cannot avoid sympathetic identification with them. The people of *Madame Bovary* are limited intellectually and culturally; they are sometimes sincere and well-intentioned, sometimes petty and vulgar, sometimes pathetic and confused, and sometimes unaware of the most obvious things or unable to take the most obvious action. They are so true to life that there are readers who resent the novel because they resent the uncomplimentary view that they are forced to take of themselves.

FLAUBERT'S REALISM

Madame Bovary is considered one of the finest "realistic" novels, and this is because of its unadorned, unromantic portrayals of everyday life and people. However, it must be understood that in literary realism one gets a view of the real world as seen through the eyes of the author. Throughout the novel there is a very carefully planned selection of episodes and incidents, so that "realism," if interpreted to mean a kind of journalistic reportage, is misleading. Every detail in *Madame Bovary* is chosen for a purpose and is closely related to everything else that precedes and follows it, to an extent that may not be evident (or possible) in real life. There is profound artistry involved in what is selected and omitted and in what weight is given to specific incidents.

The final greatness of Flaubert's realism lies in the manner in which he is able to capture the dullness of these middle class people without making his novel dull. Flaubert's minute attention to detail, his depiction of the average life, and his handling of the commonplace, all require the touch of the great artist, or else, this type of writing will degenerate into rather common dull prose. Flaubert was intent that every aspect of his novel would ring true to life. He visited the places which he wrote about to make certain that his descriptions were accurate. After he had written the Prefect's speech at the agriculture show, a speech very similar to Flaubert's was actually given by a district Prefect: both speeches were filled with the same platitudes and same cliches. And finally, Flaubert's handling of Homais is a masterful stroke of realistic description. He is able to select enough details to suggest to the reader how boring Homais' conversation is without having to repeat enough of what Homais actually said to bore the reader. And it is this selection of detail that marks Flaubert's genius.

SELECTION

An example of Flaubert's intentional selection of events takes place in III, Part I. Even that early in the novel, the reader is given a searching insight into the operation of Emma's mind and a portent of things to come, when the author comments:

> Emma, for her part, would have liked a marriage at midnight by the light of torches, but her father thought such an idea nonsensical.
>
> (trans. Gerard Hopkins)

This brief remark crystalizes the opposition between the sentimental romanticizing that will later cause Emma's downfall, and the unsympathetic real world, represented by her hard-headed peasant father.

A reporter must narrate his story as it occurs. He has no more insight or perspective than the participants, and he can only present random "slices of life," drawn out of context. Flaubert intended to illustrate a definite thesis by his story. Although his method was realistic, he determined where to place his emphasis and what to concentrate on by reference to this purpose.

SYMBOLISM

Flaubert also made extensive use of symbolism in his novel. Symbolic things are those which have an objective and limited function but which can be interpreted also to embody a wider and more profound meaning in regard to the things around them. In such a painstakingly constructed novel as *Madame Bovary*, it is rewarding to search for additional layers of meaning wherever the omission of a particular detail would not have affected the objective narration of the story. For instance, the complicated description of Charles' hat in the first chapter is not necessary to a realistic account of his school days, but has been shown to symbolize many aspects of his personality and future development. Other examples of symbols include the blind beggar, the wedding bouquet of Charles' first wife, and Emma's pet greyhound. Critics have pointed out that even the names of the characters in *Madame Bovary* have symbolic meanings; for example, Bovary is indeed bovine.

IRONY AND CONTRAST

Flaubert made use of irony and contrast on many planes, always with the intention of heightening his meaning and directing the reader's attention to his main themes. Each part of the novel contains pairs of contrasting scenes which clarify the reactions of the participants and the point of the story through their interaction. In Part I, these scenes are those describing the Bovarys' rustic wedding and the Marquis' grand ball. There are many other uses of irony, as in the contrast between the speeches of the Prefect's representative and Rodolphe at the Agricultural Show. The interrelationship of different episodes in the novel is shown at the end of Part II, where Emma develops an interest in the tenor Lagardy, emotionally preparing her and the reader for the unexpected entrance of Leon.

In terms of the entire novel, Charles had two wives who contrasted with each other. Emma had two lovers who are about as opposite as two people can be. But the greatest thematic contrast remains the contrast between Emma's idealized, fictionalized world and the realistic dull world in which she lives. This contrast embodies the differences between her hopes and her achievements. This is finally brought to an ugly conclusion when she desired a beautiful peaceful death, but instead suffered great agonies and endured great pain for hours before death finally came.

For additional analysis of this problem, consult PART II CHAPTER 8.

STYLE

Flauber was a very diligent and precise craftsman. He spent more than five years working on *Madame Bovary,* in the course of which he wrote biographies of all the characters and drew maps of the towns which were his settings. The original draft of the novel was several times longer than the completed version. Extensive research was applied to all features of the story, in order to guarantee a completely accurate picture of provincial life. While he was still writing the manuscript. Flaubert took great pride in learning that a phrase identical with one in the Prefect's speech actually appeared in a speech delivered by a government official in another part of the country.

Even the individual words Flaubert used were carefully selected, and he evoked additional subtleties of meaning and intensifications of mood from his skilled use of varied grammatical tenses and other rhetorical devices in the narrative. The pace of the novel is intricately related to the story, and the careful reader notes that events move with a speed related to the emotional feelings of the characters. When Emma is bored, her thoughts and activities are described in minute detail, and the reader becomes bored also. During Emma's frantic search for happiness in her liaison with Leon, she and the reader move through the events of several months in a bare few moments, emphasizing the transience of her pleasure.

NARRATIVE TECHNIQUE

Many of the techniques Flaubert used for descriptive purposes are cinematic in their quality, such as the flashing back and forth between the Prefect's speech and Rodolphe's flirting at the Agricultural Show. During the wild coach ride taken by Emma and Leon through the suburbs of Rouen, and at other points, the reader is made to view events from the outside. This adds to the air of reality, and it makes it necessary for the reader to call upon his own experiences to assist in understanding the experiences of the characters. The reader, in a sense, is made to participate with them. In addition, *Madame Bovary* has a formal structure that adds to the aesthetic quality of the story. Its three parts are comparable, in their development, exposition, and denouement, to the parts of a stage play, and the entire movement of the novel shows a theatrical sense of the dramatic.

SOCIAL COMMENTARY

In *Madame Bovary* Flaubert depicted an entire segment of society and unmercifully analyzed its people. He created unforgettable characters from whom our own age can learn valuable and essential lessons. Moreover, he took a mundane story and, thanks to his skill as a writer, demonstrated the potentialities of everyday life as a source of art. He was a leader in the trend towards realism in western literature. Before Flaubert, the novel was often rambling and discursive, but he helped to give it a definite structure and purpose and to make it acceptable in the canons of formal literature. There are faults in his work, for his characters are often not solid enough to bear the weight of their symbolic meanings, and Flaubert's extreme pessimism prevented him from being truly objective or fair in his evaluations and characterizations. Nonetheless, *Madame Bovary* is one of the greatest of novels and stands among the most treasured items in our living cultural heritage.

FLAUBERT'S LIFE AND WORKS

Gustave Flaubert was born December 12, 1821, in Rouen, France, and died May 8, 1880. He was the fourth child of a distinguished doctor who was the head of the hospital in that city. Gustave was a sensitive and quiet boy; he read a lot, and since the family lived in a house on the hospital grounds, he early gained a knowledge of scientific techniques and ideas. He attended a secondary school in Rouen, and in 1841 was sent, against his will, to study law in Paris. In the capital he made new friends and moved in literary circles. His talent for writing was stimulated by these experiences.

In 1844 Flaubert became the victim of a serious nervous illness, which cannot be identified precisely, but which was probably related to epilepsy. For reasons of health he retired to the family's new home in Le Croisset, a suburb of Rouen. He gladly took this opportunity to give up law and most of his time was now spent at Le Croisset where he lived quietly and devoted himself to writing and his studies.

Flaubert made a trip to the Near East in 1849-50, where he traveled widely in Egypt, Syria, Turkey, and Greece, and in 1857 he visited the site of ancient Carthage in North Africa. As the years passed, he became acquainted with most of the important literary figures of the period, including Victor Hugo, Georges Sand, Sainte-Beuve, Gautier, Turgenev, the de Goncourts, and de Maupassant. He was respected and admired by all of them.

Flaubert had few close friends, but there were two unusual relationships with women in his life. The first involved Elisa Schlessinger, a married older woman whom he met at Trouville when he was fifteen and who for many years was the object of his platonic and idealized affection. The other was Louise Colet, a poetess, who was his mistress between 1846 and 1854. She and Flaubert saw each other only very rarely, however, and their liaison existed mainly in their letters. As with so many other things, Flaubert found to his dismay that Louise in the flesh was not the same as Louise in his imagination. As a result, he usually preferred a solitary life at Le Croisset to other pursuits.

Flaubert has often been considered a misanthropic recluse. He was characterized by morbidity and pessimism, which may have been partly due to his illness, and by a violent hatred and contempt for middle-class society, derived ultimately from his childhood in bourgeois Rouen. He was often bitter and unhappy because of the great disparity that existed between his unattainable dreams and fantasies and the realities of his life; for example, his mystical and idealized love for Elisa adversely affected all his later relationships with women. Flaubert's unhappiness and loneliness is perhaps best expressed by his famous remark, "Madame Bovary, c'est moi."

Although Flaubert gained renown as a writer within his own lifetime, he was not financially successful (he made only 500 francs for the first five years' sales of *Madame Bovary),* and he was hurt by the enmity and misunderstanding of his critics and readers. At the height of public hostility, in 1857, he and the publisher of *Madame Bovary* were tried for an "outrage to public morals and religion." However, the case was finally acquitted.

Flaubert's works include *Madame Bovary* (1857); *Salammbo* (1862), a weighty historical novel about the war between Rome and Carthage; *Sentimental Education* (1869), a novel dealing again with the theme of the frustrations of middle-class life and human aspirations; and *The Temptation of Saint Anthony* (1874), a rich and evocative series of religious tableaux. In 1877 he published *Three Tales,* which contains the beautiful short stories, *A Simple Heart, The Legend of Saint Julian Hospitator,* and *Herodias.* These justly famous stories are masterpieces of short fiction and are among his finest and most moving works. Flaubert's play, *The Candidate,* failed after a few performances in 1874, and his last novel, *Bouvard and Pechuhet,* which was unfinished on his death, was published posthumously in 1881.

Flaubert was one of the most important European writers of the 19th century, and in him the French novel reached a high level of development. None of his later works, except the three short stories, ever equaled the artistic and technical quality of his first novel, and it is primarily on *Madame Bovary* that his reputation rests. Flaubert combined a feeling for the ideals of the Romantic era with the objective outlook and scientific principles of Realism to create a novel which has stood as a monument and example to writers ever since.

SUGGESTIONS FOR FURTHER READING

Brereton, Geoffrey. *A Short History of French Literatute.* Baltimore, 1954 (paperback).

Levin, Harry. *The Gates of Horn: A Study of Five French Realists.* New York, 1963.

Spencer, Philip. *Flaubert: A Biography.* New York, 1952.

Steegmuller, Francis. *Flaubert and Madame Bovary: A Double Portrait.* New York, 1957 (paperback).

_____, ed. *Selected Letters of Gustave Flaubert,* New York, 1954 (paperback).

Thorlby, Anthony. *Gustave Flaubert and the Art of Realism.* New Haven, 1957.

Turnell, Martin. *The Novel in France*. New York, 1958 (paperback).

BOOKS BY FLAUBERT AVAILABLE IN PAPERBACK EDITIONS

Madame Bovary
Salammbo
Three Tales

A Dictionary of Platitudes
Sentimental Education

SAMPLE EXAMINATION QUESTIONS

1. Discuss the attitude of Flaubert towards the middle-class society he is describing. Use illustrations from the novel to support your view.

2. Explain the use of contrast and irony in *Madame Bovary*.

3 Compare the characterizations of Homais and Bournisien. What do they each represent? What is Flaubert's reaction to them? Are they fairly portrayed?

4. In what ways is *Madame Bovary* a realistic novel? What is "realism," in a literary sense?

5. Analyze the personality of Emma Bovary. How is she responsible for her own downfall? How do the nature of provincial society and the people around her make her unhappiness inevitable?

6. Compare Emma's relationships with Charles, Rodolphe, and Leon, in terms of her attitudes and needs, the types of men they are, and the stage of her life during which she meets them.

7. Discuss the use of symbolism in *Madame Bovary,* giving examples from the text.

8. Briefly describe Flaubert's career as a writer and his place in the history of literature.

9. Analyze the personality of Charles Bovary. Why did Emma marry him? Does he contribute to her downfall? Is he a sympathetic character?

10. Identify the following characters: Lagardy, Lariviere, Justin, Felicite, Canivet, Hippolyte, Roualt.

11. Discuss the fantasies that motivate Emma and cause her unhappiness. In what way are they unrealistic? What do they indicate about her personality? Does the kind of problem that Emma suffered from still exist today, and if so, what media cater to the desires of people like her?

12. Analyze the structure of *Madame Bovary* as a novel, pointing out the major scenes, the relationships between incidents and characters, the use of theatrical techniques, and the overall dramatic form.

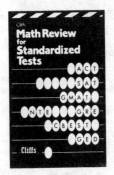

TWO CLASSICS FROM CLIFFS NOTES

*Cliffs Notes on
Greek Classics*

*Cliffs Notes on
Roman Classics*

These two publications are the definitive reference tools for students and teachers. Highly acclaimed by classical scholars, *Cliffs Notes on Greek Classics* and *Cliffs Notes on Roman Classics* aid in understanding the ideology, philosophy and literary influence of ancient civilization.

You'll find *Greek Classics* and *Roman Classics* at your local bookstore. Or to order your copies, simply return the coupon.

- Review plot summaries and characters of classical plays and epics
- Find term paper ideas and essay topics
- Check facts, dates, spelling and pronunciation
- Identify major literary movements
- Recognize literary allusions to people and events

Your Guides to Successful Test Preparation.

Cliffs Test Preparation Guides

Efficient preparation means better test scores. Go with the experts and use **Cliffs Test Preparation Guides**. They'll help you reach your goals because they're: • Complete • Concise • Functional • In-depth. They are focused on helping you know what to expect from each test. The test-taking techniques have been proven in classroom programs nationwide.

Recommended for individual use or as a part of formal test preparation programs.

NO EXIT
& THE FLIES

NOTES

including
- *Life of the Author*
- *Sartre's Major Works*
- *Sartrean Existentialism*
  Principles and Philosophies
  Existentialism Before Sartre
  Existentialism: An Overview
  Sartre's Specific Principles
- *Introduction to Each Play*
- *List of Characters in Each Play*
- *Summaries and Critical Commentaries*
  of Each Play
- *Suggested Essay Topics*
- *Selected Bibliography*

by
W. John Campbell, Ph.D.
Drama Faculty,
North Carolina School of the Arts

INCORPORATED

LINCOLN, NEBRASKA 68501

Editor

Gary Carey, M.A.
University of Colorado

Consulting Editor

James L. Roberts, Ph.D.
Department of English
University of Nebraska

Cliffs Notes, Inc.   Lincoln, Nebraska

CONTENTS

NO EXIT *(Huis Clos)*

THE FLIES *(Les Mouches)*

SARTRE NOTES

LIFE OF THE AUTHOR

Jean-Paul Sartre was a novelist, playwright, and philosopher. His major contribution to twentieth-century thinking was his system of existentialism, an ensemble of ideas describing man's freedom and responsibilities within a framework of human dignity. That is, he evolved a philosophy which concerned itself with *existence* in all its forms: social, political, religious, and philosophical.

All of Sartre's works, whether they be novels, plays, essays, or major philosophical treatises, are media through which he presented his ideas. Sartre was not a stylist, and aesthetics were of limited interest to him. His plays have even been called "black and white." More important to him than aesthetics was the *thinking* behind the works; he shifted back and forth between literary genres more to suit his ideological needs than to satisfy any aesthetic purpose. These *Notes* will show how Sartre used *No Exit* and *The Flies* to propagate his ideas. The emphasis will be placed on a firm understanding of his system — which is fairly straightforward — and then you'll see how the plays are vehicles through which this system is proffered.

Sartre was born on June 21, 1905, in Paris. The son of Jean-Baptiste Sartre, a French naval officer, and Anne Marie Schweitzer, first cousin of Albert Schweitzer, the young Sartre was to lose his father shortly after birth, making it necessary to move into the home of his maternal grandfather, Charles Schweitzer.

As a child, Sartre was small and cross-eyed — features which followed him through life — and thus he was generally unsuited for the activities of more ordinary children. Perhaps because of his physical limitations and irregular family life, he learned early to assess people and events from a detached, systematic viewpoint. He would talk with his mother in the park each day in search of new friends, and on discovering that children his age weren't much interested in him, he would return sadly to his apartment and launch into dreams. Such is the background for what would become a career based on serious and profound thinking tempered by a creative, artistic talent.

After attending the Lycée Henri IV for awhile in Paris, he transferred to the Lycée in La Rochelle after his mother remarried. Upon graduation, he entered the prestigious École Normale Supérieure in Paris and graduated first in his class – an extraordinary feat because of the demanding requirements of the school. While at the École, he formed a friendship with the young Simone de Beauvoir, who continually placed second behind him on all the exams. This friendship, which developed into a lifelong relationship of love and support, was to provide Sartre with one of his most stimulating and trustworthy colleagues and future co-workers.

Sartre did not believe in official marriage, and his friendship with Simone de Beauvoir was the closest he came to formalizing a lifestyle with another person. She provides an intimate account of their early years in two of her best-selling books, *Memoirs of a Dutiful Daughter* (1959) and *The Prime of Life* (1962).

At the École, and also at the Sorbonne, Sartre formed many important friendships with thinkers and writers who later became well known in their respective fields – people such as the anthropologist Claude Lévi-Strauss and the philosopher Simone Weil.

Between 1931 and 1934, he taught high school in Le Havre, Lyon, and Paris. It was a period during which he began to feel the need for focusing his ideas in a way that would make them accessible to large groups of people. A one-year sabbatical in 1934 at the French Institute in Berlin enabled him to immerse himself in modern German philosophy, particularly the works of Heidegger and Husserl. The atheistic nature of Heidegger's thinking was attractive to Sartre as he emerged from his Catholic background into a godless universe. Upon his return to France, he spent the years from 1934 to 1945 teaching at the Lycée Condorcet in Paris.

His first major breakthrough as a writer came in 1938 with his novel *Nausea*, which some critics feel is his best work. Based on the principle that man experiences a sensation of 'nausea' when confronted with a meaningless and irrational universe, the novel was the genesis for a series of writings in which Sartre propounds similar ideas. The literary genres vary, but the ideas are the same.

Sartre was an extremely practical man in the sense of putting into practice his thoughts and ideas. He thought nothing of becoming involved in political rallies which supported his beliefs, and the meaning of 'action,' for him, would increasingly take on a capital importance in his works. This is particularly true in the works which he produced during the World War II era. Having been drafted into the French Army in 1939, Sartre was taken prisoner-of-war in 1940 with the Fall of France. This experience was important for two reasons: (1) it sharpened his political position as a leftist thinker who decried the fascism that threatened Europe at that time, and (2) it provided the occasion for his first venture into playwriting; he wrote a Christmas play based on a biblical theme and addressed it to his fellow prisoners-of-war. He was released in 1941, and from that moment he committed himself firmly to the activities of the Resistance. In 1946, Sartre gave up teaching and devoted himself entirely to his writing; his busy schedule would no longer permit the drudgery of traditional employment.

Sartre's pre-war work is largely a defense of individual freedom and human dignity; in his post-war writing, he elaborates on these themes and strongly emphasizes the idea of social responsibility; this latter development was influenced by his growing admiration of Marxist thinking. In 1943, Sartre presented his first play, *The Flies*, as well as his monumental philosophical treatise, *Being and Nothingness*, both of which established him as one of France's most profound and gifted writers. A year later, he wrote *No Exit*, another attempt to reveal his ideas about freedom and the human condition.

As the leading French exponent of existentialism, Sartre was prepared to use any literary form or genre to communicate his ideas widely. The theater was a good way of doing this, but he also felt that the novel might also prove to be useful. So in 1945, he published the first two volumes of a proposed four-volume series entitled *The Roads to Freedom*. The first two volumes, *The Age of Reason* and *The Reprieve*, were the only ones which he completed until 1949, when he finished *Iron in the Soul*. At that time, he decided that the novel was not as effective a genre as the theater, so he abandoned plans to write a fourth installment. The years between volumes two and three were feverish ones for Sartre; he wrote plays (*The Respectable Prostitute*, 1946; *The Chips are Down*, 1947; and *Dirty Hands*, 1948), literary criticism, and a significant philosophical essay delivered originally as a lecture to the "Club Maintenant" (*Existentialism Is a Humanism*, 1946).

All of this work served to reinforce the basic principles of existential thought which Sartre had announced earlier, and it prepared him for a decade during which he again returned to the theater as a means of popularizing his ideas. He wanted to show man as he *is*, and he realized that the theater was the best place to demonstrate man in action, in dramatic circumstance, and in the midst of living. All of Sartre's plays show the raw passions of frustrated humankind – and although the plays sometime seem pessimistic, Sartre defended them vehemently on the grounds that they do not exclude the notion of salvation.

As an atheist and as a Marxist, Sartre often wrote about 'scarcity' (*la rareté*) as a motivator of human progress. He believed, as we shall see elsewhere in these *Notes*, that commitment was essential for human freedom and dignity, and that commitment was "an act, not a word." He often went out into the streets to participate in riots and protests, selling leftist pamphlets and so on, in order to verify through action that he believed in the "revolution." The war had perhaps the greatest influence on his writings of the 1940s, as Sartre moved progressively further to the left.

In 1960, he wrote the extremely dense and complicated *Critique of Dialectical Reason*, a political treatise which contains the essay "Search for a Method." This essay rivals, and even surpasses, the complexity of *Being and Nothingness*, but it is of interest today mostly to students of political science and philosophy.

In 1964, Sartre was awarded the Nobel Prize for his literary achievements. His autobiographical work, *The Words*, was hailed by readers and critics alike as being "one of the most remarkable books of the twentieth century" (*Washington Star*). But Sartre refused the Nobel Prize, eschewing it as a cultural symbol with which he did not wish to be associated.

The last years of Sartre's life were consumed with his work on Flaubert, the nineteenth-century French novelist. He sought to present a "total biography" of Flaubert through the use of Marx's ideas on history and class as well as of Freud's explorations of the psyche. At Sartre's death in 1980, only three of the proposed four volumes had been completed.

Sartre was one of the most substantial thinkers and writers of the twentieth century and will remain known for his tireless contributions to existentialism. Time will decide whether or not his plays are to survive, but regardless of their interest to future readers and/or spectators, they will always hold value as poignant illustrations of Sartre's philosophy. By writing them, he chose to create visual pictures, containing his philosophical ideas, for audiences to hear and *see*.

SARTRE'S MAJOR WORKS

1936   •*Imagination: A Psychological Critique*
1938   •*Nausea*
1939   •"The Wall" (in *Intimacy*)
       •"The Sketch for a Theory of the Emotions"
1940   •*The Psychology of Imagination*
1943   •*The Flies*
       •*Being and Nothingness*
1944   •*No Exit*
1945   •*The Age of Reason* (first volume of trilogy: *The Roads to Freedom*)
       •*The Reprieve* (second volume of trilogy)
1946   •*The Respectful Prostitute*
       •*Existentialism and Humanism*
       •*The Victors (Morts sans sépulchre)*
1947   •*The Chips Are Down (Les Jeux sont faits)*
       •*What Is Literature?*
       •*Baudelaire*
       •*Situations I*
1948   •*Dirty Hands*
       •*Situations II*
1949   •*Iron in the Soul* (often translated as *Troubled Sleep*; third volume of trilogy)
       •*Situations III*
1951   •*The Devil and the Good Lord*
1952   •*Saint Genet: Comédien et Martyr*
1954   •*Kean*
1955   •*Nekrassov*
1959   •*The Condemned of Altona*
1960   •*Critique of Dialectical Reason* (containing: "Search for a Method")
1963   •*The Words*
1971   •*Flaubert* (vols. 1 & 2)
1972   •*Flaubert* (vol. 3: *The Family Idiot*)

SARTREAN EXISTENTIALISM:

PRINCIPLES AND PHILOSOPHIES

What is it?

There is no shortage of critical material on existentialism – a term first coined by a journalist to describe Sartre's writing and later adopted by Sartre himself. But often the explanations are either confusing or incomplete, leaving one frustrated about what it all means.

Sartre was among the first to make this observation after existentialism had become widely popularized in the post-war years. In his essay "Existentialism Is a Humanism," he asserts that "the word [existentialism] has taken on such a broad meaning today that it no longer means anything. . . . People who are anxious for scandal and action embrace this philosophy, which of course can bring them nothing in this domain. In point of fact, existentialism is the least scandalous and most austere of doctrines. It is destined strictly to technicians and thinkers."

While Sartre too may be guilty of over-simplifying a bit here (he was caught up in the passion of giving a live lecture), his point is well taken: existentialism is a specific philosophy which offers practical as well as theoretical interpretations of human existence. It is not a system which seeks the endorsement of people who define themselves by fad or trend. While it was popular in the forties and fifties to label oneself an existentialist, this was by no means an indication that the person was committed to existentialist principles or even understood what they were all about.

In this section, we'll look at the basic ideas and attitudes underlying Sartrean existentialism and see how they gave rise to his philosophy. Then we'll examine the specific features of his system which appear over and over in the novels and plays, with particular reference to *No Exit* and *The Flies*. If you have not yet read the plays, it is best to read the following explanation of Sartre's system of existentialism; then you can read through the play with these points in mind. If you've already read the plays, read these *Notes*, then go back and re-read the works with this new information.

EXISTENTIALISM BEFORE SARTRE

Sartre was not the first to elaborate a system of existentialism. The question of existence has preoccupied humankind since its beginnings, and as early as the Bible, free will has been a major concern. One reads in Ecclesiasticus (15:14) (in the Apocrypha) that "God made man free in the beginning, and then left him free to make his own decisions." This notion of freedom is echoed down through the ages, from varying points of view. Rousseau's *Social Contract* (1762) revolves around his version of the above quotation ("Man is born free but is everywhere in chains"), and so do the works of the writers known to us as existentialists. The Greeks and Romans also had their own ideas concerning man's freedom, and it is still a burning issue in the writings of the twentieth century.

There are two broad categories of existentialists: Christian and atheistic. Among the Christians one finds Soren Kierkegaard, Karl Jaspers, and Gabriel Marcel; the most celebrated of the atheists, prior to Sartre, was Martin Heidegger.

Kierkegaard, A Danish philosopher of the nineteenth century, is generally regarded as one of the founders of modern existentialism. As a Christian, he claimed in his major work, *Either/Or*, that one could choose either a life with Christ or a life without Christ. He felt there were no *logical* reasons for believing in Christ and that a leap of faith – not rational proof of God's existence – was what constituted belief. He believed that, regardless of one's religious choices, man would be tormented by conscious or unconscious despair (cf. *Sickness unto Death*, 1849), and when one dwelled on this despair, it would become 'dread' (cf. *The Concept of Dread*, 1844). This idea is significant as a precursor to the Sartrean notion of 'nausea.'

Kierkegaard's beliefs brought him into direct conflict with the ideas of Hegel, the German philosopher who claimed to have rationalized Christianity. Hegel subscribed to Kant's assertion that Jesus had originally taught a rational morality and offered a religion which was suitable to the reason of all men. Hegel argued that the history of mankind was the intelligible reflection of God's will, but Kierkegaard attacked this thinking on the basis that one would have to *be* God to know what God's will was (cf. *Concluding Unscientific Postscript*, 1846). Kierkegaard was not interested in an objective, scientific proof of God; he knew that man's life, regardless of religion, was colored with despair and that a detached 'objectivity' was unable to change this. He proposed that the only way truth could be found was through one's intuitions and feelings, through the leap of faith ("truth is subjectivity"). This form of existentialism, anchored in a belief in God, was not one with which Sartre could agree.

Closer to Sartre's thinking was that of Heidegger, the German philosopher whose works had a profound influence on the budding

French writer. Heidegger's atheistic *Sein und Zeit* addressed the basic metaphysical question of: "Why is there something rather than nothing?" This will figure later in the Sartrean position on existence preceding essence, especially given Heidegger's conclusion that life is woven with care and dread, and that all man's projects come to nothingness at death. It is worth noting that Sartre's major philosophical treatise, *Being and Nothingness*, bears the very clear mark of this mode of reasoning. Sartre took from Heidegger the basic notion that life was absurd, that the universe was irrational and meaningless – and that the ultimate absurdity was death. From these ideas, he moved into his own system of thinking and evolved what is now known as Sartrean existentialism.

SARTREAN EXISTENTIALISM: AN OVERVIEW

In learning about Sartrean existentialism, it is helpful to recall data about the climate in which Sartre grew up. Recall for a moment the sadnesses of his childhood when no one wanted him for a friend. Recall his heavy dependence on a fantasy life as an escape from a world which he found hostile and offensive. Recall that his father died when he was two years old, leaving him in an environment of emotional strain and pressure. Add to this the fact that he was held prisoner-of-war in Germany and that he was forced to accept a lifestyle repugnant to human decency. By the age of thirty-five, he had known more duress than many people experience in a lifetime, and his sentiment of the absurd grew in proportion to the circumstantial hardships.

Sartre viewed the universe as an irrational, meaningless sphere. Existence was absurd and life had no sense, no purpose, no explanation. Death was the proverbially absurd icing on the cake, making life even more intolerable, more ridiculous. He felt 'nauseated' by the vastness of this empty, pointless predicament, and he wrestled many hours for a meaningful solution.

It was in this frame of mind that he produced his massive philosophical study, *Being and Nothingness*, after having already written several important books on related subjects. *Being and Nothingness* is a study of the phenomenological ontology of man (i.e., the nature of man's being). Don't be frightened off by big words. Philosophers love them, but all their polysyllabic terms have very basic meanings and can be explained within a context. Sartre was not interested in traditional metaphysics since he felt that the age-old problems of these thinkers would never be solvable by man. He suggested, for example, that the arguments for and against the existence of God were equally balanced, and that no amount of rational argumentation would provide the final word. His reasoning was simple: man is virtually unable to discover solutions to such problems, so why waste the time? Therefore, he abandoned the rational approach and opted for the phenomenological one.

Phenomenology was originated by the Moravian philosopher Edmund Husserl, in the late nineteenth century. It was a method used to define the essence of conscious data (*eidos*), and it investigated only those phenomena which could be seen, touched, verified, experienced directly by man and related in terms of his conscious experience. A fiercely logical methodology (whose name is regrettably awkward), it is based on the relation of conscious acts to meaningful objects. We'll soon see how this is relevant to Sartre's existentialism.

In *Being and Nothingness*, Sartre drew on the philosophy laid out by Husserl, but developed it further. He defined human consciousness as being a *nothingness* in the sense of *no-thingness*, and placed it in opposition to *being*, that is *thing-ness*. It is in keeping with this definition that Sartre abandons God; his decision is for moral reasons since believing in God places limits on freedom and, ultimately, on man's responsibility. God is not something that can be seen, touched, or perceived in a verifiable manner — hence, he cannot belong in the phenomenological system. *Being and Nothingness* is a psychological study, as are most of Sartre's philosophical works: he identifies the theory of freedom with that of human consciousness, showing that all objective descriptions of humankind (e.g., what he calls 'situations') fail to define man adequately. Since man's consciousness is outside the boundaries of objective inquiry, only his freedom to choose his own lifestyle allows for a definition of his essence. Within the confines of nothingness, Sartre realized that man indeed possesses freedom to choose: consciousness, being non-matter, escapes determinism, and thus permits man to make choices about the beliefs and actions of his life. This freedom of choice is at the center of Sartrean existentialism, and although it is a hopeful message, it is also tragic since death puts an end to all human efforts and achievements.

But let's move further toward finding out what this all means. Consider the political situation of the World War II years. The fascists were growing in strength, and the world was threatened by a major world war. Peace was thrown out the window and order was nowhere to be found. The very fabric of society had split at the seams, and people were groping for meaning, for security, for the comfort of lawful citizenry and the basic amenities of civilization. Instead, people were being murdered, rules were imposed by a select few, foreigners to one's own country established curfews, human rights were a thing of the past, and Sartre couldn't resist concluding that the whole thing was *madness*—completely without meaning or justification. It was one thing to disapprove of another country's political system and problems; it was quite something else to be herded by force into a prisoner-of-war camp and to be held hostage by an ugly and vile, usurping regime.

All of this left a permanent imprint on Sartre's mind. Never again, after the war, would he miss a chance to urge people away from mindless obedience. Human beings must make their own choices, reach their own decisions, think for themselves and establish their own standards of living. Conformism to the values of an outside group (e.g., the fascists) was an abomination which Sartre abhorred and condemned; it was immoral to adopt other people's beliefs if one disagreed with them internally. To act in a way which betrayed one's innermost feelings was inauthentic, irresponsible, and in 'bad faith.' All of Sartre's plays show characters who are forced to make decisions—many of which are tough ones—and the characters are often called upon to reassess the very substance of their belief systems, to adopt new personal standards by employing *responsible* choices.

Timing played a crucial role in Sartre's enormous success. Although Gabriel Marcel had been the first French writer to discuss existentialism on a large scale, Sartre benefited from the tremendously shaky emotional climate following the war. People were uncertain about their lives and were afraid. They resented what had been done to them by outside aggressors, and they were blinded by the absurdity of it all. Many people abandoned optimism and posed hard questions about the existence of a benevolent God. Among these people, Sartre attracted a vast audience by casting doubt on the heinous conformism recommended by 'official' protocol.

Sartre offered people an alternative: he prompted them to choose for themselves what their lifestyles would be, regardless of outside pressures. He encouraged them to ignore governmental threats and warnings and to place personal morality above social and political faithfulness. Most of all, he impressed upon them the need to obey their own feelings, not to conform and compromise themselves.

Since he did not believe in God, he offered what he believed to be logical conclusions based on a consistent atheism. "All possibility of finding values in an intelligible heaven" disappear, he claimed, since God does not exist. That necessitated a shift from the outside to the inside: instead of seeking answers to problems through prayer and divine intervention, one must turn inward and create one's own solutions. Sartre's notion of freedom echoes, to an extent, something of Rousseau: "Man is condemned to be free," and the only difference between this assertion and the one in Ecclesiasticus is that God has been removed from the problem—a major change—and one which rearranges all the component parts of the dialectic.

Of course, things aren't so simple. Once man has realized the need for making his own choices, Sartre proceeds to outline the responsibilities awaiting him. The universe, being irrational and absurd, has no meaning. Man is free to choose, hence to act, hence to give his life personal meaning. It is this confrontation with meaninglessness that creates a tormenting anguish which Sartre calls 'nausea.' You've probably felt it at some point in your life: all of a sudden, you realize that things don't seem to have any meaning or that your value system seems to be absurd. This is what underlies the concept of 'nausea.'

Certainly man can decide *not* to accept freedom—and we'll see how Sartre deals with this in a moment. For those who do accept it, however, this freedom brings with it considerable consequences. If the universe is absurd and without meaning, then people living in it are likewise without meaning—until *they* choose to create it. "Man is only what he does. Man becomes what he chooses to be." Sartre draws a sharp distinction between *being* and *existing*: if one chooses to act, one is said to *be*; when one chooses not to act, one merely *exists*. Hamlet's famous question of "to be or not to be" becomes, in this context, "to *be* or to *exist*, that is the question." It is an interplay of existence vs. essence, and in the next section of these *Notes*, we'll see exactly what this means. For the moment, let's finish up with our overview of Sartre's theories.

Since the act of being can only be determined through acts and deeds, man must make the active choice to follow through with his desires and intentions. This is what Sartre calls *commitment (engage-*

ment): man must be committed to his social, political, and moral beliefs, or he cannot hope to give himself definition. His acts are phenomena which can be verified, whereas intentions count for nothing. This takes us back to the principles of phenomenology.

A man who fails to choose is a man trapped in a morass of confusion. The road to freedom is through choice and action: "to do and while doing to make oneself and to be nothing but the self which one has made." Freedom, then, becomes freedom from absurdity, freedom from meaninglessness. Defining the self is tantamount to escaping one's 'nausea.' It eliminates abstraction and turns life into a series of pragmatic responsibilities. Only through this self-definition can one shape a meaningful destiny; anything short of this results in inauthenticity, 'bad faith,' and a heightened sense of 'nausea.'

The French philosopher Robert Champigny sums up this rejection of religion by pointing out that "Sartre's main objection to the more authentic brands of Christian morality is that they provide an inadequate statement of the ethical problem and can serve only as a mask for irresponsibility." In other words, by surrendering one's problems to an outside force (God), one is sacrificing the freedom to find personal solutions. One is also, in a sense, 'passing the buck' to God instead of carrying through with personal engagement – and this form of random obedience, for Sartre, is the ultimate in 'bad faith.'

SARTREAN EXISTENTIALISM: SPECIFIC PRINCIPLES

In order to simplify things even further, one should study a point-by-point list of existentialist principles. This is a summary useful for understanding several of Sartre's works, and it is representative of his major ideas. You will want to pay particular attention to these details as you examine the plays and as you prepare for essay and/or examination questions.

the problem: Existence is absurd. Life has no meaning. Death is the ultimate absurdity: it undoes everything that life has been building up to. One is born by chance; one dies by chance. There is no God.

the solution: One must make use of freedom; only freedom of choice can allow one to escape 'nausea.'

the system:

(1) *existence precedes essence:*

Our acts create our *essence*. Man alone *exists*; objects simply *are* (i.e., they do not exist per se). Animals and vegetables occupy an intermediary position. Plants grow, form fruits, live, and then die. Animals are born, chew their food, make sounds, follow their instincts, and die. Neither plants nor animals make deliberate choices or carry through with responsibility.

EXISTENCE + FREEDOM OF CHOICE
+ RESPONSIBILITY = ESSENCE

Historically, philosophy before Sartre was 'essentialist.' That is, it was concerned with defining the essence of each species, with providing details about generic traits. Existentialism, on the other hand, places existence *before* essence. Man exists (i.e., is born) before he can *be* anything, before he can become anything; therefore, his existence precedes his essence. His state of existence precedes his state of becoming. An individual is responsible for making himself into an essence, of lifting himself beyond the level of mere existence. This is where choice and action come in. Sartre offers the argument about the artisan and his craft: "When you consider a manufactured object, such as a book or a paper cutter, this object was manufactured by an artisan who started from a concept; he referred to this concept of a paper cutter and also to the technique of producing it as a part of the concept – which is basically a recipe. Thus, the paper cutter is simultaneously an object which is produced in a certain manner and which has a definite purpose; one cannot suppose a man making a paper cutter without knowing what the object will be used for. That's why we say that, for the paper cutter, essence . . . precedes existence. . . . It's a technical vision of the world in which one can say that production precedes the existence of an object. When we conceive of a God-creator, this God is usually thought of as a superior artisan. . . . In the eighteenth century, with the atheism of the philosophers, the notion of God was done away with, but not so with the idea that essence precedes existence. . . . Atheistic existentialism, which I represent, is more coherent. It declares that if God does not exist, there is at least one being in whom existence precedes essence, a being who exists before being defined by any concept, and this being is man – or, in the words of Heidegger, human reality. What does this mean, that existence precedes essence? It means that man exists first, finds himself, ventures into the world, and then defines himself. . . . Thus, there is no human nature since there is no God to conceive it. Man *is* simply, not only in the way by which he conceives himself, but as he wishes himself to be, and since he conceives himself after existence, man is nothing other than what he makes of himself."

Thus, Sartre takes the traditional assumption of "essence precedes existence" and changes it into "existence precedes essence." This is a direct result of his atheism, whereby God does *not* exist. Man is born at random, and objects such as paper cutters simply *are* (i.e., they do not *exist*). Sartre distinguishes between "to be" and "to exist." One must exist before one can have essence, but objects and animals simply *are*.

(2) *freedom:* Man's situation is an unhappy one: what is good? and what is evil? Since there is no way of separating them, man is condemned to a life of freedom in which he must choose. If one rejects the notion of God, who is to say what is good and what is evil? No one, since there are no absolutes: there is good in evil and evil in good. One cannot act and remain pure since too many fears and obstacles would present themselves; of necessity, one must make choices and assume the consequences.

Sartre delineates three categories within his definition of freedom:

(a) *the man whom he compares to a stone:* this man makes no choices and is happy in his no-choice life. He refuses to commit himself (*engagement*), to accept responsibility for his life. He continues in his passive habits. Sartre scorns him. In *The Flies*, this person is represented by the Tutor.

(b) *the man whom he compares to plants:* This man is not happy. But he lacks the courage to take responsibility for his actions. He obeys other people. He is the one who suffers from 'nausea.' Sartre scorns this man the most of all three groups.

(c) *the man* not *compared to stones or plants:* This man suffers from freedom. He has the nobility to use freedom for the betterment of his life. He is the one whom Sartre admires.

Here are a few words to watch for in your readings; when you see them (or words closely related in meaning), think back to this section and realize why Sartre is using them:

(a) *for stones:*
- stone, rock, block, object
- passivity, weakness, cowardice
- wrapped up in the self (*"en soi"*)
- oriented to the past
- solidity

(b) *for plants:*
- 'bad faith' (*"mauvaise foi"*)
- viscosity (thick, sticky)
- moisture
- softness, sponginess, swamp-like

(c) *the true person:*
- fluidity
- combat
- for the sake of the self (*"pour soi"*) – an indication that man takes action, assumes responsibility
- the future, the horizon

(3) *responsibility:* Man must be committed, engaged. He has a responsibility before other citizens for his actions. By acting, he creates a certain essence for society ("by choosing for oneself, man chooses for all men"); any action which one takes affects the rest of humanity. From the moment when man makes a choice, *he is committed*. One must not renege on one's responsibility (as does Electra in *The Flies*), nor must one place the responsibility for one's actions onto the shoulders of someone else. Man should not regret what he has done. An act is an act.

(4) *'the others'*: Other people are a torture for two reasons:

    (a) they are capable of denying one's existence and one's freedom by treating one as an object; for example, if you do a cowardly act, and another person calls you a coward, this cuts off the possibility of your doing something heroic or courageous; it stereotypes you as a coward, and this causes anguish.

    (b) others judge you, observe you without taking into consideration your intentions (either your intentions about a future act or an act which you've already committed). The image they have of you may not correspond to the one you have of yourself. But you can't do without them because only they can tell you who you are. Man does not always understand the motives behind his actions; therefore, he needs others to help in this process. But there is relief; man can say to himself: "I am torture for them, just as they are torture for me."

Sartre offers four ways of defending oneself from the torture of 'the others':

(1) *evasion or avoidance:* One can isolate oneself from them, go to sleep, commit suicide, remain silent, or live in obscurity;

(2) *disguise:* One can try to fool others, lie to them, give a false image, resort to hypocrisy;

(3) *emotions:* One can inspire emotions such as love and friendship in others, make oneself liked/loved by them: "My lover accepts me as I accept myself." Therefore, an 'other' judges you as you judge yourself;

(4) *violence:* A dictator can put people in prison to prevent them from saying what he doesn't want to hear.

Sartre concludes that if any of the above four conditions prevail(s), one finds oneself in circumstances that are hell.

(5) *commitment:* Man must not be indifferent to his surroundings. He must take a stand, make choices, commit himself to his beliefs, and create meaning through action. Sartre is in favor of *an engaged literature*, of art that has a goal, a purpose. As with a man shooting a gun in the air or directly at a target, it's better to have a target, a message. The readers

should feel their responsibilities; the author should incite the readers to action, infuse an energy into them. Sartre is interested in a "historical public" (that is, a public of a certain precise moment in history): he addresses himself to the public of his times. Ideally, an author should write for a universal audience, but this is possible only in a classless society.

But the compromise is to address all readers who have the freedom to change things (i.e., political freedom). People hostile to Sartre's writings criticized him of assassinating literature. But he replied that he would never ignore stylistics, regardless of the ideas he was developing. He claimed that a reader should not be aware of a writer's style – that this would get in the way of understanding the piece of literature. Commitment to one's writing, he argued, was as vital as commitment to all other actions in one's life.

When you read *No Exit* and *The Flies*, or any of Sartre's other works, you will see the above ideas woven throughout his thought. But before we consider the two plays in detail, let's take a look at Sartre's political ideas; they will give us even more information with which to decipher his message.

SARTRE'S POLITICAL IDEAS

Sartre was a leftist thinker throughout his entire life, and after World War II, he moved more and more to the left, expressing himself in increasingly difficult publications, and often in a language accessible only to a select few.

He rejected the idea of class and attempted to strip away the layers of bourgeois values imposed by the capitalistic society in which he lived. His major goal, politically, was to have a country in which total freedom existed – a true democracy, not a dictatorship disguised as a free society. He had good relations with the Soviet Union early in his adult life and admired the *idea* behind their society. But he later became very critical of the USSR as it spearheaded POW camps, invaded Budapest, and behaved with the kind of dictatorial will that he decried in Europe. He discusses this disagreement with the Soviets in his essay "*Le Fantôme de Staline*" in *Les Temps Modernes* and describes his condemnation of the French Communist Party for submitting to the dictates of Moscow.

This is an important factor in assessing Sartre's politics: he was *not* a Communist. Rather, he began as a believer in man's historical materialism (during the period of *The Flies*), then he moved toward Marxism, and ultimately he ascribed to what is best termed neo-Marxism. He advocated permanent progress, whereby man would correct his mistakes whenever they occurred. This is one of the reasons why he criticized the French Communists: he claimed that they acted in 'bad faith,' adhered to policies in which they did not believe, expressed a lack of honesty, used tricks and opportunism, and lacked critical perception in all their dealings with the membership.

Sartre's Marxist thinking began with a deep hatred for bourgeois values. He insisted that the bourgeois always ended in thinking about the self, selfishly, instead of thinking responsibly about individual contributions to the group, to society.

But if Sartre rejected capitalism on the one hand, and communism on the other, he found himself happily devoted to the tenets of Marxist socialism. His concept of freedom ("be free") is not at all the same as the *"Fais ce que vouldras"* ("do as you wish") of Rabelais's Abbey of Thélème, in *Gargantua and Pantagruel*, but rather a freedom based on responsibility toward society and, naturally, toward one's own growing essence. This devotion to society at large is where Sartre comes closest to Marx's thinking.

There are, however, differences between Sartre's 'system' of existentialism and Marxist politics. The differences are clearest in the early writings of Sartre: whereas Marxism is primarily interested in the biological and social condition of man (with consciousness seen as a 'superstructure'), Sartre focused originally on the individual, on his innermost thoughts about freedom and anguish, on the concept of responsibility and consciousness. The Marxists looked at the social group; Sartre narrowed in on the individual member of that group. Marxism was external to consciousness; Sartre placed consciousness at the very center. Marxism delineated the characteristics of human collectivity and class structure whereas Sartre elaborated a theory anchored in human experience and in individual choice.

The critic René Marill-Albérès explains the differences between Sartre's thinking and Marxism, as well as their eventual coming-together. "In contrast to Marxism, which has as its starting point cosmic, biological, and social elements, Sartre starts from *human experience*, from consciousness, from the individual. . . The problem is to reconcile Marxism, which explains the individual in terms of his social conditions, and Sartre's philosophy, which cannot avoid giving first place to what is actually experienced by the individual. From Marxism, Sartre borrows the notion of the dialectic – that is, the development of a reality through several stages and through several forms, each more complex than the one that preceded it. The problem of reconciliation confronting Sartre is therefore what he calls 'totalization,' or passing from the individual to the group, from consciousness to history. . . To resolve the issue, Sartre transports 'dialectical movement' from the collectivity to the individual and, in contrast to Marxism, sees in consciousness the source of the collectivity; it is the individual that experiences social realities, reacts, develops dialectically, and creates the social dialectic." This brings us right back to the essence of Sartrean existentialism, showing how Sartre's philosophical and political ideas were intimately woven into a coherent system of thinking.

Because Sartre prefers to examine the *individual*, instead of the *group*, his Marxism is actually a neo-Marxism. He does not dispute the claims of Marx about the social collectivity, but he insists that the individual must not be overlooked in the process. In this manner, he adapts Marxism to his own thinking, but he still remains committed to leftist politics. Both the individual and the group appear in his plays, and if you keep in mind Sartre's belief in the individual as a responsible contributor to the group, you will see in what way he integrates Marxism into his system.

SARTRE'S DRAMATIC FORMULA

Sartre's early plays reflect a formula which he described in a 1940 essay entitled "Forgers of Myth"; in this essay, he analyzes the French drama of the Occupation and of the post-war period. He advocates a particular type of drama, one which is short and violent and which is centered entirely around one event. It should be a "conflict of rights, bearing on some very general situation – written in a sparse, extremely tense style, with a small cast not presented for their individual characters but thrust into a conjunction where they are forced to make a choice – in brief, this is the theater, austere, moral, mythic, and ceremonial in aspect, which has given birth to new plays in Paris during the Occupation and especially since the end of the war."

Sartre's plays are characteristically classical in structure, adhering to traditional unities (time, place, action) and maintaining a fast, non-stop pace. These are not the plays of a romantic or wistful soul; rather, they fairly burst with naturalistic reality and offer the spectator a cold, often brutal encounter with Sartre's *Weltanschauung* (world view). There is little color or profusion of emotion; it is a stark universe peopled with characters who represent various 'types' in Sartre's thinking: good faith, bad faith, rocks, animals, and so on. It has often been called a "black and white" theater, one in which actions are right or wrong, acceptable or condemnable, heroic or cowardly. But traditional value judgments do *not* apply here: while there are good and bad actions, these adjectives refer more to their philosophical principle than to their moral quality.

There is much ground for comparison between the works of Sartre and the Absurdists. Sartre and Albert Camus, for example, shared many ideological viewpoints and brought to their plays, novels, and essays similar reactions concerning the universe.

But the differences are also worth noting. The epithet 'absurd' is vague and often misleading. It is used to describe the works of such varied writers as Camus, Beckett, Ionesco, Adamov, Genet, and Albee, yet the systems at work in these dramatists are unique to the writers, and even within the works of one writer, the ideas change and evolve radically. Therefore, it is of no value to apply the term 'absurd' to the works of Sartre since he is, at best, peripheral to this 'school' of drama. The absurdists, for the most part, concentrate on the irrationality of human experience. They do not suggest a path beyond this lack of rationality, and they show how cause-effect relationships deteriorate into chaos. Their dramatic structure mirrors this causal impossibility and focuses on the sense of absurdity in an irrational world. Sartre, on the other hand, begins with the assumption that the world is *irrational*.

The idea of rationalism did not interest him: what was the point, he thought, of battling with ideas which led nowhere? Who cared whether there was – or whether there was not – rationalism in the world; more important, he judged, was the concept of freedom and choice – and even more significant was the idea of creating an order out of the chaos.

So while the absurdists concentrated on the lack of order, Sartre narrowed in on the construction of order. The former were more interested in showing the absence of cause-effect situations, while Sartre demonstrated the need for making responsible choices which would effect a life based on freedom from 'nausea.'

NO EXIT *(Huis Clos)*

INTRODUCTION

No Exit is one of Sartre's finest plays; it is produced and studied more than any of his other dramas. The setting is Hell, even though it resembles the real world around us. Three characters come together in this microcosm of Hell in a way which shows their indispensability to one another: they become inextricably involved in each other's stories, and they represent the fundamental idea of the play – namely, that other people are torture for us. The question of 'the others' is integral to the works of Sartre; he describes over and over how other people can condemn us, define us, withhold love from us, murder us – in short, take the power away from us to live life as we wish.

But 'the others' cannot rob us of our freedom, and this is the central notion in Sartrean existentialism. The anguish which we feel when we are confronted with the vast and meaningless universe is something which Sartre calls 'nausea.' To combat this 'nausea,' man can use his freedom – freedom of thought, choice, and action. But once man has chosen and acted upon his choice, there is no turning back: this choice stands as an imprint on his essence, on his human makeup, and it follows him for the rest of his days. In *No Exit*, Sartre pushes this idea to its extreme, showing how the torture of looking back on our past is a form of Hell, particularly when we *fail to choose* an act when the opportunity presents itself. If man is alive, he can always choose to rearrange his life, but when he dies, the lifelong events are frozen into a mold which can never be broken. This is the atmosphere in *No Exit*, where all three characters have died and are condemned to the unmalleable truth of their past actions. Contrary to the situation in *The Flies*, this play shows what happens when people do *not* choose properly. In *The Flies*, we witness the results of correct, as well as incorrect, choices.

LIST OF CHARACTERS

Garcin

Brazilian journalist of middle age. Politically leftist, he has no problem expressing himself or making a point with passion. A very intelligent man, he is attracted to Inez. But Inez despises him, and his need for her goes unrequited.

Inez

A lesbian. Same age as Garcin. She is attracted to Estelle, but Estelle is not interested. Inez is a hard, cold woman whose experience in life has brought out the animalistic instincts in her. She will stop at nothing to get her own way.

Estelle

A pretty blonde. Younger than the other two. Estelle is very interested in being feminine, in pursuing the affections of Garcin (who is not interested in her) and in attending to her physical attractiveness.

A Valet

He ushers the characters into the room and serves no other function.

SUMMARIES AND COMMENTARIES *(while there are no divisions into "scenes" in* No Exit, *we shall break the play into subdivisions to facilitate a running commentary.)*

Summary

The play opens with Garcin and a Valet in a drawing room decorated in Second Empire style. This is no ordinary drawing room, however: it is actually Hell, and the play takes place in an afterlife following the death of its characters. The two men discuss the furniture; Garcin disdains the Second Empire furnishings, but he says that he was able, during his lifetime, to accustom himself to most styles. Actually, he is rather surprised by the decor; it is nothing like what he had expected or had been told about the afterlife. The Valet shrewdly points out that living people who have never set foot in the afterlife are not likely in a position to describe the details of it. Garcin wonders where all the instruments of torture are: Hell is supposed to have racks and "red-hot pincers." The Valet is amused by Garcin's persistence in believing the myths and the stories told by human beings about Hell. And when Garcin becomes angry over not having his toothbrush, the Valet retorts that Garcin has not yet gotten over his sense of human dignity. Human beings always ask the Valet silly questions when they arrive here. Garcin is conscious of his position and announces that he is facing up to it. He soon realizes that this Hell will be disagreeable because it is life without a break: there is no sleeping, no brushing one's teeth, no doing all the ordinary things of life—except living, non-stop. He wonders how he will endure his own company, not knowing yet that others will join him. Garcin points to a bell and asks the Valet if he will respond to it when Garcin rings for him. The Valet says that the bell is unpredictable: its wiring is faulty, and it is itself capricious.

Commentary

In these opening moments of the play, Sartre raises three fundamental matters which will underline the action of the drama: (1) religion; (2) aloneness; and (3) 'the others.' He discredits religion—particularly Western religion—by referring to life on earth as being "down there": Christian religion refers to Hell as being down below and to Heaven as being up above. Sartre reverses this notion and depicts Hell as being above earth. It's one way of upsetting stereotyped notions in the minds of spectators. As for the importance of 'aloneness,' Sartre isolates Garcin from the very start of the play; Hell is defined as being within the confines of this Second Empire structure, and beyond these limits, there is nothing. It makes for a lonely, panicky environment where hope is all but nullified. This sets the stage for Sartre's portrayal of our need for 'others' in order for us to define our *essence*: Garcin depends, from the start, on the input from the Valet. He needs answers to questions and desires instructions on how 'life' evolves in this world of Hell. The Valet is surprised by Garcin's use of the word 'life,' but he humors him throughout the conversation. This idea of 'the others' being necessary to us is the central idea of the play: *other people are our Hell.*

Summary

The Valet ushers Inez into the room. She asks for Florence, but Garcin doesn't know such a person. Inez's first reaction is that Hell is torture by separation: she obviously had a relationship with Florence during her lifetime, but changes positions quickly to inform Garcin that she won't miss Florence a bit (she assumes that Garcin is the torturer). She is cold toward Garcin, claiming that torturers look frightened. Garcin gropes to see his image in a mirror, but he finds none. Inez is annoyed that Garcin is in the same room as she; the torture has already begun for her. Garcin wishes to be polite with Inez, but she tells him that she is *not* polite. She then reproaches Garcin for twisting his mouth, and she says that he has no right to inflict his fear on her. Fear, she claims, had a purpose before death, but it is pointless now. Garcin disagrees, indicating that they still might hope for the best since *real* suffering has not yet begun.

Commentary

The little details and human foibles and peccadillos come into play here as Inez and Garcin interact with one another; she is torture for him because she is cold and inattentive to his need for sociability, and he is torture for her since she resents being subjected to someone for whom she has no fondness. Sartre draws attention to the human body, as he does in many of his other works, by singling out Garcin's mouth as the object of Inez's scorn: it is a symbol for everything human – flesh, weakness, fear, undesirable human contact. The stage is now ready for the arrival of Estelle, who will round out this trio into a perpetually vicious circle.

Summary

The Valet ushers Estelle into the room. Garcin quickly informs her that he is *not* the torturer, and she replies that she never thought that he was. She laughs at their situation, but Garcin is not amused. She worries about the color clash between her clothes and the sofa, but she quickly realizes that there is no point in worrying. Inez tells Estelle that she is pretty. They all discuss their deaths: Inez committed suicide by using a gas stove; Estelle died of pneumonia; Garcin was shot twelve times in the chest. Estelle is appalled by the discussion, and she suggests that they refer to their deaths as their 'absences.'

They are able to see their former loved ones in various states of sorrow. Garcin buries his head in his hands as he contemplates his life, while Inez mocks him, saying that her life was quite neatly put in order before she died. Estelle and Garcin think that it's mere chance that brought the three together in this room; Inez disagrees, believing that nothing has been left to chance. Estelle dislikes the idea of someone expecting something from her, but Inez tells her to do as she pleases since it is not yet clear what 'they' expect from her.

Commentary

The characters have now reached the stage where they are conscious of other people's involvement in this set-up of Hell. Their room has been carefully planned for them; "they" have assembled the three characters deliberately (according to Inez), and thus we can expect a collision of personalities — in fact, the room has become *hot*, a symbolic hint of what's to come.

Summary

The three people begin wondering why they have been sent to Hell. Estelle thinks that in her case an error was made. Inez's response is a smile, and this disturbs Estelle very much. Estelle confesses that she married a man who was old enough to be her father, but that he had money and could help her look after her delicate brother. Then, after six years of marriage, she met another man and fell in love with him. She contracted pneumonia and died. Inez thinks all three of them are criminals, murderers. Estelle shouts at her to be quiet. Suddenly, Inez realizes why the three of them are together: the "official torturer" is absent, and they shall spend eternity in the same room; "each of us will act as torturer of the two others." Garcin recommends aloneness and silence as solutions: this will give them a chance to work out their salvation, and they must not raise their heads. All three agree. Then Inez sings a song about an executioner who chops off heads for a living; Estelle powders her face, and Garcin buries his head in his hands. Estelle wants a mirror, but there are none in the room.

Commentary

The absence of a mirror is significant: it prevents the characters from being able to see themselves with an *object*; thus, they are forced to see themselves through other people's impressions about them. This places more importance on one's inner self-image than on the details of facial makeup, hair, and so on. Part of their 'Hell' process is the idea of passing through a self-examination and assessment.

Summary

Estelle is taken aback by Inez's offer to serve as her 'mirror.' She wants Garcin to intervene, but he remains buried in his hands; Inez says that he doesn't count. Inez helps Estelle with her makeup and says that it looks much better than when she entered: she now looks more "diabolical." Estelle does not respond to Inez's come-on, so Inez begins to torture her with comments about her appearance: "What's that nasty red spot . . . a pimple?" Inez reminds her that she is now Estelle's mirror. Garcin is not interested in the two women. Inez attacks Garcin because he wants passivity and silence: she claims that his presence is everywhere, and that Estelle wishes only to please him. Clearly, there is no such thing as forgetting about the others: they are present, regardless.

Inez prefers to choose her own Hell, to look Garcin in the face and fight it out with him. Garcin announces that they should tell the truth about their lives: maybe this will save them from disaster. Garcin mistreated his wife and eventually slept with another woman in his own house. Inez was living with her cousin, who was married to Florence. When the man got on their nerves, the women moved out and lived together. He was killed, and in despair, Florence turned the gas oven on one night, killing both Inez and herself. Inez had made Florence see things through her eyes, and this bitterness was too much for her. Hence, the suicide/murder; Inez is in Hell for her cruelty. Estelle had an affair with a man and became pregnant; she went to Switzerland for five months and gave birth to a daughter. Her lover, Roger, wanted the child, but Estelle didn't, so she drowned the child; later, she died of pneumonia. Roger shot himself in the head.

Commentary

The characters have now unveiled their reasons for being sent to Hell. Garcin wishes to get on with things in an effort to help each other. The damnation period is suspended for a moment while they restore peace. It comes in fits and starts; this demonstrates Sartre's theory of freedom: if they wish to create something un-hellish for themselves, they can do so. But by dwelling on the past, negative, sordid aspects of their lives, they deprive themselves of calm. Their past actions matter only insofar as their present choices are concerned. They are now becoming more and more aware of their need for one another.

Summary

Inez does not wish help from Garcin, but he argues that the three of them are inextricably linked together: if all three of them don't cooperate, they will *all* suffer. But Inez lacks sufficient "human feeling" and can no longer give anything. Interestingly, they all see what's happening on earth – in life – as their former relatives and associates continue living; this idea is interjected regularly into their conversations. Inez accepts her Hell (she says that she is "rotten to the core"), and rejects Garcin's appeal to curtail her suffering. Estelle is upset about a former lover whom she can "see" dancing with Olga, and Inez steps in to comfort her; Estelle wants nothing to do with Inez, just as the latter wants nothing to do with Garcin, nor Garcin with Estelle. Garcin agrees to pay attention to Estelle, and they begin to touch each other; Inez protests and intends to bore holes through them with her eyes.

Commentary

There are two important points in this section: (1) Part of Sartre's theory on choice and freedom states that one chooses for all of humanity when one chooses for oneself. Here, all of the choices made by each character affect the others; when Estelle fatigues of Inez, she spits in her face – and, with this, Inez directs her anger at Garcin, not at Estelle: "Garcin, you shall pay for this." Within Sartre's system, nothing can happen without influencing everything else; therefore, Estelle can't do anything without her actions also affecting Garcin. This is part of their Hell. (2) As a child, Sartre, felt the presence of God, or at least the *idea* of God, watching over his shoulder. The same silent, surveying God occurs in Sartre's "Childhood of a Leader," where God becomes something of an Orwellian Big Brother. In *No Exit*, the spiritual entity (whether this be God, Satan, or 'the others') is portrayed as a watchful eye, and this is best illustrated in the speech by Inez, in which she tells Garcin (who is about to make love to Estelle):

"Don't forget I'm here, and watching. I shan't take my eyes off you."
This is a direct reflection of the sense of a watchful God felt by young
Sartre, before he gave up religion to become an atheist: a cold, im-
personal, exacting, and critical presence which belies the claims made
in the hopeful, promising Bible. There is no hint of Christianity or
salvation in this play; its emotional and philosophical setting is a
doomed, desperate hopelessness, an *angst* par excellence, a compunc-
tion wrought out by sin.

Summary

Garcin wonders if Estelle thinks that he was a coward for being
a pacifist during the war. He wonders if he fled ("bolted" toward Mex-
ico) because he was against war or because he was afraid. He decided,
after he was caught, that his death would finally settle the matter,
but then he admits that he faced even that moment rather badly.
Again, Garcin hears his former colleagues at the newspaper talking
about him: even 'the others' from his lifetime are a torture to him,
and he cannot intervene in their conversations to defend himself. Additionally, he is not comforted by the idea that these men will eventually die because other men will replace them and *perpetuate the belief
that Garcin was a coward*. His fate is in their hands. Can Estelle love
him? Estelle says that she can love him, but only for his *body*: he has
a manly chin, mouth, voice, and head of hair. He does not *look* like
a coward. This overjoys him, and he prepares to leave Hell with her
until they hear a shrill laugh: it is Inez, who prevents them from escaping. Garcin tries to leave through the door: he is ready to put up with
red-hot tongs and molten lead – whatever torture 'they' wish to subject him to, but he *must* leave this *agony of mind*. The door opens, and
he is surprised; in fact, he is so stunned that he decides not to pass
through it. Estelle tries pushing Inez through the door so she can have
Garcin to herself, but he tells her to desist, that it's *because of Inez*
that he is *staying in the room*. This catches Inez off-guard; he says that
Inez knows what it's like to be a coward. He no longer hears the voices
of people on earth, and he realizes that Inez is the same kind of person as he: it is *she* whom he must convince that he is not a coward.
Estelle does not count: she is interested only in exterior appearances.
He says to Inez: "If you'll have faith in me I'm saved." He spent his
life trying to be a man, and Inez suggests that it was only a dream.
He retorts that he made his choice deliberately, and that a man is

what he wills himself to be. Inez enjoys her status as Garcin's torturer, and she taunts him with her evaluation of him as a coward.

Suddenly, Estelle yells at Garcin to kiss her, thereby revenging himself on Inez. As he bends over Estelle, Inez cries out, knowing that while Garcin is at her mercy, she is also at his. Garcin reaches the climactic conclusion that "Hell is – other people!" Estelle is furious that Inez has interrupted her attempt at lovemaking, so she picks up a paper-knife and stabs Inez several times. Inez laughs as she's being stabbed; she knows no harm can come to her – she is already dead. All three of them laugh at their ridiculous situation. Then they sit on the sofas, pause for a moment, and finally decide to "get on with it."

Commentary

This last section is a small capsule of the ideas contained throughout the play: other people are our torture, and once a person is dead, there is nothing to be done about changing other, living people's attitudes. Sartre stresses the negative, ugly, cold side of this Hell: it is not something to look forward to and, he implies, it can be avoided by following his system. The anxiety or hell of life (that is, 'nausea') can be combated through freedom of choice, action, responsibility and a life in 'good faith.' In *No Exit*, Sartre focuses on the negative, seamy aspects of human emotions, eliminating the positive, fulfilling, and happiness-producing effects. There is no place in his Hell for fun; it is a bleak, remote, and isolated place of horror. Good intentions count for nothing (Inez says: "It's what one does . . . that shows the stuff one's made of"), and unless man is prepared to act decisively, Sartre has nothing but scorn for him. It is this kind of man, he asserts, who is at the mercy of other people's opinions – the hell and the torture of 'the others.' This is the principal message of the play. In a historical sense, Hell is symbolic of France during World War II and 'the others' represent the Nazis.

THE FLIES *(Les Mouches)*

INTRODUCTION

Many critics consider *The Flies* to be Sartre's most effective drama. It deals with commitment and resistance, and the theme of freedom is woven throughout the play's fabric. The play was produced in 1943, during World War II, and Sartre is lauded for having gotten his play past the Nazi censors; although on the surface this is a mythological drama, it is also a political and moral play about the plight of human slavery. Sartre wrote *The Flies* in keeping with his desire to "put on the stage certain situations which throw light on the main aspects of the condition of man and to have the spectator participate in the free choice which man makes in these situations." *The Flies* is Sartre's first play, written a year before *No Exit*, and it gave him his first popular opportunity, via the stage, to communicate his ideas to large groups of people who ordinarily might not have read his other works. This, for Sartre, was the best feature of the theater: it was a tremendous forum for disseminating his thoughts. It was, in the 1940s, the medium which served something of the purpose which television serves today.

The play was produced during the Nazi occupation of France in 1943. It is an actualization of a myth (Oresteian) and came as another French contribution to the long list of Oresteian dramas. The French classical education has often led French playwrights to use Greek and Roman subject matter, and in 1873 the poet Leconte de Lisle wrote a tragedy dealing with Orestes entitled *Les Erinnyes*. After him, writers discovered the value of using myths to illustrate contemporary problems. This spawned a flow of mythologically inspired dramas, including Cocteau's *Antigone* (1922), *Orphée* (1926), and *La Machine Infernale* (1934); Giraudoux's *Amphitryon 38* (1929), *La Guerre de Troie n'aura pas lieu* (1935), and *Electre* (1937); Anouilh's *Eurydice* (1941), *Antigone* (1942) and *Médée* (1943). The idea of an American actualization of the Electra myth presented itself in Eugene O'Neill's *Mourning Becomes Electra* (1931), and this drama shows that the human aspects of mythology are relevant to the literary expression of any country.

The basic story is this: Orestes returns home after many years' absence and finds that his mother, Clytemnestra, and her lover, Aegistheus (her husband in *The Flies*), have murdered Agamemnon, Orestes' father; they now sit on the throne and have made a slave of Orestes' sister, Electra. She urges her brother to murder them, which he does, and then he is hounded for the rest of his life by the Furies of revenge.

In Sartre's version of the myth, the characters are shown as 'being' and 'becoming.' Some refuse to commit themselves to an action while others engage themselves forcefully; *responsibility* is a feature which again is shown to be necessary for escaping life's 'nausea,' and when the characters reject this responsibility, they are obliged to accept the consequences, in the form of flies. As early as the book of Exodus in the Bible, flies are used as a symbolic plague for punishment: "And there came a grievous swarm of flies into the house of the Pharaoh, and into his servants' houses, and into all the land of Egypt: the land was corrupted by reason of the swarm of flies" (Exodus 8:24). And, in the fifth century B.C., the three great Greek tragedians, Aeschylus, Sophocles, and Euripides all wrote versions of this myth. Critics have often compared the treatment of the Orestes myth by Sartre with that of Giraudoux: *The Flies* is less concerned with literary aesthetics than *Electre*, and Sartre uses it as a vehicle to elaborate his existential principles. He criticized Giraudoux for portraying human essence as a fixed commodity, as opposed to the act of becoming and, in a series of essays on theater, he described what his ideas on the theater were in terms of life's everyday situations:

(1) He was dedicated to a moral theater where there would be conflict in "the system of values, of ethics and of concepts of man." ("Forgers of Myths, The Young Playwrights in France," in *Theatre Arts*, XXX, June 1946, pp. 324-35).

(2) He rejected the realist theater and the *pièce à thèse* because man is not generally in a position to make exacting decisions between right and wrong, fact and fiction, moral and immoral, real and ideal.

(3) Theater must be seen as a religious rite where the dialogue should be dignified. There should be "a rigorous economy of words . . . through the pace of the dialogue, an extreme conciseness of statement – elipses, brusque interruptions, a sort of inner tension in the phrases."

(4) Sartre addressed the issue of choosing one's essence: "Many authors are returning to the theater of situation. No more 'characters'; the heroes are freedoms caught in a trap, like all of us. What are the issues? Each character will be nothing but the choice of an issue and will equal no more than the chosen issue. . . . Each one, by inventing his own issue, invents himself. Man must be invented each day." (*Situations III*, p. 293).

(5) He argued that the bourgeois control of the theater must end, that it be freed to the rigors of criticism and challenge from different viewpoints. He stressed the significance of the act, saying that "action, in the true sense of the word, is that of the character; there are no images in the theater but the image of the act, and if one seeks the definition of theater, one must ask what the act is, because the theater can represent nothing but the act" ("Beyond Bourgeois Theatre," translated by Rima Drell Reck, *Tulane Drama Review*, V, March 1961, pp. 3-11).

These characteristics are integrated into his plays, and each play tends to stress an individual component of his existential system while also underlining the action with his entire ideology. In *No Exit*, the specific idea stressed is: "Hell is other people," whereas in *The Flies*, the principal thought is: Only those people who choose, act, and accept responsibility can be free of 'nausea,' free of remorse, and free of the flies.

LIST OF CHARACTERS

Zeus/Jupiter

Depending on the translation you are reading, this character's name will be either Zeus (the Greek name) or else it will be Jupiter (the Roman name). He is the chief of the gods, who is said to be the son of Chronus (Saturn) and Rhea (Ops); he was educated on Mt. Ida in Crete in a cave and nourished with goat milk from Amalthaea. He conquered the Titans while he was still young, and in this play, Zeus/Jupiter represents God.

Orestes

Son of Agamemnon and Clytemnestra. His sister, Electra, saves him from being murdered by his mother (who murdered his father, Agamemnon). He later avenges his father's death by killing his mother, and he is the true hero of the play. He is the mouthpiece for the ideas which Sartre wishes to stress.

Electra

Daughter of Agamemnon, king of Argos, and sister of Orestes. She persuades her brother to avenge the murder of their father by killing Clytemnestra. In this play, she ends up adopting Zeus's attitude and, as a result, she is a traitor to the cause of the family. Sartre shows her as a woman to be pitied and hated.

Clytemnestra

Wife of Agamemnon, king of Argos. During his absence at the Trojan War, she misconducts herself with his cousin Aegistheus. When Agamemnon returns from the war (this happens before *The Flies*), she murders him and ascends to the throne of Argos. Her son, Orestes, after an absence of several years, returns home to avenge his father's death. It is Orestes, whose presence causes her remorse, who makes her realize that one must act according to one's convictions.

Aegistheus

Cousin of Agamemnon. He is an enemy of freedom and implicates himself in the crimes of Clytemnestra so that he may enjoy and usurp power. In order to make himself feared by people, he invents lies. Sartre shows how suffering and pain are inflicted on people who are against freedom; this suffering comes in the form of other people's opinions of them; by the end of the play, Aegistheus is disgusted by his own image.

The Tutor/Pedagogue

Again, the name of this character depends on which translation you are using. He falls into the group which Sartre labels 'stones': he refuses to commit himself to an action, he has no convictions, his attitude is neutral, he is satisfied with the status quo; in short, he is the kind of character whom Sartre deems to be unnoble. He is intelligent, sees things logically, and offers reasoning with a certain elegance; for this, Sartre has less scorn for him than for Electra, who is weak, trembling and cowardly.

The Furies

These are the goddesses of vengeance, of remorse. In Roman mythology, they are called the 'Furies,' whereas in Greek, the name used is the 'Eumenides,' or the 'Erinyes.'

SUMMARIES AND CRITICAL COMMENTARIES

ACT I

The play takes place in Argos, a Greek city which Sartre uses to symbolize France under the German Occupation. The action can be interpreted on three levels: (1) philosophical/moral, (2) political, and (3) the literal level of the Greek myth. There is an enormous wooden statue of Zeus, god of the flies and of death, with white eyes and blood-smeared cheeks. Already, Sartre prepares the reader/spectator for a stark, austere, and ugly drama; a procession of old women enters in black clothes, and an idiot boy squats in the background. When Orestes arrives in Argos with the Tutor, he is a mild, uncompromising young man with intelligence, wealth, culture, and a sense of sophistication. He is above the minor details of ordinary living, and he is not engaged or committed to any particular activity: he is free from caring, love, fear, or involvement. The play will trace his development from this uncommitted stance to one of serious engagement, where he is free to choose, act, and accept responsibility. He becomes Sartre's ideal man. Orestes is entering a strange community: the citizens of Argos have seemingly condoned the murder of Agamemnon by his wife, Clytemnestra, and have tolerated the tyranny of her reign, alongside her new husband, Aegistheus, a cousin of Agamemnon. It is a collective guilt that the community shares since, by not protesting or preventing the murder (i.e., by not choosing to act), they have sanctioned the evil act and must bear its responsibility. For this reason, Zeus has sent the flies to them as punishment: they are a reminder of the citizens' sinful errors and will plague them until the conditions are reversed (i.e., until responsibility for Agamemnon's death is assumed). It is for the benefit of this community that Orestes will, ultimately, perform certain acts of revenge: he will not so much be interested in slaying his mother as in restoring to the community a sense of welfare. Sartre uses the device of this unsuspecting hero (Orestes) to lead us, the spectators, along with him in his journey toward engagement.

Orestes enters, and the old women spit on the ground in front of him. His Tutor declares that the two men have lost their way and need directions. This is the perfect introduction for Sartre to exert his 'instructions' to us. The Tutor commends Orestes for choosing Argos, as opposed to the hundreds of other Greek and Roman towns where people are friendly, hospitable, and full of smiles. From the very beginning, Argos is nothing like these other towns: it is gloomy, dreary, and foreboding. Moreover, it is fiercely hot (cf. the heat of Hell in *No Exit*). The Tutor assesses Argos as a "nightmare city," a locus of horror. Orestes was born here, yet he feels lost: this situation is symbolic of the journey which awaits him – Orestes does not yet know his 'way' and will have to interact with others in order to find it. The Tutor is quickly frustrated by the townspeople's refusal to aid them and by their cowering silence; he is prepared to leave things just as they are, not to rock the boat, not to seek information from them, even though Orestes insists. The Tutor falls into Sartre's group of human beings called 'stones': he refuses to commit himself to any action, he lacks convictions, his neutral attitudes are smugly satisfied, and he believes himself to be superior by not engaging himself. Sartre does not like the Tutor, although he feels a certain admiration for his intelligence, his sense of logic.

Orestes and the Tutor are looking for Aegistheus, and while asking an idiot boy for information, they are startled to see Zeus himself, who passes by. Orestes thinks that Zeus is only a traveler like they are, but the Tutor says that this man has been following them on their trip. He does not believe it is due to mere chance that this has happened, and then he proceeds to brush the flies away from his face, claiming that the flies in Argos are more sociable than the townsfolk. The flies, meanwhile, swarm around each of the citizens and serve as a constant reminder of their collective guilt concerning Agamemnon's murder. Sartre indulges in a naturalistic, sordid description of the "yellow muck oozing out of" the idiot boy's eyes. This is indeed an ugly, hopeless town.

Zeus approaches Orestes and the Tutor, and he explains that fifteen years ago, a powerful carcass odor attracted them to the town (i.e., Agamemnon's cadaver) and that, since then, the flies have grown larger (i.e., the townspeople's guilt has assumed greater proportions). Zeus introduces himself as Demetrios from Athens. The Tutor advises Orestes that they should leave Argos but Orestes tells him to keep quiet. Zeus says they have nothing to fear, and he is quite right: until now, Orestes has had nothing to do with the death of Agamemnon or the collective silence about it – *he* is not a target of the flies, and he will remain this way unless he shows 'bad faith' and integrates himself into Argos's lifestyle. Only Zeus, however, is able to drive the flies away since he *is* the god of flies and death; the two are inextricably related. He relates the events of Agamemnon's return to Argos, after which time Agamemnon was assassinated and the people "kept silence." He describes Aegistheus as a hard, brutal man – one whom Sartre uses as a focal point of self-abasement and as the symbolic object against whom the entire people of Argos should make their appeal for divine grace (i.e., to Zeus). Zeus explains that Agamemnon's one error was in placing a ban on public executions: Zeus says that an execution now and again can entertain small-town people and rob death of its glamour. The citizens kept quiet, awaiting a violent death: they remained silent while their king, Agamemnon, entered the gates, and they said nothing when Clytemnestra greeted him warmly. They all knew her plan but said nothing, and therein lies their fault: they failed to act and to live up to their convictions. When they heard the king screaming in his death throes, they still said nothing. This is the basis for the drama of *The Flies*; everything else in the play will grow out of this 'bad faith' and will show the system which Sartre recommends for free, responsible living.

Orestes is quick to blame the gods for this crime, but Zeus admonishes him: the gods are aware of what has happened and are using this crime to "point to a moral." Moreover, Sartre seizes the occasion to show how man must accept responsibility for his own life instead of passing it off on outside authorities: God is dead in Sartrean existentialism, and the state should be cast out of one's views; one must decide for oneself how to live, then follow up with appropriate responsibility. Belief in Zeus will be a temptation throughout the entire play, but *only* Orestes will be able to resist him successfully; his sister Electra will give in to the threat of punishment and the awe of a divine authority, the likes of which Sartre condemned during his lifetime.

The flies were sent as a symbol of remorse, but the true punishment from the gods can be seen everywhere: human beings decrepit from disease, skulking in cowardice, crouching from the look of other people, and so on. Everyone wears black in Argos; everyone is in mourning in Argos. Zeus mentions the dead king, and the old woman to whom he is speaking jumps nervously; it is like salt in a wound to mention the murdered king. Zeus reminds her, however, that she actually enjoyed the thrill of Agamemnon's death ("a little tingling itch between your loins"); he tells her to earn forgiveness by repenting her sins, and the sin to which he refers is her 'bad faith' collaboration with the silent mob. She claims to be repentant, and Sartre puts in her mouth the language of Christian repentance: ". . . my son-in-law offers up a heifer every year, and my little grandson . . . never plays or laughs, for thinking of his original sin." Their 'sin' is portrayed as their constant inactivity, their refusal to have acted on their conscience, their unwillingness to change things from the way they are; they still accept their life of flies and remorse, hiding from it in weakness and relying only on 'hope' of salvation. Sartre does not espouse the Christian credo of faith in Christ as the agent for the remission of sin; rather, he accepts only action and commitment as viable means toward a free end, a life of salvation. He uses the situation in Argos to debunk what he considers to be a pointless religion: Christianity. Aegistheus feels no repentance, but it doesn't matter: the city feels it for him. They hold an annual festival of death to remind themselves of Agamemnon's murder; this is a direct parallel to the Christian Easter. Zeus makes a slip of the tongue (probably on purpose) and says that these death-driven, remorseful people are dear to him at present – it is the phrase "at present" which gives away his true sentiment: he derives fulfillment and satisfaction from their guilt and sorrow, from their *perpetual torture*. After all, he *is* the god of flies and death; without these people, what would he be? We can deduce that he is not going to want to give them up; he will do his best to keep them in his control, and, in his seductive manner, he will try to sway Orestes into believing in him.

Zeus points out Aegistheus's castle and says that Electra lives there too; her brother Orestes, it seems, is dead. Zeus then asks Orestes who he is, and the latter replies: Philebus from Corinth. He is traveling to improve his mind, which is Sartre's way of announcing that all of us will be doing this if we follow the education awaiting Orestes. Zeus says he would tell Orestes to leave Argos if ever Orestes showed up there; this is Zeus's defense against having an outsider to the crime, one who is also a rightful heir to the throne, come into town and atone for the crime, and thus set the suffering citizens free. And this is exactly what Orestes will do: he will be the Savior of Argos, assuming responsibility for their actions and taking the flies out of their lives, placing them on his own shoulders. This eventual assumption of their sins is foreshadowed in Zeus's stern, ominous words to Orestes: "Tamper with it and you bring disaster. A disaster which will recoil on you."

Zeus leaves, and the Tutor says that Zeus knows who Orestes is. Orestes retaliates and says that he also knows who *he* is, and he is in Argos as a descendant of his father. Orestes mocks the education which the Tutor has provided him, and then, for the first time, he *sees* the palace where Aegistheus lives; it is no more than a gloomy, solemn, provincial building constructed in bad taste. Orestes knows that he is "favored," that his position in life is fortunate, but he regrets that he does not possess any memories; he is "free as air, thank God," yet he admires those men who have a purpose in life which they must accomplish, and he scorns the Tutor for not sharing this admiration: "I suppose that strikes you as vulgar—the joy of going somewhere definite." The Tutor reveals that he has seen a constant change in Orestes ever since the day when he told the boy about his past. The Tutor is afraid that Orestes might have the idea of ousting Aegistheus from the throne and taking it over for himself. Orestes denies this: it would serve no purpose. But if there were something he could do in Argos, even if it were a crime, to fill the void in his mind, to give his life a meaning, then he would be ready for action, "even if I had to kill my own mother." Here, Sartre is setting up the framework for the existential act: it does not matter what traditional morals dictate, particularly within the context of Sartre's non-Christian system, murder is neither good nor bad—it is merely an act among other acts and must be judged by the people involved.

Electra enters and approaches the statute of Zeus, calling him an old swine. She claims not to be afraid of him and is disgusted by the old women who have worshipped his cold, wooden heart. She sets up the conflict between herself and Zeus: she is young and healthy, not old and decrepit (as Zeus would prefer). She tells the statue that some day Orestes will come and will chop Zeus in half, exposing his phoniness. Orestes tells her that she is beautiful, and she replies that she's only a servant, obliged to wash the dirty underwear of Aegistheus and Clytemnestra. Sartre accentuates the vile, ugly side of this life; he underlines the results of not choosing an act: one becomes a slave to 'the others' and suffers the consequences. She says, "They can't make things much worse for me," and this is the kind of attitude which Sartre criticizes: he decries the act of allowing others to define what one's essence will be; he is scornful of those who give in and accept life on other people's terms. This is what Electra has done. Orestes asks her if she has ever thought of running away, and she replies, "I haven't the courage." She says that everyone in Argos is sick with fear but that she is sick with hatred; this is significant since Electra will be the only one, alongside Orestes, who will eventually be brave enough to defy Zeus and stand up to him. She will, however, eventually give in and succumb to his threats, so her hatred of him has its origins in fear as well. The city of Argos emerges as a closed, inescapable forum of remorse, not unlike Oran in Camus' *The Plague*. It is contrasted with Orestes' professed hometown of Corinth, where life is merry and cheerful.

Queen Clytemnestra enters, and Orestes sees now what she looks like, after nights of imagining. He hadn't counted on "those dead eyes." Electra has, unknowingly, had contact with Orestes, and Clytemnestra notices a change in her; Electra is bolder and her eyes flash more. Electra reminds her mother of the ugly crime and is contemptuous of the public show of royalty which her mother wishes to present to the people. Clytemnestra claims that the rules no longer come from her—that Aegistheus is the one who reigns now. This is Sartre's way of showing Clytemnestra's 'bad faith': she has abdicated her freedom of choice and allows another person to dictate what her life will be: "It is the King's command I bring you." But Clytemnestra is aware of the fact that her crime ruined her life; she is disturbed by Electra's appearance since it reminds her of what she used to look like. In this case, 'the others' (i.e., her daughter) reinforce the torture of her crime;

her daughter, an image of her former self, hates her, so here Sartre presents us with an example of double self-hatred.

Clytemnestra is interested in Orestes; she wants to know who he is and why he has come to Argos. The Queen relates her criminal guilt to him, but Electra warns that he should pay no attention to her; everyone in Argos repents loudly for their sins on this holiday, and the Queen's sins have become boring—they are 'official' sins which everyone knows about. Clytemnestra does not regret having killed Agamemnon; in fact, she still feels "a thrill of pleasure" when she thinks about it. But she regrets having lost her son, and she doesn't realize that she's actually speaking to him right now. Electra tells Clytemnestra that she, Electra, hates Clytemnestra; moreover, she will *not* attend the death rite. She then explains to Orestes about the rite: each year, high above the city, a bottomless cavern—which Aegistheus claims leads to hell—is opened up, and the dead roam around Argos, reinforcing everyone's guilt. Twenty-four hours later, they return to the cave and remain there for another year. It's a lie, of course, fabricated by Aegistheus in order to keep people in their places. Clytemnestra says that Aegistheus will *force* Electra to take part in the ceremony, so Electra consents and invites Orestes to also partake in it with her. Clytemnestra is not pleased with Orestes' presence and requests that he leave Argos: "You are going to bring disaster on us." Zeus appears and says that he will be Orestes' host. Zeus will attempt to sway Orestes to his point of view, hoping to convince Orestes to accept him as an outside authority figure ("A man of my age can often be very helpful to lads like you"), but Orestes will not be interested.

ACT II: Scene 1

The scene begins at the mountain cavern, which is blocked at the entrance by a large black boulder; there is a crowd present for the ceremony. A woman teaches her child to cry on cue, to be frightened by the spirits who are about to exit from the cavern. This shows the extent to which Aegistheus has manipulated people into subservience through fear, and this is what Sartre attacks vehemently: no outside authority should *ever* be permitted to control our thoughts, feelings, and choices in life—and this includes political, religious, social, and other types of authority figures. Aegistheus symbolizes the state, whereas Zeus represents God and the Church: Sartre rejects them both as evils to mankind. This is an ideological play; Sartre is not concerned with developing a psychological drama (although indeed elements of psychology are part of it). He is interested in ideas, not in aesthetic beauty, and he paints the picture of gloom and doom with broad strokes of black and colorless adjectives.

Zeus enters with Orestes and the Tutor, who reacts to the ugliness of the Argos citizens. The Tutor is glad that he, unlike the citizens, still has rosy cheeks, but Zeus startles him by saying, "You're no more than a sack of dung, like all those others. These folk, at least, know how bad they smell." Sartre uses Zeus shrewdly; he is a device whose function it is to express ideas contrary to those of Sartre (and Orestes). Zeus symbolizes the enemies of freedom (e.g., the government, the Church – anything totalitarian), and he represents all those who use tricks to remove freedom from the lives of others. Since he espouses ideas opposite to Sartre's, he is used by Sartre to give Orestes the possibility to express existential ideas. Zeus, thus, becomes part of Sartre's dramatic technique: he, like other enemies of freedom, wishes for men to have remorse since the fear of remorse prevents men from acting, from choosing; this fear eliminates freedom, and if we have remorse, claims Sartre, it is because we have not acted.

Aegistheus arrives with Clytemnestra and the High Priest. Electra is not present, and Aegistheus is angry. The boulder is rolled away from the cave's entrance, and the High Priest addresses the dead spirits: "Arise, this is your day of days." All the trappings of a primitive religious ceremony are present: tom-toms, dances, gyrations, and so on. Orestes says that he cannot bear to watch them, but Zeus tells him to look in his, Zeus's, eyes; this silences Orestes. The crowd cries out for mercy, but Aegistheus tells them that they will *never* have it, that one cannot atone for sins when the person against whom a sin was committed has died. It is an ugly, hopeless atmosphere. Aegistheus announces that the ghost of Agamemnon is coming forth, and Orestes, offended by this nonsense, draws his sword and forbids him to make Agamemnon a part of this "mummery." Zeus intervenes, telling Orestes to stop, and Electra enters, dressed in white. She is quite a contrast to the black of the mob, and everyone notices her. The crowd wants to be rid of her, especially after Aegistheus reminds everyone of her treacherous blood ("the breed of Atreus, who treacherously cut his nephews' throats"). She retorts that she is happy for the first time in her life, that Agamemnon lovingly visits her by night with his secrets, and that he smiles on her present actions. The crowd isn't so sure and thinks that she has gone mad. She explains to them that there are cities in Greece where people are happy, where children play in the streets. This is a direct influence from Orestes. She tells the crowd that there's no reason to be afraid: she is the first glimpse of freedom that they've had in fifteen years, and it is only through contact with Orestes that she has been able to experience this radiance. The crowd sees that she is truly happy, and they comment on her ecstasy. They confront Aegistheus openly: "Answer us, King Aegistheus. Threats are no answer." Someone calls Aegistheus a liar. But Zeus, seeing the surge of interest in freedom, puts an end to it: he causes the boulder to come crashing against the temple steps, and this is enough to instill fear in the crowd again. Electra stops dancing. The flies swarm everywhere. Aegistheus sends everyone home and banishes Electra from the city. Orestes, furious about the turn of events, orders Zeus to leave him alone with his sister. This shows that Orestes is not afraid of Zeus and is willing to take action on his own, despite the god's interference. Orestes has been exposed to the cruelty and punishment of the townsfolk, and soon he will be committed to a new lifestyle: he will give up his detachment and will engage himself in a fight to save them.

Orestes tells Electra that she cannot stay in the city a moment longer; the two of them must flee. But she refuses and blames him for her lack of success with the crowd; she is not angry with him, but he made her forget her hatred, which was her defense against Aegistheus's tyranny. She does not want a peaceful flight with him: "Only violence can save them." She claims that her brother will come to her assistance. Orestes then identifies himself as her brother and confesses that he was reared by some wealthy Athenians, and not in Corinth, as he stated earlier. Zeus arrives to eavesdrop on them. Electra has mixed emotions about Orestes; she says that she loves him, but then she declares her fantasy-version of Orestes as being dead; the real Orestes, she claims, has not shared in her bloody, unhappy past and cannot be part of the vengeful present: "Go away, my noble-souled brother. I have no use for noble souls; what I need is an accomplice." She announces her desire: to have someone who will assist her in the murder of Clytemnestra and Aegistheus. Orestes describes how his life to date has been uncommitted to anything and that he has nowhere to go if Electra sends him away. He wants to engage himself (in an existential act): "I want my share of memories, my native soil, my place among the men of Argos." This is a difficult moment for Orestes since he has to convince Electra of his reason for staying in Argos. It is the one point along his journey to commitment where he feels an uncertainty about what to do. He hesitates for a moment, then asks Zeus what to do. "O Zeus . . . I can no longer distinguish right from wrong. I need a guide to point my way." He does not know that Zeus, the enemy of freedom, is lurking in the wings; he addresses the *legendary* Zeus who is god of all gods. He tells Zeus that, if the god wants him to remain passive and accepting of reality, he need only send a sign. The living Zeus is delighted and sends flashing bolts of light; this sign of light indicates to Orestes that he should give in, leave Argos, and not become committed. Electra laughs at Orestes for having consulted a god. Orestes quickly realizes that it is dangerous to entrust one's decisions to the feelings of other people. He recovers from his moment of weakness and decides to commit himself firmly: "It's not for me, that light; from now on, I'll take no one's orders, neither man's nor god's." Electra notices that a change has come over his face and voice. Clearly, Orestes knows that he must take on the burden of responsibility. This is the turning point of the play: Orestes says good-bye to his youth and his uncommitted days, and he launches forth into a path of action which will undo the tyrannical regime. As a Christ-like figure, he intends to take over the crimes of the suffering people of Argos. Electra shows signs already of being weak; she is not sure that she can go along with Orestes. He asks her to conceal him in the palace and, at night, to lead him to the royal bedchamber.

ACT II: Scene 2

It is the throne-room of the palace. A soldier comments on the fact that the flies are "all crazy" tonight. Clytemnestra asks Aegistheus what's wrong with *him*, and he replies that the crowd would have gone out of control if he hadn't played on their fear. He is aware of his lies and is tired of it all: "The black of my robes has seeped through to my soul." He *claims* not to have remorse; he says that he is simply very sad; then he rejects the amorous advances of Clytemnestra, calling her a *whore*. It is the gaze of Agamemnon that he fears, and he has actually begun to believe the lies about the dead spirits. This shows the weakening force of Aegistheus: he is not the tyrant he makes himself out to be, and he is now a prime target for the actions of Orestes. He sees himself as an empty shell: "I see I am more dead than Agamemnon."

Zeus enters, and Aegistheus does not recognize him. Zeus flashes lightning, and Aegistheus realizes who he is. He tells Zeus that people are afraid of the god; the latter replies: "Excellent! I've no use for love." Zeus tells him that Electra and Orestes are going to kill him. Aegistheus reacts stoically: "That's in the natural order of things." Zeus then shows his true colors: he is after Orestes' blood and would not care if he rotted to death. Zeus orders Aegistheus to have Orestes captured; the tyrant king resists, but Zeus knows that he will obey: he always does. Aegistheus then has a moment of dispute with Zeus; he wants to know what gives Zeus the right to try and save Aegistheus' life; one suspects that Aegistheus would prefer to die, and indeed he affirms this. Zeus gloats over Aegistheus's crime of fifteen years ago; for the murder of one man, twenty thousand living people have spent fifteen years in anguish, and this is real pleasure for Zeus. Aegistheus struck Agamemnon dead in a moment of rage and frenzy, not having thought out his actions with clarity. That is why he looks back now, fatigued and disgusted with his fraud. Orestes, on the other hand, is thinking everything through very carefully and, as a result, he will suffer no remorse. That's why Zeus wants to prevent the murder of Aegistheus: he wants to prolong Aegistheus's deep remorse as long as he can; when Aegistheus dies, so too does Zeus's investment in the massive remorse. Aegistheus talks about the order which he has preserved in his kingdom, knowing full well that the people are free, that they could set his palace in flames if they *knew* they were free. Zeus woos him, calling him a "mortal brother" and comparing himself to him. He convinces Aegistheus through emotional rhetoric to do his will, placing the responsibility for the deaths of Orestes and Electra on Aegistheus's shoulders. Sartre demonstrates that even gods can have 'bad faith,' shirking their responsibility.

Zeus departs as Electra and Orestes bolt into the room, barring the door before Aegistheus can call for help. Aegistheus is glad about their arrival: it is time to die, and he does not wish to resist. Death, for him, comes as a relief after fifteen years of hell on earth. Orestes strikes him down and feels no remorse: "Why should I feel remorse? I am only doing what is right." His goal is to free the people of Argos from Aegistheus' tyranny. Aegistheus rises weakly and curses them both, telling them to beware of the flies. He dies then. Orestes wants to kill the Queen next, but Electra intervenes, claiming that Clytemnestra can no longer hurt anyone. This is Electra's first step backward, into a life of subservience and fear. Orestes has come to free them from fear, yet Electra now clings to her former lifestyle. Orestes departs alone, having pointed out a change in Electra's behavior. She is the kind of person whom Sartre despises the most: she falls into the category of the 'plants' – she is unhappy about her life but lacks the courage to do something about it. She hears Clytemnestra scream in the distance and realizes that she has been murdered. Orestes returns and wishes not to speak of the death: "There are some memories one does not share." Electra has not shared in the murder and is not part of Orestes' act; she is not as free as he is. While she sees darkness, Orestes sees a new day dawning. He announces that he is free, but Electra does not feel this freedom; she suffers remorse over the murders, but Orestes feels nothing. He carries his burden with responsibility, and this is why he feels no remorse. He has earned himself the fulfillment of commitment; he possesses himself and his life. Electra loses the ability to see him and begins to suffer from an attack by the flies. But Orestes doesn't care: "What do the flies matter to us?"

ACT III

Orestes and Electra are at the Temple of Apollo. It is twilight, and the flies cannot touch them at the Temple. The flies have now become the Furies, goddesses of remorse, and they form rings around the two young people, asleep at the foot of the statue of Apollo. The Furies discuss how they will devour these new bodies; they revel in their sadistic impulses. Electra wakes up and fails to recognize Orestes. He asks what her problem is, and she tells him to go away; she is caught in the throes of her remorse, but doesn't know it. She scorns him for his crime but doesn't realize that her anguish is self-inflicted. Had she followed through in 'good faith' with her desire to see the tyrants killed, she would now be as free as Orestes. The eyes of Electra now resemble those of Clytemnestra. She too is guilty of cowardice. The Furies begin to taunt Electra, describing in detail the murder of her mother. Orestes orders her not to look at the Furies and not to ask questions; otherwise, she is lost. Electra is confused and is not sure whose side to take. Sartre criticizes those who remain on the level of intention, not daring to engage themselves in an act. So when Electra says, "I dreamt the crime, but you carried it out," we can imagine Sartre's reason for having her react this way: it shows the treachery and cowardice of her position, and at the same time, it illustrates the consequences of this 'bad faith' attitude. The Furies are 'the others' in this case, and to them, Electra screams: "Stop torturing me!" Orestes attempts to lead her to a life of freedom and peace; she resists, surrendering herself to the Furies, who swarm around her and launch their attack.

Zeus arrives, and the Furies back away from Electra. Orestes and Zeus argue over Orestes' act: it was an act of freedom, but Zeus claims that it is responsible for Electra's doom. Orestes replies that her doom comes from within and that, because she is free, only she can rid herself of it. Zeus says that he has come to save them both; he tempts them with the idea that they can be free within fifteen minutes, and this is enticing to Electra. Orestes, however, refuses to listen and cautions his sister to follow suit. Zeus makes a long speech about the goodness of the universe and of his role in it: the speech is ironical and draws on elements of Christian theology; Zeus attempts to make Orestes feel small in comparison with the universe (an argument which Sartre no doubt borrowed from Pascal). Orestes' response is: "Your whole universe is not enough to prove me wrong. . . . You are not the king of man." It now becomes an argument between the god and his creation: Orestes acknowledges that Zeus is his creator, but mocks him for having created him free. Orestes acknowledges neither right nor wrong: the only thing which has validity for him is *action*. He intends to open the eyes of the people in Argos; then, they will be able to choose their own lifestyles. Zeus leaves, warning Electra to choose between him and Orestes.

Electra says she is through with Orestes. She claims that he has robbed all of her dreams. She calls to Zeus for help, and she repents her sins, promising to be his slave. The Furies begin to pursue her, but stop and decide to torment Orestes instead. Orestes ponders his aloneness and pities Electra. The Tutor arrives and tells Orestes that the townspeople are waiting outside, anxious for Orestes' blood. Orestes orders the Tutor to open the door, and after he does so, the room is flooded with light. The people outside shout, "Kill him," but Orestes does not hear them; he sees only the sun. He stands up in full power and announces himself as their monarch: "Ah, you are lowering your tone? I know; you fear me." He tells them that they welcomed Aegistheus as their king fifteen years ago because he was of their kind: he lacked the courage of his crimes. His crime was without an owner and stalked the streets of Argos, claiming as its owner *all* the citizens of the city. But because Orestes' crime is his own, they cannot punish or pity him; that is why they are afraid of him. The bond of blood between them now intensifies his love for them: they are his subjects, and he has come to claim his kingdom. He has taken their sins onto his back, and they need no longer fear the dead or the flies. Only he will be plagued by the flies. But he has decided not to occupy his throne; he is leaving the town and wishes only that they take advantage of their new beginning. As he strides out of town, the Furies fling themselves after him. The city of Argos is now at peace.

SUGGESTED ESSAY TOPICS

NO EXIT

Long Essays:
(1) Compare and contrast the characters of Inez and Estelle, showing how they represent various aspects of Sartrean existentialism.

(2) Discuss the role of love in *No Exit*. How is it significant to the central theme of the play?

Short Essays:
(1) Show how Sartre uses the 'triangle' to create dramatic tension in *No Exit*.

(2) Inez says, "When I say I'm cruel, I mean I can't get on without making people suffer." Write a short essay on Sartre's presentation of 'the others' in *No Exit*.

THE FLIES

Long Essays:
(1) Analyze the interplay of philosophy and politics in *The Flies*.

(2) Trace the development of the Oresteian story and show how Sartre presents it in *The Flies*.

(3) In what way can *The Flies* be considered to be an existentialist drama?

Short Essays: (1) Write a short essay on the evolution of Orestes' character. How do Zeus, Aegistheus, and Clytemnestra influence this development?

(2) Show how the language of Sartre suits the character(s) speaking it.

(3) Discuss Sartre's concept of freedom and responsibility, as portrayed in *The Flies*.

SELECTED BIBLIOGRAPHY

ANDERSON, THOMAS. *The Foundation and Structure of Sartrean Ethics.* Regents, 1979.

ARONSON, RONALD. *Jean-Paul Sartre: Philosophy in the World.* Schocken, 1980.

BARNES, HAZEL. *Sartre and Flaubert.* University of Chicago Press, n.d.

BRÉE, GERMAINE. *Camus and Sartre.* Dell, 1972.

CHARLESWORTH, MAX. *The Existentialists and Jean-Paul Sartre.* St. Martins, 1976.

CONTAT, MICHEL. *The Writings of Jean-Paul Sartre.* Northwestern University Press, 1974.

CRUICKSHANK, JOHN, ed. *French Literature and its Background: The Twentieth Century.* Oxford University Press, 1970.

GREENE, NORMAN N. *Jean-Paul Sartre: The Existentialist Ethic.* University of Michigan, 1960.

HALPERN, JOSEPH. *Critical Fictions: the Literary Criticism of Jean-Paul Sartre.* (Romanic Studies, Second Series: No. 26), Yale University Press, 1976.

KERN, EDITH. *Sartre. A Collection of Essays.* (Twentieth Century Views Collection). Prentice-Hall, 1962.

MCMAHON, JOSEPH H. *Human Beings: The World of Jean-Paul Sartre.* University of Chicago, 1971.

SARTRE, JEAN-PAUL. *Sartre on Theatre.* Pantheon, 1976.

STACK, GEORGE J. *Sartre's Philosophy of Social Existence.* Green, 1978.

THODY, PHILIP. *Jean-Paul Sartre; A Literary and Political Study.* Macmillan, 1960.

WARNOCK, MARY. *The Philosophy of Jean-Paul Sartre.* Hutchinson University Press, 1972.

NOTES

NOTES

THE PLAGUE

NOTES

including
- *Life of Camus*
- *Camus and the Absurd*
- *List of Characters*
- *Critical Commentaries*
- *Character Analyses*
- *Allegory*
- *Review Questions and Theme Topics*
- *Selected Bibliography*

by
Gary Carey, M.A.
University of Colorado

INCORPORATED

LINCOLN, NEBRASKA 68501

Editor	Consulting Editor
Gary Carey, M.A.	*James L. Roberts, Ph.D.*
University of Colorado	*Department of English*
	University of Nebraska

ISBN 0-8220-1039-9
© Copyright 1967
by
C. K. Hillegass
All Rights Reserved
Printed in U.S.A.

1990 Printing

Cliffs Notes, Inc.   Lincoln, Nebraska

CONTENTS

The Plague

LIFE OF CAMUS

Albert Camus was born November 7, 1913, and reared in Algeria, a country exposed to the blistering African sun and the plain of the Mediterranean sea. These roots—the sun and the sea—have spread into all of Camus' writings—the novels, the plays, and the essays. They are a part of his lyricism, his symbolism, and his values. The universe, it seems from his early *Noces,* was mother, father, and lover for the young Camus, and from the first, Camus was aware of the paradoxical aspects of his natural world. The sensual free pleasure of swimming and hiking was in continuous contrast to the bare stony earth that made living a matter of poverty and destitution. He was early aware of the absurd condition of man's being totally alone in a resplendent universe. This concept is Camus' equivalent "In the beginning...." Against its truth, all of his writings sound revolt, for he refused to be deceived by social religions or individual submissions that ignored or defied the irreducible truth that man alone is responsible for himself, his meaning, and his measure. Camus' writings are a testament to a continuing belief in man's exiled but noble condition.

Lucien Camus, Albert's father, was killed in 1914 during World War I's Battle of the Marne and the year-old child was reared by his deaf mother. She had little money and was apparently a rather joyless and boring companion for her son. It is little wonder that he spent much of his time with athletics, studies, and necessary part-time employment. When he finished school, a university degree seemed the most important challenge available to a poverty-stricken student. Like Dr. Rieux, the narrator of *The Plague,* he was enthusiastic about studies and was ambitious. He was not able to complete his studies immediately, however. In 1930, while he was a student of philosophy at the University of Algiers, Camus almost died during a first long bout with tuberculosis, an illness which would periodically afflict him for many years. Then, after his recovery, he was beset by the constant problem of poverty and was forced to support himself for several years as variously a meteorologist, a police clerk, and a salesman. During this time he married and divorced and also joined and left the Communist party. In 1935, a year before he received his degree from the University, he founded The Workers' Theater, a group formed to present plays for Algiers' working population. Before his theater venture ended in 1939, Camus had published *L'Envers et L'Endroit (Betwixt and Between),* essays that deal with man and death in terms of his oblivious universe. They are mood pieces, written in his own mixture of irony and lyricism, describing man's defenselessness and his isolation in a splendid universe whose only rule for man seems to be death. There is an early optimism in these essays; it is here that Camus first advocates living as if man had eternal value. He believes that only in man's courageous rebellion to confront himself and his world can he begin to create a civilization that can rescue itself from a nihilistic catastrophe.

Between the years 1937 and 1939 Camus wrote book reviews and occasional essays for the *Alger-Republicain,* a left wing newspaper. Later he assumed the editorship of the *Soir-Republicain,* but for only a short time. He was severely critical of the French colonial government and after the newspaper folded, soon found himself unofficially unwelcome and unable to find a job in the country. Thus in 1940 he left Algeria and went to live in Paris. There he worked for a time with the *Paris-Soir,* but his journalistic career was once again curtailed. This time the Germans had invaded France. Much like the character Rambert in *The Plague,* Camus left the battlefield. He returned once again to North Africa, where he remarried and began teaching in a private school in Oran. He continued to write and by now had filled several notebooks with sketches and several versions of *The Stranger* and *The Myth of Sisyphus.* He also worked on background ideas for a new novel, *The Plague.*

A year later, both *The Stranger* and *Myth* were published and Camus was established as a writer of international importance. *The Stranger's* Meursault has since become a literary archetype, and the beginning sentences of *The Stranger* have become synonymous with an absurd or ironic situation. Never before had the public read about a man who was so absolutely honest as Meursault. In fact, his honesty is perhaps his only meritorious quality. Meursault is an anti-hero, an inconspicuous clerk who does not believe in God, but cannot lie. He does believe in going to the movies, swimming, and making love. He is finally beheaded because he murdered an Arab; he is condemned, however, because he seemed indifferent at his mother's funeral. Meursault becomes aware of his freedom and his happiness only after he is imprisoned, a situation similar to that of the imprisoned Oranian citizens in *The Plague.* He faces death with sensitive and joyous awareness of his last moments and hopes for a vivid end and an angry shouting crowd as witness.

In the year of *The Stranger,* 1941, Camus decided to return to France and commit himself to the French Resistance Movement. He enlisted in an organization known as "Combat," also the title of the clandestine newspaper he edited during the Occupation. After Paris was liberated in 1944,

Camus continued to edit *Combat* for four years while he published collections of his wartime essays. His plays *The Misunderstanding* and *Caligula* were presented during 1944; the latter was as well received as the former was not. In 1945, Camus toured the United States, lecturing and gathering firsthand impressions of the national power that was credited with ending the long war.

His allegory, *The Plague*, was published in June, 1947, and was immediately cited as a major literary work. The critics and the public were unanimous in their praise for this somberly narrated chronicle. As a popular book it had none of the formula gimmicks; it had no great love plot-line, no fascinating setting, or even powerfully drawn characterizations. But to a nation recovering from an enemy occupation, it was an authentic account of months during which only human dignity and survival mattered. Postwar readers were appreciative and sympathetic to this writer who had faithfully, and not melodramatically, recorded the suffering and misery of separation and exile.

In 1949, upon his return to France from a South American tour, Camus became quite ill and went into almost total seclusion, only occasionally publishing collections of more of his political essays. In 1951, when he was recovered, he published an extensive study of metaphysical, historical, and artistic revolt, *The Rebel*. It was an extremely controversial book and was responsible for breaking the friendship between Camus and Jean Paul Sartre.

After *The Rebel*, Camus began translating favorite works of international playwrights. His adaptations were rapidly produced and included Calderón's *La Devocion de la Cruz*, Larivey's *Les Espirits*, Buzzati's *Un Caso Clinico*, Faulkner's *Requiem for a Nun*, and others. More collections of his political essays appeared, plus many prefaces to contemporary writings.

In 1956 a new fictional work appeared, his novel *The Fall*. Unlike the technique of his other two novels, the narrative is not in the third person but in the first person, and the story does not take place in North Africa, but in Amsterdam. The book deals with a successful and admired lawyer who suddenly faces his conscience after he refuses to help a woman drowning in a suicide attempt. The confessions of his fraud and guilt contain precise and penetrating comments about contemporary society. It is not as ambitious or as lengthy as *The Plague*, but it is as polished a masterpiece as *The Stranger*.

The following year Camus was awarded the Nobel Prize for Literature and two years later he was dead, killed in an automobile accident on January 4, 1960. The many eulogistic essays which appeared afterward remarked on the absurdity of his death — its suddenness, its uselessness, and the lack of logic to explain why. Camus, however, was probably more aware of the significance of his individual life than any of his essayists; his meaningless death is the key witness to his body of literature.

CAMUS AND THE ABSURD

To enter into the literary world of Albert Camus, one must realize, first off, that one is dealing with an author who does not believe in God. Major characters in Camus' fiction, therefore, can probably be expected either to disbelieve or to wrestle with the problem of belief. One's first response then, as a reader, might profitably be a brief consideration of what might happen to a character who comes to realize that there is no Divinity, no God. What happens when he realizes that his death is final, that his joys, his disappointments, and his sufferings are brief flickers preluding an afterlife of nothingness? What changes in his daily pattern of work-eat-love-sleep must he now effect? Much like Kafka's Joseph K., the man in question has staggeringly comprehended that he is condemned to an eternal void — and because of no crime. Only because he is a part of a meaningless birth-death cycle is he doomed; the fact of death and his mortality is all. He sees, in short, The End focused on the screen of his future, the screen on which he used to project his dreams and hopes. Hope based on anything superhuman is now futile. He sees an end for him and for his fellowmen. So, what then? Suicide, if all is meaningless? Or a blind return flight toward an external, though ever-silent, God?

This concern with death and its abyss of nonexistence is the basis for most of Camus' literary works. Condemned to an everlasting zero of eternity, Camus' characters often suffer their author's own involvement and anguish; and, for his readers, the recognition of the fact of their own deaths is the starting point for their confronting and experiencing Camus' concept of the Absurd.

As a salvation, however, from despair and nihilism, Camus' Absurd embraces a kind of positive optimism — optimism in the sense that much emphasis is placed on human responsibility for civilizing the world. The fictional characters, therefore, who shoulder their new *mortal* responsibility, are often characterized as rebels. In revolt from both a cowardly suicide and an equally cowardly faith flight, the new optimism suggests man's returning to the center of a philosophical tightrope above an intensely physical death and, in his revolt, performing precariously. Above the threat of death, in confrontation with death, the metaphysical ropewalker acts "as if" his actions mattered. Obviously they don't in any long-range sense. And, rather than scamper to either the poles of Hope or Suicide, he knows that he will eventually fall, but stays mid-center. Obviously his life, the lives of all men do not *finally* matter. Death is definitive. But, clown-like, he creates new acts, new entertainments — reaching, gesturing. Exploiting his precarious posture in a new burst of freedom, he restructures his actions, and in vivid contrast to death, he diffuses joy and a sense of ridiculous responsibility.

Walking on this razor's edge of "as if" means that man must act to his fellowmen as though life had meaning; in short, living an absurdity. Knowing that man has only man to depend upon, however, he can take fresh courage. He is now rid of fearful superstitions and questioning theories; he can now discard the religious faiths which assume man is subservient to a Something divine and eternal. Man now has no excuse for failure, save himself. "God's Will" as a pocket excuse for failure is no longer valid. Man succeeds or fails because of the strength, or the lack of it, in himself. Each man is acting as a representative of all mankind; he is responsible for creating peace in the world. No longer will Sunday's prayers excuse Saturday's hates. He is responsible for all and is totally alone. Camus challenges man to do the work which he has hitherto assigned to God.

LIST OF CHARACTERS

Dr. Bernard Rieux
    The surgeon-narrator of *The Plague.*

Jean Tarrou
    The best friend of Rieux. His notebooks are used as part of the chronicle.

Father Paneloux
    A priest in Oran.

Raymond Rambert
    A Paris journalist trapped in Oran.

Joseph Grand
A petty official, also a writer.

Cottard
A criminal who hides from arrest in Oran.

M. Michel
A concierge, the plague's first victim.

Madame Rieux
The mother of Dr. Rieux. She comes to visit her son during the first days of the plague.

Madame Rieux
Dr. Rieux' wife, who dies in a mountain sanitarium outside Oran.

The old Spaniard
An asthmatic philosopher.

M. Othon
Oran's police magistrate.

Jacques Othon
A young victim of the plague, son of the police magistrate.

Dr. Richard
A conservative colleague of Dr. Rieux.

Prefect
The chief magistrate of Oran.

Dr. Castel
An elderly doctor who perfects a new plague serum.

Jeanne Grand
The divorced wife of the petty official.

Gonzales, Garcia, Raoul, Marcel, and Louis
Rambert's underground contacts.

CRITICAL COMMENTARIES

PART ONE

The tragedy of a plague is announced in the book's title. It is also under-scored in the first chapter. This technique, it is worth noting, is somewhat similar to that of a Greek tragedy. Here also we know in advance the horri-ble fate in store for the characters, and we watch as the scenes unfold the familiar fate and the agony of, say, Oedipus or Creon.

While reading this novel, one should remember that Camus has an initial prerequisite for an understanding of his philosophy of the absurd: a realization and a recognition of the fact of one's own death. A man only begins living, according to Camus, when he announces in advance his own death to himself and realizes the consequences. This is, in a sense, what Camus is doing in the opening scenes of *The Plague*. He is announcing the deaths of many people, common people, and as spectators, we will wait, watch, hear, and perhaps learn from the consequences of the everyday Oedipuses and Creons of Oran—citizens warned again and again of their fate to die, yet who choose to be unbelieving, antagonistic, and indifferent to the warning. The announcement of death is paramount in Camus' philos-ophy and in his novels.

In the first paragraph of the book, the ordinariness of Oran is contrasted with the extraordinary business of the plague, and on the surface the com-ment seems possibly only a bit of literary formula. Camus, however, had good reason for beginning his work with just such a contrast. In his volume of essays, *The Myth of Sisyphus*, published five years before *The Plague*, he says that contrasts between the natural and the extraordinary, the individual and the universal, the tragic and the everyday are essential ingredients for the absurd work. Camus conceived of the universe in terms of paradoxes and contrasts: man lives, yet he is condemned to die; most men live within the context of an afterlife, yet there has never been proof that an afterlife exists. Camus' idea of living meaningfully, yet knowing full well that life has no eventual meaning, is a positive-negative contrast. It is natural, then, for him to begin and set his novel in terms of an extreme contrast.

Still considering his setting, note that Camus has done two things with Oran as a stage for his chronicle. As an actual Algerian town in North Africa, it functions as an anchor of reality for the reader. The book, after all, is an allegory, but becomes more successful in all its levels partly be-cause of its existent geographic setting. *Gulliver's Travels* has improbable place names, as does *Erewhon,* and both works have a fairy tale quality, largely because of their ambiguous settings. *The Plague,* on the other hand, is more satisfying on the literal level because of its specifically placed setting, and, in addition, the literal level has more concern for the human condition than, say, the literal level of *Gulliver's Travels.*

Camus was not, however, to faithfully render Oran much further than geographically locating it for the reader. Once he set the novel in the hot, arid region of North Africa and had captured our belief in its existence, he began recreating Oran and its people in Western terms. Oran is not the typical Mediterranean town described in guidebooks as having a "delightfully sunny complexion and charming little balconies overhanging narrow streets, with delightful glimpses of shady courtyards." Camus refutes this armchair attitude; he characterizes the town as filled with bored people, people who have cultivated habits, people whose chief interest is "doing business." This is far from the romantic Mediterranean town we might expect on the shores of the sea. These people Camus describes are recognizable as Americans and as western Europeans. There are numerous articles written in popular magazines satirizing our culture as mechanistic and materialistic. And, in his quiet way, Camus is also using satire. He is showing people who choose to spend their time commercially, people who "fritter away" what time is left for living. He has, then, created a city far enough away esthetically and geographically for his artistic purposes, but one which has the tempo and coloring of our own environment.

Examining the city more closely, the narrator says that love is particularly repulsive in Oran. People either have intercourse much as robots might, or they go about it animal-like—all this, he says because they lack time and thinking. Camus has often been characterized as a godless Christian, meaning that he expounds all the Christian virtues, but only in terms of man. Love, for Camus, is a mixture of "desire, affection, and intelligence." It is given to other men instead of to God. In this sense, man is sacred, but absurdly sacred; he may die in any moment, just as love may disappear within a moment. Yet one must live committed "as if" man and love ultimately mattered. The concern with love gone wrong is a symptom of an illness within Oran even before the plague of death strikes.

Having briefly illuminated Oran's life and love, the next focus is naturally enough on the other end of the human cycle—death. Death is a "discomfort." The tone here is low-keyed because the narrator is speaking of the normal day-to-day process of dying. And if fatality is wretched normally, imagine what discomfort will be encountered during the pages of this long chronicle of death. The casual mention here is being heavily underplayed.

Even now, perhaps, one believes that the novel will not be so wholly concerned with death, but it will be. Here is a point, brief as it is, of normalcy to weigh later against the extreme. The mention of a "normal" dying man, "trapped behind hundreds of walls all sizzling with heat," suggests the mazes of Dante's hell, mazes which must be traversed before the plague's thousands of deaths are tolled. And since Camus has lamented that man's imagination has ceased to function, perhaps the reader would do well to expand it here in this trapped, sizzling, "normal" situation of death and imagine the eventual effect of the plague.

The emphasis on the habits which have been formed and cultivated by the "soulless" people of Oran are significant. Vital living can be stifled by habits: in Oran, love-making is relegated to the weekends. Camus has said in one of his essays that the absurd is often encountered when one is suddenly aware that habits have strangled natural responses and reactions, that habits have simplified one into simplemindedness. It is at this point that one should revolt against his stultifying pattern of living. Recognition of bottomless death makes a habit-bound life even more absurd. Camus seems, then, to be creating a society of habit-oriented people in order to confront them with death in its most horrible form—the plague. Then, from this confrontation, new values regarding living will emerge.

"It is impossible to see the sea," the narrator tells us. Oran turns its back on the bay. The sea, of course, is a striking symbol for life, richly and lushly lived. Camus himself loved the sea; when he swam in it, he encountered it nakedly and boldly, in a way virtually impossible to encounter society. Societies too often contain hypocrisy and jealousy; there is seldom honesty and directness. One knows what he encounters when he swims. In social waters, swimming is done blindly. Oran turns its back on nature, on sincerity, and truth; its concern is with the materialistic and the habitual. As a natural and symbolic backdrop the sea, with its unbound waves, is an ever-present, ominous comment on the action.

The narrator's insistence on the book's objectivity stresses his wish to present the truth, as nearly as possible. He lists his data and where he got them. He will tell, he says, "what happened." Knowing, of course, that he (the narrator) is Dr. Rieux, we can see a kind of scientific detachment to his style, in addition to his hope to be objectively truthful.

The style, which is semi-documentary, is reminiscent of journalism. Perhaps Camus' several years of newspaper writing were the genesis of this style or helped formulate his ideas concerning the need for careful, documented truthfulness. In any case, the reader should note that Camus does not single out lovers clinging together during a plague situation to snare his readers' attention. He hopes to tell his story authentically, directing the narrative to our intellect and our imagination rather than to our heart strings. His result has the tone of precision—much the same as Truman Capote's nonfiction novel *In Cold Blood*.

The reader should also remember that the book is not, per se, a novel; the volume is a chronicle, and thus we should not expect avant garde or impressionistic devices—nothing except, as nearly as possible, a factual account of a plague and the people affected.

In addition, Camus is striving for an esthetic distance between the reader and the novel which will keep the reader an observer. Close identification, a major objective for most fiction authors, is to be avoided because emotional involvement will keep us from seeing the book as, at least, a three-dimensional allegory. Camus' immediately attacking the problem of exposition and setting, and defining them simply and directly, establishes a tone which he will hold until the book's end. This objective tone is particularly important because by underplaying the sensationalism of the plague, he hopes to startle our intellect more completely to its lessons. In this first chapter, then, he has rather formally given us the setting, almost dryly discoursed on its features, and finished his brief, journalistically sounding framework for the action to follow.

The chronicle's action, however, develops slowly. *The Plague's* first chapter is a rather neat, concise package of setting and background, and Chapter 2 is, in a sense, another such block of writing, somewhat like a second solid step taken into the novel, but with a difference. Chapter 1 is written in a sum-up style by a narrator who slips us occasional asides throughout his short discourse. This narrator slips out of Chapter 2 and the book moves forward with conventional plot interest and the introduction of several main characters, yet it retains Chapter 1's sense of structural completeness. The chapter begins with Dr. Rieux's discovering a dead rat and a crotchety concierge's indignant and comic fussings and it ends with a total of several thousands of dead rats, plus the plague's first death—M. Michel, the concierge. The first dead rat begins the chapter; the first victim ends it.

Some of Camus' descriptions of the rats in this chapter are worth brief notice. The townspeople of Oran insist that the rats are surely meaningless, whereas the rats are extremely meaningful. Black is white to the people, and Camus' adjectives, in a parallel, often describe something quite the opposite of what is. For example, Dr. Rieux feels something "soft" under his foot. Usually *soft* is associated only with pleasant sensations, but here it is used in reverse. It describes the bloated corpse of a rat. Shortly thereafter, when a rat comes from the sewer it is described as spinning on itself with a little squeal, a sort of miniature ballet before death. In fact, Camus says later that the rats were coming out in long swaying lines and doing "a sort of pirouette." He describes the blood puddles around their noses as looking like red flowers. Again, as in Chapter 1, he uses an extreme contrast—here, to point to the absurdity of the symptoms: rats can't be seeping out of houses and sewers for a reason—rats' deaths can't be beautiful. Yet both are.

This is a small point, for there is much description of the rats as repulsive and rotting, but Camus' occasional contrasts of appearance versus reality in his description is exactly what the chapter is concerned with.

The character focus of the book is not wholly on Dr. Rieux, but because he is, in disguise, the narrator, he assumes a kind of early main-character or hero focal point. Studying his reaction to the dead rats—the symptoms of the plague—we find him to be a common-sense type of "hero." Camus does not slide him into a pivotal part to be an obvious mouthpiece for any heroics of philosophizing or, for that matter, any other kind of typical heroics. Rieux is a doctor; throughout the book, he doctors.

As a character, he is initially fleshed out with a good deal of personal preoccupation when he first encounters the dead rats. The blood leaking from their mouths reminds him of his wife's illness and her imminent trip to a mountain sanatorium. Their numbers seem only an oddity, a curiosity. He shrugs away the matter, saying "it'll pass." It is, however, Rieux's early indifference to the rats which eventually passes. With his wife away, he is left in a perspective larger than any plagued romantic tragedy. He is totally pledged to the populace, but not even yet does he divine what it is that hovers over Oran. Plague never enters his head. When the garbage cans begin filling with rats, he telephones the sanitation department—a business-like and correct way to deal with the situation. Indeed, this thorough and methodical attitude will continue throughout his dealings with the plague. His is a quiet, unsensational role, but it is exemplary in that he is totally committed to his fellow men and has "no truck with injustice or compromises with the truth."

Another character, although her part in the book is small, is introduced in this first chapter and is important because she exhibits a general Oranian attitude toward the plague's symptoms. "It's like that sometimes," says Rieux's mother, suggesting a seen-much, lived-through-much mind. She survives. She has seen depression, a loss of her husband, has surely even seen war; besides, she's with her son. She'll decide the importance of this unpleasant talk about rats when need be.

Jean Tarrou, on the other hand, is intrigued. This is a wholly new experience and he savors it.

Very briefly, we also meet in this chapter the senile, chuckling old Spaniard. Perhaps because he is so near death himself, he enjoys with relish the instinctive feeling that he will not die alone but with numerous companions.

The journalist Rambert seems, at this point, only a foil for Rieux. His role will enlarge as the story develops. At present, he admits that he works for a newspaper that compromises with truth. Rieux, of course, is intolerant of such a situation and abruptly ends their conversation.

Grand, too, seems to furnish a foil-like situation for a deeper insight into Rieux's character. Being poor, Grand is not charged for the doctor's visits. Rieux responds immediately to the old man's call for help — help for a neighbor who has tried to hang himself. Further, he says he will ask, as a favor for the man, that the police inspector hold up the inquiry for a couple of days. When Grand explains "one's got to help a neighbor, hasn't one?" the doctor's several instances of demonstrated humanity are now even more clearly emphasized.

Richard, the telephoned colleague of Dr. Rieux, exhibits an oft-used approach of intellectuals toward problems. The situation of the rats may or may not be considered "normal," he says. His defense is with a semantic shield.

In the beginning, then, the rats are a ready topic of conversation for the townspeople, drawing them together in chattery groups. Later the Oranians become vaguely uneasy. The rats, they say, are disgusting, obnoxious, and a nuisance. When a total of some 8,000 dead rats is made public, there is even a demand for some kind of action and an accusation of carelessness is made against the sanitation bureau. But, when the symptoms suddenly vanish — tritely, like the sudden calm before a storm — all concern vanishes and the people breathe, as Camus says ironically, more freely.

Considering now Chapter 3, we find yet another kind of "package" chapter than either 1 or 2. So that the book will not have a one-viewpoint narrative, the author of the chronicle offers the notebooks of — not an

Oranian – but those of an outsider, Jean Tarrou. By presenting another viewpoint, that of someone who has no family or loved ones affected by the plague to color his account in his notebooks, the truth of "what happened" will be more nearly correct. Of course, Rieux, the doctor-narrator is, as nearly as possible, scientifically objective in his reporting, but the account of Tarrou aids and insures even greater honesty in the finished statement concerning this period. It is Tarrou who will supply the details to fill in the broader narrative outlines of Rieux. These details are the gears and wheels of Rieux's project of truth; they are the bits of conversation, street-corner portraits, the city's nerve ends.

Where Tarrou has come from is a mystery, but after several days of minute observation of the city, he writes: "At last!" Thus, it seems as though he is searching for an endpoint or goal of some sort – and has found it in Oran. But what interests him most about Oran? Surprisingly, it is the town's ugliness, its lack of trees, its hideous houses, and the ridiculous layout. He takes particular delight in regularly watching an old man coax cats beneath his balcony then, ecstatically, spitting on them. Tarrou's mention of the old man's finally spitting into space one day when the cats fail to appear is another voice to convince and remind us of what Rieux has said earlier about the town. It is bound, perhaps even strangling itself, with habits.

The mercantile air of Oran also pleases Tarrou. Perhaps he is looking for an epitomy of modern foulness. If so, this amplifies the narrator's comment in Chapter 2 comparing the rats to pus, oozing from the abscesses beneath the town.

There is more, though, to Tarrou than a seemingly morbid curiosity. Rieux notes his sense of humor, his love of swimming, and his fondness for the company of dancers and musicians. More important, he is a questioner and a self-examiner. He wonders about wasting time, for example, and his present answer is "by being fully aware of it," one does not waste it. As a reader, you might consider how he would view the old Spaniard who carefully puts dried peas from one pot to another. Is the old man aware of what he is doing? Is he wasting time?

This idea of not wasting time and of infusing the utmost consciousness into the present moment is an important existential tenet. This minute – *now* – this is what matters. Tarrou's suggestion that one might profitably remain on a balcony during a Sunday afternoon is reminiscent of what Meursault of Camus' *The Stranger* does on Sunday afternoon – watching, looking, seeing. All of this can be an exercise, if done consciously, to revolt against time's silent, sure murder of the body.

Tarrou says he is only interested in acquiring peace of mind. Why, then, would he come to Oran? This is a question to speculate about after we know Tarrou more thoroughly. For the present, he records the snatches of shallow gossip in Oran: the decay of the rats' bodies is seen as the only danger. That the rats themselves mean something more serious is ignored by the general population.

Only once in his notebooks does Tarrou add a comment after his scraps of reportage. He speculates on a musician who continues to play his trombone after he knows that his lungs are dangerously weak. Why Tarrou singles out this particular instance to comment on is fairly obvious. Tarrou, besides liking musicians, sees Oran as a town built of physical ugliness and of a sterile commercial spirit. Here is a man who challenges death in this repulsive setting and accomplishes what he desires most — making music. He is somewhat of an oddity in Tarrou's album of sketches.

Rieux includes a brief physical description of himself written by Tarrou, and then ends the chapter which seems, on the whole, somewhat fragmentary. Like Meursault, Tarrou is unconcerned about most things. He seems disconnected, interested primarily in himself. But because he shows little concern for the rats, but is sufficiently fascinated by Oran to record its idiosyncrasies, he is excellent for Rieux's purpose — a substantiation in presenting as accurate a picture as possible about the first days of the plague.

As the plague gently begins its slaughter, Dr. Rieux discovers in Chapter 4 that he must battle another plague-like phenomenon — the so-called red tape of bureaucracy. The frustration is Kafkaesque. Rieux is also convinced that the victims of the unidentified fever should be put in isolation, yet he is stopped because of his colleagues' insistence that there is no definite proof that the disease is dangerously infectious. The other doctors refuse to draw conclusions or make an attempt to consider the cases. Rieux is futilely attempting a professional search for the truth. The atmosphere is as oppressive as a sickroom. Like the sudden relief from the rats before the plague sets in, the patients all seem to take a turn for the better just before their death struggles. The reality is like a bad dream — absurd. There is a breakdown in communication between Rieux and other men. Rieux seems isolated — in miniature, a situation akin to the total isolation which the plague will eventually impose upon Oran.

This isolation of Rieux and of Oran is buttressed by one of Camus' exacting images. Referring once more to Oran's position on the sea, he says that it is humped "snail-wise" on the plateau. The image expands and colors the chapter. A snail's pace is exactly the tempo that the town has taken concerning the investigation of the curious fever deaths. And a snail's shell of indifference and ignorance is hiding the townspeople and even Rieux's colleagues from the truth. Even before the crises that the plague will create, here is a crisis of major importance—a crisis for truth.

This chapter also provides a fuller treatment of the character of Grand. Earlier, he has said "one's got to help a neighbor, hasn't one?" and suggested a Samaritan attitude. This impression is now modified. He did not discover Cottard as a result of his coming for a friendly visit. He read the shocking chalk-scrawled note on Cottard's door and dashed in. Talking about Cottard, Grand says that the only previous instance of any odd behavior is that the fellow always seemed to want to start a conversation. Why didn't Grand respond then?

Grand seems paradoxical. He is sure that he is a good neighbor, but is he? On the contrary, he appears to be much more concerned with words than he does with people. His dictionaries, his blackboard, the crammed-full portfolio, his study of Latin to perfect his French—all this—his search for the basic, the Ur-origins—is admirable, but he seems, thus far, neglecting the people who speak the language he delves into. Consider, too, the fact that Grand has a "finical anxiety" about his speech. But what comes out of his mouth? Empty phrases that he gropes forward with—phrases like "his grim resolve" and "his secret grief," phrases that border on being clichés. Language is living. His search is for a knowledge that will produce a perfect prose. Again, this is a marvelous sort of endeavor, but the result will be too perfect. It will be artificial and devoid of that vital flush of life that separates an artist from a craftsman.

Leaving Grand, Rieux tends more patients. The swollen ganglia which he sees recurring are often lanced and disgorge a mixture of blood and pus. This idea of disgorging is similar to the disgorging of the bloodied, bloated rats from beneath the town—another parallel image-idea of Camus'.

And Camus proves as facile with the paradoxical. The rats were headlines in the press. The ganglia deaths are not even mentioned, and a certain knowing cynicism about journalists' reporting only what happens in the streets—not behind closed doors—reveals Camus' ever serious concern with truth.

The chapter ends with Rieux hesitating before he actually acknowledges, pronouncing the words, that this is indeed plague which is beginning to devour Oran. An older doctor is present and urges him to admit it. As he does, Rieux is staring at the cliffs, the piece of bay, the sky—at nature, at creativity; he says "plague" to himself, and his thoughts of impending death create a polar contrast with the free, natural scene before him.

Rieux's initial acceptance of the plague is a major scene in this first section, and as relief from this tension Chapter 5 briefly changes the pace. This chapter is a kind of didactic catch-all for Camus-Rieux to vent personal feelings about the plague and all its implications.

Here again we see Rieux as quite the opposite of a wily Odysseus hero-type or an undaunted chivalric figure. He is staggered by the knowledge that he has reasoned out for himself. And, if up to now he has been one step ahead of the townspeople in conscientiously trying to isolate and arrest this mysterious virus, he has never completely stopped and considered the panorama of torment which will be in store for the prey of the plague. Rieux, as narrator, castigates the townspeople for their stupidity and frivolity, these people who refuse to conjure and consider consequences. He sees them as pitiful, and universal, dupes of illusion.

The plague is an enigma to the doctor. Its death-dealing powers are so enormous that his imagination fails to respond to the figure of a hundred million deaths, a figure he reckons as the historical toll of plague.

All imaginations cope ineffectually with such a figure, but the doctor's problem is compounded by the fact that he deals daily in death and has seen the raw damage that statistics are charted from. It should be especially noted here that the doctor is attempting an emotional response to the advent of plague. His try at imagining the annihilation of five movie houses of people is an attempt to arrive at something concrete and meaningful. His thoughts of fellow Athenians fighting one another centuries ago for burial rite space for their dead foreshadows a like battle he will fight when he attempts to properly care for the sick and dying.

In contrast to his quandary in this chapter, the natural beauty of the outside beams healthily. As he watches and listens, it is the sea he hears most clearly as it murmurs with unrest, affirming "the precariousness of all things in this world." His coming-to-terms with whatever has invaded Oran must be accomplished soon, but with reason and observation. He does not undergo here a metamorphosis and emerge something much grander than before. His determination to be simply efficient and thorough is his answer for the present—doing one's job as it should be done. This is the careful, exact quality in Rieux that we have seen previously. He has considered, speculated, yet returned to his familiar role of the dedicated, common-sense doctor.

This speculation of Rieux's turns into musings throughout Chapter 6. He muses on the dimensions of Grand's character—measurements which are unexceptional, but important in their implications. Two things are done here with Grand. His unimportance is particularized and then this non-importance is generalized into symbolic significance.

First, Rieux considers Grand's occupation as clerk. He seems to manage, cheerfully enough, on what certainly can't be more than a pittance of a salary. The reader must here see Grand against the background described earlier. Most of Oran talks, scribbles, and muscles their days into ample financial rewards. Grand, in contrast, does not. He lacks almost all sense of commercial survival. Holed up in his room, he pours over volumes of philology. Ironically, Rieux remarks, just such insignificant people often escape plague. Once more, as a point of reference, Camus' earlier fictional character of Meursault won't ask for a transfer; neither does Grand ask for salary raises or advancements. To both men, their leisure time is of prime importance. For Meursault, that time is spent swimming, going to the movies, and making love. Grand struggles over perfecting the beginning of a manuscript. Both men are, strictly speaking, nobodies—statistics, figuratively; actually, counters of statistics.

This inconsequentiality, however—isn't this, in a broad sense, definitive of Oran? In spite of their greed and thrift, there are no millionaires in the city, there are no artists of repute, no statesmen or politicians—there is actually no one known outside the city walls.

Rieux considers: none of these people matter, yet such a major tragedy as plague—what possible reason could there be for its singling out Oran? What logic, he wonders, is behind the destruction of Oran? Rieux has proven himself to be a man of logic; this pondering is quite in character. And, at this point, Rieux has pronounced the word "plague," but has not wholly adjusted to its revolting reality. He is still in vague, unbelieving awe, as if the word had barely left his open mouth.

Before leaving this chapter, there are two more incidents of credit for the doctor. Exhausted and preoccupied by the fever patients, he agrees to drop by and discuss a matter with Cottard concerning something about which Cottard is irritatingly vague. Originally, the doctor had suggested that Cottard drop by during consulting hours, but clearing his head of plague thoughts, he sympathically responds to the fellow.

The doctor gives Grand credit for being a man of feelings. Is it, however, Grand who has admirable feelings toward his fellow men or is it Rieux? One should question, at this point, whether Rieux is wholly to be trusted. Making decisions about motivation and not succumbing to the evaluation of the central figure's is one of the hurdles in learning to read literature. Rieux says that Grand "confessess" to dearly loving his nephews and sisters. He even admits that his heart responds whenever he recalls his deceased parents. Rieux's observation of Grand has Oran as relief, a town which becomes uneasy at the suggestion of affection. As yet, Grand has to show us any real sympathy. Even with Rieux, on their way to the laboratory, he suddenly dashes away to spend the evening with his bookish project. Grand's character takes on ambiguous shapes.

Before Oran is finally quarantined, Dr. Rieux confronts one more tangle in the local snarl of red tape. The Prefect, or local magistrate, must be dealt with. His stand concerning the seriousness of the plague is important because he is the self-deceiver, one of the safest — and most despicable — of roles. The Prefect sounds like a Liberal, but is an arch Conservative; he imagines himself encompassing each of his city's crises with sage wisdom and acting accordingly. But when he says that prompt action should be taken but "don't attract attention," he is pitifully similar to the civil rights fighter who supports protest marches as long as they are done in good taste and don't "attract attention." The man is a coward, afraid of indiscreet remarks, and is actually very frightened of Rieux's charges of epidemic. But he is not alone. Another colleague of Rieux's loudly supports the Prefect's stand on the issue, explaining away the fever in vague, medical-book sounding generalities. Finally Rieux seems at a loss for an answer. Only old Dr. Castel says matter-of-factly that plague is their visitor. Rieux modifies his seeming indecision by saying that the symptoms are not "classic," and at this point his purist view is alarming. Is the man going to insist that definitions and clinical reports be compiled and printed? Camus is teasing our suspense. Rieux counters his introductory remarks by debunking them. He tosses semantics to the timid-tongued doctors. Word games are ridiculous now. Action is the only answer.

Irritated that Dr. Richard would sarcastically accuse him of having proven the disease to be plague, Rieux insists that he has *not* proven plague. He has simply *seen* something as deadly as plague with epidemic proportions. Rieux then insists that they must act "as if" it is plague. Only then can they perform responsibly and efficiently.

The final and short scene of the woman dripping with blood, stretching her arms in agony toward Rieux, is another incident to help us see Rieux as a man who is aware of human cries for help. He has fought throughout this chapter for official resolutions to help just such people. In the relaxingly furnished quarters of a municipal official, amid a background of professional-sounding doctors and their medical jargon, one is far from the bloody pus pockets of the city. Rieux is arguing from a distance, from scenes he witnessed on the city's outskirts, and here his opinions are so contrary to most of those assembled that he might seem absurdly radical in his insistence. He leaves the room of doctors, a room of health and sanitation and goes outside, into the fresh air — now full of disease, and he sees bloodied evidence that affirms his stand for us and stiffens his resolve for action.

In Chapter 8, the plague and municipal efforts play tick-tack-toe. The plague tallies a few more deaths, and officials respond with a brief notice or two in obscure corners of the paper and small signs at obscure city points. Officially, rats and fleas are to be exterminated; illnesses resembling the mysterious fever are to be reported and patients isolated. Cleanliness is to be observed. Perhaps, it is hoped, the plague will then take care of itself.

Cottard's character now takes on greater significance. Grand reports that a complete change has taken place in the man and Rieux does some firsthand observing. Camus delineates some of the manifestations of a guilty conscience, but does not yet answer all the why's of Cottard's behavior. The reader should imagine and reason possibilities for himself by asking such questions as: why did Cottard try to commit suicide? Why does anyone attempt suicide? Because of fear? Fear of the future? of the past? of being alone? Guilt? Why does Cottard have an irrational fear of the police? A fear that they will be "rough" with him? He is relieved, you remember, when Rieux says that he will protect him. Consider, too, the scene in which Cottard's suicide motive was discussed. He merely replied "a secret grief," and refused to look at the officer. He insists on being left in peace, yet now he effects a change. He is suddenly animated, amiable, and altogether not himself. He now eats in luxury restaurants and flourishes grand tips. His remarks about his new acquaintances being good witnesses and his unease in a gossip about a murder case — these suggest to Grand that he has something on his conscience. His uneasy glances over his shoulder and his question about patients being arrested concern Rieux. Who is this man? He has tried suicide and recovered. Now, when the plague is eroding the town's edges, he has a new surge of life. He is now concerned that he live, that the police do not arrest him, and that his rights be fully respected. The taste of death in the town has invigorated him. Camus has swollen Cottard into major proportions in this last chapter of Part I; later the man will merit even more consideration.

Rieux admits that he is afraid. His hopes for a natural cessation of the plague are of course futile. The emergency measures are insufficient. Castel says that, ironically, something as tiny as fleas are at the root of the problem.

And outside nature is serenely blue, brilliantly golden. Spring's heavy perfume is in extreme contrast to the heavy smell of death.

Tarrou continues to observe, the old man spits on the cats, Grand writes, Cottard goes his way, the Spaniard counts his peas. Nature seems indifferent to the mushrooming fungus of destruction. Even the population seem indifferent as they perform their habitual, meaningless gestures. The death figure drops, then spurts up sharply. At last word comes from the head of officialdom — Rieux's efforts to convince the proper authority that an epidemic has begun are rewarded — the town is to be severed, totally isolated. Plague is proclaimed.

PART TWO

Throughout Part I, there is a sense of urgency and frustration. Death darkens the pages and we are among the few to realize what is happening as the toll increases. The frustration, however, is not wholly a life and death matter. Now, besides lives, there are values which are being annihilated. But Camus is structuring an irony. Death does not finally seem as important as knowledge does. We do not feel horror when the plague is proclaimed; the horror of the disease has already saturated us. We have read of its ugly symptoms — the heaps of rats' bodies and the blood- and pus-swollen sores. The plague is already very real to us. When the designation is officially announced the news seems good, for it means that although death, for awhile, is the victor, at least ignorance has been defeated. We read of the acknowledgment of the plague with a sense of relief. Truth has a victory. A lucid evaluation of the crisis has been achieved, the enemy has been revealed and can now be confronted.

Part II re-begins the chronicle in a different tone and with a different sense of time. The tone is less intense. Remembering the first days after the gates were closed, Rieux pulls back the focus of his narrative for a long general view. Here and there he recalls events that link disjointedly to one another — hands scribbling last notes, the look in lost eyes, feet wandering aimlessly. This is how it was, he seems to be saying and his tone is that of a man who has survived, but only barely. As a participant, he is almost absent; he is the raconteur and he speaks of a new element of time. Previously, in many lives, there was never a definite yesterday, a definite tomorrow and today; they were all part of an ambiguous dimension. Now the plague has shut the city gates, walled out the outside, and given a name to the hours prior to closing: that time is Before. The present, the now, is particularly frightening because it is seen against and as a part of a sequence of days and nights of living and dying. At least, then, the future had always been there — somewhere — even if it hadn't been seriously considered. Now even its existence seems in doubt.

Because this first chapter of Part II is a jumble of summary, perhaps it is best to begin considering Oran's new environment and the adjustment of the townspeople toward it. Like children thrust into a dark room, they are taken by surprise and caught unprepared; perhaps "dark room" isn't an exaggerated analogy: this new environment of Oran is like a world turned upside down — by accident, loved ones are away from the city, there are no letters, no telephone calls, no word from Out There. Several times Rieux refers to the city as a "prison house" and as a "lazar-house," and of their existence as one of exile.

As for adjusting — to face a problem does not necessarily mean that one faces it honestly. Few Oranians, it would appear, do. In general, there seem to be two ways of coping with the quarantine. At first some people succumb; others invent diversionary escapes.

Rieux describes those who give up as ones re-walking where memory has now made certain streets precious. He also speaks of those who enfold themselves in nostalgia; they create new habits, slow down their pace, and orient themselves toward waiting for the inevitable. Then there are those who do not give up, but who run. They run after hope. They hope letters can be sent someday, so they continue writing. They send telegrams, but realize that clichés and platitudes are the most concise and satisfactory texts for communication. Finally they realize the futility of any messages. The telephone arteries break down early. No amount of processing can handle the swollen flow. The next step is make-believe: waiting for the renewal of train services, the jingle of the phone, of the doorbell. Why this creativity? Largely because their pasts are full of remorse. Thus, they try changing; they ritually remember a mother's face throughout the day; they become model husbands for the wives beyond the walls. All these activities are their answers for ways of living under a sentence of death.

Of particular interest is how the plague binds men together and then, ironically, cuts them apart and rebinds each man within himself. Each man is as trapped as his neighbor; no one has special consideration under the plague's regime. There is an immediate leveling of social distinctions. All are equally in trouble, but they cannot comfort one another because they have never done so before. They have never expressed conventional emotions, and thus it is frustrating and useless to speak of the extreme emotions that the plague produces. The people talk past one another. They are doubly imprisoned — within Oran and within themselves — and this double-barred atmosphere of each man is awesomely new and menacing.

Besides the Oranians, there is one more type of prisoner in Oran. Rambert is such a man. He is a journalist, trapped here without a loved one and outside his home. Rieux pities him most. But we should remember that the plague is unrespecting.

Lastly, Rieux suggests that the Oranians are lucky — a strange statement. But it has its genesis in Camus' fondness for irony. The Oranians are lucky because their suffering is selfishly and limitedly personal. Because no one feels great compassion, they escape the deepest distress; Rieux mentions indifference being taken for composure. His irony is icy when he concludes that this limited despair saves Oran from total panic.

Finishing the random rememberings of Chapter 9, Rieux now concentrates on a subject dear to the people of Oran — their commerce. And only by considering what must certainly have been one of their gravest trials can we arrive at more of the truth about those days.

The plague has sealed the harbor. Money has stopped flowing in and out of the bay, and once again there is irony as Rieux describes several Oranians gazing out at the corpse-like ships afloat. The Oranians, you remember, seldom looked at the bay or responded to the natural sea beauty on their city's edge. Now they look upon a scene of stagnation. Commerce has ceased. In comparison, people seem of lesser consequence. Perhaps this enormous natural symbol of death, more than most any other factor, staggers them. They cast about, worried and irritated, for someone to blame.

To blame the Prefect, their business leader, seems natural enough. The city's business has failed, the city's chief is to blame. They seem like children blaming their mother because rain has begun to fall. The control of gasoline and foodstuffs confuses them; their failure, however, to understand the death statistics is plausible. Before, they thought principally of themselves and of their accumulation of money and material things. Death held little interest for them — particularly when it was a numerical statistic. Now comparisons are futile. Imagination, as an antidote, is impossible because the city's supply has long since atrophied. And so most of them either run from realizing what the plague involves or give up.

Who is making money? Only someone or something able to furnish hope or illusion for the troubled: bars and movie houses. Alcohol and the silverscreen are instant relief for personal misery that is festering. Pathetically, movie house crowds do not diminish when it becomes necessary to begin showing re-runs. Nor does common sense seem to care when taverns boast that spirits are the most effective agents against infection. For some, then, there is money to be made from misfortune but, for most, commerce is indeed dead. With expected irony, Rieux remarks that the idle crowds filling the streets make the city look festive and holiday-like.

For the remainder of Chapter 10, Rieux leaves his commentary to record three conversations: one with Cottard, one with Grand, and one with Rambert, the journalist. To each of the men he is a kind of father-confessor figure.

The brief Cottard episode is disturbing. In the midst of death and confusion he is still the beaming fellow that we left pages ago. His behavior is totally incongruous. His anxiously happy questioning about the plague's getting worse, his jokes about grocers getting rich—these seem almost the actions of a madman. He could be easily tagged a psychotic if he didn't mutter that "We'll all be nuts before long." He has come back to life in the poisoned air of Oran, but what's more important—he seems to realize why he is now happy and why he must seem ludicrous and "nuts."

Why does he talk to Rieux? There are two possible reasons: first, Rieux has doctored him, shown kindness, and offered to *protect* him; second, Rieux is a doctor and can function meaningfully only when people are sick or dying. For the first time in months Cottard finds himself functioning, if not meaningfully, at least satisfactorily—and in the shadow of a plague. The values of the men are antithetical, yet Cottard is reaching for fraternity. Dr. Rieux is admirable; the plague increases his chances for stature. And because Cottard has a new sense of well-being, he resorts to a superficial analogy to provide himself with some kind of peer. Yet there are moments when he (and we) can see another analogy. If he is happy because he is surrounded by people waiting for death sentences, perhaps it is because he has his own sentence waiting for him—a legal one. His earlier fear of the police supports such a supposition. For the present we know very little about Cottard, but should be aware of his increasing uniqueness. Camus intends for this character to carry considerable symbolic weight.

Cottard meets Rieux in the morning, two days after the gates have been closed. The same afternoon Grand comes to Rieux's office and, stimulated by a picture of Rieux's wife, becomes suddenly talkative about his past.

In this scene Grand's character loses much of its previous vagueness. His mulling over of the past is exactly what some other Oranians are doing, but Rieux has said that those who suffer remorse have turned into escapists. This is not true of Grand. He has remorse, but considers and weighs the liabilities of his past actions. His wasn't a glamorous or even a happy marriage—which shouldn't surprise us, knowing Grand even as superficially as we do.

He was a shy young fellow and felt protective toward Jeanne. They shared, one day, the loveliness of a Christmas-decorated shop window and were married soon afterward. Knowing Camus' affection for natural beauty, and having Oran's commercialism as a background for Grand and Jeanne, we might wonder if their sharing of happiness—for what seems to be the first and last time—in a shop window, artificially contrived to be beautiful in order to induce people to buy, isn't a comment on the meagerness of their chances for a full, rich life together. Grand's tone is fatalistic as he continues the episode.

His wife's leaving was admirable. Here was revolt. Because her life with Grand was bleak, silent, and doomed did not mean that she had to submit to its certain fate. She did not even have a lover who promised her happiness. Her remark that one needn't be happy to make another start suggests that groundless optimism is as ridiculous as the pessimism that her marriage was fostering. The important thing is the fresh start, the refusal to be trapped by convention or environment. Man has a right to change. This is Christian and also existential. Marriage had become a habit for Jeanne and Grand; its banality became unbearable. The only honest courage was to rebel against the mores of Oran that urged acceptance of a barren marriage as inevitable and final—even good because it had been decided and contracted. A decision, in an existential sense, is never irrevocable. There is always scope for insight, growth, and change.

Grand continues that he has always wanted to write and justify himself, but he sees his failure to find the words as a flaw in his will power and in his vocabulary. Could he justify himself? His attempt to write the perfect book is cerebral, a kind of passionless fantasy. Too often, his frustrated love of words seems to be a grotesque parody of his indifferent marriage.

With both Cottard and Grand, Rieux does very little communicating. Just as Oran is sealed off, so these people seem to be fenced apart. Cottard needs Rieux for support—someone solid whom he can trust, to whom he can mutter a weakness, and as someone whom he can bounce wisecracks off. Their talk is over in minutes. Grand's contact with Rieux is a bit more fruitful. He confesses for the first time the circumstances and the consequences of his failed marriage. There may be a degree of self-deception in his narrative, but his attempt to ponder is admirable. It is, in a sense, as fresh a start as Jeanne made years ago. And Grand's story has its effect on Rieux. For days the plague has been foremost in his mind; now he sends his wife a telegram expressing his concern and hope for her recovery.

Rambert's talk with Rieux takes place approximately three weeks later than the meetings with Cottard and Grand, and it is longer than the talk with either of those. Rambert insists on being an exception, on being released from the fate imposed on the Oranians. He wants Rieux to give him a certificate of release. Rieux notes that the journalist talks "incessantly, as if his nerves were out of hand." This is significant because Grand and Cottard also talked in this fevered tempo.

There is another similarity among the three men. Within the core of each of their conversations is a secret. For Cottard, his secret is a crime; for Grand, it is his miscarried marriage. Rambert's secret is that he has discovered that love and happiness are all he really cares for. Now, as though he is asking for a parole to go back to Paris, he appeals to Rieux. The plague has stopped him in Oran and caused him to realize that he is failing to love his wife as completely as he might. As the two men talk, Rieux picks up a small boy who has tumbled down. Ironically, he cannot right matters quite so easily for Rambert. Rieux says that Rambert has an excellent subject to write about in Oran. This sounds callous and ironical, and there is probably a vein of irony here, but there is deeper truth. The future for everyone in Oran is uncertain. Today, even tomorrow, may be one's last. To escape is impossible. To plead is futile. Rambert is a journalist and, however valid and heartbreaking his discovery that he has a potential for human warmth and love, nothing can alter the black-bordered present. To write about the plague is quite a worthwhile task; in fact, for Rambert this seems his only rational course of action. He has talent and training for reporting and here is a subject for him. To try to right an unsatisfactory past is impossible for all three men. The present, as Rieux tells Rambert, is their only time. For Cottard, this means a perilous freedom and a brotherhood with the threatened populace. Grand seems to be *thinking*, if not about the plague, then at least about the past, and thinking is an Oranian rarity. Rambert has, admittedly, a larger problem. He is caught within a strange city, the probable victim of a hostile and indifferent disease. He is totally alone and must now put all of his values to test if he is to survive with his integrity intact.

After he leaves Rambert, Dr. Rieux considers the journalist's slur that medicine has hardened him and that he deals only in abstractions. Rambert's remarks stem, of course, from his disappointment and failure to get a certificate of release, but there is a certain truth in his attack. Death and sickness are both concepts and realities; Rieux deals with them in both senses. In addition, Rieux's professional pace is extremely taxing: long hours of diagnosing, of treating, and of disposing of the dead. Often one must, in such an emergency, become as abstractly enduring and as effective as one's enemy. Couple this with the temperament that originally creates a doctor and the result is an anomaly. Rieux's heart is, no doubt, more sensitive than any in Oran, yet a doctor cannot survive on onion-skin sensitivity the way a poet can. He must keep emotion alive – in spite of habitually seeing sickness and in spite of daily seeing death. Death can easily become the norm, sensitivity an outmoded burden. More than anyone else in Oran, Dr. Rieux has continued his declaration of war on death and on the plague. He honestly admits to occasional periods during which pity dies and he becomes indifferent, but it is during these times that he sleeps and forgets and heals an exhausted mind and body.

He ends the chapter with an incident which is a kind of travesty the plague has produced. Doctors must physically battle members of a family in order to remove and isolate the plague's victims. The once welcome face of a doctor is now as foreboding as though he were wearing a mask of death. Here is one more type of isolation within Oran. Already we have seen the city isolated, then large numbers of citizens isolated by selfishness and ignorance; now we have the isolation of the sick. This concept of separation is increasingly walling in the city and its prisoners.

Chapter 11 is brief but highly dramatic and most important. It concerns the role of the Church during the plague – what its attitude was and how it battled Oran's murderous enemy. More than any single scene thus far, this chapter is loud and vivid and, as a reader, you should not overlook Camus' art in readying us for its drama. In the novel, as in any other art form – music, painting, poetry – rhythm is necessary; the tempo and the modulation of mood must be in balance before an artist is satisfied. The result is beauty, but unobtrusive beauty – a whole so skillfully produced that one is usually unaware of the separate parts and their tension. A critical analysis seems the proper place to call attention to some of the mechanics of esthetic pleasure in literature.

Consider the whole of Part I. Frustration fuses the individual scenes and builds steadily until the last sentence is read with the same intensity that one feels at the culmination of a Chopin crescendo. After this emotional exercise one is not ready for an immediate, feverish movement. It is necessary now to have a breather – to relax before the next burst of theatrics. Camus gives us opportunity to do exactly this. After Part I he begins an unhurried reminiscence through Chapter 9, concentrates his recollections upon commercialism in Chapter 10, and finishes the chapter with three conversational scenes, each a little longer than the last and each more important in the quality of personal revelation. Camus moves from the general to the less general and then to various lengths of specifics before presenting again a full chapter of action.

For Chapter 11 there is special preparation because there is more than a confrontation between major characters. Camus presents Religion versus Plague. Of course the character of Father Paneloux is significant, but the Church takes precedence. Since man's beginning, he has worshiped and feared some aspect of the natural world and has hoped in terms of an Eternal. Faith in a Something larger than man has milleniums of tradition; Camus' ideas challenge all these years of seemingly instinctive faith. In this chronicle, alongside the Oranians, the Church is on trial. It is, however, not the cave of safety that critics often accuse it of being. It does not ignore Oran's epidemic. But neither does it attack it forthrightly; instead, the Church injects reason into the plague's power. Before the Week of Prayer's Sunday sermon, people had been harried by something irrational and meaningless. This is no longer true. The Church has defined: the plague has a beginning and, ostensibly, an end. It has originated in the sin of Oran, its purpose is punishment, and its termination is dependent upon repentance. The logic of religious truth is responsible for this interpretation.

Objective narrative is probably impossible when recording what Rieux (and Camus) would consider ignorant, if holy, sermon-shouting. One should be aware that this chapter is not as objective as Rieux has said his chronicle would be; there is irony shot throughout its length. In the first sentence, Rieux means that the word *truth* be understood conversely. Truth is impossible for the Church. Truth comes only after unbiased thought, repeated analyses, and admitted mistakes. The Church, never erring, once again applies its subjective, cover-all formula of "sin = punishment" to this current crisis. There is further irony in Father Paneloux's being an expert in deciphering ancient inscriptions. Deciphering hieroglyphics may be possible for the priest, but deciphering the meaning of the plague is beyond his capabilities. There is additional irony in the chapter's imagery. The church service occurs during a torrential downpour and when Rieux uses such words as the "swelling tide of prayers," the "backwash" of invocation, the "overflow" of the congregation, he is building, tongue-in-cheek, image support for a major irony. Here, in the cathedral, away from the rain and the plague, people have gathered for a rebirth of hope. But do they receive hope?

Before the congregation enters the church, they undergo a baptism of soaking rain. Then they enter, and Rieux notes the smell of their soggy, wet clothes; this suggests the soggy, wet rats of Chapter 1 which escaped from Oran's sewers to die in the streets. Now, in a reversal, the Oranians are soggily leaving the streets and going inside a church to escape the plague. They come for help and for blessing, but find themselves intimidated, brow-beaten, and charged with criminal acts; they receive spiritual death, a paral-lel to the death of the rats. The sermon will not rouse the populace to coping effectively with the physical menace which is slaughtering them. The ser-mon prescribes soul-flailing and prayer, but not practical precautions. It compounds confusion by creating guilt and fear when strength and courage are needed.

Finally, there is another example of irony. The long sermon is highly effective because it is so passionately powered with emotion. It descends with the fury of the rain outside. In fact, the pounding of the rain and the pounding of Paneloux's rhetoric join forces to drive the crowd to its knees. Yet, when Paneloux has captured their wills by emotional means, he ex-horts them to "take thought." Of course what Paneloux actually means by "taking thought" and what Camus would mean are two different concepts. Paneloux desires the congregation to take *his* thoughts. Thought, for Camus, would include thinking, not a substitution of mass confusion or mass ac-ceptance of a doctrine of punishment handed down by a furious representa-tive of the Unknown.

Besides the idea of "taking thought," there are two more ideas con-cluding Paneloux's sermon which Camus would champion, but which he would interpret antithetically. The priest charges the Oranians with "crimi-nal indifference." Camus, in his novels and essays, pleads for an end to indifference among men. Paneloux refers to man's neglecting God; Camus' concept is in terms of a conscious and intense humanism.

Paneloux concludes his sermon saying that a prayer of love might help matters. But after the orator has been so striking in his sermon about devils and bloodied spears, this suggestion is colorless and vague – a kind of post thought, a p.s. of love to soothe before he releases the congregation. Practi-cal brotherly love and love's responsibility are ideas which we have seen in use – by Dr. Rieux. For him, and for Camus, these ideas of love and re-sponsibility are primary and basic, certainly not vague and benedictional.

Before leaving the chapter, one might note that for a holy man, Paneloux's image during the service has an ironic blend of the satanic. He is described as looking massive and enormously black. His big hands grasp the pulpit; the connotation is exact. Grasp is exactly what he does to the congregation that fills his church. He seizes their minds and grips until they are united in their shame. In addition, he addresses the public as his brethren, yet he indicts them in the second person, in the "you." He does not say that "we" — if he is a brother to his brethren — have deserved the plague; he steps outside his judgment.

If there is distinction in creating a national image, Father Paneloux is responsible for a share. Rieux noted earlier that the Oranians had felt a vague sense of union because they were equally in trouble. After the Sunday sermon they increasingly see themselves as criminals — prisoners serving sentences in the prison of Oran.

In addition, after the Sunday sermon, Oran begins noticeably to change; Rieux says that panic flares up. And, in part, Paneloux is also responsible for that, but he is certainly not the only factor to consider. To blame one man would be unjust and erroneous. The priest is probably more at fault for what he failed to do than for what he actually effected. Paneloux's responsibility lies in fanning the flames of panic — of giving impassioned and unverified reasons for the deaths. To his church service came people who were directionless and questioning. He hurled to them biblical horror tales of punishment by plague, convincing them that they deserved what was happening. He cried that the Oranians were enemies of God, were proud and indifferent — charges which are necessary ingredients for regular Sunday scourging; Paneloux had only to fire these charges vocally and imagistically until he saw heightened fear and awe in their faces. It was likely terrifying, yet what takes shape within people during a harrowing Sunday sermon has partially dissolved even by Monday morning.

At the root of Oran's panic is probably the resurgence of fresh deaths. Death has vivid bloody traces; it is visual. A sharp rise in its slaughter will stir panic before preaching will. But the combination can be lethal — especially if, in Paneloux's case, the preaching is fortified with reasons that are emotional fuses. Reasons, per se, without emotional fuses, are seldom as terrifying to people as a phenomenon which seems monstrously superhuman and destructive. Reasons can be weighed by examining their validity, considering who gives the reasons, what the man's background is, and how objective he is. Rationality usually averts panic. But alarming inquisitions — emotionally colored, misunderstood, and ignorantly interpreted — can be chaotic to a people panicking in the terror of a disaster.

For an example of Oran's growing panic, Rieux tells an incident that centers upon Grand and shows us what is probably one of the less spectacular of panicky reactions. By using Grand—the petty official ("the kind of man who always escapes" plagues and wars)—as an emotional measure, our imagination can begin with him and extend up the scale of Oran's panic. Rieux therefore does not have to be encyclopedic.

Grand trembles violently, gulps his drinks, mutters, and is on edge. He is short with Rieux, who doesn't understand the writing project or the weeks spent on one word. It is not known what Rieux thinks about Grand's problem with conjunctions, but within the circumference of this special trouble is, in miniature, a parallel to his problem in living responsibly. Grand has confined himself so totally in his off hours to his room and to the numerous revisions of the first sentence of his book that he has lost real zest for living and for reality. He seems to lack a social conjunction just as he lacks the proper *and, but,* or *then.*

Grand has, besides general troubles with conjunctions, an additional problem which he explains in detail to Rieux. He has evolved a scale of difficulty in choosing conjunctions. It is hard, for example, for him to choose between *but* and *and.* He doesn't say why, but it is important to speculate about. *And* is a simple joiner, whereas *but* can imply a stand on an issue. *And* joins two ideas innocuously; *but,* however, follows a statement, qualifying it with a second statement. One cannot utter a *but* impersonally; a new dimension of the speaker is apparent. And there is even an added risk when one uses a *but. And*'s can be pedestrian; *but*'s, though, register objection, and with different motivation, can even excuse the first assertion. One has to choose then between an unassuming *and* and a more forceful *but* and, if the latter, there is the additional burden of dilemma. For a man as introspective as Grand, here in his prose problems are exactly the kinds of decisions that, in a social situation, try his courage.

And and *but* are hard to choose between, but harder yet are *but* and *then.* Remembering what has already been said of *but,* think now about *then.* The word connotes a continuance, an evolution. It has a positive, growing quality. Grand's hardest choice, however, is whether or not to use a conjunction at all. To initially commit oneself is, simply, the most difficult trial.

With Grand, Rieux is sympathetic, but no doubt the genuine tenor of his feelings is partly supported by professional poise. He listens to the constant whistling of the wind and it conjures an image of Paneloux's holy flailing, slashing the air over Oran. Rieux's mind wanders as he listens to

Grand. The assertion that he made to Rambert — that he must face actual facts — finds a humorous echo in this chapter. He thinks Grand's dream of creating the perfect prose to which publishers will say, dramatically, "Hats off!" is largely impossible on account of the fact that publishers don't wear hats in the office. This bit of faraway musing that is stimulated by Grand's repetitive gesture of "Hats off!" is one of the few touches of humor in the book.

As for imagery in Chapter 12, you might note that Grand's labored first sentence is blessed with beautiful adjectives. This is in extreme contrast to his poverty and to the plague. The morning is fine, the month is May, the rider is a lady and elegant, her horse handsome, and their path flowering and running through a park filled with greenery. The words try, in addition, to jog with the horses' trotting pace. The sentence is stuffed with superlatives and promises. And ideals. The effort Grand has set for himself needs the will to join the first sentence with the second and so on. But Grand remains with his first words. Perfection: this is his dream. He must produce a perfect work to be left behind for posterity. This will be his life's labor and, even though it may seem impossible to us, at least he has not compromised. To some, he has wasted hours and pages of paper, but he has kept a dream alive. As beset with difficulties as he is, he has worked to produce nothing less than the best. There is nothing of genius in Grand, but because he is a human being, we should see that he does possess something admirable. Absurd, perhaps, but also admirable. Even within this nobody, this drudge, there is life and an individual sense of purpose being kept alive.

Rieux makes the transition from Chapter 12 to 13 rather cleverly. While listening to Grand talk about perfecting his prose, Rieux hears a commotion outside, goes to the window and sees people racing through the streets toward the city gates. He rushes down the stairs and pauses a moment. Here is evidence of the latest gossip — the epidemic of attempted escapes. Rieux literally dashes down the stairs into Chapter 13, pausing only a moment to ponder these escapes before beginning the subject of the chapter: the escape tactics of Raymond Rambert.

On first reading, this chapter seems only one more tale of frustration, but it is more; it is one part of a principal irony Rieux is preparing. Chapters 13 and 17 will be contrasted against each other. The former recounts the numerous business-like dead ends that Rambert encounters as he tries legally to leave Oran. Chapter 17 concerns his illegal attempts. Both systems — Oran's civic structure and Oran's underground — are ironically built of similar bureaucratic labyrinths and both refuse Rambert's request with the same kinds of Kafkaesque ambiguities. In addition, Rambert's attempts to escape have a rather interesting quality of setting within this larger dimension of irony; Camus gives them a sporting image. Rambert is not the often-seen, lean journalistic type. He is a squat, powerfully built, former football player, and his refusal to accept the status quo of official and unofficial *no*'s has the kind of muscular resolution that he has surely experienced on the playing field.

Within Camus' situation of Rambert's ineffectiveness in his dealings with the city and its underground, there are smaller ironies. For example, the one official piece of paper that seems to promise most toward an official escape is finally revealed to be only a form that all strangers in Oran are requested to fill in. It has nothing of hope in it; it is information necessary for Oranian clerks should Rambert die during the plague. Its purpose deals with death, not life. The form has one function: locating his next of kin and, probably most important, determining who will pay funeral and burial costs. Living, we realize, requires many formal-looking forms, numbers, and computations, but under the new regime of plague, death demands as thorough an accounting of its citizens. There is only one word to describe such irony: absurd.

Rambert has one small reason for hoping: he *is* being considered. With everything else so topsy-turvy, he is not completely anonymous in this strange city of the dying. His name is on paper; he is calling attention to himself. Unlike so many of the townspeople, he has not given up. He is demanding recognition through perseverance. And while reading of Rambert's perseverance, remember that Rieux is telling the story and that his definition of perseverance is not the same as Rambert's. Rambert believes that perseverance can finally, literally, pay off. Rieux does not. He is a believer in perseverance, but only in this way: victory is an impossibility when one struggles almost hourly with death as Rieux does, but perseverance gains in value when one realizes it must inevitably fail—that in the darkness of an eternal nothing, it is all meaningless. To say a lifetime of *no* to death and an ever *yes* to life, with unflagging perseverance, is the essence of the revolt of Dr. Rieux. Rambert has not yet developed a philosophy concerning his perseverance; his present concept is little more than a sustained, physical endurance. Currently he is in active protest and this chapter details its intensity—for example, his satiric but accurate catalog of the guardians of the blind alleys he confronts: the sticklers, the consolers, the triflers, etc. It is a sharp focus on the ineffectiveness of his hope and perseverance versus the absurd.

Some of the chapter's other ironies are these:

There seem to be two ways of "killing time" in Oran. One way occurred earlier—an enormous spurt of energy, panic, and hope of escape. Then, when this energy was depleted, it was replaced by a lethargic drift, and hope of escape has been replaced by a hope of the plague's waning. Thus, one can kill time during a death sentence by two diametrically defined ways of hoping. There is even a kind of absurdity in the phrase "killing time." Time is killing the Oranians while they imagine that they are "killing" it.

Rieux talks again of vast nostalgia, but in this chapter uses Rambert as a particular instance. Remembering his wife, Paris, and evening walks, Rambert visits the railway station. Here you should be aware of the parallels between his faith and that of the religious townspeople. Their faith is in God's mysterious justice; Rambert's faith is in his own determination and a justice based on rational logic. He does not belong in Oran and once this error has been corrected and processed, he will be released. Only for the present is he trapped. And, in the way that churches for the faithful are places of promise, so the railway station becomes almost a holy shrine, a station of deliverance, to Rambert. Former freedom takes on a sense of the hallowed. Like the cathedral, the station affords relief from the searing midday sun of Oran. Inside, both the cathedral and the railway station are dark and cool and made of stone. Rambert studies the timetables and departures posters as though they were religious stations of the cross. The defunct iron stove is fired only by memory now; its function is ornamental during the plague's duration. But for Rambert it is as evocative as a holy statue.

Before leaving the chapter, note the poetic images Rieux records. He refers to natural beauty in the midst of Oran's dying world. The satin-white marble tops of the cafe tables have a touch of Tiffany against the pearl-colored sunset. The immensity of this beauty seems indifferent to Oran, the exiled abscess on the sea, and the universe seems at odds with civilized notions of beauty. It makes the death of the day seem flawlessly beautiful; death in Oran is torturous, ugly, and foul-smelling.

Tarrou's notebooks are once again inserted to buttress Rieux's narrative. And because there is the sense of a philosopher behind them, the sketches remain convincing. His montage of quick impressions has the same mood that Rieux sustains—that of the ironic and the objectively aloof. Mounted patrols gun down cats and dogs. Tarrou doesn't comment, yet the implication is there. These animals may be carriers of infection, but they are also pets, symbols of home. As actual homes and family living are being exterminated by something abstract, human beings are destroying abstract symbols of that home.

The newspapers reporting the death statistics change their policy. They decide to publish daily totals. Why? The figure, although high, is not as staggering as the weekly total. You should remember that this is a reversal in policy. Originally totals were published weekly to keep the plague from having pressing daily existence. Now, of course, more factors have to be weighed and, in the public's interest, the less alarming the figure, the better. You should also note that in this atmosphere of death, a birth has occurred: *The Plague Chronicle* is born, publishing speculations, tips, morale boosters, and sure-cure advertisements. The townspeople rashly turn this parasitic publication into the city's most profitable enterprise.

The closed shops Tarrou speaks of are parallels of the dead in Oran, commercial corpses. And besides the dead, he speaks of the living, especially of their habits — such as the old man waiting for the cats — the habits such people retain lest they lose their sanity. He speaks also of those who actually crack within, open their windows and scream against the sky.

Again we read of the old Spaniard counting his peas, imagining that he has accomplished a twentieth-century feat by abolishing clocks from his house. He explains that every fifteen panfuls of peas is his feeding time. He doesn't need ridiculous clocks. In bed, however, for a quarter of a century, he is little more than a verbal mainspring of his timepiece of peas.

Rieux no doubt was sympathetic to Tarrou's ironic copy. Tarrou was sensitive to such incongruities as the plague's seeming to relax at dawn. Dawn, of course, is traditionally a time of hope and promise. The description of the sun as swollen connotes the image of the large swollen buboes which Rieux is many times daily called in to lance. At midday the town has a deserted look; the people are inside and seem like animals burrowing for shelter. Then, at night, the "hectic exaltation" exists, and although Tarrou omits the analogy, it is as if the people were drugged by the presence of a deadly vapor in the air.

Plague is no longer an irritant or even a frightening, shadowy menace. It is a fact and it has firmly rooted itself around Oran's perimeter. The suburbs have steadily felt its growth and have become part of a tightening belt of death that draws together toward the center of the city. Moreover, the disease is no longer merely "plague." It begins to have a diversity and an adaptability belonging to the philosophy of adapting and surviving. The plague seems human in its individuality, in its not being unchangingly classic and therefore combatable. This new variety of plague increases its successful destructiveness by threatening the townspeople with pulmonary innovations. Even the buboes begin to diverge from their initial appearance; now they swell and harden, refusing to burst.

Rieux's task becomes more difficult. In a parallel to his belief that men have individual value, he realizes that once again evil too has its individuality. Oran's enemy is not a textbook villain. It insists on being countered on its own terms, and because of the lack of doctors, Rieux must overtax an already overworked physical endurance. After his work there is little time for his own happiness. He cannot worry his mother, who has absolute faith that her son will always return home. He tells his mother that the day has been "as usual." To his mother, this means that all is well. But imagine what the word must encompass for him. *Usual* involves agonizing dying, shrieking relatives, and an ineffectual and insufficient serum. Rieux's anxiety about his wife intensifies his exhaustion. In an ironic similarity, the doctor's wife is as inoffensively comforting to her husband as he is to his mother. His wife writes that everything is going "as well as can be expected." Her phrasing is as ambiguous and as uncommunicative as the doctor's "as usual."

For the remainder of Chapter 15 Rieux is host to Tarrou and is more explicit concerning his driving, godless optimism. He identifies his mortal foe as creation and its natural processes. Rieux rebels against death, holding it at bay as long as possible, realizing that he will eventually suffer defeat. But for the doctor, a seduction of oneself with the myth of a life beyond death or a destruction of oneself through suicide or apathy can be only the acts of a coward. Death is the adversary of man. To ignore it or to succumb prematurely to it is unworthy of man. After all, man is alone in the universe; he knows of no other worlds nor of a divinity. He is his all and at the mercy of the universe's plagues—suffering, ignorance, and death. Man is his own savior and fashions his own values in terms of intelligence, persistent courage, and a belief in the absolute value of the human individual.

Rieux has not always had these attitudes. They have developed as he began to assert responsibility. Even his doctoring did not grow from a childhood aspiration. To Tarrou, he is rather offhand when he says that he wandered into the profession much as he might have any other. Later, however, he reveals what is probably closer to the truth. Rieux was a workman's son and the medical profession was the most rigorous challenge available. It is easy to imagine a man who now pits himself against the absurdities of the universe as once accepting the challenge that medicine offered. He also confesses to Tarrou the first time he took his profession seriously: when he first watched a patient die.

It is a burden to talk to Tarrou. Rieux is terribly exhausted to try and explain himself in terms of his own values and metaphysics. But he continues and Camus offers a natural image as a kind of stimulus. Rieux stares out the window and sees the vague line of the sea. Within, he senses a vague feeling of kinship with Tarrou and so he makes himself speak seriously with this fellow. In a later chapter, the sea will consecrate this friendship between the two men.

Tarrou, up to now, has been fairly nondescript, but instead of becoming more familiar as the book progresses, he becomes more notable. He offers to organize a civilian corps to act as plague fighters. No one else, besides the doctors, has taken such moral action. Tarrou is the first nonprofessional to commit himself and offer a plan for defense. His commitment is offered at a time when he and Rieux realize that soon the plague will be out of hand and that Oran's few doctors will be obsolete. Rieux recognizes the courage behind such a proposal but he questions Tarrou concerning the "consequence," which is of course probable death. In spite of Rieux's having seen excruciating suffering and dying, he is aware that good intentions have not always considered the grisly reality involved.

Rieux also asks Tarrou to come by next day for an injection before his "adventure." His chances are 1 to 3 for coming out of this undertaking alive. Rieux's motive for offering the advice is realistic and practical, yet his tone has an ironic quality. Tarrou counters with a story about a burial overseer, the sole survivor of a historical plague. He is being ironic in return and implying that life rarely has 1 to 3 logic. To communicate like this is to be seemingly ambiguous, but both men have learned now that the other is aware of man as a being alone in an indifferent world.

Although Tarrou's plan of action is exceptional, Rieux cannot describe its members in such language. It is a fallacy to ascribe heroism to men doing only what they must. Rieux sees Oran in these terms: in an emergency, people are tried and this means that they do what they must — help others and themselves to survive. There is nothing of the heroic in this. It is man's duty to himself and he recognizes this responsibility through clearsightedness. If, because of ignorance, he shirks, then ignorance is vice. Virtue is no more than fulfillment of a commonplace obligation. Real heroics are nonexistent. Neither does Rieux believe that callousness is the general rule. On the whole, he believes that men are more good than bad.

And, as a specific, Chapter 16 offers Grand. Because he is used to dealing with statistics, he is made secretary of the sanitary squads — certainly not a heroic role even though Rieux muses that if readers seek a "hero," Grand has such merit. This is not contradictory. Rieux's values are not those of the military; awards are not given to the foolhardy who fear nothing and accidentally survive an excess of bloody skirmishes. Grand's stature as a hero is equated with his capacity for commitment and the sustaining of that commitment. The heroic is the human.

Grand is thorough in his numerical analyses; he is even creative, taking great pains to plan graphs that will be as lucid as possible. He slacks at times, but he is a man; most of all you should realize this quality about him. He is a man and he is insignificant, has failed to give love, has remorse, has a ridiculous goal, but in this emergency, with quiet courage, he has offered himself and serves as best he can. He does not neglect his writing; through his close association with Rieux, he gains even a sense of humor concerning the precision he works with. Grand is, in his small but meaningful role, more human than the radio announcers who assuringly maintain that the world Out There suffers with Oran. Rieux sees Grand as having crossed a line of indifference and, even with only his little goodness of heart, as having adhered to the human condition. He has moved from the fringes of Oran's social structure into one of its major supports by becoming a part of a common solid unit combating a common enemy.

To review, Chapter 17 is a contrast to Chapter 13. The earlier chapter dealt with Rambert's futile but legal attempts to leave Oran; this chapter is a record of his vain trys to illegally escape. The nature of the underground, Rambert discovers, has all of the intricacies of Oran's official red tape, but his discovery costs him almost all of his hope for personal happiness in escape.

Rambert begins this round of disappointments by contacting Cottard, and by trusting in Cottard, Rambert exhibits a measure of his determination. It is as though he will grasp at straws to return to Paris. Cottard's revelation that he is a blackmailer and a criminal makes little difference to Rambert. But, for Cottard, during their conversation eagerness begins to build steadily. He is anxious for Rambert's friendship and his reason seems logical. Rambert is a journalist; after the plague Cottard will be arrested and he will need all of the character references possible. A journalist in debt to Cottard for his life can be a prime asset.

Rambert's repetition of failures begins with Cottard and moves through Garcia and to Raoul, Gonzales, Marcel, and Louis; with each man's promises Rambert's hopes are bolstered and subsequently burst. Then, between links of the chain of plotting, are days of silence and suspense. Rambert's nerves are worn by the continual tension of belief and uncertainty;

they are also frayed by the heat and the rising death toll. Often his surroundings seem surrealistic: deserted cafes, a rooster defecating on his table, conversation punctuated by a parrot's squawk and interrupted by queries from the dwarf waiter. Men, even with Rambert present, speak of him as though he were a profitable commodity. The city's lazy summer dogs are gone and the streets sizzle in the noon heat. All of the places of rendezvous have this mad, surrealistic atmosphere. At one time Rambert's collaborators insist on meeting in a hospital section of Oran, a section full of wailing relatives, clotted together in hopeful masses, crying for news from within. Another time, preparing the escape plans, the plotters meet near the war memorial—a spot commemorating those who did not escape death and their duty.

Rambert's change of mind to stay in Oran and assist Rieux and Tarrou is the climax of this chapter. The journalist has had to re-evaluate things of importance to him, and Camus is thorough in convincing us that the change, although Rambert continues to nurse a flicker of hope for escape, is genuine. At first the journalist was rational and insistent that he be allowed to leave the city. Failing, he became as rash and fierce as a Don Quixotish figure fighting the quarantine's decree. His goal was to return to the woman he loved. He was never afraid of the plague; as he tells Rieux, he has seen death as a soldier in the Spanish Civil War. Only now, because of the plague, has he honestly faced "what matters." His discovery that Rieux is also without his wife is no doubt the factor that finally transforms his determination to leave immediately into a resolution to stay and help Rieux and Tarrou. For chapters, there has been a dramatic irony in which Rambert has talked to Rieux and sighed for his beloved wife and Paris, then reined in his emotions and muttered to the doctor that he wouldn't understand. Rieux never tells Rambert about his own separation. Tarrou flings the facts in Rambert's face after Rambert has been particularly ugly and maudlin. As the chapter ends, Rambert has given up almost all hope for escape. He will stay until he can find a way of leaving, he says, but he is beginning to perceive that the present requires more serious allegiance and he does, almost totally, pledge himself to it.

There is also a more subtle factor, but one which is important in Rambert's decision. He has tried desperately to escape for one reason: to return to the girl he loves; yet all the while he has been so enmeshed in the escape he has scarcely thought of her. Self-deception, of course, can only be confessed by Rambert. Rieux is the narrator and he does not comment. If Rambert realized that his concern for personal happiness was for himself, he would be making no gross discovery. At heart, most people are primarily concerned with themselves. Theology has tainted this concern with labels of pride and selfishness, but in terms of Rieux's philosophy, there is room for understanding of this desire for human personal happiness. Rieux does not, of course, place his own happiness first, but he understands this desire. He also understands and accepts that he has a different instinct—a higher loyalty to all men in theory and to all men personally. He has accepted this burden of love.

The other important decision in this chapter is made by Paneloux; he agrees to help Rieux and Tarrou. By the end of Part II, then, all of the principal characters—Rieux, Tarrou, Rambert, Grand, and Paneloux—have joined to battle together as plague fighters. The plague has separated Oran from the outside and many of the Oranians from their loved ones, but it has begun to unite men of different temperaments and philosophies and to create a feeling of common humanity among them.

PART THREE

Part III consists of only one chapter—a short, intense chronicle of the crisis weeks in Oran, the time when two natural powers—the plague's rising fever and the midsummer sun—incinerate the city's prisoners. No longer is there active revolt. The panic-generated energy of Part II is gone. Despondency has stultified the population. As the chapter builds in intensity, corpses are piled quietly in ever-higher heaps, and Rieux does not dwell with the monotonous minutes of daily living, waiting, and enduring. His concern here, for the most part, is with the dead and dying, and because most of the section deals with the details of interment, Rieux has, like the Oranians in their task of withstanding the fever and the summer heat, his own test. The dying and the burying of which he must speak have loathsome particulars. Oran's crude mass burials would have tempted most writers to create the most vividly dramatic inferno imaginable, the volume's longest chapter. Rieux, however, controls his sensational subject, writes succinctly, and reports what he saw, not lapsing into melodrama. His sense of objective purpose concerning the chronicle has the same perseverance that he has demonstrated in his doctoring.

Rather than exaggerate, Rieux uses imaginative images and factual realism for the chapter's atmosphere. Once again he uses the words "prisoners" and "prison-house," reminding us of the image most common to Oranians. He describes the summer in provocative detail: the blistering, savage heat, heightened by the dirt storms, transforms the city into a gigantic bake oven, a larger version of the recently reopened crematory on the city's outskirts. One device, he implies, burns the living; the other, the dead.

All of the prisoners' senses are attacked in this chapter. The crematory assails the city with its stench; the skin is parched by drought, the eyes are stung by the dirt, and for weeks the wind shrilly whistles above the town, at times seeming to moan, at other times seeming to wail. Plague makes direct kills on some citizens; but on others it is more devious. The latter must battle on several fronts: fear, panic, and a feeling of exile and separation drain love from the heart; the senses are physically assaulted; the mind suffers major losses of hope and logic. Even imagination fails finally to recall separated loved ones, just as memory eventually succumbs. There is a trance-like adaptation to the plague. Horror reaches a point that fails to horrify any longer; it becomes a kind of monotonous norm, a habit. The Oranians live for the present, but are so despondent and spiritless that they cannot inject their living with meaning. Rieux insists that we not interpret this state as total resignation. There were some new habits to replace the old, and only a few citizens wholly gave up; the former steadfast refusal to be coerced by death is no longer in the city, but in its place is lethargy and a limboish state of waiting and enduring.

The changes within the people and within the city are important elements in this section. The plague, for example, is no longer concentrated in the outer districts. Suddenly it strikes the center of Oran, at its heart. Civil law is no longer effective and the city is under martial law. The acts which necessitate martial law are examples of highest absurdity, only a step below murderous anarchy. The burning of homes is not spontaneous, however. There are symptoms: mounted police gun down pets, symbols of home; first, the symbol is destroyed; later, the home itself. The action of this chronicle always builds; absurdities develop logically into one another toward the final culminating of atrocities in this chapter.

As always, there is irony. Homes are burned by people living on scraps of common sense. The plague proves to be so silent, elusive, and deadly that something has to be done. If serum is not always effective, perhaps germs are harboring in the safest of places—in homes. So homes are burned in moments of breakdown and irrationality. Martial law threatens the offenders, of course, but—with imprisonment. Within the prison of Oran, if a man burns his home, he is legally imprisoned and, once behind bars, certain of death, for nowhere is plague so thorough as it is in the prison-house. The irony increases when we realize that plague initially isolated Oran from the outside world. Then, once inside the city, after it had given the town if not a responsible solidarity, at least a united sense of common trouble, it viciously attacked *not* individuals, but *groups* (prisoners, nuns, monks, soldiers) and caused the members to be in individual quarantined isolation, miniature exiles of their city's exiled state. The chapter also records the separation of Oran into habitable and off-limit districts; the various kinds of separations will increase as the chapter continues.

When Rieux turns to the changes in burial processes, he remarks that his motive for retelling what may seem excessively repulsive is not morbidity. His tone here is defensive, but justifiably so. Especially to an American audience of amateur analysts, many of whom have never seen the systematic strokes of slaughterhouses, much less the chaotic extermination and the seemingly inhuman acts Rieux means to recount, the grossness of the chapter might seem too Gothic for belief. Since Rieux has said earlier that he has told only what happened, his artistic integrity cannot be questioned. Thus an audience of today might interpret his including these scenes as traceable to morbidity or to another neurotic genesis. Freudian divining has popularly replaced the horoscope in contemporary living; each system has labeled sections with precast futures, and Rieux (Camus) was aware that many readers might — even as early as twenty years after, in a comfortable well-civilized country — evaluate this chapter as the dreams of a morbid necrophiliac. Thus his word of caution reminds us that what we are reading is based on fact.

Note particularly in this chapter the circumstances of the burials. The civic authorities, once more, are identified with their endless paper work. Official forms, Rieux says, are the most important part of burials. A satiric attitude toward the men in charge is a convenient viewpoint and perhaps too easily superficial. Although the men seem to be strangling themselves in red tape, they are fighting the plague as efficiently, and often as humanely, as possible.

To forbid vigils is to suggest a lack of feeling, but isolation of corpses is a health precaution. In a similar way, speedy funerals appear to be the end product of a speed-oriented society, but the health factor is paramount. Propriety is the principle behind separate pits for men and women after cemetery plots are filled. Then, of course, when separate pits are impossible, Oran's officials conceive of stratified burial — alternating layers of corpses and quicklime — as the most competent alternative. Even the utilization of streetcars, at night, to transport the dead en masse to the crematory has humane efficiency as its motive. All of these absurd, unbelievable acts are part of a plan to struggle against Oran's enemy; they may seem barbaric, but the plague demands such survival tactics.

And then the worst is over. When the city can withstand no more, the plague begins to level off. Had it continued its killing, Rieux projects, carloads of bodies would have been dumped into the sea. It is interesting that in 1941, when Camus was jotting ideas for the novel in his notebooks, he had decided to have a sea full of corpses. Of course, he was more of a symbolist then. Several years later, he had lived through a world war and an occupation by enemy troops. His country had been witness to bestial atrocities; these he used in this book to serve his literary purpose more effectively than the elaboration of a literary symbol. Although he intends his chronicle as an allegory, he does not sacrifice realism on the primary level for blatant symbolism. To date, man has not resorted to mass sea burials. By 1947, however, open pit interment, filled by the blades of bulldozers, had occurred under Nazi supervision. Camus does not jeopardize his book's strength with exaggeration. His realism includes only acts actually committed by man.

PART FOUR

After recording the particulars of Oranian burials in a complete chapter, in fact in a complete section, Rieux now takes up the situation of those who were living during the period of lethargy. The first half of Chapter 19 describes more fully the drugged state of general despondency, and brings us up to date on the principal characters. It especially examines Dr. Rieux's responses to the exhausting spiritual and physical fatigue. The second half of the chapter is quite different. As a contrast, Cottard, from Tarrou's notebook sketches, is presented, still happy and smiling.

The lethargy refuses to lift itself from Oran. Even the October rains do not cleanse the town of its hold and the townspeople continue to exist for the moment at hand, but see their present without a context. Rieux uses, as an analogy, soldiers held under continual fire and strain. Both suffer similar stupors, he says. This lethargic state of mind lulls Grand into sentimentality; he talks of Jeanne more often and feels deeper remorse. Rambert continues to maintain some hope for escape. Tarrou loses the colorful diversity that was in his early notebooks. Now his subject is primarily Cottard. The narrator reveals several unexpected reactions of his own — unexpected because he is usually reticent about his personal life and unexpected because they are confessions of his feelings of loss. Rieux has so successfully convinced us of his physical and mental strength, neglecting his personal complaints, that he sometimes loses a sense of human individuality. Here he modifies the impression of a superhuman with devoted perseverance. He admits that the plague has fiercely exhausted him and that he has had to harden himself as a preventive against collapse. Under the strain of growing deaths and the increasing ineffectiveness of his serum, he feels less and less competent. At the same time, he questions whether or not in the face of this growing futility, his decision to send his wife to a far-away mountain sanitarium was wise. He is certain that he could have helped her make a good recovery.

This chapter re-humanizes Rieux; he feels a lump in his throat as he stares at the collapsed sleeping position of his colleague, Dr. Castel. Rieux even talks to Grand of his personal feelings, something he has never done before. He cannot say whether or not the plague is more fierce than it was yesterday; he can only measure his own competence, and the result is negative. Medical aid grows more meager. He can only diagnose; he cannot cure. Throughout the epidemic he has resisted death as thoroughly and as rapidly as he could save his patients. Now, however, his serum is losing its strength and his own physical vigor is wasting.

Ironically, Rieux concludes that because his strength is being sapped, so he is being saved from perhaps overwhelming sentiment and pity. Confrontation with such extreme disaster might strike down a man with alert senses and sentiment. Previously, at the beginning of Part II, he had noted that most of the Oranians were saved from disastrous panic because of their lack of pity. Now he remarks that he is saved from disastrous sentiment because of exhaustion.

Rieux clarifies another misfortune of the lethargic state—the slackening of Tarrou's medical crews. No longer do they take personal precautions of hygiene and vaccination; their sense of self-preservation is slipping away.

Obviously Cottard—criminal, black marketeer, and fugitive—is a dramatic contrast to this infectious weariness, and because of Cottard's uniqueness, Rieux includes a few of the sections of Tarrou's notebooks which center on this fellow. Cottard is rather patriarchal in his pity and affection for the townspeople. He has already suffered the fear of distrust and insecurity; the present despair of Oran makes him somewhat of an elder citizen. And, like an older member of the community, he most enjoys hobnobbing with the younger set, walking at night, joining the flow of the crowds into theaters and coffeehouses.

Yet one can be somewhat objectively sympathetic toward this human rarity. He most fears what many people do: solitude and the feeling of being an outsider. For the first time, he belongs; he has a niche in the human condition. He also has a clever logic rationalizing his own immunity. He theorizes that he cannot contract the plague because he carries his own death sentence and men never die of two illnesses. One infection immunizes a man from all other infections.

The concluding scene is, somehow, amusing—perhaps because it seems so apt. Nothing less than a highly ironic Creator, in this case Camus, would have trapped the opera company of *Orpheus* within Oran when the gates were sealed. The opera contains the identical elements that the citizens are experiencing. Orpheus' laments and Eurydice's vain appeals from Hell are ordinary, common Oranian acts. The theme of lovers separated is exact, current realism. It is little wonder that the opera is performed again and again, and is popular and successful during the season of plague. Even the actor portraying Orpheus catches the rhythms of his surroundings and improvises an extreme grotesqueness for his final position of defeat. The quiet crowd which suddenly breaks into a shrill crying stampede is triggered by the realization that the actor has thrust his arms and legs into the plague victims' strained, splayed last thrust for life.

The plague, for the present, offers life to Cottard. But to no one else has it been so instantly gratuitous. It has forced Grand to reconsider his entire past, particularly his lost marriage and the values of his present daily living; it has tested Dr. Rieux's belief and devotion to his job of keeping Oran alive and it has also revealed his human failings. Tarrou's plan of the civilian sanitary squads was conceived because of the plague's dramatic emergency. All these men have changed; unlike Cottard, each of them has sworn to maintain a personal revolt against the monstrous disease that threatens their city's entire population. But two characters have yet to be fully tested: Rambert and Paneloux. Both have enlisted as plague fighters, but Rambert's offer was not quite a wholehearted pledge and Paneloux's decision came from Christian duty, not from a love for man or from a crusading spirit of Good versus Evil; his faith is tried in a later chapter. Chapter 20 is crucial to Rambert's integrity.

Chronologically, Chapter 20 precedes most of 19; the latter, however, was used as an overall review of characters after the crisis, plus the notebook jottings about Cottard, and for a graphic look at one of Oran's centers of pleasure. The brief theater scene is crucial because unhappiness, sickness, and poverty are becoming Oran's daily tenor and Oranians are therefore seeking out the last bits of pleasure in the city.

Chapter 20 is not general like 19, nor does it deal with several different matters. Rambert is stage-center throughout. The chapter is structured in this way: Rambert contacts Gonzales and his agents, then discusses his leaving with Rieux. Afterward he meets the Spanish agents and, before leaving, returns to Rieux. Returning to Rieux, of course, is synonymous with his decision to stay in Oran until the plague is defeated and the gates are once more open.

Although Rambert still retains some hope of escape, there are hints in the chapter that foreshadow his decision to stay. Another two weeks of waiting grate deeper into his residue of hope, and his long hours on the sanitation squad fatigue him but make him aware of the value of work versus a life of idleness. He now talks little about his plans of escape; no longer does he boast. When his nerves at last shatter, he runs toward the sea crying to his wife and this release of emotion is his last genuine grasp for happiness. Afterward, he walks through the last phases of the plans for escape, but silently considering, listening to others and to himself.

It is not surprising that Rambert is caught off-guard by Rieux's telling him to hurry if he means to escape. Rieux is not an absolutist in his humanitarianism. Nor has he evolved a finished philosophy concerning his actions during the plague. He has acted and has listened to his heart and his conscience. Rationally he knows he could have escaped with his wife, supervised her convalescence, and claimed that he was only doing what was his by "right of happiness." But Rieux would not have been happy; happiness is of relative value. Thus he says to Rambert that the journalist would not be happy if he stayed, that he would be dishonest with himself and with Rieux. Rambert, it seems, expected a sermon from Rieux; he wanted urging. The decision, however, to be valuable has to be Rambert's own. Rieux, an atheist, tells Rambert to claim his happiness and as a counterpoint, the mother of the two Spanish boys, a devout Catholic, gives Rambert essentially the same advice. She too understands why he must return to his wife: the girl is pretty, Rambert is sensual; he does not believe in God, man must worship and believe in something—even if it is no more than a girl, himself, and their love.

Rieux was absolutely correct to juxtapose these two scenes. Usually the abyss separating believers and nonbelievers is thought to divide two views of man, totally incompatible with one another. Yet here both sides wish Rambert to be honest and to be happy. An educated atheist and an illiterate Catholic mother elect to stay in Oran, yet they understand Rambert's desire to leave and will not damn him for preferring personal happiness.

The image Rieux uses during the suspense of Rambert's decision-making is that of a caged animal—not a particularly original image, but excellent for his purpose. Rambert is caged because he has wanted desperately to leave, but has stayed, worked with the sanitation crews, and found a value in hard work and a satisfaction in becoming part of a whole bigger than himself combatting an impartial, impenetrable, deadly plague. He is trapped within high, sealed city walls and he has tested their strength; they seem as sturdy as the plague. His animal-like qualities include the importance of sex to him. He wishes to return to Paris to make love to his wife. Until now, he had never realized how much he enjoyed and needed love-making. Rambert is physically virile, animal-like, and powerfully built. His bare chest is described as glistening with sweat, like polished wood, as he paces. In Camus' novels, sex is never the fulcrum that it is in other contemporary fiction. Either it is matter of fact or else mentioned in passing. Rambert enjoys a sensual life and it is important to realize that Rieux understands this desire. It is a fallacy to see the doctor as a valiant, asexual knight in surgeon's clothing.

The final scene in the hospital has, besides Rambert's affirmation, several other matters of importance. Tarrou has caught Rieux's frustration. Both men begin to feel that their revolts are becoming obsolete. Tarrou says that the doctors are becoming accountants. Rieux remarked similarly when he talked of the evacuations and the burials in Chapter 19.

The hospital is described as being pale green inside and the light as being like that of an aquarium. Hospitals are usually places of rest where one recovers his strength. They are like the sea in the sense that it is therapy for Rieux to swim; soon he and Tarrou will renew their determination and perseverance while swimming together, in rhythm. The hospital Rieux remembers as being not promising, not restorative and not recreative, like the sea. Instead, it is like an aquarium, like an imprisoned sea where the patients are once again locked in. Here, behind barred windows, they are imprisoned within the hospital exactly as they are imprisoned within their city. They die in the stagnant hot air that is also held prisoner.

The talk about the car running out of rationed gas and Tarrou's speculation that they'll have to walk the next day is an obvious parallel to the professional situation of Rieux and Tarrou. Their serum supply and its effectiveness is "running out of gas." They'll have to walk, might fall behind, and perhaps perish in the heat and fever of Oran's desert.

After Rambert tells Rieux that he will stay, we probably learn more about Rieux than we do about Rambert. The doctor questions him, testing his sincerity, and says that nothing is worth the exchange of whomever one loves. But this is Rieux's mind talking and he confesses that he has contradicted his statement by his actions. He doesn't know why he sent his wife away. He simply acted. There seemed to be no choice and he says that he has not examined yet why he did it. Immediately thereafter he and Tarrou assign Rambert to the surveillance of one of the city's districts. There are to be no congratulations and toasts for Rambert's conversion. The plague is still rampant and must be continuously contested.

After the chapter describing the mass burials, Chapter 21 is probably next most successful in catching our sympathy for the plague victims. It is a chapter which gives us a full-length portrait of a dying child; it is also the record of Dr. Rieux's first witnessing of the entire last stages of the disease. Never before has he so minutely observed the tortured last hours before death. He is specific about his reactions. As he searches for the child's pulse, he feels an instinctive empathy attempting to pour his own strength into the boy; he aches to scream in protest against such vile injustice. His revolt against death and disease is a kind of madness, he says, but he insists on the child's innocence. We, like Dr. Rieux, have seen until now only glimpses of death and last moments — never the full process of death.

Camus could have, without seeming awkward, described a lengthy death scene long before this. Rieux, being the narrator-doctor, might likely have sat at a bedside and early initiated us to the cries and contortions of suffering. But he deferred this scene until the reason for presenting it was crucial. The reason for this particular vigil is much more genuine than the simple disposition of Rieux into a sickroom would have been. The scene is inserted when Rieux is losing his endurance; in addition it regroups — besides Rieux — Tarrou and Rambert, plus Grand, Dr. Castel, and Father Paneloux together as multiple witnesses (and sufferers) of the death throes of M. Othon's young child. We have the opportunity to know all of their reactions, which won't be first terrified impressions, but will come from hearts already seasoned to death and suffering.

All of these characters are called to Othon's home to watch a last-resort experiment of Dr. Castel's new serum on the boy. If the serum is not effective, it is possible that plague will prove to be the victor. After the boy dies, there is general blank depression, but there is also a bit of optimism. Castel is impressed by the serum's lengthening of the suffering period. There seems to be a strengthening of resistance even if it eventually fails. This effect, you should note, also lengthens the chapter for readers, making us more exactly imagine the swelling, the convulsions, and the incessant screaming.

The young boy, even though he is unsuccessful, wages his own small revolt aginst the plague. Castel's serum gives him additional strength to endlessly scream in protest against the invisible death that burns and bites into his flesh. He fights and dies in a classroom, a room where he should have come for growing and maturing. On the blackboard, like a Camus crest, is a half-obliterated equation. Equations add up; they equilibrate and are based on logic. Nothing in Rieux's moral code will admit an equation that calls for an innocent child to suffer. The utmost in abominable evil is exactly what he is witnessing: the suffering of a young innocent child—conclusive proof for him that the universe is irrational and indifferent to man. No divine equation is possible, and so the logic of equations is almost obliterated. Paneloux's sermon linking sin with punishment will later be partially obliterated by a new philosophy after he is witness to the innocent suffering of this child in a schoolroom. At present, the priest is visibly shaken by the ordeal; Rieux's anger disturbs him, and although he answers the doctors dogmatically, the boy's death will ferment within him and he will reconsider Rieux's angry assertion that because of the child's innocence they have been joined and bonded.

The motif of separation is once again used in this chapter. The boy's parents accept Rieux's diagnoses with quiet terror and acquiescence. The father is sent to an isolation camp; the mother and daughter are confined to the quarantine hospital. Plague continues to multiply separation and exile.

Paneloux, because of the extreme philosophy in his second sermon, is even touched by this quality of the exile. We should be aware of the nurture period for this change in the man. It was not long after his "sin = punishment" sermon that the priest became a diligent member of Tarrou's plague fighters. And once at work he no longer supervised quiet last rites. Punishment, if he could still call Oran's suffering by that name, was no longer an abstract threat: it was visual, disgusting, and a fact. Rieux is aware of the priest's outer composure as well as the fear that grows beneath the skin. Death threateningly crackles around him and the priest knows that inoculations are never foolproof. His faith in divine vengeance is worn thin by the time he witnesses the death of M. Othon's child. Because he is no longer comfortable with his ready-made store of threats, he begins to question the basis of his faith. He begins to construct sermons from his doubts. Like Grand's gradual evaluation of his marriage and his literary work, Paneloux's quest for honesty begins. It is more thorough and serious in its consequences, but as necessary and as difficult as Grand's.

Paneloux was not alone in questioning his faith. The townspeople are confused and Rieux notes the reduced audience for Paneloux's sermon to the men. His congregation had generally decided in favor of prophecies, numerology, and speculative charms. The church offered little understanding and hope for their plight. The people seem to need an external order that is reassuring. If the church becomes distasteful, they turn to nature's logic and to mathematical chances and schemes. They are persistent in seeking a logical answer to their torment and a logical end to its massacre. Irrationality is generally denied.

Since his work as a plague fighter, Paneloux no longer speaks particularly loudly or distinctly. His gentle voice now says "we" instead of "you"; he has joined the ranks of his community. He is no longer one of the crimson-robed elite; his clothes have been stained by Oran's bloody suffering and Paneloux has been humbled. He has realized that death is not a symbolic angry fist in the heavens and he reminds his audience of its tangible presence. The change in Paneloux, since his earlier sermon, is largely this: suffering does not necessarily imply punishment; it is for Christian good and offers a trial during which we must continue to believe in God's plan. The plague's image has changed from that of a whip to that of a teacher. Living has been easy; this phase is for rededication. Once Paneloux would have assured the congregation of the eternal happiness waiting as the wages of suffering. No longer. He cannot loudly preach such promises because he has become uncertain. He can only believe that God has a reason that is unfathomable but that there exists a holy logic that must be trusted. He asks for complete belief in God or else a complete denial of God, an All or Nothing proposition. Paneloux's acknowledging that God is testing man's faith is akin to Rieux's viewing the plague as a test of one's humanity and integrity. Neither man asks for resignation and both desire active acts of faith. Paneloux asks that his congregation pray for a completion of the divine will, and in the meantime to trust completely in God's plan for good. He brings to his sermon many examples of the Church's reactions to previous plagues. It is evident that he has done a great deal of thinking and considering before this assessment of Oran's catastrophe. Above all, the priest maintains that God must be loved. Man must not allow unfathomable suffering to lessen his passion for God. Man must approve of God's will and make it his own.

Tarrou approves of the extreme position which Paneloux has taken for himself. In the army he has seen priests faced with Paneloux's dilemma. There too either a priest approved of the gross agony of death he saw as a part of God's good or else he denied everything.

Paneloux's faith, however, tests itself even more severely. The pamphlet mentioned by the young deacon suggests that Paneloux is considering not only the plague's illness, but simple sickness itself. His logic is this: if man is ill, then that illness is a part of God's plan. Doctors, by issuing medicine and performing surgery interrupt God's processes, a heresy. Rieux, you should note, sees his work as an interruption also — not of God's plan, however, but of death's irrationality.

When Paneloux is stricken, he abides by his city's regulations and asks to be taken to the hospital, but in the early stages of his sickness, he refuses a doctor's help. Strangely, the symptoms are not ordinary. His throat is clotted with a choking substance; later he looks as if he has been thrashed. (By the flail of God that whips the air over Oran? By his own questioning faith?)

The ambiguousness of his death is best interpreted as the result of a conscious will at work. Paneloux has seen such a variety of undeserved dying that he affirms the rightness of such suffering by joining the victims in their role in God's plan.

After three dramatic chapters, Chapter 23 begins quietly on All Souls' Day, November 1. Winter has not yet arrived to hopefully freeze the plague germs. Autumn is mild; a cool breeze replaces the hot shrill whistling of summer and the light is no longer blinding. The fall sky is pale and golden. Beauty, after being charred by the summer, surrounds the city of pestilence. Again, the irony of natural beauty is played against natural ugliness and death. This is a fairly common irony, especially in this book, but here it is used as a transition into another incongruity. The mass conversion of Oranians to superstition has clothed them even on mild days in oil-cloth raincoats because two centuries previously doctors had recommended them. Imagine how the city must have looked from above with its absurdly shiny, rubberized, uniformed citizenry.

Even a greater incongruity, however, than the raincoat costumes in the plague city is the lack of men and women carrying flowers to the cemeteries. Remembrance of death is no longer a once-a-year day. Dying has assumed such major proportions that one can almost say that life seems the exception. Absurdity, irony, and incongruity are increasingly the constant atmosphere of the city. Even Cottard, Tarrou notes, begins to toss off ironic comments. And Rieux adds his own, remarking that the crematory was blazing as merrily as ever; the plague seems as efficient as a civil servant, he says.

Dr. Richard proves in this chapter that even an educated physician can become as absurd as the plague. As the disease achieves the quality of an efficiency expert, he is relieved at its leveling out on the progress charts. The number of deaths has less importance than the fact that no longer is the toll mounting. Just as the populace looked for logic in the Church, in horoscopes, and superstitions, Richard (and the townspeople, we may assume, had he been allowed to inform them) hopes that an equation can be assumed concerning the plague's progress. His relieved optimism and his new sense of happiness in the face of plague seems impossible. Certainly absurd, but true. Dr. Castel is uncertain. His serum is being lauded, but he has learned not to trust his enemy and maintains his defense and his revolt against the illogical visitor. Castel survives, but with efficient irony the plague disposes of Richard, the optimistic doctor. Then, curiously, it allows itself to be more exactly diagnosed into two definite forms: pulmonary and bubonic. The latter is disappearing, the former becoming more frequent.

Still summarizing, Rieux notes the profiteering based on, in addition to raincoats, food supplies. A change has taken place once more in the social levels of Oran. Previously the city has been indiscriminately attacked. Now the rich can afford the steep prices, the poor cannot. Despondency naturally begins to give way to envy and protests. Journalists, as Rieux has noted, continue to defraud the public of truth. Camus, during his career as a journalist under wartime conditions, had been no doubt witness to many incidents of journalistic Yes-writers. Because Rieux uses more of Tarrou's notebooks at this point, we can probably assume that the truth about Oran is probably impossible to ascertain if one were to consult its newspapers during the plague period.

The notebook passages concerning one of the isolation camps has an interesting twist. The stadium is used as an isolation camp because it is large enough to accommodate the many quarantined family members. But remember this: the Oranians think of themselves as prisoners, encased within their city; here, they are again imprisoned. There is a coil-like pattern to their prison image, much like the maze pattern of their streets. The stadium once served as an arena for athletic events. Now it is filled with people sparring for life. Death can deliver swift punches; it is a formidable opponent. Escape is impossible; armed sentries guard the exits. The suspense is somewhat like the stadium fever of old Rome.

Tarrou visits the stadium with Rambert and Gonzales, two former football players, and the contrasts between the past and the present are more evident because of the presence of these men. The primary difference is the present lack of activity. The men in the stadium now do nothing and they are silent. The shouting football activity is gone. Instead of a rowdy, spirited comradeship, there is a core of silent distrust; anyone may be carrying death within him. There is also a feeling of futility. They can hear the sounds of life beyond the walls and, like Rambert, they have devised so many plans for escape. Then, after defeat, they have realized that they have thought so continuously of escape that they have failed to think of the loved ones they hoped to rejoin.

Tarrou's inability to tell M. Othon of his boy's suffering is humanitarian, but all men in the stadium know of the suffering that the plague produces. Othon asks for the impossible and is surely aware of what he is asking for.

Tarrou pities him; Othon is a judge and should have a measure of objectivity, but he has proven to be as vulnerable as anyone else. Staring at the setting sun he seems resigned, lost, and asking for kind favors.

Winter approaches but the plague does not abate. The only improvement seems to be the clean shine of the cold air. Rieux notes this fresh quality at the beginning of Chapter 24 and remembers the old Spaniard remarking about its pleasant coolness. The night scene on the terrace, as Tarrou and Rieux relax, is another juxtaposition of a pleasant natural world in contrast with the town, sleeping and dying during the night.

Rieux's response to the evening is given more space here than the brief, ironic asides he has earlier slipped into his narrative. The slow-paced, relaxed style also contains fewer contrasts of opposites. There seems to be a longer time for looking and contemplation. The quiet night is indeed satisfying, but not absolutely so. Sky and sea meet grayly and stars are tarnished by the lighthouse's yellow gleam. Night is beautiful, yet flawed. The universe is not always blatantly superior; it too has its moods and imperfections.

On the terrace above the city, Rieux and Tarrou share what Robert Frost speaks of in his poem "Birches." There are times when it is not cowardly, but natural and necessary to want to swing high and away on birch branches, and

> ". . . get away from earth awhile
> And then come back to it and begin over."

This isn't the desire of a recluse but of a man who needs a time-out. The doctor has spent seven months in continual taut revolt and he is aware that his perseverance is fraying. His angry lash at Paneloux, the irritation of doubts about his wife's recovery — all these he diagnoses as danger signs. There seems even to be a more satisfying act performed by Rieux and Tarrou than merely "getting away." Tarrou calls it "taking an hour off for friendship." The time away is not spent alone; it is enjoyed with someone who shares one's own values and beliefs.

Also in this chapter is more necessary background information about Tarrou. So far, we know hardly anything. Rieux has not explained; he has allowed us to know only what he knew before this night. Thus far we know that Tarrou appeared in Oran, kept notebooks, did not try to escape, and volunteered to organize the civilian plague fighters. He has been as steadfast in his struggle to cure as Rieux has been.

The father Tarrou describes to Rieux had, in Tarrou's words, a peculiarity: although he seldom traveled, he knew the arrival and departure times for all trains that stopped in Paris; in addition, he knew the changes that must be made if one wanted to go as far, say, as Warsaw. Tarrou's mention of this side of the man's personality and later Rieux's speaking of it suggest that it was not altogether an oddity. Both Tarrou and Rieux believe in and defend the value of each human individual. The hobby of Tarrou's father, insignificant and seeming strange to others, is definitive. All people have a personal "something" that might seem ridiculous to anyone else, yet it is a kernel of their individuality. Some people believe that they keep a cleaner house than anyone else on the block, others can hold their liquor better, and still others believe that they can appreciate a musical performance more sensitively than anyone else in the audience. In that same audience may be a woman who knows that she is wearing the most expensive diamonds there. All people have a sense of pride in some facet of their individuality, which if confessed to would no doubt sound peculiar, but to Rieux, they are symbolic of the valuable intrinsic worth that comes with one's birth.

Tarrou's reaction to a court trial before he actually witnessed a session was much like the Oranians' thoughts of death — vague and abstract. Even Dr. Rieux, you should remember, although he had treated victims for several months, had not fully experienced the plague's death throes until he watched the process take place within Jacques Othon. Tarrou's sympathy for the defendant was very much like that which Camus felt for a boatload of prisoners he saw in the Algerian port in 1938. Both men were confounded by the knowledge that these unfortunates had committed crimes and yet both Tarrou and Camus refused to assent to the verdict of punishment by death. Camus described his feelings in an editorial, saying that endless imprisonment was tantamount to death; thus he was grieved and felt that somehow it was as unjust to damn human beings for the rest of their lives as it was to take their lives as payment for crimes committed.

The disgust which Tarrou conveys in recounting the trial proceedings — the euphemisms for beheading, the duty of condemnation expertly pronounced by his father in a matter-of-fact fashion — is found in greater detail in Camus' essays on justice and death penalties in *Resistance, Rebellion, and Death*. Both men had early experienced the conviction that one human being may not demand the life of another. Tarrou's realization that even idealistic social revolutions shoot down the old order hardened his resolve never to harm another human being. Now that we have his story, we can understand the genesis of his early remark that he wants only to find peace of mind; he is haunted by the idea that he might be party to a kind of murder if he actively commits himself. His kindness to Cottard, his saying that he gives people chances—these few verbal hints at last take on meaning. Camus, of course, was himself troubled with Tarrou's dilemma. If he supported the French underground to demolish, for instance, a troop train he would be aiding his defeated country in its struggle against the enemy. But troop trains are full of drafted soldiers following orders and taking no pleasure in war. May one kill individually innocent human beings, even during a war, with good conscience?

Because Tarrou aids Rieux, he is often confused with the doctor. His helping Rieux stems from the monumental emergency situation and from his friendship and respect for the doctor. But Rieux wages active revolt. Tarrou's revolt consists in not joining forces with the pestilence. As nearly as possible he attempts to remain innocent. Rieux, following his conscience, cannot; he must act regardless of accidental blunders. Tarrou is attempting a mortal sainthood. Rieux says that he is attempting to be only a man. Tarrou's answer that he is less ambitious is exactly what Rieux said to Paneloux, after the priest had said that his goal was man's salvation. They are a strange kind of trinity: Paneloux, Rieux, and Tarrou. One seeks salvation for man, one seeks a definition of man through action, the other quests for a godless sainthood for himself.

Winter fails to freeze the plague germs but not the city's walls. Chinks begin to appear, metaphorically. More cases of the pulmonary type of plague become easier to treat; patients become more cooperative. M. Othon, the judge, asks to be sent back to the quarantine camp. He, too, has ceased to feel alone in his sorrow and has assumed the civic burden of a plague fighter. Letters can now be clandestinely sent and received. The outside world seems closer in spite of the dreary Christmas season with its empty shop windows, its deserted streets, and the robot-like citizens.

Grand's surviving the plague's ravishes is much like a rebirth. Plague offered crucial questions that had to be answered. The clerk does have a potential for a life beyond the boundaries of statistics and graphs. A sense of humor, objectivity, and responsibility are all tested and proven during his illness. Before the plague he had been another man, but now he has begun a letter to Jeanne, has demanded that Rieux burn years of accumulated manuscript. He makes a fresh start with his sentence.

The other recoveries in Oran are, as Rieux says, against all the rules. But this is how the plague began—against all the rules. It had been ousted from civilized countries and had no reason for attacking Oran. Nor were its symptoms exactly that of other plagues. Part IV closes with the ambiguity of the rats' return, but the implications are clear: rats are able to live again in Oran. The plague has begun its retreat.

PART FIVE

Oran does not begin to jubilate immediately at the first signs of the plague's waning. Hope has become so slender that it cannot bear the weight of sudden happiness. It must be strengthened with caution and a degree of fear. In spite of the plague's diminishing, Chapter 26 is not a cheerful one. Nursing their own hopes, the Oranians ignore the deaths of the scores of new victims. The weekly statistics remain all-important, but only as they reflect a dropping off of the total number of deaths. To be among first victims or even to be struck down at the plague's peak is to gain sympathetic thoughts, yet now that freedom and victory seem forthcoming, death appears more outrageous.

The blue winter sky may be taken as a sign of promise. Of course, had the plague still been rampant, the same sky would have seemed to be healthily jeering. But currently Castel's serum begins to be effective and the universe seems suddenly acquiescent, not almighty and indifferent.

Rieux refers in this chapter to the number of wild escape attempts that occur. Here he is being sociologically accurate. Oran had certainly been prison-like and most escape attempts occur during the last weeks of the sentence; temptation increases until common sense is overpowered. Once again the communal life of the convents is restored and although this seems very much like new pockets of self-exile, it is evidence that men are able to once more live without breathing death onto one another. Man is free to once again effect his own exile if he wishes. The plague has given him a chance for examination of his values; he must now rebuild his future in terms of what he has learned.

Rieux's images continue to be consistent. Earlier he had referred to Oran as an "island of the damned." Now he says that the inhabitants are like a "shipload of survivors." Time, he implies, isolated them, surrounding them with endless days of terror; now they are setting out on this sea of time toward the future.

Returning to thoughts of Cottard, Rieux ponders the validity of Tarrou's notes on the black marketeer, wondering at their increasing subjectivity. But Rieux himself is guilty of occasional lapses. As the plague became more abominable, he revealed himself more fully and openly. Tarrou's diaries also contain passages concerning Rieux's mother, who reminds

Tarrou of his own. He does not say that the women were saints, yet they have many qualities that Tarrou associates with his pattern of sainthood. Both women were humble, simple, gentle, and kind. They had a "dimness," he says. Perhaps this dimness is because they withdrew. Rieux's mother stays inside, is devoted to her son, and does not overly concern herself with the deaths outside. Tarrou is unable to do this, but he seeks reasons and justifications for the beauty of such withdrawal because it contains no harm for others and he is terribly afraid of committing an act against another human being.

Cottard remains unique. Rieux says that he does not share the high spirits of the city; no longer does he feel an indefinite lease on life. Death, not life, is promised him as soon as the city gates are opened. As the Oranians begin to come out of their burrows, he retreats and stays in his room more frequently.

Tarrou's remark that a return to a "normal" life means new movies is not that of a cynic. It is realistic. New movies will only be one of the many commercial changes, but he has chosen movies because of their illusion. Once more people can share someone else's life for two hours; they can leave their unexciting evenings and live through colorful, musically sung romantic ups and downs, or live the vicarious adventures of a secret service agent, even live, for two hours, within the filmed world of a plague. Whatever illusions they pay for will cost everyone the same amount of coins and at a predetermined time the illusion will be over. Life is being returned to the people and once again they can afford a variety of silverscreen illusions. After all, the return to life after the gates are opened will have all the outer aspects of Before. Yet even this will be an illusion. On each heart, in varying degrees, will be scars of the plague and each Oranian will have somewhat of a new dimension as an individual.

The chapter ends with the disappearance of Cottard. Fleeing into the night, he no doubt knows that his running is futile. Tarrou's diary ends, Rieux tells us, with his sensing an end. His tiredness is not ordinary; plague has entered his body. Both men, Cottard and Tarrou, are sensitive to the symptoms.

Rieux, in Chapter 28, relaxes and, like the Oranians, shares the prospect of a fresh start and a reunion with his wife. Absurdities will continue however. Tarrou's illness, the headache and a raging thirst are warnings that he will not survive Oran's plague. Rieux has never before refused to isolate a patient, but he keeps Tarrou in his room. Why Tarrou dies before the book's end is speculative, but perhaps this breaking of rules is significant.

Perhaps also Tarrou has always been, as he said in Part IV, too much on the "victims' side." This death, like Paneloux's is unique. The priest's death showed no definite symptoms of plague. Tarrou's, on the other hand, has an extreme conjunction of both forms—the swollen buboes and the pulmonary attacks. Just as Tarrou had advocated living—in silent courageous struggle against a murderous mankind, so he struggled against the plague. Othon's son had twisted violently. Tarrou is unmoving; he fights with silent concentration. At the bedside, Rieux notes ironically that the night sounds seem remarkably like those of a plague-free city. He imagines seeing the last flinches of the plague burning the body before him. Tarrou may be the epidemic's last victim. Perhaps this too is unlikely, absurd, and as irrational as he knew life to be.

Rieux is again reminded of his impotence to hold off the mightiest ravages of death. He has survived the plague and the rigorous exertion it demanded, but he is no more than human; he is weak, saddened, and can continue only to fight absurdly. But if Tarrou's death has saddened him, it has also raised new resolve for the doctor to continue his stopgap measures against death. His defiance has fresh conviction. It is his fresh start.

Rieux reflects on his failure to fully give and respond to love and what he says is very much like what Grand confessed—that he never was sufficiently physical and verbal to Jeanne. Rieux's and his mother's lives are somewhat like that. And neither Rieux nor Tarrou was given an opportunity to share a deep continuing friendship with each other. Perhaps, however, during the plague the two men helped each other more freely, willingly, and with more sympathy than would have otherwise been possible. Both men were of ironic temperaments, personalities which do not lend easily to simple affection. Before the plague Rieux was busy and Tarrou was aloofly inspecting the city. It is doubtful that the friendship Rieux contemplates could have been effected. The death of Rieux's wife is joined to the suffering he undergoes following Tarrou's death. He is brief about it, as he was about the worst days of the plague. Excessive grief and real love seldom find adequate words.

The remaining chapters of Part V are much like listening to the recording of a radio commentator who was present at the reopening of the city. New and old faces flow in and out of the railway arteries and Rieux especially is observant of the reunited lovers. Throughout the chronicle he has commented on the townspeople's failure before the plague to attain a more varied, joyous, appreciative sense of life. Thus if one were to paraphrase a common fault, it would be easy to say that they failed to "appreciate the moment." Now, he sees lovers wishing to slow their new moments into slow motion so as to savor all of its thrill. Memories will no longer be static faces and tableaux. They will be of flesh and blood again. Minutes are too quick for them. The slow motion of swimming through time would be more satisfying as they rush toward one another.

Rambert is used as an example of the change wrought within the people of Oran. Once an outsider, a stranger, he has become part of this community and is aware that he can no longer be oblivious to consideration beyond himself.

Rieux also describes those who returned and found no one waiting. For them the plague will remain. Like the last victims, these people are lost and ignored in the bursting of cannons and reunited love. But for the majority of Oran, today is timeless. Tomorrow clocks will cut the day into pieces, but today is a day that will never again exist. Rieux rings Oran's numerous church bells for us, colors the sky gold and blue; fraternity catches fire as was never possible during the siege. The misery of even yesterday is diminished. Someday it will be partly denied, but for the present human love is violently rekindled.

Rieux, revealing his identity, explains that perhaps his greatest temptation in writing the chronicle was to make it a record of his personal struggle. He has tried, however, to show himself as only a part of a large, suffering community.

He ends his chronicle not on the ecstatic, crowded city of new lovers, but by finishing Cottard's curious history for us. The plague-reprieved criminal has gone mad amid the loud happiness outside his window, firing into the crowd, attempting to destroy the gaiety that means his doom. The dog he kills is curiously like himself. Both have survived by being kept in hiding. Cottard is carried out loudly protesting and is vocally reminiscent of a plague victim. His arms are pinioned and he screams convulsively.

Grand has written to Jeanne, something he could never have accomplished without the plague's baring the truth about himself. His humor, as he says that he has done away with his adjectives, is also good news. His subject and verb are unburdened and can move as freely as he now seems able to.

Choosing to close the book with the old Spaniard's philosophy gives assent, at least in part, to its wisdom. The asthma patient recognizes that plague is sometimes little more than life and that combatting it is of no more importance than combatting daily injustices. He prophesies that much will be forgotten and, of course, much will. Life is always more important than the past and its dead; memorials can be erected to clear one's forgetful conscience.

The celebration's firerockets are spectacularly awesome. Only yesterdays ago death was described by such adjectives. Then the sky was colored by crematory smoke and life was razed by fiery temperatures. Rieux has written his book as a reminder of just such incongruities as a warning that "normal" times are always subject to plague, that the bacillus of tyrants and war most easily infect and destroy a nation ignorant of symptoms and consequences.

CHARACTER ANALYSES

DR. BERNARD RIEUX

The narrator is about thirty-five years old. He is a highly respected surgeon, but Tarrou thinks that he might pass more easily for a Sicilian peasant. For example, Rieux's hands are not long and sensitively surgeon-like, but broad, deeply tanned, and hairy. Rieux is of moderate height and broad-shouldered; he has dark steady eyes, a big, well-modeled nose, and thick, tight-set lips. His black hair is clipped very close.

He belongs to a small group of people whom Tarrou calls "true healers." While there is still time for him to leave Oran and join his wife, he refuses. He remains in Oran to fight the plague with all his talent and strength. There is nothing heroic about his actions. He fights death and disease because he has been trained to and because he conceives of his life having value only when he is continuing to help others combat death and achieve health. There are only two evils for Rieux — death and man's ignorance of it.

About his personal relationships with his wife and mother, Rieux has misgivings. His love for mankind is consummated daily, yet to those for whom he is husband and son, he feels that he is probably inadequate. During the plague's last stages he regrets not giving more physical and vocal affection. Rieux's flaws, including his exhaustion and his tears when Tarrou dies, are necessary for a correct interpretation of his character. He says in the chronicle that he has told only what was experienced by all, that he has not made the book a highly personal confession. He does not separate himself or his duty from that of every man. Rieux tries to be definitely human — no more, no less.

FATHER PANELOUX

The priest interprets the sudden plague as just punishment for the sins of his congregation. He is vividly adamant during his sermon and further confuses an already puzzled, fearful populace. Later, after enrolling in the plague fighters' battalion, he has direct contact with day after day of poisoned, contorted victims. Death and plague are no longer easy abstracts. After witnessing the long, agonizing death of a child, Jacques Othon, he reassesses his faith and preaches another sermon. No longer does he speak of punishment. Suffering cannot be interpreted except in the sense that it is of absolute good and part of God's will. He demands that his congregation and that he, himself, love and approve of this unexplainable curse. Either this, or man must deny God completely. His death has strange symptoms, not at all plague-like. He seems to will his own death in order to join the ranks of the victims. Assenting to the plague, convinced that it is part of a divine good, he joins the dead.

JEAN TARROU

A wanderer who comes innocuously to Oran, he stays to help Rieux battle the plague and becomes its last victim. Deeply convinced that his lawyer-father was wrong to demand the death sentence for a criminal, and later disillusioned when his revolutionary party guns down former heads of state, Tarrou believes man is too frequently a party to murder. He rejects rationalizations that include frequent execution of men in the name of justice. To Tarrou, murder is the supreme evil in the world. He refuses to be a party to it and thus is rather aloof. In Oran, he keeps notebooks about ironic curiosities which he observes.

So serious about life, he is not middle-aged, but a stocky young fellow with a deeply furrowed face. Like Camus, he is a chain smoker and greatly enjoys swimming in the sea, also a pleasure of Rieux's. He and Rieux do not essentially change during the siege. Grand, Rambert, and Paneloux are all different men afterward. Tarrou, however, dies with a strangely smiling courage, still a strongly ironic man. He sought inner peace by becoming his own moral sentry so as not to bring harm to others. During the chronicle his goal was to become, although he was an atheist, a saint. He sought an innocence impossible to achieve, quite a different kind of impossible absurdity than Rieux sought. Rieux's struggle, which he realizes will be finally futile, is not impossible. He lives ever-sympathetic with men, always aware of his human duty to heal. Tarrou's search is highly personal, highly spiritual.

RAYMOND RAMBERT

The former football player, and at present a feature writer for a Paris newspaper, is in Oran on assignment when the city is quarantined. He first tries to leave the city by appealing to the civil authorities. Then when that fails, he offers money to several shady characters belonging to Oran's underground. None of the contacts, however, are able to arrange a successful escape. Rambert feels unjustly exiled in this legally proclaimed city of exile. He has few friends, no family — in fact, no reason to be included in the quarantine; he is certain that neither Jean Tarrou nor Dr. Rieux can understand his constant demand for release. The plague changes Rambert from a hack journalist into a responsible adult. Early in the book, he pleaded to leave so that he could return to his wife. Later he willingly elects to remain in Oran and assist Rieux rather than take flight to claim a solitary happiness for himself. He has joined his conscience in a moral commitment to an allegiance higher than himself.

JOSEPH GRAND

The civil servant is fifty-ish, tall, and bent. He leads a dreary, quiet life until the plague seals off Oran from the outside world. Until then, he spends his free time polishing the first sentence of a prose-perfect book he dreams of writing. Stacks of scribbled pages do not deter him. He persists in writing and listening to the sense and the sound of his sentence number one and continues to fail. He has already failed to make a respectable income and also to hold together a marriage with a woman whom he is now sure he loved deeply. But however odd and eccentric he seems, he is among the first to volunteer to help fight the plague that threatens Oran. He contracts the disease, but recovers. Rieux had remarked offhandedly earlier in the book that he is the insignificant type that often escapes such disasters. The chronicle does not prove this though. Grand survives, not escapes. In the emergency, he reacted instinctively, doing his meager best to defend his city, and during this period of trial he gained an insight into his writing project and into the reasons why his marriage failed.

ALLEGORY

Attempts to explain an allegorical work are, at best, rarely satisfactory. Allegorical interpretations are as elusive and as tenuous as their interpreters. One critic will charge that the work has been diced into irreparable ruins; another will dismiss the same essay as superficial and general. Camus recognized this difficulty and remarked that only broad outlines should be paralleled in allegorical comment. To attempt a thorough analysis would be to suggest that the work was not art but contrived artifice. It is in this spirit of generalities that *The Plague* has been considered.

Camus' chronicle had been conceived as early as 1939, but was not begun until after France was defeated and the Germans moved their occupation troops into the country. During these years Camus kept a series of notebooks and many of the jottings in the notebooks suggest the multitude of ideas that Camus considered before his book was finally completed. Nearly all these early *Plague* ideas reveal Camus' concern for a truthful realism and a rejection of sensationalism. They also indicate his continuing insistence that his book carry his metaphysical ideas of the absurd. Initially Camus was even wary of the word *plague*. Late in 1942, he cautions himself not to include the word in the title. He considers *The Prisoners*. Later and more frequently he mentions the prisoner idea and, especially, the theme of separation.

Several kinds of separation are apparent already in the first part. Within the plot line, many of the characters are separated from one another by their small-time greeds, their lack of human love, and their indifference. There is also the separation of the living and the dead as the plague progresses into Oran. The ill are put into isolation camps and are separated from relatives and family. Finally, and of philosophical interest, is the separation of nature and the Oranians. The setting is awesome and beautiful — on the sea. Throughout the sick-tainted days of the epidemic, nature is radiant. Man's plight seems nonexistent. Here is Camus' crux. Man wants and prays fervently to be important to some guiding force in the heavens — something larger than himself. Yet there is only beautiful, sun-warmed silence; there is only separation between man and his universe.

What supreme irony that man should be in such total isolation and long most for the impossible. The universe is indifferent to us, to our plagues of whatever magnitude. Nothing is certain but death. We are isolated. Alone. These are the truths which Camus believed about existence and which he hoped to parallel in Oran's situation, cut off from the outside world and imprisoned by the plague. And, in this extreme situation, he created characters who would be forced to think, reflect, and assume responsibility for living. Death is faced by many of the Oranians for the first time — and with all the horror of a plague. This confrontation with death is mandatory for experiencing the Absurd. The symbol of the plague can, of course, represent any hardship or disaster, but rationally facing our existence is probably one of the most extreme of metaphysical trials. One never fully experiences until he has gone through a struggle for self-understanding and, in *The*

Plague, the symptoms of the rats suggest the confusion one undergoes before this long struggle. The symptoms of distress — of this need to understand oneself and one's universe — can of course be ignored, but finally one does have to face himself honestly and endure a plague-like period of readjustment to the truths one must live with. Within existential philosophy this examination period is mandatory. It is actually a reassertion of Socrates' "the unexamined life is not worth living."

There seem, however, to be few positive or concrete symptoms of distress before man comes to terms with his existence in the universe. On the contrary, there seem to be only negatives and nothings to confirm this distressed feeling. One must reach rock bottom and begin questioning a faith that began long ago to cope with the revelation of the frauds of Santa Claus, of stork-delivered babies, and the perfection of, at least, one of our parents. Everyone finally seemed composed of a measure of hypocrisy, greed, and selfishness. People become, simply, human. And with honest consideration even the superhuman becomes suspectedly human. The universe is ever silent. Prayer seems much less than even 50-50 certain. God's whimsy confuses.

Awareness of a godless universe and a thorough re-evaluation of one's life and one's civilization is of prime importance within the existential context. Man's struggle to adjust to his new vision, his guilty relapse into easeful hope for eternal life, and his fleeting thoughts of suicide — all these will plague him until he will, with new insight, re-emerge to live with the absurd vision, with spiritual hope, or self-impose his own death.

The plague is also a useful symbol for all evil and suffering. The old Spaniard suggests that life is plague-like and Rieux seems to argue for this possibility of interpretation. Facing a plague's problems is no more than facing the problem of man's mortality. Camus' atheism may at first seem repugnant, but it is affirmative because it stresses each man's role as representative in its responsibility and commitment. Camus does not tempt man to endure suffering or evil for promised rewards in the hereafter. He denounces evil and offers human dignity to men who will end suffering through action, not through prayer. He offers man the awful burden of total freedom to determine the fate of mankind — with no recourse to an always, all-forgiving deity. God can too easily become last-minute insurance. His forgiveness entitles man to exist in the lifeless monotony of Oran, living life selfishly and indifferently until crisis time.

Leaving the metaphysical and turning to the concrete, remember that while he was writing *The Plague,* Camus was living in a homeland occupied by German conquerors. His country was imprisoned as completely as plague might seal off its borders. There was destruction, death, and suffering. The cruel violence of this was as unjust as the cruelty of a plague. And Camus' chronicle is a personal affirmation of the worth of human beings and life *despite*—despite being exiled in the universe, despite being ravaged by disease and tyrants. It is a belief in life's potential for multiple meaning and fullness.

This belief is especially remarkable because Camus realized that the world was not conscientiously reacting to the symptoms of war. France, particularly, has been criticized by historians for succumbing too easily to the Nazis and delivering their country into German hands. But France was not alone. These symptoms were known to all countries, and because Part I of Camus' book deals with symptoms of the plague and the reaction of the populace to them, we might now consider the symptoms that preluded World War II and some of the national reactions. Further, we might recount some of the major national deaths before the United States actively entered the fight against the Axis powers.

Aggression was first initiated by Japan in September, 1931, when she moved into Chinese Manchuria. The trouble spot was oceans away. The Chinese made appeal to the League of Nations, who appointed a committee to study the problem. The committee verbally condemned the aggression, but no active measures were taken to repel Japan. Her next move was a deeper penetration into northern China.

The actions taken against the enemy, then and in Camus' book, were on paper—compiling, counting, suggesting. To combat either a plague or a hungry aggressor, piles of study reports often amount to the same kind of ashcan effectiveness.

The Chinese Nationalist government recognized Japan's conquests, but the rebelistic Chinese Communists refused, demanding that the invaders be driven out. They finally kidnaped Nationalist leader Chiang Kai-shek and demanded immediate military action against the enemy. But the Chinese continued to retreat and in 1938 Japan openly proclaimed a New Order. Chiang Kai-shek's empire was to be annihilated and all Occidentals were to be removed so that a new and completely Oriental government might be established.

Here was solid proof of aggression that should be halted, but because Japan had not declared war, could another nation label her actions aggressive? The policy of look-see (the same as that of Dr. Richard, Dr. Rieux's opponent, in *The Plague*) was generally agreed to at this time.

Meanwhile, happenings in Europe were somewhat parallel. In 1936, Hitler had sufficiently mesmerized the German people into a growing Nazi war machine. His first move was to march into the Rhineland. After World War I, this area had been a kind of no-man's land. Originally it was to have been ruled by France; later decisions filled it with Allied occupation troops. It was to be strictly demilitarized. Hitler's invasion was in gross violation of the Treaty of Versailles. Further, it violated the Locarno treaty, which reaffirmed the zone as demilitarized and which France, Germany, and Belgium agreed not to invade. Any offender would be attacked by the other two signers.

Camus could be justifiably proud of his nation in this crisis. While the rest of the world looked on at the Rhineland, France mobilized 150,000 troops. She alone responded. Other nations thought it unwise to engage in militaristics; some feared the label of "warmonger"; others simply saw Germany as arming her borders, a rather natural thing for a country to want to do.

In 1936, Italy overran Ethiopia. France, Britain, and the United States seemed indifferent.

Meanwhile, Hitler continued his expansion. Austria was swallowed in March, 1938; a year later, Czechoslovakia was overwhelmed by the Nazis. In America people went to their jobs, hoping for the best. Enjoying relief from the earlier Depression, they were not anxious to face the horrors of war.

During this time President Roosevelt delivered his "quarantine speech," stating that peace was being jeopardized by a small portion of the world. Later in 1939 he speculated that "in case of war" the Germans and the Italians might win.

Even earlier than Roosevelt's quarantine speech, however, Winston Churchill (a Rieux or Castel figure) had the reason and the imagination to consider what confronted the world. "Do not suppose that this is the end," he said. "This is only the beginning of the reckoning...which will be proffered to us year by year unless, by a supreme recovery of moral health and martial vigor, we arise again and take our stand for freedom...."

United States armed soldiers came to Europe late. Only in December, 1941, when the Japanese attacked Pearl Harbor, did the United States officially enter the world conflict. Before this entry the Nazis had invaded Poland, conquered Denmark and Norway, defeated Holland and Belgium, driven through France, captured Paris, annexed Rumania, Bulgaria, and Hungary. Finally they threatened Britain with successive air raids. Then they turned toward the Soviet Union.

Throughout these years, the people of the United States had commented on these tragedies to each other over bowls of breakfast cereal. And, as the Nazi machine devoured the houses of European neighbors, the United States continued to go its way—like Grand, Cottard, Rambert, and many others of the Oranians. We hoped for the best, that this plague would sate itself and relent. Ironically, after we quarantined ourselves from the European conflict, we found ourselves in a kind of quarantine after Pearl Harbor. Our Allies lay wounded at the Nazis' heels and we were surrounded by enemies.

Thus not only can one see parallels in the French people's failure to curb German encroachment and occupation, but a general reluctance on the part of people everywhere to recognize the germination of the plague of war. Finally, of course, must come the formal declaration.

Even before their country was occupied by *la peste brune* (the brown plague), as the brown-uniformed Nazis were called, the French people did not consider the mobilization orders serious. Sisley Huddleston, in his book *France, the Tragic Years,* reports that the general comment was "It will be like last year." The people thought it silly to cry "Wolf!" when there was no real danger.

When war was official, there was the same sense of incredulity that Oran suffered. There was also death, but it was not caused by the kind of war fought in 1914. This time war was mechanized. Nazis parachuted their troops, had amphibious craft, and Panzer divisions. The French were ill-equipped and fear was as destructive as the Nazis' machines. This fear, plus the lack of any cohesion weakened the country. By degrees, waves of panic, dejection, and indifference swept the trapped people. At the war's beginning, even Camus was rather unbelieving; later he was morose when the conflict could not be averted. He blamed both the masses and the leaders for their weaknesses, just as in *The Plague,* he attacks the indifferent citizens and their wishy-washy officials.

The plague lasts almost a year; the Occupation of France lasted four years. During those years the majority of the French people clung instinctively to life, seeking out small pleasures, praying intermittently, hoping for signs but, largely, neither aiding nor resisting the enemy. The Resistance was not a large organization, just as Rieux's team was also not large. But they persevered, believing in the rightness of their efforts. It was not easy to murder men merely because they were Occupation troops. Tarrou's philosophy seemed most humane, but Camus and others finally took the stand that he writes of in his "Letters to a German Friend." Here he confesses the difficulty he had in affirming violence to counter the enemy. He stresses the agony that intelligence burdens one with, especially when one is fighting savage violence and aware of consequences of which the enemy is ignorant.

The despair and the separation were endured by the French people until the Allied troops liberated the country trapped behind the Occupational walls. And, like all men, like even those survivors of World War I, the French swore never again to let tragedies like this happen. Mankind, however, is free. Camus believes in the potential of the human race to avoid destroying itself. But he offers it the freedom to do so — under one condition: that each man assume his guilt for the holocaust.

REVIEW QUESTIONS

1. Considering only the remarks about Oran in Chapter 1, what can you say concerning the character of the anonymous narrator?

2. Rambert insists on leaving Oran; is it because he fears death? Why or why not?

3. What events prompt Tarrou to try to live as a saint? How does he define "sainthood"?

4. In general, what are the differences between the two sermons of Paneloux? What is responsible for the change?

5. Why does Rieux not consider himself a hero?

6. Why does Rieux say that Grand might be considered hero-like?

7. What is the function of Rieux's mother in the chronicle?

8. Account for Rieux's sympathy toward Cottard.

9. Of the many reunited Oranian lovers, why does Rieux single out Rambert as representative?

10. In terms of Rieux's objective narrative, do you think it necessary to describe so minutely the suffering of Jacques Othon? Why or why not?

11. What is accomplished by having Rieux and Tarrou take a night swim together?

12. What prompts Grand to ask Rieux to burn his years of accumulated manuscript?

13. Before he dies, does Tarrou find the peace of mind that he has said he seeks?

14. Does the book seem an obvious allegory? Why or why not?

SUGGESTED THEME TOPICS

1. Attitudes toward death in *The Plague*.

2. The advantages or disadvantages of an ironic tone (or irony) in *The Plague*.

3. Optimism and pessimism in *The Plague*.

4. Camus' ideas concerning religion in *The Plague*.

5. Imagery and symbolism in *The Plague*.

6. Happiness in Oran, before and after the plague.

7. A definition of humanism in terms of *The Plague*.

8. *The Plague:* an anti-Christian novel.

9. Characterization: successful or unsuccessful in *The Plague*.

10. Realism in *The Plague*.

SELECTED BIBLIOGRAPHY

WORKS BY ALBERT CAMUS

(In English Translation)

Fiction

The Stranger, trans. Stuart Gilbert. New York: Vintage Books, 1946.

The Plague, trans. Stuart Gilbert. New York: The Modern Library, 1948.

The Fall, trans. Justin O'Brien. New York: Vintage Books, 1956.

The Exile and the Kingdom, trans. Justin O'Brien. New York: Vintage Books, 1965.

Drama

Caligula and 3 Other Plays, trans. Stuart Gilbert. New York: Vintage Books, 1958.

The Possessed, trans. Justin O'Brien. New York: Vintage Books, 1964.

Essays

The Rebel, trans. Anthony Bower. New York: Vintage Books, 1956.

The Myth of Sisyphus and Other Essays, trans. Justin O'Brien. New York: Vintage Books, 1959.

Resistance, Rebellion and Death, trans. Justin O'Brien. New York: Alfred A. Knopf, 1960.

Notebooks 1935-42, trans. Philip Thody. New York: Alfred A. Knopf, 1963.

Notebooks 1942-51, trans. Justin O'Brien. New York: Alfred A. Knopf, 1965.

BOOKS ON CAMUS

Brée, Germaine. *Camus*. New Brunswick, New Jersey: Rutgers University Press, 1959. Revised Edition, 1961. A basic study of Camus' writings.

—— (ed.). *Camus: A Collection of Critical Essays*. Twentieth Century Views Series. Englewood Cliffs, New Jersey: Prentice-Hall, 1962. A valuable combination of reviews and critical articles written in the 1940's and 50's and scholarly estimates written after Camus' death.

Cruickshank, John. *Albert Camus and the Literature of Revolt:* New York and London: Oxford University Press, 1959. Camus' philosophical ideas are examined within the philosophical background of Kierkegaard, Nietzsche, Dostoievsky, and Jaspers.

Hanna, Thomas C. *The Thought and Art of Albert Camus*. Chicago: Henry Regnery, 1958. Analyses of Camus' essays, plays, and novels.

Maquet, Albert. *Albert Camus: The Invincible Summer,* trans. Herma Briffault. New York: George Braziller, 1958. A study of Camus' publications, delineating Camus' increasing concern with optimistic humanism.

Parker, Emmett. *Albert Camus, the Artist in the Arena*. Madison, Wisconsin: The University of Wisconsin Press, 1965. An extensive examination of Camus' journalistic essays, editorials, and articles from the 1930's until his death.

Thody, Philip. *Albert Camus: A Study of His Work*. London: Hamish Hamilton, 1957. An assessment and detailed interpretation of Camus' fiction and nonfiction.

NOTES

NOTES

NOTES

NOTES

NOTES

THE RED AND
THE BLACK

NOTES

including
- *Stendhal's Life and Work*
- *List of Characters*
- *Synopsis of the Novel*
- *Chapter Summaries and Commentaries*
- *Analysis of Main Characters*
- *Stendhal's Romanticism and Realism*
- *Review Questions and Theme Topics*
- *Selected Bibliography*

by
D. L. Gobert, Ph.D.
Department of Foreign Languages
Southern Illinois University

Cliffs Notes
INCORPORATED
LINCOLN, NEBRASKA 68501

Editor

Gary Carey, M.A.
University of Colorado

Consulting Editor

James L. Roberts, Ph.D.
Department of English
University of Nebraska

ISBN 0-8220-1111-5
© Copyright 1967
by
C. K. Hillegass
All Rights Reserved
Printed in U.S.A.

1988 Printing

Cliffs Notes, Inc.   Lincoln, Nebraska

CONTENTS

ANALYSIS OF MAIN CHARACTERS

The Red and the Black

STENDHAL'S LIFE AND WORK

Henri Beyle (Stendhal) was born in 1783, in Grenoble, into a respectable, middle-class family. Chérubin Beyle, Stendhal's father, a reactionary in politics, was an industrious, narrow-minded bourgeois, whom Henri detested and to whom he later referred as the "bâtard." Stendhal loved his mother tenderly, but this delightful woman, whose origin Stendhal liked to think was Italian, died when he was only seven. Later, he idealized her memory just as he exaggerated the mediocrity of his father. Of a fiery and rebellious nature, Stendhal declared himself early to be an atheist and "jacobin," or liberal—an expression of revolt, no doubt, against his father.

Stendhal studied at the Ecole Centrale in Grenoble until 1799, excelling in mathematics and art. Thirsting for adventure, he went to Paris, and securing a commission in the army, sojourned briefly in Italy, a country he came to love above France. Back in Paris, Stendhal resigned from the army, and from 1802 until 1806, he studied the eighteenth-century materialistic philosophers, Helvétius and Cabanis, and aspired unsuccessfully to become a playwright. A highly placed relative obtained for Stendhal an administrative position in the army that took him to Germany, with periodic trips back to Paris. In 1812, he participated in Napoleon's Russian retreat.

Stendhal's first literary endeavors were biographies, *Vies de Haydn, de Mozart, et de Métastase,* written in 1815 in Milan, where he lived as a dilettante, fraternizing with Italian liberals, delighting in Italian art and music. He was so taken with Italy, and in particular with Milan, that he requested that his epitaph read: "Henri Beyle, Milanais." He believed that Italy afforded a more propitious atmosphere for the pursuit of the cult of energy than did more prosaic, post-Napoleonic France. Turning to art criticism, he wrote *Histoire de la Peinture en Italie* (1817), and addressing himself to tourism, *Rome, Naples, et Florence* (1817).

Stendhal's unsuccessful love affair with Méthilde Dembowski inspired him to write the autobiographical treatise, *De l'Amour* (1822). Méthilde served as a model for various of Stendhal's subsequent heroines. The treatise analyzes the mechanism of love as Stendhal had observed it operating in himself. The second part of the work is a pseudo-sociological study purporting to show how national temperament influences and modifies the love mechanism. Stendhal was forced to leave Milan in 1821 because of his liberal political beliefs.

Back in Paris from 1821 until 1830, Stendhal experienced financial hardships. In 1823 and 1825, he published parts I and II, respectively, of *Racine et Shakespeare,* in which he praised Shakespeare as superior in psychological analysis to the classical Racine. The work elaborates the prevailing romantic view in esthetics that proclaimed the relativism of beauty. Stendhal saw in Romanticism the latest manifestation of the beautiful. In Part II of the work, Stendhal addressed himself to the comic, attempted to define it, and proclaimed Molière, the French classical comic genius, to be a literary anachronism. Stendhal seemed to favor Shakespeare only when the latter italianized his plays. Stendhal's cult of energy caused him to execrate contemplatives such as Hamlet.

At the age of forty-four, Stendhal wrote his first novel, *Armance,* which neither his friends nor the public acclaimed. It was intended as a psychological study of Octave, an impotent who ultimately commits suicide. Octave's physical anomaly prefigures and is symbolic of the Stendhalian hero's inability to accept life as offered by Restoration society. The Stendhalian theme of the pursuit of individual happiness is already apparent, but Octave is unsuccessful in his search, preferring suicide to compromise as a solution to his dilemma. Stendhal's own reserve and the prevailing mores prevented him from clarifying the nature of Octave's affliction for the reader, and the resulting ambiguity was the reason that the public found the hero enigmatic. The society that Octave opposes with such violence is not minutely described by the novelist, therefore the social dimension of the novel is unconvincing.

Turning away from the novel, Stendhal composed *Promenades dans Rome* (1829), utilizing surplus material from his earlier travelogs and notes offered by a cousin. The work has been called a glorified guidebook, by which is meant that Stendhal's original perceptions and impressions illuminate many pages of what would otherwise simply be a book of tourism. In this work Stendhal again exposed the concept of relativism in esthetics, proclaiming that the concept of the beautiful varies from age to age and among cultures.

The realistic note that runs through Stendhal's literary endeavors — fictional, biographical, documentary, critical, and journalistic — stems from his need to anchor himself solidly in reality as a point of departure. Everything he wrote begins in the realm of facts. He imposes his impressions and transforms reality, but it is a reality exterior to himself that furnishes the plot or subject matter.

Thus, *The Red and the Black, Chronicle of the XIX Century,* written in 1829 and published in 1831, fictionalizes and elaborates an actual happening of which Stendhal had read in records of court proceedings.

The historical person who served as a model for Julien Sorel was a certain Antoine Berthet, convicted, like Julien, of murder in December, 1827, at Grenoble. Berthet was the son of a Brangues blacksmith. At twenty, he became preceptor in the home of a local dignitary, M. Michoud, and probably became the lover of Mme. Michoud. Leaving the Michoud home, Berthet entered a seminary at Belley, from which he was dismissed as undesirable. From there, he went as preceptor to the home of M. de Cordon. He had an affair with the latter's daughter and was sent away. Now desperate, without a future or position, but still in love with Mme. Michoud, Berthet began writing threatening letters to Mme. Michoud, accusing her of infidelity toward him and of calumny, holding her responsible for his failure. His intimidations and threats finally caused M. Michoud to find a position for Berthet in the home of some cousins. One Sunday, however, Antoine returned to Brangues, followed Mme. Michoud to church, and shot her during the service.

Berthet's story, reduced to this pattern, is the story of Julien Sorel, hero of the novel. The three successive stages in Julien's adventure have their counterparts in Berthet's life. Few details about the third phase of Berthet's life were available from the Grenoble trial records, and Stendhal was forced to stray from the facts in his creation of Julien's experiences with Mathilde in the Mole episode. Critics still debate as to how successfully Stendhal extricated himself from the dilemma resulting from the implicit divergency in the careers of Julien and Antoine in the third phase. (See Commentary, Part II, Chapters 33-35.)

The novel has political and social dimensions also. The story of the individual, Julien, is narrated against a background of contemporary events. A variation of the subtitle given by Stendhal to the novel—*Chronicle of 1830* —calls attention to the circumstances of the composition of the novel and to its political implications. Stendhal conceived the novel at the end of the autocratic reign of Charles X, and although the novelist foresaw the revolution that overthrew the Bourbon dynasty in 1830, he dared not publish it until the following year. (See Commentary, Part II, Chapters 21-23.)

Just as Stendhal's position vis-à-vis his time was one of revolt, his protagonists, as projections of himself, are portrayed as being in conflict with their milieu. Julien Sorel is an outsider, a peasant, nurtured by the example of Napoleon, the army officer become emperor, who would become an aristocrat in a caste society where the equality promised by the revolution was no longer a possibility.

The Stendhalian hero without insuperable obstacles would no longer be a hero, nor for that matter, would he be worthy of portrayal through analysis at all. Since the Stendhalian ideal of the superior man engaged in the elaboration of an art of living to assure him happiness is only conceivable in a negative posture of revolt, society presents itself quite naturally in the role of the obstacle. Julien has not only the exterior world as an obstacle, he is likewise endowed with a contradictory nature that compounds his dilemma. His extreme sensibility, virtue, and generosity will prevent him from succeeding like the unscrupulous, calculating bourgeois parvenu, Valenod.

The novel presents conflict on two levels: Julien's inner struggle is waged between ambition and a predisposition to an idyllic happiness; and his conflict against society engages both aspects of his nature.

The social and political aspects of the novel are inseparably fused with the psychological study of a superior being, and this fusion constitutes the artistic unity of the work. Such an organic unity was lacking in *Armance.*

This novel demonstrates Stendhal's belief that art is the expression of intense emotion, presented with simplicity and directness. The reader, Stendhal hoped, would be jolted by what he read and would participate by visualizing, by experiencing the narration personally. Although Stendhal possessed the extreme sensibility of a woman, as he put it, he reacted violently against the personal effusions and unbridled subjectivity of the Romanticists. He believed that even passion has its modesty. Therefore, Stendhal carefully checks and controls the expression of Julien's emotions as he does his own.

Stendhal's character presentation alternates omniscient analysis and interior monolog. Both methods are characterized by transitional omissions, which betoken Stendhal's "pudeur," his refusal to be penetrated by another consciousness, and by sudden, seemingly spontaneous, affective reactions that startle the characters themselves as much as the reader, and that demonstrate realistically the autonomy of the emotions. These sudden jolts experienced by the characters as they discover themselves and Stendhal's rapid narration create an air of tension that intrigues the reader.

A disciple of the eighteenth-century materialists and a precursor, in this respect, of the determinism of Naturalism, Stendhal conceived the formation of mind and character of man as resulting from experiences he undergoes with external reality. He puts his characters, therefore, in typical situations of everyday life and watches them react.

After the ascension to the throne of Louis-Philippe, the bourgeois king, Stendhal secured an appointment as consul in Civita-Vecchia, Italy, where he served from 1831 to 1836. During this time, he wrote his autobiographies, *Souvenirs d'Egotisme,* the *Vie de Henry Brulard,* and an unfinished novel, *Lucian Leuwen.* These were all published posthumously.

Henry Brulard is just one of the dozens of pseudonyms that Stendhal adopted and discarded during his life. The work investigates his early life through adolescence and was prompted by his need to know himself. It is the antithesis of Rousseau's *Confessions*, in that Stendhal, typically rigorously self-demanding, is frank and truthful to the point of deprecating himself. He reconstitutes his intellectual and emotional formation in Grenoble. Although the work is full of historical inaccuracies, it presents an accurate account of the psychological reactions of the child and adolescent.

The *Souvenirs d'Egotisme* recalls later years, specifically the last years of the Restoration. Stendhal abandoned his autobiographical attempts because of his inability to resolve the inner conflict that they inspired. Although he felt the imperious need to know himself, he was constantly checked by his strong sense of modesty and reserve.

Lucien Leuwen again satirically opposes a protagonist to the contemporary scene, the politically and socially corrupt France of Louis-Philippe. The melancholy and calm of the novel contrast in mood with the tense *Red and the Black*. The hero, Lucien, is not motivated by passion or energy. Rather than imposing himself on the world, he seems to undergo influence more passively, and with aloofness scorns those with whom he must interact. He would seem to exemplify Stendhal's thirst for freedom from restraint. Like Julien, Lucien is in search of an identity and happiness. He is not orphaned or alienated from society, but is protected by his father in a political career, and had Stendhal finished the novel, Lucien would have ultimately married his only love, Bathilde, patterned after Méthilde, and presumably, would have found happiness. In this novel, Stendhal took greater pains to render in depth the lesser characters. His inspiration for the novel went beyond contemporary events. The plot he plagiarized from a work that a friend had written with the request that Stendhal criticize it. Stendhal, no more so than the classicists of the seventeenth century, did not feel scruples about plagiarism.

Temporarily abandoning fiction, Stendhal turned again to biography, *Vie de Napoléon* (1839), to tragic adventure stories, *Chroniques italiennes* (1837-39), and to another travelog, *Mémoires d'un touriste* (1839). The latter is a satire of customs and mores of provincial French life.

Within a period of two months at the end of 1839, Stendhal improvised his second masterpiece in the novel, *The Charterhouse of Parma*. The source was again historical, an old Italian chronicle narrating the life of Alexandre Farnèse. Although the action of Stendhal's novel is placed during the first third of the nineteenth century, the violent passions and fierce individualism of the Italian Renaissance motivate the characters. Love is the theme of the *Charterhouse*, as it had been the major preoccupation of Stendhal's life, although political intrigue and heroic adventures abound.

Fabrice del Dongo follows somewhat the pattern of the Stendhalian hero — he seeks happiness — but in his adventurous pursuit, he is joined and protected by three other chosen creatures. Fabrice does not, therefore, know the social solitude of Julien. He is loved by his aunt, Sanseverina, and protected by her husband, Count Mosca. While imprisoned, Fabrice falls in love with the jailor's daughter, Clélia, and it is this love that changes him profoundly, as it does the other "elect." Fabrice does not repeat the projected denouement of Lucien, however, by an idyllic marriage. Like Julien, Fabrice is allowed but a glimpse of happiness on this earth and he dies young. In Fabrice's separation from Clélia, there is glory and the hope that a final union beyond this life will occur. Rather than being a creature of egotism, such as is Julien, Fabrice is a more generous soul. Even though society is opposed to Stendhal's ideal of individualism, the forceful alliance of these four exceptional beings — Fabrice, Clélia, La Sanseverina, and Mosca — would seem to represent a sort of triumph over society. Balzac commented that this novel could only be truly appreciated by the diplomat, statesman, or man of the world, so intricate are its political innuendos.

Stendhal returned to his consular post in Italy in 1839, where he began his last novel, *Lamiel*, destined never to be completed. Instead of a hero, here he presents a heroine, Lamiel, who further differs from Stendhal's previous protagonists in that she is driven only by an avid curiosity and meets with success by yielding to the expression of spontaneity. She is the most successful adventurer of Stendhal, the most primitive of his protagonists in her amorality, rising from the peasant class to become the queen of Paris.

When Stendhal died in Paris in 1842, his burial in the Montmartre cemetery was attended by three faithful friends, one of whom was Mérimée. Stendhal had written for himself and for the "happy few," and his prediction that he had taken a ticket in a lottery that would be drawn in 1935 has proven accurate, since his most appreciative audience has been that of the twentieth century.

LIST OF CHARACTERS

Julien Sorel

The hero of the novel; peasant son of a provincial sawyer, who, by means of hypocrisy and of the women who love him, driven by insatiable ambition, briefly succeeds in penetrating into the aristocracy. His failure and subsequent death are caused by society's punishment of the parvenu and by the consequences of his own impetuosity.

Mme. de Rênal

Thirty-year-old wife of the ultra mayor of Verrières, and the first and only real love of Julien; she becomes his mistress and through jealousy he shoots her in church. Ultimately, the lovers are reconciled, although she does not long survive Julien's death.

M. de Rênal

Prototype of the provincial petty aristocracy, the ultra, wealthy mayor of Verrières. Blinded by his exaggerated self-esteem, he is the easy dupe of everyone — thus a ridiculous character.

Mme. Derville

Pretty cousin of Mme. de Rênal; one of the happy threesome with Julien and her cousin in Vergy. She helplessly watches her cousin fall in love with Julien, innocently and unknowingly.

Abbé Chélan

Jansenist priest of Verrières, destituted by the intrigues of the Congrégation; first mentor of Julien.

Abbé Maslon

Jesuit priest, tool of the Congrégation, who replaces Chélan as priest in Verrières after the latter's disgrace.

Old Sorel

The crafty, greedy, peasant father of Julien; responsible for his son's unhappy childhood, and at the news of Julien's imminent death, more interested in a possible inheritance than moved by his death.

Abbé Pirard

Jansenist director of the Besançon seminary that Julien attends; old friend of Chélan; Julien's mentor at the seminary, then in Paris: Pirard is instrumental in placing Julien in the Mole household as the marquis' secretary.

Fouqué

Childhood friend of Julien, whose mountain retreat is a refuge for the hero. Fouqué offers Julien a partnership in his sawmill, visits him during imprisonment, and manages his friend's burial.

Valenod

Rênal's assistant and successor as mayor; scheming pawn of the Congrégation; rival of Julien for Mme. de Rênal and instrumental in Julien's death. Prototype of the unscrupulous, bourgeois parvenu.

Marquis de la Mole

Peer of France, powerful, ultra aristocrat, who employs Julien as secretary; later treats him as a portégé, and confers nobility on Julien, after the latter has compromised his daughter Mathilde.

Mathilde de la Mole

Impetuous, proud, haughty daughter of the marquis, and second mistress of Julien; after seducing Julien, she becomes pregnant and frantically attempts to save him from the guillotine, although Julien no longer loves her.

Abbé Frilair

Jesuit leader of the Besançon Congrégation; enemy of Chélan, of Pirard, and for different reasons, of the marquis. Mathilde bargains with Frilair to win the freedom of Julien, awaiting trial.

Norbert de la Mole

Son of the marquis; prototype of the colorless, unheroic, conformist young aristocrat of the period. Neither his father nor his sister Mathilde find him worthy of the illustrious Mole ancestry. Julien usurps his role of son of the marquis.

Mme. de la Mole

Wife of the marquis and the prototype of the nullity and sterility of the Restoration aristocracy; holds her court at the Hôtel de la Mole, enforcing an empty decorum and banishing any signs of intelligence and spontaneity; a snob whose only interest is the genealogy of nobility.

Mme. de Fervaques

A prude whom Julien pretends to court to awaken Mathilde's jealousy. She is of Jesuit leaning and of mystical bent. Her bourgeois lineage makes her an uncomfortable aristrocratic parvenue.

Altamira

A liberal, expatriated aristocrat, condemned to die. Julien makes his acquaintance in Paris and idolizes this idealist.

Croisenois

An aristocrat of the ilk of Norbert de la Mole, and his friend; aspires to the hand of Mathilde and dies in a duel defending her honor after the scandal.

Géronimo

Italian singer, bon vivant, adventurer, vagabond; frequents the aristocracy and puts to advantage his social connections.

M. de Beauvoisis

A dandy of the lesser nobility; befriends Julien and serves as a model for the hero in manners and dress.

Prince Korasov

A Russian whom Julien meets in London and in Strasbourg; serves as another mentor for Julien. Korasov, himself a great lover, inspires Julien with the plan to awaken Mathilde's jealousy.

Bishop Agde

Young, successfully arrived, reactionary churchman; Julien serves as his messenger during a religious ceremony of great pomp in Verrières; they meet again at the secret meeting in Paris.

Abbé Castanède

Spy, Jesuit henchman of Frilair. He is a menace to Julien in the seminary and on the secret mission.

Tanbeau

Unsuccessful rival of Julien for the position of secretary to the marquis. Another example of the would-be parvenu.

SYNOPSIS OF THE NOVEL

M. de Rênal, ultra mayor of the small provincial town of Verrières, hires Julien Sorel, a young peasant who aspires to the priesthood, as tutor for his children. The hiring of Julien is calculated to enhance Rênal's prestige among the wealthy liberals. Julien, ambitious and amoral, had hoped to pursue a military career but has decided to enter the priesthood, as the most likely means to success. He chooses hypocrisy as his weapon in his encounter with society. He sees his position as tutor as the first step in his ascension, which will culminate, he hopes, in Parisian aristocracy.

Mme. de Rênal innocently falls in love with Julien after he has lived in the Rênal country home for some time. When Julien discovers that he is loved, he decides that he will seduce Mme. de Rênal, as an expression of the scorn he feels for her husband. His plan of seduction would have failed miserably, so awkwardly does he execute it, were Mme. de Rênal not hopelessly in love with him. Succumbing to Julien's natural charm, which he displays in unguarded moments, Mme. de Rênal becomes, in fact, Julien's mistress. She educates him socially and in the local political intrigues. She succeeds in having Julien awarded a much coveted place in the guard of honor, on the occasion of a visit by Charles X.

Their love affair is idyllic until one of the Rênals' sons falls gravely ill, which Mme. de Rênal interprets as divine punishment for her adultery. Soon M. de Rênal receives an anonymous letter accusing Julien of having seduced his wife. Mme. de Rênal succeeds in duping her husband into believing that the accusation is false. She convinces him that the letter comes from Valenod, Rênal's rival and assistant, who has attempted in the past to court Mme. de Rênal. Her husband believes her because he is comfortably established and is horrified at the thought of a scandal. In order to quiet the rumors, Julien moves into the Rênals' townhouse in Verrières. Because of his brilliant reputation as a tutor, he is invited to dinner by Valenod, who would hope to hire Julien as the tutor for his own children.

A servant girl from the Rênal household, also in love with Julien but spurned by him, denounces the lovers to the former village priest, Chélan, who insists that Julien leave Verrières to enter the seminary in Besançon. Through Chélan's influence with Pirard, rector of the seminary, Julien is awarded a scholarship. Julien's affair with Mme. de Rênal is temporarily ended, but he visits her room for a final rendezvous.

Julien's first attempts to succeed as a student meet with failure because he excels as a scholar, and the Church's reactionary influence that prevails in the seminary requires of its future priests docility and intellectual conformity in mediocrity. Julien's superiority, however, is appreciated by Rector Pirard, who makes Julien his protégé. One day as Julien is assisting in the decoration of the Besançon cathedral, he encounters Mme. de Rênal, who promptly faints at the sight of him.

Pirard obtains a position for Julien as secretary to a powerful aristocrat in Paris, the Marquis de la Mole, to whom Pirard has been of invaluable assistance in a lawsuit. Pirard also leaves Besançon for a comfortable parish in Paris.

Before going to Paris, Julien pays a last visit to Mme. de Rênal, presenting himself at her window late at night. At first rebuffed by his mistress' virtue, Julien artfully destroys her resistance by announcing that his departure for Paris is imminent and that they will never see each other again. Mme. de Rênal acquiesces and Julien remains hidden to spend the following day with her.

Book II finds Julien in Paris as secretary to the Marquis de la Mole. Soon Julien makes his services indispensable to his employer, although his provincial manners and inexperience in high society cause him constant embarrassment. The marquis' proud daughter, Mathilde, takes an interest in Julien when she overhears the latter denouncing the sterility of the Mole's salon. Mathilde is bored with the convention and barrenness of the aristocracy of which she is a part. She is in need of diversion and Julien will provide it for her. The marquis finds Julien's intelligence and wit very refreshing, and ultimately Julien becomes almost a son to the marquis. The latter sends Julien to London on a diplomatic mission in order that he may gain experience and as a pretext to have Julien awarded a decoration.

At the behest of Mathilde, Julien attends a ball, where he makes the acquaintance of a liberal aristocrat condemned to die. Mathilde is the most sought after beauty of the season, but Julien hardly notices her, so inspired is he by the hero he has met. Mathilde, on the other hand, sees in Julien a reincarnation of her illustrious ancestor, Boniface de la Mole, a queen's lover who was beheaded. Mathilde falls in love with Julien.

Julien is unable to decide if he is loved or if Mathilde and her brother and their friends are trying to make of him a dupe. Julien's attempt to leave Paris on a business trip for the marquis moves Mathilde to a declaration of love. Julien, still distrustful, takes precautions to safeguard his reputation, sending Mathilde's avowal to his friend, Fouqué. Alleging another business trip, Julien receives an invitation from Mathilde to visit her in her room late at night. Still convinced that he is being tricked, Julien nonetheless appears at the appointed hour, and after much mutual embarrassment, Mathilde becomes his mistress.

Mathilde now fears that she has given herself a master and she repents of having compromised herself. Julien discovers that he is desperately in love with Mathilde, but her ardor has cooled. Unfortunately for Julien, Mathilde is only capable of loving him when she thinks that she is not loved by him. When in a moment of anger, Julien one day appears to threaten her life, she is in love again. Their second rendezvous occurs, but Mathilde again repents immediately after.

Julien, tormented by passion, is called upon by the marquis to serve as secretary at a secret meeting of reactionary aristocrats and to deliver a secret message to London. Successfully fulfilling his mission, Julien then goes to Strasbourg, where he meets a former acquaintance from London, who advises him how to reawaken Mathilde's love by jealousy. Julien returns to Paris to execute his plan, choosing a prude to court by means of love letters furnished to him by his friend.

Mathilde responds to the stratagem, but Julien realizes that to keep her love alive he must love her at a distance. Mathilde is pregnant, and after the marquis' rage has subsided at the announcement of this news, the latter finally agrees to obtain an army commission for Julien and to encourage his career. Julien occupies his new post in Strasbourg but receives word from Mathilde to return to Paris, that all is lost. In checking on Julien's past, the marquis has learned from Mme. de Rênal, in a letter dictated by her confessor, that Julien is an opportunist who succeeds by seducing women.

Learning this, Julien hurries to Verrières, arms himself, and shoots Mme. de Rênal at church. Imprisoned and awaiting trial for attempted murder, Julien is visited by Mathilde, who attempts to negotiate his acquittal with the Jesuits. Julien is resigned to die and in the solitude of his prison cell discovers that he is still in love with Mme. de Rênal, whom he had only wounded, and that his love for Mathilde has disappeared.

During the trial, in spite of his resolution not to speak in his own defense, Julien informs the court that he is not being tried for attempted murder, but for having attempted to rise above his social class. The jury finds Julien guilty and he is sentenced to be guillotined.

During his last days in prison, Julien finds peace and happiness in his reflections and through the reunion with Mme. de Rênal, who visits him daily. Julien faces death courageously, and after the execution, Mathilde, in a re-enactment of a scene from the Mole family history, furtively steals Julien's severed head and lovingly buries it with her own hands. Mme. de Rênal follows Julien in death.

SUMMARIES AND COMMENTARIES
PART I
CHAPTERS 1-3
Summary

M. de Rênal is the mayor and wealthy owner of the nail factory in the small mountain village of Verrières in the eastern province of Franche-Comté. Situated above the river Doubs, the village owes the prosperity of its peasant citizenry to sawmills and to the manufacture of calico. The sudden arrival of M. Appert, sent from M. de la Mole in Paris to inspect the municipal workhouse and prison administered by M. Valenod, the mayor's assistant, has erupted on the otherwise peaceful existence of the village.

The village, a microcosm of Paris and of all of France in this respect, is politically divided into two camps: royalists like the mayor and a liberal element dissatisfied with the Restoration. They are in agreement, however, upon the importance that they attribute to money and in their slavish respect for small-town public opinion. Father Chélan, Jansenist and village priest for many years, takes M. Appert on a tour of the workhouse and prison, thereby disobeying the wishes of M. Valenod, who risks being exposed for misuse of funds, given the pitiable conditions existing in these institutions. Rênal and Valenod have, in fact, visited Chélan and reprimanded him for this action. This is the subject of the conversation between M. and Mme. de Rênal one day as they are strolling with their three children on the "Cours de la Fidélité," a public promenade sustained by an enormous retaining wall, the glory of Verrières, the construction of which is due to the administration of Mayor de Rênal. The latter then proposes to his wife that they hire Julien Sorel, student priest of Chélan, as tutor for their children, a move destined to increase his own social prestige, since it will cause envy among the liberal textile mill owners. Julien's father, a crafty sawyer, has already, in the past, outwitted Rênal in a land transaction.

Commentary

Note that Stendhal does not rely for his exposition on many pages of description and documentation. His method might be called "free associational" and characterizes the entire novel, since the exposition never ends. It is clearly not that of his famous contemporary Balzac or of the latter's predecessor Scott. (Balzac quite often utilizes the "in medias res" technique of the epic: short dramatic scene, followed by pages of description explaining the initial glimpse, which then re-catches that glimpse and develops it into dramatic narrative.) Stendhal moves rather swiftly back and forth from background description to an action scene as the need arises, after an initial five pages of introductory setting.

Chapter divisions are entirely arbitrary: Chapter 1 situates Verrières, characterizes the economy of the town, then introduces a hypothetical Parisian visitor who will encounter the mayor, giving Stendhal the opportunity to present him for the first time. Most of the short chapter is, in fact, devoted to M. de Rênal, to his home, his past, and his relationship with Sorel, even before Stendhal reaches Chapter 2, which as the title indicates, is to be devoted to M. de Rênal.

Stendhal does not exhaust the description of a newly introduced character upon initial presentation, but rather he returns periodically to "round it out," having been led astray into digressions. Nothing is seen out of relation to other considerations: describing Rênal physically leads Stendhal to ascribe to the passerby a moral judgment about Rênal, condensing time; this then leads Stendhal to Rênal's home; then a parenthetical note about his ancestry; next Rênal's imposing "retaining walls" are evoked; then a comparison with gardens of other manufacturing towns; this leads the author to mention Sorel, since it is through him that the land was acquired; follows a necessary remark about the shrewdness of Sorel; and finally an incident which illustrates that M. de Rênal suspected that he had been bettered in the bargain. Had Stendhal followed the path into Verrières consistently as his means of introduction, the reader would have been enlightened about Sorel's sawmill at an earlier point.

This omission is not an oversight, however. Before Sorel and especially his son Julien, the hero of the novel, can be introduced, the Adversary against which Julien will pit himself in its various forms must be defined. The Adversary will be all of society as it incarnates the corruption and stagnation of the Restoration, thereby oppressing a superior being.

Chapter 1 thus gives us a sweeping, superficial tour; Chapter 2 repeats this gesture, now evoking Valenod and Maslon by the same "afterthought" technique before introducing the action proper: the Rênals' conversation on the promenade. The last few lines of this chapter begin the conversation, the meaning of which escapes the reader, and Stendhal must reappear to furnish more background details at the beginning of Chapter 3. The latter, in turn, involves a "flashback" to an episode having occurred the day before — this before we hear the end of the conversation between the Rênals. Thus, we hear briefly of Julien for the first time in Chapter 3 and we see him through the eyes of M. de Rênal, whose judgment we have already learned to question. Julien can't be a liberal, reasons Rênal, since he has been studying theology for the last three years.

These recurring views of M. de Rênal in interaction with other people permit us to judge him as pretentious, vain, easily duped, proud, and avaricious. Stendhal next turns to Mme. de Rênal and devotes a page to her character and history, taking care to emphasize her virtue and resignation to her lot. She is unaware that life holds anything better than what her husband offers her. Even the method of exposition fits a description of Stendhal's style as that of "improvisation." It suggests the image of ever-widening, superimposed circles.

CHAPTERS 4-5

Summary

M. de Rênal proposes to Sorel the next day that Julien come live with them and tutor their children. Old Sorel, a crafty peasant, meditates the conditions but refuses to answer before he has consulted his son Julien. Returning to his sawmill, Sorel finds Julien reading, sitting astride a beam above the saw he should be tending. Infuriated by his useless son, Sorel brutally knocks the book into the stream. Julien is saddened by the loss of this book, a cherished possession from the legacy his army surgeon friend had left him. His father demands an explanation of the strange offer from Rênal, but Julien is unable to account for it. In solitude, Julien decides that rather than submit to the humiliation of eating with the Rênals' servants, he will run away and enlist in the army. He abandons this plan immediately, however, since it would require that he renounce his ambitions for the priesthood, where success would be certain.

The next day, the bargain is struck, and Sorel has again outwitted Rênal, obtaining as much as he can for his son's services. Julien, meanwhile, has entrusted his possessions—books and military decoration—for safekeeping to his friend Fouqué. On his way to the chateau, Julien judges it wise for his hypocrisy to stop by the church. There he feels his courage waning, but reassures himself with a Napoleonic "To Arms!" and resolutely goes forth to battle in his first encounter at the Rênal home.

Commentary

Stendhal continues alternating exposition and dramatic action in these two chapters. We are not surprised that Sorel outwits Rênal in his two encounters, since we have been prepared for it. Of main interest here is Julien, first seen in his characteristic stance—reading, and in a relatively "high place." This is the first of many times that Stendhal will set Julien physically above his fellows, emphasizing Julien's superiority and solitude and providing him with a secret refuge from society.

The fall from the rafter foreshadows Julien's ultimate fall. He is persecuted then, even by his family because he is different. This aspiring "pariah" will be forever excluded because of his superiority. Note Julien's response to brutality and ugliness: tears. His is a very sensitive nature. It is fitting that Stendhal first presents Julien physically at a moment when he is emotionally moved. Normally pale, his cheeks are flushed with anger, his dark eyes burning with hatred, revealing a reflective and passionate nature. Julien's eternal struggle to control his sensibility by self-mastery and discipline will characterize his future conduct. His hypocritical air helps ward off the blows of his father and will serve as a defense against society.

Julien's dual formation—by the military, through the old surgeon who has inculcated him with respect for Napoleon, and by the Church, through Father Chélan, who has found in him a quick intelligence, readily grasping theology and easily memorizing the Bible—is alluded to in these two chapters, reiterating the novel's title and sketching Julien's situation as representative of the youth of France during the Restoration: born too late to achieve greatness in Napoleon's military endeavors, they must seek it through the Church.

During the interrogation by his father, Julien betrays his pride and ambition in three short, almost automatic utterances: "What will I get for that? . . . I don't want to be a servant. . . . But whom will I eat with?"

We learn that his aristocratic pride is acquired from Rousseau, whose Saint-Preux he also resembles in his extreme sensibility.

Julien's ability to memorize will be an asset both in his success as a preceptor and later, when he plays the same role, that of subservient secretary, but in the highest circle of political intriguers. Another quality of Julien that is sketched is his distrustfulness — of youth, of his peasant heritage. He will not speak to Father Chélan of his new position, since he suspects a trap.

In Chapter 5, Stendhal again takes up Rênal's fear of losing Julien to Valenod — a misunderstanding that will later justify Rênal's blindness to Julien's affair with Mme. de Rênal. It is Sorel who, quite by chance, hits upon the threat of a better offer for Julien elsewhere, which gives the old sawyer the upper hand in his bargaining with Rênal. Mme. de Rênal had already suggested this threat in Chapter 3. On that occasion, Rênal seized the danger as an argument — cleverly contrived, he congratulated himself — for moving ahead with his plan to hire Julien.

The church visit adds to the elaboration of Julien's character, permitting Stendhal to speak of his hero's hypocrisy, his best weapon. This permits more exposition, first of the Congrégation, then of more details of Julien's relationship with Chénal and of his decision to use the priesthood as a means to success. Julien had witnessed the persecution of Napoleon sympathizers and was forced to keep silent on that subject. In alliance with the "ultra" monarchy, the all-powerful Congrégation, a clandestine Jesuit organization, held absolute sway and did not permit dissension.

The art of hypocrisy requires complete self-control. Julien punishes himself for having openly defended Napoleon at a gathering of priests with Chélan. The manner of narration is characteristic of Stendhal: "At one point in the conversation he began fervently to praise Napoleon. He tied his right arm to his chest." Stendhal's psychological analysis sometimes omits transitional thoughts. The causal relationship between the two statements quoted must be supplied by the reader.

A final, very important trait of Julien is his personal honor, his only moral principle. It is called into play when he asks himself in the church if he could be a coward. Here he begins his ritual of self-imposing obstacles which his honor requires that he overcome.

The forewarning that Stendhal intercalates in the form of a scrap of paper (recalling the execution of the historical character who inspired the novel) bearing the ominous warning "the first step" on the other side, cannot be taken seriously by the sophisticated reader. It is simply indicative of Stendhal's penchant for the secretive, the mysterious. Its presence cannot be logically explained, since Julien's fate is realized without recourse to any supernatural powers. It also underlines Stendhal's intention to be closely inspired by reality in writing fiction.

Stendhal turns briefly to Mme. de Rênal, who is having her own doubts about the imminent arrival of Julien. Her initial and ultimate reception of him will be the subject of the next three chapters, so that this final paragraph is transitional.

CHAPTERS 6-8

Summary

Mme. de Rênal receives Julien, and after their mutual embarrassment has changed — for Mme. de Rênal to relief and for Julien to a beginning of composure — he is outfitted in a new suit and presented to the children. Now in complete command of himself, Julien recites at random entire passages of the Bible in Latin, earning the respect and admiration of all. Within a month, he is considered as a real prize by M. de Rênal.

During the next five weeks, Julien engages in petty negotiations beginning his scheme of success through hypocrisy. The self-righteousness that this society feels causes him to feel superior to it, and this, in turn, alienates him from it. His utter ignorance of most matters prevents him, at this stage, from understanding much of what he hears. He craftily convinces Rênal of the necessity of taking out a subscription with the liberal bookseller, presenting the matter in such a way that it will not offend the vanity of the Royalist.

Julien is extremely wary of Mme. de Rênal, since her beauty caused him to stumble when he first arrived. She, on the other hand, is becoming increasingly drawn to this charming and intelligent young man. Unaware of what love is, she gives no thought to the fact that she is attentive to his needs and that her husband is becoming increasingly unbearable to her.

Mme. de Rênal's maid, Elisa, has designs on Julien, and Father Chélan urges him to consider favorably the possibility of such a match and discourages him from entering the priesthood. Julien's burning ardor makes Chélan fear for his salvation should he pursue a career in the Church. Julien retreats, then returns to try to impress the priest by a new tactic. To no avail, for Chélan is not fooled. This is a defeat for Julien.

Mme. de Rênal is overjoyed to hear Elisa confess tearfully that Julien has rejected her. Soon Mme. de Rênal becomes aware that she is in love with Julien.

In the spring, the family moves to the summer home in the neighboring village of Vergy. Animated by a fresh outlook, Mme. de Rênal agrees to Julien's suggestion to create a meandering path "à la Julie," among the walnut trees. Catching butterflies provides a new activity and topic of conversation for the inexperienced couple. Mme. de Rênal changes clothes two or three times a day, unaware, however, of what prompts this interest in her appearance. The arrival of Mme. Derville creates a happy threesome. Julien relaxes to the point of reading, not only at night in the solitude of his room but during the day. This increased reading finally gives him some ideas about women.

The three begin to assemble at night outside in the darkness for conversation. One evening, in his animated gesticulation, Julien happens to touch Mme. de Rênal's hand. When it is instantly withdrawn, he decides it is his duty to hold it. A new challenge disturbs his peace.

Commentary

In these chapters Stendhal brings Julien and Mme. de Rênal together for the first time, then concentrates on their separate progression. As will be typical of Julien's character, he reacts spontaneously when surprised by Mme. de Rênal. An aspiring hypocrite must learn to control his reactions. He hates her "because she is beautiful"—that is, her beauty produces a violent reaction in him, a superior being born to exalt in beauty and to be offended by ugliness, but his reaction is spontaneous, and in betraying it, he ruins his "pose."

His pride is offended when she expresses amazement at his knowledge of Latin. Her supplicating tone causes him momentarily to forget his pride, and as his self-confidence becomes progressively stronger, he dares himself to kiss her hand. This daring act he accomplishes. His composure is shattered again when he gives way to the expression of joy, caused by his new clothes, but once again, after collecting himself in his room, he reassumes the calm and dignity befitting a tutor.

The scene relating Julien's arrival is important for several reasons. It establishes the pattern of conduct that will characterize him throughout the novel. In him there seethes a conflict between spontaneous expression of joy associated with happiness and the hypocritical wearing of a mask imposed by ambition. The scene illustrates the tender irony that characterizes Stendhal's attitude toward his "chosen" characters. He deliberately places them in awkward situations that will challenge and embarrass them, after already creating them with a contradictory nature that will cause them to stumble. He has great affection for his "chosen" characters, but he demands of them as much as he demands of himself.

Julien's petty maneuvering wins him minor triumphs in this household which he disdains. Throughout the novel his prodigious memory will be a sure means of winning for him the admiration of others, but it seems to produce a special effect on the provincial bourgeois, incapable, says Stendhal, of appreciating intelligence in any other form. The almost photographic memory that Julien possesses would seem to serve in place of keen reasoning and eloquence to convince the reader of Julien's superior nature, as we will see.

Misunderstanding it, Julien rebuffs Mme. de Rênal's offer of money and succeeds in tricking the mayor on two occasions. His social behavior is quite unacceptable and his efforts to play a role accentuate his ineptness. On the other hand, he unknowingly charms Mme. de Rênal with his eyes. He is unable to deceive Chélan, and the great emotion he experiences at the love and concern shown him by the priest betrays an ardent soul thirsting for friendship and happiness. Thus, to enjoy this emotion completely, Julien takes refuge in the mountains, where his superior soul may not be surprised — unguarded — by the watchful eyes of society.

Stendhal intervenes at this point to assure the reader that Julien will succeed as a hypocrite — he is only a beginner. This intervention betrays the sympathy of the author for his amoral hero and dictates the reader's reaction. Since the novel is also the story of the education of Julien, Stendhal will intervene periodically to praise or censure the conduct of his hero.

For the first time in his life Julien is happy — interestingly enough, only when he momentarily forgets his relentless ambition and hypocrisy. His ambition reawakens at a gesture of Mme. de Rênal: when she withdraws her hand, Julien vows, in a chivalric way, to force her to leave her hand in his. His code of honor is very demanding and depends entirely upon personal criteria. For Julien, personal honor replaces morality.

The chapters advance Mme. de Rênal toward her role as mistress more so than Julien toward his of lover, although the affair will necessarily begin awkwardly and almost by accident, both parties lacking experience and even a conception of what love is.

The awakening and development of love in his characters is illustrative of the crystallization process that Stendhal elaborated in *De l'Amour*. The feeling manifests itself autonomously of will and, after a preliminary stage of admiration and hope, soon crystallizes in the mind of the lover. This means that it becomes the exclusive obsession of the victim smitten, and every subject, no matter how far removed in appearance, ultimately leads one back to discover new perfections in the loved one.

Mme. de Rênal has never before been so deeply moved by a purely agreeable sensation as when she learns that this delightful young man is the stern priest she had anticipated. Note that only when her mind is at ease over the fate of her children does she notice Julien's good looks. She will remain in the early stages of "admiration" for a seemingly long period of time because of utter inexperience and ignorance of love.

She feels in Julien a kindred spirit and she has never imagined that such a man existed, so different from the husband whom she has considered the prototype of manhood. She involuntarily conceals her pleasure at the prospect of Julien's staying, her subconscious forcing the opposite reaction in the conscious.

Mme. de Rênal is greatly moved when she finds Julien beaten by his brothers. She notices the attentiveness that Elisa shows him, then wants to show him kindnesses. Increasingly she disapproves of the lack of delicacy and tact in her husband. Leaning on Julien's arm during a walk, she offers him the gift. His refusal leaves her t embling, and she takes some pleasure in his reprimand. She redoubles her attentions, giving herself the pretext that she has offended him. She becomes physically ill when Elisa speaks to her of Julien's refusal. At this point, Mme. de Rênal becomes consciously aware that she is in love; and what pleasure it is to plead the cause of Elisa, to speak of Julien knowing that he has refused. She actually faints from the joy that the interview causes her. With this realization does not come guilt, since Mme. de Rênal is unaware of what love implies. Thus she plunges head on, in her innocence, attending to her toilette with unprecedented care.

CHAPTERS 9-15

Summary

Julien plans his campaign and, after much anguish, takes Mme. de Rênal's hand the next evening. Although she at first withdraws, he insists, and ultimately, she offers it freely. Rênal offends Julien by accusing him of neglecting the children, but Julien's sullen mood is suddenly changed by the imminence of a catastrophe: Rênal might find his hidden picture of Napoleon as the mayor and the servants change the mattress stuffing. Mme. de Rênal rescues it for Julien, unaware of whose picture the box contains. Rênal, on the other hand, misinterprets Julien's pride for the cunning of the peasant demanding more wages. When he grants Julien a raise, the latter is abashed and scorns the mayor even more for measuring everything in monetary terms. Julien gives expanse to the joy of victory in the solitude of the mountains as he goes to visit Chélan.

The next night Julien dares to show his scorn of Rênal by taking Mme. de Rênal's hand in his very presence, albeit under the cover of dark, and he covers it with passionate kisses. Julien contemplates his campaign against this contemptible bourgeois, while Mme. de Rênal is torn between her jealousy and anguish at the first pangs of guilt, imagining herself to be a fallen woman. Her agitation is so great that she almost betrays her passion by asking Elisa abruptly if it is she, Elisa, whom Julien loves. Mme. de Rênal resolves to treat Julien coldly.

Julien takes offense and does not confide to her his plans to leave for a three-day trip. He stops off again in the mountains to enjoy his freedom in solitude. During their visit, Fouqué offers Julien a partnership that would assure the latter of financial success. After deliberation, Julien rejects the offer, since the success he envisages must be gained through hardship and it must be accomplished by means of the Church. His friendship itself is instrumental in his rejection of the offer. He would not choose to betray Fouqué later, once his education had been financed. Fouqué confides to Julien the tales of his amorous conquests.

Upon his return, Julien discovers that Mme. de Rênal is in love with him, and he decides that his duty requires that he make her his mistress. He announces that he must leave, since he loves her desperately. This avowal sends her into ecstasy, but she innocently assures herself that their relationship will be a platonic one. Julien awkwardly begins his seduction.

His absence caused by another trip to Verrières, where he witnesses the disgrace into which Chélan has fallen, causes his awkward attempts of the previous day to be forgotten. He announces quite abruptly to Mme. de Rênal that he will visit her room at two o'clock in the morning. The declaration is met with an indignant reprimand. He forces himself to carry out this, the most daring of his exploits, and it succeeds only because he forgets his plan and throws himself at Mme. de Rênal's feet. He is unable to enjoy the experience, however, since he is so occupied seeing himself in the role of lover. Returning to his room, Julien's only thought is whether he played his role well.

Commentary

In spite of the obvious earnestness of the characters, the reader cannot help but be amused at the "comedy of errors and cross purposes" that is played out in these chapters, having its climax in Chapter 15 with the seduction of Mme. de Rênal.

This triumph is not due to Julien's art, but rather to his charm, which erupts in unguarded moments; to Mme. de Rênal's love for him, which by this time has become passion; and to the unknowing collaboration of the mayor. Stendhal manipulates the episodes in such a way that each of the three characters acts independently of the others, yet almost by chance they contribute by their convergence to the fortuitous victory of Julien.

This unwitting conspiracy is apparent upon analysis. Julien's ambition to seduce Mme. de Rênal does not result from love for her, but from his sense of duty toward himself. He owes it to himself to take her hand, but he has forgotten the incident the next morning. To motivate this "de-motivated" campaign, Stendhal then utilizes the mayor, whose reproach to Julien for his idleness provokes the latter to avenge his wounded pride by demanding an apology. To the amazement of Julien, the mayor grants him a raise. Julien realizes, however, that this second victory has not been earned, but the elation of the victories must be expressed in the solitude of the mountains.

Julien's next step is again motivated by his scorn for the mayor. What an expression of ridicule to take Mme. de Rênal's hand in the presence of her husband! That evening, Julien relaxes enough to actually enjoy the unknown pleasure that her beauty causes him. Planning his strategy according to Napoleon, he will further crush the mayor by requesting a three-day leave. Already, in spite of himself, however, a feeling for Mme. de Rênal is autonomously manifesting itself. Stendhal comments that Julien longed to see her again, in spite of his expectations. The mutual coldness of their interview summarizes their dilemma: it moves them apart in order, ultimately, to unite them.

The numerous absences of Julien ripen Mme. de Rênal for the ultimate conquest, although Julien does not absent himself for that specific purpose. The tranquility enjoyed by Julien during his second retreat to the mountains is disturbed by Fouqué's offer. Even this obstacle advances Julien's cause, unbeknownst to him: it frees his mind to think of her. Fouqué's amorous affairs teach Julien something about women. Upon his return, therefore, he comes "naturally" to the realization that Mme. de Rênal loves him. This proves to be the greatest step in his progression, since when she herself initiates the hand-clasp ritual, Julien "ups the ante" in his self-imposition of obstacle pattern, deciding that it is his duty to seduce her, to make her his mistress. This decision, then, is made in all lucidity.

With no love yet prompting him, only his ambition and pride, Julien announces hypocritically that he loves her passionately. As he executes his plan, he falls from blunder into blunder, and his attempts at paying court are climaxed by his brutal announcement of the early morning visit he will pay. Had Mme. de Rênal not been moved by Julien's tears of confusion and had her love not progressed to its paroxysm, she would never have given herself. Julien's conquest of Mme. de Rênal and his love for her at this point take the form of a military assault on society.

Mme. de Rênal, on the other hand, already painfully knows the bliss of love. But it has developed in these chapters. She allies herself unknowingly more and more closely with Julien against her husband. The sweet complicity into which she enters with Julien has a twofold importance: it is a sign of a greater degree of involvement with Julien and a means to the realization of a further step in the crystallization of her love because it contains the seeds of jealousy which will torment her.

At first her conflict is between the fear of not being loved and the shame of becoming an adultress. Then when she permits herself to enjoy the thought of happiness with Julien, she is tormented by jealousy, by the fear that he loves another. Soon fear of Julien's departure overcomes any thought she has of resisting him. His hypocritical confession of love for her sends her into a blissful state, although she continues to delude herself as to the future of their relationship, which she can only see as platonic.

The final blunder that precipitates the seduction again reproduces in miniature their entire experience: he clumsily tries to make contact with her foot; she reproaches him, ordering him to be careful; he is offended by the tone and leaves for a day; this absence prepares her to accept him.

In the two studies of love that the novel presents, with Mme. de Rênal, and in Part II, with Mathilde, Stendhal is not only contrasting two types of love — passionate and intellectual — but he is focusing different stages of the love experience, and the two are presented in a complementary way. Julien and Mme. de Rênal are united through blunder and by accident, and separation brings about the union. Julien and Mathilde will both calculate, and Julien will succeed in keeping her love alive only through imposing separation and distance.

CHAPTERS 16-23

Summary

Now their love idyll begins: Julien loves her madly, says Stendhal, but his love is still a form of ambition. Mme. de Rênal's great joy is clouded only by the fear that she is too old for Julien. The second night finds Julien forgetting his role and enjoying his experience. Mme. de Rênal takes great pleasure in educating Julien in social manners and in all the political intrigue that reigns in Verrières, of which Julien has been completely ignorant.

The town is honored by a visit of the king, and Mme. de Rênal succeeds in having a place in the guard of honor awarded to Julien. From his role of dashing, handsome officer, Julien moves to that of attendant priest to Chélan in a religious ceremony honoring the local saint. Other important personages to whose presence his role gives him access are the young

Bishop Agde, officiating prelate, and M. de la Mole, influential and powerful Parisian aristocrat, Peer of France, in the king's entourage.

When one of her sons falls seriously ill, Mme. de Rênal is convinced that God is punishing her adultery. Witnessing her anguish and torment, Julien finds new reasons to love her. When Stanislas is well, her anguish nevertheless remains, since the experience has made her aware of guilt. Their love, however, becomes deeper, more desperate, and somber.

M. de Rênal receives an anonymous letter denouncing Julien as his wife's lover. Julien senses what the letter is and warns Mme. de Rênal not to come to his room that night. She, however, constantly wary that Julien is looking for an excuse to abandon her, comes to his room anyway but is not received. She writes Julien a long letter, elaborating her doubts and reiterating her undying love for him. At the same time, however, she is capable of devising a plan, in the event that there does exist an anonymous letter denouncing them. She will pretend also to have received such a letter, will deliver it to her husband to confound him and to allay his doubts.

M. de Rênal is suffering greatly from wounded pride, anger, and self-pity. He is unable to bring himself to take any decisive step. His wife arrives, hands her letter to him, and in the next breath requests that Julien be sent away for a time until the scandal dies down. This represents exactly the solution Rênal would have wanted. It relieves him of the necessity of finding out the truth, since it is an avowal of innocence on her part. She furnishes him with further evidence in the form of old love letters written to her by Valenod. She succeeds masterfully in putting him on the wrong track, thereby saving appearances and her affair with Julien.

In order to prove to the town that all is well in the Rênal household, Julien lives in their townhouse. There he is visited by the sub-prefect, M. de Maugiron, who, on the behalf of another, sounds out Julien on the possibility of leaving the Rênal household for a new position. Julien congratulates himself on his ability to satisfy Maugiron with a long-winded answer that constitutes, in effect, no answer to his proposition. Invited to dinner at the home of Valenod, Julien inwardly condemns the vulgar ostentation and bad taste of his hosts. When Valenod silences one of the inmates of the workhouse, Julien finds further grounds to feel superior to Valenod and to scorn him. Julien is invited everywhere, he is held in such esteem as a learned and talented tutor.

When the Rênals come for the day to Verrières, mother and children form a happy family group with Julien, and their happiness irks the mayor, who interrupts the scene. The mayor has been forced by the Congrégation to rent out a property at a much lower sum than he could have asked. Valenod, his subordinate whose trickery and intriguing with the Congrégation have brought about the downfall of the Jansenist Chélan, has played a role in this intrigue. Valenod is indebted to the Vicar Frilair of the Congrégation, and at the same time he is ingratiating himself with the liberals, in the event that he falls out of favor with the conservatives and that M. de Rênal takes steps to disgrace him.

Julien learns of these machinations from Mme. de Rênal, and since he attends the mysterious auction, he is taken for the Rênals' spy.

The gloom that reigns in the Rênal household is momentarily dispelled by the unexpected arrival of an Italian singer, recommended highly to Rênal and seeking further recommendations to the French court. His gaiety, exuberance, and talent provide a welcome interlude for the family, and his mission further edifies Julien as to how influence assures promotion and personal advancement.

Meanwhile, several factors precipitate Julien's departure to Besançon. The town is scandalized that M. de Rênal has ignored the talk about the affair in his household. Through Valenod's machinations, Elisa has related to the Jesuit Maslon and to Chélan what is going on between Julien and Mme. de Rênal. Chélan therefore requires of Julien that he either enter the seminary at Besançon, the director of which is Chélan's lifelong friend, or that Julien become the partner of Fouqué. M. de Rênal agrees that Julien must leave. Julien accepts the ultimatum but volunteers, to the great joy of Mme. de Rênal, to return after three days for a last farewell. If Julien goes to Besançon, his education must be financed; if he stays, Valenod will engage him as tutor.

Another anonymous letter received by Rênal presents the occasion for the final intervention of Mme. de Rênal to convince her husband of the necessity of offering money to Julien. At first, Julien accepts the money as a loan, but ultimately, to the joy of the mayor, he refuses it because of his great pride.

Mme. de Rênal, paradoxically, lives only for the last night's rendezvous with Julien, but when it arrives, she is cold and lifeless, anticipating the future emptiness of her life. Julien departs for Besancon.

Commentary

In these chapters, Julien plays a relatively passive role, since his education requires that his experience be enlarged, and this requires that through his teacher, here for the most part Mme. de Rênal, fresh insights into the local political situation be managed for Julien and for the reader. It is as if by seducing Mme. de Rênal, Julien has displayed sufficient initiative, so that he may now sit back, without having to play an active role himself. He will have only to feel the effects of his relationship with Mme. de Rênal and of other conditions existing in Verrières.

Besides, this is also a political novel, and Stendhal takes time out to add to his scornful exposé of the evils of the Restoration on the local level.

It is mainly to Mme. de Rênal that the initiative falls because her love has taught her the necessity of ruse. Julien's earlier petty scheming seems even more ludicrous judged against Mme. de Rênal's daring and heroic strategems inspired by love. Her love has crystallized to the point where she would make any sacrifice for Julien: she educates him socially and, at the risk of scandal, obtains for Julien the position in the guard of honor. It is likewise she who takes the initiative to skillfully dupe her husband about the anonymous letters. Their love is that of mother and son, at the same time that it is of mistress and lover. Julien has never had a mother or the love of a family, and Stendhal remedies this lack by the insertion of an idyllic family scene in which Julien displaces completely Mayor Rênal in Chapter 22. The conclusions to be drawn about Stendhal's own childhood are obvious.

Note that it is mainly on faith that we must believe in Julien's superior intelligence, for Stendhal will rarely permit us to witness any examples of his brilliance and articulate eloquence. The author intervenes to assure us of Julien's superiority, others acclaim him (the Valenods and their guests), and Mme. de Rênal herself predicts a great future for such a brilliant man. His inexperience, at this stage, accounts somewhat for the lack of indications, it is true, but in his later experiences in Paris, the same absence of proof will be noticeable. Julien out-jesuits the sub-prefect when the latter attempts to enlist him in the service of Valenod, but we hear none of his brilliant conversational digressions to avoid an answer. Stendhal simply tells us that his reply was perfect, as long-winded as a pastoral letter in that it suggested everything and stated nothing. Since Stendhal was, in a sense, writing the novel for himself and for the "happy few," he evidently felt no need to demonstrate a superiority of which he was convinced. His modesty was another factor in this reticence.

Thanks to the love that Mme. de Rênal has for him, Julien has made two noticeable strides ahead in his onslaught on society: he enjoys a vicarious military experience in the guard of honor, and because of his roles that day, is soon sought after by all of Verrières. He makes progress, profits from his education, in spite of the generally passive role he assumes. He has progressed in the art of hypocrisy: when he lets slip praise of Napoleon and is rebuked for it by Mme. de Rênal, his pride does not incapacitate him, and he is even adroit enough to dodge responsibility for the statement.

Julien's self-appointed role as messenger to Bishop Agde previews his later roles as secretary and as spy. Julien will never attain a position of independence vis-à-vis society, rather he will always be a protected and cherished instrument of others. He actively compares the success of alternative ways of action as he sees them in others. He prefers the refined manners of Bishop Agde to those he has found in the province. He sees everywhere examples of compromise in order to succeed: the letter left in the room occupied by M. de la Mole; the mission of the Italian singer. The latter he compares favorably to M. de Rênal, who is forced to humiliate himself before the Congrégation.

At the Valenod's dinner, Julien is horrified at the ill-treatment the workhouse inmates receive, although he is able to contain his true feelings. In the face of the ultimatum given him by Chélan, Julien debates as to whether he should take offense, but again he remains master of himself, silent in a feigned attitude of humility. It must be reiterated that Stendhal does not condemn Julien's hypocrisy. A nature as sensitive, generous, and spontaneous as Julien's is forced to this extremity to survive.

The playing out of the novel's title in Chapter 18 will not have been missed by the reader: Julien plays alternately the role of soldier, then priest. It will be, of course, the latter vocation that he will choose as a means to success, since Napoleon's disappearance has rendered the former impossible. Nonetheless, the spurs that he wears under the priest's cassock indicate that his career in the priesthood will be marked with the ruthlessness and dashing of the soldier.

Although Julien is capable of more love for Mme. de Rênal than before his seduction of her, he is far from being a victim of it. Goaded by ambition, Julien's mind is not yet a fecund "theater" where this imperious emotion may manifest itself and thrive. Stendhal makes passing allusions to the "mad" love Julien has for her and to the fact that he finds new reasons to love her, but we are hardly convinced. His love for Mme. de Rênal must await the end of the novel for its full development. It might be argued that in making Julien master of the love experience, Stendhal is getting his revenge on all of the women with whom he had been unsuccessful.

Julien's love brings him, at this stage, contentment and a peace and happiness he has never known. He seems to love her more as he sees more and more how much she loves him—particularly when Mme. de Rênal's son is critically ill. At that moment, Julien realizes how completely his mistress is a helpless, suffering victim of love. He feels only momentarily the doubts and torments that continue to plague her and that move her love to constant renewal in new crystallizations. It is quite possible that it is Stendhal's own sensibility, modesty, and need for privacy that prevent him from disclosing much of what Julien's love for Mme. de Rênal entails. For Julien is a projection of what Stendhal would like to be, as are all his protagonists.

It will be obvious to the reader at this point in the novel that Stendhal does not take great pains to conceive an overall view of the action in which subsequent events are mutually interdependent and which would seem to be "necessary" as logical and expected results of previous causes. On the contrary, he invents incidents as he needs them, and the resulting haphazard nature of succession results from an almost improvisational technique of composition and it is one of the meanings of his definition of the novel as a "mirror which is carried along the road."

He needed, for example, the sudden grave illness of Stanislas to permit a further crystallization of Mme. de Rênal's love for Julien and an intensification of his love for her. The unannounced arrival of Géronimo is a fortuitous event needed to alleviate the series of defeats that M. de Rênal has just undergone and that have plunged the household into gloom. In Chapter 23, almost without any warning, the reader learns that because of the scandal of Julien's affair with Mme. de Rênal, a scandal hardly surprising but heretofore not even alluded to by Stendhal, a decision must be made as to Julien's future. Obviously, Stendhal wants to move him on to Besançon, and this is the logical means. Similarly, Elisa chooses this moment to inform Chélan of Julien's conduct, and it is this "father-figure" alone who can prevail on Julien to leave.

CHAPTER 24

Summary

Julien visits the military installation in Besançon before reporting to the seminary. He stops at a cafe, and his fancy is taken by the barmaid, Armanda, who recognizes his obvious embarrassment at the strangeness of this large city. The arrival of one of her lovers nearly incites Julien to challenge him to a duel, but on the insistence of Armanda, Julien leaves the cafe. He stops at an inn to leave his clothes in the safekeeping of the landlady, then courageously starts out for the seminary.

Commentary

This transitional chapter introduces Julien to the city of Besançon, where the next stage of his education will take place. The cafe scene will reappear in the second part of the novel in a slightly different form but producing the same effect. Here, the young, inexperienced country boy ventures into a big city cafe. Stendhal creates for him an almost quixotic episode, where Julien may give heroic proportions to a trivial incident: drawing from his experience as lover, Julien places himself abruptly in the role of Don Juan with Armanda, and his sudden declaration of love to the barmaid is reminiscent of a previous one, pronounced with less sureness but with as much hypocrisy to Mme. de Rênal.

After his brief and audacious visit to the fortress overlooking Besançon, where he has again evoked an imaginary military career, it is here in a cafe that he almost spontaneously gives form to his aggressiveness in an imagined amorous adventure. The arrival of Armanda's lover is but a part of this mock-heroic adventure, immediately awakening in Julien the sense of honor of the knight errant, who, without the intervention of Armanda, would have challenged his supposed "rival." The scenes preliminary to Julien's arrival at the seminary should recall to the reader Julien's visit to the church prior to his entrance at the home of the Rênals. In both, Julien is play-acting, rehearsing, in a sense, for his big scene. He musters up his courage, measures it, or rather "takes its temperature," to assure himself in advance that he will not fall short of the ideal performance required in a new and challenging situation.

Note that the "glance" is the basis of the real and imagined adventure that Stendhal narrates, and he gives Julien almost magical powers of self-extrication. Communication by the "glance" seems to be one of the secretive codes designed to protect the integrity of the superior being.

As was predicted by the priest Chélan, Julien's merit will endanger him because of the envy it inspires in others. Therefore, it is not surprising that Julien seeks protection in women from his enemies. In this short chapter, the two incidents present women as a defense against the world. Lover (Armanda) and Mother (the landlady) are irresistibly attracted to Julien and would protect him.

Even though his method is improvisational, Stendhal relies on "preparation" for the development of plot: this interlude will have served also as the basis of a subsequent plot devised by Julien's enemies to destroy him in the seminary.

CHAPTERS 25-27

Summary

Julien is admitted to the presence of the rector, Father Pirard, by an extremely ugly porter. This impression of ugliness and the fright given by the sternness of Pirard cause Julien to faint. Pirard agrees to give him a full scholarship in recognition of the recommendation from his dear friend Chélan. Julien obviously impresses Pirard favorably by his knowledge of scripture and Latin and by the clarity and insight of his answers. Julien is taken to his cell, where he falls into a deep sleep. His first meeting with Pirard has given him to believe that the seminary is taken seriously by the students. Julien fails miserably in his attempt to succeed by brilliant achievement. He also has erred by requesting Pirard as his confessor, instead of the rector's Jesuit enemy. Julien learns that to distinguish himself and gain acceptance among his fellows he must appear stupid, materialistic, and docile.

The Jesuit Castanède has found Armanda's address in Julien's luggage and has denounced him to Pirard. Confronted by the rector, Julien lies successfully and exonerates himself. It is the baseness, vulgarity, and ugliness of his adversaries—his fellow seminarians—that cause him to flinch and become discouraged in his struggle. His attempts to win them are without success. The description of the ideal awaiting the young priests as preached by Father Castanède revolts Julien: it consists of being well-fed, of vegetating in a parish surrounded by all the physical comforts. His eloquence proves to be another reason for alienation from his fellows, and he must often defend himself against physical attacks.

Commentary

Verrières was protected by walls, figuratively speaking, that Julien succeeded in climbing; now he enters another "prison," the seminary, which he must also conquer. In direct contrast to his imagined conquest of Armanda in the cafe, Julien's interview with Pirard is a confrontation that overwhelms and terrifies him. His sensitive nature shuts out ugliness by rendering him unconscious. Again Stendhal omits Julien's brilliant, concise answers to Pirard's interrogation, although we learn that Julien's answers evoke Pirard's admiration for him.

The keenness of Stendhal's psychological observation is noted in the brief statement occurring at the end of the interview, which casts light on Julien's frame of mind in retrospect: "Julien looked down and saw his trunk directly in front of him; he had been looking at if for three hours without recognizing it." Moments of intense emotional strain prevent us from evaluating objectively a situation except in retrospect.

The prison-like nature of the seminary is emphasized by fleeting views of the outside world, caught by Julien through a window, both during the grueling interview with Pirard and later in his cell. This glimpse of "high places"—mountains, in this instance—serves to reassure Julien, is inspirational to him in this crisis.

Just as Julien blundered in his attempt to seduce Mme. de Rênal, he will blunder in his attempt to succeed in the seminary. The cafe scene served to mark his progress as a seducer, evidence that he had gained experience and wisdom from the experiences in Verrières. Here, however, is a new field of experience, and his evaluation of the interview with Pirard gives him a false sense of security, causing him to fail miserably in his first few weeks in the seminary. He thought that his usual hypocritical mask was the one to assume, but he soon discovers that he has assumed the wrong mask. It is not excellence that is required of the young, would-be priests, rather submission, obedience, and docility. Even in the seminary, Julien is an outsider, a pariah, because of his superior nature. He has great difficulty trying to perfect a mask of stupidity.

Note, however, his progress in the second interview with Pirard. Stendhal admits the reader into a complicity with Julien in the following way: Julien cleverly utilizes the two incidents that had occurred during his first day in Besançon, taking from each what he needs to substantiate his lie to Pirard. Stendhal does not make any comment on this operation. Julien utilizes, then, the potential of Stendhal's logic. Julien's self-imposed campaign of austerity has borne fruits, however, since in not leaving the seminary, he has avoided a worse fate. He has succeeded, again, in spite of himself.

CHAPTERS 28-29

Summary

One priest, however, befriends Julien, Father Chas-Bernard, master of ceremonies of the cathedral. Julien is selected to aid the latter in an important ceremony in the cathedral in Besancon. There he distinguishes himself for his physical prowess and agility in decorating pillars. Here, Julien is also glimpsed by Mme. de Rênal, who promptly faints at the sight of him. He, similarly, is violently moved by this encounter.

Pirard sends Julien as his messenger to the bishop with Pirard's letter of resignation. Julien also learns from Pirard that he is being named tutor in the Old and New Testaments, a signal honor proving Pirard's esteem for him. Contrary to Julien's expectations, the other seminarians accept his advancement as evidence of his merit, that is, they recognize him as one whom they must fear.

Stendhal fills in the political intrigue that has prompted Pirard's resignation: Pirard has allied himself with M. de la Mole in a lawsuit the latter has against Frilair, the powerful Jesuit vicar and organizer of the Besançon Congrégation. Pirard has accepted the generosity of his friend Mole's influence: responsibility of a very wealthy church in the vicinity of

Paris, since he knows that Frilair will succeed in divesting him of his position at the seminary. Julien receives an anonymous gift of money from Mole, who has chosen to honor Pirard's prize student, since the rector himself will not accept recompense for his services in Mole's lawsuit.

Julien receives a wild boar from Fouqué, and this gift further wins the esteem of his fellows, since they believe that Julien's parents have sent the boar and, therefore, must be rich. Julien performs brilliantly in his examinations, but he is tricked by Frilair into displaying his knowledge of Latin poets, poets whose works are banned at the seminary. Julien delivers the letter to the bishop and is invited to dinner. In Frilair's presence he provides a stimulating discussion of the arts for the bishop of Besancon. As a reward, the bishop makes him a gift of the complete works of Tacitus. News of this gift soon circulates in the seminary and adds to the high esteem in which the others now hold Julien.

Commentary

These chapters narrate Julien's success at the seminary. The beginning of Chapter 28 illustrates Stendhal's improvisational technique. The "event" —the protection offered by Father Chas, thus the beginning of his success—needs an introduction to "precipitate" it. The method of having the event happen is Julien's question: Surely among all these learned professors, one at least has noticed my willingness and has been taken in by my hypocrisy?

Julien has overevaluated Father Chas, however. Stendhal. it will be remarked, does not state this fact; the reader must draw the conclusion. Julien is so accustomed to hypocrisy and ruse that he sees it where it isn't. He imagines in this simple priest (the projection in the future of what the materialistically oriented fellows of Julien will become) a very shrewd man with some ulterior motives beneath conversation entirely devoted to revelings in the rich furnishings of the cathedral. In reality, Father Chas-Bernard is only what he appears to be. The priest's disinterestedness gives a certain gratuitousness to Julien's success.

We learn that Pirard is taking Julien more and more into his confidence from his passing warning to the hero concerning his mission into Besancon to aid in the adornment of the cathedral. This isolated note of confidence is a preparation for Julien's future in Paris.

Note again that Julien's physical ascension betokens his aspirations and destiny. He alone is daring enough to risk his neck forty feet off the ground to pose the feathers. The ecstatic reverie that the solemnity of the surroundings inspires in Julien is reminiscent of the scene in Chapter 18 where he watches in ecstasy the ceremony of the ardent chapel. Both scenes betray his highly sensitive, superior nature and contrast his emotional, authentic religious response to the baseness of the Church, no longer a divine instrument, but perverted to political ends during the Restoration.

The unexpected appearance of Mme. de Rênal should not completely surprise us. We know that she has become extremely pious and that, refusing to make Father Maslon her confessor, she frequents the confessional at Besançon. It is also obvious why she comes to Besançon—her passion for Julien is the only justification for her piety. We will find another important encounter between Julien and Mme. de Rênal in a church later in the novel. Her fainting in this scene foreshadows her fate in that later scene, for which Julien will be more directly responsible.

The cathedral episode is the first step in Julien's success at the seminary.

Julien's mentors are kindred souls: noble, of great principle, who have refused to compromise. The austere Jansenist Pirard, just as Chélan, recognizes Julien's nobility of soul and protects him. The touching "communion of souls" that takes place in this scene between Pirard and Julien, two rebels who finally let down their guard and console each other, is reminiscent of Julien's escape sought in high places and solitude in earlier chapters. Note the philosophy of Pirard, similar to Julien's, that has helped to strengthen the latter's character: Pirard has tested Julien by creating insurmountable obstacles in his path. It is Pirard's belief that only the noblest of men could prove themselves by overcoming these obstacles. Pirard tests Julien in this episode, just as Stendhal "tests" his hero throughout the novel.

Julien still interprets incorrectly the attitudes of his fellows. On various occasions during his rapid advancement, he expects hate and receives respect from the seminarians. Stendhal benefits from a certain ambiguity of presentation to maintain the reader's sympathy for Julien. It is uncertain as to how aware of the political maneuvering Julien is; Stendhal chooses not to elaborate this point. It is to be presumed that Julien is as informed as are the others about the rivalry between the Jansenist Pirard and the Jesuit Frilair. The reader is completely informed, however, and our superiority over Julien encourages an indulgent attitude toward his mistakes.

The bishop has no future, and his awareness of this accounts in part for his fair treatment of Julien. He is a power, and independent, but his old age relieves him of the need to intrigue. He is another "father-figure" for Julien, albeit his role is short-lived.

Again, it is by feats of memory, by "bon mots" which we do not hear, and by brilliant discussion, likewise unrecorded, that Julien charms the bishop.

Note the brief allusion to the "Red" in this chapter: Julien is quickly consoled at not being able to enlist as he overhears two old troopers lament the present state of command and the absence of the great Napoleon.

CHAPTER 30

Summary

Pirard refuses to serve as Mole's secretary but recommends Julien for the post. The latter is notified by Pirard to come to Paris but visits Verrières before his departure. Chélan requires that he not see Mme. de Rênal. Julien obtains a ladder, however, and courageously presents himself at Mme. de Rênal's window, not knowing who might be awaiting him there, or how he would be received by Mme. de Rênal. She admits him with reluctance; and after three hours of conversation, he succeeds in overcoming her remorse. She has given herself with a certain gaiety and abandon, an attitude that she retains the next day while she hides Julien in her room and, in spite of endless perils, until the next night. The arrival of M. de Rênal, who has discovered the "thief's" ladder, pounding on her door, causes Julien to leap from her window and to take flight to Paris, on the road to Geneva, however, to avoid capture.

Commentary

It is obvious that Pirard's journey to Paris is a means to get Julien there, and with a position, that is, protected by the powerful M. de la Mole. Julien can only assume that the gift he has received comes from Mme. de Rênal. The superiority of the reader invites our complicity with Julien's other mentors. It is fitting that Julien returns to Verrières before undertaking the next stage in his education in Paris. We are thereby made more aware of the distance covered in his formation. Fourteen months have passed, we are told, but we are not noticeably aware of the passage of time with Stendhal. We have, rather, the impression of a non-ending present. Contrast Julien's attitude as he undertakes with premeditation the seduction of Mme. de Rênal to his awkwardness on the first occasion. A refusal on her part would have been a disgrace for his honor, and he is forced to cold calculation to overcome her remorse. The ruthlessness with which Julien calculates this seduction shows us the extent to which the hypocrisy of the seminary has permeated his character. His threat to leave and the avowal that he will be going to Paris never to return force her consent.

Note the means employed by Julien to gain access to Mme. de Rênal's room prior to their last meeting. It is possible that Julien recalls his meeting with Mme. de Rênal in the Besançon cathedral, a scene in which he had utilized a ladder to perform another act of daring: the decoration of the church. Stendhal flatters the intelligence of his reader by not making explicit this associational mechanism in the mind of Julien. In both incidents Julien distinguishes himself by a spirit of adventure, a necessity to engage his entire existence in a single act, regardless of the consequences.

What of Julien's love for Mme. de Rênal? Once again he is able to appreciate her greatness of soul as he witnesses her courage and gaiety in the face of danger. They are worthy of one another in their heroism. The dangers to which his visit exposes Mme. de Rênal, both real and in the form of remorse which will no doubt follow, and Julien's insistence — everything indicates that although Stendhal says that Julien "adores" her, his love is rather a need to be loved, to be preferred, to be the object of sacrifice for another.

PART II

CHAPTERS 1-4

Summary

Julien's voyage to Paris is enlivened by the conversation of his fellow travelers — a Bonapartist, former friend of M. de Rênal, and a newly formed liberal, Saint-Giraud, who is fleeing the pettiness and intrigue of provincial life for the calm of Paris. The latter had sought peace in the provinces, but because he refused to take sides in the great debate between ultras and liberals, he was persecuted by both. The conversation reflects their opposing political views: Saint-Giraud maintains that the present disorder is due to Napoleon's desire to revive the monarchy. Such strong argumentation does not prevent Julien, upon his arrival in Paris, from making a pilgrimage to Napoleon's palace at Malmaison.

Pirard describes to him in detail the new life he will lead at the home of the Marquis de la Mole. Pirard warns Julien of what to expect from this aristocratic and haughty family.

Chapter 2 is devoted to Julien's arrival and few days in the Mole household. He is first presented to the marquis, who has him outfitted and finds it necessary, in order to improve Julien's grace, to have him take dancing lessons. Invited for dinner in the salon, Julien meets Mme. de la Mole and Mathilde. The latter he finds uninteresting and even unattractive, in comparison to Mme. de Rênal. He finds Norbert, the marquis' son, charming. At dinner, Julien succeeds in making a favorable impression by his knowledge of the classical writers.

Julien takes his working post in the library, where the vast array of books dazzles and inspires him. Mlle. de la Mole enters to smuggle out a copy of Voltaire, and this encounter strengthens Julien's impression of her as a cold-hearted, uninteresting woman. Norbert, on the other hand, continues to delight Julien by his kindness, and he accepts Norbert's invitation to go riding. A mishap while riding is later related at dinner, and Julien's good grace and innocence in the avowal of his awkwardness cause the marquis to look favorably upon him and incite the curiosity of Mathilde.

Further equestrian attempts on Julien's part elicit the remark from Norbert at dinner that Julien is very courageous. Julien's many mishaps are especially relished by the servants of the household.

Chapter 4 describes a typical evening in the salon of the Mole family. Julien reacts as violently to what he witnesses as he did in the Verrières home of Valenod, and the scenes are, in fact, similar. Court at the Mole's is strongly reminiscent in its sterility of the court of Louis XVI. There reigns an air of decorum, politeness, and cruelty. Only insignificant subjects are discussed, nothing controversial, and the barrenness of the conversation inevitably leads to calumny, derision, and mockery, by those in favor with M. de la Mole, directed at those out of his favor. Admitting to Pirard how distasteful he finds these evenings, Julien is overheard by Mathilde, who admires this courage and sincerity.

Commentary

Stendhal loses no opportunity to further the education of Julien, rendering, at the same time, a view of the political situation of the period. Julien would seem by nature and inclination to be a liberal, although he frequents only ultra milieus: the Rênals and the Moles. Julien is, in fact, an opportunist—he has no allegiance, except to himself and to others of the "happy few" who befriend and love him. The only reaction that Julien registers at this revelatory discussion during the coach journey is one of astonishment, and Napoleon remains his idol.

Saint-Giraud's situation is an ironic preview of what Julien's future holds, but in reverse. Saint-Giraud is returning to Paris, after having vainly sought peace in the provinces. He apparently considers Paris as the lesser of the two evils. Julien will follow the reverse route—arriving at the same conclusion: present happiness is not appreciated.

The scene is an effective transition between the scenes of action from another point of view. It indicates that France's lamentable situation during the Restoration is localized neither in Paris nor in the provinces—it is ubiquitous. We have seen corruption and compromise as it operates on the local level, in the grass-roots, then in the seminary, where the purveyors of weakness are formed. Now we will witness the motor source of France's sickness in the aristocratic and ecclesiastical powers in Paris.

Note the father-function of Pirard, whose kind intervention will minimize Julien's chances of being ridiculous in the Mole household.

Although the other members of the Mole family are cruelly and concisely described by Pirard, Mathilde is only briefly mentioned at this point.

Compare Julien's wary but self-assured air upon introduction to the Mole household to his awkwardness and intimidated state upon arrival at the Rênal home, fifteen months before. Stendhal tells us that Julien has come to expect the worst from people; therefore, he is not easily intimidated.

Note, however, how astutely Stendhal renders, almost in passing, a psychologically convincing detail describing Julien's manner of confronting a new situation, where he must find some weakness in his adversary, the discovery of which will bolster Julien's own confidence. (The same mechanism functioned for Julien as he met Mme. de Rênal, whose beauty had intimidated him.) It seems to Julien that M. de la Mole's wig is much too thick. Thanks to this observation, he is not at all intimidated. That is, observing no matter how slight a deficiency in a superior, Julien is able to derive confidence from it. At dinner, his self-assurance does not falter, this time because he decides that Mathilde de la Mole will never be a woman in his eyes.

Mathilde takes an interest in Julien for the first time in Chapter 3, and it is his uniqueness and candor, in contrast to the stereotyped characters to whom she is accustomed, that will constitute much of the basis of her interest and subsequent love for Julien.

Julien must undergo a social metamorphosis as part of his education, and learning to ride a horse is part of this training. Stendhal notes, at the end of the chapter, that Julien already feels himself to be an outsider in this family, the customs and manners of which are strange to him. This concluding remark serves as a transition to the subject matter of the following chapter.

Stendhal benefits from Julien's role of outsider to view the sterility of this social institution, the aristocratic salon of 1830. Pirard's austere presence and conspicuous isolation contrast with the habitués' obsequious conduct, their superficial and docile character, as they mingle and assume their roles in their respective sub-circles. Julien does not fail to note this contrast. Julien's violent disapproval of the cruel derision of merit, especially by his rival secretary, Tanbeau, is reminiscent of his reaction at the Valenod's dinner party. It is by means of this device that Stendhal elicits the reader's sympathy for his hero: Stendhal satirizes Julien's adversaries through ridicule; the reader, therefore, naturally allies himself with Julien.

Admitted as a silent spectator into Mathilde's circle, Julien observes her suitors, the most favored of whom is the Count de Croisenois. In passing, Stendhal observes that Mathilde admires Julien's courage in denouncing this type of social gathering to Pirard—a second hint at the future relationship of Julien and Mathilde. The description of the salon no doubt inspired Proust in his own vivid and satirical depiction of early twentieth-century salon mores. It was Proust, incidentally, who first called attention to the recurrent theme of "high places" in the works of Stendhal.

CHAPTERS 5-7

Summary

After several months, Julien has made his services very valuable to M. de la Mole, although, socially, he has fallen from favor in the household. He applies himself tirelessly to his work, and to escape the discouragement that his exile causes him to feel, he devotes his leisure time entirely to fencing and riding. Norbert is estranged from him, and Mme. de la Mole finds Julien's impetuosity and sensitivity repugnant to decorum.

Julien is offended by a rude individual in a cafe one day, and he immediately challenges the man to a duel. Going the following morning to the address indicated on the offender's card, Julien finds, to his surprise, that the Chevalier de Beauvoisis, whose name is on the card, is the master of the coachman who had offended Julien. Julien promptly punishes the coachman for his insolence, and the chevalier agrees to a duel. Julien is slightly wounded, but the new acquaintance soon becomes friendship. The chevalier is a model aristocrat whom Julien imitates in manners and attitude, accompanying him to the opera. In order to escape the ridicule that would result from public knowledge that he had dueled with a sawyer's son, the chevalier spreads the rumor that Julien is the natural son of a close friend of the Marquis de la Mole. The latter, upon hearing this rumor, is greatly amused.

Bedridden with gout, the Marquis de la Mole is reduced to the company of Julien during the absence of his family. The marquis discovers in Julien a man of ideas and of quick wit. The marquis makes Julien a gift of a blue coat, and when Julien visits him in the evenings wearing the garment, the marquis treats him as an equal. Julien introduces efficiency into the marquis' business affairs, and his innovations are so much appreciated that the marquis wants to reward him with a gift of money. This Julien declines, pretending that the gift would ruin the relationship with the man in blue, since it is to that man and not to the man in black that it is made.

Recognizing the inborn nobility of Julien, the marquis devises a plan to confer upon him the cross of the *Légion d'Honneur*, which will constitute an exterior acknowledgment of Julien's inner nobility. He sends Julien to England, where he is introduced to various notables in the highest circles. Upon his return, Julien is told that when he wears his decoration, he will be, in the eyes of the marquis, the son of the Duc de Retz, a friend of the marquis. The decoration makes Julien more confident.

A visit is paid to Julien by Valenod, recently made a baron. Valenod has replaced Rênal as mayor of Verrières. Ironically, Valenod was the ultra candidate, and Rênal the candidate of the liberals. The marquis agrees to receive the mayor and intends even to encourage his political career. Benefiting from his more intimate relationship with the marquis, Julien succeeds in having his own father named director of the workhouse and Cholin named as director of the lottery. Julien learns later that his intervention has thwarted the candidacy of an honest man, M. Gros, who, Julien recognizes, really deserved and needed the appointment to the lottery post. This causes Julien some remorse, which is quickly stilled, however, by a rationalization that expediency sometimes brings about injustice.

Commentary

These chapters constitute a further stage in the education of Julien, specifically as the protégé of M. de la Mole. Chapter 5 is preparatory to the subsequent development of the father-son relationship, in that it points up Julien's success and failure: success as a prized secretary; failure as a social creature in this blasé aristocracy in which he moves.

Note again Stendhal's tenderly ironic treatment of his hero in the cafe scene. Stendhal will make a fool of Julien by exploiting his hero's basically contradictory nature, causing his impetuosity to play out another mock-heroic adventure. Julien is "unmasked" by a less glorious counterpart: the "gentleman" whom he challenges turns out to be a lackey, like himself. Typically, however, Stendhal takes care not to exploit the ridiculousness that would be inherent in such a situation. Stendhal permits himself to make light of Julien, delicately, but the reader may not take this liberty. The same restraint is apparent in the handling of the encounter with the chevalier. Instead of taking offense, the latter, another of the "happy few," befriends Julien and plays the role of fairy godfather.

Stendhal calls to our attention the resemblance between the two café scenes. He utilizes repeatedly the recurrence of similar situations at different points of the narration, and such a device is particularly effective in a novel describing the formation of an individual. An event that repeats itself calls our attention to the distance covered by the character. In this instance, we note that Julien's pride has not weakened but that he is now more highly placed on the social ladder.

The duel episode serves also to further the relationship between Julien and the marquis. The rumor of noble but illegitimate birth circulated by the chevalier "suggests" to the marquis, without his own awareness of it, the action he takes to confer a kind of nobility on Julien in Chapter 7. By the end of Chapter 6, the fatherly interest felt by the marquis in Julien has progressed to the point where the marquis wants actively to "form" his secretary. Hence, he stations Julien at the Opéra to study another spectacle, the impressive entry and departure of the aristocracy, in order that Julien may imitate their ways and rid himself of his remaining provincialisms.

Betraying his negligence in plot manipulation and preparation, Stendhal feels obliged, in Chapter 7, to justify the familiar tone in which the marquis has just addressed Julien at the end of the preceding chapter. Such an intervention Stendhal would no doubt justify by evoking his realistic pretention and his definition of the novel—he is not inventing, he is only reporting the truth, and this detail he had forgotten to mention. Stendhal indicates to the reader to what extent Julien has actually replaced Norbert as a worthy son for the marquis, both in the eyes of the latter and in those of Stendhal.

"Play acting" recurs as a theme in these chapters, and the deliberate insincerity that it implies is a necessary quality of the nobility to which Julien aspires. The marquis, another fairy godfather, intervenes as for Cinderella, outfitting Julien and casting him in a dual role. A truly noble soul is capable of effecting metamorphosis by will. Thus, the marquis is "magically" empowered to transform Julien into the gentleman in the blue coat by night and into the black-coated secretary by day.

That Julien is making progress is obvious by the fact that he surpasses his master's performance. By proudly refusing the well deserved gift, Julien intimates that the marquis is violating the rules he has established himself. This performance inspires the marquis to bring about the next transformation: Julien's diplomatic mission to London, which will serve as a pretext for a decoration. Julien's frequenting London's high society is the culminating phase in the stage of his formation related in these chapters.

Valenod's reappearance and his victory over Rênal serve to remind the reader of the changing fortunes on the political scene. Valenod's ascendancy had been predicted in Chapter 1 of Part II. Stendhal is careful to note that antipathy and rivalry still exist between Julien and Valenod. This fact will be utilized in the ultimate determination of Julien's fate.

The close of Chapter 7 reminds us that Julien's experiences have taken their toll on his principles and innocence. In short, he is being corrupted but, fortunately, this change is reversible. In the incident in question, Julien has occasion only to rationalize his remorse. One cannot help but wonder which would have won out, expediency or principle, had Julien known earlier that Gros was also aspiring to the position in which Julien's intervention has established Cholin.

CHAPTERS 8-9

Summary

Julien sees Mathilde after a period of separation, and she commands him to attend a ball with her brother. Julien is dazzled by the magnificence of the Hôtel de Retz and by the brilliance of the aristocracy in attendance. Although Mathilde is the center of attraction, she is bored with the lack of color that characterizes all of her suitors. Julien and Altamira, a liberal condemned to die, are the only men present who intrigue her, and they seem unmoved by her charm, unlike Croisenois and the others of his ilk.

In her boredom and because of her fascination with the unconventional, the exciting, the unusual, Mathilde seeks out the company of Julien and Altamira, who are deeply engrossed in a conversation about political expediency and idealism. They remain oblivious to her presence. Piqued, Mathilde seeks to tire herself by dancing and engages in a verbal bout with the impertinent Fervaques, a bout in which she is pitilessly victorious. Julien's admiration for Altamira is unbounded, and the day after the ball, as he works in the library, he is still engaged in an endless inner debate between expediency and idealism. Mathilde appears and reappears, hoping to attract his attention. When Julien deigns to answer her question about the object of his thoughts, he overwhelms her with his reflections. Mathilde hastily retires, realizing that she has interrupted his thoughts.

Commentary

These chapters serve as preparation for the beginning of Julien's affair with Mathilde. Unaware that she is doing so, she will instinctively seek out Julien, as a potential realization of the ideal she seeks—a noble soul, capable of self-sacrifice for great ideals.

The chief point of view of narration is that of Mathilde. Stendhal's artistry as a psychological novelist requires that the reader supply the explicit formulation of the characters' motivation. Why does Mathilde command Julien's presence at the ball? We are to conclude that this is precipitated by her boredom and by the conversation she has had with her father concerning Julien. In that conversation, the marquis praised Julien for being capable of the unexpected and found his own son inferior by comparison. Stendhal transforms psychological analysis into action, expecting the reader to supply the explicit description of the psychological movement. Not even Mathilde arrives at an awareness of her own motivation.

Stendhal creates the ball, in all its sterile glitter, as a fitting stage where Mathilde's boredom may be displayed as having reached its paroxysm. In this regard, the ball scene is the culmination of the salon scenes in the Hôtel de la Mole.

Stendhal takes little interest in describing the ball as such. He presents no exhaustive description of costumes, physical surroundings, or of guests. We have the impression of crowds mainly because Mathilde seems endlessly searching for Julien. Stendhal limits the point of view to that of Mathilde and Julien. The reader's appreciation of the ball is, therefore, limited to that of the characters. This represents a partial abandonment of the traditional omniscient point of view and previews more radical innovations in technique by late nineteenth- and twentieth-century novelists.

Were Mathilde less appealing to her suitors, she would be less bored. Stendhal emphasizes her role as the most sought-after beauty of the season in order to put her boredom in relief. Any unearned victory, rather victory as such, is considered by Mathilde as a defeat, since it supposes an end to battle. Happiness, for the "beyliste," is no more than the search for happiness. Ironically, only those potential realizations of Mathilde's ideal are indifferent to her—Altamira and Julien.

It would be inexact to say that Mathilde is, at this stage, directing her attentions exclusively toward Julien as an individual. Julien and Altamira appear, not as individuals, but as a human type, a realization of her ideal. Mathilde's ideal will ultimately individualize itself into Julien.

Julien finds a kindred soul in Altamira, the only individual in the novel who earns the hero's unreserved admiration. In these chapters, Stendhal gives more ample consideration to the conflict between idealism and expediency. Ironically, Julien aspires to revolutionary liberalism, but he is becoming more firmly entrenched in the home of an ultra. He, an ambitious pariah, idolizes Altamira, a liberal whose idealism has condemned him to death. This, Stendhal is saying, is the lamentable state to which the glorious revolutionary principles have degenerated during the autocratic Restoration. Altamira is Julien's double. Because of her pride and superiority, Mathilde is very worthy of Julien, although he continues to find her unattractive, and her pride offends his. Julien has become a dandy, Stendhal tells us, and he conducts himself coldly as a defense against Mathilde's haughtiness. He will not fail to notice, however, that others admire her, that, in fact, she is the attraction of the ball. He will begin to see her differently, since prized by others, she must be worthy. Note that Julien disagrees with Altamira, although the reader realizes that Julien is really undecided as he defends so forcibly the position of expediency.

The graphic image of character disposition that may be seen in the ball scene is the following: Altamira is impassioned by his ideal of freedom; Julien shares this ideal and is only attentive to its exponent, Altamira; Mathilde instinctively pursues both as representatives of her own heroic ideal. The result, temporarily, is parallel and unfulfilled aspirations.

CHAPTERS 10-12

Summary

As Julien's ardor cools, he is able to reflect on Mathilde's attitude toward him, and he begins to see her in a new light. The academician tells Julien the story of Boniface de la Mole, ancestor of Mathilde, who was beheaded in the Place de Grève defending his friends, and whose lover was the Queen Marguerite. The latter heroically retrieved Boniface's head and lovingly buried it. Mathilde reveres this ancestor and wears mourning on the anniversary of his death. This knowledge evokes Julien's admiration for Mathilde, and in subsequent conversations with her in the garden, he finds that she is intelligent and charming. Finding himself treated kindly by Mathilde, Julien wonders whether she loves him. Then his suspicious nature sees a plot being perpetrated by Mathilde and her brother to make him look ridiculous. Julien decides to seduce her, then to flee. He is tormented by the suspicion that she loves him. Mathilde, on the other hand, has arrived at the discovery that she must be in love with Julien.

Mathilde praises Julien in the presence of her brother, Caylus, and Croisenois, and, to their surprise, ridicules them in Julien's defense. She attributes their condemnation of Julien to the jealousy they must feel for a man of genius. One evening, Julien hears his name mentioned in an argument between Mathilde and her brother, and when he joins them, silence falls, and Caylus, Croisenois, and de Luz treat him coldly.

Commentary

Julien discovers immediately how to have a successful relationship with Mathilde. He must remain cool and never permit her momentary sympathy to lull him into complete confidence. He notices that their conversations seem to begin as a duel, and he realizes that, in order to command her respect, thus her admiration, he must maintain a certain distance between them. Later, as their relationship becomes more involved, Julien will forget this discovery momentarily. His ultimate success with Mathilde will depend upon his rediscovery and utilization of this strategy.

Julien is still master of himself. He suspects that Mathilde loves him, but he is not the victim of any passion for her. Here reawakens the peasant's distrust and suspicion. Julien's fear of ridicule (a trait of Stendhal's heroes) conflicts with his growing admiration for Mathilde, and the resulting decision to seduce her indicates the victory of his suspicious nature. According to Stendhal's theory of love, some assurance and encouragement that one is loved are necessary before one's own feelings progress in the crystallization process.

Chapter 11 is an exploration of Mathilde's character and presents the culmination of the various preoccupations she has had since Chapter 8. Stendhal describes typical incidents that illustrate her pride, the command she has over others, her boredom with the ordinary; and he continues the self-analysis she made at the ball. Mathilde arrives at the discovery that she must be in love with Julien and is overjoyed at this prospect. In reality, she is in love with the idea of being in love. Hers is a love in the Cornelian sense: it depends upon her intellectual approval of it, and it is necessary that the object of the love prove himself worthy of it. She projects its future course: "I've already shown boldness and greatness of heart by daring to fall in love with a man so far below me in social position, I wonder if he'll continue to be worthy of me. At the first sign of weakness I see in him, I'll abandon him."

Chapter 12 is but the continuation of the preceding, in that Mathilde continues to subject her love for Julien to cold intellectual analysis. She rationalizes it, justifies it, and revels in it. Here for the first time, Mathilde verbalizes the association between Julien and herself and Boniface and Marguerite, an association she has unconsciously forged since Chapter 8.

Mathilde has arrived at that stage in crystallization in which every virtue and perfection is attributed to the object, once the realization of love has come to awareness. She sees Julien as a superior man who despises others, and that is why she doesn't despise him. Doubtless, she defends Julien with greater vigor because of the overwhelming disgust that her brother and suitors inspire in her, as the epitome of the commonplace. Even Norbert's warning that Julien is a future revolutionary who would see them to the guillotine is simply another reason for Mathilde to love him. What does worry her, however, is the possibility that Julien does not love her. At any rate, Mathilde has escaped her boredom by deliberating about this decision to indulge in a great passion.

Julien still wavers between his doubts and hopes concerning Mathilde's intentions. In this respect, Julien would seem to be experiencing a variation of the crystallization process, although Stendhal's modesty prevents him from showing Julien as a victim of this emotion.

CHAPTERS 13-16

Summary

Julien finds himself in love with the beauty and charm of Mathilde, and even his previous, black vision of her as a Catherine de Medici forms part of the ideal she is becoming for him. Convinced, however, that he will be made a dupe, Julien pretexts a business trip to Mole's estates in the Languedoc. This threat of departure moves Mathilde to action, and in the declaration of love that she writes him, she states that it would be beyond her strength to be separated from him.

Julien is overjoyed at this avowal and convinces Mole that the latter's affairs in Normandy now require a change in plans and Julien's presence in Paris. Mole's joy at Julien's plans causes a conflict to rise for Julien. How can he seduce the daughter of a man who has been so kind and who is so attached to him? He silences this scruple and, still driven by his mistrust of these aristocrats, devises a plan whereby, if need be, there will exist proof of Mathilde's attempt to seduce him. He copies the letter, sends it in a Bible to his friend Fouqué for safekeeping. Then he composes a truly diplomatic letter as an answer to Mathilde, an answer that does not compromise him.

Mathilde writes Julien a second letter, impatiently demanding an answer. Julien complies, but admits nothing and announces his imminent departure from Paris. In order to deliver it to her, he strolls in the garden, and there he catches her eye as she watches him from her room. The next exchange contains her queenly command that Julien is to come to her room by means of a ladder at one o'clock.

The evening before the rendezvous finds Julien still debating over Mathilde's intentions. Prepared for the worst, Julien imagines the various means at the disposal of the conspirators to capture, murder, and disgrace him. He sends more copies of Mathilde's letters to Fouqué, together with a sealed denunciation to be circulated to various newspapers in the event of a catastrophe. Julien tries, in vain, to read betrayal on the face of the servants and of Mathilde during dinner. He strolls in the garden, wishing that she would appear to reassure him. He then reproaches himself for having stooped to ingratitude that would compromise the honor of such a noble family. He regrets having mailed the letters to Fouqué.

At the appointed hour Julien climbs the ladder to Mathilde's window. Their first moments of conversation are forced, and both are very ill at ease. Julien stealthily inspects the premises, searching for concealed enemies. Finally he confesses his suspicions to Mathilde. They search desperately for subjects of conversation. Julien's evident assurance as he projects future meetings causes Mathilde to realize with horror that she has given herself a master. After much hesitation, Mathilde decides that she owes it to Julien, who has displayed much courage by appearing, to give herself to him. Neither finds pleasure, however, in the act of love. Julien departs before dawn, riding to the heights of Meudon, where at last he finds happiness. Mathilde asks herself whether she loves Julien, after all.

Commentary

These chapters relate the development, manifestations, and expressions of the duel of love that is waged between Julien and Mathilde. Chapter 16 culminates in the first rendezvous in her room, representing a definitive victory for Julien. Although Julien has certainly been formed by the action since his days in Verrières, his success with Mathilde depends on his own blundering, which is reminiscent of his affair with Mme. de Rênal. It is his distrust, his suspicion that he will be made a dupe that prevent him from accepting Mathilde's overt advances. This coldness, on the other hand, is exactly what encourages Mathilde, and her fear of losing Julien prompts her to make the first written avowal. In spite of Stendhal's ironic treatment of the lovers' dilemma, Julien remains the fictitious Stendhal who coolly puts into operation what Stendhal himself had learned about the mechanism of love, as expressed in *De L'Amour*.

As it has been shown, Julien is vaguely aware of the uniqueness of the psychology of this haughty Mathilde, but he is unable yet to exploit his knowledge efficaciously. The element of gratuitous victory is also present in his evaluation of her character. He sees her as machiavellian, exaggerating her duplicity. She is, in fact, complex and strange, but not in that way. He is, therefore, right and wrong simultaneously. Stendhal gives to Julien an awareness of his own crystallization process. Julien attributes to Mathilde all qualities; he imagines her to be Catherine de Medici. "Nothing was too profound or too criminal for the character he ascribed to her." Julien, like Mathilde, seems to be in love with an ideal. Mathilde is undergoing the same torment, fearing that Julien feels nothing for her. The theme of self-delusion, manifest here in the area of love, is one of the dominant Stendhalian themes and constitutes part of his uniqueness as a psychological novelist.

The rationalization that Julien makes of the affront of which he is guilty toward M. de la Mole is a very convincing demonstration of the title of the novel. Julien vindictively shouts his battle cry: it's every man for himself in this desert of selfishness known as life. Why should providence have given him such a noble soul and not the material success that should accompany it? He has been denied the brilliant uniform that Croisenois wears, but he has known how to choose the uniform of his time—the priest's cassock that could ultimately become a cardinal's robe. Julien sees the necessity of a strategic campaign, cloaked in duplicity, as the only means to success. He begins the attack by composing his diplomatic letter to Mathilde.

Chapter 14 illustrates again Stendhal's concentric-circle technique of narration. He now returns to a description of the circumstances surrounding the delivery of the first letter to Julien, this time from Mathilde's point of view. Like Julien, Mathilde has undergone a conflict as her love has progressed. She has feared that she is not loved, and the new fear is born, to become stronger later, that she has given herself a master. Stendhal then shifts to Julien's point of view, proceeding to the second and third letters from Mathilde. Still undecided as to the reality that confronts him, Julien plans for both eventualities: either Mathilde's love for him, regulated by her pride; or the comedy in which his adversaries would make him the dupe. He realizes that he made a mistake by not leaving as he had threatened; therefore, his answer to Mathilde's second letter announces, in effect, that this time he will leave. The result in this comedy of errors is that Mathilde gives him a rendezvous. Without really being conscious of it, Julien has successfully used, on two occasions, a threat of departure to bring about the seduction of Mathilde. He is re-enacting his experience with Mme. de Rênal.

In the interior monolog preceding the rendezvous, Julien sees himself as most assuredly a victim of his imagined conspirators. The scene is perhaps the most exemplary in the novel of the almost paranoic state into which the hero is capable of working himself. It is hardly a question of withdrawing, at this point. Things have progressed too far, and honor forbids him from shirking his duty. A bust of Richelieu silently reproaches him and rids him early of any doubt but that the rendezvous will take place. What he debates is how to rehabilitate his personal honor, how to justify himself after the scandal, the eruption of which looms as a certainty.

That nothing could convince him of the contrary is evidenced by the fact that he "sees" conspiracy in the servants' faces and a medieval grandeur in the face of Mathilde. He is imposing his own fears on reality.

Note how even this impending doom for himself that he sees on Mathilde's face is intimately related with his love for her. "He nearly fell in love with her." The Stendhalian hero permits himself to be afraid without shame, because he has resolved to have the courage before the event itself. This attests to the self-imposed honesty and astringent morality by which Julien lives. He is presented truly as the military commander surveying the battlefield, anxiously awaiting the offensive.

Julien is capable of detachment and of a sort of ironic self-scrutiny. This is a kind of insurance against ridicule that Stendhal permits Julien to create. After all, Julien does not take himself too seriously, just as Stendhal has not been his own dupe.

Julien repents for having sent the letters to Fouqué. He sees the possible circulation of the documents as a base action on his own part, since posterity would see in him an ingrate who would resort to attacking a woman's honor. He is now at the point of preferring to be a dupe, his personal honor requiring self-immolation in silence. Note the rapidity of Stendhal's pace in narration, imitating, thereby, the mental processes of Julien.

Chapter 16 begins without a break from the end of the preceding by the running interior monolog of the hero. Although Julien has never been so afraid in his life, waiting at any moment for the conspirators to strike, he assures himself that he has left no eventuality without consideration, so that he will not be able to reproach himself in the event of a blunder. Arriving at Mathilde's window with his pistol in hand, Julien goes to battle.

The rendezvous scene is rightly reputed as one of Stendhal's masterpieces in psychological analysis. The scene is very dramatic and fast moving. These effects are achieved by the use of short, terse sentences, both by Stendhal in commenting and by the characters in dialog. A second contributing factor is the structure: Stendhal alternates consistently in his presentation first, of Julien's, then of Mathilde's view of the situation, adding commentaries and making analysis after the remarks of each character.

Alternation is necessitated by the nature of the characters and of their love. Both have conceived a role that they are playing, and the roles prove inadequate to the occasion. Such a rendezvous demands passion, spontaneity, forgetfulness of self. Both are self-conscious, scheming, suspicious, acting out a preconceived conduct. It is the bifurcation of two characters into an identical role and their own individual "doubling" in the presence of the other that make the scene basically comic-heroic.

A rapid sketch of their respective states — internal and the manner in which they find external expression — follows: Mathilde has been observing Julien for an hour and is now very emotional. Nonetheless, she addresses him as "Monsieur." Julien has thought only of the ambush he expects, therefore, he is ill-prepared. He remembers, in his embarrassment, that his role requires that he be romantic; therefore, he attempts to embrace Mathilde. Her refusal, stemming, no doubt, from timidity and from her preference of the ideal to the real, puts Julien back on the defensive. This explains his reaction: ". . . overjoyed at being repulsed, he hastened to look around."

Mathilde is delighted to find a topic of conversation, she is so unprepared for this "real" situation. She asks what Julien has in his pockets. Julien, likewise embarrassed, is pleased to have conversational subject matter and explains that he is carrying an "arsenal." Then it is a question of how to dispose of the ladder. Mathilde adopts a tone of normal conversation, admonishing Julien not to break the windows, lamenting over the flowers crushed as the ladder falls.

Julien, seemingly dedicated to the idea of self-defeat, sees Mathilde's supply of rope as proof that Croisenois has triumphed over him after all, since he, Julien, must not be the first to have visited her room. Julien becomes suspicious again, but he has enough resourcefulness and presence of mind to playfully adopt a Creole accent. This effort does not escape Mathilde's attention, and she joins in the game, seeing this as a manifestation of Julien's superiority, thus justifying, in her own eyes, her love for him.

When she takes his arm, his violent reaction is one of suspicion again, and he draws his dagger. There reigns a complicity of silence, as they are listening for a menacing noise. Then returns the embarrassing silence. Julien busies himself with measures of security; Mathilde has just awakened to the compromising situation her daring has put her into. This leads her to ask what has happened to her letters.

Julien, still distrustful, explains the measures he has taken to safeguard himself, believing that his hidden enemies will hear his words. Mathilde's amazement calls forth a sincere avowal on Julien's part of his suspicions. Mathilde has now switched to "tu," but her tone belies this familiarity. This encourages Julien to embrace her, and she only half repulses the embrace.

Now Julien is more the master of himself and, relying on recollection of his past successes, begins reciting love passages from Rousseau. Mathilde, not even hearing them, but carrying on her own mental debate, announces that she finds his courage in coming proof that he merits her love.

Each is attempting to capture reflections of the "self," not to direct attention to the "other." Therefore, what is actually occurring are two separate monologs: Mathilde looking for evidence that Julien is worthy of the sacrifice she has made; Julien looking for encouragement, which in turn will bolster his self-esteem and courage. Stendhal is showing vanity, an early stage of love.

Sensing the emptiness of the familiar address, Julien falls back on his reason, and he is content, momentarily, to found his happiness simply on being preferred by this haughty aristocrat. Now he is searching for a plan of conduct, making conversation to fill the silence; Mathilde joins in this "substitute" action, covering her horror at her own indiscretion by prattle about when they can meet again.

In narrating their conversation, Stendhal has recourse to a method of narration called later "style indirect libre," the initiation of which is attributed to Flaubert. It consists of quoting the words of the characters out of quotes, of narrating as if the characters were speaking. Julien offers his plan, not directly quoted as dialog, but as part of the narration: "What could be easier for them than to meet in the library and make arrangement for everything?" and again: "If Mathilde thought it better for him always to come by means of a ladder, he would expose himself to that slight danger with a heart overflowing with joy. . . ."

Instead of helping to create an air of complicity, thus furthering their rendezvous and speeding it on to its climax, Julien's brilliance and self-assurance awaken Mathilde's pride and make her ask herself again whether Julien is now her master. "If she had been able, she would have annihiliated herself and Julien," says Stendhal, in an abrupt manner, startling the reader. Stendhal prefers classical litotes to romantic hyperbole.

Mathilde had not predicted this attitude of hers; thus do Stendhal's characters watch themselves develop, surprised at what they become. Eventually, her will silences her remorse, timidity, shyness, and wounded modesty, and she notes that she is not fulfilling her role: one speaks to one's lover. She therefore speaks tender words in a cold tone. She forces herself to permit herself to be seduced. From this act, typically hardly alluded to because of Stendhal's great modesty, neither feels pleasure.

Their reactions are different, yet consistent with their character: Julien feels happiness only in retrospect as he rides in "high solitude"; Mathilde wonders why there has been such a distance between her ideal and the real, and she asks whether she really loves Julien. The reaction of both characters echoes Stendhal's own, at his persistent disappointment with reality: N'est-ce que ça? (Is that all it is?) Mathilde has emptied the act of pleasure for Julien because she has undertaken it as a duty to him and to herself. Julien had felt the same reaction after his first rendezvous with Mme. de Rênal. He notices again, however, how inferior is this happiness with Mathilde to that which he knew with Mme. de Rênal.

CHAPTERS 17-20

Summary

In the days following the rendezvous, Mathilde is distant and cold toward Julien. He is perplexed and discovers that he is hopelessly in love with her. Confronting her one day in the library, Julien asks directly if she does not love him any more. Mathilde answers that she is horrified at having given herself to the first one to come along. Julien's reaction is spontaneous: he rushes upon a medieval sword hanging in the room, and after unsheathing it, stops, checks his impulse to kill Mathilde, examines the blade curiously and puts it back. Mathilde sees in the act a truly heroic gesture, worthy of her ancestors. In desperation, Julien announces to the marquis that he is going on a business trip to Languedoc. The marquis has other plans for Julien, who is confined to his quarters to be available at any time for an important mission.

Mathilde now considers Julien worthy of being her master and for a week permits him to walk with her in the garden, while she passionately talks of the love she felt in the past for his rivals. This is torture for Julien, who is suffering all the pangs of jealousy and unhappiness, thinking himself not loved. Blurting out his love for her, Julien finds himself hated again. The course of events increasingly depends upon Julien's imminent departure on the marquis' mission.

By a happy accident, Julien and Mathilde come quite independently to a state of mind propitious to a second midnight rendezvous. Mathilde begins to reproach herself for having been so unkind, then is carried away by the mood and sentiment that an opera inspires in her. Julien, for his part, is in the depths of despair and contemplates suicide as he daringly puts up the ladder and presents himself uninvited at Mathilde's window. Their second rendezvous is less studied and more successful than the previous one. Soon thereafter, however, Mathilde regrets having succumbed and having shorn her locks and presented them to Julien in a submissive gesture. Julien has again known, but lost, happiness.

At dinner, Julien finds that he has lost favor at court. He rides all day in an effort to numb his mind through physical exhaustion. As she confronts him one morning in the library, Mathilde tells him pitilessly that she does not love him. She overwhelms him with her vehemence. Julien accidentally breaks an antique Japanese vase, and his apology to Mme. de la Mole, made in the presence of Mathilde, intimates that his love, like the vase, has been irreparably shattered.

Commentary

This four-chapter episode might well have been subtitled their war in love. Viewed as a whole, it consists of the ups and downs of the stormy relationship between Julien and Mathilde. Their love undergoes a reversal from the previous stage. Here, Julien falls madly in love with Mathilde because of her continued coldness and unavailability. He undergoes all the anguish, uncertainty, and torment that Mme. de Rênal felt in his affair with her. Julien has lost his advantage; his triumph has turned to ashes.

Several explanations are possible. Both egotists, the two are so similar in nature that they are bound to experience love unsuccessfully. Then, too, this is how love develops, according to Stendhal: it is an autonomous emotion that reserves unexpected developments for us. It dies, is revived, overpowers the victim. It is true that in this couple Stendhal has chosen extreme examples for the demonstration of love.

Mathilde, previously so ardent and the initiator of the rendezvous, flees Julien, insults and humiliates him. She denies even that she loves him. Paradoxical in nature, their love resembles that between Rodrique and Chimène in Corneille's *Cid:* at moments when they are farthest apart and when their love seems impossible, they love each other most, since it is during these moments that they are the most worthy of each other. Again, Stendhal reminds us that happiness is the energy expended in the pursuit of happiness.

Unwittingly, Julien has magically dispelled the idealization that constituted Mathilde's love for him. Since Mathilde has ceased to feel boredom for the last few months, Stendhal explains, she forgets what it was like and is now bored by Julien. Mathilde exists only for "magic moments" of paroxysm when she is placing her entire existence at stake. Once happiness is realized, it ceases to be interesting. In such a proud soul as Mathilde, the idea that another would be her master is unbearable. This fear of domination is another reason for Mathilde's rejection of Julien.

The sword incident demonstrates the paradoxical nature of their relationship: Mathilde scorns Julien and insults his honor. Julien reaches blindly for the sword to do her harm, so great is his anger. From this act of malicious intent results a temporary advantage in Mathilde's estimation of Julien, thus in her love for him. She is able to relegate this scene to the medieval past that is the basis of her idealization of their love. She is overjoyed at being on the verge of being killed by her lover. Hurriedly, however, she flees after having recaptured her vision, lest Julien destroy it. Note that the entire dramatic effect of the scene depends upon the image of the sword, chosen with care by Stendhal to jolt the reader.

No novelist succeeds as well as Stendhal in forcing the reader's complicity, unless it be the "new novelists" of contemporary France who are writing what some critics call the "do-it-yourself-novel." In effect, appreciation of Stendhal depends upon the active participation of the reader, who must himself supply the motivation for the acts that Stendhal has his characters commit. The resulting complicity between Stendhal and the reader is particularly operative in episodes such as the love duel between Julien and Mathilde.

Her ideal partially salvaged, Mathilde now readmits Julien to her presence for walks in the garden, where she sadistically forces Julien to listen to her passionate narration of feelings she has felt for his rivals. Mathilde must keep the upper hand, with herself as master and Julien as victim. Only by seeing herself as the master is she able to permit herself to love him. Julien's admission of love to her is a blunder on his part. Sure that he loves her, Mathilde utterly despises him. Mathilde resorts instinctively to these stratagems to keep her love alive in its ideal state. She half hopes that Julien doesn't love her any more, since that would furnish her with a new adventure, permitting her to experience new emotions. The two characters seem to be looking for a safe way to love themselves through the eyes of the other.

Julien has never known such unhappiness. The jealousy that he feels is reminiscent of that felt by Mme. de Rênal. And just as the latter felt pleasure pleading the cause of her rival's, the servant girl's, love for Julien, the hero now praises his rivals in order to "share" the love he thinks Mathilde feels for them.

Stendhal is preparing for Julien's departure, which will occur at the end of Chapter 20, the lowest point and end of Julien's subordinate role in their hateful love. Mathilde projects the future of their relationship, trying to see it as a glorious one, worthy of the ancestry she reveres.

Chapter 19 portrays another partially gratuitous victory for Julien. The thought of suicide inspires him with a courageous act. He will visit Mathilde's room again, then kill himself after she has rebuffed him.

Mathilde might well have rebuffed him, had she not been once again at the "high point" of the idealization cycle.

Mathilde arrives at this point of intoxication in three ways: she continues to project a glorious future for Julien in which she will play a part, then reproaches herself for having acted so cruelly toward him. Second, her idle daydreaming prompts her unconsciously to draw a sketch of Julien. Such an imaginative and romantic nature as Mathilde's could only see this as an almost supernatural sign and proof of her love. The third event congenial to the creation of a receptive frame of mind is the opera that she attends, where again she is able to participate safely, at a distance, idealizing her own love by seeing it in the opera. Stendhal himself sees Mathilde's love as intellectual and contrasts it unfavorably with that felt by Mme de Rênal. The latter's love comes from the heart and does not need to see itself, to examine itself.

Stendhal's intervention to justify Mathilde's character represents an ironic way of condemning those who would condemn his portrait of the times. Mathilde's adventurous and fanciful flights are certainly not to be found in the conduct of the young ladies of his age, he continues, since nineteenth-century France is incapable of great passion. Then, in an apparent contradiction, he introduces his definition of the novel as a mirror carried along a highway. Should it reflect the mire it encounters, the novelist is not to blame, but the mire. Balzac, Stendhal's great contemporary, defends his realism on similar grounds, as had the eighteenth-century French realistic novelists. The point is that even though Mathilde cerebrates her passion, she is capable of one. She, like Stendhal, scorns the apathy and sterility of society.

Discreetly, Stendhal hardly alludes to the rendezvous. By chance, the lovers' exalted moments coincide, and Julien knows happiness reminiscent of that with Mme. de Rênal. The unsolicited avowal of servitude made by Mathilde, betraying her chief concern, Julien will find almost immediately afterward disavowed by her. After having almost half shorn her head and thrown him the locks in a romantic gesture symbolic of her submission, Mathilde, by the next evening, regrets her conduct. She is again at another low ebb in her love, having found only banal reality, much to the bewilderment of Julien.

Chapter 20 confirms the view that Mathilde is playing a game with herself, and Julien is but an instrument. She congratulates herself on the power of her will, which has dominated her love and which has finally permitted her to announce to Julien that she was only deluded into believing that she loved him. Although a conflict is waged in Mathilde's mind between her love and her pride and modesty, she does not appear to be a real victim of love at this stage in their relationship.

Julien's symbolic remark about the vase represents another accidental, clever move. He regrets later having claimed that he no longer loves her, but the avowal, no matter how feigned and insincere, is actually the type of strategy needed to revive Mathilde's love for him.

CHAPTERS 21-23

Summary

The marquis prepares Julien for his role as scribe and spy. Julien will accompany the marquis to a meeting of a group of ultras, where he will take notes on the conversation, condense them with the help of the marquis, memorize the contents, and, inconspicuously dressed, start out on a mission to London. On the way to the meeting, Julien recites a page from the newspaper to the marquis to demonstrate his photographic memory. At the place of rendezvous, the room gradually fills with the plotters. Julien sharpens numerous quills waiting for further orders.

The marquis introduces Julien to the conspirators, and Julien demonstrates to them his prodigious memory. The twelve conspirators would plot means of strengthening the ultras' position against the ever-increasing threat of liberalism, or, as it was termed, jacobinism. The question is whether to ask England to intervene in order to strengthen the ultra monarchy. The marquis is of the opinion that England will help only if the French help themselves by galvanizing their ultra supporters at every level of society. He would recommend severe curtailment of the liberty of the press in an effort to control public opinion.

A cardinal supports the proposal of the marquis, adding the necessity of relying on the power of the Church, whose 50,000 priests have the ear of the people. He suggests that the cabinet minister, M. de Nerval, resign, since he is compromising their cause. Nerval, present among the conspirators, presents himself as favoring the ultra cause against the liberal monarchy. The discussion becomes heated and lasts until three in the morning. The minister leaves, then the Bonapartist, and the remaining conspirators conjecture that the Bonapartist might betray them in an attempt to ingratiate himself with the minister.

Later, Julien and the marquis edit the notes, which Julien memorizes, and the next morning Julien departs on his mission. Stopping at an inn near Metz, Julien encounters the Italian singer Géronimo, who informs Julien that their innkeeper has detained them in order to find a spy who must be apprehended. Julien awakens to find the Jesuit leader of the Besançon Congrégation searching his effects. It is Géronimo who is suspected of being the spy. The singer has been drugged, having fallen into the trap that Julien has avoided.

Arriving in London, Julien finally succeeds in meeting the Duke of Wellington, to whom he recites the message in the secrecy of a shabby inn. Julien follows the duke's instructions to go to Strasbourg, then return within twelve days. Julien arrives in Strasbourg, eluding the watchful Jesuits.

Commentary

The mission to which Stendhal has previously alluded is conveniently introduced to create suspense, of course, but also to separate the lovers in order to reverse their roles. Upon his return, Julien will take the offensive. The transition between what preceded and the spy episode was constituted by Mathilde's musings on Julien's future.

Julien has definitely replaced Norbert as a son worthy of the Marquis de la Mole, and for the first time, the marquis explicitly states this preference. Freudians would see in this a disavowal by Stendhal of his own father and a legitimization of his view of himself as one of the "happy few."

Julien gains admittance to the inner sanctum of reactionary power, but he is still an outsider, a role to which he is condemned. He is made painfully aware of this role of outsider-inside by his isolation, obvious only to himself, before the meeting begins. His embarrassment, which he aggravates by endlessly sharpening quills, aptly characterizes Julien as a very self-conscious being. The presence of the Bishop of Agde serves to remind the reader again of the distance covered by our hero, since Julien was also in the role of messenger when the bishop appeared in Verrières.

The affair of the secret note affords another insight into the manner in which Stendhal utilizes actual happenings as a basis for fiction. Although the novel is set in 1830, at the end of the autocratic reign of Charles X, this episode is based upon incidents that took place during the reign of Louis XVIII (1815-24), the more liberal brother of Charles. The memory of Napoleon's One Hundred Days in 1815 and Louis' liberalism actually caused the ultras to plot with foreign powers in an effort to re-establish the reactionary spirit of the "ancien régime." Stendhal's conspirators are speaking "historically," without naming him, of Louis XVIII, although they are "living" under the reign of Louis' successor, Charles X. The "Ordonnances de Juillet" by which Charles X attempted to revoke the Charter embodying the principles of the Revolution of '89 and to stifle freedom of the press precipitated the July Revolution of 1830, which hailed the "bourgeois king," Louis-Philippe, who re-established liberalism and reigned until 1848.

This incident and others of political inspiration in the novel were added by Stendhal after the July Revolution. He could hardly have included them with impunity before that date.

Stendhal has a predilection for the mystery of clandestine operations, of spy intrigue, including secret rendezvous to which only the initiated are admitted. It is at once related to his own adventures (he was pursued by the Austrian police for his liberal views) and simply an indication of the exclusiveness of the "happy few," the elite of whom Stendhal counted himself as one.

Although Julien has definite republican sympathies, he is in the service of legitimists. Aside from aptly describing this social pariah—the idealist who champions the revolutionary cause but who traffics with the enemy out of necessity—Julien's paradoxical position betrays the political ambiguities of Stendhal himself. Defender of liberalism and, at the same time, aspiring to the good old days of the monarchy, Stendhal nonetheless abhorred the idea of a democracy.

Stendhal's apology for inclusion of the political discussion should not be taken too seriously by the reader. Furthermore, the political and social substrata of the novel are the context in which Julien's individual adventure is realized. This is the most illustrious role that Julien will play as an individual subservient to others. His next brief "position" will seem to grant him a momentary social independence. The power hierarchy, so ubiquitous in the novel, is apparent even in this assemblage of the summit. Some are deferential to others, some can be outspoken and ironic, others must be silent.

It should be noted that Stendhal limits the narration strictly to Julien's perception and comprehension of the mysterious proceedings. The reader has the impression that he, too, is an outsider privileged to eavesdrop. We are rarely told any more than Julien knows. When Julien is excluded briefly during the course of the meeting, the reader is also excluded. And we take our cues from Julien, who takes his from interpreting the facial expressions and tone of voice of the Marquis de la Mole.

Three minor characters have reappeared in these chapters: Castanède, Agde, Géronimo. Their reappearance reminds us of Julien's progress: he is now the very successful protégé of the Marquis de la Mole, and he fulfills his mission without a hitch.

CHAPTERS 24-28

Summary

Smitten by love, Julien is unable to amuse himself in Strasbourg. He encounters his London friend, the Russian Prince Korasov, who befriends and undertakes to cheer him. The prince advises Julien how to proceed in his love affair with Mathilde. He must resort to inspiring jealousy in the woman he loves by courting another. The prince gives Julien a series of love letters with directions as to how and when they are to be delivered to the lady. Julien intends to court Mme. de Fervaques, a beautiful widow of a marshal of bourgeois lineage, a prude who is influential in the Congrégation. Julien agrees to the stratagem. At the same time, he turns down an offer made by Korasov for the hand of the latter's cousin, a match that would facilitate a glorious military career for Julien in Russia.

Upon returning to Paris, Julien asks advice of Altamira in his courting of Mme. de Fervaques. Altamira introduces him to Don Diego Bustos, who had unsuccessfully attempted to court this lady. From Bustos, Julien learns how to go about the conquest. At the Moles', Julien must exert much self-control to begin his campaign. Civil but not attentive to Mathilde, he seeks out Mme. de Fervaques and spends the evening in conversation with her. At the theater, his eyes remain fixed on Mme. de Fervaques. Upon seeing Julien again, Mathilde, who has sworn to forget him, to return to virtue, and to hasten her marriage to Croisenois, now reverses her position, seeing in Julien her real husband.

Mathilde is consternated by Julien's indifference for her. Mme. de la Mole now looks upon Julien more favorably, since he seems to be interested in Mme. de Fervaques. Julien copies the first letter and delivers it, following the directions of the prince. During his evening conversations, Julien places himself in such a way that he can observe Mathilde without being seen. Mme. de Fervaques is quite favorably impressed with Julien, in whose eloquence, metaphysical bent, and mystical preoccupation she thinks she sees the making of a great churchman.

Two weeks and many letters later, Julien receives an invitation to dinner at the home of Mme. de Fervaques. Julien finds the dinner, the conversation, and the guests insipid. Tanbeau, his rival at the Hôtel de la Mole, encourages him in his conquest of Mme. de Fervaques.

One evening at the opera, Mme. de Fervaques intimates that whoever loves her must not love Napoleon. Julien interprets this as an avowal of a certain success in his campaign. Julien's carelessness in copying a letter almost causes Mme. de Fervaques to doubt his sincerity, but he succeeds in excusing the blunder. Mathilde is succumbing to his strategy. She admires his machiavellianism in telling Mme. de Fervaques things he obviously does not believe. Mathilde's marriage with Croisenois is imminent, and Julien thinks again of suicide.

Commentary

These chapters relate the next stage in the love of Julien and Mathilde, in which Julien initiates action and painfully gains an ascendancy over Mathilde.

In the form of Korasov, another father-image reappears to take Julien in hand and teach him the art of seduction. Korasov sees Julien's problem immediately. It will be necessary to attract Mathilde's attention to himself away from herself. Julien must make Mathilde see him not as an ideal she has created, but as he is. Korasov's offer to Julien should remind the reader of a similar one made by Fouqué in Part I. The identity of circumstances points up Julien's contrasting situations: in Verrières he refused happiness because he was goaded by ambition; here, he refuses to satisfy that ambition, now silenced by a love of which he is the victim.

Julien is so much the victim of his love that he adopts the point of view of the woman who scorns him to deprecate himself pitilessly. This period of depression that Julien is experiencing Stendhal had analyzed in his treatise on love. Julien sees himself as the most abject of beings, as inferior to Korasov, and at fault for not being loved by the perfect Mathilde.

It is not by chance that Julien chooses Mme. de Fervaques as his instrument. He admits that her beautiful eyes remind him of those loving and passionate eyes of Mme. de Rênal. He longs unconsciously for that experience where he was loved.

Two more mentors are introduced to guide Julien. Altamira and Bustos provide Julien with the necessary information for a seduction. Note that Julien is hypocritical even with his friend Altamira, who is not advised of Julien's stratagem. Stendhal doubtless delights in the dissection of the prude. It is reminiscent of the seduction undertaken in Laclos' *Liaisons Dangereuses* by Valmont of his prudish victim, more sincere, however, in her religious principles than is Mme. de Fervaques. Stendhal's portrayal of the latter as somewhat of an imposter absolves Julien of any guilt, since she is not truly a victim.

The abrupt images betraying Julien's extreme sensibility are meant to convince the reader of the hero's great effort in playing his role. Julien is moved by the sight of the sofa and ladder in the true romantic tradition. Note, however, that the rapid narration and abrupt sentences betoken restraint and a refusal on the part of Stendhal to fall into the raptures and effusiveness of the hyperbole à la Chateaubriand. Julien remains the passive actor of the role carefully outlined by Korasov, acting as a sort of robot. Another note is inserted by Stendhal to show to what extent Julien's ambition is dead. The possibility that the marquis might be named as a minister would give Julien an opportunity to become a bishop. Such a possibility is very far from Julien's present aspiration.

Julien's return has sufficed to change the impetuous Mathilde's plans completely. Mathilde has rationalized her interpretation of virtue to justify her reversal in position. She had decided to return to virtue, but now virtue means legitimizing her love for Julien through marriage: "He's my real husband," blurts out Mathilde.

Note Stendhal's "peeping Tom" tendency (which he has in common with Balzac). The privilege of the superior soul is that he may observe others observing him without their knowledge. Julien is protected by hat brims, his own and that of Mme. de Fervaques, as he observed Mathilde watching him.

Although his love at first incapacitates him for creative action, Julien nonetheless makes progress as an actor and conversationalist. Again, Stendhal states this fact, without offering a demonstration of it. Profiting from his knowledge of Mathilde's character, Julien decides that she will admire him for uttering absurdities with eloquence.

The dinner at the home of Mme. de Fervaques is similar to the one Julien attended in Part I, at the Valenods'. Both present Julien appearing in the enemy camp, and his refusal to take a stand politically is thereby underlined. In Verrières, Julien frequented the society of both liberal and monarchists; here, in spite of his Jansenistic mentor, Pirard, Julien is frequenting the Jesuit milieu. Julien experiences the same feeling of superiority at the two dinners. He had scorned the materialism and bad taste of the Valenods; here, he is disgusted by the pompousness of the guests and by the sterility of the conversation.

Stendhal again underlines Julien's lack of ambition by intimating how he could, were he so inclined, profit from his relationship with Mme. de Fervaques to have himself named a bishop. One aspect of the tragedy of Julien Sorel begins to become apparent. Ironically, he abandoned the tender love of Mme. de Rênal because of his insatiable ambition. He is now reaping the fruits of this ambition — or he could, but he no longer hears that voice — in favor of a love inferior to the one he abandoned.

There is another advantage to feigning a courtship, other than the obvious purpose, which is to inspire jealousy in the real love object. If the victim responds, one may observe the mechanism of love and its progress objectively and with a cool head, hardly possible if one is really in love. Stendhal's own ambition was to achieve an impossible synthesis: to love passionately but without the enslavement of his will and mind.

Mathilde is being taken in by Julien's stratagem, in a different way than he had anticipated, however. She admires his duplicity as she observes him courting Mme. de Fervaques. This means simply that she sees through the stratagem, but that it is nonetheless successful because she is able to relegate this newly discovered quality of Julien to her idealization of him.

Julien's despair reaches its greatest intensity as he again contemplates suicide. Even if he succeeds in reviving Mathilde's love, he knows that it will not produce a lasting effect. He concludes by condemning himself: Why am I myself?

CHAPTERS 29-32

Summary

Mme. de Fervaques is beginning to respond and finally answers Julien's letters. Ultimately, she is writing him a letter daily, which Julien doesn't open and answers with the letters from Korasov. Mathilde, finding the present state of affairs unbearable, encounters Julien one day in the library. She reproaches him from having neglected her, his wife, then collapses in tears. Julien initiates no action in the way of response. Mathilde then reproaches herself for having forgotten her pride, and finding Mme. de Fervaques' letters to Julien all unopened, she is beside herself with rage, insults him, then confessing her love, begs for mercy and faints at his feet. Julien has triumphed.

Mathilde asks Julien if Mme. de Fervaques has shown him proof of her love. Julien answers no, indirectly and diplomatically. He demands guarantees from Mathilde that she will not continue this cruel game with him. She has nothing but the "intensity of her love and her unhappiness if he no longer loves her." Julien withdraws respectfully, requesting time to reflect. Mathilde has found happiness in renouncing her pride. Julien feels obligated to appear in Mme. de Fervaques' box at the opera. The latter mistakenly believes that the tears in Julien's eyes are shed for her. Julien catches sight of Mathilde in another box, weeping.

Going to her box, Julien hears Mathilde murmur tearfully "guarantees." Giving himself over to the expansive joy of his love in the solitude of his room, Julien hits upon a new stratagem to perpetuate Mathilde's love: he must frighten her. The next day she offers to elope with him. He rejects the offer, reminding her that this mood would soon pass. Walking in the garden with Mathilde, Julien confesses how he used to watch for her there, but he then denies immediately the truth of this avowal. He continues to write to Mme. de Fervaques, despite Mathilde's disapproval.

Mathilde is now truly in love. She acts recklessly, but Julien maintains caution. She announces triumphantly, to Julien's consternation, that she is pregnant, and that this is the guarantee which he demanded. She insists on informing her father, but defers to Julien's view that it would be better to delay in writing the letter. In her letter, Mathilde assumes all blame and expresses the hope that her father will forgive both of them. She announces her intention of marrying Julien, and she suggests that their future situation will depend upon how M. de la Mole receives this news.

Commentary

These chapters narrate the victory that Julien wins over Mathilde as his stratagem succeeds. It is here that the Cornelian nature of their love is most fully exemplified: they are nearest when farthest apart. Julien can force an avowal from Mathilde only by refusing to respond in any way to her successive anger, tears, scorn, then tenderness. Note that Julien does not utter a word in this interview. He must not betray his extreme joy, and they seem condemned to love each other separately.

This scene in Chapter 29 is the exact antithesis of a normal love scene. Instead of mutual tenderness and intimacy leading to a reciprocal avowal, there is a progression in hostility and silence leading to an avowal of defeat and submission. Mathilde's initial eruption is spontaneous—she reproaches Julien for having neglected her. Her next reaction is equally spontaneous, but results from the first—she has humiliated herself and weeps tears of shame. Julien proves that he has progressed in controlling his sensibility by treating her with impassive coldness. His lack of response intensifies her shame to the point that she explodes in anger. Opening the drawer and finding the letters unopened, Mathilde next resorts, in her uncontrollable rage, to insults. Instantly repenting, however, she avows her love and faints. Julien can only enjoy his love as a triumph when his victim is reduced to unconsciousness, as an object. This scene no doubt inspired Proust in his demonstration of the impossibility of possessing another through love. Stendhal's portrayal of Mathilde in this scene is an excellent example of the author's unique character presentation. The reader seems to witness at first hand a process of becoming that is simultaneous with the character's acts. It has been said that the words as Stendhal uses them do more than they say. Mathilde faints because she is one of those superior beings whose emotional makeup is so intense that beyond a certain point, it shuts out reality. Julien reacted similarly in his initial interview with Pirard.

Note the Mme. de Fervaques remains hypocritical, even toward herself. She does not admit to herself that she is beginning to love Julien, and since her pride would suffer by addressing letters to him, she is reduced to requesting that he give her self-addressed envelopes. There is a faint glimpse of the role played by Mme. de Rênal as confidante to Elise; however, Stendhal chooses not to exploit it. Mme. de Fervaques confides in Mathilde and asks her advice on how to deal with Julien.

Stendhal utilizes chapter division to isolate and put into relief a scene, or part of a scene, as is evidenced by the artificial chapter division between 29 and 30. The latter in fact continues the previous scene, but the dramatic effect inherent in 29 would not have been otherwise achieved. Chapter 30 rounds out Julien's victory. He continues to exert incomparable self-control, to the point of hypocritically telling Mathilde that he loves Mme. de Fervaques. Finally, he comes to the conscious awareness of the necessity of maintaining a distance in order to continue to be loved by Mathilde. The reader has long since been aware of this fact.

The short scene that concludes Chapter 30 represents a different angle of vision from which to see the situation between Julien and Mathilde. They appear at the opera separately, yet in their separateness they are similarly affected. Both are reduced to tears; both are enjoying their love vicariously by association with the spectacle itself. Julien is permitted to maintain the superiority of the unobserved observer.

The glance that the eyes bestow is a means of communication between the elect, believes Stendhal. Thus, he gives much importance to the role of Julien's eyes in his adventures. In 31, Julien hides his eyes as he sits near Mathilde at the opera, lest they betray his true feelings.

Note in Stendhal's intervention to express approval of Julien's progress, the use of the present tense and "may." These are intended to convince the reader of the veracity of the narrative and is a much abused device to which eighteenth- and nineteenth-century novelists resort. The result is the complicity so vehemently denounced by the "new French novelists": the omniscient novelist would pass off fiction as truth; and in this complicity, the public agrees to pretend that what it is reading is indeed fact. It might be argued that Stendhal in particular needs to establish such a complicity, since his practice of withholding proof of his hero's superiority might alienate the reader.

Stendhal prefers the garden as a setting for amorous adventures. Julien's affair with Mme. de Rênal began and progressed in the garden. The garden scene in 31 evokes Julien's solitary anguish as he watched for Mathilde when he thought he wasn't loved. It is also the setting of the reversal of a previous meeting between them: Mathilde tortured Julien to maintain her ascendancy by telling him of her past loves; now, Julien, momentarily giving way to an expression of his "past" love for her, uses the same stratagem to maintain his present supremacy over Mathilde. He brutally denies the veracity of the words he has just spoken. Julien is testing Mathilde to ascertain to what degree his unchecked sincerity has dampened her love. His own "guarantee" consists of continuing to write the letters. He realizes that he must keep Mathilde in constant doubt as to whether he loves her.

Chapter 32 presents at once the culmination of their conflict, the transformation of Mathilde's love, and it puts into motion the subject matter to be fully developed in the next few chapters.

Circumstances somewhat beyond Julien's control seem to give a new direction to their relationship. Things are getting out of hand for Julien. Mathilde has accepted him as her master, it is true. Her proud nature requires that she continue the struggle elsewhere, however. First, by her reckless, almost promiscuous conduct with a social inferior, she flouts respectability. Mathilde's pregnancy is the beginning of the end for Julien. For Mathilde, it is the renewal in a different form of her dream of heroism and martyrdom. Her duty, she informs Julien, is to inform her father of this turn of events, and joyfully, she sees this heroic act as a way of proving her merit in Julien's eyes and as a way to compete with him in bravery.

Julien has succeeded in convincing Mathilde that her love for him is stronger than his for her. This satisfies Mathilde, giving her a kind of superiority over him. The letter to her father, her "best friend," is certainly consistent with Mathilde's character. Love is for her so intimately associated with the infliction of pain on herself and others that she logically turns to the person she loves best after Julien to initiate a new conflict. A "great soul" requires that others of the elect participate in a kind of ritualistic sacrifice. Fabrice in *The Charterhouse of Parma* has a similar demanding relationship with the other elect in that novel.

The next three chapters recount a struggle of wills between Mathilde and M. de la Mole.

CHAPTERS 33-35

Summary

After reading Mathilde's letter, the marquis is beside himself with rage and hurls every insult at Julien. Julien offers to commit suicide or to be killed by the marquis' men. He goes to Pirard for advice. Mathilde learns of Julien's suicide note, resolutely tells her father that if Julien dies, she dies, and that she will appear as Julien's widow to society. When Julien returns to Paris, Mathilde convinces him to leave and to let her manage her father. The latter only shows indecision. Mathilde refuses to negotiate other than on the condition of a marriage with Julien, heedless of what their future might be. In a moment of tenderness, the marquis gives shares worth 10,000 francs to Mathilde for Julien. Julien stays with Pirard, who has become Mathilde's best ally in trying to convince the marquis of the necessity of a public marriage.

The marquis cannot bring himself to act. He alternately envisions Julien's accidental death, then entertains the wise counsel of Pirard. Above all, he refuses to believe that his ambition for Mathilde's brilliant future has been thwarted. Mathilde has been seeing Julien almost daily at Pirard's. Finally, the marquis gives the couple an estate in Languedoc as a means to put off making a final decision. By letter, Mathilde begs her father's permission to marry Julien. This causes the marquis to consider the possibility of protecting Julien, of helping him to build a brilliant career. He has a doubt, however, about Julien's sincerity. Has he merely used Mathilde as a means to get ahead in society? Rather than give his permission for the marriage, he gives Julien a title and a commission in the army. Mathilde replies by trying to bargain. She will not communicate news of the title to Julien, unless her father agrees to the marriage. The marquis refuses categorically, demands that Julien leave for Strasbourg or all will be rescinded.

Julien prepares to leave for Strasbourg. Pirard explains how the marquis has bought Frilair's silence in order to gain acceptance of the fictitious noble ancestry he has devised for Julien. For five days the latter is in Strasbourg, where his calm dignified bearing, elegance, daring, and ability with arms inspire admiration in his men. Then a letter from Mathilde arrives announcing that all is lost and calling for Julien's immediate return to Paris. There Julien learns that the marquis has inquired of Mme. de Rênal about Julien's past. The answer she has written confirms the fears of the marquis. The letter accuses Julien of making a practice of insinuating himself into respectable families, of seducing the womenfolk, then of ruining them. Julien leaves immediately for Verrières, arriving on a Sunday morning. He buys revolvers, goes to the church, and shoots Mme. de Rênal.

Commentary

In a crisis Julien's women are able to act more efficaciously than he is. Mme. de Rênal resolutely initiated the deception of her husband; Mathilde confronts her father successfully. She is more resolute than her father and turns his indecision to her advantage. The passivity that Stendhal bestows on Julien provides the opportunity for enjoyment of maternal affection that the premature death of Stendhal's own mother denied him.

Twice in Chapter 33 Stendhal describes Julien's conduct as tartuffian. As a defense against the marquis' anger, Julien tries to justify his action, all the while expressing his gratitude to the marquis. Then, Julien adopts the required air of contrition to confess his situation to Pirard, in the hope of getting advice. In Julien's initial confrontation with the marquis, the only solution the former can hit upon is suicide, or letting himself be killed, a solution he doubtlessly offers without reflection. The thought of his "son" comes to him for the first time, however, and this thought checks his willingness to be killed. Julien plays an extremely passive role in Chapters 33 and 34.

Chapter 34 narrates the give and take between Mathilde and her father. He sits in irresolution; Mathilde presses him by letter. The marquis grants a concession, and this encourages Mathilde to ask for more. Another concession is forthcoming from her father, rather than a definitive action that would condone their marriage. Although the marquis is more sympathetically treated by Stendhal than was M. de Rênal, both have the same role in the author's playing out of his oedipus complex.

The marquis' doubting of Julien's motivation is a preparation for the event that will bring about the latter's downfall. A parallel development to this preparation, however, is the momentary "taste" of success that Stendhal will allow his hero to have. Stendhal will accord a title and a regiment to Julien. This is typical treatment by Stendhal of his superior beings. They are not destined for a permanent, commonplace happiness, which would, in fact, become vile to them.

Note that Julien already seems far away from the action. His thoughts are absorbed completely by the future of his child. Stendhal begins attenuating Julien's love for Mathilde, and his ambition is reappearing. Stendhal mentions Julien's ambition twice in this chapter. Julien's joy is boundless at the news that he is an officer of the Hussars. He is aware, however, of the ephemeral nature of this goal attained, as he remarks that his story has reached its climax. Julien still misunderstands situations, however, as he attributes his success to himself alone. He has succeeded in making himself loved by this monster of pride. And he summarizes his present situation astutely when he muses that Mathilde cannot live without him, nor M. de la Mole without her.

How many events, and of what moment, Stendhal crowds into Chapter 35. He moves Julien to the pinnacle of success, lets him revel in this glory for the duration of one page, then precipitates events that will divest him of this worldly glory and ultimately destroy him. The marquis has again been Julien's fairy godfather who conjures up the illusion of success and glory, then takes it from him abruptly.

The scene sketched by Stendhal of Julien in all his equestrian glory evokes briefly the same scene in Part I where Julien played a role in the honor guard. The scenes have in common their illusory nature: then, Julien was merely in the costume of a soldier; now, the abrupt ending of the real role makes its very existence seem doubtful.

Proof of the fact that Julien himself almost believes in his fictitious nobility is furnished by the letter he sends to Chélan, together with money to be distributed to the poor. This is the noble gesture of an aristocrat. Julien wants to believe in his nobility, since he would not consider himself a monster if Sorel, a man whom he despises, were not his father. In this way, the tragic contradiction he has been forced to live — a superior soul stifled by mediocrity — would be reconciled.

Happiness, for the superior being, is simply not available except in small, almost unbearable doses. The proximity of Stendhal to his hero is again underlined. Stendhal is self-demanding, almost masochistic, and his hero, to whom he denies happiness, is superior because of the denial.

We have noted that Stendhal has already begun to exclude Julien's intimate reactions. This tendency is even more pronounced in Chapter 35 as Julien returns hurriedly to Paris, learns what the catastrophe is, takes to the road again, arrives in Verrières, arms himself, and shoots Mme. de Rênal. It is partially Stendhal's reserve, his timidity, his refusal to let himself be seen that has dictated his attitude in narrating these events almost devoid of reference to the psychology that prompts Julien to act. This ambiguity has given rise to a literary debate that continues to our day. Is this act, the attempted murder of Mme. de Rênal, consistent with the character of Julien? Is Stendhal betraying that psychology in an effort to remain faithful to the historical episode that inspired the novel, and is the denouement therefore artificial? Here are some of the critics' views.

Emile Faguet, noted nineteenth-century critic, saw Julien as committing a senseless act that contradicts his character as established by Stendhal. Faguet denies Stendhal a great degree of intelligence, moreover. He sees Julien as the ruthless, ambitious man, coldly calculating and of unshakable will. The character thus conceived, continues Faguet, Julien should have realized that within a short time the marquis, already having accepted many compromises, would have reversed his decision and sanctioned the marriage. Julien seems to have forgotten that he is master of the situation. The denouement, concludes Faguet, seems a little more false than is permitted.

A contemporary critic, M. Henri Rambaud, defends Faguet's interpretation, seeing Julien simply as the "arriviste" type. These critics would see, therefore, the rapidity and incomplete nature of the narration of these events as evidence of Stendhal's dilemma, his avowal, by omission, of the contradiction he was creating in Julien's character.

On the other hand, the contemporary critic Henri Martineau sees this act and the dry, sketched narration leading to it as logical, given the character of Julien. Here is the extremely sensitive, impetuous hero who has throughout the novel attempted, with varying degrees of success, to submit his spontaneity to the discipline of self-control, to disguise his true feelings by hypocrisy. Such a type is capable, as his past conduct has shown, of seeing his discipline thwarted by the sudden eruption of his passion. When this occurs, the act is but the next movement from its inspiration. Therefore, Stendhal is obliged to reduce the narration to its barest elements, to get Julien there, to have him commit the act. The narration reflects the motivation: Julien is in a semi-somnambulistic state. He has but one idea — revenge on Mme. de Rênal — and any other detail would be extraneous.

And why does Julien want revenge? Herein lies the psychological insight of Stendhal. Julien both hates and loves Mme. de Rênal. He has never reached the end of his love for her, yet she has apparently deliberately lied about his conduct. She has ruined his success. His pride and sense of honor have also been wounded. He must avenge himself. Julien's sudden awakening after the act, his long sleep in the jail resulting from excessive tension — these, argues Martineau, are proof that Julien has acted consistently with his character.

Note the scene of the attempted murder. Julien is unable, at first, to fire on Mme. de Rênal because he recognizes her. The bell rings at that moment marking the Elevation of the Host. Mme. de Rênal bows her head, and he no longer recognizes her so clearly. He fires. Only when she ceases to exist momentarily, as herself, defined as an individual whom he loves, is he capable of the act. The ringing of the bell might be instrumental also in the very commission of the act. Its abrupt occurrence, followed by another action, the bowing of heads, calls for another: the firing of the pistol. This would constitute a sort of demotivation of the act, reminiscent of Gide's attempts to produce the gratuitous act in *Les Caves du Vatican* and of Camus' scene in *L'Etranger,* where Meursault through the complicity of things — the sun's reflection, heat — fires on the Arab. Here, there is a "chain of events," one producing another, an inexorable rhythm created thereby, to which Julien almost involuntarily and mechanically contributes.

CHAPTERS 36-39

Summary

Julien is imprisoned in Verrières, unaware that Mme. de Rênal has miraculously escaped death and that the kind treatment he receives in prison is due to her intervention. He writes his farewell to Mathilde, requesting that she never attempt to see him again. Julien is overjoyed to learn that Mme. de Rênal is not dead. He has confessed numerous times to the public prosecutor who visits him, and he hopes, by this means, to simplify the procedure and to be left alone. He is moved to another prison in a gothic tower in Besançon. He begins to relive his past with Mme.

de Rênal and finds that there was happiness. He contemplates suicide, then rejects the idea.

Julien receives the visits of Chélan and Fouqué. Chélan disheartens him, weakening his courage. Fouqué cheers him. The interrogations continue, in spite of Julien's frank avowal of guilt. Fouqué attempts to intervene by means of a visit to Frilair. The latter is increasingly intrigued by the mystery of the Sorel affair, and he will attempt to benefit from it. Julien hopes not to have to endure a visit from his father, and Fouqué is horrified at this lack of filial love.

Mathilde visits Julien, disguised as Madame Michelet. She has made overtures everywhere to gain Julien's release. Of these attempts she tells him nothing. Julien finds her extremely attractive, and, out of respect and admiration, he abandons himself with ecstasy to her love. Mathilde has visited Frilair, leader of the Besançon Congrégation, erstwhile enemy of her father. She discloses to Frilair enough information to arrive at a sort of bargain: she will exercise her influence in Paris to Frilair's advantage, in exchange for Frilair's assurance that he will work for the acquittal of Julien.

Mathilde has requested that Mme. de Fervaques use her influence with a bishop to negotiate with Frilair. Mathilde has bribed the guards to gain constant access to Julien. The latter reproaches himself for not appreciating Mathilde's superhuman efforts to save him or her passionate ecstasies. He proposes that she turn over their child to Mme. de Rênal. Mathilde, offended at this suggestion, finds that she is increasingly obliged to fight against Julien's growing inclination for solitude and against an awakening of affection for Mme. de Rênal. He returns to the subject of his child's future, but approaches it more diplomatically.

Commentary

From this point on, Julien's life will be lived in the jail cell. Although his physical life will be severely limited, his mental and psychological life will be very active, and he will ultimately know the happiness he has sought, once the voice of ambition stills itself, out of necessity. Julien will arrive at a sort of self-knowledge. Here begin to unfurl the various preoccupations of Julien that will be fully developed in later chapters: his decreasing interest in Mathilde and the ever-increasing thought of Mme. de Rênal; his meditations on death, courage, and happiness.

Let us analyze one of Julien's states of mind. Finally emerging from his hypnotic state, Julien's first comment is that it is over, there is only death awaiting him, either by the guillotine or by suicide. Then he falls asleep. It is as if he realizes the necessity of steeling himself, of adopting an attitude, in order to avoid falling into the anguish of fear. His defiant confession to the judge is simply a refusal to submit to the humiliation of being judged, reserving this right for himself. Next he feels the tiresome duty of reporting to Mathilde, to inform her of his act of vengeance, to request that she forget him. It is not only an accounting to his partner in heroism to prove that he is worthy, but also the expression of an unconscious wish to be rid of her.

Then comes the first awesome realization of the death that awaits him. At the hint of the appearance of fear, Julien rallies his courage, rejects the idea of remorse by rationalization: he has been wronged; he has wronged: he must be punished. He rounds out this reasoning by scorning society, which might see some glory in his execution only if he were to scatter gold among the people on his way to the scaffold. Stendhal's presentation of Julien as the victim of society, condemned not for the crime of attempted murder but for not accepting his place in that society, no doubt inspired Camus in his portrayal of Meursault in *L'Etranger*. Meursault killed an Arab, but he is found guilty because he did not weep at his mother's funeral. Meursault's acceptance of the verdict echoes many of Julien's thoughts of these final chapters.

Julien's carefully constructed mask is completely destroyed when he learns that Mme. de Rênal is not dead at all. At this news, Julien is reduced instantaneously to a simple, defenseless child in tears, and he sees the will of God in his act. Only now does Julien permit himself to feel repentance for his crime, and it is his own renewed love for Mme. de Rênal that prompts his joyous cry that she will live, then, to love him still. Momentarily, he thinks now of escape, but dismisses the idea, since it would depend upon bribing the ignoble jailor.

Julien's prison tower cell affords him a beautiful view. It is another of the symbols of the elevated isolation of the superior soul. Stendhal puts Fabrice in a similar situation in *The Charterhouse*. Moreover, Fabrice comes to prefer the prison to freedom, since he has fallen in love with the jailor's daughter. It will be only in such solitude, safely shut off from the world, that Julien will find happiness. Note that in Stendhal's view the hero is less excluded from society by his imprisonment than is society denied access to the hero.

Julien resigns himself again, however, to the justice of the death penalty. Life is not boring for him, since he begins to see it from a new slant. Julien is amazed at what is happening to him inwardly. Stendhal's heroes watch themselves, discover themselves. There is nothing predetermined about them, in the sense that characters are often "flat" and never surprise us. Balzac tends to create flat characters; Stendhal's are round, using the terminology of E. M. Forster *(Aspects of the Novel)*. It is this aspect of Stendhal's character portrayal that has found much favor with contemporary existentialistic critics. The Stendhalian hero is forced to be free, is condemned to the eternal state of becoming. He discovers himself daily in order to remake himself.

What are these perceptions of his glorious future in prison? Julien's rediscovery of the happiness he had with Mme. de Rênal and of the fact that he still loves her. Stendhal's analysis of Julien operates by the associational method: remorse makes Julien think of Mme. de Rênal and of his past happiness; at other times, thinking that he might have killed her, Julien swears that, in that event, he would have committed suicide; suicide, an imagined consequence of that past possibility, then looms as a possibility in the present. Still measuring himself against Napoleon, Julien rejects suicide, since Napoleon went on living. The end of Chapter 36 finds Julien temporarily happy with his present surroundings.

Julien's imprisonment will be punctuated by intermittent visitors. Even here he cannot escape the outside world. Note the contrasting effects that his visitors have on him: the aged Chélan presents to Julien only the image of death and decay, in spite of his reasoning that his own death in the prime of life ought to dispel such a vision; the antidote is the vision of the sublime afforded by the simplicity, sincerity, and artless friendship of Fouqué.

Part of Stendhal's uniqueness for his age as a psychological novelist is obscured to us by the developments in the novel posterior to Stendhal, and to which we are very much accustomed. Stendhal was one of the first novelists to portray how the individual is altered by the influence exerted upon him from surrounding reality. In this respect, he antidates naturalism. Such alternations have in fact, been carefully noted throughout the novel be Stendhal, but they are particularly noticeable during the episode relating Julien's imprisonment. Here, any intrusion on Julien's isolation produces dramatic reactions in his soul.

Julien hits upon the idea of the thermometer to measure his courage, and this gives rise to his resolution to be courageous when it will be required of him. We have already witnessed Julien's tendency to bolster his courage in the present by assuring himself of his future self-control.

Although he is safely imprisoned, Julien is still the victim of society and of its intrigues. This theme is taken up again by Stendhal and will be amplified in what follows.

Julien plays almost no role in Chapter 38. More hints are given that he is losing interest in Mathilde. The time has come for Mathilde to play out in reality her ideal dream of heroic self-sacrifice for her own version of Boniface de la Mole. The Julien-Mathilde continues to be Cornelian: Julien now really merits her love, since Mathilde may assume that what prompted his crime was love for her. This incarnation in Julien of her ideal plus his increasing indifference toward her will intensify Mathilde's love. She seems in fact to love Julien desperately, even though Stendhal will tell us that this love needs the third party to witness it. That is, Mathilde's heroic efforts to save Julien at the risk of loss of her own reputation are partially inspired by her need to impress the world, to be admired by others. She aspires to see herself loving Julien as others would see her. Hers is still an intellectual love.

Mathilde's visit to Frilair is reminiscent of Julien's entrance into the seminary. Both must screw up their courage as they approach the lion in his den. The confrontation between Mathilde and Frilair might be considered a battle in ruse in which Mathilde will not have the upper hand. Nevertheless, Frilair and Mathilde are fairly evenly matched as adversaries, and, in the end, both will be duped.

The action in Chapter 39 takes place wholly in Julien's cell. At first there is not one specific incident narrated; rather several visits, all similar, are fused to comprise a typical one in which the attitude of Mathilde and Julien are contrasted. The final conversation closing the short chapter becomes the result of what precedes and stands for one specific visit. Here is represented one of Stendhal's typical methods of narration.

Julien is tired of heroism. He is more virtuous now than at any time in his life, since ambition no longer goads him. Therefore, he reproaches himself for what he has done to the marquis and Mathilde de la Mole. It is here that Stendhal advises us that Julien, unwittingly, is hopelessly in love with Mme. de Rênal. Julien's awareness of this fact is dim, expressing itself only in his desire to give his offspring to Mme. de Rênal. Rebuffed by Mathilde, Julien artfully returns to the same subject, expressed in terms that would appeal to Mathilde's turn of mind. Note that Stendhal does not comment on Julien's stratagem. His conduct toward Mathilde is reminiscent of that which he adopted in his "seduction" of Mme. de Fervaques. This is the first manifestation of Julien's new attitude toward Mathilde. He relies on duplicity to convince her. Later, as he becomes increasingly irked by her presence, he will punish her somewhat sadistically.

Note, in Julien's presentation, Stendhal's own preoccupation with the future. Stendhal was convinced that his real public would be that of the twentieth century. The appearance of the idea of abolishment of capital punishment, a burning issue today, would bear out Stendhal's conviction that he was writing for the future.

CHAPTERS 40-42

Summary

Just before his trial, Julien pleads guilty of premeditated attempted murder to the judge and to his own defense lawyer, who visit his cell. Mathilde has succeeded in establishing a contact between Mme. de Fervaques and M. de Frilair, with the result that promise has been intimated of a bishopric for Frilair in exchange for his willingness to influence the jurors. Frilair is certain of being able to control the votes of Valenod, de Moirod, and of Cholin, and of being able to bring about an acquittal. In spite of the protests of her husband, Mme. de Rênal has come to Besançon and has personally written a plea of mercy for Julien to each of the thirty-six jurors.

All of Besançon has turned out for the trial. Mathilde makes a final tearful visit to Frilair, who assures her that all has been arranged, that the jurors will vote as Valenod votes. Julien has decided not to speak out in his own defense at the trial. The trial begins. The audience, mostly women, is obviously sympathetic toward the defendant. The trial lasts far into the night with no recess. Julien delivers a final oration after the summation, in spite of his resolve not to speak. The jury returns with a verdict of guilty with premeditation. Julien's only comment to the court is that he has been justly condemned to death.

Julien is moved to the death cell. His thoughts are only of Mme. de Rênal, whom he would hope to see before he dies. Mathilde disturbs his peaceful sleep to plead that he appeal for another trial. Julien stands firm in his refusal, in spite of Mathilde's entreaties. Julien gives the same answer to his lawyer, and he feels more kindly disposed toward the lawyer as they depart than he does toward Mathilde.

Commentary

These chapters relate the trial and the events immediately anterior and posterior to it.

Julien's soliloquy reveals his calm acceptance of the inevitability of his death. This attitude is in marked contrast to the frantic activity of Mathilde and Mme. de Rênal to bring about his acquittal. Julien remains ignorant of their attempts, and the ironic result is that they are working at cross purposes: Julien admits premeditation; but Mme. de Rênal urges the jurors not to find premeditation; Julien refuses to consider a plea of jealousy, as Mathilde, swallowing her pride, urges him to plead.

Chapter 40 brings Mme. de Rênal back into focus, in preparation for the final role she will play in the last chapters. The movement of the short chapter shifts from Julien's cell to the final efforts of Mathilde with Frilair, and finally to the passionate plea for mercy that is Mme. de Rênal's letter. In passing, Stendhal alludes to the effect that the trial has had on Besancon. This adds to the brief, but complete and suspenseful, summing up of everyone's pretrial state.

Note the point at which Julien has arrived in his elaboration of an "art of living." In his own mind, his affair is already classified. He is finally enjoying a life in which he may give himself over completely to contemplation, to dreams of past happiness with Mme. de Rênal, to an objective, dispassionate self-scrutiny and evaluation. Any invasion of his privacy by sordid details of life outside his cell is painful to him. Freudians would see in the Stendhalian hero's passive, blissful state achieved in the protectiveness of prison Stendhal's desire to return to the womb. When maternal Mme. de Rênal finally joins Julien in this happy seclusion, such a view is even more convincing.

We witness the trial scene from Julien's point of view. Thus, the reader adopts Julien's physical vantage point, and he observes not individual faces in the courtroom, but groups of faces, mostly feminine, localized only generally by their position vis-à-vis Julien. Across from the dock above the jurors and judge, twelve to fifteen pretty women occupy three galleries. In the circular gallery overhanging the crowded courtroom are more young, pretty faces. Just as he enters the courtroom, Julien glimpses the gothic pillars, an isolated and clear detail of the blurred scene that surrounds him. After his initial view, by means of a wide sweep Julien's attention is attracted to the galleries above the jury, where he sees Mme. Derville. Only once does the point of view stray—to appreciate Julien's simple elegance as viewed by the ladies of the courtroom. The description is incomplete and fragmentary, but in that respect realistic. It is a foretaste of Stendhal's great battle scene in the *Charterhouse* in which the battle of Waterloo is seen from the point of view of an individual soldier, who is never quite sure of what is transpiring. This realistic technique was admired and imitated by the great Tolstoy. *The Red Badge of Courage,* by Stephen Crane, portrays war realistically in much the same way that Stendhal had done.

Is it accurate to say that Julien commits suicide? Again, Stendhal does not offer an explicit answer. The answer lies partially in another question: would Valenod have betrayed Julien had the latter not denounced the society that condemns him? Stendhal has been careful to reintroduce Valenod intermittently and to assert Valenod's jealousy of Julien, who had succeeded in making Mme. de Rênal his mistress. Would this hatred and desire for vengeance have sufficed to cause Valenod to instruct the jury to condemn Julien, or was Julien's brutal condemnation of the aspiring bourgeoisie the final blow that precipitated the betrayal?

At any rate, it is because of his accurate evaluation of the situation, and because of his courage in proclaiming it to others, that Julien plays a truly heroic role in the court scene. Julien tells the jury that he will be condemned not for having committed the crime, but for having violated the social hierarchy, for having risen above his class. Julien, like Camus' Meursault, executes a reversal in position: the accused condemns the accuser. In a sense, Julien assumes the way in which he will die: he rejects the death penalty unless he, first, has admitted its justice. In this regard, he is the ancestor of Malraux's heroes, who do not undergo death passively, but who assume their death.

To what extent is Julien aware of the gravity of the consequences of his oration, assuming that it did incite Valenod to betrayal? It would not appear to have been a deliberate attempt to bring about his own condemnation, rather it is prompted by his sense of duty, which arises spontaneously. His manner during the trial is one of dignity and courage, although he has difficulty at times in controlling his emotions. During his emotional moments, Julien is seeing himself as the lady spectators see him. The oration would simply be another of those moments when Julien's sensibility betrays him. An impulsive awakening of emotion catches his mask of self-control and calm off guard. That Julien is aware of how others are viewing him during this trial when his life is in the balance should not surprise us too much. This is another faithful rendition of psychological truth by Stendhal. In crucial moments, immediate reactions will many times be quite far from the vital issue. Julien seems to view his trial with a certain objectivity.

One critical view holds that Julien unconsciously harbors a death wish. Such a view would give more responsibility to Julien in the resulting verdict of guilty.

Another view would see in Julien simply another example of the fate of the Stendhalian creature who, having lived so intensely, has burned himself out. It would be the extension on a grander scale of such phenomena as Mathilde's involuntary fainting, of Julien's loss of consciousness in the presence of Pirard, of La Sanseverina's falling asleep while seated in the *Charterhouse*. Such an interpretation of Julien's role in his own condemnation would be in keeping with Stendhal's romantic conception of character.

Even after the death sentence is read, Julien keeps his aplomb and inner calm. He lucidly examines the act of vengeance that Valenod has committed and muses momentarily on what will await him after life. Recalled to reality by Mathilde's cry, Julien's thoughts come with haste and confusion, but he contains these and expresses outwardly only his approval of the death penalty.

Note that the most strained emotional moments undergone by the characters are related with the most clipped, terse, and abrupt prose by Stendhal.

Stendhal continues to "detach" Julien from the action, a tendency we first noticed when the hero left to assume his commission in the army. Now that he is condemned to death, Julien's detachment is even more strongly pronounced. In musing about himself, Julien utilizes the past tense. He sees himself as having already been guillotined, which produces the effect of an even greater degree of objectivity achieved by Julien. This approach and the ironic self-detachment characterizing his interior monolog are no doubt a sort of defense mechanism. Julien is steeling himself in order not to give way to the horror of death. At the same time, it is part of the new happiness, the "art of living" that Julien has perfected now that he is in the seclusion of the prison cell.

Unconsciously, Julien is punishing Mathilde for all the humiliations she has imposed on him, as he refuses to give serious thought to her appeals. He even solicits her praise at his courtroom heroism, which is reminiscent of the ideal that characterized their love. In a sense, Julien has been victorious in their heroic rivalry: he has invited death and refused to appeal the sentence. It is quite possible that Mathilde feels somewhat cheated. Julien is destroying her own heroic role.

Stendhal depicts for us here a truly superior soul. Julien is moved by genuine suffering, sensitive, but proud to the point of refusing to expose his suffering to the view of others, thus to debasement. The tiresome presence of Mathilde succeeds only intermittently in piercing the reverie that increasingly characterizes the mental life of Julien. He imagines Mme. de Rênal's reaction after his death. Stendhal is preparing for the long-awaited arrival of Julien's first and only love.

CHAPTERS 43-45

Summary

Julien is overjoyed by a visit from Mme. de Rênal. He agrees to appeal if she will visit him every day in his cell. They know complete happiness. After three days, M. de Rênal has ordered that his wife return to Verrières. An ambitious priest has undertaken the conversion of Julien and has posted himself in all weather outside the prison, where much to Julien's annoyance, he attracts a great crowd. In desperation, Julien admits him, then rids himself of the troublesome priest by sending him to say masses for the poor.

Mathilde arrives on the heels of the departing priest to relate the treachery of Valenod and to try to convince Julien of the necessity of requesting a reprieve. Julien finally sends her away, requesting that she listen to a mass for him. The much dreaded visit of his father occurs. Sorel ceases his reproaches when Julien suggests that he will bequeath his money to his father and brothers. Julien then shares a bottle of champagne with two other prisoners and listens to the life story of one. Finally, Julien is left to his gloomy meditations.

Julien submits to confession, and provincial public opinion is thereby satisfied. Mme. de Rênal has left Verrières and, living with her aunt in Besançon, visits Julien twice a day. This bliss is interrupted by the daily visits of Mathilde. M. de Croisenois has been killed in a duel defending the honor of Mathilde. Julien angrily rejects a Jansenist's entreaties that he make a spectacular conversion, which, according to the priest, would encourage many lost souls to return to the Church. Julien must dissuade Mme. de Rênal from begging a reprieve from the king at Saint-Cloud. After the execution, Mathilde visits the cell and carries off Julien's head. Fouqué, carrying out Julien's last wishes, negotiates his burial on a high hill overlooking Verrières. Mathilde accompanies the procession and with her own hands buries Julien's head. Mme. de Rênal dies three days after the death of Julien.

Commentary

In the time of the novel, the action of Chapter 43 occurs only one hour after Mathilde had left Julien's cell in the preceding chapter. In 43, the incident of greatest importance is, of course, Mme. de Rênal's visit with Julien. Then in almost a sentence, Stendhal indicates that "three days after these visits had been taking place," M. de Rênal recalls her home. The end of the chapter elaborates another short incident, the interview of the priest, and Chapter 44 opens with the immediate reaction of Julien after the priest has left. This is typical of Stendhal's treatment of time and events. A single chapter develops one incident (already begun in what precedes), culminates it (indicating that this incident was in fact typical by multiplying its occurrence, condensing time by an allusion to its passage), and introduces a second (to be enlarged in the following chapter).

The long awaited event is the reunion of Mme. de Rênal with Julien. Stendhal tells us that Julien has never known such happiness, although the author's "pudeur" prevents him, as usual, from elaborating the ecstatic happiness that both enjoy during this supreme moment. He passes over it with: "much later, when they were able to speak." Mme. de Rênal loves Julien as a human should love only God. This is no doubt the love that Stendhal would have wanted to receive. Mme. de Rênal's sadness and admission of her disgrace prompt a "new happiness" in Julien. In Stendhal's conception of love, one constantly makes new discoveries in the object, which increases one's love for her.

We are now aware of the extent of Julien's love for Mme. de Rênal and of how instrumental it has been in his calm acceptance of the death penalty up to this point. Imagining himself bereft of her love, Julien was prepared for death. Now, a new possibility of happiness opens up before him, and he will really know the terror of the condemned man. The priest's visit serves to materialize Julien's despair, and thereafter, he sees death as horrible.

It was no doubt Stendhal's "pudeur" that prevented him from giving titles to the last four chapters in the original version of the novel. It is as if the suggestion of privacy were thus made after Julien has been condemned to death. Within one short chapter, Julien moves from the heights of bliss to the depths of despair.

Weeping about his own death, Julien will be visited, in Chapter 44, by three more "misfortunes": the visits of Mathilde and of his father, and exposure to the criminals with whom he shares a bottle of champagne.

From these he will draw food for meditation. During these meditations, the reader will witness, for the last time, Julien's solitude. There exists in this chapter the same movement as in the preceding one, but in reverse: from the depths of despair, Julien will emerge "strong and resolute, as a man who sees clearly into his own heart."

Julien finally learns about the machinations of Mathilde and Frilair. The latter, no doubt in an effort to mitigate the betrayal he has suffered personally from Valenod, has tried to shift the blame for Julien's conviction to Julien himself. Frilair sees the courtroom oration as an invitation for condemnation to death. Julien has great difficulty in concealing his despair from Mathilde. His remark concerning the prisoner's public situation vis-à-vis the world sets the tone for the chapter. Just as in life outside, Julien is forced to adopt a hypocritical air in dealing with his visitors to protect what remains of his courage.

The interlude of the prisoners is at once a moment of respite, of relief — an escape from the horror of the present moment — thereby permitting Julien to transform his self-reproach and grief into a more objective melancholy, and a pendant to the visit by his father. Both incidents are inspirational to his musings in the latter part of the chapter. The prisoner episode is reminiscent of the appearance of Géronomo at the Rênal home in Part I, which constituted a sort of poetic escape from the misfortunes of the family. Here, there is a more macabre note. Greed for money has motivated the life of this criminal, otherwise endowed with a brave heart.

Thus taken out of himself, Julien is able to recapture the necessary detachment to arrive at the re-creation of the required attitude before death. From Julien's meditations result some of the very important ingredients of beylism: the need to see man for what he is, not to be taken in, not to betray one's real nature; the danger of trading the present moment of happiness, so hard to come by, for sterile meditations about the unfathomable; in the absence of any ethical basis of society, the necessity of the creation of and adherence to a private code of morality based upon the most exigent criterium—duty toward oneself.

Five days elapsed during Chapter 44. Stendhal terminates his novel with rapidity. One would be hard put to say over what extent of time the action takes place in the final chapter. It opens as a continuation of the final scene of the preceding chapter: Fouqué awakens Julien, the latter having regained his composure and resolution. Stendhal is winding up, moving from Julien's relationship to Mme. de Rênal, to Mathilde, almost without transition.

Julien admits to Mme. de Rênal that he mistook, at the time, the real happiness he had known with her in Vergy. Mathilde is insanely jealous of Mme. de Rênal's visits, and Julien's own role toward Mathilde has now become almost paternal, just as Mme. de Rênal's love for him still has a maternal character.

Stendhal's refusal to indulge in hyperbolic description and pathos is evidenced by his very sparse treatment of the execution of Julien, which has been termed literary euthanasia. We are told that the weather was beautiful, that Julien was poetic, courageous, observant of decorum. Stendhal even makes Julien "speak" after the narration of his death, as instructions to Fouqué concerning burial are given.

Note the final utilization of the "high place" motif in the burial of Julien. The cell has been the scene of his last happiness, and the heights culminate this representation beyond death. It is fitting that Mathilde be portrayed in this macabre scene retrieving Julien's head. It permits her to play the final scene in the drama from the past which she has re-enacted in her affair with Julien. There is likewise a kind of poetic justice attained thereby—her "amour de tête" is recompensed.

One wonders at the future of Mathilde de la Mole. Stendhal has hinted, in a previous chapter, that Frilair's attempts to replace Julien had not yet been noticed by Mathilde. As for Mme. de Rênal, her death is the logical consequence of her character and conduct. She and Julien have shared a more vital identity. Mathilde and Mme. de Rênal, each reflecting aspects of Julien, are complementary.

ANALYSIS OF MAIN CHARACTERS

JULIEN SOREL

Stendhal's depiction of Julien betokens his art in conceiving beings where contradictory impulses and qualities coexist. Julien shares his gentle qualities and sentiment with Mme. de Rênal and his aggressiveness and egotism rival Mathilde's, but Julien remains, necessarily, a solitary figure whose existence is to be enjoyed by himself alone. It is the solitude, imposed from within and without, of the superior individual who requires of others their generous and voluntary self-sacrifice for his sake that emerges as the dominant trait of the Stendhalian hero, in spite of his dichotomy.

Such a hero proves himself worthy of the sacrifice made by others of the "happy few" by his observance of an ascetic personal code of honor and morality, born of and nurtured by revolt. Julien would have found lasting happiness with Mme. de Rênal, were he not a Stendhalian hero. He faces death resolutely, having arrived at the certainty that he has been faithful to his code.

From several points of view, Julien is a twentieth-century hero. He represents the individual alienated from and pitted against society, whose vileness and corruption offend his idealism and integrity as an individual. For in the last analysis, Julien chooses idealism as opposed to compromise. He is a tragic figure in that he is superior to the force that destroys him, and to the extent that he has assumed his own death, he cheats the guillotine. It is possible that Julien's amoral pose may be more acceptable than the immorality of the society that has forced him to adopt it.

MATHILDE DE LA MOLE

Mathilde is a female Julien, except that her rebellion is sterile, motivated only by a thirst for the novel, the bizarre, the unusual. In a sense, she is as much the victim of the reigning social order as is Julien, since it stifles her imagination and potential of energy. Her aggressiveness and domineering nature cause her, in effect, to play a masculine role, which explains in part the impression she gives as Julien's rival.

Her romantic temperament has been aggravated by the absence of any outlet in which to express itself. After conceiving the thought that only the death sentence could distinguish a man, she resorts to the attempt to live out this thought in real life. Her aristocratic pride is as great as Julien's fear of ridicule, and this clash proves to be an almost insurmountable obstacle to the realization of their love. Her pride and vanity thwart the expression of her romantic nature, which is somewhat the reverse of Julien's dilemma: his sensitivity constantly erupts to thwart his preconceived conduct.

Paradoxically, the character flaws that prevent them from achieving happiness are the necessary flaws of the superior being. Mathilde should not have intellectualized her passion, implies Stendhal disapprovingly, yet because of this defect, Mathilde may count herself among the "happy few." Her passion controlled by reason represents another variation of Stendhal's own impossible ideal: to love and not lose control. Like Julien, she lives in accordance with her own demanding morality. All in all, since Mathilde has fully realized her romantic dream at the end of the novel, one can visualize her as unhappy only after her last raptures have ceased, and, finding herself back in the banality of reality, she searches for a new adventure.

MADAME DE RENAL

Mme. de Rênal contrasts with Mathilde in age and in nature. The two further reflect different aspects of Julien's nature: Mme. de Rênal is spontaneous, sensitive, tenderhearted, as is Julien; Mathilde shares his pride. Mme. de Rênal awakens to a new existence when she falls in love with Julien. It is as if her previous thirty years had not existed. This sudden, overwhelming blossoming of her being explains the violence and permanence of her passion.

Her love sharpens her intelligence and endows her with momentary cunning and daring, making her again the reverse of Mathilde. At first a very moral person and somewhat naive, she sacrifices every scruple to her love for Julien. She is incapable of self-scrutiny, so instinctive a creature is she. Mme. de Rênal never achieves the amoral freedom that typifies the "happy few," although her existence on the instinctive level approximates amorality.

From her son's illness, which she sees as divine punishment, to her death following Julien's own, she is constantly tossed between passion and guilt. This fluctuation is not as obvious as it is in the case of Mathilde, but it is nonetheless basic to her nature. Mme. de Rênal can make claim to be of the "happy few," however, in that her happiness is found in love and it is doomed to failure. It is the happiness of the moment and of eternity. The maternal nature of Mme. de Rênal's love for Julien is complemented by the latter's paternal concern for Mathilde.

M. DE RÊNAL

M. de Rênal appears as the unsympathetic dupe and answers to the definition of the ridiculous character in that he contributes to his own downfall. His materialistic values are the antithesis of those of the "happy few." In Stendhal's view, the French of his time played the role of duped or of duper. M. de Rênal is, of course, in the former category. M. de Rênal is doubtless Stendhal's repudiation of his own father.

MARQUIS DE LA MOLE

Although the marquis, like the mayor, prepares his own misery in that he makes Julien his protégé, he is treated with more deference and respect by Stendhal than is the mayor. He would represent the father Stendhal would have wanted. Julien first usurps the role of son from Norbert, then that of father of Mathilde. The same pattern is visible in both families into which Julien enters: M. de Rênal cannot forsake his wife, who in turn loves Julien; M. de la Mole cannot get along without Mathilde, who is hopelessly in love with Julien. In his role of the generous father vis-à-vis the hero, M. de la Mole prefigures the same role to be played by Mosca in the *Charterhouse*.

STENDHAL'S ROMANTICISM AND REALISM

Labels always prove to be inaccurate, and at best they signal tendencies by which individuals may be grouped as more different than similar. This is particularly true of writers like Stendhal, in whom mutually exclusive tendencies coexist but achieve a kind of synthesis in the author's artistic creations. Although *The Red and the Black* appeared during the heyday of French Romanticism and the novel and Stendhal are in many ways "romantic," Stendhal seems to absent himself from his time, and while writing for the twentieth century, perpetuates the rationalism of the seventeenth century, the empiricism of the eighteenth, and announces the re-emergence of this "scientific" spirit of later nineteenth-century Realism and Naturalism.

Beylism itself, Stendhal's personal "system of happiness," shows a curious combination of romantic and realistic influences. Its ideal is romantic and, at the same time, a modification of eighteenth-century epicureanism. It assumes the existence of a superior elite, dedicated to the enjoyment of happiness, consisting of the "combined satisfaction of the intellect, imagination, and the will," as Léon Blum expresses it. Stendhal's confidence in man's ability to "systematize" happiness through experimentation announces the optimism of Comte's positivism, which, in turn, is influential in the formulation of Naturalism's scientific pretentions.

Stendhal's romantic tendencies are: the cult of the superior individual in revolt against society and its ideology; the presentation, albeit indirect, of himself idealized in his protagonists, indicating a basic subjectivity; the portrayal of sensitive, passionate souls on the quest for happiness — happiness, again, such as the author himself conceives.

These romantic traits are constantly subdued, however, by traits that make Stendhal a realist or classicist. He is attached to reality, specifically to contemporary reality, which he would render with scrupulous honesty and exactness. Julien is what Stendhal would want to be, but at the same time Julien is Antoine Berthet, and the society he encounters is that which confronts Berthet. Although many of Stendhal's characters are "beylistes," they are formed by their environment, as registered by their sensorial impressions, and this psychological process is portrayed as such by the author. In true classical tradition, Stendhal's study is of man's inner life, fraught with conflict, although Stendhal has no didactic aims, except perhaps as manifested in his desire to reach the "happy few."

Stendhal's own hypercritical attitude toward himself dictates his treatment of his characters, whom he "puts to the test," throwing them into predicaments where their worth may be measured. Stendhal's resulting detachment from his creatures creates the air of an ironic objectivity.

He forged his style in direct reaction to the lyrical, hyperbolic, flowery style of Romanticism. Constantly checking his own extreme sensibility, Stendhal trusted only the authenticity of spontaneity and created a style, which in its directness, approximates the immediacy of the spoken language. The Stendhalian sentence is clipped, dry, terse, and has an irregular cadence in its rapidity. Although it is as far from Flaubert's laboriously wrought prose as from the hyperbole of the romantics, Stendhal's style is realistic in a broader sense of the term, in that it communicates a direct impression of life being lived at the present moment.

REVIEW QUESTIONS AND THEME TOPICS

1. Justify, if possible, the political episodes as not being extraneous to Julien's individual drama.

2. Exemplify Stendhal's "tender irony" toward his "happy few."

3. Does the attempted murder of Mme. de Rênal by Julien contradict his character or is it consistent with the hero's nature?

4. What could be an explanation for Stendhal's use of epigraphs preceding every chapter?

5. Is it the realism or romanticism of the novel that appeals to the contemporary audience of Stendhal?

6. Determine to what extent Julien is an aggressive protagonist, actively responsible for his successes and failures.

7. Compare the two parts of the novel from the point of view of structure and recurrence of motifs.

8. How does Stendhal maintain the reader's sympathy for his hero?

9. Which character—Mme. de Rênal or Mathilde de la Mole—do you find more convincing?

10. How does Julien's affair with Mathilde reflect the political conflict exposed in the novel?

11. Does Julien commit suicide?

12. In what ways is Stendhal's improvisational technique apparent in the novel?

13. To what extent are the characters the victims of self-delusion?

14. Define Stendhal's method of psychological analysis.

SELECTED BIBLIOGRAPHY

In English

Adams, Robert M. *Stendhal: Notes on a Novelist.* New York: The Noonday Press, 1959. An amusing, highly original work which confronts influences that Stendhal underwent, with their reflection in his novels. The author gives the impression of imitating Stendhal's improvisational technique.

Brombert, Victor. *Stendhal, a Collection of Critical Essays.* Englewood Cliffs, N.J.: Prentice-Hall, Inc., 1962. A very useful collection of essays with an equally informative preface by the editor. Six of the essays treat various aspects of different novels; five are devoted to the novelist, alluding directly to his philosophy or style. The essays are excerpted from entire works.

Dutourd, Jean. *The Man of Sensibility,* (translated from the French by Robin Chancellor). New York: Simon & Schuster, 1961. An original and unique approach to Stendhal that embraces both Stendhal and his good friend Mérimée, by using the latter's essay on Stendhal ("H.B.," 1850) as a point of departure for each chapter of his own criticism. Dutourd emphasizes Stendhal's modernity.

Green, F. C. *Stendhal.* Cambridge: Cambridge University Press, 1939. A solid interpretation of the works of a very contradictory author.

Recommended for the individual who is baffled by the enigmatic Stendhal and is looking for some clear interpretations.

Levin, Harry. *The Gates of Horn.* New York: Oxford University Press, 1963. (The chapter herein contained was originally published as *Toward Stendhal;* New Directions, 1945.) A very provocative study of Stendhal's works as an expression and representation of his time. Levin sees Stendhal as a reformed idealist, the first in the current of bourgeois literature that is Realism.

In French

Bardèche, Maurice. *Stendhal romancier.* Paris: La Table ronde, 1947. Bardèche treats Beyle principally as a novelist. He probes the circumstances and sources of composition and offers helpful interpretations of the novels.

Caraccio. Armand. *Stendhal, L'Homme et L'Oeuvre* (Connaissance des Lettres series). Paris: Boivin et Cie., 1951. The first part is devoted to the author's life, the second to his works. Caraccio's concluding chapter reviews briefly Stendhal criticism. Although the work is not exhaustive, it is reliable and entertaining.

Marill-Albérès, Francine. *Stendhal* (Classiques du XIXe Siècle series). Paris: Editions Universitaires, 1959. A short work devoted to Stendhal's works and offering a poeticized interpretation of the "Stendhalian universe."

Martineau, Henri. *L'Oeuvre de Stendhal.* Paris: Le Divan, 1945. The great French Stendhal scholar presents an authoritative, basic study of the works and thought of Stendhal. He traces the author's thought by chronologically following his works. It is primarily a study in literary history rather than in interpretation.

————. *Le Coeur de Stendhal.* 2 vols. Paris; A. Michel, 1952, 1953. Rated as the best biography of Stendhal.

Prévost, Jean. *La Création chez Stendhal.* Paris: Mercure de France, 1951. As the title indicates, the work is devoted to an investigation of the creative process of the author as deduced from his works, and to a very imaginative analysis of style: character presentation and utilization, narrative techniques, and stylistic devices.

NOTES

NOTES

NOTES

NOTES

NOTES

NOTES

NOTES

THE STRANGER

NOTES

including
- *Life of Camus*
- *Camus and the Absurd*
- *List of Characters*
- *Critical Commentaries*
- *Character Analyses*
- *Review Questions*
- *Selected Bibliography*

by
Gary Carey, M.A.
University of Colorado

INCORPORATED

LINCOLN, NEBRASKA 68501

Editor	Consulting Editor
Gary Carey, M.A.	*James L. Roberts, Ph.D.*
University of Colorado	*Department of English*
	University of Nebraska

ISBN 0-8220-1229-4
© Copyright 1979
by
C. K. Hillegass
All Rights Reserved
Printed in U.S.A.

1990 Printing

Cliffs Notes, Inc.   Lincoln, Nebraska

CONTENTS

THE STRANGER NOTES

LIFE OF CAMUS

Albert Camus was born November 7, 1913, and reared in Algeria, a country exposed to the blistering African sun and the plain by the Mediterranean sea. These roots—the sun and the sea—have spread into all of Camus' writings—the novels, the plays, and the essays. They are a part of his lyricism, his symbolism, and his values. The universe, it seems from his early notebook, *(Noces),* was mother, father, and lover for the young Camus, and from the first, Camus was aware of the paradoxical aspects of his natural world. The sensual free pleasure of swimming and hiking was in continuous contrast to the bare stony earth that made living a matter of poverty and destitution. He was early aware of the absurd condition of man's being totally alone in a resplendent universe. This concept is Camus' equivalent of "In the beginning. . . ." Against its truth, all of his writings sound revolt, for he refused to be deceived by social religious or individual submissions that ignored or defied the irreducible truth that man alone is responsible for himself, his meaning, and his measure. Camus' writings are a testament to a continuing belief in man's exiled but noble condition.

Lucien Camus, Albert's father, was killed in 1914 during World War I's Battle of the Marne, and the year-old child was reared by his deaf mother. She had little money and was apparently a rather joyless and boring companion for her son. It is little wonder that he spent much of his time with athletics, studies, and necessary part-time employment. When he finished school, a university degree seemed the most important challenge available to a poverty-stricken student. Camus was enthusiastic and ambitious about his studies, but he was not able to complete them immediately. In 1930, while he was a student of philosophy at the University of Algiers, he almost died during a bout with tuberculosis, an illness which would periodically afflict him for many years. Then, after his recovery, he was beset by the constant problem of poverty and was forced to support himself for several years as a meteorologist, a police clerk, and a salesman. During this time he married and divorced and also joined and left the Communist party. In 1935, a year before he received his degree from the University, he founded The Workers' Theater, a group formed to present plays for Algiers' working population. Before his theater venture ended in 1939, Camus published *L'Envers et L'Endroit (Betwixt and Between)*, essays that deal with man and death in terms of an oblivious universe. They are mood pieces, written in Camus' mixture of irony and lyricism, describing man's defenselessness and his isolation in a splendid universe whose only rule for man seems to be death. Yet there is an optimism in these essays; it is here that Camus first advocates living *as if* man had eternal value. He believes that only in man's courageous rebellion to confront himself and his world can he begin to create a civilization that can rescue itself from a nihilistic catastrophe.

Between the years 1937 and 1939, Camus wrote book reviews and occasional essays for the *Algier-Republicain*, a left-wing newspaper. Later he assumed the editorship of the *Soir-Republicain*, but for only a short time. He was severely critical of the French colonial government and after the newspaper folded, he soon found himself unofficially unwelcome and unable to find a job in the country. Thus in 1940 he left Algeria and went to live in Paris. There he worked for a time with the *Paris-Soir*, but his journalistic career was once again curtailed. This time the Germans had invaded France.

Camus returned once again to North Africa, where he remarried and began teaching in a private school in Oran. He continued to write and filled several notebooks with sketches and several versions of *The Stranger* and *The Myth of Sisyphus*, and he also worked on ideas for a new novel, *The Plague*.

A year later, both *The Stranger* and *The Myth of Sisyphus* were published, and Camus was established as a writer of international importance. *The Stranger*'s Meursault has now become a literary archetype, and the beginning sentences of *The Stranger* have become synonymous with an absurd or ironic situation. Never before had the public read about a man who was so absolutely honest as Meursault. In fact, his honesty is perhaps his only meritorious quality. Meursault is an anti-hero, an inconspicuous clerk who does not believe in God, but cannot lie. He does believe in going to the movies, swimming, and making love. He is finally beheaded because he murdered an Arab; he is condemned, however, because he seemed indifferent at his mother's funeral. Meursault becomes aware of his freedom and his happiness only after he is imprisoned, a situation similar to that of the imprisoned Oranian citizens in *The Plague*. He faces death with sensitive and joyous awareness of his last moments and hopes for a vivid end and an angry shouting crowd as a witness.

In the year of *The Stranger*, 1942, Camus decided to return to France and commit himself to the French Resistance Movement. He enlisted in an organization known as Combat, also the title of the clandestine newspaper he edited during the Occupation. After Paris was liberated in 1944, Camus continued to edit *Combat* for four years while he published collections of his wartime essays. His plays, *The Misunderstanding* and *Caligula*, were presented during 1944; the latter was as well received as the former was not. In 1945, Camus toured the United States, lecturing and gathering firsthand impressions of the national power that was credited with ending the long war.

His allegory, *The Plague*, was published in June, 1947, and was immediately cited as a major literary work. The critics and the public were unanimous in their praise for this somberly narrated chronicle. As a popular book it had none of the formula gimmicks; it had no intense, romantic plot-line, no fascinating setting, nor even a powerfully drawn characterization of its main character. But to a nation recovering from an enemy occupation, it was an authentic account of months during which only human dignity and survival mattered. Postwar readers were appreciative and sympathetic to this writer who had faithfully, and not melodramatically, recorded the suffering and misery of separation and exile.

In 1949, upon his return to France from a South American tour, Camus became quite ill and went into almost total seclusion, only occasionally publishing collections of more of his political essays. In 1951, when he was recovered, he published an extensive study of metaphysical, historical, and artistic revolt, *The Rebel*. It was a controversial book and was responsible for breaking the friendship he had with Jean Paul Sartre.

After *The Rebel*, Camus began translating favorite works of international playwrights. His adaptions were rapidly produced and included Calderón's *La Devocion de la Cruz*, Larivey's *Les Espirits*, Buzzati's *Un Caso Clinico*, Faulkner's *Requiem for a Nun*, and others. More collections of his political essays appeared, plus many prefaces to contemporary writings.

In 1956, a new fictional work appeared, his novel *The Fall*. The book deals with a successful and admired lawyer who suddenly faces his conscience after he refuses to help a woman drowning in a suicide attempt. The confessions of his fraud and guilt contain precise and penetrating comments about contemporary society. It is not as ambitious or as lengthy as *The Plague*, but it is as polished a masterpiece as *The Stranger*.

The following year Camus was awarded the Nobel Prize for Literature, and two years later he was killed in an automobile accident on January 4, 1960. The many eulogistic essays which appeared afterward remarked on the absurdity of his death — its suddenness, its uselessness, and the lack of logic to explain why. Camus, however, was probably more aware of the significance of his individual life than any of his essayists: his meaningless death is the key witness to his body of literature.

CAMUS AND THE ABSURD

To enter into the literary world of Albert Camus, one must realize, first off, that one is dealing with an author who does not believe in God. Major characters in Camus' fiction, therefore, can probably be expected either to disbelieve or to wrestle with the problem of belief. One's first response then, as a reader, might profitably be a brief consideration of what might happen to a character who comes to realize that there is no Divinity, no God. What happens when he realizes that his death is final, that his joys, his disappointments, and his sufferings are brief flickers preluding an afterlife of nothingness? What changes in his daily pattern of work-eat-love-sleep must he now effect? Much like Kafka's Joseph K., the man in question has staggeringly comprehended that he is condemned to an eternal void — and because of no crime. Only because he is part of a meaningless birth-death cycle is he doomed; the fact of death and his mortality is all. He sees, in short, The End focused on the screen of his future, the screen on which he used to project his dreams and hopes. Hope based on anything superhuman is now futile. He sees an end for himself and his fellowmen. So, what then? Suicide, if all is meaningless? Or a blind return flight toward an external, though ever-silent God?

This concern with death and its abyss of nonexistence is the basis for most of Camus' literary works. Condemned to an everlasting zero of eternity, Camus' characters often suffer their author's own involvement and anguish; and, for his readers, the recognition of the fact of their own deaths is the starting point for their confronting and experiencing Camus' concept of the Absurd.

As a salvation, however, from despair and nihilism, Camus' Absurd embraces a positive optimism—optimism in the sense that much emphasis is placed on human responsibility for civilizing the world. The fictional characters, therefore, who shoulder their new *mortal* responsibility, are often characterized as rebels. In revolt from both a cowardly suicide and an equally cowardly flight from faith, the new optimism suggests man's returning to the center of a philosophical tightrope above an intensely physical death and, in his revolt, performing precariously. Above the threat of death, in confrontation with death, the metaphysical ropewalker acts "as if" his actions mattered. Obviously they do not in any long-range sense. And, rather than scamper to either the poles of Hope or Suicide, he knows that he will eventually fall, but stays mid-center. Obviously, his life, the lives of all men do not *finally* matter. Death is definitive. But, clown-like, he creates new acts, new entertainments—reaching, gesturing. Exploiting his precarious posture in a new burst of freedom, he restructures his actions, and in vivid contrast to death, he diffuses joy and a sense of ridiculous responsibility.

Walking on this razor's edge of "as if" means that man must act to his fellowmen as though life had meaning; in short, living an absurdity. Knowing that man has only man to depend upon, however, he can take fresh courage. He is now rid of fearful superstitions and questioning theories; he can now discard the religious faiths which assume that man is subservient to a Something divine and eternal. Man now has no excuse for failure, except himself. "God's will" as an excuse for failure is no longer valid. Man succeeds or fails because of the strength, or the lack of it, in himself. Camus challenges man to do the work which he has, too often, assigned to God.

LIST OF CHARACTERS

Meursault
    The narrator, an Algerian clerk who is sentenced to death for murdering an Arab.

Céleste
    Meursault's friend and owner of a restaurant where he usually dines.

Warden
    In charge of the old age home in Marengo where Meursault's mother dies.

Gatekeeper
    Inmate and employee in the same institution.

Pérez
    Close friend of Meursault's mother at the old age home.

Marie Cardona
    Meursault's mistress, formerly a typist and a stenographer in Meursault's office.

Emmanuel
    Another worker in Meursault's office.

Salamano
    Lives with his grotesque spaniel on Meursault's floor.

Raymond Sintès
    Lives on the same floor, reputed to be a pimp.

"Robot-woman"
    Woman who shares Meursault's table at Céleste's one day and later attends his trial.

Masson
    Owner of the cottage at the beach visited by Raymond, Meursault, and Marie on the day of the murder; friend of Raymond.

Examining Magistrate
    Conducts the preliminary interrogations.

CRITICAL COMMENTARIES

PART ONE

CHAPTER I

The Stranger is a very short novel, divided into two parts. In Part One, covering eighteen days, we witness a funeral, a love affair, and a murder. In Part Two, covering about a year, we are present at a trial that recreates those same eighteen days from various characters' memories and points of view. Part One is full of mostly insignificant days in the life of Meursault, an insignificant man, until he commits a murder; Part Two is an attempt, in a courtroom, to judge not only Meursault's crime but also to judge his life. Camus juxtaposes two worlds; Part One focuses on subjective reality; Part Two, on a more objective, faceted reality.

The novel opens with two of the most quoted sentences in existential literature: "Mother died today. Or, maybe, yesterday; I can't be sure." The impact of this indifference is shocking, yet it is a brilliant way for Camus to begin the novel. This admission of a son's unconcern about his mother's death is the key to Meursault's simple, uneventful life as a shipping clerk. He lives, he doesn't think too much about his day-to-day living, and now his mother is dead. And what does her death have to do with his life? To Meursault, life is not all that important; he doesn't ask too much of life, and death is even less important. He is content to, more or less, just exist. But by the end of the novel, he will have changed; he will have questioned his "existing" and measured it against "living" — living with an awareness that one can have and demand for himself — that is, a passion for life itself.

Today's readers of this novel have usually been exposed to such an anti-hero as Meursault, but to those who read this novel when it was first published, Meursault was a most unusual man. They were confronted with a man who has to attend to the details of a death — and not just a death, but the death of his mother. And the tone of what Meursault says is: so, she's dead. This tone is exactly what Camus wanted: he calculated on its shock value; he wanted his readers to examine closely this man who does not react as most of us are expected to do. Meursault is very matter-of-fact about his mother's death. He does not hate his mother; he is merely indifferent to her death. She lived in a nursing home not far from him because he didn't have enough money to pay the rent and buy food for them both, and also because she needed somebody to be with her a great deal of the time. They didn't see each other very often because, in Meursault's words, they had "nothing else to say to each other."

Camus is challenging us, in effect, with this idea: Meursault has a unique freedom; he does not have to react to death as we are taught by the church, by novels, movies, and cultural mores. His mother gave him birth; she reared him. Now he is an adult; he is no longer a child. Parents cannot remain "parents"; children, likewise, at a certain point, are no longer "children." They become adults, and when Meursault became an adult, he and his mother were no longer close. Eventually, they had "nothing else to say to each other." Meursault is no longer responsible to his mother for his actions. He defines himself and his own destiny. And, at this moment in his life, Meursault cannot succumb to the rituals of frantic, emotional breast-beating because of his mother's death. Meursault is not rebellious; he has simply discarded burdensome gestures. He cannot exaggerate his feelings.

Meursault has a special kind of freedom; he has made a commitment, an unconscious commitment, really; he has committed himself to living his life his way, even though it is dull, monotonous, and uneventful. He has no desire, no driving ambition, to prove his worth to other people. To most people, a funeral is an emotional trauma; for Meursault, note that his mother's wake is so insignificant that he borrows a black tie and armband for the funeral: why spend money for them when he would use them only one time? And he almost misses his bus for the funeral. He will bury his mother with church rites, but his sense of freedom is his own; he will physically do certain things, but he cannot express emotions which do not exist.

Thus we see Meursault's reaction to death. Consider, then, after the funeral, his attitude toward life. Meursault enjoys life. One can't say that he has a rage for living, but he affirms simple physical pleasures — swimming, friendships, and sex — not spectacularly, but remember that he is not a hero, just a simple shipping clerk. Note, too, that on the way to the funeral, during the vigil, and during the funeral itself, Meursault's reactions are mostly physical. When he enters the mortuary, for example, his attention is not on the wooden box that holds his mother's corpse. He notices, first, the skylight above and the bright, clean whitewashed walls. Even after the mortuary keeper has left, Meursault's attention is not on the coffin; instead, he reacts to the sun, "getting low, and the whole room was flooded with a pleasant, mellow light."

During the funeral procession, Meursault is not concerned with his mother's existence in an afterlife. She is dead; he is alive, and he is sweaty and hot, and doing what he is expected to do for a funeral, but these are all physical acts. Physically, he experiences the "blazing hot afternoon," the "sun-drenched countryside . . . dazzling," a "shimmer of heat," and he is "almost blinded by the glaze of light." This is what is painful to Meursault; he is not torn by religious agony or by a sense of loss. And besides Camus' showing us Meursault's physical responses to living, as opposed to his feelings about death, he is preparing us for the climax of Part One: Meursault's murder of the Arab. Again, the sun will be glaring, dazzling, and blinding; in fact, one of Meursault's defenses in court as to why he shot the Arab will be: "because of the sun."

In contrast to Meursault's reactions to the funeral and the heavy heat of the sun is Thomas Pérez. Old Pérez was a friend of Meursault's mother; they had a kind of romance. He follows the funeral procession, limping in the broiling sun, sometimes dropping so far behind that he has to take shortcuts to rejoin the procession. At the funeral, he faints.

Meursault, not Camus, tells us these facts. Meursault's narrative is documentary, objective, like a black-and-white photograph. He is not effusive when he tells us of Pérez's aged, wrinkled face and the tears streaming from his eyes. There is no attempt for sympathy. Meursault states facts, then tells us that his own thoughts are focused on getting back to Algiers and going to bed and sleeping for twelve hours.

Can we condemn Meursault? Should he have shed tears? Should he have thrown himself on his mother's casket? Or should we recognize his honesty? In Part Two, a jury will judge him and will find him guilty, not because he murdered an Arab, but mainly because he could not and did not weep at his mother's funeral. Shall we also condemn him? Camus says No; a man must be committed to himself, to his own values, and not be confined by certain value judgments of others. It is important to be a physical, *mortal* man, as opposed to being a half-man, living with the myth of someday becoming an immortal spirit.

Meursault's philosophy is, despite its unusual nature, very positive. He cannot live with illusions. He will not lie to himself. This life now is more important than living for a mythical then. When, according to Camus, one has seen the value of living with no illusion of an afterlife, he has begun to explore the world of the Absurd. Values must be, ultimately, self-defined, and certainly not by the church. Why fake an emotion because society says that it is proper etiquette? A lifetime is only so long and can end very suddenly. Camus would have us ask ourselves: why am I living a life that I have not structured? How old is the universe and who am I amidst the millions of people who are dead in the earth and the millions who are still living on this earth? There is no Holy One who cares about me; the whirling universe is alien, uncaring. Only *I* can try to determine my significance. Death is ever-present and, afterward, nothing. These are all questions and issues that Meursault, by the end of the novel, will have examined. He will have become an Absurd Man, and Camus has shown us the genesis of this philosophy in this opening chapter. Slowly, we will see how this rather simple shipping clerk will change, how he will gain immense insight into the importance of his life, and how he will learn to enjoy it passionately, ironically, as he faces death.

CHAPTER II

After showing us Meursault's reaction to death, Camus shows us a day during which Meursault reacts to life. Meursault wakes up and realizes how exhausting the funeral has been, physically. It would be nice to go swimming. There are no introspective feelings about his mother, about how she looked when she was alive, how she smiled, the expression in her eyes, the things which she and he talked about years ago, his childhood with her—or even her absence, forever. Right now, swimming would be pleasant.

By chance, on the swimming raft, Meursault meets a girl who worked for a short time in his office and they go to a film that night, a comedy of all things, and then they go home and have sex.

We have seen Meursault's casual reaction to his mother's death; now, we see him manage a casual pickup. Marie knows that Meursault's mother has just been buried because she asks him about his black tie, but she's unconcerned, for the most part. Note, too, that Meursault tells Marie that his mother "died yesterday." It's of so little importance to him that he confuses, absently, the day of her funeral with the day of her death. Today is Saturday. Meursault's mother died, probably, Wednesday or Thursday; she was buried "yesterday."

Next morning, Meursault awakens; it is Sunday. There is nothing very exciting or special about Sundays, except for the fact that he dislikes Sundays. He has awakened after having had sex with Marie, but he is not disappointed about Marie's not being there when he wakes up. And he does not tell us how satisfying their lovemaking was. Yet he is responsive to the smell of the salt from Marie's hair. He falls asleep again and, when he wakes again, he smokes in bed until midday.

Recall that on the bus, traveling to his mother's funeral, Meursault was so sleepy he could hardly keep his eyes open; in fact, he thinks he dozed off for a while. He lives rather like an animal; if he's sleepy, he dozes. Remember, too, that Meursault had fleeting guilt feelings about dozing off during the ordeal of the vigil and during the funeral itself, but today, he stays in bed because it is pleasant to lie there and smoke.

When Meursault does get up, he doesn't know what to do. He wanders around the apartment, reads an old newspaper, and cuts out an advertisement for a scrapbook that he keeps of amusing things. Then he goes out on the balcony. He is uneasy, unhappy on Sundays. Sundays are unstructured. Weekdays may be monotonous but there are certain things to do at certain times; Saturdays are for fun. But then comes Sunday, completely unstructured.

Depicting this kind of mechanical, day-to-day living is important for Camus' purpose. In his *Myth of Sisyphus,* he said that the discovery and the disgust of this monotony — "rising, tram, four hours in the office or the factory . . ." — is absolutely essential for an understanding of the Absurd. Meursault has not yet made this discovery, but Meursault is not, by nature, introspective; he likes small pleasures — sex, swimming, a good night's sleep, and smoking. He will eventually make his discovery about the meaningless routine of his life, but it will come later in the novel. For the present, Camus wants us to see Meursault's restlessness on a day when there is no routine — no "rising, tram, four hours in the office . . ."

When Meursault goes out on the balcony, he observes the people below him. Sundays, for them, seem to have a routine: young men going to the movies, a waiter sweeping sawdust, a tobacco seller bringing a chair out onto the pavement, and the empty streetcars going by. This has happened many Sundays. Meursault watches during the afternoon, he smokes, he watches the evening come, and then he eats some bread and macaroni. He says that he's "managed to see another Sunday through . . ." In a word, he is bored.

The tone of this chapter is, again, largely a tone of indifference, except that today Meursault enjoys smoking in bed and smelling the salt from Marie's hair on the pillow beside him. But read again the passage describing his perception of this Sunday afternoon. He is aware, even if passively, that the street lights reveal "little pools of brightness," that the lights of the streetcars shine, "lighting up a girl's hair, a smile, or a silver bangle"; the sky becomes "velvety black." These fragments of sensitivity might go almost unnoticed. Meursault enjoys basic pleasures, but he also has a poetic perceptiveness within him—despite his passive reaction to his mother's death and his having had sex with Marie and his comment that "nothing had changed."

Yet what meaning has Meursault given to this Sunday? He has slept and smoked and sat on his balcony, and watched—alone. He is not deeply troubled about such things as—my life is wasted; I am bored; or I am lonely; in contrast, he has an ability to sit and watch, delighting, in small degrees, to colors, to the sky, and to the feel of the air. Meursault is not like an ordinary major character in a novel, and this "sitting and doing nothing" will be used in Part Two to condemn him. But one must still deal with the present, for this is what matters most to Meursault. Has Meursault done anything that has been especially enjoyable today? Has he chosen to make this day, in any way, significant, even in a small way, memorable? No. It has been just another Sunday and Meursault has "gotten through it." As he says, "It's all the same to me: makes no difference much." Life. Death. He faces them with the same easy indifference. Just as his mother's death was meaningless, so is his life, except for the few sensual pleasures and the fact that he lives the way he wants to. Meursault has yet to realize that he can make his life have meaning, that it can have intensity. Before that happens, however, he must confront this monotonous, meaningless routine day-to-day living and be disgusted by the waste he has made of each day, even Sundays, in order to be liberated. When this awakening comes, it will shatter the drifting rhythm of his life. But Camus must show us, first, Meursault's going through the empty motions of living so that we will have a perspective of Meursault's realizing and becoming aware of the possibilities of what life can contain.

CHAPTER III

Camus moves us in this chapter through one of Meursault's work days. It opens on a Monday and there are references to the age of Meursault's mother. Meursault does not know how to answer when he is asked how old she was; it is a matter that never seemed of importance to him. But do not label Meursault a nihilist or a cynic. He is indifferent to his mother's age and he is probably ignorant of how old she really was. And he can't understand why his employer looks relieved when Meursault answers, without any knowledge, "round about sixty." Moreover, why his employer would ask such a question is a mystery to Meursault. He could have answered fifty, and he would have heard "how terrible; so young." Had he said that she was eighty, he would have heard, "well, she led a long life." The age of his mother is simply of no consequence to Meursault.

Note what Camus is doing here; he is showing us that Meursault, instead of bothering with deep guilt about not knowing his mother's age, is annoyed. And, in contrast, he is happy and enjoys the physical pleasure of washing his hands at work and he enjoys this act less at the end of the day because the roller towel is sopping wet. This small act is what is important to Meursault. In fact, he has mentioned this business of the soggy towel to his employer, who considers it a mere detail; to Meursault, the age of his mother is a "mere detail."

In the same way that Meursault, rather impulsively, thought that swimming would be pleasant, after leaving work for a lunch break, he and another employee, Emmanuel, pause a moment to look at the sea, an ever-fascinating phenomenon for Meursault; they endure the "scorching hot" sun for a moment, then decide to do something irrational; they run, half-dazed by the heat, and madly jump onto a big firetruck coming toward them. They achieve a small goal, a fun game, following a child's instinct to dare to do something wild and sudden. What they accomplish makes them feel proud. Who else that afternoon decided to run and jump on a fast-moving firetruck? Probably only Meursault and Emmanuel. This is another facet of Meursault's uniqueness; his job as a shipping clerk may be dull, but, spontaneously, he acts without thinking, doing something which is both physical and satisfying.

After a nap and a cigarette, Meursault endures the rest of the afternoon in an office that is "stifling," making his slow, cool evening stroll home even more satisfying; again, Camus focuses on Meursault's physical reactions rather than on an introspective analysis about himself or his relationship with Marie or with his mother.

There is a bit of black humor injected into the novel when Meursault reaches his apartment. A neighbor of his, Salamano, and a dog also lead a routine life. But, unlike Meursault's life, which is usually solitary, Salamano is, as it were, almost married in a love/ hate relationship with his dog. And, Meursault tells us, they resemble one another (hairless, scabby, and hunched up) and, most important, they seem to fiercely detest one another.

This routine of living together has lasted eight years, the dog being walked regularly and beaten regularly. This does not particularly matter to Meursault; they are merely a curious couple of neighbors. Unlike Meursault, Raymond Sintès, an acquaintance of Meursault's, is disgusted by Salamano's living eight years with his dog—loving him, hating him, and beating him. But not Meursault. Salamano and his dog choose to live that way; otherwise, the dog would run away. At any rate, it would be ridiculous to worry a lot or try to solve a situation that has lasted eight years.

A rebel, without knowing or caring about being one, Meursault enjoys listening and talking with Raymond Sintès, a pimp who is disliked in the neighborhood. When asked what his profession is, Raymond says that he is a warehouse man. It makes no difference to Meursault that Raymond lies, or that Raymond is a pimp. He likes him; that's reason enough for their casual friendship.

Unlike Meursault, Raymond is a violent person. One can almost see him pacing the room, ready to smash his fist into a wall to release his frustrated anger, while Meursault sits this evening, enjoying some wine, half-listening to Raymond's harangues. Meursault seems to be in the room and, yet, not in the room. He is an observer (remember, for example, how he noted that the sky was "green" on his way home from work, as he also notes the color of the scabs on Salamano's dog), and he is an outsider to Raymond's intensity. Raymond, on the other hand, says that he's merely short-tempered, but admits that he has just fought with a fellow who annoyed him and, while the man was lying on the ground, Raymond continued kicking him: "He was bleeding like a pig when I'd done with him." Besides being somewhat of an outcast in this neighborhood, it would seem that he does not have many friends at all. Thus he comes to Meursault, only a casual friend, for advice and says that if Meursault will help him, he will be Meursault's "friend for life." Meursault's lack of a comment is typical; he has no objection to helping the fellow and has already agreed to eat supper and have some wine with Raymond.

Raymond's desire for revenge against his girlfriend is revealed as soon as supper begins. Like the man whom he continued kicking, even though the man was lying beaten on the ground, Raymond now says that he wants to further punish this girl, whom he has beaten on occasion until "the blood came," but, he adds, he beat her "only affectionately-like."

To say that Raymond is violent is an understatement; he is a sadist. Because the girl slept with someone else, he wants to turn her in to the police as a common prostitute, and he has also considered branding her. Once more, Meursault offers no opinion as to a course of action. What is Meursault's opinion? In his own words, "I said I hadn't any," continuing, however, that he finds the story interesting.

Meursault does not judge; he has no strongly positive or negative reactions to the girl's plight. One can never be sure what to do — this is Meursault's comment, as he drinks more wine. And, with more wine shared between the two men, Meursault agrees to write a scathing letter, making the girl repent of her unfaithfulness; then if she does, Raymond will spit in her face and throw her out of the room. Meursault agrees that such a plan would punish her, but he writes the letter mainly to satisfy Raymond. Why not? Meursault has no reason not to satisfy Raymond because Meursault doesn't really care one way or the other.

For Meursault, what he has done is merely a gesture; it takes no trouble to write such a letter and, besides, Raymond has been generous with his wine and food and cigarettes. Thus we view two very different men as the chapter closes: one is full of fury and revenge; the other has just composed a "real stinker" of a letter, with no personal malice.

At this point, one might ask himself why Meursault writes a letter discrediting the girl. Raymond, we must remember, is not a close friend; the letter is an attempt at deep revenge. This act is unlike Meursault, for usually he is a truthful man, yet here he fabricates a letter to be used for one purpose: to humiliate a girl. Meursault is not, we realize, a thoroughly honest man. His indifference, in this case, is an indifference to truth, for Raymond asks him to write a letter "that'll get her on the raw." Meursault does so, with the help of Raymond's wine; he composes a letter that states not facts, but a letter that will arouse violent emotions. And why? For Meursault, what he has done is a simple act, seemingly, of no great importance; for Raymond, what Meursault has helped him accomplish is monumental. In fact, what Meursault has done, is, indeed, very monumental, for had he not written the letter, he would not have found himself later intertwined in Raymond's problems; he would not have shot an Arab friend of the girl, and he would not have been guillotined.

The chapter ends poetically; whether this is Camus or Meursault commenting, one cannot be certain for Meursault describes the "sleep-bound" house and the moans of Salamano's dog rising slowly "like a flower growing out of the silence and darkness." We have seen rare moments of deeply poetic sensitivity within Meursault, so perhaps Meursault is far more intelligent and sensitive than we have seen until now. Yet this sentence is almost startling, coming from a man who says, in effect, frequently, that most things "don't matter much." If the night moans are compared to fruitful beauty, surely Camus intends irony for this chapter initiates Meursault's doom.

CHAPTER IV

A work week passes and Camus resumes his story on Sunday. It has been a busy week, the letter which Meursault wrote for Raymond has been sent, and Meursault has seen two movies with Emmanuel. Emmanuel doesn't seem too bright because Meursault has to explain what is happening on the screen. Remember, too, that in the last chapter, it was Emmanuel who suggested that he and Meursault try and run fast enough to jump on the fire truck, a rather foolhardy, impulsive act, even if they did it for sheer fun. Meursault, though, doesn't complain that he has to explain to

Emmanuel throughout the movies; likewise, he didn't consider the danger of jumping on a fast-moving fire truck. In both cases, Meursault enjoys himself—the physical exertion of running for the truck and the quiet, monotonous, running analysis of the movies.

Meursault remembers the day before, Saturday, primarily because of Marie's sensuality. Her bright-colored dress, her leather sandals, her breasts, and her tanned face remind him of a "velvety brown flower." Meursault's sensitivity is sensual as he recalls their sucking foam from the sea waves and spouting it toward the sky. This is not the indifferent Meursault of so many situations. This is a man who has an authentic, almost spiritual intimacy with the world. What he describes is a game that he and Marie played, but it was a game of much value for Meursault. Marie and the sea are, in a sense, both sexual partners for him. But, instantly, when the sea becomes too salty, Meursault reacts; he does not enjoy it any longer. And when Marie's kiss is finished, he is ready to swim back to the beach, catch the bus and, at home, make love, feeling the cool air on their sun-brown bodies. Stimulating moments, like these, are rare for Meursault, but they have a richly primitive and personal value for him and enable us to understand this man.

Later, when Marie asks him if he loves her, Meursault answers, honestly, that he supposes that he does not; he says, "that sort of question [has] no meaning, really." The sea, the sun, the waves, kisses, sex—Meursault can touch and feel, but love is too abstract, too ambiguous, and too all-encompassing to ponder. When Marie laughs, Meursault wants to kiss her; that he can understand and delight in. Love, however, is only a word, an over-used word, defined with a sense of permanence. Meursault is permanently bonded to no one—except with moments of spontaneous joy.

Following this scene, centering on love and love-making, Camus juxtaposes a violent battle scene between Raymond and his girlfriend. This becomes a loud battle that quickly gathers a crowd of people. Marie, seeing the woman being knocked about, reacts as most people would. She thinks that this is horrible and that someone should call for a policeman. Quite in character, Meursault observes the battle and comments that he isn't going for a policeman; he doesn't like them. Meursault doesn't care if the girl is being beaten up. Furthermore, it was Meursault who wrote the letter that caused this quarrel. The fate of the girl is of no concern to him. What matters to Meursault is that he dislikes policemen. Note also that the girl is an Arab. Meursault and Raymond and Marie are French. The girl is a native; the police are native; why inject oneself, a Frenchman, into a stormy lovers' quarrel with an Arab?

When a policeman does arrive to settle the argument, he makes a telling observation about Raymond. He accuses Raymond of having drunk so much that Raymond cannot stand steady. Raymond admits that he is trembling, but denies that he has been drinking. His rage has so infuriated him that he has become like a madman. He is, in fact, a man of uncontrollable urges and temper.

There is also a short, revealing scene following the battle. Marie is so upset that she has no appetite for eating her lunch; Meursault eats nearly all of his lunch. Earlier, when Raymond explained to the policeman that his trembling was "only natural," we realized that it indeed was. Now, Meursault's appetite, after just witnessing the end of a fight has not changed and this does not bother him, nor is he bothered that Marie has no appetite. Meursault would say of his actions and attitude exactly what Raymond told the policeman, "That's only natural."

Still later, when Raymond is discussing the fight and Raymond questions Meursault as to whether Raymond should have hit the policeman for knocking a cigarette out of Raymond's mouth, Meursault can only verbally shrug: "I told him I hadn't expected anything whatsoever and, anyhow, I had no use for the police." This is a typical reply for Meursault. His lack of interest, however, does not disturb Raymond, who suggests their taking a stroll, then confesses that he wants Meursault to act as his witness.

Meursault's answer is exactly the same as when Raymond asked if the two men could be friends: "I had no objection." Meursault didn't know what to expect the policeman to do and he doesn't know what Raymond expects him to say. He is not a "programmed" individual, in the social sense. He does not envision or consider the varying consequences of a given situation.

Raymond's pleasure at Meursault's reply is evident. He has a witness for himself; he punished his girlfriend and feels absolutely justified and Meursault will bear witness that the girl provoked and deserved the beating. Raymond is even happier later in the evening when he wins a game of billiards with Meursault. And he laughs when Salamano tells them that he has lost his dog at the fair and that he, Salamano, will *not* pay for a dog he hates—even if the dog dies at the dog pound.

Later, while Salamano paces his room, wheezing, even weeping, there appears a crack in the often abstracted neutrality of Meursault's character. He thinks of his mother and he has no appetite and goes to bed without supper. This is all we know. He tells us no more. Like the staccato-worded telegram which Meursault received at the beginning of the novel, we feel a sense of loss at not knowing more. But Camus' novel is not a journal of Meursault's feelings; it is not an illuminating confession; instead, it is often more like an album of black-and-white snapshots.

CHAPTER V

After a Sunday that was more unusual than most of his Sundays, Meursault begins another week of work, another week of monotony, doing the robot-like actions that most people perform in order to make a living, the same monotony that Camus despises because of its intoxicating, suffocating effect on the human soul. Meursault, as we see from the beginning of this chapter, is what one might call a "good employee." He is annoyed that Raymond telephones him about a personal matter; this is not done. Such telephoning is frowned on by Meursault's superior and Meursault wants to have no trouble with him. He is not free, as he was at the beach, as he was when he ran to catch the fire truck, or when he leaves work and leisurely strolls home. Meursault's work may be dull, but it must be done, and he becomes, at the office, uneasy that he is violating office rules and wasting time. At home, he would not give the idea of chatting on the phone, or of wasting time, a second thought, but his freedom is restricted here.

Raymond's call has two purposes; first, he invites Meursault to spend next Sunday at the seaside with a friend; and, naturally, Meursault, as we have seen, is delighted at the prospect of swimming and sunning and also happy when he learns that he can bring Marie with him. Raymond's second reason for calling is typical of something Raymond might do; he thinks that he is being followed by some Arabs. Raymond, as we have seen, is highly emotional and would be fascinated by the thought of a threat to him by some Arabs. One of them, he tells Meursault, is surely the brother of the girl whom he beat up.

At this point, Meursault is summoned to his employer's office and he becomes queasy, sure that he is to be reprimanded for his personal telephone conversations. Meursault, for the present, is not the unemotional and indifferent Meursault whom we have seen so frequently. He wants no trouble at work. But he quickly meta-morphoses into the familiar Meursault when he is told that his com-pany is opening a branch office in Paris and that Meursault has been selected, if he chooses, to work in the Paris office. Most people would be ecstatic, if offered the opportunity to move from Algiers to Paris, but Meursault's reply to his superior is that he is "prepared to go." To us, Meursault seems to be saying that he doesn't care much one way or the other. We puzzle at his reaction — until we read farther and discover what Meursault was really thinking during his conversation with his superior.

Thus, already this morning, Meursault has two promises — one that includes good friends and swimming, and the other, a move to Paris. Most people associate Paris with romance, love, music, gaiety, and reveries. Not Meursault. He reacted to his superior as if his present life suited him and that one life is as good as another. Paris or Algiers — it would, seemingly, make no difference where Meursault worked and lived. It is probably true that he has no in-tense ambition to receive new promotions and amass a fortune by working his way up through the business ranks of his firm, but we do know that Paris is antithetical to everything we know about Meursault. The city would be repugnant to him; it is bleak, rainy, the sun is rare, and warmth and swimming are very important to Meursault's moments of happiness.

For the first time, we have a small nugget of Meursault's past slipped to us. He remembers once that he did have ambition, but that when he had to drop his studies, he gave up and decided that all of his ambitions were futile. Seemingly, from that time on, he has been the come-what-may, indifferent Meursault.

This nonchalance is emphasized even further when Marie asks Meursault to marry her. He says that he doesn't mind; if she wants to get married, he will marry her "if it will give her pleasure." This attitude is almost identical to Raymond's proposal that he and Meursault become friends. At that time, Meursault replied that he "had no objections."

Meursault's honesty is disarming, for whereas he did not mind one way or the other about writing a letter for Raymond that would punish a girl, fattening the letter, in all probability, with insinuations and, perhaps, even lies, Meursault cannot lie about his own feelings.

He cannot please Marie by saying that he loves her; he will marry her, perform this physical and legal act, but he cannot lie and say that he loves her. Marriage, to him, is of no great importance, just as the exact day on which his mother died is of no great importance. Meursault is an unusually taciturn man. Raymond offered friendship; Marie herself, and now Meursault is offered a new position in Paris. And it all makes no difference, he says; he doesn't object.

Meursault's attitude confuses Marie and it seems a bit unusual to Raymond, but Raymond doesn't mull over the matter as Marie does. Marriage, for her, is a very serious business. She is most ordinary and is described in the most matter-of-fact terms. She likes sex and wants a home and a husband and children. She is unusual only in that she is willing to marry Meursault even after he admits that he would marry any girl that he had been sleeping with and who proposed to him. She rationalizes that perhaps it's Meursault's strangeness that fascinates her, but she is not truly satisfied with the explanation. She threatens Meursault that she may hate him one day, but even that taunt has no emotional thrust, for Meursault says nothing, for a while, until he tells her of the move to Paris, which he describes as dingy, full of masses of pigeons and dark courtyards and pasty-faced people.

Marriage and Paris! Marie's evening is complete. She has her ambitions fulfilled. But she cannot dine with Meursault and wonders why he doesn't ask her why, implying that she might have a date with another man. Meursault merely looks embarrassed and admits to us that he *did* want to know. It is one of the few times that we see him being dishonest.

Camus finishes the chapter with two episodes—one, involving a woman who eats at Meursault's table in Céleste's restaurant and, afterward, Meursault's conversation with Salamano about the lost dog. Camus gives a great deal of attention to this woman and to Meursault's observation of her. Meursault is curious, fascinated by the woman. She is robot-like, moving jerkily, raptly attentive, adding up the bill in advance, wolfing down her food voraciously and checking off from a radio magazine which programs she intends to listen to (which seem, to Meursault, to be practically every one). Robot-like, in fact, is the word which Meursault uses to describe her exit from the cafe. On the surface, this is an incident with no meaning, a strange person who shares his table and whom he watches and someone whom he says he will soon forget about.

Later, in Part Two of the novel, she will be watching Meursault himself as he stands trial for the murder of an Arab.

The love-hate relationship between Salamano and his dog is an illustration of how very different, emotionally, old Salamano is from Meursault. Because Meursault has nothing to do, he listens to the old man's tale. In fact, Meursault offers to the grieving old man a gesture of a so-called white lie: he tells Salamano that his dog looked "well bred." This is not how Meursault described the dog heretofore. Salamano's grief over the dog is a contrast to Meursault's lack of grief over his mother's dying and, in both cases, there are uncertainties. Salamano does not know if his dog is dead, found and housed by someone else, or merely lost; Meursault isn't sure when his mother died. But he listens to Salamano, not because he was concerned about the dog but because, he says, he wasn't sleepy anyway.

Salamano acquired the dog after his wife died; he didn't get along well with her either. To Salamano, who fed the dog, at first from a bottle, the dog was like a child or a baby, but because a dog's life is short and the man was getting old, they both became very old at the same time. Once, he had taken pride in the dog's appearance (and probably in his own), then the dog developed skin trouble that was incurable. When Salamano leaves, Meursault tells us that he "could feel the scales on his skin." The old man hopes that the dogs won't bark in the night, for he always thinks of the dog barking as possibly being his. He wants no false hopes, no false promises that the dog will return. This time the chapter ends on a sad note of resignation, rather than earlier, when the dog's moan was described as being like "a flower growing out of the silence and the darkness."

Perhaps one of the most important, but small bits of information that we receive in this chapter is Salamano's off-hand comment that some of the people in the neighborhood have begun to say nasty things about Meursault, now that his mother is dead. Meursault is not an invisible man anymore. He is already marked as someone who cared so little for his mother that he sent her away. Salamano's affirmation of his friendship and his saying that he knows that Meursault was devoted to his mother is of little comfort to Meursault. The man is clearly disturbed. He tries to explain that he could not afford to keep her any longer and that, for years, they hadn't spoken to one another and that at the Home, he hoped that perhaps she could make friends. Here, in a capsule form is an important part of Meursault's defense in Part Two. Salamano only half-listens to Meursault; he has his own troubles. It will not be an easy night for either man.

CHAPTER VI

Sundays, for Meursault, are usually stagnant days — no routine, no fun, no impromptu outings. This Sunday, however, is the climax of the novel's action, leading us to Meursault's philosophical insight and conversion and, then, to his decapitation. Other than Meursault's mother's funeral, which was described somewhat journalistically, nothing much has happened in the novel until now; thus, Meursault's opening comment in this chapter, describing what an effort it was to get up this morning is ironically comical, reminding one, if he knows anything at all about this novel, of the old saying, "It was one of those mornings when I should have stayed in bed." Certainly this is true in Meursault's case. Marie has to shout at him to rouse him, and as they want to get to the beach early, they don't bother to prepare any breakfast, which is of little concern to Meursault: he has a headache, his first cigarette tastes bitter, and he feels limp and drained. Marie comments that he looks "like a mourner at a funeral," a remark that is part of Camus' irony. During his mother's wake and funeral, Meursault looked the least like a mourner of all those who came to the long vigil around his mother's coffin. If, in fact, someone mistakenly believed that Meursault's behavior was that of a mourner, he was mistaken; Meursault, during those long hours, was not in mourning; he was uncomfortable and embarrassed. He was mourning only in the sense that he was wasting the day and that he had to endure the lengthy and boring ordeal.

Marie's mood this Sunday morning is in direct contrast with Meursault's; she is happy and laughing; Meursault comments that she looked quite ravishing.

This day, as we will discover, is Meursault's last day of physical freedom, his last day to enjoy swimming and sunning and being with Marie, and Camus has already prepared us for this most unusual and fateful day by blackening Meursault's waking mood and accentuating it with the brightness of Marie's gaiety.

After knocking on Raymond's door, letting him know that they are ready to leave, Meursault and Marie go on down the street, but, again, Camus has Meursault remind us that he feels "rather under the weather." It is important that this chapter is studied carefully, for its climax, Meursault's murder of the Arab, should contain a motive for killing the Arab, a key issue. It is extraordinary that Meursault feels particularly bad, most unusual for someone who was eagerly anticipating this bit of a holiday. This day was looked forward to, providing Meursault a chance to get away to the beach and do some swimming and sunning with Marie.

Moments later, Meursault describes himself as not only feeling rather ill, physically, but as if he were struck down, smashed by the glare of the morning sun. Camus is presenting us here with more irony, for if there is anything that Meursault loves, it is the sun. The sun, indeed, has already become almost a character in this novel; we have seen Meursault's delight in its warmth. Today, however, it is too strong and too powerful for him. It hits him in the eyes "like a clenched fist." Once again, Camus stresses and accents Meursault's condition by repeating Marie's reactions to the Sunday morning. To her, the day is glorious. She keeps repeating, "What a heavenly day!" Heavenly is the antithesis of hellish, and hellish the day will certainly become prior to the murder. There is a constant negative-positive counterpoint in this chapter as it builds slowly and tensely towards its climax.

Like Marie, Raymond is in high spirits, addressing Marie in mock graciousness as "Mademoiselle"; he is wearing sports clothes that Meursault finds unattractive and is also wearing a straw hat that makes Marie giggle. In addition, he is wearing a short-sleeved shirt that exposes his rather hairy, white forearms. Meursault is truly in a bad mood to make note of such inconsequential matters.

After commenting on Raymond's outing clothes, Meursault partially explains his feeling of depression. He tells us that the previous evening he had gone to the police station and had testified that Raymond's explanation about beating the Arab girl because of her infidelity was true. The police chose to believe Meursault and, as a result, they released Raymond with merely a warning. Meursault says, "They didn't check my statement." He is saying, in effect, that he lied. Meursault does not know if the girl was actually unfaithful to Raymond; he is indifferent to whether or not she had sex with someone else. He simply had no objection to writing a "real stinker" of a letter for Raymond and testifying that Raymond's reason for the brawl was due to infidelity. Meursault, Camus is stressing, has lied and this is unusual for a man who refuses to lie about his own feelings and actions. He, therefore, is not the one-dimensional victim of this novel, as he is sometimes characterized, nor is he a martyr who has done no wrong (other than shedding no tears at his mother's funeral) and yet is guillotined.

The action quickens even before the trio board the bus, for Raymond points out to Meursault that some Arabs are watching them. Meursault sees them and says that the Arabs looked at them as though they were blocks of stone or dead trees. Raymond even knows which Arab is the brother of the girl whom he abused. Raymond's moods fluctuate, at this point. He is, at least to Meursault, seemingly worried, yet he laughs and says that the brawl is "ancient history," but halfway to the bus stop, he glances back for reassurance that the Arabs are not following them. He does this as a man, fearful of death, might look toward the sky for buzzards circling overhead.

On the bus, Raymond's nervousness becomes flirtatious; he "kept making jokes," Meursault says, in order to amuse Marie, although she seemed unaware of him, nodding at Meursault every now and then and smiling at him. There is a tenseness at this point; we wait for something to happen as they journey toward the beach, the scene of the murder.

The three have left the city and are alone as they walk toward the beach; they are far removed from even the Sunday business of Algiers. Wild lilies are snow-white against the sky, which Meursault describes as being so blue that it has a "metallic glint." During Meursault's silent observations, Marie, child-like, amuses herself by swishing her bag against the flowers and showering their petals. The landscape is described here in portent fragments. As Marie innocently destroys the flowers, Meursault notes that some of the houses are "half-hidden," and that others are "naked from the stony plateau." When at last they reach the beach, a big headland juts out over the sea's "black reflection."

After meeting Raymond's friend, Masson, and his wife, Meursault notices Marie chatting with Masson's wife, laughing, and he tells us that, for the first time, he "seriously" considers the possibility of his marrying her. Remember that he promised her that he would marry her earlier. Now, he "considers" the "possibility" of marrying her. Meursault promised that he would marry Marie, meaning that, for him, at that moment, he "had no objection." He is, above all, a man of present moments, and this present revelation, when he tells us of his actually considering marrying Marie is quite important in understanding this enigmatic man.

Meursault is happy, at this present moment, on the beach. He basks in the sunlight and feels better. The sun, in fact, is a restorative to Meursault, as it usually is. We have heard him speak of it often and we have seen how he reacts to it and how he reacts to his memories of Paris and its lack of sun.

Swimming makes Meursault presently feel even better, particularly the physical contact of his body against the cold water beneath him and the hot sun above him, when his arms and shoulders emerge. There is much emphasis here on this series of present moments, as Meursault and Marie swim, side by side, in rhythm, matching their movements, enjoying, as Meursault says, "every moment."

Meursault eventually becomes so completely relaxed that, after swimming back to the beach and drying in the warmth of the sun and Marie's body, he naps for a short time. Then he rouses at Marie's insistence and the two swim awhile longer, twining around one another. Meursault is so physically satisfied that his senses tingle. He is "ravenously" hungry for lunch and eats much bread and fish and steak and potato chips. Masson, the host, enjoys Raymond's friend and is quick to refill Meursault's wine glass whenever it is empty.

By the time that coffee is being poured, Meursault describes himself as feeling "slightly muzzy," and he starts smoking one cigarette after another. The two couples and Raymond feel deep, empathetic rapport as they discuss spending the entire month of August on the beach together, sharing expenses.

One might think that after Meursault and his friends have spent time on the bus to the beach, swimming, napping, lunching, and discussing plans to summer in the bungalow during August, that it must be mid-afternoon by now. It is not: Marie announces that it is only half-past eleven, which causes her to laugh again. And it is then that Masson proposes that the men take a stroll on the beach while the women clean up the luncheon dishes.

Leaving the house, Meursault first notices the sun, just as he first noticed it when he emerged from his apartment house in Algiers. This time, however, he describes it not as a fist smashing against him, but he comments on its glare; this, combined with the reflection from the water sears his eyes, he says. By now, high noon is approaching, and Meursault sees shimmers of heat rising from the rocks, the beach deserted, and he tells us that one can hardly breathe.

While his attention is paralyzed by the heat of the sun, the glare from the sea, and the intoxicating effect of the wine, Raymond and Masson talk together, Meursault sensing that the two men have known each other for a long time. They walk by the water's edge and, one more time, Meursault mentions the heat and glare on the sea as the sun "beats down" on his bare head. The effect is numbing. Meursault feels half-asleep.

A moment later, he notices two Arabs coming toward them from a long way down the beach. Raymond is immediately apprehensive, as is his nature, sure that one of the Arabs is his girl friend's brother. Meursault says nothing, as is his usual nature. Raymond is ready for a scuffle, planning to fight one Arab himself and the hefty Masson taking the other. Meursault is to stand by to help if another Arab appears. The sun broils on the two clusters of men approaching one another along the edge of the sea. And, besides the sun blazing from above them, below them the sand is "as hot as fire." Meursault swears that it is "glowing red."

The confrontation occurs when the men are only a few steps apart. Raymond steps forward and when one of the Arabs lowers his head, Raymond lashes out, shouting at Masson. Masson throws his appointed Arab into the sea, and Raymond, proud of punishing "his" already bleeding Arab, foolishly breaks for a moment to shout to Meursault that he "ain't finished yet," hoping to beat this Arab the same way that he did the Arab's sister. In that moment, the Arab reaches for his knife and slashes Raymond on the arm and on the mouth.

Frightened by Masson's hulking appearance, both Arabs begin to back away slowly, the knife held before them; when they are a distance from the Frenchmen, they begin to run.

Raymond seems to be wounded badly; blood is running from his arm and when he tries to talk, blood bubbles from his mouth. By chance, however, once they are back at the bungalow, they discover that the wounds are not deep and that Raymond will be able to walk to a nearby doctor.

Masson accompanies Raymond and Meursault is left behind with the women; Marie is quite pale and Mme. Masson is crying. Ostensibly, Meursault is left behind to guard the women and also to explain to them what has happened. It is difficult to imagine him as a proficient guard and, as he admits, he doesn't say much about what has happened. He prefers to stare at the sea.

Raymond is unhappy when he returns, even though he has been assured by the doctor that his wounds are not serious and he is emphatic when he says that he is going for a walk on the beach, that he wants to be alone, and that he wants *no one* to accompany him. In fact, he "flies into a rage." Meursault, however, as we have often seen, does as he pleases. He follows Raymond, despite Masson's objections.

It is approaching two o'clock now, and Meursault describes the afternoon as feeling like a furnace, the sunlight splintering into "flakes of fire" on the sand and on the sea. Meursault continues to follow Raymond, and Raymond continues to walk until he finds what he has been seeking—the two Arabs, who seem quite docile now, one staring without speaking, the other playing three notes on a little reed flute. This, then, is Camus' tableau: no one moving and no one speaking. All is hot sunlight and heavy silence, and the reed flute and a tinkling sound from a small stream. The scene seems almost idyllic.

Without warning, Raymond asks Meursault if he should shoot the girl's brother. Meursault explains to us that he says the first thing that comes into his head; this is usually what he has always done. This time, though, his answer is tempered, for he knows that Raymond's ire might well be responsible for a murder. Meursault says it would be a "low-down trick" to shoot the Arab "in cold blood." Raymond is not to be so easily persuaded; he will say something sufficiently provocative that he will have a chance to gain revenge on the man who has maimed him. This was his same tactic with the girl; he wrote a note which so provoked her that he was able to further punish her.

Again, Meursault warns Raymond that he should not fire unless the Arab draws his knife, but Raymond is beginning to fidget. Both of the Arabs watch them like cautious, alert animals, revealing no emotion or movement, yet watching Raymond and Meursault all the time and observing Raymond's building excitement and Meursault's hesistancy. When Meursault asks for the gun, we instinctively feel that if Meursault has the gun, he will not use it. We are certain that Raymond needs little reason for using it.

The sun glints on the revolver. Again, as though it is a character in this drama of death, the sun asserts itself. Then all is silence and during the silence, Meursault comes to the conclusion that "one might fire, or not fire – " and it "would come to absolutely the same thing." Recall that when he was offered a position in the Paris office, his thoughts were similar: he "didn't care much one way or the other." When the subject of a "change of life" was introduced by his employer, he answered that "one life was as good as another," and that his present life suited him quite well. Later, when Marie asked him to marry her, he said he "didn't mind; if she was keen on it, [they would] get married." Meursault has been mesmerized by the heat into his former, almost total, indifference to matters at hand. Here he stands with a gun, able to kill another man and he thinks, "it would come to absolutely the same thing." The situation has no meaning, no importance to him. The Arabs are not really men to Meursault; a death, a marriage, a move to Paris – nothing is of absolute importance to him.

Suddenly the Arabs vanish. So quickly do they accomplish this that it is as though they were like lizards, slipping under the cover of a rock. So, it would seem, ends the stand-off duel, and Raymond and Meursault turn and walk back, Raymond talking about taking the bus back to Algiers.

But while Raymond seems happier, Meursault has changed. The light thuds within his head and he feels that he hasn't the energy to walk up the steps to the bungalow. He stresses continuously that the heat is too great. He cannot move; it is "blinding light falling from the sky. And his leitmotif occurs again: "To stay, or to make a move – it came to much the same." He does not know what to do and it is purely by chance that his decision is not one that he has reasoned. He simply starts walking – returning to the beach. For no reason, with no stated intent, other than a vague recollection of the coolness behind the rock, a retreat from the fiery afternoon, he returns to the beach. As he walks slowly ahead, there is a red glare as far as he can see and he can hear small waves lapping at the hot sand. Meursault's temples are throbbing and he feels that the heat is trying to force him back, pressing on him, trying to check any progress that he might attempt to make. Hot blasts strike at him repeatedly as he grits his teeth and clenches his fist in defiance of a universe that he will not allow domination over him. Camus' description of Meursault's walk toward the beach becomes almost like that of a battle – Meursault pitted against the sun. He clenches his fists, he grits his teeth; blades of light shoot toward him from broken glass and shells. His jaw sets more firmly, more determinedly. We have never seen Meursault so intent, so purposelessly intent on accomplishing nothing other than reaching the cool stream. He is, very simply, defying a force that opposes him.

When he sees a small black hump of rock, he can think only of one thing—the cold, clear stream behind it and his longing to hear the tinkling of running water. His goal is finally definite: to be rid of the sun, the women in tears, and retrieve the cool silence behind the shadow of the rock.

Someone else has done the same thing; the brother of Raymond's girl friend has reclaimed his spot behind the rock. Meursault had completely forgotten about the Arabs. Not once while he was staggering toward the rock had he thought about the Arabs; now Raymond's enemy has possessed the cool safety from the sun. Both men react immediately and naturally. Despite Meursault's weariness, one cannot say now that Meursault is totally indifferent to the Arab; this is mutual fear that we view, each of the men simultaneously reaching for their weapons when they encounter one another. Meursault grips Raymond's pistol in the pocket of his coat and the Arab's hand goes to the pocket of his coat, where he keeps his knife. To Meursault, the Arab, even though only ten yards away, is only a blurred, dark form, wobbling in the heat haze. At times, Meursault can see glimpses of the Arab's eyes, glowing against the sound of the waves and the weight of the molten sun.

A sense of the rational returns to Meursault. He has no quarrel with this Arab; their relationship seems an empty, meaningless one. But Meursault *did* write the letter; he has forgotten that fact as he thinks that all he need do is turn his body around, move his feet, and walk away and think no more about the Arab. But he cannot. He feels the sun pulsing within the sand beneath his feet, pressing up the length of his body and, instead of turning, Meursault moves toward the stream and toward the Arab. The heat scorches his cheeks and sweat gathers in his eyebrows; this heat is akin to the smothering heat during his mother's funeral. Then, as now, especially in Meursault's forehead, he feels as though he cannot bear for another instant the heaviness of the sun; a moment more and his veins will burst through the skin. He takes a step forward and, at that moment, the Arab draws his knife, holding it up, causing the sun to travel the length of the blade and "pierce" Meursault's forehead, transfixing him. Sweat splashes down his eyelids, veiling his eyes with salty brine. Meursault is conscious of nothing except the sun on his skull and the blade of knife-light, "slicing" into his eyeballs.

He begins to reel as he describes the fiery gust that comes from the sea, the sky cracking in two and a great sheet of flame "pouring down." Meursault tells us that at that moment "the trigger gave, and the smooth underbelly of the butt jogged my palm." Reality, at this point, has vanished for Meursault. There is no conscious gripping the trigger, aiming and firing; the trigger "gave way" and, as it were, the gun fired and Meursault heard a "crisp, whipcrack sound." He does not tell us that he saw the Arab's body fall; he does not tell us much more at all, only that he fired four more shots into the dead body and yet could see no visible trace of the bullets entering the body. We have witnessed a murder. There is a dead body which Meursault continues to fire into, yet there seems to be no evidence of a murder, no visible signs of a murder.

The chapter ends with the emphasis not so much on the murder of the Arab, but on Meursault's return to consciousness. He is aware that he has committed an act that is of prime importance. For once in his life, which heretofore had been assembled of meaningless acts, he has acted so definitely that the consequences will not be meaningless, will matter one way or another. He knows, he says, that he has destroyed the "balance of the day." Until Meursault composed the letter for Raymond, he simply lived; nothing very exciting ever happened to him; days began and days ended and these days added up into monotonous years. This was not so following the letter and the beating of the Arab girl. The Arabs have a natural resentment for their French colonial invaders and a human desire for revenge. Meursault, by chance, by "having no objection," became involved in Raymond's emotional escapades and, by chance, Meursault murders the man who once stalked Raymond.

Meursault is jolted, knowing that he has desecrated the calm of the beach on which he had been so happy. It is then that he fires four more shots into the dead Arab, knowing that each successive shot is undoing a life of rhythmic drifting. He is creating for himself his own "undoing," as he puts it. The cymbals of the sun clashing inside his head have climaxed a former life which drifted toward an uncertain death. Now he faces a life directed toward a certain death.

PART TWO

CHAPTER I

The first chapter of Part Two is narrated in Meursault's frequent matter-of-fact tone, describing his first interrogation by police officials. At first, he says, nobody seemed to have much interest in his case. Interestingly, this attitude is, more or less, how Meursault views the matter. He is not deeply concerned about his case or the possibility that he has committed the ultimate of crimes — murder. Instead of his telling us about his internal feelings, which he seems to ignore or lack, he describes, in bare outlines, the boredom of the police official's questioning and the repetition of giving again and again his name and address and occupation. Meursault has so little comprehension of what is happening that he is surprised when an examining magistrate asks him if he has obtained a lawyer. Meursault's answer is succinct and honest: no, of course not. To Meursault, it didn't seem necessary to find a lawyer, consult with the lawyer, and pay this man a large fee for defending him. That would be too much trouble and Meursault is not sure that it is necessary for him even to have a lawyer. He is, in fact, pleased to learn that the court will appoint a lawyer for the defense; all the bothersome details will be taken care of. To him, this is "an excellent arrangement"; he won't have to waste his time with petty trivials.

Whereas Meursault's first examination took place at the police station and was uneventful, the examination, a week later, before a magistrate is different. To the earlier police officers who questioned Meursault, he was faceless; he was simply a Frenchman who had shot an Arab. This new magistrate, however, eyes Meursault with distinct curiosity. This magistrate recognizes that Meursault is not a typical murderer. From the first, he is curious and even amused at Meursault's naivete when he is queried about a lawyer. Meursault blandly answers again that he hadn't thought about obtaining the services of a lawyer. Meursault still does not know whether or not a lawyer is necessary, for a lawyer still seems superfluous; we know Meursault killed an Arab and he knows that he killed an Arab. He is confronted with legal mechanics and is a stranger in this new world, without any knowledge of this foreign, legalistic environment.

Whereas his former life had been lived in fragments, this new life is a highly regimented system.

To Meursault, his case is simple. Lawyers are only necessary when a case contains a multiplicity of details, ambiguities, and there is a reasonable doubt as to the seriousness of the crime. There is nothing to argue about when Meursault's case is on the docket; he is not callous or being canny in displaying such an attitude. It is only a formality that he be required to have a lawyer and he is again relieved to hear that he will not have to bother with certain prescribed formalities.

There is a sense of the examination being surreal to Meursault. He finds himself concentrating on the room where he is being questioned. It is more like a living room than a questioning room for murderers. There is an absurdness about the bourgeois curtains, the dumpy armchair and the simple lamp. Once more, Meursault seems to have removed himself from the scene and seems to be viewing it from another point of view, watching another man answer questions in this "ordinary sitting room." He admits that he doesn't listen to the magistrate very seriously because he has read descriptions of how such examinations are held and this does not conform to the stark, brutal descriptions in novels. This examination, to Meursault, seems "like a game." This is a telling statement. In a preface to the British edition of this novel, Camus states that Meursault is condemned and guillotined because "he doesn't play the game." Meursault dies because he refuses to lie in a court of law; he dies, says Camus in the same preface, "for the sake of truth."

There are no anguished feelings of guilt within Meursault as he relates the details of his interview; instead, he tells us about the physical features of the magistrate, who gives the impression of being highly intelligent except for one small aspect—his mouth has a rather ugly, nervous tic. Camus combines this stroke of description with the ridiculousness of an examination for murder taking place in a living room, suggesting further absurdness when Meursault admits that, when leaving, he does so almost as if he had finished a chat. He is ready to extend his hand and say good-by to the magistrate. Then, momentarily, Meursault remembers that he has killed a man. Yet his use of the word "man" is not wholly convincing. If he felt that he had actually murdered another human being, surely there would be more internal struggling within himself as to why he did it. There seems to be none. And his admission that he remembered "just in time" about the murder is almost an aside, as though he had forgotten something far less important than taking the life of another man.

When Meursault talks with the lawyer that the court has appointed, he agrees to follow the lawyer's advice. The lawyer already knows that Meursault's case is not the simple case that Meursault is convinced it is. For example, he does not like the possibility that he will have to explain Meursault's attitude toward his mother's death. He tells Meursault that the police know that, according to rumors, Meursault showed "great callousness" during his mother's funeral. This matter of Meursault's callousness bothers the lawyer. If Meursault evidenced a lack of feeling during his own mother's funeral, what defense can the lawyer use when he must explain the actions of his client who has murdered a stranger, without motive? He tries to make certain that Meursault realize the seriousness of this charge of callousness. Only Meursault can help himself in this court of law, he says.

Asking Meursault if he felt any grief at all during the funeral, the lawyer is distraught when Meursault replies that the question is terribly odd. Meursault would have been embarrassed to ask anyone such a personal question. He admits that he doesn't think much about his feelings and that his "detachment" has increased in recent years. Most questions are difficult for Meursault to answer, as we have seen, unless he can answer them with a simple yes or no. When a question requires thinking and considering, Meursault becomes confused and wonders why he is being asked such a question, particularly questions with philosophical dimensions. Truthfully, he knows that he was quite fond of his mother. But note that he does not say that he loved her. At this point, Meursault says only that he was "quite fond" of his mother. This is the most positive statement he can make, which does not carry much legalistic clout, especially when one is considering a charge of callous, cold-blooded murder.

Meursault considers himself just a normal man, yet note that the magistrate looks at Meursault with much curiosity and even Marie earlier wondered if Meursault's oddness was one of the reasons she had fallen in love with him. All of the accumulated evidence convinces us that Camus is showing us that Meursault is certainly not "just a normal man." In another example, Meursault reveals something to his lawyer that an ordinary man, in a cell waiting for a trial, would not utter. Meursault says that *all* normal people probably have, at one time or another, wished the death of those they loved. He adds that his thought occurred to him as sort of an afterthought; he does not realize the potential gravity of what he has said. To him, it is just an after-thought, a harmless musing.

It is little wonder that Meursault's lawyer is greatly perturbed. He begs Meursault not to make such damning statements during the trial. And Meursault promises—for one reason: "to satisfy him." He has done this repeatedly; he helped Raymond because he wanted to satisfy him; he promised to marry Marie to satisfy her. But now he warns the lawyer that his promises are not iron-bound. He explains that his "physical condition at any given moment" usually influences what he says and does and how he feels. This is rare insight for Meursault to realize about himself and it is rarer still for him to admit such a statement, when his life depends on convincing a jury that he should not be executed for murdering another man.

With almost child-like innocence, Meursault tells the lawyer that he'd rather that his mother had *not* died. Meursault considers this a strongly positive statement. Merely because he did not weep carries no importance because he was hot and tired that day; were it up to him, his mother would be alive today. But she died. It was not his fault and it is astonishing that the lawyer can place so much importance on the fact that, because of the heat and Meursault's fatigue, that he did not weep at the funeral.

The lawyer, who is what most readers would probably consider "normal," feels sure that Meursault will want to say that on the day of the funeral that he managed to keep his feelings "under control." This is impossible for Meursault to do. It would be a lie. We are not surprised when Meursault says that the lawyer looked at him queerly and seemed slightly revolted, saying that the head of the Home and some of the staff would be witnesses, proving that Meursault was devoid of feelings for his mother. The prosecution has powerful weapons to use against Meursault.

It is beyond Meursault's comprehension what the death of his mother and the death of the Arab have in common. To him, they are two totally unrelated events. The lawyer, however, knows how facts can be twisted and misinterpreted; in this particular case, the prosecution wouldn't even have to make sly, subtle charges. Meursault's attitude toward his mother's death can be used with blatant reminders in order to convince the jury that, before them, is a man who has no feelings, evidenced by witnesses, for his own mother's death. Thus he is capable of killing—because of his lack of feeling. The lawyer warns Meursault that it is evident that the prisoner has never had any dealing with the law. Meursault notes that the lawyer looked "vexed" when he left.

Meursault does not want understanding and sympathy from the lawyer and he admits being tempted, at times, to assure the lawyer that he is only "an ordinary person." But he does not because, as he says, he is too lazy to do so.

Later that day, when Meursault is taken to the examining magistrate's office, he notes, first of all, the intense heat in the room and that it seems to be flooded with light. Already we have seen how sensitive Meursault is to heat and light and so this visit begins badly. The heaviness of the heat is an omen, presaging the magistrate's statement that the lawyer cannot be present and that Meursault may, if he wishes, reserve answering any questions. There is little doubt as to what Meursault will do; he will answer for himself. From the beginning, he saw little use for a lawyer, other than the fact that the Code demanded he have one.

The interrogation is brusque. Meursault, the magistrate says, has the reputation of being taciturn and somewhat self-centered. These charges are negative; one might use other words and say that Meursault is a man who minds his own business and gives nobody any trouble. Meursault's answer to the magistrate's question as to whether or not the charges are true is, one might say, taciturn. Meursault rarely has much to say, so naturally he doesn't say much. He is very logical and very honest as he answers the magistrate. Again, the naivete of Meursault amuses the magistrate, who smiles at the answer, adding that his question, at any rate, has little or no importance, which is exactly what Meursault has said—why say—or ask—anything when there is nothing of importance to be said?

Meursault's uniqueness intrigues the magistrate, who, Meursault notes, leans forward, fastening his eyes deeply and raising his voice a little. The magistrate, obviously, has never interrogated a man who was so bluntly honest. Or perhaps stupid. He admits the charge of murder doesn't interest him as much as Meursault, himself, does. He is puzzled about Meursault's participation in the crime more than he is in the crime itself. Meursault is not puzzled; he assures the magistrate that what happened is quite simple and he is puzzled only that the magistrate wants to hear the story again, for he says that he has told the magistrate about Raymond, the beach, the swimming—all the details—during their first interview. But Meursault consents, rather unwillingly, to retell the story and when he finishes, it is with a sense that he has wasted time repeating what he already has said and that he feels as though he has never talked so much in his life.

The magistrate promises to help Meursault, partly because Meursault interests him, but he questions him, as did the lawyer, about Meursault's relationship with his mother. As to his loving his mother, Meursault says that he did, "like everybody else." There is a noise behind him when the clerk pushes the typewriter carriage back and seems to be crossing something out. This is a moment in which Camus foreshadows the irony of Meursault's discussing love "like everybody else" and his eventual fate, which will be determined by the jury's failure to believe that he can love "like everybody else." As a result, because of an error (the murder) and Meursault's failure to weep at the funeral, he will be crossed out, executed, as efficiently as the typist here corrects an error.

The magistrate's next question causes Meursault to pause before he answers. He emphasizes that he did not shoot five consecutive shots. He tells the absolute truth. He fired one shot, killing the Arab, and then, after a short interval, he fired four more shots. And he cannot explain the interval between the first shot and the others, but he re-lives that instant, probably due to the intense heat and light in the magistrate's room. He sees the glow of the beach hovering again before his eyes. He cannot answer the magistrate's question, even after the magistrate waits, fidgets, half-rises, sits down again and asks for an answer. He insists on an answer, but Meursault remains silent.

Meursault's silence transforms the magistrate, whom Meursault once thought looked like a most intelligent man, into a madman. Waving a silver crucifix, he rants that he believes in God Almighty and that even the worst of sinners (presumably, Meursault) can obtain forgiveness. But, first, the magistrate says, there must be repentance and the sinner must become "like a little child." Again we encounter irony, as we have viewed Meursault's child-like behavior and responses to the magistrate. The madness of the magistrate, in turn, transforms Meursault. He becomes alarmed. This supposedly sane judge of men is brandishing a silver crucifix before Meursault's eyes—a weapon very similar to the knife which the

Arab flashed before Meursault and on which the light blazed. Meanwhile the office is becoming more stiflingly hot and big flies are buzzing on Meursault's cheeks. It is a scene of punishment—by the heat, the flies, and by the magistrate. Meursault realizes that such odd behavior is far more typical of a criminal, and Meursault, enduring silently, is the criminal. Furthermore, he becomes truly criminal to the magistrate when he admits to a disbelief in God. In despair, the magistrate says that if he ever doubted that God existed, his life would have no meaning; it is as though he is accusing Meursault of trying to convert him to being a non-believer, asking Meursault if he wishes the magistrate's life to have no meaning. Child-like, Meursault cannot follow the logic of the magistrate; how could his wishes have any effect on the magistrate's faith in God?

Meursault has had enough and is willing to lie in order to escape from this asylum of heat and talk of sin, but, instinctively, he says that he must have shaken his head, meaning No, when the magistrate asked him a final time if he believed in God.

The silence that follows is similar to the silence between the first shot and the following four shots. The magistrate is convinced, he says, that Meursault is the most hard-hearted criminal he has ever known. Everyone else has wept at the magistrate's performance with the crucifix, the symbol of Christ's suffering. As he did not at his mother's funeral, Meursault does not weep now.

The lawyer and, especially, the examining magistrate have struggled to find and give meaning to their lives. Meursault never bothered to consider whether or not his life had "meaning." His attitude is frightening and threatens the philosophy of society: once one is born, life must be lived and suicide is a sin and one's life must be governed by principles and purposes. This kind of reality, however, is not Meursault's and, for that reason, he is accused of lacking "feeling." Meursault has feelings, but his feelings are not coalesced into a systematic, moral unity.

The interview ended, Meursault admits that he does not feel total regret for what he has done; what he feels is "less regret than a kind of vexation." Subsequently, during the many interrogations with the magistrate, the lawyer accompanies Meursault, attempting to have Meursault amplify his previous statements. And, sometimes, Meursault notices, they take very little notice of him. The magistrate seems to have lost interest in this queer, hard-hearted man who denies the existence of God. To them, Meursault becomes a non-person; neither man is hostile toward him. Ironically, Meursault says that he felt that sometimes he was "one of the family."

The interrogations last eleven months and Meursault is transformed into almost enjoying the ordeals. He takes delight in the magistrate's dismissing him and addressing him as "Mr. Antichrist." Any semblance of reality has been reversed within this court of which is supposedly stark reality.

CHAPTER II

Chapter I of Part Two focused on Meursault's changing relationship with the magistrate and with the lawyer and with his own attitude toward himself during the eleven months of the legal conferences. Chapter II takes those same eleven months and reveals what Meursault did when he was not being interrogated. It focuses on his day-to-day living while in prison. In addition, it illuminates various comments made by Meursault in Chapter I. For example, Meursault said that at times, he felt as though he and the examining magistrate were playing games. Here, he says that despite not wanting to talk about some things that happened, he has decided to recount them. The first which he mentions concerns his sense of unreality. During his early days in prison, he could not comprehend that he was actually being held prisoner. He was hardly conscious of what had happened and that prison was the result of an act which he performed. He had a child-like hope that something would happen, something agreeable and surprising.

Now, matters have changed and Meursault can pinpoint when he lost his reluctance to talk about what happened to him in prison. The change occurred when he received a letter from Marie stating that she would not be able to visit him anymore. She had come to see him only once. But because they were not married, she was denied a wife's privilege. It was on that day, Meursault tells us, that he realized that his cell was his "last home," and, as he puts it, "a dead end."

When he was first arrested, he was taken to a large room filled mostly with Arabs — that is, natives. Meursault is a Frenchman, one of the occupiers of the Algerian colony. It is not surprising that the natives are reluctant to say much to him when he tells them that he has killed an Arab. Afterward, he recounts being put in a small cell with a little window, through which he has glimpses of the sea. He is denied all but a single visitation from Marie, and he is teased by glimpses of the sea he loves to swim in, where he can see sunlight playing on the waves. Here, Camus shows us the ever-present dual role of the sun; at times, it is murderous, while at others it is warming and playful.

Meursault describes his new surroundings almost clinically, detailing the flights of steps, the room, the windows, the grilles, the thirty feet of "no man's land" between the prisoners and their visitors. There, he must face Marie and raise his voice in order for her to hear him. This is a vastly different world for Meursault. Formerly, he spoke only rarely; now, he must raise his voice, among the babel of voices of Arab natives. And even here, he cannot escape the torture of the white, glaring sunlight covering the two groups of desperate people, trying to be heard above the other voices, battling for one another's messages under the sunlight that floods the stark room. Meursault admits that, at first, he felt dizzy, for his cell had been very dark and very silent. Then he was thrust into a world of panic, harshly lit, and peopled with murmurs and whispers of Arabs. For some time, he could not say anything of importance. The reality of prison was beginning to tighten. Marie was pressed against bars, looking pretty, and Meursault wanted to tell her so, give her a simple compliment, yet he was too embarrassed to say so, surrounded by the Arabs. Likewise, Marie's questions are commonplace; she wonders if he is all right and if he has everything he wants. Not only are the questions commonplace; they are ridiculous. Yet he answers affirmatively and quickly. The two become even more separated when the Arabs closest to them begin to interrupt them and comment about their own troubles, and Marie shouts that Raymond sends greetings. Meursault's thanks are drowned by the voice of the man next to him. Meursault desires so much to be free now, to be able to embrace Marie, despite this sea of confusion, to feel her body through her thin dress. She assures him that he will be acquitted and that they will go swimming together again, and says that he must not give up hope. But as one reads of the chaotic shouting and of the drone of the Arabs among themselves, we know that Meursault can have little hope. Even the light outside the window seems to become evil, smearing the faces of the people with a coat of yellowish oil. He feels sick, yet he wants to remain and absorb as much as he can of a single moment of Marie's presence. She continues to smile and talk about her work, and all of Meursault's attention is on her and not on what she is saying. Then he is led away, leaving Marie pressed to the rails, trying to smile.

With Marie's first letter comes Meursault's sharp realization that he must, to keep his sanity, stop thinking like a free man. All of his life he has yielded to impulses; we saw this clearly in Part One of the novel. Now he can no longer go down to the beach for a swim in order to feel the cold water against his body after a hot day at the office. This is no game. He is locked within a narrow cell. This phase of being reminded that he is no longer a free man lasts for a few months only, he says. Then another change occurs.

Meursault began having a "prisoner's" thoughts. Being no longer free to do what he wishes to do on impulse, he looks forward to the few things that he is allowed to do. Small ventures, such as a daily walk in the courtyard of the prison or even a visit from his lawyer become of prime importance. His adjustment pleases him, even though it also surprises him. He likens his imprisonment to being held within the trunk of a tree and being able to see only a patch of sky. Even tortured by that, he is sure that he can adjust. He imagines that if such were the case, he would find pleasure in watching for the passing of birds overhead or watching for drifting clouds. Camus' comments in his *Myth of Sisyphus* are pertinent to Meursault's comments here.

Although condemned to rolling an enormous boulder up a hill, only to watch it tumble back down, Sisyphus adjusted. His mind was his own, although his body was forced to repeat again and again, throughout eternity, the same action. Camus says that when one begins to realize a sense of the absurd, he places a great value on "a single impression, like Proust lingering over the scent of a rose." This is step one: valuing the depth of a single sensation, adjusting to the intoxication of a new lucidity. Here, Meursault is newly aware that if it were possible to claim only a scrap of sky for himself, he could be satisfied. He could define that sky and those moments as absolutes and be content with them. Later, Meursault will change because Camus goes one step further: the absurd man will, finally, abandon single moments, single sensations, and limited visions. He will see the need of "accumulating as many as possible." Yet, for the present, Meursault is excited that he can envision being satisfied with a single patch of sky. It would be reason enough for him to rebel and transcend his punishment. Man has always looked to the heavens for help; and Meursault would be sustained by a corner of the sky for it would infuse within him a desire to continue to live. Death is an absolute end and as long as Meursault had his portion of sky (or, as in reality, his sliver of sea), he has hope, a new awareness of life, and the knowledge that he has the strength to struggle against an incomprehensible court and, ultimately, an incomprehensible world.

Meursault also realizes that, simply, matters could be worse. At least, he is not, literally, bound within the trunk of a tree. He does have the freedom of his narrow cell and the anticipation of wondering what kind of odd necktie his lawyer will appear in next, and it is during these thoughts that he remembers the words of his dead mother. She was frequently saying that "in the long run, one gets used to anything." This is Meursault's first thoughts of his mother that have been positive and not associated in some way with her death or her funeral.

Sex—the lack of it—bothers Meursault, but he has memories of the many women he has had sex with and he can fill his small cell with their faces. Although it may seem a torment to realize that he is no longer free to have sex when he pleases, his memories serve to blot out boredom and time.

Meursault also misses smoking. Cigarettes are forbidden and he tells us that that particular deprivation was "what got me down the most," describing tearing off splinters from his plank bed and sucking on them. He describes in detail the physical symptoms of withdrawal, the feeling of faintness and the biliousness that was constantly with him. He cannot understand why he is not allowed to smoke. It is only when he realizes, again, that he is a prisoner that he understands. He is a prisoner and a prisoner is a person who is being punished. His punishment is a denial of women and cigarettes. But Meursault almost smiles as he admits that when this revelation comes to him, he had lost the craving for cigarettes, so the authorities who denied him cigarettes were no longer able to punish him.

He confesses to being not absolutely unhappy. He quickly learns the trick of defeating boredom by exercising his memory, recounting his apartment's bedroom, for instance, and visualizing every single object in every detail—tiny dents in the woodwork, chipped edges, the exact grain and color of the woodwork. All of these things he had never noticed before. They had simply existed, as he had simply existed. He was as unaware of their importance as they were unaware of him.

He discovers that the more he remembers, the more he is able to remember and concludes that even after a single day's experience in the outside world, if a man were imprisoned for the rest of his life, if he could recall, in the minutest detail, everything about that day, he could fill all his time with memory and not be defeated by boredom. This is compensation, he says. It is also more; it is a victory over the system that hopes to stifle hope and humanity. By remembering, Meursault discovers again a world that did not exist when he lived in it. Now it has come alive for him, but this miracle of sorts was only possible because he is not allowed to live in it.

In addition, Meursault sleeps, and sleep can also blot out the monotony of time. Meursault sleeps so well, in fact, that he has only six hours to fill with memories and fantasies.

He then stops telling of how he spent his time during those eleven months and describes an incident when, one day, while he was inspecting his straw mattress, he found a bit of yellowed newspaper stuck on the underside. Part of the paper is missing, but the newspaper contains the story of a crime, committed in a village in Czechoslovakia. The story is a short one, one in fact that Camus later enlarged into a play, *The Misunderstanding*. The play recounts the story of a young man who leaves home, makes a fortune, and after twenty-five years, returns, hoping to surprise his mother and sister. The two women manage an inn and murder their guest during the night for his money. When the dead man's wife explains what has happened, the mother hangs herself and the sister throws herself into a well. The story intrigues Meursault; he says that he read and re-read the story thousands of times, determining finally that perhaps one shouldn't play tricks of that sort. Perhaps one, indeed, should not play tricks, even tricks that include writing vicious letters that lead to brawls and, in Meursault's case, a murder.

The Misunderstanding was first produced in 1944, several years following the publication of *The Stranger*. Obviously, Camus was very much intrigued with the irony of a mother and a daughter murdering a rich stranger, who, by chance, is their son and brother. The women, it is assumed, have probably murdered other rich strangers who have come to their inn; this particular guest, being alone in the inn, is an easy victim. Thus, as readers, we are confronted with another murder—a murder of, presumably, a stranger.

Unlike Meursault, however, the mother and daughter kill themselves in fits of madness and guilt when they discover the identity of the dead man, whereas, in contrast, Meursault does not fully comprehend his own murder of a stranger.

Camus also teases us with yet another murder and with the philosophical question as to whether or not it makes any difference whether one kills a stranger or, in this case, a son and a brother. Even the title of Camus' play, based on this short tale is ironic. Murder, can under no circumstance, ever be excused as the result of a mere misunderstanding. In the next chapter, Meursault's old friend Céleste will defend Meursault by saying that the murder of the Arab was just an accident, a stroke of bad luck. Likewise, Raymond will defend Meursault by stating that "chance" and "mere coincidence" are to blame. Such statements are true, but are they reason enough to excuse a man for taking another man's life and then firing four additional bullets into the dead corpse? And, in turn, we must ask ourselves if the murderer must pay with his life and be murdered for "the good of society" by the state.

From a former existence of living only for present moments, as a prisoner Meursault is able to comprehend only yesterday and tomorrow with meaning. When the jailer informs him that he has been six months in jail, the words have no meaning; they convey nothing to him. He studies his face in his little tin pannikin to see if he has changed, holding it at various angles, but his face always has the same mournful, tense expression. Watching the sun setting, he hears his voice and realizes that lately he has been talking to himself; he has been unaware that this has been happening. A free man cannot, Meursault says, imagine what evenings are like in prison.

In this new world, where freedom does not exist, time becomes of prime importance for Meursault because it seems endless. The uniformity is unrelieved until Meursault discovers that he can challenge his punishment with memory, with sleep, and the intriguing re-creation in his mind of the account of the murder in the scrap of newspaper clipping. Thus he "murders" time in order to retain a semi-sense of life. *Inside* the walls of his cell, Meursault is, literally, an *outsider,* a stranger to society *(The Outsider,* interestingly, is the British title of this novel). Yet, it is only within his cell that Meursault learns for the first time to fathom that life is valuable and that it can have quality.

CHAPTER III

Because of Meursault's ability to cope with the usual boredom that accompanies imprisonment, he tells us early in this chapter that, in truth, the eleven months he spent in his cell did not pass slowly. He adds that as his trial approaches, another summer has come. Almost a year has passed since he shot the Arab.

On the day Meursault's trial begins, Camus colors it, characteristically, with "brilliant sunshine." Sunshine has been described, metaphorically, in many various guises throughout the novel but, on this particular day, it is "brilliant." There seems to be added hope in the remark of Meursault's lawyer, during which he assures Meursault that the trial will be brief, lasting only two or three days. Meursault's case, it seems, is not important because the case immediately following his deals with the murder of a father by his own son, a trial which probably will take some time.

Meursault is almost relaxed; the sense of game-playing returns as he describes the noises of the courtroom, reminding him of small-town "socials," when a room is being cleared, after a concert, for dancing. He even refuses an offered cigarette, once his greatest deprivation and, further, he anticipates the prospect of witnessing a trial. His own trial does not seem to trouble him at all; he is far more interested in the spectacle of being a witness to another device of the legal machinery that has attempted to control his world for these eleven months. This is a novelty to a man who has had—except in a single instance—no visitors, other than legal interrogators, for almost a year, living in a narrow cell with memory, sleep, and innumerable recreations of a clipping about a murder in Czechoslovakia.

Once inside the prisoner's dock, however, the atmosphere of the court changes. Although the blinds are down, light filters through them and the air becomes "stiflingly hot," especially since the windows are closed. Only then does Meursault see the row of faces opposite him. Earlier he had considered that he would be "witnessing" a trial; now he is confronted with the prospective jurors, who will be witnessing his trial, listening to witnesses for and against Meursault. But, like the Arab, they are nameless, almost faceless; at this point, they are merely a body of people. He does not comprehend that they are individuals with names and private lives and emotions. He is amused at their stares because he realizes that they are looking at him for signs of criminality. He feels the absurdity and the almost comic aspects of the situation, the unreality of his being confronted by strangers, intently analyzing him as an object on display.

Slowly, as he has done on previous occasions, when he becomes too warm, he begins to feel dizzy. Time becomes heavy once more as he finds that he must continue to endure being the focus of attention by a sea of faces that he cannot recognize. Never before has Meursault been such a focal point. Before the murder, he was, we have to suppose, sufficiently ordinary looking that no one took a second glance, either admiringly or disparagingly. He – a nobody – is, suddenly, someone vastly important. The policeman, to the left of Meursault, explains that the newspapers are responsible for the dense, crowded courtroom. He even points out the press reporters sitting at a table, just below the jury box. One journalist knows the policeman and shakes hands, seems friendly and, later wishes Meursault good luck. When Meursault looks out upon the courtroom, he senses that, perhaps, he should not be here, for the people beyond him are exchanging remarks and seem to belong to a club; he feels ill at ease only because he is alone, an outsider, a stranger, or, as he puts it, a "gate-crasher."

Meursault's case, he discovers, is not as simple as he thinks and, we are led to believe, the crowded courtroom is particularly fascinated by Meursault. The journalist friend of the policeman beside Meursault says that because news was scarce, the journalists have been featuring Meursault's murder of the Arab, along with the news and the gossip surrounding the patricide. Thus the amplification has already begun and Meursault has been ignorant of the fact that his name and his murder of the Arab have been written about by journalists. Since the two murder trials are scheduled one after another, they have, by chance, become linked into a grotesque curiosity. One of the correspondents, it is noted, even came from Paris to cover the patricide, but was asked, as long as he was present, to cover the details of Meursault's trial.

All of this is said to Meursault thoughtlessly, and Meursault, in turn, does not understand the interest in himself and his trial, for he almost comments that it was kind of the Parisian reporter to spend time listening to Meursault's trial; but he stops short when he realizes that it would sound silly. The journalist goes back to his colleagues, with another friendly wave of his hand, and the journalists again chatter and laugh together, all seeming "very much at home." Camus is emphasizing the coziness, the sense of comradship on the part of the press, in addition to that of the crowd in order to point out Meursault's feeling of aloneness and the feeling that he is an outsider, a stranger in their midst.

The account of the trial's opening is discussed quickly because Meursault does not understand the legal maneuvering and rules of order and is conscious, mainly, of a single journalist who is eyeing him but betraying no emotion.

Meursault's consciousness of being an outsider in a courtroom linked by a strange common bond disappears as soon as the witness list is called. Raymond, Masson, Salamano, the doorkeeper from the Home, old Pérez (his mother's closest friend), and Marie slowly emerge from the faceless blur of people, standing, then filing out of the room through a side door. Céleste, the owner of a restaurant that Meursault used to enjoy drinking and eating in is the last to leave. And, by chance, Meursault is startled for a moment at the woman who is beside Céleste. It is the robot-woman whom he observed one evening, but Meursault has little time for thinking about her, for his trial begins immediately. With a touch of black humor, Camus has the Judge describe himself as a "sort of umpire," recalling what Camus said about Meursault's being finally condemned because he "wouldn't play the game." The Judge vows to be scrupulously impartial. This is nonsense, as we well know, for no one is able to be impartial, to any great extent, about a death or, in this case, a murder. He closes by citing that the case will be handled "in the spirit of justice," another ironic comment for justice will not enter into Meursault's trial. His trial will not be impartially viewed, argued about, or judged, and his sentence will not be the result of impartial justice.

After a brief reference to the heat and the public fanning themselves with newspapers and the three judges fanning with plaited straw fans, the Judge begins his questioning of Meursault.

Like a child, Meursault is vaguely annoyed that he must once again answer questions about his identity and give particulars about the crime; but he reasons, like a child, that perhaps this might be the best procedure; it would be wrong if the wrong man were on trial. His innocence mocks the idea of justice having begun, for in a sense, Meursault is being tried for a wrong which he committed, and he will be sentenced for the wrong reasons. His attitude, at this point, is as though he is a spectator, viewing himself, reciting names and places which he has done so many times previously. Indeed, even as the Judge questions Meursault about the account of the murder, it is as though another person were answering "Yes, sir," as instructed by his lawyer to do. Instead of listening to the Judge's questions, Meursault allows himself to concentrate on the youngest journalist whose eyes are fixed on him and, at the same time, he notices the little robot-woman.

When the Judge finishes his routine questioning, he launches into matters which he says might seem irrelevant, but which are in his opinion, highly relevant. Remember, at this point, that the Judge promised to be impartial. Thus Meursault is prepared for what he describes as the "odious" matter of his mother's death.

To the questions about his mother, Meursault is very honest. The questions are, to him, simple. He sent her away because there was not enough money for them both and neither he nor his mother was particularly distressed at the parting. Neither he nor his mother, he adds, "expected much of one another" — or anybody else. Therefore, the new condition and the adjustment was easy.

The Prosecutor is quick to take advantage of Meursault's simple explanations. It is easy for Meursault to explain to him that he had no intention of killing the Arab and, as for his carrying a revolver, that was merely a matter of pure chance. This is the truth, we know, because we are certain of the truth of this man's first-person narrative.

The truthfulness of Meursault's explanations helps confirm what he says happened after the Prosecutor has finished. When he says that he couldn't "quite follow what came next," we are sure that he could not. Meursault is easily and often confused. We observed several instances of this in Part One and especially in the first two chapters of Part Two.

The call for adjournment bewilders Meursault, as does his being hustled into the prison van and given a midday meal. He is tired when he is returned to the courtroom, confronting the same faces and starting the trial over again. This is, in a sense, punishment for Meursault, for, in addition to his being tired and disconcerted by the court proceedings, the heat has increased; Meursault is sweating, barely conscious, and now all of the people in the courtroom have fans and everyone is fanning themselves — except the young journalist and the steel-eyed robot-woman.

The evidence against Meursault's rumored callousness is first confirmed by the warden of the Home. He swears that Meursault's mother complained about her son's conduct and that she reproached him for sending her to the Home. Meursault fails to comprehend the importance of what has been uttered to the jury. To him, the warden of the Home has not qualified his answers and, in addition, it is natural for old people in Homes resenting, at one time or another, being sent there. This fact does not surprise or alarm him.

The warden becomes embarrassed when he has to explain, however, Meursault's "calmness." Calm, normally, is a word with positive connotations; here, it is damning as the warden explains that Meursault's calmness consists of not wanting to see his mother's body, not shedding a tear and not even knowing his mother's age. According to the Code, the Judge asks that the warden identify the man so described as the prisoner Meursault. It is a formal question, but one which the Prosecutor relishes. Meursault is riveted now even more tightly into his role of an unfeeling man, a man who could kill in cold blood. Meursault notes the look of triumph on the man's face. It would be foolish for him to burst into tears, but being the focal point of so much hate as he feels bearing upon him, he does want to cry. He has never before sensed such loathing by another person.

The doorkeeper at the Home adds to the warden's damning evidence, adding that Meursault declined to see the corpse, that he smoked cigarettes and slept and even drank coffee with cream. Of course Meursault is "guilty" of that. Those facts are truth. The frightening aspect of this testimony is that Meursault begins to feel guilty and becomes even more aware that he is being condemned on false charges when the doorkeeper is asked to repeat his statements about smoking and about drinking coffee. A heat of indignation encases the courtroom. Guilty as charged, one might say. But the murder of the Arab has scarcely been touched on; little mention is made of Meursault's killing the native. The focus of the trial, thus far and throughout the remainder of the day, will be on Meursault's behavior during the weekend after his mother's burial.

Embarrassment follows the doorkeeper's statement when Meursault's counsel asks the doorkeeper if, in fact, he too did not smoke. He did, he confesses, but he took the cigarette "just out of politeness." Meursault confirms the truth of giving the cigarette, which gives the doorkeeper so much relief from being accused of also smoking that he confesses that it was he who suggested that Meursault have some coffee.

The statements made by old Pérez are even more damning for Meursault, for the old man recounts that he himself fainted during the funeral and speaks of his being "a great friend" of Meursault's mother and that his grief and his shock were so intense during the funeral that he barely noticed Meursault. He also says that he did not see Meursault shed a tear, but he cannot "swear" to such a statement.

Céleste's testimony begins on a positive note; he admits that Meursault was a customer of his and also a friend; when asked whether or not Meursault was a "secretive" sort of man, Céleste answers instead that Meursault "isn't one to waste his breath, like a lot of folks," meaning the Prosecutor. Clearly, he is trying to help Meursault, saying that he paid his bills. When asked about his opinion of the murder, he says that, in his opinion, it was a stroke of bad luck, an accident, and is abruptly dismissed when the Judge observes that this trial is being held for just such reasons: to judge such "accidents."

Marie's testimony is ripe for the Prosecutor as he draws forth that she and Meursault made love the day following Meursault's mother's funeral; in addition, he forces her to confess that they met while swimming and that they attended a movie together before having sex. Then the Prosecutor brings the trial to a halt with a startling silence, following his statement that the movie they attended was "a comedy film." He pleads with the jury to remember, foremost, that the man they are to judge did these three acts on the very day following his mother's funeral.

Marie's tears and pleas for understanding are of no help; she is led away and the hearing continues, with scarcely anyone paying any attention to the testimony of Masson or Salamano. Salamano, like Marie, asks for understanding, but it is obvious that his attempt is as futile as Marie's tears were.

Raymond, the last witness, states that Meursault is innocent. This is a rash statement, but one typical of the volatile Raymond Sintès. One might think that he protests too quickly. He does explain that Meursault had no motive for killing the Arab, that it was he, Raymond, who had the grudge against the Arab. Meursault's presence, he says, on that particular day was due to "pure coincidence." This is true, but the Prosecutor knows a great deal about this murder, for he asks Raymond about Meursault's writing the defaming letter to the dead Arab's sister. To this question, Raymond can answer only that it was mere chance, which gives the Prosecutor an opportunity to chant "chance" and "mere coincidence" as playing much too large a role in the murder. For example, he points out that Meursault did not interfere when Raymond beat up his mistress, that Meursault swore falsely to the police about Raymond, and points out that this man, who states, unequivocally, that Meursault is innocent is well known as a pimp, as a man who makes a living on the prostitution of women. Meursault is, therefore, pinned against a sordid backdrop of prostitution, brutal fights, a liaison of his own, and a perverted "calmness" during his mother's funeral. The Prosecutor describes Meursault as inhuman, a monster, wholly without morals, a man who indulged himself in an orgy following the death of his mother, and killing a man as part of a vendetta for his best friend, a pimp.

When Meursault's lawyer protests that his client is on trial for murder and not for his associations with certain types of friends or matters happening during and after his mother's funeral, there are a few titters from the courtroom audience. When he tries to gain understanding for his client, the lawyer's gestures are awkward and the Prosecutor is fast on his feet to emphasize that the two elements mentioned are the vital link in this case: Meursault is a criminal at heart. And Meursault notices that "these words seemed to take much effect on the jury and the public."

This statement is certainly true, for if it was the doorkeeper who is the blame for Meursault's drinking coffee, he is guilty of defaming Meursault's character, which the Prosecutor is attempting to do also. And, if the doorkeeper is guilty, then Raymond, by extension, is guilty for suggesting that Meursault write the letter, and Marie is guilty for suggesting the comic movie that she and Meursault attended together. But, remember that in each case, Meursault was given a choice; he could have said no. He must now assume the responsibilities for his actions. One cannot define his actions as models of behavior and the Prosecutor is alert to this, damning Meursault's moral sense, logically, but for the wrong reasons. Later, Meursault will be labeled a monster because he disobeys conventions; that is, he does not "play the game." Clearly this is the Prosecutor's most valuable weapon against Meursault and he uses it repeatedly and stunningly.

The first day of the trial finished, Meursault is conscious, first of all, of a summer evening out-of-doors; later, sitting in the darkness of the truck, memories return to him of things which had mattered, but things which he had never given value to before—sounds of a town which he had loved, a certain hour of the day, the languid air, birds calling, and streetcar noises. Once, he was unconsciously content with life, but he did not know that he was content or that he was "living"; only now, in this prison of the moving vehicle does he realize what has been taken away—forever—from him.

CHAPTER IV

Camus has altered the tone of his narrative slowly as Meursault has, after a fashion, somewhat adjusted to prison life and is now on trial for his life. In Part One, Meursault reacted either positively or negatively or was confused by questions and decisions which he alone could answer or make. Numerous times, the first-person narrative focused on the simplicity of Meursault's reactions. Now, however, even Meursault is aware of the sense of detachment which has grown within him. It was especially evident in the last chapter, and Camus emphasizes it even more in this chapter.

Meursault, for example, is vaguely aware that he is being thoroughly condemned by the Prosecutor, yet he himself senses a new, far-reaching indifference to his fate. He is intrigued by the trial. He finds it "interesting," although he is the prisoner who is hearing himself discussed. He is a focal point and, as almost an afterthought, he is aware that more is said about *him* than is said about his crime. Camus' understatements here confirm what we have seen happening in this so-called court of justice. It is, for Meursault, absurd that both his own lawyer and the Prosecutor have come to almost the same conclusion after having argued about Meursault's character. They agree: Meursault is guilty. Meursault's lawyer differs only in that he raises his arms to heaven and pleads Meursault's guilt with extenuating circumstances.

Normally, as has been noted, Meursault is a man of few words, but he finds himself, at the present, eager to speak out, to add more to his lawyer's defense. This he has been advised not to do and so he remains silent. To him, it seems as though he has been excluded from the trial entirely and that his fate is to be decided with his having little to do with the matter.

Tide-like, Meursault's fascination with the trial ebbs and recedes; he listens intently, wanting to protest, then drifts away, only half-hearing the vindictive voice of the Prosecutor. Meursault is aware of the Prosecutor's gestures and his elaborate phrases, but even these, he admits, catch only isolated moments of his attention. It is with almost a sense of impatience that Meursault waits for the Prosecutor to continue as he tries to prove to the jury that the murder was obviously premeditated and that it can be summarized as being the "dark workings of a criminal mentality." Camus' ironic sense of comedy is included in the Prosecutor's tirades. For the Prosecutor, the facts of the crime are "as clear as daylight." Recall that when Meursault fired the shots, he was mesmerized by the daylight. But the sun itself was *not* clear; it was thickly clotted by Meursault's mental state. And note also that Camus has the Prosecutor, in another stroke of ironic comment, add that Meursault's criminal mentality might be called the "dark side of this case." The sun, as we have seen, did darken, blinding Meursault, literally and figuratively. It was so intense that Meursault was blinded by the stinging sweat in his eyes, the blurry vision of the Arab, and he was blinded by the enormity of what was happening. As he said in Part One, the trigger of the pistol simply "gave." Meursault's daylight was so blackened by the sun that he was not even conscious of firing the first shot into the Arab.

Camus' having the Prosecutor reiterate the facts of the crime increases our sense of what Meursault must be feeling as he hears again and again the sequence of, for him at least, "chance" events that occurred, culminating in what the Prosecutor describes as "cold blooded murder." Underscoring his summation, the Prosecutor cites Meursault's education, logically proving that the crime was done by a man capable of premeditation. Had Meursault been a simple, passionate man, perhaps he could have killed the Arab in a moment of madness. But, the Prosecutor tells the jury, this is not the case: Meursault had all his faculties and wits about him when he fired the shots and was quite aware of what he was doing. This, we know, is not so. It is, seemingly logical, but it is false. Meursault was totally unaware of what he was doing and, later, the reason why he did it. Even now, he cannot explain why he murdered the Arab and, especially, why he fired the four extra shots. To the Prosecutor, the four extra shots prove that Meursault was being thorough; to this charge, Meursault has no answer, other than knowing that the Prosecutor is wrong.

Meursault admits to himself that he feels little regret; after all, the man whom he shot was a stranger; he was only an Arab, and, to Meursault, the Prosecutor is overdoing the emphasis on Meursault's regret. Camus, here, is placing Meursault in the position of a judge — listening, watching, observing, and making decisions as to justice being done.

Meursault tells us that he is a man incapable of regret. To regret, philosophically, includes in its definition a re-thinking and contemplation about past actions — these do not exist within Meursault. He is a man of present moments and considers only briefly the immediate future and if the future will contain pleasure. He has never looked backward and contemplated the past, and, for this reason, the entire trial has been an enormously new experience for Meursault. He has had to endure re-hearing the past, depicted by the Prosecutor, and by his own counsel, and judging their versions of the past with his own.

The Prosecutor is a thorough villain; Camus is quite clear in his portrayal of the man, parading him and prancing him before the jury as he states that Meursault clearly lacks a soul and although it would be wrong to condemn a man for something that he lacks, it is logical, and just, that justice cannot tolerate the lack of a soul. Logically, therefore, Meursault is a menace to society. And, although he does not say so at the moment, logically, he could conclude that if one is a menace to society, then, for society's sake, that menace should be done away with — burned, executed, or beheaded.

Consider, also, in this chapter that Camus manipulates the Prosecutor's oratory so that when the man is condemning Meursault, he continually refers to the case following Meursault's — the murder of a father by his son. He links, within the consciousness of the jury, the idea that extenuating circumstances are no excuse. A murder is a murder and an execution is a murderer's just reward. He preys upon the jury, trapped in their seats, in order to construe a physical murder of a father by a son with a "moral" murder of a mother by her son.

The Prosecutor adds that when he asks for the death penalty, he has never asked for a capital sentence with so little pain. Because Meursault is heartless, the Prosecutor feels no qualms because, being a religious man, he is following not only his own conscience, but his sacred obligation. He is now dealing with a criminal who lacks a "spark" (a light image, again) of human feeling.

Meursault's reaction is both physical and one of anguish. When the Prosecutor sits down, Meursault is quite overcome, he says, but he is not wholly defeated because of what the Prosecutor has said. Meursault is suffering terribly from the heat, he tells us first, and then adds that he is also amazed at what he has been hearing.

Meursault, given a chance to speak, says briefly that he had no intention of killing the Arab. After the long harangue, the contrast between his defense and the Prosecutor's defamation is striking. Meursault's only defense for his act was "because of the sun." That is all: "because of the sun." Meursault adds that he spoke too quickly and ran his words together; actually, what he said is of little importance for we are sure what the verdict will be.

Court is adjourned and is continued the following day with no hint of what Meursault thought about during the evening as he waited for the trial to resume. Whether or not he has changed during the interval, we see that little has changed when he is brought back into the courtroom. The fans are still waving before the faces of the jury and the speech by the defense seems as endless, if not more so, than that of the Prosecution. Meursault removes himself from the proceedings, as he has done before; in effect, this is what has happened to him, by order of the court. His lawyer has been used, instead of Meursault himself, to explain the murder and its circumstances. This is particularly vivid to Meursault when he realizes that the lawyer is so enthralled in recounting the murder that he becomes confused and says "I killed a man."

Meursault realizes that he is judging his lawyer and he also realizes that the man is not nearly as "talented" as the Prosecutor. This is appallingly evident in the lawyer's failing to summon to the attention of the jury the issue of the trial: Meursault is on trial for killing an Arab—not for his actions at his mother's funeral and certainly not for any of his adventures with Marie and Raymond. In addition, Meursault tells us nothing of his lawyer's defense concerning why Meursault was carrying the gun in the first place. Thus we must assume that the lawyer did not mention the subject. Further, the lawyer fails to grasp the easiest explanation possible for

Meursault's shooting the Arab: Meursault saw that the Arab had a knife; the initial shot was fired in self-defense and the ensuing shots were fired because of panic and fright. This makes absolutely good sense and is logical and carries sufficient persuasiveness that the jury probably would accept the truth of such statements. But such explanations are not even brought to their attention. At times, therefore, Meursault's lawyer seems to be a dolt, feeble and ridiculous, especially when he counters the Prosecutor's arguments concerning Meursault's soul.

To our dismay, we listen to him return to the matter, once more, of Meursault's mother. This is rhetorical quicksand, a subject that has engulfed the entire trial and has been given a thorough damnation by the Prosecutor. The defense says proudly that such institutions as the Home are excellent and are promoted and financed by the government. His logic is absurd: Meursault's soul exists because he was sufficiently humane to put his mother into a "government" Home.

It seems, at times, that Meursault can bear hearing no more, for not only can he not defend himself, he cannot explain his actions. The repetitious recreation of the past sickens him; he feels as though he could vomit because of the rush of memories flooding over him. And, in his remembering, consider that Meursault remembers the physical, not the philosophical, aspects of scenes — the warm smells, the color of the sky at evening, the feel of Marie's dress, and the sound of her laughter. These sensations are denied to him and never before has Meursault been confronted with the disappearance of an entire world. Formerly, his life was composed of warm skies, swimming, and sex, and little thought was given to one day following another and the disappearence, forever, of present moments that he was delighting in.

The trial over, Meursault is so exhausted that he utters a naked, blatant lie; he says that his defense has been fine. His insincerity troubles him a bit, but he is far too tired to judge whether or not it could be labeled, decisively, "fine." Ironically, we pause and consider that had Meursault "played the game" — had he wept during the trial, wrung his hands, exhibited any emotion or remorse, the Prosecutor's case would have failed.

Even Marie's presence cannot rouse Meursault now from his stupor as he awaits the verdict. He reveals that he feels as though his heart had "turned to stone," leaving us with an ironic affirmation that Meursault is, indeed, heartless.

When he hears that he is to be decapitated in "some public place," he says that he sensed a respectful sympathy within the courtroom and then he "stopped thinking altogether." We do not; we cannot. We continue thinking and questioning the justness of such a verdict.

CHAPTER V

At the beginning of this chapter, Meursault very briefly notes that he has refused to see the prison chaplain for the third time; then he dismisses the subject as quickly as he dismissed the chaplain, and turns to another subject. He speaks of hope. There has been an element of hope within him despite his knowledge that death is a soon certainty, and caught between his hope for life and his certainty of death, Meursault's thoughts have become wild and random. He grasps for the impossible: freedom *must* be possible, he thinks, if for no other reason than that of chance. (Remember that chance is largely responsible for his being in prison.) He remarks that had he —just once—read an escape story and discovered at least one instance in which chance saved a man from execution, he would be satisfied. But he cannot cling to hope for long, and so these paragraphs of doubt and hope counterpoint one another. As soon as Meursault envisions the possibility of escape, he confronts himself with the fact that he is caught in "a rattrap, irrevocably." The ebb and flow of his contrasting emotions are evocative of the movement of the sea, yet they resemble more the intake and gasping for breath of a drowning man.

Even one of Meursault's former consolations is of little comfort to him now. Earlier, Meursault imagined being imprisoned within a tree, able to see only a piece of sky; in his new cell, he can, in fact, see nothing but the sky, but circumstances have changed. His punishment now is not mere imprisonment. Here he must face not an endless punishment; he must cope every morning with the fear of hearing footsteps, the prelude to his beheading. Prisoners in Algiers are never told when they are to be executed; thus Meursault has no opportunity to adjust for an eternity of punishment as, for example, Sisyphus had.

These desperate moments of hope, of escape, flow through a mind that cannot fathom fully, with certitude, that this imprisonment, this waiting to be killed, is happening to him—a nobody of a person, a clerk, a man who has asked nothing from life other than a few pleasures and that he be left alone. It is probably impossible for Meursault, as it would be for any man, to fully realize death's nothingness. For this reason, Meursault's imagination is released and allowed free rein to comfort him. Formerly, imagination was of no use to Meursault. His life consisted of whatever was occurring to him at any given moment. His current "present" however is unbearable and so he must find an alternative, another way of existing, moment to moment, as he awaits the certain, yet unknown, dawn when he will be led to the guillotine.

Even Meursault's imagination fails, though, for the most part, because he is basically a practical man. He cannot even romanticize that he will ascend majestically a flight of stairsteps above a crowd of people awaiting his beheading. He remembers, oddly, in this chapter, some things his mother used to tell him — some old, philosophical homilies, but because he has always lived without much forethought or hindsight, his agony is scarcely relieved by remembering his mother's platitudes. Clearly, Meursault is able to measure his own degree of panic. He is frightened and repelled by his thoughts of dying and he realizes at the same time how absurd such panic is. Man must eventually die and, in addition, the world will continue — without any man, many men, and certainly without Meursault.

It is interesting that Meursault refuses "to play *the* game" by seeing the chaplain, confessing his sins and asking for prayers and consolation. Yet he allows his imagination to play *a* game with chance and possibility. At the same time, he keeps, with effort, some control on his thoughts, for he knows that his execution is probably inevitable. But is there an alternative? Perhaps he can appeal, successfully. He sustains himself by thinking, constantly thinking: if he is able to maintain control over his thoughts, he can gain some semblance of peace of mind.

But his peace of mind, even if achieved, is brief. His thoughts return too quickly to a familiar groove — to Marie — and he considers her feelings about being labeled the mistress of a man who murdered another man; she is the mistress of a man who is sentenced to die. He wonders about her. She is alive now. If she were to die, her memories of Meursault die also. And, if she is dead, and once Meursault is dead, he will be absolutely forgotten. No trace of him will remain, even in a memory.

When the prison chaplain walks in, unannounced, Meursault's

shock is evident. He has been caught off guard: he has been caught thinking. One senses that Meursault has been surprised when he is naked; he is vulnerable, for normally he clothes himself in indifference, passivity, or physical activity.

Meursault describes the chaplain's behavior as an attempt to be friendly, and he describes the chaplain, himself, as a mild, amiable man. Knowing that the chaplain has not come to offer last words, the quiet within the cell allows Meursault to drift outside himself, observing the chaplain's eyes, his knees, and his sinewy hands. Meursault is a master at this kind of observation, admitting that for awhile he almost forgets that the chaplain is there, a live human being, sitting on Meursault's bed. Like the examining magistrate, the chaplain cannot accept Meursault's statement that God does not exist; he has come to Meursault's cell to assure him that his doubts about God are too certain and, therefore, might be wrong. When he questions Meursault about a belief being too thorough and the possibility that the reverse is true, Meursault answers that the chaplain may be right, but, most of all, Meursault is sure that he is *not* interested in discussing God.

The chaplain is unwilling to accept Meursault's lack of spiritual interest, saying that Meursault's feelings are fostered because of desperation, which, we realize, is most unlikely. Meursault feels fear—not desperation; in fact, he lacks the time to even begin a discussion about God because any discussion of God would involve sin and guilt and, although Meursault has been pronounced guilty, he emphatically does not accept that guilt. He also refuses to be consoled with the chaplain's observation that "all men are under a sentence of death." Meursault has already considered this notion himself and it is futile to philosophize about "death" and "all men." Meursault is undaunted by the chaplain's standing suddenly and sternly staring him in the eyes; it is, he says, a trick he himself has played.

Meursault drifts away as the chaplain laments about the suffering of a man who does not believe in an afterlife; he is roused only when the chaplain becomes so agitated that he professes a belief in the possibility that Meursault's appeal will succeed. Meursault is convinced that he has *not* sinned: a man of God has no business in his cell. He committed a criminal offense, not a sin, and God's laws should have no dimension in civil matters. He may be guilty of a civil offense but he is not guilty of sinning. Meursault is incapable of imagining the face of God on the stone walls, as the chaplain suggests. He wants only to conjure, before him, Marie's face, "sun-gold, lit up with desire."

Like the examining magistrate, the formerly "mild, amiable" man is metamorphosed into a madman, swinging around and crying out in defiance against Meursault's staunch refusal to believe in an afterlife.

In contrast, Meursault is calm and bored; of course he knows that one might wish, perhaps at times, for an afterlife, but such wishes are a waste of time. Man cannot change death's being an eternal void.

Meursault's request that the chaplain leave is not granted. The man is determined to squeeze out of Meursault some piece of his humanity that *must* be spiritual — which, in a sense, he does manage to accomplish. Meursault's imagination *can* picture an afterlife, but only an afterlife in which he can remember this life on earth. For Meursault, a spiritual existence is absolutely impossible unless it consists of a mind, residing in eternity, and doing one thing: remembering the pleasure of a man's former, physical life. Meursault has no use for any spiritual "present" moments in a vaporous spiritual world. Meursault is an active, physical man and the constant memory of such things as swimming and sex is the only kind of an afterlife possible for him.

When the chaplain begins to pray, Meursault is transformed into a madman himself, yelling, hurling insults, and grabbing the chaplain by the neckband of his cassock. He is desperate; he has precious few moments left to him and yet he is still being punished, even now, by a man who wants to be called Father and who wants to pray for his "son." Meursault describes his joy and rage as he attacks the certainty of the chaplain's beliefs; none of this man's spiritual certainties is comparable to a physical strand of a woman's hair. The only certainty important at this moment is the surety of Meursault's pending death, and his mind reels as his hands tighten on the chaplain. Meursault is so wrought with rage that several jailers finally have to rescue the chaplain.

Afterward, in the calm of the night, Meursault is able to fall asleep, until just before daybreak; then he is flooded by smells and sounds, physical responses during what he fears might be his last moments on earth. The sound of a steamer reminds him of his anonymity; not a single person on the boat knows or cares about

Meursault's fate, and it is at that moment that he understands the odd behavior of his mother as she approached death. She succumbed to a game of sorts, playing as though she were young once more, delighting in the interest that Old Pérez offered to her. Pérez cared.

Meursault realizes that his mother rebelled against dying. She "played" at beginning again. Likewise, so will Meursault. At last he is drained. He is emptied of all hope. And he is free. He can face the universe, alone — without fearing any man or any god. The "benign indifference" of the universe is no threat to him. He is, at last, able to defy everything and everybody because he has gained the knowledge that his indifference is akin to that of the universe. He is not to be pitied because he is a victim of a prejudiced jury. He has determined his own value to himself and, in addition, has realized an entirely new sense of self value: he knows how deeply his indifference and disbelief disturb society. One must "play the game" if he is to live within society. But in order to do this, one must give up being absolutely true to himself and acting according to his conscience. Society cannot afford to harbor strangers or outsiders who live by other rules. Society demands obedience. Meursault cannot be subservient to the emotional mores of the Algerian masses. Meursault's truth is his only companion, and he will die, defending his right *not* to cry at his mother's funeral and his right *not* to profess a belief in God. What good is it to attempt tears or swear beliefs in the name of truth when they would be melodramatically fraudulent?

Meursault has confronted the absurdity of his life and of life itself. In Part One, he lived without pausing to consider the meaning of his present moments, his past, or his future. He was either satisfied, or content, or bored. He placed no emphasis on his life's significance. Now, he realizes that the universe and most of the world are indifferent to his fate. So he *will* play the game of the Absurd; he himself will live as long as he can — giving his life *his* meaning, even though he knows that ultimately, it has no meaning. He will watch and measure his life's meaning as he faces what he hopes to be a howling mob. If he is so hated and such a threat to that mob of people, he will be able to laugh at their fear of him. He does not fear their hatred. He can determine the extent of his importance by measuring how thoroughly he is a threat to them. Meursault can imagine dying, enjoying the absurdity of his rejection. The crowd that howls for his blood are *not* free; they have not been forced to question their existence. They are governed and bound by secular and sacred laws which Meursault will not accept. He realizes that nothing—no value—is lasting or eternal. His former indifference was mute; now he can articulate and justify his new indifference and, with this insight, he is able to attain ecstatic peace.

CHARACTER ANALYSES

Meursault

Because so much time has been spent throughout the discussion of this novel, analyzing Meursault's character, there is little elaboration that would be more than speculation. Basically, one should remember that Meursault is a man who will not lie about himself, a man who cannot accept the formulas by which his society convinces itself it is happy. He will not look forward to a life after death, he will not use religion as a vehicle to avoid facing the fact that he must die, and he refuses to mask his calm acceptance of his mother's death. He defies all judges, except himself: he will not play the hypocritical penitent for his interrogators and prosecutors.

Perhaps one of the most valuable ways to understand Meursault is to quote what Camus has said about him:

"Meursault for me," writes Camus, is "a poor and naked man, in love with the sun which leaves no shadows. He is far from being totally deprived of sensitivity for he is animated by a passion, profound because it is tacit, the passion for the absolute and for truth. It is still a negative truth, the truth of being and feeling, but a truth without which no conquest of the self or of the world is possible." That is why, until the very end, "Meursault is the man who answers but never asks a question, and all his answers so alarm a society which cannot bear to look at the truth."

Marie

The few clues that we have about Marie's personality come from Meursault and he is not given to analyzing himself or other people and so we know little other than she seems, basically, an uncomplicated middle-class young woman. She wants marriage, children, enjoys casual sex, swimming, movies, and outings to the beach. She is frightened and terrified when Meursault is arrested; her life, one would guess, has never been confronted with such drama. Like Meursault, she has had rather unimportant jobs; he is a clerk, she was a typist. She is attracted to Meursault because he enjoys many things that she does and also because he is a little "different." When Meursault agrees to marry her, Marie is happy. Meursault will probably be an adequate husband; he will probably have a steady job, an income that she needn't worry about, and she doesn't ask much more from a man. Like Meursault, she does not demand much from life or from other people.

Marie is on the fringe of this novel, even though Meursault has agreed to marry her. But one should remember that she had great hope for her new life in Paris with Meursault. She is much more of a romantic than he is. She has her daydreams and is happier than we have ever seen her. When Meursault is arrested and sentenced to death, her dreams also die. Later, she is obscured by Meursault's introspection and she drifts away, from the plot, from Meursault, to everyday life and everyday routine.

Raymond

Even before we see Raymond in action we can infer a great deal about his personality. He is short and thick-set and has a flattened nose. He wears flashy clothes, but his room is unclean and the walls are covered by pinup pictures. His reputation as a pimp never is much of a problem for him; most of his friends are pumps, except Meursault and Masson. He repeatedly seeks reassurance, usually by violence, and thus we can be fairly sure that his macho pose is just a front for insecurity. He struts, is a tough guy, but isn't intelligent enough to realize how easily even Meursault sees through his veneer. He is humiliated more than physically harmed when he is wounded by the Arab's knife. He is not a close friend of Meursault; Meursault simply has no objection to spending time in the evenings with Raymond, sharing wine and food and listening to Raymond rant about the newest crisis in his life. And yet Meursault stands trial for a crime that Raymond may well have committed had Meursault not gone to the beach that particular Sunday.

68

REVIEW QUESTIONS

1. Meursault is a Frenchman living in Algeria; of what importance is this fact?
2. Describe the wake and the funeral of Meursault's mother, detailing Meursault's reactions and impressions.
3. The sun is a complex symbol in this novel. Describe the dual role that it plays, noting particularly the role in the climactic murder.
4. Discuss Camus' literary style in *The Stranger*.
5. How does Camus employ cause-and-effect in this novel?
6. In terms of Camus' philosophy of the Absurd, of what significance is the prison?
7. Why does Meursault place such a high value on the sea? What does it mean to him?
8. How would you have defended Meursault?
9. Compare the judicial character of the examining magistrate and the spiritual character of the priest.
10. Relate Meursault's interest in the robot-woman to his scrapbooks. How does his interest in her help us understand more about him?
11. What role does hope play in the second half of the novel?
12. What is Meursault's idea of an afterlife?
13. Evaluate the justice that was accorded Meursault during his trial and his sentencing.
14. Which played the greater role—emotion or reason—during Meursault's trial? In what way was each employed?
15. Explain Meursault's passivity during his interrogation and imprisonment.
16. Describe Meursault's moment of genuine revolt.
17. Do you think that Meursault is capable of love?
18. Meursault is often characterized as a man who makes no choices. Yet Meursault makes a single very important choice. What is it?
19. Contrast Meursault's view of society with society's expectations of Meursault.
20. How does *The Myth of Sisyphus* explore and expand the significance of *The Stranger*?

SELECTED BIBLIOGRAPHY

Abel, Lionel. "Albert Camus, Moralist of Feeling," *Commentary*, Vol. 31, No. 2 (Feb. 1961), pp. 172-75.

Barnes, Hazel E. *Humanistic Existentialism: The Literature of Possibility*. Lincoln, Nebraska: University of Nebraska Press. 1962.

Beebe, Maurice. "Criticism of Albert Camus: A Selected Checklist of Studies in English," *Modern Fiction Studies*, Vol. 10, No. 3 (Autumn 1964), pp. 303-14.

Bittner, William. "The Death of Camus," *Atlantic Monthly*, Vol. 207, No. 2 (Feb. 1961), pp. 85-88.

Brearley, Katherine. "The Theme of Isolation in Camus," *Kentucky Foreign Language Quarterly*, Vol. 9, No. 3 (1962), pp. 117-22.

Brée, Germaine. "Introduction to Albert Camus," *French Studies*, Vol. 4, No. 1 (Jan. 1950), pp. 27-37.

_____. *Camus*. New Brunswick: Rutgers University Press. 1959.

_____. "The Genesis of *The Stranger*," *Shenandoah*, Vol. 12, No. 3 (Spring 1961), pp. 3-10.

Bruckberger, Raymond-Leopold. "The Spiritual Agony of Europe," *Renascence*, VII, No. 2 (Winter 1954), pp. 70-80.

Cruickshank, John. *Albert Camus and the Literature of Revolt*. London: Oxford University Press. 1959.

Frank, Waldo. "Life in the Face of Absurdity," *New Republic*, CXXXIII, No. 12 (Sept. 19, 1955), pp. 18-20.

Frohock, W. M. "Camus: Image, Influence, and Sensibility," *Yale French Studies*, II, No. 2 (Fourth Study), pp. 91-99.

Gershman, Herbert S. "On *L'Etranger*," *French Review*, XXIX, No. 4 (Feb. 1956), pp. 299-305.

Hanna, Thomas. *The Thought and Art of Albert Camus*. Chicago: Henry Regnery Co. 1958.

Harrington, Michael. "The Despair and Hope of Modern Man," *Commonweal*, LXIII, No. 2 (Oct. 1956), pp. 224-33.

John, S. "Image and Symbol in the Work of Albert Camus," *French Studies*, IX, No. 1 (Jan. 1955), pp. 42-53.

King, Adele. *Camus*. London: Oliver and Boyd. 1964.

Mason, H. A. "M. Camus and the Tragic Hero," *Scrutiny*, XIV, No. 2 (Dec. 1946), pp. 82-89.

70

Rolo, Charles. "Albert Camus: A Good Man," *Atlantic*, Vol. 201, No. 5 (May 1958), pp. 27-33.

Scott, Nathan H. *Albert Camus*. London: Bowes and Bowes. 1962.

Theody, Philip. *Albert Camus: A Study of his Works*. London: Hamish Hamilton. 1957.

Viggiani, Carl A. "Camus in 1936: The Beginnings of a Career," *Symposium*, Vol. 12, Nos. 1-2 (Spring-Fall 1958), pp. 7-18.

_____. "Camus' *L'Etranger*," *PMLA*, Vol. 71, No. 5 (Dec. 1956), pp. 865-87.

NOTES

NOTES

TARTUFFE, THE MISANTHROPE, & THE BOURGEOIS GENTLEMAN

NOTES

including
- *Introduction*
- *List of Characters*
- *General Plot Summaries*
- *Summaries and Commentaries*
- *Character Analyses*
- *Review Questions*
- *Selected Bibliography*

by
Denis M. Calandra, Ph.D.
Department of Theater
University of South Florida
  and
James L. Roberts, Ph.D.
Department of English
University of Nebraska

Cliffs ® **Notes**

INCORPORATED

LINCOLN, NEBRASKA 68501

Editor

Gary Carey, M.A.
University of Colorado

Consulting Editor

James L. Roberts, Ph.D.
Department of English
University of Nebraska

CONTENTS

"THE BOURGEOIS GENTLEMAN" 83

SELECTED BIBLIOGRAPHY 106

Introduction

LIFE AND BACKGROUND

Molière is the pseudonym for Jean Baptiste Poquelin, one of the greatest comic geniuses the world has seen, and undoubtedly the master of "social comedy." Almost single-handed, he prompted international acclaim for French social comedy, and established the form as one of the more enduring types of comedy. In the plays, he analyzed many aspects of his contemporary society and penetrated into the essential characteristics of various types of people. His critical insights into the nature of types like the hypocrite, the misanthrope, and the miser remain almost as urbane today as they were when written.

Molière was born in Paris, France, in 1622, the son of rather prosperous middle-class parents, who sent him to good schools to be trained in law. However, somewhere along the way, Molière fell in love with the theater and was to devote his entire life to the theatrical profession.

He probably received a law degree in about 1641-42, but thereafter he joined three other people to form a theater company called *L'Illustre Théâtre*. At this time acting was not held in the highest esteem, to begin with, so when Molière consorted with a woman in his troupe named Madeleine Béjart, it only proved to his bourgeois parents that their son was lost. Molière was actually to remain acquainted with this woman for the rest of her life. In 1662, he married nineteen-year-old Armande Béjart, a vivacious flirt who gathered numerous admirers around her, much to the chagrin of her husband. Legend has it that four years later, Armande would become the model for the capricious and flirtatious Célimène in *The Misanthrope*. She did however, bear him three children before his untimely death in 1673, the third child being born in 1672, the year before Molière's death.

The company Molière helped establish did not fare too well and went bankrupt during its second season. During this time, he was often plagued by creditors and it was also then that he began to use the name "Molière."

He continued in his career as an actor in another company for about ten more years before he turned his hand to playwriting. In the interim years, he also gained experience in directing and managing. By the time he began to write, he was known as one of the greatest comic actors of his time, and the experience he gained by acting, managing, and directing contributed to his understanding of what was theatrically effective and provided him with a thorough knowledge of the theater.

The production of Molière's first play, *The Romantic Ladies*, established a reputation for him that was to endure for the rest of his life. Since this play, like his later ones, dealt rather severely with certain aspects of society, satirizing affectations of speech, among other things, many people of high society objected to the portrayal because it hit too close to home. Almost every play that Molière wrote met objections, usually from the faction in society which he ridiculed. The most open and hostile objections centered upon the production of *Tartuffe*, a play which satirizes religious hypocrites and certain aspects of the church. *Tartuffe* was perennially banned, and Molière had to resort to using his influence with the king to get permission for the play to be produced.

Even after Molière became a successful and rather wealthy playwright because of his shrewd business ability, he continued acting in his own plays. It was during a production of his last play, *The Imaginary Invalid*, in which Molière had a part, that he complained of ill health; he died the same night.

Because of his criticism of many aspects of life, Molière was denied a proper burial and was only grudgingly allowed a burial plot in sanctified ground. His plays, however, have transcended the times and the society for which they were written; and the very probes into human nature which caused him such difficulty during his lifetime have gained for him a lasting reputation as dramatist and satirist.

NEOCLASSICAL COMEDY

The "romantic comedy" (Shakespeare's variety) of the period directly preceding Molière's emphasized a kind of plot development which was to be rejected by Molière. Comedies written during the Renaissance period were often similar in outline: a complex situation involving a number of characters, misunderstandings, mistaken identities, and the like is created, then an element of suspense is added, and finally all of the complications are unraveled to the satisfaction of most of the characters. "Romantic comedy" had nothing directly to do with contemporary society; indeed, the settings of most of the plays are in faraway kingdoms or "exotic" foreign countries. Any immediate social reference would usually be embedded in the fanciful story of the play.

In the neoclassical period, however, contemporary society became one of the central concerns of the comic dramatist. An age of balance, precision, and regularity — as the neoclassical age is generally considered — insists upon certain norms of behavior in society. The "irregular," eccentric individual had to be laughed back to normalcy. While the same principle may have applied to Shakespearean comedy in general, the identification of actual social types in the plays was not quite so obvious as it became with Molière. The very subject matter for neoclassical comedy became problems implicit in society. Although this type of drama, "social comedy," necessitates a certain faith in the value of society, the dramatist does not necessarily condone all of the aspects of his particular contemporary society. Laughter is evoked when a character departs in his behavior from the sanctioned norms of society, but it is also evoked often enough from the very "norm" itself.

Repeated emphasis in neoclassical comedy is placed upon "rational" perspective and behavior. As late as Voltaire's

Candide the irrational acceptance of a popular philosophy is ridiculed. In England, earlier, Jonathan Swift was concerned with rationality in a similar fashion. In many of Molière's plays the characters, even when they are in error, maintain that they are acting from purely rational motives and in a most collected manner. They repeatedly express the exasperated wish that the rest of the world would act equally as rationally. A reader might be surprised at the number of times the word "reasonable" appears in this context in Molière's plays. It is often used by opposing characters to add strength to their own contradictory points of view.

Neoclassical comedy also calls for a degree of intellectual detachment from the audience which other types of plays do not. Tragedy demands sympathy for the protagonist; other kinds of comedy — like "Romantic comedy" — individualize characters and allow for a certain identification with them. This detachment forces us to see a fop as a fop (the type) and thus comic, rather than as an individual evoking pity. The more complex of Molière's characters verge on winning our sympathies for the moment — but more in the sense that we can see his point of view in ridiculing society than in feeling a deep pity for him as a suffering human being.

MOLIERE'S COMIC TECHNIQUE

Molière was a master of the neoclassical comedy. He possessed a wide knowledge of the society in which he lived, and had long training in the theater before he ever began writing. As an actor, he knew the various technical difficulties connected with acting and he understood all the various problems connected with staging a play. His sense of theater was unsurpassed.

As a peak representative of neoclassical comedy, Molière apparently accepted the importance of society and emphasized throughout his plays a concern for man in the social order of things. He was also a shrewd observer of the varying manners of his age and was able to present his plays with an intellectual detachment and sanity which has preserved the plays through the centuries. To use terms associated with the period, Molière possessed that "sweet reasonableness" and "critical serenity" which allowed him to view mankind with enough detachment to see both the comic foibles inherent in the individual and the flaws also inherent in the society in which man must function.

Molière's technique, therefore, grows out of those qualities emphasized for all neoclassical comedy. First, his characters were chosen to represent types of people or some generalized aspect of human nature. Thus, in his plays we have the "misanthrope" or the man who despises people, the "religious hypocrite" in *Tartuffe* or the new enthusiastic convert in the same play, the "miser" as a type, or the middle-class bourgeois who has pretensions to being a gentleman.

Second, after choosing the type of character, Molière would create certain situations which would illustrate the absurdities of this type. He exposes the character to situations which demonstrate the character's deviation from the normal, socially accepted behavior. By this method, the audience soon becomes aware of both the nature of the type and the nature of his incongruity with society. One of the most apparent uses of this technique would be in *Tartuffe* or *The Bourgeois Gentleman.* In both plays, there is a series of scenes in which the actions of the main character are seen to be totally absurd and totally in opposition to the general accepted behavior of the society at large.

These situations must continue until the audience is able to completely evaluate both the type and his deviations from the norm. On this point, there is critical disagreement as to how successfully Molière accomplishes his aim. For example, in *The Misanthrope,* the full extent of Alceste's absurdity is not completely revealed until the final and closing scenes. However in *The Bourgeois Gentleman,* the absurdity of the type is fully revealed by the midpoint of the play, and it is questionable whether the last part of the play can be justified as necessary in terms of this theory.

Fourth, in continuation of the above point, the play should end when the characters have been fully exposed and we can sufficiently evaluate their absurdities. In a play like *Tartuffe*, however, Molière, for varied reasons, continues the play for an entire act longer than is often thought necessary. The fifth act of *Tartuffe* contributes little or nothing to the total view of the play and is a blatant piece of flattery to the king.

Last, since Molière's aim was to reveal characters in exemplary situations and expose their absurdities, he never included any background on the characters. All we know of the person consists of those basic traits seen operating at the moment on the stage. Molière's purpose, then, was to have characters who exemplify certain human traits and no additional background material is necessary. For example, in *Misanthrope*, we know that there is an impending lawsuit which later in the play is decided against Alceste, but we are never given any clear notion of what the suit is all about.

Tartuffe

LIST OF CHARACTERS

Orgon

The central character who comes under the influence of the hypocrite Tartuffe.

Elmire

Orgon's second wife who represents a reasonable attitude toward life.

Damis

Orgon's son and Elmire's stepson who tries to prove Tartuffe a hypocrite and succeeds only in having himself disinherited.

Mariane

Orgon's daughter who is in love with Valère and who is being forced to marry Tartuffe.

Madame Pernelle

Orgon's mother who is totally deluded by Tartuffe.

Valére

Mariane's suitor who is rejected by Orgon in favor of Tartuffe.

Cléante

Orgon's brother-in-law who tries to get everyone to view things with calm and reason.

Tartuffe

The religious hypocrite who weasels his way into Orgon's confidence and then betrays him.

Dorine

Mariane's maid who functions as a cunning manipulator and commentator on the actions of the play.

Flipote

Madame Pernelle's maid.

M. Loyal

An officer of the law who serves Orgon's eviction papers.

GENERAL PLOT SUMMARY

Madame Pernelle is visiting her son's house and uses the opportunity to criticize all the members of the house and to praise their boarder, Tartuffe, because he is a man of such holiness and zeal. The others present offer objections to Tartuffe, maintaining that he is false and hypocritical, but Madame Pernelle will not entertain such thoughts. As she leaves, she admonishes everyone to follow Tartuffe's precepts.

After Madame Pernelle's departure, Cléante and Dorine talk about Tartuffe and both agree that he has beguiled Orgon. Damis wonders if his father will still allow Mariane to marry Valère; Damis must know Orgon's feelings because he wants to marry Valère's sister. He asks Cléante to question Orgon about his promise to allow the marriage to take place.

Orgon arrives and seems much more concerned about the welfare of Tartuffe than he is about his wife's illness. Cléante tries to discuss Tartuffe with Orgon, but fails and discovers that Orgon is only interested in singing Tartuffe's praises. When Orgon is questioned about the intended wedding, he dodges the issues and refuses to give a direct answer. When his daughter arrives, Orgon tells her that he wants to ally Tartuffe with his house; this he can best do by Mariane's marrying Tartuffe. Mariane is so shocked that she cannot believe her ears.

After Orgon departs, Dorine, the maid, reprimands Mariane for not having refused to marry Tartuffe. Mariane's beloved, Valère, arrives and accuses her of consenting to the marriage. Dorine listens to them argue and then, after they are reconciled, she promises to help them expose Tartuffe's hypocrisy.

Damis, incensed about Tartuffe, is also determined to reveal Tartuffe's hypocrisy, and, as he hears Tartuffe's approach, he hides in the closet. Elmire, Orgon's wife, arrives and Tartuffe, thinking that they are alone, makes some professions of love to Elmire and suggests that they become lovers. Having heard Tartuffe make such a proposition, Damis reveals himself and threatens to expose Tartuffe. When Orgon arrives, Damis tries to inform his father about Tartuffe's proposition, but Orgon is so blind that he thinks his own son is evil in trying to defame Tartuffe's good name and he immediately disinherits his son. Alone with Tartuffe, Orgon reveals that he plans to make Tartuffe his sole heir and also his son-in-law. They leave to execute this plan.

Cléante later confronts Tartuffe and tries to reason with him, but Tartuffe will only respond in religious clichés, and as soon as the opportunity presents itself, he hastily excuses himself from the room. Orgon and Elmire arrive, and when she hears Orgon's plans, she extracts a promise from him to hide in some concealed place and observe Tartuffe's actions. Orgon consents and Elmire sends for Tartuffe. When he arrives, he is accosted by Elmire, and soon he begins to make not only his declarations of love to Elmire but also derogatory comments about Orgon.

Finally convinced of Tartuffe's hypocrisy, Orgon emerges and orders him from the household. Tartuffe then reveals that legally he is now the owner of the house, since Orgon has signed over all his property. Alone with his wife, Orgon reveals that he is frightened because, earlier, he had entrusted some secret documents to Tartuffe's care — documents which could ruin Orgon's trusted position in the court.

When Orgon's mother arrives, he cannot convince her that Tartuffe is a hypocrite; it is only when news arrives that Tartuffe is having the entire family evicted that Madame Pernelle is convinced. Tartuffe brings with him officers of the court, but, as the family is about to be evicted, the officer reveals that the king has seen through the hypocrisy of Tartuffe and has ordered him to be imprisoned for this and for other crimes. The king has also restored to Orgon all of his rightful property.

SUMMARIES AND COMMENTARIES

ACT I – SCENE 1

Summary

Madame Pernelle is ready to leave her son's house because she finds it appalling that no one pays any attention to her. She offers everyone her good advice and everyone tends to contradict or ignore her. She tells her grandson, Damis, that he is a dunce; her granddaughter, who seems so shy and demure, is censured for being so secretive. She accuses her daughter-in-law, Elmire, of being too free with money, and she accuses Cléante, Elmire's brother, of being too worldly. The only person who has her approval is Tartuffe — to her, the epitome of perfection.

Damis and the maid Dorine both argue that Tartuffe is a bigot and a hypocrite, but Madame Pernelle is unconvinced; she thinks that the others don't like Tartuffe because this "good man" reminds them of their sins and reveals their moral flaws. She also maintains that there are too many visitors who come and, upon leaving, gossip about the family. Dorine snaps that the old woman condemns out of jealousy; before Madame Pernelle grew old, she was a part of the world and now, fearing that the world is going to drop her, she spends her time criticizing it. Madame Pernelle will not tolerate such comments and upon leaving, reminds the company that they are lucky to have such a holy man as Tartuffe dwelling beneath their roof.

Commentary

First of all, the reader should note the division of the scenes. It was a tradition in the French neoclassical theater for a scene to end when a new character appeared on stage or when a character left the stage. Sometimes when the entrance or exit occurs within the length of a few short exchanges of dialogue, this practice seems highly artificial; however, in the actual production of the play, none of these scene divisions interfered with the continuity of the action, since the curtain was never lowered except at the end of an act. Some modern editions do not adhere to these divisions, but the reader can use the above explanation to determine the scene divisions.

In the early history of the theater and well past Molière's time, the audience was not the attentive and polite audience which we expect in today's theater. Instead, it was often an unruly group; many of the public came to the theater to be seen rather than to see a play. In addition, often there were prostitutes and vendors moving among the audience. The author, therefore, had to find some dramatic way of capturing his audience's attention. In Shakespeare's *Hamlet* or *Macbeth*, for example, remember that the play opens with the appearance of a ghost in one case and with witches in the other. These were dramatic ways of immediately catching the attention of the audience. Thus, Molière must also create a dramatic and theatrical way of opening his play. He does this by having Madame Pernelle ready to leave as the curtain opens, and constantly throughout the scene, she is on the point of leaving, but then feels the necessity of coming back to admonish or criticize one more person.

Consequently, the play opens with several people (seven) on the stage amid a flurry of activity.

The comedy of this first scene is based partly upon the physical activity on the stage. One must visualize the flustery and overbearing woman dominating all conversation and forcing her own egotistical opinions upon the others. Intellectually, the comedy is based upon the anticipation of seeing this woman proven wrong—an expectation which will not be satisfied until the third act. By this, we mean that part of Molière's comic technique is to set up a character or characters who are deviations from the norm of behavior and gradually reveal the absurdity of these characters.

Consequently, we must observe how Molière is able to convey to the audience that Madame Pernelle is the absurd deviation from the norm. First, Molière has subtitled his play "The Hypocrite" (or as it is sometimes translated "The Impostor.") Thus, from the mere subtitle, we know that Madame Pernelle is praising a man unworthy of praise.

Second, when there is a stage filled with characters and only one person is holding the opinion that Tartuffe is a holy and pious man, then the tendency is to side with the many and not with the one. Third, the manner in which Madame Pernelle defends Tartuffe automatically makes the audience doubt both her credibility and his honesty. That is, she is so overbearing, so talkative, and so superficial that we immediately tend to dismiss her opinions as absurd.

Finally, when each person on the stage is criticized for the most minute aspect of his behavior and when we know that Madame Pernelle's advice to the people on the stage is absurd, then we tend to doubt the validity of all her advice. She tells her grandson that he is a fool; she accuses her granddaughter of being secretive; she reprimands Elmire for dressing elaborately; she dislikes Cléante because he is filled with worldly counsel; the maid Dorine is too impudent; in other words, the entire world is wrong and only she and Tartuffe are right. Thus, to conclude, since everyone on stage who seems normal and rational is against Tartuffe and the only person who praises him is a blustery and talkative old woman, the audience would immediately sense Tartuffe's true character. And, if we examine the comments of the other characters on the stage, the things they say seem to represent good logic and a good evaluation of society in general.

Cléante, who will function throughout the play as the voice of reason, tries to get Madame Pernelle to see that one cannot stop foolish gossip however much one tries. To refuse to have guests would only cause another type of gossip to arise.

In conjunction with Cléante's sound reasoning is the equally sound and realistic voice of the maid Dorine. She functions as a practical, common-sense viewpoint; she calls a spade a spade. If there is gossip, she feels that it has to come from someone named Daphné who gossips about other people only in order to conceal her own indiscretions. Furthermore, Dorine points out the psychologically sound idea that Daphné was once a great flirt until she began to lose her own beauty. Dorine reminds Madame Pernelle that as long as that woman could attract people she was a great flirt, but now that she is no longer captivating, she retires and condemns others for the same vice which she practiced.

Madame Pernelle, however, has a closed mind and insists only that people should be proud to have such a virtuous man as Tartuffe living with them. Of course, later, she will have to eat these words, and she will have to acknowledge that she has been deluded. The audience now can easily see that she is deceived. She has talked about the virtues of Tartuffe, but at the same time she has not demonstrated a single virtue of her own; this is seen especially in the crude manner in which she orders her own servant about.

One of the interesting techniques in this first act is the use of the maid, Dorine. She is the source of much of the comedy and she is also the voice of practical reasoning. It has since become a traditional stage technique in comedy to have a servant who can get the best of his so-called superiors.

ACT I – SCENES 2-3

Summary

When Madame Pernelle leaves, Cléante refuses to see her to the door because he has heard enough of her foolish prattle. He cannot understand how Tartuffe has so totally deceived her, but then Dorine points out that her master, Orgon, is even more deceived: one would actually have to see for himself in order to believe what great folly Orgon has fallen into. She explains the many ways in which Tartuffe has already duped Orgon and the many tedious sermons which they all have to listen to constantly.

Elmire returns and tells Cléante that, since her husband is coming, she feels the need of a rest before seeing him. Damis requests Cléante to question Orgon about Mariane's wedding because if Mariane is not allowed to marry Valère, Damis would not be received as a suitor for Valère's sister.

Commentary

These two short scenes serve mainly to establish the influence which Tartuffe has over Orgon and to push the plot forward by introducing the matter of the wedding.

In Dorine's analysis of the influence which Tartuffe has over Orgon, we see again that she is the shrewd, practical realist who sees directly into the fundamental principles of things. Her explanation of Tartuffe's effect allows the reader to side with Dorine and, when Orgon appears on the stage, we are then prepared for Dorine's interpretation of her master. In other words, Molière is making certain that we have the right perspective.

In characterizing the influence which Tartuffe has over Orgon, Dorine says that Orgon loves Tartuffe better than "mother, child, or wife." This statement will appear several more times in the play, and in its purest sense characterizes the religious man who will give up all earthly ties in order to follow a saintly life. At this point, the idea is not fully developed; it will be later on. At present, it is enough to note that the idea surely applies to Orgon, because in the next scenes, he shows no concern for the wishes of his own daughter.

In a sense the only plot element in the play is the question of whether or not Mariane will be allowed to marry Valère. It is typical in Molière that the actual plot of the drama is considerably less important than his intent to satirize certain types of individuals. Consequently, the plot, for what it is, is not established until the third scene when Damis asks Cléante to inquire about the forthcoming wedding between his sister and Valère.

ACT I – SCENES 4-5

Summary

When Orgon arrives from the country, he immediately inquires about his household. But he ignores Dorine's report of his wife's indisposition and, instead, inquires about the health of Tartuffe. Each time he shows concern for Tartuffe, Dorine tells him more bad news about his wife. Totally unresponsive to his wife's problems, Orgon continually feels sorrow for Tartuffe, who has fared well in his host's absence.

After Dorine leaves, Cléante tries to get Orgon to be more reasonable. Orgon, however, will hear no criticism against Tartuffe and characterizes him as an excellent man. Orgon describes some of the pious things which have endeared Tartuffe to him and, when Cléante tries to point out that some of these acts are obviously false piety, Orgon accuses Cléante of being too much a part of the current rage against true piety. Cléante points out that good deeds characterize a religious man, not loud protestations of devotion.

Orgon listens to Cléante, but ignores every word and is about to leave when Cléante detains him to ask about the forthcoming wedding between Mariane and Valère. He points out that Orgon has already given his word of honor that the marriage will take place. Orgon, rather than answering Cléante directly, maintains that he will be guided by the will of heaven in this and all other undertakings. Cléante senses that something is going wrong and plans to warn Valère.

Commentary

Scene 4 is a highly comic scene which leaves no doubt in anyone's mind that Orgon is completely duped and is also blinded in his devotion to Tartuffe. The comic technique of this relies basically upon the servant-master relationship in which we have the shrewd servant who ridicules the stupid master and the master who is never aware that he is being ridiculed. The other comic technique is simply the use of repetition. That is, when Orgon shows no interest in his wife's condition, she then tells him how content and well off Tartuffe is. That Orgon then feels sorry for Tartuffe and ignores his wife's condition indicates the extent of his folly. This lack of concern verifies Dorine's statement earlier that Orgon does not care for his wife or children and could easily dispose of them in his enthusiastic attention to Tartuffe. Dorine's closing remarks carry a sharp point of wit as she laughs in her master's face without his knowing it.

In Scene 5, Cléante tries to admonish Orgon for being so wrapped up in Tartuffe that he does not even realize that the servant is ridiculing him, but at the same time he admits that Orgon is deserving of the ridicule.

Orgon's first attempted defense of Tartuffe is highly revealing in that, when he tries to explain exactly what virtues Tartuffe possesses, he can only stutter, "He's a man . . . a man who . . . an excellent man." Obviously, Orgon is so influenced by this man that he has apparently lost all ability to evaluate anything rationally.

Orgon's speech also sets the tone for all of the objections to the play during Molière's times. It should now be apparent that the clergy and others did not object to the obvious portrayal of a hypocrite in religious matters. Even though it was true that in the earliest productions, Tartuffe was often depicted as a member of the clergy, such forthright satire would not be highly objectionable, even to the clergy. Ironically, the objections rested upon Orgon's ready acceptance of many of the Christian doctrines and on his perversion of these basic doctrines. When Orgon says that Tartuffe "has taught me to view this dunghill of a world with scorn," he is expressing one of the cardinal principles of a saintly man. Many of his other expressions are also those which are admired in the saints of the church. The behavior of Orgon is revered when that same behavior is evinced by one of the church's saints. For example, a saint is a person who would despise the world and spend all of his time learning to reject the things of this world. Orgon thus exhibits the qualities which would define a saint.

Orgon also says that his soul has been freed from all earthly ties or loves. If his brother, mother, wife, or children were to die, it would not matter to him. Again, the saint is often seen as a person who puts aside his earthly cares and allegiances in favor of more spiritual matters. This stems from the very roots of Christian doctrine, since the true saint cannot allow any earthly loves to interfere with his divine mission.

Finally, in terms of the norm in society, a saint is a person who by definition is abnormal. He is separated from the mainstream of society and stands apart from the average person. Consequently, for Molière to choose a person such as Orgon to adopt the language of the saint and then to have him mouth certain basic Christian doctrines while at the same time acting so foolish and contrary to common sense—the combination of these qualities caused many people to react strongly against the play and demand that it be banned.

We should also remember that Molière wrote in an age that demanded a certain adherence to common sense, good conduct, and rational behavior. Even though Orgon is advocating important Christian principles, we cannot say that he is conducting his life by any principles of good sense, thus causing the audience to condemn not only his actions but the very Christian doctrines which he advocates. For example, note how often Cléante exclaims, "Good God, have you lost all of your common sense!"

What becomes apparent to the audience in Orgon's description of Tartuffe is that he is a person who plays upon the outward acts of religion. Orgon describes how loudly Tartuffe prays in church, how obsequious he is in performing minor tasks in the church, and what humility he has in accepting only small gifts. These descriptions make it obvious that Tartuffe is using the outward acts of religion to appear religious.

Cléante, who has never met Tartuffe, recognizes the hypocrisy in such acts and tries to reason with Orgon. Cléante suggests that even in religious matters a man must employ common sense and criticizes the apparent "affected zeal" and the "pious hypocrisy" practiced by Tartuffe. He suggests that the truly religious person has no desire to parade his "holiness" before the world for all to see. Furthermore, Cléante points out that the truly religious man does not spend his time chiding and criticizing others; instead, he is moderate and humane, trying to teach by good examples rather than by vituperative criticism. Cléante concludes that Orgon has been greatly deluded by Tartuffe.

Orgon, however, is so deluded that he cannot listen to any criticism. The high degree of his absurd deviation from the norm of behavior is rapidly becoming apparent to the audience and we now observe how far he will go in his absurdities before regaining his rationality.

Act I closes with Cléante inquiring about Orgon's promise that his daughter could marry Valère. To the right-thinking religious man, a word of honor is binding. Yet Orgon, who has previously given his word of honor that the marriage can take place, begins now to retract. The first act, which opened with the blustering of Orgon's mother, closes with the fickle equivocations of Orgon.

ACT II — SCENES 1-2

Summary

Orgon finds his daughter alone and asks her if she will obey him in all things. Being a dutiful daughter, she tells him it is her pleasure always to please her father. Therefore, Orgon instructs her to say that she finds Tartuffe to be a very worthy man and that she would be delighted to be his wife. Mariane then points out that if she said such a thing, she would be lying. Orgon, howered, announces that he is determined to have Tartuffe allied to the family by marrying Mariane.

Dorine, the maid, interrupts the conversation by arriving unexpectedly. She is laughing about a joke she has heard — a joke concerning Orgon's plan to allow Tartuffe to marry Mariane. When Orgon tells her that it is no joke, that it is the truth, Dorine laughs harder, thinking that it is still a joke; she refuses to believe her master.

When Orgon refuses to retract, Dorine points out that Tartuffe has no property and no social alliances; such a man should be content to devote his time to his prayers. She also points out that Tartuffe, who theoretically brags about his poverty, also brags about his lands and birth — a matter which seems, for Dorine, a contradiction. Failing to convince Orgon, she then suggests that if a girl is forced to marry a man whom she dislikes, she is sure to be unfaithful.

Orgon tries his best to ignore her, but finally orders her to be quiet, and Dorine goes to the side as Orgon continues to try and influence his daughter. Then Dorine comments to herself about the absurdity of the situation until Orgon is so infuriated that he has to go out for a walk to calm himself.

Commentary

As Act I closed with the exposure of Orgon's wrongheaded obstinacy, Act II opens with his putting into action his plans to marry his daughter to Tartuffe. And, without having met Tartuffe yet, the audience immediately recognizes this as an absurd act; immediately, we wonder how much more ridiculous Orgon will become before he regains his sanity. Thus, again, we see that Molière's technique is one of exposing a character's deviation from the norm of behavior until the audience is ready to thoroughly condemn his absurd behavior.

By trying to make Mariane say that she thinks highly of Tartuffe, Orgon takes advantage of the fact that his daughter is a dutiful daughter, who would obey him. It is paradoxical that Orgon, in his enthusiasm, would actually have his daughter lie about her feelings, merely because he is determined to have the wedding take place. At the end of this scene, Orgon has gone to a further ridiculous extreme in determining to force Mariane to marry Tartuffe.

In terms of the development of character and plot, the reader should be aware that Mariane only functions as a convenient vehicle for the other characters. As a person, she merely functions as an intermediary between the other, more central, characters.

When Dorine enters, we have some delightful comic techniques developed. One of the principal comic devices throughout the drama is the incredible statements made by a character and the absolute wonder of the other characters. Orgon finds himself now in a position of being laughed at because Dorine feels that his suggestions are so absurd that he could not be serious and, instead, is making a joke involving the entire family. The difficulty Orgon has in convincing Dorine of his serious intent is inherently comic and also functions as a commentary on the absurdity of trying to get Mariane to marry Tartuffe.

The second comic technique involves the wise servant contradicting and ridiculing the master. That Dorine is a wise servant is shown in the logical arguments she puts forth against the marriage: (1) she suggests that Tartuffe is not a pious person who worships poverty; this cannot be because he is constantly bragging about his lands and his noble birth. Such wordly pride does not blend with his pretended piety; (2) if Tartuffe really cared for only saintly matters, he would not be interested in marriage or finances; and (3) if one marries a girl to someone whom she detests, this is the easiest way to make a wife violate her marriage vows.

Orgon, in the grips of his absurd proposal, cannot listen to rational arguments. Consequently, Dorine begins to ridicule him. The comic technique then involves the master making a serious assertion only to be cut by a sarcastic observation from the maid. Furthermore, the exasperation which Orgon causes by his proposal is then reversed as Dorine exasperates him. She pretends that she cannot be silent because she loves her master so much that she can't let him make such a dreadful error.

Throughout the scene, we note then that the servant is in control of the situation—and the master. Consequently, since Orgon cannot control even his servant, he is then exposed as being even more ridiculous.

ACT II – SCENES 3-4

Summary

After Orgon leaves to recover his composure, Dorine immediately begins to attack Mariane, who did not stand up to her father and openly refuse to marry Tartuffe. Mariane defends herself by saying that she has lived for so long under her father's strict control that she can't oppose him now. Dorine then begins to paint a picture of what it will be like to marry Tartuffe. She is realistic enough to reject Mariane's idea that she will kill herself rather than marry Tartuffe or disobey her father; such talk is sentimental drivel. When Mariane protests that she knows of no way to defy her father, Dorine then begins to depict all of the horror of what it would be like to be Madame Tartuffe. Mariane is then so horrified of the possibility of having to marry Tartuffe that she is in total despair. Dorine consoles her by promising that they will find some line of action to prevent this absurd situation.

Valère, Mariane's betrothed, arrives and asks Mariane if it is true that she will marry Tartuffe. Mariane responds that it is her father's wish and innocently says that she does not know what to do. Valère interprets this as meaning that she is not seriously opposed to the marriage and then he insultingly advises her to enter into the marriage. Mariane then thinks that Valère no longer cares for her. The two then enter into a ridiculous lovers' quarrel until Dorine can no longer stand it. Just as Valère is about to leave, she drags him back, then stops the departing Mariane and forces them both to admit their love for each other.

Dorine's advice is to pretend to go along with Orgon's plan but to keep postponing the wedding until something can be devised. She says that she is going to enlist the help of anyone she can find.

Commentary

In this scene between Dorine and Mariane, we come to understand that Mariane is the pliable daughter who finds it impossible to defy her father. She does not have the basic common sense of Dorine so as to understand that her father has become an unreasonable tyrant and thus she views her predicament as hopeless.

When Mariane cannot bring herself to oppose her father, then Dorine begins to depict the horrors of being married to Tartuffe. By showing her the distasteful details of marriage to Tartuffe, Dorine is then able to get Mariane to become more firmly resolute in opposing Orgon.

The comedy of Scene 4 depends largely upon physical actions. Dorine retires to the back of the stage, and as we observe the childish arguments between Mariane and Valère, we are constantly aware that Dorine is viewing the entire scene with comic detachment. She is merely waiting to see how absurd the two lovers can become before she steps in to reconcile them. Consequently, the comedy is that of the crossed lovers at cross-purposes, and then the entire scene is lightened by the reconciliation.

To bring about the reconciliation, Dorine must be physically alert and the reader should imaginatively re-create the physical actions called for in this particular scene. For example, Valère is about to exit from one side of the stage when Dorine has to run over and tug him back and, just as she has accomplished this, Mariane is about to exit from the other side, forcing Dorine to rush over and bring her back.

In bringing the lovers together, Dorine is the practical person who tells them that they can argue later but for the present they have to conceive some plan to stop Orgon from carrying out his project. For the present, Dorine gives them sound advice: to pretend to go along with the wedding until they can think of some way of bringing Orgon to his senses.

ACT III – SCENES 1-2

Summary

Orgon's son Damis is raving because he has just heard of his father's plan to force Mariane to marry Tartuffe. He tells Dorine that he is determined to expose Tartuffe as a hypocritical scoundrel. Dorine wants Damis to calm down because she has already arranged for Orgon's wife, Elmire, to talk with Tartuffe, and she furthermore believes that Tartuffe is very much taken with Elmire's charms. The hot-tempered Damis is determined to hear the conference, and when Dorine cannot get rid of him, she hides him in the closet when she hears Tartuffe coming.

Tartuffe arrives, spouting forth pious comments and when he sees Dorine he will not look at her until she takes his handkerchief and covers her bosom with it because "the flesh is weak" and cannot withstand too many temptations. Dorine tells him that she could see him completely naked and not have any unclean thoughts. She then announces that Elmire is coming and she excuses herself.

Commentary

As was noted in the preceding act, Mariane represents the simple, sweet, demure, and obedient daughter. In contrast, we see that the son represents the typical hot-tempered young man whose anger interferes with the trap being set for Tartuffe.

In this opening scene, Dorine is seen setting her plan into motion. As the wise and observant maid, she has noted that in the past Tartuffe seemed smitten with Elmire, and she now feels that Elmire might be able to persuade Tartuffe to reject the proposed marriage. Dorine, then, sets the plan in motion without having any idea that Tartuffe will later trap himself by his infatuation with Elmire. In other words, even though Dorine is responsible for beginning the revelation, not even she is aware of the exact nature of events about to occur.

When Damis hides in the closet to listen to the conversation between Elmire and Tartuffe, Molière is using one of the oldest devices in the theater; that is, the idea of having a person concealed and listening to some type of revelation. This same technique will become the method later by which Orgon is awakened to Tartuffe's hypocrisy.

Scene 2 presents the arrival of Tartuffe. The reader should be aware that Molière has held off presenting this central character until the third act. This is technically called "the delayed emergence." We have now heard about Tartuffe from all sorts of people and we have been anticipating his appearance. Now his actual arrival lives up to our expectations. He walks onto the stage spewing out pious clichés and announcing his intentions very loudly for Dorine and anyone else to hear. His opening remark, "Hang up my hairshirt" sets the tone for his character, in that a hairshirt would be the apparel of penance which a person would never reveal if he actually wore one. Thus when Tartuffe loudly announces that his is to be hung up, we are immediately aware of his hypocritical nature.

As a historical note, when Tartuffe asks Dorine to cover her bosom, and earlier when he loudly proclaims that he is going to the prison to share his money with the prisoners, Tartuffe reveals that he is aligned with a group called The Company of the Holy Sacrament, which undertook to help prisoners and which acted as self-appointed critic of women's dress. The audience in Molière's day would immediately have associated Tartuffe with this organization. And this brotherhood was instrumental in getting the play banned in 1664 and constantly strove to keep it from being produced.

Dramatically, Tartuffe's admonition to Dorine suggests that he is aware of lustful instincts and thus prepares us to accept his downfall because of his lustful desires for Elmire. Dorine's witty repartee places her as the sensible one who sees through Tartuffe's affectations and who understands now that Elmire will have some influence over him.

ACT III—SCENES 3-4

Summary

After Tartuffe inquires about Elmire's health and pays her some obvious compliments, he then expresses his joy at being alone with her. She tells him that she wants to discuss something confidential with him and he responds by saying that he has long wanted to open his heart to her. He takes her hand and expresses his great admiration for her and Elmire draws back. She moves her chair just as he begins to feel her knee and to comment upon the softness of her gown.

Tartuffe pursues, declaring his passion for Elmire. She reminds him that such declarations ill become a pious man, but he replies by pointing out that even religious men can feel the power of such charms as those of Elmire. He then offers her his love with the assurance that she will be safe from gossip and slander because he also will want to protect his name; she can feel quite secure, he says, in having an affair without being discovered.

Elmire rebukes him and tells him that if he does not put an end to the forthcoming marriage between himself and Mariane, she will inform her husband of his proposal.

At this moment, Damis cannot restrain himself any longer and comes forth, asserting his determination to expose Tartuffe for the hypocrite he is. Elmire tries to restrain him, but his hot temper and hatred for the hypocrite are too strong for him to listen to reason.

Commentary

The reader of the play sometimes forgets that the audience would be fully aware that Damis is hiding during this scene and is thus overhearing everything that Tartuffe says to Elmire. This comic technique, called the comedy of concealment, is often used by Molière.

Molière is careful here not to make Tartuffe a hypocrite in the abstract. Tartuffe is very human, a man who has all the basic impulses of any person, and the interest of the play lies partly in the fact that his own passion and desire for Elmire is the flaw that lets him forget his ultimate plan and causes him to abandon the careful disguise he has so far maintained.

Earlier in the play, Dorine had hoped that Elmire could have some influence over Tartuffe, but Tartuffe's passion for

Elmire comes as a surprise to us. The manner in which he cannot control his passion and the way he pursues Elmire, who constantly rebuffs him, constitute the essential comedy of this scene. Tartuffe's hypocrisy—once vicious—now becomes comic as we see the absurd manner in which he uses reverse logic to suggest that a woman is safe in having an affair with a pious man because the pious man himself must be careful to protect his name. Tartuffe's passion, furthermore, is so intense that he cannot discern that Elmire finds him repulsive.

Elmire's primary role is to get Tartuffe to repudiate the marriage between himself and Mariane. To accomplish this, she allows Tartuffe to proceed so far in revealing his love, but rather than making a scene about it or actually revealing his hypocrisy to her husband, her first desire is to prevent the impending marriage. Damis' arrival, with his hot-tempered determination to reveal Tartuffe's treachery, spoils the more reasonable plan put forward by Elmire. Elmire's view is the more rational view as she maintains that a woman should not run and tattle to her husband every time a man makes an overture to her.

ACT III — SCENES 5-7

Summary

Orgon arrives at the opportune moment and Damis tries to reveal that Tartuffe has been trying to seduce Elmire and is thus filled with treachery. He explains that Elmire was not going to reveal the offense because of her gentility, and Elmire responds that she sees no need of ruining her husband's peace of mind when her own sense of honor does not demand it. Then she leaves.

Orgon turns in wonder to Tartuffe, who exclaims in the most religious language that he is wicked, depraved, and deserving of being driven from the house. He would not defend himself against any charge Orgon or Damis wish to level against him.

Immediately, Orgon turns on Damis and reproaches him for trying to impugn a good man's name. Tartuffe suggests that

Orgon should believe Damis' story because while the world takes him to be a good man, he feels that he is the most worthless and the most sinful man in this world. He kneels down and tells Orgon to heap upon him all of the abuse in the world.

Orgon, instead, turns against his son, calling him a villain and an ingrate. Tartuffe, on bended knees, implores that Orgon be gentle with Damis and not harm him. The more Tartuffe begs for tolerance for Damis, the more Orgon turns against his son. Damis refuses to ask pardon of Tartuffe and immediately Orgon disinherits him and throws him out of the house.

Alone with Orgon, Tartuffe offers to leave the house, but Orgon will not hear of it. Instead, he is determined to make his family jealous and to vex them by making Tartuffe his heir and son-in-law. As they leave to draw up the proper documents, Orgon reasserts his belief that Tartuffe is worth more than his wife, his children, or his relatives.

Commentary

When Damis tries to reveal that Tartuffe has tried to make Orgon a cuckold, Elmire does not either affirm or deny the accusation, but merely puts forward the proposition that a wife should not always be running to her husband with tattle (particularly when her husband probably would not believe her). Here, at the close of the third act, Orgon is revealed in his total absurdity. This is the turning point of the drama and the last two acts will be devoted to forcing him to see his own mistakes.

Orgon's absurdity is almost unbelievable, and it shows how completely he is deceived by Tartuffe's hypocrisy. The reader, to fully appreciate this scene, must understand that during the accusation, it is traditional to have Tartuffe assume a most pious attitude, and in some productions he would be reading piously from his prayer book during the entire accusation.

In asking Orgon to believe all the dreadful things about him, he is adopting a basic religious attitude in which the saintly person overexaggerates his own sins. Here, the irony occurs because Tartuffe is guilty of all the crimes he confesses to, yet Orgon refuses to believe him and immediately turns on his son Damis.

In an age in which rational behavior was extolled, this irrational behavior of Orgon's is the height of madness. As Cléante said earlier, even the religious man must, at times, exhibit good common sense and have a practical side to his nature. Orgon, in his enthusiasm for his newfound religion will not even listen to his own son; he angrily disinherits him—an act which might suggest a saint who would deny his family for the sake of spiritual values. However, driving one's son from the house and cursing him can hardly be called the acts of either a religious man or a sane man. Finally, as Orgon plans to sign away all of his property, partly to vex his own family, we see illustrated for us the extent of his religious fanaticism; in other words, such absurdity as can hardly be believed.

ACT IV—SCENES 1-3

Summary

Cléante confronts Tartuffe and suggests that it is not the act of a religious man to cause such strife in a family and to allow a father to disinherit his son. Tartuffe argues that he would love to see Damis reinstated, but he is afraid that people would then interpret his act incorrectly. Cléante points out the warped reasoning in this argument and suggests that he leave vengeance to God. Tartuffe maintains that he has forgiven Damis but finds it wrong to live with someone who smears his name. He also explains that he despises wealth and the only reason he allows Orgon to transfer his property to him is so that it will not fall into wicked hands where it might be used for crime and sin. When Cléante begins to point out the fallacy in this argument, Tartuffe leaves abruptly, saying that he has to attend to certain pious offices.

Elmire, Mariane, and Dorine arrive, asking Cléante to stay and help them convince Orgon of his errors. When Orgon arrives, he presents Mariane with the marriage contract. She pleads on her knees that he not force her to marry Tartuffe; she says she does not resent her father's love for Tartuffe and, if he wishes, Orgon can take all of her property and bestow it on Tartuffe, but she requests that she be left free to choose a husband for herself.

Orgon argues that the more one loathes a man the more noble it will be to marry him because, by so doing, one will be able to mortify one's flesh and make it pure. Cléante starts to offer advice, but Orgon tells him that even though his advice is sound, he will not follow it. Elmire is astounded at Orgon's ability to be continually wrong. She wonders if he would believe his eyes and challenges him to become a part of a plot which would reveal Tartuffe's hypocrisy. Orgon has such faith in Tartuffe that he accepts the challenge.

Elmire sends the others away and tells Orgon to hide under the table and to observe what is about to take place. She asks him to interrupt the interview between her and Tartuffe at any moment that he is convinced that Tartuffe is not the man he pretends to be.

Commentary

In all of Molière's plays there is always at least one character who represents the voice of moderation and rationality, qualities which were greatly admired by the age during which Molière lived. At the beginning of Act IV, it is obvious that Cléante functions as the expression of the reasonable view. In talking with Tartuffe, Cléante displays unassailable logic. He points out that Tartuffe is not acting as a truly religious person should and also demonstrates that Tartuffe's logic is faulty. For example, when Tartuffe tries to justify his taking Orgon's money and property so as to keep it from falling into wicked hands, the irony is double here because there are no more wicked hands than his for it to fall into; then, when Cléante reasons that the burden of handling such money should belong to Damis, that the son should be allowed to bear the burden, and that true religion does not demand that a person be disinherited, Tartuffe is unable to withstand this onslaught of logical consistency. Thus, as Cléante begins to trap Tartuffe by sound reasoning, Tartuffe suddenly realizes his danger and leaves with the hypocritical statement that he has to attend to some pious duties.

Throughout the scene, Cléante does not realize that he is dealing with an unmitigated scoundrel and part of the comedy of this scene depends upon how the scoundrel cleverly escapes the rationalist's traps.

The entire situation becomes more desperate as Orgon insists upon the marriage taking place that very night. This forces everyone concerned to create some plan of action so as to undeceive Orgon.

Mariane's plea to her father to be spared such horror as marriage with Tartuffe arouses the first real note of feeling in Orgon. But, like a true religious fanatic, he forces himself to put aside his more humane values and adhere absolutely to his own religious views. Ironically, his statement that one should mortify the flesh in order to purify it is a strong principle of many religions. The intentional mortification of the flesh is often one of the customs of some monasteries and nunneries and is consistent with many other religious practices. Such statements as these spoken in such an absurd context also contributed to the censoring of the play.

This scene (Scene 3) also contributes to the exposure Orgon's absurdity. For example, when he tells Cléante that though Cléante's advice is correct, he will not follow it, then we begin to doubt Orgon's sanity.

Elmire, who, along with Cléante, represents the true voice of reason, must now step in and bring an end to the absurdity. When she says that she is astounded at Orgon's capacity to be wrong, she expresses the thoughts of all the readers and the audience. Orgon refuses to believe her accusations about Tartuffe because, earlier, Elmire had refused to be indignant. In true rational fashion, Elmire explains that she dislikes the type of prudish woman who screams about any flirtation. She herself offers a polite and distant rebuff and, therefore, is never involved in an embarrassing position.

In spite of all of Elmire's explanations, Orgon refuses to accept her story. When she challenges him to be present at a scene where she can reveal the fact that Tartuffe is a hypocrite, Orgon accepts the challenge only because he is certain that he is right. Elmire is, however, confident of the outcome because she knows that lustful men such as Tartuffe can easily be trapped by their passions.

ACT IV – SCENES 4-8

Summary

Alone with her husband, Elmire instructs Orgon to hide under a table and not to be surprised by some strange behavior on her part. She informs him that she will be only too glad to drop the entire act whenever he is fully satisfied that Tartuffe is a hypocrite who is determined to seduce her. She also reminds Orgon to save her in case Tartuffe advances too far too rapidly.

When Tartuffe arrives, Elmire has him close the door so that they will not be caught as they were earlier by Damis. She then confesses how glad she is to see him. Tartuffe is at first confused by her change until Elmire explains that women are by nature reluctant to confess their love and that her objection to the marriage with Mariane was caused by jealousy. Tartuffe says that he will not be fully convinced until he has more concrete proof and advances toward Elmire. She restrains him by asking time to catch her breath. In order to delay his advances, she inquires if her love might not be offensive to Heaven, toward which Tartuffe professes such reverence. Tartuffe assures her that his purity of intent will be accepted in Heaven's eyes and that there is not sin when that sin committed in secret. Only the scandal of having the sin known can make the act a sin.

Elmire says loudly that she will have to yield to his desires, and if it is a sin for her to yield, then the person who drove her to the sin must be held responsible. She delays him by asking him to open the door and look out to see if anyone is around, especially her husband. Tartuffe says disparagingly that Orgon is so stupid that even if he saw them he would doubt his sight. Nevertheless, Elmire insists that he go out to look.

After he is gone, Orgon emerges from his hiding place, completely astounded. Elmire tells him to return to hiding until he is completely satisfied, but Orgon is now convinced of Tartuffe's hypocrisy. As Tartuffe is returning, Orgon hides behind Elmire and then immediately accosts Tartuffe and orders him from the house. Tartuffe then reminds Orgon that the house now belongs to him and that Orgon — not Tartuffe — is the one who must leave.

When Orgon is alone with his wife, he confesses that he is frightened about the deed he signed and also about a certain strongbox that should be in Tartuffe's room upstairs. They leave to ascertain its whereabouts.

Commentary

During the entire episode concerning Elmire's exposure of Tartuffe, the reader must remember that the comedy is more apparent to the viewing audience than it is to the reader because the audience is constantly aware that Orgon is hiding under the table, and, at various moments, the audience would have glimpses of Orgon as he momentarily emerges from his hiding place.

When Elmire tells her husband to stop her whenever he has seen enough to satisfy his doubts and when he has been completely convinced, the situation illustrates Molière's general view of comedy as explained elsewhere. Molière, for example, would always show his main character in suffient episodes until that character's total absurdity was exposed. Here, Elmire will continue in her charade with Tartuffe until her husband cries "enough." Her final remonstrance to him is that he is to save her from her plight because she does not want to carry the pretended rendezvous too far.

Consequently, part of the comedy of the scene relies upon Orgon's refusal to be convinced. For example, after a couple of speeches, Elmire feels that Tartuffe has already said enough to prove that he is out to seduce her. She constantly coughs and talks to the table in a very loud voice, hoping that her husband will put an end to the farce. It is, however, even more comic when Orgon refuses to believe what he hears and allows his wife to be subjected to further indignities. However, from the perspective of the audience, the comedy lies in the way that Elmire holds off Tartuffe's advances while her husband remains stupefied under the table. The scene could be played with a great deal of physical action as Elmire verbally expresses her devotion for Tartuffe, but continually moves away from him.

Furthermore, Elmire feels that Tartuffe's religious hypocrisy is fully revealed in the manner that he suggests that he will be responsible for any sin which they might commit.

After coughing loudly a number of times and still not being rescued by her husband, Elmire finally pretends to consent to the seduction, but conceives of another ruse to gain time by asking Tartuffe to see if anyone is watching. She pretends to be afraid that her husband might catch them. At this point, Tartuffe finally seals his fate by saying that Orgon is too stupid to understand—even if he caught them.

It seems that only when Tartuffe insults Orgon personally does he finally enrage Orgon sufficiently to make him emerge from his hiding place and denounce his friend. The irony is that he would allow his wife to be put in a compromising position, but only when *he* was the subject of a personal affront would he denounce Tartuffe as a scoundrel. Consequently, the comedy stems from a type of delayed emergence as we notice Orgon taking so long to be convinced and, finally, being convinced only when he is revealed as an object of contempt.

In Scene 6, after Orgon has been so adamant in his view that only *he* is correct, we delight in Elmire's sarcasm when she tells him to go back to his hiding place until he is completely convinced. Dorine will later chide him for being too stubborn for too long.

In Scene 7, we take delight in finally having the scoundrel Tartuffe confronted with his own hypocrisy. But when Orgon says that he has long suspected Tartuffe and thought that he would soon catch him in some type of hypocrisy, there is no evidence to support Orgon's claim. In fact, since he was so hard to convince in the preceding scenes, we must assume that he cannot accept all of the indications about his own stupidity.

The scene offers another reversal. After Tartuffe's hypocrisy is exposed, the tables are turned when Tartuffe reveals that he is now master of the house and that it will be Orgon who will have to leave.

Molière's technique here is not to dwell upon Orgon's stupidity — it would be too easy to merely make him the butt of more sarcasm. Instead, once illuminated, Orgon then feels the weight of his own stupidity by being made the victim of Tartuffe's machinations. Molière does not allow us to revel in Orgon's mortification, but immediately makes us feel a bit sympathetic for him, since he now stands in danger of losing everything.

The final scene of the act offers one more bit of suspense as Orgon states his concern about a certain strongbox which we later discover contains some important papers pertaining to the State.

ACT V — SCENES 1-2

Summary

Orgon explains that the strongbox contains some papers which were left in his keeping by a friend. If the papers were made public, both Orgon and his friend would be in serious trouble. Earlier, Tartuffe had persuaded Orgon to allow him to keep the entire strongbox and now Tartuffe has taken the secret papers and left.

Orgon cannot understand how anyone could be so base and wicked as Tartuffe; he vows to hate the entire race of men. Cléante advises him to learn to practice restraint. At this point, Orgon's son, Damis, rushes in and tells his father that he will be only too glad to put an end to Tartuffe's life. Again, Cléante has to recommend restraint and moderation.

Commentary

These opening scenes are devoted to pushing the plot forward and explaining the amount of difficulty Orgon has gotten himself into as a result of his devotion to Tartuffe. It is ironic that earlier Orgon was not concerned about money—said to be the root of all evil—but, having now been enlightened he is suddenly very much concerned about worldly things. And, in the same way that Orgon was a fanatic about his devotion to Tartuffe and his religious feelings, now he is seen as being equally fanatic about his hatred of all pious men.

Cléante, who, as noted previously, represents the voice of reason in an age devoted to reason, offers the advice which everyone in the audience in Molière's day would recognize as the ideal of the century. The point of Molière's comedies was to ridicule any type of extravagant emotion and to emphasize the rational middle course. The person who goes to absurd extremes is to be ridiculed and Cléante explains this to Orgon. He advises him to learn to distinguish between the true man of worth and the charlatan, and to be cautious in bestowing his admiration.

As Cléante speaks of the need for a reasoned view of life, Damis runs in, impetuous and hot-tempered, determined to kill Tartuffe. Again, Cléante has to calm him, with words which were obviously spoken to flatter the King of France and the aristocracy in the audience. Cléante maintains that murder is not the proper way of handling things in this enlightened age, and that in a just kingdom such as France, one does not resort to violence.

If we remember that Molière was under the protection of the king and often had to appeal directly to him in order to get his plays produced, then it is understandable why he included such blatant flattery as this.

ACT V — SCENES 3-5

Summary

Madame Pernelle, Orgon's mother, arrives and hears her son explain that he has been the victim of the hypocrite Tartuffe. Madame Pernelle reminds her son that the righteous are always maligned and that the people of the house have been slandering the dear, pious Tartuffe. Orgon tries to explain that he was present and saw everything, but Madame Pernelle refuses to believe anything unfavorable about a man so pious and worthy as Tartuffe. Orgon is at his wits' end when suddenly there appears an officer at the door.

The officer, M. Loyal, announces that he comes with news about Tartuffe. He says that he served Orgon's father and he regrets having to give Orgon an order of eviction. But he explains further that, since everything in the house now belongs to Tartuffe, surely Orgon will honor the law and leave immediately with his family; he hopes that Orgon will honor justice and leave peacefully. He will allow him until tomorrow morning, but he and ten men must stay in the house until then.

When M. Loyal leaves for a moment, Orgon confronts his mother with Tartuffe's treachery, but Dorine reminds Orgon of what he had just said earlier in the day — that material things enslave the spirit and that one's salvation can be endangered by money and property. In a state of confusion, each person maintains that some desperate course of action must be undertaken.

Commentary

The comedy of Scene 3 relies upon a subtle reversal. Earlier, Orgon had refused to believe anything evil about Tartuffe. Now the entire position is reversed and he cannot convince his own

42

mother of Tartuffe's hypocrisy. The utter exasperation which he feels delights the audience because he had earlier so exasperated everyone else by his stubbornness. Note also that the clichés which Madame Pernelle recites about Tartuffe and all righteous men in general are almost exactly the same clichés which Orgon used earlier. The entire episode is summed up for us when Dorine says, "You wouldn't trust us earlier; now it's your turn not to be trusted."

M. Loyal, both by his name and his deportment, is highly comic. He arrives thinking naively that he brings good news because any subject is anxious to obey the law, even if the law is dispossessing him of his house. He is also proud to have been a loyal servant to Orgon's father and he is continuing his loyalty by evicting Orgon. It is indeed comic that every time Orgon starts to object, M. Loyal reminds him that a man so esteemed as Orgon would never think of trying to obstruct justice and a man so upright as Orgon must be pleased to help the law function without difficulty.

Again, Dorine makes Orgon the butt of her sarcasm when she explains that Tartuffe is doing him a favor because only yesterday Orgon said that material things enslave the soul and for salvation one should look to Heaven and not the possessions of this world. She stands as a constant reminder to Orgon of his own stupidity and gullibility.

ACT V – SCENES 6-7

Summary

Mariane's fiancé, Valère, arrives and explains that he has heard in confidence that Orgon is in dire trouble concerning some secret documents which Tartuffe turned over to the king. Tartuffe, he says, has denounced Orgon as a traitor to the king and, since there is a warrant out for Orgon's arrest, Valère has brought money and a carriage and will help Orgon take refuge in the country.

As they are about to leave, officers, accompanied by Tartuffe, arrive. Tartuffe announces that Orgon is now under arrest and the only journey he is going to take is to prison. When Orgon reminds Tartuffe of his indebtedness, Tartuffe merely replies that his first duty is to serve the king and to do that he would sacrifice anything. Cléante tries to use logic against Tartuffe, but Tartuffe only tells the officers to carry out their duty.

The officers, however, perform their duty by arresting Tartuffe and then explain to the rest of the company that the king, who sees into the hearts of all his subjects, knew that Tartuffe was a hypocrite and a liar. The wise and judicious king could never be deluded by such an imposter. Furthermore, the king has invalidated the deed and has pardoned Orgon for keeping the documents of an exile. The wise king thinks much more of a man's virtues than he does of a man's mistakes; Orgon's past loyalty to the king is rewarded and his mistakes are now forgiven.

As Orgon is about to say something to Tartuffe, Cléante advises him to forget the poor wretch and turn his attention to better things. Orgon then gives his daughter Mariane to Valère to be his wife.

Commentary

The arrival of Valère with the news that Tartuffe is closing in thickens the plot and brings everything to a climax. Orgon is suddenly the recipient of a kindness from Valère which he does not deserve in view of the way he has previously treated Valère.

Tartuffe's last chance to be hypocritical occurs when he is faced with his devious ways and he can only respond that his first duty is to his king. In order to serve his king, he would sacrifice anyone. These are almost the same words which Orgon used earlier in the play concerning his newfound religion. Thus, the repetition of these same ideas give a final ironic twist to the situation.

The final scene in the drama has been severely objected to on occasion by critics as being extraneous to the plot. In other words, there is nothing in the earlier parts of the play to indicate that the king will play any role in the play. The ending of a drama should arise out of the parts of the drama which have preceded it and should never be imposed upon the drama in such an artificial manner.

One of the purposes of this ending, however, was to flatter the king, who was Molière's patron. In view of the fact that this particular play was banned several times, it seems necessary that Molière try to offer some type of flattering ending.

The flattery is quite blatant when we realize that the qualities attributed to the king are in direct contrast to those exhibited by Orgon. While Orgon was hasty, domineering, and tyrannical over his family, the king is reported to be judicious and forgiving. And whereas Orgon was completely duped by Tartuffe, the king sees through Tartuffe's hypocrisy immediately. In other words, all of the qualities attributed to the king in the speech by the officer are qualities which were missing in Orgon.

CHARACTER ANALYSES

M. ORGON

Whereas Tartuffe is the obvious hypocrite and scoundrel, Orgon is a much more complex character. In the past he obviously had served the king honorably and had tended to his estates in a rational and dignified manner. It is indicated that prior to the opening of the play, he was a sane man who was respected by his family and friends. The question, therefore, arises as to why he has become such an absurd and ridiculous person.

Some critics have suggested that Orgon, having reached middle age, now needs to attach himself to some type of a religious person and Tartuffe is the most readily accessible. Many scenes in the play ridicule the type of character who can no longer participate successfully in society and who then retires from society and attacks it. Orgon's religious fanaticism, however, seems more directly correlated to his basic nature, which is characterized by Cléante as being extravagant and uncontrolled in all respects.

Having once adopted a life of piety, Orgon tries to become the epitome of the pious person and goes to absurd extremes both in his words and deeds. In contrast, when he discovers the hypocrisy of Tartuffe, he reverses himself and determines to hate and persecute all pious men. Orgon, then, seems to be a man of extravagant excesses who never steers his course along a rational, middle course, but instead, fluctuates between absurd extremes.

It is interesting to note that part of the objection to the play was that Orgon, while expressing many of the basic tenets of the church and, while performing deeds consistent with the devout man, was presented as a dupe whose actions demonstrated that he did not live by the standards of common sense, good taste, moderation, and the other qualities admired by Molière's age.

TARTUFFE

In various editions of the play, Tartuffe is called "The Impostor" or "The Hypocrite." He is a superb scoundrel who can don any pose and become a master of it. As a religious ascetic, he convinces Orgon and Madame Pernelle that he is a devoutly pious and humble man; his obvious hypocrisy, however, is apparent to the reader and to the audience.

Tartuffe's superiority lies in the fact that he can accurately analyze the weaknesses of his victims and then exploit these flaws for his own advantage. He is no simple or ignorant charlatan; instead, he is an alert and adept hypocrite who uses every means to bring about his success.

Molière humanizes Tartuffe by endowing him with one other flaw. His eventual downfall is caused by his lust. Instead of making Tartuffe into an inhuman monster, Molière shows how lust causes the clever hypocrite to lower his mask and reveal his hypocrisy.

DORINE

Dorine is a stock character found in many of Molière's comedies and, in fact, has become a type found in comedies of all periods. She is the wise servant who sees through all pretense, and while being the inferior, in terms of social position, she is the superior in any contest of wits. Surrounded by the deluded and tyrannical Orgon, the hypocritical Tartuffe, and the ineffectual Mariane, Dorine appeals to us through her winning wholesomeness, her directness, and her simple honesty.

In the social structure of the day, Dorine would be part servant and part companion to Mariane. This accounts for her open manner in contrast to a typical servant. She always comes across as the person highly capable of perceiving the truth amid hypocrisy and fanaticism; she is the person who satirically expresses much of the exasperation felt by the audience.

REVIEW QUESTIONS

1. What factors account for Orgon's devotion to Tartuffe?

2. What is gained by having Tartuffe appear for the first time in the third act?

3. Why do Orgon's comments on religion create such a sense of absurdity?

4. How is Dorine indispensable to the plot of the play? How would the play be affected if her part were omitted?

The Misanthrope

LIST OF CHARACTERS

Alceste

The misanthrope who is in love with the flirtatious Célimène and who believes that people should be completely honest at all times.

Philinte

A friend of Alceste's who can see the frailty in man, and who advises tolerance and reasonableness in human relationships.

Oronte

A gentleman-about-town who is also in love with Célimène and who lodges a complaint against Alceste for criticizing a poem he has written.

Célimène

A beautiful young flirt who enjoys gossiping about everybody and who might be said to epitomize the insincerity of this society.

Eliante

A friend and cousin of Célimène's who admires Alceste for his honesty.

Arsinoé

A lady past her prime who tries to intervene in Célimène and and Alceste's relationship.

Acaste

A marquis who considers himself to be very fortunate and well-liked by society.

Clitandre

Another fop who is also in love with Célimène.

GENERAL PLOT SUMMARY

Alceste, the misanthrope, explains to Philinte that he hates mankind because there is so much hypocrisy, deceit, and false flattery in the world that he can't find a man who will speak the truth openly. He asserts that all people should be completely frank and honest with one another. Philinte asks Alceste to be more tolerant because it is a part of human nature to flatter other people and to enjoy a certain amount of gossip. At this point, a fashionable man about town, Oronte, appears and asks Alceste to evaluate a poem he has just written. Alceste reads the poem and gives Oronte an honest answer—the poem is wretched and Oronte should give up trying to write poetry. Oronte, who has asked for an honest answer, is insulted when Alceste speaks frankly, and leaves in an indignant huff. Philinte points out to Alceste that his honesty has created an enemy, when a little innocent flattery would have won him a friend.

When Alceste meets Célimène, the woman he loves, he immediately begins to reproach her for her coquettish and flirtatious behavior. He dislikes the fact that she treats all people with the same charm and grace. She tells him that it is better to treat all people equally than for her to closet herself and heap all her favors on one person. In the midst of the argument, two fops, Acaste and Clitandre, arrive, followed by Philinte and Eliante, a woman of good reasonable sense. The fops immediately begin gossiping about various members of the court, and to Alceste's chagrin, Célimène joins in the gossip by castigating every person who is mentioned. Alceste cannot tolerate this, and tries to stop the performance. Shortly afterward, an officer arrives with a summons for Alceste. He is to appear before the court of the marshals because of his comments about Oronte's poem.

Later at Célimène's house, the two fops talk about her, but abruptly cease when she appears. Soon afterward a servant announces the arrival of Arsinoé, a lady of society. When the fops leave, Arsinoé pretends to inform Célimène of the gossip being spread about her. In turn, Célimène tells Arsinoé what is being said about her. When Alceste arrives, Célimène excuses herself and leaves Arsinoé and Alceste together. Immediately, Arsinoé begins flattering Alceste and offers to show him proof that Célimène is false to him.

In the following scene Philinte reports to Eliante that Alceste would not retract what he had said about Oronte's poem. Eliante admits that she must admire a man who sticks to his opinion so firmly; in fact she would not mind having him as a suitor. Philinte then confesses his love for Eliante and his own desire for her hand if she does not become involved with Alceste. When Alceste arrives, he is in a rage against Célimène for being false. Arsinoé has given him a love letter which appears to be from Célimène to someone else. When he confronts Célimène with the proof, she simply ignores it and suggests that it might have been written to a woman and not a man. She then accuses Alceste of being too strict and of not caring for her. Before the argument is settled, Alceste is reminded of a lawsuit against him, which he is apparently about to lose and which must be tended to immediately.

Later, Alceste is complaining to Philinte about the injustice in human society: he has indeed lost his lawsuit even though his case was a just one. He decides that he will retire from mankind and live in solitude. When Célimène comes in accompanied by Oronto, both men insist that she choose one of them. She avoids making a choice and before the two men can force her, the two fops, Clitandre and Acaste, arrive with incriminating letters which Célimène has written. In these letters, she made derogatory remarks about all of the gentlemen. The fops leave, promising to publish her perfidy to all of society. Oronte also gives up his suit to Célimène. Left alone with Alceste, Célimène acknowledges her mistake and offers her hand to Alceste if he will still have her. He then tells her that he wants to retire from society and wants her to join him in solitude. But Célimène cannot forego society, and at this point Alceste is cured of his love for Célimène and dismisses her. He then promises to live alone and rail against all of society and mankind.

SUMMARIES AND COMMENTARIES

ACT I – SCENE 1

Summary

The scene opens in a seventeenth-century drawing room in Paris. Alceste is reprimanding his friend Philinte for constantly betraying his integrity by conforming to the hypocritical uses and customs of polite society. An extended debate occurs between Alceste and Philinte. They argue about how genuinely and honestly a man can conduct his affairs in society. Alceste believes that a man must at all costs be honest with himself and with all of his acquaintances. Alceste maintains that no self-respecting man can accept a compliment as genuine when he is perfectly aware that all compliments are paid equally without distinction as to merit. He insists that quality be considered before people praise their fellows and that honesty dictate all judgments. Philinte argues that compliments are merely tactful maneuvers to ease the strain of getting along with people. One cannot speak his mind openly in all situations and must yield at times to the general customs prevailing in society.

Philinte asks Alceste to stop criticizing mankind and turn his attention to his impending lawsuit. He recommends that Alceste pay a visit to the judge or send someone who will solicit the judge's favor for him. Alceste adamantly refuses to stoop to such devices and insists that his suit must be tried purely on the basis of justice.

Philinte then asks Alceste if he perceives those values which he so highly esteems in the woman he loves. Philinte goes on to say that this lady, Célimène, is just as much a coquette and as much affected by the manners of the age as anyone whom Alceste criticizes. Alceste admits that he sees her faults, but he is still bewitched by her.

Commentary

Note the division of the scenes. It was a tradition in the French neoclassic stage for a scene to end when a new character appeared onstage or when a character left the stage. Sometimes when the entrance or exit occurs within the length of a few short exchanges of dialogue, this practice seems highly artificial; however, in the actual production of the play, none of these scene divisions interfered with the continuity of the action, since the curtain was never lowered except at the end of an act.

Early in the first scene Molière establishes certain dramatic tensions which will continue throughout the play: Alceste and the contrasting Philinte appear together onstage. We can clearly see from the start that Alceste is an intemperate person, as he immediately complains about people betraying their integrity. There is a heavy tone to most of the raving Alceste does, whereas Philinte seems much more reasonably contained, allowing his friend to spurt forth his rage before saying much. Alceste's language is characterized by harsh and bitter castigation of his fellow man: "shameful," and "disgraceful." He says "what a base degrading infamous thing it is to stoop to betraying one's integrity like that." Alceste exclaims that he would hang himself if ever he stooped to such a point, but Philinte answers that he will spare his own neck for a time while he attempts to correct Alceste's views.

In this first exchange between these two characters, Molière sets up the dialectic which will dominate the entire play. We see that Alceste and Philinte are friends in spite of the language that Alceste uses. We get the impression that Philinte is tolerating his friend's idiosyncrasies, while not entirely contradicting them.

A duality in our opinion toward Alceste crops up this early in the play. Although we feel that he is a bit radical in his opinions, we cannot completely reject all of his statements: "I expect you to be sincere and honorable and never utter a single word you don't mean."

In any comedy, a norm of opinion is often established, against which we can see various comic deviations. It is interesting to note that Molière does not set up a definite norm in the beginning of this play, but instead, offers a picture ambiguous enough to give the audience reason to sympathize with both Philinte and Alceste. As noted above, we do agree with Alceste's ideas about sincerity and honesty, but then we must also agree with Philinte when he complains "This philosophic rage is a bit overdone." Perhaps Alceste's idealism, admirable as it may first seem, overextends itself when he reaches the point of loathing mankind because of it. Philinte astutely remarks that Alceste has deviated from the norm: "It's wrong to be too high principled." One of the moral problems with which Molière is dealing, and with which the reader must come to terms, is just this: can one ever really be "too high principled?" A different statement of the same problem as it appears in the play is just how far can man be tolerant with a corrupt, false, and artificial society. In Molière's terms, how much "can we yield to the times."

Molière's own position is difficult to determine in this first scene. Certainly he would not agree with Alceste, who wants to flee from all of mankind, but just how much would he accept Philinte's view that we must be "a bit merciful to human nature" and not "judge it with the utmost rigor." In the final analysis, Molière is criticizing both the society which breeds such behavior, but at the same time, he is disdainful of a man like Alceste who takes such strident measures against the society.

In connection with the lawsuit with which Alceste is involved, Philinte asks Alceste what he will bring to court in his behalf. Alceste answers that he will bring reason, justice, and the rightness of his cause. Philinte wants Alceste to call on the judges and pay his respects to them, but Alceste refuses because he feels that the case should be judged entirely by its merits. In terms of the French society of the times, Philinte is, of course, correct. Alceste refuses to pay court to the judge because he sees such an action as a bribe. But in fact, the judge might be perfectly honest and just, and the act of calling on the judge was a custom of courtesy. Refusal to do so would probably be interpreted as an act of rudeness in the same way as a prisoner's refusal to stand up in an American law court when the judge enters would be considered disrespectful.

Alceste, who would appear to be setting himself up as the perfect rational being, is in actuality thoroughly irrational in matters of love. He has fallen in love with the most famous flirt and tease of the town, and he even admits that he cannot justify his emotions as anything except irrational. In the final section of this scene, we learn that two other characters, Eliante and Arsinoé, are also in love with Alceste but that he refuses to acknowledge their affections, since he is so completely in love with Célimène. These facts will have a bearing on the development of the plot.

ACT I – SCENE 2

Summary

Oronte, a rival suitor for the hand of Célimène, interrupts the discussion between Alceste and Philinte. He praises Alceste highly and pledges everlasting friendship. Alceste refrains from entering into a pledged bond of friendship, maintaining that the two men should get to know each other somewhat better. Oronte then suggests that by way of establishing their friendship Alceste should evaluate a sonnet he (Oronte) has just written. As he reads the poem, Philinte praises certain parts while Alceste recoils from both the poem and the praise. Finally, Alceste is so

54

angered at the false praise that he has difficulty in restraining himself. As Oronte forces Alceste to make an evaluation of the poem, Alceste cannot bring himself to flatter such a piece of nonsense. He eventually tells Oronte that the poem, style, and subject matter are sheer affectation. He advises Oronte to put the poem away and never read it again in public. When Oronte realizes that Alceste will not praise the poem according to the custom of society, Oronte becomes highly indignant and leaves in a fit of rage.

Commentary

In the first scene, Molière set up his dialectic between the completely frank view and the tactful view. In the second scene, he introduces a character which will test the two viewpoints. The entrance of Oronte brings the abstract ideas to a practical test. Oronte is obviously the type of dissimulating fop which Alceste was decrying in the first scene. Consequently, the appearance of Oronte openly supports Alceste's argument.

It is further established in this scene that Alceste does not know how to function in his role of "social animal." As Oronte talks to Alceste, the latter seems to take no notice of Oronte's presence. He makes only a mild effort to be tolerant. Yet, Alceste does not immediately reject Oronte and attempts to back out gracefully. He does not openly reject Oronte's friendship, but tries to get around accepting his friendship. And later, he does not openly criticize Oronte's poem until he is forced to pronounce an opinion. Alceste is infuriated that Philinte will *volunteer* praise when it is not asked for. Actually, Alceste tries to present an analogy of another person who wrote poetry, hoping that Oronte will see the connection and thus relieve him from making a pronouncement. Only when he is pressed by this pest, who simply wants to receive the same flattery, does Alceste actually tell him that the poem is trite and insignificant.

The poem illustrates all the flaws which Alceste objects to in the society. The poem is filled with affectations and elaborate similes, thus showing a fondness of elegant and false language.

These are the basic qualities which Alceste objects to in his society. He prefers a type of poem which expresses a simple emotion in a straightforward manner.

Toward the end of the scene, we see the result of Alceste's adherence to his viewpoint: that is, he has made an enemy by refusing to praise Oronte's poem. Alceste will be summoned to appear before the marshals because of his refusal to compliment Oronte's poem. Both viewpoints will later be exposed to be ridiculous, but for the final actions of Scene 2, it is enough to note the anger caused by Alceste's honest criticism.

ACT I – SCENE 3

Summary

Philinte points out the trouble with being too sincere: "Now you've got an ugly quarrel on your hands." Alceste refuses to budge from his position and maintains that he will renounce all of mankind. He even wants to escape from Philinte.

Commentary

The final scene brings to a close the first act and shows essentially the same relationship between the friends. Only Philinte can recognize the possible danger of making someone like Oronte into an enemy.

ACT II – SCENES 1-4

Summary

Alceste and his beloved Célimène are squabbling over her encouragement of rival suitors. Alceste is jealous and cannot tolerate competitors for Célimène's affections or attentions. He is especially disturbed by favors bestowed on one Clitandre, with his blond periwig, frills at his knees, and his affected falsetto voice. Célimène merely thinks that Alceste is becoming jealous of the entire universe.

While Alceste and Célimène are talking, the servant, Basque, announces the arrival of another suitor, Acaste, and then the arrival of still another, Clitandre. Alceste tries to escape because, as he says, "these conversations only bore me." Célimène begs him to stay but when he refuses her, she tells him to "be off! Do as you please!"

Commentary

At the beginning of this act, we see that Alceste is putting his theories to the test; or as Philinte had said in the end of the last act, proving his "precious sincerity." This desire for absolute honesty on Alceste's part urges him to approach Célimène and openly tell her her faults.

The basis for Alceste's criticism of Célimène is that she has too many admirers and that she treats all people with the same degree of courtesy. She refuses to deny her presence to anyone and "gives any and everyone too easy access to" her heart. Browning's poem "My Last Duchess" aptly suggests the exact nature of Alceste's objections:

> She had
> A heart—how shall I say?—too soon made glad,
> Too easily impressed; she liked whate'er
> She looked on, and her looks went everywhere.

In general, Alceste makes the unreasonable request of almost all lovers in wanting the lady to have no acquaintances other than himself.

Unlike Alceste, Célimène's arguments do not stem from any particular points of integrity. She argues like a coquette. First she asks if she can be blamed for her beauty. She is so naturally beautiful that men are automatically attracted to her. When Alceste spurns this, she then argues that these suitors can advance her interest in society. Finally, she is reduced to illogical but witty rebuttals against Alceste's objections. Isn't it better for her to have many suitors than to bestow her affections on one particular person. Finally, she complains that if he is so jealous then he really can't be in love with her.

Each of the characters is acting in terms of his own version of "reasonable" behavior. The disparity between the two vividly indicates two different opinions on how man should function in society. Throughout the discussion, we should be aware that Célimène is trying to pacify Alceste's arguments, which suggests that she is concerned about their relationship. Even though it will be revealed more fully in later scenes, the reader should now be aware that Célimène's arguments are the cleverer of the two.

Molière somewhat undercuts Alceste's position by the exaggerated language he provides him. When Alceste cries out "No man has ever loved as I do!" he is the picture of a stock romantic lover. In the mouth of this eccentric "rationalist" these words are even more absurdly comic than usual. Honest Alceste is thus not so reasonable at all times as he would have himself seem.

On Alceste's words to Célimène, "Let us be entirely open with each other," Basque interrupts to announce the arrival of the type of fop about whom the lovers have been arguing. Alceste is left totally exasperated with her. The technique used in these scenes is similar to that used in Act I. Two characters argue a particular point, then the argument is put to the test by the entrance of a third party. In Act I, Alceste and Philinte argue the relative merits of social amenities and personal sincerity in dealing with undesirable but influential people one is acquainted with. Each takes his stand—Alceste for strict honesty, Philinte for a necessary flexibility in conduct. Immediately, Oronte, an influential but extremely foppish character, enters and acts as a catalyst for each character to test his position. In Act II, Célimène and Alceste argue about her numerous suitors. He believes that she should not be so readily accessible to them and should not treat them with such easy familiarity; she believes in being polite and responsive to them. Then the suitors arrive and the audience may observe how the expressed opinions meet the test.

Finally, Alceste admits for the first time that he is trying to break his infatuation with Célimène. Since Alceste's final actions in the play will be his break with Célimène, we should be aware that Molière has begun to prepare us for this idea.

In Scene 3, Molière ironically undercuts Alceste's sense of exaggerated integrity. For a man who stands for complete honesty and who has just been arguing the value of always being completely frank, suddenly to have him ask Célimène to lie is a clever undercutting of his character. He asks "Can you never bring yourself to say you are not at home for one single moment." This rings false from a champion of truth and integrity, and is therefore comic.

ACT II – SCENES 5-7

Summary

Almost as if to vex Célimène, Alceste decides that he will stay while she is entertaining her other suitors. He furthermore announces that he will force her to "declare yourself. – For their satisfaction or mine." Along with Acaste and Clitandre, Célimène's cousin Eliante, and Alceste's friend, Philinte, enter the room. The two fops proceed to gossip with Célimène about several mutual acquaintances, much to the disgust of Alceste, Philinte, and Eliante.

Finally, unable to bear it any longer, Alceste speaks out and criticizes them for slandering their friends: "But let any one of them appear on the scene and you would all rush to meet him, offer him your hands in fulsome greeting, and protest your eternal devotion." Then Clitandre tells Alceste that he should not so much berate the men because his fiancée, Célimène, is more to blame for the gossip. Then the conversation turns to the subject of the sincerity of the man-woman relationship. Alceste claims that the man and woman must always speak the plain facts to each other. Eliante explains that love is blind, and flattery is an essential part of any love relationship.

The servant Basque announces the arrival of another guest, an officer of the court of the marshals. The officer tells Alceste that he must appear before the marshals on account of his quarrel with Oronte, the author of the sonnet which Alceste had criticized. Alceste comments as he is leaving that Oronte should be hanged for writing such bad verse.

Commentary

At the end of the last scene, Alceste had announced that he was going to leave because he could not tolerate the presence of the dandies who were about to arrive. However, at the beginning of Scene 5, he changes his mind, partly to spite Célimène. His decision to stay perhaps smacks a bit of pettiness—he seems to stamp his foot and refuse to leave simply because Célimène told him to leave.

Among the "social types" being criticized in this scene Célimène should be a major culprit, as she gossips at length about her acquaintances. However, she is such a fascinating coquette, who amuses us with her wit and her verbal portraits, that we can hardly bring ourselves to condemn her. When she is fed a line of gossip by one of the fops, she transforms it into an extended stinging portrait of the hapless object. Her performance delights all of the fops while it disgusts Alceste. What Célimène is doing is playing the game of society; she is practically the epitome of this type of society.

Throughout these verbal characterizations, part of the reason we do not condemn Célimène as much as Alceste does is the fact that she is not being intentionally malicious; instead, she is merely functioning in the role that society has created for this type of person. Furthermore, there is an irony in each of her characterizations because she is guilty of every fault that she criticizes in other people. For example, she charges one of the people with being too conceited for words. Yet her very performance demonstrates that she is also conceited, and earlier she had told Alceste that she is so beautiful that men are helplessly drawn to her. She also talks of people being obsessed with rank and position, yet she cultivates a number of friends simply because these people can help her attain a higher rank and position.

One touch of Molière's greatness is his complex characters: they are rarely totally black or totally white. While we must condemn what Célimène does as wrong because it does no good, yet she does it with such vivacity, such charm and such wit, that we cannot totally reject her. She has such virtuosity in her characterization that we admire her ingenuity while condemning her purpose. Then when Alceste decries her actions as being pure hypocrisy, we must also agree with him.

Immediately after we sympathize with Alceste, Molière qualifies our view by having him act in ways that we cannot accept. For example, by dint of a clever equivocation, Alceste rebuts the arguments of the foppish suitors and claims that what Célimène is guilty of is not really Célimène's fault. The fault lies mainly with the foppish suitors who, by flattering her, really encourage her to participate in such slanderous sallies.

Throughout the play Molière introduces Alceste as the perfectly rational man who can see the faults in all of his acquaintances and in all levels of society. Then, throughout the play, point for point, Molière undercuts Alceste's opinion of himself and of others by showing him up as being often irrational in many of his actions. First, his reason is obviously blinded by his irrational love for Célimène. Second, his arguments are often based on the most dubious logic. Third, in her characterization of him, Célimène indicates that Alceste is often ruled by a certain spirit of contrariety in that he enjoys contradiction. This aspect of his character will be dramatically indicated in Act IV in the scene in which Alceste presents a letter to Célimène that she had written to Oronte and accuses her of perfidy. The scene concludes with Alceste on the defensive. For a further illustration of this idea, consult the Commentary after Act IV.

Célimène does see the contradiction in his character in that he speaks one way and acts another. Her view of Alceste attests to her understanding of his nature: He can never agree with other people's opinions. He must always maintain the contrary view. "He would think he was cutting a very ordinary figure if he were found to agree with anyone else." It is true throughout the play that he proves himself wrong. In this very scene he tells the group that "the proof of a true love is to be unsparing in criticism." But although he is the only person who does not find true love, yet he dwells on criticism. Likewise, in the preceding speech, he had not criticized Célimène, but shifted the fault to the flatterers.

Célimène's response is closer to a norm. However noble Alceste might sound when he advocates that one must be unsparing in criticism for whomever one loves, in society one cannot function in these terms. Célimène then takes Alceste's argument to his own extreme, and says that to prove her love she would have to be constantly criticizing him.

In this scene, Eliante and to a lesser degree, Philinte, stand as reasonable voices. Philinte tries to point out to Alceste that he is being unreasonable for criticizing Célimène for her verbal portraits because the people that Célimène is castigating are the same people whom Alceste also castigates; so it is not logical for Alceste to raise such strong objections. Likewise, at the end of the act, Alceste maintains that he will not "budge an inch," and Philinte tries to make him "be reasonable." Similar to Philinte, Eliante realizes that Alceste's criticism of flattery is justified, but she also realizes that human nature is imperfect and that lovers will always be flatterers.

The closing scene of the act—Alceste summoned to court—aptly illustrates the trouble his honesty can get him into. Richelieu and Louis XIV had taken stern measures to suppress the deadly prevalence of dueling among the nobility. To this end, a special court, the *tribunal de marechaux,* had been established to arbitrate quarrels that might otherwise terminate in bloodshed.

ACT III – SCENES 1-4

Summary

The fop, Acaste, is telling Clitandre about his own merits. He can find no reason to be discontent with himself, since he is rich, young, and of a good family, and furthermore, he exhibits a certain style in everything he does. He always sits on the stage during productions of plays and acts as the self-appointed critic. In conclusion, he can say "without conceit" that he dresses well and is admired by all of the fairer sex.

Clitandre wonders why Acaste, who has so many easy conquests elsewhere, spends so much time trying to win Célimène's affections. In response to Clitandre's inquiry about his relationship to Célimène, Acaste at first says that he has reason to believe that he is favored by the lady, but then pretends that he is deceived in thinking so. He refuses to admit the extent of his relationship. The two fops then make a pact whereby if one does receive definite proof of Célimène's affections, the other will automatically withdraw.

Célimène returns and is surprised to find them both still present. At this moment, the servant, Basque, announces the arrival of Arsinoé. Acaste and Clitandre make some slanderous remarks about Arsinoé, and Célimène soon picks up the refrain. She complains about such a person as Arsinoé, who would like very much to have a lover but being unable to get one, pretends to be such a prude. Just as Célimène is disparaging her, the lady arrives and immediately Célimène changes her tone and tells the new guest how pleased she is to see her.

Commentary

Acaste's "frank" estimate of himself at the beginning of this act contrasts excellently with Alceste's estimate of himself. The fop's opinion of himself illustrates the very things that Alceste objects to in society. In reality, Acaste is a rather slight, one-dimensional character, whose purpose in the play is to represent one aspect of society which the misanthrope justifiably detests.

Embedded in his opinion of himself is an interesting reference to a habit which Molière objected to. During this era of theater there was actually room on the stage for a certain number of people to sit while a play was being produced. The type of person who occupied these places was often the man-of-mode or fop—who generally had an exaggerated opinion of his critical abilities. Molière undoubtedly disliked this interfering fop, and used such speeches to ridicule just that type who would be sitting on the stage during the presentation of *The Misanthrope*.

Act III opens in a manner parallel to Act I. In the earlier act, we saw the two friends, Alceste and Philinte, talking and discussing certain problems. In Act III, we have another set of acquaintances, but this time they are fops, Acaste and Clitandre. One of the main concerns in the play is sincerity in human relationships. In Act I, Alceste represents one view in stating that one must be completely frank at all times, whereas Philinte suggests that other people's feelings must be taken into consideration. For all the ostensible antagonism between Alceste and Philinte in Act I, however, we can see that beneath the exterior arguments, there is a true friendship. Although the parallel between Act I and Act III is largely on the surface, in the third act, we do not have the sense that the two fops possess that essential quality of true friendship. There is a difference in the depth of character, and the subject matter is considerably more superficial than was the subject of the conversation between Philinte and Alceste. The scene in the third act, furthermore, ends with a bit of clever dialogue wherein both characters feign their real views and content themselves with expressing the artificial superficialities associated with society. The implicit contrast between the two sets of characters serves to raise Alceste and Philinte in our estimation.

The technique of the scene where Célimène characterizes Arsinoé is the same technique used earlier in Act II, where people are ridiculed but when they appear are then welcomed with exuberant graciousness. In the speech just prior to Arsinoé's arrival, Célimène launches into another of her verbal portraits as she paints a picture of Arsinoé as the insidious hypocrite. Yet Célimène's views and her subsequent actions prove her to be just as hypocritical. In the actual stage presentation, we would see that Célimène is being very spiteful and nasty about Arsinoé, but when the character actually arrives, there would be a sudden transformation in the physical actions of Célimène. She would then be all smiles and would flutter around the new arrival, trying to show how utterly concerned she is with Arsinoé; therefore, in addition to the hypocrisy of her statements, her actions would reveal even more of the hypocrisy to the audience.

ACT III – SCENES 5-6

Summary

Arsinoé immediately tells Célimène that she has come to prove her love and affections for the younger person by telling her all of the gossip that has been circulating about her. She explains that Célimène's conduct is beginning to win a certain amount of notoriety, and that recently in several conversations, she has tried to stand up for Célimène by explaining to others that Célimène meant no harm in the things she did. However, Arsinoé is finally compelled to admit that Célimène's conduct must be wrong because so many people have criticized it. She concludes by saying that only the purest and best motives cause her to repeat what the various gossips are saying about her.

Célimène wants to repay the "favor," so she proceeds to tell Arsinoé what the town is saying about her. Generally, Célimène says, people think Arsinoé acts too much the part of the prude. She pretends to have virtues which she does not really possess. She makes an "outward show of virtue and modesty" but then paints herself in a disgraceful fashion by her actions. Célimène advises Arsinoé to "meddle less with other people's conduct, and look a bit more closely to your own." She ends by explaining that she has only said these things because of her concern for Arsinoé.

Arsinoé is offended, and reprimands Célimène for being so frank. Célimène, however, maintains that such mutual warnings are good and "dispel that blindness most of us suffer as regards ourselves." She also says that when she is older she will then perhaps become a prude, but "it's not time to be a prude at twenty." Furthermore, she doesn't like to be blamed for all of Arsinoé's disappointments.

Arsinoé maintains that she could have as many admirers as does Célimène if she lowered her standards enough to attract men. Célimène challenges her to do so, and as Alceste arrives at this minute, she excuses herself to go write some letters, thus leaving Alceste to entertain Arsinoé.

Commentary

This scene, one of the most masterful in the play, is concerned with the social shams which masquerade as true human relationships. Each of the women claims to be telling the other one the prevailing gossip for her benefit. Arsinoé says that she has heard that Célimène is being talked about in many circles as being a gossip. What she says may be true enough, though we even doubt that, but the motive behind her telling is far from noble. In the same way, Célimène says that she has heard that Arsinoé is being talked about as being a meddler and ostentatious person. Actually the two women are speaking the truth as Alceste would have true friends do. But the truth is here disguised behind the facade of pretense; the purpose is not really to improve their relationship, but to antagonize and spite the other person.

The general purpose of social comedy is to point out the foibles of individuals so that they can reform. In this short scene Molière ironically presents two characters who are apparently trying to point out each other's failings—an admirable thing in comedy. But by using this traditional device in reverse—the two women *are not* reforming one another—he sharpens his criticism of the two women themselves.

Although in this particular scene Célimène and Arsinoé are not particularly admirable characters, Molière has them mouth certain general truths about each other's character. Neither of them, however, recognizes such as meaningful because of the purpose for which it is being told. For example, there are many stock phrases stated by each character: that we should judge ourselves before we judge others, that a woman becomes a prude only when she is too old to attract men, that we should clean our own backyard before we criticize our neighbors, etc. But the characters mouth these statements only as social formulas and are totally unaware of the truth behind the statements.

We have so far in the play seen Célimène functioning as a superb example of the society in which she lives. Now in this scene with Arsinoé, we see her feeling the pinch of criticism of the malicious side of society which she herself has helped support. By the end of the play, she will be trapped by the society which she represents; we get an intimation of that in this early scene.

The basic antagonism between Célimène and Arsinoé is the result of several factors. First, Arsinoé is jealous of the younger beauty. Célimène has taken away several of Arsinoé's admirers, and out of bitterness, Arsinoé has been telling people of her own virtue and suggesting that Célimène attracts suitors by being a loose woman. Célimène resents the slander and therefore accuses Arsinoé of starting the slander because she is too old to attract men herself.

ACT III – SCENE 7

Summary

Arsinoé immediately begins to flatter Alceste by telling him that his merits are not justly appreciated and that he should be more in favor with the court. Alceste, however, points out that he has done absolutely nothing to warrant the attention of the court, and, furthermore, the court should be involved in more important matters than trying "to bring to light the worth of everybody." Arsinoé maintains that Alceste's virtues are praised in certain houses, but Alceste is not interested because the "present age has no distinction left" and everyone is praised with equal fervor. He will not allow Arsinoé to "set intrigues at work" to get him into the court; quite the contrary, he points out that he has no qualities that would make him congenial enough for life at the court.

Arsinoé drops the subject of the court and turns her attentions to Alceste's relationship with Célimène. She tells him that his beloved is unworthy of him. Alceste tries to remind Arsinoé that she is maligning her friend, but she continues to insist that Célimène has betrayed Alceste. She offers to prove the accusation if Alceste will accompany her to her own house, where she will show him "faithful proof of Célimène's unfaithfulness."

Commentary

As her character is built up to this point, it would seem that Célimène would take delight in leaving Arsinoé and Alceste together because she knows that the older woman has a crush on Alceste and she also knows that Alceste is interested only in her. The impending confrontation would surely amuse her. On the basic plot level, she goes off to write letters (perhaps the ones which will trap her later in the play).

Arsinoé commits the obvious error of trying to sidle up to Alceste and to offer him the most blatant and false compliments. At first she tries the most obvious method of winning his favor — speaking of the need of the court to recognize Alceste. To any other person, this connection with the royal court would make a great impression, but to Alceste, any honors from the court would be superficial, and as he honestly evaluates himself, he tells Arsinoé that he has done nothing to warrant the esteem of the court. He has performed no brilliant deeds and therefore has no right to distinction in anyone's eyes.

When Arsinoé tries to say how she has heard men at court praise Alceste, he is once again true to his principles by saying that it is the custom today to praise a man whether he deserves it or not, and he himself is, therefore, not impressed by the praise.

68

He puts an end to this hypocrisy by telling her that his nature is not the type which could even endure a life at the court. Thus, throughout the conversation, we must admire Alceste to a limited degree for being honest in evaluating himself and his merits as far as his association with the court is concerned.

Again in this scene, when Alceste's frankness and sincerity are put to a test as far as Célimène is concerned, he falters. Although he claims that he is sincere and although Arsinoé is essentially telling him the truth, Alceste is annoyed that he is being told the truth. He would have preferred to be deceived and remain in the dark concerning Célimène's activities. Consequently, even though Alceste maintains that one must always be honest, and even though he is honest as far as his own merits are concerned, he is not consistent as far as Célimène is concerned. Throughout the play, his nature is contradictory when it comes to his love for Célimène.

In general, by the end of the first three acts we have had presented to us numerous pictures of fops, of flirts, of hypocrites, etc. Each has been exposed to show exactly what his nature is. Even Alceste cannot remain consistent to his philosophy when Célimène is concerned.

ACT IV – SCENE 1

Summary

Philinte recounts to Eliante the settlement of the quarrel between Oronte and Alceste and the latter's unbending obstinacy. Alceste would not change his opinion about Oronte's verses. The best he would do was to wish "that I could have thought better of your sonnet." On this note, Alceste and Oronte were directed to embrace, and the proceedings were concluded.

Philinte and Eliante next discuss Alceste's relationship with Célimène. Eliante admires Alceste for his honesty, and though it seems strange to her that Alceste should fancy such a coquette as Célimène, she reverts to something she said at the end of

Act II: "love is blind and is not always a matter of temperamental affinities." Philinte craftily expresses the wish that Eliante's affection for Alceste be requited, but, then he goes on to show his true intentions by saying that if Alceste refuses her, he would be glad to accept her hand for himself.

Commentary

After the favorable picture of a sincerely principled man is drawn of Alceste in the court, Eliante speaks up and expresses a certain admiration for Alceste: "There's something in its way noble and heroic in this sincerity he so prides himself on. It's a rare virtue in these days. I only wish there were more people like him." This comment functions as a type of sounding board for the audience. We have to join with Eliante in applauding Alceste's honesty and sincerity after having been exposed to so much hypocrisy in the other characters.

In this opening scene, we are given to understand for the first time that Philinte is also in love with Eliante. In contrast to Alceste, who speaks directly and frankly, Philinte uses much more tact and consideration — one is tempted to say dissimulation — in declaring his love for Eliante. Such tactics do, however, succeed in winning his loved one; Alceste, for failure to act similarly, loses his woman. Together, Philinte and Eliante will come to represent the closest there is to a norm in the play.

ACT IV — SCENE 2

Summary

At the moment that Philinte is making advances to Eliante, Alceste enters ranting that Célimène has been unfaithful to him. He claims to have in his possession a love letter which Célimène has written to Oronte. Philinte tries to calm him, saying that the letter simply might have given the wrong impression, but Alceste refuses to listen. Then Alceste offers his devotion to Eliante in order to get vengeance on Célimène. Eliante stays him with the words: "guilt in loved ones soon turns to innocence again, resentment quickly vanishes; we all know what lovers' quarrels are." Alceste claims undying antagonism toward Célimène.

Commentary

Alceste's entrance on the scene emphasizes again that he is the "spleen" character, a man given to obsessions and intemperate behavior. He enters in a rage and has to be calmed by Philinte. His language is comically hyperbolic, and his actions are similarly exaggerated. Feeling betrayed by Célimène, he immediately proposes to Eliante, saying: "Accept my heart, Accept it, in that faithless woman's place; Only in that way will I be avenged. I'll punish her by the sincere attachment, profound affection, worshipful attentions, eager devotion and assiduous service my heart will henceforth offer at your shrine." This honest man is driven to extremes in promising to idolize one woman simply to make another jealous. This is incongruous with the rational behavior Alceste has been advocating throughout the earlier parts of the play. The rational misanthrope is now seen as the not so admirable man of confused ideas.

ACT IV—SCENES 3-4

Summary

At the very moment that Alceste is decrying the faithless Célimène, she enters the room. Alceste begins a lengthy tirade about Célimène's perfidy, the blows he has been dealt by fortune, and the inability of his reason to restrain his passions. He presents the letter to Célimène with a melodramatic flair and she seems to glance at it, amused, saying "you are indeed a strangely foolish man!" The lovers' quarrel jumps back and forth as Alceste accuses Célimène of perfidy, and she accuses him of not loving her. At one moment Alceste is angry and at another he is apologetic. Finally the coquette wins out; she pouts and says "no, you don't love me as you should." Alceste exclaims "Ah! my love is beyond all comparison."

The conversation is interrupted by the entrance of Alceste's stumbling manservant, DuBois. The servant hems and haws and then finally tells the exasperated Alceste that a strange man "with a face as black as his coat" came and left some papers about the lawsuit process. An hour later another man came and warned DuBois that his master was in danger. He left a written message to be delivered to Alceste. Alceste, disturbed by the fact that he has been interrupted in his conversation with Célimène, goes off to see what it all means.

Commentary

There is both comic reversal and comic discrepancy illustrated in this scene. At first, we see Alceste raging with anger and in contrast, a serene, coy, and clever Célimène. Alceste's actions are typical here: he is repeatedly exasperated with Célimène and can never really function as the perfectly rational man. Gradually during the scene, there is a comic reversal as Célimène's ire grows in tempo until Alceste is forced to try and placate her. The exchange of roles by the characters within this one scene adds to the comedy of the situation. Furthermore, this entire scene seems to substantiate Célimène's characterization of Alceste in Act II. That is, he seems to be contrary for its own sake; first he berates Célimène, then when she counters and berates him he takes the opposite role and swears innocence.

Alceste finally recognizes what she is doing; he is the would-be rational man who has lost control and has to admit it: "Perfidious creature, how well you know how to turn my weakness against me and exploit it to your own purposes the fatal and excessive love those faithless eyes inspire!" Ironically, he progresses from being accusing and spiteful toward her to being the supplicant who is apologetic. The basis of the scene is that he wants her to prove to him that she has not been unfaithful, yet she never cares to.

Before Alceste can bring Célimène to some type of terms, he is interrupted by his servant, who brings news that he has lost his long-pending lawsuit. The servant here is a stock figure who

72

cannot manage to deliver the message until his master is totally exasperated. The reader should remember that Alceste is already exasperated by Célimène, who would not give him any direct answers; the appearance of the servant who can't deliver a straight message is a further means of exasperating Alceste and of evoking laughter. Alceste takes out his anger against Célimène by being harsh with his servant.

Molière ends the act by having Alceste's philosophical honesty interfere with his life because once again he must interrupt his life to tend to a lawsuit against him. His unswerving honesty does not allow him to live without the constant harassment by the society which he ultimately rejects.

ACT V – SCENE 1

Summary

Alceste has lost the court case which was first mentioned in Act I. He rants on about it to Philinte: "By dint of sheer hypocrisy, of opened and most palpable fraud, right is overthrown and justice perverted!" Alceste vows to accept his punishment to prove himself a living example of one victimized by this wicked age, and further vows to withdraw from society. Philinte calmly says "I think your intentions are a little rash." He then explains that the weakness of human nature from which this injustice and evils of all kinds spring, is merely something that we must learn to live with. Alceste dismisses this and says that he will test Célimène's reaction to his decision. Philinte leaves to visit Eliante and Alceste waits for Célimène.

Commentary

As the play began with Alceste and Philinte discussing sincerity and honesty, the final act begins with an almost identical discussion. Molière has balanced the play by placing the characters in essentially the same situation, with Alceste fuming and raging, and Philinte trying again to make him look at things reasonably. We can also say that Alceste has learned virtually nothing of the ability to adapt to society during the play and has become now more and more the misanthrope.

At this point in the play, we discover that Alceste has just lost his lawsuit. There is no evidence that Alceste's case was the right one and that it was unjust for him to lose, but because of his character and because of the reactions of the other characters, we can reasonably well assume that Alceste's was a just cause. A reader's first impression would be that Alceste should win, perhaps simply because he is such a brutally honest person.

Alceste cuts a ridiculous figure in this scene because of his obvious posing and the melodramatic air about him. He strikes the pose of the martyred innocent, crucified by society. He is even determined to buy his own cross by paying the 20,000-franc judgment. He almost seems delighted to have lost the case because this gives him the right to rail against mankind and to reject society.

Molière has created a delicate balance here between what Alceste says and the manner in which he says it. What he actually says is true, but his manner of stating it makes it impossible for the audience to sympathize with him completely. For example, Alceste says that "there is too much baseness in the world today." We categorically agree with this statement, but the manner in which Philinte frames the problem sets us to wondering: "The world *is* governed by intrigue and self-interest; fraud *does* carry all before it nowadays. Men *ought* to be different from what they are. But is the prevalence of injustice among them a reason for withdrawing from their society?" Embedded in this statement is the philosophical tone of the entire play: that is, Molière is criticizing the type of society which exists, but at the same time he is ridiculing someone like Alceste who cannot function in that society. On the other hand, even Philinte's statement—that one should welcome the bad society because only in the presence of baseness can his own true virtue shine forth—somewhat undercuts his "reasonable" stand. The logic is at best dubious.

At the end of the scene, the hater of mankind is left sulking in the corner of the stage awaiting the vibrant social butterfly, Célimène.

ACT V – SCENES 2-3

Summary

Oronte and Célimène arrive and Oronte requests Célimène to make a choice between him or Alceste; if she chooses him, he does not want her to see Alceste any more. Célimène does not understand, since recently Oronte had praised Alceste. As Oronte is awaiting Célimène's decision, Alceste steps forward and affirms that he wants a similar decision in his favor. The two men agree that Célimène must choose and each is shocked that she seems to hesitate in making her decision.

Célimène thinks it would be rude to openly express her preference. Both men avow that her silence indicates that she likes the other; both demand a decision.

At this point Eliante and Philinte arrive, and Célimène appeals to Elinate for help. Eliante, however, says that she is "on the side of those who speak their mind." Again both men demand an answer from Célimène.

Commentary

The comedy of this scene is based upon the fact that Alceste and Oronte—two archenemies in the play—are both demanding the same thing. They are in a sense allied. The comedy also lies in the rapid delivery of the repetitive lines. One character makes part of a statement, the other picks it up and finishes or modifies it; then the other goes on with the modification, and so on.

Throughout the scene, Célimène is adeptly able to avoid giving an answer. It is also ironic that Célimène refuses to answer because she claims the requests are "unreasonable," whereas the two suitors are for once making a reasonable request. Again, throughout the play, almost every character's actions are motivated by what he considers to be reasonable. The repetition of this word becomes comic in view of all the unreasonable actions committed by almost every character.

Eliante is seen in direct contrast to Célimène; Célimène is embarrassed to have to make a choice, but Eliante is on the side "of those who speak their minds."

ACT V — SCENES 4-6

Summary

Arsinoé, Acaste, and Clitandre enter "to clear up a little matter" with Célimène. It concerns all who are present, says Clitandre. Acaste first reads from a letter which Célimène had sent to Clitandre. In it she expressed her opinions of each of her suitors. The "little marquis" (Acaste) is a person of no significance; "the man with the green ribbons" (Alceste) is often the most bothersome bore in the world; Oronte is as dull as his verse. Then Clitandre reads Célimène's equally disparaging opinion of himself from a letter she sent to Acaste. Acaste and Clitandre exit with plans to "publish abroad this portrait" of Célimène's true nature.

Oronte quickly follows suit, by condemning Célimène for making the same specious promises of love to everyone. Arsinoé is indignant that Célimène has so thoughtlessly trod on the feelings of Alceste. Alceste says that he does not want any sympathy from Arsinoé and dismisses her by saying that if he were to seek vengeance by transferring his affections elsewhere, she would be the last person he would turn to. Arsinoé is highly insulted; she points to Célimène and says: "This lady's leavings are not a commodity I should prize as highly as all that!" She reproves Alceste's vanity and struts off the stage.

Commentary

Scene 4 brings together all the personages of the play as Molière once again uses the device of the discovered letters to bring about this confrontation scene.

Part of the purpose of the scene is to show how Célimène, the superb example of her society, is trapped by the very factors in society which she has encouraged.

By the end of Scene 6, the stage is cleared except for four main personages. The fops desert Célimène, promising to publish her behavior to all of society; Oronte gives up his pretensions to Célimène; Arsinoé is rapidly dismissed by Alceste and only the four main characters are left on the stage.

ACT V – SCENES 7-8

Summary

Alceste has waited for the others to leave before speaking his mind. But before he can say anything, Célimène admits that she has wronged him. She does not care for the anger of the others, but her betrayal of Alceste, she feels, is deserving of his hatred. Alceste, however, finds that he cannot hate her and is willing to forget her crime if she will consent to "flee from all mankind" and follow him into retirement. Célimène, however, says that "solitude has terrors for a soul of twenty." But if her hand in marriage would soothe Alceste she will suffer herself to be married.

Suddenly Alceste is disgusted by Célimène and tells her that now in her refusal to deny society, she has destroyed all love he previously had for her. He sends her away from his presence. Then he apologizes to Eliante, telling her that he has decided that he is not fit for marriage. Eliante explains that she has a promise from Philinte. He wishes them happiness and plans now to retire from the world and live in solitude, "where one is free to be an honest man." Philinte and Eliante hope that they can change his mind.

Commentary

In the final analysis, Alceste offers Célimène a life of the misanthrope totally isolated from society. Since she has been presented as the epitome of all that society stands for, it is indeed an unreasonable request. As she points out, at twenty solitude is frightening for one who is accustomed to moving in the sphere of high society. In spite of the fact that she has just been trapped by the artificialities of that particular society, she does recognize that her position is as a member of society and that she cannot function as a misanthropic hermit.

Alceste does not realize that he has demanded the impossible from Célimène. He is egotistic enough to want her to conform completely to his personal specifications and live according to his rules. She is, of course, willing to modify some of her behavior and marry him, but she would indeed be unreasonable to deny completely her own personality simply to satisfy Alceste's exaggerated opinion of what constitutes proper conduct.

It is perhaps slightly difficult to believe in Alceste's sudden disapproval of Célimène. Simply because she won't conform to his ideas, he suddenly despises her and sends her away.

The comedy ends on a slight note of hope as Philinte and Eliante form an alliance which could offer some relief from the society presented so far in the play. The ending is not, however, the perfectly happy ending of the usual comedy.

CHARACTER ANALYSES

ALCESTE

Alceste is the main character in the play; he is, in fact, the "misanthrope" from whom the play derives its name. From the beginning to the end of the action, we witness no real change for the better in his character. Rejecting all the usual types of social amenities as well as the uglier forms of social hypocrisy, he repeatedly insists upon the strictest honesty in all situations between people in society. His unbending opinions often evoke laughter in the play as they manage to get him into difficulty after difficulty. He loses a case at court because he won't compromise. He also loses his loved one, Célimène, because of his insistence that society thrives on hypocrisy, and his ultimate desire to withdraw completely from the world of men. The irony implicit in Alceste's affair with Célimène is a further source for ridiculing the misanthrope's position. Throughout the play his own cry, not unlike the cries of other morally "rigid" comic characters, is that the rest of the world is "unreasonable."

While Alceste claims to be the only man governed solely by his rational faculties, he is also the one who has practically become a slave to his passion for Célimène. This contradiction troubles Alceste, and affords the audience a chuckle, for Célimène is the epitome of all the hypocrisy which disguises itself with the name "social etiquette."

But for all of Alceste's eccentricity—and it *is* the "eccentric" which comedy tries to cure in man—and for all the tomfoolery he engages in as a "matter of principle," we do feel a certain pity for him. Molière's comic technique in ridiculing the young man acts as a two-edged sword. Alceste is absurd in the society simply because he has scruples about such things as hypocrisy, lying, and skirting the law. Alceste is surely not the only one to be criticized; Parisian society, and human nature in general, which in fact does tolerate the existence of the numerous vices Alceste decries, are equally taken to task. Indeed, part of the greatness of Molière's play is its complexity; the author never gives the impression that any one point of view is the unquestionably "correct" one. We must join in with society at the conclusion of the play in rejecting an Alceste who has chosen to separate himself from man's company, but there remains something within us which perceives the scrap of wisdom in Alceste's symbolic action.

CELIMENE

Célimène epitomizes the society of the age and represents almost everything which Alceste finds objectionable in this society. She is young and vivacious and enjoys being a part of the social world. The setting for the play is in her house and by this means we get to know everyone who visits her. These include some of the most absurd fops found in the society.

Célimène is only twenty years old, but in spite of her youth she has learned all the tricks which are needed to be successful in society. She receives everyone without distinguishing their attributes. She would rather associate with the worse fop than to be denied any visitors at all.

She treats all people alike and seems to enjoy the company of the fops as much as she does Alceste's presence. She is deliberately flirtatious and attempts to ensnare a large number of suitors. She is able to castigate another person if he is not present, but when the same person appears, she is hypocritically delighted to see the person. She puts into practice all the deceit and hypocrisy which Alceste rails against.

PHILINTE AND ELIANTE

These two characters serve generally as foils to the main pair of "lovers," Alceste and Célimène. Philinte's role, more important than Eliante's, exists largely as a voice of reason, especially in scenes with Alceste. He is a good friend of Alceste's and can see both the folly and the reason behind the "misanthrope's" carryings-on. He is finally of the opinion, however, that to live in this world one must be able to put up with man's shortcomings — something Alceste refuses to do.

Eliante's most important contribution in the play is the commentary she makes on the process of man pursuing women, and indirectly on the relationship between Alceste and Célimène. She is of the opinion that honesty is desirable in all their dealings, but she also understands the weakness of man which makes such a condition impossible.

The union of Philinte and Eliante by the end of the play suggests if not the triumph, then at least the durability, of rational but not overly scrupulous people in society.

A GENERAL VIEW

In the closing scenes of the drama, Alceste makes an offer to Célimène which involves her retiring from society and joining him in a life of solitude. To become a hermit as he suggests to Célimène is, however, a negation of society. This is a flat denial by Alceste, then, that man is essentially a social animal. His request also presents an alternative that is the reverse of the traditional end of comedy: comedy usually celebrates man in society.

Célimène will not go with Alceste to live as a recluse because she is too much of a vibrant member of a living society, and her spirit in the play, though several times condemned for its apparent facade, has to be celebrated by the audience. She is left to be exposed by the fops because she must suffer for her falseness.

Society is affirmed at the end of the play in the persons of Philinte and Eliante, two of the more reasonable characters in the play. By their marriage, society is carried on after the turmoil of the exposures and expulsions in the last act.

Molière seems to be judging human behavior, which word implies *Man in Society*, as if it were on a linear scale. The extremes of behavior—too scrupulous and too unscrupulous—are equally execrable. Alceste cannot exist in society because he does not allow for man's being a fallen creature, weak in many ways. Célimène and her ilk cannot, or rather should not, survive because they are nothing *but* "fallen" creatures. Each group, of course, has to be judged in terms of the other, and since we know that Célimène (and her group) are the majority in the social system, a great deal of the criticism Molière metes out is directed at the particular society of his day, as somehow violating the principles of the generic thing, Society with a capital "S" which is affirmed in the comedy.

Philinte and Eliante are the closest thing we have to "normal" characters in the play. By their union at the end Society is rejuvenated. But it should be noted that even these two have weaknesses — Philinte is at times too compromising (Act IV, he lets his friend be slandered by Célimène), and Eliante is too weak. Molière, however, seems to recognize that man does have weaknesses — and so must those who carry on Society.

REVIEW QUESTIONS

1. Contrast the very first scene in the play with the final scene. Which characters are involved? Have they changed at all in the course of the action? Why does Molière "contain" the play in this kind of structure?

2. Think of man as a creature which exists in "society," and comment on the "rightness" and "wrongness" of Alceste's ideas and behavior.

3. To what effect do the two "love affairs" — Alceste and Célimène, and Philinte and Eliante — parallel each other? Think in terms of "rational" and "irrational" behavior.

4. In what particular ways do Alceste's beliefs hinder him in his efforts to woo Célimène?

5. What are the atitudes toward the man-woman relationship expressed in the play?

6. How does the type of language used by Alceste, and his obvious method of delivering his lines express his character? Contrast Alceste's speech with Philinte's in the scenes they share.

7. What is Molière's attitude toward Célimène? Look closely at the way she comports herself in Act II.

8. In what particular ways does the society in which Alceste lives soften our ridicule of him? Consider Oronte, Clitandre, and the other minor characters.

9. What kind of devices does Molière utilize to move the plot of the play along? Is "plot" particularly important in this play?

10. What possible norm of behavior would Molière advocate?

The Bourgeois Gentleman

LIST OF CHARACTERS

Monsieur Jourdain

A bourgeois who has pretensions to becoming a gentleman.

Madame Jourdain

His practical wife, who prefers to keep within her station in life.

Lucile

His daughter who wants to marry Cléonte.

Cléonte

A respectable young man who is in love with Lucile but who is not "noble" enough for M. Jourdain.

Dorimène

A marquise whom M. Jourdain is infatuated with.

Dorante

A titled gentleman who cheats M. Jourdain out of sums of money.

Nicole

Monsieur Jourdain's shrewd servant, who ridicules his foolish antics.

Covielle

Cléonte's shrewd servant, who is able to manipulate other people.

Dancing Master, Music Master, Fencing Master, Philosophy Master, Master Tailor, etc.

Various people whom M. Jourdain has hired to help him become a gentleman.

GENERAL PLOT SUMMARY

Monsieur Jourdain, a tradesman who has made an immense fortune, has aspirations to become a gentleman and move in the higher circles of society. He has hired a number of people to teach him the proper things that a gentleman should know. The Music Master, the Dancing Master, the Fencing Master, and the Philosophy Master all recognize that their employer is a man without taste and a buffoon, so they use their knowledge to ridicule him and cheat him out of everything they can.

Wanting to be accepted in society, M. Jourdain is flattered when the count, Dorante, pretends to be his friend. He never realizes that the count is merely using him so as to cheat him out of large sums of money. Furthermore, the count is in love with a wealthy marquise, Dorimène, and he uses M. Jourdain's money to buy her gifts and then tells Jourdain that the marquise thinks the gifts come from him.

Cléonte, a respectable young man of the middle class, wants to marry M. Jourdain's daughter, Lucile; but M. Jourdain wants his daughter to marry nobility. Madame Jourdain, a sensible and practical person, tries to arrange the marriage, but her husband is so obsessed with his folly that he will not agree to the match. Therefore, a fantastic plot is conceived whereby Cléonte will appear as a royal person from Turkey, and will make M. Jourdain a fictitious "mamamouchi" and then will ask for the daughter's hand. Monsieur Jourdain is simple enough to fall for the ruse, and allows his daughter to marry the disguised Cléonte.

SUMMARIES AND COMMENTARIES

NOTE: Because of the sketchiness of the dialogue in the play, summary divisions are made between acts rather than between scenes. The interval between each act is regularly marked by an "interlude," or stylized dance. For example, Act I concludes with a performance by four dance pupils executing their various steps; after Act II four journeymen tailors dance to express their joy over the money M. Jourdain has given them. Six cooks enter dancing with "banquets for Dorimène between Acts III and IV, and Act IV ends with six Turks dancing in the ceremony to ennoble Jourdain as a "mamamouchi." The play ends with the grand "Ballet of the Nations."

ACT I

Summary

After a musical overture the curtain rises to reveal the Music Master's pupil working by himself. The Music Master with three singers and two violinists enters from one side of the stage and a Dancing Master with four pupils from the other side.

The two masters greet each other and proceed to discuss their mutual student and benefactor, M. Jourdain. The Music Master is delighted to have someone like Jourdain as a student because he pays well, but the Dancing Master has reservations, exclaiming that "the best payment we can receive is to see our work appreciated," and Jourdain is hardly capable of that. The Music Master remains convinced that "his [Jourdain's] money purifies his bad taste."

Dressed in a gaudy striped dressing gown, lined with green and orange, M. Jourdain arrives attended by two lackeys. Monsieur Jourdain struts about the stage, exercising his power by snapping his fingers to test the attentions of his lackeys, by calling for the Dancing Master and the Music Master to show him their "little thingamajig," and finally by calling for their praise after "improving on" one of their songs.

Next the Music Master and the Dancing Master argue the relative merits of their respective arts, each claiming the world is somehow sustained by the art he practices. The act draws to a close with the performance of a pastoral operetta, and Jourdain's inane critical appraisal of it: "A neat job."

The act ends with the four dancing pupils presenting an interlude.

Commentary

This is not a straight realistic play, but is an entertainment composed of dance, song, and general buffoonery. Thus, at times, the plot and character delineation suffer at the expense of concentration on the dance and song. The musical overture at the beginning gives the audience a hint of the type of entertainment in store for them. However, this play is often presented with only the minimum amount of music and dance, emphasizing instead Molière's satire.

At the time of the play, the middle class was rising in importance, owing to the increase in commercial trading. There were appearing in seventeeth-century society people of immense newly acquired wealth who would want to buy a place in the social or aristocratic world with their money. Molière, then, is satirizing the pretensions of the type of person who because of his money thinks he can achieve a certain social status.

The above idea is suggested in the first scene, which functions as exposition. We find out how M. Jourdain's instructors feel about him as they discuss their employer before he arrives.

The Music Master says: "This M. Jourdain is a very nice property, with his visions of nobility and gallantry." As these two characters discuss their relationship with M. Jourdain, it becomes increasingly evident that they are silly fops. They talk about M. Jourdain's lack of taste and inflate their own sense of what constitutes good taste. The irony involved here lies in the fact that if M. Jourdain did possess any taste he would not have hired these charlatans. So it is that their jobs depend upon the fact that the employer they ridicule is indeed a man without any taste.

When M. Jourdain first appears onstage, he is dressed in ridiculous garb. He wears "a gorgeous striped dressing gown, lined with green and orange." This is a physical symbol of his extreme folly. His first actions are equally indicative of his folly. He has two lackeys following him and he suddenly calls them for no other purpose than to see if they are attentive.

A typical Molière technique is apparent between Scenes 1 and 2: the two "masters" are talking about M. Jourdain in derogatory terms, but as soon as he appears onstage they become very ingratiating. Also, they had earlier said that the only thing an artist wants is an appreciative audience, but when M. Jourdain sings his ridiculous song, both fops are excessive in their praise of this absurd ditty.

Besides satirizing Jourdain and the Music Master, Molière seems to be poking a bit of fun at some traditional ideas. The Music Master extols his particular art as that which is most important to the world because it is "a way to harmonize everything and bring universal peace into the world." The conception of the "harmony of the spheres" and the great unity in the universe becomes an amusing cliché in the mouth of this fop. The Music Master presents a brief entertainment for M. Jourdain in a pastoral setting. Jourdain then claps his hands to his head and cries, "Why are they always shepherds? All I ever see around is shepherds." This is a dig at the type of popular pastoral masques in which shepherds are always seen. Furthermore, it indicates the prosaic mind of the Music Master, who can only offer bad imitations of what is popularly successful. Even the words of the song suggest how trite and unoriginal the Music Master is.

The act ends with the dance prepared by the Dancing Master and with M. Jourdain wondering if there are to be more shepherds.

By the end of the first act, part of Molière's comic technique is apparent. He is gradually exposing M. Jourdain to situations which will then point out clearly how absurd this man is. The technique will continue until Jourdain is fully exposed and the audience can evaluate his extreme deviation from the norm of behavior.

ACT II

Summary

The dancers retire as M. Jourdain continues his lessons from the masters. When convinced that "people of quality" hold musicales at home every Wednesday or Thursday, he agrees to have them arranged for himself, provided they "put in an accordion too."

Two physically exhausting lessons for M. Jourdain ensue: one is in the minuet and the other is in fencing from the Fencing Master who has just arrived. The Fencing Master explains that the whole secret of swordplay consists in two things—"to give and not to receive."

The Fencing Master rekindles the broil of the first act by claiming the ultimate superiority of his profession over all others. The mishmash only thickens when the Philosophy Master arrives and, by ostensibly setting out to arbitrate the difficulty between the Music Master, Dancing Master, and Fencing Master, degrades these three professions in favor of his own. All three set on him and the melee is at full tilt.

When the other masters retire, the Philosophy Master begins M. Jourdain's instructions. Jourdain says he wants to learn "everything I can," but is taught nothing more than how to pronounce the vowels and consonants. He is overjoyed at learning that all his life he has had the eminent distinction of speaking "prose" and never knowing it.

Monsieur Jourdain's tailor arrives to dress him in his newly ordered suit. The suit is rather silly-looking, covered with upside-down flowers, but M. Jourdain is convinced it is the proper attire, because "all the people of quality wear them [their flowers] this way."

The act ends with Jourdain being dressed to music and showering gratuities on those dressing him because they address him as "Monsignor" and "your grace." The four journeymen tailors dance with glee as an interlude.

Commentary

In the first scene, when M. Jourdain suggests that an accordion should be used in the musicales, the Music Master, in what must be a very condescending and patronizing voice, puts him off by saying "just let us arrange everything." Obviously, the accordion has no place in a musical presentation.

Often the comedy depends upon slapstick and buffoonery rather than on fine lines of characterization. In the first scene, the farce is implicit in the manner in which M. Jourdain leaps about the stage trying to learn to dance. What would be obvious to the audience must be imagined by the reader of the play.

Immediately after the dancing lesson, the Fencing Master arrives to give a lesson. Again, the comedy lies in the ridiculous manner in which M. Jourdain practices his lessons. In the actual presentation, the actor would have to present this buffoon in exaggerated mannerisms and ridiculous antics. These scenes then gain in the amount of farce and slapstick comedy. Everything is absurd; the argument about whose art is superior reaches ridiculous proportions when the Fencing Master stubbornly insists that his own art is superior to all others.

We can anticipate the joke when the Philosophy Master arrives and tries to arbitrate the dispute by saying that "the grand answer one should make to all affronts, is moderation and patience." Within minutes we know that he will be frothing at the mouth as he calls the others infamous dogs and rogues, and insolent curs, and claims that his profession is the single most important profession.

When the Philosophy Master begins his instruction by asking M. Jourdain what he wants to learn, Jourdain answers "everything I can." This sentiment of wanting to learn is admirable, but the motive behind Jourdain's desire, linked with the particular situation of the farce, renders the sentiment purely ludicrous.

A large part of the comedy depends upon brief one-line, witty gags. For example, M. Jourdain asks: "What are the operations of the mind?" The Philosophy Master answers "The first, the second, and the third." The lessons actually deal with no more than learning how to speak the vowels. The farce will probably at least in part derive from the ridiculous faces that M. Jourdain makes as he tries to pronounce these letters (which he has naturally been pronouncing all his life anyway). In his mad desire for knowledge, he does not realize that he is being taught things which he already knows and furthermore which are useless. But when he finds out that he has been speaking "prose" all his life, he feels that he is amply rewarded by the Philosophy Master's instruction.

When the tailor appears, he is wearing a coat made out of the same material as that used to make a coat for M. Jourdain previously. Beside the fact that he is blatantly stealing from M. Jourdain, we see in his wearing the same ridiculous material that Jourdain has chosen a tailor with no taste and no honesty.

By the end of the first two acts, we have seen very little in the traditional sense of plot development. So far, Molière has been exposing his main character, M. Jourdain, to all types of absurdities so that the audience can fully evaluate his ridiculous behavior. Most of these people who are with him, however, are as absurd as he is. Consequently, we have not yet seen a norm of behavior by which to completely judge Jourdain's deviations.

ACT III

Summary

When the tailors exit, M. Jourdain and his lackeys are left alone onstage until Nicole shows up and bursts out laughing at the ridiculous sight of M. Jourdain in his new suit of clothes. He threatens to beat her if she doesn't stop laughing but she doesn't care: "That will do me more good." Madame Jourdain soon joins in the effort to persuade her husband that he is making a complete fool of himself, but he only persists in impressing her with his newly acquired knowledge: he asks if she has any idea that what she is speaking is "prose," and then he gives a fencing demonstration.

While Mme. Jourdain and Nicole are trying to tell the "bourgeois gentleman" that his friend, Dorante, is only his friend so that he can leech money from him, the count arrives and flatters M. Jourdain on the beauty of his new suit. Dorante claims to have come so they "can go over their accounts together." They figure that Dorante owes M. Jourdain 15,800 francs, and decide to add 200 pistoles and make it exactly 18,000 francs.

While M. Jourdain is fetching the money, Dorante tries to flatter Mme. Jourdain, but doesn't get very far. Dorante then takes M. Jourdain aside and tells him of arrangements that have been made for a private little banquet in honor of a certain marquise whom Jourdain fancies.

When Jourdain and Dorante leave, Mme. Jourdain first voices her suspicion of her husband, then turns to thoughts of her daughter's (Lucile's) relationship with Cléonte. Both she and Nicole approve, with Nicole expressing an interest in Cléonte's manservant. Nicole is sent to arrange for a meeting while exclaiming to the audience: "I think I'm going to make some people very happy."

Nicole rushes to tell Cléonte and Covielle (his servant) the good news, but they act disdainfully toward her, claiming to have been ignored by Lucile and Nicole when they last ran into one another in the street. Nicole retreats and the two men enter into an extended lament over the ill-treatment their loved ones have afforded them. "Tell me, please, all the evil you can about her [Lucile]," asks Cléonte of Covielle, but Covielle in a few minutes' time discovers that his friend finds Lucile perfect.

The two girls—Lucile and Nicole—arrive and try to soften the opinions of the men. In a brief time the roles are reversed with the men begging the girls to be forgiven for thinking ill of them. After the men threaten to leave, the women admit that they didn't acknowledge the men in the street because of the presence of Lucile's stern old aunt, "who is convinced that the mere approach of a man dishonors a girl."

The next scene is a confrontation between M. and Mme. Jourdain and the suitors. Jourdain asks Cléonte if he is a gentleman. Cléonte describes himself as a good bourgeois, but thinks that "any imposture is unworthy of a decent man." He then admits that he is not a gentleman. Thereupon, M. Jourdain dismisses him as a possible husband for his daughter. Madame Jourdain argues that Jourdain himself is as bourgeois as one can get, and is answered with a resounding "slander!" from her husband. He will have nothing less than a "gentleman" for his daughter.

When they are left alone, Covielle berates Cléonte for disrupting their plans for marriage—"You've got yourself into a nice mess with your high principles." Covielle then hatches a plan to play a practical joke on Jourdain with the help of an acting troupe. The subject is dropped as Jourdain enters. After mumbling something to his lackey about nobles having "the monopoly of honors and civility," Jourdain leaves.

Dorante enters with Dorimène, the "certain marquise" Jourdain fancies, but acts more like the suitor himself than as Jourdain's go-between. Dorimène thanks Dorante for all the lavish gifts (which Jourdain actually paid for), but tries to put him off as a suitor.

Jourdain comes in and makes an abortive attempt at a bow he had learned in his "education." In "asides" to Dorimène, Dorante comments on Jourdain as a bourgeois. Dorante warns Jourdain not to even mention any of the gifts he has bought for Dorimène, for it would be vulgar to do so.

The act ends with six cooks dancing as they bring in a table and several dishes.

Commentary

The opening conversation between M. Jourdain and Nicole at the beginning of the act gives us another figure typical in comedy: the clever servant who is in many ways superior to the master. Shortly, when M. Jourdain tries to teach her to fence so that he can show off his newly acquired knowledge, she masters the lesson rather rapidly and ends by being the superior fencer.

With the appearance of Nicole and Mme. Jourdain, we have the first rational characters to appear. Both see through M. Jourdain's absurdity at once and try to correct him. As Nicole laughs at him, we see that one of the purposes of comedy is to cure man of his foibles by laughter. Thus, Nicole is willing to take a beating from her master if he will allow her to continue laughing at him.

Madame Jourdain recognizes her husband's folly immediately, and her advice is perfectly rational. She is not impressed by all the lessons he receives because it does not help "run the house." She presents the sane and sensible view and tells her husband that he ought to think more of getting their daughter married than of learning these newfangled ideas.

As Jourdain shows Nicole how to fence, we must imagine what he looks like on the stage. We have the physical picture of a simpleton dressed in a gaudy, nonsensical costume and prancing about the stage fencing. His wife tries to bring him to his senses by saying "You are a fool, husband, with all these whims, and this is come to you since you have taken upon you to keep company with quality." Her statement prepares us for the entrance of Count Dorante in the next scene.

When Dorante arrives, the staging of the characters is expressive of the themes of the play. The sensible realists — Mme. Jourdain and Nicole — are placed to one side, and Dorante and M. Jourdain are together in a separate place. Dorante flatters Jourdain about being a gentleman so that he can fleece him of his money while the two realists stand aside and comment sanely on the situation. When Dorante blatantly flatters M. Jourdain, Mme. Jourdain says: "He scratches him where it itches."

The implicit irony in the situation is that M. Jourdain is flattered to have someone like Dorante visit him and he wants to emulate Dorante, but in reality, Dorante is nothing but a cheat and a thief. Madame Jourdain easily sees through Dorante's facade and will have nothing to do with him.

In this act the love intrigue is first presented. First, M. Jourdain is seen as the typical comic fool, that is, the old man (December) who is in love with a beautiful young woman (May). This subject is a perennial comic theme. Thus, M. Jourdain as the old man "December" figure will make a fool of himself.

Following the introduction of M. Jourdain's infatuation with the marquise, the true romance between Cléonte and Lucile is presented. This is Molière's use of balance to show the absurdity of M. Jourdain's infatuation. Furthermore, he introduces a third pair of lovers in the clever servants, Covielle and Nicole. Thus, with these diverse couples, the deviation of Jourdain is further demonstrated.

The manipulating type of servant who often advances the intrigues of plot in comedy is evident in both Nicole and Covielle. In the scene where Mme. Jourdain sends Nicole to see about matters pertaining to the wedding between Cléonte and Lucile, the servant alone onstage announces her role: "I think I'm going to make some people very happy." Later we shall see Cléonte's servant, Covielle, in a similar role when he arranges the scheme to "ennoble" M. Jourdain and marry the lovers.

The extended lamentation by Cléonte and Covielle over their perfidious lovers almost parallels in exaggeration the pastoral love scene arranged by the Music Master in Act I. Molière could surely be making the point that if the conception of pastoral lovers is ridiculous, the usual behavior of the real lovers is just as ridiculous. For example, his exaggerated statement: "I am going far away to die of grief and love," could be found in the most sentimental pastoral love scene. The behavior is exaggerated, but comedy often uses exaggeration to show the deviation from the norm of behavior.

If, however, everything in comedy were exaggeration and deviation from the norm, the audience would have difficulty determining the norm. Therefore, while Cléonte is ridiculous in some of his behavior, his expressions about imposture, honesty, and worthiness come close to being the norm to which we can react. Along with Mme. Jourdain, who supports Cléonte's claim, he seems to represent a rational voice which is the furthest removed from M. Jourdain's absurd actions and ideas.

Much of the staging of the play is stylized rather than realistic. For example, the scene between the four lovers is presented in terms of balance and contrasts, with two men and two women back to back hurling insults at one another. The comedy is in the fact that none of them *really* cares to be at odds with any of the others. They seem to be playing a game, taking turns accusing and entreating—the stylized game of pursuit and re-treat which characterizes the man-woman relationship and in which Molière sees the seeds for laughter.

Although Cléonte is somewhat ridiculed as a lover, in the scene where he refuses to lie to M. Jourdain, he does appear as the stable figure in the comedy. When asked if he is a gentleman, he states: "I look upon all imposture as unworthy of an honest man." But Molière seldom allows a character to come off scot free. Cléonte then is somewhat similar to Alceste in *The Misanthrope* in totally refusing to bend his views, and insisting upon total honesty when a little flattery would help him gain his ends.

While supporting him, Mme. Jourdain is seen as the practical person. Her advice constantly emphasizes the practical attitude toward any situation. She would not like her daughter to marry a man who would be ashamed of her; the idea that her daughter "should have children who should be ashamed to call me grandmother" upsets her. Instead, she says: "I'll have a man who shall be beholden to me for my daughter, and to whom I can say, 'Sit down, there, son-in-law, and dine with me.'"

When the marquise, Dorimène, appears, M. Jourdain tries to practice accomplishments that he has learned earlier and again makes a fool of himself. It is basically comic that he has to have the lady back up so that he can bow to her properly.

Whereas Acts I and II had confined themselves to presenting M. Jourdain in his absurd relations with the various "masters," Act III introduces subplots and shows M. Jourdain being even more ridiculous in the midst of society than he was when merely with his hirelings. By the end of this act, his absurdity has been almost completely revealed.

ACT IV

Summary

The stage is clear after the interlude except for Dorimène, Dorante, Jourdain and his lackeys, and a few singers. Dorimène praises the feast, but is told by Jourdain it is nothing at all, and by Dorante that it is completely unworthy of her. A tense moment for Dorante occurs when Jourdain remarks on the beauty of Dorimène's hands and she turns the subject to the beautiful diamond on her finger (which Jourdain paid for, but which Dorante took the credit of giving Dorimène).

Two singers then sing several drinking and love songs accompanied by an orchestra. After the songs Jourdain makes several not so artful advances toward Dorimène, but abruptly breaks off as his wife arrives. Madame Jourdain, who was supposed to have been off dining with her sister, scolds her husband for such extravagance in this dinner; Dorante happily relieves M. Jourdain of all the blame for having arranged and paid for the feast (and thus takes all the credit in Dorimène's eyes). Madame Jourdain remains irate, and so angers her husband to say: "These are nice tricks of yours! You come and insult me before everybody, and you drive people of quality out of the house!" But she doesn't care a straw for their quality, and claims "I'm defending my rights; and every woman will be on my side."

When Mme. Jourdain leaves, Cléonte's servant, Covielle, arrives dressed in oriental costume and claiming to have been away on distant journeys. He flatters M. Jourdain, telling him that he knew his father to be a gentleman of great renown. He further tells him that the son of the Grand Turk (Cléonte in disguise) desires to marry Lucile, his daughter, and furthermore that the Turk wants to do Jourdain the great honor of making him a "mamamouchi." Cléonte shows up and some joking ensues in a type of gibberish which M. Jourdain thinks is Turkish. All leave the scene except for Covielle, who explains to Dorante the purpose of the ruse.

The fourth interlude is the elaborate ennobling ceremony of M. Jourdain, a ceremony complete with Turkish musicians, dervishes, and a pagan religious dignitary known as a Mufti. The language of the celebrants is again the pseudo-sounding Turkish of the previous scene. By the time the Mufti reaches the point where he reads an invocation from a Koran which is placed on the prostrate Jourdain's back, the "bourgeois gentleman" is practically frightened out of his wits. After the final "presentation of the turban" to Jourdain, the Mufti is led from the stage, exhausted, by Turks and dervishes. M. Jourdain is left alone on the stage.

Commentary

The first striking thing about the opening of Act IV is the exaggerated language used by another pair of suitors—this time Jourdain and Dorante, seeking the favors of Dorimène. Each of the men belittles the feast before them as not worthy for such a personage as the marquise. Dorante only wishes it could have been a more "learned feast" with such things as "bread *de rive,* with the golden kissing-crust, raised all round with a crust that crumples tenderly in your teeth."

The opening scene of Act IV develops neatly with first one character, Dorante, having a close call with being discovered as a cheat; and then the other, Jourdain himself, with being found out by his wife. When Jourdain is admiring Dorimène's hand and she calls attention to the diamond, Dorante has an anxious moment; and then when Mme. Jourdain bursts in and interrupts the dinner, M. Jourdain is rescued by Dorante taking all the credit for the feast. The comedy of the scene is the complications caused by Mme. Jourdain's sudden appearance. The comedy also exists in the misunderstanding resulting when Mme. Jourdain begins to complain to Dorimène about M. Jourdain because, as we know, Dorimène is not aware that she is also being pursued by M. Jourdain. The common device of the "misunderstanding" to evoke laughter is thus also used by Molière.

Covielle appears in the ridiculous Turk's costume to advance the intrigue which he had planned in the previous act. Unlike his master, he knows exactly how to get what he wants from M. Jourdain. He simply "scratches the old man where he itches," by telling M. Jourdain that his father was a gentleman.

Jourdain fails to recognize any type of ruse going on, and completely ignores the nonsensical oriental costume. He cannot see through Covielle because of his obsessive desire to be flattered.

The reader should be aware that the King of France, Louis XIV, had invited the sultan to Versailles. The king had himself ordered a special suit of clothes in exceptional splendor and since the Turks expressed no admiration for either the magnificent palace or for the king's royal appearance, the king became piqued at the Turks and suggested to Molière that he write a comedy in which the Turks were to be ridiculed. Therefore, the appearance of the Turks in this act was an especially comic scene, since most of the audience knew of the king's annoyance at the Turks.

ACT V

Summary

Madame Jourdain comes onstage, sees her recently "mamamouchied" husband, and asks him: "You're dressing up for Hallowe'en at this time of year?" When her husband tries to explain the honor conferred on him, and begins to chant some "Turkish" and dance offstage, she is convinced that he has gone completely mad. She follows him offstage.

In the next scene Dorante professes to Dorimène that they ought to help Cléonte in his scheme to marry Lucile. She changes the subject to the lavish spending Dorante has supposedly been doing for her sake. She says they must put an end to it by getting married. He agrees with vigor.

Jourdain comes onstage, spouting "mamamouchi phrases" to Dorimène and Dorante: "I wish you the strength of serpents and the wisdom of lions." They play along with him in his folly.

When Cléonte arrives Jourdain does his best to introduce the "Turkish noble" to the two "French mamamouchis." Covielle enters and acts as "interpreter," and is soon followed by Lucile. When Jourdain first informs her that she is to marry this son of a Turk, she is horrified, bellowing that she will have no one other than Cléonte. When she recognizes the Turk as Cléonte she vows obedience to her father's wishes. Madame Jourdain then enters and is next to protest against her daughter's marriage to a "circus clown." Monsieur Jourdain pleads with her, of all things, to be "reasonable" about it and consent to the wedding. Madame Jourdain's cries abate when Covielle draws her aside and informs her of the trick and asks her as well to "fall in with your husband's mania" for the moment.

Madame Jourdain goes as far as to have a notary sent for to seal her daughter's marriage with the Turk (Cléonte). Dorante adds that the same notary can seal his contract with Dorimène. Monsieur Jourdain sees this merely as a trick on Mme. Jourdain. Nicole, Lucile's servant, is given to the Turk's interpreter (Covielle) to round off the series of marriages, as the play draws to a close with the grand Ballet of the Nations.

Commentary

The picture of M. Jourdain in Act V is another physical manifestation of the dunce he has been making of himself all along. Again, his dress is ridiculous; his wife asks him if he is dressed for Hallowe'en. Ironically, he has attained what he has always wanted—to be received into the nobility (any nobility)—and the fact that it is all a farce never enters his head. He is now content to be a mamamouchi. But equally comic is the fact that he makes a bad mamamouchi. He unwittingly reverses the "traditional" greeting of the mamamouchis by saying "I wish you the strength of the serpent and the wisdom of the lion" instead of "the strength of the lion and wisdom of the serpent."

With the perennial cry of a man obsessed with one passion or idea, M. Jourdain remains to the very end a fool, claiming that the rest of the world is being perfectly "unreasonable" for not agreeing with him. The play ends in a typically comic fashion with the pairing off of the three sets of lovers.

CHARACTER ANALYSES

JOURDAIN

The central character of the play is a wealthy bourgeois Parisian whose one aspiration in life is to educate himself in the ways of a gentleman, and by so doing elevate his position in society. In the abstract such an aspiration appears admirable, but as it turns out with M. Jourdain, the aspiration—even at the beginning of the play—is an obsession which blinds him to everything else.

His folly is perfectly obvious to everyone, audience included, but not to himself. In the first act his foolishness is physically displayed by the very "stylish" coat he wears, complete with upside-down floral designs; in the last act, we see him "beturbaned as a mamamouchi."

As an older man, he cuts an equally absurd figure in his pursuit of Dorimène. The irony implicit in this pursuit is the fact that his go-between, Dorante, a member of the noble class which Jourdain aspires to, shows himself as a culprit by cheating the bourgeois of his money and doing his best to court Dorimène for himself.

Jourdain, like the other characters in the play, is not a complex figure. He is a man who, by his obsession, has set himself off from society, and is consequently ridiculed by society. His plight is not pitiful because he is such an unthinking person. He never has the slightest impression that he is the butt of laughter. His single cry to all the other characters is that they are "unreasonable," while in reality he is the most unreasonable character in the play.

MADAME JOURDAIN

Her practical attitude toward life, evidenced by her efficient summary in Act III of what a woman should look for in a husband, sets her at odds immediately with the folly of her own husband. Her task throughout the play is to try to rescue his sanity. She is generally a favorable character in the eyes of the audience, both as a mentally stable personality in a world of fops and flatterers, and as a woman of sprightly intelligence in her own right. She adeptly puts the wily Dorante in his place in Act III when he tries to sidle up to her; she seems to see through all the pretense of the play. Yet, she is wise enough to go along with some form of pretense to bring about the marriage which she strongly desires.

CLEONTE

Cléonte functions in a role similar to M. Jourdain's when he shows up the idiocy of M. Jourdain's aspirations: Cléonte refuses to have anything to do with being a "gentleman" himself. As the lover of Jourdain's daughter, Lucile, however, he is represented as a bit of a fool himself. He is spoofed as the conventional young man in love whose speech is syrupy and whose actions are exaggerated. In the end, however, his marriage to Lucile functions as the happy continuation of the social order despite the folly of some of its more important members.

NICOLE AND COVIELLE

The relationship between these two servants parallels that between their masters, and the consummation of it in the end parallels the function of the marriage on the higher level of society. Significant about Nicole and Covielle is their role as traditional clever servants who act in some ways as foils to their masters. Nicole tries to laugh Jourdain out of his folly the first time she sees him; Covielle at one point remarks on Cléonte's stubbornness in his attitude toward M. Jourdain. Both servants also manipulate the action of the play to bring it to its happy conclusions.

DORANTE

Dorante deserves mention as the single representative of that order of society to which Jourdain aspires. Without stretching the idea too far, we can almost perceive Molière presenting this noble as a liar and cheat to indicate that in some ways Jourdain is better off as a "mamamouchi" of the "Turkish court" than as a real French noble.

A NOTE ON THE TITLE

For those unfamiliar with the historical backgrounds, some explanation may be in order concerning the implications of Molière's title *Le Bourgeois gentilhomme*. A modern reader accustomed to a theoretically classless society wherein position in the social structure is loosely determined by education, occupation, or income may find it difficult to comprehend seventeenth-century attitudes conditioned by centuries of adherence to the doctrine of fixed classes.

In our day the large, vaguely defined segment of population called the "middle class" is sometimes termed the *bourgeosie*. Today "gentleman" has become a general designation, which may have connotations of respect and special courtesy, but often does not.

But this was not always the case; originally only members of the upper classes were gentlemen. The plain, untitled "gentleman" stood on the lowest rung among those held to be distinguished by "gentility," but he was nevertheless unmistakably elevated above those deemed beneath him in rank. Thus when John Shakespeare was officially granted permission to display a coat of arms, the privilege was automatically conferred on his son, who was thenceforeward invariably known as "William Shakespeare, gentleman."

The urban dwellers comprised of artisans, professionals, and merchants constituted the bourgeois class. Their status was not merely a matter of custom and tradition, but was expressly regulated by law. Each level had its particular rights, privileges, and obligations that had evolved during the Middle Ages.

By Molière's time, however, the medieval hierarchy had begun to creak under various strains. Among other things, many of the nobility and gentry were experiencing severe financial adversity. On the other hand, prosperous bourgeois were accumulating great wealth, with its attendant power and influence. So it was becoming common for highborn offspring to be married to the children of rich bourgeois in order to restore declining fortunes. The practice was, nevertheless, still regarded with distaste, and such a match was a *mésalliance*.

In this manner, a bourgeois might contrive to insinuate his descendants into a more illustrious class. But he himself could in no way escape from his niche, except by some official act, or possibly by the purchase of an estate that might have a title attached to it.

Accordingly, it was manifestly impossible for a man to be a "bourgeois" and a "gentleman" at one and the same time, which is what M. Jourdain was innanely trying to do. We might casually characterize someone of the middle class or a businessman as a gentleman, but for Molière's audience "bourgeois gentleman" would be an absurdity only to be applied in jocularity.

Therefore the literal translation of *Le Bourgeois gentilhomme* as *The Bourgeois Gentleman* loses some of the sharp irony that Molière intended. For that reason, in an attempt to convey the the sense explicit in Molière's title, it is often rendered, somewhat awkwardly, as *The Would-be Gentleman*.

REVIEW QUESTIONS

1. In your opinion, what characteristics in this play appeal strongly to the audience—the plot? the ideas? the farce? the characters?

2. Considering his association with Dorante, what is the irony implicit in M. Jourdain's aspirations to be a gentleman?

3. How do you justify the first two acts of the play? After all, nothing much happens to advance the plot.

4. In terms of all five acts, how important is the plot?

5. If Molière's purpose was to expose the Bourgeois Gentleman in all of his absurdities, does it take five acts to accomplish this? Would you consider the last act superfluous?

6. How does Cléonte represent the voice of normalcy? How does he vary from normalcy?

7. Comment on the function of the various masters and then on the function of the servant, Nicole.

8. What advice does Mme. Jourdaine contribute to the play which entitles her to be called the voice of practicality?

Selected Bibliography

CHATFIELD-TAYLOR, HOBART C. *Molière: A Biography.* New York: Duffield & Co., 1906. A basic factual account of Molière's life that takes into consideration various discrepancies.

FERNANDEZ, RAMON. *Molière.* Tr. WILSON FOLLET. New York: Hill & Wang, 1958. This book tries to come to an understanding of the personality of Molière through a close reading of his plays.

GUICHARNAND, JACQUES. *Molière: A Collection of Critical Essays.* Englewood Cliffs, N.J.: Prentice-Hall, 1964.

HUBERT, JUDD DAVID. *Molière and the Comedy of Intellect.* Berkeley: University of California Press, 1962. Examines the intellectual basis of Molière's great plays.

MANTZIUS, KARL. *History of Theatrical Art.* London: Duckworth & Co., 1908. Attempts to place Molière's works in the long tradition of the theater, beginning with the earliest Greek plays.

MOORE, W. G. *Molière: A New Criticism.* Oxford: Clarendon Press, 1949. This book is another close reading of the internal structure and meaning of the plays as approached from a textual critical viewpoint.

TURNELL, MARTIN. *The Classicial Moment.* New York: New Directions, 1948. Includes essays on Molière, Racine, and Corneille, and discusses Molière in terms of the neoclassical period in France.

WILCOX, JOHN. *The Relation of Molière to Restoration Comedy.* New York: Benjamin Blom, 1962. This is a specialized study of the influence of Molière on Restoration comedy in England.

WRIGHT, C. H. C. *French Classicism*. Cambridge, Mass.: Harvard University Press, 1920. A good survey of the classical period which touches upon the type of social milieu in which Molière wrote.

NOTES

NOTES

NOTES

NOTES

NOTES

THE THREE MUSKETEERS

NOTES

including
- *Life of the Author*
- *Introduction to the Novel*
- *List of Characters*
- *Brief Plot Synopsis*
- *Selected Genealogies*
- *Summaries & Commentaries*
- The Three Musketeers *as Film*
- *Suggested Essay Questions*
- *Selected Bibliography*

by
James L. Roberts, Ph.D.
Department of English
University of Nebraska

Cliffs Notes

INCORPORATED

LINCOLN, NEBRASKA 68501

Editor

Gary Carey, M.A.
University of Colorado

Consulting Editor

James L. Roberts, Ph.D.
Department of English
University of Nebraska

ISBN 0-8220-1300-2
© Copyright 1989
by
C. K. Hillegass
All Rights Reserved
Printed in U.S.A.

1989 Printing

Cliffs Notes, Inc.   Lincoln, Nebraska

CONTENTS

THE THREE MUSKETEERS
Notes

LIFE OF THE AUTHOR

Alexandre Dumas was perhaps the most popular author of the nineteenth century, and his best works continue to be popular today. Two of his novels, *The Three Musketeers* and *The Count of Monte Cristo,* are ranked among the best adventure stories of the world and have been read by countless thousands. *The Three Musketeers* has also been the subject of many movies and has inspired many similar types of swashbuckling films.

Born on July 24, 1802, Dumas was one of the most prolific writers of the nineteenth century. His father, a mulatto, was somewhat of an adventurer-soldier and was not a favorite of Napoleon because of his staunch republicanism. When his father died, young Dumas was only four, and the family was left in rather severe financial straits. The young boy's formal education was scanty, most of it provided by a priest, and as soon as he could qualify, Dumas worked in the office of a lawyer. As he grew older, he became close friends with the son of an exiled Swedish nobleman, and the two of them began to dabble in vaudeville enterprises.

As a young man, Dumas went to Paris and secured a position as a clerk to the Duc d'Orleans; this was a marvelous stroke of good fortune, for the Duc would soon become king, and Dumas would write a superb memoir about his many and varied mishaps while he was employed by the future king. At the same time, Dumas and an old friend, Adolphe de Leuven, produced several melodramas.

When Dumas was twenty-two, his life underwent a drastic change: first, he wrote and produced his own melodrama which was a popular success and, second, he became the father of an illegitimate son by a dressmaker. When the boy was seven, Dumas went to court to get custody of the boy and succeeded.

Professionally, these years were extremely happy times for Dumas; for six years, he and Leuven had been collaborating on plays, and their legitimate dramas had been staged to much popular acclaim. In 1829, Dumas' *Henry III et sa Cour* (Henry III and his Court) was produced; it was Dumas' first spectacular triumph. The Duc was so fond of it that he appointed Dumas the librarian of the Palais Royale.

The Revolution of 1830 interrupted Dumas' playwriting, and for a pleasant and amusing account of these years, one should consult Dumas' memoirs for many richly humorous anecdotes (don't worry unduly about the degree of truth in them). Later, because Dumas was implicated in some "irregularities" during a noted general's funeral, he decided to "tour" Switzerland; as a result, we have another long series of memoirs, this time issued as travel books. It should be noted, though, that Dumas always retained his affectionate relationship with the Duc and that he eventually returned to France, where he composed many first-rate, long-running plays.

Dumas' well-known collaboration with Auguste Maquet began in 1837 and resulted in a series of historical novels in which Dumas hoped to reconstruct the major events of French history. For example, in *The Three Musketeers,* the musketeers are united in order to defend the honor of Anne of Austria (the queen of France) against Cardinal Richelieu's schemes. This particular novel was so popular that Dumas immediately composed two sequels and, by coincidence, his other great novel, *The Count of Monte Cristo,* was also written during this same creative period, even though the time periods of the two novels vary greatly.

With the aid of collaborators, Dumas turned out so much fiction and miscellaneous writing that it has been remarked that "no one has ever read the whole of Dumas, not even himself." We know now, however, that Dumas' assistants provided him with only rough plotlines and suggested incidents. He himself filled in the outlines, and all of his manuscripts are in his handwriting.

Like so many creative and productive men, Dumas' life ended in a series of personal and financial tragedies. He built a strangely beautiful and impressive French Gothic, English Renaissance hybrid mansion and filled it with a multitude of scavenger-friends; both his home and his hangers-on were tremendous drains on his purse, as was the construction and upkeep of his own theater, the Theatre Historique, built specifically for the performance of his own plays.

In 1851, Dumas moved to Brussels, as much for his political advantage as to escape creditors – despite the 1,200 volumes which bore his name – and he died not long after a scandalous liaison with an American circus girl, a situation that he might well have chosen as a fictional framework for his demise.

Dumas' son, Alexandre ("Dumas *fils*"), is remembered today chiefly for his first novel, *The Lady of the Camellias,* which was the basis for the libretto of Verdi's opera *La Traviata,* as well as the plot of one of Hollywood's classic films, *Camille,* starring Greta Garbo.

INTRODUCTION TO THE NOVEL

In order to understand and enjoy this novel to the fullest, one should be acquainted with a special kind of novel – the "swashbuckling novel," a novel which is filled to the brim with intrigue, adventure, and romance. One rarely, if ever, encounters this kind of novel in contemporary fiction, and it was very popular during the nineteenth century. Dumas was a master of this genre.

Basically, the swashbuckling novel combines the best elements of the novel of intrigue, the novel of adventure, and the novel of romance. The novel of intrigue involves plots and sub-plots in which one person or a group of people are involved in elaborate plots or schemes of one nature or another. This kind of novel is often, but need not be, about love and is frequently concerned with the intrigues of spies, the takeover of some enterprise, or political intrigue.

The novel of adventure is, as the term suggests, one which involves all kinds of adventures, most commonly those which take place on the highroads. For example, d'Artagnan's trip to London to retrieve the diamond tags for the queen and his various adventures and encounters with the enemy along the way constitute a novel of adventure. Usually, a main character's life is at stake, but this need not be necessarily so.

The novel of romance involves a simple love story of some nature, and there are several basic love stories in *The Three Musketeers* – for example, the duke of Buckingham's love for Anne of Austria, the queen of France; he will do anything for the pleasure of being in her presence. D'Artagnan is continually astonished at the duke's extravagant sacrifices – merely to please this lady. Likewise, d'Artagnan will undertake a dangerous journey solely because of his love for and devotion to Constance Bonacieux, a love that is, as we see toward the end of the novel, deeply reciprocated.

The term "swashbuckling" refers most often to a combination of the above three elements, accompanied by extreme histrionics – fantastic dueling and hair-raising escapades, narrow escapes, and desperate situations. These escapades are often seen as heroics – such as the episode where d'Artagnan and the three musketeers make a bet to stay in the bastion for an hour, and during this time, they stave off a number of the enemy.

Most often, the term "swashbuckling" is associated with dueling, especially when the hero is outnumbered by lesser swordsmen or when he encounters a superb opponent and yet easily disarms or conquers him. There is a good deal of swaggering (especially by Porthos); there is also a good amount of bantering, bragging, bravado, and exaggeration (by all three of the musketeers and d'Artagnan), and, of course, d'Artagnan is the perfect example of the swashbuckler because he is handsome, an expert dueler, and a superb swordsman. D'Artagnan is a young man captivated by love and romance and willing to undertake any type of adventure merely for the sake of adventure – but certainly for the sake of the woman he loves.

LIST OF CHARACTERS

D'Artagnan (där·tàn yän')

The main character of the novel, d'Artagnan was raised in the French province of Gascony, an area known for its courageous and brave men. The novel begins with his departure from home and his arrival in Paris, taking with him virtually nothing but his good looks, his honesty and integrity, his loyalty to both the king and the cardinal, and his expert swordsmanship. Despite initial blunders and difficulties, d'Artagnan quickly makes friends with the three musketeers, and later he finds himself in a position to do a great service for the queen of France. D'Artagnan's name has become synonymous with a fearless adventurer and a swashbuckling swordsman. At the end of the novel, d'Artagnan's dream of becoming a member of the King's Musketeers is fulfilled, and he is given a commission in the company.

THE THREE MUSKETEERS

Athos (à·tôs′)

Wounded when d'Artagnan first meets him, Athos will later prove to be the person who wrote his memoirs about these adventurers. He is the most aristocratic of the three musketeers and also the oldest, but d'Artagnan feels closer to Athos than to the other two. Long before Athos reveals that he is the young nobleman who married the wicked Milady (Lady de Winter) during his youth, d'Artagnan is deeply impressed by him. Athos′ real name is Count de La Fère.

Aramis (à·rà·mē′)

He is supposedly passing his time as a musketeer until the queen provides France with an heir, at which time Aramis will enter the priesthood. He was brought up in a monastery, and it was assumed that he would become a priest, but when he was nineteen, he met a young lady and became extremely devoted to her. An officer ordered him never to speak to her again, and so Aramis left the monastery, took fencing lessons for a year, and eventually challenged and killed the haughty officer. Even though we are never told so directly, the lady in question is apparently Madame de Chevreuse, a close friend to the queen. She now lives in exile in Tours.

Porthos (pôr·tôs′)

The most worldly of the three musketeers, Porthos is extremely proud of his worldly good looks and his fine physique, which he shows off to its best advantage by dressing to impress the women of society, who seem to fully appreciate his good looks and his courtly attentions. He is devoted to good food and comfortable surroundings. At the end of the novel, Porthos gives up musketeering in order to marry an older woman who has inherited a fortune.

THE MUSKETEERS′ SERVANTS

Planchet (plän·shā′)

D'Artagnan's servant. He is ultimately the sharpest of the servants and serves his master well on many dangerous occasions. Unlike d'Artagnan, Planchet is prudent, but still exhibits moments of great courage and ingenuity. Planchet is able to make a long and dangerous trip to England by himself, and at the end of the novel, he is rewarded for his daring and made a sergeant in the guards.

Grimaud (grē·mō')

Athos' servant. Because his master is mannerly and rather reticent, Grimaud is also rather reserved. One of the comic incidents in the novel focuses on Athos' forbidding Grimaud to speak unless it is an absolute emergency. A dignified silence passes between them, and thus Grimaud upholds the quiet nobility of his master.

Bazin

Aramis' servant. Because Aramis is planning to enter the priesthood, it is only fitting that Bazin should also contemplate a future devoted to the religious life. His utmost desire is to be the servant of a high church official. Bazin believes that Aramis is capable of attaining the rank of cardinal.

Mousqueton (müs·kə·tōn')

Porthos' servant. Like his master, Mousqueton is the most knowledgeable about worldly things. For example, when his master is wounded and is confined to an inn with no money, Mousqueton is able to poach some choice wild game and fish, and he is extremely clever about Western-style roping, a talent he puts to good use when his master needs wine. Cunningly, Mousqueton lassos bottles of wine like an expert and hauls them back to Porthos.

OTHER CENTRAL CHARACTERS

Monsieur de Tréville (də trə·vēl')

The captain of the King's Musketeers, he is an old friend of d'Artagnan's father; thus he will be a special protector of the youthful and impulsive d'Artagnan. He also acts as d'Artagnan's special confidant and advisor and, being genuinely fond of the young man, he watches over him carefully.

Monsieur Bonacieux (bô·nän·syoe′)

D'Artagnan's unprincipled landlord who seeks d'Artagnan's help when his young wife is kidnapped; later, he becomes one of the cardinal's toadies, and he even assists in the kidnapping of his own wife.

Constance Bonacieux (kōn·stäns′ bô·nän·syoe′)

Bonacieux's wife; she is more than thirty years younger than her husband. Through the influence of her godfather, she has become the queen's linen maid; she is fiercely loyal to the queen. When d'Artagnan first rescues her from the clutches of the cardinal's men, he falls madly in love with her. Consequently, she is able to convince him to go to London in order to save the queen's reputation. Constance eventually realizes that she is in love with d'Artagnan.

Milady, alias Lady de Winter

She represents the quintessence of evil in the novel; she is d'Artagnan's wicked nemesis (someone bent on revenge). At first, d'Artagnan is deeply attracted to her physical beauty and charm; however, even after he hears how much she despises him and how she plans to have him murdered, he is still captivated by her loveliness. She acts as the cardinal's personal spy and is responsible for the deaths of (1) a young priest; (2) the duke of Buckingham; (3) de Winter's assistant, John Felton; (4) Constance Bonacieux; and (5) she is probably responsible for her husband, de Winter's, death. In all probability, she is responsible for the deaths of many other innocent, insignificant people who got in the way of her crafty machinations. Milady is finally tracked down by d'Artagnan, the three musketeers, and her brother-in-law, and she is tried and beheaded for her numerous and brutal crimes.

Lord de Winter

Lady de Winter's brother-in-law; he suspects that Milady killed his brother in order to inherit vast family properties. When she arrives in England, he knows of her intent to murder Buckingham and himself, so he has her imprisoned. After Felton helps free her and Buckingham is murdered, de Winter joins the others who are determined to punish her. He accuses her of the deaths of his brother, of Buckingham and John Felton, and he votes for her beheading.

King Louis XIII

The king of France—but not a very strong or effective king. He resents Cardinal Richelieu, but he recognizes his dependence on this powerful man.

Queen Anne, or Anne of Austria

The king's Spanish queen; she is romantically involved with the duke of Buckingham, a powerful politician in England. Since France is at war with England, Buckingham is an enemy of France; nonetheless, Anne is in love with him, and it is her intrigue with Buckingham which causes d'Artagnan to go on his first adventure to London to retrieve a gift that the queen made to the duke. Despite her love for the masterful Buckingham, Anne is faithful and loyal to her husband, the weak and incapable king of France.

Cardinal Richelieu (rē shə·lyoe')

Historically, he was one of the most powerful diplomats of his time, controlling both individual people and nations with his clever and astute machinations. In this novel, he is presented as the antagonist to the queen—primarily, we are led to believe, because she rejected his romantic advances. Richelieu has spies throughout the country, constantly monitoring the activities of the musketeers, yet he clearly respects their bravery and courage—especially d'Artagnan's, to whom he offers a commission, a lieutenancy.

George Villiers, duke of Buckingham

Next to the king of England, he is the most powerful man in England; just as the cardinal controls France, so the duke controls England. These two powerful men once vied for the love of Queen Anne, but since the duke won, he has been an enemy to the cardinal—in matters of politics *and* love. Buckingham is reputed to be the most handsome man in Europe, besides being one of the most powerful and wealthy, and he is willing to use all of his power, wealth, and influence simply to be near the queen. His love for Anne is so great that he would make any compromise for her. The cardinal knows about this devotion and uses it to his advantage. Buckingham is killed by John Felton, a puritan fanatic.

John Felton

A neurotic puritan whom Milady is able to manipulate by pretending to be a "persecuted puritan." Felton's blind devotion to his religion renders him impossible to judge the greatness of Buckingham or to look upon Buckingham as anything but a libertine who should be put to death. Felton is Milady's instrument whereby she can bring about the duke's death.

"The Man from Meung" (Count de Rochefort) (də rôsh·fôr')

This man, the personal representative of the cardinal, is also d'Artagnan's nemesis. He is the man who steals d'Artagnan's introduction to Tréville while d'Artagnan is on his way to Paris, and it is de Rochefort who continually appears at various places at unexpected times. He is the man who is twice in charge of abducting Constance Bonacieux, and he is the man who finally tries to arrest d'Artagnan for the cardinal, who ultimately orders the two men to become friends.

MINOR CHARACTERS

Bernajoux

One of the most gifted swordsmen in the cardinal's guards. He insults d'Artagnan at a tennis game, and during the ensuing duel, he is defeated by d'Artagnan, thereby making d'Artagnan's name known throughout Paris.

Count de Wardes

He first appears as a man with permission to cross the English channel when the ports have been closed by the cardinal's order. D'Artagnan wounds de Wardes, and later, in Paris, d'Artagnan discovers through Milady's maid, Kitty, that Milady is in love with the count. D'Artagnan then poses as the count in order to make love to Milady.

The Executioner of Lille

Athos discovers this man in his laboratory, piecing together a human skeleton. He shows him the piece of paper which the cardinal once gave to Milady, authorizing its bearer to demand any request. When Athos returns with the executioner, the man is wearing a mask and a large red cloak.

During the "trial scene," the executioner reveals that Milady seduced his fifteen-year-old brother into stealing church relics. Both were caught, but Milady escaped, and the boy was convicted as a common criminal; thus the executioner of Lille had to burn the fleur-de-lis onto the shoulder of his own young brother—all because of Milady's evil power. The executioner vowed to find Milady and brand her—and eventually he found her and branded her. Afterward, the brother escaped, hoping to find Milady, and the executioner had to serve out his brother's prison term. Meanwhile, Milady seduced the lord of the province (Athos; de La Fère) and spurned the runaway priest. Dejected, the young man surrendered to the authorities, and during his first evening in jail, he hanged himself.

Monsieur de La Porte

The queen's gentleman-in-waiting; he is also Constance Bonacieux's godfather. Because of his influence, Constance becomes the queen's linen maid.

Kitty

Milady's lovely and attractive maid who is infatuated with d'Artagnan and, consequently, helps him get revenge against Milady.

Chancellor Seguier

The man whom the king assigns to search the queen's room and her person, believing that she has written a love letter to the duke of Buckingham.

Monsieur des Essarts

The captain of the king's guards and d'Artagnan's superior, who urges d'Artagnan to volunteer for important missions.

Madame Coquenard

Porthos' mistress; she is about fifty – very rich and very miserly. Porthos uses his good looks and charm to get her to buy him equipment for the siege of La Rochelle.

Brisemont

Milady's hired assassin who fails in his attempt to kill d'Artagnan, but because his life is spared, he becomes d'Artagnan's devoted servant until he accidentally tastes the poisoned wine sent by Milady and dies, thus saving d'Artagnan's life.

The Queen's Ladies-in-Waiting

- Madame de Chevreuse has been exiled to Tours because the king thinks that she is conspiring against him; she is Aramis' beloved.
- Madame de Lannoy is one of the cardinal's spies; she reports all of the queen's activities to him; in this way, the cardinal knows about the diamond tags which the queen gave to Buckingham.
- Madame Bois-Tracy is a trusted friend of the queen.

BRIEF PLOT SYNOPSIS

D'Artagnan, a poor but noble young man from Gascony, leaves his home to make his fortune in Paris; he is carrying a letter of introduction to his father's friend, Monsieur de Tréville, captain of the King's Musketeers. On the way to Paris, d'Artagnan's impulsive nature gets him into trouble; he is beaten and the letter of introduction is taken from him. In Paris, he nevertheless is granted an interview with Monsieur de Tréville and is promised acceptance in the Royal Academy free of charge, where he can learn fencing, riding, and good manners; later, with experience, d'Artagnan can expect to become a musketeer.

While Tréville is writing a new letter of introduction, d'Artagnan glances out the window and, by accident, sees the person who robbed him. He runs after him, and while pursuing him, he offends three musketeers: first, he collides with Athos, reinjuring Athos' wounded shoulder; then he jostles Porthos and reveals a partly counterfeit golden shoulder belt that he is wearing; and finally, he offends Aramis by ungallantly and unintentionally bringing attention to a lady's

ROYAL GENEALOGY

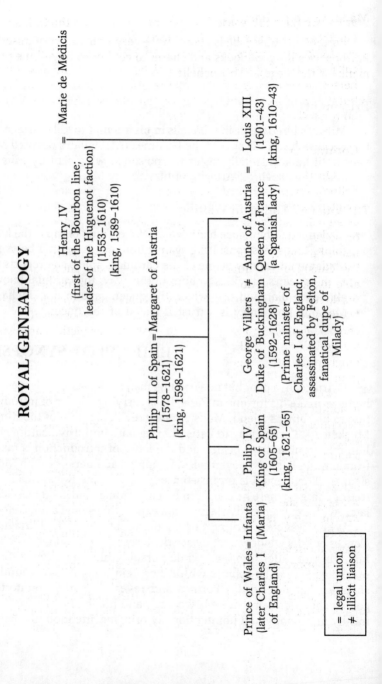

Henry IV
(first of the Bourbon line;
leader of the Huguenot faction)
(1553–1610)
(king, 1589–1610)

= Marie de Médicis

Philip III of Spain = Margaret of Austria
(1578–1621)
(king, 1598–1621)

George Villers ≠ Anne of Austria = Louis XIII
Duke of Buckingham   Queen of France   (1601–43)
(1592–1628)   (a Spanish lady)   (king, 1610–43)
(Prime minister of
Charles I of England;
assassinated by Felton,
fanatical dupe of
Milady)

Philip IV
King of Spain
(1605–65)
(king, 1621–65)

Prince of Wales = Infanta
(later Charles I   (Maria)
of England)

= legal union
≠ illicit liaison

MILADY'S GENEALOGY

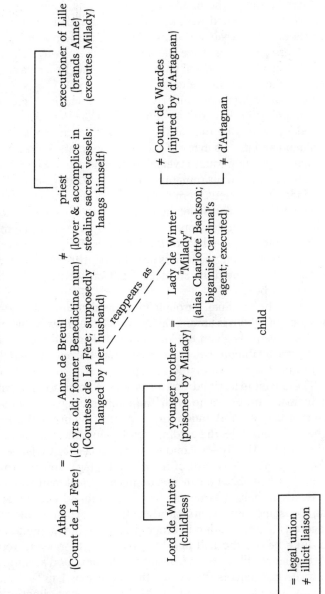

handkerchief. He is challenged to a duel by each of the musketeers.

After he meets the musketeers and begins dueling with Athos, they are all threatened with arrest by the dreaded cardinal's guards because of a law against dueling. D'Artagnan joins forces with the musketeers and helps drive the cardinal's men away. Thus, almost immediately after his arrival in Paris, d'Artagnan becomes an intimate friend of the three musketeers.

One day, d'Artagnan's elderly landlord, Bonacieux, comes to ask him for help; the landlord's young wife, Constance, has been kidnapped – probably by the cardinal's men because she is the queen's linen maid and knows many of the queen's secrets, secrets which the cardinal desperately wants revealed so that he can discredit the queen, who earlier rejected his romantic advances. D'Artagnan is able to rescue Madame Bonacieux from her abductors and, while doing so, falls in love with her. Later, when he inadvertently sees her cross a bridge with a strange man, he stops them and discovers that the man is an English nobleman, the duke of Buckingham, the queen's secret lover; being an Englishman, the man is also an enemy of France. That night, the queen gives the duke an elegant gift of twelve diamond tags in a rosewood box.

When the cardinal, through his extended and vast network of spies (one of whom is among the queen's ladies-in-waiting) discovers that the queen has given Buckingham the diamond tags, he asks the king to give a fabulous ball and demand that the queen wear the king's gift to her: the twelve diamond tags.

The queen is terrified when she learns about the ball and hears her husband order her to wear the diamond tags. She knows very well that they are in London, in the possession of the duke of Buckingham. Meanwhile, the cardinal sends one of his spies – the elegant and beautiful Milady – to London; he instructs her to dance with the duke, snip off at least two of the diamond tags, and return them to the cardinal so that he can use them in a blackmail scheme.

Ready to help the queen regain the diamond tags, whatever the cost, Constance Bonacieux pleads with d'Artagnan to undertake the dangerous trip to London in order to retrieve the diamond tags from the duke before the ball and thereby save the queen's reputation. D'Artagnan readily accepts Constance's request, and accompanied by the three musketeers, he begins the hazardous trip to London. On the way, they are continually ambushed by the cardinal's spies, and one by one, the musketeers are foiled from accompanying d'Artagnan to London.

When d'Artagnan reaches London, he reports the situation to Buckingham, who discovers in horror that two of the tags are missing. Immediately, he calls in his personal jeweler and instructs him to work furiously in order to make exact copies. He gives the copies to d'Artagnan, along with the remaining ten tags, and a superb, prearranged series of horses that will take d'Artagnan from London to Paris in twelve hours. Thus, the queen is able to appear in what seems to be all twelve of the diamond tags – to the utter astonishment of the cardinal. For d'Artagnan's heroic efforts, the queen secretly presents him with a large, magnificent diamond ring.

After agreeing to a rendezvous with Constance (which never takes place because she is again abducted by the cardinal's men), d'Artagnan is told that it is dangerous to remain in Paris: the cardinal knows everything that happens in Paris; it will not be long before he learns about d'Artagnan's role in the diamond tag escapade. D'Artagnan therefore decides that this would be a good time to discover what happened to his musketeer friends.

He returns to each of the places where he left them, and finding them all safe, they return to Paris – only to discover that they must buy equipment for the king's next military maneuver: the siege of La Rochelle. Each of the musketeers must find some way of getting money – something they are always short of.

While pondering how to get some cash, d'Artagnan sees Milady by accident and is overwhelmed by her beauty; he follows her and tries to protect her from a bothersome man who turns out to be her brother-in-law. The brother-in-law challenges d'Artagnan to a duel and they fight. D'Artagnan overpowers him, but spares his life. In appreciation for his life, the brother-in-law – Lord de Winter – introduces d'Artagnan to Milady, Lady de Winter. Meanwhile, Milady's maid sees d'Artagnan and falls in love with him, and later she tells him that Milady is madly in love with Count de Wardes, the man whom d'Artagnan wounded just before sailing to London. She also gives d'Artagnan a love note which Milady has written to de Wardes. D'Artagnan is so furious that he forges de Wardes' signature on a return letter to Milady, arranging a dark, nighttime rendezvous with Milady. While she thinks that she's making love to de Wardes, d'Artagnan will be making passionate love to her.

The plan works, and afterward Milady is so satisfied that she gives d'Artagnan an elegant sapphire ring surrounded with diamonds, promising to have "that stupid d'Artagnan" killed for having wounded de Wardes, the man she thinks she's been making love to in the darkness.

Later, d'Artagnan is furious, and, in order to get revenge against her, he answers another love note of hers to de Wardes, signing de Wardes' name under a flippant reminder that Milady has to "wait her turn." Milady is so incensed that she asks d'Artagnan to kill de Wardes, and as prepayment she goes to bed with him. D'Artagnan is so enamored by Milady's loveliness that he impulsively reveals that this is not the first time that he has made love to her: earlier, when she thought that she was making love in the dark to de Wardes—she wasn't. D'Artagnan was in bed with her.

Milady rears up and tries to kill d'Artagnan, and as they scuffle, her nightgown is torn and d'Artagnan sees the mark of a convict branded on one of her shoulders. The discovery of this secret is so terrible that Milady vows that d'Artagnan will die. By a stroke of good fortune, however, and some help from Kitty, d'Artagnan escapes.

Relating the adventure to Athos later, the two men discover that Milady is Athos' wife, a woman whom he thought he hanged after *he* discovered that she was a branded criminal. Athos and d'Artagnan decide to sell Milady's "tainted" ring—which originally belonged to Athos' family—and now they are both able to buy their equipment for the siege of La Rochelle. Meantime, Porthos has obtained his equipment from his aging, miserly mistress, and Aramis has obtained his equipment from his beloved friend, Madame de Chevreuse.

Before d'Artagnan and the musketeers leave in their separate regiments for the siege, the king becomes ill, and d'Artagnan's group moves out first, leaving the musketeers behind for the time being to await the king. D'Artagnan is lonesome for his friends and, one day, he wanders off alone—not a wise decision, because he is fired at by two of Milady's hired assassions. Later, during a dangerous mission that d'Artagnan is leading, the same two assassins again try to kill him. When this attempt fails, Milady decides to have some poisoned wine delivered to d'Artagnan—compliments of "the three musketeers." D'Artagnan does not realize that the wine is poisoned, and he is so busy talking that he fails to drink the wine immediately. Instead, another soldier drinks the wine—and falls dead.

Meanwhile, the three musketeers are enjoying their leisure time, drinking and joking, and, by chance, they meet the cardinal, who is going to a meeting with Milady, who is staying at the inn which the musketeers just left. The musketeers accompany the cardinal and listen through a broken stovepipe to the conversation.

Milady, they learn, is going to London to make sure that the duke of Buckingham is killed; in return, the cardinal will take revenge against d'Artagnan. The musketeers immediately decide on a plan to warn d'Artagnan and Buckingham. Thus, when Milady arrives in England, she is taken prisoner by her brother-in-law, de Winter. However, she cleverly corrupts her jailer, convinces him (a religious puritan fanatic) that Buckingham deserves to be put to death, and he obeys her.

She then escapes to France, where she is determined to complete her revenge against d'Artagnan. She goes to the convent where the queen has placed Constance Bonacieux, d'Artagnan's beloved, for protection, and there Milady wins the young girl's confidence. Precisely when d'Artagnan and the musketeers arrive to rescue Constance, Milady poisons her and escapes.

D'Artagnan and the musketeers track her down, accuse her of her many crimes – and execute her. When the entire story is revealed later to the cardinal, he is horrified at the extent of Milady's evil web of death, and he is extremely impressed with d'Artagnan's laudable actions. Consequently, he writes out a commission for d'Artagnan to become a lieutenant in the King's Musketeers. After offering the commission to Athos, Porthos, and Aramis and being refused by all three, d'Artagnan accepts the prestigious commission at the early age of twenty-one.

SUMMARIES AND COMMENTARIES

Part 1

PREFACE

This novel is one of the world's most famous adventure novels and is often referred to as the quintessential "swashbuckling" novel. Most readers throughout the Western world know something about the exploits of "the three musketeers."

In his preface, Dumas uses a literary device that was common

22

during the romantic period in literature. That is, in order to give his novel a sense of being authentic, rather than a work of fiction, Dumas pretends that he discovered two old manuscripts, each of them written by a main character in this story. These old manuscripts, which were found in the Royal Library, supposedly tell the history of the three musketeers. The first manuscript, *Memoirs of Monsieur d'Artagnan,* was supposedly written by the most famous musketeer of all time, and the other manuscript, *Memoirs of Count de La Fère* (the novel we are about to read), was supposedly written by the musketeer Athos who was, in reality, the Count de La Fère. Thus, Dumas' *Three Musketeers,* using the device of being an old, authentic manuscript, gains credibility and immediacy by purporting to be a factual account of the daring, adventurous deeds of d'Artagnan and three of the most famous of the King's Musketeers.

CHAPTER 1

Summary

In the year 1625, in Gascony, a province of France, a young man named d'Artagnan is taking leave of his father to journey to Paris, where he will seek out the prestigious Monsieur de Tréville, captain of the King's Musketeers and a childhood friend of d'Artagnan's father.

D'Artagnan's father has only three gifts which he can give to his son: fifteen ecus in money, a ridiculous-looking horse about thirteen years old, and a letter of introduction to Monsieur de Tréville. If d'Artagnan can convince Tréville to allow him to become a musketeer, he believes that he will have his fortune made because the musketeers are a select group of swordsmen highly favored by the king.

After a sentimental leave-taking from his mother, d'Artagnan begins his journey to Paris. He arrives at the market town of Meung, where he sees an unknown nobleman who he believes is laughing at him, or at least at his horse. D'Artagnan's impetuous temper causes him to insult the nobleman and pick a quarrel with him. D'Artagnan is outnumbered, however, and before long he is carried unconscious into the inn. Learning from the innkeeper that d'Artagnan has a letter to the powerful Monsieur de Tréville, the nobleman steals it from d'Artagnan's doublet.

When d'Artagnan recovers, he goes downstairs in time to see the nobleman talking with someone whom he addresses as "Milady." Later, d'Artagnan discovers that his letter of recommendation to Tréville is missing, and after threatening the innkeeper and his servants, he learns that the mysterious nobleman ransacked his belongings and apparently stole the valuable letter of introduction. D'Artagnan departs, and when he arrives in Paris, he rents a room that he discovers is near the home of Monsieur de Tréville.

Commentary

This first chapter moves quickly. We see that our hero is a country boy, unaccustomed to the sophisticated ways outside of his little town; he is also from a section of France which is famous for its brave and daring young men. Throughout the novel, d'Artagnan's birthplace will be referred to as a place famous for producing men of exceptional courage, military valor, and quick tempers. D'Artagnan possesses all of these qualities – especially the latter. In fact, in the opening chapters of this novel, we see that d'Artagnan is so impetuous that he quickly embroils himself in a series of duels with three of the king's best swordsmen.

D'Artagnan's encounter with the as-yet-unnamed Count de Rochefort introduces us to the man who will become d'Artagnan's mysterious nemesis (enemy). However, until the end of the novel, Rochefort will be referred to only as "the man from Meung." At the end of the novel, when ordered to do so by Cardinal Richelieu, Rochefort and d'Artagnan will put aside their differences and become allies and friends.

The puzzling appearance here of "Milady" will become even more important to the plot than d'Artagnan's chance encounter with Rochefort; Milady will play a major, pivotal role later in the novel. The ultimate importance of both of these mysterious characters suggests that Dumas had the plot of his novel well outlined before he began writing it.

CHAPTERS 2–4

Summary

Monsieur de Tréville, the captain of the King's Musketeers, is a genuine and loyal friend to the king, who in turn thoroughly values Tréville's loyalty and devotion. Tréville began his career as a brave, loyal young Gascon, one very much like d'Artagnan, and now, as captain of the King's Musketeers, he holds one of the country's most powerful and prestigious posts. In fact, the King's Musketeers have become so famous that Cardinal Richelieu, not to be outdone by the king, has established his own company of guards; both men, the king and the cardinal, searched throughout the French countryside for the bravest and most courageous men.

When d'Artagnan calls upon Monsieur de Tréville, he finds a number of musketeers awaiting audiences with this powerful man, and he listens in particular to two musketeers who are bantering with each other in a friendly manner. One of them is Porthos, dressed rather pompously; the other is Aramis, dressed more conservatively. Aramis states that he is waiting for the queen to have an heir to the throne; afterward, he will resign from the musketeers and begin studying for the priesthood. Their conversation is interrupted when it is announced that Monsieur de Tréville will receive d'Artagnan.

As d'Artagnan enters, he sees that Monsieur de Tréville is in a bad mood. The exalted gentleman immediately calls for Athos, Porthos, and Aramis. Porthos and Aramis enter and are told that the cardinal informed the king that they, as well as Athos, were arrested by the cardinal's guards in a tavern where they were causing a disturbance. Coolly, but inwardly enraged, Tréville vows that he "won't have [his] musketeers going to low taverns, picking quarrels, fighting in the street, and being laughed at by the cardinal's guards."

Porthos explains that they were taken by surprise, that two of their group were killed, and that Athos was wounded before they had a chance to draw their swords—thus, it was six against three. Yet even with those odds, Aramis killed one of the cardinal's guards with the guard's own sword. At that moment, the wounded and pale Athos appears, but before he can say much, he collapses. Tréville sends for doctors to have Athos tended to and dismisses the two musketeers.

Alone with Tréville, d'Artagnan describes his desire to be a musketeer, the letter of introduction that was stolen, and the mysterious nobleman who stole it. Tréville is curious; he asks d'Artagnan to describe the man, and afterward Tréville is sure of the man's identity: the unidentified nobleman is none other than the cardinal's right-hand man (later identified as Count de Rochefort). D'Artagnan asks for the name of the mysterious nobleman, but Tréville refuses to reveal it.

He tells d'Artagnan to forget the man and to walk on the other side of the street – if necessary – to avoid him.

D'Artagnan then describes the woman whom the nobleman referred to as "Milady," and it is obvious that Tréville also knows the identity of the mysterious lady. Tréville turns to write a letter commending d'Artagnan to the Royal Academy when d'Artagnan suddenly spies the mysterious "man from Meung" across the street. Without waiting for the letter of recommendation, he rushes out.

Running after the mystery man, d'Artagnan inadvertently collides with Athos, reinjuring Athos' wounded shoulder; Athos is furious and challenges d'Artagnan to a duel at noon. Still chasing the mysterious "man from Meung," d'Artagnan runs headlong into the pompous Porthos and discovers that his magnificent golden shoulder belt is a fraud; it is only partly gold. Infuriated, Porthos challenges d'Artagnan to a duel at 1 P.M. Again, d'Artagnan takes up the pursuit, only to discover that he has lost his man. At this very moment, though, he sees Aramis talking to some other musketeers, and he notices that Aramis is standing on a lady's elegant handkerchief. D'Artagnan retrieves the handkerchief and gives it to Aramis, who glares at him. After the guards leave, Aramis reprimands d'Artagnan for being so "ungallant" and bringing attention to the lady's handkerchief. He promises to teach d'Artagnan a lesson; he challenges him to a duel at 2 P.M.

Commentary

Dumas stresses the importance of d'Artagnan's being a Gascon by paralleling his early years with Tréville's early years. Like d'Artagnan, Tréville is also a Gascon. Possessing the same courageous and adventuresome qualities that d'Artagnan possesses, Tréville has risen to be one of the most powerful men in France. Thus we can anticipate that d'Artagnan, who is also endowed with quick-witted daring, shrewd, intelligent bravery, and courageous loyalty, will use these qualities to become a success in Paris.

In this world of the 1620s, perhaps the most significant attribute that both Tréville and d'Artagnan possess is their absolute sense of loyalty and devotion to either a person or a cause. Indeed, Tréville's absolute devotion to his king is part of his power. Likewise, we will soon see that d'Artagnan is the type of man who is absolutely loyal to his friends; in the upcoming episode when the king gives d'Artagnan forty pistoles, d'Artagnan immediately divides the money with Athos,

Porthos, and Aramis because of his instantaneous sense of loyalty to them. Later, d'Artagnan's devotion and loyalty to the queen will motivate many of his actions.

Since Athos, Porthos, and Aramis – the three musketeers – share many similarities, it is important to note their differences. All of them have assumed aliases, but we sense that only Athos has noble blood; he conducts himself as a young nobleman might. Porthos, on the other hand, relishes in the intrigues of society, and he prides himself on his many romantic conquests; later, when he is in need of money, he will use his charm and good looks to obtain money from a wealthy woman. In contrast, Aramis is passing his time as a musketeer only until the queen provides an heir for the realm; afterward, Aramis will enter the priesthood. There are many other differences in the men that will be noted later, but, for the present, these differences are sufficient to help us readily distinguish one from the other.

Ironically, just as d'Artagnan is about to receive Tréville's recommendation for the Royal Academy, the mysterious "man from Meung" reenters d'Artagnan's life – causing d'Artagnan to dash out of Tréville's house without the new letter of recommendation. In only minutes, d'Artagnan re-wounds Athos, rushes into the proud Porthos and reveals the man's fraudulent golden shoulder belt, and, finally, he contradicts Aramis about the ownership of a lady's batiste handkerchief. In less than twenty-four hours after arriving in Paris, d'Artagnan finds himself challenged to duels by three of the greatest swordsmen in France.

CHAPTER 5

Summary

On his way back to meet Athos, d'Artagnan ponders his situation. If he wounds the already-wounded Athos, he will look bad; yet if he himself is wounded by the already-wounded Athos, he will be doubly disgraced. He searches for a way out of the dilemma. Arriving on time for the duel, he finds that Athos' seconds have not arrived. Meanwhile, Athos' shoulder has begun to throb painfully, so d'Artagnan offers him some of his mother's miraculous salve. This generosity impresses Athos. Afterward, the seconds arrive: Porthos and Aramis. D'Artagnan registers great surprise when he learns that these gentlemen are known as "the three inseparables," or "the three musketeers."

Just as Athos and d'Artagnan have their swords in position for the duel, they are interrupted by five of the cardinal's guards and are ordered to yield to arrest because of the edict against dueling. D'Artagnan has to decide whether he will support the cardinal's men (after all, the cardinal is more powerful than the king) or whether he should side with the King's Musketeers. Immediately, he decides on the musketeers. During the encounter, the cardinal's guards are soundly defeated, and d'Artagnan is accepted into the close camaraderie of Athos, Porthos, and Aramis.

Commentary

Prior to each of d'Artagnan's dueling encounters with the three musketeers, Dumas creates tension by making us guess how the hero will confront each of them and yet emerge with honor from each encounter. This question, of course, is ultimately obviated by the appearance of the cardinal's guards and by d'Artagnan's decision to fight on the side of the musketeers. His brilliant although unorthodox swordsmanship wins him the respect of the musketeers, and thus through a stroke of luck, d'Artagnan becomes, as it were, an unofficial "fourth musketeer." Not until later in the novel, however, will he become an official musketeer.

CHAPTERS 6–7

Summary

Hearing how the three musketeers and d'Artagnan fought with five of the cardinal's guards and left four of them lying on the ground, King Louis calls in Monsieur de Tréville for an explanation. The king pretends to be angry, but he is secretly pleased that his musketeers defeated the cardinal's guards. In particular, he wants to have an audience with d'Artagnan, the young Gascon who fought so daringly.

The next day, the three musketeers and d'Artagnan spend the morning playing tennis. D'Artagnan doesn't know how to play the game, and after retiring to the sidelines, he is insulted by one of the cardinal's most gifted swordsmen, Bernajoux. During a duel, d'Artagnan overpowers the superior swordsman, but he is attacked by others, and soon, musketeers and cardinalists are embroiled in a free-for-all brawl. The three musketeers, however, are able to extract themselves because they have a noontime meeting with the king; unfortunately, His Majesty went hunting that morning after one of the cardinal's men told him that there was a magnificent stag in a neighboring woods.

By the time that Tréville is able to have an audience with the king, Louis has heard about this new brawl with the cardinal's guards. Tréville is able to prove, though, that the cardinal's men provoked the quarrel and were soundly defeated. The king then has an audience with the three musketeers and d'Artagnan and hears d'Artagnan describe in detail the events of the preceding days. Satisfied, the king rewards d'Artagnan with forty pistoles, which d'Artagnan divides with the three musketeers.

In Chapter 7, d'Artagnan asks for advice concerning how he should spend his share of the forty pistoles; Athos tells him to have a good meal, Porthos tells him to hire a servant, and Aramis tells him to take a mistress. D'Artagnan hires a servant named Planchet, who serves them all a fine meal. We then learn more about the musketeers.

Athos, although handsome and intelligent, lives a quiet life with Grimaud; they virtually never speak to one another. Porthos, however, is different; he is loud and outgoing, and his servant Mousqueton is also loud and rough. Aramis is the most reserved of the three, and his servant, Bazin, is a pious fellow who looks forward to Aramis' entering the priesthood.

When d'Artagnan enters the king's company of guards, under Monsieur des Essarts, the three musketeers often accompany d'Artagnan on his guard duties. Very soon, the four are constantly seen together.

Commentary

As stated earlier in the novel, the only way for a poor young man from Gascony to make his fortune is to have the courage, daring, and bravery to attract the attention of powerful people. Fortunately, fate arranges matters so that d'Artagnan is confronted by members of the cardinal's guard, who have the reputation of being expert swordsmen. The fact that so young a man defeats so experienced and polished a swordsman as the cardinalist Bernajoux attracts the attention of the king himself, who rewards d'Artagnan and requests that the young Gascon be placed in special troops, an honor which will lead to d'Artagnan's later becoming a musketeer.

The modern reader is often perplexed at the blatant disregard for human life that is so often found in this "swashbuckling" type of novel, but it is a common characteristic of the genre; d'Artagnan himself seems to have little or no regard for his own life as long as he dies an honorable death at the hands of someone whom he considers noble.

Part 2

CHAPTERS 8–9

Summary

The forty pistoles received from the king are soon spent, and although the musketeers receive an advance on their pay from Tréville, they are soon broke. Thus they start enumerating people whom they have entertained in the past in order to be invited to meals. When they are beginning to become desperate, d'Artagnan receives an unusual visitor. His landlord, Monsieur Bonacieux, seeks help; his wife, Constance, the queen's linen maid, has been mysteriously abducted— probably for political reasons. Constance is the goddaughter of Monsieur de La Porte, the queen's gentleman-in-waiting; it was through this powerful and influential gentleman that Madame Bonacieux received her position. Both Constance and La Porte are known to be extremely devoted and loyal to the queen (whose heritage is Spanish, whose husband is French, and whose title is Anne of Austria).

During d'Artagnan's discussion with Monsieur Bonacieux, we learn that Bonacieux is d'Artagnan's landlord and that d'Artagnan is several months behind with his rent. But Bonacieux has another reason for coming to see d'Artagnan; Bonacieux is a coward, and he has often seen d'Artagnan duel in the company of the three musketeers, who are known to be brave and expert with their swords.

As they are discussing Bonacieux's predicament, d'Artagnan suddenly sees "the man from Meung" across the street and dashes out to confront him, but returns half an hour later, having had no success.

D'Artagnan explains to Athos and Porthos that "a woman has been abducted . . . and probably threatened and may be tortured, and all because she is faithful to her mistress, the queen." We then learn that the queen is being persecuted by the cardinal for being loyal to her native Spain (an enemy of France); in addition, she is in love with the duke of Buckingham, an Englishman (England is also an enemy of France). Nonetheless, the musketeers agree: the queen, despite her emotional and political bonds, must be defended.

Guards appear and arrest Bonacieux, and rather than defend him and cast suspicion on himself, d'Artagnan allows Bonacieux to be arrested. The musketeers and d'Artagnan agree to try to free Madame Bonacieux because she is loyal to the queen and is the goddaughter of Monsieur de La Porte.

Commentary

The title of Chapter 8, "A Court Intrigue," characterizes the action of much of this novel. For many of Dumas' early readers, a court intrigue was as exciting as a salacious story in today's *National Enquirer,* or some other gossip tabloid. Court intrigues and gossip have always fascinated many readers—in Dumas' day as well as in the present.

At the beginning of this chapter, Dumas again emphasizes the motto of the three musketeers; each shares whatever money he has with the others and thus fulfills their motto: "All for one, one for all." By now, d'Artagnan knows that if any difficulty or need arises, he can count on the three musketeers.

The introduction of Constance Bonacieux begins one of the many sub-plots of the novel. She will move in and out of the action until her untimely death late in the novel. She will be d'Artagnan's first love, creating resolute loyalty and adoration in the young Gascon.

Chapter 8 ends with the sudden reappearance of the mysterious "man [in a cloak] from Meung," an appearance which neatly fits the "cloak and dagger" type of novel, another category into which this novel readily belongs.

For d'Artagnan and the three musketeers, the mere fact that a lady who is close to the queen has been abducted is reason enough for them to pledge their talents to solving the mystery of her disappearance. And to facilitate matters, they allow her older husband to be arrested on false charges so that he won't interfere with their actions (and won't be bothering d'Artagnan with such "insignificant" matters as the rent). The chapter concludes with their agreeing on the motto, "All for one, one for all."

CHAPTERS 10–12

Summary

The term "mousetrap" is explained as being a method whereby the police trap friends and/or associates of a person who has been arrested for political reasons. Here, the authorities have placed four guards at Monsieur Bonacieux's house, and they plan to arrest anyone who knocks. Meanwhile, upstairs, d'Artagnan has removed most of the first section of the flooring in his apartment so that he can hear the entire proceedings. When he hears the guards manhandling Constance Bonacieux, he sends his servant, Planchet, to enlist the aid of the three musketeers, and grabbing his sword, he flies to Constance's rescue. Only one of the guards is armed, and after a short time, d'Artagnan is able to drive all four men from the premises in a manner so dashing and thrilling that Constance is marvelously impressed and eternally grateful.

Constance Bonacieux turns out to be young (in her early twenties), charming, and beautiful. When she describes the man who abducted her, d'Artagnan recognizes him as "the man from Meung." She tells d'Artagnan about her escape: she was left alone, so she immediately tied some sheets together and let herself down from a window. She feels so deeply grateful to d'Artagnan that she entrusts him with a secret password which will gain him entrance into the palace to see Monsieur de La Porte, whom he is to send to her. When d'Artagnan delivers the message to La Porte, the gentleman advises him to find someone whose clock is slow and go there and establish an alibi.

Afterward, d'Artagnan daydreams about a romantic love affair with Constance Bonacieux, and while wandering idly through the Paris streets, he finds himself outside Aramis' house, where he sees a lady in a cloak knocking at what appears to be Aramis' window. He sees the woman talking to another woman, and when she leaves, he discovers that it is Constance Bonacieux. He follows her and accosts her. She denies knowing Aramis, and when she refuses to reveal the secret of her mission, d'Artagnan offers to escort her to her destination. She permits him to do so on condition that he leave and not follow her. D'Artagnan promises and returns home, where he learns that Athos has been arrested by authorities who thought that they were arresting d'Artagnan.

D'Artagnan sets out for Tréville's house to tell him about the arrest and other events. On a bridge, he sees two figures – one is dressed exactly like Constance Bonacieux and the other is in a musketeer's uniform; his appearance resembles Aramis. When d'Artagnan brashly stops them, calling out Aramis' name, he discovers that Constance Bonacieux is escorting the duke of Buckingham to the Louvre Palace. D'Artagnan is pleased to escort them safely to the palace.

At the palace, Constance leads the duke through a series of corridors and leaves him in a private anteroom. Soon, Anne of Austria, the queen of France, appears, and the duke makes his protestations of love to her, but she continually and sadly rejects his overtures, even though she is obviously in love with him. As a parting gift for him, she goes to her chambers and returns with a rosewood box as a token of her love. Inside the rosewood box are twelve diamond tags, or studs (button-like ornaments).

Commentary

Here, as part of the novel of intrigue, we are introduced to the villainous "authorities" who set a trap and arrest anyone – innocent or guilty – who enters the "mousetrap." In modern terms, this is similar to police entrapment, a technique whereby the police use an officer to trap someone into violating a law so that the police can arrest that person. It is by this method that d'Artagnan meets Constance Bonacieux, who becomes his first love.

Constance Bonacieux's escape from her captors (by tying sheets together and letting herself down from a window) and d'Artagnan's rescue of her are in the best swashbuckling, romantic tradition, as is the scene where the four guards battle against d'Artagnan and d'Artagnan overcomes these odds and rescues the fair damsel in distress.

Also in the tradition of the troubadors and other devoted cavaliers who love for-the-sake-of-love, d'Artagnan immediately falls in love with Constance Bonacieux; she will be d'Artagnan's beloved for whom he will perform valorous deeds. His relationship with Constance Bonacieux will, of course, eventually cause him to volunteer to perform a great service for the queen, thereby saving her honor and virtue. Ultimately, then, d'Artagnan's love and devotion to Constance Bonacieux will be one of the causes for his own advancement in society and will tightly entangle him in the deadly political intrigues of France. In other words, the relationship established here and intensified when d'Artagnan helps Constance Bonacieux slip the duke of Buckingham into the Louvre are sufficient for Constance to trust d'Artagnan to go on the dangerous and highly secret mission for the queen.

The importance of this love affair is a commentary on the times. Dumas writes that Constance Bonacieux was an amorous ideal, that she knew the secrets of the court and was not insensitive to masculine attentions, even though she was married. Furthermore, it was the custom of the time for a young and handsome man to take money or other gifts from his mistress, and the young and handsome d'Artagnan is always in need of money.

The scene where d'Artagnan sees the mysterious woman in a cloak, knocking at what he thinks is Aramis' window is an example of a scene which allows the reader to classify this novel as a "cloak and dagger" novel—that is, mysterious people are often seen half-concealed by cloaks, and they do not reveal themselves until someone has drawn his sword, as does d'Artagnan in this scene.

Chapter 12 presents our first view of George Villiers, the English duke of Buckingham—an extremely handsome and sophisticated man. The love which Buckingham has for the French queen is depicted in terms of his desperate need to be with her. There is no compromise of the queen's honor—except, at the end of the interview, she gives him a gift as a token of her love for him. This gift, a monogrammed, gold-inlaid jewel box made of rosewood, is, as we later discover, filled with diamond tags, or studs, which will become the object of the first real adventure in the novel, when the king demands that the queen wear the jewels to a ball. The king, however, demands that the queen wear the diamonds only because the cardinal tells him that the jewels are in Buckingham's possession; the cardinal wants to prove that the queen is untrue so that he can gain even more power over the king.

CHAPTERS 13–16

Summary

We return to the fate of Monsieur Bonacieux, who has been taken to prison and questioned by the authorities about his wife. As it turns out, Bonacieux is much more concerned about his own avarice and safety than he is about his wife. He explains that his only interest in d'Artagnan was that he needed someone who could help him find his wife. When Athos is brought in, Bonacieux tells them that this man is *not* d'Artagnan. Bonacieux is then taken from the prison, placed in a carriage, and taken for a trip which he assumes is a ride to the gallows.

Later, Bonacieux is questioned by someone whom he discovers to be the powerful and imminent Cardinal Richelieu. While interrogating Bonacieux, the cardinal discovers that the houses which Bonacieux visited with his wife – houses which Constance Bonacieux had said were merchants' houses – are, in reality, the two houses where the duke of Buckingham and the queen's trusted friend, Madame de Chevreuse, have been hiding. When the cardinal calls in Count de Rochefort, Bonacieux immediately cries out that Rochefort is the man who abducted Constance.

Rochefort reports that the cardinal's spy in the queen's inner circle, Madame de Lannoy, has reported that the queen left her ladies-in-waiting and was gone for awhile. When she returned, she was carrying a rosewood box containing the diamond tags which the king gave her. She went into the antechamber and when she returned, she was empty-handed. The cardinal is certain that the duke of Buckingham has the coveted box and the diamond tags.

When Bonacieux is recalled and questioned further by the cardinal, the old man becomes putty in the hands of the honey-tongued cardinal; Bonacieux pledges everlasting loyalty to him. The cardinal then sends one of his men with a letter to be delivered to a woman in England, a certain Milady, who is to dance with Buckingham and secretly snip off two of the diamond tags that he will be wearing.

The next day, d'Artagnan tells Tréville about Athos' mistaken arrest. Tréville goes to see the king about Athos' arrest and discovers that the cardinal is already there; after much discussion, during which Tréville vouches for the whereabouts of both Athos and d'Artagnan during the fracas with Bonacieux, the king and the cardinal both agree to let the matter rest.

Immediately after Tréville leaves, the cardinal informs the king that Buckingham is in Paris. The king is certain that with the help of Madame de Chevreuse, the queen and the duke are seeing one another. When he hears that the queen has been writing letters that very morning, he is determined to have her searched and have the letters brought to him. He goes to see the queen and informs her that his chancellor, Seguier, will visit her soon and, at his command, will make a request of her. When Chancellor Seguier appears and searches the queen's room and desk and finds nothing, he prepares to search her person. The queen indignantly refuses, and he is about to use force when she reaches into her bosom and gives him a letter.

When the king opens the letter, he discovers that it is not a love letter to Buckingham; it is a political letter. The queen is asking her brother in Spain and her brother, the Emperor of Austria, to demand the dismissal of Cardinal Richelieu. The cardinal, upon reading the letter, cleverly offers to resign, but the king knows that he cannot manage France without the cardinal's powerful influence.

To make peace with the queen, the cardinal suggests that since the queen loves to dance, the king should give a big ball, and he tells the king that he should *insist* that the queen wear the diamond tags that he gave her as a present. On returning home, the cardinal hears from Milady that she has secured two diamond tags; she needs money to get to Paris, and as soon as she gets the money, she will be in Paris in four or five days. The cardinal then plots the date of the ball so that he might trap the queen.

Commentary

In Chapter 13, we find out that Constance Bonacieux is only twenty-three years old; since she is married to a fifty-one-year-old stingy, selfish husband, she would naturally make a likely candidate for a love affair with d'Artagnan, especially since we also learn that her husband thinks of his love for his wife as being secondary to his love for money and influence. Bonacieux is thus an easy prey for the powerful cardinal, and he quickly becomes the cardinal's dupe. Later, when Constance asks him to do a service for the queen, he will *not* consent to it; thus, she turns to our hero, d'Artagnan, and asks him to perform this crucial deed for the queen.

In his questioning of Monsieur Bonacieux, the cardinal is seen to have an acute sense of the intrigues of the court. He knows that the duke of Buckingham is in Paris, and he is able to discover where both the duke and Madame de Chevreuse are staying—that is, in the houses that Constance Bonacieux often visited, pretending to her husband that she was visiting "tradesmen." Through his spies, the cardinal is able to deduce that the queen gave Buckingham the rosewood box containing the diamond tags. Knowing this, he requests the king to give a ball and *demand* that the queen wear the diamond tags. This demand, as we soon will see, will require d'Artagnan to go on his first adventure. He will have to get the diamond tags and return them to the queen *before* the date of the ball, a date which the cardinal sets as soon has he hears that his spy, Milady, has stolen two of the diamond tags – snipped them off while she was dancing with Buckingham.

In an earlier chapter, when d'Artagnan helped get a message to Monsieur de La Porte, the gentleman told d'Artagnan to find someone with a slow clock who could provide him with an alibi. D'Artagnan went to see Tréville and reset his clock; now, when Tréville has to give his word of honor that d'Artagnan was with him at a precise hour, he can do so – fully believing that he is telling the truth. Consequently, d'Artagnan is freed from all accusations by the cardinal.

Until Chapter 16, the reader might have wondered why the queen is such an enemy of the cardinal. It has been suggested that there are two reasons: (1) she is Spanish and Spain is France's enemy, and (2) she loves Buckingham, an Englishman, and England is an enemy of France. However, in Chapter 16, the real reason appears: ". . . the queen [Anne of Austria] was persecuted by the cardinal because he could not forgive her for having rejected his amorous advances."

Because of the cardinal's accusations about Anne's affair with Buckingham, the king is certain that his wife is untrue. He orders that her person be searched, and in those days, a gentleman's having his wife searched for a love letter was a dastardly thing, but a *king's* having the *queen* searched was beyond comprehension. Thus, the cardinal, whose rumors cleverly prompt the search, now urges the king to be reconciled with the queen. Cunningly, he suggests a festive ball so that the queen will *have* to wear the diamond tags, which are – he feels sure – in the possession of the duke of Buckingham. Now the trap for the queen is set, and to counteract this trap, d'Artagnan will have to undertake the journey to recover the diamond tags and return them to the queen.

CHAPTERS 17–19

Summary

The king wonders briefly why the cardinal is so insistent that the queen wear the diamond tags, but he nevertheless tells the queen about his plans for the ball and instructs her to wear the diamond tags. On further questioning, the queen learns that the idea of having a ball was the cardinal's idea; furthermore, it was the cardinal who suggested that she wear the diamond tags.

After the king leaves, the queen is filled with fear. Suddenly, Constance Bonacieux enters from the closet and reveals that she knows the entire story; furthermore, she promises that she will find someone to go to the duke of Buckingham and retrieve the diamond tags. The queen reminds Constance that a letter would have to accompany the messenger and, if intercepted, she (the queen) would be ruined— divorced and exiled. Constance, not knowing of her own husband's allegiance to the cardinal, swears that her husband will do anything for her. Relieved, the queen gives Constance a jewel to sell in order to defray the expenses of the journey.

At home, Constance discovers that her husband has become an ardent cardinalist and will have nothing to do with her intrigues: "Your queen is a treacherous Spanish woman, and whatever the cardinal does is right," he says. Constance also discovers that her husband is in league with Count de Rochefort, even though he knows that Rochefort is the person who abducted Constance. Monsieur Bonacieux leaves and Constance is certain that he will betray her.

D'Artagnan overhears the entire conversation between husband and wife, and later he is delighted to assert that her husband is a wretch. He then offers himself at her service. When Constance is reluctant to tell d'Artagnan all of the details about the mission, he reminds her that she was about to tell her traitorous husband everything, and furthermore, d'Artagnan loves her more than her husband does.

Constance relents and tells him all about the secret mission, and d'Artagnan promises to obtain a leave of absence and be on his way to London. Constance suddenly remembers the three hundred pistoles that the cardinal gave her husband, and she gives the money to d'Artagnan for the journey. D'Artagnan is delighted: "It will be twice as amusing to save the queen with His Eminence's [the cardinal's] money."

At that moment, they hear her husband returning with someone. D'Artagnan recognizes the person as "the man from Meung," and he is ready to attack him when Constance stops him because of his duty to the queen; in other words, first things first. They listen and overhear her husband's plan to supposedly relent and agree to go on the errand for his wife; then, after he has the queen's letter to Buckingham, he will take it to the cardinal.

On his way to Tréville's house, d'Artagnan wonders if he should tell Tréville about the secret mission; interestingly, Tréville tells d'Artagnan to keep the details of the mission secret and, instead, to ask for whatever favors he needs. D'Artagnan says that the cardinal will do anything to keep him from getting to London, and Tréville suggests that at least four people should go on the journey so that one of them might succeed in actually getting there. D'Artagnan says that Athos, Porthos, and Aramis will accompany him without demanding to know the nature of the secret mission. Accordingly, Tréville writes out passes, and d'Artagnan goes to each of the musketeers and tells them to get ready for the trip. They discuss several tactics for successfully accomplishing the mission, but d'Artagnan tells them that they must all go together, not in separate directions, because if one of them is killed, the others can make certain that the letter is finally delivered to London. They agree and begin to make preparations to leave.

Commentary

When the queen is instructed to wear her diamond tags to the ball, she is also told that it was the cardinal who proposed having the ball. Constance quickly realizes that the idea of her wearing the diamond tags was also the cardinal's idea. As a consequence, she knows that the cardinal has a spy among one of her ladies-in-waiting, but she does not know which one. Therefore, when Constance Bonacieux appears from the closet, where she has been tending to the linen, she could have overheard the conversation between the queen and the king; therefore, the queen is not sure, at first, if she can trust Constance. But after Constance's protestations of loyalty and her reminder that she is the person who brought Buckingham to her, the queen is finally convinced that she can trust Constance. Now we can see that these earlier episodes function as a basis for Constance's loyalty and are proof that the cardinal is indeed a powerful enemy of the queen.

In a similar way, we can now look back at other scenes. For example, when we read that Constance Bonacieux discovered that her husband was a cardinalist—totally devoted to and committed to the cardinal—we realize now how the cardinal used his interview with

Constance's stupid husband in order to gain another loyal adherent.

Dumas closes Chapter 18 with a brilliant stroke of irony: the old miser Bonacieux is howling for his missing money. D'Artagnan's trip to London will be financed by money which the cardinal gave to Bonacieux.

Clearly, Dumas delights in d'Artagnan's heroics. In the scene where Constance is in despair, fearing that the mission for the queen is doomed to fail, Dumas uses the romantic device of having d'Artagnan overhear the entire conversation between Constance and her husband; then, suddenly and romantically, d'Artagnan presents himself as her rescuer and savior. The queen's honor can be preserved.

Note too how Dumas uses a combination of circumstances in order for d'Artagnan to be fully characterized as the romantic hero: he is in the right place at the right time and overhears the right kind of intrigue so that he can become involved in the affairs of great people. Dumas also stresses that it is *d'Artagnan's* plan for the mission that the older, more experienced musketeers finally accept. D'Artagnan is younger than the other men, but already he seems to have a natural talent for intrigue and adventure; in fact, Buckingham will later marvel at d'Artagnan's being so young, yet so dashing, brave, and inventive.

CHAPTERS 20–22

Summary

At 2 A.M., the four adventurers, accompanied by their armed servants, ride out of Paris. At the first inn where they stop, Porthos gets into an argument with a stranger; his companions are anxious to be on their way, so they tell him to "kill that man and rejoin us as soon as you can." They continue on their journey and decide to wait two hours for Porthos, but he never appears.

Later, they encounter eight or nine men working on the road, and suddenly the workmen race for the ditch, pick up their muskets, and begin firing. D'Artagnan realizes that they have ridden into an ambush, so he warns the others, urging them back. Mousqueton falls, wounded. Aramis receives wounds and can't ride any farther, so they leave him at an inn in Crèvecoeur, tended to by his servant, Bazin.

The original party of eight is now reduced to four: d'Artagnan and his servant Planchet, and Athos and his servant Grimaud. At midnight they reach Amiens and stop at the Lis d'Or inn. Grimaud guards the horses while Planchet sleeps in front of the door so that d'Artagnan and Athos won't be taken by surprise. Two hours later, they are awakened by noises, and at 4 A.M., they hear more loud noises in the stable. They investigate and discover Grimaud lying unconscious with a bleeding head. Planchet goes to saddle the horses but they are still too exhausted to go any farther. Mousqueton's horse has even been bled, mistakenly, by the local veterinarian.

When Athos goes to pay the bill, the innkeeper looks at the money and declares it to be counterfeit. At this moment, four armed men rush toward him, but Athos holds them off while yelling to d'Artagnan to escape.

Outside Calais, both d'Artagnan's and Planchet's horses collapse when they are only a hundred paces from the town gates. They dismount and begin following a young nobleman and his servant. By accident, they overhear a ship's captain stating that he will take no one to England without the written permission of the cardinal. The young nobleman presents a paper signed by the cardinal and is told that the paper must be endorsed by the harbor master.

D'Artagnan and Planchet continue following the two men, pick a quarrel with them, and while Planchet duels with the servant, d'Artagnan duels with the young nobleman. Defeating him, even though he is wounded while doing so, d'Artagnan steals the traveling permit, which is made out to Count de Wardes. He gets the permit signed by the harbor master, takes it to the ship's captain, and he and Planchet sail for England.

For a moment in London, d'Artagnan is at a loss: he knows no English. Nonetheless, he writes the duke of Buckingham's name on a piece of paper and is immediately directed to the duke's residence. The duke's servant, who speaks French, takes d'Artagnan to the field where the duke is hunting with the king. When the duke reads the letter that d'Artagnan gives him, he turns pale and immediately returns to London.

On the ride back to London, d'Artagnan relates his exploits, surprising the duke that someone so young could be so brave, resolute, and resourceful. The duke takes d'Artagnan through many rooms and finally to a concealed chapel, where he shows him a life-sized portrait of the queen of France. Then, as he takes the diamond tags out of their box, he is horrified to see that two of them are missing. He instantly realizes that the ribbons have been cut, and he knows that the diamonds were taken by Milady – Lady de Winter – obviously an agent for the cardinal. Immediately, he sends for his jeweler and his secretary.

He instructs his secretary to have all the English ports closed so that Milady cannot return to France with the diamond tags. When d'Artagnan reveals his astonishment at the duke's enormous, unlimited power and his use of it – all for the sake of his beloved, Anne of Austria, queen of France – Buckingham acknowledges that "Anne of Austria is my true queen. At a word from her, I'd betray my country, my king, even my God." D'Artagnan marvels at such total devotion.

The jeweler arrives and tells Buckingham that duplicating copies of the missing diamonds will take a week; Buckingham offers him double the price if he can finish the job in two days, and he agrees to do so. Since speed is of the utmost importance, the jeweler immediately goes to work in the duke's palace. D'Artagnan is again impressed by the duke's power and his ardent love for the French queen.

After the fake diamond tags are made, the duke wants to reward d'Artagnan, but d'Artagnan reminds the duke that he, d'Artagnan, is serving the queen of France and that some day in the future, he and the duke might be enemies on the battlefield. However, because Buckingham sincerely wants to reward him and because d'Artagnan needs some good horses in order to return to Paris in time for the ball, d'Artagnan accepts four magnificent horses – one for d'Artagnan himself and one for each of the three musketeers. D'Artagnan is also given the secret password that will enable him to change horses. Twelve hours later, he is in Paris.

Next day, all of Paris is talking about the upcoming ball. That night, the king is especially pleased to see that the queen is wearing her diamond tags. The cardinal, however, calls the king's attention to the fact that the queen has only *ten* tags. He gives two diamond tags to the king and tells him to inquire of the queen about the two tags which are missing. During their next dance together, the king is unable to count the number of diamond tags on his wife, so at the end of the dance, he tells her that two of her tags are missing – and he gives her two more. The queen triumphantly announces that now she has fourteen! The king counts the tags: she is wearing twelve – and now she does have two more diamond tags. The cardinal is stunned at the news, but recovers from his astonishment and explains to the king that the two extra diamond tags are his way of making a gift to the queen. Anne is not fooled, however, and she subtly lets the cardinal know that *his* two diamond tags probably cost him *more* than the king's original twelve.

Later, d'Artagnan is rewarded for his success in returning the tags; Constance Bonacieux leads him down a series of corridors where the queen presents her hand to be kissed. As d'Artagnan does so, she presses a magnificent ring into his hand. Constance then returns and tells d'Artagnan that she left a note for him at his house.

Commentary

Again, we can see why this novel is called one of the best swash-buckling, "cloak and dagger" adventure novels. In Chapter 20, the four adventurers embark on a mission and encounter all sorts of un-expected obstacles. Without a doubt, the cardinal seems to be able to know exactly what everyone in the kingdom is doing. Remember that Tréville warned d'Artagnan about this very possibility.

On the trip to London, the musketeers and d'Artagnan encounter difficulty at the first inn and leave Porthos. Then during an ambush along the road, they believe that Mousqueton is killed; they know that Aramis is wounded, so they leave him at an inn, tended by his servant, Bazin. Later, Athos is falsely accused by an innkeeper of try-ing to pass counterfeit money and is attacked by four men. Finally, when d'Artagnan and his servant reach the port of Calais, they dis-cover that the cardinal has had the port closed and is sending one of his men, Count de Wardes, with a special permit to London. Clearly when this novel was written, episodes such as these were truly adven-tures on the highroads.

The story then continues with d'Artagnan's encounter with the duke of Buckingham and the revelation of the duke's power. Since this novel is also a romantic novel, Dumas' emphasis is often on the power of love. D'Artagnan is in awe of the duke's willingness to use all of his power in the service of his beloved Anne of Austria, queen of France. However, we should remember that this adventure which d'Artagnan undertakes (during which he proves himself to be reso-lute, brave, and ingenious) is undertaken because of his own devoted love for Constance Bonacieux. Thus we have two plots of love and adventure: one centering on court intrigues; the other, on the romantic intrigues of a daring adventurer and his beloved.

Earlier in the novel, it seemed a superficial scene when d'Artagnan accosted Constance Bonacieux on the Pont-Neuf bridge while she was accompanying a disguised man. Then we learned that the man was the duke of Buckingham; now we can see that Dumas created this unlikely encounter in order for d'Artagnan – a common, foreign soldier – to get an interview with the most powerful man in England. He can identify himself now as "the young man who nearly fought you one night on the Pont-Neuf."

During the queen's encounter with the cardinal, concerning the diamond tags, the cardinal displays his brilliance in the way that he is able to "explain" his motives, but the queen is equally clever; she lets the cardinal know that she is aware of all his secret machinations against her.

These chapters also anticipate future chapters in that we hear more about Milady, a woman who will prove to be the very blackest quintessence of evil, a character responsible for the deaths of many people later in the novel. Likewise, Count de Wardes will also appear later, although in a lesser role than Milady.

Part 3

CHAPTERS 23–24

Summary

Arriving home, d'Artagnan learns from Planchet that a letter has mysteriously appeared. D'Artagnan anxiously opens the letter and discovers that Constance Bonacieux requests a rendezvous with him for ten o'clock that night. Ecstatic, he tells Planchet to meet him at seven that night with two horses (Note: at the end of the chapter, the two men meet at nine P.M. instead of seven, a minor slip by Dumas).

Leaving the apartment, d'Artagnan meets Monsieur Bonacieux, who questions him about his recent absence from Paris. D'Artagnan then contacts Monsieur de Tréville who, upon hearing about d'Artagnan's adventures in England, strongly advises d'Artagnan to sell the diamond ring which the queen gave him and leave Paris for awhile in order to avoid the cardinal's wrath: "The cardinal has a long memory and a powerful hand. He'll do something against you, you can be sure of that." D'Artagnan promises to leave the next day, but tonight he has other plans. Tréville is sure that a woman is involved.

At nine o'clock, d'Artagnan and Planchet wend their way toward the bungalow designated by Constance Bonacieux. Planchet complains of the cold and stops at an inn; meanwhile, d'Artagnan arrives at the bungalow. He waits until ten, then ten-thirty, and then he waits until eleven before climbing up a tree to look through a window. There, he discovers a room in total disarray. "Everything in the room bore witness to a violent, desperate struggle."

D'Artagnan awakens an old man who lives behind the bungalow, and after pleading with him, he softens the old man's sympathies and learns that three men came to his shack and borrowed a ladder. The old man saw a distinguished gentleman take a key and open the door to the bungalow. A woman screamed loudly and tried to climb out of the window, but her escape was blocked by two men on the ladder. They forcibly took the lady to a waiting carriage and left. After d'Artagnan listens to a description of the men, he is sure that one of them is "the man from Meung"; the other description fits the despicable Monsieur Bonacieux. However, he can do nothing until next morning, when Planchet arrives with the horses.

Commentary

In these chapters we move away from the world of adventure and into the world of romance and intrigue. When d'Artagnan reads Constance Bonacieux's letter, he is elated; no amount of personal danger can prevent him from keeping his rendezvous. Tréville warns him to leave Paris that very night, but d'Artagnan will not leave until his rendezvous with Constance Bonacieux, the woman for whom he completed the arduous and dangerous mission to London. D'Artagnan's elation is particularly evident when he impulsively and impetuously gives his servant, Planchet, an "ecu" (about $8.00, probably equal to more than two or three months' salary).

These two chapters continue to present Monsieur Bonacieux as a slimy, distasteful person. We first saw his spitefulness when he refused to go to London to aid the queen. Now we see something so despicable as his helping "the man from Meung" (actually, Count de Rochefort) kidnap Bonacieux's own wife, Constance. No doubt Dumas

intended this scene to justify Constance's decision to have a romantic liaison with d'Artagnan.

These chapters also focus again on the immense power which
the cardinal wields. Seemingly, Cardinal Richelieu is omnipresent and
omniscient – a very dangerous combination. Dumas' precise characterization of Richelieu will justify d'Artagnan's later adventures – particularly when he realizes that he must leave Paris immediately and
remain out of reach of the cardinal and his spies.

CHAPTERS 25–27

Summary

D'Artagnan decides to tell Tréville the entire story of Constance
Bonacieux's abduction. Afterward, Tréville is certain that the entire
matter was conceived by the cardinal. He tells d'Artagnan to leave
Paris as soon as possible.

When d'Artagnan returns to his apartment, he is accosted by old
Bonacieux, who tries to question him about his recent whereabouts.
D'Artagnan notices the mud on Bonacieux's boots and is convinced
that Bonacieux did indeed aid in kidnapping his own wife. Upstairs,
Planchet tells d'Artagnan that the cardinal's captain of the guard, Monsieur de Cavois, stopped by to extend an invitation to d'Artagnan to
visit the cardinal. Planchet wisely told the captain that d'Artagnan was
out of town. They decide to leave immediately.

At the inn where they left Porthos, d'Artagnan orders some wine,
which he shares with the innkeeper while discreetly trying to learn
the whereabouts of Porthos. He learns that Porthos fought a duel and
was seriously wounded, that he lost all of his money gambling, and
that he has run up a large bill which he can't pay. In addition, Porthos
gave the innkeeper a letter to be posted to Porthos' "duchess." The
innkeeper ordered his servant to deliver the letter in person and discovered that the "duchess" was only Madame Coquenard – a plain,
fiftyish, lawyer's wife.

When d'Artagnan goes to see Porthos, he pretends that he knows
nothing about the dueling wound and listens attentively as Porthos
fabricates a story about his tripping and hurting his knee. Obviously,
he is being well cared for by his servant, Mousqueton, who knows
all about poaching and getting wine by lassoing it through a small

window. D'Artagnan bids farewell and tells Porthos that he will be back, about eight days later.

Lost in thought, d'Artagnan arrives at the inn in Crèvecoeur where they left Aramis. He is told by the congenial hostess that Aramis is still there – at present, entertaining the local curate and the superior of the local Jesuits. When d'Artagnan approaches, Aramis' servant tries to block the door; Bazin is anxious to serve a religious master, and he fears that d'Artagnan will lure Aramis away from his current religious meditations and commitments.

When d'Artagnan enters the room, he is stunned by the stark simplicity of the room – only religious objects are to be seen. Aramis tries to draw d'Artagnan into a ridiculously esoteric religious question concerning whether a priest should bless the congregation with one hand, with two hands, or with his fingers. After the priests leave, Aramis tells d'Artagnan that he has foresworn the world, that he hates all wordly ties, that his friends are but shadows, that love has no meaning to him, and that the world is a tomb.

Aramis then confesses to d'Artagnan that he was brought up in a seminary and that everyone fully expected that he would become a priest. When he was nineteen, however, while he was reading to a beautiful young lady, he was ordered out of the house and threatened by another guest, a young officer who was jealous of the attention which the young lady bestowed upon Aramis. Aramis left the seminary, took fencing lessons for a year, tracked down the officer, challenged him and killed him. Now he plans to return to the seminary.

Teasingly, d'Artagnan tells Aramis that if he is determined to return to a life of celibacy, he probably won't be interested in a perfumed letter that is sealed with a duchess' coronet and comes from the household of Madame de Chevreuse. Suddenly, Aramis has a change of heart. He grabs the letter, reads it, and becomes ecstatic. He embraces d'Artagnan – and all worldly matters. He can hardly wait to rejoin the musketeers. He tries to mount the magnificent horse that d'Artagnan brought him, but he is still too weak to ride, so d'Artagnan leaves him at the inn to practice riding until he is stronger.

D'Artagnan then rides on to find Athos, the musketeer for whom he has a special liking because Athos carries himself with such proud, noble grace and conducts himself with such aristocratic authority.

Remembering that the innkeeper accused Athos of trying to pass counterfeit money, d'Artagnan is filled with fresh indignation and anger when he arrives. The innkeeper begs to be listened to; he explains that he had been forewarned by the authorities that some men who fit the musketeers' descriptions were expected in the neighborhood and that they were criminals disguised as musketeers. He received a description of their uniforms, their servants, and their facial features. He tells d'Artagnan that Athos killed one of the men in the inn and seriously wounded two more; then he barricaded himself in the basement and threatened to kill anyone who tried to get near him. The innkeeper went to the police, but they wouldn't help him because the instructions concerning the fraudulent musketeers did not come from them. They refused to interfere and arrest someone who might be one of the King's Musketeers.

Athos remained in the basement, and now he has drunk over a hundred and fifty bottles of wine, he has eaten all the hams and sausages in the basement, and the innkeeper is almost financially ruined. Amends are finally made, however, and d'Artagnan and Athos leave Athos' old horse with the innkeeper to compensate his losses.

At supper that night, Athos becomes very drunk and tells d'Artagnan, who is bemoaning the fate of his beloved Constance Bonacieux, about his own misfortunes in love. Pretending that he is telling the story of "a young friend," he explains that this "friend" once met a beautiful sixteen-year-old girl, fell in love with her and married her; later, while the "friend" and his young wife were out riding, she fell and, while trying to help her regain consciousness, the "friend" loosened the upper part of her dress and discovered that she had been branded on the shoulder with a fleur-de-lis, a sign that she was a convicted criminal. Athos says that his "friend" immediately hanged his young wife.

Commentary

Essentially these three chapters serve to tell us more about each of the three musketeers. Chapter 25 gives us additional information about the vain Porthos, Chapter 26 shows us Aramis' conflict between love and religion, and Chapter 27 tells us more about Athos' past, which haunts him and drives him to excessive drinking.

While reading Chapter 25, we should remember that d'Artagnan first encountered Porthos when he collided with him on a stairwell and, by accident, it was revealed that Porthos was wearing a golden shoulder belt that was only half gilded. In that encounter, injured vanity was the principal reason why Porthos challenged d'Artagnan to a duel. Likewise, in this chapter, the emphasis is again on Porthos' extreme vanity. As noted in the summary, Porthos cannot admit that he was bested in a duel. Likewise, he feels that he needs to brag about his young and beautiful "duchess" when, in reality, his "duchess" is a fiftyish wife of a lawyer. Yet note that d'Artagnan, although a young man, is astute enough not to mention the truth to Porthos; he allows Porthos to continue with his fantasies.

Although Dumas revealed to us earlier that Monsieur Bonacieux assisted in his wife's abduction, it is only in Chapter 25 that d'Artagnan becomes fully aware of this fact. Remembering the description given to him of the fat little man, he looks at Bonacieux's shoes and realizes that he and Bonacieux have the same kind of red mud on their shoes. "At the same time he also noticed Bonacieux's shoes and stockings: they were spotted with exactly the same kind of mud. An idea flashed into his mind: that short, fat, gray-haired man, treated without respect by the noblemen who abducted Madame Bonacieux, was Bonacieux himself! The husband had taken part in his wife's abduction!" D'Artagnan concludes that Bonacieux is a miserable scoundrel.

Chapter 26 reveals the whereabouts of Aramis and focuses on the conflict between love and religion. As long as a person loves, and is loved in return, and knows the whereabouts of his beloved, religious matters rarely fill one with anguish. But if one feels rejected in love, as does Aramis, then a viable alternative to love in this world is a religious life in a monastery. That is, when Aramis thinks that he has been rejected, he turns to religion for solace.

However, when Aramis receives a letter from his beloved — Madame de Chevreuse, the friend of the queen whom the king suspected of connivance and banished to Tours — Aramis becomes ecstatic. He immediately disavows his religious plans and tells d'Artagnan that he is bursting with happiness. He rejects the religiously correct meal of spinach and eggs, and, instead, he orders meat, game, fowl, and the bottle of wine which he rejected only moments earlier. Here, in this typical romantic novel, the power of love once again triumphs.

While d'Artagnan is on his way to find Athos, he wonders why he feels closer to Athos than he does to the other two musketeers; clearly he and Athos are the furthest apart in age. He concludes that he is attracted to Athos because Athos seems so noble in his conduct, has such a distinguished air, and has such sudden flashes of grandeur.

Also, Athos' face suggests a striking sense of majesty combined with graciousness. At this point, d'Artagnan does not know that Athos is descended from nobility, but he can nevertheless recognize that Athos seems to have noble heritage. Later in the novel, d'Artagnan will not be too surprised when he learns about Athos' nobility.

Athos, however, does not always "act noble." Dumas continually characterizes him as a heavy drinker, and part of the humor in Chapter 27 is derived from Athos' barricading himself, by accident, in a *wine* cellar. Clearly, Athos does not suffer unduly during his two weeks there; we see that he survives on hams and sausages and consumes over one hundred and fifty bottles of wine. (His servant drinks only from the casks.)

Later, when Athos tells d'Artagnan a story about a young lord who once married a beautiful sixteen-year-old girl, he is, of course, telling his own story. But not until the last part of the novel will we discover that this beautiful girl is Milady, Lady de Winter – the evil nemesis to all of the loyalists. The only false part of Athos' story is his report that he hanged her and that she is dead. Foreshadowings such as this are virtual proof that Dumas had his novel well plotted and did not write, as some critics believe, without knowing where he was going next.

CHAPTERS 28–29

Summary

Next morning, Athos maintains that everything he told d'Artagnan the night before was only the ramblings of a drunken musketeer; there was no truth to any of it. He also confesses that when he got up that morning, he was somewhat muddle-headed and gambled away his magnificent horse. D'Artagnan is deeply disappointed. Then Athos reveals that he also gambled away d'Artagnan's horse as well. D'Artagnan believes that Athos has lost his mind. Then Athos further confesses that he gambled – and lost – the silver harnesses, saddles, and other elegant trappings.

D'Artagnan is speechless. Then comes the bitterest blow of all: Athos says that he gambled away d'Artagnan's diamond ring, the one which the queen gave him. D'Artagnan can only exclaim "My God" in total disbelief. Athos then says that he gambled for his servant, Grimaud – and won back the diamond ring, Then, using the ring, he won back the harnesses. And then he quit. Now they have harnesses – but no horses.

Athos convinces d'Artagnan that he should try a toss of the dice – that he should at least *try* to win back his horse, or 100 pistoles. When d'Artagnan wins, Athos talks him into accepting the 100 pistoles, rather than the horse, because he will need the money to continue his search for Constance Bonacieux. D'Artagnan agrees, and they set off on their servants' old horses to meet Aramis.

Aramis confesses to his friends that he sold his magnificent English horse to pay for some masses that he had earlier contracted for, and now he has only the harness left. When they meet Porthos, he asks them to sit down to a magnificent and extravagant meal. Shortly thereafter, Athos asks them to identify what they are eating, and after one of them names an elegant dish, he tells them that they are all eating, as it were, "horse." He realizes that Porthos had to sell his horse in order to pay his debts and eat well. "But," Porthos explains, "I saved the harness."

Arriving in Paris, they learn from Tréville that d'Artagnan has been admitted to the King's Musketeers, but no date has been set for the formal ceremony. They also learn that they *must* have their equipment ready in two weeks because they will be leaving for battle. At present, none of them has enough money to buy equipment, and they each need about 2000 livres each. Athos hopes that they can talk d'Artagnan into selling his diamond ring.

While pondering how to get some money, d'Artagnan notes that Porthos is curling his mustache; moments later, Porthos slips into a church. D'Artagnan follows him and watches as Porthos goes quietly up to a middle-aged woman (whom he intentionally ignores) and deliberately flirts with a beautiful and obviously wealthy lady at the front of the church. D'Artagnan recognizes the beautiful lady as Milady, the woman whom he saw at Meung. The middle-aged woman turns out to be Madame Coquenard, the mistress whom Porthos wrote to for money and who ignored his request. As d'Artagnan leaves, he notices that Madame Coquenard is pleading with Porthos for forgiveness. He is fairly sure that Porthos will get his musketeer supplies and a horse.

Commentary

D'Artagnan was rewarded so richly with the magnificent horses for his friends that he is deeply hurt when he learns that the horses have been sold. He is additionally horrified to learn that Athos dared to gamble with d'Artagnan's diamond ring. But we should remember that d'Artagnan took a great deal for granted when he told the three musketeer friends that they were going to accompany him on his trip to London—that is, they all risked their lives for him without even knowing or questioning why he demanded such dedication from them. Now they have all sold or lost their horses, even though they have the harnesses. This fact is fortunate because in Chapter 29, they learn that they must have full equipment ready in two weeks, and their harnesses are one less thing that they will have to buy.

Chapter 29 also includes mention of Milady, or as we come to know her, Lady de Winter, the person who snipped the diamond tags from Buckingham's suit so that the cardinal could try to entrap the queen. As d'Artagnan increasingly begins to follow her, the novel will frequently focus on her influence over him. Similarly, we see that Porthos has successfully established himself in Madame Coquenard's affections.

CHAPTERS 30–33

Summary

D'Artagnan follows Milady and hears her tell the coachman to go to Saint-Germain, a neighborhood too distant for him to follow on foot. Therefore, he decides to visit Athos; he tells him about Milady, but Athos is not sympathetic. Athos is cynical about all love affairs; he sarcastically tells d'Artagnan, "Go have an adventure with Milady. I wish you success with all of my heart."

D'Artagnan finds Planchet, they borrow two horses from Tréville, and ride to Saint-Germain. There, Planchet sees a man whom he recognizes: the servant to Count de Wardes—the same servant whom Planchet fought outside Calais. D'Artagnan sends Planchet to the servant to see if Planchet will be recognized, and if he isn't, to find out if the count survived. After talking with Planchet for awhile, the count's servant leaves, and suddenly Milady's maid appears. She gives Planchet a note intended for the servant of Count de Wardes. The maid says, "For your master." Planchet takes the piece of paper to d'Artagnan, and they discover that it is a love note: Milady is asking the count for a rendezvous.

Later, while he is following Milady's carriage, d'Artagnan overhears Milady in a heated argument with a man. Impulsively, d'Artagnan comes to her rescue, but is told by Milady that she is not in danger; she is only arguing with her brother-in-law. After she leaves, the two men agree to a duel, along with a free-for-all with three friends to be brought by each duelist. The gentleman introduces himself as Lord de Winter. D'Artagnan returns home and tells the three musketeers that he has committed them to a duel. All three are excited at the prospect.

Before the duel, the Englishmen are clearly concerned that they are titled members of society and perhaps should not be fighting with mere "commoners." Therefore, Athos takes one of them aside and tells him who he really is. He also tells him that because he now knows Athos' true identity, Athos will have to kill him—and he does so only moments into the duel. Meanwhile, Porthos wounds his opponent in the thigh, picks him up, and carries him to the carriage. Aramis traps his opponent momentarily before the Englishman manages to escape. D'Artagnan fights Lord de Winter with cool detachment until he is able to unarm him; then graciously, he spares his life. In appreciation, de Winter arranges to introduce d'Artagnan to Milady, his sister-in-law, Lady de Winter.

When the two men arrive, Milady seems momentarily unhappy to learn that d'Artagnan spared de Winter's life, but quickly recovers her composure. She becomes gracious to d'Artagnan, and soon d'Artagnan becomes a daily visitor to Milady's house.

Meanwhile, Porthos goes to his dinner engagement with Madame Coquenard, posing as her cousin. Her miserly husband is there, and their dinner is the poorest excuse of a meal that Porthos, a fastidious gourmet, has ever tried to eat. In addition, he is served the most foul-tasting wine that can be imagined. After the meal, he discovers that Madame Coquenard is as miserly as her husband; she almost faints when she hears how much money Porthos needs to buy new musketeer equipment for himself. Nonetheless, she promises to get most of the equipment (a horse, a mule, and some other things) from business acquaintances, and she further promises Porthos some money. Disappointed, hungry, and morose, Porthos goes home.

Hourly, d'Artagnan is falling more in love with Milady. He is not even aware that the lady's exceptionally pretty maid, Kitty, takes every opportunity to rub against him. Finally one day, Kitty takes d'Artagnan aside and tells him that her mistress does not love him. D'Artagnan, being young and ardent, does not believe Kitty, so she takes him up to her private room, next to her mistress' chamber. There, she gives d'Artagnan a note that Milady has written to Count de Wardes. D'Artagnan reads the note, an open plea for the count to take advantage of Milady's love for him.

After reading the note, d'Artagnan pleads with Kitty to help him take revenge on Milady, but Kitty refuses; she says that in matters of love, it's "everyone for herself." Just then, d'Artagnan recalls Kitty's languishing glances, her flirtatious greetings in the antechamber, the corridor, and on the stairs, those touches of the hand every time she meets him, and her deep, warm sighs. D'Artagnan is shrewd enough to realize how advantageous it would be to have Kitty as a mistress; therefore, for the rest of the evening, he turns his attentions to her.

When Milady calls to Kitty, d'Artagnan hides in a closet where he can overhear their conversation. He learns that Milady knows that d'Artagnan has foiled her plots; she says that she detests him, that he is a simple country fool, and that she hates him most for not killing Lord de Winter, her brother-in-law. Had d'Artagnan killed de Winter, Milady would have inherited an extremely large fortune. D'Artagnan realizes that Milady is utterly corrupt, a monster.

Because d'Artagnan has won Kitty's love, she is eager to please him, so she brings him another letter that Milady has written to Count de Wardes. D'Artagnan forges an answer, setting up a rendezvous for 11 P.M., and signs the count's name. Kitty fears the consequences, and she doesn't want to deliver the letter, but she is finally persuaded to — especially after he reminds her what vengeance Milady would take against her if she ever found out about Kitty's betrayals.

Commentary

When Athos tells d'Artagnan to go and amuse himself with Milady, little does Athos realize that he is telling d'Artagnan to amuse himself with the woman whom he once married — the woman whom he believes he murdered. This coincidence is, of course, one of the romantic ironies of this loose and seemingly rambling novel, but a novel which is nevertheless well-plotted. One would have thought that d'Artagnan would have recognized the name "Lord de Winter" since he had heard from Buckingham that it was "Lady de Winter" who cut off the diamond tags—but Dumas explains this puzzling detail by having d'Artagnan admit that de Winter's English name is so strange-sounding that he can't even pronounce it. Ultimately, all of these unlikely coincidences—that is, the accidental sighting in the church, the inadvertent interception of Milady's note to Count de Wardes, the duel with Milady's brother-in-law, and d'Artagnan's sparing his life—prepare us for the actual introduction of d'Artagnan to the beautiful Lady de Winter herself, the infamous Milady.

Chapter 31 presents another exciting duel scene, the type of scene that makes this novel a favorite of Hollywood filmmakers. Here, it is worth noting that the only Englishman killed is Athos' opponent; Athos, remember, confided his real name and social status to the Englishman. Athos' secret is so personal at this point in the novel that it is necessary that Athos kill the Englishman to make sure that his secret will not be revealed. Thus, for the present, Athos' real identity continues to be a secret, and his origins and background become even more intriguing.

Chapter 32 presents an entertaining interlude. It is an established comic device to pit an extreme miser (Madame Coquenard) against an extreme libertine and spendthrift (Porthos). We have continually seen that Porthos puts great emphasis on fine and delicate foods prepared to perfection. In earlier chapters, Porthos was the one who suggested spending money on good meals. Earlier too, he sold his beautiful English horse so that he could enjoy an elegant repast. Therefore, when we now see the finicky Porthos being subjected to watery soup, the wing of a scrawny chicken, inedible green beans, undrinkable wine, and a dessert that clogs the throat—all for the sake of getting Madame Coquenard to provide new musketeer equipment— this is an extremely comic situation from an author who is not particularly known for his comic touch. Dumas even satirically compares Madame Coquenard to Moliere's famous character Harpagon in *The Miser*, but points out that Madame Coquenard lived many years before Moliere created his now-archetypal skinflint.

In Chapter 33, Dumas begins building suspense for one of the novel's most significant intrigues. We know that d'Artagnan has a great deal of pride and ambition, so it is not surprising that he realizes that Kitty is an exceptionally pretty mistress who can satisfy his immediate needs and whom he can use to revenge himself on Milady. This reasoning is prudent because without Kitty's help, d'Artagnan could never effect his long-range plans. He desperately lusts for Milady – even though he knows of her hatred for him – and yet, at the same time, he is desperate for revenge. He knows what a monster Milady is, but he cannot rid himself of his passionate desire to possess her: "He knew her to be treacherous in matters of more importance, and he had no respect for her, yet he felt an uncontrollable passion for this woman boiling in his veins – passion drunk with contempt but passion and desire nevertheless." Throughout d'Artagnan's relationship with Milady, we should be aware of Dumas' use of the modern-day love/hate dichotomy.

CHAPTERS 34–38

Summary

Next day, d'Artagnan visits the three musketeers in Athos' apartment and finds them all in vastly different moods. Mousqueton arrives and tells Porthos to return home for a very important matter. Then Bazin comes in and tells Aramis that there is a beggar from Tours waiting to talk to him (Tours, remember, is the town where Aramis' beloved Madame de Chevreuse lives in exile). Both Porthos and Aramis leave immediately. Alone with Athos, d'Artagnan tells him about the romantic escapades with Milady.

Meanwhile, Aramis arrives home, and the beggar gives him a letter which says, "It is the will of fate that we should still be separated for some time, but the wonderful and happy days of youth are not lost beyond recall." Madame de Chevreuse has sent money by the beggar, who is really a Spanish nobleman in disguise. Thus, Aramis now has enough money to buy first-rate musketeer equipment, and he also has enough money to buy his friends a splendid dinner.

Athos, however, still refuses to leave his apartment; he says that he will have his dinner sent up. D'Artagnan, on his way to see Porthos, notices Porthos' servant leading an old nag and a disreputable mule. D'Artagnan recognizes the nag as the one which his father gave him, the one which he sold for three ecus. He is told that Porthos' mistress' husband is responsible for the insult and that Porthos is sending the animals back to be tied to the Coquenards' front door.

Later, Porthos confronts Madame Coquenard, and using his most disdainful, lordly, and aristocratic manner, he orders her to meet him later, letting her know the utter contempt he has for such a disgraceful horse. Madame Coquenard promises to make amends if Porthos will come to her house when her husband is gone. Porthos now feels certain that she will soon open her secret treasure chest and he will have a chance to view all of its fabulous contents.

Early in the evening, d'Artagnan visits Milady and immediately notices that she is impatient; he knows that she is anxious for him to be gone so that she can (she thinks) receive Count de Wardes. D'Artagnan leaves and goes to Kitty's room, where he waits for the hour assigned for Count de Wardes' visit. The only way he can console Kitty is to keep reminding her that he is acting solely out of his desire for revenge. Later, he hears Milady wildly delirious with happiness, instructing Kitty to make sure that all of the lights are out when the count arrives.

When it is dark within, d'Artagnan enters Milady's room. She presses his hand and asks for a token of love from him tomorrow. As proof of her own love for him tonight, she gives him a magnificent sapphire ring surrounded by diamonds, a ring that she suggests is a relief to be rid of. He then hears her refer to himself, d'Artagnan, as "that Gascon monster"; she vows to revenge herself against him. When d'Artagnan hears himself referred to with such derogatory names, he realizes the hate and contempt that she has for him; yet this woman has an "incredible power" over him. He hates and adores her at the same time.

Next morning, wearing the sapphire ring, d'Artagnan visits Athos. Athos examines the ring and turns pale. He is certain that he recognizes the ring; it is exactly like the one which once belonged to his family, the ring which he gave to his wife during a night of love. Finding a unique scratch on one of the stone's facets, Athos is certain that it is the same ring. Yet it is a mystery how Milady, Lady de Winter, happened to have this ring.

When d'Artagnan arrives home, Kitty is waiting for him with a note to de Wardes; Milady is asking de Wardes to come back sooner than he said he would. D'Artagnan begins plotting his revenge. He writes a note to Milady, stating that he ("de Wardes") is involved with other mistresses and that she (Milady) will have to wait her "turn." He signs the note, "Count de Wardes." When Milady reads the note, she vows revenge against de Wardes.

For two days, d'Artagnan stays away from Milady; on the third day, Milady sends Kitty with a note asking d'Artagnan to call. That night, he goes to her house and instantly he notices that her face seems ravaged with torment. Even though he knows that she is a wicked woman who casts evil, hypnotic spells on men, d'Artagnan finds himself once again under her spell. He believed that his love for her was extinguished, but now he knows that it was only smoldering. Now he feels as if he would risk damnation for her smile. Milady, knowing that he loves her, asks if he will do something for her, and d'Artagnan promises that he will do anything for her.

Milady says that she has an enemy ("a mortal enemy") — but just as she is about to speak the enemy's name, d'Artagnan speaks it for her. When she inquires how he knows the man's name, he lies to her. He says that de Wardes was bragging about his seductive success with Milady and showing everyone the ring that she gave him. This revelation incenses Milady, but since d'Artagnan is going to kill de Wardes in a duel, she promises d'Artagnan sexual satisfaction that evening at eleven.

Milady's kisses are as cold as stone, but d'Artagnan is nonetheless passionately and blindly in love with her. His youth, his pride, his vanity, and his mad passion make him believe that Milady loves him. Later, after they have made love for two hours, Milady wants to discuss her revenge against de Wardes. At this point, d'Artagnan reveals that it was *he* and *not de Wardes* who made love to her in the dark last week, and that it is *he* who has the valuable ring.

D'Artagnan has never seen such violent hatred in a woman as that which erupts within Milady. She attacks him and during a struggle, her negligee is torn, revealing a fleur-de-lis, the mark of a convicted criminal, indelibly branded on one of her smooth white shoulders. Milady has only one thought: "Now he knew her secret, her terrible secret that no one else knew." Knowing that d'Artagnan must be killed, Milady attacks the half-naked youth with a knife. D'Artagnan is terror-stricken at Milady's face, now contorted by hatred, fury, and revenge; her lips are blood-red and her pupils are horribly dilated. Suddenly Kitty opens the door and d'Artagnan is able to escape — after quickly slipping into women's clothes.

Despite the fact that d'Artagnan is wearing a woman's dress, he goes immediately to Athos' house, where he tells Athos that Milady has a fleur-de-lis branded on one of her shoulders — just like Athos' late wife, the woman whom Athos believes he hanged. Comparing notes, the two men realize that Milady and Athos' wife are the same person. Athos knows how evil and dangerous Milady can be, and he warns d'Artagnan.

They send Grimaud to ask Planchet to bring clothing for d'Artagnan, and meanwhile, d'Artagnan tries to give Athos the diamond and sapphire ring which rightfully belongs to him. Athos, however, will not take back his mother's ring because it has been sullied by Milady. He can't bring himself to sell it, so he asks d'Artagnan to pawn it so that they can split the money. D'Artagnan tries to refuse his half of the money, but Athos tells him that he must accept half of the money or he, Athos, will throw the ring in the river. Hearing this threat, d'Artagnan agrees to take it.

Kitty enters, begging for help. By now, Milady is sure to know that Kitty is d'Artagnan's accomplice, and Kitty is convinced that her life is in danger. D'Artagnan recalls Aramis' friend in Tours and asks him to write a letter to this noble woman, asking her to protect Kitty. Aramis agrees and hands Kitty a sealed letter for the mysterious lady in Tours.

The ring is pawned, and they buy equipment for Athos; Athos, however, realizes that he never wants to see the ring again, so he tells d'Artagnan to go back and get two hundred more ecus for the ring and sell it outright. Now Athos has his equipment—and money to spare.

Commentary

These chapters include some of the most exciting intrigues in the entire novel. They are compellingly narrated, demonstrating Dumas' genius as a storyteller.

Chapter 34 is constructed like an interlude, showing how Aramis receives a mysterious letter delivered by a beggar who demands that Aramis show proof of identification. It turns out that the beggar is really a Spanish nobleman. Remember that the queen (Anne of Austria) is Spanish and that her closest friend, Madame de Chevreuse, has been exiled to Tours; since the Spanish noblemen are enemies of France, we must assume that the beggar is also a close friend of the queen and Madame de Chevreuse. Aramis is ecstatic over the letter and declares his love for her. Once again, love and intrigue are inextricably intertwined in this novel.

Meanwhile, love has also entangled the usually placid Porthos. He has "used" love to threaten his mistress who, in her miserliness, tried to give Porthos an ugly nag, the one that belonged to d'Artagnan when he first came to Paris. Finally, however, her infatuation, devotion, and love for Porthos makes her relent and, through the power of love, both Aramis and Porthos obtain their military equipment, even though the means are quite different.

D'Artagnan's entanglement with love is also comic — even if his life is at stake. Before de Wardes is due to rendezvous with Milady, she insists that all of the lights be out. This might seem like an amateurish way for Dumas to have d'Artagnan accomplish his deception, but ultimately, Dumas is creating this scene exactly as a shrewd woman might prepare for a rendezvous. Milady wants the room darkened so that her lover will not be able to see that she has a fleur-de-lis branded on one of her shoulders; she musn't allow anyone to know that she is a branded, convicted criminal. Only later, when Milady and d'Artagnan make love until daylight and he accidentally tears her gown, is her dreadful secret exposed. Furiously, she vows to kill d'Artagnan — primarily so that she can protect her dreadful secret. Most men would not be so obsessed with such a wicked woman, but d'Artagnan is entrapped in a typical love/hate dichotomy wherein he is so strongly attracted to Milady's physical beauty that he cannot face the reality of her corruption. He is a very young man, and he wants Milady to love him for himself. He is sure that he is more handsome than de Wardes — he has a better body, he is stronger, prouder, and he is a better swordsman. In his youth and vanity, d'Artagnan cannot believe that Milady would really prefer someone else.

In Chapter 35, when Athos realizes that the sapphire ring with the diamond facets is the same one that he gave to his late wife (don't forget that he thinks he hanged her), he can surmise only that either she sold the ring or that, somehow, Milady gained possession of it. At this point, it does not occur to him that Milady is his wife. It is only after d'Artagnan describes her and the fleur-de-lis branded on her shoulder that Athos realizes that this evil, wicked woman is the same evil woman whom he cast aside long ago.

60

CHAPTERS 39-40

Summary

Planchet brings d'Artagnan two letters, a small one in a simple envelope and a large, imposing one with the cardinal's coat-of-arms on it. The small letter, although unsigned, is from Constance Bonacieux, instructing him to be on a certain road at 7 P.M. The other letter instructs d'Artagnan to be at the cardinal's palace at 8 P.M. D'Artagnan arranges for his three friends to be posted outside the cardinal's house, and then he purchases one of Aramis' elegant horses that was "mysteriously" sent to him by an unknown benefactoress and rides out to keep the seven o'clock appointment with Constance Bonacieux. Fleetingly, Constance appears at the window of a heavily guarded carriage; she throws him a kiss and gives him a sign not to acknowledge her.

D'Artagnan then returns in time for his eight o'clock appointment with the cardinal. At the beginning of the interview, the cardinal demonstrates that he knows many things about d'Artagnan—for example, he knows about d'Artagnan's first encounter with "the man from Meung," his losing the letter of introduction to Tréville, his trip to England, his meeting with the duke of Buckingham, and his meeting with the queen and her gift of the diamond ring. The cardinal assures d'Artagnan that he respects him highly, and he then offers him a position as lieutenant in his own guards—a very distinguished post. He also lets d'Artagnan know that he is aware of d'Artagnan's nocturnal activities, and he suggests that d'Artagnan needs protection from ladies who love him. He cautions d'Artagnan that if he were in the cardinal's service, he would have that protection. D'Artagnan refuses the offer because all of his friends are musketeers; he feels that he couldn't fit in with members of the cardinal's guards. The cardinal warns d'Artagnan that if something unfortunate should happen to him, it won't be the cardinal's fault. However, the cardinal does promise d'Artagnan that, for the time being, his feelings toward him are neutral; he is waiting to see how d'Artagnan conducts himself during the siege of La Rochelle.

Next day, during the inspection of the troops, all of the musketeers are magnificent in their new trappings. In fact, d'Artagnan is so concerned with his own appearance that he does not see Milady pointing him out to some sinister-looking, low-class rogues.

Commentary

In Chapter 39, d'Artagnan believes that Constance Bonacieux is still in captivity because she will not acknowledge him and his actions; later, however, we discover that she is being secretly transported according to the instructions of the queen to a rural convent for her protection.

Chapter 40 gives us one of the few favorable views of the cardinal. This is also the scene of the long-awaited meeting between d'Artagnan and the cardinal, and we are anxious to see how d'Artagnan conducts himself during the confrontation. Historically, Cardinal Richelieu was a superb diplomat, one of the most powerful men of his era; today, his name is far more famous than that of his king, Louis XIII.

In this scene, we see that the cardinal is fair; he respects virtue and loyalty, and he acknowledges d'Artagnan's superior qualities by offering him a promotion in the guards. Earlier, this offer would have been an undreamed-of opportunity for a young man from Gascony, but now d'Artagnan has formed his own allegiances. He refuses the cardinal's offer with a subtle and effectively diplomatic answer, proof that he has learned a great deal during his short stay in Paris. The cardinal's promise to be neutral, that he won't personally persecute or hound d'Artagnan, gives us a fuller perspective of Cardinal Richelieu. We are being prepared for d'Artagnan's ultimate alignment with the cardinal at the end of the novel.

Part 4

CHAPTERS 41–42

Summary

The siege of La Rochelle allows the cardinal an opportunity to fulfill two aims. First, he wants to rid France of its enemies, and second, he wants to take vengeance on a rival. That is, the cardinal was once in love with the queen, Anne of Austria, but she rejected him and accepted the romantic overtures of the duke of Buckingham, who is now declaring war on France, hoping to return triumphantly to Paris and rendezvous with the queen.

Since the king has a fever and cannot go to the battlefront, the musketeers are forced to remain behind with him. Thus, for the first time, d'Artagnan is separated from his friends. Since he has made no friends among the guards of his own division, he is out walking alone on an isolated road at twilight when he suddenly sees the end of a musket on one side of the road and another musket on the other side. He quickly and instinctively takes cover when both muskets are fired at him and he manages to escape before the ambushers can reload. He ponders the meaning of the attack and rejects the idea that it was the enemy who fired on him because the muskets were not military weapons. D'Artagnan cannot fathom the cardinal's stooping to ambush; finally, he decides that Milady was involved.

Two days later, Monsieur des Essarts, commander of the guard, informs d'Artagnan that the commander-in-chief is going to call for volunteers for a dangerous mission. D'Artagnan volunteers and, not surprisingly, he is made leader of the expedition. Two other officers and two ordinary soldiers also volunteer. The mission is to discover whether the enemy, on recapturing a bastion, left it guarded or unguarded. They will have to get dangerously close to the bastion. When they are approaching it, a volley of shots rings out, wounding one of the officers. Then two more shots ring out, and d'Artagnan is very nearly killed. He realizes instantly that the shots did *not* come from the enemy but that they came from *behind* him. He also realizes that the two common soldiers are trying to kill him and make it seem as though the enemy killed him. In fact, d'Artagnan believes, the two traitorous soldiers are the same two men who tried to ambush him earlier; he is absolutely certain that Milady conceived this plot.

D'Artagnan attacks and disarms the two soldiers. One of them manages to escape toward the bastion, but is shot by the enemy. The other soldier begs for mercy and confesses that they were indeed hired by Milady and that the wounded soldier has a letter from her. The letter chides the two soldiers for allowing Constance Bonacieux to escape and warns them *not* to allow d'Artagnan to escape.

Even though the letter isn't signed, d'Artagnan knows that it is from Milady, and he realizes anew what a terrible craving for revenge she has. Back at camp, he is accorded the reception of a hero, and his exploits are extolled by the entire command.

One morning in early November, d'Artagnan receives a letter telling him that the three musketeers are confined to quarters because of rowdy behavior, but that they have sent him twelve bottles of Anjou wine. D'Artagnan offers to share the wine with one of the guards, but just as they are about to drink up, a commotion announces the arrival of the king and the cardinal, and also – the three musketeers.

D'Artagnan thanks his friends for the wine and asks them to join him in drinking it. The musketeers tell him that *they* didn't send the wine, and all four of them simultaneously realize that Milady is responsible for the gift. At that moment, one of the guards who drank some of the wine falls down, poisoned. The four friends realize again that Milady is a worse threat than the enemy, and they decide to try to do something about her. D'Artagnan tells them that Constance Bonacieux is in a convent somewhere, but he doesn't know where. Aramis assures him that he will find the woman soon.

Commentary

These two chapters reveal to the reader what a powerful enemy d'Artagnan made when he saw the branded fleur-de-lis on Milady's naked shoulder. The extent of her drive for revenge is enormous. Three separate attempts on d'Artagnan's life have been made, and it is only because of d'Artagnan's alertness and daring during the first two attempts, and purely by accident during the incident of the Anjou wine that he is still alive. Even though these attemps to kill d'Artagnan are foiled, we will see in future chapters that Milady will never give up. She has vowed to see d'Artagnan dead – or die trying.

The beginning of Chapter 41 again emphasizes that the cardinal's persecution of the French queen is partly a result of jealousy: the queen prefers Buckingham to the cardinal. Dumas is insistent that the cardinal not be seen as merely a clever manipulator of people, but as a three-dimensional man, one spurned by the queen of France.

It is also worth noting that the separation of d'Artagnan from his friends sets the stage for several attempts on his life. Since his only close friends until now have been the three musketeers, it is believable that he would go for solitary walks. Were his three friends with him, d'Artagnan would never have been attacked by two cowardly dastards. However, because he is alone, he is attacked. Similarly, because he is alone and bored and eager to put some adventure into his life, he volunteers for a dangerous mission. D'Artagnan is continually trying to establish his own sense of identity and display leadership qualities – apart and separate from the three musketeers.

Lest someone think that d'Artagnan would not likely know that the unsigned letter in the wounded solder's uniform was from Milady, remember that he is familiar with Milady's handwriting. He has received love notes from her and, because of Kitty, he has been able to intercept love notes which she wrote to Count de Wardes. Dumas ties up most of his complicated plot elements very neatly and effectively.

CHAPTERS 43-45

Summary

The three musketeers have little to do because they are not yet involved in the siege, so they ride out to a neighboring inn. On the way back, they challenge an approaching rider who, in turn, challenges them with a voice of absolute authority. It is the cardinal. Surprisingly, he knows the names of each of the three musketeers; because his mission is secret, he asks them to accompany him in order that his safety be guaranteed. He knows their reputations for bravery, loyalty, and trustworthiness.

They learn that he is going to the inn which they just left, and they tell him about some rogues who tried to break into a lady's room. The musketeers were obliged to disperse these unsavory characters. The cardinal is pleased; the lady is the very person whom he is to meet. He asks the musketeers to wait for him in a room below while he goes up to talk to the lady.

In the musketeers' room, there is a broken stovepipe and, by accident, Athos discovers that he can hear the conversation between the cardinal and Milady. Porthos and Aramis also draw up their chairs and listen. They hear the cardinal tell Milady that she is to go to London to contact Buckingham and let him know that as soon as he attacks France, the cardinal will bring about the queen's ruin. Milady is also to tell Buckingham that the cardinal knows about his activities with the queen, and he describes each meeting which the duke has had with the queen, including a description of the clothes that the duke wore on each occasion. The cardinal also knows the truth about the diamond tags.

Furthermore, the cardinal's men have intercepted an Englishman who had letters on him (one from Madame de Chevreuse, Aramis' beloved) which compromise the queen because they prove that the queen is capable of loving the king's enemies and of conspiring with the enemies of France – charges which could imprison the queen for life. The cardinal is aware that the duke will do almost anything to protect the queen, but if the duke refuses, the cardinal indicates to Milady that she is to kill him – and make it look like the work of a fanatic. Milady agrees and, in return, she requests that *her* enemies be killed – first, Constance Bonacieux; and then, and even more important, she wants d'Artagnan killed. She will provide evidence that d'Artagnan has been in collusion with Buckingham; afterward, the cardinal will see to it that d'Artagnan disappears forever. Then she asks for, and receives, a valuable letter from the cardinal stating that whatever the bearer of the letter does, that person is doing so for the benefit of the cardinal and for France.

After hearing this, Athos makes ready to leave. He tells Aramis and Porthos to tell the cardinal that he has gone forward to scout the road – just in case there are unknown dangers. After the cardinal and the two remaining musketeers have left the inn, Athos returns to Milady's room and confronts her. She is horrified when she realizes that Athos is Count de La Fère, her husband, the man who tried to hang her and left her for dead.

Athos charges her with all of the vile, infamous things she has done and reviews her recent vengeful actions. Milady is stunned by his minutely detailed knowledge of her evil machinations, and Athos threatens her life if she doesn't cease trying to kill d'Artagnan. Milady defies Athos and vows that d'Artagnan will certainly die after she has made certain that Constance Bonacieux is dead. Athos draws his pistol and is about to kill her, but instead, he takes the letter which the cardinal wrote for her, and leaves.

Commentary

In these chapters, we have an ambiguous view of the cardinal. His request to the three musketeers, his acknowledgment that they are loyal and brave men, and his affirmation of the trust he has in them indicate that he is a man who recognizes good qualities in others. However, when the cardinal learns from Milady that d'Artagnan has been in collusion with Buckingham, he is determined to make sure that d'Artagnan is punished.

In Chapter 44, the device of having the three musketeers overhear the conversation between the cardinal and Milady is an easy, often-used fictional gimmick that good writers rarely use. In the romantic fiction of the nineteenth century, however, it was a favorite device. Sometimes a person hid behind a screen in the same room, or behind a shrub outside, or listened through a broken stovepipe, as we see here. (Actually, this "stovepipe device" is an anachronism on Dumas' part because the time period for the novel is the 1620s, and the stovepipe was not invented until the 1760s, by Benjamin Franklin in America. Dumas' novel was written in 1843–44, when the stovepipe was an established feature of many households.)

While the cardinal is giving Milady instructions, we are once again aware of how all-powerful and omniscient he is. He reveals that he knows almost every movement which the duke has ever made in France, including the duke's role in the intricate misadventures of the diamond tags. The cardinal is a shrewd diplomat; he knows that the duke will go to almost any length to protect Anne of Austria, the queen of France, and since there is an allegiance between England, Spain, Austria, and Lorraine against France, he must take drastic measures to assure France's safety and protect her powers. His ability to find the right methods to accomplish these things is what makes him such a powerful and feared man.

In Chapter 45, we learn Athos' real name—Count de La Fère— and we should recall that in the preface, Dumas wrote that he found a manuscript by Count de La Fère that recounts the events of this novel. During Athos' confrontation with Milady (alias Anne de Breuil, alias Countess de La Fère, alias Lady de Winter), he is stunned at the depths of her evil nature, her vile soul, and her infamous behavior. He thought he had killed her once and although he is on the verge of killing her now, he relents. He merely takes away her valuable "letter of protection," a letter which d'Artagnan will put to profitable use later on in the novel.

CHAPTERS 46–48

Summary

When the three musketeers meet d'Artagnan, they want to go someplace where they cannot be overhead as they make plans. They decide on an inn, but have no privacy there; they are continually bombarded with questions about d'Artagnan's exploits. When they hear some soldiers talking about a bastion that the enemy has taken and temporarily abandoned, Athos makes a bet that they can eat their breakfast there and remain safely in the bastion for one hour. The other soldiers bet against him.

Initially, d'Artagnan, Porthos, and Aramis are perplexed about Athos' ridiculous bet, but are reminded that they need privacy to discuss some very important matters that must remain absolutely secret. In the bastion, they will have complete privacy. Porthos wishes that they had remembered to bring their muskets, but Athos reminds them that when the bastion was stormed, twelve men and their muskets and powder were left lying there. They can use these weapons and receive even greater glory when their colleagues realize what a dangerous mission they went on, theoretically armed only with swords.

In Chapter 47, they enter the bastion, and Athos announces that he saw Milady the previous night. While d'Artagnan is registering surprise, Athos explains to the others what a wicked and evil woman she is and that she tried to have d'Artagnan shot and poisoned during the last two weeks.

Suddenly the musketeers see four soldiers and sixteen workmen approaching. Using the twelve muskets, they take careful aim, killing some of the soldiers and wounding the rest. The workmen flee. Resuming their talk, the musketeers and d'Artagnan decide that they must warn Buckingham against Milady's treachery, but since they are officially at war with England, they decide to warn Lord de Winter and tell him that he is about to be killed by his sister-in-law and that he should protect himself and Buckingham as well. Their next goal will be discovering the whereabouts of Madame Bonacieux before Milady and the cardinal do. Athos shows them the cardinal's "protection letter" which he took from Milady, signed by the cardinal and insuring absolute protection and permission to the bearer of the note. They decide to send Planchet to London and Bazin to Aramis' countess, but unfortunately, they realize, they need money to carry out their plans.

Grimaud abruptly announces that about twenty-five men are approaching. Athos has Grimaud place all the dead bodies outside and put muskets in their hands. Meanwhile, they finish their breakfast and see that they have probably ten more minutes before they can win their bet. They conceal themselves and carefully take aim at the approaching soldiers, kill several of them, and then, as the rest try to approach the bastion, they push over a rotting wall on them – killing or drowning most of them in the moat. Then they return gloriously to camp.

On the way, they wonder how they will get some money – and at this point they remember d'Artagnan's diamond ring. They convince him that since the queen gave it to him, it would be an honor to the queen if he were to sell it to help Buckingham, the queen's lover, and the money could also help rescue Constance Bonacieux, the queen's loyal servant.

They persuade Aramis to write a letter to de Winter and one to Madame de Chevreuse, using elegant, arabesque phrases so if the letter is confiscated or captured, the enemy (or the cardinal) will not understand the contents. Then they send Planchet and Bazin on the important errands, promising them extra money if they return at a specifically designated time. D'Artagnan has now been officially declared a musketeer, so the *four* musketeers while away their time, waiting for the servants to return. Not long afterward, both servants return on the designated day at the designated time.

Commentary

The episode in the bastion does little to advance the plot, but it does emphasize the daring and inventive bravado of the musketeers and d'Artagnan. Of course, the purpose of their going to the bastion, apart from its being a daring excursion, is to find a place where they can discuss secret strategy without being overheard. We know that the cardinal has spies in every nook and cranny of France – if not in all of Europe – therefore, only in a captured and temporarily abandoned bastion can they find sufficient privacy to make plans to thwart Milady's scheme to kill Constance Bonacieux and d'Artagnan.

Athos is characterized in this episode as a true leader: he knows that the muskets belonging to the dead soldiers are still beside their bodies, and by placing the dead men and their muskets on the bastion's parapet, he shows great ingenuity: the attacking soldiers will be firing at dead bodies while the musketeers will be taking direct aim at the attacking soldiers.

Once again, during their discussion about Milady, we realize that she is one of the most villainous and crafty women imaginable. She is totally amoral; she will sacrifice anyone to her deadly, vengeful schemes.

It is interesting to see how several earlier adventures prepared the way for these present adventures. For example, if Planchet had not accompanied d'Artagnan on the trip to England, he would not know how to get there now. Likewise, because Bazin is known by Madame de Chevreuse as Aramis' servant, he will be recognized and trusted.

CHAPTERS 49–51

Summary

Milady's ship is detained by a storm, and when she finally reaches England, Planchet has already warned de Winter of Milady's wicked plans; meanwhile, Planchet is now boarding a ship heading back to France. Therefore, when Milady's ship docks, she is received by an austere English officer who, with utmost politeness, escorts her to a castle some distance away and places her in a locked room. Milady is livid with anger and indignation, but after awhile, Lord de Winter appears. To her horror, she learns that she is a prisoner.

She tells her brother-in-law that her only reason for coming to England was to see him. De Winter is not fooled. He sarcastically acknowledges that her reason for coming is now fulfilled: she is a "guest" in his castle and they can visit together every day. Slyly, de Winter lets Milady know that he is aware of her first husband (Athos), as well as her recent plottings. And when he mentions her branded shoulder, she is ready to kill him—but he warns her not to try, for if she does he will either kill her or send her to the public executioner.

De Winter then calls for his assistant, John Felton, and tells him to guard this wicked woman. He recounts many of the immoral and evil things she has done, and he warns Felton not to be deceived by her. Felton, who is deeply indebted to de Winter for many favors, promises to obey his master's instructions to the letter.

Meanwhile, back in France, the cardinal is wandering around the campgrounds, waiting for Milady's report. By accident, he encounters the four musketeers, who are reading a letter. Richelieu approaches them and engages in a rather guarded political conversation, during which Athos gets the better of the cardinal, who grudgingly leaves.

Commentary

These chapters further reveal the dark and murky depths of Milady's vile nature. For example, other people might have committed some of her immoral acts for the sake of money, but we hear from de Winter that Milady is already wealthy. Milady's desire for de Winter's money is simply another aspect of her enormous greed and lust for power. De Winter finally concludes that her only reason for doing evil is for the sheer pleasure she receives when she is doing it. She can be compared to Shakespeare's Iago (in *Othello*); both Iago and Milady enjoy evil for the sake of evil.

Nonetheless, we should note that in spite of Milady's evil nature, she is treated politely and accommodatingly as a lady should be — rather than being thrown into a dungeon, where she belongs. This politeness is part of the nineteenth century's code of gentlemanly respect for womanhood — even though in this case, Milady's "womanhood" is indelibly corrupt and evil.

In Chapter 51, Athos is rather forward with the cardinal; he suggests that the letter he is reading is from his mistress, and he takes an even more dangerous chance when he says that the letter is not from either of two ladies who have been the cardinal's mistresses. The letter, of course, must be concealed at all costs because it contains the location of the secret whereabouts of Madame Bonacieux — and the cardinal wants this information badly.

CHAPTERS 52–57

Summary

Milady spends her first day in captivity brooding on her fierce hatred for d'Artagnan, Buckingham, and Constance Bonacieux. She wishes them all dead. Her eyes glow with murderous hatred, and she makes elaborate plans for revenge against them. When she finally calms herself, she decides that she should probably study the characters of the men who are guarding her. Foremost, there is John Felton, a seemingly strict disciplinarian.

She pretends to faint, but this ploy doesn't soften Felton's heart, and, to make matters worse, de Winter walks in during the fraudulent fainting fit and tells Felton that Milady's swoon is only her first dramatic performance: she will give many more performances, all demonstrating her considerable talents as an actress. Milady is furious. She grabs a dinner knife—only to discover that it has been blunted. De Winter points out Milady's fury to Felton and again warns him, but this time, Milady notices that Felton seems to have a tiny bit of pity for her.

On the second day, Milady feigns illness, and this time Felton responds sympathetically. He gives her a Catholic missal (a book of masses), and as he does so, she notes that Felton handles the book with distaste, signifying to Milady that he is not a Catholic—he is a Puritan. Thus she pretends to be a victimized Puritan, suffering from Catholic persecution. She summons up all of the pious knowledge that she has accumulated about the Puritans and begins to rant about persecution, martyrdom, and suffering—ideas that are close to a Puritan's heart. She also reads her prayers loudly and fervently, and she sings Puritan hymns like a steadfast victim might. By chance, her voice is so beautiful that Felton is deeply moved and distracted.

On the third day, Milady tries to conceive of a way to make Felton linger in her room. She knows when Felton is coming, so she makes sure that she is ardently praying for the strength to bear her sufferings. In particular, she asks God if the enemy is to be allowed to succeed in his abomination. This show of spiritual earnestness deeply touches young Felton because his religion embraces repentent sinners and elevates martyrs. Milady asks Felton for a favor which he is quick to deny, but he continues to listen to her story, especially when she suggests that de Winter plans to plunge her into shame with Buckingham. Felton can't believe such injustice from de Winter; yet, Milady notices, Felton *is* willing to believe anything derogatory about Buckingham. Felton is surprised to learn that Milady knows Buckingham.

At this point, Milady asks Felton for a knife, promising not to hurt him and promising to return the knife immediately. Felton is convinced that she plans to commit suicide and refuses to give her a knife, but clearly he does believe in her sincerity and goodness. When he leaves, Milady feels that she has Felton within her power.

When de Winter arrives and offers Milady exile or death, she does not choose death. Instead, she begins singing a Puritan hymn so loudly that she can be heard by all the guards.

On the fourth day, young Felton finds Milady playing with a rope made of batiste handkerchiefs. He assumes that she plans to hang herself. She, in turn, accuses him of protecting her body while being an accomplice to the slaughter of her soul. Felton is visibly shaken and tells her that earlier he doubted her sincerity; now, he believes her. Indeed, he is suddenly so fascinated by her that he cannot turn his eyes away from her. As she pleads with him for death, Felton feels the magic of her beauty, her irresistible attraction of sensuality, and her vibrant religious fervor.

Without warning, de Winter enters and breaks Milady's spell. Later, Felton tells Milady that he will return to hear all of her story. She is overjoyed; now she has Felton – "that brainless fanatic" – in her power.

On the fifth day, Milady has her plans prepared; her fictional autobiography is ready. Felton reenters and puts a sharp knife on the table; Milady is further convinced that she has Felton in her power. She tells Felton a long, dramatic story about a nobleman who once tried to seduce her because she was so young and beautiful; she rejected his advances, but he drugged her and then he raped her. Later, she awoke and he stood before her, offering a fortune for her love. She refused and threatened to stab herself. He left, and again she was drugged and raped. Afterward, she still refused – despite threats of more punishment. She vowed that someday she would publish his vile crimes throughout the world. At this point, he threatened to brand her with the mark of a criminal if she murmured a word.

Felton is so moved that he can hardly stand. Milady continues her fictitious story, providing all of the graphic, emotional details, particularly about the sadistic branding. Then, removing just enough of her clothing to entice Felton, Milady reveals the hideous brand, the fleur-de-lis.

When Felton sees the dreadful mark, he is so overcome with passion and fury that he will do anything for her. He demands to know who is responsible for such a crime. Before Milady can answer, though, Felton himself speaks: "Buckingham." He insists on knowing how de Winter is involved. Milady explains that de Winter's brother (her late husband) learned about her past, but married her and promised to kill Buckingham. Yet before he could, he mysteriously died. Buckingham then fabricated stories to her brother-in-law, de Winter, about Milady's shameful past, persuading him that Milady was never in love with de Winter's brother, that she was interested only in the family money. Finishing up, Milady falls dramatically into Felton's arms. He feels the warmth of her breath and the throbbing within her breasts. He has never felt such passion.

De Winter enters, and when Milady threatens to kill herself, he calls her bluff. She takes sudden, drastic measures and cleverly stabs herself in such a superficial way that she draws only a little blood — but it is enough to convince Felton that she is an innocent victim of both de Winter and Buckingham.

Commentary

On the first day of her imprisonment, Milady tries to arouse Felton's sympathy by pretending to faint; the ploy doesn't work. De Winter warns Felton that she will continue to use her immense talents as an actress to gain his sympathy. Later, however, when she puts on a grand performance for Felton, she is so superb that the young, naive Puritan falls for her ruse and also for her beauty and sensuality. Thus, Dumas prepares us for the likelihood that Milady will be able to deceive almost anyone else she wishes to deceive. Clearly, we do not have merely an ordinary villainess here; we have a skillful, talented woman who is the quintessence of evil, possessing the psychological insight to know how to evaluate her victims and how to determine their weak points. She is a magnificent adversary, stunningly powerful and gifted — no match for the naive and sympathetic John Felton.

Note too that Dumas has endowed Milady with all sorts of talents; in addition to her intellectual perceptions, her acting, and her superb deceptions, Milady is endowed with a lovely and piously beautiful voice which converts not only Felton, but also her guards. Yet, never should we forget that at the core of this beautiful body and angelic voice beats the heart of a corrupt and destructive woman. Milady recognizes that a man like Felton can't be tempted by ordinary feminine wiles, and she is astute enough to know that when a man displays extreme piety, he is usually suppressing a secret, passionate nature. Accordingly, she plays on his pity, confessing a multitude of lies about being abducted, drugged, raped and finally branded. Then, playing on his suppressed sensual nature, she reveals to him a lovely naked shoulder, scarred indelibly with a hateful brand.

Her plan is successful: "The enchantress had again taken on the magic power of her beauty and distress, heightened by the irresistible attraction of sensuality mingled with religious fervor." Thus, Dumas, like many modern writers, presents a close correlation between religious fanaticism and sexual passion.

It is to Milady's evil credit that she can seduce Felton's compassion and sympathy so quickly, especially after he has been warned repeatedly about her evil nature – and even after he has seen evidence of her duplicity. However, since Buckingham is known to be something of a "libertine" and a "ladies man," as the Puritans have labeled him, Felton is ready to believe anything about Buckingham; thus, Milady's story of sadistic lust appeals to him. He *wants* to believe wicked things about Buckingham.

The story that Milady tells Felton is filled with stock melodramatic elements, cliches which the innocent Felton readily believes – sleeping potions, drugs, poison, and a virgin deflowered and scarred for life. Ultimately, the dramatic actress finishes her story and pretends to collapse in his arms. Felton gathers up her sensuous body, and apparently this is the first time that he has held such loveliness. He no longer feels pity for her; he worships her.

CHAPTERS 58–59

Summary

De Winter, suspecting that Felton is under Milady's influence, sends him on an errand – away from the castle. That night, Milady hears a tap at the window; it is Felton. He has chartered a boat to take them to France, and he plans to file through the bars on her window and help her escape.

Felton is successful and helps Milady climb down a rope ladder. They board the boat and he tells her that he has to debark at Portsmouth in order to take his revenge on Buckingham before Buckingham leaves for France. Milady is convinced that Felton will be able to dispose of Buckingham; her vengeance will be fulfilled. It is agreed that she will wait for Felton until 10 o'clock before setting sail.

Felton's mind seethes with all of the horrible things he has heard about Buckingham. His strange, maniacal devotion to Milady, together with his fanatical religious notions, make him totally irrational. When he is allowed into Buckingham's office, he pleads for Milady's freedom, but Buckingham absolutely refuses. Crazed, Felton pulls out a dagger and stabs Buckingham. He tries to flee, but he is apprehended by de Winter.

As Buckingham is dying, he learns that Queen Anne's friend, Monsieur de La Porte, is outside; La Porte has a letter from the queen which he reads to the dying Buckingham, assuring Buckingham of Anne's love for him. After Buckingham dies, de Winter questions Felton, who maintains that he killed Buckingham only because of a matter concerning promotions. Then Felton sees the sloop with Milady on it sailing out to sea. Obviously she heard the cannon alerting the nation that something extraordinary had happened, and she surmised that Buckingham was dead. Instantly, she set sail — alone. Felton has been betrayed and abandoned.

Commentary

These two chapters bring to an end the "English episodes" concerning Milady and the puritanical fanatic, Felton, whose religious blindness allowed him to become her dupe. Ironically, the cardinal casually remarked earlier: if all else fails, maybe some fanatic will rid the world of Buckingham. The cardinal was brilliantly prophetic. Dumas has arranged his material so carefully that neither author nor reader wishes to dwell upon the particulars of Felton's religious views; we are content to leave him to his destiny.

Part 5

CHAPTERS 60–63

Summary

After the death of Buckingham, the king of England closes all the ports, but Milady has already escaped, *and* one other ship *also* left. Dumas comments cryptically, "We will later see who was aboard it and how it left."

In France, everyone — including the king — is bored with the siege of La Rochelle. The musketeers, meanwhile, receive a letter from Aramis' ladyfriend, Madame de Chevreuse, with a note that gives freedom to Constance Bonacieux and puts her in their care; the note is signed "Anne."

The king, being bored, needs an escort to Paris, and the four musketeers are among those chosen. In Paris, because they have no pressing duties, they obtain a leave of absence so that they can go to the convent. Once there, d'Artagnan again sees his nemesis, "the man from Meung." As the man rides away, he drops a piece of paper which d'Artagnan retrieves from his servant; on it is written one word, "Armentiers."

Meantime, Milady has also wended her way toward the convent, where she is received as a gracious lady since she has the blessing of the cardinal. However, she senses that the Abbess is not a cardinalist, so she pretends to be a victim of the cardinal (instead of a friend of the cardinal), thereby hoping to gain favor with the Abbess. By chance she learns that another "persecuted person" is at the convent, a woman named Kitty. Milady is anxious to meet this "Kitty," because her own maid Kitty helped d'Artagnan deceive her.

After a brief nap, Milady awakens to discover a beautiful novice standing at her bedside. After they talk, they discover that they are both victims of the cardinal's persecution; Milady, of course, is lying, but she shrewdly questions the other woman and, to her astonishment, she realizes that she is talking to Constance Bonacieux—the very woman she wants killed. Immediately, she ingratiates herself into Constance's confidence, and Constance innocently shares a letter from Madame de Chevreuse. The letter says that d'Artagnan will be arriving for her very soon. At that moment, a man on horseback arrives, asking for "a lady who just came from Boulogne."

The visitor is Count de Rochefort, the cardinal's right-hand man, the person whom d'Artagnan always refers to as "the man from Meung." Milady immediately tells him three important matters: (1) Buckingham is either dead or seriously wounded; (2) she has become a close confidante to Constance Bonacieux, whom the cardinal is searching for; and (3) the four musketeers will be arriving soon. The count is to report immediately to the cardinal, but Milady asks that he leave his chaise, his servant, and his money at her disposal. He is also to instruct the Abbess that Milady is to be allowed to walk in the woods.

Milady then plans her revenge. She pretends that the visitor was her brother, and she convinces Constance Bonacieux that the letter from Madame de Chevreuse is a forgery and that they must flee to a secret cottage that Milady knows about. Suddenly they hear hoofbeats and, leaving Constance seated, Milady peers through the window and sees the musketeers approaching. She tells Constance that it is the cardinal's men and they must escape through the woods. Constance is so paralyzed with fear that she can't move, so Milady pours her a glass of wine, while opening a secret ring and pouring poison into the wine. Then she makes the innocent and trusting Constance drink the wine. Afterward, she flees for her life.

D'Artagnan and the others arrive and find Constance weak and dying. With her last bit of strength, Constance embraces d'Artagnan and tells him that she loves him. As he holds her tenderly in his arms, she is able to remember the name of the woman who gave her the poison. Then she dies, and d'Artagnan "now held only a corpse in his arms." At this moment, de Winter enters, identifies himself and explains that he has been following close behind Milady ever since the death of Buckingham.

D'Artagnan is prostrate with grief, but is comforted by Athos, who tells him to "weep, weep, young heart filled with love, youth, and life!" The other musketeers want to take revenge against Milady immediately, but Athos insists that *he* be in charge because "she is my wife."

Commentary

The king's boredom allows the musketeers the opportunity to accompany him to Paris and, from there, to continue to the convent with the letter from Queen Anne authorizing the release of Constance Bonacieux.

In a romantic novel such as this one, coincidences often play a large part in the plot. Thus, the piece of paper with only the name of a town, "Armentiers," written on it, proves to be a very valuable find because the musketeers feel sure that this is the town where they will be able to find Milady.

At the convent, we again witness Milady's knowledge of psychology and her ability to win the confidence of such different people as the Abbess and Constance Bonacieux. We also see additional proof that Milady is corrupt to the core; she does not even know the young and innocent Constance Bonacieux, but she fiercely desires her death – in order to get even with d'Artagnan. A woman who would sacrifice the life of an innocent victim only to satisfy her own selfish lust for revenge deserves the worst punishment available.

The death of Constance Bonacieux at the very moment that her supposed savior, d'Artagnan, arrives is typical of nineteenth-century melodramatic romanticism. This scene is one that still affects most readers — in spite of its overt use of sentimentalism and contrived timing. The death of this young woman causes Athos, who earlier had been so secretive about his past, to reveal that the scheming, vicious Milady is his wife and that he will take personal charge of punishing her.

CHAPTERS 64–66

Summary

After Athos sends the others to bed, he sends the four servants on four different roads to discover the whereabouts of Milady. Meanwhile, he goes for a walk and begins questioning some late wanderers. Each one of them is so frightened when they hear his question that they cannot speak; they can only point him in a certain direction. Finally, Athos finds an old beggar who is too frightened to accompany him but agrees to do so after Athos gives him a silver coin.

At the small house to which he has been directed, Athos is admitted by a tall, powerful man who shrinks in terror at Athos' request. However, when Athos shows him a piece of paper with the cardinal's signature and seal, the tall man recognizes the seal and agrees to accompany Athos.

Next day, after attending Constance's funeral, Athos investigates the garden and discovers Milady's footsteps. Shortly, Planchet returns with the news that Milady is staying at an inn and that the servants are keeping her under surveillance. That night, they prepare to leave, accompanied by the mysterious tall man, who is wearing a mask and a big red cloak.

Amidst a raging storm, they approach the inn and are led to a cottage, where Athos sees Milady. As she suddenly sees them, Athos breaks through a window, and d'Artagnan comes through the door. Then Porthos, Aramis, de Winter, and the man in the red cloak enter. Athos announces that Milady is to be tried for vile, innumerable crimes — in particular, for poisoning Constance Bonacieux, sending poisoned wine with the intent of killing d'Artagnan, and trying to coerce d'Artagnan to kill Count de Wardes. Then de Winter accuses Milady of corrupting John Felton, of being responsible for the deaths of Buckingham and Felton, and of being responsible for the mysterious death of his own brother – her husband, the first Lord de Winter. Athos then condemns her further because of her deceit in their marriage.

At this point, the executioner – the man in the red cloak – speaks; he reveals her origins and tells how she seduced his brother, a convent priest, to a life of crime. When the crime was discovered, he (as official executioner) had to brand his own brother. Milady escaped, he says, by seducing the jailer's son. She also helped the priest to escape. The executioner managed to track her down and brand her. He himself had to serve his missing brother's remaining prison term. Later, after Milady abandoned the priest for Athos (Count de La Fère), the priest surrendered, then hanged himself.

Athos asks each of the men for a verdict. Each one of them asks for the death penalty. Milady is carried to the edge of a river where she is tied hand and foot, and once again her crimes are recounted as she begs for her life. The executioner takes her across the river, and in the boat she frees her feet and tries to escape, but she cannot get up. The executioner cuts off her head, wraps her body and head in his cloak and dumps them in the river, crying out loudly, "God's justice be done."

Commentary

These chapters bring to an end the horrible injustices of Milady – Lady de Winter. As in most nineteenth-century novels, justice triumphs and evil is destroyed. But not before Dumas introduces one last mystery. In Chapter 64, he creates a wonderful sense of suspense when he has everyone who is quizzed by Athos quail before him, afraid to tell him where a certain person lives. As we discover later, Athos is looking for an executioner, and most simple and superstitious people fear such a man – even though he is only doing his job. It is poetic justice that Milady loses her life at the hands of an "official" executioner – especially since he suffered so terribly as a result of her evil conniving.

Moviemakers often revel in filming this final scene, where the climax of raging emotions and passions parallel the raging storm outside, suggesting the furious storms within the protagonists.

When the various men gather to denounce Milady's numerous and infamous sins, the list is truly impressive – a list that chills most people, but note that Milady feels that she is being treated unfairly. Even though she herself has just killed Constance Bonacieux, a young, innocent woman, Milady pleads that she herself is "too young" to die. Milady's death fits the crimes that she committed: her head, the source of all her conniving, is severed from her body and both pieces are thrown into the river. With her death, justice has been done, and the novel can now draw rapidly to an end.

CONCLUSION & EPILOGUE

Summary

The French king is overjoyed to learn that Buckingham is dead; in addition, he is finally able to return to the siege. On the way, he and the musketeers stop at an inn where "the man from Meung" appears and tells d'Artagnan that he is under arrest. He identifies himself as Count de Rochefort, Cardinal Richelieu's agent. D'Artagnan's three comrades will not allow him to be arrested; they promise to deliver him to the cardinal at the appointed time.

Later, the cardinal tells d'Artagnan that he is accused of conspiring with enemies of France, intercepting state secrets, and attempting to thwart his general's plans. D'Artagnan defies the cardinal to name his accuser. He states that his accuser is a woman branded by French justice, a bigamist who poisoned her second husband, tried to poison d'Artagnan, poisoned Constance Bonacieux, and was guilty of many other crimes.

When d'Artagnan finishes the tangled story of Milady's web of crimes, including her being sentenced to death, a shudder runs through the cardinal's body. Still, though, he thinks that d'Artagnan should be tried. It is then that d'Artagnan shows the cardinal the carte blanche "paper of protection" which the cardinal himself gave to the wicked Milady, stating, "The bearer of this letter has acted under my orders and for the good of the State. Richelieu."

The cardinal pauses, sits and writes. D'Artagnan wonders if it is his death sentence. It is not. The cardinal has written out a commission for "someone" to serve as a first lieutenant in the musketeers; d'Artagnan can fill in any name he chooses. The cardinal reminds d'Artagnan, however, that the opportunity is given to *him*. D'Artagnan first offers the commission to Athos, but Athos refuses it because he has inherited some money. Then Porthos turns it down because his mistress has inherited a fortune. Aramis refuses it because he is finally entering a monastery. Thus, d'Artagnan has to accept the commission.

The novel ends with d'Artagnan's fighting three duels with Count de Rochefort. Then Cardinal Richelieu orders them to become friends. To seal the friendship, Count de Rochefort makes Planchet a sergeant in the guards.

Commentary

After only a short time in Paris, our young Gascon has evolved, as did Monsieur de Tréville, from being a country boy to being a power to be reckoned with in the King's Musketeers. He is now a friend of the cardinal and also a defender of the queen. The other musketeers are happy and living their own individual lives. Here, as in most nineteenth-century novels, all's well that ends well.

CRITICAL ESSAY

THE THREE MUSKETEERS AS FILM

Dumas' novel has appealed to filmmakers of the world ever since the beginning of commercial cinema. In this country alone, there have been many different films based on Dumas' masterpiece. Some versions remain reasonably faithful to the novel, while other versions use some of Dumas' general plot outlines, or the characters, or the era, and then stray variously from the novel itself.

One of the early films which was based on *The Three Musketeers* starred Douglas Fairbanks, probably the most famous "swashbuckling" actor of the silent film industry. In fact, this movie almost singlehandedly set the tone for the Douglas Fairbanks–style of acting which has, in one way or another, influenced later productions and acting styles for similar movies. That is, Fairbanks was filmed swinging from chandeliers, brandishing swords, perilously crossing deep, craggy ravines, fighting against insurmountable odds, and performing other improbable feats of bravado and bravery. The film is 186 minutes long, an extremely long movie for a silent film; usually silent films lasted 60 to 90 minutes.

Another film version of *The Three Musketeers* was released in 1933. This cinematic treatment of the novel contained sound, but was a rather brief, truncated version of the story. The director terribly mis-cast a youthful John Wayne as one of the musketeers.

The 1935 version of the novel starred Walter Abel, an actor known for his dignity and reserve; not surprisingly, he made d'Artagnan one of the most boring swordsmen ever. Not recommended.

The 1939 *Three Musketeers* film starring the Ritz Brothers – Al, Jimmy, and Harry – used Dumas' title as a vehicle for the rich comic talents of the three zany brothers. Very little attention was given to Dumas' plot; Don Ameche (a recent Oscar winner) was cast as d'Artagnan, but he failed to make the role memorable. The movie should be seen only for the antics of the three Ritz Brothers as the three irrepressible musketeers.

Recently, there have been efforts to create sequels for Dumas' original novel. Among them, *The Fifth Musketeer* has been given a screen treatment, as well as a movie featuring d'Artagnan as an aging swordsman, still gallant and dashing, but now more of a Don Quixote figure.

Of all the movie versions, however, most movie critics agree that the best were released in 1949 and 1974. The 1949 *Three Musketeers* featured an all-star cast of MGM notables. Director George Sidney cast Gene Kelly as d'Artagnan; Van Heflin as Athos; June Allison as Constance; Lana Turner as Milady; Vincent Price as Richelieu; and Angela Lansbury as Queen Anne. This film version, unlike the 1974 production by Richard Lester, is unusually faithful to Dumas' novel. Consider, for instance, the fidelity of the film to the novel in the following key scenes.

Scene 1. As d'Artagnan departs from home, he is cleanly and neatly dressed, although he is a peasant lad; he receives gifts from his father and departs on a very comic-looking horse. In contrast, this same scene in the 1974 Richard Lester film, starring Michael York as d'Artagnan, shows the hero dressed in dirty, ragged clothes, conducting himself rather basely and departing on a perfectly acceptable-looking horse.

Scene 2. D'Artagnan's arrival in Meung is memorable because of his impetuous attack on "the man from Meung"; d'Artagnan attempts to duel with the stranger, but is defeated, beaten and robbed. In Lester's film, the duel scene and the fighting are played wholly for comedy.

Scene 3. D'Artagnan's arrival in Paris and his admittance to Tré-ville's house shows him overhearing Athos, Porthos, and Aramis being reprimanded for dueling in a tavern. This scene is omitted in Lester's film.

Scene 4. D'Artagnan catches sight of "the man from Meung," runs after him, bumps into Athos and agrees to a 12 o'clock duel; he knocks Porthos down, revealing a half-golden (instead of an entirely golden) shoulder belt, and agrees to a 1 o'clock duel; then he enrages the usually quiet Aramis and agrees to a 2 o'clock duel. In the Lester film, there are so many extraneous things happening that one loses all sense of any individuality among the three musketeers.

Scene 5. During d'Artagnan's duel with Athos, while the other two musketeers wait their turn, the duel is interrupted by the appearance of the cardinal's men, who arrive to arrest them; d'Artagnan sides with the musketeers and thereby becomes an unofficial "fourth" musketeer.

While this is a rather short scene in the novel, it is usually presented in the movies in the grand tradition of the great dueling scenes established by Douglas Fairbanks. In the Sidney film, it is a continuous, running scene, marvelously orchestrated and brilliantly choreographed. Each of the duelists is individualized with the ultimate and final attention focused on the magnificent performance by Gene Kelly as d'Artagnan. In his heyday, Kelly was one of the finest dancers on the silver screen, and this particular scene emphasizes his masterful ability to move and dance.

The three musketeers finally retire to the background and function merely as an appreciative audience as this fantastic peasant lad from Gascony deliciously combats with finesse and, at times, with humor—always in control of the situation. The entire scene functions as a complete cinematic unit.

In contrast, the Lester version is filmed as though it were a back street brawl, with no continuity of camera work; each short, jerky shot has little or no relation to the next short, jerky shot. Instead of long, lyric passages of classic dueling, Lester has his swordsmen doing karate chops, kicking, gouging, jumping, bludgeoning with rakes and poles, and other such related nonsense. There is absolutely no sense of d'Artagnan's being a superior swordsman.

Scene 6. After Tréville reprimands the four men and they are summoned to an audience with the king, the scene of them marching through the elegant throne room and up to the king is a classic scene which is often used or recreated for advertising purposes. Curiously, this entire scene is deleted from the Lester film and replaced with odd doings of street people and gratuitous acrobats, circus-like activities, and other visual diversions inserted to create a sense of "atmosphere."

From this point on, the Sidney film varies only slightly from the novel. However, note that Constance Bonacieux becomes Monsieur Bonacieux's adopted *daughter;* thus the love affair between her and d'Artagnan was more acceptable to the moral code of the late '40s than d'Artagnan's having an affair with his landlord's *wife.* In the Lester movie, the young and beautiful Constance is played by an aging but voluptuous Raquel Welch, who is immediately attracted to d'Artagnan; the two are in bed within minutes of meeting one another.

From this point on in the Lester film, there is little similarity to Dumas' novel. The Sidney film, however, continues to follow Dumas' novel almost scene for scene. Admittedly, there are some "adjustments"—such as placing Milady under the guard of Constance, instead of introducing a new character (John Felton in the novel), and later, there is a serious divergence from the novel when Milady goes to her death proud and defiant, rather than pleading and conniving, as she does in the novel.

In conclusion, the 1949 movie is a very close rendering of Dumas' literary masterpiece, whereas the 1974 movie uses the basic plotline of the novel, but creates an entirely different sort of finished product.

SUGGESTED ESSAY QUESTIONS

1. The three musketeers—Athos, Porthos, and Aramis—are often thought of collectively, yet each of them is a unique individual. Discuss their individual differences and show how these differences are reflected in their choice of servants—for example, in Athos' Grimaud, Porthos' Mousqueton, and Aramis' Bazin.

2. Write on the relationship between adventure, intrigue, love, and mystery throughout the novel.

3. Discuss the significant occurrences (events, happenings, adventures, coincidences) which allow d'Artagnan, a simple young eighteen-year-old boy, to become a twenty-one-year-old man of position and power.

4. How does Cardinal Richelieu affect d'Artagnan's rise to fame more than do d'Artagnan's friends?

5. Discuss the correlation between the duke of Buckingham's love for Queen Anne and d'Artagnan's love for Constance Bonacieux.

6. Discuss Milady as the pure essence, or quintessence, of evil.

SELECTED BIBLIOGRAPHY

BASSAN, FERNANDE. *Alexandre Dumas, pere, et la Comedie-Francaise.* Paris: Lettres Modernes, 1972.

BELL, A. CRAIG. *Alexandre Dumas, a Biography and Study.* London. Cassell, 1950.

COOK, MERCER. *Five French Negro Authors.* Washington, D.C.: Associated Publishers, 1943.

GORMAN, HERBERT SHERMAN. *The Incredible Marquis, Alexandre Dumas.* New York: Rinehart, 1929.

HEMMINGS, FREDERICK WILLIAM JOHN. *The King of Romance: A Portrait of Alexandre Dumas.* London, 1929.

LUCAS-DUBRETON, JEAN. *La Vie d'Alexandre Dumas, pere.* Paris: J. Lucas-Dubreton, 1916.

MAUROIS, ANDRE. *Alexandre Dumas: A Great Life in Brief.* New York: Knopf, 1955.

MUNRO, DOUGLAS. *Alexandre Dumas, pere.* New York: Garland, 1981.

PARIGOT, HIPPOLYTE LOUIS. *Alexandre Dumas, pere.* Paris, 1902.

REED, FRANK WILD. *Alexandre Dumas, Benefactor.* New York: Colophon, 1935.

Ross, Michael. *Alexandre Dumas.* London: Newton Abbot, 1981.

Schop, Claude. *Alexandre Dumas: Genius of Life.* New York: Franklin Watts, 1988.

Simon, G. M. *Histoire d'une Collaboration.* Paris, 1919.

Stowe, Richard. *Alexandre Dumas.* New York: Twayne, 1976.

Thompson, John A. *Alexandre Dumas, pere, and the Spanish Romance Drama.* Louisiana State University Press, 1938.

NOTES

NOTES

BECKETT'S
WAITING FOR GODOT, ENDGAME, & OTHER PLAYS

NOTES

including

- *Brief Life of the Author*
- *Samuel Beckett and the Theater of the Absurd*
- **Waiting for Godot**
    - *List of Characters*
    - *Dramatic Divisions*
    - *Critical Analysis*
    - *Circular Structure*
    - *Character Analyses*
- *Critical Analyses of*
    - **Endgame**
    - **All That Fall**
    - **Act Without Words I**
    - **Krapp's Last Tape**

by
James L. Roberts, Ph.D.
Department of English
University of Nebraska

INCORPORATED

LINCOLN, NEBRASKA   68501

Editor

Gary Carey, M.A.
University of Colorado

Consulting Editor

James L. Roberts, Ph.D.
Department of English
University of Nebraska

ISBN 0-8220-1354-1
© Copyright 1980
by
C. K. Hillegass
All Rights Reserved
Printed in U.S.A.

1990 Printing

Cliffs Notes, Inc.   Lincoln, Nebraska

CONTENTS

BECKETT NOTES

BRIEF LIFE OF SAMUEL BECKETT

Samuel Beckett was born in Dublin, Ireland, in 1906, the second son of comfortable middle-class parents who were a part of the Protestant minority in a predominantly Catholic society. He was provided with an excellent education, graduating from Trinity College, Dublin, with a major emphasis in French and Italian. His first job was as a teacher of English in the Ecole Normale Superiéure in Paris. In 1931, he returned to Ireland as a lecturer in French literature, and he received his masters degree in French from Dublin and subsequently returned to Paris as a teacher in 1932. He has made Paris his home since that time, except for visits abroad and a retreat to the Unoccupied Zone in Vichy, France, during 1942-44.

Beckett found teaching uncongenial to his creative activities and soon turned all of his attention to writing. During the 1930s and 1940s, his writing consisted of critical studies (Proust and others), poems, and two novels (*Murphy* and *Watt*), all written in English. In the late 1940s, he changed from writing in English to writing in French. Part of the reason for this was his basic rejection of Ireland as his homeland. When asked why he found Ireland uncongenial, he offered the same explanation that has been given by other famous Irish expatriates, such as Sean O'Casey and James Joyce. He could not tolerate the strict censorship of so many aspects of life, especially the arbitrary censoring of many works of literature by the Catholic clergy. In addition, the political situation created an oppressive anti-intellectualism. Even after he became famous, he refused to allow some of his plays to be presented in Ireland. In 1958, during the International Theater Festival in Dublin, a play of his compatriot O'Casey was banned, and Beckett, in protest, withdrew his plays, which have not been seen in Ireland since then.

Since the major portion of his dramas were composed in French and first presented in Paris, many critics find difficulty in classifying Beckett's works: should he be considered a French or an Irish writer? The nature of his characters, even when named Vladimir and Estragon, seems to be more characteristically Irish than any other nationality. Essentially, it should be a moot question because Beckett, when composing in French, was his own translator into English and vice versa. Thus his works do not suffer from another translator's tampering with them, and his great plays now belong to the realm of world literature.

SAMUEL BECKETT AND THE THEATER OF THE ABSURD

With the appearance of *En Attendant Godot* (*Waiting for Godot*) at the Théâtre de Babylone in Paris in 1953, the literary world was shocked by the appearance of a drama so different and yet so intriguing that it virtually created the term "Theater of the Absurd," and the entire group of dramas which developed out of this type of theater is always associated with the name of Samuel Beckett. His contribution to this particular genre allows us to refer to him as the grand master, or father, of the genre. While other dramatists have also contributed significantly to this genre, Beckett remains its single, most towering figure.

This movement known as the Theater of the Absurd was not a consciously conceived movement, and it has never had any clear-cut philosophical doctrines, no organized attempt to win converts, and no meetings. Each of the main playwrights of the movement seems to have developed independently of each other. The playwrights most often associated with the movement are Samuel Beckett, Eugene Ionesco, Jean Genet, and Arthur Adamov. The early plays of Edward Albee and Harold Pinter fit into this classification, but these dramatists have also written plays that move far away from the Theater of the Absurd's basic elements.

In viewing the plays that comprise this movement, we must forsake the theater of coherently developed situations, we must forsake characterizations that are rooted in the logic of motivation and reaction, we must sometimes forget settings that bear an intrinsic, realistic, or obvious relationship to the drama as a whole, we must forget the use of language as a tool of logical communication, and we must forget cause-and-effect relationships found in traditional dramas. By their use of a number of puzzling devices, these playwrights have gradually accustomed audiences to a new kind of relationship between theme and presentation. In these seemingly queer and fantastic plays, the external world is often depicted as menacing, devouring, and unknown; the settings and situations often make us vaguely uncomfortable; the world itself seems incoherent and frightening and strange, but at the same time, it seems hauntingly poetic and familiar.

These are some of the reasons which prompt the critic to classify them under the heading "Theater of the Absurd"—a title which comes not from a dictionary definition of the word "absurd," but rather from Martin Esslin's book *The Theatre of the Absurd*, in which he maintains that these dramatists write from a "sense of metaphysical anguish at the absurdity of the human condition." But other writers such as Kafka, Camus, and Sartre have also argued from the same philosophical position. The essential difference is that critics like Camus have presented their arguments in a highly formal discourse with logical and precise views which prove their theses within the framework of traditional forms. On the contrary, the Theater of the Absurd seeks to wed form and content into an indissoluble whole in order to gain a further unity of meaning and impact. This theater, as Esslin has pointed out, "has renounced arguing *about* the absurdity of the human condition; it merely presents it in being—that is, in terms of concrete stage images of the absurdity of existence."

Too often, however, the viewer notes only these basic similarities and fails to note the distinctive differences in each dramatist. Since these writers do not belong to any deliberate or conscious movement, they should be evaluated for their individual concerns, as well as for their contributions to the total concept of the Theater of the Absurd. In fact, most of these playwrights consider themselves to be lonely rebels and outsiders, isolated in their own private worlds. As noted above, there have been no manifestoes, no theses, no conferences, and no collaborations. Each has developed along his own unique lines; each in his own way is individually and distinctly different. Therefore, it is important to see how Beckett both belongs to the Theater of the Absurd and, equally important, how he differs from the other writers associated with this movement. First, let us note a few of the basic differences.

8

Differences

One of Samuel Beckett's main concerns is the polarity of existence. In *Waiting for Godot, Endgame,* and *Krapp's Last Tape,* we have such characteristic polarities as sight versus blindness, life—death, time present—time past, body—intellect, waiting—not waiting, going—not going, and dozens more. One of Beckett's main concerns, then, seems to be characterizing man's existence in terms of these polarities. To do this, Beckett groups his characters in pairs; for example, we have Vladimir and Estragon, or Didi and Gogo, Hamm and Clov, Pozzo and Lucky, Nagg and Nell, and Krapp's present voice and past voice. Essentially, however, Beckett's characters remain a puzzle which each individual viewer must solve.

In contrast to Beckett, Eugene Ionesco's characters are seen in terms of singularity. Whereas Beckett's characters stand in pairs *outside* of society, but converse with each other, Ionesco's characters are placed in the midst of society—but they stand alone in an alien world with no personal identity and no one with whom they can communicate. For example, the characters in *The Bald Soprano* are *in* society, but they scream meaningless phrases at each other, and there is no communication. And whereas Beckett's plays take place on strange and alien landscapes (some of the settings of his plays remind one of a world transformed by some holocaust or created by some surrealist), Ionesco's plays are set against the most traditional elements in our society—the standard English drawing room in *The Bald Soprano,* a typical street scene in *Rhinoceros,* and an average academic study in *The Lesson,* etc.

The language of the two playwrights also differs greatly. Beckett's dialogue recalls the disjointed phantasmagoria of a dream world; Ionesco's language is rooted in the banalities, cliches, and platitudes of everyday speech; Beckett uses language to show man isolated in the world and unable to communicate because language is a barrier to communication. Ionesco, on the other hand, uses language to show the failure of communication because there is nothing to say; in *The Bald Soprano,* and other plays, the dialogue is filled with cliches and platitudes.

In contrast to the basic sympathy we feel for both Beckett's and Ionesco's characters, Jean Genet's characters almost revile the audience from the moment that they appear on the stage. His theme is stated more openly. He is concerned with the hatred which exists in the world. In *The Maids,* for example, each maid hates not just her employer and not just her own sister, but also her own self. Therefore, she plays the other roles so as to exhaust her own hatred of herself against herself. Basically, then, there is a great sense of repugnance in Genet's characters. This revulsion derives partially from the fact that Genet's dramatic interest, so different from Beckett's and Ionesco's, is in the psychological exploration of man's predilection to being trapped in his own egocentric world, rather than facing the realities of existence. Man, for Genet, is trapped by his own fantastic illusions; man's absurdity results partially from the fact that he prefers his own disjointed images to those of reality. In Genet's directions for the production of *The Blacks,* he writes that the play should never be played before a totally black audience. If there are no white people present, then one of the blacks in the audience must wear a white mask; if the black refuses, then a white mannequin must be used, and the actors must play the drama for this mannequin. There must at least be a symbol of a white audience, someone for the black actors to revile.

In contrast to Beckett, Arthur Adamov, in his themes, is more closely aligned to the Kafkaesque, existentialistic school, but his technique is that of the Theater of the Absurd. His interest is in establishing some proof that the individual does exist, and he shows how man becomes more alienated from his fellow man as he attempts to establish his own personal identity. For example, in *Professor Taranne,* the central character, hoping to prove his innocence of a certain accusation, actually convicts himself through his own defense. For Adamov, man attempting to prove his own existence actually proves, ironically, that he does not exist. Therefore language, for Adamov, serves as an inadequate system of communication and, actually, in some cases serves to the detriment of man, since by language and man's use of language, man often finds himself trapped in the very circumstances he previously hoped to avoid. Ultimately, Adamov's characters fail to communicate because each is interested only in his own egocentric self. Each character propounds his own troubles and his own achievements, but the words reverberate, as against a stone wall. They are heard only by the audience. Adamov's plays are often grounded in a dream-world atmosphere, and while they are presenting a series of outwardly confusing scenes of almost hallucinative quality, they, at the same time, attack or denounce the confusion present in modern man.

Characteristic of all these writers is a notable absence of any excess concern with sex. Edward Albee, an American, differs significantly in his emphasis and concern with the sexual substructure of society. The overtones of homosexuality in *The Zoo Story* are carried further until the young man in *The American Dream* becomes the physical incarnation of a muscular and ideally handsome, young sexual specimen who, since he has no inner feelings, passively allows anyone "to take pleasure from my groin." In *The Sandbox,* the angel of death is again seen as the musclebound young sexual specimen who spends his time scantily dressed and performing calisthenics on a beach while preparing for a career in Hollywood.

Similarities

Since all of the writers have varying concerns, they also have much in common because their works reflect a moral and philosophical climate in which most of our civilization finds itself today. Again, as noted above, even though there are no manifestoes, nor any organized movements, there are still certain concerns that are basic to all of the writers, and Beckett's works are concerned with these basic ideas.

Beyond the technical and strange illusionary techniques which prompt the critic to group these plays into a category, there are larger and, ultimately, more significant concerns by which each dramatist, in spite of his artistic differences, is akin to the others. Aside from such similarities as violation of traditional beginning, middle, and end structure (exposition, complication, and denouement) or the refusal to tell a straightforward, connected story with a proper plot, or the disappearance of traditional dramatic forms and techniques, these dramatists are all concerned with the failure of communication in modern society which leaves man alienated; moreover, they are all concerned with the lack of individuality and the overemphasis on conformity in our society, and they use the dramatic elements of time and place to imply important ideas; finally, they reject traditional logic for a type of non-logic which ultimately implies something about the nature of the universe. Implicit in many of these concerns is an attack on a society or a world which possesses no set standards of values or behavior.

Foremost, all of these dramatists of the absurd are concerned with the lack of communication. In Edward Albee's plays, each character is existing within the bounds of his own private ego. Each makes a futile attempt to get another character to understand him, but as the attempt is heightened, there is more alienation. Thus, finally, because of a lack of communication, Peter, the conformist in *The Zoo Story*, is provoked into killing Jerry, the individualist; and in *The Sandbox*, a continuation of *The American Dream*, Mommy and Daddy bury Grandma because she talks incessantly but says nothing significant. The irony is that Grandma is the only character who does say anything significant, but Mommy and Daddy, the people who discard her, are incapable of understanding her.

In Ionesco's plays, this failure of communication often leads to even more drastic results. Akin to the violence in Albee's *Zoo Story*, the professor in *The Lesson* must kill his student partly because she doesn't understand his communication. Berenger, in *The Killers*, has uttered so many cliches that by the end of the play, he has convinced even himself that the killers should kill him. In *The Chairs*, the old people, needing to express their thoughts, address themselves to a mass of empty chairs which, as the play progresses, crowd all else off the stage. In *Maid to Marry*, communication is so bad that the maid, when she appears on the stage, turns out to be a rather homely man. And ultimately in *Rhinoceros*, the inability to communicate causes an entire race of so-called rational human beings to be metamorphosed into a herd of rhinoceroses, thereby abandoning all hopes of language as a means of communication.

In Adamov's *Professor Taranne*, the professor, in spite of all his desperate attempts, is unable to get people to acknowledge his identity because there is no communication. Likewise, Pinter's plays show individuals grouped on the stage, but each person fails to achieve any degree of effective communication. This concern with communication is finally carried to its illogical extreme in two works: in Genet's *The Blacks*, one character says, "We shall even have the decency—a decency learned from you—to make communication impossible." And in another, Beckett's *Act Without Words I*, we have our first play in this movement that uses absolutely no dialogue. And even without dialogue, all the action on the stage suggests the inability of man to communicate.

Beckett's characters are tied together by a fear of being left entirely alone, and they therefore cling to one last hope of establishing some kind of communication. His plays give the impression that man is totally lost in a disintegrating society, or, as in *Endgame*, that man is left alone after society has disintegrated. In *Waiting for Godot*, two derelicts are seen conversing in a repetitive, strangely fragmented dialogue that possesses an illusory, haunting effect, while they are waiting for Godot, a vague, never-defined being who will bring them some communication about—what? Salvation? Death? An impetus for living? A reason for dying? No one knows, and the safest thing to say is that the two are probably waiting for someone or something which will give them an impetus to continue living or, at least, something which will give meaning and direction to their lives. As Beckett clearly demonstrates, those who rush hither and yon in search of meaning find it no quicker than those who sit and wait. The "meaning" about life that these tramps hope for is never stated precisely. But Beckett never meant his play to be a "message play," in which one character would deliver a "message." The message here is conveyed through the interaction of the characters and primarily through the interaction of the two tramps. Everyone leaves the theater with the knowledge that these tramps are strangely tied to one another; even though they bicker and fight, and even though they have exhausted all conversation— notice that the second act is repetitive and almost identical—the loneliness and weakness in each calls out to the other, and they are held by a mystical bond of interdependence. In spite of this strange dependency, however, neither is able to communicate with the other. The other two characters, Pozzo and Lucky, are on a journey without any apparent goal and are symbolically tied together. One talks, the other says nothing. The waiting of Vladimir and Estragon and the journeying of Pozzo and Lucky offer themselves as con- trasts of various activities in the modern world—all of which lead to no fruitful end; therefore, each pair is hopelessly alienated from the other pair. For example, when Pozzo falls and yells for help, Vladi- mir and Estragon continue talking, although nothing is communi- cated in their dialogue; all is hopeless, or as Vladimir aphoristically replies to one of Estragon's long discourses, "We are all born mad. Some remain so." In their attempts at conversation and communi- cation, these two tramps have a fastidious correctness and a grave propriety that suggest that they could be socially accepted; but their fastidiousness and propriety are inordinately comic when con- trasted with their ragged appearance.

Their fumbling ineffectuality in their attempts at conversation seems to represent the ineptness of all mankind in its attempt at communication. And it rapidly becomes apparent that Vladimir and Estragon, as representatives of modern man, cannot formulate any cogent or useful resolution or action; and what is more pathetic, they cannot communicate their helpless longings to one another. While failing to possess enough individualism to go their separate ways, they nevertheless are different enough to embrace most of our society. In the final analysis, their one positive gesture is their strength to wait. But man is, ultimately, terribly alone in his waiting. Ionesco shows the same idea at the end of *Rhinoceros* when we see Berenger totally alone as a result, partly, of a failure in communication.

Each dramatist, therefore, presents a critique of modern society by showing the total collapse of communication. The technique used is that of evolving a theme about communication by presenting a series of seemingly disjointed speeches. The accumulative effect of these speeches is a devastating commentary on the failure of communication in modern society.

In conjunction with the general attack on communication, the second aspect common to these dramatists is the lack of individuality encountered in modern civilization. Generally, the point seems to be that man does not know himself. He has lost all sense of individualism and either functions isolated and alienated, or else finds himself lost amid repetition and conformity.

Jean Genet's play *The Maids* opens with the maid Claire playing the role of her employer while her sister Solange plays the role of Claire. Therefore, we have Claire referring to Solange as Claire. By the time the audience realizes that the two sisters are imitating someone else, each character has lost her individualism; therefore, when Claire later portrays Solange, who portrays the employer, and vice versa, we gradually realize that part of Genet's intent is to illustrate the total lack of individuality and, furthermore, to show that each character becomes vibrantly alive only when functioning in the image of another personality.

Other dramatists present their attack on society's destruction of individualism by different means, but the attack still has the same thematic intent. In Albee's *The American Dream,* Mommy and Daddy are obviously generic names for any mommy and daddy. Albee is not concerned with individualizing his characters. They remain types and, as types, are seen at times in terms of extreme burlesque. So, unlike Beckett's tramps, and more like Ionesco's characters, Albee's people are seen as Babbitt-like caricatures and satires on the "American Dream" type; the characters remain mannequins with no delineations. Likewise in Ionesco's *The Bald Soprano,* the Martins assume the roles of the Smiths and begin the play over because there is no distinction between the two sets of characters.

Perhaps more than any of the other dramatists of the absurd, Ionesco has concerned himself almost exclusively with the failure of individualism, especially in his most famous play, *Rhinoceros.* To repeat, in this play, our society today has emphasized conformity to such an extent and has rejected individualism so completely that Ionesco demonstrates with inverse logic how stupid it is *not* to conform with all society and be metamorphosed into a rhinoceros. This play aptly illustrates how two concerns of the absurdists—lack of communication and the lack of individualism—are combined, each to support the other. Much of Ionesco's dialogue in this play seems to be the distilled essence of the commonplace. One cliche follows another, and yet, in contrast, this dialogue is spoken within the framework of a wildly improbable situation. In a typically common street scene, with typically common cliches about weather and work being uttered, the morning calm is shattered by a rhinoceros charging through the streets. Then two rhinoceroses, then more. Ridiculous arguments then develop as to whether they are African or Asiatic rhinoceroses. We soon learn that there is an epidemic of metamorphoses; everyone is changing into rhinoceroses. Soon only three individuals are left. Then in the face of this absurd situation, we have the equally appalling justifications and reasons in favor of being metamorphosed advocated in such cliches as "We must join the crowd," "We must move with the times," and "We've got to build our life on new foundations," etc. Suddenly it seems almost foolish *not* to become a rhinoceros. In the end, Berenger's sweetheart, Daisy, succumbs to the pressures of society, relinquishes her individualism, and joins the society of rhinoceroses—not because she wants to, but rather because she is afraid not to. She cannot revolt against society and remain a human being. Berenger is left alone, totally isolated with his individualism. And what good is his humanity in a world of rhinoceroses?

At first glance, it would seem obvious that Ionesco wishes to indicate the triumph of the individual, who, although caught in a society that has gone mad, refuses to surrender his sense of identity. But if we look more closely, we see that Ionesco has no intention of leaving us on this hopeful and comforting note.

In his last speech, Berenger makes it clear that his stand is rendered absurd. What does his humanity avail him in a world of beasts? Finally, he wishes that he also had changed; now it is too late. All he can do is feebly reassert his joy in being human. His statement carries little conviction. This is how Ionesco deals with the haunting theme of the basic meaning and value of personal identity in relationship to society. If one depends *entirely* upon the society in which one lives for a sense of reality and identity, it is impossible to take a stand against that society without reducing oneself to nothingness in the process. Berenger instinctively felt repelled by the tyranny that had sprung up around him, but he had no sense of identity that would have enabled him to combat this evil with anything resembling a positive force. Probably any action he could have taken would have led to eventual defeat, but defeat would have been infinitely preferable to the limbo in which he is finally consigned. Ionesco has masterfully joined two themes: the lack of individualism and the failure of communication. But unlike Beckett, who handles the same themes by presenting his characters as derelicts and outcasts from society, Ionesco's treatment seems even more devastating because he places them in the very middle of the society from which they are estranged.

Ultimately, the absurdity of man's condition is partially a result of his being compelled to exist without his individualism in a society which does not possess any degree of effective communication. Essentially, therefore, the Theater of the Absurd is not a positive drama. It does not try to prove that man can exist in a meaningless world, as did Camus and Sartre, nor does it offer any solution; instead, it demonstrates the absurdity and illogicality of the world we live in. Nothing is ever settled; there are no positive statements; no conclusions are ever reached, and what few actions there are have no meaning, particularly in relation to the action. That is, one action carries no more significance than does its opposite action. For example, the man's tying his shoe in *The Bald Soprano*—a common occurrence—is magnified into a momentous act, while the appearance of rhinoceroses in the middle of a calm afternoon seems to be not at all consequential and evokes only the most trite and insignificant remarks. Also, Pozzo and Lucky's frantic running and searching are no more important than Vladimir and Estragon's sitting and waiting. And Genet presents his blacks as outcasts and misfits from society, but refrains from making any positive statement regarding the black person's role in our society. The question of whether society is to be integrated or segregated is, to Genet, a matter of absolute indifference. It would still be society, and the individual would still be outside it.

No conclusions or resolutions can ever by offered, therefore, because these plays are essentially circular and repetitive in nature. *The Bald Soprano* begins over again with a new set of characters, and other plays end at the same point at which they began, thus obviating any possible conclusions or positive statements. *The American Dream* ends with the coming of a second child, this time one who is fully grown and the twin to the other child who had years before entered the family as a baby and upset the static condition; thematically, the play ends as it began. In all of these playwrights' dramas, the sense of repetition, the circular structure, the static quality, the lack of cause and effect, and the lack of apparent progression all suggest the sterility and lack of values in the modern world.

Early critics referred to the Theater of the Absurd as a theater in transition, meaning that it was to lead to something different. So far this has not happened, but the Theater of the Absurd is rapidly becoming accepted as a distinct genre in its own right. The themes utilized by the dramatists of this movement are not new; thus, the success of the plays must often depend upon the effectiveness of the techniques and the new ways by which the dramatists illustrate their themes. The techniques are still so new, however, that many people are confused by a production of one of these plays. Yet if the technique serves to emphasize the absurdity of man's position in the universe, then to present this concept by a series of ridiculous situations is only to render man's position even more absurd; and in actuality, the techniques then reinforce that very condition which the dramatists bewail. In other words, to present the failure of communication by a series of disjointed and seemingly incoherent utterances lends itself to the accusation that functionalism is carried to a ridiculous extreme. But this is exactly what the absurdist wants to do. He is tired of logical discourses pointing out step-by-step the absurdity of the universe: he begins with the philosophical premise that the universe is absurd, and then creates plays which illustrate conclusively that the universe is indeed absurd and that perhaps this play is another additional absurdity.

In conclusion, if the public can accept these unusual uses of technique to support thematic concerns, then we have plays which dramatically present powerful and vivid views on the absurdity of the human condition—an absurdity which is the result of the destruction of individualism and the failure of communication, of man's being forced to conform to a world of mediocrity where no action is meaningful. As the tragic outcasts of these plays are presented in terms of burlesque, man is reminded that his position and that of human existence in general is essentially absurd. Every play in the Theater of the Absurd movement mirrors the chaos and basic disorientation of modern man. Each play laughs in anguish at the confusion that exists in contemporary society; hence, all share a basic point of view, while varying widely in scope and structure.

Waiting for Godot

LIST OF CHARACTERS

Vladimir (Didi)
An old derelict dressed like a tramp; along with his companion of many years, he comes to a bleak, desolate place to wait for Godot.

Estragon (Gogo)
Vladimir's companion of many years who is overly concerned with his physical needs, but is repeatedly told by Vladimir that, above all, they must wait for Godot.

Pozzo
A traveling man dressed rather elaborately; he arrives driving another man (Lucky) forward by means of a rope around the latter's neck.

Lucky
The "slave" who obeys Pozzo absolutely.

Boy Messenger I and Boy Messenger II
Each is a young boy who works for "Mr. Godot" and brings Vladimir and Estragon news about "Mr. Godot"; apparently he takes

messages back to "Mr. Godot."

Godot
He never appears in the drama, but he is an entity that Vladimir and Estragon are waiting for.

DRAMATIC DIVISIONS

Even though the drama is divided into two acts, there are other natural divisions. For the sake of discussion, the following, rather obvious, scene divisions will be referred to:

ACT I: (1) Vladimir and Estragon Alone
(2) Arrival of Pozzo and Lucky: Lucky's Speech
(3) Departure of Pozzo and Lucky: Vladimir and Estragon Alone
(4) Arrival of Boy Messenger
(5) Departure of Boy Messenger: Vladimir and Estragon Alone

ACT II: (1) Vladimir and Estragon Alone
(2) Arrival of Pozzo and Lucky
(3) Departure of Pozzo and Lucky: Vladimir and Estragon Alone
(4) Arrival of Boy Messenger
(5) Departure of Boy Messenger: Vladimir and Estragon Alone

The above divisions of the play are Beckett's way of making a statement about the nature of the play—that is, the play is circular in structure, and a third act (or even a fourth or fifth act, etc.) could be added, having the exact same structure. For further discussion, see the section on Circular Structure.

CRITICAL ANALYSIS

ACT I: VLADIMIR AND ESTRAGON

The rising curtain exposes a landscape that is strange and alien. It most resembles some strange place in outer space with its haunting and brooding sense of despair. A country road or an actual lonely road is the main setting, and there is a single tree. We know there is a ditch on the other side of the road because immediately Estragon tells Vladimir that he slept last night in the ditch. The loneliness and the isolation of the setting sets the tone for the play. The idea of a road implies a journey, a movement, a purpose to life, but we see, instead, two deserted, isolated figures with no place to go and with no journey to look forward to. These figures are dressed in rags and tatters, clothes that would be worn by two tramps in an old, second-rate burlesque production. Thus the setting and the clothing make an ominous comment before we are too far into the drama.

The play opens with Estragon involved in a tremendous struggle —but not a struggle of a highly metaphysical nature; instead, it is a physical struggle to get his stuck boot off his sore foot. The struggle has literally exhausted him, and he gives up the struggle with the opening words of the play: *"Nothing to be done"* (emphasis ours). Estragon's words are repeated two more times by Vladimir in the next moments of the play, and variations of this phrase become one of the central statements of the drama. The phrase is innocent enough in itself and obviously directed toward a specific struggle— the removal of the boot. But as frustrating as the boot is, this is still a minor concern when compared to what Estragon and Vladimir are to do with the problem of waiting for Godot. In response to Estragon's struggle with his foot, Vladimir ignores the immediate physical problem but agrees with Estragon metaphysically that there is "nothing to be done," even though he has not "yet tried everything."

Thus the two opening speeches, innocent and simple enough in themselves, set the tone for the entire drama. The words carry a foreboding overtone which will be later associated with the word "appalled," or as Vladimir calls it, "AP-PALLED," and also the two tramps' inability to laugh.

After the opening words, we find that the two tramps are linked to each other in some undefined, ambiguous way. Vladimir greets Estragon with the comment "I thought you were gone forever," and since they are "together again at last," they will "have to celebrate." Vladimir then discovers that Estragon spent the night "in a ditch . . . over there" and that he was beaten by "the same lot as usual." This reference to a beaten man in a ditch carries overtones of other matters, but cannot be definitely correlated. For example, this could be an oblique reference to the biblical story of the Good Samaritan who finds a man beaten, robbed, and thrown into a ditch and rescues him. But no Good Samaritan has come to Estragon's rescue. Instead, he has apparently spent the entire night alone in the ditch, which means that both of them are, as their clothes indicate, in the most extreme, impoverished condition that they have ever known.

Estragon remains concerned with his boots; Vladimir, however, is extremely impatient and finds the conversation about the boots to be profitless. He turns the conversation to more abstract matters. Very early in the play, then, the difference between the two tramps is established: Estragon is concerned about immediate, practical problems—the removal of his boots, the beating, and now his aching foot; Vladimir, in contrast, laments the general nature of their sufferings by remembering better days that used to be. Whereas Estragon's foot *hurts,* Vladimir is concerned with suffering of a different nature.

The philosophical concept of the nature of suffering is first introduced here by the contrasting physical ailments of each character: Estragon has sore feet which *hurt* him, and Vladimir has some type of painful urinary infection which causes him to suffer; one character *hurts* and the other one *suffers.* Ultimately, the physical disabilities characterize the two men (an aching foot is easier to locate and describe than is a painful urinary infection) and also symbolize the various spiritual disabilities of the two characters.

Vladimir's thoughts shift from his urinary problems to the biblical concept of "Hope deferred maketh the something sick . . ." but he is unable to complete the proverb. (See *Proverbs* 13:12: "Hope deferred maketh the heart sick, but a desire fulfilled is a tree of life.") The proverb fits Vladimir and Estragon's condition perfectly since we will see them in a state of sickness of heart; their hopes are constantly deferred as they continually wait for Godot, and their desires are never fulfilled since Godot never arrives. Vladimir then concludes as did Estragon: "Nothing to be done."

Estragon has not gotten his boot off, and he looks inside it to see what was causing the difficulty. Vladimir then chastises Estragon for one of man's most common faults: blaming one's boots for the faults of one's foot. This accusation, of course, refers to the tendency of all of mankind to blame any external thing—boots, society, circumstances, etc.—for deficiencies in one's own nature. It is easier for Estragon to blame the boots for his aching feet than to blame his own feet.

The idea of Estragon's foot hurting and Vladimir's suffering, combined with their appalling human condition, causes Vladimir to realize again that there is "nothing to be done." This suffering and lack of hope turn Vladimir's thoughts to the suffering of the two thieves on the cross and their lack of hope. Then from the Old Testament proverb about hope, Vladimir's thoughts turn to the New Testament and the possibility of hope expressed in the story of Christ and the two thieves on the cross. There were *two* thieves, as there are now *two* tramps, and *one* of the thieves was saved; therefore, maybe there may be hope for either Vladimir or Estragon if they repent—but there is nothing to repent of, except being born. This remark causes "Vladimir to break into a hearty laugh which he immediately stifles," and he reminds Estragon that "one daren't even laugh any more"; one may "merely smile." This comment is another early indication of the seriousness of their condition. Vladimir's apprehension over laughing suggests that they both have a nagging awareness of the precariousness and insecurity of their condition, a condition that extends beyond their physical concerns.

In the discussion of the thieves, Estragon is unable to participate fully because he can't remember the details. In frustration, Vladimir yells to Estragon: "Come on . . . return the ball can't you, once in a way?" Vladimir's complaint is descriptive of much of the dialogue in the remainder of the play; it is very much like two people playing a game with one another and one is unable to keep the ball in play. Estragon constantly fails to "keep the ball in play"; that is, throughout the drama, he is unable to sustain his end of the conversation. Even in response to the matter of being saved "from hell" or "from death," Estragon merely replies, "Well what of it?" Therefore, even if they were to repent, Estragon can't understand what they might be saved from, who their savior would be, and, furthermore, why the four Gospels differ so significantly. The discussion is brought firmly to a close with Estragon's pronouncement: "People are bloody ignorant apes."

From this discussion, the two tramps confront the central problem of the play. Estragon looks about the bleak, desolate landscape and tells Vladimir: "Let's go." The recurring thematic refrain is then put forth: they can't leave because they are "waiting for

Godot." They are not sure they are in the right place; they are not sure they are here on the correct day; they are not sure what day of the week it is (maybe it is yesterday); they think they were to meet Godot on Saturday, but if today is Saturday, is it the right Saturday? At least, they are fairly certain that they were to meet by a tree, and there is only one tree on the horizon, but it could be either a bush or a dead tree. The tree, whatever its symbolic value (the cross, the hanging tree, spring's renewal), is a rather pathetic specimen and cannot be a very hopeful sign. Completely frustrated, they resign themselves to waiting. Vladimir paces, and Estragon sleeps.

Suddenly, Vladimir, feeling lonely, awakens Estragon, who awakens from his dream with a start. Estragon wants to tell about his dream (or nightmare), but Vladimir refuses to listen to it. Estragon's nightmare, even without its subject being revealed, symbolizes the various fears that these tramps feel in this alienated world. Vladimir's refusal to listen suggests his fear and apprehension of all of life and of certain things that are best left unsaid. Estragon, then, unable to tell about his nightmare, tries to tell a joke about an Englishman in a brothel. Again Vladimir refuses to listen and walks off.

Estragon's attempt to tell his nightmare and then his attempt to tell the joke about the Englishman—a story that is never finished—represent an effort to pass the time while the two are waiting for Godot. Since they have been waiting and will be waiting for an indeterminate time, the essential problem is what to do with one's life while waiting, how to pass the time while waiting.

When Vladimir returns, the two embrace and then they try to decide what they are going to do while waiting. During the embrace, the tender, fraternal rapport of the moment is suddenly broken by Estragon's mundane observation that Vladimir smells of garlic. This technique is typical of Beckett's method of deflating man's pretensions by allowing the absurd and the vulgar to dominate the action.

The eternal question returns: what to do while waiting? Estragon suggests that perhaps they could hang themselves. That would certainly put an end to their waiting. Hanging also has another incentive: it would excite them sexually and cause each to have an erection and an ejaculation. But the matter of hanging creates some problems. Vladimir should hang himself first because he is the heaviest. If the straggly tree does not break under Vladimir's heavier weight, then it would be strong enough for Estragon's lighter weight. But if Estragon went first, the tree might break when Vladimir tried it, and then Estragon (Gogo) would be dead, and poor Vladimir (Didi) would be alive and completely alone. These considerations are simply too weighty to solve. Man's attempts to solve things rationally bring about all types of difficulties; it is best to do nothing—"It's safer." Accordingly, they decide to "wait and see what [Godot] says," hoping that he, or someone, will make a decision about them or that something will be done for them. They will make no effort to change their rather intolerable and impossible situation, but, instead, they will hope that someone or some objective event will eventually change things for them.

Having resolved to wait for Godot, they then wonder what he might offer them and, even more important, "what exactly did we ask him for?" Whatever it was they asked him for, Godot was equally vague and equivocal in his reply. Maybe he is at home thinking it over, consulting friends, correspondents, banks, etc. The tramps' entire discussion about Godot indicates how little, if indeed anything at all, they know of this Godot. The fact that Vladimir can't remember what they asked of Godot indicates that they are unable to understand their own needs. They rely on someone else to tell them what they need. Similarly, the request and the possible response are discussed in terms of a person requesting a bank loan or some type of financial transaction. A philosophical question then begins to emerge: how does one relate to Godot? If he is God, can one enter into a business contract with this person? And if so, where is He? If Godot (or God) has to consult many outside sources before replying or appearing, then Vladimir and Estragon's condition is not very reassuring. And, if, as it now begins to become obvious, Vladimir and Estragon represent modern man in his relationship with God (Godot), then the modern condition of man is disturbingly precarious.

What, then, is man in this modern world? He is a beggar or a tramp reduced to the most dire circumstances: he is lost, not knowing where to turn. He is denied all rights, even the right to laugh:

ESTRAGON: We've no rights anymore?
VLADIMIR: You'd make me laugh if it wasn't prohibited.

Furthermore, they are reduced to crawling "on [their] hands and knees." Of course, in ancient cultures, man always approached a deity on his hands and knees. But in Beckett's dramas, a character's physical condition is correlated with his spiritual condition; all outward aspects of the two tramps reflect man's inward condition.

In a feeble attempt to assert their freedom, Estragon murmurs that they are not tied, but his assertion does not carry much conviction. The assertion, however feeble, that they are not tied might suggest man's revolt from God, because as soon as the idea of revolt is verbalized, they immediately hear a noise as though someone is approaching—Godot or God—to chastise them for heresy. They huddle together in fear:

> ESTRAGON: You gave me a fright.
> VLADIMIR: I thought it was he.
> ESTRAGON: Who?
> VLADIMIR: Godot.

After the discussion of whether or not they are tied has occupied their thoughts, Vladimir gives Estragon their last carrot to eat. Now they have only a turnip left to eat, and these reduced circumstances make it necessary for them to continue to wait for Godot—and possible salvation.

While eating his carrot, Estragon ruminates further about being "tied" or "ti-ed." Even though Vladimir feebly asserts that they are not tied, we noted that they are indeed tied to the idea of waiting. They cannot assert themselves; they have ceased struggling; there is even "no use wriggling." They are merely two stranded figures on an alien landscape who have given up struggling and are dependent upon waiting for Godot, realizing there is "nothing to be done." Thus, the play opens, and this section closes on the same note: *nothing to be done.*

ACT I: ARRIVAL OF POZZO AND LUCKY

As Vladimir and Estragon sit in peaceful resignation to their condition, a loud cry destroys the quietness and terrifies them. They immediately run to hide, huddling together and "cringing away from the menace." Suddenly Pozzo and Lucky arrive on the scene. Lucky has a rope around his neck and is being driven forward by Pozzo, who is brandishing a whip. This sudden, surprise entrance lacks only the flair of a drum roll and a band to give the entrance a highly theatrical, circus atmosphere. In the same way that Vladimir and Estragon are parodies of the circus clown or burlesque tramp, we now have the appearance of a character resembling a circus ringmaster and his trained animal. Throughout this scene, circus imagery is used to suggest that life itself can be seen as a circus, and one which will soon be brought to an abrupt end.

Vladimir and Estragon are in awe of the forceful manner in which Pozzo seems to be in control of Lucky; he seems to absolutely dominate the poor creature. Noting his *omnipotence* and *authority,* they inquire about the possibility of this man's being Godot. The mere fact that they have to ask, however, emphasizes their ignorance about the identity and true nature of Godot, the entity whom they are waiting for. They can't even explain Godot to Pozzo:

> VLADIMIR: . . . he's a kind of acquaintance.
> ESTRAGON: Personally, I wouldn't even know him if I saw him.

Throughout the scene, Pozzo conducts himself not only as a ringmaster, but also as a person far superior to the two tramps whom he condescends to spend some time with, even though he barely recognizes them as belonging to the same species. Furthermore, Vladimir and Estragon recognize Pozzo's seeming superiority and are dutifully obeisant to him, even after they discover that he is not Godot.

With the arrival of Pozzo and Lucky, we see how two people are *physically* tied to each other. Estragon and Vladimir are tied to each other by abstract bonds and also by their common act of waiting for Godot, but Lucky is literally and physically tied to Pozzo. And whereas Vladimir and Estragon are *waiting,* Pozzo and Lucky seem to be *going*—but where they are going is not stated.

After denying all knowledge of Godot, Pozzo magnanimously decides to rest for awhile. Even though Vladimir and Estragon are terribly inferior to him, Pozzo recognizes that they are "human beings none the less . . . of the same species as Pozzo! Made in God's image!" Thus, Pozzo recognizes these clowns (tramps) as belonging to the same species, albeit they are very imperfect specimens of the species, and he condescends to rest because he has been traveling for six hours without seeing a soul.

After rather elaborate preparations for settling himself, involving his ordering Lucky to set up a stool and picnic, Pozzo sits down to enjoy a meal of chicken and wine. Vladimir and Estragon begin an investigation of Lucky. Pozzo had earlier called the poor fellow "pig" and "hog." Vladimir, in particular, is appalled by Pozzo's treatment of Lucky and is quick to discover a running sore on Lucky's neck. The two conclude that Lucky is a "halfwit . . . a cretin." The irony here lies in the levels of humanity which Estragon and Vladimir fail to grasp—that is, Lucky is very much like Pozzo, and he is also very much like the tramps; he is a member of the same species, and his predicament emphasizes the essential oneness of us all.

After Pozzo has finished eating his chicken, Estragon notices the bones lying inthe ditch and, to Vladimir's embarrassment, asks Pozzo if he can have the bones. Pozzo refers the matter to Lucky since Lucky has the first right to the bones. Lucky, however, ignores all the questions, and Estragon receives the bones. Meanwhile, Vladimir continues to be shocked by Pozzo's treatment of Lucky. He tries to express his horror over the situation only to be ignored. Vladimir wants to leave, but he is reminded that they must meet Godot.

Pozzo justifies his treatment of Lucky by maintaining that Lucky wants to impress him with his ability to carry things; yet, in reality, Lucky is very bad in that capacity. A basis of any relationship can be seen in Pozzo and Lucky's relationship, where one person has a desire to dominate and command and the other person craves to be dominated and to be a slave. Pozzo points out that the reverse could have easily been true—that he could have been, in other chance situations, Lucky's slave.

As Lucky begins to weep upon hearing that he might be sold at the fair and that the world would be a better place without him ("the best thing would be to kill . . . such creatures"), Pozzo notes that tears in themselves are not unusual: "The tears of the world are a constant quality. For each one who begins to weep, somewhere else another stops." Basically, for Beckett, the misery of human existence will always exist, and man must learn to live with his tears and his misery. For example, when Estragon tries to wipe away Lucky's tears, Lucky rewards him with a tremendous kick in the shins.

Estragon, Pozzo, and Vladimir talk in circles with images of the circus and the music hall dominating their conversation. Pozzo, feeling the need of leaving if he is to keep on his schedule, undertakes a lyrical explanation of "what our twilights can do." His recitation goes from lyrical enthusiasm about the nature of the gentleness of the "sky at this hour of the day" to a realization that more ominous matters lurk "behind this veil of gentleness and peace" and that, eventually, night "will burst upon us . . . when we least expect it . . . that's how it is on this bitch of an earth." The seriousness of this speech and its contents are then undermined when Pozzo lets it be known that he was merely delivering a pompous, memorized oration.

Before leaving, Pozzo wishes to express his appreciation to Vladimir and Estragon and wonders if they have any requests of him. Estragon immediately asks for ten francs (or even five, if ten is too much), but Vladimir interrupts and asserts that he and Estragon are not beggars. Pozzo then offers to let Lucky entertain them by dancing, singing, reciting, or thinking. They decide first on dancing and then on thinking.

ACT I: LUCKY'S DANCE AND SPEECH

Lucky's dance is merely a clumsy shuffling, which is a complete disappointment to Vladimir and Estragon. Thus they decide to have Lucky think. They give him his hat, and after protesting Pozzo's brutality, they arrange themselves for Lucky's performance of thinking. It takes the form of a long, seemingly incoherent speech. The speech is delivered as a set piece, yet it is anything but a set piece. Under different directors, this scene can be variously played. For example, Lucky most often speaks directly to the audience with the other characters at his back, while Vladimir and Estragon become more and more agitated as the speech progresses. Often Vladimir and Estragon run forward and try to stop Lucky from continuing his speech. As they try to stop Lucky, he delivers his oration in rapid-fire shouts. At times, Pozzo pulls on Lucky's rope, making it even more difficult for him to continue with his speech. The frenzied activity on the stage, the rapid delivery of the speech, and the jerking of the rope make it virtually impossible to tell anything at all about the speech and, consequently, emphasize the metaphysical absurdity of the entire performance. Lucky's speech is an incoherent jumble of words which seems to upset Vladimir and Estragon, for sporadically both rise to protest some element of the speech. Therefore, the speech does communicate *something* to the two tramps or else they would not know to protest. The form of the speech is that of a scholarly, theological address, beginning "Given the existence . . . of a personal God," but it is actually a parody of this kind of address since the nonsensical and the absurd elements are in the foreground and the meaningful aspects of it are totally obscured, as is the God whom Lucky discusses. Here, we have a combination of the use of scholastic, theological terminology along with the absurd and the nonsensical. For example, the use of *qua* (a Latin term meaning "in the function or capacity of") is common in such scholarly addresses, but Lucky's repetition of the term as *quaquaquaqua* creates an absurd, derisive sound, as though God is being ridiculed by a quacking or squawking sound. Furthermore, the speech is filled with various academic sounding words, some real words like *aphasia* (a loss of speech; here it refers to the fact that God from his divine heights now has divine aphasia or a divine silence) and some words like *apathia* or *athambia* which do not exist (even though *apathia* is closely aligned to *apathy* and thus becomes another oblique comment on the apathy of God in the universe). Other absurd terms are used throughout the speech, and there is also a frequent use of words which sound obscene, interspersed throughout the speech. As an example, the names of the scholars Fartov and Belcher are obviously created for their vulgarity.

Therefore, the speech is filled with more nonsense than sense—more that is illogical than that which is logical. If, however, we remove the illogical modifiers, irrelevancies, and incomprehensible statements and place them to the side, the essence of the speech is as follows in the left-hand column:

THE ESSENCE OF LUCKY'S SPEECH	THE IRRELEVANCIES, THE ABSURDITIES
"Given [acknowledging] the existence . . .	
	as uttered forth in the public works of Puncher and Wattmann
of a personal God . . .	with white beard quaquaquaqua
[who exists] outside [of] time . . .	
	without extension
[and] who . . .	from the heights of divine apathia divine athambia divine aphasia with some exceptions . . .
loves us dearly . . .	
	but time will tell [etc.]
and [who] suffers . . .	like the divine Miranda [etc.]

	for reasons unknown, but time will tell
with those who . . .	
are plunged in torment . . .	in fire [etc.] [that will] blast hell to heaven so blue . . . so calm [etc.]
it is established beyond all doubt . . .	all other doubt than that which clings to the labors of men that as a result of the labors [etc.]
that man . . .	in short
that man . . .	in spite of the strides of alimentation and defecation, wastes [etc.]
for reasons unknown . . .	no matter what the facts [etc.]
for reasons unknown . . .	in spite of the tennis [etc.]
for reasons unknown . . .	in spite of the tennis on on the beard [etc.]
[our] labors abandoned left unfinished . . .	graver still [etc.]
abandoned unfinished . . .	the skull the skull in Connemara [etc.]

Lucky's speech is an attempt, however futile, to make a statement about man and God. Reduced to its essence, the speech is basically as follows:

> acknowledging the existence of a personal God, one who exists outside of time and who loves us dearly and who suffers with those who are plunged into torment, it is established beyond all doubt that man, for reasons unknown, has left his labors abandoned, unfinished.

It is significant that the speech ends at this point because man can make certain assumptions about God and create certain hypotheses about God, *but* man can never come to a logical conclusion about God. One must finish a discourse about God, as Lucky did, by repeating "for reasons unknown . . . for reasons unknown . . . for reasons unknown. . . ." And equally important is the fact that any statement made about God is, by its nature, lost in a maze of irrelevance, absurdity, and incoherence—without an ending. Therefore, man's final comment about God can amount to nothing more than a bit of garbled noise which contains no coherent statement and no conclusion. Furthermore, Lucky's utterances are stopped only after he is physically overpowered by the others.

After the speech, Pozzo tries to revive Lucky, who is emotionally exhausted, completely enervated by his speech. After great difficulty, Pozzo gets Lucky up, and amid protracted adieus, he begins to go, albeit he begins to go the wrong way. Pozzo's inability to leave suggests man's reliance upon others and his natural instinct to cling to someone else. But with one final adieu, Pozzo and Lucky depart.

ACT I: DEPARTURE OF POZZO AND LUCKY: VLADIMIR AND ESTRAGON ALONE

With the departure of Pozzo and Lucky, Vladimir realizes that he is glad that the episode helped pass the time. Constantly, the two are faced with finding some way of passing the time while waiting, even though Estragon philosophically points out that time "would have passed in any case." Thus the entire episode seemingly has no real significance to them. They return to wondering what they can do now—besides wait for Godot. Since they can do nothing, they decide to make a little conversation about whether or not they had previously known Pozzo and Lucky, but no agreement is reached. Estragon then returns to tending his aching feet.

ACT I: ARRIVAL OF BOY MESSENGER

Out of nowhere a boy with a message from Mr. Godot appears, but the boy is too frightened to come close to the tramps. They question the boy about his fears and ask him if he has been here before. Suddenly, the boy delivers his message: "Mr. Godot told me to tell you he won't come this evening, but surely to-morrow." The tramps question the boy about Mr. Godot and discover that the boy tends the goats for Mr. Godot, that Mr. Godot does not beat him, but that he does beat the boy's brother, who tends the sheep. Both of the brothers sleep in the hayloft of the barn. The boy then leaves.

The main significance of the arrival of the boy lies in what light he can shed on the figure of Godot. By the way the tramps question the boy about Godot, we now realize that Vladimir and Estragon know very little, if anything, about Godot. Apparently, Godot keeps sheep and goats and is good to the boy who tends the goats but beats the brother who tends the sheep. The reasons for beating the brother are unknown. If, therefore, Godot is equated with God, then Godot's behavior would suggest an Old Testament God who accepts the offering of one brother (Abel) and rejects the offering of the other brother (Cain). God's rejection of Cain's offering is difficult or impossible to explain. Thus Godot's actions are as incomprehensible as some of the actions of the Old Testament God.

ACT I: VLADIMIR AND ESTRAGON ALONE

After the boy leaves, Vladimir and Estragon are left alone. Night has fallen and the moon has risen. The two tramps resolve to leave since there is "nothing to do here," but then, hopefully, Vladimir reminds Estragon that the boy said "Godot was sure to come to-morrow." Thus, they must wait—even though nothing is certain. Impulsively, they decide to leave—but do not do so.

The first act ends as it began. Estragon is still concerned about his feet and his boots, which he is now carrying. Vladimir reminds Estragon that he can't go barefoot because it's too cold, and Estragon compares his going barefoot with Christ's going barefoot. Vladimir can't see the comparison; Christ went barefoot in a *warm* climate. Yet Estragon is quick to point out that it was precisely because of that warm climate that Christ was crucified quickly, whereas here and now, man, by implication, must suffer for an extended time. The futility of their situation makes Estagon wish for some rope so that he can hang himself. The thought of death reminds him of a time about fifty years ago when he threw himself in the Rhone River and was "fished out" by Vladimir. This allusion reminds us of the Christian symbols of baptism, cleansing, and renewal. Yet the incident occurred fifty years ago, so now it is "all dead and buried." In other words, there is no more hope of baptism and renewal—instead, they must face the coldness and the darkness of the world alone.

The first act began with the line "Nothing to be done." Nothing has been done. Now Vladimir and Estragon realize that "nothing is certain," and that "nothing is worth while now." Consequently, they decide: "Let's go." But instead, according to the stage directions, *They do not move.* The act ends, therefore, with a contradiction between their words and their actions. All they can do now is simply wait.

ACT II: VLADIMIR AND ESTRAGON ALONE

The second act begins almost exactly as the first act did—with one exception: there are now four or five leaves on the once barren tree. As in Act I, Estragon is alone and Vladimir enters, singing some repetitious doggerel about a dog which was beaten to death because he stole a crust of bread. The repetition of the doggerel is typical of the repetition of the entire drama, and the condition of the dog in the doggerel is similar to the condition of the two tramps. Again, as in Act I, Vladimir wonders where Estragon spent the night and discovers that Estragon has again been beaten. Thus, the dog in the doggerel was beaten to death, and now we hear that Estragon is suffering from a beating. Consequently, the second act begins on a note of death, but one that is doubly ominous.

After a moment, the two tramps are reconciled and embrace each other, pretending that all is right between them. However, Estragon immediately reminds Vladimir that he was singing all the while that he (Estragon) was being beaten. Vladimir can only respond that "one is not master of one's moods." Vladimir's remarks characterize the actions of the first act—especially where it was evident that the two tramps were not in control of their lives, that they were unable to determine what was going to happen to them.

We now discover part of the reason for Vladimir's singing. He is happy because he slept all night long. The urinary trouble that he had in the first act did not force him to get up during the night and, therefore, he enjoyed a complete night's sleep. But then, if Vladimir had been with Estragon, he would not have let the people beat Estragon. Vladimir assumes a traditional philosophical position, a position that goes back to the writer of the Book of Job in the Old Testament. If Estragon was beaten, it was because he was guilty of doing something wrong and, had Vladimir been with Estragon, he would have stopped him from doing whatever it was that caused Estragon to get a beating. This scene reminds one of Franz Kafka's *The Trial*; there, the main character is punished for a crime and is never able to discover what his crime was and feels increasingly more guilty by asking what he is accused of.

After the two convince each other that they are happy, they then settle down to wait for Godot, and the basic refrain of the drama reemerges: the two tramps can do nothing but wait. Suddenly, Vladimir is aware that "things have changed here since yesterday." The change that Vladimir notices (and note that it is always Vladimir who is the most perceptive of the two, even though in the final analysis he is also incapable of changing their predicament) concerns the tree. Later, the change in the tree will be more fully appreciated, but for now, Estragon is not convinced that it is the same tree; he does not even remember if it is the same tree that they nearly hanged themselves from yesterday. In addition, Estragon has almost forgotten the appearance of Pozzo and Lucky, except for the bone he was given to gnaw on. Blankly, he asks, "all that was yesterday, you say?" For Estragon, time has no real meaning; his only concern with time is that it is something to be used up while waiting for Godot. He dismisses the discussion by pointing out that the world about him is a "muckheap" from which he has never stirred.

The world-as-a-muckheap is a central image in Beckett's work—for example, in *Endgame*, one of the central images is garbage cans as symbols of the status of man, who belongs on the refuse heap of the world. Estragon solidifies the image of the world-as-a-muckheap by asking Vladimir to tell him about worms.

In contrast to the landscape, or world which they now inhabit, Vladimir reminds Estragon of a time once long ago when they lived in the Macon country and picked grapes for someone whose name he can't remember. But it has been so long ago that Estragon can't remember and can only assert that he "has puked [his] puke of a life away here . . . in the Cackon country!" The oblique reference to another time and place where apparently grapes (the biblical symbol of fertility) could be harvested contrasts with this barren landscape where they now eat dried tubers of turnips and radishes. If Estragon and Vladimir are representatives of mankind waiting for God to appear to them, then we realize that possibly they are in this barren land because they represent man as fallen man—man who has been cast out of the Garden of Eden, man who originally was picking the grapes of God has now incurred the wrath of God, who refuses to appear to them any more.

Vladimir and Estragon make a desperate attempt at conversation in order to make time pass "so we won't think." Their efforts at conversation are strained and useless, and each time after a few meaningless words, they obey the stage directions: *Silence*. This is repeated ten times within the passing of a minute or so—that is, a few meaningless phrases are uttered, followed by "silences." The two even contemplate trying to contradict each other, but even that fails. The entire passage is characterized by a brooding sense of helplessness and melancholy. The images are those of barren, sterile lifelessness—the falling of leaves, ashes, dead voices, skeletons, corpses, and charnel-houses, etc. All of these images are juxtaposed to the background idea of a once-fertile life "in the Macon country" that can no longer be remembered and the idea that they are constantly involved in the sterile, unprofitable endeavor of waiting for Godot. The entire conversation is absolutely pointless, and yet Estragon responds, "Yes, but now we'll have to find something else." The only effect, then, of their banter was to pass the time.

With nothing else to do, the two tramps are momentarily diverted when Vladimir discovers that the tree which was "all black and bare" yesterday evening is now "covered with leaves." This leads to a discussion of whether or not the two tramps are in the same place; after all, it would be impossible for a tree to sprout leaves overnight. Perhaps it has been longer than just yesterday when they were here. Yet Vladimir points out Estragon's wounded leg; that is proof that they were here yesterday.

The confusion about time and place is typical of Beckett's dramas. How long the two tramps have been in this particular place can never be determined. The fact that Estragon has a wound proves nothing because man is eternally wounded in Beckett's dramas and, furthermore, can show proof of his injuries. The leaves on the tree, which earlier was black and bare, astonish Vladimir. It would indeed be a miracle if such an event could occur in a single night, and this would open up all types of opportunities for miracles to occur. But the discussion of a miracle is rejected by Estragon because the leaves have no mystical appearance. They could be a manifestation of spring, or else this could be an entirely different tree. Consequently, their conversation is inconclusive, and we never know if this is the same tree in the same place or not. This confusion is characteristic of Vladimir and Estragon's inability to cope with life.

As Vladimir is trying to prove to Estragon that Pozzo and Lucky were here yesterday, he makes Estragon pull up his trousers so that they can both see the wound which is "beginning to fester." This scene is especially significant in the manner that it is staged because the actions of the two tramps are those found in a burlesque comedy house, with Vladimir holding up Estragon's leg while Estragon can hardly keep his balance, and against this background of farcical comedy is the contrasting intellectual idea of the metaphysical and spiritual wounds that man carries about with him.

The wound on Estragon's leg, in turn, causes Vladimir to notice that Estragon does not have his boots on. Coincidentally, there is a pair of boots lying on the ground, but Estragon maintains that his boots were black and this pair is brown. Maybe someone came and exchanged boots. Are they the same boots or someone else's boots?

As with the tree, the confusion about the boots is a further indication of the inadequacy of Estragon and Vladimir's logic and reasoning. They are unable to find anything which will help "give us the impression that we exist." The boots were to be objective proof of their particular existence on this particular bit of landscape at this particular time, but in an absurdly tragic manner, they cannot even determine if the boots are the same boots that existed yesterday. They are unable to find within themselves or outside themselves anything which is helpful in establishing their existences. There is no hope within or without. Therefore, even the attempt to arrive at a conclusion totally exhausts them, and with the familiar refrain "we are waiting for Godot," they abandon the problem.

But the boots are still there, and Vladimir convinces Estragon to try them on. Even though they are too big, Estragon grudgingly admits that the boots do fit him. Then with his new boots on, Estragon wishes that he could sleep. "He resumes his foetal posture" and to the accompaniment of a lullaby sung by Vladimir, Estragon is soon asleep, only to be awakened shortly by the recurrence of a nightmare. Frightened, Estragon wishes to leave, but Vladimir reminds him that they can't leave because they are "waiting for Godot."

Estragon's assuming the fetal position suggests his complete resignation and despair, his defeat in the face of such staggering, unsolvable metaphysical problems as the significance of the tree and the mysterious boots. Obviously, too, this is a "return-to-the-womb" situation wherein Estragon can escape from the responsibilities of life. His security in the womb, however, does not last long because he is awakened by a nightmare about falling. Whether it is a nightmare involving falling from the womb (man's most traumatic physical experience) or falling from God's grace (man's most traumatic spiritual experience), we are never sure.

Suddenly, Estragon can bear no more. He is going and tells Vladimir that he will never see him again. Vladimir doesn't pay attention, for he has found a hat, Lucky's hat; and so, in the midst of all these ambiguous physical and philosophical considerations, we have another burlesque interlude. In the tradition of the old burlesque theater, a tramp (Vladimir) in an old bowler hat discovers another hat on the ground. There follows an exchange-of-hats act between himself and his partner that could be found in many burlesque acts. The hat is apparently the one that Lucky left the day before, during the scene when he was silenced after his speech. The comic exchange begins when Vladimir gives his own hat to Estragon and replaces it with Lucky's. Estragon then does the same, offering his hat to Vladimir, who replaces it for Lucky's, and hands Lucky's hat to Estragon, who replaces it for Vladimir's and so on until they tire of the interchange. And then there is silence.

Once more the two tramps must pass the time while waiting. They decide to play a game of pretending to be Pozzo and Lucky, but this game lasts only a moment because they think that they hear someone approaching. After a frantic search for some place to hide, they decide that there is no one coming. Vladimir then tells Estragon: "You must have had a vision," a phrase that is reminiscent of T. S. Eliot's *The Love Song of J. Alfred Prufrock*, a long poem in which the main character, an ineffectual intellectual of the twentieth century, cannot do anything, much less have the strength to have visions. Furthermore, visions are associated with people entirely different from these two tramps. To think that they could have a vision is absurd.

One more game is attempted. Remembering Pozzo's calling Lucky ugly names and recalling the anger and frustration of the master and his slave, they begin a game of name-calling. It is Vladimir who suggests the idea of the game: "Let's abuse each other." There follows in rapid succession a series of name-calling:

> VLADIMIR: Moron!
> ESTRAGON: Vermin!
> VLADIMIR: Abortion!
> ESTRAGON: Morpion!
> VLADIMIR: Sewer-rat!
> ESTRAGON: Curate!
> VLADIMIR: Cretin!

After this, they make up, and then they decide to exercise, mutually relieved by the discovery that time flies when one "has fun!"

> VLADIMIR: We could do our exercises.
> ESTRAGON: Our movements.
> VLADIMIR: Our elevations.

ESTRAGON: Our relaxations.
VLADIMIR: Our elongations.
[etc., etc.]

The name-calling, the embracing, and the exercising are finally over; they have been no more than futile attempts to pass the time while waiting for Godot, and Estragon is reduced to flailing his fists and crying at the top of his voice, "God have pity on me! . . . On me! On me! Pity! On me!"

ACT II: ARRIVAL OF POZZO AND LUCKY

Suddenly and without warning, as in the first act, Pozzo and Lucky come back on stage. Their arrival puts an end to Vladimir and Estragon's games. Things have changed significantly for Pozzo and Lucky. The long rope which bound them together is now much shorter, binding them closer together and suggesting that however much man might consider himself to be different from others, ultimately he is drawn or bound closer and closer. Furthermore, Pozzo and Lucky are physically changed: Pozzo is blind and Lucky is dumb (i.e., mute). But the entire scene is played without the audience's knowing that Lucky is now dumb. As they enter, staggering under their load, Lucky now carries suitcases filled with sand (symbolically, perhaps, the sands of time). Lucky falls and drags Pozzo down with him.

With the arrival of Pozzo and Lucky, Vladimir and Estragon think that help ("reinforcements") have arrived from Godot. But they soon realize that it is just Pozzo and Lucky. Estragon wants to leave then, but Vladimir must remind him once again that they cannot go; they are "waiting for Godot." After some consideration, Vladimir decides that they should help Pozzo and Lucky get up. But Estragon wants to consider an alternative plan. After all, he was wounded by Lucky the day before. Vladimir reminds him, however, that "it is not everyday that we are needed." This is one of the most profound comments of the drama. Vladimir realizes that Pozzo's cries for help were addressed to "all of mankind," and "at this place, at this moment of time, all mankind is us, whether we like it or not." This statement certainly clarifies the idea that Vladimir and Estragon represent all mankind in its relationship to God (Godot). Realizing this, Vladimir also realizes that man's fate is to be a part of "the foul brood to which a cruel fate consigned us."

Instead of Hamlet's "To be or not to be, that is the question," Vladimir asks, "What are we doing here, *that* is the question." Again, his problem is more akin to the dilemma of T. S. Eliot's Prufrock (who is also faced with an "overwhelming question": should he marry or not?) than it is to the predicament of Shakespeare's Hamlet. Vladimir concludes: "We [all mankind] are waiting for Godot to come." Hamlet's metaphysical question about existence is reduced to a Prufrockian decision to do nothing but wait.

At the end of Vladimir's speech, Pozzo's call for help loses importance as Vladimir once again asserts his pride in the fact that they have at least kept their appointment to meet Godot; not all people can make such a boast. Vladimir's confusing the metaphysical with the practical anticipates the confused actions that are to immediately follow—that is, Vladimir decides that they should help Pozzo and Lucky get up, and the result is that all four of the men ultimately end up on the ground. Thus their cries for help fall on deaf ears.

The entire scene in which the two tramps try to help two equally distraught figures get up returns the drama to the burlesque house. The scene is a parody of many similar types of scenes found in burlesque theaters, thus emphasizing again the absurdity of man's actions, or in the words of Estragon: "We are all born mad. Some remain so."

Immediately after the above statement, Estragon leaves off with philosophy and becomes very practical; he wants to know how much Pozzo is willing to pay to be extricated from his position. Meanwhile, Vladimir is concerned with finding something to do to pass the time: "We are bored to death"; he begins his efforts to help Pozzo, but, as noted above, they all end up in a heap on the ground, and Pozzo, in fear, "extricates himself," then crawls away. This incident also serves as a contrast to Pozzo's actions in the first act; there, he was proud and disdainful and asserted himself with aloofness and superiority. Now he has lost all his previous qualities and is simply a pathetic, blind figure crawling about on the ground. Like Job or Sophocles' blind Oedipus, Pozzo seems to suggest that no man's life can be secure since tomorrow might bring incalculable catastrophes.

Lying on the ground, Vladimir and Estragon try to call to Pozzo, who doesn't answer. Then Estragon decides to call him by some other name:

> ESTRAGON: . . . try [calling] him with other names. . . . It'd pass the time. And we'd be bound to hit on the right one sooner or later.
> VLADIMIR: I tell you his name is Pozzo.
> ESTRAGON: We'll soon see. (*He reflects.*) Abel! Abel!
> POZZO: Help!
> ESTRAGON: Got it in one!
> VLADIMIR: I begin to weary of this motif.
> ESTRAGON: Perhaps the other is called Cain. Cain! Cain!
> POZZO: Help!
> ESTRAGON: He's all humanity.

Beckett's use of the names of Abel and Cain stresses the universality of the characters since Pozzo answers to both names. According to some interpretations of the scriptures, all of mankind carries with it both the mark of Cain and the mark of Abel; thus Pozzo can answer to both names because "He's all humanity!"

To pass the time, Estragon suggests that they stand up. They do. Then Estragon suggests once again, "Let's go," only to be reminded once again that they must remain because "we're waiting for Godot."

Since there is nothing else to do, Vladimir and Estragon help Pozzo get up. It is then that they discover that he is blind. In contrast to the Pozzo of the first act, we now see a pathetic figure leaning on the two tramps for physical support and pleading for help because he is blind. For Estragon, there is hope in Pozzo's blindness because the prophets of old, such as the Greek Tiresias, were often blind but could "see into the future," exactly what Estragon hopes Pozzo can do. But there is no hope for Vladimir and Estragon. Carrying through with the Greek imagery, Estragon tires of holding Pozzo, especially since he can't prophesy for them. Pozzo wants to drop him since he and Vladimir "are not caryatids" (caryatids were statues of Greek goddesses used to hold up temples; why Estragon uses this word instead of "telamons," the male equivalent, is confusing).

Because of his blindness, Pozzo has also lost all contact with time. He even refuses to answer questions about what happened yesterday: "The blind have no notion of time." This confusion over time is symptomatic of his changed condition; just as he has lost all contact with life, so also has time lost all significance for him. When Vladimir hears that Lucky is dumb, he inquires, "Since when?" The question incenses Pozzo and causes him to violently reject Vladimir's concern with time: "Have you not done tormenting me with your accursed time! It's abominable! When! When! One day, is that not enough for you, one day he went dumb, one day I went blind, one day we'll go deaf, one day we were born, one day we shall die, the same day, the same second, is that not enough for you?" For Pozzo, one day at a time is enough for him to cope with. All he knows now and all that he "sees" now is the misery of life. Life itself is only a brief moment—that flash of light between the darkness of the womb and of the tomb. "They give birth astride of a grave, the light gleams an instant, then it's night once more." Thus the grave-digger is the midwife of mankind. Ending on this note of utter despair, Pozzo arouses Lucky and they struggle off to continue on their journey.

ACT II: DEPARTURE OF POZZO AND LUCKY: VLADIMIR AND ESTRAGON ALONE

While Vladimir and Pozzo have been talking, Estragon has been sleeping again in his fetal position. Vladimir, feeling lonely, awakens him. Significantly, since Estragon was sleeping in his fetal position, his dreams were happy ones; but even so, Vladimir refuses to listen to them. Vladimir's final speech before the entrance of the Boy Messenger suggests that he feels a deep estrangement from the universe. Something tells him that there should be some reason for him to be here—at this place, at this time, with his friend Estragon while waiting for Godot. Furthermore, he is aware of a misery, a disquietness which he cannot understand. Life seems as though it is "astride of a grave," and there is to be a "difficult birth," for the "grave-digger puts on the forceps." Vladimir senses that life is filled with the cries of a suffering humanity, but he has used "a great deadener" (boredom) as a barrier to these cries. Suddenly, in complete despair, he cries out: "I can't go on." But the alternative to his despair is obviously death; therefore, he immediately rejects his despair by asking, "What have I said?" There is left only man's stubborn, useless clinging to a meaningless life.

ACT II: ARRIVAL OF BOY MESSENGER

Vladimir's depression is suddenly interrupted by the appearance of a boy. Since this boy asserts that he was not here yesterday, he has to be a different one. However, the message that he brings is identical to the one brought yesterday by a boy: Mr. Godot will not come this evening but he will surely come tomorrow, without fail. Thus Vladimir finds that there is absolutely nothing to do but wait for Godot. But in view of the message from the boy of the preceding day, the assurance that Godot will come tomorrow is lacking in conviction.

Upon questioning the boy further, Vladimir discovers two things —that Mr. Godot "does nothing" and that he has a white beard. Since God is sometimes viewed as a Supreme Entity doing nothing and possessing a long white beard, then if Godot is God, there can be little or no hope for God's intervention in the affairs of men. Instead, man must continue to stumble through this muckheap, this ash can of a world. Vladimir tells the boy to inform Mr. Godot that "you saw me." Vladimir is so insistent on the fact that the boy has indeed seen him that he makes "a sudden spring forward." This frightens the boy, and he quickly runs offstage.

ACT II: DEPARTURE OF BOY MESSENGER: VLADIMIR AND ESTRAGON ALONE

After the boy leaves, the sun sets and the moon rises, indicating that another day of waiting for Godot has passed. Estragon awakens and wants to leave this desolate place, but Vladimir reminds him that they have to wait for Godot. When Estragon suggests that they "drop Godot" and leave, Vladimir reminds Estragon that if they did, Godot would "punish us."

As he did at the end of Act I, Estragon once again brings up the subject of their hanging themselves. But Estragon forgot to bring the rope. They decide to hang themselves with the cord that holds up Estragon's trousers, but when tested, the cord breaks. This misadventure returns us to the world of the circus and the world of the burlesque house, and this rare, decisive action to kill themselves is rendered ludicrous since in the process of testing the cord, Estragon suffers the indignity of having his trousers fall down. Thus we see again Beckett's notion of the incongruity between what man attempts (and longs to be) and the absurdity of his position and his actions.

Since they have to come back tomorrow to wait for Godot, Estragon once again proposes that they bring "a good bit of rope" with them; Vladimir agrees:

> VLADIMIR: We'll hang ourselves tomorrow. (Pause) Unless Godot comes.
> ESTRAGON: And if he comes?
> VLADIMIR: We'll be saved.

The question then is: if Godot doesn't come, will Vladimir and Estragon be damned?

After telling Estragon to put on his trousers, which are still around his ankles since the cord that held up his trousers is now broken, Vladimir suggests that they leave:

> VLADIMIR: Well? Shall we go?
> ESTRAGON: Yes, let's go.
> *They do not move.*

Curtain

The ending of Act II is exactly the same as was the ending of Act I, and we have one final example of the disparity between the characters' words and the characters' actions. And since both acts are so identical and so circular, it should be obvious that tomorrow will find the two tramps back at the same place waiting for Godot, who will not come but who will send a boy messenger to tell them that Godot will surely come tomorrow and they must come back to wait for Godot, etc., etc.

THE PLAY'S CIRCULAR STRUCTURE

"But what does it all mean?" is the most frequent statement heard after one has seen or finished reading a play from the Theater of the Absurd movement. Beckett's plays were among the earliest and, therefore, created a great deal of confusion among the early critics.

No definite conclusion or resolution can ever be offered to *Waiting for Godot* because the play is essentially circular and repetitive in nature. Once again, turn to the Dramatic Divisions section in these Notes and observe that the structure of each act is exactly alike. A traditional play, in contrast, has an introduction of the characters and the exposition; then, there is a statement of the problem of the play in relationship to its settings and characters. (In *Waiting for Godot*, we never know where the play takes place, except that it is set on "a country road.") Furthermore, in a traditional play, the characters are developed, and gradually we come to see the dramatist's world view; the play then rises to a climax, and there is a conclusion. This type of development is called a linear development. In the plays of the Theater of the Absurd, the structure is often exactly the opposite. We have, instead, a circular structure, and most aspects of this drama support this circular structure in one way or another.

The setting is the same, and the time is the same in both acts. Each act begins early in the morning, just as the tramps are awakening, and both acts close with the moon having risen. The action takes place in exactly the same landscape—a lonely, isolated road with one single tree. (In the second act, there are some leaves on the tree, but from the viewpoint of the audience, the setting is exactly the same.) We are never told where this road is located; all we know is that the action of the play unfolds on this lonely road. Thus, from Act I to Act II, there is no difference in either the setting or in the time and, thus, instead of a progression of time within an identifiable setting, we have a repetition in the second act of the same things that we saw and heard in the first act.

More important than the repetition of setting and time, however, is the repetition of the actions. To repeat, in addition to the basic structure of actions indicated earlier—that is:

> Vladimir and Estragon Alone
> Arrival of Pozzo and Lucky
> Vladimir and Estragon Alone
> Arrival of Boy Messenger
> Vladimir and Estragon Alone

there are many lesser actions that are repeated in both acts. At the beginning of each act, for example, several identical concerns should be noted. Among these is the emphasis on Estragon's boots. Also, too, Vladimir, when first noticing Estragon, uses virtually the same words: "So there you are again" in Act I and "There you are again" in Act II. At the beginning of both acts, the first discussion concerns a beating that Estragon received just prior to their meeting. At the beginning of both acts, Vladimir and Estragon emphasize repeatedly that they are there to wait for Godot. In the endings of both acts, Vladimir and Estragon discuss the possibility of hanging themselves, and in both endings they decide to bring some good strong rope with them the next day so that they can indeed hang themselves. In addition, both acts end with the same words, voiced differently:

ACT I: ESTRAGON: Well, shall we go?
        VLADIMIR: Yes, let's go.

ACT II: VLADIMIR: Well? Shall we go?
        ESTRAGON: Yes, let's go.

And the stage directions following these lines are exactly the same in each case: "*They do not move.*"

With the arrival of Pozzo and Lucky in each act, we notice that even though their physical appearance has theoretically changed, outwardly they seem the same; they are still tied together on an endless journey to an unknown place to rendezvous with a nameless person.

Likewise, the Boy Messenger, while theoretically different, brings the exact same message: Mr. Godot will not come today, but he will surely come tomorrow.

Vladimir's difficulties with urination and his suffering are discussed in each act as a contrast to the suffering of Estragon because of his boots. In addition, the subject of eating, involving carrots, radishes, and turnips, becomes a central image in each act, and the tramps' involvement with hats, their multiple insults, and their reconciling embraces—these and many more lesser matters are found repeatedly in both acts.

Finally, and most important, there are the larger concepts: first, the suffering of the tramps; second, their attempts, however futile, to pass time; third, their attempts to part, and, ultimately, their incessant waiting for Godot—all these make the two acts clearly repetitive, circular in structure, and the fact that these repetitions are so obvious in the play is Beckett's manner of breaking away from the traditional play and of asserting the uniqueness of his own circular structure.

CHARACTER ANALYSES

Vladimir and Estragon

In spite of the existential concept that man cannot take the essence of his existence from someone else, in viewing this play, we have to view Vladimir and Estragon in their relationship to each other. In fact, the novice viewing this play for the first time often fails to note any significant difference between the two characters. In hearing the play read, even the most experienced theater person will often confuse one of the characters for the other. Therefore, the similarities are as important as the differences between them.

Both are tramps dressed in costumes which could be interchanged. They both wear big boots which don't necessarily fit and both have big bowler hats. Their suits are baggy and ill-fitting. (In Act II, when Estragon removes the cord he uses for a belt, his trousers are so baggy that they fall about his feet.) Their costumes recall the type found in burlesque or vaudeville houses, the type often associated with the character of the "Little Tramp," portrayed by Charlie Chaplin.

The Chaplinesque-type costume prepares us for many of the comic routines that Vladimir and Estragon perform. The opening scene with Estragon struggling with his boots and Vladimir doffing and donning his hat to inspect it for lice could be a part of a burlesque routine. The resemblance of their costumes to Chaplin's supports the view that these tramps are outcasts from society, but have the same plucky defiance to continue to exist as Chaplin's "Little Tramp" did.

Another action which could come directly from the burlesque theater occurs when Vladimir finds a hat on the ground which he tries on, giving his own to Estragon, who tries it on while giving his hat to Vladimir, who tries it on while giving the new-found hat to Estragon, who tries it on, etc. This comic episode continues until the characters—and the audience—are bored with it. Other burlesque-like scenes involve Vladimir's struggles to help Estragon with his boots while Estragon is hopping awkwardly about the stage on one foot to keep from falling; another scene involves the loss of Estragon's pants, while other scenes involve the two tramps' grotesque efforts to help Pozzo and Lucky get up off the ground and their inept attempts to hang themselves. Thus, the two characters are tied together partly by being two parts of a burlesque act.

Vladimir

In any comic or burlesque act, there are two characters, traditionally known as the "straight man" and the "fall guy." Vladimir would be the equivalent of the straight man. He is also the intellectual who is concerned with a variety of ideas. Of the two, Vladimir makes the decisions and remembers significant aspects of their past. He is the one who constantly reminds Estragon that they must wait for Godot. Even though it is left indefinite, all implications suggest that Vladimir knows more about Godot than does Estragon, who tells us that he has never even seen Godot and thus has no idea what Godot looks like.

Vladimir is the one who often sees religious or philosophical implications in their discussions of events, and he interprets their actions in religious terms; for example, he is concerned about the religious implications in such stories as the two thieves (two tramps) who were crucified on either side of Jesus. He is troubled about the fate of the thief who wasn't saved and is concerned that "only one of the four evangelists" speaks of a thief being saved.

Vladimir correlates some of their actions to the general concerns of mankind. In Act II, when Pozzo and Lucky fall down and cry for help, Vladimir interprets their cries for help as his and Estragon's chance to be in a unique position of helping humanity. After all, Vladimir maintains, "It is not everyday that we are needed . . . but at this place, at this moment in time," they are needed and should respond to the cries for help. Similarly, it is Vladimir who questions Pozzo and Lucky and the Boy Messenger(s), while Estragon remains, for the most part, the silent listener. Essentially, Vladimir must constantly remind Estragon of their destiny—that is, they must wait for Godot.

In addition to the larger needs, Vladimir also looks after their physical needs. He helps Estragon with his boots, and, moreover, had he been with Estragon at night, he would not have allowed his friend to be beaten; also, he looks after and rations their meager meals of turnips, carrots, and radishes, and, in general, he tends to be the manager of the two.

Estragon

In contrast, Estragon is concerned mainly with more mundane matters: he prefers a carrot to a radish or turnip, his feet hurt, and he blames his boots; he constantly wants to leave, and it must be drilled into him that he *must* wait for Godot. He remembers that he was beaten, but he sees no philosophical significance in the beating. He is willing to beg for money from a stranger (Pozzo), and he eats Pozzo's discarded chicken bones with no shame.

Estragon, then, is the more basic of the two. He is not concerned with either religious or philosophical matters. First of all, he has never even heard of the two thieves who were crucified with Christ, and if the Gospels do disagree, then "that's all there is to it," and any further discussion is futile and absurd.

Estragon's basic nature is illustrated in Act II when he shows so little interest in Pozzo and Lucky that he falls asleep; also, he sleeps through the entire scene between Vladimir and the Boy Messenger. He is simply not concerned with such issues.

Estragon, however, is dependent upon Vladimir, and essentially he performs what Vladimir tells him to do. For example, Vladimir looks after Estragon's boots, he rations out the carrots, turnips, and radishes, he comforts Estragon's pain, and he reminds Estragon of their need to wait for Godot. Estragon does sometimes suggest that it would be better if they parted, but he never leaves Vladimir for long. Essentially, Estragon is the less intelligent one; he has to have everything explained to him, and he is essentially so bewildered by life that he has to have someone to look after him.

Pozzo and Lucky

Together they represent the antithesis of each other. Yet they are strongly and irrevocably tied together—both physically and metaphysically. Any number of polarities could be used to apply to them. If Pozzo is the master (and father figure), then Lucky is the slave (or child). If Pozzo is the circus ringmaster, then Lucky is the trained or performing animal. If Pozzo is the sadist; Lucky is the masochist. Or Pozzo can be seen as the Ego and Lucky as the Id. An inexhaustible number of polarities can be suggested.

Pozzo

Pozzo appears on stage after the appearance of Lucky. They are tied together by a long rope; thus, their destinies are fixed together in the same way that Pozzo might be a mother figure, with the rope being the umbilical cord which ties the two together.

Everything about Pozzo resembles our image of the circus ringmaster. If the ringmaster is the chief person of the circus, then it is no wonder that Vladimir and Estragon first mistook him for Godot or God. Like a ringmaster, he arrives brandishing a whip, which is the trademark of the professional. In fact, we hear the cracking of Pozzo's whip before we actually see him. Also, a stool is often associated with an animal trainer, and Pozzo constantly calls Lucky by animal terms or names. Basically, Pozzo commands and Lucky obeys.

In the first act, Pozzo is immediately seen in terms of this authoritarian figure. He lords over the others, and he is decisive, powerful, and confident. He gives the illusion that he knows exactly where he is going and exactly how to get there. He seems "on top" of every situation.

When he arrives on the scene and sees Vladimir and Estragon, he recognizes them as human, but as inferior beings; then he condescendingly acknowledges that there is a human likeness, even though the "likeness is an imperfect one." This image reinforces his authoritarian god-like stance: we are made in God's image but imperfectly so. Pozzo's superiority is also seen in the manner in which he eats the chicken, then casts the bones to Lucky with an air of complete omnipotence.

In contrast to the towering presence exhibited by Pozzo in Act I, a significant change occurs between the two acts. The rope is shortened, drawing Pozzo much closer to his antithesis, Lucky. Pozzo is now blind; he cannot find his way alone. He stumbles and falls. He cannot get along without help; he is pathetic. He can no longer command. Rather than driving Lucky as he did earlier, he is now pathetically dragged along by Lucky. From a position of omnipotence and strength and confidence, he has fallen and has become the complete fallen man who maintains that time is irrelevant and that man's existence is meaningless. Unlike the great blind prophets of yore who could see everything, for Pozzo "the things of time are hidden from the blind." Ultimately, for Pozzo, man's existence is discomforting and futile, depressing, and gloomy and, most of all, brief and to no purpose. The gravedigger is the midwife of mankind: "They give birth astride the grave, the light gleams an instant, then it's night once more."

Lucky

As noted above, Lucky is the obvious antithesis of Pozzo. At one point, Pozzo maintains that Lucky's entire existence is based upon pleasing him; that is, Lucky's enslavement is his meaning, and if he is ever freed, his life would cease to have any significance. Given Lucky's state of existence, his very name "Lucky" is ironic, especially since Vladimir observes that even "old dogs have more dignity."

All of Lucky's actions seem unpredictable. In Act I, when Estragon attempts to help him, Lucky becomes violent and kicks him on the leg. When he is later expected to dance, his movements are as ungraceful and alien to the concept of dance as one can possibly conceive. We have seldom encountered such ignorance; consequently, when he is expected to give a coherent speech, we are still surprised by his almost total incoherence. Lucky seems to be more animal than human, and his very existence in the drama is a parody of human existence. In Act II, when he arrives completely dumb, it is only a fitting extension of his condition in Act I, where his speech was virtually incomprehensible. Now he makes no attempt to utter any sound at all. Whatever part of man that Lucky represents, we can make the general observation that he, as man, is reduced to leading the blind, not by intellect, but by blind instinct.

Endgame

"Nothing to be done" are the opening words of *Waiting for Godot*, and the line characterizes the entire drama. Likewise, the opening words of *Endgame*: "Finished, it's finished . . ." set the theme for this drama. These are the last words that Christ murmured on the cross: "It is finished." It is the end of the game. Beckett himself once described *Endgame* as being "rather difficult and elliptic" and as "more inhuman than *Godot*."

Part of the difficulty of the play lies in the condensation of the language. *Act Without Words I*, of course, has no language in it, but in *Endgame*, Beckett reduces language to its smallest denominator. It is even difficult for many to glean even the barest essentials of the drama. First, we cannot even be certain as to the nature of the setting itself. On the stage, we see a rather sparse, dim room with two small, high windows, one that looks out on land and the other on sea. There are two "ashbins" (ash cans) and a large object covered with a sheet. At first, the ash cans are also covered with a sheet, and thus the opening setting resembles a furniture storage house without any sign of life. The setting alone suggests various approaches to the play. The characters are confined to this bare room, which could suggest such diverse things as the inside of the human skull with the windows being the eyes to look out onto the world, or as one critic has suggested, we are within the womb. Outside the room, there is only devastation, with no sign of life (except maybe a small boy, if he exists, who (perhaps) appears towards the end of the play). The setting, therefore, is typical of Beckett; it is bizarre and unfamiliar, one that can evoke multiple associations and interpretations.

Against this decaying setting, the action (or non-action) of the drama is enacted, and it begins as it ends, with the words "it is finished," and the rest of the play deals with the end of the game. Unlike traditional drama, *Endgame* has no beginning and no middle; it opens at the end of a chess game, or at the end of life, or at the end of the world, and there is only "the impossible heap" that is left outside. In addition to the biblical echoes of Christ's last words, there are also various allusions throughout the play to the Christian story and to other biblical parallels. There are also Shakespearean allusions, along with multilingual puns and various, strategic chess moves. (For example, at the end of a chess game, only a few pieces remain on the board. Clov, with his cloven feet, hops about the stage as does the chess knight (or horse), and he is seen moving the "king" (Hamm) about the board one square at a time, but essentially he allows the king to remain stationary (whenever possible). Consequently, among the difficulties of the play are the non-action and the language, which has been reduced to a virtual non-language, but which is nevertheless filled with allusions to a great body of diverse literature.

At the opening, Hamm, who is blind, and Clov, who cannot sit, speak disjointedly about their life together; they are bored with one another and have lived together too long, but Clov can't leave because there is "nowhere else," and he can't kill Hamm because "I don't know the combination of the cupboard." Hamm controls what food or sustenance there is—thereby forcing the others to be subservient to his wishes. After Hamm inquires about his pain-killer and asks some seemingly irrelevant questions about some nonexistent bicycle wheels, Clov departs; the lid on one of the ash cans lifts, and Nagg, Hamm's father, looks out and asks for food. We hear that Nagg has no legs, only stumps, and is always kept in one of the ash cans. Clov returns, gives Nagg a biscuit, and as Nagg begins to nag about the biscuit, Clov forces him back into the ash can and closes the lid. After a brief discussion about Clov's seeds, which "haven't sprouted" (an allusion to Eliot's *Wasteland*), Clov departs.

Nagg reappears in his ash can and knocks on the adjacent ash can. Nell, Nagg's wife and Hamm's mother, appears and they reminisce about how they lost their legs in an accident on a tandem bicycle in northern France. Then they remember another incident which happened long ago, when they were engaged and were rowing on Lake Como. Then, Nagg told a story about a tailor who took longer to make a pair of striped trousers than it took God to make the world. But, according to the tailor, the trousers were better made than is the world. Hamm then whistles for Clov, who returns, and Nagg and Nell are forced back into their ash cans and the lids are replaced.

After Clov takes Hamm for a spin about the room and returns him to the exact center of the room, Hamm wants Clov to look out a window and report to him. Clov must get the stepladder (he has either shrunk or else the windows have risen) and the telescope. He looks out and reports that there is "Zero . . . (*He looks*) . . . zero . . . (*He looks*) . . . and zero."

After a discussion about the state of the earth (they wonder what would happen if a rational being came back to the earth), Clov discovers a flea on himself, which occupies his complete attention. Afterwards, Hamm wants to get on a raft and go somewhere, and he reminds Clov that someday Clov will be "like me. You'll be sitting there, a speck in the void, in the dark, forever." (The blind Pozzo in *Waiting for Godot* also says approximately the same thing: "One day I went blind, one day we'll go deaf . . . one day we shall die . . . is that not enough . . .") Hamm then promises to give Clov the combination to the cupboard if Clov will promise "to finish me." When Clov refuses, Hamm reminds Clov of the time long ago when Clov first came here and Hamm was "a father" to him. This thought causes Hamm to ask for his toy dog to play with.

Suddenly, Hamm asks about Mother Pegg and if her light is on and whether or not she is buried, but Clov replies that he has had nothing to do with her or her burial. Then Hamm wants his "gaff," or stick, to move the chair; also, he wants the wheels (casters) oiled, but they were oiled yesterday, and yesterday was like all other days —"All life long the same inanities." Hamm wants to tell his story, but when Clov refuses to listen to it, Hamm insists that he awaken Nagg to listen to the story.

Hamm's story involves a man who comes crawling towards him on his belly. The man wants "bread for his brat." Hamm has no bread, but maybe there is a pot of porridge. The man asks Hamm to take in his child—if the child is still alive. Hamm can still see the man, "his hands flat on the ground, glaring . . . with his mad eyes." The story will soon be finished unless Hamm decides to "bring in other characters."

Hamm whistles for Clov, who excitedly exclaims that he's found a rat in the kitchen. Despite the fact that Clov has only exterminated "half the rat," Hamm says that can wait; for the present, they must all "pray to God." After several futile attempts to pray, Hamm concludes: "The bastard! He doesn't exist."

When Hamm's father begins wailing for a sugar plum, he reminds his son of how he used to cry in the night. Nagg and Nell let him cry, even moved him "out of earshot" so they could sleep in peace. Someday, Nagg warns, Hamm will cry out again for his father. He then sinks back into his ash can and closes the lid behind him.

Clov begins to straighten up the room ("I love order"), and he wonders how Hamm is progressing with his story (his chronicle). Hamm says that he has made some progress with the story—up to the point where the man wants to bring a small child with him to tend Hamm's garden, but the creative effort has exhausted him.

Hamm then inquires about his parents. Clov looks into the ash cans and reports that it looks as though Nell is dead, but Nagg is not; Nagg is crying. Hamm's only reaction is to ask to be moved by the window where he wants to hear the sea, but Clov tells him that this is impossible. After he checks on Nagg once again, refusing to kiss Hamm or even to give a hand to hold, Clov exits to check on the trapped rat in the kitchen.

Alone, Hamm ruminates almost incoherently about life and possible death and then blows his whistle for Clov; he inquires whether or not the rat got away and about his pain-killer. It is finally time for it, he says, but now "there is no more pain-killer." Hamm then wants Clov to look through the windows and give him a report. Clov looks out "at this muckheap," but it is not clear enough to see anything. Hamm wonders "what happened." For Clov, whatever happened doesn't matter, and he reminds Hamm that when Hamm refused to give old Mother Pegg some oil for her lamps, he knew that she would die "of boredom."

Clov, when ordered to get something, wonders why he always obeys Hamm, and Hamm suggests that perhaps it's because of compassion. As Clov is about to look out through the telescope, Hamm demands his toy dog. When Clov throws it to him, Hamm tells Clov to hit him with an axe or with his stick, but not with the dog. He would like to be placed in his coffin, but "there are no more coffins." Clov looks out the window toward "the filth" and says that it will be the last time; this is to be the end of the game. Suddenly, he sees something that "looks like a small boy." Clov wants to go see, but Hamm is against it. Hamm then announces that "it's the end, Clov; we've come to the end." Hamm says he doesn't need Clov anymore, and Clov prepares to leave. He makes a final speech to Hamm: "You must learn to suffer better . . . if you want them to weary of punishing you." Clov then exits while Hamm asks one last favor, but Clov doesn't hear it. In a few moments, Clov reenters, dressed for traveling. He stands impassively while Hamm continues his chronicle about the man coming to him, wanting to bring a child. At the end, Hamm calls out to Nagg and then to Clov. With no answer, he then covers his face with his handkerchief as the curtain falls.

One could easily conclude from the above that nothing happens, and this is part of Beckett's purpose. The world ends, according to T. S. Eliot, not with a bang but with a whimper. In this play, most of the things that Western civilization has stood for seem no longer to matter—God, family ties, respect for parents, love, prayer, loyalty, and religion—everything is meaningless here as the end of the game is being played; everything outside is *zero*. The only people remaining are sterile and despairing (one rotting); they "have had enough of this thing."

In *Endgame,* as in so many of his other plays, Beckett utilizes several sets of polarities which characterize most of his plays (*Act Without Words I* is something of an exception to the rule). Among the most obvious polarities here are (1) Hamm versus Clov: Hamm, when he is uncovered, is seen immediately to be a mass of decaying flesh in contrast to Clov, whose name is the same of a preservative spice—thus (2) decay versus preservative; (3) standing versus sitting: Clov must constantly move about the stage to preserve the status quo of the situation, giving us the polarity of (4) movement (Clov) versus non-movement (Hamm); (5) sight versus blindness: not only is Hamm decaying, but he is also blind and must rely upon Clov to see all things for him. The (6) master versus slave polarity is similar to the Pozzo-Lucky polarity; Pozzo and Hamm as masters are blind and must be led (or attended to) by the slaves, Lucky and Clov; (7) inside versus outside polarities are emphasized by the (8) left and right windows, through which Clov is able to report what is going on outside; (9) Nagg and Nell, the parents of Hamm, seem to suggest the muckheap which Beckett sees mankind as being. Ultimately, the concept (10) of life versus death informs most of the play. Whereas twice in *Waiting for Godot,* Vladimir and Estragon consider suicide by hanging, the idea of death pervades this entire play, from its title (the End of the Game) to the presumed death of Nell during the play and includes death images throughout the play —all indicating the possible death and fall of civilization as we know it. These, at least, are part of the complex polarities and images which Beckett uses in investigating man's absurd existence in an absurd world.

All That Fall

Unlike Beckett's other works, *All That Fall* was commissioned by the British Broadcasting Corporation (BBC) explicitly for radio presentation. This work can be considered as a type of contrasting companion piece to *Act Without Words I,* a play that has no dialogue, no spoken words, and no sound effects except the sound of a whistle; the play relies entirely on mime. In contrast, *All That Fall* relies a great deal for its impact on sound effects and a very careful attention to the spoken word and the various death images that run throughout the play.

In outline form, the play could be said to most resemble the structure of *Don Quixote*—that is, it is picaresque; in the same way that the old, decrepit Don Quixote sallied forth and encountered a series of adventures, usually of an absurd nature, in *All That Fall*, Mrs. Maddy Rooney (in her seventies) is found to be on a difficult journey to the train station to meet her blind husband. On the way, she has a series of ludicrous or absurd adventures. First, she meets the local dung carrier, who tries to sell her a load of dung which she does not need. After he drags his "cleg-tormented" hinny (a sterile, hybrid animal resembling a mule) and dung wagon away, we hear the sound of a bicycle bell, and Mr. Tyler, a retired bill-broker squeaks to a stop. While telling how his daughter's operation rendered her barren, he is almost killed by a passing motor van, which covers them "white with dust from head to foot," making them interrupt their journey until "this vile dust falls back upon the viler worms." As the two travel onward, she bemoans the death of her only daughter, Minnie.

After Mr. Tyler pedals off on his bicycle, Mr. Slocum (slow come), a clerk of the racecourse, draws up beside her in his automobile and offers her a ride. She is, however, too old and fat to climb in alone, and Mr. Slocum has to push her in. He tries to start the car, but it has died. After finally getting it started again, he drives over a hen, killing her. Arriving at the station, the porter, Tommy, tries to help Mrs. Rooney down, but she is stuck. After great effort, Tommy and Mr. Slocum free her, and the latter drives away, "crucifying his gearbox."

The station master, Mr. Barrell, inquires about Mrs. Rooney's health and hears from her that she should still be in bed: "Would I were still in bed, Mr. Barrell. Would I were lying stretched out in my comfortable bed, Mr. Barrell, just wasting slowly, painlessly away...." We then hear of the death of Mr. Barrell's father, a story which reminds Mrs. Rooney of many of her own sorrows. Miss Fitt is then seen approaching, but she is so absorbed in humming a hymn that she does not see Mrs. Rooney, who reminds her that they worshipped together the preceding Sunday. Miss Fitt, a misfit, asserts strongly that she does not notice things of this world, and she does not help Mrs. Rooney up the station stairs.

The train is late, an occurrence that has not happened within the memory of any of the characters. An explanation is demanded of the station master, Mr. Barrell: "Please a statement of some kind.... Even the slowest train on this brief line is not ten minutes and more behind its scheduled time without good cause." At last, the train arrives, and Mr. Rooney (Dan), who is blind, is helped from the train by a small boy, Jerry, whom they immediately dismiss with a small tip. The Rooneys carefully descend the steps and begin the arduous journey home. Mrs. Rooney then stops to inquire about the reason for the lateness of the train. Her husband refuses to discuss the subject, and they continue on their journey.

Suddenly they feel threatened by two children hiding and jeering at them. Mr. Rooney wonders if Mrs. Rooney has ever wished "to kill a child." He speaks of his desire to live at home, simply, with no cares or tribulations. On the way, he explains how he got on the train, how it started, and then stopped. Being blind, he could see no reason for it to stop unless it had reached a station, but this was not true. After some time, the train moved on and he arrived at his home station.

Mr. Rooney then requests, "Say something, Maddy. Say something." Mrs. Rooney, to pass time, tells about a specialist on "the troubled mind" who treated a "very strange and unhappy" little girl: "The only thing wrong with her as far as he could see was that she was dying. And she did, in fact, die, shortly after he washed his hands of her." Mrs. Rooney went to the specialist, she says, because of her "lifelong preoccupation with horses' buttocks." Her concern was directly correlated with the sexual nature of the ass (or hinny) that Christ rode into Jerusalem.

In the distance, they hear faint strains of Shubert's "Death and the Maiden" song, which prompts Mr. Rooney to inquire about the text of Sunday's sermon: it is "The Lord upholdeth all that fall and raiseth up all those that be bowed down."

Jerry suddenly catches up with them in order to return something that Mr. Rooney dropped; as Jerry is about to leave, Mrs. Rooney asks about "the hitch . . . what kept the train so late." Jerry explains that it was "because a little child fell out of the carriage, Ma'am. On the line, Ma'am. Under the wheels, Ma'am."

As the action denotes, the most commonplace events are constantly surrounded by death or signs, symbols, and reminders of death. The absurdity of the play lies partly in the comic, grotesque nature of Mrs. Rooney and the other characters in the drama. But even in the most grotesque, there is something of the commonplace and even in the most common and vulgar, there is an element that transcends the ordinary. Mrs. Rooney's speech, which is ordinary and common, is sprinkled with unusual expressions and bizarre syntax. Early in the play, she tells Christy to "climb up on the crest of your manure and let yourself be carried along." Later in the play, Mr. Rooney comments on Mrs. Rooney's speech:

MR. ROONEY: I speak—and you listen to the wind.
MRS. ROONEY: No no, I am agog, tell me all, we shall press on and never pause, never pause till we come safe to haven.
MR. ROONEY: Never pause . . . safe to haven. . . . Do you know, Maddy, sometimes one would think you were struggling with a dead language.

Likewise, there are not many things more commonplace than the fact that a chicken is often run over and killed by a car on a country road. Yet, Mrs. Rooney's language becomes a literary eulogy in praise of the dead chicken:

What a death! One minute picking happy at the dung, on the road, in the sun, with now and then a dust bath, and then— bang!—all her troubles over. [*Pause.*] All the laying and the hatching. [*Pause.*] Just one great squawk and then . . . peace. [*Pause.*] They would have slit her weasand in any case. [*Pause.*]

Thus, we have on the one hand, the most common and elemental figures—characters one would find in any low comedy—yet on the other hand, these same characters are in constant confrontation with death. Images of a barren, sterile, and death-like world are constantly evoked. The uniqueness of the characters is that they continue to exist or endure (as did Vladimir and Estragon in *Waiting for Godot*) in an absurd world such as theirs, and the absurdity is emphasized by the juxtaposition of their ignorant commonplace natures in a world where death is indeed the most commonplace occurrence.

Among the images of barrenness, sterility, or death which are either evoked or used thematically are some of the following:

1. "Death and the Maiden" is the Schubert song which opens and closes the drama, thereby setting a death tone which is carried throughout.

2. Since this is a radio drama, various other sounds are constantly evoked, only to die slowly away.

3. In the first scene, Mrs. Rooney encounters the dung carrier, Christy, whose animal is a hinny, a hybrid between a horse and an ass, which is sterile; being unable to procreate, it dies with itself.

4. The encounter with the sterile hinny reminds Mrs. Rooney that her daughter, Minnie, also died barren, and there is no issue from her to survive.

5. Mr. Tyler arrives, and we hear that his daughter is barren and, therefore, he will always be grandchildless.

6. The flat tire on Mr. Tyler's bicycle becomes significant in the barrenness of the world around him.

7. Mrs. Rooney meets Mr. Slocum (slow come) and hears that his mother is dying and is usually in great pain.

8. Mr. Slocum's car dies, and he can get it started again only with difficulty.

9. Then Mr. Slocum runs over and kills the hen, allowing Mrs. Rooney to deliver her eulogy on the dead hen, an ode that is a parody on grandiose literary rhetoric.

10. Arriving at the station, Mrs. Rooney describes her condition in such a way as to evoke the image of a corpse being shrouded for burial: "Would I were lying stretched out in my comfortable bed. . . . "

11. Mrs. Rooney then hears about the death of Mr. Barrell's father, who died only a short time after receiving the job of station master.

12. Miss Fitt, a misfit in this world, believes herself to belong to a heavenly world and "left to myself would soon be flown home."

13. While Miss Fitt is helping Mrs. Rooney up the stairs, she begins to hum John Henry Newman's hymn "Lead, Kindly Light," which was sung on the *Titanic* as it was sinking.

14. Suddenly a female voice warns young Dolly not to stand close because "one can be sucked under." This, of course, anticipates the death of the young maiden at the end of the drama.

15. Mr. Tyler thinks that Miss Fitt has lost her mother, but it turns out that Miss Fitt simply cannot find her because the mother was to arrive on the last train, and Miss Fitt does not yet know that the last train has been detained; thus, since the mother is bringing fresh sole (soul), there is still hope that the mother is not lost.

16. Mr. Rooney (Dan) arrives, and he is blind and suffers from an old wound and a coronary.

17. Going home, the old man inquires of his old wife if she has ever had the desire to kill a child.

18. Mr. Rooney even sees the two of them in terms of Dante's great lovers, Paolo and Francesca, who were doomed to hell for adultery and were constantly locked in each other's arms. Thus, Mr. Rooney, who is blind, is locked to Mrs. Rooney, who is so decrepit that she can hardly move, an ironic reversal of the great lovers of Dante's *Inferno,* but the evocation reminds one of the sterility of the entire *Inferno.*

19. Mr. Rooney, in commenting on his wife's strange speech, thinks sometimes that she is "struggling with a dead language." Mrs. Rooney agrees, believing that her language will "be dead in time, just like our poor dear Gaelic" language is already dead.

20. Mrs. Rooney remembers a time when she went to a lecture about a cure for her "preoccupation with horses' buttocks," but she heard at the lecture, instead, a story about a young girl who had only one thing wrong with her—"the only thing wrong with her . . . was that she was dying." This then anticipates the death of the young maiden under the wheels of the train at the end of the drama.

21. As the drama nears its close, many death images converge —the leaves falling and rotting, the dead dog rotting in the ditch, the concern over whether Jesus rode a sterile hinny into Jerusalem, the wind and the rain, and the recurrence of the Schubert song "Death and the Maiden."

22. The text of the sermon thus furnishes the title for this drama: "The Lord upholdeth *all that fall.*" This is immedi-

ately followed by the reason for the train's being late: "It was a little child fell out of the carriage, Ma'am . . . on the line, Ma'am . . . under the wheels, Ma'am."

The above list contains some of the more prominent concerns with death or death-like images in the drama. From the comic eulogy on the dead hen to the horror of the innocent child being killed under the wheels of the train, the entire drama abounds in orchestration on the theme of death—some ludicrous and some filled with solemnity. The various sounds of the play contribute to the eerie effects and also remind us that among the familiar sounds, death is as commonplace as a hen crossing the road.

Act Without Words I

Whereas the characters in Beckett's plays usually exist in terms of pairs, *Act Without Words I* has a single figure upon an alien, desert landscape. This setting aligns it with *Waiting for Godot*, which also has a barren landscape and a single barren tree. In *Act Without Words I*, among the things that descend on the stage is a single tree with "a single bough some three yards from the ground and at its summit a meager tuft of palms." Against a barren desert landscape with "dazzling light," a single individual, "The Man," is thrown backwards upon the stage. The rest of the drama simply shows the actions (or the *acts*) of the man without any word spoken. There is, of course, the sense of another presence (another distant Godot or God) which is controlling "The Man's" actions, but we are never made aware of the nature of this other presence.

Act Without Words I can be seen as a contrasting piece to *All That Fall* in terms of pure dramatic technique. *All That Fall* relies totally upon voice and sound effects for its meaning and, in contrast, *Act Without Words I* is purely visual. It has no spoken word nor any sound effects, except the sound of a whistle. Some critics have debated whether or not *Act Without Words I* should be considered as drama. In traditional terms, it should not be, but it is definitely a work of the Theater of the Absurd. For example, since so many plays in this tradition have emphasized the failure of communication, Beckett has simply gone a step further and has written a play in which there is no dialogue whatsoever, yet this is a play in which significant intellectual concerns are suggested by the actions we observe.

The play opens with "The Man" being thrown *backwards* onto the stage. This action is repeated two more times to the accompaniment of a whistle and then later is repeated some more, for a total of four times. There is no visible sign of confinement; nor is there any indication that "The Man" is being flung backwards by a person, yet he is not allowed to leave the stage. Then other things begin to appear: a tree and a carafe of water. He can't reach the carafe, and some cubes begin to appear. After attempting to reach the carafe of water by stacking the cubes, only to have the cubes pulled from under him and the carafe moved beyond his reach, he then takes a rope which has descended, arranges one of the cubes next to the tree, and makes plans for suicide before he "hesitates, thinks better of it." Between each action, a whistle either directs his actions or calls attention to some aspect of the stage. Finally, "The Man" no longer hears the whistle, and he no longer responds to any outside stimuli. Like Vladimir and Estragon, who also reject suicide at the end of *Waiting for Godot* and are seen sitting perfectly motionless, so also is "The Man" inert at the end of *Act Without Words I*.

The most obvious intellectual analogy, of course, is to the ancient Greek myth of Tantalus, who was a mortal favored by the gods. The gods allowed Tantalus to dine with them on nectar and ambrosia, but he violated their trust by feeding these divine foods to his mortal friends. Later, he became so arrogant that he committed the ultimate atrocity: he killed his own son and served him to the gods, who recoiled in horror. For his sins, Tantalus was sentenced to eternal torment: he was placed in a pool of water, and whenever he tried to drink, the water receded. Above him were clusters of grapes (or fruit), and whenever he reached up, they receded. Thus, we have the English verb "to tantalize."

We must ask ourselves if "The Man" is being punished by some God, since, like Tantalus, each time he reaches for the carafe, it recedes. But unlike Tantalus, who seemingly continues throughout eternity to reach for the water and fruit, "The Man" abandons all efforts and at the end is content to lie on his side and stare at his hands, totally ignoring the whistle which earlier controlled his life. And unlike Tantalus who defied the gods, "The Man" does not defiantly shake his fist at God; he is content to stare at his hands and ignore all else. He might even be god-like, since the typical Deist depicts God as One sitting apart from the world with nothing to do but pare his fingernails. In addition, "The Man" is somewhat like God—silent and solitary.

As in *Waiting for Godot*, the use of the burlesque here undermines man's attempt to assert himself in an absurd world. The entire *Act Without Words I* could easily be part of any burlesque theater; it employs, as did *Waiting for Godot*, many of the Chaplinesque or burlesque techniques. "The Man" is flung backwards on the stage four different times, and each time he has the plucky courage of the little man who refuses to give up, who gets up from an undignified fall in order to confront again the opposing force. The comic element is there, despite the tragic emphasis on man's fallen state. The fact that the little man can do nothing about it is both laughable and pathetic, as was Chaplin. But neither the tragic element nor the comic element is allowed to dominate. A seat is pulled out from under "The Man," a rope which he climbs breaks, and again we realize that we are in the presence of the comic and the burlesque, yet "The Man" is pathetic and trapped. Thus Beckett's statement: man is comic and, at the same time, he is trapped and pathetic. Yet like Vladimir and Estragon, there is a sense of enduring; "The Man" ultimately refuses to play the game any longer; he refuses to respond or to reflect. He has silenced the whistle and is content with his inertia. Thus man's *act* without words is his *non-act* of doing absolutely nothing and saying absolutely nothing. In existential terms, a refusal to choose is a choice; here, "The Man's" refusal to *act* is in itself an *act*.

Krapp's Last Tape

Beckett was constantly experimenting with new forms of expression. After *All That Fall* (a radio drama largely dependent upon many sound effects) and *Act Without Words I,* he experimented further with a form often characterized as a "monodrama" and gave us the uniquely different *Krapp's Last Tape*. The title implies that Krapp, an old man who is hard of hearing and whose eyesight is failing, is making his last recorded tape soliloquy. (Some critics prefer to use the more vulgar suggestion that Krapp is crapping his last turd.) We later discover that through the years, he has been constantly recording observations about his life on tape; now, he sits in his rather sparsely furnished apartment listening to old tapes and making new ones. In fact, most of the play consists of listening to the voice of Krapp, recorded on a tape thirty years earlier. This is another dramatic *tour de force* in terms of structural concepts—that is, Krapp's present voice, taping a tape for the future, is juxtaposed against Krapp's past voice, recorded on a tape thirty years ago. And to make the situation even more complicated, the present voice is supposed to be set in the future, thus making the past voice actually in the present.

Like many other Beckett characters, Krapp belongs to the world of the outcasts. He is dressed in "rusty black" trousers and waistcoat with a dirty white shirt. He looks rather like one of the derelicts in Beckett's other plays. The emphasis on the white face and purple nose suggests that he is another of Beckett's "music hall" characters. Similar to the munching of turnips and carrots which Vladimir and Estragon eat in *Waiting for Godot*, here Krapp eats bananas during the scene and, from the voice on the tape, we know that he ate bananas thirty years earlier.

The tape which he chooses to listen to was recorded when he was thirty-nine years old, and as he moves the tape on fast forward, we hear in disjointed segments, references to the three bananas that he has just eaten, to his mother's dying after a long "viduity" (widowhood), to a dog, to a storm and darkness, and to various descriptions of the progress and dissolution of a love affair when "I lay down across her with my face in her breasts and my hand on her." Ultimately, the love affair dissolves, and its dissolution becomes central to the past tape.

In listening to the voice of the tape of the past and hearing Krapp's present voice utter the same longing (Krapp's present voice says: "All that old misery. Once wasn't enough. Lie down across her."), we realize that the passing of thirty years has been insignificant. Krapp is still troubled by this love affair, which he tried unsuccessfully to dismiss thirty years ago, but he still returns to listen again and again about its dissolution and failure.

The suggested failure of the love affair was a failure of communication. Krapp tries to discover his own identity in the image that he finds in the eyes of his beloved, but in staring into her eyes, he sees only a reflection of himself. His insistent plea—"let me in"—is not a sexual plea so much as it is a metaphysical plea to be accepted into her world. (The sexual imagery, especially that of their moving "up and down," and other movements is obvious, as is the pun upon Krapp's name, but the imagery throughout transcends the purely physical in the manner that John Donne's poetic sexual imagery is also metaphysical.) Since his romantic breakup, Krapp's world has been aligned to his mother's world, and both have existed in a "viduity" for years. Krapp's only communication now is with the spool of his last tape.

Just as nothing changes in the lives of Vladimir and Estragon during *Waiting for Godot*, nothing has changed in the thirty years between Krapp's last tape and the present moment. He still eats bananas, he still voices the same concerns, he is still isolated from the world, and he is still plagued by his same hopes and despairs. As the tape ends, the voice of thirty years ago maintains that "My best years are gone. . . ." But the irony is that thirty years have passed and he is still playing the tape, still living in the same world, and as the curtain falls, "The tape runs on in silence." As we leave the theater, neither Krapp nor his tape is heard. Man can no longer communicate—even with himself.

SELECTED BIBLIOGRAPHY

CHEVIGNY, B. G. (ed.). *Twentieth Century Interpretations of Endgame: A Collection of Critical Essays*. Prentice-Hall, 1961.

COE. R. N. *Beckett*. Oliver and Boyd, 1964.

COHN, RUBY. *Beckett: The Comic Gamut*. Rutgers University Press, 1962

———. *(ed.). A Casebook on Waiting for Godot*. Grove Press, 1967.

ESSLIN, MARTIN. *The Theater of the Absurd*. London, 1968.

———. *Samuel Beckett: A Collection of Critical Essays*. Prentice-Hall, 1965.

HOFFMAN, FREDERICK J. *Samuel Beckett: The Language of Self*. New York, 1964.

This is the TITLE INDEX, indexing the over 200 titles available by Series, by Library and by Volume Number for both the BASIC LIBRARY SERIES and the AUTHORS LIBRARY SERIES.

This is the AUTHOR INDEX, listing the over 200 titles available by author and indexing them by Series, by Library and by Volume Number for both the BASIC LIBRARY SERIES and the AUTHORS LIBRARY SERIES.

AUTHOR	TITLE(S)	SERIES	LIBRARY	Vol
Aeschylus	Agamemnon, The Choephori, & The Eumenides	Basic	Classics	1
Albee, Edward	Who's Afraid of Virginia Woolf?	Basic	American Lit	7
Anderson, Sherwood	Winesburg, Ohio	Basic	American Lit	3
Aristophanes	Lysistrata * The Birds * Clouds * The Frogs	Basic	Classics	1
Aristotle	Aristotle's Ethics	Basic	Classics	1
Austen, Jane	Emma	Basic	English Lit	1
	Pride and Prejudice	Basic	English Lit	2
Beckett, Samuel	Waiting for Godot	Basic	European Lit	1
Beowulf	Beowulf	Basic	Classics	3
Beyle, Henri	see Stendhal			
Bronte, Charlotte	Jane Eyre	Basic	English Lit	3
Bronte, Emily	Wuthering Heights	Basic	English Lit	4
Brown, Claude	Manchild in the Promised Land	Basic	American Lit	7
Buck, Pearl	The Good Earth	Basic	American Lit	4
Bunyan, John	The Pilgrim's Progress	Basic	English Lit	2
Camus, Albert	The Plague * The Stranger	Basic	European Lit	1
Carroll, Lewis	Alice in Wonderland	Basic	English Lit	3
Cather, Willa	My Antonia	Basic	American Lit	3
Cervantes, Miguel de	Don Quixote	Basic	Classics	3
Chaucer, Geoffrey	The Canterbury Tales	Basic	Classics	3
Chopin, Kate	The Awakening	Basic	American Lit	2
Clark, Walter	The Ox-Bow Incident	Basic	American Lit	7
Conrad, Joseph	Heart of Darkness & The Secret Sharer * Lord Jim	Basic	English Lit	5
Cooper, James F.	The Deerslayer * The Last of the Mohicans	Basic	American Lit	1
Crane, Stephen	The Red Badge of Courage	Basic	American Lit	2
Dante	Divine Comedy I: Inferno * Divine Comedy II: Purgatorio * Divine Comedy III: Paradiso	Basic	Classsics	3
Defoe, Daniel	Moll Flanders	Basic	English Lit	1
	Robinson Crusoe	Basic	English Lit	2
Dickens, Charles	Bleak House * David Copperfield * Great Expectations * Hard Times	Basic	English Lit	3
	Oliver Twist * A Tale of Two Cities	Basic	English Lit	4
	Bleak House * David Copperfield * Great Expectations * Hard Times * Oliver Twist * A Tale of Two Cities	Authors	Dickens	1

AUTHOR	TITLE(S)	SERIES	LIBRARY	Vol
Dickinson, Emily	Emily Dickinson: Selected Poems	Basic	American Lit	2
Dostoevsky, Feodor	The Brothers Karamazov * Crime and Punishment * Notes from the Underground	Basic	European Lit	3
	The Brothers Karamazov * Crime and Punishment * Notes from the Underground	Authors	Dostoevsky	2
Dreiser, Theodore	An American Tragedy * Sister Carrie	Basic	American Lit	3
Dumas, Alexandre	The Count of Monte Cristo * The Three Musketeers	Basic	European Lit	1
Eliot, George	Middlemarch * The Mill on the Floss * Silas Marner	Basic	English Lit	4
Eliot, T.S.	T.S. Eliot's Major Poets and Plays: "The Wasteland," "The Love Song of J. Alfred Prufrock," & Other Works	Basic	English Lit	6
Ellison, Ralph	The Invisible Man	Basic	American Lit	7
Emerson, Ralph Waldo	Emerson's Essays	Basic	American Lit	1
Euripides	Electra * Medea	Basic	Classics	1
Faulkner, William	Absalom, Absalom! * As I Lay Dying * The Bear * Go Down, Moses * Light in August	Basic	American Lit	4
	The Sound and the Fury * The Unvanquished	Basic	American Lit	5
	Absalom, Absalom! * As I Lay Dying * The Bear * Go Down, Moses * Light in August The Sound and the Fury * The Unvanquished	Authors	Faulkner	3
Fielding, Henry	Joseph Andrews	Basic	English Lit	1
	Tom Jones	Basic	English Lit	2
Fitzgerald, F. Scott	The Great Gatsby	Basic	American Lit	4
	Tender is the Night	Basic	American Lit	5
Flaubert, Gustave	Madame Bovary	Basic	European Lit	1
Forster, E.M.	A Passage to India	Basic	English Lit	6
Fowles, John	The French Lieutenant's Woman	Basic	English Lit	5
Frank, Anne	The Diary of Anne Frank	Basic	European Lit	2
Franklin, Benjamin	The Autobiography of Benjamin Franklin	Basic	American Lit	1
Gawain Poet	Sir Gawain and the Green Night	Basic	Classics	4
Goethe, Johann Wolfgang von	Faust - Parts I & II	Basic	European Lit	2
Golding, William	Lord of the Flies	Basic	English Lit	5
Greene, Graham	The Power and the Glory	Basic	English Lit	6
Griffin, John H.	Black Like Me	Basic	American Lit	6

AUTHOR	TITLE(S)	SERIES	LIBRARY	Vol
Haley, Alex see also Little, Malcolm	The Autobiography of Malcolm X	Basic	American Lit	6
Hardy, Thomas	Far from the Madding Crowd * Jude the Obscure * The Mayor of Casterbridge	Basic	English Lit	3
	The Return of the Native * Tess of the D'Urbervilles	Basic	English Lit	4
	Far from the Madding Crowd * Jude the Obscure * The Mayor of Casterbridge The Return of the Native * Tess of the D'Urbervilles	Authors	Hardy	4
Hawthorne, Nathaniel	The House of the Seven Gables* The Scarlet Letter	Basic	American Lit	1
Heller, Joseph	Catch-22	Basic	American Lit	6
Hemingway, Ernest	A Farewell to Arms * For Whom the Bell Tolls	Basic	American Lit	4
	The Old Man and the Sea	Basic	American Lit	7
	The Sun Also Rises	Basic	American Lit	5
	A Farewell to Arms * For Whom the Bell Tolls The Old Man and the Sea The Sun Also Rises	Authors	Hemingway	5
Herbert, Frank	Dune & Other Works	Basic	American Lit	6
Hesse, Herman	Demian * Steppenwolf & Siddhartha	Basic	European Lit	2
Hilton, James	Lost Horizon	Basic	English Lit	5
Homer	The Iliad * The Odyssey	Basic	Classics	1
Hugo, Victor	Les Miserables	Basic	European Lit	1
Huxley, Aldous	Brave New World & Brave New World Revisited	Basic	English Lit	5
Ibsen, Henrik	Ibsen's Plays I: A Doll's House & Hedda Gabler * Ibsen's Plays II: Ghosts, An Enemy of the People, & The Wild Duck	Basic	European Lit	4
James, Henry	The American * Daisy Miller & The Turn of the Screw * The Portrait of a Lady	Basic	American Lit	2
	The American * Daisy Miller & The Turn of the Screw * The Portrait of a Lady	Authors	James	6
Joyce, James	A Portrait of the Artist as a Young Man * Ulysses	Basic	English Lit	6
Kafka, Franz	Kafka's Short Stories * The Trial	Basic	European Lit	2
Keats & Shelley	Keats & Shelley	Basic	English Lit	1
Kesey, Ken	One Flew Over the Cuckoo's Nest	Basic	American Lit	7
Knowles, John	A Separate Peace	Basic	American Lit	7

AUTHOR	TITLE(S)	SERIES	LIBRARY	Vol
Lawrence, D.H.	Sons and Lovers	Basic	English Lit	6
Lee, Harper	To Kill a Mockingbird	Basic	American Lit	7
Lewis, Sinclair	Babbit * Main Street	Basic	American Lit	3
	Babbit * Main Street	Authors	Lewis	7
Little, Malcolm see also Haley, Alex	The Autobiography of Malcolm X	Basic	American Lit	6
London, Jack	Call of the Wild & White Fang	Basic	American Lit	3
Machiavelli, Niccolo	The Prince	Basic	Classics	4
Malamud, Bernard	The Assistant	Basic	American Lit	6
Malcolm X	see Little, Malcolm			
Malory, Thomas	Le Morte d'Arthur	Basic	Classics	4
Marlowe, Christopher	Doctor Faustus	Basic	Classics	3
Marquez, Gabriel Garcia	One Hundred Years of Solitude	Basic	American Lit	6
Maugham, Somerset	Of Human Bondage	Basic	English Lit	6
Melville, Herman	Billy Budd & Typee * Moby Dick	Basic	American Lit	1
Miller, Arthur	The Crucible * Death of a Salesman	Basic	American Lit	6
Milton, John	Paradise Lost	Basic	English Lit	2

Moliere, Jean
  Baptiste
	Tartuffe, Misanthrope &
	  Bourgeois Gentleman
		Basic	European Lit	1

More, Thomas	Utopia	Basic	Classics	4
O'Connor, Flannery	O'Connor's Short Stories	Basic	American Lit	7
Orwell, George	Animal Farm	Basic	English Lit	5
	Nineteen Eighty-Four	Basic	English Lit	6
Paton, Alan	Cry, The Beloved Country	Basic	English Lit	5
Plath, Sylvia	The Bell Jar	Basic	American Lit	6

Plato	Plato's Euthyphro, Apology,
	  Crito & Phaedo * Plato's
	  The Republic
		Basic	Classics	1

Poe, Edgar Allen	Poe's Short Stories	Basic	American Lit	1
Remarque, Erich	All Quiet on the Western Front	Basic	European Lit	2
Rolvaag, Ole	Giants in the Earth	Basic	European Lit	4
Rostand, Edmond	Cyrano de Bergerac	Basic	European Lit	1
Salinger, J.D.	The Catcher in the Rye	Basic	American Lit	6
Sartre, Jean Paul	No Exit & The Flies	Basic	European Lit	1
Scott, Walter	Ivanhoe	Basic	English Lit	1
Shaefer, Jack	Shane	Basic	American Lit	7

Shakespeare,
  William
	All's Well that Ends Well & The
	  Merry Wives of Windsor * As
	  You Like It * The Comedy of
	  Errors, Love's Labour's Lost, &
	  The Two Gentlemen of Verona *
	  Measure for Measure * The
	  Merchant of Venice * Midsum-
	  mer Night's Dream * Much Ado
	  About Nothing * The Taming
	  of the Shrew * The Tempest *
		Basic	Shakespeare	1

AUTHOR	TITLE(S)	SERIES	LIBRARY	Vol
Steinbeck, John	The Grapes of Wrath * Of Mice and Men * The Pearl * The Red Pony	Authors	Steinbeck	12
Stendhal	The Red and the Black	Basic	European Lit	1
Sterne, Lawrence	Tristram Shandy	Basic	English Lit	2
Stevenson, Robert Louis	Dr. Jekyll and Mr. Hyde *	Basic	English Lit	3
	Treasure Island & Kidnapped	Basic	English Lit	4
Stoker, Bram	Dracula	Basic	English Lit	3
Stowe, Harriet Beecher	Uncle Tom's Cabin	Basic	American Lit	2
Swift, Jonathan	Gulliver's Travels	Basic	English Lit	1
Thackeray, William Makepeace	Vanity Fair	Basic	English Lit	4
Thoreau, Henry David	Walden	Basic	American Lit	1
Tolkien, J.R.R.	The Lord of the Rings & The Hobbit	Basic	English Lit	5
Tolstoy, Leo	Anna Karenina * War and Peace	Basic	European Lit	3
Turgenev, Ivan Sergeyevich	Fathers and Sons	Basic	European Lit	3
Twain, Mark	A Connecticut Yankee * Huckleberry Finn * The Prince and the Pauper * Tom Sawyer	Basic	American Lit	2
	A Connecticut Yankee * Huckleberry Finn * The Prince and the Pauper * Tom Sawyer	Authors	Twain	13
Virgil	The Aeneid	Basic	Classics	1
Voltaire, Francois	Candide	Basic	European Lit	2
Vonnegut, Kurt	Vonnegut's Major Works	Basic	American Lit	7
Walker, Alice	The Color Purple	Basic	American Lit	7
Warren, Robert Penn	All the King's Men	Basic	American Lit	6
West, Nathanael	Miss Lonelyhearts & The Day of the Locust	Basic	American Lit	5
Wharton, Edith	Ethan Frome	Basic	American Lit	3
Whitman, Walt	Leaves of Grass	Basic	American Lit	1
Wilder, Thornton	Our Town	Basic	American Lit	5
Williams, Tennessee	The Glass Menagerie & A Streetcar Named Desire	Basic	American Lit	6
Woolf, Virginia	Mrs. Dalloway	Basic	English Lit	5
Wordsworth, William	The Prelude	Basic	English Lit	2
Wright, Richard	Black Boy	Basic	American Lit	4
	Native Son	Basic	American Lit	5

INDEX OF SERIES

<u>BASIC LIBRARY (24-0)</u>

THE SHAKESPEARE LIBRARY: 3 Volumes, 26 Titles (25-9)
    V. 1 - The Comedies 12 titles (00-3)
    V. 2 - The Tragedies, 7 titles (01-1)
    V. 3 - The Histories; The Sonnets, 7 titles (02-X)

THE CLASSICS LIBRARY: 4 Volumes, 27 Titles (26-7)
    V. 1 - Greek & Roman Classics, 11 titles (03-8)
    V. 2 - Greek & Roman Classics, 2 titles (04-6)
    V. 3 - Early Christian/European Classics, 7 titles (05-4)
    V. 4 - Early Christian/European Classics, 7 titles (06-2)

ENGLISH LITERATURE LIBRARY: 6 Volumes, 55 Titles (29-1)
    V. 1 - 17th Century & Romantic Period Classics, 7 titles (07-0)
    V. 2 - 17th Century & Romantic Period Classics, 7 titles (08-9)
    V. 3 - Victorian Age, 11 titles (09-7)
    V. 4 - Victorian Age, 10 titles (10-0)
    V. 5 - 20th Century, 10 titles (11-9)
    V. 6 - 20th Century, 10 titles (12-7)

AMERICAN LITERATURE LIBRARY: 7 Volumes, 77 Titles (33-X)
    V. 1 - Early U.S. & Romantic Period, 11 titles (13-5)
    V. 2 - Civil War to 1900, 11 titles (14-3)
    V. 3 - Early 20th Century, 9 titles (15-1)
    V. 4 - The Jazz Age to W.W.II, 11 titles (16-X)
    V. 5 - The Jazz Age to W.W.II, 10 titles (17-8)
    V. 6 - Post-War American Literature, 13 titles (18-6)
    V. 7 - Post-War American Literature, 12 titles (19-4)

EUROPEAN LITERATURE LIBRARY: 4 Volumes, 29 Titles (36-4)
    V. 1 - French Literature, 12 titles (20-8)
    V. 2 - German Literature, 7 titles (21-6)
    V. 3 - Russian Literature, 7 titles (22-4)
    V. 4 - Scandinavian Literature, 3 titles (23-2)

<u>AUTHORS LIBRARY (65-8)</u>

    V. 1 - **Charles Dickens** Library, 6 titles (66-6)
    V. 2 - **Feodor Dostoevsky** Library, 3 titles (67-4)
    V. 3 - **William Faulkner** Library, 7 titles (68-2)
    V. 4 - **Thomas Hardy** Library, 5 titles (69-0)
    V. 5 - **Ernest Hemingway** Library, 4 titles (70-4)
    V. 6 - **Henry James** Library, 3 titles (71-2)
    V. 7 - **Sinclair Lewis** Library, 2 titles (72-0)
    V. 8 - **Shakespeare** Library, Part 1 - The Comedies, 12 titles (73-9)
    V. 9 - **Shakespeare** Library, Part 2 - The Tragedies, 7 titles (74-7)
    V. 10 - **Shakespeare** Library, Part 3 - The Histories; Sonnets, 7 titles (75-5)
    V. 11 - **George Bernard Shaw** Library, 2 titles (76-3)
    V. 12 - **John Steinbeck** Library, 4 titles (77-1)
    V. 13 - **Mark Twain** Library, 4 titles (78-X)

Moonbeam Publications ISBN Prefix: 0-931013-

CLIFFS NOTES

HARDBOUND LITERARY LIBRARIES

INDEX OF LIBRARIES

This is the INDEX OF LIBRARIES, listing the volumes and the individual titles within the volumes for both the BASIC LIBRARY SERIES (24 Volumes, starting below) and the AUTHORS LIBRARY SERIES (13 Volumes, see Page 6).

BASIC LIBRARY SERIES (24 Volumes)

THE SHAKESPEARE LIBRARY: 3 Volumes, 26 Titles

Vol 1 - The Comedies (12 titles)
*All's Well that Ends Well & The Merry Wives of Windsor * As You Like It * The Comedy of Errors, Love's Labour's Lost, & The Two Gentlemen of Verona * Measure for Measure * The Merchant of Venice * A Midsummer Night's Dream * Much Ado About Nothing * The Taming of the Shrew * The Tempest * Troilus and Cressida * Twelfth Night * The Winter's Tale*

Vol 2 - The Tragedies (7 titles)
*Antony and Cleopatra * Hamlet * Julius Caesar * King Lear * Macbeth * Othello * Romeo and Juliet*

Vol 3 - The Histories; The Sonnets (7 titles)
*Henry IV Part 1 * Henry IV Part 2 * Henry V * Henry VI Parts 1,2,3 * Richard II * Richard III * Shakespeare's Sonnets*

THE CLASSICS LIBRARY: 4 Volumes, 27 Titles

Vol 1 - Greek & Roman Classics Part 1 (11 titles)
*The Aeneid * Agamemnon * Aristotle's Ethics * Euripides' Electra & Medea * The Iliad * Lysistrata & Other Comedies * Mythology * The Odyssey * Oedipus Trilogy * Plato's Euthyphro, Apology, Crito & Phaedo * Plato's The Republic*

THE CLASSICS LIBRARY (cont'd)

Vol 2 - Greek & Roman Classics Part 2 (2 titles)
*Greek Classics * Roman Classics*

Vol 3 - Early Christian/European Classics Part 1 (7 titles)
*Beowulf * Canterbury Tales * Divine Comedy - I. Inferno * Divine Comedy - II. Purgatorio * Divine Comedy - III. Paradiso * Doctor Faustus * Don Quixote*

Vol 4 - Early Christian/European Classics Part 2 (7 titles)
*The Faerie Queene * Le Morte D'Arthur * New Testament * Old Testament * The Prince * Sir Gawain and the Green Knight * Utopia*

ENGLISH LITERATURE LIBRARY: 6 Volumes, 55 Titles

Vol 1 - 17th Century & Romantic Period Classics Part 1 (7 titles)
*Emma * Frankenstein * Gulliver's Travels * Ivanhoe * Joseph Andrews * Keats & Shelley * Moll Flanders*

Vol 2 - 17th Century & Romantic Period Classics Part 2 (7 titles)
*Paradise Lost * Pilgrim's Progress * The Prelude * Pride and Prejudice * Robinson Crusoe * Tom Jones * Tristram Shandy*

Vol 3 - Victorian Age Part 1 (11 titles)
*Alice in Wonderland * Bleak House * David Copperfield * Dr. Jekyll and Mr. Hyde * Dracula * Far from the Madding Crowd * Great Expectations * Hard Times * Jane Eyre * Jude the Obscure * The Mayor of Casterbridge*

ENGLISH LITERATURE LIBRARY (cont'd)

Vol 4 - Victorian Age Part 2 (10 titles)

*Middlemarch * The Mill on the Floss * Oliver Twist * The Return of the Native * Silas Marner * A Tale of Two Cities * Tess of the D'Urbervilles * Treasure Island & Kidnapped * Vanity Fair * Wuthering Heights*

Vol 5 - 20th Century Part 1 (10 titles)

*Animal Farm * Brave New World * Cry, The Beloved Country * The French Lieutenant's Woman * Heart of Darkness & The Secret Sharer * Lord Jim * Lord of the Flies * The Lord of the Rings * Lost Horizon * Mrs. Dalloway*

Vol 6 - 20th Century Part 2 (10 titles)

*Nineteen Eighty-Four * Of Human Bondage * A Passage to India * A Portrait of the Artist as a Young Man * The Power and the Glory * Shaw's Man and Superman & Caesar and Cleopatra * Shaw's Pygmalion & Arms and the Man * Sons and Lovers * T.S. Eliot's Major Poems and Plays * Ulysses*

AMERICAN LITERATURE LIBRARY: 7 Volumes, 77 Titles

Vol 1 - Early U.S. & Romantic Period (11 titles)

*Autobiography of Ben Franklin * Billy Budd & Typee * The Deerslayer * Emerson's Essays * The House of Seven Gables * The Last of the Mohicans * Leaves of Grass * Moby Dick * Poe's Short Stories * The Scarlet Letter * Walden*

AMERICAN LITERATURE LIBRARY (cont'd)

Vol 2 - Civil War to 1900 (11 titles)
*The American * The Awakening * A Connecticut Yankee in King Arthur's Court * Daisy Miller & The Turn of the Screw * Emily Dickinson: Selected Poems * Huckleberry Finn * The Portrait of a Lady * The Prince and the Pauper * Red Badge of Courage * Tom Sawyer * Uncle Tom's Cabin*

Vol 3 - Early 20th Century (9 titles)
*An American Tragedy * Babbitt * Call of the Wild & White Fang * Ethan Frome * The Jungle * Main Street * My Antonia * Sister Carrie * Winesburg, Ohio*

Vol 4 - The Jazz Age to W.W.II Part 1 (11 titles)
*Absalom, Absalom! * As I Lay Dying * The Bear * Black Boy * A Farewell to Arms * For Whom the Bell Tolls * Go Down, Moses * The Good Earth * The Grapes of Wrath * The Great Gatsby * Light in August*

Vol 5 - The Jazz Age to W.W.II Part 2 (10 titles)
*Miss Lonelyhearts & The Day of the Locust * Native Son * Of Mice and Men * Our Town * The Pearl * The Red Pony * The Sound and the Fury * The Sun Also Rises * Tender is the Night * Unvanquished*

Vol 6 - Post-War American Literature Part 1 (13 titles)
*100 Years of Solitude * All the King's Men * The Assistant * The Autobiography of Malcolm X * The Bell Jar * Black Like Me * Catch-22 * The Catcher in the Rye * The Color Purple * The Crucible * Death of a Salesman * Dune and Other Works * The Glass Menagerie & A Streetcar Named Desire*

AMERICAN LITERATURE LIBRARY (cont'd)

Vol 7 - Post-War American Literature Part 2 (12 titles)

*The Invisible Man * Manchild in the Promised Land * O'Connor's Short Stories * The Old Man and the Sea * One Flew Over the Cuckoo's Nest * The Ox-Bow Incident * A Separate Peace * Shane * To Kill a Mockingbird * Vonnegut's Major Works * Walden Two * Who's Afraid of Virginia Woolf?*

EUROPEAN LITERATURE LIBRARY: 4 Volumes, 29 Titles

Vol 1 - French Literature (12 titles)

*Candide * The Count of Monte Cristo * Cyrano de Bergerac * Les Miserables * Madame Bovary * No Exit & The Flies * The Plague * The Red and the Black * The Stranger * Tartuffe, Misanthrope & Bourgeois Gentlemen * The Three Musketeers * Waiting for Godot*

Vol 2 - German Literature (7 titles)

*All Quiet on the Western Front * Demian * The Diary of Anne Frank * Faust Pt. I & Pt. II * Kafka's Short Stories * Steppenwolf & Siddhartha * The Trial*

Vol 3 - Russian Literature (7 titles)

*Anna Karenina * The Brothers Karamozov * Crime and Punishment * Fathers and Sons * Notes from the Underground * One Day in the Life of Ivan Denisovich * War and Peace*

Vol 4 - Scandinavian Literature (3 titles)

*Giants in the Earth * Ibsen's Plays I: A Doll's House & Hedda Gabler * Ibsen's Plays II: Ghosts, An Enemy of the People & The Wild Duck*

AUTHORS   LIBRARY

Vol 1 - Charles Dickens Library (6 titles)
*Bleak House * David Copperfield * Great Expectations *
Hard Times * Oliver Twist * A Tale of Two Cities*

Vol 2 - Feodor Dostoevsky Library (3 titles)
*The Brothers Karamazov * Crime and Punishment *
Notes from the Underground*

Vol 3 - William Faulkner Library (7 titles)
*Absalom, Absalom! * As I Lay Dying * The Bear * Go
Down, Moses * Light in August * The Sound and the Fury
* The Unvanquished*

Vol 4 - Thomas Hardy Library (5 titles)
*Far from the Madding Crowd * Jude the Obscure * The
Major of Casterbridge * The Return of the Native * Tess
of the D'Urbervilles*

Vol 5 - Ernest Hemingway Library (4 titles)
*A Farewell to Arms * For Whom the Bell Tolls * The Old
Man and the Sea * The Sun Also Rises*

Vol 6 - Henry James Library (3 titles)
*The American * Daisy Miller & The Turn of the Screw *
The Portrait of a Lady*

Vol 7 - Sinclair Lewis Library (2 titles)
*Babbitt * Main Street*

Vol 8 - Shakespeare Library, Part 1 - The Comedies (12 titles)
*All's Well that Ends Well & The Merry Wives of Windsor
* As You Like It * The Comedy of Errors, Love's Labour's
Lost & The Two Gentlemen of Verona * Measure for
Measure * The Merchant of Venice * A Midsummer
Night's Dream * Much Ado About Nothing * The Taming
of the Shrew * The Tempest * Troilus and Cressida *
Twelfth Night * The Winter's Tale*

Vol 9 - Shakespeare Library, Part 2 - The Tragedies (7 Titles)
*Antony and Cleopatra * Hamlet * Julius Caesar * King
Lear * Macbeth * Othello * Romeo and Juliet*

Vol 10 - Shakespeare Library, Part 3 - The Histories; The Sonnets (7 titles)
*Henry IV Part 1 * Henry IV Part 2 * Henry V * Henry VI
Parts 1,2,3 * Richard II * Richard III * Shakespeare's The
Sonnets*

Vol 11 - George Bernard Shaw Library (2 titles)
*Pygmalion & Arms and the Man * Man and Superman &
Caesar and Cleopatra*

Vol 12 - John Steinbeck Library (4 titles)
*The Grapes of Wrath * Of Mice and Men * The Pearl *
The Red Pony*

Vol 13 - Mark Twain Library (4 titles)
*A Connecticut Yankee in King Arthur's Court * Huckle-
berry Finn * The Prince and the Pauper * Tom Sawyer*